Women of South Asia

A Guide to Resources

Women of South Asia

A Guide to Resources

by

Carol Sakala

with
a Foreword by

Maureen L. P. Patterson

Kraus International Publications
Millwood, New York

A U.S. Division of Kraus-Thomson Organization Limited

The author gratefully acknowledges The Committee on the Status of Women in Asian Studies, of the Association for Asian Studies, for its sponsorship.

First printing

Printed in the United States of America

Library of Congress Cataloging in Publication Data

Sakala, Carol.
Women of South Asia.

Includes indexes.
1. Women — South Asia — Bibliography. I. Title.
Z7964.S65S23 [HQ1735.3] 016.3054'0954 79-28191
ISBN 0-527-78574-1
ISBN 0-527-78575-X (pbk.)

Contents

Foreword / Maureen L.P. Patterson vii

Preface xi

Acknowledgments xiii

Note on Transliteration xv

Abbreviations xvii

Introduction: Resources and Their Uses 3

Part One: Published Resources

Outline of Headings 17

Bibliographic Entries 31

I. Perspectives unbounded by time and space 31

II. Perspectives in temporal and spatial contexts 63

A. Roots of the Hindu tradition 63

B. Sixth century B.C.E. to sixth century C.E. 66

C. Seventh century to 1820 C.E. 79

D. South Asian women in the modern period 103

1. History and culture of the subcontinent as a whole 103

a. The colonial experience 103

b. Continuity and change in contemporary South Asia 166

2. History and culture of the regions of South Asia 275

a. Indic cultural region 275

(1) Sri Lanka 275

(2) South India 286

(3) West India 308

(4) Lowland East India 328

(5) Bangladesh 349

(6) North/Central India 360

b. Northwestern Islamic cultural region 400

c. Nepal/high Himalayan cultural region 411

d. Eastern highland tribal cultural region 418

e. The diaspora 420

Part Two: Libraries, Archives and Other Local Resources

Libraries, Archives and Other Resources in India for the Study of Women / Geraldine H. Forbes 425

Libraries, Archives and Other Resources in Pakistan for the Study of Women / Emily Hodges 437

Libraries, Archives and Other Resources in Bangladesh for the Study of Women / Sirajul Islam 448

Library Resources in the United Kingdom for the Study of Women in South Asia / Maureen L.P. Patterson 455

Indexes

Author Index 475

Subject Index 501

Foreword

In North America, the study of most aspects of South Asia is just emerging from its infancy. Aside from teaching and research in classical Indology (primarily through Sanskrit, Pali and Prakrit texts), which has continued since the late nineteenth century, few academics here worked outside this narrow field until shortly after World War II. The University of Pennsylvania established the first large-scale program in 1949 under W. Norman Brown's direction. It comprised modern language teaching, plus courses in both the social sciences and humanities, as well as in classical Sanskrit and the Vedas. Foundations began to support similar programs at Berkeley and Chicago in the 1950s, and many more centers sprang up after the National Defense Education Act of 1958. US federal aid and substantial Ford Foundation support helped establish South Asian studies in a dozen major universities and, eventually, on a smaller scale but with significant programs at other graduate institutions and colleges.

In this mushrooming of programs, the development of teaching materials and reference works was underemphasized, if not virtually neglected. The exception was those linguistic volumes that offered modern methods for teaching the many and unfamiliar subcontinental languages. But supporting materials such as up-to-date dictionaries and bibliographies received little emphasis. These indispensable works too often seemed dispensable when it came to funding. They were slow and therefore costly to prepare, and, when complete, not nearly as flashy as a new-method Hindi text replete with "cultural" slides, or a series of lectures on religion accompanied by a spectacular film and exotic music. Dictionaries, glossaries, and bibliographies remain, nonetheless, indispensable and must be encouraged.

While a number of general and specialized bibliographies have appeared both in the subcontinent and outside, their quality is uneven and their usefulness quite varied. With the exception of two or three recent works, even those which do exist and are both relatively comprehensive and up to date, have a striking and important bias: they tend to exclude entries on women in South Asia, except for perfunctory and short "status" or "position" of women sections. Little attempt is made to ferret out and include material that would provide information on the life and activities of this half of the 800 million population of South Asia, itself about one sixth of all the people on this planet. The two or three bibliographies on women which appeared in South Asia as a result of International Women's Year — 1975 — tend to restrict themselves to the nation in which they were produced, rather than dealing with women throughout the subcontinental civilization. When viewed vis à vis the neighboring Chinese or Middle Eastern civilizations, differences among these national and regional groups are less meaningful than commonalities within the subcontinent.

In a decade when studies of women are just beginning to be legitimate and accepted in academic circles in this country, it is time to attempt to make South Asian women more visible, both in the study of the subcontinent itself and in comparative studies of women. To date, comparative studies of women do not do justice to South Asia for lack of adequate and available reference materials. If South Asian studies have emerged from infancy, studies of women in general and women in the nonwestern world in particular are still in that stage.

Foreword

I became aware of this "woman gap" in 1975 in the course of preparing my overall bibliography on South Asian civilizations. Hanna Papanek and Carolyn Elliott, while planning the Wellesley Conference on Women and Development, asked me for sources on South Asian women. It was to be an opportunity to introduce students to the role women have played in Indian civilization, to present their problems in the present context of rapid modernization and to put into perspective such well-known and perhaps overstressed customs as suttee, female infanticide, child marriage, the dowry system and purdah.

In looking for materials to assemble for the Wellesley Conference (which took place in 1976), it became clear that few reference works were available, even on women in developing countries as a whole, and certainly nothing on South Asian women. By the time of the conference, I had accumulated a large number of references to South Asian women. I considered typing these in a long list and presenting them as "Materials Towards a Bibliography . . ." but rejected this idea because, without a carefully constructed framework, such a list can be frustrating and misleading. Instead I set about looking for a better solution, which I found, though not in time for the Wellesley Conference.

The solution lay in the aims and efforts of the Committee on the Status of Women in Asian Studies, a subgroup of the Association for Asian Studies. One of its early commitments was support for preparing a basic bibliography on women for each of the four regional subdivisions of the AAS. Charlotte Furth, then committee chair, had already organized work on a bibliography of women in China. Late in 1975, Furth and her committee held a meeting to consider extending this type of work to the other regions. The South Asianist at that meeting, Karen Leonard, reported that I was already doing some bibliographic work on women. After discussing the possibilities, the committee decided to encourage the work I had started. Since I could not then spare the time to do the work myself, I recommended an editor who would work under my informal supervision, and the committee funded our proposal.

Carol Sakala had been on my staff working on the overall South Asian bibliography. She accepted the task of compiling additional entries, organizing materials and making annotations. Sakala began by applying the chronological and spatial framework of the overall bibliography, which she had played a significant role in helping develop. She has found it necessary to modify the framework somewhat, to combine certain sections and expand others. The basic conceptual framework, however, combining time, space and topic, appears to work well for this and probably other single subject bibliographies focusing on South Asia, since it transforms an "A to Z" list into an intellectually stimulating and satisfying research guide. While it takes time — lots of time — to organize materials in this way, and virtually requires examination of the books and articles to be included, its end result justifies the time and the effort. I would commend this approach to others who would prepare other topically focused bibliographies either at the South Asian or regional levels, and either in western languages or the many regional languages.

This bibliography was intended to be a project for the summer of 1977, but as the summer drew to a close, Sakala had turned up so much more material that it became clear she would need considerably more time and money. The Committee on the Status of Women in Asian Studies of the AAS, under the succeeding chairperson, Hanna Papanek, continued to support the project and persuaded both the AAS and its South Asia Council, the Ford Foundation and the US Agency for International Development to come through with funds. In 1978, a fortunate set of circumstances brought the Kraus-Thomson Organization publishers into contact with me. When I mentioned the women's bibliography project, they were immediately interested. KTO editor Mrs. Marion Sader was quick to see the merit and magnitude of Carol Sakala's work, which in due course, KTO offered to publish. I am sure that Mrs. Sader and KTO take both pride and pleasure in their decision.

The finished product is testament to Carol Sakala's enthusiastic and imaginative editorship, and to her tenacity and industry in the face of long hours and the postponement of personal career goals. I am confident that all who have supported her in this endeavor will welcome the appearance of a volume of top-notch quality and multi-leveled utility. This is truly a path-breaking reference work in both the South Asian field and women's studies as a whole.

Maureen L. P. Patterson
Chicago, 30 September 1979

Preface

This book organizes an unprecedented and perhaps unanticipated wealth of materials related to South Asian women. The materials cover both historical and contemporary South Asia, which includes India, Pakistan, Bangladesh, Sri Lanka and Nepal. The range is from primary source materials to scholarly interpretations and analyses. The abundant amount of clearly identified material and the excellent prospects for locating additional sources challenge the widely-held view that women are invisible and their lives are undocumented. Such an assessment may seem to be particularly accurate in the context of social systems like the South Asian ones in which sex segregation and forms of female seclusion are widespread. But as the bibliography shows, resources are extensive and accessible.

As I prepared this volume my focus shifted from a largely retrospective one to a predominantly prospective one. Despite the sheer mass of available material much remains unknown. A large amount of primary source material is still unexamined and a high degree of emotionalism — explicable historically and psychologically — characterizes much of the material. In addition, many works purporting to be analytical are superficial, and some topics are covered only minimally. Thus in the course of this work my view of my task has changed from merely presenting what has been done to providing a guide for those interested in closing gaps and producing materials of higher quality. I would like to mention some specific aspirations.

I hope that these materials on South Asian women, as well as the limited coverage of particular topics, will inspire others to prepare similar and complementary compilations of materials available in South Asia's regional languages. Many topics cannot adequately be covered by using western-language materials. For example, although elite women are prominent in the present work, writings on the lives of peasant and tribal women and the urban poor are limited. The reports on local resources in Part Two suggest some regional-language materials, but detailed coverage of these will require intensive efforts.

I would like this volume to facilitate the inclusion of the experiences of South Asian women in on-going works by scholars in the humanities and the social sciences. Women's studies and fields that include the study of women overwhelmingly focus on western women, yet new syntheses cannot afford to ignore the richness of nonwestern experiences and traditions. Similarly, this work will make it more convenient for South Asian scholars to incorporate women into those research problems which, while not focusing on gender and sexuality per se, involve women.

For those specifically interested in South Asian women, this work will decrease time spent locating resources and increase time spent working with them. The panoramic perspective that this book affords will help such scholars delineate research problems and gain access to resources.

In nonacademic spheres, this work should help staff members of foundations and government agencies include in their proposals and action programs reference to South Asian women.

Preface

The consideration of women in fields or programs where they have not or have been superficially represented is not merely a question of including them in present paradigms, policies and programs. This book is also an invitation to rethink these issues: some aspects of present systems will be appropriate and others will not. My greatest hope is that we will come closer to a time when issues of sex and gender as well as the participation of women in all spheres of social and cultural life will be considered as a matter of course. Then a reference work of this type will be obsolete, and isolation of materials on women as a category will be unnecessary.

The book is divided into two parts. "Published Resources," Part One, is the major section of the volume, and is the bibliography. It contains over 4,600 entries to western-language books, book segments, articles, serials, dissertations, films and recordings. Most titles are accompanied by annotations based on examination of the works. Bibliographic information of works not available for examination was verified in catalogs and bibliographies.

The entries in Part One are presented according to an outline, called an "Outline of Headings," which organizes such features as major social movements, traditional literary forms, prominent personalities and cultural regions. All headings appear in the Outline of Headings and each precedes an appropriate section of entries. Entries follow the format of the outline, which is intended to be both referential and provocative. The bibliography is based on the substantial South Asian collection in the University of Chicago's Regenstein Library; it is not, however, limited to its holdings.

Part Two, "Libraries, Archives and Other Local Resources," contains a series of reports that discuss identified and potential resources on South Asian women in India, Pakistan, Bangladesh and England. Prepared by scholars who have first-hand experience with these materials, the papers describe research sources, including court records, private papers, organizational records and newspapers. In addition they offer valuable advice on gaining access to materials and making use of them.

The Introduction reviews trends in the published literature available regarding women of South Asia, and discusses the scope and organization of the entries in Part One and the reports in Part Two.

Acknowledgments

This volume is sponsored by the Committee on the Status of Women in Asian Studies of the Association for Asian Studies. Several members in particular, including Charlotte Furth, former committee chair, and Karen Leonard, were instrumental in setting the project in motion and have maintained an ongoing interest in it. Current chair Hanna Papanek offered notes regarding recently published and forthcoming materials, especially on issues relating to development. She has, in addition, been an enthusiastic fund-raiser and publicist.

Maureen Patterson, South Asia Bibliographer at the University of Chicago, supplied me with initial references to women in South Asia, collected in the course of work on her bibliography of South Asian civilizations. She provided work space at the University of Chicago's South Asia Reference Center, access to indispensable reference works, and a wide range of essential facilities and equipment, in addition to her time, information and advice at many stages. My work has greatly benefited from so qualified a personal guide to South Asian materials.

I would like to thank Michael Seadle, assistant at the South Asia Reference Center, who worked on many reference questions, and offered advice on translation of German titles and the content of German works. My excellent coworker Stephen Kontos researched references, and Rama Jha, Ray Gude and Carol Prindle helped prepare annotations. Beth Hawrylo was the book's manuscript editor, designer, proofreader and production manager, and I appreciate her personal interest and commitment to a large and demanding task. Shiona Grant typed from thousands of handwritten cards with incredible speed and accuracy, and Deborah Peterson did a fine job of typing the remaining sections. Barbara Sakala arranged for the headings to be typeset and pasted up the bibliographic entries, an enormous task. I am grateful to these people for their dedication.

C.M. Naim, Professor of Urdu, gave advice on Urdu transliterations and Muslim name breaks. Frances Pritchett assisted with Urdu transliterations and suggested important clarifications in the Outline of Headings. Clinton Seely, professor of Bengali, helped with Bengali transliterations. Ephraim Miller, formerly Outreach Coordinator at the University of Chicago's South Asia Language and Area Center, provided film sources. The editorial skills of current Outreach Coordinator Joan L. Erdman brought greater coherence to the organization of contents and introductory materials. Lark Zonka offered solutions to thorny design problems. My parents, Jane Sakala and Joseph Sakala, were tremendously supportive.

Many persons throughout the world, too numerous to name here, sent copies of articles and references to important publications, and suggested people to contact and potential contributors for Part Two. With their help, much information has been included that would otherwise have been overlooked.

I wish to thank the Regents of the University of Minnesota for permission to adapt sections of the outline of Part One according to information contained in "Plate X.D.I Culture Realms, Regions and Areas, c.1961" of *A Historical Atlas of South Asia*, edited by Joseph E. Schwartzberg (Chicago: University of Chicago Press, 1978).

Acknowledgments

Marion Sader, Editor-in-Chief, and the staff at Kraus International Publications provided help and advice at crucial junctures, and I thank them for their patience.

At various times the following divisions within the Association for Asian Studies allocated substantial portions of their resources to this work: Committee on the Status of Women in Asian Studies, South Asia Council and Executive Committee. Carolyn Elliott, past chair, and Barbara Ramusack, current chair of the South Asia Council, were especially helpful in securing AAS funding. With the help of Warren Ilchman, the Ford Foundation provided an interim grant. The United States Agency for International Development, through its Women in Development division and the perseverance of Elsa Chaney, provided production funds. I wish to acknowledge the indirect contribution of the National Endowment for the Humanities to this book: the endowment funded Maureen Patterson's bibliography on South Asian civilizations on which I worked as a research assistant and where I gained valuable experience that I have been able to apply to this project.

And finally, this book owes much to the multifaceted support of my husband, Dan Dick, whose encouragement, advice, labor and sense of humor have been of immeasurable help.

Note on Transliteration

I have used standardized orthographic transliterations for the words from more than a dozen South Asian languages that appear in this volume, with two exceptions. First, vowels that are not expressed in the Urdu writing system are supplied in transliterated Urdu words. Secondly, the inherent final *a* in many words of Sanskrit origin has been sometimes omitted. Romanized conventions and diacritical marks are based upon the systems used in Monier Monier-Williams' *A Sanskrit-English Dictionary* (with the substitution of ś for ṡ and ṣ for sh), John T. Platts' *A Dictionary of Urdū, Classical Hindī, and English* (with the substitution of c for c', ch for c'h and <u>gh</u> for g̶) and the University of Madras' *Tamil Lexicon*. Platts was also the source for Urdu vowels that are not orthographically expressed. Names of nineteenth and twentieth century persons and widely-used South Asian words, such as names of languages and places, are spelled according to anglicized conventions. Names of deities, and of persons who lived before the nineteenth century, are transliterated and appear in regular type. Other South Asian words are transliterated and appear in italic type.

Abbreviations

The following works verified bibliographic information:

ALB UNITED STATES. LIBRARY OF CONGRESS. LIBRARY OF CONGRESS OFFICE, DELHI. Accessions list, Bangladesh. v1- (1972-). New Delhi.

ALI ________. Accessions list, India. v1- (1962-). New Delhi.

ALN ________. Accessions list, Nepal. v1- (1966-). New Delhi.

ALP UNITED STATES. LIBRARY OF CONGRESS. LIBRARY OF CONGRESS OFFICE, KARACHI. Accessions list, Pakistan. v1- (1962-). Karachi.

ALS UNITED STATES. LIBRARY OF CONGRESS. LIBRARY OF CONGRESS OFFICE, DELHI. Accessions list, Sri Lanka. v1- (1967-). New Delhi.

BAS Bibliography of Asian Studies. v1- (1956-). [Ann Arbor?]: Association for Asian Studies.

BMG BRITISH MUSEUM. DEPARTMENT OF PRINTED BOOKS. General catalogue of printed books: photolithographic edition to 1955. London: Trustees of the British Museum, 1959-66. 263v. *And supplements.*

BP PUBLISHERS' TRADE LIST ANNUAL. Books in print: an author-title-series index to the Publishers' Trade List Annual, 1948-. New York: R.R. Bowker Company, 1948-.

BUP British union-catalogue of periodicals: a record of the periodicals of the world, from the seventeenth century to the present day, in British libraries. Ed. by James D. Stewart. London: Butterworths Scientific Publications, 1955-58. 4v. *And supplements.*

CF INDIA (REPUBLIC). MINISTRY OF INFORMATION AND BROADCASTING. Films Division catalogue of films, 1949-1972. Bombay: Films Division, Ministry of Information and Broadcasting, Government of India, 1974. 655p.

DAI Dissertation abstracts international. v1- (1938-). Ann Arbor: University Microfilms International.

IBP Indian books in print. 1st ed.- (1955/67-). Delhi: Indian Bureau of Bibliographies.

IOL GREAT BRITAIN. OFFICE OF COMMONWEALTH RELATIONS. INDIA OFFICE LIBRARY. Catalogue of European printed books. Boston: G.K. Hall, 1964. 10v.

IPP GANDHI, H.N.D., JAGDISH LAL and SUREN AGRAWAL. Indian periodicals in print, 1973. Delhi: Vidya Mandal, [1973]. 2v.

MRL NEW YORK (CITY). MISSIONARY RESEARCH LIBRARY. Dictionary catalog of the Missionary Research Library. Boston: G.K. Hall, 1968. 17v.

NST New serial titles: a union list of serials commencing publication after December 31, 1949; 1950-1970 cumulative. Washington, D.C.: Library of Congress and New York: R.R. Bowker Company, 1973. 4v. *And supplements.*

NUC National union catalog, pre-1956 imprints: a cumulative author list representing Library of Congress printed cards and titles reported by other American Libraries. London: Mansell, 1968-. v1-. *And supplements.*

ULS Union list of serials in libraries of the United States and Canada, 3d ed. Ed. by Edna Brown Titus. New York: H.W. Wilson Company, 1965. 5v.

Women of South Asia

A Guide to Resources

Introduction: Resources and Their Uses

This introduction consists of a note on "Writing about Women of South Asia," a discussion of the scope of this book, and a description of the organization and use of the bibliographic entries.

WRITING ABOUT WOMEN OF SOUTH ASIA

Widespread interest in South Asian women predates the interest in women's issues that arose and spread to many areas of the world in the 1960s. In pre-independence India and Ceylon the confrontation of eastern and western values is evidenced in social reform issues relating to women, such as widow-burning (suttee), female infanticide, age of consent (for marriage), widow marriage, female seclusion (purdah), health care, temple prostitution (***devadāsīs***) and legal rights for women. From the early nineteenth century well-intentioned reformers, who were both westerners and South Asians who had accepted western values, worked to eliminate what they perceived as "social evils." British officials and missionaries used their evaluations of the condition of women as a justification for intervention.

Some South Asians responded with vehemence and indignation in support of their social institutions and beliefs. The social reform issues stimulated a historical consciousness: What do sacred texts have to say about these issues? What had women's lives been like in earlier times? If there are undesirable aspects of society, what are their origins?

In the early twentieth century the Indian nationalist movement also focused attention on South Asian women. Accommodations to the sphere of women's work within the context of prevailing norms for women, encouraged them to undertake public activities. Mahatma Gandhi was instrumental in bringing about women's participation in this movement. Towards the end of the colonial period, the Muslim separatist movement for the state of Pakistan had a similar effect on certain Muslim women in India.

The Indian women's movement, which arose in the context of reformist and nationalist politics, was led by both Indian and British women. They espoused many causes: social and political equality for women, "women's uplift," general "social uplift," and nationalism. Activities of this movement were conducted through a large network of national and local women's associations, which maintained records of proceedings and sponsored publications.

Throughout colonial India, issues of western (particularly British) versus Indian values and social institutions arose. Simultaneously, leaders and writers examined Hindu versus western, Muslim versus western, Muslim versus Hindu and other perspectives on social change. When challenged, both Hindu and Muslim communities turned to the authority of sacred texts. Hindus postulated an ideal Golden Age in their past, which was much like contemporary western society, and

Muslims compared the earlier doctrines of Islam to western social ideals. Many Hindus who accepted criticism of their society traced problems to Muslim influence in the subcontinent; many Muslims argued that Islam had become adulterated through contact with Hinduism. Fundamentalist movements arose in both communities. Some who charged that the colonial power was responsible for social problems argued for a socialist system. Still others did not accept the western criticisms at all.

To a great extent, South Asian women served as a focus for attempts to establish the relative merit of these values and ideals. The maxim, "The measure of a society is in the position of its women," was repeatedly evoked in writings of the period. Most of the entries in the bibliography from this time are assessments of the "status" or "position" of women or reports of activities to alter it. An insightful picture of the texture of women's lives is the exception rather than the rule, for these discussions focus upon a limited and recurrent set of topics that are typically presented without reference to their social or cultural context. Issues of sexuality and sex roles came to represent the social and political struggles of the time, and gained heightened emotional meaning. Very little of the writing is scholarly and balanced. This literature is frequently more informative about the writer and his or her social context than about the ostensible subject of women themselves.

Interest in the condition of women was overshadowed by massive political and economic problems in the years preceding and following independence. Many changes sought by reformers were or were believed to be taking place. The issue of whether South Asian nations were fit for self-rule had been resolved, and the nationalist movement had accomplished its primary goal. Events no longer necessitated a focus on women.

The women's movement that arose in western nations in the 1960s stimulated interest in women of many areas of the world, including South Asia. International Women's Year in 1975 brought forums and reassessments of the changes that had occurred, along with the establishment of programs in the subcontinent. Interest in South Asian women is again vigorous.

The Shreemati Nathibai Damodar Thackersey (SNDT) Women's University in Bombay recently established a Research Unit on Women's Studies. The Indian Council of Social Science Research (ICSSR), New Delhi, created an Advisory Committee on Women's Studies, which sponsors a large research program. In Pakistan, the Shirkat Gah/Women's Resource Center in Karachi and the Pakistan Women's Institute in Lahore facilitate research on women. The Women for Women collective in Dacca, Bangladesh, conducts research concerning the women of that country. Local programs, facilities and associations for women exist in all South Asian countries. The steadily increasing production of western-language works on South Asian women that began in the 1960s continues.

Much of the contemporary literature on women from the post-independence period resembles that which appeared before independence. Frequently, research topics are identical to those that received attention during the earlier period, and research questions ask whether particular groups demonstrate continuity or change when compared to the past. What is the rate of increase of female age at marriage? Do brahman widows marry again? Do urban middle-class women have traditional or modern values? How does education influence Muslim women's attitudes toward and practice of seclusion? These "social reform" topics relate to crucial aspects of women's lives. Yet they are often treated from a narrow and limited perspective, which lacks a sensitive and detailed appraisal of their significance. Furthermore, recurrent focus on these issues obscures other areas of study and research.

The increasingly complex social setting with conflicting identities and authorities helps account for circumstances under which earlier western-language literature arose, and for its past and present forms. However, some writing within this tradition is more substantive than is suggested above, treating its subject matter with balance and objectivity, perception and detail. Furthermore, much writing does not come from within this tradition at all, including most works that consider women incidentally. A closer view of who studied what, and of potential areas for future studies is one of the rewards of working with the material offered in the present volume.

THE SCOPE: INCLUSIONS AND LIMITATIONS

Three questions must be discussed with respect to the scope of this volume. First, what topics have been included, and how are women considered in them? Secondly, what is the range of space, time and quality covered herein? And thirdly, what sources have been used for the resources listed here as entries of Part One and in the reports of Part Two?

The Topics of Women

With respect to topics covered, these principles have governed the selections: 1) works that focus directly on women, 2) works that incidentally relate to or refer to women, and 3) works that refer to associations with women, especially the primary sources listed in the Part Two reports. While the works that focus explicitly on women are most clearly delineated, some points may be made regarding the latter two categories.

Works in such fields as kinship, demography, family planning and law consider women incidentally, as do many biographies, bibliographies and ethnographies. These works have been included as interpretations of women within broader contexts and as resources for more specific studies on women. For many topics, more explicit works are not available.

Topics that relate to women by virtue of symbolic and psychological associations, most notably goddesses and feminine cosmological principles, are also included. Some observers have noted that Hindu South Asia is profoundly feminine; thus the section on "manifestations of the feminine in South Asian philosophy, theology and social structure" is within the scope of this work. A male or female devotee's identification with the female consort or beloved of the male god is common in South Asia. The female divinity is prominent in the Hindu tradition. Such topics help to reveal the meaning of male and female in South Asia.

Also among the entries are creative writing and literary criticism. Both female writers in general and male writing on women have been included. The inclusion of works by female writers is not intended to perpetuate the view that they be considered primarily as women. Creative writing comes from personal experience, however, and poetry, short stories, novels, plays and essays should be counted among the resources relating to South Asian women. The distinction between fiction and nonfiction is often not clear. A number of the works in the entries that could be classified as "nonfiction" are highly emotional pieces, better considered as primary sources than as scholarly interpretations of social conditions. Conversely, authors can often speak more freely about sensitive topics in creative writing than in other media. In short, there's fact in fiction and fiction in fact.

Another topic included in both parts of this volume is the experiences and activities of western women in South Asia during the British raj. There are dozens of primary sources: letters, diaries, memoirs and autobiographies, as well as contemporaneous biographies and reports of organizational activities. Scholars have not yet examined the great majority of these for insights into social history; the men who have written the history of the British and other westerners in India and Ceylon have produced highly skewed accounts without the perspectives of the wives, daughters and female missionaries. Feminists will welcome recurring displays of strength and ingenuity often not associated with western women of this period. In the segregation of South Asian men and women, western women found a rationale for doing philanthropic work and entering professions, particularly medicine, that was unavailable at home; many South Asian women could only be educated, given medical treatment or provided with other services by other women.

Range of Materials

Given the broad range of pertinent materials, truly comprehensive coverage has been impossible. Entries cover standard, classical works and recent first-rate scholarly works on South Asian women, and provide examples of peripheral but pertinent works. Bibliographies serve as bridges to additional materials. The PL480 *Accessions Lists* for the five South Asian countries (see Abbreviations) provide a convenient listing of many new publications from the subcontinent; one should scan the lists for titles in the languages of interest instead of relying on the subject index.

The bibliographic entries of Part One refer only to western-language materials. Because the British ruled most of the subcontinent, nearly all western-language materials relating to South Asia are in English. Although some research problems can be examined well with western-language materials alone, for others use of sources in South Asian regional languages is essential. Certain biases have been imposed by the exclusion of works in South Asian languages. Without assessments of these materials, it is not possible to know whether they offer more balanced and varied perspectives than do western-language works alone. The very medium of the written word, as opposed to oral traditions, brings with it its own biases. The systematic identification of material on women in the regional languages would be a valuable complement to this work, as would an inventory of collections of recorded oral materials, such as songs and folk tales.

Geographically, the entries and reports cover present-day India, Pakistan, Bangladesh, Sri Lanka and Nepal. Although these countries share linguistic, religious and artistic cultural traditions, scholarship relating to South Asia is often compartmentalized, not crossing international boundaries. Previous bibliographies on South Asian women have been limited to one or another of the countries. The available literature reveals that similar issues and problems relating to women recur throughout the subcontinent.

The bibliographic entries consist of works published from the late eighteenth century through mid-1979. A few references to forthcoming works are also included. Although only published works are listed, some may be difficult to locate. Sources for verification of the entries are listed in the Abbreviations. If a bibliography listed as an entry includes unpublished papers, the annotation notes this, and they appear in the subject index category "unpublished papers, sources for." Unpublished theses and dissertations are not entered individually, but the subject index identifies works that list them under "theses, sources for" and "dissertations, sources for."

The original and naive conception of this work was to include only the best works available on various topics, and in order to pursue this goal, letters soliciting recommendations on the most important works in particular fields were sent to scholars in South Asia, Europe, the United States, Australia and Japan. But for many topics and research problems, excellent and scholarly interpretations are unavailable. There are vast technical fields (e.g., family planning and demography) where selection of entries proved difficult. Thus the emphasis changed from presenting only selected scholarly works to offering such works as are available and encouraging future studies by highlighting research topics, presenting reports on primary source materials and including references to less scholarly published works as primary sources. The quality of the works included is therefore variable.

There is another important reason for including entries that could be considered marginally qualified. Issues of gender and sexuality are inherently emotional topics. They speak to investigators' personal experiences and evoke strong feelings, as the social reform references in particular affirm. Sophisticated understanding of such topics is impossible without first grasping the dynamics of the experience of observation. The distortion brought to emotional issues can be transcended only by accepting and interpreting this distortion; to ignore it or deny that it exists merely perpetuates the problem. Therefore issues of "studying women and women's studies" appear as a subject index category and as a section of entries.

Since India is by far the largest and most complex country included, there was more material to choose from on Indian women than on women of the other countries. In order to provide entries on varied topics for those countries, some works of lesser quality were included. Similarly, certain aspects of Indian women's lives are poorly documented, in which case standards are also reduced. Rather than omit a particular topic, I chose to represent the problem or facet of women's lives with brief and often popular works or single-entry sections. A paucity of sources attests to the need for further work on that particular topic.

Media of the Materials

Entries in Part One are scholarly and popular books, parts of books, journal articles, dissertations, serials, films and recordings, either published or forthcoming. Only dissertations published by University Microfilms International have been entered.

Serials listed as entries include publications of women's organizations, popular women's magazines, social welfare journals and religious publications about spiritual leaders or goddess worship. Many serials printed in small numbers or of a popular nature were unavailable for examination in the University of Chicago library. However, serials catalogs allowed us to verify publication information.

Most of the several dozen films were also unavailable for examination. Information in their annotations comes from film catalogs and directories, distributors' promotional literature, the ***National Union Catalog*** and personal communications. Films range from didactic works issued by the government of India as part of development programs, through ethnographic works, to the full-length feature films of Satyajit Ray. Evaluation of South Asian films for their content regarding women awaits a search for additional sources and a review article or directory for the films.

Audio recordings, primarily records, and some cassette tapes, are provided in the entries. Most are recordings of performances of vocalists and dancers. There are also records of folk songs and cassettes of poets reading their own and others' works. Films and recordings are entered according to subject matter and listed in the subject index.

The field reports in Part Two are a special kind of medium that discuss the holdings of major libraries, relevant contents of government archives, records of women's organizations and the location of rare periodicals. Beyond these categories the reports vary in content, reflecting materials found in the respective countries and the individual interests of the contributors. Each contains suggestions, leads and references to resources that might be pursued in the other countries as well.

During her research in numerous Indian cities in 1975-76, Geraldine Forbes located rare and unique resources regarding the activities of Indian women and western women in India in the first half of this century. Subsequently several persons planning research in India asked to share her knowledge of these resources. Recognizing that the work of future researchers could be facilitated if such information were more readily available, she agreed to prepare a report for this volume. In turn, I decided to look for other contributors to report and reflect upon similar resources in other countries. Maureen Patterson, who was planning a tour of South Asian libraries and research centers in England, offered to investigate their holdings on South Asian women and western women associated with South Asia, and to prepare a report of her findings. Through recommendations I was able to contact Sirajul Islam and Emily Hodges, who agreed to prepare reports on Bangladesh and Pakistan, respectively. I received brief statements about some relevant material in Sri Lanka and Nepal but not enough to prepare reports on these countries.

These reports provide information and advice that will help users gain access to the resources and make good use of them: addresses of collections, procedures for securing permission to see materials, hours open to the public, photocopying facilities and restrictions. Patience and consideration are necessary virtues in pursuing these resources, but the reports point the way.

ORGANIZATION AND SUGGESTIONS FOR USE

In this volume I have, to the extent possible, presented materials in their own terms. Serious constraints to such an approach include the use of the English language, the discrete and absolute categories necessary for outline form, concepts and methodology in the works themselves, and my own biases and limitations. Despite these limitations, it has been possible to adopt as standards usages that preserve the intent and integrity of the subject matter to a greater extent than would more ordinary bibliographic conventions. The major divisions of the outline, for example, do not correspond to western academic categories, but describe historical periods and cultural areas significant for South Asia and South Asians. Several calendrical systems are used in the subcontinent. I have chosen to use the western frame of reference here, but to give it a secular rather than religious meaning. Thus the terms B.C.E., "before the common era," and C.E., "of the common era," replace the more customary B.C. and A.D.

The Outline of Headings

The organization of entries is not an outline of South Asian women per se, for it is dependent upon the materials themselves. Furthermore, it is one interpretation; another person organizing the works with similar aims would probably have produced a substantially different outline. The question of context and meaning is subtle and complex. Time and space are the grossest of contextual variables, and headings at lower levels also reflect relatively crude factors. Many of the contextual subtleties are beyond the scope of a manageable outline, and others remain to be established. Despite these limitations, I believe that the outline reflects some of the major dimensions of the lives of South Asian women.

The most general distinction made in the outline is between unbounded time and space, on the one hand, and temporal and spatial contexts, on the other.

The section entitled "I. Perspectives on South Asian women unbounded by time and space" includes entries for items that lack particular historical and, with limited exceptions, spatial contexts. It includes, for example, general statements of the position of women in various religious traditions, collected biographies, discussions of feminine cosmological principles, and collections of references to ***satīs*** and female seculsion, when not limited to a particular time period. The section entitled "II. Perspectives on South Asian women in temporal and spatial contexts," which is much larger, organizes material in chronological and, at lower levels in the outline, geographic contexts. Its most general subdivisions relate to four historical periods appropriate to the history of the subcontinent. The headings are as follows:

A. Roots of the Hindu tradition: archeological and textual evidence to third century B.C.E.

B. Sixth century B.C.E. to sixth century C.E.: heterodox challenges, development of Vedic tradition and earliest Tamil literary record

C. Seventh century to 1820 C.E.: *bhakti* movement, development of *Śākta* traditions, coming of Islam, regional states and more

D. South Asian women in the modern period: ca. 1820 to the present.

Western-language writing on South Asian women focuses on the nineteenth and twentieth centuries, beginning with the anti-*satī* movement of the 1820s. Thus, approximately four-fifths of the entries are located under "II.D." in the outline, which includes two parts:

1. History and culture of the subcontinent as a whole
2. History and culture of the regions of South Asia and South Asian immigrants in other countries.

The Outline of Headings, which contains many additional subdivisions, appears following this introduction, preceding the entries themselves.

The distinction noted above, between "1." and "2.", which deal with the subcontinent and the regions respectively, requires some explication. The large subcontinental section is residual, as it contains those materials that transcend the scope of particular regions. Since this part includes entries for India as a whole from the early nineteenth century to the present, most topics are covered in greater detail in this section than in any other. This part also contains entries related to both East and West Pakistan, after the partition of India in 1947 and up to the secession of East Pakistan to form Bangladesh in 1971. Material relating to post-1971 Pakistan and Bangladesh, or to either East or West Pakistan from 1947 to 1971, is located in separate sections.

Some examples will illustrate the basis for assigning materials to subcontinental or regional categories. Sarada Devi and Anandamayi Ma both grew up in Bengal and have large Bengali followings, but they have many followers in other areas as well, and have thus been classified here as "subcontinental." Creative writing in English and Urdu is directed toward audiences who are not limited to a particular region, and is "subcontinental"; creative writing in regional languages is "regional."

The major divisions of "II.D.2. History and culture of the regions of South Asia ..." were established by adapting information contained in "Plate X.D.1 Culture Realms, Regions and Areas, c.1961" of ***A Historical Atlas of South Asia***, edited by Joseph E. Schwartzberg. "Realms" from the Schwartzberg plate are here designated "regions," and "regions" from that plate are here simply designated according to conventional names of political units and areas. In order to reserve judgment on the question of Kashmir, the Northwestern region, which includes all of present-day Pakistan, is not named as synonymous with Pakistan. Several territories of the Schwartzberg map are designated as transitional areas between two or more zones. For practical purposes I have used the boundary that works best with the literature. Unambiguous placement is difficult with respect to prepartition Punjab and Bengal. In these cases entries relating to the colonial experience and to Panjabi or Bengali literature are in the North/Central India and Lowland East India sections respectively, with cross-references from the Northwestern and Bangladesh divisions. Entries relating to a religious community of prepartition Punjab or Bengal are located according to the area in which it now predominates.

The problem of deciding upon a work's topic for placement purposes occurred at the lower outline divisions, which are exclusively topical. Here the aim of presenting indigenous perspectives and experiences was greatly compromised because the works themselves tend to be organized according to western ideas and categories. However, some South Asian notions and experiences could be conveyed. For example, the idea of an "inner" domestic sphere as opposed to an "outer" sphere where formal education and employment take place, and the interrelationship of social reform, nationalist and women's movements are shown. Other organizing concepts were selected for their relative universality, such as the idea of the life cycle.

Categorizing by content rather than form was the choice when the problem of entries fitting into more than one category arose. For example, an entry for a general bibliography on Indian women is found with key reference tools, but an entry for a bibliography on prostitution is with entries on prostitution. An entry for a paper on folk literature illustrating diverse topics is found with folk literature, but an entry for a paper on family relationships in folk literature is with other materials on the family. A survey of legislative provisions is found with legislation; entries with material on legislation relating to family life or employment benefits are with other works on family life or employment. The subject index provides access to topics, which are dispersed by time and area throughout the bibliography. In addition, some headings have been cross-referenced.

Works not available for examination were classified on the basis of title, date and place of publication, and authors' other writings. Question marks in annotations indicate assessments based largely on conjecture.

In order to limit its categories, the outline does not follow the conventional practice of listing entries only at lowest levels. For example, in the case of

(d) English literature by South Asians

i) Toru Dutt, 1856-1877,

anthologies and general criticism have been placed at the "(d)" level to eliminate the need for an additional intervening outline level that opposes general and particular categories.

Entries

Individual entries consist of bibliographic information, or its equivalent, and annotations.

Bibliographic information for books includes, where relevant and available:

name(s) of author(s)
title and subtitle
edition if other than the first
translator and original language
place of publication, publisher, date

pagination
series name and number

Entries for journal articles include similar author information, title, name of journal, volume number, issue number (or where unavailable, month or quarter), year and pagination. References to book segments, serials, dissertations, films and recordings contain information appropriate to these media. Additional information, which includes alternate publication information, dates of first editions if the interval between later and already-entered edition date is substantial, and the order number of University Microfilms International dissertations, follows in brackets.

Authors' names are entered as they appear on a given work. In many cases, the name an author uses or is known by differs from the name that later appears in card catalogs, published catalogs and other listings. Because of the vicissitudes of women's names and the corporate identity of women with their husbands, official cataloging procedures alter their names frequently. In the present volume, providing names as they appear on works frequently sheds additional light on the author's view of herself and society. These circumstances include:

1) author widely known by pseudonym, e.g., Kamala Markandaya as opposed to Kamala (Purnaiya) Taylor;

2) author evoking maiden name regardless of married name, e.g., Krishna Nehru as opposed to Krishna (Nehru) Hutheesing:

3) author writing under personal name alone, e.g., Rukmini Devi as opposed to Rukmini Devi Arundale;

4) author using husband's personal name, e.g., Mrs. Samuel Newell as opposed to Harriet (Atwood) Newell;

5) author using compound surname, e.g., Amy Wilson-Carmichael as opposed to Amy (Wilson) Carmichael;

6) author marrying and changing her name after her association with South Asia, e.g., Fanny Parks as opposed to Fanny (Parks) Parlby; and

7) author widely known as member of a religious order, e.g., Sister Nivedita as opposed to Margaret Elizabeth Noble.

Where "official" or "real" names, as in above examples, have come to my attention, I have included them in brackets following the name as it appears on the work. The subject and author indexes follow a similar system. Works in translation by a single author are entered by the author's name, and the translator's name follows the title.

Bibliographic information has been treated as a quotation; thus ungrammatical or awkward titles of works and inconsistent or nonstandard transliterations have been maintained. Although a publisher may be located in New Delhi, the place name "Delhi" has been maintained when that appears in the book itself. In addition, no attempt has been made to standardize place names and publishers' names.

The contents of the annotations reflect various standards appropriate to different kinds of materials. Annotations are descriptive, and note main topics covered, theoretical and methodological approaches, locality, significant identity of author and chief conclusions. In addition the annotations identify supplementary matter, such as photographs and other illustrations, contents of appendixes, tables where extensive and bibliographies when notable. While annotations avoid explicit evaluations, they frequently provide a quotation of the author's own conception of the work or its conclusions, which can reveal whether the work is scholarly and precise, emotional and polemical, or inconclusive and weak. Each quotation given is the author's own unless another source, such as a book jacket or foreword, is specified. I apologize to any authors who feel that the annotations misrepresent their works and ask that they recognize that a careful reading of all works in their entirety was impossible.

Entries for those works that I did not personally examine are marked "[Unexamined]." These entries frequently contain annotations based on secondary sources, such as book reviews, personal communications and texts of other works. Information from such sources was also used to decide the section in which an unexamined work would appear. Such information should be considered to be unconfirmed. Since the sources initially used contained a high rate of error in bibliographic citations, bibliographic information for unexamined works was later supplemented, corrected or verified in reputable catalogs and bibliographies, whenever possible. Some unexamined works, particularly those not verified in this way, contain incomplete and undoubtedly erroneous bibliographic information. The annotations of verified works identify the source of verification with an abbreviation.

Indexes

For users who approach this work with traditional disciplinary perspectives the subject index provides access to materials by such categories. Authors have been listed in a separate index.

Author index and subject index listings for individuals in the present volume use as listings any popular, common or public names that may appear on works. Cross-referencing directs users to listings under the popular name of an author. Some official names are provided as alternatives following main listings. This provides names that may be necessary to gain access to the works themselves. License is taken with main entry names where a full given name may be substituted for an initial. This may reveal the author's gender, but otherwise does little to alter original context or intent. These names were included to provide access for users, particularly to works of authors with common surnames.

The author index contains references to the bibliographic entry numbers of Part One; it contains no listings for Part Two. Most author index listings are derived from the bibliographic information of the entries. One, two or three authors of a work are indexed; a work with more than three authors is entered in Part One as "[First author] et al." and indexed by this author alone. The author index lists the editor of a multi-author volume of collected papers, compiler of a reference work, translator of an anthology, director of a film and performer on a recording. It does not list the editor of a work with a single specified author or the translator of a single-author work. In two situations, author index listings are derived from information provided in annotations: 1) an annotation for collected papers may list complete or partial contents by title and author, in which case individual authors are indexed, and 2) an annotation may note the existence of a substantial introduction prepared by someone other than the work's author, in which case the main author and the author of the introduction are indexed.

The subject index contains listings for items in both Parts One and Two. Listings for the Outline of Headings of Part One and the Part Two reports are in italic numbers, which indicate pages. Listings for the bibliographic entries in Part One are in standard type and refer to entry numbers.

The subject index was especially constructed to complement the access to published resources entered via the outline structure of Part One. Major divisions of Part One, categorized by time and cultural region, do not afford access by traditional western fields of study. Works concerning "religion," for example, appear in many sections of the outlined entries. Subject index listings for major topics and disciplines bring together related materials in sublistings and sub-sublistings. Cross-references direct users to listings with many such divisions. These listings are easily noted, due to their length and indentation. They include:

arts
associations, programs
castes, communities
child bearing
development
education
folklore
goddesses
health
kinship
law
life cycle
motherhood/child rearing
politics
population studies
psychodynamics
religion
seclusion, modesty, veiling
social change
social welfare
western women in South Asia
work.

In addition to providing access to topics not available through the Outline of Headings, such expanded listings bring together related materials which a user might otherwise find cumbersome to assemble.

The subject index provides personal and other dates where they have been available. In some cases the dates given result from a single unverified source. Although some dates undoubtedly remain incorrect, substantial effort has been made to assure accuracy.

Outline of Headings

Numerals in righthand column indicate initial entry number of each section

I. PERSPECTIVES ON SOUTH ASIAN WOMEN UNBOUNDED BY TIME AND SPACE

A. Key reference works
1. Selected South Asian reference tools 1
2. Bibliographies of South Asian women 12

B. Collected biographies: admirable and heroic women 19

C. Interpretations of "The Position of Women"
1. General statements from a variety of perspectives 33
2. Historical perspectives
a. Demarcating and characterizing historical periods 46
b. Women through the expanse of the "ancient" period 61
3. Collected papers 72
4. Major religious traditions of South Asia 74
a. Hindu tradition
(1) Various interpretations 80
(2) Legal position 90
(3) Ideal Hindu women 94
b. Buddhist tradition 96
c. Jaina tradition 97
d. Parsi tradition 101
e. Islamic tradition
(1) Various interpretations 104
(2) Ideal Muslim women 107
f. Sikh tradition 111

D. Manifestations of the feminine in South Asian philosophy, theology and social structure 115
1. Philosophical perspectives
a. *Śākta* doctrines 117
b. Cosmology 125
2. Goddess traditions: the one and the many 131
a. Histories of goddess worship in South Asia 138
b. The many forms: dictionaries and surveys 143
c. The many forms: particular manifestations of the goddess
(1) The Great Goddesses 148
(a) Sarasvatī 149
(b) Durgā-Kālī 154
(c) Lakṣmī 159
(2) Others
(a) Goddess forms 163
(b) Goddess temple traditions 178
(c) *Yakṣiṇīs*, *apsarās*, various *devatās* 188
3. Matrilineal systems and matriarchal tendencies 192

E. The life cycle
1. Childhood 195
2. Puberty 196
3. Marriage 199
a. Rites 207
b. Female age at marriage 211
4. Reproductive life
a. Pregnancy and birth 214
b. *Niyoga*: assuring continuity of the family line 220
c. Preventing pregnancy 221
5. Widowhood 222

F. Women's power and sexuality, women's danger to others and seclusion 227
1. Pursuit of *kāma*, sexual love
a. As art and science 230
b. In legend: Rādhā 243
2. Forbidden sexual unions 246
3. Prostitutes and courtesans: history, typology, images 247
4. *Devadāsīs*, "servants of god": history, typology, interpretation 256
5. *Satīs*: history, legends, interpretation 258
6. Histories of female seclusion 274
7. Various types of evil women 277
8. Fantasies of *strīrājya*, a land of women 281
G. The spiritual life and religious observances 283
1. Performance of Vedic rites: rights and obligations 286
2. Spiritual enlightenment: education in "ancient" South Asia 295
3. Lives of female saints 297
4. Devotees' attitude toward god: the model of lover toward beloved 300
H. Economic position: property and maintenance rights 302
I. Clothing, adornment, beauty 312
1. Clothing: history, typology, bibliography 316
2. Jewelry: history, typology, bibliography 321
3. Hairstyle variations 326
4. Personal names, a feminine adornment 328
J. Artistic traditions 329
1. Music/dance/drama traditions 330
2. Visual arts: sculpture, painting, decorative arts and crafts 336
3. Literary traditions 344
a. Female writers of, images in Sanskrit and Prakrit literature 346
b. Other traditions: Pali, Tamil, Bengali, Oriya, Sinhala, Urdu 354
c. Poetry and poets: surveys and anthologies 359
d. Folk literature traditions 362

II. PERSPECTIVES ON SOUTH ASIAN WOMEN IN TEMPORAL AND SPATIAL CONTEXTS

A. Roots of the Hindu tradition: archeological and textual evidence to third century B.C.E.

1. Indus valley civilization, ca. 3000-1500 B.C.E., and evidence of a Mother Goddess cult 364
2. Aryan migrants and their Vedic, *śruti* literature "heard" by seers, ca. 1200-300 B.C.E.
a. Vedic position of women: honored as scholars and in other capacities 370
b. Goddesses and feminine cosmology in Vedic literature 389
c. Women in selected *vedāṅga* disciplines, "limbs of the Veda"
(1) *Kalpasūtra*, guides for ceremonies 397
(2) *Vyākaraṇa*, grammar 400
(3) *Nirukta*, etymology 401

B. Sixth century B.C.E. to sixth century C.E.: heterodox challenges, development of Vedic tradition and earliest Tamil literary record

1. Women and society: general interpretations and artistic representations 402
2. Heterodox challenges to Brahmanism organized by 6th century B.C.E. contemporaries, Buddha and Mahāvīra 411
a. Early Buddhism: ambivalence toward and cautious increase in opportunities for lay and ascetic women
(1) Position of women in early Buddhism: evidence and interpretation 413
(a) Lives of lay women: adherents and patrons 426
(b) *Bhikṣuṇīs/bhikkhunīs*, "almswomen," and the early Buddhist order for women 433
i) Structure and laws of the order 437
ii) Biographical details of early *bhikkhunīs* 442
iii) The early *bhikkhunī* order in Sri Lanka 452
(2) Feminine aspects of early Buddhist cosmology 453
b. Early Jainism: ambivalence toward and cautious increase in opportunities for lay and ascetic women 455
3. Classical Sanskrit literature 456
a. Late *śruti* literature: *āyurveda*, "science of life," medical texts 459
b. Early *smṛti* literature: a "recollection" and elaboration of the Vedic tradition 463
(1) *Dharmaśāstra*, law codes, and the *Mānava Dharmaśāstra* 466
(2) The epics: major sources for Hindu tradition from ca. 400 B.C.E. to 200 C.E., pervasive influences until the present 474
(a) *Mahābhārata*: vast storehouse of Hindu lore 477
(b) *Rāmāyaṇa*: tale of Rāma and Sītā, an ideal king and an ideal wife 489

(3) Early *purānas*, encyclopedic sources for social history, and the chaste, devoted feminine ideal 500
c. Sanskrit "secular" literature 501
(1) *Kāvya*, a class of ornate poetry: early works 502
(a) Kālidāsa, master of *kāvya*, ca. 400 C.E. 504
(b) Śūdraka's *Mṛcchakaṭika*: images of urban life, ca. 3rd to 4th centuries C.E. 508
(2) Selected *śāstras*, scientific treatises
(a) The *Nāṭyaśāstra*: earliest extant treatise on music/dance/drama 509
(b) Vātsyāyana's *Kāmasūtra*: early treatise on sexual love, model for later works 511
(c) Kauṭilya's *Arthaśāstra*: early treatise on statecraft 514
4. Classical Tamil literature: earliest written record of Dravidian peoples 518
a. The *Caṅkam*/Sangam tradition: *Eṭṭuttokai*, eight anthologies; *Pattuppāṭṭu*, ten songs; and a grammar
(1) Women's lives in the poetry, particularly the *akam*, "interior," love poetry 523
(2) The great scholar Auvaiyār, writer of *puṟam*, "exterior," heroic poetry 534
b. *Cilappatikāram*, Iḷaṅkōvaṭikaḷ's Jaina-influenced epic, 5th to 6th centuries C.E. 536

C. Seventh century to 1820 C.E.: *bhakti* movement, development of *Śākta* traditions, coming of Islam, regional states and more

1. Biography: notable women 537
2. Social life and women's lives
a. General interpretations 550
b. Various social institutions 565
3. Later *smṛti* literature and its social contexts
a. *Bhakti* movement: opportunities for women in its unmediated worship, egalitarian values and use of regional languages 570
(1) Emergence in the South: the Tamil saints, 7th to 12th centuries 571
(a) *Śaiva Nāyaṉmār* tradition: the saint Kāraikkālammaiyār, other spiritual women, conceptions of the goddess 573
(b) *Vaiṣṇava Āḻvār* tradition: the saint Āṇṭāḷ, consort of Lord Kṛṣṇa 577
(2) Various Kerala *Vaiṣṇava* saints: without an organized regional tradition 582
(3) Karnataka *Vīraśaiva* tradition: Akkamahādēvi's *vacanas*, leader Basavaṇṇa on women, 12th century 583
(4) The many female saints of Maharashtra, 13th to 17th centuries
(a) Bahiṇābāī: issues of her womanhood and other concerns, 1629?-1700 588
(b) Other saints of the Marathi tradition 590
(5) Kashmiri devotionalism: synthesis of *Śaiva bhakti* and Islamic *ṣūfī* traditions
(a) The mystic Lal (Lal Dyad, Lalīśvarī, Lallā), 14th century 593
(b) Rūpa Bhavānī, 1625?-1721 600
(6) Tradition of Mīrābāī, ca. 1500-1546, in the North: *padas* in honor of her beloved Kṛṣṇa 601
(7) *Vaiṣṇava* traditions in the Bengal area: identification with Rādhā as lover of Kṛṣṇa 622
(a) Inspiration from Jayadeva's 12th century Sanskrit lyric poem, the *Gītagovinda* 624
(b) Maithili poetry of Vidyāpati (early 15th century?) and the tradition of Caitanya, 1485-1533, in Bengali and Sanskrit 629
(8) The Gujarati saint Gaurībāī, 1759-1809: a widow turned to spiritual pursuits 631
b. Development of the *Śākta* tradition
(1) Feminine elements of various philosophies 632
(2) Rise of *Śākta* and *tāntrika* cults 638
(3) Particular forms of the goddess 644
(4) Later *Śākta* and non-*Śākta purāṇas* 655
(a) The *Devī Māhātmya/Durgā Saptaśatī/Caṇḍī* of the *Mārkaṇḍeya Purāṇa*, ca. 550 C.E. 659
(b) The *Devī Purāṇa*, ca. 550-650 C.E. 664
(c) The *Devībhāgavata Purāṇa*, ca. 850-1350 C.E. 665
(d) The *Kālikā Purāṇa*, ca. 1350 C.E. 670
4. Sanskrit "secular" literature
a. Continuing the *kāvya* tradition 673
b. Narrative literature: *kathā*, "tale"
(1) *Pañcatantra* didactic tales of *nīti*, "conduct of life," date unknown 674
(2) Somadeva's *Kathāsaritsāgara*, "Ocean of Story Streams," 11th century 675
(3) The *Śukasaptati*, seventy tales of a parrot, date unknown 678
c. Sanskrit drama, *nāṭaka* 680

d. Lyric poetry 681
e. Continuing Vātsyāyana's love treatise, *kāmaśāstra*, tradition: the works of Kokkoka, Jayadeva, Kalyāṇamalla, Padmaśrī, Devarāja, Nāgārjuna Siddha and others 682
f. Historical writing 693
5. Themes of love and devotion in painting, sculpture and regional literature 694
6. Coming of Islam as a major influence in the subcontinent, from the 11th century
a. Muslim influence on North Indian social life 706
b. The Delhi Sultanate and the brief reign of Raẓiyya Sulṭān, 1236-40 712
c. The Mughal Empire, 1526-1707
(1) Women and society: general statements 715
(2) Women of the Mughal court 720
(a) Women associated with Bābur, 1494-1530 725
(b) The age of Humāyūn, 1508-1556, through the eyes of his sister, Gulbadan Begam 726
(c) Women during the life of Akbar, 1542-1605 727
(d) Political and cultural contributions of Nūr Jahān, 1577?-1646?, wife of Jahāngīr, 1569-1627 730
(e) Mumtāz Maḥal, 1593-1631, and Jahānārā, 1613-1683, wife and daughter of Shāh Jahān, 1592-1666 736
(f) Zīb-un-Nisā, 1639-1702, daughter of Aurangzīb, 1619-1707 738
7. Regional states and ruling families
a. Women in inscriptions of the Kalacuri dynasty, 8th to 12th centuries 742
b. Women of the Cōḻa dynasty, 10th to 13th centuries: temple patrons 743
c. Naikīdevī: 12th century Caulukya queen 744
d. Cānd Bībī of Ahmadabad Niẓām Shāhīs and her struggle against the Mughals, 16th century 745
e. Rūpamatī of the Khaljī dynasty, 16th century: legendary for her devotion 752
f. Women of the Maratha kingdoms, 17th to early 19th centuries 753
(1) Jijābāī Bhosale, 1596?-1674, mother of Maratha hero Śivājī 754
(2) Tārābāī Bhosale, 1675-1761, and the defense of the Deccan against the Mughals 757
(3) The *satī* Ramābāī, d.1771 758
(4) Ahalyābāī Hoḷakar, 1725?-1795, noble and exemplary ruler 759
g. Begams of 18th and early 19th century Oudh 768
h. Begams of 18th century Bengal 771
i. Women connected with various lesser territories
(1) The spirited queen of Gondwana, Durgāvatī, 16th century 775
(2) The renowned Begam "Sumroo" of Sardhana, ca. 1750-1836 777
(3) Various others 783
8. The coming of Europeans
a. Early missionary women 787
b. Travelers, relatives of civil servants and others 790

D. South Asian women in the modern period: ca. 1820 to the present

1. History and culture of the subcontinent as a whole

a. The colonial experience
(1) "The Position of Indian Women": a subject of great debate
(a) Statements by South Asians 800
i) On Hindu women 818
ii) On Muslim women 828
iii) On women of princely families 831
(b) Statements by westerners 836
(c) "Mother India" attacked as non-nurturant, particularly regarding females 864
i) The critic: Miss Katherine Mayo, an American journalist 866
ii) A rapid series of replies, pro and con, from Indians and westerners 869
(2) Three intertwined movements: social reform, nationalist and women's 889
(a) The social reform movement 920
i) *Satī*, "a woman who is true," versus suttee, "widow-burning" 955
ii) Female infanticide 987
iii) Family and marriage patterns attacked and defended 996
iv) The "age of consent" issue: minimum legal age of females at marriage consummation 1019
v) The unfavorable position of widows and prohibitions against widow marriage 1035
vi) Female education 1044

vii) Adequate health care and its obstacles: funds, female seclusion and "superstition" 1105
viii) Dancing ("nautch") girls, ***devadāsīs*** and prostitution 1140
ix) Female seclusion — ***pardā***/"purdah" — and zenana life 1148
x) Economic position of women: property rights and employment opportunities 1164
xi) Conditions among rural women 1177
xii) Origins of the birth control movement in the subcontinent 1181
xiii) Legal rights: legislation and accessibility 1187
xiv) Hindu Code Bill, 1937-1956: whether to codify, how to codify, women's legal rights 1205
xv) Christian "women's work" and conversions 1215
(b) Nationalist movements
i) The Indian freedom movement 1225
ii) The Pakistan Muslim separatist movement and Hindu-Muslim communalism 1240
(c) The Indian women's movement 1244
(3) Political participation: rapid strides within limited sectors 1270
(4) Prominent personalities of the period: autobiographies, biographies and writings
(a) Collected biographies, directories 1287
(b) Particular persons 1295
i) The Sorabji family — Franscina and Kharsedji and their daughters, Susie and Cornelia 1295
ii) Mohandas Karamchand Gandhi, the Mahatma, 1869-1948 1298
iii) Kasturba Gandhi, "Ba," 1869-1944 1320
iv) Sarojini Naidu, 1879-1949 1326
v) S. Muthulakshmi Reddy, 1886-1968 1335
vi) Kamaladevi Chattopadhyaya, 1903- 1338
vii) Jawaharlal Nehru, 1889-1964 1341
viii) Vijaya Lakshmi (Nehru) Pandit, 1900- 1344
ix) Indira (Nehru) Gandhi, 1917- 1353
x) Other Nehrus — Kamala Nehru, Krishna (Nehru) Hutheesing, Nayantara (Pandit) Sahgal 1376
xi) Other participants in the Indian freedom movement, women's movement and much else 1381
xii) Participants in the Muslim League, Pakistan movement and Pakistani women's movement 1395
(5) The myriad roles and activities of western women in colonial South Asia
(a) Assessments of their lifestyle: primarily a dreary picture 1404
(b) Guides for domestic arrangements: cookery, servants, health, travels, etc. 1418
(c) Personalities: autobiographies, biographies, writings 1425
i) Emily Eden: travels in India as Lord Auckland's sister 1427
ii) The Kinnairds: aristocratic Scottish family dedicated to social service 1431
iii) Mary Carpenter: an English social worker promoting female education 1434
iv) Annie Besant: interpreter of India to the West, theosophist, nationalist leader 1439
v) Sister Nivedita: disciple of Swami Vivekananda, educator, nationalist sympathizer 1463
vi) Margaret Cousins: champion of Indian women's advancement 1477
vii) Wives of officials and civil servants 1479
viii) Various travelers and a theosophist 1493
ix) Women in India as relatives of Indians 1501
(d) Writing inspired by the experience of India 1503
i) Flora Annie Steel and her works 1504
ii) The fiction of Fanny Emily Penny 1518
iii) The fiction of Maud Diver 1523
iv) The novels of Rumer Godden 1530
v) Fiction by other western women 1539
(e) Christian missions: "women's work" and other tasks
i) On women as missionaries, women as missionaries' wives and work among women 1556
ii) Mission organizations devoted to women's work: histories and programs 1574
iii) Firsthand accounts and contemporaneous biographies: rich sources for social history 1596

b. Continuity and change in contemporary South Asia
(1) The interest persists: studying women and women's studies 1644

(2) Biography: dictionaries, directories, sketches of contemporary women 1657
(3) "Status of Women": many contemporary statements
(a) Women of particular nations — statements by South Asians 1661
i) Indian women 1663
ii) In depth investigation by the Committee on the Status of Women in India 1704
iii) Pakistani women 1711
(b) Women of particular nations — statements by westerners 1725
i) Indian women 1727
ii) Pakistani women 1734
(c) Women of particular nations — collected papers 1736
(d) Women of the subcontinent's major religious traditions 1760
i) The Hindu tradition — encompassing about 68% of the South Asian population 1762
ii) The Islamic tradition — encompassing about 25% of the South Asian population 1767
(e) Women of rural and urban areas
i) The rural majority: about 82% of the South Asian population 1791
ii) Women in towns and cities: about 18% of the South Asian population 1797
(f) Women of other communities and groups
i) India's tribal women: *ādivāsīs*, the "original dwellers" 1802
ii) India's scheduled caste women: former "untouchable" communities 1810
iii) Sanskritizing and westernizing groups 1811
(4) The life cycle 1812
(a) Growing up female: socialization, ideals, self-images, roles 1813
(b) Marriage 1823
i) Arrangements: matrimonial advertisements, advantageous unions, love marriages 1829
ii) Rites 1842
iii) Economics of marriage: dowry and inheritance 1846
iv) The increasing female age at marriage: its causes and effects 1851
v) Polygamous marriages 1869
vi) Marriage legislation 1872
(c) Reproductive patterns 1892
i) Onset of menstruation 1894
ii) Fertility studies 1897
iii) Fertility differentials and correlates 1901
iv) Maternity data 1925
v) Midwifery 1929
vi) Birth rites and "female horoscopy" 1931
vii) Abortion, infanticide 1936
viii) Menopause 1945
(d) Motherhood and child rearing 1946
(e) Adult and unmarried: a small minority with unique problems 1962
(f) Widowhood: status, rates, remarriage 1963
(5) The "inner" world: home and family life, often considered women's sphere par excellence 1971
(a) Overviews: the Hindu family 1984
(b) Overviews: the Muslim family 1990
(c) Relationships within the family 1995
(d) Domestic problems: family and marriage disorganization, divorce 2002
(e) Legislation concerning family life 2013
(f) Home science, family life education 2029
(g) Matrilineal systems and matriarchal tendencies 2033
(6) Women's power and sexuality, women's danger to others and seclusion
(a) Women inspiring reverence and fear 2040
(b) Aspects of sexuality 2042
(c) Female seclusion 2050
(7) The spiritual life and religious observances 2059
(a) Spiritual leaders: Sarada Devi, The Mother, Anandamayi Ma and others
i) Sarada Devi/Sri Ma/the Holy Mother: spiritual consort of Sri Ramakrishna 2063
ii) La Mère/The Mother: spiritual consort of Sri Aurobindo 2075
iii) Anandamayi Ma, a saint fully realized from birth 2094
iv) Various other female spiritual leaders 2110
v) Sri Ramakrishna: his femininity, female devotees and attitudes toward women 2116
(b) Worship of the Goddess, Devī, and her manifestations in contemporary South Asia 2122

(8) The "outer" world and issues and patterns of female employment
(a) Should women work outside the home? Some opinions 2133
(b) Labor force participation, occupational distribution 2138
i) In villages 2155
ii) In towns and cities 2157
(c) Surveys of employment patterns and problems 2163
(d) Employment patterns in various occupations and professions 2183
i) Agriculturalists: the majority of female workers 2188
ii) Women in village industries 2191
iii) Women in factories and mines 2196
iv) Women in service and professional occupations 2206
(e) Participation in cooperatives and trade unions, legislative protection 2220
(f) Vocational guidance for women 2226
(g) Employment and other roles: conflicts and compatibilities 2231
(9) The "outer" world and issues and patterns of female education
(a) The merits of female education, some opinions 2235
(b) Comprehensive surveys, reports, collected papers and a bibliography 2238
i) Histories of female education in 19th and 20th century India 2248
ii) Official reports 2251
(c) Formal education 2256
i) Secondary education 2261
ii) Higher education 2262
(d) Adult/nonformal education 2276
(e) Reaching rural girls and women 2283
(f) Literacy rates 2288
(g) Sex education 2289
(h) Physical education and sports participation 2292
(i) Education as a profession for women 2298
(10) Hand in hand: women as agents in the development process and beneficiaries of social welfare measures 2300
(a) India: accomplishments, tasks and facilities 2308
i) Women's and girls' organizations 2333
ii) Social welfare policy, programs and organizations 2354
iii) Reaching the rural sector 2365
iv) International Women's Year (IWY) and India 2380
(b) Pakistan: accomplishments, tasks and facilities 2389
i) Women's and girls' organizations 2398
ii) Participation in military services 2406
(c) Social welfare issues 2409
i) Problems of poverty 2410
ii) Health care and problems, participation in the medical profession 2411
iii) Issues relating to sexuality: prostitution, rape, VD and moral danger 2423
iv) Crime and imprisonment 2437
v) Alcoholism 2440
vi) Housing needs 2441
(11) The demographic perspective 2442
(a) The sex ratio issue — why do women constitute only 48% of South Asia's population? — and differentials. 2459
(b) Female mortality rates , 2474
(12) Problems of family planning and population control 2477
(a) Relationship between status of women and fertility control 2490
(b) Government programs and policies
i) India 2498
ii) Pakistan 2505
(c) Practice of family planning: motivations and obstacles
i) Family dynamics: communication channels, desire for sons, etc. 2511
ii) KAP (Knowledge, Attitudes, Practices) studies 2517
iii) Programs of women's organizations 2526
iv) Religious principles: Islam 2527
(13) Legal rights and the legal profession
(a) Legislative provisions for women 2530
(b) The effectiveness of legislative provisions 2540
(c) Law as a profession for women 2543
(14) Political participation 2546
(a) National and state levels 2552
i) Indian National Congress 2560
ii) Communist Party of India 2563
(b) Women's movements and women's liberation: socialist and other perspectives 2564

(15) Fine, folk and performing arts 2580
(a) Classical dance forms and performers
i) Forms 2589
ii) Life and work of performers 2595
(b) Classical vocalists
i) Life and work of performers 2610
ii) Selected recordings 2618
(c) Life and work of painters 2632
i) Zubeida Agha 2634
ii) Amrita Sher-Gil 2636
(d) Folk art forms 2640
i) Domestic ritual designs 2643
ii) Henna hand and foot designs 2646
iii) Embroidery traditions 2648
iv) Folk dance traditions 2653
v) Folk literature 2655
(16) Mass media and literary arts 2657
(a) Women and the film industry
i) Opportunities and problems for actresses and others 2662
ii) Images: issues of exploitation, sexuality and censorship 2666
(b) Journalism
i) Selected popular English-language magazines for women 2671
ii) Images of women in popular magazine fiction 2689
(c) Women and literature 2690
(d) English literature by South Asians 2697
i) Toru Dutt, 1856-1877 2712
ii) Sarojini Naidu, 1879-1949 2722
iii) Lila Ray, 1910- 2743
iv) Bharati Sarabhai, 1912- 2746
v) Attia Hosain, 1913- 2749
vi) Monika Varma, 1916- 2751
vii) Nergis Dalal, 1920- 2754
viii) Zaib-un-Nissa Hamidullah 2759
ix) Rama Mehta, d.1978 2764
x) Santha Rama Rau, 1923- 2766
xi) Kamala Markandaya, 1924- 2772
xii) Nayantara Sahgal, 1927- 2790
xiii) Mrinalini Sarabhai, 1928- 2802
xiv) Punyakante Wijenaike, 1933- 2805
xv) Kamala Das, 1934- 2808
xvi) Anita Desai, 1937- 2818
xvii) Bharati Mukherjee 2828
xviii) Meena Alexander, 1951- 2832
xix) Various other female writers 2835
xx) Men writing about women 2863
(e) Urdu literature: criticism and in translation 2887
i) Ismat Chugtai, 1915- 2895
ii) Razia Sajjad Zaheer, 1918- 2903
iii) Qurratulain Hyder, 1927- 2905
iv) Mumtaz Shirin 2909
v) Other female writers 2914
vi) Men writing about women 2918
(17) Clothing, adornment, beauty 2930
(a) Clothing: communicator of levels of modesty and modernity and other kinds of identity 2938
(b) Jewelry: important source of status and wealth for women 2945
(18) Western women in postcolonial South Asia
(a) Writers
i) Ruth Prawer Jhabvala, 1927- 2951
ii) Others 2976
(b) Women in social service: missionaries and a Peace Corps volunteer 2979
(c) Wives of South Asians 2987
(d) Travelers, a student and others 2989

2. History and culture of the regions of South Asia and South Asian immigrants in other countries

a. Indic cultural region

(1) Sri Lanka: area of Sinhala and island-Tamil languages

(a) The colonial experience: social reform issues
i) Education 2994

ii) Health 2999
iii) Prostitution 3000
iv) Enfranchisement 3001
(b) The colonial experience: western women in Ceylon
i) Missionaries 3002
ii) Travelers and others 3008
(c) General statements: ethnographic and other 3012
(d) The life cycle 3023
i) Puberty rites, menstruation 3026
ii) Marriage age and arrangements 3029
iii) Marriage ceremonies 3034
iv) Polyandrous marriages 3044
v) Marriage law 3047
vi) Fertility patterns 3057
vii) Pregnancy and childbirth 3064
viii) Motherhood and child rearing 3070
ix) Rebirth accounts 3072
(e) Domestic sphere and family life 3074
(f) Women's sexuality, seclusion, spirit possession 3078
(g) The spiritual life and religious observances
i) Goddess Pattini and her cult 3082
ii) Sītā in Lanka 3092
iii) Images of women in Sinhalese Buddhism 3093
iv) Our Lady of Lanka 3095
(h) Employment
i) Patterns and opportunities 3096
ii) Particular occupations 3101
(i) Education 3106
(j) Development and social welfare
i) Women's associations 3109
ii) Family planning 3111
(k) Political participation
i) Leadership and elections 3114
ii) Sirimavo Bandaranaike, prime minister 1960-65, 1970-77 3116
(l) Popular magazines for women 3119
(m) Jewelry 3123
(n) Western women in independent Sri Lanka 3125

(2) South India: area of mainland-Tamil, Malayalam, Kannada and Telugu languages

(a) The colonial experience: social reform issues 3130
i) Widow marriage 3132
ii) Education 3133
iii) Health 3146
iv) *Devadāsīs, basavis* and "nautch girls" 3147
v) Christian conversion 3161
(b) The colonial experience: western women in South India
i) Dr. Ida and the Scudder family 3164
ii) Amy Wilson-Carmichael's mission work 3169
iii) Other missionary and social service work 3174
iv) Impressions of a resident and a traveler 3186
(c) General statements: ethnographic and other 3188
(d) Autobiography, biographies 3200
(e) The life cycle 3203
i) Puberty and menstruation 3207
ii) Marriage rules, age and arrangements 3213
iii) Marriage ceremonies and definitions 3220
iv) Fertility patterns 3223
v) Pregnancy, childbirth and motherhood 3228
vi) Widowhood and aging 3233
vii) Rebirth account 3235
(f) Domestic sphere and family life 3236
i) Family relationships 3241
ii) Domestic rites 3245
iii) Inheritance 3252
iv) Continuity and change 3255
v) Nayars of Kerala and other matrilineal communities 3261
(g) Women's power, sexuality, dangers 3273
(h) The spiritual life and religious observances 3281
i) Spiritual leaders 3282
ii) Goddesses 3286

(i) Employment
i) Patterns and problems 3295
ii) Particular occupations 3301
(j) Education 3306
i) Adult/nonformal education 3308
ii) Higher education 3309
(k) Development and social welfare
i) Associations, programs, agencies 3314
ii) Health 3319
iii) Prostitution 3320
iv) Housing 3322
v) Mother-child welfare program of Mahbubnagar District, Andhra Pradesh 3325
vi) Family planning 3328
(l) Political participation and issues 3334
(m) Arts 3337
i) Folk literatures 3338
ii) Tamil literature 3347
iii) Malayalam literature 3356
iv) Kannada literature 3361
v) Telugu literature: male writer P. Padmaraju 3363
vi) Dance forms 3365
(n) Adornment: saris and personal names 3367

(3) West India: area of Marathi and Gujarati languages

(a) The colonial experience: social reform issues 3369
i) *Satī*/suttee 3376
ii) Female infanticide 3380
iii) Widow marriage, age of consent 3395
iv) Education 3403
v) Health 3418
vi) Prostitution and dancing girls 3422
vii) Female seclusion 3426
viii) Property rights 3427
ix) Christian conversion and missions 3428
x) Pandita Ramabai Sarasvati's work for women 3430
xi) Dhondo Keshav Karve's work for women 3451
xii) Behramji M. Malabari's and Karsondas Mulji's work for women 3463
(b) The colonial experience: autobiographies documenting social history 3465
(c) The colonial experience: mission and medical work by western women 3473
(d) General statements: ethnographic and other 3483
(e) The life cycle 3488
i) The natal home 3490
ii) Puberty rites, adolescence 3491
iii) Marriage: social structure and demography 3493
iv) Marriage ceremonies 3497
v) Marriage compatibilities and conflicts 3505
vi) Fertility patterns 3509
vii) Pregnancy, childbirth, gender preference 3516
viii) Widow marriage 3518
(f) Domestic sphere and family life 3519
i) Family roles and relationships 3525
ii) Family in folk literature, domestic rites 3531
(g) The spiritual life and religious observances 3535
(h) Employment
i) Employment patterns 3542
ii) Particular occupations 3545
(i) Education 3549
i) Attitudes of educated women 3550
ii) SNDT Women's University 3552
(j) Development and social welfare
i) SEWA of Ahmedabad and other organizations 3559
ii) Poverty 3562
iii) Prostitution and crime 3564
iv) Family planning 3567
(k) Political participation
i) Organizing rural women 3577
ii) Candidates and elections 3584
(l) Arts
i) Folk literatures 3587
ii) Popular magazines for women 3594
iii) Marathi literature 3595

iv) Gujarati literature 3600

(4) Lowland East India: area of Oriya, Assamese and western Bengali languages

(a) The colonial experience: social reform issues 3602
i) *Satī*/suttee 3614
ii) Female infanticide and human sacrifice 3622
iii) Widow marriage 3627
iv) Education 3630
v) Enfranchisement 3653
vi) Work 3654
vii) Contributions of various reformers 3656
viii) Contributions of Brahmo Samaj 3660
ix) Christian conversion 3663
(b) The colonial experience: ruling families of native/princely states 3665
(c) The colonial experience: freedom movement and World War II 3667
(d) The colonial experience: autobiography documenting social history 3671
(e) The colonial experience: western women in lowland East India 3672
i) Missionaries 3674
ii) Mary Frazer Campbell/Mrs. Monkland 3693
(f) General statements: ethnographic and other 3697
(g) The life cycle 3701
i) Puberty and menstruation 3703
ii) Marriage ceremonies 3713
iii) Fertility patterns 3714
iv) Pregnancy and childbirth 3723
v) Abortion 3726
vi) Rebirth account 3728
(h) Domestic sphere and family life 3730
i) Family relationships 3736
ii) Domestic rites/arts 3746
(i) Witchcraft 3757
(j) The spiritual life and religious observances
i) Spiritual leaders 3759
ii) *Devadāsīs* 3761
iii) Goddesses 3765
(k) Employment 3781
i) Problems and solutions 3782
ii) The jute industry 3788
(l) Sex ratio 3789
(m) Arts
i) Dance traditions 3790
ii) Folk literatures 3793
iii) Oriya literature: Nandini Satpathy 3800
iv) Bengali literature: female writers 3803
v) Bengali literature: male writers 3819
(n) Women's language: Bengali dialect 3844

(5) Bangladesh: Islamic area of eastern Bengali language

(a) General statements: ethnographic and other 3845
(b) The life cycle 3859
i) Fertility 3860
ii) Pregnancy, childbirth and motherhood 3867
iii) Widowhood 3873
(c) Domestic sphere and family life 3874
(d) Work: as employment and without remuneration 3882
i) Rural women 3884
ii) Urban women 3896
(e) Education 3900
(f) Development and social welfare, legal provisions 3906
i) Associations, programs, agencies 3914
ii) Development and welfare through the law 3924
iii) Family planning 3926
(g) Political participation 3945
(h) Arts
i) Folk literature 3947
ii) Reading interests 3951
(i) Experiences of 1971 Bangladesh war of liberation 3952

(6) North/Central India: area of Hindi-Urdu, Central Pahari and eastern Panjabi languages

(a) The colonial experience: social reform issues 3954

i) *Satī*/suttee 3956
ii) Female infanticide 3961
iii) Education and health 3976
iv) Village uplift 3984
(b) The colonial experience: autobiography documenting social history 3985
(c) The colonial experience: ruling families of native/princely states
i) Royal women of Oudh 3986
ii) Bhopal Begam-Nawabs 3988
iii) Rajputana princesses 3993
iv) Sikh princesses of the Punjab 3995
(d) The colonial experience: women and the Mutiny of 1857-58
i) The Rani of Jhansi 3999
ii) Accounts by and of westerners 4010
(e) The colonial experience: western women in other capacities
i) Missionaries 4032
ii) Relatives of civil servants 4054
(f) General statements
i) Ethnographic contexts 4057
ii) Collected papers 4069
iii) Patterns of social change 4071
iv) Case studies of Delhi and Bihari women 4076
v) Santal and Bhil tribal women 4078
(g) The life cycle 4080
i) Youth and adolescence 4088
ii) Marriage systems 4091
iii) Marriage rules and types 4096
iv) Marriage age and arrangements 4101
v) Marriage ceremonies 4104
vi) Dowry 4112
vii) Polyandrous and polygynous marriages 4114
viii) Fertility patterns 4120
ix) Pregnancy and childbirth 4133
x) Motherhood and child rearing 4151
xi) Barrenness 4156
xii) Widowhood, aging, menopause 4158
xiii) Rebirth account 4164
(h) Domestic sphere and family life 4165
i) Marriage networks, kin groups, prestations 4172
ii) Family relationships: social science perspectives 4179
iii) Family relationships: in folk literature 4192
iv) Continuity and change 4201
(i) Women's sexuality, seclusion, dangers
i) Ideals of chastity 4208
ii) Seclusion 4210
iii) Witchcraft 4224
iv) Women's response to social constraints 4227
(j) Ceremonial friendship 4232
(k) The spiritual life and religious observances 4233
i) Spiritual leaders 4236
ii) Goddesses 4239
iii) The Rādhā-Kṛṣṇa legend 4246
(l) Work and economic position
i) Jewelry and other resources 4248
ii) Participation in agriculture and other occupations 4251
iii) Attitudes, activities and conflicts of women at work 4259
(m) Education
i) Attitudes of educated women toward family life, *pardā* and other topics 4267
ii) Attitudes toward female education 4275
iii) Educational institutions and programs 4277
(n) Development and social welfare
i) Understanding sex ratio differentials 4281
ii) Programs and institutions for women 4283
iii) Khanna rural population study, 1953-60 and 1969, Ludhiana District, Punjab 4286
iv) Family planning knowledge, attitudes and practices 4287
v) Poverty 4309
vi) Prostitution 4310
vii) Crime and imprisonment 4315
viii) Health 4318
(o) Political participation 4320

(p) Arts
i) Folk literatures and oral traditions 4323
ii) Domestic folk arts of Mithila: printed sources 4340
iii) Domestic folk arts of Mithila: film sources 4349
iv) Rajasthani literature: work of Rani Laxmi Kumari Chundawat 4360
v) Hindi literature: images of women 4361
vi) Hindi literature: female writers 4365
vii) Hindi literature: male writers 4370
viii) Panjabi literature: work of Amrita Pritam 4385
ix) Panjabi literature: male writers 4399

b. Northwestern Islamic cultural region: area of western Panjabi, Sindhi, Baluchi, Pushto, Urdu and Kashmiri languages

(1) The colonial experience: western women in Northwest India
(a) Missionaries 4403
(b) Others 4414
(2) General statements
(a) Ethnographic contexts 4417
(b) Collected papers and a bibliography 4429
(3) The life cycle
(a) Marriage 4433
(b) Fertility 4438
(c) Pregnancy and childbirth 4440
(4) Domestic sphere and family life
(a) The family and social change 4442
(b) Legislation 4449
(5) Sexuality, honor/shame and seclusion 4452
(6) Work and economic position
(a) Property 4457
(b) Labor force participation 4458
(c) Job opportunities 4464
(d) Attitudes and problems of women at work 4466
(7) Education
(a) Overviews, problems, statistics 4474
(b) Attitudes and experiences of educated women 4479
(c) Physical education and sports 4483
(8) Development and social welfare 4486
(a) Associations, programs and agencies 4489
(b) Family planning 4495
(c) Various problems: the poor, the infirm, runaways 4505
(9) Political participation: Sindhi nationalist movement 4508
(10) Arts
(a) Painters 4509
(b) Reading interests 4510
(c) Sindhi literature: work of Popti Hiranandani 4511
(11) Clothing, adornment, beauty 4513

c. Nepal/high Himalayan cultural region: area of Nepali and northern Tibeto-Burman languages

(1) General statements
(a) Ethnographic contexts 4515
(b) Collected papers and a photo essay 4520
(2) The life cycle
(a) ***Rodī***, Gurung youth association 4523
(b) Courtship and marriage 4524
(c) Fertility and motherhood 4528
(3) Domestic sphere and family life
(a) Overviews, marriage stability, family relationships 4530
(b) Property rights 4535
(4) Sexuality, witchcraft 4537
(5) The spiritual life and religious observances
(a) Ascetic communities 4539
(b) A women's festival: ***Tīja/Ṛṣi Pañcamī*** 4541
(c) ***Kumārī*** worship, ***devīkī*** tradition 4543
(d) Goddesses, Newar ***tāntrika*** tradition 4550
(6) Education 4552
(7) Development and social welfare 4553
(8) Political participation: Queens Ratna and Aishwarya 4562
(9) Arts: children's drawings of man, woman and self 4568
(10) Western women in the Himalayas 4570
(11) Mountaineering
(a) Mrs. Bullock Workman 4576

(b) Others 4583

d. Eastern highland tribal cultural region: area of eastern Tibeto-Burman and Mon-Khmer languages

(1) Ethnographic contexts 4588
(2) Fertility and reproduction 4596
(3) The political leader Rani Gaidinliu 4599
(4) Western women 4600

e. The diaspora: South Asian women abroad

(1) South Africa 4602
(2) The Caribbean 4605
(3) Britain 4610
(4) North America 4625
(5) The Middle East 4628
(6) New Zealand 4629

Bibliographic Entries

I. Perspectives on South Asian women unbounded by time and space

A. Key reference works

1. Selected South Asian reference tools

1 BHATIA, KANTA. Reference sources on South Asia. Philadelphia: South Asia Regional Studies, University of Pennsylvania, 1978. 77p.
Bibliography of 671 works based on the University of Pennsylvania South Asia reference collection. Organized by topic. Detailed index.

2 GIDWANI, N.N. and K. NAVALANI, comps. and eds. A guide to reference materials on India. Jaipur: Saraswati Publications, 1974. 2v.
Over 50,000 sources. Attempts to include "all the reference material issued anywhere in the world, in any language and at any time since the invention of printing." Detailed subject organization and index, brief annotations. Includes selected works on other South Asian countries.

3 NUNN, G. RAYMOND. South and Southeast Asia: a bibliography of bibliographies. Honolulu: East-West Center Library, East-West Center, University of Hawaii, 1966. 59p. (*Its* Occasional Paper 4).
Lists 186 bibliographies of published material relating to Asia as a whole and South Asia.

4 PATTERSON, MAUREEN L.P. South Asian civilizations: a synthesis of selected resources. Chicago: University of Chicago Press, forthcoming.
Compilation of over 10,000 of the most basic and authoritative sources in the social sciences and humanities for the study of historical and contemporary South Asia. Entries are arranged according to a structure of temporal, spatial and topical dimensions and presented with informative headings.

5 PEARSON, J.D., ed. South Asian bibliography: a handbook and guide. Hassocks, Sussex: Harvester Press, 1979. 381p. [*Also* Atlantic Highlands, New Jersey: Humanities Press].
Series of contributions prepared and revised under the auspices of the South Asia Library Group. Focuses on access to published and unpublished materials on South Asia (excluding Nepal) in South Asia, Europe and North America. Types of materials considered include manuscripts, archives, theses, newspapers, periodicals, maps, official publications and bibliographies. Although material on women is not highlighted explicitly, certain of the source materials discussed are undoubtedly quite relevant to the topic.

6 SCHWARTZBERG, JOSEPH E., ed. A historical atlas of South Asia. Chicago: University of Chicago Press, 1978. 352p., 149 plates. (Association for Asian Studies Reference Series, 2).
Attempts to "provide a comprehensive cartographic record of the history of South Asia from the Old Stone Age to the present day. . . . History we take . . . to include not merely the recounting, analysis and interpretation of political events, but also the consideration of cultural, social, demographic, and economic developments." Over 650 detailed maps and accompanying texts, charts, tables, photographs, bibliography and index.

7 SPATE, O.H.K. and A.T.A. LEARMONTH. India and Pakistan: land, people and economy, 3d ed. London: University Paperbacks, Methuen and Company, Ltd., 1972. 439p. [*1st ed.* 1954].
A geography, broadly defined. This volume has three main sections — "The Land," "The People" and "The Economy" — and covers what are now India, Pakistan and Bangladesh.

8 ________ and B.H. FARMER. India, Pakistan and Ceylon: the regions, 3d ed. London: University Paperbacks, Methuen and Company, Ltd., 1972. pp.407-862. [*1st ed.* 1954].
This second volume divides the South Asian subcontinent (including present-day Bangladesh, India, Nepal, Pakistan and Sri Lanka) into 37 regions and numerous subregions. Details of physical features, climate, economy, settlement, cultural patterns, etc., are discussed for each.

9 TINKER, HUGH. South Asia: a short history. London: Pall Mall Press, 1966. 287p.

Book jacket calls this the first history of South Asia as a whole. Women are inconspicuous; the book is included here because its subcontinental focus is akin to the spirit of the present work.

10 WAGLE, IQBAL, comp. Reference aids to South Asia. Toronto: University of Toronto Library, 1977. 133p. (*Its* Reference Series, 22).
Annotated bibliography of 439 items based on University of Toronto holdings. Material is organized by topic and country.

11 ZBAVITEL, DUŠAN, ed. Dictionary of oriental literatures, v2: South and South-east Asia. New York: Basic Books, Inc., 1974. 191p.
Concise articles by eminent scholars describe the life and work of particular writers, literary terms, schools, movements, genres, etc. Articles discuss aesthetic and historical merits and points of scholarly debate and include dates, references to published works and standardized transliterations of South Asian words. From Vedas to present, "sacred" and "secular."

2. Bibliographies of South Asian women

12 DASGUPTA, KALPANA, ed. Women on the Indian scene: an annotated bibliography. New Delhi: Abhinav Publications, 1976. 391p.
References for 822 books, articles and reports, with annotations. Prefaced by essay, "Research on Status of Women in India: a Trend Survey." Appendixes list 1) relevant theses and dissertations and 2) major pieces of legislation, in chronological order.

13 JACOBS, SUE-ELLEN. Afghanistan, Bangladesh, Pakistan. *And* Ceylon, India, Nepal. *In her* Women in perspective: a guide for cross-cultural studies. Urbana, Illinois: University of Illinois Press, 1974. pp.39-48.
Lists of references, most regarding contemporary topics.

14 LAKHANPAL, SARV KRISHNA. Indian women: a bibliography. Saskatoon: University of Saskatchewan, 1967. 14p. (Bibliography Publication 2).
[Unexamined. NUC].

15 LYTLE, ELIZABETH. Women in India: a comprehensive bibliography. Monticello, Illinois: Vance Bibliographies, 1978. 29p. (*Its* Public Administration Series, P-109).
Bibliography of 386 references without annotations, organized according to 23 categories. Contains many of the standard monographs and many very brief articles which have not been included in the present work. The majority of the entries refer to events and personalities of the 19th and 20th centuries.

16 NIGHAT, AYUB, researcher and annotator, and ABAN MARKER, ed. Women in Pakistan and other Islamic countries: a selected bibliography with annotations. Karachi and Islamabad: Najma Sadeque for the Women's Resource Centre/Shirkat Gah, 1978. 203p.
Section on Pakistan contains 478 concisely annotated entries. A large portion of these are for unpublished papers, reports and theses with indications of where they are available. Remaining 422 entries are unannotated and grouped according to various other Islamic countries and a "Women and Islam" category.

17 SHREEMATI NATHIBAI DAMODAR THACKERSEY WOMEN'S UNIVERSITY. RESEARCH UNIT ON WOMEN'S STUDIES. A select bibliography on women in India. Bombay: Allied Publishers, 1975? 131p.
Bibliography of about 1,000 books, articles (many very short), theses and reports based upon the holdings of the principal libraries of western India.

18 YOUNG, KATHERINE K. and ARVIND SHARMA. Images of the feminine — mythic, philosophic and human — in the Buddhist, Hindu and Islamic traditions: a bibliography of women in India. Chico, California: New Horizons Press, 1974. 36p.
Several hundred books, articles and unpublished papers relating to the religious traditions of India, broadly interpreted. A few sources in Indian languages. A to Z listing with no index.

B. Collected biographies: admirable and heroic women

19 BHATTACHARYYA, PANCHANAN. Ideals of Indian womanhood. Calcutta: Goldquin and Company, 1921. 365p.
Biographical sketches of 20 renowned and idealized women in India's history. Each represents a particular virtue, e.g., fidelity, renunciation, honor, love of country.

20 DUTT, MANMATHA NATH, ed. Heroines of India, 2d ed. Calcutta: H.C. Dass, 1897. 40, 183p.
Women of India's history. [Unexamined. BMG].

21 HEMACHANDRA, NARAYANA, comp. Noble deeds of women and girls. Ahmedabad: "Gujarat Gazette" Press, 1895. 116p.
[Unexamined. BMG].

22 KINCAID, CHARLES AUGUSTUS. Heroines of India. Bombay, 1941. 139p.
[Unexamined. IOL].

23 MADHAVANANDA, SWAMI and RAMESH CHANDRA MAJUMDAR, eds. Great women of India. Mayavati, Almora: Advaita Ashrama,

1953. 551p.
Most articles are collections of biographical sketches of women of a particular region, religion, time period or literary genre. Also includes several general survey papers and a lengthy article on the Holy Mother, Sri Sarada Devi (the volume commemorates her birth centenary). Illustrated. For contents see entries 24, 29, 46, 53, 100, 139, 295, 375, 415, 456, 479, 481, 491, 500, 538-9, 541-2, 545-6, 1289, 1680, 2069 and 2121.

23a MALLESON, G.B. Famous women of India. *In* Asiatic Quarterly Review 3,5 (1887) 57-76.
Biographical sketches of three women whom the author considers to be "illustrative of the real women of India" — the 18th century Hoḷakar ruler Ahalyābāī, the early 19th century Hoḷakar ruler Tulasībāī and Sikandar Begam who ruled Bhopal in the mid-19th century.

24 NILAKANTA SASTRI, K.A. et al. Great women in South India (c. 400 B.C. to 1300 A.D.). *In* Swami Madhavananda and Ramesh Chandra Majumdar, eds. Great women of India. Mayavati, Almora: Advaita Ashrama, 1953. pp.298-319.
Biographical details of various saints and mystics, pious devotees, poets and queens.

25 PEACE, M.L. Our Hindu and Sikh heroines. Jullundur: Rattan Kaur, n.d. 126p.
Biographical sketches of 23 prominent women.

26 POOL, JOHN J. Famous women of India, 2d abr. and rev. ed. Calcutta: S. Gupta, 1954. 150p. [*1st ed.* Woman's influence in the East: as shown in the noble lives of past queens and princesses of India. London: Elliot Stock, 1892. 283p.].

Biographical sketches of 16 ideal and heroic women of ruling families, from Sītā to Tārābāī.

27 SALETORE, R.N. Unread leaves of Indian history, I: women in arms. *In* Illustrated Weekly of India 91, 12 (29 Mar 1970) 26-7.
Briefly mentions some female warriors from the Mauryan court to the mutiny of 1857-58.

28 SIMHARAY, DIANA. Warring women of India: lives of Rani of Jhansi; Zeb-un-Nisa, daughter of Aurangzeb; Tarabai; Bahinabai; and Mira. Bombay: Colour Publications, 1973. 136p.
[Unexamined].

29 SIRCAR, D.C. Great women in North India (c. 400 B.C. to 1200 A.D.). *In* Swami Madhavananda and Ramesh Chandra Majumdar, eds. Great women of India. Mayavati, Almora: Advaita Ashrama, 1953. pp.285-97.
Biographical details of queens, poets and scholars.

30 Some illustrious women of India: with special reference to Tamilnadu. Madras: Asian Book Company, 1975.
Published under auspices of International Women's Year Celebration Committee, Tamil Nadu. [Unexamined].

31 SWAMIVADIVU. Great women of India. Madras: Arunodayam, 1969. 94p.
[Unexamined. IBP].

32 VERMA, HARI NARAIN and AMRIT VERMA. Indian women through the ages. New Delhi: Great Indian Publishers, 1976. 203p.
Briefly identifies several thousand eminent women.

C. Interpretations of "The Position of Women"

For temporally circumscribed "status" statements see entries 370-88, 402-7, 550-64, 706-11, 715-18, 800-88 and 1661-1811

1. General statements from a variety of perspectives

33 ANAND, MULK RAJ. The bride: an essay on the status of woman in India. *In his* Lines written to an Indian air: essays. Bombay: Nalanda Publications, 1949.
A noted 20th century author writes of Indian women, past and present. [Unexamined. Book in NUC].

34 BANERJI, O.N. Ideals of Indian womanhood in Sanskrit kāvya-sahitya. *In* Poona Orientalist 26, 3/4 (1961) 105-15.
Image of women in Kālidāsa's work is shown to be much like that in both earlier epics and the work of Rabindranath Tagore in the present era. All have a similar concern with ideals. The "craze for 'Realism' which is against the very spirit of Indian soil, has never been indulged in as is being done today under the sophisticated influence of Western civilization."

35 BAZAZ, PREM NATH. Daughters of the Vitasta: a history of Kashmiri women. New Delhi: Pamposh, 1959. 279p.
Introductory survey chapter argues that Kashmiri women have enjoyed greater social and political freedoms than many women elsewhere in South Asia. The main body of the book consists of numerous biographical sketches of Kashmiri queens, women accomplished in poetry and other arts, military leaders and others, based primarily on the *Rājataraṅgiṇī* (12th century) and other historical documents. Con-

cluding chapters discuss the position of Kashmiri women in recent centuries.

36 BESANT, ANNIE. Womanhood. *In her* Ancient ideals in modern life: being the four Convention Lectures delivered at the twenty-fifth anniversary of the Theosophical Society, at Benares, December, 1900, 2d ed. Adyar: Theosophical Publishing House, 1925. pp.98-131. [*1st ed.* 1901].
Argues that women in ancient India were accorded a favorable position that was "natural" and "wise;" in contemporary India their lives are undeveloped and restricted and they are treated in an "artificial" and "foolish" way.

37 DERRETT, J. DUNCAN M. The legal status of women in India from the most ancient times to the present day. *In* Recueils de la Société Jean Bodin pour l'Histoire Comparative des Institutions II (1959) 237-67.
Considers the history of women's rights in the areas of marriage and divorce law, inheritance and property rights, criminal law and criminal and civil procedure. Begins with a statement on the foreignness of the notion of equality between the sexes in India: "They are unequal because they are dissimilar, and girls' inequality may in fact be a sign of their superiority: in other words females may be given special treatment not because they are despised, but because they are peculiarly honoured and protected."

38 ________. Religion, law and the state in India. London: Faber and Faber, 1968. 615p. [*Also* New York: Free Press].
Traces interplay of religion, primarily of Hindus and Muslims, and the state with respect to law from ancient times to the present. Includes references to many articles and contemporary cases involving women.

39 INDRADEVA, SHRIRAMA. Woman in folk and elite traditions: a comparative study. *In* Folklore [Calcutta] 10,3 (1969) 101-8. [*Reprint in* Sankar Sen Gupta, ed. Women in Indian folklore. Calcutta: Indian Publications, 1969. pp.286-94. (*Its* Folklore Series, 15)].
Concludes that "though the basic ideal for woman is the same in the elite and the folk traditions, the folk woman appears to be more vigorous in her protests against injustice."

40 JACOBSON, DORANNE and SUSAN S. WADLEY. Women in India: two perspectives. Columbia, Missouri: South Asia Books, 1977. 144p.
Contains Jacobson's introduction reviewing recent studies of women in general and Indian women in particular, her paper "The Women of North and Central India: Goddesses and Wives" (entry 4059), and Wadley's unabridged paper "Women and the Hindu Tradition" (entry 89a).

41 JACOLLIOT, LOUIS. La femme dans l'Inde: la femme au temps Védiques, aux temps Brahmaniques et dans l'Inde de la décadence [Woman in India: woman in Vedic times, in Brahmanic times and in decaying India]. Paris: A. Lacroix, 1877. 348p.
Argues against idea that the emancipation of women in India has only been brought about by Christian influence by showing that women in ancient India were respected, enjoyed much freedom, functioned in a variety of roles and so forth. The assorted materials in this book include translations of numerous Vedic hymns about women, a chapter on ***devadāsīs*** and a critique of contemporary "decay."

42 MARRIOTT, MC KIM and RONALD B. INDEN. Caste systems. *In* Encyclopaedia Britannica, macropaedia, v3, 15th ed. Chicago: Helen Hemingway Benton, 1977. pp.982-91.
Attempts to understand caste phenomena in South Asia in terms of cognitive assumptions of South Asians themselves. With some brief comments on women as a ***jāti***, "genus" (i.e., the ***strījāti***), as opposed to the "male genus" and much that implicitly relates to this concept.

43 NANDY, ASHIS. Woman versus womanliness in India: an essay in social and political psychology. *In* Psychoanalytic Review 63,2 (1976) 301-15. [*Also in* B.R. Nanda, ed. Indian women: from purdah to modernity. New Delhi: Vikas Publishing House, 1976. pp.146-60].
Attempts to "identify the structure of defences, individual as well as cultural, which has given meaning to the role of woman in Indian society and which has been challenged in recent times by new waves of social consciousness." Considers feminine cosmological principles, mother-son relationships, the feminine in men, the particularly strong force of womanliness in Bengali identity and 19th and 20th century reform movements as a major challenge to traditional concepts of womanhood.

44 SEN GUPTA, SANKAR. A study of women of Bengal. Calcutta: Indian Publications, 1970. 349, 62p. (*Its* Monograph Series, 12).
Included are chapters on the general South Asian and Bengali backgrounds, the status of "Women from Vedic to Modern Period," women in early and oral literature, marriage and matrimonial advertisements, working women and political participation. The study cites many examples from folklore, with Bengali original included. Appendixes on women in nursery rhymes and in folklore.

45 VINOBA [VINOBA BHAVE]. The women of India. *In* Sarvodaya 20,7 (1971) 294-9.
Various thoughts on the attitudes of Śrī Kṛṣṇa, Mahāvīra, Buddha and Gandhi toward women. From a 1958 address to Kasturba workers.

2. Historical perspectives

a. Demarcating and characterizing historical periods

46 ALTEKAR, ANANT SADASHIV. Ideal and position of Indian women in social life. *In* Swami Madhavananda and Ramesh Chandra Majumdar, eds. Great women of India. Mayavati, Almora: Advaita Ashrama, 1953. pp.26-48.
Historical survey. Delineates early Vedic period, ***brāhmaṇa-upaniṣad*** age (ca. 1000 to ca. 500 B.C.E.) and ***smṛti-purāna*** period (ca. 500 B.C.E. to ca. 1800 C.E.). Picture of general decline.

47 ANAND, MULK RAJ. The Indian woman through the ages. *In* Eve's Weekly 29, 18-19 (3-10 May 1975) 16-7ff.
Well-known writer reviews the vicissitudes of women's status in Indian history from the Vedas to the present.

48 AUBOYER, JEANNINE. La femme en Inde des origines au XIXe siècle [Woman in India from earliest times to the 19th century]. *In* Histoire mondiale de la femme, v3. Paris: Nouvelle Librairie de France, 1967. pp.215-336.
Discusses diverse aspects of lives of women during two historical periods: the Vedic era to the Muslim conquest and the middle age to the 19th century.

49 CHAUDHURI, ROMA. The position of women in medieval India. *In* Modern Review 93,6 (1953) 457-60.
Offers a threefold scheme of periodization: 1) Vedic "golden age of women's all-around progress and emancipation;" 2) ***smṛti*** age of limited freedom for women, beginning with Manu and going through the 18th century; and 3) "the upward trend in women's progress and emancipation" initiated by Rammohun Roy. Presents evidence from Sanskrit literature showing an upper class unaffected by ***smṛti*** laws.

50 FAROOQI, VIMLA. Position of women in different stages of society. *In* Vimla Farooqi and Renu Chakravartty. Communism and women. New Delhi: Communist Party of India, 1973. pp.1-26. (Communism Today, 5).
Socialist interpretation of women in history with some attention to the particularities of South Asia. "Women must participate actively in the struggle for the national-democratic revolution which will raise their social and economic status and enable them to participate more effectively in the production of national wealth which will be distributed on the basis of just principles."

51 GUPTA, S.L. Status of women in India. *In* India Cultures Quarterly 26,3 (1970) 90-5.
Sketch of the changes in women's status from the "pedestal of glory" and reverence in the Vedic age to the decline and confinement instituted by foreign invaders to the new political reforms that, however, should not obliterate the "ancient ideal of womanhood." With Sanskrit quotations, some translated.

52 LAJPAT RAI. The woman in India: a historical review. *In* Modern Review 27,5 (1920) 523-30.
Periodization of ancient history: the Vedic period (up to 1500 B.C.E.) in which women were so esteemed that the relative position of man and woman was not even an explicit issue; the epic period (1500 to 500 B.C.E.), perhaps the "high watermark" in the status of Indian womanhood; and the ***sūtra*** period (beginning at about 500 B.C.E.) in which "there was a strange conflict of opinion between jurists and lawyers about the rights and position of women."

53 MAJUMDAR, RAMESH CHANDRA. Ideal and position of Indian women in domestic life. *In* Swami Madhavananda and Ramesh Chandra Majumdar, eds. Great women of India. Mayavati, Almora: Advaita Ashrama, 1953. pp.1-25.
Status of women in ancient India. Focuses on favorable position portrayed in ***Ṛgveda*** and decline in the ***smṛti*** period.

54 MOOKERJI, RADHA KUMUD. Women in ancient India. *In* Tara Ali Baig, ed. Women of India. Delhi: Publications Division, Ministry of Information and Broadcasting, Government of India, 1958. pp.1-8.
Emphasizes the high status accorded to women in Vedic texts and in early Buddhist religious orders. Urges that "these forgotten ideals of ancient Indian womanhood" be recaptured. Photographs of art works.

55 RAI, KUMARI S. Women in medieval India. *In* Indo-Asian Culture 19,2 (1970) 33-5.
Brief periodization statement: women in ancient India "enjoyed a high social status and economic freedom;" medieval invasions "led to their intellectual and social deterioration;" during British rule "along with the whole nation, women too were awakened."

56 SATTHIANADHAN, KAMALA. The position of woman in ancient and modern India. *In* C. Yajneswara Chintamani, ed. Indian social reform: being a collection of essays, addresses, speeches, etc., with an appendix. Madras: printed at the Minerva Press, 1901. First part, pp.335-61.
The author, editor of the ***Indian Ladies' Magazine***, takes the position that women enjoyed a high and ideal status in Vedic and epic times. By 1000 C.E. the "pride of Brahmanism" resulted in their complete subordination to men. The Muslim conquest "completed the degradation." She investigates the ideas that men and women are complementary and that they are equivalent. To reach "the possibilities of womankind" Indian women are urged to gain in-

dependence and education, leave seclusion, marry later and remarry when widowed.

57 SENGUPTA, PADMINI. The story of women of India. New Delhi: Indian Book Company, 1974. 273p.
Broad historical panorama with major sections on ancient, medieval, British and independent Indias.

58 SHARMA, I.D. Western ideas and the awakening of Indian women. *In* East and West n.s. 13,1 (1962) 41-8.
Argues that women generally had a low position in the "ancient period" of history, which further deteriorated in the "Muslim period." Western education and ideas, through the media of missionaries, the government, internal reform movements and so forth, are helping to remove "the age old evils and handicaps."

59 THOMAS, PAUL. Indian women through the ages: a historical survey of the position of the women and the institutions of marriage and family in India from remote antiquity to the present day. Bombay: Asia Publishing House, 1970. 392p.
[Unexamined. IBP].

60 Women of India. Produced by Mohan Wadhwani. Directed by Ramesh Gupta. 1964. 17 min. Black and white. 16 and 35 mm. [*Distributed by* Films Division, Ministry of Information and Broadcasting, 24 G. Deshmukh Marg, Bombay 400 026].
Film about the history of Indian womanhood. Portrays their honored position in ancient times. Medieval decline and restoration via modern reform movements. [Unexamined. CF].

b. Women through the expanse of the "ancient" period

61 BADER, CLARISSE. Women in ancient India: moral and literary studies, [2d ed.]. Tr. from French by Mary E.R. Martin. Varanasi: Chowkhamba Sanskrit Series Office, 1964. 338p. (Chowkhamba Sanskrit Studies, 44). [*Reprint of* 1925 English ed. *1st ed.* La femme de l'Inde antique. Paris: Asiatic Society, 1867].
Based on wide variety of Sanskrit sources, from Vedas to epics. Primarily a collection of legends.

62 BHARADWAJ, S.K. 'Woman' in Veda and Aryan Scriptures. *In* S.A.J. Zaidi, ed. Malik Ram felicitation volume. New Delhi: Malik Ram Felicitation Committee, 1972. pp.135-54.
Selections from variety of Sanskrit texts showing that the ancient scriptures present woman in "glorious colours." Author believes both women and men have today fallen from their previous positions of having recognized great potentialities.

63 INDRA, V.V. The status of women in ancient India. Lahore, 1940. 324p.
[Unexamined. IOL].

64 INDRADEVA, SHRIRAMA. The status of woman in ancient India: compulsives of the patriarchal order. *In* Diogenes 93 (1976) 67-80.
Argues that womanhood was stigmatized from an early period in South Asia. Many Aryan invaders married indigenous women who, by virtue of their foreignness and the greater freedom for women in their society, were threatening. Heterodox threats, particularly Buddhism, encouraged further rigidity. Points out misogynous aspects of Vedic literature (most interpreters view this as a Golden Age) and the continuation of this attitude in the early *smṛti* literature.

65 MAJUMDAR, R.C. Position of women in ancient India. *In* Bulletin of the Ramakrishna Mission Institute of Culture 5,12 (1954?).
[Unexamined].

66 PINKHAM, MILDRETH WORTH. Woman in the sacred scriptures of Hinduism. New York: Columbia University Press, 1941. 239p.
Nine chapters on images of women in various Sanskrit texts and genres. Concludes: "Hindu women, then, should realize that antiquity reveals both greatness and limitations."

67 ROW, KSAMABAI. The cultural and social status of Indian women in Vedic and mediaeval times. *In* Aryan Path 16,5 (1945).
Argues that Aryan women in South Asia enjoyed greatest freedom in Vedic times. [Unexamined].

68 SARKAR, SUBIMAL CHANDRA. Some aspects of the earliest social history of India (pre-Buddhistic ages). London: H. Milford, Oxford University Press, 1928. 225p.
Study based on Vedic and Brahmanic literatures, the epics and the *purāṇas*.

69 SASTRI, SHAKUNTALA RAO. Women in the Vedic age, 4th ed. Bombay: Bharatiya Vidya Bhavan, 1969. 187p.
Chapters on *Ṛgveda, Atharvaveda,* Avestan scriptures, *brāhmaṇas, upaniṣads, Mantrabrāhmaṇa, śrautasūtras* and *gṛhyasūtras.*

70 SUBRAMANIA SASTRI, N. Women in ancient India as reflected in Sanskrit texts. *In* Sri Venkateswara University Oriental Journal 4,1/2 (1961) 55-74.
Discusses many topics. Based on Vedas, epics, *Mānava Dharmaśāstra* and other sources.

71 WINTERNITZ, MORITZ. Die Frau in den indien Religionen, I. Teil: die Frau im Brahmanismus [Woman in Indian religions, part I: woman in Brahmanism]. Leipzig, 1920.
[Unexamined].

3. Collected papers

72 Indian womanhood through the ages. Vivekananda Kendra Patrika 4,2 (1975) 378p.
Eighty-seven brief articles on wide range of topics relating to historical and contemporary women. Most are extracted and reprinted from other sources.

73 JAIN, DEVAKI, ed. Indian women. New Delhi: Publications Division, Ministry of Information and Broadcasting, Government of India, 1975. 312p.
Numerous brief articles by a distinguished group of authors. Wide variety of topics. For contents, see entries 89, 95, 335, 1234, 1248, 1645, 1656, 1776, 1803, 1816, 1985, 2140, 2444, 2542, 2552a, 3198, 3301, 3320, 3563, 4077, 4228 and 4269.

73a Part I: Indian women — yesterday, today and in 2000 A.D. *In* B.K. Vashishta, ed. Encyclopaedia of women in India, 1976. New Delhi: Praveen Encyclopaedia Publications, 1976. First part, pp.1-224.
Twenty articles on various topics including rural women, legal rights, dowry, family and marriage, development, art, statistics, work, International Women's Year and the future. Several general survey papers.

4. Major religious traditions of South Asia

74 CARMODY, DENISE LARDNER. The religions of India. *And* Islam. *In her* Women & world religions. Nashville: Abingdon, 1979. pp.39-65, 137-55.
First selection traces Hindu and Indian Buddhist images of and influences upon women through the centuries. Second selection examines images of women in Islamic thought without special reference to South Asia.

75 GOVINDA, LAMA. Position of women in Hinduism and Buddhism. *In* J. of the Maha Bodhi Society 58 (1950).
[Unexamined].

76 GUPTE, B.A., comp. Notes on the position of women among Hindus, Muslims, Buddhists, and Jains. Calcutta: Superintendent Government Printing, 1910. 30p.
Compiled for the Ethnographic Survey of India. [Unexamined. NUC].

77 KIDWAI, M.H. Woman under different social and religious laws: Buddhism, Judaism, Christianity, Islam. Delhi: Seema Publications, 1976. 167p.
Brief treatments of Buddhism and Judaism, longer treatment of Christianity, detailed treatment of Islam, by topic. "Of the four great religions which still have sway over by far the major portion of the world . . . it is only [Islam] which was the final religion, that acceded right, dignity and equality for women." Examples from British India. Edition cited is a reprint of an edition published in London as the second volume in the Central Islamic Society Series.

78 NANAVUTTY, PILOO. The influence of religion. *In* Tara Ali Baig, ed. Women of India. Delhi: Publications Division, Ministry of Information and Broadcasting, Government of India, 1958. pp.131-52.
Brief survey of women's place within the major religions of South Asia. Considers Hindu woman as Śakti and "custodian of religion," rural *kathā* recitation, goddesses, *bhakti* movement and Mīrābāī, Islamic *ṣūfī* tradition and, briefly, other religious traditions of India. Photographs.

79 TRIBHUWAN, JYOTSNA. Law relating to women in India. Ahmednagar: the author, 1965. 112p.
Considers Hindu, Muslim, Christian and Parsi religious and civil laws. Major sections on marriage and property law; smaller sections on immoral traffic, dowry and labor.

79a WHITE, E.M. Hinduism. *And* Buddhism. *And* Mohammedanism. *In her* Woman in world history: her place in the great religions. London: Herbert Jenkins Limited, 1924. pp.76-115, 116-32, 133-65.
Interpretation of the position of women in the various major religions based on 1) sayings and actions of founders, 2) sacred literature, 3) associated legends, poetry, customs and institutions and 4) social conditions of contemporary adherents.

a. Hindu tradition

(1) Various interpretations

80 ALTEKAR, A.S. The position of women in Hindu civilization: from prehistoric times to the present day, 2d ed. Delhi: Motilal Banarsidass, 1959. 380p. [*Also* Rev. ed. Mystic, Connecticut: Lawrence Verry, 1962. *1st ed.* Benaras: Benaras Hindu University, 1938].
Survey of the position of women in various times and contexts. Organized according to life cycle (childhood, marriage, married life, widowhood) and various topics (public life, religion, property rights, dress and adornment). Concludes with chapters that review the variety of attitudes toward women and the main historical periods pertaining to women in the Hindu tradition.

81 CHAUDHURY, ROMA. Some reflections on the ideals of Indian womanhood. *In* Cultural heritage of India, 2d ed., v2. Calcutta: Ramakrishna Mission Institute of Culture, 1962. pp.601-9.
Examines ways that ideals of the ***brahmavādinī***, or ascetic type, and the ***sadyovadhū***, or domestic type, have influenced the lives of Indian women. Considers women in Vedic literature, grammatical literature, epics, ***purāṇas***, other ***smṛti*** literature and the modern age.

82 FANE, HANNAH. The female element in Indian culture. *In* Asian Folklore Studies 34,1 (1975) 51-112.
Survey paper with sections on Indus valley goddesses; matriarchal matrix and patriarchal overlay; legal position; female elements in ***Śākta***, ***Śaiva*** and ***Vaiṣṇava*** traditions; village religion; and low-caste and tribal women. Author's thesis is that the essence of Indian culture is female-oriented but invaders have injected a patriarchal overlay.

83 GANGULY, D.C. Some aspects of the position of women in ancient India. *In* Cultural Heritage of India, v2. Calcutta: Ramakrishna Mission Institute of Culture, 1962. pp.594-600.
General survey based on Vedic to epic and ***dharmaśāstra*** literatures.

84 HEIMSATH, CHARLES H. Shakti: the female component of Indian culture. *And* Shakti 2: conflict of Aryan and non-Aryan cultures. *In* Illustrated Weekly of India 93,23-24 (4-11 Jun 1972) 26-9, 32-5ff.
Observations regarding the power of women and feminine cosmological principles in historical and contemporary South Asia and conflicts with alternate traditions. Drawn from various types of materials and observers. "The female power of India, never squelched under the ludicrous brahmanic attempts to Aryanise native mother-right customs, will be harnessed to restorative and innovative public tasks as women recognise themselves and are recognised by men as equals."

85 MATHUR, RAMESH. Women in Hindu society: status and image, parts one through four. *In* J. of Intercultural Studies 1-4 (1974-1977) 21-42, 42-50, 46-56, 55-64.
Part one traces the decline in status from time of Vedas to time of ***purāṇas*** and argues, citing the power and glory of mothers and chaste wives, that the ideals should not be taken as a sign of inferiority. Part two discusses the brother-sister relationship in historical and contemporary India. The third part examines sensual images of women in Indian literature. Part four considers ideals of feminine beauty and physical charm in literature and art.

86 MAZUMDAR, VINA. Comment on suttee. *In* Signs: J. of Women in Culture and Society 4,2 (1978) 269-73.
Author reflects upon an account of a 19th century ***satī*** in her own family and upon the various ideal figures held up to Hindu women. She argues that the concept of personal freedom in the Hindu tradition is only conceivable in limited circumstances such as worldly renunciation in old age. Finally, she points to the "staying power that women could draw from traditional values" to explain the strength and integrity so often found in Hindu women in spite of unkind treatment they may have received.

87 MUKHERJEE, PRABHATI. Hindu women: normative models. Calcutta: Orient Longman, 1978? 118p.
Considers Hindu ideal of womanhood, the chaste woman devoted to family and domestic duties. Considers social structural reasons for such an ideal and means by which the ideal is actualized in Hindu women. Cites various textual authorities to document argument. [Unexamined. ALI].

88 RAMA KRISHNA, T. The Hindu ideal of womanhood. *In* Asiatic Quarterly Review, 3d series, 23,46 (1907) 98-107.
Argues that Hindu ideal of womanhood is above all to respect, honor and obey the husband.

89 RUDRA, ASHOK. Cultural and religious influences. *In* Devaki Jain, ed. Indian women. New Delhi: Publications Division, Ministry of Information and Broadcasting, Government of India, 1975. pp.37-49.
Notes various misogynist and glorifying aspects of the conception of women in the Hindu tradition. The contemporary "emergence of the Indian woman, like lotus out of the mire, has to be treated as a gift of the goddesses."

89a WADLEY, SUSAN S. Women and the Hindu tradition. *In* Signs: J. of Women in Culture and Society 3,1 (1977) 113-25. [***Also in*** Doranne Jacobson and Susan S. Wadley. Women in India: two perspectives. Columbia, Missouri: South Asia Books, 1977. pp.113-39].
Women and the Hindu tradition from various perspectives. Discusses the feminine concepts of ***Śakti*** and ***Prakṛti***, prominent images of women (with examples drawn from myths), ideals held to women as wives and mothers, religious activities of women and potential for change in traditional conceptions.

(2) Legal Position

90 BANERJEE, GOOROODASS. The Hindu law of marriage and stridhana: being the Tagore Law Lectures for 1878. Calcutta: S.K. Lahiri, 1923. 550p.
Six lectures on marriage and six lectures on ***strīdhana***. Discusses various topics in terms

of traditional legal texts and contemporary court cases and legislation.

91 MITTER, DWARKA NATH. The position of women in Hindu law. Calcutta: University of Calcutta, 1913. 707p.
Reviews general position of women in Hindu law and position with respect to topics of marriage and the status of a wife, widows, inheritance and status of courtesans and dancing girls. Based on numerous authoritative texts and hundreds of contemporary court cases. Suggests that Jaimini's *Mīmāṃsā* aphorisms offer traditional legitimation for an improved legal position of Hindu women.

92 MITTRA, PEARY CHAND. A few desultory remarks on the "Cursory Review of the Institutions of Hindooism affecting the interest of the Female Sex," contained in the Rev. K.M. Banerjia's prize essay on native female education. *In* Goutam Chattopadhyay, ed. Awakening in Bengal in early nineteenth century: selected documents, v1. Calcutta: Progressive Publishers, 1965. pp.273-97.
Attempts to summarize the laws enjoined upon women in the *śāstras*. Author concludes that in England "they exhibit a partiality or even fairness toward the fairer sex" and the *śāstras*, written when they were, should not be judged harshly.

93 SASTRI, SHAKUNTALA RAO. Women in the sacred laws. Bombay: Bharatiya Vidya Bhavan, 1953. 193p. (Bhavan's Book University, 13).
[Unexamined. NUC].

(3) Ideal Hindu women

94 BOSE, KUNJABIHARI. The model Hindu ladies. Benares: B.K. Chakravarti, 1918. 159p.
Biographical sketches of 13 Hindu women who have served as ideals through the ages.

95 SREENIVASAN, M.A. Panchakanya, an age-old benediction. *In* Devaki Jain, ed. Indian woman. New Delhi: Publications Division, Ministry of Information and Broadcasting, Government of India, 1975. pp. 51-7.
Biographical details of "five maidens" invoked in a blessing for girls (Ahalyā, Sītā, Draupadī, Tārā, Maṇḍodarī). Briefly mentions a ritual context in which this blessing is bestowed.

95a SUNITI DEVI, MAHARANI OF COOCH BEHAR. Nine ideal Indian women. Calcutta: Thacker, Spink, 1919. 214p.
On ideal women from the Hindu tradition. Probably Sītā, Satī, Sāvitrī, etc. [Unexamined. NUC].

b. Buddhist tradition

96 PEIRIS, W. Women in Buddhism. *In* Ceylon Today 9 (Sep 1960) 6-9.
[Unexamined].

c. Jaina tradition

97 JAIN, KAMTA PRASAD. Marriage in Jaina literature. *In* Indian Historical Quarterly 4,1 (1928) 146-52.
Compares various aspects of marriage customs as recorded in Jaina *purānas* with contemporary Jaina practices.

98 KAPADIA, HIRALAL RASIKDAS. Women in Jainism. *In* All-India Oriental Conference 7, 1933, Baroda. Proceedings 7. pp.259-92.
[Unexamined].

99 MAHAPATRA, PIYUSHKANTI. Jaina women and their folk-life through ages. *In* Folklore [Calcutta] 10,1 (1969) 26-33. [*Reprint in* Sankar Sen Gupta, ed. Women in Indian folklore. Calcutta: Indian Publications, 1969. pp.33-40 (*Its* Folklore Series, 15)].
Briefly presents materials from texts, epigraphs and oral tradition to discuss women in Jaina religious orders, women of rank and the social and folklife of Jaina women.

100 SHAH, UMAKANT PREMANAND. Great women in Jainism. *In* Swami Madhavananda and Ramesh Chandra Majumdar, eds. Great women of India. Mayavati, Almora: Advaita Ashrama, 1953. pp.275-84.
Brief biographical details of many women, classed as 1) mothers and daughters, 2) chaste women and 3) nuns and lay devotees.

d. Parsi tradition

101 DASTOOR, ALOO J. Woman in Zoroastrianism. *In* J. of the Gujarat Research Society 37,3 (1975) 2-16.
Gives examples of high status of women in Persia in the Kayanian period (ca. 2000 to 700 B.C.E.), a decline in the Achaemenian period (558 to 330 B.C.E.) and renewal in the Sassanian age (226 to 651 C.E.). Reviews changes that followed migration to western India and surveys progressive position of Parsi women in recent times.

102 MODI, JIVANJI JAMSHEDJI. The Parsee purificatory ceremonies: purificatory processes in daily life. *In* J. of the Anthropological Society of Bombay 11, 4 (1918) 364-75.
Focuses on menstrual pollution and purification in Iranian texts and according to contemporary practice.

103 _______. The religious ceremonies and customs of the Parsees, 2d ed. Bombay: Jehangir B. Karani's Sons, 1937. 555p. [*1st ed.* 1922. *Reprint* New York: Garland Publishing Company, forthcoming].
Detailed presentation of Zoroastrian ceremonies as prescribed in ancient texts and as practiced by 20th century Parsis. Of particular relevance to women's lives are chapters on birth ceremonies, marriage ceremonies and certain purificatory ceremonies.

e. Islamic tradition

(1) Various interpretations

104 BAVEJA, MALIK RAM. Women in Islam. Tr. from Urdu by M. Abdul Ali. Hyderabad, India: Institute of Indo-Middle East Cultural Studies, 1964? 138p.
Exposition on the place of women in Islamic culture and law. Major topics treated are daughter, wife, mother, divorce, inheritance. "The Traditions can guide us only where the Quran is not explicit, or where an order is laid down in the Quran but is vague . . . . clearly, Traditions cannot supersede the Quran, nor can we give precedence to Traditions over the Quran."

105 HAQUE, MOZAMMEL. Status of women in Islam. *In his* Islam, socialism and women. Dacca: Society for Pakistan Studies, 1970. pp.22-33.
"Islam does not make any distinction between man and woman except in consideration of the nature of their constitution. They are equal intellectually, morally and spiritually and this equality has been proclaimed by the Holy Quran in chapter 33, verse 35."

106 ZAIDI, SYED M.H. Position of women under Islam. Calcutta: Book Tower, 1935. 154p.
Considers many topics as revealed in the *Qor'an*, other material from the time of the Prophet, material from 20th century India and other contexts. [Unexamined].

(2) Ideal Muslim women

107 ALI, AMEER. The influence of women in Islam. *In* Nineteenth Century 45,267 (1899) 755-74. [*Reprint in* Syed Razi Wasti, ed. Syed Ameer Ali on Islamic history and culture. Lahore: Peoples Publishing House, 1968. pp.50-73.
Biographical details of some of the many prominent Muslim women through the ages. Their position in British India is considered to be depressed. Asserts that the West offers a model of "civilized life," but that endeavors to improve the condition of Muslim women must come from within.

108 AZMAT, TAHERA. Women mentors of men. Ujjain: Siddhartha Prakashan, 1970. 139p.
Biographical sketches of ten women. Most belong to "medieval" Muslim ruling families, although some are Hindu and/or from 19th century. Does not, as title would imply, focus on these women as inspirations for their menfolk.

109 MASUD-UL-HASAN. Daughters of Islam: being short biographical sketches of 82 famous Muslim women. Lahore: Hazrat Data Ganj Baksh Academy, 1976? 171p.
This collection is arranged chronologically from the time of the Prophet to the present and includes about 20 sketches relevant to South Asia.

110 PAUL, S.K. Muslim ladies in India. *In* Indian History Congress 21, 1958, Trivandrum. Proceedings 21. Bombay: the Congress, 1959. pp.399-400.
Summary of the paper presented. Names various Muslim women who "cast tremendous influence in politics in India" from the 14th through 19th centuries.

f. Sikh tradition

111 DEBNATH, DHIRENDRA. Sikh women in religion and customs. *In* Folklore [Calcutta] 10,2 (1969) 55-62. [*Reprint in* Sankar Sen Gupta, ed. Women in Indian folklore. Calcutta: Indian Publications, 1969. pp.277-85. (*Its* Folklore Series, 15)).
Brief survey of women's position in the Sikh religion from its founding by Gurū Nānak (1469-1539) to the present.

112 GILL, PRITAM SINGH. Social status of women. *In his* Heritage of Sikh culture: society, morality, art. Jullundur: New Academic Publishing Company, 1975. pp.91-7.

Reviews Guru Nānak's teachings about women and the Sikh heritage for women, both of which are said to contrast favorably with the Hindu tradition. "With Guru Nanak's teachings the woman felt a sigh of relief . . . . In Sikhism woman is not considered to be a source of sin, vice or dishonour for man as assumed by Manu, Buddhism and Christianity."

113 SINGH, PURAN. The sisters of the spinning wheel and other Sikh poems. Tr. from Panjabi by the author. Patiala: Punjabi University, 1977. 144p. [*1st ed.* New York: J.M. Dent, 1921].
Translations of original poems and selections from the central Sikh corpus, the *Gurū Granth Sāhib*. Many feminine images, including the title piece.

114 SINGH, TEJA. What Sikhism did for womankind. Lahore: Sikh Tract Society, 1921. 16p. [*Also* Amritsar: Star Press].
[Unexamined. IOL].

D. Manifestations of the feminine in South Asian philosophy, theology and social structure

115 MANGAHAS, ANNA F. Eternal dryad of the Indian forest. *In* Asian Studies 9,2 (1971) 114-25.
On the Dravidian aspects of womanhood and the feminine in pre-Vedic and post-Vedic ancient India: ". . . our discussion will deal with woman as the universal Earth Goddess, woman of the matriarchate, woman as worshipped by the *Shaktas*, and woman's symbols, and woman at the time of male ascendancy and her eventual subjugation."

115a MUKHERJEE, GOVINDA GOPAL. Śākta literature. *In* Suniti Kumar Chatterji, ed. The cultural heritage of India, 2d ed., rev. and enl., v5: languages and literatures. Calcutta: Ramakrishna Mission Institute of Culture, 1978. pp.130-40.
Reviews *Śākta* images in Vedas, *upaniṣads*, epics, *purāṇas* and *upapurāṇas*, *kāvya* literature and *tantras* and *āgamas*.

116 Sakti or woman power. *In* Illustrated Weekly of India 96,41 (12 Oct 1975) 8-15.
Explores various concepts related to *Śakti* and goddesses in history of Hindu thought and relation of these to attitudes toward women. Photographs and illustrations.

116a SIRCAR, D.C., ed. The Śakti cult and Tārā. Calcutta: University of Calcutta, 1967. 189p. (*Its* Centre of Advanced Study in Ancient Indian History and Culture, Lectures and Seminars, II-B (Seminars)).
Proceedings of a seminar concerned with the origins and evolution of the *Śākta* cult and the iconography of the goddess Tārā. Eighteen papers, summary of proceedings and plates.

1. Philosophical perspectives

a. *Śākta* doctrines

117 BAKE, A.A. The appropriation of Śiva's attributes by Devī. *In* Bulletin of the School of Oriental and African Studies 17,3 (1955) 519-25.
Illustrates process of Devī's annexation of Śiva's attributes and prerogatives via field of music. Traces development from Bharata's *Nāṭyaśāstra* (dated variously from second century B.C.E. to fifth century C.E.) in which Śiva is without consort through *Saundaryalaharī* hymn of praise to the goddess (sixth to eighth centuries) in which melody is rediscovered with the emergence of the female principle and to later texts, which continue the predominance of the goddess.

118 CHAKRAVARTI, PRABHAT CHANDRA. Doctrine of Śakti in Indian literature. Calcutta: General Printers and Publishers, 1940? 123p.
Project to investigate in detail *Śākta* doctrine in Indian philosophical literature. Was interrupted by author's death. [Unexamined. NUC].

119 DAS, SUDHENDU KUMAR. Śakti or divine power: a historical study based on original Sanskrit texts. Calcutta: University of Calcutta, 1934. 298p.
Development of concept of *Śakti* in Vedic corpus, in the *Trikaśāsana Śaiva* philosophical tradition of Kashmir and in the South Indian *Vīraśaiva* tradition.

120 MOOKERJEE, AJIT. Tantra art: its philosophy and physics. New Delhi: Kumar Gallery, 1966. 152p.
A straightforward text accompanies 96 plates of art works dating from the 11th century to the present. With notes on plates and lengthy bibliography.

121 PAYNE, ERNEST A. The Śāktas: an introductory and comparative study. Calcutta: Y.M.C.A. Publishing House, 1933. 153p. (Religious Life of India).
Traces growth of *Śākta* thought from Vedas to *tantras*, describes non-Aryan and Aryan influences, traces development of *Śākta* tradition in Bengal and presents comparative material from other religious traditions.

122 SEN GUPTA, SUDHIR RANJAN. Mother cult Calcutta: Firma KLM, 1977. 112p.
Interpretive study of the *tāntrika Śākta* tradition by a student of Swami Purnananda. *Śāktas* call God 'Mother' "as the relation between the mother and her child is the closest

and most cordial [and as] the universe with all its diversity evolves in God just as a child with its organism evolves in the womb of the mother. The Mother is Omnipotent, Omniscient, All-pervading and Ever-effulgent." Sections on *tantra, mantra, yantra, devatā* and mother worship.

123 TUCCI, GIUSEPPE. Rati-līlā: an interpretation of the tantrik imagery of the temples of Nepal. Tr. from Italian by James Hogarth. Geneva: Nagel Publishers, 1969. 165p.
Wide ranging discussion of *tantra* tradition of Nepal. Considers iconography, cosmology, ritual and so forth. Photographs (230).

124 WOODROFFE, JOHN. The garland of letters: studies in the mantra-śāstra, 6th ed. Madras: Ganesh and Company, 1974. 318p.
Series of lectures and essays on various concepts as they relate to *Śākta* doctrine.

b. Cosmology

125 AGRAWALA, VASUDEVA SHARANA. Mother earth. *In* Néhru abhinandan granth: a birthday book presented to Jawaharlal Nehru, Prime Minister of India, on completion of his sixtieth year, November 14, 1949. Calcutta: Aryavarta Prakashan Griha, 1949? pp.490-6.
On the "divine conception of the Mother Land" in India. Various textual references are interpreted and much else is briefly related to this concept.

126 BHATTACHARYYA, NARENDRA NATH. Earth and woman: a study in the cults and rituals of fertility. *In his* Ancient Indian rituals and their social contents. Delhi: Manohar Book Service, 1975. pp.97-113.
Discussion of historical and contemporary symbolism associating the fertility of the earth with the fertility of women in India and throughout the Indo-European world.

127 EVOLA, JULIUS. The "mysteries of woman" in East and West. *In* East and West n.s. 9,4 (1958) 349-55.
Cross-cultural examination of female cosmological principles, including those of the Buddhist and Hindu *tantras*.

128 INDRADEVA, SHRIRAMA. Correspondence between woman and nature in Indian thought. *In* Philosophy East and West 16,3/4 (1966) 161-8.
"A metaphor persistently occurs in Indian thought. Woman is compared in innumerable ways to *prakṛti* (Nature), *māyā* (illusion), and earth. This correspondence. . . . seems to be one of the basic modes of perception and understanding with regard both to woman and to Nature." Gives examples of these related concepts and of feminine attributes from numerous textual genres.

129 SASTRI, T.V.G. General concepts of māyā and its applications. *In* J. of the Oriental Institute of Baroda 24, 3/4 (1975) 343-56.
Discusses development of the concept of *māyā* from Vedas to *purāṇas* and in sculpture. Considers its relation to feminine cosmological principles and symbolic representations.

130 SHASTRI, PRABHU DUTT. The doctrine of māyā in the philosophy of the Vedānta. London: Luzac, 1911. 138p.
[Unexamined].

2. Goddess traditions: the one and the many

131 BHATTACHARYYA, NARENDRA NATH. Indian Mother Goddess. *In* Indian Studies: Past and Present 11,4 and 12,1 (1970) 327-98, 65-124.
Wide-ranging essay. Major sections consider association of earth with women, sacred aspects of birth and fertility, various manifestations of the Goddess, "mother right," Aryan and pre-Aryan dimensions of the goddess tradition and the overall historical development of goddess worship in South Asia.

132 _______. The Indian mother goddess, 2d rev. and enl. ed. New Delhi: Manohar Book Service, 1977. 319p. [*1st ed.* 1970].
Indian Mother Goddess in comparative perspective with a focus on the social basis of religious ideas. An encyclopedia of sorts, this book includes sections on categories of goddesses (earth, city, war, disease, etc.), goddesses in literary records from Egypt to South Asia, goddesses in the archeological record of South Asia and goddesses in "advanced religious systems." Appendixes on regional distributions in South Asia, female-dominated societies and fertility and *tantra*.

133 GOPALAKRISHNAN, M.S. The cult of the Mother-Goddess. *In* L.K. Bala Ratnam, ed. Anthropology on the march: recent studies of Indian beliefs, attitudes and social institutions. Madras: Book Centre *and* Social Sciences Association, 1963. pp.334-43.
On the origin, development and contemporary expressions of Mother Goddess worship in South Asia.

134 JAMES, E.O. The cult of the Mother-Goddess. London: Thames and Hudson, 1959. 300p.
Comparative examination of Mother Goddess cults, forms, rites and beliefs from eastern Mediterranean to Asia. Uses archeological and other data from the paleolithic age through the Common Era. Several sections on goddess cults in South Asia (pp.31-6, 99-127, 242-5).

135 PRZYLUSKI, JEAN. The great goddess in India and Iran. *In* Indian Historical Quarterly 10,3 (1934) 405-30.
Asserts historical connection of geographically distant goddesses in South Asia and the Middle East. Linguistic, mythical and ritual evidence.

136 WOODROFFE, JOHN. Hymns to the Goddess. Madras: Ganesh and Company, 1973. 335p.
English translations of the *Karpūrādistrotra* to Kālī and Sanskrit texts selected from the *tantras, purāṇas, Mahābhārata* and writings of Śaṅkarācārya. With prefaces, introductions and substantial commentary. Reprinted from earlier works.

137 ZIMMER, HEINRICH. The Indian world mother. *In* Joseph Campbell, ed. The Mystic vision: papers from the Eranos Yearbooks, v6. Princeton, New Jersey: Princeton University Press, 1968. pp.70-102. (Bollingen Series, 30-6).
On the Goddess and her many forms throughout the Hindu tradition, including Jaina and Buddhist variants. Philosophy, psychology, iconography, etc.

a. Histories of goddess worship in South Asia

138 BHATTACHARYYA, NARENDRA NATH. History of the Śākta religion. New Delhi: Munshiram Manoharlal Publishers, 1974. 188p.
The "cult of the Female Principle," chronologically from pre-Vedic times to the present.

139 DAS GUPTA, SHASHI BHUSAN. Evolution of mother worship in India. *In* Swami Madhavananda and Ramesh Chandra Majumdar, eds. Great women of India. Mayavati, Almora: Advaita Ashrama, 1953. pp.49-86.
A survey, from the Vedas to the present.

140 DUDLEY, ROSEMARY J. She who bleeds, yet does not die. *In* Heresies: a Feminist Publication on Art and Politics 5 (Spr 1978) 112-6.
Interpretation of vicissitudes of Goddess worship and symbols of womanhood in South Asia from Indus Valley civilization to the present. Other articles in this special issue of feminist views of the Goddess refer briefly to South Asia in comparative perspective.

141 MOTI CHANDRA. Studies in the cult of the Mother Goddess in ancient India. *In* Bulletin of the Prince of Wales Museum of Western India 12,1/2 (1973) 1-47.
Reviews textual and iconographic characterizations of the Mother Goddess in her many forms from the chalcolithic epoch to the *purāṇas*. Discusses symbolism of various associated plants, animals and birds.

142 SRIVASTAVA, M.C.P. Mother Goddess in Indian art, archaeology and literature. Delhi: Agam Kala Prakashan, 1979. 231p.
Traces history of Mother Goddess worship in South Asia from prehistoric times through the *tantras*. Photographs and drawings.

b. The many forms: dictionaries and surveys

143 DURDIN-ROBERTSON, LAWRENCE. The goddesses of India and Tibet. *In his* The goddesses of India, Tibet, China and Japan. Clonegal, Ireland: Cesara, 1976. pp.1-221.
Dictionary of goddesses with such information as etymology of name, epithets, genealogy and locality. Many entries briefly cite comments of various scholars.

144 KRAMRISCH, STELLA. The Indian Great Goddess. *In* History of Religions 14,4 (1975) 235-65.
Iconographic and textual characterizations of Devī and her manifestations as Saraṇyū, Saramā, Sarasvatī, Vāc, Mother Earth (Padmā, Śrī, Lakṣmī, Kṣamā), Uṣas, Śivā (Satī, Umā, Pārvatī) and others.

145 KRISHNA SASTRI, H. South-Indian images of gods and goddesses. Madras: Government Press, 1916. 292p. [*Reprint* Delhi: Bhartiya Publishing House, 1974].
Considers iconography and, to a lesser extent, worship modes. Based mainly on Sanskrit sources. Latter chapters describe variety of South Indian goddesses. Numerous photographs and drawings.

146 SRIVASTAVA, BALRAM. Iconography of Śakti: a study based on Śrītattvanidhi. Varanasi: Chaukhambha Orientalia, 1978. 173p. (Chaukhambha Oriental Research Studies, 9).
Survey of *Śākta* iconography as detailed in various *purāṇas*, the *śilpa* and *āgama* texts and, particularly, the *śaktinidhi* section (reproduced as an appendix) of the *Śrītattvanidhi* of Krishnaraja Wodeyar III, Raja of Mysore. This 19th century text summarizes previous texts on Hindu iconography. Drawings and photographs.

147 STUTLEY, MARGARET and JAMES STUTLEY. Harper's dictionary of Hinduism: its mythology, folklore, philosophy, literature and history. New York: Harper and Row, Publishers, 1977. 372p.
Many entries succinctly identify various forms of the Goddess and provide bibliographic references. See also Devī, Śakti *māyā, prakṛti* and other entries.

c. The many forms: particular manifestations of the goddess

(1) The Great Goddesses

148 SIRCAR, D.C., ed. Foreigners in ancient India and Lakṣmī and Sarasvatī in art and literature. Calcutta: University of Calcutta, 1970. 192p. (*Its* Lectures and Seminars, Centre of Advanced Study in Ancient Indian History and Culture, 5-B (Seminars)).
Proceedings of a 1969 seminar at the University of Calcutta. [Unexamined. NUC].

(a) Sarasvatī

149 DAVANE, G.V. The goddess Sarasvatī in Sanskrit literature. *In* J. of the University of Bombay, Arts 37,73 (1968) 70-7.
Qualities, iconography and development of Sarasvatī from the *Ṛgveda* through the *purāṇas.*

150 GUPTA, ANAND SWARUP. Conception of Sarasvatī in the purāṇas. *In* Purāṇa 4,1 (1962) 55-95.
Historical development and images of goddess Sarasvatī in the *purāṇas*. Discusses accounts of her origin, etymologies of her name, iconography, synonyms and epithets and modes of worshiping her.

151 ________. Sarasvatī as the river-goddess in the purāṇas. *In* All-India Oriental Conference 22, Gauhati, Jan. 1965. Proceedings and transactions 22, v2. Gauhati: A.K. Borkakoty, 1966. pp.68-80.
Legends, qualities and rites associated with Sarasvatī as a river goddess in the *purāṇas.*

152 KHAN, MOHAMMAD ISRAIL. Sarasvatī in Sanskrit literature. Ghaziabad: Crescent Publishing House, 1978. 238p.
Development of Sarasvatī from the Vedas to the *purāṇas*: as a river, a river goddess, the goddess of speech and as an anthropomorphic figure. Appendixes compare her forms with those in Greek and Roman mythology and give important selections from Sanskrit texts (no translations). Plates (16).

153 YASODADEVI, V. Sarasvati through the ages. *In* J. of Indian History 41,3 (1963) 681-97.
Traces development and representations of Sarasvatī from Vedic literature to the 16th century. Considers Hindu, Buddhist and Jaina traditions.

(b) Durgā-Kālī

154 BEANE, WENDELL CHARLES. Myth, cult and symbols in Śākta Hinduism: a study of the Indian mother goddess. Leiden: Brill, 1977. 288p.
Study of Durgā-Kālī with respect to cosmology (*Kālī Śakti*), ritual (*Kālī pūjā*) and eschatology (*Kālī yuga*). These aspects are examined as "a potentially unified structure of thought and expression. . . .focusing upon this goddess as the prototypical image par excellence in the religious tradition of *Śākta* Hinduism."

155 CHOUDHURI, NARENDRA NATH. Mother goddess Durgā. *In* Poona Orientalist 15,1/4 (1950) 32-8.
Character of Durgā as revealed by selections from the Vedas, *purāṇas, tantras* and other Sanskrit texts.

156 KINSLEY, DAVID R. Freedom from death in the worship of Kālī. *In* Numen 22, 3 (1975) 183-207.
Traces the history of Kālī from her prototypes in Vedic literature to contemporary worship in Bengal. Attempts to reconcile her ferocity and maternal grace.

157 ________. The sword: Kālī, mistress and death. *And* The sword and the flute: conclusion. *In his* The sword and the flute: Kālī and Kṛṣṇa, dark visions of the terrible and sublime in Hindu mythology. Berkeley: University of California Press, 1975. pp.79-159.
The phenomenology and history of Kālī from Vedic prototypes to devotional worship in contemporary Bengal. Notes her relatively late arrival in the Hindu tradition, her peripheral position in the Hindu pantheon, her exceptional popularity in Bengal and the "softening" of her qualities, which occurred with her *tāntrika* and Bengali popularity. Considers her as embodying for the worshipper such central Hindu themes as *mahāmāyā*, *prakṛti*, *duḥkha*, time and death; yet in the end "she grants her boon of freedom and reveals herself as Mother."

158 RAYCHAUDHURI, ARUN KUMAR. A psychoanalytic study of the Hindu mother goddess (Kali) concept. *In* American Imago 13,2 (1956) 123-46.
Historical survey of Kālī cult, including origins and textual references and psychoanalytic interpretation of her role in oedipal conflicts. [Unexamined].

(c) Lakṣmī

159 COOMARASWAMY, ANANDA K. Early Indian iconography II: Śrī-Lakṣmī. *In* Eastern Art 1,3 (1929) 175-89.
"To sum up: Śrī-Lakṣmī combines an abstract

Vedic terminology with a concrete Indian mother-goddess of abundance; her special associations are with the Waters and the lotus. A definite iconographic type, very early developed has persisted almost unchanged to the present day."

160 DHAL, UPENDRA NATH. Goddess Laksmi, origin and development: a study of the Hindu goddess of beauty and wealth. New Delhi: Oriental Publishers, 1978. 229p. (World's Wisdom Series, 7).
Development of Lakṣmī and her inauspicious aspect (Alakṣmī) and her festivals and rites in the Vedas and classical Sanskrit literature.

161 MOTI CHANDRA. Our lady of beauty and abundance: Padmāśrī. *In* Nehru abhinandan granth: a birthday book presented to Jawaharlal Nehru, Prime Minister of India, on completion of his sixtieth year, November 14, 1949? Calcutta: Aryavarta Prakashan Griha, 1949? pp.497-513. [*Also in* J. of the United Provinces Historical Society 20 (1948) 15-42].
Development and characteristics of Lakṣmī in literature and iconography from Indus valley Mother Goddess antecedents to the Gupta period.

162 SIVARAMAMURTI, C. Goddess Lakṣmī and her symbols. *In* J. of the United Provinces Historical Society 14 (1941) 21-4.
[Unexamined].

(2) Others

(a) Goddess forms

163 BHATTACHARYYA, ASUTOSH. Cult of the smallpox goddess of West Bengal. *In* Quarterly J. of the Mythic Society 43,1 (1952) 55-69.
Origin and antiquity of the Śītalā cult and the history of her legend. Sources include meditative verses, Buddhist *tāntrika* literature and Bengali folk literature.

164 ________. Serpent stories in Bengal and its comparative study. *In* Folklore [Calcutta] 2,2-3 (1961) 97-104, 169-77.

Contemporary (Bengali, Bihari, Assamese) and historical legends of various serpent goddesses. Author is concerned with origins and cultural diffusion.

165 DHAVALIKAR, M.K. The origin of Saptamātṛkās. *In* Bulletin of the Deccan College Research Institute 21 (1963) 19-26.
Attempts to trace origin of the "Seven Mothers" through examination of texts and images. Argues that Vedic literature reveals seven rivers revered by Indo-Aryans as mother goddesses or water deities, a tradition that has survived to the present.

166 ________. "Eye goddesses" in India and their West Asian parallels. *In* Anthropos 60 (1965) 533-40.
Regarding a series of figures found in South Asian excavations from the Madhya Pradesh area north and west. They date from the end of the second millenium to the second century B.C.E. and are characterized by a "dot-in-circle" motif also found in the Middle East. Considers appearance, origin, function and possible identity as precursor of present day Śītalā. Illustrations.

167 DIEHL, C.G. The goddess of forests in Tamil literature. *In* Tamil Culture 11, 4 (1964) 308-16.
Compares qualities of Tamil and Sanskritic goddesses associated with forests.

168 GUPTA, PARMESHWARI LAL. Ekānaṁśā and her images. *In* J. of the Bihar Research Society 54, 1/4 (1968) 229-44.
Development, worship and iconography of goddess Ekānaṃśā who appears frequently in first to twelfth century C.E. literature but is little known in iconography and art. From literature and sculpture. With two plates.

169 JOSHI, J.R. Idā. *In author's* Some minor divinities in Vedic mythology and ritual. Pune: Deccan College Postgraduate and Research Institute, 1977, pp.50-4.
Reviews interpretations of and references to this female divinity associated with nourishment, abundance and progeny.

170 ________. Pṛthivī and Dyāvāpṛthivī. *In author's* Some minor divinities in Vedic mythology and ritual. Pune: Deccan College Postgraduate and Research Institute, 1977. pp. 109-20.
Traces references to, rituals associated with and interrelationship of "the divine parents, Heaven and Earth," in various texts and according to various scholars.

171 MAITY, PRADYOT KUMAR. Historical studies in the cult of the goddess Manasā: a socio-cultural study. Calcutta: Punthi Pustak, 1966. 377p.
Considers serpent worship in ancient India, the Bengali Buddhist and Hindu context out of which Manasā developed, Manasā in *kāvya* and *purāṇa* literature, origin and development of the main legend, development of the cult, Manasā's relationship to other "cult-divinities," her iconography and her rituals. Plates (26).

172 MEERWARTH-LEVINA, LUDMILA. The Hindu goddess Pattini in the Buddhist popular beliefs of Ceylon. *In* Ceylon Antiquary and Literary Register 1,1 (1915) 29-37. *And* W.A. de Silva. Pattini Devi. 1,2 (1915) 127-8.

Relates a story of Pattini as evidence of a Buddhist veneer on "popular belief," which includes Vedda, Aryan and Tamil elements. De Silva's reply argues that Pattini worship in Sri Lanka is of Tamil origin, introduced probably in the 15th century, and thus is not pre-Buddhistic. Disputes other points as well.

173 MUNDKAR, BALAJI. The enigma of Vaināyakī. *In* Artibus Asiae 37,4 (1975) 291-302.
Examines origins and representations in literature and art of an elephant-headed goddess, first century B.C.E. to tenth century C.E. At various periods she is worshipped as a consort of Gaṇeśa, as one of Śiva's Śaktīs and independently.

174 PALIT, D.R. Sapta-matrkas or the seven mothers from Besnagar. *In* Indian History Congress 12, 1949, Cuttack. Proceedings 12. Allahabad: the Congress, 1950. pp.109-12.
Describes goddess images found at Besnagar excavations and compares them to generally later references to and images of Saptamātṛkās. The Besnagar figures are assigned to circa fourth century C.E.

175 RAGHAVAN, M.D. The cult of the goddess Pattini. *In his* Ceylon: a pictorial survey of the peoples and arts. Colombo: M.D. Gunasena and Company, 1962. pp.69-73.
Short sketch of the life of Kaṇṇaki, her deification as Pattini, the inauguration of Pattini worship in Sri Lanka by King Gajabāhu in the second century C.E. and various rituals associated with her worship.

176 SANKALIA, H.D. The nude goddess or "shameless woman" in western Asia, India and south-eastern Asia. *In* Artibus Asiae 23 (1960) 111-23.
Regarding a number of nude goddess images distributed over a wide geographical area. Their vulvas are often displayed and they are frequently headless. Numerous photographs and diagrams.

177 YASODADEVI, V. Ganga and Yamuna. *In* Sri Venkateswara University Oriental Journal 4,1/2 (1961) 44-54.
History and iconography of these twin rivers as goddesses.

(b) Goddess temple traditions

178 BALARAM IYER, T.G.S. and T.R. RAJAGOPALAN. History and description of Sri Meenakshi temple, 2d ed. Madurai: Sri Karthikeiya Publication, 1976. 42p., 64 plates.
Physical description, historical background and legends of this major goddess temple in Madurai, Tamil Nadu.

179 BARUA, B.K. and H.V. SREENIVASA MURTHY. Temples and legends of Assam. Bombay: Bharatiya Vidya Bhavan, 1965. 136p. (Bhavan's Book University, 132).
History, iconography, rituals, legends and so forth of various Assam temples. Discusses several *Śākta* sites.

180 GANHAR, J.N. Jammu: shrines and pilgrimages. New Delhi: Ganhar Publications, [1975]. 180p.
Survey of sacred sites, festivals and arts in Jammu. Section on goddess temples (pp.1-27) describes legends, geography, rites and so forth.

181 JHA, MAKHAN. The sacred complex in Janakpur: Indological, sociological, anthropological and philosophical study of Hindu civilization. Allahabad: United Publishers, 1971. 152p. (Social Studies, 1).
History, geography, legends, rituals and so forth of the pilgrimage center at Janakpur in southeastern Nepal. The site is considered to be Sītā's birthplace and the preeminent temple is her Jānakī temple. Photographs.

182 KAKATI, BANI KANTA. The mother goddess Kāmākhyā: or, studies in the fusion of Aryan and primitive beliefs of Assam. Gauhati: Lawyer's Book Stall, 1948. 83p. [*3d ed.* 1967].
Considers contemporary Kāmākhyā worship near Gauhati and history and legends associated with site; textual references, predominantly from the *Kālikā Purāṇa* and the *Yoginī Tantra*; and dynastic inscriptions.

183 PALANIAPPAN, K. The great temple of Madurai. Tr. from Tamil by K. Thiagarajan. Madurai: Sri Meenakshi-sundareswarar Temple Renovation Committee, 1963. 152p.
History of the Mīnākṣī temple in the context of Tamil political history. With various legends, description of physical site and photographs.

184 RAJAGOPALAN, T.R. Key to Sri Meenakshi temple: a self-explanatory description. Madurai: Sri Karthikeiya Publication, 1975. 32p., 32 plates.
Guide to the architecture and sculpture of this well-known Madurai temple. With some Mīnākṣī legends.

185 ROY CHOUDHURY, P.C. Temples and legends of Bihar. Bombay: Bharatiya Vidya Bhavan, 1965. 189p. (Bhavan's Book University, 127).
Reviews major temples of Bihar, providing histories, legends, physical descriptions, discussion of major festivals, photographs and so forth. Includes several goddess temples.

186 SARAF, SURAJ. Vaishno Devi, Jammu. Jammu: Raj Mahal Publishers, 1976? 52p.
Guide to a goddess pilgrimage site by a journalist. Discusses origin, associated legends,

geography of site, its various attractions and accommodations. Numerous photographs.

187 THIAGARAJAN, K. Meenakshi temple, Madurai. [Madurai]: Meenakshi Sundareswarar Temple Renovation Committee, 1965? 81p.
Historical background, legends, maps and photographs of the Mīnākṣī temple in Madurai city, Tamil Nadu.

(c) *Yakṣiṇīs, apsarās, various devatās*

188 BANERJEA, JITENDRA NATH. Some folk goddesses of ancient and mediaeval India. *In* Indian Historical Quarterly 14,1 (1938) 101-9.
Regarding examples of the *devatā* class of beings. Notes the "great similarity as regards origin, character as well as the method of worship" of the *rākṣasī* Jarā from the *Mahābhārata* and the *yakṣiṇī* Hārītī from Buddhist texts and describes Jyeṣṭhā as an antecedent of present-day Śītalā.

189 COOMARASWAMY, ANANDA K. Yakṣas. New Delhi: Munshiram Manoharlal, 1971. 84p., 73 plates.
Concerning *yakṣas* and their female counterparts, *yakṣīs* or *yakṣiṇīs*, a complex class of deities frequenting forest and jungle and prominent in folklore. *Yakṣiṇīs* are associated with fertility, having tapped the life of trees in which they dwell. They are prominent in Buddhist and Jaina traditions.

190 JOSHI, J.R. Apsaras. *In author's* Some minor divinities in Vedic mythology and ritual. Pune: Deccan College Postgraduate and Research Institute, 1977. pp.39-49.
On a class of female spirits associated with water and progeny. Reviews scholars' conceptions and textual representations, discusses derivation of the name *apsarā* and notes several particular *apsarās* named in the literature.

191 TAVARKAR, NARAYAN GOPAL. The apsarases: the perfect women of the ancient world. *In his* The essays throwing new light on the gandharvas, the apsarases, the yakshas and the kinnaras. Bombay: Tavkar Prakashan, 1971. pp.27-54. (Fog of Myths and Legends, 1).
Essay on diverse topics relating to this class of celestial singers and dancers found throughout Sanskrit literature.

3. Matrilineal systems and matriarchal tendencies

192 EHRENFELS, UMAR ROLF VON. Mother-right in India. Hyderabad: printed at the Government Central Press, 1941. 229p. (Osmania University Series).
Historical and contemporary survey of "mother-right" in South Asia in its active and passive forms and as disparate elements or pervasive systems. Extensive use of ethnographic materials available at the time of writing.

193 ________. Matrilineal family background in South India. *In* J. of Educational Sociology 26,8 (1953) 356-61.
Brief article that reviews the scope — in time and space — of matriliny in South India, describes the main social structural and psychological features associated with matriliny and comments on the transition to patriliny.

193a PATIL, SHARAD. Some aspects of matriarchy in ancient India: clan mother to tribal mother. *In* Social Scientist 2,4 (1973) 42-58.
Examines references to social structural units from the Vedas through Buddhist Pali literature to evaluate women's social position. Considers earth and fertility symbolism, courtesans, Buddhist orders for women and other topics.

194 SCHNEIDER, DAVID M. and KATHLEEN GOUGH, eds. Matrilineal kinship. Berkeley: University of California Press, 1961. 761p.
This book consists of an introductory theoretical statement about matrilineal descent groups by Schneider, ethnographic accounts of nine matrilineal groups, an examination of various hypotheses about matriliny by Gough and a statistical cross-cultural analysis by David F. Aberle. Of the ethnographic presentations, four, by Gough, concern "traditional," pre-British systems and British period changes of Kerala communities — the Nayar of Central Kerala and the Nayar, Tiyyar and Mappilla of North Kerala. Other sections consider Kerala data in comparative perspective.

E. The life cycle

1. Childhood

195 STERNBACH, LUDWIK. Infanticide and exposure of new-born children in ancient India. *In* Poona Orientalist 13, 1/2 (1948) 79-87.
"All these quotations show that in Ancient India [Vedas through *sūtras*] foeticide, infanticide and exposure of new born boys were prohibited, and certainly unknown and the same of new born girls, prohibited but, perhaps, secretly practised. The custom of infanticide of girls and their exposure became known and practised in Mediaeval India." Refutes Westermark's assertion that the *Ṛgveda* refers to female infanticide.

2. Puberty

196 BHATTACHARYYA, NARENDRA NATH. Indian puberty rites. *In* Indian Studies: Past and Present 9,3-4 (1968) 271-302, 303-42.
Making extensive use of religious texts and early ethnological and ethnographic sources, the author discusses menarche rites in various parts of India; ceremonial defloration; the association of puberty with marriage; initiation of boys; and various elements of puberty rites: tatooing, hair-shaving, ear-piercing, forms of mutilation and taboos. Appendixes give selections from various authorities on menstruation, age at marriage for girls and other topics.

197 _______. Sacred and accursed: a study in the menstrual rites of ancient India. *In his* Ancient Indian rituals and their social contents. Delhi: Manohar Book Service, 1975. pp.85-96.
Reviews menarche rites as detailed in various Sanskrit texts and as practiced by various contemporary peoples.

198 THANKAPPAN NAIR, P. Defloration and couvade in Kerala. *In* J. of Kerala Studies 3, 3/4 (1976) 457-77.
An assortment of references, historical and contemporary, to premarital defloration and couvade in various parts of India.

3. Marriage

199 BANDYOPADHYAY, SAMARESH. Foreign accounts of marriage in ancient India. Calcutta: Firma K.L. Mukhopadhyay, 1973. 76p.
Compares accounts of marriage by Greek, Chinese and Arab travelers, ca. 300 B.C.E. to ca. 1100 C.E., with those in Sanskrit, and particularly *dharmaśāstra*, literature. Organized by topic, e.g., polyandry, divorce, dowry.

200 DERRETT, J. DUNCAN M. The death of a marriage law: epitaph for the rishis. New Delhi: Vikas Publishing House, 1978. 228p.
History of Hindu marriage law in India up to the present, with comments about the future. In presenting recent cases the author is "concerned with society's dilemma in the face of a law which it has given to itself in one of its many bursts of optimism." Considers problems of women in detail.

201 KANE, PANDURANG VAMAN. Marriage. *And* Polygamy, polyandry and rights and duties on marriage. *In his* History of dharmaśāstra: ancient and mediaeval religious and civil law, v2, part 1, 2d ed. Poona: Bhandarkar Oriental Research Institute, 1974. pp.427-541, 550-82. (Government Oriental Series, Class B, 6). [*1st ed.* 1941].
Legal treatment of marriage from Vedas through later *dharmaśāstras*. Topics include: purpose of marriage, choosing a bride, female age at marriage, intercaste marriage, meaning of *sapiṇḍa*, mother's brother's daughter marriage, marriage and *sapiṇḍa* relationship, *gotra*, *pravara*, marriage prohibitions, marriage guardians, sale of girls, infanticide, auspicious times, forms, ceremonies, polygamy, polyandry, rights and duties, position of women and dependence of women.

202 KAPADIA, K.M. Marriage and family in India, 3d ed. Bombay: Oxford University Press, 1966. 395p.
Brahmanic texts and their influence upon various aspects of marriage and the family in contemporary India. Chapters with much information on women are "Polyandry," "Polygamy," "Age at Marriage," "Hindu Marriage a Sacrament," "Marriage in Islam," "The Status of Woman" and "The Matrilineal Family."

203 MAHADEVA SASTRI, ALLADI. Vedic law of marriage or the emancipation of women. Madras: V. Ramaswamy Sastrula, 1918. 255p.
Collected lectures and papers on marriage in the *śruti* and *smṛti* literatures. Includes debate with Dewan Bahadur R. Raghunatha Rao.

204 MITRA, VEDA. Happy married life in ancient India. New Delhi: Arya Book Depot, 1965. 176p.
Various aspects of marriage as described in *śruti* and *smṛti* texts.

205 RADHAKRISHNAN, S. Women in Hindu Society. *In his* Religion and Society. London: George Allen and Unwin, 1947. pp.139-98. (Kamala Lectures).
Essay on love and marriage in Hindu thought. Based on lecture notes.

206 SUR, A.K. Sex and marriage in India: an ethnohistorical survey. Bombay: Allied Publishers, 1973. 194p.
History of marriage in India up to Kauṭilya and survey of contemporary marriage by community (Hindu, Muslim, tribal) and by topic (rites, pre- and extra-marital sexuality, etc.), which show that "India is almost an ethnic museum of marital forms and patterns."

a. Rites

207 CHATTERJEE, KRISHNA NATH. Hindu marriage: past and present. Varanasi: Tara Publications, 1972. 397p.
Marriage in the Hindu tradition, organized by topic. Sources range from Vedas to contemporary legislation. Includes chapters on women's position in this marriage system, remarriage of women and divorce, and *satīs*.

208 MODI, JIVANJI JAMSHEDJI. Marriage customs amongst the Parsees and their comparison with similar customs of other nations. *In* J. of the Anthropological Society of Bombay 5,4 (1900) 242-82. [Unexamined].

209 Patterns of marriage in Tamil society: old and new. *In* Bulletin of the Institute of Traditional Cultures, Madras (Jan/Jun 1973) 151-227.
Proceedings of a seminar. Participants, papers and commentary. Focuses on marriage ceremonies and ritual.

210 SENGUPTA, NILAKSHI. Evolution of Hindu marriage: with special reference to rituals, c. 1000 B.C.-A.D. 500. Bombay: Popular Prakashan, 1965. 191p.
Discusses emergence of child marriage, diversity of marriage forms, concern with *varṇa* intermarriage, prohibition of widow marriage, *satīs* and other marriage features, which signify the "great deterioration" of the position of women in this period.

b. Female age at marriage

211 ABEILLE, MIREILLE. Age at marriage: historical obstacles to needed reforms. *In* George Kurian, ed. The family in India: a regional view. The Hague: Mouton, 1974. pp.263-75. (Studies in the Social Sciences, 12).
Discusses problems of acquiring accurate age-related data in India. Reviews the vicissitudes of expected age of women at marriage in the Hindu tradition and points to its relation to religious beliefs and other social factors.

212 ALTEKAR, A.S. The vicissitudes of the marriage age of girls in Hindu society. *In* Indian Culture 4,4 (1938) 455-66.
History of views on the desired marriage age of girls from the Vedas through the Sarda Act of 1929. Primarily based on texts and other literary evidence.

213 RAGHUNATHA RAO, R. The Aryan marriage, with special reference to the age question: a critical and historical study. Delhi: Cosmo Publications, 1975. 280p. [*Reprint of* 1908 ed.].
"I have endeavored to depict the Aryan Ideal of Marriage as found in the Sāstras, and I have entered into historical considerations to show how the modern Hindu marriage has come to be but a sad travesty of the Grand Old Ideal." Argues that prepubescent marriage is "unvedic."

4. Reproductive life

a. Pregnancy and birth

214 BLOOMFIELD, MAURICE. The dohada or craving of pregnant women: a motif of Hindu fiction. *In* J. of the American Oriental Society 40 (1920) 1-24.
Regarding the motif of "two-heartedness," the will of an unborn child expressed in the cravings of its pregnant mother, in Sanskrit and Pali literature and contemporary South Asian folk tales. Surveys numerous occurrences under six rubrics: injures or endangers husband, prompts husband to heroism or superior action, takes form of pious acts or aspirations, is ornamental and without consequence to plot, is feigned to accomplish woman's aspirations and is obviated by deception and not fact.

215 MEHTA, S.S. Pregnancy (fecundity) amongst ancient and modern races. *In* J. of the Anthropological Society of Bombay 10,5 (1915) 400-9.
Draws parallels between western and Indian beliefs that a pregnant mother's experiences can create physical or mental "impressions" upon the fetus. With examples from Sanskrit texts, ancient Greece, a British medical journal, etc.

216 MITRA, SARAT CHANDRA. Note on clay-eating as a racial characteristic. *In* J. of the Anthropological Society of Bombay 7,4 (1905) 284-90.
Discusses a pregnant woman's craving for clay as exemplified in Kālidāsa's *Raghuvaṃśa* and in various areas of contemporary India.

217 ________. On some ancient Indian beliefs about the origin of child birth. *In* J. of the Anthropological Society of Bombay 15,2 (1932) 178-84.
Discusses the disregarding of the male's contribution to conception and birth, which occurs in the *Kādambarī* of Bāṇa (7th century C.E.) and in various contemporary folk materials. Describes women's rituals that aim to induce conception and birth without intercourse.

218 MODI, JIVANJI JAMSHEDJI. Birth customs and ceremonies of the Parsees. *In* J. of the Anthropological Society of Bombay 9,8 (1912) 568-78.
Discusses ceremonies and customs of pregnancy, birth, naming and childhood. Based on author's experiences and Zoroastrian texts.

219 PENZER, N.M. Appendix III: on the dohada or craving of the pregnant woman as a motif in Hindu fiction. *In* Charles Henry Tawney, tr., and N.M. Penzer, ed. The ocean of story, vI. Delhi: Motilal Banarsidass, 1968.

pp.221-8. [*Reprint of* London: Charles Sawyer, 1924].

Reviews Bloomfield's essay on pregnancy cravings and presents some supplementary material

b. *Niyoga:* assuring continuity of the family line

220 KANE, PANDURANG VAMAN. *Niyoga. In his* History of dharmaśāstra: ancient and mediaeval religious and civil law, v2, part 1, 2d ed. Poona: Bhandarkar Oriental Research Institute, 1974. pp.599-607. (Government Oriental Series, Class B, 6). [*1st ed.* 1941].

Historical development and various opinions regarding the "appointment of a wife or widow to procreate a son from intercourse with an appointed male" in legal texts of the Hindu tradition. Considers eligible persons and status of child.

c. Preventing pregnancy

221 DASH, BHAGWAN. Methods for sterilization and contraception in ancient and medieval India. *In* Indian J. of History of Science 3,1 (1968) 9-24.

Discusses earlier ideals for family size and composition and reviews range of techniques used for controlling births. Sources range in time from the Vedas to the 20th century.

5. Widowhood

222 COLEBROOKE, H. On the duties of a faithful Hindu widow. *In his* Essays on history, literature and religion of ancient India, v1. New Delhi: Cosmo Publications, 1977. pp.114-22. [*Reprint from* Asiatic Researches 4 (1795) 209-19].

Collection of injunctions for widows translated from Vedic and classical Sanskrit works.

223 DUTT, N.K. Widow in ancient India. *In* Indian Historical Quarterly 14,4 (1938) 661-79. [*Also in* Woolner commemoration volume. Lahore, 1940. pp.77-87].

Collection of references to widowhood in Vedic and classical Sanskrit literature and in dynastic records.

224 KANE, PANDURANG VAMAN. The duties of a widow, some privileges of women and the *purda* system: vidhavādharmāḥ. *In his* History of dharmaśāstra: ancient and mediaeval religious and civil law, v2, part 1, 2d ed. Poona: Bhandarkar Oriental Research Institute, 1974. pp.583-98. (Government Oriental Series, Class B, 6). [*1st ed.* 1941].

Prohibitions and prescriptions applied to widows by the various legal texts in the context of recent social reform efforts. Discusses general demeanor and lifestyle, property rights and various opinions on tonsure. Brief attention to decline of position of women after Vedas and history of *pardā* observance.

225 ________. Remarriage of widows. *In his* History of dharmaśāstra: ancient and mediaeval religious and civil law, v2, part 1, 2d ed. Poona: Bhandarkar Oriental Research Institute, 1974. pp.608-23. (Government Oriental Series, Class B, 6). [*1st ed.* 1941].

Remarried widows as one category of *punarbhū* in Hindu legal texts. Discusses opinions on remarriage of widows and others and on divorce.

226 MITRA, TRAILOKYANATH. The law relating to the Hindu widow. Calcutta: Thacker, Spink and Company, 1881. 480p. (Tagore Law Lectures, 1879).

From traditional law texts and contemporary court cases. Lectures address right of succession, obligations as heiress, remarriage, widow's estate, alienations, rights of reversioners, suits by reversioners and maintenance. Reviews Hindu law sources and condition of women and widows in ancient India.

F. Women's power and sexuality, women's danger to others and seclusion

227 BROWN, W. NORMAN. Change of sex as a Hindu story motif. *In* J. of the American Oriental Society 47 (1927) 3-24.

Gives many examples from the entire historical range of Indic fiction to illustrate five means by which change of sex is effected: bathing in enchanted water, a curse or a blessing, exchanging sexes with a superhuman being, magic objects and charms and the power of righteousness or wickedness. Discusses origin of notion of sex change and some of the contexts in and purposes for which it occurs.

228 KRISHNAMURTI, Y.G. and CHANDRAKANTA SHARMA. Samudrika: the Hindu art of sex and body-signs predications. Delhi: Asia Press, 1971? 100p.

Meaning of palm lines, moles, various forms of body parts, etc. From two manuscripts and various other texts. Much on women, including the chapter "Anatomy of Eve" (pp.11-37). Popular, familiar tone.

229 SPRATT, P. Hindu culture and personality: a psycho-analytic study. Bombay: Manaktalas, 1966. 400p.
Interpretation based exclusively on the male point of view. Much on women as men relate to them (see especially chapters entitled "Tapasya and Yoga," "Caste," "The Mother Fixation," "Goddess Worship" and "Village Goddesses"). Attributes men's interest in controlling women to 1) the "narcissistic pollution complex," including the fear of others' semen, and 2) the "mother fixation," the son's identification with his mother. Discusses both concepts in depth.

1. Pursuit of *kāma*, sexual love

a. As art and science

230 BASU, NRIPENDRA KUMER. The art of love in the Orient, 2d ed. Calcutta: Medical Book Company, 1947. 266p.
[Unexamined. NUC].

231 BHATTACHARYYA, NARENDRA NATH. History of Indian erotic literature. New Delhi: Munshiram Manoharlal, 1975. 135p.
First part discusses Indian attitudes toward sex and attributes extreme ambivalence to extreme patriarchy. Considers alternatives of "primitive sex rites," matriarchy and erotica in art. Second part deals with the erotic in pre-*Kāmasūtra* literature. Final section deals with *Kāmasūtra* and later *kāmaśāstra* texts.

232 CHAKRAVARTI, CHANDRA. Sex life in ancient India: an explanatory and comparative study. Calcutta: Firma K.L. Mukhopadhyay, 1963. 167p.
[Unexamined. IBP].

233 DE, SUSHIL KUMAR. Ancient Indian erotics and erotic literature. Calcutta: K.L. Mukhopadhyay, 1959. 109p.
[Unexamined. NUC].

234 ________. Indian erotics (kama-sastra) in its origin and development. *In* H.L. Hariappa and M.M. Patkar, eds. Professor P.K. Gode commemoration volume. Poona: Oriental Book Agency, 1960. Second part, pp.75-89. (Poona Oriental Series, 93).
Traces erotic love from the first appearance of *kāma* in the *Ṛgveda* through Vātsyāyana's *Kāmasūtra*. Includes summary of the latter.

235 GONDA, JAN. Ascetics and courtesans. *In* Adyar Library Bulletin 25, 1/4 (1961) 78-102. (Silver Jubilee Volume).
Alternation of chastity and licentiousness as a recurring strategy for acquiring power (often to promote crop fertility) from the Vedas to the present.

236 KANNOO MAL, LALA. Kāma-kalā: a comprehensive survey of erotics, rhetorics and science of music with special reference to sex psychology. Lahore: Punjab Sanskrit Book Depot, 1931. 114p.
The "art of love," a general survey. Illustrated. [Unexamined. NUC].

237 KHAZAN CHAND. Indian sexology. New Delhi: S. Chand, 1972. 449p.
Material on sexuality from various Vedic and classical Sanskrit texts. Major sections are: "General," "Coital," "Relating to Girls," "About a Wife," "Regarding Others' Wives," "Prostitution," "Religion and Indian Sexology (Dharm)," "Sexology and Exchequer (Arth)," "Moksha," and "Ayurved and Indian Sexology." Photographs of temple sculpture.

238 LEESON, FRANCIS. Kama shilpa: a study of Indian sculpture depicting love in action. Bombay: D.B. Taraporevala Sons, 1962. 132p.
Historical survey, ranging from the Indus valley civilization to the 19th century. Reviews eight propositions regarding the portrayal of the *mithuna*, or amorous couple, in sculpture. 96 plates.

239 SCHMIDT, RICHARD. Beiträge zur indischen Erotik: das Liebesleben des Sanskritvolkes nach den Quellen dargestellt [Contributions to Indian eroticism: the love life of the Sanskrit peoples as represented according to the sources]. Leipzig: Lotus-Verlag, 1902. 976p. [*Abridged reprint* Berlin: Hermann Barsdorf Verlag, 1911. 691p.].
Attempts to present a complete and orderly synopsis of love and sexuality in Sanskrit literature. Extensive excerpts are transliterated and translated into German.

240 TAMBIMUTTU [THURAIRAJAH TAMBIMUTTU], ed. and tr. India love poems: selected and with an essay on woman in India. Mount Vernon, New York: Peter Pauper Press, 1954. 121p.
Translated in collaboration with four others. Wood engravings. [Unexamined. NUC].

241 THOMAS, P. Kāma kalpa or the Hindu ritual of love: a survey of the customs, festivals, rituals and beliefs concerning marriage, morals, women, the art and science of love and sex symbolism in religion in India from remote antiquity to the present day; based on ancient Sanskrit classics, *Kama Sutra, Ananga Ranga, Rati Rahasya,* and modern works, 4th Indian ed. Bombay: D.B. Taraporevala Sons and Company, 1959? 151p.
Four parts: 1) periodization of women in South Asian history (Indus valley, Vedic, epic, medieval and modern periods); 2) con-

ceptions of woman and her power; 3) erotic poetry, art and sciences and 4) erotic element in religion (*Śaiva* cult, *Śākta* cult, love attitudes to God, temple art, *devadāsīs* and bacchanalian festivals). 224 photographs and drawings.

242 UPADHYAYA, S.C. Literary sources for a study of Indian erotics. *In* J. of the Gujarat Research Society 16,3 (1954) 230-43.
Reviews the major erotic genres, authors and treatises, providing such information as dates, size, patrons, contents and references elsewhere in literature. Does not give location of texts and availability of translations.

b. In legend: Rādhā

243 MAJUMDAR, A.K. A note on the development of the Rādhā cult. *In* Annals of the Bhandarkar Oriental Research Institute 36 (1955) 231-57.
[Unexamined].

244 MILLER, BARBARA STOLER. Rādhā: consort of Kṛṣṇa's vernal passion. *In* J. of the American Oriental Society 95,4 (1975) 655-71.
Attempts to trace origins and development of Rādhā and her association with Kṛṣṇa up to Jayadeva's *Gītagovinda* (12th century). Cites references to her in numerous works and suggests an earlier springtime celebration of the secret love of Rādhā and Kṛṣṇa.

245 PATIL, VIMLA and SUNIL KOTHARI. Radha in Indian song and dance. *In* Times of India Annual (1972) 19-26.
Text gives examples of the variety of literary references to Rādhā and her representation in several dance traditions. Plates (18) show her as depicted in various painting and contemporary dance traditions.

2. Forbidden sexual unions

246 KANE, PANDURANG VAMAN. Strīsaṅgrahaṇa: adultery or unlawful intercourse with a woman. *In his* History of dharmaśāstra: ancient and mediaeval religious and civil law, v3, 2d ed. Poona: Bhandarkar Oriental Research Institute, 1973. pp.531-7. (Government Oriental Series, Class B, 6). [*1st ed.* 1946].
Categories of and punishments for "the unlawful coming together of a man and a woman for sexual enjoyment" in various texts. Includes rape, adultery and devious seduction. Section on duties of a husband and a wife. Footnotes give original Sanskrit injunctions.

3. Prostitutes and courtesans: history, typology, images

247 BULLOUGH, VERN L. Hinduism. *In his* The history of prostitution. New Hyde Park, New York: University Books, 1964. pp.79-90.
Discusses images of women in traditional Hindu texts, courtesans and prostitutes in classical India, indigenous classification of prostitutes, *devadāsīs* and the double standard applied to men and women.

248 CROOKE, W. Prostitution (Indian). *In* James Hastings, ed. Encyclopaedia of religion and ethics, v10. New York: Charles Scribner's Sons, 1919. pp.406-8.
Concise history of prostitution. Considers the Vedic age, the *dharmaśāstra*, the Buddhist age, the period of Muslim rule, temple dancers and the British period.

249 EDWARDES, S.M. Prostitution in India. *In his* Crime in India: a brief review of the more important offences included in the Annual Criminal Returns, with chapters on prostitution & miscellaneous matters. London: Humphrey Milford, Oxford University Press, 1924. pp.71-98.
Reviews the prominent place of courtesans in much of Indian history and discusses contemporary *devadāsīs* and commercial prostitution.

250 HENRIQUES, FERNANDO. Classical India. *In his* Prostitution and society, a survey, v1: primitive, classical and oriental. London: MacGibbon and Kee, 1962. pp.140-203.
Reviews information on prostitution in Kauṭilya's *Arthaśāstra*, Vātsyāyana's *Kāmasūtra*, the *Mahābhārata* and *Rāmāyaṇa*, Daṇḍin's *Daśakumāracarita*, the *Mānava Dharmaśāstra*, *tantra* texts, Buddhist texts, the *Qo'rān*, reports of various travelers and social observers and other sources through the 20th century. Includes material on *devadāsīs*.

251 KANE, PANDURANG VAMAN. *Veśyā*. *In his* History of dharmaśāstra: ancient and mediaeval religious and civil law, v2, part 1, 2d ed. Poona: Bhandarkar Oriental Research Institute, 1974. pp.637-9. (Government Oriental Series, Class B, 6). [*1st ed.* 1941].
Discusses law relating to courtesans, prostitutes and concubines in the Hindu legal tradition, including their rights to maintenance.

252 LAURENT, EMILE. Die Prostitution in Indien: eine kulturhistorische Studie [Prostitution in India: a cultural-historical study]. Tr. from French? by G. Montanus. Frieberg im Breisgau, 1901.
[Unexamined].

253 MOTI CHANDRA. The world of courtesans. Delhi: Vikas Publishing House, 1973. 245p.
History of courtesans from Vedic to medieval periods. Material, based on primary and secondary sources, is arranged by literary genre, dynastic period and region. Photographs of sculptures of courtesans.

254 MUKHERJI, S.K. Prostitution in India. Calcutta: Das Gupta and Company, 1934. 528p.
[Unexamined. BMG].

255 SINHA, S.N. and N.K. BASU. History of prostitution in India . . . Calcutta: Bengal Social Hygiene Association, 1933. 229p.
This volume apparently deals with "ancient India" and was the first in a planned series. [Unexamined. BMG].

4. *Devadāsīs*, "servants of god": history, typology, interpretation

256 PATIL, B.R. The devadasis. *In* Indian J. of Social Work 35,4 (1975) 377-89.
History of the institution from about the third century C.E. to its present degeneration. Discusses distinctions between types of *devadāsīs*, regional variants of the institution and its positive and negative influences on Indian civilization.

257 PENZER, N.M. Appendix IV: sacred prostitution. *In* Charles Henry Tawney, tr., and N.M. Penzer, ed. The ocean of story, v1. Delhi: Motilal Banarsidass, 1968. pp.231-80. [*Reprint of* London: Charles Sawyer, 1924. *Rev. ed. in his* Poison-damsels and other essays in folklore and anthropology. London: privately printed for Charles J. Sawyer, Ltd., 1952. pp.129-84].
"In view of the anthropological importance of the connection of religion and prostitution, and of the interesting ritual, customs and ceremonies which it embodies, I shall endeavour to lay before my readers what data I have been able to collect, with a few suggestions as to the possible explanation of the curious institution of the *dēva-dāsīs*." Based on historical sources and contemporary ethnographic accounts.

5. *Satīs:* history, legends, interpretation

258 AHUJA, S.K. The legend that was sati. *In* Folklore [Calcutta] 11,3 (1970) 77-85. [*Also in* Triveni 38,4 (1970) 48-56].
History of widow immolation from literary sources and as contemporary social reform issue.

259 DESHPANDE, V.V. Comments on "A note on the origin of sati" by Shri Bani Prasanna Misra. *In* Hindutva 7,11 (1977) 18-28.
Reviews several mutually confirming legends taken by Misra to be essentially factual. Argues that these are based upon the erroneous assumption of a degraded society. Influenced by foreign ideas, Sri Misra is not able to appreciate that sacred customs have developed "naturally" and for positive reasons. Cites authoritative texts in support of this point of view.

260 GANDHI, RAJ S. *Sati* as altruistic suicide: beyond Durkheim's interpretation. *In* Contributions to Asian Studies 10 (1977) 141-57.
Argues that altruistic explanations alone are inadequate. The role of Brahmanical ideology and ideologies of dominant caste and sex are equally as important. However, warns against an "over-socialized" conception of women. Notes variations in practice of widow immolation.

261 GOPINATHA RAO, T.A. Ancient memorial stones in India. *In* Ceylon Antiquary and Literary Register 1,2 (1915) 77-82.
One category of memorial stones discussed. *mahāsatikaḷ*, have been established to honor "great *satīs*." Describes their form and establishment ceremonies. Primarily with reference to Tamil Nadu Photograph.

262 JACKSON, A.V. WILLIAMS. The practice of suttee, or widow-burning, in India, according to Greek, Latin, Arabic, Persian, Italian, Dutch, French and English accounts. *In his* History of India, v9. London: Grolier Society Publishers, 1907. pp.68-120.
A 2,000-year history of "widow-burning," beginning with the Greek historian Nikolaos Damaskenos (1st century B.C.E., who wrote that, "when Hindus die, they cause to be burned with them the most devoted one of their wives . . ."

263 JOSHI, P.B. The festival of the cuckoos and the origin of the name and practice of sati. *In* J. of the Anthropological Society of Bombay 9,8 (1912) 554-67.
The origin of the name *satī* and practice of widow immolation is said to be found in the story of the self-immolation of Satī, the wife of Śiva, in the sacrificial fire of Dakṣa. Describes Satī as the contemporary cuckoo goddess and the ritual of the festival of the cuckoos (place unidentified).

264 KANE, PANDURANG VAMAN. *Satī*, self-immolation of widows. *In his* History of dharmaśāstra: ancient and mediaeval religious and civil law, v2, part 1, 2d ed. Poona: Bhandarkar Oriental Research Institute, 1974. pp.624-36.

(Government Oriental Series, Class B, 6). [*1st ed.* 1941].
History of and opinions regarding *satīs* in the Hindu legal tradition and epigraphic record. Discusses rewards promised to a *satī*, the opposition of some commentators to the practice, ritual relating to it and its former disproportionate prevalence in Bengal.

265 KRISHNASVAMI AIYANGAR, S. Self-immolation which is not sati. *In* Indian Antiquary 35 (May 1906) 129-31.
Examples from history to demonstrate that women and men have frequently immolated themselves for reasons other than a spouse's death. Widow *satīs* as one variant among many showing "depth of devotion and a sacrifice of that most precious legacy, life in this world . . ."

266 MODI, JIVANJI JAMSHEDJI. The antiquity of the custom of sati. *In* J. of the Anthropological Society of Bombay 13,5 (1926?) 412-24.
Relates various historical accounts of *satīs*, including a Greek account dating from the 4th century B.C.E., and cross-cultural parallels within the Indo-Aryan tradition. Considers the motivation, "the high ideal of love and affection among some wives," which should be appreciated, although not justified. Describes Parsi double funeral ceremonies when either spouse dies, which similarly evokes high devotional ideals without entailing death of the remaining spouse.

267 MURTHY, K.K. The sati sacrifice and its lithographic vestige at Nagarjunakonda, Andhra Pradesh. *In* Orissa Historical Research Journal 11 (1963) 201.
Memorial stones honoring *satīs*? [Unexamined].

268 PENZER, N.M. Appendix I: widow-burning. *In* Charles Henry Tawney, tr., and N.M. Penzer, ed. The ocean of story, v4. Delhi: Motilal Banarsidass, 1968. pp.255-72. [*Reprint of* London: Charles Sawyer, 1924].
Concerning widow immolation through the ages in South Asia with comparative data from other civilizations.

269 RAHMAN, MUQADDESUR. The custom of widow-burning in India. *In* Itihāsa Samiti Patrikā: J. of the Bangladesh Itihas Samiti 2 (1973) 111-43.
Reviews history of the practice from its early development to its legal abolition in the 19th century. Summarizes textual, traveler and other references to *satīs* and tries to identify the socio-economic reasons for its existence, growth, decline and eventual prohibition. Traces British policy. Appendixes give statistics on number of reported *satīs* in various political units for the years preceding abolition.

270 RAO, SAKUNTALA [SHAKUNTALA RAO SASTRI]. Suttee. *In* Annals of the Bhandarkar Oriental Institute 14, 1/2 (1932/33) 219-40.
History of widow immolation in South Asia. Considers texts from Vedas until the 13th century and argues that the practice "was coming into vogue about the beginning of the 6th century A.D."

271 THAKUR, UPENDRA. Satī and jauhar. *In his* The history of suicide in India: an introduction. Delhi: Munshi Ram Manohar Lal, 1963. pp.126-84.
Considers textual, epigraphic and secondary source evidence regarding the history of widow sacrifice during the British period and reviews movement to abolish it in the 19th century. Notes some 20th century *satīs*. With photographs of memorial stones honoring *satīs*. Brief section describes *jauhar*, a mass suicide among a defeated people "to avoid intolerable shame, and thereby escape sexual dishonour." Although this practice was primarily undertaken by Rajput women in "medieval" India, the author presents evidence for a wider distribution through region and time.

272 THOMPSON, EDWARD. Suttee: a historical and philosophical enquiry into the Hindu rite of widow-burning. Boston: Houghton Mifflin Company, 1928. 165p. [*Also* London: G. Allen and Unwin].
Monograph by an ardent anti-*satī* crusader. Chapters are: "Origin of Suttee," "Prevalence and Area of the Rite: Suttee Memorials," "The Form that Suttee Took," "Reasons for Suttee," "Was Suttee Voluntary," "Attempts at Prohibition: Last Years of Legal Suttee in British India," "Prohibition in British India," "The Suppression of Suttee in Native States," "Illegal Suttee," "Legal Suttee Today" and "Concluding Considerations." With "Appendix: Some Accounts of Suttee."

273 YULE, HENRY and A.C. BURNELL. Suttee. *In their* Hobson-Jobson: a glossary of colloquial Anglo-Indian words and phrases, and of kindred terms, etymological, historical, geographical and discursive, 2d ed. Delhi: Munshiram Manoharlal, 1968. pp.878-83. [*Reprint of* 1903 ed.].
This entry includes the etymology of the word *satī* and the history of its use and the practice as exemplified in selected quotations from 317 B.C.E. to 1872 C.E. Quotes many firsthand observers and provides references.

6. Histories of female seclusion

274 ALTEKAR, A.S. The purda system. *In* Indian History Congress 2, 1938, Allahabad. Proceedings 2. Allahabad: the Congress, 1939? pp.47-54.
Argues that female seclusion came into practice in South Asia early in the common era but only became prevalent at about 1200 C.E. Discusses various references through the 16th century.

275 JAFRI, S.N.A. Purdah in India. *In* Asiatic Review n.s. 33 (Jul 1937) 533-8.
References to *pardā* in South Asian history, from the epics to the present.

276 SASTRI, SAKUNTALA RAO. The purdah. *In* J. of the Ganganatha Jha Research Institute 7, 2/4 (1950) 109-24.
Historical review of early references to various forms of seclusion in South Asia.

7. Various types of evil women

277 BLACKWELL, FRITZ. Misogyny and philogyny: the bifurcation and ambivalence of the stereotypes of the courtesan and the mother in literary tradition. *In* Feminine sensibility and characterization in South Asian literature. Guest ed: Fritz Blackwell. J. of South Asian Literature 12,3/4 (1977) 37-43.
The courtesan as a representative of *rāga*, or sensual desire, in the Sanskritic tradition; the mother as a representative of *tyāga*, or renunciation, in this tradition; and the wife as the ambivalent mother/whore.

278 BLOOMFIELD, MAURICE. On false ascetics and nuns in Hindu fiction. *In* J. of the American Oriental Society 44 (1924) 202-42.
Notes that evil doers in legends of the Hindu tradition are often Śaiva, Jaina or Buddhist ascetics. Section six (pp.236-42) treats wicked female ascetics in particular.

279 BOAZ, G.D. The terrible mother. *In* J. of the Madras University 16,1 (1944) 62-74.
Reviews numerous theories explaining attribution of both positive and negative qualities to mothers and goddesses.

280 PENZER, N.M. Appendix III: poison-damsels. *In* Charles Henry Tawney, tr., and N.M. Penzer, ed. The ocean of story, v2. Delhi: Motilal Banarsidass, 1968. pp.275-313. [*Reprint of* London: Charles Sawyer, 1924. *Rev. ed. in his* Poison-damsels and other essays in folklore and anthropology. London: privately printed for Charles J. Sawyer, Ltd., 1952. pp.1-71].
The motif of a woman who poisons in comparative perspective. Gives "facts and . . . references" to support the argument that the motif "originated in India at a very early period before the Christian era" and "travelled slowly westwards."

8. Fantasies of *Strīrājya*, a land of women

281 CROOKE, W. The land and island of women. *In* Man in India 2,4 (1922) 216-9.
Collection of references to places populated by women alone in South Asia and elsewhere. Includes event from *Mahābhārata* legend of Naga community.

282 SALETORE, R.N. Unread leaves of Indian history 3: strirajya. *In* Illustrated Weekly of India 91,14 (12 Apr 1970) 22-3.
Reviews various legends told by historical travelers and writers regarding past "kingdoms of women" in South Asia.

G. The spiritual life and religious observances

283 ASHA. Women and Hindu monasticism. *In* Vedanta Kesari 41,3 (1954?) 149-53.
[Unexamined].

284 GHANANANDA, SWAMI. Spiritual tradition among Hindu women: introductory. *In* Women saints of East and West: Śrī Sāradā Devī (the Holy Mother) birth centenary memorial. London: Ramakrishna Vedanta Centre, 1955. pp.1-8.
Historical survey of women and spirituality in the Hindu tradition. Delineates Vedic period, *smṛti-purāṇa* period (500 B.C.E. to 600 C.E.), epic-*purāṇa* period (600 to 1800 C.E.) and modern period.

285 KANE, PANDURANG VAMAN. Vratas (religious vows) and utsavas (religious festivals). *In his* History of dharmaśāstra: ancient and mediaeval religious and civil law, v5, part 1, 2d ed. Poona: Bhandarkar Oriental Research Institute, 1974. pp.1-462. [*1st ed.* 1958].
Deals with some major vows and festivals in depth and briefly treats about 1,100 others. Discusses general concepts and reviews the extensive textual literature on the topics. Texts prescribe many as particularly relevant for women and certainly today women are far more concerned with these observances than men.

1. Performance of Vedic rites: rights and obligations

286 BHANDARKAR, DEVADATTA RAMKRISHMA. Can women perform śrauta sacrifices of their own accord? *In* D. Bhandarkar et al., eds. B.C. Law volume, part 1. Calcutta: Indian Research Institute, 1945. pp.159-63.
Cites various proponents, opponents and examples of women who perform sacrifices in a variety of Sanskrit texts.

287 BHATTACHARYYA, N.N. The priest and the queen: a study in the rituals of

Asvamedha. *In* J. of the Oriental Institute 21, 1/2 (1971) 1-21. [*Reprint in his* Ancient Indian rituals and their social contents. Delhi: Manohar Book Service, 1975. pp.1-24].
History and analysis of the "horse sacrifice" in Vedic and post-Vedic literature. This rite, performed by kings, culminates with ritualized sexual intercourse between the queen and the horse.

288 CHAUDHARI, JATINDRA BIMAL. The position of mother in the Vedic ritual. *In* Indian Historical Quarterly 14,4 (1938) 822-30.
"Thus it is seen that in the pre-birth Saṃskāras, in the afterbirth Saṃskāras, in the Aurdhva-daihika rites, and in every other Vedic rite, the position of the mother is a very important one. In fact she seems to hold a more honourable position than the father in Vedic rituals." Essentially regarding the mother of sons.

289 _______. Initiation of women. *In* Indian Historical Quarterly 15,1 (1939) 101-21.
Argues, citing wide range of Sanskrit texts, that girls are entitled to initiation (*upanayana*), to wear the sacred thread and to utter *mantras*.

290 _______. Wife in the Vedic ritual. *In* Indian Historical Quarterly 16,1 (1940) 70-98.
Reviews position of first wife and cowives in various rituals as detailed in the Vedas, *gṛhyasūtras*, *śrautasūtras* and other Sanskrit texts.

291 _______. The position of wives other than the first in the Vedic ritual. *In* Indian Historical Quarterly 17, 2 and 4 (1941) 180-95, 492-505.
"Though the wives other than the first have no right to participate in those rites which are meant for Supreme Bliss, they are, however, allowed to participate in those acts which are considered as Saṃskāras, and those which are meant only for earthly bliss (ārād upakārika)." Reviews Sanskrit textual references to such rites.

292 _______. The widow in the Vedic ritual. *In* Prabuddha Bharata 47 (Feb 1942). [*Also in* Modern Review 70 (Nov? 1941) 472ff].
Widows as husbands' coequals in Vedic ritual. [Unexamined].

293 _______. Position of women in the Vedic ritual, 2d ed. Calcutta: Pracyavani, 1956. 268p.
[Unexamined. IBP].

294 VENKATARAMA DIKSHITAR, T. Women's rights in the performance of dharma. *In* B.V. Narayanaswamy Naidu, ed. Rajah Sir Annamalai Chettiar commemoration volume. Madras: Annamalai University, 1941. pp.878-87.
Briefly considers significance of *dharma* and related concepts. Reviews arguments against women's performance of sacrifices; these "will not stand scrutiny." The *śruti* texts, which allow all to perform *dharma*, are more authoritative than the *smṛti* texts, which limit women. Asserts that women have joint rights with their husbands in the performance of *śrautakarma* and independent rights in *dāna* and *pūrtakarma*.

2. Spiritual enlightenment: education in "ancient" South Asia

295 CHAUDHURI, ROMA. Women's education in ancient India. *In* Swami Madhavananda and Ramesh Chandra Majumdar, eds. Great women of India. Mayavati, Almora: Advaita Ashrama, 1953. pp.87-111.
Reviews educational patterns and opportunities for women and girls in the Vedas, epics, Jaina and Buddhist literature and early *smṛtis*. Education was essentially for self-realization and "ethical and religious in its tone and contents," although it was recognized that inclinations and capacities vary. It was free and based on long term residence with a teacher. Men and women were given equal opportunities in both sacred and secular education.

296 DEVI, SUSHIL MALTI. Girls' boarding houses and their management in ancient India. *In* Dr. Satkari Mookerji felicitation volume. Varanasi: Chowkhamba Sanskrit Series Office, 1969. pp.386-403. (Chowkhamba Sanskrit Studies, 69).
Study of references in Sanskrit texts to lodging arrangements, chiefly *āśramas*, for girl students.

3. Lives of female saints

297 ARUNACHALAM, M. Women saints of Tamilnad. Bombay: Bharatiya Vidya Bhavan, 1970. 59p. (Bhavan's Book University, Rupee Series, 69).
Biographical details and legends of eleven saints from the first through eleventh centuries.

298 GOPALAKRISHNA NAIDU, G.T. The holy trinity, the three saintly ladies of ecstatic mysticism: Divine Mother Sri Sarada Devi, Sri Mira Bai and Sri Andal. Coimbatore: Mercury Book Company, 1974. 58p.
Life sketches of Sarada Devi and Mīrā and teachings of Āṇṭāḷ. "Our purpose will be amply served if our readers get an insight into the Beauty and Truth inherent in the three Lady Saints whose innate glory is delineated in the following pages."

299 RAMAKRISHNA VEDANTA CENTRE. Women saints of East and West: Srī Sāradā Devī (The Holy Mother) birth centenary memorial. London: Ramakrishna Vedanta Centre, 1955. 274p.
Biographies of Hindu, Buddhist, Jaina, Christian, Jewish and *Ṣūfī* saints. Contributors were requested to discuss "the struggles and difficulties, the spiritual disciplines and realizations, of the women saints portrayed, so that the reader might feel drawn to the divine ideal which they attained, and glimpse their fervour of soul." For contents relevant to South Asia, see entries 284, 411-2, 534, 575, 581-2, 587-8, 590, 594, 607, 631, 2064, 2117 and 3283.

4. Devotees' attitude toward a personal god: the model of lover toward beloved

300 SANYAL, NISIKANTA. The erotic principle and unalloyed devotion, 4th ed. Calcutta: Gaudiya Mission. 36p.
Essay is largely devoted to the concept of *kānta bhāva* (the attitude of loving devotion), which a woman has for a lover or husband and a devotee has for a deity. [Unexamined. NUC].

301 SARABHAI, MRINALINI. Longing for the beloved: songs to Siva-Nataraja in bharata natyam. Ahmedabad: Darpana, 1976? 1v.
Compares and contrasts attitudes of saint or devotee toward God and lover toward beloved. Describes representation of these images in *bhakti* movement and dance traditions. Presents series of translated song texts that express these attitudes.

H. Economic position: property and maintenance rights

302 ALTEKAR, A.S. The daughter's right of inheritance. *In* P. Seshadri, ed. Har Bilas Sarda commemoration volume: presented on the occasion of his completing seventy years. Ajmer: Vedic Yantralaya, 1937. pp.217-23.
Its "vicissitudes in the course of Hindu civilization," from the Vedas to the 20th century.

303 ________. The history of the widow's right of inheritance. *In* J. of the Bihar and Orissa Research Society 24, 1/2 (1938) 4-28.
Asserts that no jurist prior to ca. 300 B.C.E. recognized the Hindu widow's right of inheritance and most of the *dharmasūtra* writers were in accord. Traces a rise of more sympathetic attitudes toward widows. Jurists were divided on the issue in the 5th to 10th centuries. While the period ca. 1200 to 1800 C.E. was generally conservative in the Hindu tradition, there is evidence of attempts to liberalize widows' rights of inheritance. Discusses variations in regional traditions.

304 CHAUDHARY, ROOP L. Hindu woman's right to property: past and present. Calcutta: Firma K.L. Mukhopadhyay, 1961. 156p.
Major topics: classical origins of Hindu woman's limited property rights, her rights of alienation, her rights of surrender, reversioners' rights with respect to her estate and the Hindu Succession Act of 1956.

305 KANE, PANDURANG VAMAN. Strīdhana. *In his* History of dharmaśāstra: ancient and mediaeval religious and civil law, v3, 2d ed. Poona: Bhandarkar Oriental Research Institute, 1973. pp.770-802. (Government Oriental Series, Class B, 6). [*1st ed.* 1946].
Concerns development of various conceptions of women's property rights in the Hindu legal tradition. Treats three aspects: what constitutes *strīdhana*, woman's control over her *strīdhana* and inheritance of *strīdhana*.

306 ________. Maintenance and other topics. *In his* History of dharmaśāstra: ancient and mediaeval religious and civil law, v3, 2d ed. Poona: Bhandarkar Oriental Research Institute, 1973. pp.803-24. (Government Oriental Series, Class B, 6). [*1st ed.* 1946].
Summarizes various textual injunctions upon a householder regarding maintenance obligations. Discusses widows, concubines and others. With commentary on the contemporary efforts at codification of Hindu law relating to maintenance.

307 MC CREERY, JOHN L. Women's property rights and dowry in China and South Asia. *In* Ethnology 15,2 (1976) 163-74.
Refutes notion that female inheritance and dowry are substantially related "different ways of implementing the same basic rights," using legal data from China, India and Sri Lanka. In these countries "dowry has been associated with women's property rights which have ranged from virtually non-existent to essentially the same as those enjoyed by men. In Ceylon and China, moreover, rights to inherit have been legally defined while rights to dowry have not."

308 MADAN, ATAM PRAKASH. Strīdhana or woman's property in Indian law: an appraisal of its concept and contents. *In* Vishveshvaranand Indological Journal 9,1 (1971) 85-108.
". . . Sanskrit law-books. . . . enumerate and mark out different kinds of *strīdhana* without aiming at any logical classification. However, the details given there provide ample basis for the analysis and classification of the concept of woman's property rights in India." Author attempts such a classification, based on Sanskrit texts and contemporary court cases.

309 SIRVYA, BHAGWAN DAS. Hindu woman's estate: non-technical stridhana. Calcutta: Butterworth, 1913. 418p.
Extensively documents Hindu women's property rights as in traditional legal texts and "all available cases up to the end of August 1913."

310 SIVARAMAYYA, B. Women's rights of inheritance in India: a comparative study of equality and protection. Madras: Madras Law Journal Office, 1973. 215p.
"The primary aim of this study is to investigate the position of women in the Hindu and Muslim laws of inheritance and to suggest the means of achieving equality between the sexes with respect to inheritance in India." Major topics: concept of joint family in the ***Mitākṣara*** legal tradition, Hindu Succession Act (1956), laws in Quebec and New York, the *Qor'ān* on inheritance, ***Sunnī*** and ***Shī'a*** laws and trends of and recommendations for Muslim law reform.

311 TAMBIAH, STANLEY J. Dowry and bridewealth, and the property rights of women in South Asia. ***In*** Jack Goody and Stanley J. Tambiah. Bridewealth and dowry. Cambridge: Cambridge University Press, 1973. pp.59-169. (Cambridge Papers in Social Anthropology, 7).
Major sections discuss 1) modalities of bridewealth and dowry and their relationship; 2) Hindu legal concepts relating property ownership and transmission and female property to the familial context; 3) contemporary ethnographic examples from North, Central and South India; 4) Jaffna Tamils and Kandyan Sinhalese of Sri Lanka as related to Indian historical and contemporary findings; and 5) the pattern in Burma as related to those of India and Kandyan Sri Lanka.

I. Clothing, adornment, beauty

312 ACHAREKAR, M.R. Rupadarsini: The Indian approach to human form. Bombay: Taraporevala, 1972. 63p.
[Unexamined. IBP].

313 ANAND, MULK RAJ and KRISHNA HUTHEESING. The bride's book of beauty. Bombay: Kutub, 1947. 125p.
This book was compiled by "eliciting information from our friends about the potions and perfumes and necklaces and stones which decked them from the tips of their heads to their painted feet . . ." as well as by consulting earlier texts. Includes many recipes, techniques and illustrations.

314 GHOSH, D.P. Kama ratna: Indian ideals of feminine beauty. New Delhi: R & K Publishing House, 1973. 69p.
Subsumes information relating primarily to historical sources under the categories "The Ideal Beauty," "Cosmetics and Coiffures," "Costume and Jewellery," "Music and Dance" and "Love and Lovers." Plates (67) of art works and contemporary photographs.

315 SAHAY, SACHIDANAND. Indian costume, coiffure and ornament. New Delhi: Munshiram Manoharlal Publishers, 1975. 206p.
". . . an account of Costume, Coiffure and Ornament of the people of North-Eastern India from c. 325 BC to c. 1200 AD with particular reference to Bihar, on the basis of archaeological evidences . . . . corroborated by the literary and foreign accounts of the period." Separate chapters on male and female dress, headdress, hairstyles and ornament. Photographs, drawings, bibliography.

1. Clothing: history, typology, bibliography

316 BRIJ BHUSHAN, JAMILA. The costumes and textiles of India. Bombay: D.B. Taraporevala Sons and Company, 1958. 92, 87p., 144 plates.
Traces historical development of male and female garments and presents various aspects of textiles: embroidery, printing and dyeing, weaver's craft and textile industry. Profusely illustrated with colored half-tone plates and line drawings.

316a CHANDRA, JAGDISH, comp. Indian costumes. ***In his*** Bibliography of Indian art, history and archaeology, v1: Indian art. Delhi: Delhi Printers Prakashan, 1978. pp.260-1.
Fifty-five references, many particularly related to women's apparel.

317 DAR, S.N. Costumes of India and Pakistan: a historical and cultural study. Bombay: D.B. Taraporevala Sons, 1969. 244p.
Survey of clothing by historical period and by various topics, i.e., main types and forms, aesthetics, in arts, in magic and religion, erotics of dress, future trends and philosophy. Many illustrations.

318 FABRI, CHARLES. Indian dress: a brief history. New Delhi: Sangam, Orient Longman, 1977. 92p. [***First published as*** A history of Indian dress. 1960].
Historical survey of male and female clothing styles from 150 B.C.E. to the 19th century by a conservator of Indian archaeology. With 30 plates.

318a GHURYE, G.S. Indian costume, 2d ed. Bombay: Popular Prakashan, 1966. 302p. [***1st ed.*** 1951].
Reviews historical development of male and female clothing to circa 1800 and presents recent and contemporary clothing patterns by geographical area. Numerous illustrations.

319 Indian costumes: a select bibliography. *In* Cultural News from India 3,2 (1962) 27-30.
Forty-two references, some briefly annotated.

320 TAGORE, PROTIMA. The sari: past and present. *In* Asiatic Review n.s. 31,107 (1935) 522-7. ***And*** Saral C. Ghosh. Correspondence: "The Sari: Past and Present." 31,108 (1935) 842-3.
Brief survey of the sari through the ages. The correspondent offers a number of alternate views.

2. Jewelry: history, typology, bibliography

321 BRIJ BUSHAN, JAMILA. Indian jewellery, ornaments and decorative designs, 2d ed. Bombay: D.B. Taraporevala Sons, 1964. 189p.
This wide-ranging survey has chapters on jewelry in ancient India, Muslim jewelry, modern trends, craft of the goldsmith, precious stones and hints to the collector. With an inventory of ancient and contemporary ornaments, bibliography of 97 items and numerous drawings and photographs.

322 DONGERKERY, KAMALA S. Jewelry and personal adornment in India. New Delhi: Indian Council for Cultural Relations, 1970. 77p.
Broad treatment of the design and uses of jewelry from the Indus Valley civilization to the present, including folk and tribal jewelry. Photos and drawings.

323 HENDLEY, THOMAS HOLBEIN. Indian jewellery. J. of Indian Art and Industry 12,95/107 (1909). 189p.
Large format volume that considers men's and women's jewelry of 19th century India, by regions, and "antique" jewelry. Considers historical factors, mode of wearing, stylistic qualities, construction and materials. Based on personal survey and published materials. Full-page plates (167), many in color and full-scale.

324 Indian jewellery. Mārg 17,4 (1964). 59p.
Extensively illustrated issue has articles on historical development, aesthetics, flower motifs, various local folk traditions, tribal jewelry, goldsmith traditions, Indian jewelry for contemporary elegance and jewelry as a development and export industry. Much specifically relating to women.

325 A select bibliography on Indian jewellery. *In* Cultural News from India 8, 5-6 (1967) 49-53, 43-7.
Eighty references, with brief annotations.

3. Hairstyle variations

326 PALCHOUDHURI, ILA. Ancient hair styles of India. Calcutta: Rupa, 1974. 44p.
Drawings of 15 women's hairstyles (most based on temple sculpture) with photographs of contemporary adaptations of the same, along with brief commentary.

327 Shringar. 1960. 29 min. Color. 16 and 35 mm. [***Distributed by*** Films Division, Ministry of Information and Broadcasting, 24 G. Deshmukh Marg, Bombay 400 026].
Survey of historical and contemporary hairstyles of Indian women. [Unexamined. CF].

4. Personal names, a feminine adornment

328 BHATTACHARYA, SIBESH. Some aspects of female names in eastern India of Gupta and post-Gupta periods. *In* K.C. Chattopadhyaya memorial volume. Allahabad: Department of Ancient History, Culture and Archeology, Allahabad University, 1975. pp.127-36.
Data on naming patterns and particularly meaning of names themselves from inscriptions. Essentially concerns elite, royal and brahman families.

J. Artistic traditions

329 BHAVNANI, ENAKSHI. Creative and fine arts. *In* Tara Ali Baig, ed. Women of India. Delhi: Publications Division, Ministry of Information and Broadcasting, Government of India, 1958. pp.161-76.
Reviews contributions of many notable female artists (poets, temple patrons, calligraphers, painters, dancers, actors, etc.) from the Vedic age to the present. With photos.

1. Music / dance / drama traditions

330 BHAVNANI, ENAKSHI. The dance in India: the origin and history, the art and science of dance in India — classical, folk and tribal. Bombay: D.B. Taraporevala Sons, 1965. 261p.
Survey of main classical and folk dance forms.

With material on dance images in sculpture and painting, divine aspects of dance, components, music, apparel and revival. Photographs, glossary, bibliography.

331 Mohini attam. Guest ed: Kanak Rele. Mārg 26,2 (1973) 55p.
Special issue devoted to various aspects of an essentially secular dance form that is about 300 to 600 years old. It is derived from ***bhārata nāṭyam*** and ***kathākali*** and performed by women. Discusses origin and history, associated myths, technique, repertoire, main performers, costume and make-up, music and other topics. Many photographs.

332 SATHYANARAYANA, R. Bharatanāṭya: a critical study. Mysore: Sri Varalakshmi Academies of Fine Arts, 1969. 400p. (Sri Varalakshmi Academy Publication Series).
An attempt to fill the need for "a systematic approach to the principles and philosophy of bharatanāṭya based on original source material as well as on current practice." Considers history, technique, teaching, performance and so forth. A section entitled "Dedication of Dancer to God" reviews the ***devadāsī*** tradition, by region. Extensive bibliography.

333 SEETA, S. Role of women in the preservation of Carnātic music during the late medieval period. *In* Bulletin of the Institute of Traditional Cultures, Madras (Jul 1975) 224-31.
Past and present contributions of women to devotional and folk music; as court poets, composers, musicians and dancers; and as professional artists.

334 VAN ZILE, JUDY. Dance in India: an annotated guide to source materials. Providence, Rhode Island: Asian Music Publications, 1973. 129p. (*Its* Bibliographies and Research Aids, 3).
Bibliography of 839 briefly annotated English sources for dance. See especially sections on temple dancers, individual biography and particular dance forms for materials concerning women.

335 VATSYAYAN, KAPILA. In the performing arts. *In* Devaki Jain, ed. Indian women. New Delhi: Publications Division, Ministry of Information and Broadcasting. Government of India, 1975. pp.289-97.
Survey of women's involvement in the music/dance/drama traditions of India, including historical and contemporary trends.

2. Visual arts: sculpture, painting, decorative arts and crafts

336 CHANDRA, JAGDISH, comp. Bibliography of Indian art, history and archaeology, v1: Indian art. Delhi: Delhi Printers Prakashan, 1978. 316p.
Numerous entries (8,329) subsumed under six major divisions (art, architecture, sculpture, painting, handicrafts, greater India) and various subdivisions. Among the many topics relating to women are artistic representations of many types, goddess images and myths, female artists, folk arts and feminine handicrafts. Title page indicates: "Dr. Anand K. Coomaraswamy Memorial Volume."

337 DAS GUPTA, CHARU CHANDRA. Bibliography of ancient Indian terracotta figurines. *In* J. of the Asiatic Society of Bengal, Letters 4 (1938) 67-120.
Annotated bibliography of 175 books and articles on terracottas published through 1936. Subject and location indexes. Large number of specimens are feminine figures.

338 _______. Supplement to bibliography of ancient Indian terracotta figurines. *In* J. of the Asiatic Society of Bengal, Letters 10,1 (1944) 61-75.
Forty-one annotated references to books and articles, published 1937-42.

339 INDIA (REPUBLIC) OFFICE OF THE REGISTRAR GENERAL. Bibliography of Indian arts and crafts. Compiled by Suman Chandna. New Delhi: Office of the Registrar General, Ministry of Home Affairs, Government of India, 1967. 71p. (Census of India, 1961, v1, part II, 2).
Over 1,400 items classified according to medium (textiles, ceramics, metal, stone, ivory, horn and shell, wood, bamboo and grass, sola-pith and wicker work, leather, glass, laquer work) and use (jewelry and ornaments, floor covering, dolls and toys, musical instruments). While many of these objects are important to women's lives, few writings have been organized from this perspective.

340 MEHTA, RUSTAM J. Masterpieces of the female form in Indian art. Bombay: D.B. Taraporevala Sons, 1972. 56p.
Enthusiastic and admiring text touching on various aspects of classical and medieval sculptures of female forms — nature of ideal forms, attitudes expressed, concepts of love, etc. Sculptures in the 100 plates date from second century B.C.E. to sixteenth century C.E.

341 MODE, HEINZ. The woman in Indian art. Tr. from German by Marianne Herzfeld. Revised by D. Talbot Rice. New York: McGraw-Hill Book Company, 1970. 51p. [*Tr. of* Die Frau in der indischen Kunst. Leipzig: Edition Leipzig].
"Indian art is a mirror of Indian femininity . . . . Surely nowhere in the world than in India can women be better entitled to claim higher rank than men in art, whether through the quantity of representations, the quality of their execution or the importance of their symbolic content." Text considers women in Indian art as celestial or terrestial, mother or lover/beloved, active and charm-displaying. Discusses character and moods,

portraits and overall conception. Illustrations range historically from Indus Valley civilization to modern art. Plates (118).

341a SCHMITT-MOSER, ERIKA [ERIKA MOSER-SCHMITT]. Die Frau als „Künstlerin" in der traditionellen indischen Gesellschaft [Woman as artist in traditional Indian society]. *In* Indo-Asia 21,2 (1979) 175-87.
Examines legend of the artist Citralekhā, feminine aesthetic standards, women as professional artists, women as domestic artists and women's work and the contemporary art market. Focuses on pictorial arts.

342 Terracottas. Mārg 23,1 (1969) 54p.
Special issue on terracottas in South Asia from the Indus valley civilization to the advent of Muslim rule. A large proportion of these are female images and they are well-represented in the illustrations and discussed in the text. Organized by excavation area and dynasty.

343 UPADHYAYA, PADMA. Female images in the museums of Uttar Pradesh and their social background. Varanasi: Chaukhambha Orientalia, 1978. 322p. (Chaukhambha Oriental Research Studies, 8).
Attempts to "describe these sculptures in their respective secular or nonsecular settings . . . during the various chronological epochs; to assess their artistic techniques and aesthetical merits, to dwell on the variety of their form; to bring out their social importance, and reflect on their relation to life; and finally to catalogue them." Hindu, Buddhist and Jaina traditions. Thirty-two plates.

3. Literary traditions

344 Feminine sensibility and characterization in South Asian literature. Guest ed: Fritz Blackwell. J. of South Asian Literature 12,3/4 (1977). 155p.
Wide variety of topics. Most concern 20th century literature. For contents see entries 277, 503, 508, 1317, 2689, 3693-4. 2702, 2865-6, 2882, 2886, 2914, 3347, 3791, 3830, 4363-4 and 4375.

345 RAY, LILA. Women writers. *In* Tara Ali Baig, ed. Women of India. Delhi: Publications Division, Ministry of Information and Broadcasting, Government of India, 1958. pp.177-92.
Capsule profiles of important writers of prose and poetry from the Vedic period to the present. With excerpts in English and photos.

a. Female writers of, images in Sanskrit and Prakrit literature

346 BANERJI, SURES CHANDRA. Contributions of women to Sanskrit literature. *In his* A companion to Sanskrit literature; spanning a period of over three thousand years, containing brief accounts of authors, works, characters, technical terms, geographical names, myths, legends, and twelve appendices. Delhi: Motilal Banarsidass, 1971. pp.599-602.
[Unexamined. Book in NUC].

347 CHAUDHURI, JATINDRA BIMAL. . . . Sanskrit poetesses . . . Tr. by Roma Chaudhuri. Calcutta: J. Chaudhuri, 1941. lv.
First part contains selected verses and a piece on female Prakrit poets. Second part contains *Vaidyanāthaprāsādapraśanti* attributed to Devakumārikā and *Santānagopālakāvya* by Lakṣmī Rājñī. Introduction in English by Roma Chaudhuri. [Unexamined. NUC].

348 DIKSHIT, RATNAMAYIDEVI. Women in Sanskrit dramas. Delhi: Mehar Chand Lachhman Das, 1964. 495p.
History of female characterization in Sanskrit drama from Kālidāsa's predecessors to the present. With a chapter on the influence of Sanskrit drama on the portrayal of women in plays written in the various regional languages of India today. General assessment is a "more potential and influential position in the classical period," an unenviable position in the "medieval" period and "gallant efforts made by play-wrights of the 19th and 20th centuries at bringing the concept of ***Aryan womenhood*** to the fore-front once more."

349 JAIN, J.C. and MARGARET WALTER, trs. The gift of love and other ancient Indian tales about women. Delhi: Bell Books, Vikas Publishing House Pvt. Ltd., 1976. 99p.
Nine tales from Jaina Prakrit literature from the second through twelfth centuries C.E. "The tales were mainly intended for the purpose of spiritual edification" and concern prostitutes, courtesans, "procuresses," wives and others as examples of virtuous and unvirtuous women.

350 PARADKAR, M.D. Contributions of women to ancient and medieval Sanskrit literature. *In* Bhāratīya Vidyā 26,1/4 (1966) 29-33.
Briefly mentions numerous female contributors from the *Ṛgveda* through classical Sanskrit literature.

351 RAGHAVAN, V. Sanskrit and Prākṛt poetesses. *In* Quarterly J. of the Mythic Society 25,1/3 (1934/35) 49-74.
Names 31 Sanskrit and 8 Prakrit poets. Describes poetic style and gives biographical details and source of information. Provides some verses in original Sanskrit or Prakrit and in translation.

352 SHARMA, D.D. The concept of heroine in Sanskrit drama. *In* Panjab University Research Bulletin, Arts n.s. 6,2 (1975) 89-100.
[Unexamined].

353 _______. Sociological aspect of the Sanskrit drama with special reference to the status of women. *In* Vishveshvaranand Indological Journal 15,2 (1977) 202-10.
Reviews types of female characters in Sanskrit plays, patterns in their social position and changing trends toward the end of the classical Sanskrit dramatic tradition.

b. Other traditions: Pali, Tamil, Bengali, Oriya, Sinhala, Urdu

354 CHITTY, SIMON CASIE. The Tamil plutarch: containing a summary account of the lives of the poets and poetesses of southern India and Ceylon from the earliest to the present times, with select specimens of their compositions. Jaffna: Ripley and Strong, 1859. 122p.
Short biographies and selected translations of their works. [Unexamined. NUC].

355 JAHAN, ROUSHAN. Women in Bangla literature. *In* Women for women: Bangladesh, 1975. Dacca: University Press Limited, 1975. pp.217-46.
Reviews the changing images of women in the essentially male-produced Hindu Bengali literature (religious and secular) from the 13th century to the present. With comments on the interaction of particular ideals and social realities.

356 MATTHEWS, D.J. and C. SHACKLE. An anthology of classical Urdu love lyrics: text and translations. Delhi: Oxford University Press, 1972. 283p.
Reader of *ghazals* and related poems by 22 major poets from the 17th through 20th centuries. Includes introduction, poetry in English translation and Urdu original, biographical notes and vocabulary.

357 ROUT, SAVITRI. Women pioneers in Oriya literature. Cuttack: Manorama Rout, 1971. 136p.
Reviews life and work of notable extant and present female writers of Orissa. With section on folk literature and excerpts variously translated, transliterated or in the original Oriya.

358 TOUSSAINT, J.R. Women's contribution to Ceylon literature. *In* J. of the Dutch Burgher Union of Ceylon 30,3 (1941) 93-105.
[Unexamined].

c. Poetry and poets: surveys and anthologies

359 Indian poetesses: past and present. Delhi: Ministry of Education, Social Welfare and Culture; Government of India, 1976-77. 2v.
Brief articles on contemporary and historical poets in various traditions.

360 MACNICOL, MARGARET, ed. Poems by Indian women: selected and rendered by various translators. Calcutta: Association Press, 1923. 98p. (Heritage of India). [*Also* London: Oxford University Press, 1923].
Poetry of 56 women in 14 languages, arranged according to historical period — Vedic, early Buddhist, medieval and modern. With an introduction, a chronology of the poets and lists of poets and translators by language.

361 MEHTA, HANSA. Literary achievements of Indian women. *In* Evelyn C. Gedge and Mithan Choksi, eds. Women in modern India: fifteen papers by Indian women writers. Bombay: D.B. Taraporewala Sons and Company, 1929. pp.78-102. [*Reprint* Westport, Connecticut: Hyperion Press, 1976. (Pioneers of the Women's Movement)].
Reviews better known female poets and their works from the Vedas to Sarojini Naidu. Includes Vedic seers, Buddhist nuns, *bhakti* saint poets, Mughal women and their Muslim predecessors, Hindi writers influenced by the Muslim tradition and western-influenced English writers. With excerpts in translation and in English original.

d. Folk literature traditions

362 HANDOO, JAWAHARLAL. Bibliography of Indian folk literature. Mysore: Central Institute of Indian Languages, 1977. 421p. (*Its* Folklore Series, 2).
Numerous sources (4,252) in many Indian languages, each with mention of relevant folk genres and linguistic traditions. No index. Organized alphabetically by authors.

363 SEN GUPTA, SANKAR. Women in ancient literature and folklore. *In* Folklore [Calcutta] 10,9-12 (1969) 332-45, 374-89, 394-422, 464-85. [*Reprint in his* A study of women of Bengal. Calcutta: Indian Publications, 1970. pp.69-106, 113-53].
Bits and pieces on many aspects of women's folklife. Examples are primarily taken from the Bengali.

II. Perspectives on South Asian women in temporal and spatial contexts

A. Roots of the Hindu tradition: archeological and textual evidence to third century B.C.E.

1. Indus valley civilization, ca. 3000-1500 B.C.E., and evidence of a Mother Goddess cult

364 BILLIMORIA, N.M. Worship of the Mother-Goddess and the bull in Mohenjo-daro and Baluchistan. *In* J. of the Sind Historical Society 3 (1938) 84-93.
[Unexamined].

365 CHAUDHURI, NANI MADHAB. The worship of the Great Mother in the Indus region. *In* Calcutta Review 117,3 (1950) 151-67 and 118,1 (1951) 1-17.
Argues against Marshall's assertion of the importance of the Indus valley Mother Goddess cult. Considers most female figurines found there to have been toys. Based on archeological evidence and comparative data from the Middle East.

366 MACKAY, ERNEST. Religion. *In his* Early Indus civilizations, 2d ed., rev. and enl. by Dorothy Mackay. London: Luzac & Company, Ltd., 1948. pp.52-76. [*1st ed.* The Indus civilization. 1935].
Argues that various female figures from Indus valley excavations are remnants of a Mother Goddess cult, citing features of Hindu civilization to the present day and comparative data from the ancient Near and Middle East.

367 MARSHALL, JOHN, ed. Mohenjo-daro and the Indus civilization: being an official account of archaeological excavations at Mohenjo-daro carried out by the Government of India between the years 1922 and 1927. Delhi: Indological Book House, 1973. 3v. [*Reprint of* London: A. Probsthain, 1931].
See chapters on "Religion" and "Figurines and Model Animals" in the first volume and relevant plates in the third for Mother Goddess cult evidence and interpretations.

368 NEOGI, HARAN CHANDRA. The dancing girl of Mohenjodaro. *In* J. of Indian History 48,3 (1970) 559-64.
Proposes that a slim bronze image found at Mohenjodaro is a mother goddess and links image with later goddess iconography.

369 PURI, BAIJ NATH. Can we identify the Mother Goddess cult at Mohenjodaro? *In* Quarterly J. of the Mythic Society 34, 2/3 (1943-44) 159-64.
Indus valley Mother Goddess cult identified with Nāna-Ambā cult of the Kuṣāṇa period.

2. Aryan migrants and their Vedic, *śruti* literature "heard" by seers, ca. 1200-300 B.C.E.

See also interpretations of Vedic literature relating to 19th and 20th century reform issues within "(a) The social reform movement," entries 920-1224

a. Vedic position of women: honored as scholars and in other capacities

370 BASANA DEVI. Great women of Vedic times. *In* Prabuddha Bharata 59 (1954) 162-5.
[Unexamined].

371 BASU, JOGIRAJ. The education of women in Vedic India. *In* Visvabharati Quarterly 37,2 (1971/72) 121-33. [*Also in* Bulletin of the Ramakrishna Mission Institute of Culture 10,7 (1959) 160-5].
References from Vedic literature demonstrate value placed upon female education "in all its varieties — intellectual, moral, spiritual, aesthetic, and physical."

372 BHANDARKAR, D.R. Were women entitled to perform śrauta sacrifices? *In* All-India Oriental Conference 12th, Benares, 1943-44. Proceedings and transactions 12, v2. Benares: printed at the Benares Hindu University Press, 1946. pp.345-8.
In *śruti* literature a woman "can have her own wealth but can also participate in the possession of her husband's wealth . . . . if she has but the desire of attaining the fruit of a Śrauta Sacrifice, she can very well do so alone and on her own behalf or jointly with her husband . . ."

373 CHAKLADAR, HARANCHANDRA. Early Indian poetesses. *In* Sir Asutosh memorial volume, part 2. Patna: J.N. Samaddar, 1928. pp.65-74.
Biographical details and literary contributions of eight *brahmavādinīs*, female seers, of the *Ṛgveda*.

374 CHATTOPADHYAY, APARNA. The women in the upanisads. *In* Prabuddha Bharata 72,5 (1967) 223-6.
Argues that women were glorified in the *upaniṣads* as 1) scholars ("The age of the Upaniṣads had discovered the highest truth that knowledge of Brahman alone gives immortality and beatitude."), 2) wives and 3) mothers.

375 DE, SUSHIL KUMAR. Great women in Vedic literature. *In* Swami Madhavananda and Ramesh Chandra Majumdar, eds. Great women of India. Mayavati, Almora: Advaita Ashrama, 1953. pp.129-39. [*Reprint in* S.K. De, ed. Aspects of Sanskrit literature. Calcutta: Firma K.L.M., 1976. pp.177-86].
Chiefly biographical information about women seers, *brahmavādinīs*, in the *Ṛgveda* and *upaniṣads*.

376 DEVI, AKSAYA KUMARI. Female seers of ancient India. Calcutta: Vijaya Krishna Brothers, 192_. 44p.
On Ghoṣā, Sūryā, Yamī, Gārgī and Maitreyī from Vedic literature. With textual selections. [Unexamined. NUC].

377 DHARMA, P.C. The status of women in the Vedic age. *In* J. of Indian History 26,3 (1948) 248-68.
Survey covering variety of topics. Positive overall assessment.

378 DIWAKAR, R.R. Woman in the upanishads. *In* Prabuddha Bharata 59,3 (1954) 168-71.
[Unexamined].

379 HANDIQUI, KRISHNAKANTA. The women poets of the Rig-veda: a study. *In* Indian Antiquary 50 (Apr 1921) 113-7.
Translations of and commentary on verses of the *Ṛgveda* attributed to various women.

380 OMANANDA PURI, SWAMI. Women in the Brihadaranyaka Upanishad. *In* Modern Review 86,3 (1949) 238-9.
The accomplishments of two respected scholars, Gārgī and Maitreyī.

381 RAHURKAR, V.G. The Ṛṣikās (female seers) of the Ṛgveda. *In* Indian Antiquary, 3d series 3,1/4 (1969) 41-55.
Biographical sketches of various women who appear in the *Ṛgveda*. Not limited to seers.

382 RAJA, C.K. Womanhood as a spiritualizing and unifying force in Indian tradition. *In* Prabuddha Bharata 59,3 (1954) 186-90.
Discusses high status of women during the Vedic period in various spheres, including the significance of the term *dampatī*.

383 ROY, MIRA. Methods of sterilization and sex-determination in the *Atharvaveda* and in the *Bṛhadāraṇyakopaniṣad*. *In* Indian J. of History of Science 2,1 (1966) 91-7.
Reviews various surgical techniques, herbal drugs and dietary measures for both sterilization and influencing qualities of unborn child.

384 RUKMINI, M.A. Glory of womanhood in the Upanishadic Age. *In* Prabuddha Bharata 59,3 (1954) 175-9.
[Unexamined].

385 SASTRI, P.S. Two women thinkers of the Upanishadic Age. *In* Prabuddha Bharata 59,3 (1954) 171-4.
Maitreyī and Gārgī. [Unexamined].

386 SASTRI, SAKUNTALA RAO. Position of women in the Ṛgveda. *In* Indian Culture 11,4 (1945) 185-224.
Various topics. Cites many verses.

387 UPADHYAYA, BHAGWAT SARAN. Women in Ṛgveda, 3d rev. ed. New Delhi: S. Chand, 1974. 243p. [*1st ed.* 1933].
Various aspects of women's lives in *Ṛgveda*. Author has also consulted later Vedic commentaries.

388 VENKATARAMA SASTRI, T.R. Vedic attitude to satī. *In* J. of Oriental Research 20,1/4 (1953) 1-4.
Examines Vedic words and verses and concludes that a widow is enjoined to live as head of the family. A symbolic *satī* rite seems to have been practiced at the time.

b. Goddesses and feminine cosmology in Vedic literature

389 AGRAWALA, VASUDEVA S. Vedic conception of the motherland: a study in the Pṛthvī sūkta of the Atharvaveda. *In* D.R. Bhandarkar et al., eds. B.C. Law volume, part 1. Calcutta: Indian Research Institute, 1945. pp.368-76.
On the "earth hymn," an early manifestation of the conception of earth as mother in the Hindu tradition.

390 BANERJEA, J.N. Some aspects of Śakti worship in ancient India. *In* Prabuddha Bharata 59 (1954) 227-32.
In Vedic literature. [Unexamined].

391 BROWN, W. NORMAN. The creative role of the goddess Vāc in the Rig Veda. *In* J.C. Heesterman, G.H. Schokker and V.I. Subramoniam, eds. Pratidānam:

Indian, Iranian and Indo-European studies presented to Franciscus Bernardus Jacobus Kuiper on his sixtieth birthday. The Hague: Mouton, 1968. pp.393-7. (Janua Linguarum, Studia Memoriae Nicolai van Wijk Dedicata, Series Maior, 34).
"Vāc produced the raw material of the universe, the means for organizing it, and taught Agni, who taught the gods, how to use that means. The capstone of that process was the provision that the instruction should be imparted to men so that they could constantly renew creation . . ."

392 CHAUDHURI, NANI MADHAB. Mother-goddess conception in the Vedic literature. *In* Indian Culture 8,1 and 2/3 (1941/42) 65-83, 159-74.
Asserts that although a greater number of female deities and spirits are named in the *Ṛgveda* than male deities, Vedic scholarship has largely ignored them. Classifies the female deities and spirits, considers those invoked as mothers and discusses the female cosmological principle as the source of all creation (the "culmination" of the mother goddess conception). Points out attributes of the more prominent goddesses and their relations to gods. With a short summary of goddesses in later Vedic literature.

393 DUTT, K. GURU. Sakti in the Veda. *In* Triveni 14 (1945).
Concepts related to the idea of ***Śakti*** as subtly present in the ***Ṛgveda***. [Unexamined].

394 KANTAWALA, S.G. The hymn to Araṇyānī: a study. *In* J. of the Oriental Institute of Baroda 20,1 (1970) 1-11.
On a hymn to the goddess of the forest in the *Ṛgveda* and subsequent Vedic commentary on this passage.

395 RAGHAVAN, V. Mother worship: Vedic concept. *In* Vedanta Kesari 39,7 (1952?) 310-5.
[Unexamined].

396 WILLMAN-GRABOWSKA, HELENA. Sarasvatī-Anāhita et autres déesses: étude de mythologie indo-iranienne [Sarasvatī, Anāhita and other goddesses: a study in Indo-Iranian mythology]. *In* Rocznik Orientalistyczny 17 (1951/52) 250-72.
Vedic nature of goddess Sarasvatī compared with Iranian goddess Anāhita.

c. Women in selected *vedāṅga* disciplines, "limbs of the Veda"

(1) *Kalpasūtra*, guides for ceremonies

397 DUTT, RUBY. The property rights of women in the sutra period. *In* Modern Review 118,3 (1965) 239-46.
Rights of women to various types of property at various stages in the life cycle. Based on *dharmasūtra* texts.

398 GONDA, J. The sīmantonnayana as described in the Gṛhyasūtras. *In* East and West 7,1 (1956) 12-31.
Author argues that previous interpretors of this rite have not recognized its importance. He demonstrates the centrality of the parting of the wife's hair to marriage and conception in a detailed discussion from a comparative, Indo-European point of view.

399 WINTERNITZ, M. Das altindische Hochzeitsrituell nach dem Āpastambīya-Gṛihyasūtra und einigen anderen verwandten Werken: mit Vergleichung der Hochzeitsgebräuche bei den übrigen indogermanischen Völkern [The old Indian marriage ritual according to the *Āpastamba Gṛhyasūtra* and some other related works: with comparison to the marriage customs of the other Indo-German peoples]. *In* Denkschriften der Kaiserlichen Akademie der Wissenschaften 40 (1892) 1-114.
Detailed study based on a domestic rites text.

(2) *Vyākaraṇa*, grammar

400 CHATTOPADHYAY, APARNA. A note on the term 'Asūryampaśyā' in Pāṇini. *In* J. of Indian History 45,2 (1967) 535-9.
Argues that in spite of Pāṇini's reference to a woman who is not seen by the sun, female seclusion was not in practice at the time of this Sanskrit grammarian (ca. 500 to 300 B.C.E.).

(3) *Nirukta*, etymology

401 BHAWALKAR, VANAMALA. Disposal of girls in Yāṣka's time. *In* Indian Culture 3,1 (1936) 198-202.
Briefly discusses three forms of "disposal" of a girl by her family to others as enumerated in the ***Nirukta***, a commentary on difficult Vedic words compiled under the patronage of Yāska: *dāna*, *vikraya* and *atisarga*.

B. Sixth century B.C.E. to sixth century C.E.: heterodox challenges, development of Vedic tradition and earliest Tamil literary record

1. Women and society: general interpretations and artistic representations

402 AUBOYER, JEANNINE. Daily life in ancient India: from approximately 200 BC to AD 700. Tr. from French by Simon Watson Taylor. London: Weidenfeld and Nicholson, 1965. 344p. [*French ed.* La vie quotidienne dans l'Inde ancienne. Paris: Librairie Hachette, 1961. 400p.].
General survey with interspersed material about the lives of women.

403 CHATTERJEE, A.K. Misogynistic ideas in ancient Indian literature. *In* D.C. Sircar, ed. Social life in ancient India. Calcutta: University of Calcutta, 1971. pp.39-44. (*Its* Lectures and Seminars, Centre of Advanced Study in Ancient Indian History and Culture, VI-B (Seminars), part 2).
Reviews misogynist ideas expressed in the epics, the *Mānava Dharmaśāstra*, Pali Buddhist texts and other works. "Our discussion would show that the Hindus had a deep-seated prejudice against women and it would be [difficult] to find a single work which is entirely free from misogynic ideas."

404 GLADSTONE, SOLOMAN W.E. Women of the Ajanta caves. Bombay: Times of India, 1937. 29p.
Female figures in the murals of Buddhist cave temples at Ajanta. [Unexamined].

405 MAITY, SACHINDRA KUMAR. The imperial Guptas and their times, cir. AD 300-550. New Delhi: Munshiram Manoharlal, 1975. 286p.
Chapter on "Social Life" (pp.101-55) in particular contains perspectives on women's lives within general social and political context of the age.

406 MUKERJEE, SANDHYA. Some aspects of social life in ancient India, 325 B.C.-A.D. 200. Allahabad: Narayan Publishing House, 1976. 309p.
Social life from Mauryas to fall of Kuṣāṇas based on wide variety of sources. Much on women including the chapter "Status of Women" (pp.124-73).

407 MUKHERJEE, PRABHATI. Some notes on the study of the 'woman question' in ancient India. *In* Man in India 44,3 (1964) 264-74.
Argues that women can only be adequately understood in the context of the socio-economic system in operation, a quite heterogeneous system in "ancient" India. Gives examples of some elements of the socio-economic system of the period from about 400 B.C.E. to 500 C.E. and how they affected women.

408 SPINK, WALTER. Female figures. *In* Ajanta to Ellora. Mārg 20,2 (1967) 32-7.
Photographs and brief identification of selected sculpture from the cave temples of western India. "The female [figure] did not evolve in very easily definable ways during the course of the evolution of the Vakataka caves. This is partly because Indian sculptors had already achieved an eminently satisfactory canon for the female form long before the mid-fifth century, so the type appears at the new sites already full-blown."

409 Terra-cotta figurines in Patna Museum, Patna. Patna: S.A. Shere, 1961? lv.
Photographs of figurines, most feminine, dating from Maurya to Gupta dynasties. Brief identifying notes.

410 YAZDANI, G. Woman in sculpture of the Deccan: an artistic study. *In* Annals of the Bhandarkar Oriental Research Institute 23,1/4 (1942) 678-86.
"The object of the present article . . . is to judge the merits of Deccan sculpture, particularly of female figures, in the light of the universal criterion of beauty of form, naturalness of pose, and expression of inner feeling." From about the third century B.C.E. to the eighth century C.E. With plates.

2. Heterodox challenges to Brahmanism organized by 6th century B.C.E. contemporaries, Buddha and Mahāvīra

411 GHANANANDA, SWAMI. Improved status of women in Jainism and Buddhism: introductory. *In* Ramakrishna Vedanta Centre. Women saints of East and West: Śrī Sāradā Devī (The Holy Mother) birth centenary memorial. London: Ramakrishna Vedanta Centre, 1955. pp.139-43.
Mahāvīra, founder of the Jaina religion (599-

527 B.C.E.) and Buddha (ca. 560-480 B.C.E.) "stood for *social* equality amongst the people of all communities and classes, extending it also *to all women* of the country" in response to Brahmanic orthodoxy. Gives some examples of opportunities given to women early in these two traditions.

412 HANDOO, CHANDRA KUMARI and SWAMI GHANANANDA. Women saints of Buddhism and Jainism. *In* Ramakrishna Vedanta Centre. Women saints of East and West: Śrī Sāradā Devī (The Holy Mother) birth centenary memorial. London: Ramakrishna Vedanta Centre, 1955. pp.144-58.
Gives brief biographical details of the Buddhist *bhikkhunīs* Gopā, Gotamī (Mahāpajāpatī), Kisā Gotamī, Suppiyā, Paṭācārā, Ambapālī and Saṅghamittā and mentions notable Jaina women: mothers (notably, Marudevī), princess Mallinātha, who became the 19th *Tīrthaṃkara*, and numerous renowned nuns.

a. Early Buddhism: ambivalence toward and cautious increase in opportunities for lay and ascetic women

(1) Position of women in early Buddhism: evidence and interpretation

413 AMBEDKAR, B.R. The rise and fall of Hindu woman. Jullundur: Bheem Patrika Publications, 1970. 28p. [*Reprint from* J. of the Maha Bodhi Society 59 (May/Jun 1951)].
Article written in response to charge that Buddha was responsible for the downfall of women in India. Examines Pali Buddhist literature to demonstrate Buddha's favorable attitudes toward women and blames Manu for the decline in female status. Author was the main leader in the massive 20th century conversion of untouchables to Buddhism.

414 DHIRASEKARA, JOTHIYA. Women and the religious order of the Buddha. *In* Maha Bodhi 75,5/6 (1967) 154-61.
Discusses ambivalence about nature and potential of women in early Buddhist writings. While the Pali canon is frequently hostile to women, the general community seems to have been more hospitable.

415 DUTT, NALINAKSHA. Great women in Buddhism. *In* Swami Madhavananda and Ramesh Chandra Majumdar, eds. Great women of India. Mayavati, Almora: Advaita Ashrama, 1953. pp.253-74.
Biographical details of nuns — Mahāpajāpatī Gotamī, Khemā, Paṭācārā, Bhaddā Kuṇḍalakesā, Ambapālī and Isidāsī — and lay devotees — Sāmāvatī, Khujjuttarā and Visākhā. Argues that "there was some improvement in [women's] condition, due primarily to the basic principles which Buddha laid down in his teachings."

415a FALK, NANCY. An image of woman in old Buddhist literature: the daughters of Māra. *In* Judith Plaskow and Joan Arnold, eds. Women and religion, rev. ed. Missoula, Montana: Scholars Press, 1974. pp.105-12. (Aids for the Study of Religion, 1).
Attempts to explain the transition from the predominantly favorable early Buddhist view of women to the predominantly negative view around the time that the first Buddhist literature was written. Acknowledges changing parallel attitudes among Hindus during the same period and the influence of ascetic expectations upon monks, who produced the Buddhist literature. Proposes that in addition the "close association between women and the whole realm of natural generative productivity" conflicted with the Buddhist goal of release from worldly existence. Buddhism came to be hostile to woman "on a personal level, as an individual source of temptation, but also on a cosmic level, as representation and summation of the processes binding all men."

416 HORNER, I.B. Women under primitive Buddhism: laywomen and almswomen. Delhi: Motilal Banarsidass, 1975. 391p. [*Reprint of* London: G. Routledge, 1930].
First part, "The Laywomen," is based on canonical literature, later commentaries, *Jātaka* tales and the *Milindapañha*. Second part, "The Almswomen," is based on the *Vinaya Piṭaka* and *Bhikkhunī Vibhaṅga* rule books, the *Therīgāthā* and its commentaries and other Pali literature. Comprehensive discussion of many aspects of the lives of these women.

417 The Jātaka or stories of the Buddha's former births. E.B. Cowell, ed. Tr. from Pali by various persons. London: Luzac and Company, 1969. 5v. [*Reprint of* 1895-1905 ed.].
Hundreds of popular tales combining Buddhistic concepts with pre-existing folklore. Important source for daily life of period from which they date (ca. third century B.C.E. to third century C.E. or later). View of women in the *Jātakas* is especially negative.

418 LAW, BIMALA CHURN. Female characters as depicted in the Pali texts. *In* All-India Oriental Conference 4, 1926, Allahabad. Proceedings 4. pp.383-99. [Unexamined].

419 ________. Women in Buddhist literature. Colombo: W.E. Bastian and Company, 1927. 128p.
First "systematic and comprehensive treatment" of women as portrayed in Buddhist Pali literature. Chapters discuss marriage, slaves, dancing girls and courtesans, female

character, education, influence of Buddhism on women's lives, the *bhikkhunī* order and the lives of prominent Buddhist women.

420 ______. Buddhist women. *In* Indian Antiquary 58, 3-5 (1928) 49-54, 65-8, 86-9.
Who's who of about 75 early Buddhist women, mostly *bhikkhunīs*.

421 MUDIYANSE, NANDASENA. Some women in Buddhist literature appearing in popular Sinhalese poetry. *In* The Buddhist 42,4/7 (1971) 130-3.
References to well-known early Buddhist women in popular Sinhala poetry of the 13th through 20th centuries. Sinhala excerpts.

422 SEELANANDA BRAHMACHARI. Buddha, the friend of women. *In* J. of the Maha Bodhi Society 42 (Aug 1934).
[Unexamined].

423 SUBRAMANIAM, V. Pañcakanyātaraṅginī; Pancha Kanya Tarangini: a book of five dance dramas on five women who played a part in Buddha's life. Bangalore: the author, 1975? 82p.
Contemporary composition of five dance dramas that suggest the "mental transformation" of a series of lay women and *bhikkhunīs* who influenced and were influenced by the Buddha: Ambapālī, Yasodharā, Sujātā, Mahāpajāpatī and Māyā.

424 SUNITY, DEVEE [SUNITI·DEVI, MAHARANI OF COOCH BEHAR]. The life of Princess Yashodara, wife and disciple of the Lord Buddha. London: E. Mathews and Marrot, 1929. 75p.
[Unexamined. NUC].

425 TALIM, MEENA. Women in early Buddhist literature. Bombay: University of Bombay, 1972. 242p.
Details of monastic life, lay life and women and Gautama Buddha, "the motive underlying the study being to get a clear idea of the environments and atmosphere in which the Buddhist woman lived and was brought up." Concluding chapter discusses women in the Brahmanical, epic and Jain literatures and in travelers' accounts contemporary with the Buddhist material consulted.

(a) Lives of lay women: adherents and patrons

426 AŚVAGHOṢA. The lady Āmra (Āmrapālī) sees Buddha. *In his* Fo-sho-hing-tsan-king. Tr. from Sanskrit into Chinese by Dharmarakṣa and from Chinese into English by Samuel Beal. Delhi: Motilal Banarsidass, 1966. pp.249-56. (Sacred Books of the East, 19). [*Reprint of* 1883 ed.].
Story of Buddha's visit to a rich courtesan and influential lay woman of early Buddhism.

427 BARUA, DIPAK KUMAR. Folklife of women as revealed in the early Buddhist texts. *In* Folklore [Calcutta] 9,5 (1968) 161-73. [*Reprint in* Sankar Sen Gupta, ed. Women in Indian folklore. Calcutta: Indian Publications, 1969. pp.116-28. (*Its* Folklore Series, 15)].
Various aspects of women's lives from early Buddhist sources. Primarily considers lay women.

428 ______. Secular life of women in the Pāli texts. *In* Maha Bodhi 76,11/12 (1968) 333-7.
Brief review based on Pali texts and commentaries. Positive assessment.

429 DUTT, SUKUMAR. Nāgārjunakoṇḍa: an aftermath of Sātavāhana culture. *In his* Buddhist monks and monasteries of India: their history and their contribution to Indian culture. London: G. Allen and Unwin, 1962. pp.126-37.
Account based on inscriptions that show extensive patronage of monastic order by a queen mother, queens and princesses of the Ikṣvāku royal house in the third century B.C.E. While the Ikṣvāku kings were of the Brahmanical faith, many women were pious Buddhists.

430 The lion's roar of Queen Śrīmālā: a Buddhist scripture on the Tathāgatagarbha theory. Tr. by Alex Wayman and Hideko Wayman. New York: Columbia University Press, 1974. 142p.
Semi-historical text by anonymous author placed tentatively in third century C.E. Andhra Pradesh, a context where "prosperity of the Buddhist congregation depended heavily on the patronage of one or more Buddhist queens and contributions by ladies of high social rank." An early text to profess that "all sentient beings . . . have the potentiality of Buddhahood," the *Śrīmālā* contrasts with many previous Buddhist texts on the spiritual potentialities of women. With introduction and notes by Alex Wayman and Hideko Wayman. Recension based upon fragments of original Sanskrit text and Chinese, Japanese and Tibetan translations.

431 PAUL, DIANA MARY. A prolegomena to the *Śrīmālādevī Sūtra* and the tathāgatagarbha theory: the role of women in Buddhism. Ph.D. dissertation, Department of Religion?, University of Wisconsin, Madison, 1974. 299p. [University Microfilms 74-30,123].
Central figure of this text is an ideal Buddhist laywoman/teacher/philosopher. The study attempts to delineate the text's social and geographical context, its Buddhist philosophical antecedents and its place within *tathāgatagarbha* literature. [Unexamined. DAI].

432 ______. The Buddhist feminine ideal: Queen Srimala and the Tathagatagarbha. Missoula, Montana: Scholars Press, forthcoming. (American Academy of Re-

ligion, Dissertation Series, 30). Includes annotated translation of the *Srīmālādevī Siṁhanāda Sūtra*. Based on author's dissertation. [Unexamined].

(b) *Bhikṣuṇīs / bhikkhunīs*, "almswomen," and the early Buddhist order for women

433 BARUA, RABINDRA BIJOY. Bhikkhuni saṅgha and its repercussion on the society. *In his* The Theravāda saṅgha. Dacca: Asiatic Society of Bangladesh, 1978. pp.179-227. (*Its* Publication 32).
Describes establishment, structure and rules of Buddhist order for nuns and compares these with those of order for monks. Discusses inferior status of nuns to monks and notes that texts contain many references to substantiate Buddha's prediction that the institution would greatly endanger the ideal of *brahmacarya*. Gives examples of spiritual and scholarly accomplishments of nuns. Discusses significance of the *bhikkhunī* order for Buddhist expansion and the close relationship of nuns to laity via social service, spiritual guidance, need for patronage and other means.

434 DUTT, S. Buddhist nuns of India. *In* March of India (Aug 1956). [Unexamined].

435 MITRA, K.P. About Buddhist nuns. *In* J. of the Bihar and Orissa Research Society 7,4 (1921) 55-9.
Argues that female ascetics predated Buddhism in South Asia and that Buddha's aversion to the creation of an order of nuns was well-founded for, "The later Sanskrit literature bears testimony to the depth of immorality to which the Bhikkhunīs had fallen."

436 RAO, K.V. LAKSHMAN. Did Pāṇini know Buddhist nuns? *In* Indian Antiquary 50 (Mar 1921) 82-4.
Argues that the great Sanskrit grammarian must have been in contact with Buddhist nuns and, in doing so, contrasts Hindu and Buddhist attitudes toward female asceticism.

i) Structure and laws of the order

437 BHAGWAT, DURGA N. Early Buddhist jurisprudence (Theravāda Vinaya laws). Poona: Oriental Book Agency, 1939. 204p. (Studies in Indian History and Culture, Heras Institute of Indian History and Culture, St. Xavier's College, 13).
Has section (pp.158-90) on participation of women in monastic life, including various rituals. Revision of author's Master's thesis. [Unexamined. Book in NUC].

438 Bhikkhunivibhaṅga ("Nun's Analysis"). *In* The book of the discipline (Vinaya-Pitaka), v3: Suttavibhaṅga. Tr. from Pali by Isaline Blew Horner. London: Humphrey Milford, Oxford University Press, 1942. pp.156-426. (Sacred Books of the Buddhists, 13).
Rules and their interpretation regarding restraint and training of nuns with introduction (pp.xxix-lix) and notes. Major sections are "Defeat," "Formal Meeting," "Forfeiture," "Expiation," "Confession," "Training" and "Legal Questions."

439 Bhikṣuṇī-Vinaya: including Bhikṣuṇī-Prakīrṇaka and a summary of the Bhikṣu-Prakīrṇaka of the Ārya-Mahāsāṃghika-Lokottaravādin. Tr. from Sanskrit and ed. by Gustav Roth. Patna: K.P. Jayaswal Research Institute, 1970. 61, 413p. (Tibetan Sanskrit Works, 12).
Regarding a manual of discipline for Buddhist nuns dating from about the third or second century B.C.E. Detailed introduction by editor, critical notes, indexes and transliteration of text.

440 The Lesser Division (Cullavagga) X: on nuns. *In* The Book of the Discipline (Vinaya-Piṭaka), v5: Cullavagga. Tr. from Pali by Isaline Blew Horner. London: Luzac and Company, 1952. pp.352-92. (Sacred Books of the Buddhists, 20).
Gives account of formation of order, eight important rules, a variety of lesser regulations and methods of ordination.

441 TALIM, MEENA V. Buddhist nuns and disciplinary rules. *In* J. of the University of Bombay 34,2 (1965) 98-137.
Documents various motivations of early Buddhist women for renouncing worldly life. Briefly reviews controversy over Buddha's attitudes toward women. Lists and discusses various classes of rules for *bhikkhunīs*. Argues that although there were 311 laws for nuns as opposed to 227 for monks, the former were not degraded and the latter were not favored.

ii) Biographical details of early *bhikkhunīs*

442 BODE, MABEL. Women leaders of the Buddhist reformation. *In* J. of the Royal Asiatic Society 25 (1893) 517-66, 763-98.
Pali transliterations and English translations of the stories of 13 important early *bhikkhunīs* from Buddhaghoṣa's *Manoratha Pūraṇī* (fifth century), a commentary on the

Aṅguttaranikāya.

443 DE SARAM, C. 13 eminent female disciples of the Buddha. *In his* The pen portraits of ninety three eminent disciples of the Buddha. Colombo: Ceylon Readers Bookshop, 1971? pp.143-67.
Adapted chiefly from Ratmalane Piyaratna's Sinhala *Śrāvaka Śrāvikā Carita*, this book contains brief biographical sketches based ultimately on Pali texts. Each of the 13 *bhikkhunīs* discussed embodies a particular virtue.

444 The Elder's Verses 2: Therīgāthā. Tr. from Pali by K.R. Norman. London: Luzac and Company, Limited, 1971. 91, 199p. (Pali Text Society Translation Series, 40).
Translation of canonical work ascribed to various women mendicants. They describe their lives before joining the order and their experiences as *bhikkhunīs*. With lengthy literary-oriented introduction and extensive notes.

445 FOLEY, CAROLINE A. [CAROLINE AUGUSTA FOLEY RHYS DAVIDS]. Women leaders of the Buddhist reformation: as illustrated by Dhammapāla's commentary on the Therī-Gāthā. *In* International Congress of Orientalists 9th. Transactions 9, vl. London: Committee of the Congress, 1893. pp.344-61.
Translates and discusses selections from the *Therīgāthā* and Dhammapāla's commentary on it (ca. sixth century). Focuses on circumstances under which women joined early Buddhist order.

446 LAW, BIMALA CHURN. Buddhist Bhikshunis in inscription. *In* Epigraphica Indica 25,1 (1939) 31-4.
Briefly compares information on Buddhist *bhikkhunīs* in inscriptions with that in texts and travelers' accounts.

447 MÜLLER, E. Introduction. *To* Eduard Müller, ed. Paramatthadīpanī: Dhammapāla's commentary on the Therīgāthā. London: Oxford University Press, 1893. pp.vii-xxviii. (Pali Text Society, 30).
"I have . . . briefly examined all the historical and mythological matter contained in Dhammapāla's introductions and in the Therī Apadāna as far as the therīs of the Therī Gāthā collection are concerned. Only a small number of them has been left out, as about these there was nothing particular to say." Precedes transliterated version of Dhammapāla's commentary.

448 Psalms of the early Buddhists 1: Psalms of the Sisters. Tr. from Pali and ed. by Mrs. Rhys Davids [Caroline Augusta Foley Rhys Davids]. London: Henry Frowde, 1909. 42, 200p. (Pali Text Society Translation Series, 1). [*Reprint* 1964].
Translation of *Therīgāthā* with introduction and notes. These autobiographical verses, ascribed to various early *bhikkhunīs*, are a part of the Pali canon.

449 Psalms of the early Buddhists 2: Psalms of the Brethren. Tr. from Pali and ed. by Mrs. Rhys Davis [Caroline Augusta Foley Rhys Davids]. London: Henry Frowde, 1913. 52, 446p. (Pali Text Society Translation Series, 4). [*Reprint* 1964].
Translation of *Theragāthā* from the Pali canon with introduction and notes. The verses, attributed to various monks, describe their experiences as laymen and as members of the Buddhist order.

450 RAINA, VIMALA. Ambapali. Bombay: Asia Publishing House, 1962. 439p.
Historical novel about a wealthy court dancer who joined the Buddhist community.

451 SHARMA, ARVIND. How and why did the women in ancient India become Buddhist nuns. *In* Sociological Analysis 38,3 (1977) 239-51.
Examines autobiographical material in the *Therīgāthā* of women who joined the Buddhist order. Rejects notion that most women were moved toward the order by unsatisfactory personal and social circumstances. In at least 42 of 68 cases "it can be reasonably asserted that it was the spiritual attraction of Buddhism which led women to become nuns . . . . the positive appeal of . . . its founder, its doctrines and its Order."

iii) The early *bhikkhunī* order in Sri Lanka

452 WEERARATNE, AMARASIRI. The bhikkhuni order in Ceylon. *In* Maha Bodhi 78,10/11 (1970) 333-7.
Discusses the founding (by Saṅghamittā, King Aśoka's daughter) and early history of the *bhikkhunī* order in Sri Lanka. Based on Pali literature, Sri Lanka chronicles and inscriptions.

(2) Feminine aspects of early Buddhist cosmology

453 MACY, JOANNA ROGERS. Perfection of Wisdom: Mother of all Buddhas. *In* Rita M. Gross, ed. Beyond androcentrism: new essays on women and religion. Missoula, Montana: Scholars Press, 1977. pp.315-33. (American Academy of Religion, Aids for the Study of Religion, 6). [*Reprint from* Anima 3,1 (1976) 75-80].
Regarding *Prajñāpāramitā*, who has received little scholarly attention, and the *Mahāyāna* Buddhist literature so named. She is a personification of "the fundamental and saving wisdom. Imaged as light and space, pregnant

zero and matrix of dimension, this clear-eyed, compassionate Mama was, at a key point in the Dharma's history, its channel and its symbol." Based on the first text of this group, the *Aṣṭasāhasrikā Prajñāpāramitā*, ca. 100 B.C.E.

454 WAYMAN, ALEX. Female energy and symbolism in the Buddhist Tantras. *In* History of Religions 2,1 (1962) 73-111.
Detailed study of the meaning of the feminine in those *anuttara yoga tantra* Buddhist texts originally edited in Sanskrit. This class of texts deals with higher mysticism. Argues for the legitimacy of *tāntrika* scholarship and the genuine insights the subject matter may afford.

b. Early Jainism: ambivalence toward and cautious increase in opportunities for lay and ascetic women

455 JAIN, JAGDISH CHANDRA. Life in ancient India as depicted in the Jain canons, with commentaries: an administrative, economic, social, and geographical survey of ancient India based on the Jain canons. Bombay: New Book Company, 1947. 420p.
See interspersed material throughout but especially "Position of Women" chapter (pp.152-68) for an assessment of ambivalent attitudes toward women and their place in social life as revealed in the Jain canonical literature.

3. Classical Sanskrit literature

456 BHATTACHARYYA, SIVAPRASAD. Great women in Sanskrit classics. *In* Swami Madhavananda and Ramesh Chandra Majumdar, eds. Great women of India. Mayavati, Almora: Advaita Ashrama, 1953. pp.238-52.
Biographical details of numerous figures in Sanskrit literature, including Sītā, Draupadī, Pārvatī, Mahāśvetā, Śakuntalā, Vāsavadattā, Vasantasenā, Damayantī, Rādhā and Cūḍālā. Emphasizes virtues of female control, submission and dependence.

457 MUKHERJEE, PRABHATI. Property rights of women as recorded in Kauṭilīya Arthaśāstra and Manusmṛti. *In* Our Heritage 9,1 (1961) 47-60.
Discusses numerous categories of property and the circumstances under which each is regulated.

458 ________. Widowhood and niyoga in the Arthaśāstra and Manusmṛti. *In* Our Heritage 11,1 (1963) 1-11.
". . . *vedana*, *niveśa* and *niyoga* in the Arthaśāstra denoted three distinct customs; namely, remarriage, levirate, and temporary 'appointment' for raising *kṣetraja* sons, respectively. In the Manusmṛti, on the other hand, such permanent unions (in the forms of remarriage or levirate) were not encouraged."

a. Late *śruti* literature: *āyurveda*, "science of life," medical texts

459 BHAGAVAT SINH JEE [BHAGAVAT SIMHAJI, MAHARAJA OF GONDAL]. Hindoo practice during the period of nubility. *In his* A short history of Aryan medical science. Delhi: New Asian Publishers, 1978. pp.45-55. [*Reprint of* London: Macmillan, 1896?].
Reviews women's reproductive lives as characterized by *āyurveda* texts.

460 CARAKA. The Caraka Saṃhitā: expounded by the worshipful Ātreya Punarvasu, compiled by the great sage Agniveśa and redacted by Caraka and Dṛḍhabala. Tr. from Sanskrit and ed. by Shree Gulabkunverba Ayurvedic Society. Jamnagar: the editor, 1949. 6v.
Important medical text, which is still in use for instruction and consultation. Author was perhaps a physician of the Kuṣāṇa court in the first century C.E. This elaborate edition includes the original Sanskrit text and translations into Hindi, Gujarati and English as well as an extensive introduction (all of v1, 625p.). Material on women is interspersed throughout. *Śārīra Sthāna* section contains much on conception, pregnancy and birth.

461 RANADE, H.G. Women in ayurvedic literature. *In* Bulletin of the Deccan College Research Institute 31/32 (1970/72) 317-22.
Various comments about women's nature, health problems, roles and relationship with physicians. Based on *Suśruta Saṃhitā* and *Caraka Saṃhitā*.

462 SUŚRUTA. An English translation of the Sushruta Samhita based on original Sanskrit text. Tr. from Sanskrit and ed. by Kunja Lal Bhishagratna. Calcutta: the editor [v1-2] and S.L. Bhaduri [v3], 1907-16. 3v.
One of most important *āyurveda* medical texts, belonging perhaps to the second century C.E. Material on women is interspersed throughout but is especially concentrated in the *Śārīra Sthāna* section (v2, pp.113-238).

b. Early *smṛti* literature: a "recollection" and elaboration of the Vedic tradition

463 PINKHAM, MILDRETH WORTH. The status of women in Hinduism as reflected in the purāṇas, the Mahābhārata, and the Rāmāyaṇa. New York: Columbia University Press, 1941. lv.
Four chapters taken from her *Woman in the Sacred Scriptures of Hinduism* (entry 66).

464 SHAMA SHASTRI, R. Women's rights in the smṛitis. *In* All-India Oriental Conference 7, 1933, Baroda. Proceedings 7. pp.303-37.
[Unexamined].

465 SHARMA, RAM SHARAN. Some joint notices of women and property in the epics and puranas. *In his* Light on early Indian society and economy. Bombay: Manaktalas, 1966. pp.28-33.
[Unexamined. Book in BMG].

(1) *Dharmaśāstra*, law codes, and the *Mānava Dharmaśāstra*

466 CHATTERJEE, HERAMBA. Position of women as reflected in the forms of marriage. *In* Calcutta Review 145,1 (1957) 67-72.
Reviews eight forms of marriage described by Manu and their respective implications for the status of women.

467 ________. Studies in the social background of the forms of marriage in ancient India. Calcutta: Sanskrit Pustak Bhandar, 1972-74. 2v.
Discusses eight forms of marriage in detail. Based on *dharmaśāstra* texts and their commentaries.

468 DAS, R.M. Women in Manu and his seven commentators. Varanasi: Kanchana Publications, 1962. 288p.
Woman in *Mānava Dharmaśāstra* (primarily as daughter, wife, mother and widow) and ninth to seventeenth century commentaries. Takes general position that Manu has great reverence for women yet "is not blind to their defects and shortcomings."

469 GAUTAM, K. Concept of womanhood in Manusmṛti. *In* Agra University J. of Research 14,1 (1966).
[Unexamined].

470 JOLLY, JULIUS. Ueber die rechtliche Stellung der Frauen bei den alten Indern nach den Dharmaçāstra [About the legal status of women according to the *dharmaśāstra* of ancient Indians]. München: K. Akademie, 1876. 59p. [*Also in* Sitzungsberichte der Philosophische-Philologischen und Historischen Classe der K.B. Akademie der Wissenschaften zu München (1876) 420-76].
Position of women in *dharmaśāstras* as maidens, as wives and as widows. Sanskrit selections with German translations.

471 MANU, supposed author. The laws of Manu. Tr. from Sanskrit by G. Bühler. Delhi: Motilal Banarsidass, 1964. 620p. (Sacred Books of the East, 25). [*Reprint of* 1886 ed.].
Among the most important of the *dharmaśāstra* law code texts. Much on women.

472 RANGASWAMI AIYANGAR, K.V. Aspects of the social and political system of Manusmṛti. Lucknow: Lucknow University, 1949. 204p. (Radha Kumud Mookerji Lectures, 1946).
Said to contain a succinct statement of the Hindu view of males and females as unequal, including the idea that females may be superior (pp.162-6). [Unexamined. Book in NUC].

473 ROCHER, LUDO. The theory of matrimonial causes according to the *dharmaśāstra*. *In* J.N.D. Anderson, ed. Family law in Asia and Africa. London: George Allen and Unwin, 1968. pp.90-117. (School of Oriental and African Studies, Studies on Modern Asia and Africa, 6).
Compilation of *dharmaśāstra* material relating to grounds for legal action in marital disputes. Considers rights and procedures for redress. Notes tension between views of marriage as a community matter and as a private affair between two people.

(2) The epics: major sources for Hindu tradition from ca. 400 B.C.E. to 200 C.E., pervasive influences until the present

474 DHARMA, P.C. The status of women during the epic period. *In* J. of Indian History 27,1 (1949) 69-90.
Review organized by topic. "The transition from the Vedic to the Epic period is characterized by restricted freedom for women."

475 JAYAL, SHAKAMBARI. The status of women in the epics. Delhi: Motilal Banarsidass, 1966. 335p.
Introductory chapter regards epics as sources of history. Six chapters on various life stages and chapters on *niyoga*, adultery and extramarital relations, general attitudes toward women and central female characters. Brief appendixes review some kinship problems in epics.

476 MEYER, JOHANN JAKOB. Sexual life in ancient India: a study in the comparative history of Indian culture, 2d English ed. Tr. from German. New York: Barnes and Noble, 1953. 2v. [*1st German ed.* Das Weib im altindischen Epos: ein Beitrag zur indischen und zur vergleichenden Kulturgeschichte. Leipzig: von Wilhelm Heims, 1915. 440p.].
Most chapters discuss the various life cycle stages of a woman as portrayed in the *Mahābhārata* and *Rāmāyaṇa*. Concluding chapters discuss various topics: women's misfortunes and sorrows, ideal women, their powers, their worth and nature, their general position and women as chattel. English title is sensational rather than descriptive of content.

(1) *Mahābhārata:* vast storehouse of Hindu lore

477 AGRAWAL, CHANDRA P. Draupadi: a female hero. *In* New Quest 7 (Jan 1978) 33-7.
Examines Draupadī's structural position in the story of the *Mahābhārata*, her qualities and her deeds. Asserts that she lacks unity of character, representing the double matrix of old matriarchal values and new patriarchal values.

478 ALPHONSO-KARKALA, JOHN B. Woman as man's resurrection in Kalevala and Mahabharata. *In* Indian Literature 16, 1/2 (1973) 70-83.
Compares the *Mahābhārata* Sāvitrī legend to a similar legend from the Finnish *Kalevala*.

479 CHAKRAVARTI, TRIPURARI. Main women characters in the Mahābhārata. *In* Swami Madhavananda and Ramesh Chandra Majumdar, eds. Great women of India. Mayavati, Almora: Advaita Ashrama, 1953. pp.169-81.
Biographical details of three heroines: Gāndhārī, Kuntī and Draupadī.

480 FALK, NANCY. Draupadī and the dharma. *In* Rita M. Gross, ed. Beyond androcentrism: new essays on women and religion. Missoula, Montana: Scholars Press, 1977. pp.89-114. (American Academy of Religion, Aids for the Study of Religion, 6).
Relates contradictions in the *Mahābhārata* character Draupadī (e.g., she is a classical submissive ideal type yet sharp-tongued) to the evolution of the epic during a period when the position of women was in flux. Discusses Draupadī's role in central plot and as a vehicle for reflecting upon the central issue of *dharma*.

481 GUPTA, SUNITI BALA. Women characters in the stories of the Mahābhārata. *In* Swami Madhavananda and Ramesh Chandra Majumdar, eds. Great women of India. Mayavati, Almora: Advaita Ashrama, 1953. pp.182-220.
Biographical sketches of Sukanyā, Jaratkāru, Pativratā, Śakuntalā, Lopāmudrā, Sulabhā, Vidurā, Damayantī and Sāvitrī.

482 ________. Women characters in the Mahābhārata. *In* Vedanta Kesari 41,8-9 and 11-12 (1954/55) 271-2, 319-23, 405-7, 441-5.
On Gāndhārī, Kuntī, Draupadī, Sāvitrī, Vidulā and Sulabhā. [Unexamined].

483 HOPKINS, EDWARD W. Appendix on the status of woman. *In his* The social and military position of the ruling caste in ancient India: as represented by the Sanskrit epic. Varanasi: Bharat-Bharati, 1972. pp.274-316. [*Reprint from* J. of the American Oriental Society 13 (1889) 330-72. *Also reprinted in* J. of Ancient Indian History 2,1/2 (1968/69) 360-423].
Reviews position of women in the *Mahābhārata* and compares this to images in various sources from the same period. "The woman of the Mahābhārata in its completed form is best described in short by [negating] most of the description taken from the earliest Vedic age."

484 The Mahābhārata. Tr. and ed. by J.A.B. van Buitenen. Chicago: University of Chicago Press, 1973-. v1-. [3v published to date].
Among the most important texts of the Hindu tradition. Many of its female characters are presented to and by South Asian women as ideal figures. With volume three of the present recommended translation, five of eighteen major divisions are published. Of note in the material published to date is the story of Nala (v2, pp.319-64). The translator says, "Quite striking is the humanity of its characters, especially of the women . . . . the story's femininity . . . . The entire concatenation of events is treated strictly from a woman's point of view."

485 NÈVE, FÉLIX JEAN BAPTISTE JOSEPH. Des portraits de femme dans la poésie épique de l'Inde: fragments d'études morales et littéraires sur le Mahabharata [Images of women in Indian epic poetry: selections from moral and literary studies of the *Mahābhārata*]. Brussels: Librairie Polytechnique d'A. Decq, 1858. 123p.
[Unexamined. NUC].

486 SANDESARA, UPENDRARAY J. Terms of address to men and women in the Ādiparvan of the Mahābhārata. *In* J. of the Oriental Institute of Baroda 13,1 (1963) 21-5.
Primarily a list of the Sanskrit words and the *ślokas* in which they are found. Gives 68 terms of address to women. Excludes personal names and clan names.

487 SUR, ATUL KRISHNA. Sex and marriage in the age of Mahābhārata. *In* Man in India

43,1 (1963) 42-54.
Ethnography of sex and marriage as presented in the *Mahābhārata*.

488 THOMAS, P. Kama katha: tales of love, womanly wiles and devotion from the ancient Indian classic. Bombay: D.B. Taraporevala, 1969. 170p.
From the *Mahābhārata*? Illustrations (52). [Unexamined. IBP].

(b) *Rāmāyaṇa:* tale of Rāma and Sītā, an ideal king and an ideal wife

489 DHARMA, P.C. Women during the Ramayana period. *In* J. of Indian History 17,1 (1938) 1-28.
"It is possible to glean from the epic, many interesting bits of information about the habits, customs, education, accomplishments, toilette, status and rights of women during the Epic period."

490 KUMAR, ARVIND. A study in the ethics of the banishment of Sita, 2d ed. New Delhi: Sarita Magazine, 1975? 68p.
Examination of *Rāmāyaṇa* that (from jacket) "analyzes threadbare its sanctity, inquires into the minds of its main characters, indicates the place of women in that society . . ." The book is a study of the "genesis of the greatest malady which Hindu society today is suffering from — the deliberate suppression and humiliation of the Hindu woman."

491 NIHSHREYASANANDA, SWAMI. Great women in the Rāmāyaṇa. *In* Swami Madhavananda and Ramesh Chandra Majumdar, eds. Great women of India. Mayavati, Almora: Advaita Ashrama, 1953. pp.140-68.
Biographical details concerning numerous women in the *Rāmāyaṇa*, classed in two groups—those who are retired from worldly life and practicing asceticism and those who remain amidst society and are active in family life.

491a PANDURANGA RAO, I. Women in Valmiki. Hyderabad: Andhra Mahila Sabha, [1978]. 143p.
Study of outstanding women in the *Rāmāyaṇa*. Includes Sanskrit and Telugu quotations. [Unexamined. ALI].

492 VYAS, SHANTIKUMAR NANOORAM. Woman as chattel in the Rāmāyaṇa. *In* Poona Orientalist 13,3/4 (1948) 64-7.
"The practice of beautiful women being presented as gifts to others is found time and again in the ancient literature of India."

493 ________. Treatment of abducted women in the Rāmāyana Age. *In* Poona Orientalist 14,1/4 (1949) 85-8.
Concludes that female characters forcibly abducted and raped in the *Rāmāyaṇa* are rejected by most of society.

494 ________. Polygamy and polyandry as depicted by Valmīki. *In* J. of the Oriental Institute of Baroda 2,3 (1952). 22-31.
[Unexamined].

495 ________. Position of the daughter in Rāmāyaṇa society. *In* J. of the Oriental Institute of Baroda 3,1 (1953) 72-83.
Examines *Rāmāyaṇa* for what it reveals about the position of women as daughters, sisters, wives and mothers.

496 ________. The widow in the Rāmāyaṇa. *In* J. of the Oriental Institute of Baroda 6,2/3 (1956/57) 75-8.
Attitudes toward and practices of widows among various communities in the *Rāmāyaṇa*. Generally widows of higher groups are subject to greater restrictions. Some may remarry; others may not. Some become *satīs*; others do not. "There is no evidence to indicate that the presence of the widow was held undesirable on auspicious or festive occasions."

497 ________. Measure of freedom accorded to women in the Rāmāyaṇa. *In* J. of the Oriental Institute of Baroda 7,1/2 (1957) 1-6.
Explores the actions permitted and prohibited to women in the *Rāmāyaṇa*. Notes relative freedom permitted to women of warrior nobility and relative constraints of women of the harem.

498 ________. India in the Rāmāyaṇa Age: a study of the social and cultural conditions in ancient India as described in Vālmīkī's Rāmāyaṇa. Delhi: Atma Ram, 1967. 358p.
Has two chapters and much other interspersed material relating to women.

499 WAGLE, N.K. A study of kinship groups in the Rāmāyaṇa of Vālmīki. *In* George Kurian, ed. The family in India: a regional view. The Hague: Mouton, 1974. pp.17-42. (Studies in the Social Sciences, 12).
Descriptive study of kin group structures. Discusses such categories as *gṛha*, *kula*, *bandhu*, *bāndhava*, *jñāti*, *jāti* and *varṇa*, noting, among other things, women's place in them.

(3) Early *purāṇas*, encyclopedic sources for social history, and the chaste, devoted feminine ideal

For later purāṇas *(including* Śākta) *see entries 655-72*

500 HAZRA, RAJENDRA CHANDRA. Great women in the purāṇas. *In* Swami Madhavananda and Ramesh Chandra Majumdar, eds. Great women of India. Mayavati, Almora: Advaita Ashrama, 1953. pp.221-37.
Biographical sketches of mothers (Madālasā and Devahūti), wives (Satī, Umā, Śaibyā, Sunīti and Bhāminī) and an unmarried girl (Śarmiṣṭhā) from the earlier *purāṇas*. The author states that the later *purāṇas* passed into "the hands of inferior classes of people" who eliminated many exemplary female characters of the later period.

c. Sanskrit "secular" literature

501 GODE, P.K. The role of the courtezan in the early history of Indian painting. *In* Annals of the Bhandarkar Oriental Research Institute 22,1/2 (1941) 24-37.
References in the *Kāmasūtra*, *Arthaśāstra*, *Mṛcchakaṭikā* and other works demonstrate a period (ca. 500 B.C.E. to 800 C.E.) when courtesans were encouraged to cultivate the art of painting, *ālekhya*. In more recent times courtesans have concentrated on music/dance/drama arts.

(1) *Kāvya*, a class of ornate poetry: early works

502 Glimpses of sexual life in Nanda-Maurya India, translation of the Caturbhāṇī: together with a critical edition of the text. Tr. from Sanskrit by Manomohan Ghosh. Calcutta: Manisha Granthalaya, 1975. 181,56, 144p.
Four one act monolog plays of the *bhāṇa* type, satirical and comical in tone. [Unexamined. ALI].

503 ROBINSON, RICHARD H. Humanism versus asceticism in Aśvaghoṣa and Kālidāsa. *In* Feminine sensibility and characterization in South Asian literature. Guest ed: Fritz Blackwell. J. of South Asian Literature 12,3/4 (1977) 1-10.
Compares treatment of tension between erotic passion and asceticism in Aśvaghoṣa's *Buddhacarita* ("Career of the Buddha," ca. 100 C.E.) and Kālidāsa's *Kumārasambhava* ("The birth of Kumāra," ca. 400 C.E.). In the former austerities are performed out of compassion and, while the Buddha is truly human, women are objectified. In the latter, Pārvatī performs austerities to attain erotic love and is "consummately human and utterly feminine."

(a) Kālidāsa, master of *kāvya*, ca. 400 C.E.

504 DHAR, SHAILENDRANATH. The women of the Meghadūta. *In* Indian Historical Quarterly 4,2 (1928) 297-305.
". . . the very charm of the poem lies mainly in its description of the fair objects of nature and the fair sex." Discusses association of women with nature, the prominence of courtesans, eight different types of women and images of the ideal woman.

505 RADHAKRISHNAN, S. Women and marriage in Kālidāsa. *In* Bhavan's Journal 4 (1957) 70-6.
[Unexamined].

506 RAMACHANDRA RAO, VISARADA. The heroines in the plays of Kalidasa. Bangalore: Indian Institute of World Culture, 1951. (*Its* Transaction 7).
[Unexamined].

507 SUMMER, MARY [MARIE FOUCAUX]. Les héroines de Kalidasa et les héroines de Shakespeare [Heroines of Kālidāsa and Shakespeare]. Paris: Ernest Leroux, 1879. 142p. (Bibliothèque Orientale Elzévirienne, 24).
Essay appreciative of Kālidāsa's portrayal of women.

(b) Śūdraka's *Mṛcchakaṭika:* images of urban life, ca. 3rd to 4th centuries C.E.

508 HAGMAN, LORRI. Two famous courtesans: Vasantasena and Miss Tu. *In* Feminine sensibility and characterization in South Asian literature. Guest ed: Fritz Blackwell. J. of South Asian Literature 12,3/4 (1977) 31-6.
Compares Vasantasenā of the Sanskrit play *Mṛcchakaṭikā* ("The Little Clay Cart," attributed to Śūdraka, ca. 400 C.E.) and Miss Tu of the 16th century "Courtesan's Jewel Box" by Feng Meng-lung.

(2) Selected *śāstras*, scientific treatises

(a) The *Nāṭyaśāstra:* earliest extant treatise on music/dance/drama

509 BHARATA, supposed author. The Nāṭyaśāstra: a treatise on Hindu dramaturgy and histrionics. Tr. from Sanskrit by Manomohan Ghosh. Calcutta: Asiatic Society, 1950-61. 2v. (Bibliotheca Indica, 272).
Important, influential and earliest extant text on poetics, dramaturgy, music, body gestures, temple architecture and so forth in South Asia. Material about women is primarily found in the chapters on "The Costumes and Make-up," "Dealings with Courtezans," "Types of Character" and "Distribution of Roles." Dated variously from second century B.C.E. to fifth century C.E.

510 VARADPANDE, M.L. Stree preksha: female theatre in India. *In* Indian Horizons 27,2/4 (1978) 58-65.
Statement in Kauṭilya's *Arthaśāstra* "indicates that plays used to be performed by the dramatic parties consisting exclusively of female artistes . . ." Reviews references to women's cultivation of theatrical arts in various classical Sanskrit works, particularly the *Nāṭyaśāstra*.

(b) Vātsyāyana's *Kāmasūtra:* early treatise on sexual love, model for later works

For later kāmaśāstra *literature see entries 681-92*

511 CHAKLADAR, HARAN CHANDRA. Social life in ancient India: a study in Vatsyayana's Kamasutra, 2d rev. ed. Calcutta: Sushil Gupta, 1954. 193p. [*1st ed.* Calcutta: Greater India Society, 1929. 212p.].
Chapters on date of *Kāmasūtra*; its geography; general picture of social life, marriage and courtship; life of town dweller; position of women; and arts and crafts.

512 PETERSON, P. Vatsyayana on the duties of a Hindu wife. *In* J. of the Anthropological Society of Bombay 2 (1889) 459-66.
Lists 34 of Vātsyāyana's injunctions for wives and 4 for widows. Includes some interpretive comments.

513 VĀTSYĀYANA. Kama Sutra. Tr. from Sanskrit. Delhi: Asia Press, 1967. 181p. 42 photographs.
Early treatise on sexual love, both within and outside of marriage. Major sections include: "Of Sexual Union," "About the Acquisition of a Wife," "About the Wives of other Men," "About Courtesans" and "About the Means of Attracting others to Yourself." Numerous other editions are available.

(c) Kauṭilya's *Arthaśāstra:* early treatise on statecraft

514 CHUNDER, PRATAP CHANDRA. Kauṭilya on love and morals. Calcutta: Jayanti, 1970. 208p.
Family, marriage and sexual morality in the *Arthaśāstra*.

515 DAS, SUDHIRRANJAN. The position of women in Kauṭilya's Arthaśāstra. *In* Indian History Congress 3, 1939, Calcutta. Proceedings 3. Calcutta: Bhupendralal Banerjee, 1940. pp.537-63.
Considers aspects of marriage, seclusion, widowhood, prostitution, asceticism, sexual crimes against women, service occupations, property rights and maintenance rights. Concludes that "Kauṭilya was born in an age when morality was to a great extent degraded" leading him to "frame stringent rules restricting the liberty and the freedom" that women had previously enjoyed.

516 SINHA, B.P. Readings in Kauṭilya's Arthaśāstra. Delhi: Agam Prakasham, 1976. 184p.
"Social Life" chapter in particular discusses views on women expressed in this important treatise on polity and statecraft.

517 STERNBACH, LUDWIK. Legal position of prostitutes according to Kautilya's Arthasastra. *In* J. of the American Oriental Society 71 (1951) 25-60.
"Kauṭilya's Arthaśāstra is a unique source for the comprehension of the legal position of prostitutes, particularly from the point of view of the State, and for the introduction of State prostitution in ancient India."

4. Classical Tamil literature: earliest written record of Dravidian peoples

518 MANICKAM, J.T. Harlots in ancient Tamil culture. *In* International Conference Seminar of Tamil Studies I, Kuala Lumpur, Apr 1966. Proceedings I, vI. Kuala Lumpur: International Association of Tamil Research, 1968. pp.338-45.
"The aim of this paper is to present the institution of harlotry . . ., the place of harlots in the society, the various grades of

harlots, their different roles in the town-life, their inquisitiveness and artistry in fine arts like music and dance, their sports and other pastimes etc." Based upon numerous classical Tamil sources.

519 NADARAJAH, DEVAPOOPATHY. The mullai and the tulaci as symbols of chastity. *In* International Conference Seminar of Tamil Studies I, Apr 1966, Kuala Lumpur. Proceedings I, vl. Kuala Lumpur: International Association of Tamil Research, 1968. pp.314-9.
Describes association of a set of correspondences — a flower, a landscape, an emotion and so forth — with feminine chastity in classical Tamil literature.

520 _______. Women in Tamil society: the classical period. Kuala Lumpur: University of Malaya, [1969]. 189p. (*Its* Department of Indian Studies, Monograph Series, 15).
Considers various aspects of lives of women as reflected in classical Tamil literature.

521 _______. The Tamil ideals of female beauty. *In* R.E. Asher, ed. International Conference Seminar of Tamil Studies 2, 1968, Madras. Proceedings 2. Madras: International Association of Tamil Research, 1971. pp.34-40.
In classic Tamil literature the physical features and qualities of women are compared with such things as flowers, gems, cities of historic importance and goddesses. Factors such as shape, texture, color, aroma and temperature underlie the comparisons. The ideal woman of the Tamils was supposed to "please and gratify in every sense."

522 SUBRAHMANIAN, N. The status of women in ancient Tamilaham. *In* J. of Indian History 38,3 (1960) 487-95.
Surveys classical Tamil literature to show that the social philosophy of the ancient Tamils "was not particularly solicitous to women, though it cannot be called misogynic."

a. The *Caṅkam*/Sangam tradition: *Eṭṭuttokai*, eight anthologies; *Pattuppāṭṭu*, ten songs; and a grammar

(1) Women's lives in the poetry, particularly the *akam*, "interior," love poetry

523 ARUNACHALAM, M. The role of women in India: through history and literature. *In* Bulletin of the Institute of Traditional Cultures (Jul 1975) 191-205.
Images of women in classical Tamil literature to refute the frequent conception of Indian women as without power or rights.

524 BALASUBRAMANIAN, C. The status of women in Tamilnadu during the Sangam Age. Madras: University of Madras, 1976. 83p. (Diwan Bahadur K. Krishnaswami Rao Endowment Lectures, 1971/72).
Organized according to various topics. Many citations from primary sources. "The Sangam literature uniformly praises the womanhood of Tamil Nadu. The women of the Sangam period had distinguished themselves in their cultural attainments and virtuous living."

525 HART, GEORGE L. Woman and the sacred in ancient Tamilnad. *In* J. of Asian Studies 32,2 (1973) 233-50.
Asserts that one of two foci of early Tamil literature is women, as reflected in *akam* poetry; the other focus is the king who is reflected in *puṟam* poetry. Discusses the characterization of women and suggests some Dravidian contributions to widespread and enduring conceptions of womanhood in South Asia.

526 _______. Some aspects of kinship in ancient Tamil literature. *In* Thomas R. Trautmann, ed. Kinship and history in South Asia: four lectures. Ann Arbor: Center for South and Southeast Asian Studies, University of Michigan, 1974. pp.29-60. (Michigan Papers on South and Southeast Asia, 7).
Examines and supports Beck's thesis (entry 3241) on the centrality of women to the Tamil kin nucleus and the need to direct their power, using *akam* poetry about love relationships between men and women.

527 _______. The poems of ancient Tamil: their milieu and their Sanskrit counterparts. Berkeley: University of California Press, 1975. 308p.
Much on women. See especially major section (pp.93-119) about the power of women and Tamil contributions to widely held South Asian views of women from post-Vedic times to the present.

528 MANICKAM, VALLIAPPA SUBRAMANIUM. The Tamil concept of love. Madras: South India Saiva Siddhanta Works Publishing Society, 1962. 339p.
Psychological and social analysis of love in the *akam* poetry of the *Eṭṭuttokai* and *Pattuppāṭṭu* collections.

529 MANICKAVASAGAM, M.E. Patterns of early Tamil marriages. *In* Tamil Culture 11, 4 (1964) 329-38.
Forms of marriage and courtship in ancient Tamil Nadu as revealed in the *Eṭṭuttokai* and the *Pattuppāṭṭu*.

530 NADARAJAH, DEVAPOOPATHY. Courtship and marriage in the classical period. *In* J. of Tamil Studies 1,2 (1969) 19-42.
Describes courtship, mate choice, marriage ceremony and widowhood in ancient Tamil society, drawing mainly on the classical Tamil anthologies.

531 RAJALAKSHMI, S. Women in the age of the Saṅgam. *In* Bulletin of the Institute of Traditional Cultures, Madras (Jul 1975) 205-10.
Attitudes toward women and aspects of their lives in classical Tamil literature. ". . . the position of women in general was honorable but they had no property or political rights in the age of the Saṅgam."

532 RAMANUJAN, A.K., tr. The interior landscape: love poems from a classical Tamil anthology. Bloomington: Indiana University Press, 1975. 125p. (UNESCO Collection of Representative Works, Indian Series).
Translations of 76 Tamil ***akam*** love poems of the ***Kuṟuntokai*** anthology. Includes interpretive essay.

533 SUBRAHMANIAN, N. Śaṅgam polity: the administration and social life of the Saṅgam Tamils. Bombay: Asia Publishing House, 1966. 424p.
"Social Life" chapter includes discussion of the status of women, marriage, ***satīs***, widowhood, courtesans, dress and pastimes. Remaining sections contain scattered, brief references to women.

(2) The great scholar Auvaiyār, writer of *puṟam*, "exterior," heroic poetry

534 AVINASHILINGAM, T.S. Avvaiyār. *In* Ramakrishna Vedanta Centre. Women Saints of East and West: Śrī Sāradā Devī (The Holy Mother) birth centenary memorial. London: Ramakrishna Vedanta Centre, 1955. pp.9-14.
Details of her life story and 22 brief selections from her works. In legend, Auvaiyār prayed to her chosen deity to remove her beauty in order to avoid marriage and pursue learning. Her request was granted and, for the rest of her long life, she wrote ethical works and went about imparting wisdom.

535 RAJAGOPALACHARI, C. Avvaiar: a great Tamil poetess. Bombay: Bharatiya Vidya Bhavan, 1971. 32p.
Biographical details interspersed with translations of 55 poems. This "most popular figure" of classical Tamil literature is worshipped as an ***avatāra*** of the goddess of learning. Appendix of poetry in original Tamil.

b. *Cilappatikāram*, Iḷaṅkōvaṭikaḷ's Jaina-influenced epic, 5th to 6th centuries C.E.

536 HESSNEY, RICHARD C. The women in the Shilappadikaram. *In* Literary Half-Yearly 12,2 (1971) 98-104.
Argues that this Tamil epic is unique among epics of the world in its extensive concern with women. Discusses several of its female characters.

C. Seventh century to 1820 C.E.: *bhakti* movement, development of the *Śākta* tradition, coming of Islam, regional states and more

1. Biography: notable women

See also entries 712-86

537 CHAUDHURI, J.B. The authoress Bīnabāyī. *In* Indian Historical Quarterly 16,3 (1940) 580-5.
Bīnabāyī is said to be the only woman whose contribution to *paurāṇika* literature is extant today. Summarizes her text, the *Dvārakā Pattalā* (a summary of the *Dvārakā Māhātmya* of the *Skanda Purāṇa*) and the biographical details therein. The work reveals her to be a writer of "poetic genius."

538 DATTA, KALIKINKAR. Great Hindu women in North India, c. 1201 to 1800 A.D. *In* Swami Madhavananda and Ramesh Chandra Majumdar, eds. Great women of India. Mayavati, Almora: Advaita Ashrama, 1953. pp.320-31.
Biographical sketches of Rajput heroines (Saṃyogitā, Kurmādevī, Padminī, Tārābāī, Rani Durgāvatī and Dhātrī Pānnā), religious devotees (Lallā, Mīrābāī and various others) and numerous women distinguished in the arts.

539 DESHPANDE, KAMALABAI. Great Hindu women in Mahārāṣhṭra. *In* Swami Madhavananda and Ramesh Chandra Majumdar, eds. Great women of India. Mayavati, Almora: Advaita Ashrama, 1953. pp.343-61.
Biographical sketches of saints and poets (Mahadambā, Muktābāī, Janābāī, Kānhopātrā, Bahiṇābāī, Veṇābāī and Akkābāī) and women in politics and administration (Jijābāī, Tārābāī and Ahalyābāī).

540 KESHAVIAH, M. Life of Nacharamma: history of her migration. Mysore: Sree Panchacharya Electric Press, 1936. 99p.
Biography of a brahman female saint who led the first migration of Sanketi brahmans from Tamil Nadu to Karnataka in the mid-14th century. Interspersed with wide-ranging philosophical musings and Sanketi history.

541 MIRZA, MOHAMMAD WAHID. Great Muslim women of India. *In* Swami Madhavananda and Ramesh Chandra Mujumdar, eds. Great women of India. Mayavati, Almora: Advaita Ashrama, 1953. pp.378-94.
Brief biographies of queens and princesses (Raẓiyya Sulṭān, Gulbadan Begam, Nūr Jahān, Jahānārā and Zīb-un-Nisā), religious women (Bībī Fātima Sām and Bībī Zulaikhā) and heroic women (Cānd Bībī and Ṣaḥibjī).

542 NILAKANTA SASTRI, K.A. et al. Great Hindu women in South India, c. 1301-1800 A.D. *In* Swami Madhavananda and Ramesh Chandra Majumdar, eds. Great women of India. Mayavati, Almora: Advaita Ashrama, 1953. pp.332-42.
Sketches of the lives of poets (Gaṅgadevī, Molla, Oduva Tirumalāmbā, Honnamma, Celuvāmbā,Heḷavanakaṭṭe Giriyamma, Tarigoṇḍa Veṅgamāmbā, Madhuravāṇī, Rāmabhadrāmbā, Raṅgajamma and Muddupaḷani) and queens (Cennammāji, Umayamma and Maṅgamma).

543 RAGHAVACHARYULU, K. Some South Indian poetesses. *In* Quarterly J. of the Mythic Society 26,1 (1935) 41-8.
Discusses six women and their work, from the 14th through 18th centuries. Provides some untranslated selections of their poetry.

544 RAGHAVAN, V. Some more Sanskrit and Prākṛt poetesses. *In* Quarterly J. of the Mythic Society 27,3/4 (1937) 279-90.
Author points out that four poets mentioned as female in his previous article (entry 351) were found to have been male. Discusses life and work of "one Apabhramśa poetess, Āyiccāmbā by name, a Sanskrit poetess, Padmāvatī, and a woman writer on a religious subject, Bīnabāyī, who was a queen." With some untranslated selections from their poetry.

545 SANDESARA, BHOGILAL J. Great Hindu women in Gujarāt and Saurāṣhṭra. *In* Swami Madhavananda and Ramesh Chandra Majumdar, eds. Great women of India. Mayavati, Almora: Advaita Ashrama, 1953. pp.362-8.
Biographical sketches of three distinguished women (Mayaṇallā/Mīnaladevī, Naikīdevī and Anupamā). Briefly mentions several saint poets.

546 SEN, SUKUMAR. Great Hindu women in East India. *In* Swami Madhavananda and Ramesh Chandra Majumdar, eds. Great women of India. Mayavati, Almora: Advaita Ashrama, 1953. pp.369-77.
Biographical information on rulers and administrators (Viśvāsadevī, Caucing, Candraprabhā and Rani Bhavānī), *Vaiṣṇava* devotees (Sacīdevī, Viṣṇupriyā, Jāhnavā, Sītā, Icchādevī and Hemalatā) and literary women (Candrāvatī, Gaṅgāmaṇi and Haṭī Vidyālaṅkāra).

547 SENAVERATNE, ANNA P. Some notable Sinhalese women in history. *In* Ceylon Antiquary and Literary Register 1,2-3 (1915/16) 140-4, 212-5.
Biographical sketches of ten women; based primarily on the *Mahāvaṃsa*.

548 SENEVIRATNE, MAUREEN. Some women of the Mahavamsa and Cūlavamsa. Colombo: H.W. Cave, 1969. 186p.
Biographical accounts of twelve women drawn from the Sri Lanka chronicles, *Mahāvaṃsa* and *Cūlavaṃsa*.

549 SHANTAKUMARI, S.L. Some women administrators in ancient and medieval Karnataka. *In* Sarojini Shintri, C.R. Yaravintelimath and S.L. Shantakumari, eds. Woman: her problems and her achievements. Dharwar: Karnatak University, 1977. pp.72-8.
"Some [Karnataka] women belonging to the royal families as well as the noble class wielded the reins of administration of big and small territories either as queens or as officers, some jointly with their husbands and some independently." Lists and briefly describes several such women.

2. Social life and women's lives

a. General interpretations

550 ARIYAPALA, M.B. Society in medieval Ceylon: the state of society in Ceylon as depicted in the Saddharma-ratnāvaliya and other literature of the thirteenth century. Colombo: Department of Cultural Affairs, 1956. 415p.
Interspersed with miscellaneous details relating to women's lives.

551 CHAKRABARTY, TAPO NATH. Women in the early inscriptions of Bengal. *In* D.R. Bhandarkar et al., eds. B.C. Law volume, part 2. Poona: Bhandarkar Oriental Research Institute, 1946. pp.243-60.
Life of and attitudes toward women as revealed in Bengali inscriptions of the fifth through twelfth centuries.

552 DATTA, KALIKINKAR. Position of women in Bengal in the mid-eighteenth century. *In* Calcutta Review 37,1 (1930) 17-32.
Presents material from reports of contemporary Europeans and Bengali literature to describe the position of women in family life and community affairs in the mid-18th century. Wide range of topics. Author is not committed to an overwhelmingly positive or negative view as are many who write such "position of women" papers.

553 GANGULY, D.C. Some aspects of the position of women in ancient India. *In* Cultural heritage of India, 2d ed., rev. and enl., v2. Calcutta: Ramakrishna Mission Institute of Culture, 1962. pp.594-600.
Various aspects of women's lives, primarily in the eighth through twelfth centuries. Considers achievements of women of letters and women of politics, marriage, legal rights, enjoined conduct and recreation.

554 GHOSHAL, U.N. The position of women in early medieval Hindu society. *In* Bulletin of the Ramakrishna Mission Institute of Culture 9,8 (1958) 180-4.
States that later *smṛti* works are generally harsh and constraining. [Unexamined].

555 GODAKUMBURA, CHANDRA. Women in early Sinhalese society. *In* New Lanka 4,2 (1953) 54-61.
[Unexamined].

556 HUSAIN, SHAHANARA. Life of village women in early medieval Bengal. *In* J. of the Asiatic Society of Bangladesh 19,2 (1974) 1-9.
Miscellaneous details drawn from inscriptions, texts, literature, sculpture and so forth. Some photographs and drawings.

557 ________. The position of women in pre-Muslim society, 700 - 1200 A.D. *In* J. of the Institute of Bangladesh Studies 1,1 (1976) 155-68.
Discusses marriage, family and widowhood as detailed in texts, literature and inscriptions.

558 MAJMUDAR, M.R. Cultural history of Gujarat: from early times to pre-British period. Bombay: Popular Prakashan, 1965. 364p.
Chapters on marriage and family, religion and pleasure arts have much on women. Topics include widowhood, female infanticide, seclusion, child marriage, *satī*, goddess worship, dress and erotic literature.

559 PANIKKAR, K.M. The Middle Period. *In* Tara Ali Baig, ed. Women of India. Delhi: Publications Division, Ministry of Information and Broadcasting, Government of India, 1958. pp.9-13.
Traces the gradual, but not equivocal, decline in the status of women from the Islamic invasions through the 18th century. Notes the relative stability of women's position in South India and the "revival of Hindu life" in the 15th century as exceptions to the trend. Briefly discusses various notable women and various social institutions. Photographs of art works.

560 PIERIS, RALPH. Kinship and marriage. *In his* Sinhalese social organization: the Kandyan period. Colombo: Ceylon University Press Board, 1956. pp.193-230.
Sections on "Marriage," "The Sinhalese Kinship System" and "The Family and the Crises of Life" are the only ones with substantial material on women in this book dealing with the period 1591 to 1815.

561 ROWLANDS, J. HELEN. La femme Bengalie dans la littérature du moyen-âge [The Bengali woman in medieval literature]. Paris: A. Maisonneuve, 1930. 241p.

[Unexamined. NUC].

562 TRAKROO, P.L. Position of Kashmiri women in Nilamatapurana. *In* S.M. Iqbal and K.L. Nirash, [eds]. The culture of Kashmir. New Delhi: Marwah Publications, 1978. pp.110-2.
Argues that the ***Nīlamata Purāṇa*** offers a pleasant and casual image of women and lacks the extreme glorification/depreciation ambiguity of many other texts of the Hindu tradition.

563 UPADHYAY, VASUDEV. The socio-religious conditions of North India, 700 - 1200 A.D. Varanasi: Chowkhamba Sanskrit Series Office, 1964. 388p. Chowkhamba Sanskrit Series, 39).
Primarily male-oriented, but miscellaneous brief references scattered throughout regarding clothing, ***Śākta*** cult, dancing girls, courtesans, etc.

564 VAIDEHI KRISHNAMOORTHY, A. Position of women. *In her* Social and economic conditions in eastern Deccan, from A.D. 1000 to A.D. 1250. Madras: printed at Kabeer Printing Works, 1970. pp.51-73.
Discusses three classes of women in the literary works and inscriptions of the period — the family woman, the courtesan (including *dāsīs* attached to temples) and the prostitute — and occupational categories and educational opportunities for women.

b. Various social institutions

565 DIXIT, S.C. An account of widow immolation in Gujarat in 1741 A.D. *In* J. of the Anthropological Society of Bombay 14,7 (1931) 830-3.
Translation of a Gujarati poem describing the ***satī*** Śivābāī of Surat's Nagar brahman community.

566 NAGASWAMI, R. A 13th century sale deed on rights of women. *In his* Studies in ancient Tamil law and society. Madras: Institute of Epigraphy, State Department of Archaeology, Government of Tamilnadu, 1978. pp.84-8.
Discusses a Tamil inscription that concerns land sales and the rights of inheritance of women in the 13th century. It suggests that "women had equal rights to property but the transactions were made through the male members" of the family who acted as guardians.

567 RAIKAR, Y.A. Prostitution during the Yadava period. *In* J. of the Oriental Institute of Baroda 13,2 (1963) 124-33.
Social organization of prostitution in the 12th through 14th century Deccan. Based upon early Marathi ***Mahānubhāva*** cult literature and the ***Jñāneśvarī***.

567a SALETORE, R.N. Sex in Indian harem life. New Delhi: Orient Paperbacks, 1978. 181p.
Considers history and social structure of the Indian harem, sexuality and intrigue, the harem during war and various pastimes and practices.

568 THAKUR, UPENDRA. Self-immolation in early mediaeval India. *In his* Some aspects of ancient Indian history and culture. New Delhi: Abhinav Publications, 1974. pp.219-40.
Reviews widow immolation and ***jauhar*** in the "medieval" period of Indian history. The author says of ***jauhar***: "The loss of a battle or the capture of a city was a signal to avoid captivity and its horrors which to the Rajput ladies was worse than death: to avoid such degradation they took recourse to ***Jauhar*** or immolation of every female of the family or even the whole tribe if the occasion so demanded."

569 YESUDAS, R.N. Pulappēḍi in Kerala. *In* J. of Kerala Studies 2,1 (1975) 41-54.
Women of Kerala's higher castes had, until the end of the 17th century, "a certain dread toward the underprivileged classes in certain seasons of the year known variously as Pulappēḍi (fear of Pulayas), Parappēḍi (fear of Parayas) and Maṉṉāppēḍi (fear of Maṉṉān or washerman)." Attempts to analyze this phenomenon. Argues that the tension is important in social history as a sign of a move toward greater egalitarianism.

3. Later *smṛti* literature and its social contexts

a. *Bhakti* movement: opportunities for women in its unmediated worship, egalitarian values and use of regional languages

570 DESAI, NEERA. Impact of bhakti movement on the status of Indian woman. *In her* Woman in modern India. Bombay: Vora and Company, 1957. pp.34-47.
The ***bhakti*** movement, with its emphasis on humanism, lack of ceremonialism, vernaculars and direct approach to God, offered new and expanded opportunities "in a period when Hindu society was rigid and callous to lower castes and women." However, the ***bhaktas'*** "total conception of woman's status was not quite free from the admixture of the then prevailing attitude toward womanhood" and the overall effect of the movement on women was rather limited.

(1) Emergence in the South: the Tamil saints, 7th to 12th centuries

571 KAMALIAH, K.C. Women saints of Tamilnad. *In* Indian Literature 20,2 (1977) 46-65.
Briefly treats the lives and works of Kāraikkālammaiyār, Āṇṭāḷ, Maṅkaiyarkkaraciyār and Tilakavatiyār.

572 SCHOMERUS, HILKO WIARDO. Die Frau und die Religion südindien. *And* Kāraikkāl Ammaiyār: Aṟpudattiruvandādi, Kompendium der Wunder. *And* Āṇḍāḷ-Ālvār: Tiruppāvai [Woman and South Indian religion. *And* Kāraikkālammaiyār's *Aṟputattiruvantāti*, Compendium of Wonder. *And* The *Ālvār* Āṇṭāḷ's *Tiruppāvai*]. *In his* Indien und das Christentum, vI: Indische frommigkeit. Halle-Salle: Buchhandlung des Waisenhauses, 1931. pp.159-76, 177-89, 190-8.
First section discusses historical context of South Indian *bhakti* and its opportunities for women, in contrast to Brahmanism. Remaining sections contain translations of 101 poems of the *Vaisnava* devotee Kāraikkālammaiyār and 30 poems of *Śaiva* devotee Āṇṭāḷ from Tamil into German.

(a) *Śaiva Nāyanmār* tradition: the saint Kāraikkālammaiyār, other spiritual women, conceptions of the goddess

573 NALASWAMI PILLAI, J.M. Mother of Karaikal. *In* Siddhanta Deepika 13,4 (1912) 151-60.
Details of her life taken from her works and the 12th century *Periyapurāṇam*. With translations of some of her verses. [Unexamined].

574 SARASWATHI, M.E. Women in *Periyapurāṇam*. *In* Bulletin of the Institute of Traditional Cultures, Madras (Jul 1975) 211-23.
Notes positive references to women in Cēkkiḻār's *Śaiva* text. Gives biographical details of two female *Śaiva* revivalists, Maṅkaiyarkkaraciyār and Tilakavatiyār, and the saint poet Kāraikkālammaiyār.

575 SATCHIDANANDAM PILLAI, S. Kāraikkāl Ammaiyār. *In* Ramakrishna Vedanta Centre. Women saints of East and West: Śrī Sāradā Devī (The Holy Mother) birth centenary memorial. London: Ramakrishna Vedanta Centre, 1935. pp.15-22.
Account of her life taken from Cēkkiḻār's 12th century *Periyapurāṇam*. With 12 verses translated from her *Aṟputattiruvantāti*.

576 YOCUM, GLENN E. The goddess in a Tamil Śaiva devotional text, Māṇikkavācakar's *Tiruvācakam*. *In* J. of the American Academy of Religion 45, supplement (Mar 1977) K: 369-88.
Regarding attention to Śiva's spouse in this poetry collection, considered to be among the best Tamil *Śaiva* devotional literature. Goddess as 1) coparticipant in Śiva's gracious actions for the world, 2) a paradigm of devotion to Śiva and 3) the female half of his androgynous manifestation. Discusses her characterization, attitudes of the male author, Māṇikkavācakar, and related aspects of Tamil culture and the theology expressed in the *Tiruvācakam*.

(b) *Vaiṣṇava Āḻvār* tradition: the saint Āṇṭāḷ, consort of Lord Kṛṣṇa

577 ĀṆṬĀḶ. The maiden's vow. *In* Hymns of the Āḻvārs. Tr. from Tamil by J.S.M. Hooper. Calcutta: Association Press, 1929. pp.49-58. (Heritage of India).
Translation of Āṇṭāḷ's *Tiruppāvai*, a poem that describes fulfillment of a vow as a mode of realization of the divine presence. She identifies herself as the consort of God.

578 ________. Thiruppavai, with an English rendering, 2d ed. Tr. from Tamil by D. Ramaswamy Iyengar. Madras: Sri Visishtadvaita Pracharini Sabha, 1967. 35p. [*1st ed.* 1946].
Miscellaneous introductory comments about Āṇṭāḷ, her best known work and their significance for Tamils. Juxtaposes Tamil original and English translation of each of the 30 stanzas of the *Tiruppāvai*.

579 FILLIOZAT, JEAN. Un texte Tamoul de dévotion Vishnouite: le Tiruppāvai d'Āṇṭāḷ [A Tamil *Vaiṣṇava* devotional text: Āṇṭāḷ's *Tiruppāvai*]. Pondichéry: Institut Français d'Indologie, 1972. 120p. (Publications de l'Institut Français d'Indologie, 45).
Contains introduction that discusses the author, her work and commentaries on it; a bibliography; the text in Tamil and in French translation; extensive notes; Śrīraṅgarāmānuja's Sanskrit translation in transliteration and French translation; another Sanskrit version, the *Śrīvrata*, in transliteration and French translation; and a series of plates, including many illustrations of the *Tiruppāvai*

580 MAHADEVAN, T.M.P. Āṇḍāḷ. *In his* Ten saints of India. Bombay: Bharatiya Vidya Bhavan, 1971. pp.70-5.
Biographical legends and a drawing.

581 PARAMATMANANDA, SWAMI. Āṇḍāḷ. *In* Ramakrishna Vedanta Centre. Women saints of East and West: Śrī Sāradā Devī (The Holy Mother) birth centenary

memorial. London: Ramakrishna Vedanta Centre, 1955. pp.23-9.
Aspects of her life story, with six poems translated from her works, *Tiruppāvai* and *Nāyacciyār Tirumoḻi*, and a tribute poem by a contemporary Bengali devotee, Sri Devendranath Sen.

(2) Various Kerala *Vaiṣṇava* saints: without an organized regional tradition

582 SESHADRI, P. and K.S. NILAKANTAN UNNI. Some women saints of Keraḷa. *In* Ramakrishna Vedanta Centre. Women saints of East and West: Śrī Sāradā Devī (The Holy Mother) birth centenary memorial. London: Ramakrishna Vedanta Centre, 1955. pp.80-5.
Mentions some available fragments of the life stories of three Malayalam saints: Chaṅkrottu Amma (8th century?), devoted to Śrī Vallabha (Viṣṇu); Vaḍakkēḍattu Naṅga Peṇṇu (date unknown), devoted to Lord Viṣṇu; and Kurūr Amma (late 16th century), devotee of Bālakṛṣṇa.

(3) Karnataka *Vīraśaiva* tradition: Akkamahādēvi's *vacanas*, leader Basavaṇṇa on women, 12th century

583 AKKAMAHĀDĒVI. Mahādēviyakka. *In* Speaking of Śiva. Tr. from Kannada by A.K. Ramanujan. Baltimore, Maryland: Penguin, 1973. pp.111-42.
Brief biographical notes and translations of 48 *vacanas*.

584 ________. Vacanas of Akkamahadevi. Tr. from Kannada by Armando Menezes and S.M. Angadi. Dharwar: Manohar Appasaheb Adke, 1973. 173, 119p.
Three hundred fifteen *vacanas* in English and in Kannada original subsumed under divisions "Devotion," "Divinity," "Grace Abounding" and "Community." Includes a brief introduction about Mahādēvi's life and devotion, notes to poems and indexes (English and Kannada) to first lines.

585 HUNASHAL, S.M. Women saints of Karnatak. Raipur: Taranath Prakashan, 1971.
Akkamahādēvi and others. [Unexamined. IBP].

586 SAMARTHA, MICHAEL PRAKASH. The role and status of women. *In his* The compassionate Basava: an evaluative study of a medieval saint-reformer of Karnātaka, India. Ph.D. dissertation, Hartford Seminary Foundation, 1972. pp.167-74. [University Microfilms, 73-15,937].
Brief documentation of the striking inclusion of women in the ***bhakti*** movement as demonstrated in the life of a twelfth century male *Śaiva* saint poet: "Basava's view of the totality of the devotional life, encouraged an equal status of women in all 'religious' activities."

587 SREEKANTAIYA. Akka Mahādevī. *In* Ramakrishna Vedanta Centre. Women saints of East and West: Śrī Sāradā Devī (The Holy Mother) birth centenary memorial. London: Ramakrishna Vedanta Centre, 1955. pp.30-40.
Stories from Mahādēvi's life interspersed with some of her *vacanas*.

(4) The many female saints of Maharashtra, 13th to 17th centuries

(a) Bahiṇābāī: issues of her womanhood and other concerns, 1629?-1700

588 ANANDKAR, PIROJ. Bahiṇābāī. *In* Ramakrishna Vedanta Centre. Women saints of East and West: Śrī Sāradā Devī (The Holy Mother) birth centenary memorial. London: Ramakrishna Vedanta Centre, 1955. pp.64-72.
Legends from the life of a disciple of Tukārāma in the 17th century.

589 BAHINĀBĀĪ. Bahiṇā Bāī: a translation of her autobiography and verses. Tr. from Marathi by Justin E. Abbott. Poona: Scottish Mission Industries, 1929. 301p. (Poet-Saints of Maharashtra, 5).
Bahiṇābāī's autobiography recounts experiences of her early years. She addresses many philosophical problems that troubled her, including the nature of womanhood. Includes 473 selected verses in English translation and Marathi original and a glossary.

(b) Other saints of the Marathi tradition

590 KHER, B.G. Mahārāshṭra women saints. *In* Ramakrishna Vedanta Centre. Women saints of East and West: Śrī Sāradā Devī (The Holy Mother) birth centenary memorial. London: Ramakrishna Vedanta Centre, 1955. pp.58-63.
Brief survey of Marathi female saints. Gives dates, connection to Marathi saint tradition, anecdotes, sources of information and so forth.

591 MAHĪPATI. Stories of Indian saints: an English translation of Mahipati's Marathi *Bhaktavijaya*. Tr. from Marathi by Justin E. Abbott and Narhar R. Godbole. Poona: Aryabhushan Press, 1933-34. 2v. (Poet Saints of Maharashtra, 9-10).
Late 18th century compilation of legends of the Marathi saints. Includes examples of the distinctive Maharashtrian *bhakti* focus on the god Viṭhobā at Pandharpur and the conception of him as "Mother." Miscellaneous references throughout to issues concerning women and *bhakti* values. Does not treat female Marathi saints in detail.

592 ________. Nectar from Indian saints: an English translation of Mahīpati's Marāthī Bhaktalīlāmrit, chapters 1-12, 41-51. Tr. from Marathi by Justin E. Abbott, N.R. Godbole and J.F. Edwards. Poona: J.F. Edwards, 1935. 498p. (Poet Saints of Mahārāshtra, 11).
Volume of stories of *bhakti* saints and their devotees (mostly Maharashtrian) composed in 1774. Includes stories of the female saints Muktābāī (including "Muktābāī teaches the equality of man and woman") and Premābāī and other material relating to particular biographical events and moral questions concerning women.

(5) Kashmiri devotionalism: synthesis of Śaiva *bhakti* and Islamic Ṣūfī traditions

(a) The mystic Lal (Lal Dyad, Lalīśvarī, Lallā), 14th century

593 BAZAZ, PREM NATH. Lalla: harbinger of a new age. *In his* Daughters of the vitasta: a history of Kashmiri women from early times to the present day. New Delhi: Pamposh Publications, 1959. pp.123-38.
Depicts Lal as having provided a synthesis of Islamic and Brahmanic elements at a time when Kashmir was experiencing the conflict of these two cultures. Describes her spiritual quest and various biographical details (e.g., of her education and marriage). Discusses her monotheistic philosophy and presents several *vākhs* in translation and transliteration.

594 HANDOO, CHANDRA KUMARI. Lalleśwarī or Lāl Diddi of Kashmir. *In* Ramakrishna Vedanta Centre. Women saints of East and West: Śrī Sāradā Devī (The Holy Mother) birth centenary memorial. London: Ramakrishna Vedanta Centre, 1955. pp.41-50.
Life sketch of Lal Dyad as detailed in Anand Koul's pamphlet *Lalla Yogīśwarī: Her Life and Sayings*. With translations of many of her *vākhs*, "sayings."

595 KAUL, JAYALAL [JAI LAL KAUL]. Lal Ded. New Delhi: Sahitya Akademi, 1973. 147p.
Detailed "reappraisal" of Lal Dyad's life and work in the context of her times. Based extensively on primary sources. With translations of 138 *vākhs* and bibliography.

596 KOUL, ANAND. Life sketch of Laleshwari: a great hermitess of Kashmir. *In* Indian Antiquary 50 (Nov - Dec 1921) 302-12.
Legends about Lal Dyad's life.

597 ________. Some additions to the Lallā-Vākyāni (the Wise Sayings of Lal Ded). *And* Lallā-Vākyāni (the Wise Sayings of Lal Ded). *In* Indian Antiquary 59 (Jun - Jul 1930) 108-13, 127-30; 60 (Oct 1931) 191-3; 61 (Jan 1932) 13-6; 62 (Jun 1933) 108-11.
Translations and transliterations of 85 of Lal Dyad's *vākhs*.

598 LAL. Lallā-Vākyāni, or the wise sayings of Lal Dĕd, a mystic poetess of ancient Kashmīr. Tr. from Kashmiri by George Grierson and Lionel D. Barnett. London: Royal Asiatic Society, 1920. 225p. (Asiatic Society Monographs, 17).
In the form of a Kashmiri language text? [Unexamined. NUC].

599 ________. The word of Lalla the prophetess, being the sayings of Lal Ded or Lal Diddi of Kashmir (Granny Lal) known also as Laleshwari, Lalla Yogishwari and Lalishri; between 1300 and 1400 A.D., done into English verse from the Lallavakyani or Lal-wakhi and annotated by Sir Richard Carnac Temple. Cambridge: the University Press, 1924. 292p.
[Unexamined. NUC].

(b) Rūpa Bhavānī, 1625?-1721

600 KOUL, ANAND. Life of Rūpa Bhawānī, a great hermitess of Kashmir. *In* Indian Antiquary 60 (Jul 1932) 127-34.
Tales of her life with correspondence from and to her brother in Persian original and English translation and several of her verses transliterated and translated.

(6) Tradition of Mīrābāī, ca. 1500-1546, in the North: *padas* in honor of her beloved Kṛṣṇa

601 BANKEY BEHARI. Bhakta Mira, 2d ed. Bombay: Bharatiya Vidya Bhavan, 1971. 190p. (Bhavan's Book University, 81). [*1st ed.* The story of Mira Bai. Gorakhpur: Ghanshyamdas Jalan, 1937. 150p.].
Life of Mīrā with a fervent introduction. English translations and Hindi dialect original of 112 of her *padas*.

602 BASU, ANATH NATH. Mirabai, saint and singer of India: her life and writings. London: G. Allen and Unwin, 1934? 71p.
An essay on Mīrā and translations of her poems based upon an earlier Bengali work by the author. [Unexamined. NUC].

603 Bhajans of Juthika Roy: Juthika Roy, songs of devotion. Gramophone Company of India ECLP 2278. [*Distributed by* Peters International, Inc., 619 West 54th Street, New York, New York 10019].
Juthika Roy sings five Mīrā *bhajanas* and seven by other saints. *Tablā* accompaniment. [Unexamined. Verified with distributor].

604 GOETZ, HERMANN. Mirabai: her life and times. Bombay: Bharatiya Vidya Bhavan, 1966. 45p. [*Reprint from* J. of the Gujarat Research Society (1956)].
Attempts to sort historical fact from fictional legend regarding Mīrā's life by critically analyzing all available sources. Bibliography lists numerous primary and secondary sources.

605 Lata Mangeshkar sings Meera bhajans. Gramophone Company of India ECSD 2371. [*Distributed by* Peters International, Inc., 619 West 54th Street, New York, New York 10019].
Eight *bhajanas*. [Unexamined. Verified with distributor].

606 MACAULIFFE, M. Legend of Mira Bai, the Rajput poetess. *In* Indian Antiquary 32 (Aug 1903) 329-36.
Biographical sketch with poetry selections.

607 MADAN, LAJWANTI. Mīrā Bāī. *In* Ramakrishna Vedanta Centre. Women saints of East and West: Śrī Sāradā Devī (The Holy Mother) birth centenary memorial. London: Ramakrishna Vedanta Centre, 1955. pp.51-7.
Her life story (with comments about the broader social setting of 16th century North India) and translations of numerous verses.

608 MAHĪPATI. Mirabai. *In his* Stories of Indian saints: an English translation of Mahipati's Marathi Bhaktavijaya, v2. Tr. from Marathi by Justin E. Abbott and Narhar R. Godbole. Poona: Aryabhushan Press, 1934. pp.66-77. (Poet Saints of Maharashtra, 10).
Selection from the late 18th century Marathi compilation of the lives of saints (most from Maharashtra). Details various events in Mīrā's life.

609 Meera bhajans, Smt. M.S. Subbulakshmi. Gramophone Company of India EALP 1297. [*Distributed by* Peters International, Inc., 619 West 54th Street, New York, New York 10019].
M.S. Subbulakshmi sings ten Mīrā *bhajanas* accompanied by violin and *mṛdaṅga*. [Unexamined. Verified with distributor].

610 MĪRĀBĀĪ. Songs of Mirabai. Tr. from Hindi dialect by R.C. Tandon. Allahabad: Hindi Mandir, 1934. 72p.
[Unexamined. NUC].

611 _______. Six padas of Mirabai. Tr. from Hindi dialect by S.M. Pandey and Norman Zide. *In* Mahfil 1,4 (1964) 23-6.
Includes brief introduction.

612 _______. The devotional poems of Mirabai. Tr. from Hindi dialect with introduction by Shreeprakash Kurl. Calcutta: Writers Workshop, 1973. 87p.
Introduction discusses *bhakti* as a movement and as a devotional attitude, form and style of Mīrā's poetry, her life and legends and the message of her poetry. Translations of 50 poems. Glossary.

613 _______. The songs of Mirabai. Tr. from Hindi dialect by Pritish Nandy. New Delhi: Arnold-Heinemann Publishers, 1975. 71p.
English translations of several dozen of Mīrā's *padas*. The translator found her songs comforting during a period of grief and says that she wrote and he translates for "those who have loved and suffered."

614 _______. Songs of Meera: lyrics in ecstasy. Tr. from Hindi dialect by Baldoon Dhingra. New Delhi: Orient Paperbacks, 1977. 135p.
Translations of 96 selections from Mīrā's devotional poetry with a brief introduction on her life and poetry and a discography.

615 NILSSON, USHA S. Mira Bai. New Delhi: Sahitya Akademi, 1969. 70p. (Makers of Indian Literature).
Discusses Mīrā's life, legends, devotional worship attitudes and poetry and presents translations of 50 *padas*.

616 PANDEY, S.M. Mīrābāī and her contributions to the bhakti movement. *In* History of Religions 5,1 (1965) 54-73.
Treats her life and *padas*, expressions of *bhakti* in her work and her marriage with Kṛṣṇa. With some translated poems.

617 RAMASWAMI AIYAR, C.P. Mirabai. *In his* Biographical vistas: sketches of some eminent Indians. Bombay: Asia Publishing House, 1968. pp.34-40.
A summary of the events in Dilip Kumar Roy's play, *The Beggar Princess*. Portrays Mīrā's early spiritual experiences and longing for

Kṛṣṇa, her constrained marriage and her husband's family's disapproval of her spiritual behavior and her eventual meeting with her Lord.

618 ROY, DILIP KUMAR. Mira in Brindavan: a play in two acts. Poona: M.J. Shahani, 1961. 66p.
The last two acts of *The Beggar Princess*? [Unexamined. IBP].

619 ________ and INDIRA DEVI. The beggar princess: a historical drama in five acts. Allahabad: Kitab Mahal, 1955. 178p.
Prose poem about the life of Mīrā. Portrays her as defying convention in her devotion to Lord Kṛṣṇa. She forsakes her status as a princess and ignores her duties as a wife in search of spiritual union with her Lord. [Unexamined. NUC].

620 SCOTT, DAVID. Mirabai. *In* Bhavan's Journal 22, 7-10 (26 Oct and 9-23 Nov and 7 Dec 1975) 217-27, 57-9, 49-53, 52-7.
Attempts to demonstrate the great extent to which ideas found in the *Nārada Bhaktisūtra* are also found in Mīrā's concepts of *prema-bhakti* and her view of Kṛṣṇa as her lover.

621 VASWANI, T.L. Saint Mira, 2d ed. Poona: St. Mira's English Medium School n.d. 88p.
Stories of her life with English translations of many verses.

(7) *Vaiṣṇava* traditions in the Bengal area: identification with Rādhā as lover of Kṛṣṇa

622 DIMOCK, EDWARD C., JR. The place of the hidden moon: erotic mysticism in the Vaiṣṇava-Sahajiyā cult of Bengal. Chicago: University of Chicago Press, 1966. 299p.
Theology, literature, philosophy, history and so forth of a Bengali cult (dating from at least the eighth century) that intermingled with Caitanya's *Vaiṣṇava* tradition. Interspersed throughout is material on women: as *nāyikās*, as embodiments of Rādhā, as gurus, etc. See especially "Women in the Vaiṣṇava-Sahajiyā Movement" (pp.96-102).

623 ________ and DENISE LEVERTOV, trs. In praise of Krishna: songs from the Bengali. Garden City, New York: Anchor Books, Doubleday and Company, Inc., 1967. 95p. (UNESCO Collection of Representative Works, Indian Series).
Translations of Rādhā-Kṛṣṇa devotional lyrics of nine Bengali poets. Introduction discusses Bengali *Vaiṣṇava* tradition and describes a contemporary *kīrtana* at which such songs are sung.

(a) Inspiration from Jayadeva's 12th century Sanskrit lyric poem, the *Gītagovinda*

624 JAYADEVA. Love song of the dark lord: Jayadeva's *Gītagovinda*. Barbara Stoler Miller, ed. and tr. New York: Columbia University Press, 1977. 225p. (UNESCO Collection of Representative Works, Indian Series).
Sanskrit text and English translation "based on a critical edition of the text and an extensive study of the traditions associated with the poem at various levels of Indian culture." Introduction attempts to "analyze and trace the sources of formal and thematic elements that have been relevant to [Miller's] understanding of Jayadeva's poetic creation." With extensive critical material.

625 MOTI CHANDRA. Gītagovinda. New Delhi: Lalit Kalā Akademi, 1965. 12 plates. (Lalit Kalā Series, Portfolios 2 and 3).
Portfolios contain brief introduction to Jayadeva's poem and to paintings depicting it, twelve color plates of paintings from ca. 1775 and original text and translation of segments depicted in plates.

626 RANDHAWA, M.S. Kangra paintings of the Gīta Govinda. New Delhi: National Museum, 1963. 132p.
Twenty color plates of 18th century paintings, Sanskrit text excerpts depicted in paintings, complete text of *Gītagovinda* and discussion of poem and paintings.

627 SIEGEL, LEE. Sacred and profane dimensions of love in Indian traditions as exemplified in the Gītagovinda of Jayadeva. Delhi: Oxford University Press, 1978. 328p.
Considers: the *Gītagovinda* as a work relating to secular and religious love, concepts of love therein, Rādhā and Kṛṣṇa as lover and beloved and their relationship to the messenger, love in separation and in union, love as allegory and symbol and Jayadeva as poet and saint. Much on conceptions of womanhood. Includes complete translated and transliterated text.

628 SINHA, R.P.N. Geeta Govind in Basohli school of Indian painting. New Delhi: Oxford Book and Stationery Company, 1958. 15p., 9 plates.
Introduction focuses on concept of love in Jayadeva's poem: ". . . to love God as a woman loves her beloved is considered the highest form of worship. This attitude has . . . several names . . . dampatyabhava, kantabhava, gopibhava, madhuryabhava, parkiyabhava etc. all of which . . . mean the sweet feeling which a woman has for the object of her love. The highest personification of it is Radha." Eight of the paintings are reproduced in color.

(b) Maithili poetry of Vidyāpati (early 15th century?) and the tradition of Caitanya, 1485-1533, in Bengali and Sanskrit

629 KARUN KRISHNA. The concept of ŚrīRādhā as the embodiment of Mahābhāva in Bengal Vaiṣṇavism. *In* Calcutta Review n.s. 2,4 (1971) 451-60.
As expounded by Caitanya's devotee, Śrī Rūpa Gosvāmin, and the latter's nephew, Śrī Jīva Gosvāmin. "The superiority of the Gopīs to every other beloved of Śrī Kṛṣṇa lies in the fact that in them is prominently displayed a particular essence of the love-laden rasa which in its turn is the quintessence of the Ṣupreme Hlādinī-Śakti (The ecstatic energy) of Srī Kṛṣṇa Bhagavat . . . . Śrī Rādhā represents among the Gopīs the culmination of supreme love."

630 VIDYĀPATI. W.G. Archer, ed. Love songs of Vidyāpati. Tr. from Maithili by Deben Bhattacharya. London: George Allen and Unwin, 1963. 148p.
Translations of 100 poems. Aims to convey atmosphere over literalness. Introduction and notes by editor. Introduction focuses on Sanskrit love poetry, Jayadeva's *Gītogovinda* and Vidyāpati's life and work.

(8) The Gujarati saint Gaurībāī, 1759-1809: a widow turned to spiritual pursuits

631 MEHTA, SAROJINI. Gaurībāī. *In* Ramakrishna Vedanta Centre. Women saints of East and West: Śrī Sāradā Devī (The Holy Mother) birth centenary memorial. London: Ramakrishna Vedanta Centre, 1955. pp.73-9.
Gaurībāī's life story, based upon a biography written in the 19th century, which involved interviews with two of her descendents.

b. Development of the *Śākta* tradition

(1) Feminine elements of various philosophies

632 BROWN, CHEEVER MACKENZIE. God as mother: a feminine theology in India: an historical and theological study of the Brahmavaivarta Purāṇa. Hartford, Vermont: Claude Stark and Company, 1974? 264p.
In this *purāṇa*, "we see various attempts to come to terms with the bi-sexual nature of reality . . . . historically, [it] seems to reflect a stage in transition from a basically masculine-oriented theology, centered upon Viṣṇu or Kṛṣṇa, to a feminine theology, centered upon Kṛṣṇa's consort Rādhā." The study seeks to illuminate this transition as it appears in the text. Major sections examine "The Krsnaite Theological Framework" and "The Theology of Rādhā as Prakṛti."

633 GOMBRICH, R. Feminine elements in Sinhalese Buddhism. *In* Wiener Zeitschrift für die Kunde Südasiens 16 (1972) 67-93.
Part one examines the equation/metaphor "Buddha-mother" that seems to be absent from the Pali canon and its commentaries but present in Sinhalese Buddhist thought since the 13th century. With various textual references and translations including the *Mātṛ Upamāva*, "Mother Simile," ca. late 18th century. The second part examines an oral pamphlet poem of perhaps the last two hundred years, the *Manopraṇidhānayē Sirpada*, which deviates from classical Buddhist doctrine in suggesting that "the greatest enterprise the world has ever known might have failed without a mother's blessing." With segments translated and transliterated.

634 SINHA, JADUNATH. The cult of divine power: "sakti-sadhana." Calcutta: Sinha Publishing House, 1977. 128p.
Śākta philosophy drawn from *tantras*, *Śākta purāṇas* and other sources.

635 WOODROFFE, JOHN. Shakti: the world as power. *In* The Quest 11? (Jul 1920) 451-64 and 12? (Oct 1920) 24-39.
Outlines "a few of the more important principles of the Shakti-doctrine."

636 ________. Shakti and Shākta: essays and addresses on the Shākta tantrashāstra, 4th ed. Madras: Ganesh and Company, 1951. 734p. [*1st ed.* 1919].
Although quite detailed, the author considers this collection of essays and addresses to be a "popular" exposition of the *Śākta tantraśāstra*, this being the "first attempt to give an authenticated and understanding general account, from the Indian standpoint, of the chief features of the Doctrine and Practice of . . . Shāktas . . ." Main sections concern doctrine, ritual and *yoga*. With introductory and concluding matter.

637 ________. The serpent power, 11th ed. Madras: Ganesh and Company, 1978. 500p.
On the important *tantaśāstra* topic, "the Serpent Power (Kuṇḍalini-Śakti), and the Yoga effected through it . . . . consists of a translation of two Sanskrit works . . . . 'Ṣaṭcakra-Nirūpaṇa' ('Description of and Investigation into the Six Bodily Centres') has as its author the celebrated Tāntrik Pūrṇānanda-Svāmī [15th century] [and] 'Pādukā-Pañcaka' ('Five-fold Footstool of the Guru') . . ." With a 315-page introduction.

(2) Rise of *Śākta* and *tāntrika* cults

638 CHANDRA, PRAMOD. The Kaula-Kāpālika cults at Khajurāho. *In* Lalit Kalā 1/2 (1955/56) 98-107.
On Śaiva cults that flourished in the tenth and eleventh centuries. "The aims of the Kaula adept and the Yogi are similar, and only the means adopted . . . are different. To the Kaula the path is one of controlled enjoyment of the objects of the senses, for he realises that in the ultimate analysis *yoga* and *bhoga* are one and the same thing." Discusses Candella dynasty patronage, philosophy of the cult and the 20 figures that accompany the text.

638a CHAKRAVARTI, CHINTAHARAN. Śakti-worship and the Śākta saints. *In* Haridas Bhattacharyya, ed. Cultural heritage of India, 2d ed., rev. and enl., v4: the religions. Calcutta: Ramakrishna Mission Institute of Culture, 1956. pp.408-18.
Briefly reviews prominent *Śākta* and *tāntrika* saints and literary works.

639 GHOSHAL, U.N. The oldest representation of the Śākta cult in Bengal art. *In* Indian Historical Quarterly 16,3 (1940) 489-96.
Considers earliest Bengali example of the offering of a head and other blood sacrifices, a characteristic of the *Śākta* cult, to be a terra-cotta plaque of the eighth century. Reviews subsequent examples of this motif and a historical incident of the mid-19th century.

640 KARAMBELKAR, V.W. Matsyendranātha and his Yoginī cult. *In* Indian Historical Quarterly 31,4 (1955) 362-74.
Regarding a cult (ca. 700 to 900 C.E.) said to represent a transition from the *Śaiva* to the *Śākta* traditions.

641 LORENZEN, DAVID N. The Kāpālikas and Kālāmukhas: two lost Śaivite sects. New Delhi: Thomson Press (India) Limited, 1972. 214p. (Australian National University Centre of Oriental Studies, Oriental Monograph Series, 12). [*Also* Berkeley: University of California Press, 1972. 214p.].
Study of two *tāntrika* sects based primarily on epigraphic record and images in contemporary works. Attempts "to gather together for the first time all the available source materials on the Kāpālikas and Kālāmukhas and to extract a coherent account of their history, doctrines and religious practices."

642 RĀMAPRASĀDA SENA. Rama Prasada's devotional songs: the cult of Shakti. Tr. from Bengali by Jadunath Sinha. Calcutta: Sinha Publishing House, 1966. 175p.
Author was 18th century Bengali goddess devotee. Introduction discusses Durgā/Kālī mother worship. [Unexamined. ALI].

643 SHARMA, R.K. The temple of Chaunsaṭha-yoginī at Bheraghat. Delhi: Agam Kala Prakashan, 1978. 184p.
Historical study of the temple of the 64 *yoginīs* in present-day Jabalpur District, Madhya Pradesh. Examines literary and archeological sources in an effort to trace the rise and fall of the *yoginī* cult in this region. Concludes that this temple was the greatest center for the *Yoginī Kaula* sect, which arose in about the eighth or ninth century C.E. With iconographic descriptions of nearly 100 images and 113 plates.

(3) Particular forms of the goddess

644 AR CY DAE [ROMESH CHUNDER DUTT]. Makunda Ram Chakravarti. *In his* The literature of Bengal: being an attempt to trace the progress of its national mind in its various aspects, as reflected in the nation's literature from the earliest times to the present day, with copious extracts from the best writers. Calcutta: I.C. Bose and Company, 1877. pp.107-38.
Biographical sketch of this 16th century Bengali poet and a summary of his two surviving poems, both about the glories of Caṇḍī. Concludes with observations about the poetry, including its conception of the goddess. The people for whom this has meaning must "be in constant need of the support of a mother, and such a mother is Chandi." Bengali excerpts.

645 CAKRAVARTĪ, MUKUNDA RĀMA. Three episodes from the old Bengali poem "Caṇḍī." Tr. by E.B. Cowell. *In* J. of the Asiatic Society of Bengal 71, supplement 1 (1902) 1-46.
Selections from the late 16th century poem of Mukunda Rāma Cakravartī, known as the "Ornament of Poets." This goddess myth is read today in some Bengali households during goddess worship.

646 CLARK, T.W. Evolution of Hinduism in medieval Bengali literature: Śiva, Caṇḍī, Manasā. *In* Bulletin of the School of Oriental and African Studies 17,3 (1955) 503-18.
Examines development of the *maṅgalakāvya* literature of medieval Bengal to elucidate the poets' intention to provide formulae whereby the earlier popular cults of Caṇḍī and Manasā could be admitted within the canon of Hinduism. Discusses the powers, activities and rites of worship of Caṇḍī and Manasā and the evolution of their cults.

647 DIMOCK, EDWARD C., JR. The goddess of snakes in medieval Bengali literature. *In* History of Religions 1 (Win 1962) 307-21.
Qualities of *Manasā* (including the two most prominent, destruction and regeneration) in Bengali *maṅgalakāvya* literature.

648 ________ and A.K. RAMANUJAN. The goddess of snakes in medieval Bengali literature, part II. *In* History of Religions 3,2 (1964) 300-22.
". . . we shall examine in more detail the myth of Manasā, with attention to the elements of folklore which are found in it, the relationship of mythic elements to the myths of other gods and goddesses, and the ways in which various characteristics have accreted to the goddess." Outlines the Manasā myth from texts and variants dating from the late 15th to mid-18th centuries and analyzes the chief characteristics of the myth's main characters.

649 HARLE, JAMES C. Durgā, goddess of victory. *In* Artibus Asiae 26,3/4 (1963) 237-46.
Interprets iconography of three tenth century South Indian Durgā images. Studies the relationship between Durgā worship and figures depicting self-mutilation. Photographs of figures.

650 MAJMUDAR, MANJULAL R. Treatment of goddesses in Jaina and Brahmanical pictorial art. *In* J. of the Uttar Pradesh Historical Society 23 (1950) 218-27.
Discusses various Jaina goddesses and their iconographic representations in Gujarati palm leaf and paper miniatures. Draws parallels with Brahmanic iconography.

651 NAGARAJA RAO, M.S. The aṣṭamātṛkās from Haveri. *In* Bulletin of the Deccan College Research Institute 23 (1962/63) 78-82.
Iconographic description of a relief panal of the "eight mothers" in a temple in Haveri, Karnataka, ca. eleventh century.

652 PAREKH, KISHOR. Sensuous women of Sigiriya. *In* Orientations 1,8 (1970) 30-9.
Regarding paintings of 21 *apsarās* on the Sigiriya rock in central Sri Lanka. King Kāśyapa I built a palace and fortress on this site in late fifth century C.E., evoking images of heaven with paintings of various heavenly beings. [Unexamined].

653 SHAH, UMAKANT P. Yakṣiṇī of the twenty-fourth Jina Mahāvīrā. *In* J. of the Oriental Institute of Baroda 22,1/2 (1972) 70-8.
Iconography of Jaina *yakṣiṇīs*, a class of beings that served as attendants to the *tīrthaṃkaras*. Thirteen photographs.

654 SIRCAR, DINES CHANDRA. The Śākta pīṭhas. *In* J. of the Royal Asiatic Society of Bengal, Letters 14,1 (1948) 1-108. [*Also* Delhi: Motilal Banarsidass, 1950?].
On sites of goddesses. Includes a reconstruction (from ten sources) of the Sanskrit *Pīṭhanirṇaya* or *Mahāpīṭhanirūpaṇa* and a translation of it. This "late medieval" text describes 51 centers of goddess worship. Traces the history of such *pīṭhas* in the *purāṇas* and from local sources. With lists of goddess centers from various sources and numerous appendixes.

(4) Later *Śākta* and non-*Śākta purāṇas*

655 GIRI, RAGHUNATH. Śakti (the power) in the philosophy of the purāṇas. *In* Purāṇa 12,2 (1970) 231-51.
Distinguishes four stages in development of *Śakti* concept in *purāṇas*: 1) as identified with supreme reality, undifferentiated from Brahman; 2) as the inseparable power of supreme reality, Śiva; 3) as the "unwarranted command" of Śiva, instrument of his sport; and 4) as primal nature, *prakṛti*, material cause of all conscious beings.

656 HAZRA, R.C. The Śākta upapurāṇas. *And* The lost Sākta upapurāṇas. *In his* Studies in the upapurāṇas, v2. Calcutta: Sanskrit College, 1963. pp.1-361, 466-89. (Calcutta Sanskrit College Research Series, 22).
First section contains an introduction and summaries and discussion of the four *Śākta upapurāṇas* available in printed form: *Devī Purāṇa*, *Kālikā Purāṇa*, *Mahābhāgavata Purāṇa* and *Devībhāgavata Purāṇa*. With a lengthy discussion of language of the *Devī Purāṇa*. The other section describes available information on nine *Śākta purāṇas* that have not been found.

657 O'FLAHERTY, WENDY DONIGER, tr. Devī, the goddess. *In her* Hindu myths: a source book translated from the Sanskrit. Middlesex: Penguin Books, 1975. pp.238-69.
Notes and text excerpts from various *Śākta* and non-*Śākta purāṇas*. ". . . when the goddess came into her element in the medieval period, these early myths were retold in a new light, with the goddess using the gods to serve her higher purposes."

658 SHARMA, PUSHPENDRA KUMAR. Śakti cult in ancient India: with special reference to the Purāṇic literature. Varanasi: Bhartiya Publishing House, 1974. 317p.
Reviews goddess worship preceding period of *purāṇas* and discusses philosophy, ritual, particular incarnations and *tāntrika* aspects of the goddess in the *mahāpurāṇas* and the *upapurāṇas*. Extensive use of original texts.

(a) The *Devī Māhātmya / Durgā Saptaśatī / Caṇḍī* of the *Mārkaṇḍeya Purāṇa*, ca. 550 C.E.

659 AGRAWALA, V.S. The Glorification of the Great Goddess. *In* Purāṇa 5,1 (1963) 64-89.
Interpretation of the meaning of the *Devī Māhātmya*.

660 The Devī-Māhātmyam or Śrī Durgā-Saptaśatī. Tr. from Sanskrit by Svami Jagadisvarananda. Madras: Sri Ramakrishna Math, 1955. 170p.
Translation of the *Devī Māhātmya* with Sanskrit original.

661 MAJMUDAR, M.R. Earliest Devī-Māhātmya miniatures with special reference to Śakti worship in Gujarat. *In* J. of the Indian Society of Oriental Art 6 (1938) 118-36.
[Unexamined].

662 ______. Two more manuscripts of Durgā Māhātmya miniatures of the Gujarāti school of painting. *In* J. of the University of Bombay 18,2 (1949) 83-97.
[Unexamined].

663 PRABHAKAR, C.L. Goddess Durgā (Durgā Saptaśatī). *In* Bharatiya Vidya 31,1/4 (1971) 22-38.
Discusses style and content of the *Devī Māhātmya*.

(b) The *Devī Purāṇa*, ca. 550-650 C.E.

664 HAZRA, R.C. The Devī-Purāṇa, a work of Bengal. *In* Purāṇa 5,1 (1963) 351-9.
Author is primarily interested in demonstrating the Bengali origin of the *Devī Purāṇa*; some additional material is to be found amidst the argument.

(c) The *Devībhāgavata Purāṇa*, ca. 850-1350 C.E.

665 CHEMBURKAR, JAYA. Umā Haimavatī myth in the Devī Bhāgavata: a study. *In* Purāṇa 18,1 (1976) 93-100.
Compares *Kenopaniṣad* and *Devībhāgavata Purāṇa* versions of a myth to show *Śākta* influences upon the latter.

666 LALYE, P.G. Studies in Devī Bhāgavata. Bombay: Popular Prakashan, 1973. 400p.
Multifaceted study of the *Devībhāgavata Purāṇa*. Puts text in context of Vedic and other preceding literature. Discusses literary, philosophical and mythological aspects.

667 SANYAL, NIRMAL CHANDRA. The Devī-Bhāgavata as the real Bhāgavata. *In* Purāṇa 9,1 (1969) 127-58.
Argues that the *Devībhāgavata Purāṇa* rather than the *Bhāgavata Purāṇa* is the primary one, the *mahāpurāṇa*. Includes references to previous participants in the ongoing debate.

668 SRIKANTHA SASTRI, S. The two Bhāgavatas. *In* Annals of the Bhandarkar Oriental Research Institute 14,1/2 (1932/33) 241-9.
Regarding the dispute between *Śākta* and *Vaiṣṇava* proponents over whether the *Devībhāgavata Purāṇa* or the *Bhāgavata Purāṇa* is the true *mahāpurāṇa*. Author argues that former is the *mahāpurāṇa* and latter is the *upapurāṇa*.

669 TADPATRIKAR, S.N. Devī-Bhāgavata or Bhagavatī-Purāṇa? *In* Annals of the Bhandarkar Oriental Research Institute 23,1/4 (1942) 559-62.
Brief contribution to the dispute over whether the *Devībhāgavata Purāṇa* or *Bhāgavata Purāṇa* is the *mahāpurāṇa*. From manuscript evidence.

(d) The *Kālikā Purāṇa*, ca. 1350 C.E.

670 BARUA, B.K. *Kālikā Purāṇa* on iconographical representations of some Sakta goddesses and their worship in medieval Assam. *In* H.L. Hariyappa and M.M. Patkar, eds. Professor P.K. Gode commemoration volume. Poona: Oriental Book Agency, 1960. Third part, pp.1-18. (Poona Oriental Series, 93).
Sanskrit excerpts and English discussion of aspects of various goddesses as portrayed in the *Kālikā Purāṇa*. Author argues that some iconographical details allow speculation about locality of origin of this text.

671 HAZRA, R.C. The Kālikā-Purāṇa. *In* Annals of the Bhandarkar Oriental Research Institute 21,1/2 (1941) 1-23.
History, summary of contents and estimated date of this *purāṇa* about Kālī or Kālikā worship.

672 KOOIJ, K.R. VAN. Worship of the goddess according to the Kālikāpurāṇa. Leiden: E.J. Brill, 1972-. v1-. [1v published to date, 2v planned].
Translation and study of selections of the *Kālikā Purāṇa* about worship. Inspired by desire to clarify context of human sacrifices that have made the text "more or less notorious." "The first [volume] comprises chapters 54-69 . . . together with a general introduction. In the second volume . . . the remaining part, chapters 70-80, will be preceded by a study of the iconographic evidence found in this Purāṇa."

4. Sanskrit "secular" literature

a. Continuing the *kāvya* tradition

673 HANDLER, ESTHER. The feminine paradigms of the Gadya Kāvyas: a study in literary convention. Ph.D. dissertation, University of Pennsylvania, 1966. 261p. [University Microfilms 67-3076].
Delineation, *varnaṇa*, of women in four *kāvya* works: Subhandu's *Vāsavadattā*, Bāṇa's *Harṣacarita* and *Kādambarī* and Daṇḍin's *Daśakumāracarita*. [Unexamined. DAI].

b. Narrative literature: *kathā*, "tale"

(1) *Pañcatantra* didactic tales of *nīti*, "conduct of life," date unknown

674 STERNBACH, L. Legal rules in the Pañcatantra: obligation of the father to marry his daughter at the proper time. *In* Bharatiya Vidya 7,3/4 supplement (1947?) 51-70.
[Unexamined].

(2) Somadeva's *Kathāsaritsāgara*, "Ocean of Story Streams," 11th century

675 CHATTOPADHYAY, APARNA. Life of a maiden in the Kathāsaritsāgara. *In* Bharati 6 (1961/62) 157-69.
[Unexamined].

676 ________. The institution of 'devadasis' according to the Kathasaritsagara. *In* J. of the Oriental Institute of Baroda 16,3 (1967) 216-22.
[Unexamined].

677 ________. Position of widows in early medieval India in the light of the Kathāsaritsāgara. *In* J. of the Oriental Institute of Baroda 24,3/4 (1975) 393-402.
Incidents in Somadeva's *Kathāsaritsāgara* suggest three options for widows of the period: 1) become *satīs* (common), 2) remarry (infrequent) or 3) lead the harsh life of a widow.

(3) The *Śukasaptati,* seventy tales of a parrot, date unknown

678 The enchanted parrot: being a selection from the "Suka Saptati," or, The Seventy Tales of a Parrot. Tr. from Sanskrit by B. Hale Wortham. London: Luzac and Company, 1911. 127p.
Erotic tales told on 70 consecutive nights to prevent a listless young wife from seeking a lover while her husband is away on a journey. Author and date unknown.

679 Erotic Indian tales from the Sanskrit classic Suksaptati. Tr. from Sanskrit by G.L. Mathur. Delhi: Orient Paperbacks, Hind Pocket Books, 1971. 202p.
From introductory note: "Seductive Prabhavati's adulterous liasion [sic] was frowned upon by the grandfatherly parrot (India's classical symbol of wisdom) .... Seventy times the bewitching Prabhavati tries to meet her lover and each time the garrulous parrot discourages her from precipitate action by explicitly describing the pleasures and also the consequences of adultery." Author and date of *Śukasaptati*, the "Parrot's Seventy," are not known.

c. Sanskrit drama, *nāṭaka*

680 CHAUDHURI, JATINDRABIMAL, ed. The contribution of women to Sanskrit literature. Calcutta: Calcutta Oriental Press, 1943. lv. (Calcutta Oriental Series, 30).
Volume on drama. Apparently contains translations of Rājeśekhara's *Viddhaśālabhañjikā*, a comedy of palace intrigue by a man of the ninth and tenth centuries; the *Camatkārataraṅgiṇī* of Sundarī and Kamalā, a commentary on Rājeśekhara's drama; and another commentary, the *Prāṇapratiṣṭhā* by their husband, Ghanaśyāma. The latter was a minister at Thanjavur in the 18th century. [Unexamined. NUC].

d. Lyric poetry

681 DĀMODARAGUPTA. The art of the temptress: translation of the 1200 year old Sanskrit classic the Kuttni Mahatmyam of Damodara Gupta. Tr. from Sanskrit by B.P.L. Bedi. Bombay: Pearl Publications, 1968. 218p.
The author (fl. 779-813), prime minister to a Kashmiri king, wrote the *Kuṭṭanīmata* in order to educate the young prince in his care about the nature and arts of courtesans.

e. Continuing Vātsyāyana's love treatise, *kāmaśāstra*, tradition: the works of Kokkoka, Jayadeva, Kalyāṇamalla, Padmaśrī, Devarāja, Nāgārjuna Siddha and others

682 DEVARĀJA. K. Rangaswami Iyenger, ed. Ratiratnapradīpikā. Tr. from Sanskrit by the editor. Mysore, 1923.
Devarāja's erotic treatise, the "Jewel Lamp of Rati," is perhaps an amplification of the *Ratirahasya* of Kokkoka. The work discusses classifications of women, love-making techniques and other topics. Its date is unknown and has been tentatively ascribed to the 17th century. [Unexamined].

683 _______. Liladhur Sarma, ed. Ratiratnapradīpikā of Mahārāja Devarāja. Calcutta: Benkateswar Book Agency, 1930.
[Unexamined].

684 JAYADEVA. The Ratimañjarī of Jayadeva. Tr. from Sanskrit by Alex Comfort. *In* Alex Comfort, tr. The Koka Shastra: being the Ratirahasya of Kokkoka and other medieval Indian writings on love. London: George Allen and Unwin, 1964. pp.88-94.
This brief text, "Blossoms of Love," is complete in only 125 *ślokas*. It consists primarily of a series of classifications of types of women and men, times, body parts, techniques, positions and so forth. The author lived perhaps in the 15th century and is not the well-known Jayadeva who composed the *Gītagovinda*.

685 KALYĀṆAMALLA. Ananga Ranga: stage of the bodiless one; the Hindu art of love. Tr. from Sanskrit by F.F. Arbuthnot and Richard F. Burton. New York: Medical Press of New York, 1964. [*Reprint of* 1885 ed?].
Translation of the 16th century *Anaṅgaraṅga*, "Stage of the God of Love." Topics include classifications of men and women according to a host of criteria; coital postures and amorous gestures; aphrodisiacs and remedies and so forth. Includes photographs of erotic sculpture and an appended "Pharmacopeia 'Ars Amoris Indica'."

686 KOKKOKA. Kokkokam, by Ativira Rama Pandian, translated from the Tamil by Yato Dharma Tato Jaya; Ratirahasyam, translated from the Sanskrit by Richard Schmidt. Calcutta: Medical Book Company, [1949]. 224p.
Includes English translations of Kokkoka's *Kokaśāstra* (also known as the *Ratirahasya*, "Secrets of Love") and of Varakuṇarāma Pāṇṭiyaṉ's Tamil rendering, the *Kokkōkam.* Kokkoka's work dates to about the 12th century and Pāṇṭiyaṉ's to the 16th. [Unexamined. NUC].

687 _______. Kokkokam and Ratirahasyam. Tr. from Sanskrit by T.L. Ray. Calcutta: Medical Book Agency, 1960.
Manual instructs husbands how to please their wives sexually. Major sections discuss physical types of women, various other categories of women (e.g., by age and locality), the lunar calendar and love-making, embraces, kisses, love marks, intercourse, blows and cries, approaching a bride, wives, extramarital relations, spells and concoctions. [Unexamined].

687a _______. The Koka Shastra: being the Ratirahasya of Kokkoka and other medievil Indian writings on love. Tr. from Sanskrit with introduction by Alex Comfort. Preface by W.G. Archer. London: George Allen and Unwin, 1964. 171p. [*Also* New York: Stein and Day].
Archer's preface (pp.11-41) discusses 19th century British interest in *kāmāśāstra* literature, the third century C.E. social context ("bland and sensuous") and contents of the *Kāmasūtra*, the "new severity" of medieval Indian society and its reflection in the *Anaṅgaraṅga* and *Kokaśāstra*. Comfort's introduction (pp.43-100) examines various aspects of the Sanskrit erotic treatise tradition as a whole and the *Kokaśāstra* text in particular and reviews the contents of other major later texts. *Kokaśāstra* translation does not include concluding sections on love spells and recipes, which vary from manuscript to manuscript. See also entry 684.

688 NĀGĀRJUNA SIDDHA. Ratiśāstra. Tr. from Sanskrit by A.C. Ghose. Calcutta: Seal, 1904.
The "Science of Love" is a discourse by Śiva to his consort. The work includes material on classifications of women and prenatal and astrological influences. It is more Brahmanical than most of the *kāmaśāstra* literature. Date unknown. [Unexamined].

689 _______. Science of life: or, Hindu system of sexual secrets . . . Tr. from Sanskrit. Calcutta: Ganguly and Company, 1909. 143p.
Sanskrit text and English translation of the *Ratiramaṇa* or "Pleasure of Love," date unknown. [Unexamined].

690 [NĀGĀRJUNA SIDDHA?]. Ratisastram: or, the Hindu system of sexual science, with text in Devanagari. Tr. from Sanskrit by Abinash Chandra Ghose, [2d rev. ed.]. Delhi: Nag Publishers, 1977. 84p. (N.P. Series, 19). [*Reprint of* 1895? ed.].
Nāgārjuna's *Ratiśāstra*? Contains information on healthy progeny, astrological influences, matching of parents, rules for sexual unions relating to menstruation and other topics. [Unexamined. ALI].

691 PADMAŚRĪ. Tansakhram Sarma, ed. Nāgarasarvasva of Padmaśrī. Bombay: Gujrati Press, 1921.
Translation of "The Townsman's All," date unknown. Some consider Padmaśrī to have been a woman and others a Buddhist monk. Thirty-

eight major sections discuss wide range of topics, including classifications of women, erotic techniques, prostitutes (unusual in post-*Kāmasūtra* erotic literature) and jewels. Buddhist in orientation. [Unexamined].

692 PARAJULI, DEVIDATTA, ed. Kokkoka's Ratirahasya with Kāñcīnātha's commentary Ratirahasyadīpikā. Tr. from Sanskrit. Lahore: Punjab Sanskrit Book Depot, n.d. 228p.
[Unexamined].

f. Historical writing

693 KALHANA. Rājataraṅgiṇī: the saga of the kings of Kaśmīr. Tr. from Sanskrit by Ranjit Sitaram Pandit. New Delhi: Sahitya Akademi, 1968. 56, 783p.
Social history of Kashmiri upper classes by a twelfth century historian. Contains interspersed material about lives of women of this strata. Introduction and notes by the translator.

5. Themes of love and devotion in painting, sculpture and regional literature

694 BROWN, W. NORMAN, ed. and tr. The Vasanta Vilāsa: a poem of the spring festival in old Gujarātī accompanied by Sanskrit and Prakrit stanzas and illustrated with miniature paintings. New Haven: American Oriental Society, 1962. 251p. (American Oriental Series, 46).
Gujarati poem of the *phāgu* genre celebrating vernal passion. Probably from the 15th century. "The text takes many ideas from the common Indic storehouse respecting the beauties of spring and the sway of love . . . but all is used with greater simplicity and naturalness . . . . there are new elements, notably a slender — and rather charming — plot . . . . the tone is innocent and guileless, even naive, rather than sensual." With introduction, text and translation of a long recension, text of a short recension, attempted reconstruction of original text, critical apparatus, linguistic details and reproductions of 78 early secular miniature paintings of western India.

695 COOMARASWAMY, ANANDA K. The eight nāyikās. *In* J. of Indian Art and Industry n.s. 16,128 (1914) 99-112.
On classification of the heroine who "occupies considerably more space than the Hero (*Nāyaka*) in the literature of Dramaturgy and Erotic." Reviews various three-, four- and six-fold classifications. Presents selections about the eight, *aṣṭanāyakā* from the late 16th century Hindi *Rasikapriyā* by Keśavadāsa in transliteration and in translation. Reviews references to these heroines by other Hindi poets. Briefly describes the accompanying plates of 16 Pahari paintings of *nāyikās* inspired by the poetry.

696 DESAI, DEVANGANA. Erotic sculpture of India: a socio-cultural study. New Delhi: Tata McGraw-Hill Publishing Company, 1975. 269p., 155 figures.
Descriptive survey and critical interpretation of erotic representations in South Asia from ca. 500 to 1400 C.E.

697 EASTMAN, ALVAN CLARK. The Nala-Damayantī drawings: a study of a portfolio of drawings made for Rājā Saṁsār Cand of Kāṅgṛā (1774-1823), illustrating an early Indian romance; twenty-nine drawings now in Museum of Fine Arts, Boston, with the addition of nineteen drawings from other American museums and from a private collection. Boston: Museum of Fine Arts, 1959. 119p, 48 plates.
Reproduces and discusses 48 early 19th century drawings that fuse a 12th century version of the Nala-Damayantī romance with features of court life in the Kangra region of the Punjab where the paintings were commissioned. While not stressed in the text, the paintings contain much information on ideals of romantic love.

698 Eroticism in Hindu sculpture. 1968. 20 min. Color. 16 and 35 mm. [*Distributed by* Kevin Duffy Productions, 10616 Blythe Avenue, Los Angeles, California 90064].
Film. Describes scenes of sculpture from Puri, Konarak, Khajuraho, Belur, Halebid and Bhubaneswar in relation to texts of the Hindu tradition and popular belief. [Unexamined].

699 KANNOOMAL. Some notes on Hindu erotics. *In* Rupam 4 (Oct 1920) 20-7.
Discusses various sets of categories relating to the moods and psychology of love in the Hindu tradition. Accompanying plates of miniature paintings illustrate several of the categories.

700 KRISHAN, Y. The erotic sculptures of India. *In* Artibus Asiae 34,4 (1972) 331-43.
Suggests that erotic temple sculpture executed in various parts of India, primarily in the tenth to thirteenth centuries, may have been associated with the *devadāsī* institution.

701 MUKTĀNANDA. L'épouse idéale: la Satī-Gītā de Muktānanda [The ideal wife: Muktānanda's "*Satī* Song"]. Tr. from Gujarati by Françoise Mallison. Paris: l'Institut de Civilisation Indienne, 1973. 184p. (*Its* Série 8, fascicule 35).
Muktānanda's (1757-1829) adaptation of his guru's poem on moral and religious feminine ideals. Includes Gujarati original and English translation of this song sung by fe-

male members of the Swami Narayani sect and interpretive chapters on both the *satī* theme and the sect.

702 Radha and Krishna. Produced and directed by Jehangir Bhownagary. 1957. 22 min. Color. 16 and 35 mm. [*Distributed by* Films Division, Ministry of Information and Broadcasting, Government of India, 24 G. Deshmukh Marg, Bombay 400 026. *And* Information Service of India, 975 National Press Building, 529 14th Street NW, Washington, D.C. 20004].
The Rādhā-Kṛṣṇa legend as illustrated by 18th century Pahari miniature paintings. [Unexamined].

703 RANDHAWA, M.S. Kangra paintings on love. New Delhi: National Museum, 1962. 209p., 89 figures, 25 plates.
Interpretive discussion, textual selections and artistic representations of various love themes in paintings from Kangra valley and related traditions. Chapters discuss Kangra paintings on theme of erotic love, *śṛṅgāra*; background in Hindi love literature and particularly the *Rasikapriyā* of Keśavadāsa; moods and meeting places of lovers; external indications of love's emotions, *hāva*; the eight heroines, *aṣṭanāyikā*; love in separation, *vipralambha*, *māna* and *pravāsa*; love in union, *saṃyoga*; and the twelve month, *bārāmāsā*, sequences.

704 ________. Eight nayikas from Arki. *In* Times of India Annual (1962) 28-39.
Reproductions, some in color, of paintings on the theme of a woman separated from her lover. From the collection of the Raja of Arki (in present-day Himachal Pradesh). Perhaps from early 19th century.

705 SARABHAI, MRINALINI. The eight nayikas: heroines of the classical dance of India. New York: Dance Perspectives, 1965. 49p. (Dance Perspectives, 24).
Illustrations accompanied by poetic text. [Unexamined. BAS].

6. Coming of Islam as a major influence in the subcontinent, from the 11th century

a. Muslim influence on North Indian social life

706 ASHRAF, MOHAMMAD. Life and conditions of the people of Hindustan, 2d ed. New Delhi: Munshiram Manoharlal, 1970. 312p. [*1st ed.* 1959. *Originally* Life and conditions of the people of Hindustan, 1200-1550 A.D.: mainly based on Islamic sources. *In* J. of the Asiatic Society of Bengal, Letters I (1935) 103-359].
Multifaceted description of society in North India under the Delhi Sultanate and early Mughal rule. Interspersed material on women; see especially "Haram" (pp. 53-7), "Domestic Life" (pp.164-94, considers general position of women, female seclusion, marriage, *satīs* and *jauhar*), "Prostitution" (pp.264-7) and "Hindu Women" (pp.271-2).

707 HABIB, MOHAMMAD. Indian culture and social life at the time of the Turkish invasions. *In his* Politics and society during the early medieval period: collected works of Professor Mohammad Habib, v1. Ed. by K.A. Nizami. New Delhi: People's Publishing House, 1974. pp.152-228.
Social life in ca. eleventh century North India as revealed in various primary sources. Documents extent and nature of segregation of the sexes and absence of veiling. Briefly describes marriage practices and status of widows.

708 LAW, NARENDRA NATH. Female education. *In his* Promotion of learning in India during Muhammadan rule by Muhammadans. London: Longmans, Green, 1916. pp.200-5.
Briefly surveys educational opportunities available to upper-class Muslim women in North India during Delhi Sultanate and Mughal periods.

709 RIZVI, ATHAR ABBAS. Appendix A: female sufis. *In his* A history of sufism in India, v1. New Delhi: Munshiram Manoharlal, 1978. pp.401-3.
Briefly names some exemplary personages and their contributions to show that women played "an important role in the movement both as sufis and as the mothers of leading sufis." However, "Muslim women who became deeply committed to mysticism and a life of asceticism did so in spite of a lack of encouragement and assistance from their male counterparts and from Islam in general."

710 SAHU, KISHORI PRASAD. Some aspects of North Indian social life, 1000-1526 A.D. (with a special reference to contemporary literatures). Calcutta: Punthi Pustak, 1973. 306p.
Focuses on cultural interaction of Hindus and Muslims. Based primarily on original sources. Has interspersed material on women and a section "Social Status of Women" (pp.184-233).

711 SRIVASTAVA, M.P. Society and culture in medieval India, 1206-1707. Allahabad: Chugh Publications, 1975. 219p.
Examines cultural trends in subcontinent from time when Delhi Sultanate came to be regarded as an Indian state through reign of Aurangzīb. Considers mutual influence of Muslim and Hindu cultures. Interspersed brief comments relating to women throughout (e.g., on *satīs*, *jauhar*, Mīrābāī, marriage, dress and education).

b. The Delhi Sultanate and the brief reign of Raẓiyya Sulṭān, 1236-40

712 ELLIOT, H.M. and JOHN DOWSON. Sultān Raziya, daughter of the Sultān. *In their* The history of India as told by its own historians, v2. Allahabad: Kitab Mahal Private Ltd., n.d. pp.332-7.
Translation of excerpt from 13th century chronicle. Describes events of Raẓiyya's life and rule and her admirable qualities.

712a HABIBULLAH, A.B.M. Sulṭānah Rāziah. *In* Indian Historical Quarterly 16,4 (1940) 750-72.
Details of Raẓiyya's rule, including her scandalous descarding of the veil, and information on the context in which she, as a woman, was appointed to rule.

713 MINHĀJ-UD-DĪN, ABŪ-'UMAR 'UṢMĀN [MINHĀJ SIRĀJ JUZĀNĪ]. Sulṭān Raẓiyyat-ud-Dunyā wa ud-Dīn, daughter of Sulṭān I-Yal-Timish. *In his* Ṭabakāt-i-Nāṣirī: a general history of the Muhammadan dynasties of Asia, including Hindustan from A.H. 194 (810 A.D.) to A.H. 658 (1260 A.D.) and the irruption of the infidel Mughals into Islam, v1. Tr. from Persian by H.G. Raverty. New Delhi: Oriental Books Reprint Corporation, 1970. pp.637-48. [*Reprint of* Calcutta: Asiatic Society of Bengal, 1881. (Bibliotheca Indica Series)].
Regarding her family background and personal qualities, along with the character and particular events of her reign and defeat. Details of her experiences as a female ruler. From Persian manuscripts. Extensive notes.

714 ZAKARIA, RAFIQ. Razia: Queen of India. Bombay: Popular Prakashan, 1966. 159p.
Fictionalized biography. The only woman to hold the throne at Delhi, Raẓiyya reigned from 1236 until her death in 1240. Based on 13th century sources listed in introduction. Focuses on progressive policies Raẓiyya followed as ruler.

c. The Mughal Empire, 1526-1707

(1) Women and society: general statements

715 CHOPRA, PRAN NATH. Life and letters under the Mughals. New Delhi: Ashajanak Publications, 1976. 439p.
Social life in North India during the Mughal period, extensively documented from primary sources. See chapter entitled "The Position of Women in Society" (pp.108-30) and miscellaneous references throughout on education, dress and ornaments, marriage, particular poets, etc.

716 MISRA, REKHA. Women in Mughal India: 1526-1748 A.D. Delhi: Munshiram Manoharlal, 1967. 177p. [*Also* Mystic, Connecticut: Lawrence Verry].
Social life and biography of noble women with one chapter devoted to middle- and lower-class women in North India of the same period. Primarily drawn from Persian sources and travelers' accounts.

717 MUKHERJEE, ILA. Social status of North Indian women, 1526-1707 A.D. Agra: Shiva Lal Agarwala, 1972. 172p.
Various aspects of lives of women in North India of all social classes, Hindu and Muslim, from reign of Bābar through reign of Aurangzīb. Chapter topics are birth and marriage; food, adornment and pastimes; education; widows, ***satīs*** and *jauhar*; and prostitutes. Women's lives in this period were "full of colourless and pathetic events."

718 OJHA, P.N. Education of North Indian women under the Great Moghuls, 1556-1707 A.D. *In* Indian History Congress 20, 1957, Vallabh Vidyanagar, Gujarat. Proceedings 20. Bombay: the Congress, 1958. pp.208-12.
Asserts that historical references suggest that many well-to-do Muslim and Hindu women received education by private tutors in this period. Public women and dancing girls became accomplished in the arts.

719 ________. North Indian social life during Mughal period. Delhi: Oriental Publishers and Distributors, 1975. 182p.
Survey of social conditions based primarily on travelers' accounts and contemporary poetry (Hindi, Bengali, Oriya and Maithili). Scattered references to women; see especially chapter on "Social Status of Women."

(2) Women of the Mughal court

720 BEVERIDGE, ANNETTE S. Appendix A: biographical notices of the women mentioned by Babur, Gul-Badan and Haidar. *In* Gulbadan Begam. The history of Humāyūn (Humāyūn-nāma). Tr. from Persian with introduction and notes by Annette S. Beveridge. London: Royal Asiatic Society, 1902. pp.203-97. (Oriental Translation Fund, n.s. 1). [*Reprint* Delhi: Idarah-i Adabiyāt-i Delli, 1972. (Oriental Translation Series, 1)].
Partial list of women mentioned by three important chroniclers of early Mughal history. Provides information such as ties to Mughal families, significant dates, significant life events and references in Persian sources for 203 women.

721 GANGOLY, ORDHENDRA C. On the authenticity of the feminine portraits of the Mughul School. *In* Rupam 33/34 (Jan/Apr 1928) 11-5.
Considers the possibility, as some have suggested, that due to strict rules of seclusion supposed portraits of Mughal women were in fact modeled after substitutes. References to female artists and a miniature of a woman sketching other women suggest that genuine portraits could have been done by women. Proposes that several Nūr Jahān portraits are authentic as they bear a common resemblance. By the same criterion, judges Zīb-un-Nisā's portraits to be inauthentic. Plates of eleven paintings and drawings.

722 LAL, K.S. The Mughal harem. *In* J. of Indian History 53,3 (1975) 415-30.
Descriptive account based, in large part, upon primary sources.

723 RAJPUT, A.B. The contribution of Mughal princesses to architecture. *In* Pakistan Quarterly 11,4 (1963) 48-54.
Discusses important role of Mughal wives, daughters and consorts as patrons of or inspiration for many notable architectural works.

724 SUNITY DEVI, MAHARANI OF COOCH BEHAR [SUNITI DEVI, MAHARANI OF COOCH BEHAR]. The beautiful Mogul princesses. Calcutta: Thacker, Spink, 1918. 128p.
Fiction. [Unexamined. NUC].

(a) Women associated with Bābur, 1494-1530

725 BANERJI, S.K. Some of the women relations of Bābur. *In* Indian Culture 4,1 (1937) 53-60.
Biographical sketches of Bābur's chief queen, his sister, his daughter, two wives of his maternal grandfather and a woman who taught the women and children of the palace.

(b) The age of Humāyūn, 1508-1556, through the eyes of his sister, Gulbadan Begam

726 GULBADAN BEGAM. The history of Humāyūn (Humāyūn-nāma). Tr. from Persian by Annette S. Beveridge. London: Royal Asiatic Society, 1902. 331, 95p. (Oriental Translation Fund, n.s. 1). [*Reprint* Delhi: Idarah-i Adabiyāt-i Delli, 1972. (Oriental Translation Series, 1)].
Sister of Emperor Humāyūn and witness to reigns of Bābur, Humāyūn and Akbar, Gulbadan Begam has written a detailed account of her perspective on Mughal famililal and political life. Includes much on activities of royal women. The translator has supplied a lengthy and detailed "Introduction: Biographical Account of the Princess and her Family" (pp.1-77), a brief discussion of the Persian manuscript (pp.77-9) and extensive notes. Original Persian text appended.

(c) Women during the life of Akbar, 1542-1605

727 ABŪ AL-FAẒL IBN MUBĀRAK. Ain-i-Akbari. Tr. from Persian by H. Blochmann. Calcutta: Asiatic Society of Bengal, 1927. 741p. (Bibliotheca Indica, 61). [*Reprint* Lahore: Qausain, 1975].
Emperor Akbar's life and times by his contemporary biographer. Contains many references to lives of noble women, including organization of the harem.

728 MUḤAMMAD RIẒĀ, called NAU'Ī. Burning and melting: being the Sūz-u-gudāz of Muhammad Rizā Nau'ī of Khabūshān. Tr. from Persian by Mirza Y. Dawud and Ananda K. Coomaraswamy. London: printed at Old Bourne Press, 1912. 65p.
Persian *ṣūfī* poem concerning a woman who, desiring to burn with her beloved on his funeral pyre, acquires permission from Akbar. In his introduction Coomaraswamy notes that Muḥammad Rizā "writes throughout as Sufī, and finds in this burning human love a symbol of the affection of the soul towards God." His interest in bringing the poem into English was in order to demonstrate to western readers the courageous, committed and passionately loving spirit with which *satīs* mount the pyre. Persian work was commissioned by a son of Akbar early in the 17th century.

729 RAHIM, M.A. Maham Anaga, the nurse-prime minister of Akbar. *In* J. of the Asiatic Society of Bangladesh 19,2 (1974) 37-51.
Biographical details of Māham Anaga who tended Akbar in his youth and was powerful in the early period of his reign. Based on primary sources.

(d) Political and cultural contributions of Nūr Jahān, 1577?-1646?, wife of Jahāngīr, 1569-1627

730 FAROOQI, H. ABBADULLAH. Nur Jahan. *In* J. of the Research Society of Pakistan 12,1 (1975) 21-39.
Biographical sketch of Nūr Jahān based upon and citing contemporary and secondary sources. Focuses on her political ambitions and literary talents. Describes her tomb, which has recently been restored.

731 HASAN, S. NURUL. The theory of the Nur Jahan 'junta': a critical examination. *In* Indian History Congress 21, 1958, Trivandrum. Proceedings 21. Bombay: the Congress, 1959. pp.324-35.
Argues, using Persian sources, against a theory that Nūr Jahān was actively involved in a particular political faction during Jahāngīr's reign.

732 PANT, CHANDRA. Nur Jahan and her family. Allahabad: Dandewal Publishing House, 1978. 199p.
Presents extensive primary source material to negate the claim that Jahāngīr yielded his power to Nūr Jahān who used it for the benefit of her family members. Sections discuss women of the family and Nūr Jahān's cultural contributions. Appendixes reproduce numerous documents, variously in Persian, in transliteration and in English translation.

733 SHUJAUDDIN, MOHAMMAD and RAZIA SHUJAUDDIN. The life and times of Noor Jahan. Lahore: Caravan Book House, 1967. 146p.
Detailed and multifaceted biography. Based on extensive use of primary sources, Urdu and Persian writings and travelers' accounts.

734 SINGH, JOGENDRA. Nur Jahan: the romance of an Indian queen. London: James Nisbet, 1909. 260p.
Historical novel concerning Nūr Jahān and Mughal court life. [Unexamined. NUC].

735 STEEL, FLORA ANNIE. Mistress of men: a novel. London: John Lane, 1917. 368p. [*Also* New York: Frederick A. Stokes Company].
Novel recounting the life of Nūr Jahān. [Unexamined. NUC].

(e) Mumtāz Maḥal, 1593-1631, and Jāhānarā, 1613-1683, wife and daughter of Shāh Jahān, 1592-1666

736 BOGA, RUSSI. "The beloved of the palace." *In* Onlooker, annual number (1977) 60-5.
Biographical sketch of Mumtāz Maḥal. Discusses circumstances surrounding her husband Shāh Jahān's building of the Taj Mahal in her honor.

737 JAHĀNĀRĀ. The life of a Mogul princess: Jahānarā Begam, daughter of Shāh Jahān. Tr. from Persian by Andrea Butenschön. London: George Routledge and Sons, Ltd., 1931. 221p.
Long sections of Jahānārā's text are devoted to longing for a lover (Akbar had proclaimed that Mughal princesses should not be given in marriage): "Man guards the purity of woman, in order that he may enjoy it, but does he ever think of the fire that runs through her blood?" Her account chronicles her interest in and the political turmoils of her father, Emperor Shāh Jahān, and her brothers. A visit to Akbar's palace evokes a long passage on Jahānārā's perspective of the Mughal past. Some explanatory notes; no introduction.

(f) Zīb-un-Nisā, 1639-1702, daughter of Aurangzīb, 1619-1707

738 FAROOQI, HAFIZ ABBADULLAH. Zebun Nisa and her tomb. *In* J. of the Research Society of Pakistan 12,4 (1975) 25-50.
Biographical material from original and secondary sources, interspersed with selections from her verses in Persian and in translation. Considers her literary skills, her thwarted relationship with a noble and poet of her father's court, the influence of court politics on her life, the possibility of other historical personages being the princess under ficticious names, details of her tomb and other topics.

739 MOHAMED, SYED. The romance of Zaib-un-Nessa. *In* Rupam 25,1 (1926) 18-22.
Identifies the subject of a miniature portrait painting as Zīb-un-Nisā and discusses the legend from her life that is depicted. With translations of various verses found on the painting.

740 ZĪB-UN-NISĀ. Translations from the Diwan of Zib-un-Nissa Begum, poetically styled Makhfī, daughter of the emperor, Aurangzib. Tr. from Persian by P. Whalley. *In* J. of the Asiatic Society of Bengal 45,3 (1876) 308-11.
Translations and original Persian text of three poems. No interpretive commentary.

741 ________. The diwan of Zeb-un-nissa: the first fifty ghazals. Tr. from Persian by Magan Lal and Jessie Duncan Westbrook. London: John Murray, 1913. 112p. (Wisdom of the East). [*2d ed.* Lahore: Orientalia, 1954. 100p.].
Selections from "Book of the Hidden One," Zīb-un-Nisā's posthumously compiled *ṣūfī* poetry. Westbrook's introduction reviews biographical details in the context of the political and artistic climate of the 17th century.

7. Regional states and ruling families

a. Women in inscriptions of the Kalacuri dynasty, 8th to 12th centuries

742 LAL, R.K. Women in the Kalacuri inscriptions. *In* Madhya Bharati, Arts? 2,2 (1953?) 13-25.
The Kalacuri dynasty ruled from areas of Central India in the eighth through twelfth centuries. [Unexamined].

b. Women of the Cōḻa dynasty, 10th to 13th centuries: temple patrons

743 VENKATARAMAN, B. Temple art under the Chola queens. Faridabad: Thomson Press (India) Limited, 1976. 154p.
Presents the contributions of Cōḻa queens and princesses to South Indian temple art and architecture. Three patrons are discussed in detail and several others more briefly. "We are . . . dealing . . . with the provenance, growth and characteristics of religious monuments . . . . The emphasis is on the fact of contribution by them and their participation in the endeavour and activities of their spouses." Photographs (71).

c. Naikīdevī: 12th century Caulukya queen

744 SASTRI, HIRANANDA. A brave queen of Gujarat. *In* P. Seshadri, ed. Har Bilas Sarda commemoration volume: presented on the occasion of his completing seventy years. Ajmer: Vedic Yantralaya, 1937. pp.231-8.
Account, drawn from Muslim sources, of a Muslim invasion of 1178 successfully defended by Naikīdevī, mother of the Caulukya kings, Mūlarāja II and Bhīmadeva II. The victory is said to have been significant in securing Gujarat from further serious attacks in the next century.

d. Cānd Bībī of Ahmadabad Niẓām Shāhīs and her struggle against the Mughals, 16th century

745 GRIBBLE, J.D.B. The story of Queen Chand and the fall of Ahmadnagar. *In his* A history of the Deccan, v1. London: Luzac and Company, 1896. pp.211-41.
Much extracted from Taylor (entry 751). [Unexamined. Book in NUC].

746 KNIGHT, HENRY. A noble queen: Chand Bibi. *In* Times of India Annual (1959) 19-21, 76-80.
[Unexamined].

747 KULKARNI, V.B. Chand Bibi. *In his* Heroes who made history. Bombay: Bharatiya Vidya Bhavan, 1965. pp.53-9.
Brief biographical sketch stressing political and military accomplishments.

748 PATEL, TONI. Chand Bibi. Bombay: India Book House Education Trust, n.d. 32p. (Amar Chitra Katha, 54).
Comic book that portrays Cānd Bībī's coming to power, unification of the feuding factions of Ahmadnagar and defense of that city against the Mughals. Also issued in several South Asian languages.

749 QADRI, SAYYID AHMAD-ULLAH. Memoirs of Chand Bibi: the princess of Ahmednagar. Tr. from Urdu by Mohammad Hayat Quraishi. Hyderabad, India: Tarikh Office, 1939. 128p. (Nawab Lutf ud-Dawlah Memorial Series, 2).
Political biography of Cānd Bībī. Contains extracts from Persian sources, dynastic genealogies and tables and plates of paintings and her tomb.

750 SHERWANI, H.K. Political and military aspects of the reign of Muhammad-Quli Qutb Shah. *In* J. of Indian History 39, 3 (1961) 503-33.
Includes extensive and detailed information about Cānd Bībī's political and military acumen and her intricate relationships with three Deccan dynasties.

751 TAYLOR, MEADOWS [PHILIP MEADOWS TAYLOR]. The noble queen: a romance of Indian history. London: C.K. Paul and Company, 1878. 3v in 1. [*Also* New ed. London: Kegan Paul, Trench, Trubner and Company, 1892. 486p.].
Novel. Historical romance about the life of Cānd Bībī. [Unexamined. NUC].

e. Rūpamatī of the Khaljī dynasty, 16th century: legendary for her devotion

752 AḤMAD-UL-'UMRĪ. The lady of the lotus: Rūp Mati, queen of Māndu; a strange tale of faithfulness. Tr. from Persian by L.M. Crump. London: Oxford Univer-

sity Press, 1926. 96p.
Translation of a Persian tale, written in 1599, about "Rup Mati, queen of Māndu, in her chaste devotion to Bāz Bahādur, the last king of that doomed city, through life and unto death . . . one who, despite all trials and temptations, lived and died faithful to husband and ideal." With translations of 26 verses attributed to Rūpamatī, photographs of the fortress at Mandu where she lived and reproductions of eight miniature paintings depicting her life. Introduction by translator.

f. Women of the Maratha kingdoms, 17th to early 19th centuries

753 PADHYE, K.A. A few notes as regards the custom of wearing garments peculiar to the Deccani females. *In* J. of the Anthropological Society of Bombay 15,5 (1933/34) 396-400.
The traditional Maharashtrian sari style — wrapped between the legs and tucked into the back at the waist — is traced historically to the necessity of protecting the honor of women who rode horses in the Maratha empire. Portrays Maratha women as sharing the warlike qualities of their husbands.

(1) Jijābāī Bhosale, 1596?-1674, mother of Maratha hero Śivājī

754 BISEN, MALINI. Rajmata Jijabai. *In* Lok Rajya 30,3/4 (1974) 84-7.
Life of Jijābāī, in brief, including her relationship with her son, Śivājī, and her role in his development and later successes.

755 Indian mothers must follow Jijamata. *In* Lok Rajya 30,5 (1974) 12-5.
Summarizes remarks made at various functions in Maharashtra and Goa to honor Jijābāī, mother of the Maharashtrian national hero Śivājī, on the 300th anniversary of her death. With photographs of participants and audiences at the various functions.

756 OTURKAR, R.V. Part played by Jijabai, the mother of Shivaji, in the foundation of the Maratha state. *In* Indian History Congress 21, 1958, Trivandrum. Proceedings 21. Bombay: the Congress, 1959. pp.361-4.
Maratha historical sources reveal that "she was not simply a mother that gave good training to her illustrious son [as in her popular image], but she actually participated in a variety of activities concerning the administration of the Maratha State." Reviews evidence for this position in various papers and letters and names other influential Maratha women.

(2) Tārābāī Bhosale, 1675-1761, and the defense of the Deccan against the Mughals

757 KISHORE, BRIJ. Tara Bai and her times. Bombay: Asia Publishing House, 1963. 232p.
Detailed political biography with extensive use of original Marathi and Persian sources. The wife of Śivājī's younger son, Rājārāma, Tārābāī played an active role in the political and military activities of the family.

(3) The *satī* Ramābāī, d.1771

758 ACWORTH, H.A. On the Marathi ballad written on the suttee of Ramabai, widow of Madhavrao Peshwa. *In* J. of the Anthropological Society of Bombay 2 (1889) 179-92.
This paper, read before the Anthropological Society of Bombay, includes the original Marathi ballad, a translation into "rough English verse" and miscellaneous comments about Marathi ballads, the Marathas and their bards.

(4) Ahalyābāī Hoḷakar, 1725?-1795, noble and exemplary ruler

759 ANAND, MULK RAJ. Homage to Ahilya Bai. *In* Onlooker, annual number (1977) 56-9.
Biographical sketch of her adult life. Discusses her problems with her son, accession to throne and able and benevolent leadership.

760 GARG, R.S. An inscription in the temple of Ahalyabai Holkar at Maheshwar. *In* J. of Indian History 48,3 (1970) 657-60.
Translation of the Sanskrit inscription that describes the circumstances surrounding the erection of a temple in honor of Ahalyābāī Hoḷakar. Begun in 1799 by her husband's brother's son, it was completed by the latter's wife in 1833.

761 KIBE, M.V. Fragments from the records of Devi Shri Ahilya Bai Holkar. *In* India. Historical Records Commission 13th meeting, Dec 1930, Patna. Proceedings 13. Calcutta: Government of India Central Publication Branch, 1932. pp.132-9.
Six documents in Marathi and English translation relating to Ahalyābāī and dated 1765-66. Four are letters from her father-in-law, Malhār Rāo. The letters are concerned with political, military and financial matters of the state of Indore and demonstrate the extent of Ahalyābāī's responsibilities.

762 ________. The cultural Indian empire of the saintly Queen Ahilyabai Holkar *In* Indian History Congress 3, 1939, Calcutta. Proceedings 3. Calcutta: Bhupendralal Banerjee, 1940. pp.1330-3.
Ahalyābāī as the "embodiment of non-violence and renunciation." Discusses in brief her just rule and charitable acts and the widespread respect she received.

763 RAJWADE, MADHAV. Rani Ahilyabai Holkar. *In* Illustrated Weekly of India 94,32 (12 Aug 1973) 22-3, 25, 27.
Brief biographical sketch.

764 RANADE, MEENA. Ahilyabai Holkar. Bombay: India Book House Education Trust, n.d. 31p. (Amar Chitra Katha, 74).
Comic book. Ahalyābāī's life story in skeletal form.

765 SHARMA, HIRA LAL. Ahilyabai. New Delhi: National Book Trust, 1969. 123p. (National Biography).
Detailed and admiring biography based on Hindi and Marathi sources.

766 THAKUR, V.V. A short note on the charities of Devi Shri Ahilya Bai Holkar: based chiefly on the state records. *In* India. Historical Records Commission 13th meeting, Dec 1930. Patna. Proceedings 13. Calcutta: Government of India Central Publication Branch, 1932. pp.139-43.
Author classifies her charities as 1) "personal" — twelve *Śaiva jyotirliṅga* sites, seven cities and four quarters; 2) "national" — various sects; and 3) "rational" — various Islamic causes.

767 VAIDYA, G.M. Ahalyadevi Holkar. Poona: Vidarbha Marathwada, 1965. 32p. (Makers of India, 9).
[Unexamined. IBP].

g. Begams of 18th and early 19th century Oudh

See also entries 3986-87

768 'ABD AL-AḤAD. Tarikh Badshah Begam: a Persian manuscript on the history of Oudh. Tr. from Persian by Muhammad Taqi Ahmad. Delhi: Idarah-i Adabiyat-i Delli, 1977. 98p. (IAD Oriental Series, 45). [*Reprint of* 1938 ed.].
Biography of Bādshāh Begam, consort of Ghāzī-ud-dīn Ḥaidar, King of Oudh, fl. 1794-1837. [Unexamined. ALI].

769 ABDUL ALI, A.F.M. The last will and testament of Bahu Begum. *In* India. Historical Records Commission 6th Meeting, 10-11 Jan 1924, Madras. Proceedings 6. Calcutta: Central Publication Branch, Government of India, 1924. pp.149-56.
Short account of the life and will of Ammat-uz-Zahrā or Bahū Begam, wife of Shujā'-ud-Daulah, Nawab of Oudh from 1754 to 1775. Describes the political events of North India that she witnessed and participated in during her 88 years, including relations with the Mughals and the British.

770 SINGH, SHILENDRA K. Minto and the Begums of Oudh. *In* Proceedings of the Indian History Congress 14 (1951) 295-301.
Regarding the part played by Bahū Begam of Faizabad (widow of Shujā'-ud-Daulah) and her daughter-in-law, Bhābhī Begam (widow of Āṣaf-ud-Daulah), in Anglo-Oudh diplomatic relations during the Governor Generalship of Lord Minto in the early 19th century. Encouraged by their supportive gestures, Minto's relations with Oudh represent a break with his predecessors' tradition of nonintervention.

h. Begams of 18th century Bengal

771 ABDUL ALI, A.F.M. Munny Begum: the "Mother of the Company." *In* Bengal: Past and Present 29 (Apr/Jun 1925) 148-54.
[Unexamined].

772 BANERJI, BRAJENDRANATH. The Mother of the Company: compiled from original sources. *In* Bengal: Past and Present 32 (Jul/Sep and Oct/Dec 1926) 37-48, 136-40.
[Unexamined].

773 ________. Begams of Bengal: based mainly on state records. Calcutta: S.K. Mitra and Brothers, 1942. 64p.
Biographical sketches of six women connected with the 18th century Nawabs of Murshidabad as either daughter, wife, aunt, mother or consort. Based on Muslim court chronicles and British records of the period. Some "exerted a salutory influence . . . . others were not a credit to their sex . . . their life-sketch brings out. . . .the cause of the decline of the independent Muslim Kindgom of Bengal. . . . Their Sultans became pleasure-seekers and mere tools in the hands of their Begams, who virtually ruled the destiny of the people from behind the *pardah*."

774 BHALLA, P.N. The Mother of the Company. *In* J. of Indian History 22,2/3 (1943) 128-44.
Life and activities of Munnī Begam, consort of Nawab Mīr Ja'far Khān and mother and guardian of later Nawabs. Focuses on the power she exerted in the management of the Nawabs' household affairs and on her relationship with the British Government. From original documents.

i. Women connected with various lesser territories

(1) The spirited queen of Gondwana, Durgāvatī, 16th century

775 KULKARNI, V.B. Rani Durgavati. *In his* Heroes who made history. Bombay: Bharatiya Vidya Bhavan, 1965. pp.60-7.
Brief biographical sketch of a queen of Gondwana of the 16th century. Portrays her as a rebel valuing personal character qualities over birth ascription, as a loyal and devoted leader and as courageous in battle against the Mughals.

776 Rani Durgavati. Bombay: India Book House Education Trust, n.d. 31p. (Amar Chitra Katha, 104).
Her life story in comic book form.

(2) The renowned Begam "Sumroo" of Sardhana, ca. 1750-1836

777 BANERJI, BRAJENDRANATH. Some original sources for a biography of Begam Sombre. *In* India. Indian Historical Records Commission 6th meeting, 10-11 Jan 1924, Madras. Proceedings 6. Calcutta: Central Publication Branch, Government of India, 1924. pp.96-9.
Lists and describes published and unpublished English, Marathi and Persian materials relating to Begam Sumroo. With a reproduction of a portrait of the Begam.

778 _______. Begam Samru. Calcutta: M.C. Sarkar, 1925. 228p.
Regarding a North Indian woman who played a predominant role in politico-military events of the late 18th century. Attempts "to produce an authentic and as far as possible complete history of this remarkable lady" from original Persian, Marathi and English documents. Illustrated, with numerous documents reproduced in appendixes.

779 _______. A chapter of the East India Company's diplomacy: the Begam of Sardhana, based on unpublished records. *In* Modern Review 37,5 (1925) 521-30.
Discusses Begam Sumroo's relations with British officials and gives specific examples based on original sources from 1790 to 1805. Excerpts reproduced.

780 DYER, A. SAUNDERS. The Begum of Sardhana. *In* Calcutta Review 98 (1894) 310-26.
Relates incidents from the life and rule of Begam Sumroo, a Christian "woman of bold and masculine spirit" who ruled Sardhana from 1778 to 1836. Includes a tourist-style description of her palace and cathedral as they appeared in the late 19th century.

781 H.,G. [GEORGE HUDDLESTON]. A Calcutta benefactress. *In* Bengal: Past and Present 1,2 (1907) 137-47.
Account of the life of Begam Sumroo. Addresses her marriage to foreigners, command of troops and allegiance to the British, conversion to Christianity and philanthropic activities. Based primarily on contemporary documents, including many firsthand accounts.

781a HENNESSY, MAURICE. The rajah from Tipperary. London: Sidgwick and Jackson, 1971. 183p.
Biography of George Thomas, an Irishman who conquered large areas of the Punjab in the late 18th century. The work documents in detail his military and romantic alliances with Begam Sumroo.

782 KEEGAN, W. Sardhana and its Begam, 6th ed. Agra: St. Francis' Orphan Press, 1932. 78p. [*1st ed.* 1879].
Story of the Christian colony of Sardhana near present-day Meerut and its Begam Joanna Ziboolnissa Sumroo who was born a Muslim but "embraced the Catholic Faith when she was at the zenith of her glory and power in 1781." Discusses the church she had built (including the physical site), circumstances of her marriages to and identities of two European husbands, her friendships and alliances with the British and her political and military activities.

(3) Various others

783 DESHPANDE, Y.K. Raya Bhaghinis: the brave brahmin ladies of India. *In* Indian History Congress 8, 1945, Annamalainagar. Proceedings 8. Allahabad: the Congress, 1947. pp.298-302.
Two little-known women who have been designated "tigresses among rulers." Bhavaśaṃkarī of 16th century Bengal led the defeat of an Afghan raid from Orissa for which she received her epithet from emperor Akbar. Sāvitrībāī, deputed by Emperor Aurangzīb, fought bravely against Sivājī in the 17th century. Aurangzīb conferred the "tigress" title upon her.

784 IBRAHIM KUNJU, A.P. Umayamma Rāṇi, 1677-1684 A.D.: the first woman ruler of Vēṇāḍ (Travancore). *In* J. of Kerala Studies 2,1 (1975) 17-24.
Her seven-year reign, including circumstances leading to her ascension to the throne, military turmoil in this critical period in Venad history and legends are discussed.

785 LAL, LAKSHMI and ASHOK. Nildevi. Bombay: India Book House Education Trust, n.d. 32p. (Chaturang Katha, 510).
Comic book concerning the defense of the

Himalayan kingdom of Nurpur from a Mughal invasion. Plans to abduct the queen, Nīladevī, were successfully foiled.

786 WODEYAR, SADASHIVA. Rani Chennamma. New Delhi: National Book Trust, 1977. 153p. (National Biography).
Biography of Cennamma, ruler of the Karnataka state of Kittur, which was annexed by the British in 1824. Focuses on struggles with the British. Based largely on archival materials.

8. The coming of Europeans

a. Early missionary women

787 MORGAN, LADY SYDNEY. The missionary: an Indian tale. New York: Franklin and Butler and White, 1811. 279p.
Novel? [Unexamined. NUC].

788 NEWELL, H.A. Memoirs of Mrs. Harriet Newell, wife of the Rev. S. Newell, American missionary to India, who died at the Isle of France, Nov. 30, 1812, aged nineteen years, 5th ed. Edinburgh: Ogle, 1817. 228p.
[Unexamined. MRL].

789 ________. The life and writings of Mrs. Harriet Newell, rev. ed. Philadelphia: American Sunday School Union, 1831. 267p.
[Unexamined. MRL].

b. Travelers, relatives of civil servants and others

790 COTTON, H.E.A. An echo from Old Bengal. *In* Blackwood's Magazine 182,1103 (1907) 419-24.
The life and times of "Begam" Johnson (1725-1812), known "for her longevity, her influence and popularity in Calcutta society and her four weddings." She "preferred the certainty of a reign in Calcutta to the possibilities of a life in England, which she had already tasted and not relished."

791 D.,A. [MRS. A. DEANE]. A tour through the upper provinces of Hindostan: comprising a period between the years 1804 and 1814, with remarks and authentic anecdotes, to which is annexed a guide up to the River Ganges with a map from the source to the mouth. London: printed for C. and J. Rivington, 1823. 291p.
[Unexamined. NUC].

792 DA CUNHA, J. GERSON. Madame Dupleix and the Marquise de Falaiseau. *In* J. of the Bombay Branch of the Royal Asiatic Society 18 (1890/94) 370-401.
Personalities and social contexts of two prominent ladies of 18th century French India. Mme. Dupleix was the daughter of a surgeon in the Royal Company of France at Pondichery and the wife of the General Commandant of French Possessions in India. The Marquise de Falaiseau was Dupleix' grand-niece, born in Pondichery (as Adelaide de Kerjean) while her father was serving there.

793 GRAHAM, MARIA [LADY MARIA (DUNDAS) GRAHAM CALCOTT]. Journal of a residence in India. Edinburgh: A. Constable and Company, 1812. 211p. [*Also* Journal d'un séjour fait aux Indes orientales, pendant les années 1809, 1810 et 1811. Tr. from English. Genève: J.-J. Paschoud, imprimeur-libraire, 1818. 300p.].
Travel and description. [Unexamined. NUC].

794 HYDE, H.B. The first marriage of Warren Hastings. *In* Proceedings of the Asiatic Society of Bengal (Jul 1899) 79-81.
Brief attempt to establish the identity of Warren Hastings' first wife and the probable place of their meeting.

795 MORENO, H.W.B. Woman's place in the Anglo-Indian (Eurasian) community. *In* Muslim Review 4,1 (1929) 38-45.
Biographical details of South Asian women who married western men in India in the 18th and 19th centuries.

796 ________. Anglo-Indian women of the past. *In* Bengal: Past and Present 39 (Jan/Jun 1930) 53-8.
Women of 19th century Eurasian community. [Unexamined].

797 NUGENT, MARIA. A journal from the year 1811 till the year 1815, including a voyage to, and residence in, India, with a tour to the north-western parts of the British possessions in that country, under the Bengal government. London: printed by T. and W. Boone, 1839. 2v.
[Unexamined. BMG].

798 RAWLINSON, H.G. The Englishwoman in India. *In* Eastern World 4,1 (1950) 10-2.
Biographical details of two of the earliest Englishwomen in India, Mrs. William Hawkins (later Mrs. Gabriel Towerson) and Eliza Draper of the 17th and 18th centuries, respectively.

799 WRIGHT, ARNOLD and WILLIAM LUTLEY SCLATER. Sterne's Eliza: some account of her life in India with her letters written between 1757 and 1774. London: William Heinemann, 1922. 199p.
Eliza Draper's letters and an interpretation of them. The chief interest of the letters will likely be "in the sketches of Anglo-Indian life which Eliza so deftly draws. These, with her own dramatic life story . . . constitute a record of the manners and habits of expatriated Britons in India a century and a half since, which is equal to anything that the literature of that period furnishes."

D. South Asian women in the modern period: ca. 1820 to the present

1. History and culture of the subcontinent as a whole

For corresponding developments within cultural regions and areas of South Asia see "2. History and culture of the regions of South Asia. . .," entries 2994-4629

a. The colonial experience

(1) "The Position of Indian Women": a subject of great debate

(a) Statements by South Asians

800 ALL-INDIA WOMEN'S CONFERENCE. The Indian woman's charter of rights and duties. Calcutta, 1946. 14p.
[Unexamined. NUC].

801 CHATTOPADHYAYA, KAMALADEVI. The status of women in India. *In* Evelyn C. Gedge and Mithan Choksi, eds. Women in modern India: fifteen papers by Indian women writers. Bombay: D.B. Taraporewala Sons and Company, 1929. pp.1-13. [*Reprint* Westport, Connecticut: Hyperion Press, 1976. (Pioneers of the Women's Movement)].
Argues that the common occidental image of Indian women as degraded until the period of British influence is misconstrued. It is "the last hundred years which have marked the rapid decline of India and consequently a deterioration in the position of women. Reviews the reawakening of Indian womanhood in such areas as politics, education, social reforms, women's associations and legal rights.

802 DUTT, MOHENDRA NATH. Basanta Kumar Chatterjee, ed. Reflections on woman. Calcutta: Seva Series Publishing House, 1923. 111p. (Seva Series, 2).
[Unexamined. NUC].

803 MENON, LAKSHMI N. The position of women. London: Oxford University Press, 1944. 32p. (Oxford Pamphlets on Indian Affairs, 2).
Reviews their contemporary position, briefly addressing numerous topics – health, birth control, education, work, legal rights and so forth.

804 RAJAGOPAL, T.S. Indian women in the new age: or, women in young India. Mysore: printed at the Jaya Stores, 1936. 246p.
Foreword by the Maharani of Baroda. [Unexamined. NUC].

805 REGE, Y.M. Whither woman? a critical study of the social life and thought of the western woman. Bombay: Popular Book Depot, 1938. 292p.
Revision of author's thesis on the history and condition of womanhood. [Unexamined. NUC].

806 ROY, M.N. The ideal of Indian womanhood. *In his* Crime and karma, cats and women: fragments from a prisoner's diary, vI, 2d ed. Calcutta: Renaissance Publishers, 1957. pp.101-76. [*1st ed.* 1940?].
Selection from a collection of essays, based on the prison diary of a 20th century Marxist, humanist intellectual from Bengal. Criticizes the traditional role of women in India, discusses the problem of family planning and espouses economic freedom as a basic condition for giving modern direction to women in India. Criticizes Gandhian concept of ***brahmacarya*** as outmoded.

807 SEN, HANNAH. Our own times. *In* Tara Ali Baig, ed. Women of India. Delhi: Publications Division, Ministry of Information and Broadcasting, Government of India, 1958. pp.32-53.
A general statement of the changing position of Indian women in the 19th and 20th centuries. Stresses social reform efforts, women's organizations and post-independent programs. Photographs.

808 SEN, MRS. N.C. The future of Indian women. *In* Asiatic Review n.s. 15,44 (1919) 552-67. *With* Discussion on the foregoing paper, pp.568-73.
In fact, author discusses the past of Indian women, stressing the civilization's refinements and the accomplishments of many notable women. She suggests that pity and other condescending western attitudes are inappropriate, that there are good and bad in all peoples and that westerners have been slow to realize positive aspects of Indian womanhood. Paper read before the East India Association.

809 SETHNA, H.D., ed. 15 years ahead. Bombay: Bombay Radio Press, Division of Fazalbhoy Ltd., 1946. 261p.
Has some material on Indian women. Illustrated. [Unexamined. MRL].

810 SORABJI, CORNELIA. Between the twilights: being studies of Indian women by one of themselves. London: Harper, 1908. 191p.
". . . a great yearning was in my heart that others should know [my friends of the Zenana] as I did, in their simplicity and their wisdom." Sketches of various common traditional

women and typical events in their lives, along with depictions of goddesses.

811 ________. India recalled. London: Nisbet and Company, 1936. 287p.
Social life and customs in India. Much on women. [Unexamined. NUC].

812 TAGORE, RABINDRANATH. Woman. *In* Mentor 9,4 (1921) 5-12.
On various attributes and qualities of woman and the important differences between the natures of man and woman: womanliness as saintliness of love, woman worshipped as Devī, spiritual character of woman's life work, moral qualities, home as an eternal moral idea, women of epic legends as ideals for conduct, woman as an inspiration to artists. Photographs and illustrations.

813 ________. Woman and home. *In his* Creative unity. New York: Macmillan, 1922. pp.149-60.
Argues that woman's place at home and in society is a function of her special and distinct nature. Laments intrusion of western ideas about the sameness of men and women.

814 VIVEKANANDA, SWAMI. Our women. Almora: Advaita Ashrama, 1946. 59p.
Includes replies to disciples' questions on a variety of topics. [Unexamined].

815 ________. Women of India. *In his* Complete works of Swami Vivekananda, v8, 5th ed. Calcutta: Advaita Ashrama, 1971. pp.53-72.
Lecture delivered in Pasadena, California in 1900. Contrasts ideals of Indian womanhood with those of the West.

816 WADIA, A.R. The ethics of feminism: a study of the revolt of women. New Delhi: Asian Publication Services, 1977. 256p. [*Reprint of* London: G. Allen and Unwin, 1923].
Largely a discussion of 19th and early 20th century feminist ideas in the West. Concluding chapter, "Womanhood in the East," discusses position of contemporary Hindu, Muslim and Parsi women. Barring the latter group, problems of feminism in East and West are quite different. Although Parsis have been "pioneer feminists" in India, the "influence has not been of a universally healthy character."

817 ZAIN-EL-ABIDIN. Die Stellung der Frau in Indien [The position of woman in India]. Tr. by O. Rescher. Berlin, 1918.
[Unexamined].

i) On Hindu women

818 BOSE, PRAMATHA NATH. The social position of women. *In his* History of Hindu civilisation during British rule, v2. Calcutta: W. Newman, 1894. pp.107-22. [*Reprint* New Delhi: Asian Publication Services, 1978].
Briefly considers history of position of women in South Asia, achievements of Ahalyābāī Hoḷakar of Indore state and Rani Bhavānī of Natore state and effects of British influence. Reproduces a selection from a Madras newspaper by an unnamed conservative Hindu.

819 COOMARASWAMY, ANANDA K. Status of Indian women. *In his* The dance of Shiva, rev. ed. New York: Noonday Press, Farrar, Straus and Giroux, 1957. pp.98-123. [*Reprint of his* Sati: a vindication of the Hindu woman. *In* Sociological Review 6,2 (1913) 117-35].
Reply to would-be reformers and emancipators of Indian women. Argues that westerners have misunderstood the actual position of Indian women and attempts to present various issues (e.g., arranged marriages, *satīs*, wifely devotion) from the Indian point of view. Notes various aspects of Indian womanhood that are superior to circumstances for western women.

820 DEVI, SUSHILA. The ideal of Hindu womanhood: with practical suggestions for its realization. Lahore: Union Steam Press, 18__. 53, 11p. [Gaekwar Prize Essay].
[Unexamined. NUC].

821 GHOSHA, JOGESACHANDRA. The daughter of Hindusthan or the Hindu woman of India. Calcutta: Sen Brothers, 1928? 140p.
"The author's main task has been to help to understand the Hindu woman rightly." Defends orthodox Hindu attitudes toward widowhood, marriage, feminine ideals and so forth.

822 GIDUMAL, DAYARAM [DAYARAM GIDUMAL SHAHANI]. The Hindu woman: our sins against her. *In* C. Yajneswara Chintamani, ed. Indian social reform: being a collection of essays, addresses, speeches, etc., with an appendix. Madras: printed at the Minerva Press, 1901. First part, pp.97-106.
Emotional essay concerning sins perpetrated against women by Hindu society throughout the stages of their lives.

823 KESHAWAJI, HARI and DADOBA PANDURANG. Prize essays on the condition of Hindu females. Bombay, 1840?
[Unexamined. BMG].

824 PAL, DHIRENDRA NATH. The Hindu wife: a few sketches from her life. Calcutta: Phanindra Nath Pal, 1911. 65p.
[Unexamined. NUC].

825 RAMABAI SARASVATI, PANDITA. The high-caste Hindu woman. New York: F.H. Revell, 1901. 42p. [*1st ed.* 1887. *Also* Pandita Ramabai. The widows' friend: an Australasian edition of The

high-caste Hindu woman by Pandita Ramabai, with a sequel by her daughter, Manoramabai . . ., 2d ed. Melbourne: George Robertson and Company, 1903. 195p. *Reprint* The high-caste Hindu woman. Westport, Connecticut: Hyperion Press, 1976].
A description of the difficult condition of high-caste Hindu women in India written as a plea to Americans. "Will you not, all of you who read this book, think of these, my countrywomen, and rise, moved by a common impulse, to free them from life-long slavery and infernal misery?" Major chapters on childhood, married life and widowhood. Photographs of Ramabai and her work.

826 SHRIDHARANI, KRISHNALAL. Grand old Mother India. *And* Modern Mother India. *In his* My India, my America. New York: Duell, Sloan and Pearce, 1941. pp.197-242. [*Also published as* My India, my West. London: V. Gollancz, 1941].
Interpretation of Hindu womanhood and effects of modern movements on women's lives that is directed toward the West. "The Indian woman's subtle supremacy in social and private matters generally escapes the notice of Westerners . . ." Argues that Indian women do not feel oppressed and that they are generally better off than prevailing conceptions would suggest. Defends practices that may appear strange to Western eyes.

827 SORABJI, CORNELIA. Zenana-dwellers: the selfless women of Hinduism, keepers of the god-rules. *In* Asia 24,3 (1924) 171-6.
Description of some typical experiences in the lives of Hindu girls and women. "The fact of orthodoxy follows a woman relentlessly, from birth to the burying-ground." With anecdotes from the author's many years' work on behalf of secluded women.

ii) On Muslim women

828 HUSSAIN, IQBALUNNISA. Changing India: a Muslim woman speaks. Bangalore: Hosali Press, 1940. 236p.
On Muslims, women and social life in India. [Unexamined. NUC].

829 WAZIR HASAN, SAKINATUL FATIMA. Indian Muslim women: a perspective. *In* Shyam Kumari Nehru, ed. Our cause: a symposium by Indian women. Allahabad: Kitabistan, 1938? pp.22-6.
Decries the backward condition of Muslim women in India, calling for "constant activity on a national plane" in order to achieve emancipation. Reviews some social reform efforts that have affected Muslim women.

830 ZAIDI, M.H. The Muslim womanhood in revolution . . . Calcutta: the author, 1937. 140p.
Plates. [Unexamined. BMG].

iii) On women of princely families

831 BAIG, TARA ALI. The moon in Rahu: an account of the Bhowal Sannyasi case. Bombay: Asia Publishing House, 1968. 371p.
True tale of Bibhavati Devi, a rani of Bhowal in present-day Bangladesh, and her 25-year fight to repudiate the statements of a man who appeared in 1921 claiming to be her husband, a kumar of Bhowal, who had died in 1909. Based in part on discussions with the rani. Includes details of zamindari life.

832 BRINDA, MAHARANI OF KAPURTHALA. Maharani: the story of an Indian princess. New York: Henry Holt and Company, 1953? 246p.
Autobiography of a Rajput princess of Jubbal. Tells of her childhood in Jubbal, her marriage to Tika Raja of Kapurthala and her cosmopolitan, worldwide travels. Much of the narrative concerns her father-in-law's wrath and her own anxiety over the lack of a male heir. Photographs.

833 DASS, JARMANI and RAKESH BHAN DASS. Maharani: love adventures of Indian maharanis and princesses. New Delhi: S. Chand and Company, 1972. 259p.
A diwan writes of his experiences in India and abroad with members of princely families. Focuses on intrigue and alliances in these families and their contacts with Europeans. Compares princely women to western women. Discusses ways that values relating to women have changed with their emancipation and the largely negative effect these changes have on society. Gossipy tone.

834 GAYATRI DEVI, MAHARANI OF JAIPUR and SANTHA RAMA RAU. A princess remembers: the memoirs of the Maharani of Jaipur. Philadelphia: J.B. Lippincott Co., 1976. 335p.
Account of her family background and childhood in the royal family of Cooch Behar, her adult life as Maharani of Jaipur, and her very cosmopolitan lifestyle in the rapidly changing world of many princely states in the 20th century. Many photographs.

835 ONE OF THEM. The status of Indian princesses. *In* Indian Social Reformer 37, 19 (8 Jan 1927) 295-6.
Anonymous article lamenting the restrained and humiliating circumstances of Indian princesses by "One of Them." Reprinted from the *Bombay Chronicle*.

(b) Statements by westerners

836 BILLINGTON, MARY FRANCES. Woman in India. New Delhi: Amarko Book Agency, 1973. 269p. [*Reprint of* London: Chapman and Hall, 1895. 342p.].
From a series that appeared in the *Daily Graphic*, for which Billington toured India. Distinguished among the "status of Indian women" pieces of the period, this work compares them to the English working class, considers missionaries and social reformers to frequently be sentimental and egocentric, and examines some topics that were rarely considered at the turn of the century. She discusses birth and infancy, education, marriage, health care, widow marriage, work, dress, needlework, jewelry, amusements, crime and criminals, and death and funerals. Numerous drawings. Two chapters, "Anglo-Indian Society" and "Notes on Travelling and Outfit," are not included in the reprint edition.

837 BRADBURY, JAMES. The women of India. *In his* India: its condition, religion, and missions. London, 1884. pp.143-69.
[Unexamined. Book in NUC].

838 BURR, AGNES RUSH. The status of women. *In her* Neighbour India: changing days in an age-old land. New York: Fleming H. Revell Company, 1929? pp.85-112.
[Unexamined. MRL].

839 BUTLER, MARGUERITE L. Hindu women at home. London: London Missionary Society, 1921. 34p. (World Womanhood Series, 5).
[Unexamined. BMG].

840 CAMPBELL, MARY JANE. Daughters of India. Monmouth, Illinois: Republican-Atlas Printing Company, 1908. 121p.
By a missionary who worked in the Punjab. Illustrated. [Unexamined. NUC].

841 CATON, A.R. Appendix II: summary of the report of the Indian Statutory Commission, 1930, in reference to women. *In* A.R. Caton, ed. The key of progress: a survey of the status and conditions of women in India. London: Humphrey Milford, Oxford University Press, 1930. pp.218-26.
Summarizes main findings of the commission regarding the need for advancement of women in the areas of enfranchisement and political participation, education, health and social welfare.

842 COELHO, MARCEL ANTHONY FRANCIS. The question: whither India? Bombay: Thacker, 1946. 185p.
On political and social conditions in India, with material on women. [Unexamined. NUC].

843 COOPER, ELIZABETH. The harim and the purdah: studies of oriental woman. London: T. Fisher Unwin, 1915. 309p.
Survey of the lives of women from Egypt to Japan with numerous chapters relating to South Asia. With photographs.

844 D.,A. [MRS. A. DEANE?]. The Indian child's mother. London: Church Missionary Society, 1922. 150p.
Contains major sections on Hindu, Muslim and Christian women with anecdotes, descriptive material and biographical details of ideal and notable examples of these women.

844a DENNING, MARGARET B. Mosaics from India: talks about India, its peoples, religions and customs. Chicago: Fleming H. Revell Company, 1902. 296p.
Mission work and impressions of India and its peoples. Chapters with substantial material on women are "Child-Widows," "Stories of Little Girls," "Behind the Purdah," "The Iron Bracelet," "Lower Caste Women," "Famine" and "A Country Wedding in India."

845 F.,F.E. North India. *In* T. Athol Joyce and N.W. Thomas, eds. Women of all nations: a record of their characteristics, habits, manners, customs and influence, v4. London: Cassel and Company, 1915? pp.585-604. [*Also* New York, Funk and Wagnall Company, 1915].
Addresses various topics, e.g., hill tribes, "curious marriage customs," "life behind the *Purdah*," music and dance, the rani of Sikkim, magic and witchcraft. With numerous photos.

846 GIBSON, JULIA R. A cry from India's night. Kansas City, Missouri: Publishing House of the Pentecostal Church of the Nazarene, 1914? 216p.
Dr. Gibson graduated from the Woman's Medical College of Pennsylvania and subsequently worked in India. The book considers Indian womanhood and other topics. Photos. [Unexamined. NUC].

847 Indian women through alien eyes. Calcutta: Information Research Academy, 1977. 173p.
Western writers describe the status of Indian women in the 19th and 20th centuries. Articles are reprinted; identity of authors and original publication information are not supplied.

848 JACOLLIOT, LOUIS. Les moeurs et les femmes de l'extrême Orient: voyage au pays des bayadères [The manners and women of the Far East: voyage to the land of the dancing girls]. Paris: Dentu, 1873. 376p.
[Unexamined. NUC].

849 _______. Voyage au pays des jungles: les femmes de l'Inde [Voyage to the land of jungles: the women of India]. Paris: E. Dentu, 1889. 384p.
Travel and description. [Unexamined. NUC].

850 LLOYD, HARRIETTE. Hindu women: with glimpses into their life and zenanas. London: J. Nisbet and Company, 1882. 143p.
[Unexamined. NUC].

851 MAC KAY, JEAN SINCLAIR. Voices from India. Toronto: Woman's Missionary Society of the United Church of Canada, 1934. 141p.
Voices of Indian women. [Unexamined. MRL].

852 NIVEDITA, SISTER [MARGARET ELIZABETH NOBLE]. The web of Indian life, 2d ed. London: William Heinemann, 1906. 276p.
Discusses ethical and social ideas embodied in ideals of Indian womanhood (pp.17-94), social philosophy and religious beliefs. Directed toward Europeans.

853 On the state of female society in India. *In* Essays relative to the habits, character, and moral improvement of the Hindoos. London: Kingsbury, Parbury, and Allen, 1823. pp.163-84.
Scathing critique. Originally published in the ***Friend of India***, a periodical of the Serampore missionaries.

854 PINCH, TREVOR. Stark India. London: Hutchinson and Company Ltd., 1930? 288p. [*Also* New York: D. Appleton and Company, 1931].
Includes observations on social life and conditions, women and religion in India. [Unexamined. NUC].

855 ROBINSON, EDWARD JEWITT. The daughters of India: their social condition, religion, literature, obligations and prospects. Glasgow: Thomas Murray and Sons, 1860. 308p.
[Unexamined. NUC].

856 ROTHFELD, OTTO. Women of India. London: Simpkin, Marshall, Hamilton, Kent and Company, 1920. 222p.
Survey of various topics – marriage, "ladies of the aristocracy," the middle classes, working and aboriginal classes, the dancing girl, dress and ideals – that is both romanticized and critical. With 48 color illustrations of women from various communities throughout South Asia by M.V. Dhurandhar.

857 SHEATSLEY, CLARENCE VALENTINE. Women in India. *In his* Our mission field in India. Columbus, Ohio: Lutheran Book Concern, 1921. pp.44-54.
Status paper regarding Hindu women with a dim outlook.

858 STORROW, E. Our Indian sisters. London: Religious Tract Society, 1898. 256p. [*Also* Our sisters in India. Boston: United Society Christian Endeavor, 1899?].
[Unexamined. NUC].

859 UNDERHILL, MURIEL M. Some aspects of Hinduism as seen in the lives of Hindu women. *In* Student Movement 17? (May 1914) 179-82.
[Unexamined].

860 WILKENS, W.J. Woman. *In his* Modern Hinduism: being an account of the religion and life of the Hindus in northern India. London: T. Fisher Unwin, 1887. pp.323-91.
A minister's interpretation of Hindu womanhood. Following a review of the position of women in the *śāstras*, he discusses the lives of middle- and upper-class women in late 19th century North India with special attention to the preference for sons, religious activities, marriage ceremonies and marriage. Concluding chapters discuss widowhood and *satīs*.

861 WILLIAMS, GERTRUDE MARVIN. Women. *In her* Understanding India. New York: Coward-McCann, Inc., 1928. pp.241-85.
The author, who considers her view of India to be much more sympathetic than certain western critics, nonetheless presents a dim view of Indian womanhood. She discusses child marriage, female seclusion, *satīs*, widowhood and women of princely families.

862 The women of Hindostan, parts 1-6. *In* Asiatic Journal n.s. 29, 114-6, and 30, 118-20 (1839) 129-40, 208-17, 291-301, 115-26, 207-18, 247-55.
Rambling and romantic impressions of an anonymous Briton.

863 The women of India. *In* Asiatic Journal n.s. 18,72 (1835) 268-77 and 19,73 (1836) 17-26.
Rambling and romantic impressions of various aspects of women's lives in (North?) India by a Briton.

(c) "Mother India" attacked as non-nurturant, particularly regarding females

864 JHA, MANORANJAN. Katherine Mayo and India. New Delhi: People's Publishing House, 1971. 128p.
Report of research into the story behind Mayo's journalism in India, based largely upon her private papers. Concludes that "there is no doubt that the motives were primarily political: to discredit India and the Indian nationalist movement in international opinion, particulary American opinion; to win American support for the British cause in India; and to frighten even British liberals into giving up the constitutional reforms they had envisaged for India."

865 ROSENTHAL, A.M. 'Mother India' thirty years after. *In* Foreign Affairs 35,4 (1957) 620-30.

Notes the profound influence ***Mother India*** has had on foreign impressions of India and describes India's "split personality" or simultaneous commitment to traditional and contemporary values. "The country's chief psychological problem at the moment is not the sloth of the mind about which Miss Mayo wrote but something quite the reverse . . . . There is an impatience . . . with parliamentary change, a reluctance to wait."

i) The critic: Miss Katherine Mayo, an American journalist

866 MAYO, KATHERINE. Mother India. New York: Harcourt, Brace and Company, 1927. 440p.
The antagonistic book by an American journalist that triggered a fiery debate about social reform issues and Indian versus western values and social systems. It has been accused of having been commissioned by British authorities. The title is a mocking usage of an age-old cultural image, which was employed by contemporary nationalists to describe their cause and appeal to the masses. Prominent throughout the debate are the attack and defense of both India as "Mother" and the conditions of Indian women.

867 _______. Slaves of the gods. London: Jonathan Cape, 1929. 242p.
Twelve fictional narratives based on actual episodes to further illustrate and reemphasize some of the main points of ***Mother India***. Includes Mayo's assessment of the course of the debate she started.

868 _______. The face of Mother India. London: Hamish Hamilton, 1932? 41p., 406 photos.
"This book is a story-picture book. Its aim is to give eyewitness of India as India stands today." The photos, captions and introduction serve mainly to substantiate Mayo's view of India as a "land of internal antagonisms" and lend credence to her other works. Includes photos of ***devadāsīs***, prostitutes, holy women and others.

ii) A rapid series of replies, pro and con, from Indians and westerners

869 ANDREWS, CHARLES FREER. The true India: a plea for understanding. London: G. Allen and Unwin, 1939. 251p.
Argues that attacks of Mayo and others from the West are one-sided and have obscured the real India, which in fact has much to offer the West. Treats various social reform issues. Author was a missionary.

870 CHAKRAVARTY, SYAM SUNDER. My mother's picture: an attempt to get at the Hindu spirit in connection with the Mayo challenge. Calcutta: Sanjiboni Book Depot, 1930? 226p.
This "poor Brahmin" says, "The evils to which Miss Mayo refers, and worse . . . are really the outcome not of the orthodox Hindu creed, but of a fall from that creed . . . . these evils can only end if India recovers her ancient ideals . . . . shallow, soulless mimicry [of western modes of life and thought] is responsible for these."

871 CHAPMAN, J.A. The character of India: a reply to Mother India, 2d ed., rev. and enl. Oxford: Basil Blackwell, 1928. [***1st ed.*** India, its character: a reply to Mother India. Oxford: B. Blackwell, 1928. 84p.].
[Unexamined. NUC].

872 COUSINS, JAMES HENRY. The path to peace . . . an essay on cultural interchange and India's contribution thereto, with a prefatory note on "Mother India." Madras: Ganesh and Company, 1928. 60p.
[Unexamined. BMG].

873 CRASKE, M. EDITH. Sister India: one solution of the problems of "Mother India." London: Religions Tract Society, 1930. 106p. [***Also*** Grand Rapids, Michigan: William B. Eerdmans Publishing Company, 1930. 106p.].
Asserts that Mayo's exposure of "India's suffering womanhood" was essential but that she offered no solutions. Discusses work of the church in this respect. Based on travels with Dr. Edith Brown, founder and principal of the Women's Christian Medical College, Ludhiana, Punjab. With photographs.

874 DEVI, CHARULATA. The fair sex of India: a reply to "Mother India." Calcutta: Ramkrishna Cottage, 1928? 151p.
Collection of short biographies of Indian women who provided social services in refutation of Mayo's critique. [Unexamined. NUC].

875 FIELD, HARRY H. After Mother India: being an examination of ***Mother India***, of the first nine volumes written in reply thereto, and of other criticisms; together with certain new evidence mostly from Indian sources. London: Jonathan Cape, 1929. 299p.
A contemporary documents the debate. Author argues that Mayo's assessment was essentially correct and is substantiated by newer materials. Much varied information and a good bibliography of the response to the original book.

876 GAUBA, KANHAYA LAL. Uncle Sham: the strange tale of a civilization run amuck. New York: Claude Kendall, 1929.

261p. [*Also* 30th ed. Ludhiana: Kalyani Publishers, 1972? 212p.]. Critical exposé of evils in the United States as a response in kind to Mayo. "I write that the truth about American life may be made known as fearlessly and as fully as Miss Mayo has made known what she only believed to be the truth about India." Includes extensive criticisms about woman and family that make the South Asian circumstances appear favorable.

877 Indian Social Reformer 37 and 38 (1926/27 and 1927/28).
Editorials on Mayo's *Mother India* begin in volume 37, number 50 (page 785) and discussion and debate follow.

878 LAJPAT RAI. Unhappy India, 2d rev. and enl. ed. Calcutta: Banna, 1928. 565p.
Author is "writing a book in defence of my motherland, in refutation of the calumnies invented and circulated throughout the world from base motives . . ." Discusses women-related and other social reform issues and criticizes aspects of American life as perceived during a residence of five years.

879 Miss Katherine Mayo's book. *In* Indian Social Reformer 46,21 (25 Jan 1936) 321.
Protests the government's banning of *Face of Mother India* in India. "By banning her book, the Government of India have effectively banned the exposure of the palpable and malignant falsehoods in which the book evidently abounds on their own showing. Such an exposure can be made only in India and by Indians."

880 MUKERJI, DHAN GOPAL. A son of Mother India answers. New York: E.P. Dutton, 1928. 119p.
Criticizes Mayo for rousing anti-Indian sentiments in the West and anti-West sentiments in India. Refutes many of Mayo's specific arguments. Appendixes reproduce opinions of Tagore, Gandhi and others regarding *Mother India* and social reform in general.

881 NATARAJAN, K. Miss Mayo's *Mother India*: a rejoinder, 2d ed. Madras: G.A. Natesan and Company, 1928. 126p.
Collected articles from the *Indian Social Reformer* by its editor. Argues that Mayo's view of India is highly selective, unnecessarily negative, politically motivated, a racial slur, full of half-truths or untruths and so forth. With an appendix of statements that support this general position.

882 PANDIT, S.G. Mother India's answer. *In* Sociology and Social Research 12,6 (1928) 535-42.
Refutes Mayo's apolitical claim, her ethical stance and particular statements she makes.

883 RANGA IYER, C.S. Father India: a reply to *Mother India*. London: Selwyn and Blout, 1927. 207p.
Considers Mayo's book to be merely a justification of India's colonial status. *Father India* refutes many of her statements — one by one — concluding, "East *plus* West is much the best."

884 RATHBONE, ELEANOR F. Has Katherine Mayo slandered "Mother India"? *In* Hibbert Journal 27,2 (1929) 193-214.
Argues that Mayo's apparent bias should not detract from her facts, which are largely substantiated by the data of independent observers.

885 S., C. India as it is: *Mother India* by Katherine Mayo. *In* New Statesman 29, 742 (16 Jul 1927) 448-9.
Favorable review of Mayo's book in a relatively liberal publication. Was inflammatory in India. "It is certainly the most fascinating, the most depressing and at the same time the most important and truthful book that has been written about India for a good deal more than a generation." Suggests that, as an American, Mayo can expose the extent of Indian evils that English officials and missionaries could not, for fear of repercussions.

885a The truth about "Mother India": answers to an infamous slander. Vancouver, Canada: by the authority of Khalsa Diwan Society, 1927? 8p.
Opinions of M.K. Gandhi, Annie Besant, Rabindranath Tagore, Lala Lajpat Rai and others. [Unexamined. NUC].

886 TURNBULL, H.G. DALWAY. Miss Mayo and her critics. *In* Fortnightly Review 131 (Mar 1929) 355-69.
Examines the ongoing debate. "Miss Mayo's book, in spite of its misleading perspective and its occasional exaggerations," nonetheless presents a well-taken argument for the colonial power's responsibility regarding social reforms.

887 WOOD, ERNEST. An Englishman defends Mother India: a complete constructive reply to "Mother India," 2d rev. ed. Madras: Ganesh and Company, 1930. 475p.
"As to facts [this book] will show that [Miss Mayo] is generally wrong, and as to deductions from facts, that she is almost entirely wrong. While thus vindicating the real Mother India (as the Indians affectionately call their country) I hope this book will [also give] a true picture of Indian life and conditions." Much on women. Many photographs. Author is former principal of Sind National College, Hyderabad, and a translator of Sanskrit texts.

888 WORLD-CITIZEN [S.G. WARTY]. Sister India: a critical examination of and a reasoned reply to Miss Katherine Mayo's "Mother India." Bombay: S.G. Warty, Sister India Office, 1928? 242p.
Attempts to portray Indian life as a self-respecting Indian views it, so as to make it understandable to unbiased outsiders. "If all the faces and peoples of the world outside India would understand India rightly, they would all treat her as a 'sister' country, to

whom some affectionate service and assistance from them are due." The aim of Mayo's book is said to be the vindication of British rule in India and "to humiliate India in the eyes of the world." Author refutes Mayo issue by issue. With appendixes of Gandhi's and Tagore's reviews of *Mother India*.

(2) Three intertwined movements: social reform, nationalist and women's

889 ASTHANA, PRATIMA. Women's movement in India. Delhi: Vikas Publishing House, 1974. 175p.
Concise survey of the history of and major forces behind the 19th and 20th century changes for Indian women. Considers early 19th century western impact, leading male Indian reformers, the female "pathfinders," the expansion to the level of a movement, the growth of women's organizations, social legislation, political participation and educational progress. Concluding chapter summarizes range of opportunities open to contemporary Indian women. Extensive use of primary documents.

890 CATON, A.R., ed. The key of progress: a survey of the status and conditions of women in India. London: Humphrey Milford, Oxford University Press, 1930. 250p.
Handbook designed to educate the British public. "In dealing with social evils, we have . . . allowed the facts to speak for themselves." The book aims to give a full account of the organizations and movements in operation in India. "To supplement published material we [circulated] in India a comprehensive Questionnaire, which invited both information on points of fact and constructive suggestions for improvement." For contents, see entries 841, 891, 999, 1074, 1130, 1144, 1152, 1164, 1173 and 1177.

891 CATON, A.R., anonymous and A. YUSUF ALI. Women in public life. *In* A.R. Caton, ed. The key of progress: a survey of the status and conditions of women in India. London: Humphrey Milford, Oxford University Press, 1930. pp.80-100.
The changing position of and opportunities for women in India in the context of the various movements.

892 CHATTOPADHYAYA, KAMALADEVI et al. The awakening of Indian women. Madras: Everymans Press, 1939. 78p.
Essays by prominent women on changing opportunities for Indian women. [Unexamined. NUC].

893 COUSINS, MARGARET E. Indian womanhood today, rev. and enl. Allahabad: Kitabistan, 1947. 205p. (Kitabistan Series, 5). [*1st ed.* 1941].
A history of the interrelationship of the nationalist and Indian women's movements. Focuses on political participation and changes effected.

894 DESAI, A.R. Movement for the emancipation of women. *In his* Social Background of Indian nationalism. Bombay: Popular Prakashan, 1966. pp.273-80.
Brief discussion of the transition of Indian women within the social movements of the 19th and 20th centuries.

895 DESAI, NEERA. Woman in modern India. Bombay: Vora and Company, 1957. 314p. [*2d ed.* 1977. 334p.].
History of the changing status of Indian women in the 19th and 20th centuries and the political and social reform movements that led to these changes. Background chapters discuss pre-British period history and the effects of the *bhakti* movement. The 1977 edition includes updated statistical tables.

896 DE SÉLINCOURT, AGNES. The place of women in the modern national movements of the East. *In* International Review of Missions 1,1 (1912) 98-107.
General statement about the rapidly changing position of women in India. Discusses ways that missionary work among them might most effectively be carried out.

897 GEDGE, EVELYN C. and MITHAN CHOKSI, eds. Women in modern India: fifteen papers by Indian women writers. Bombay: D.B. Taraporewala Sons and Company, 1929. 161p. [*Reprint* Westport, Connecticut: Hyperion Press, 1976. (Pioneers of the Women's Movement)].
Prominent Indian women speak to westerners on their own behalf. Considers achievements of and for women and problems remaining in areas of social work, medicine, higher education, literature, arts, law and seclusion. Oriented toward conditions in western and southern India. For contents, see entries 361, 801, 1061, 1115, 1120, 1122, 1158, 1176, 1204, 2587, 3373, 3375, 3442 and 3470.

898 GHOSE, LOTIKA. Social and educational movements for women and by women, 1820-1950. *In* Kalidas Nag and Lotika Ghose, eds. Bethune School and College centenary volume, 1849-1949. Calcutta: Bethune College, 1951. pp.132-69.
[Unexamined. Book in NUC].

899 GIDUMAL, DAYARAM [DAYARAM GIDUMAL SHAHANI]. The status of women in India: or, a handbook for social reformers. Bombay: Fort Printing Press, 1889. 102, 337p.
Catalog of data and opinions from numerous officials and others arranged by presidency. Chapter topics include facts, causes, laws and proposed solutions to the problems of infant marriage and enforced widowhood, along with reasons for non-interference. Prefaced by a 102-page "Symposium of Hindu Domestic Reform-

ers and Anti-reformers." Includes appendixes on aspects of infant marriage and Vedic authorities for widow marriage.

900 GRAY, MRS. R.M. The advance of Indian women. *In* Asiatic Review n.s. 28,96 (1932) 559-69. *With* Discussion, pp.570-81.
Reviews the changing position of women in India since the First World War in the context of the women's and the nationalist movements. Distinguished discussants.

901 GUHA, PHULRENU. Women in political and social reform movements. *In* B.N. Ganguli, ed. Social development: essays in honour of Smt. Durgabai Deshmukh. New Delhi: Sterling Publishers, 1977. pp.91-106.
Reviews the social reform movements for and by women of the 19th and 20th centuries and women's participation in India's freedom struggle.

902 HAUSWIRTH, FRIEDA [FRIEDA MATHILDA (HAUSWIRTH) DAS]. Purdah: the status of Indian women. New York: Vanguard Press, 1932. 289p.
Reviews the impact of the nationalist and social reform movements on women against a background survey of the history of women in India. Based in part on eight year's residence as wife of an Indian, the author aligns herself with the views of Sister Nivedita and opposes herself to the views of Katherine Mayo: there is a strength and integrity to Indian womanhood often misapprehended in the West.

903 HEIMSATH, CHARLES H. Indian nationalism and Hindu social reform. Princeton, New Jersey: Princeton University Press, 1964. 379p.
Considers the relationship of the two movements through World War I. Includes material on women's issues, most notably on age at marriage and widow marriage.

904 HUME, ELIZABETH C. Women's part in modern movements in India. *In* Moslem World 22,4 (1932) 361-73.
Briefly surveys the changing circumstances for women in India; focuses on the participation of Muslim women in these changes.

905 MC DOUGALL, ELEANOR. The preparation of Indian women for public service. *In* Church Missionary Review (Dec 1920) 307-18.
[Unexamined].

906 MENON, LAKSHMI. Women in India and abroad. *In* Tara Ali Baig, ed. Women of India. Delhi: Publications Division, Ministry of Information and Broadcasting, Government of India, 1958. pp.54-71.
Places the changes relating to Indian women in the past century in the context of worldwide movements and trends. With tables on comparative political representation and voting rights. Photographs of several Indian women of international stature.

907 Modern Review. v1-. (1907-). Calcutta. Monthly.
This journal has taken a particular interest in women's issues, organizations, etc.

908 NEHRU, SHYAM KUMARI, ed. Our cause: a symposium by Indian women. Allahabad: Kitabistan, 1938? 419p.
Prominent participants in the Indian women's movement discuss issues subsumed under: "Retrospect," "Home," "Health," "Education," "Arts," "Industry," "Rural Life," "Social Evils," "Marriage and Divorce," "Legal Rights," "Political Struggle," and "Future of Indian Women." For partial contents see entries 829, 909, 927, 949, 952, 1006, 1011-2, 1026, 1038, 1098, 1128, 1131, 1143, 1150, 1157, 1165, 1174, 1178, 1245, 1247, 1270, 1280, 1957, 2586 and 2664.

909 NEHRU, UMA. Whither women? *In* Shyam Kumari Nehru, ed. Our cause: a symposium by Indian women. Allahabad: Kitabistan, 1938? pp.403-19.
Considers inherent versus socially-based factors that have determined the conditions of women in the past and present. Considers the religious and emotional aspects of the old social system to be giving way to a new rationality that recognizes the crucial relevance of an enlightened womanhood in society as a whole.

910 PAUL, GLENDORA B. Emancipation and education of Indian women since 1829. Ph.D. dissertation, Department of Education?, University of Pittsburgh, 1970. 220p. [University Microfilms 71-8006].
Argues that influences of English education and mission work are the significant factors in the changing circumstances for Indian women in the 19th and 20th centuries. Discounts role of nationalist movement in effecting significant change. Based primarily on secondary sources, a basic list of which are provided in bibliography. [Unexamined. DAI].

911 RUNGANADHAN, S.E. Indian women of today. *In* Asiatic Review n.s. 38,135 (1942) 236-44. *With* Discussion, pp.244-5.
Reviews the changing position of women in India in light of cooperation of women's organizations, missionary work and so forth. Author comments on the fact that the women's movement in India is free from communalism and welcomes the efforts of British women.

912 SEN, ELA. Women's movements. *In her* Testament of India. London: George Allen and Unwin, 1939. pp.227-55.
Reviews effects of social reform and nationalist movements on Indian women. Concludes with discussion of achievements of several prominent Indian women.

913 SEN, HANNAH. Problems of women's welfare. *In* India (Republic). Planning Commission. Social Welfare in India. Edited by Durgabai Deshmukh. New

Delhi: Publications Division, Ministry of Information and Broadcasting, Government of India, 1955. pp.135-47.
Assessment of changes taking place in women's lives due to the movements of the 20th century.

914 SHRIDEVI, S. A century of Indian womanhood. Mysore: Rao and Raghavan, 1965. 161p.
Presents the changing position of Indian womanhood from 1857 to 1957. Principal topics are reform movements, nationalism, education and participation in fine arts. Speculates about the future.

915 THARPAR, ROMILA [ROMILA THAPAR]. The history of female emancipation in southern Asia. *In* Barbara E. Ward, ed. Women in the new Asia: the changing social roles of men and women in South and South-east Asia. Paris: UNESCO, 1963. pp.473-99.
Traces changes in women's rights, status and roles from Vedic times to the present with an emphasis on the 19th and 20th centuries. Considers reform movements and the issues of marriage, widowhood and education; women's organizations; and the Indian independence movement. Also deals with 20th century Southeast Asia.

916 UNDERHILL, MRS. L.A. Women and new movements in India. *In* Asiatic Review n.s. 26,85 (1930) 117-29. *With* Discussion, pp.130-40.
Lecture given at a meeting of the East India Association. Details the changing position of women in India due to the social reform and other movements. Discussion includes the comments of such distinguished persons as Lady Rama Rau and Lady Hartog.

917 WILSON, DAGMAR CURJEL. The women's movement in northern India. *In* Asiatic Review n.s. 25,83 (1929) 373-80.
From a series of articles considering women's movements throughout the world. One "cannot help noticing the rapidity with which, in so many directions" women's lives are changing in northern India. Attributes this to influence of women's movements in other countries; improved economic conditions due to the "beneficent departments" of government; and health, educational and legislative provisions.

918 The women's movement. *In* Indian Social Reformer 37,14 (4 Dec 1926) 211-2.
Assesses changes in women's attitudes and activities in the context of the contemporary social milieu.

919 YOUNG, RUTH. Women's work in India: a quarter of a century of progress. *In* Asiatic Review n.s. 32,111 (1936) 555-70. *With* Discussion on the foregoing paper, pp.571-82.
Address to the East India Association notes the changes in opportunities for Indian women in the past 25 years in the areas of education, the All-India Women's Conference, politics, social work, medicine and population control. Argues that English women should be friends and supporters rather than leaders of the Indian women's movement.

(a) The social reform movement

See also social reform material in regional contexts within "2. History and culture of the regions of South Asia. . .," entries 2994-4629

920 ASTHANA, PRATIMA. The leading reformers and the cause of women. *In* Agra University J. of Research, Letters 22, 1 (1974) 81-94.
Attitudes and contributions, in brief, of Rammohun Roy, Debendranath Tagore, Iswar Chandra Vidyasagar, Swami Dayanand Saraswati, Huzur Maharaj Rai Saligram Bahadur, Keshab Chandra Sen, Mahadev Govind Ranade, Behramji Malabari, Dhondo Keshav Karve, Rabindranath Tagore, Swami Vivekananda, Viresalingam Pantulu, R. Venkata Ratnam Naidu, Gopal Krishna Gokhale and Mohandas Karamchand Gandhi.

921 BESANT, ANNIE. Wake up, India: a plea for social reform. Madras: Theosophical Publishing House, 1913. 303p.
Lectures delivered in 1913 designed to help the Freethinkers and Theosophists in their social reform efforts. Topics are foreign travel for Indians, child marriage, depressed classes, Indian industries and self-government, mass education, education of Indian girls, color bar in England and its colonies and caste system.

922 Chapter VI: sex. *In* India. Census Commissioner. Census of India, 1911, v1: India, part 1, report. Calcutta: Superintendent Government Printing, India, 1913. pp.205-34.
Describes sex ratio patterns from 1911 census by province and state. Discusses general reasons for a low proportion of females to males and particular reasons that affect interregional variation. Considers female infanticide, neglect of female infants, early marriage, death in childbirth, bad treatment of women and hard work. Tables.

923 CHIMNABAI II. MAHARANI OF BARODA and S.M. MITRA. The position of women in Indian life. New York: Longmans, Green and Company, 1911. 358p.
An account of "some Western feminine institutions, the adaptation of which to suit Eastern requirements is likely to help Indian women to achieve a higher position in public life than they at present hold." By two persons with considerable firsthand experience in the West.

924 CHINTAMANI, C. YAJNESWARA, ed. Indian social reform: being a collection of essays, addresses, speeches, etc., with an appendix. Madras: printed at the Minerva Press, 1901. 369, 363p.
Collection of statements highly critical of Indian, primarily Hindu, traditions by a distinguished group of Indians. In four parts: "Original Papers," speeches of M.G. Ranade, presidential addresses of the Indian National Social Conference and "Miscellaneous Papers." For contents with greatest relevance to women, see entries 56, 822, 1010, 1016, 1031-2, 1135, 1147 and 3397.

925 DATTA, KALIKINKAR. Education and social amelioration of women in pre-Mutiny India. Patna: Patna Law Press, 1936. 126, 31p.
History of female education, widow marriage and anti-*satī* movements from mid-18th century to 1857. Numerous appendixes reproduce statistics and documents relating to *satīs*. Largely based on primary sources.

926 DENNY, J.K.H. Toward the sunrising: a history of work for the women of India done by women from England, 1852-1901. London: Marshall Brothers, 1901? 262p.
Illustrated. [Unexamined. NUC].

927 DEULGAONKAR, SULOCHANA. The Hindu woman's struggle. *In* Shyam Kumari Nehru, ed. Our cause: a symposium by Indian women. Allahabad: Kitabistan, 1938? pp.312-7.
Deals with social problems of Hindu women of the 19th century, and efforts of social reformers of that period.

928 FISHER, FRED B. Lifting the purdah. *In his* India's silent revolution. New York: Macmillan, 1919. pp.116-44.
Reviews progress of the social reform movement in India, touching briefly on the various topics. Little about *pardā* per se.

929 GRAY, H. The progress of women. *In* L.S.S. O'Malley, ed. Modern India and the West: a study of the interaction of their civilizations. London: Oxford University Press, 1941. pp.445-83. [*Rev. ed.* Indian women and the West . . . London: Zenith Press, 1944? 63p.].
Argues that western impact has brought to India a new conception of women's worth, has challenged their remediable suffering and has encouraged their adaptation to changing economic conditions. Discusses social reform movement and particular issues of education, religious reform, Christian mission work and western health services and participation in industry, politics and the arts.

930 GREAT BRITAIN. PARLIAMENT. HOUSE OF COMMONS. Annual lists and general index of the Parliamentary Papers relating to the East Indies published during the years 1801 to 1907 inclusive. London: Eyre and Spottiswoode, 1909. 194p.
Indispensable source for material concerning British colonial administration and policy during the 19th century, including documents relating to social reform issues. Although the organization of these House of Commons and House of Lords materials is somewhat complicated for one not familiar with the papers, all are indexed by subject.

931 Hindoo women. *In* Calcutta Review 40, 79 (1864) 80-101.
Enumerates the causes of the low status of Hindu women as "1st, idolatrous rites and antiquated customs; 2nd, early marriage; 3rd, polygamy; and 4th, the utter want of education." Prescribes western-style education "to produce a class of intelligent and cultivated wives and mothers." Presents data on women's schools, including female enrollment, in mid-19th century Bengal.

932 Indian Social Reformer. v1-63 (1894?-1952). Founded in Madras, moved to Bombay. Weekly.
Launched during age of consent debates in the 1890s, this journal gave prominence to women's reform issues. When taking up the "Mother India" debate the editor comments: "The abolition of child marriage, enforced widowhood, and dedication of women as *devadāsīs*, purity, total abstinence, removal of caste restrictions on sea voyages, inter-dining and intermarriage, the removal of untouchability, women's education, the abolition of animal sacrifices — all these and other social and moral reforms have been advocated and, in some cases, initiated by this paper." Thoroughly covered various social reform issues and provided notices of conferences and other events, primarily in brief articles (including extracts from contemporary newspapers). The journal was in touch with current events and one can generally find topical discussions concurrent with legislative and other events.

933 INGHAM, KENNETH. Reformers in India, 1793-1833: an account of the work of Christian missionaries on behalf of social reform. Cambridge: Cambridge University Press, 1956. 150p.
Largely based on archival materials. Major sections on *satīs* and various other issues involving women.

934 KAYE, JOHN WILLIAM. The suppression of human sacrifice, suttee, and female infanticide. *In his* The administration of the East India Company: a history of Indian progress, 2d ed. London: Bentley, 1853.
[Unexamined. Book in NUC].

935 LAKSHMANA, GANPAT. An essay on the promotion of domestic reform among the natives of India, 3d ed. Bombay: printed at Dnyan Mitra Press, 1881. 229p. [*1st ed.* 1843].
Prize-winning essay treats 20 reform topics, most centrally related to women's issues.

Presents a scathing critique of the status quo, along with a program for improvement. Sponsor of the competition is unclear.

936 MAHARANI OF BARODA [CHIMNABAI II. MAHARANI OF BARODA]. The first All-India Women's Conference: Her Highness the Maharani of Baroda's presidential address. *In* Indian Social Reformer 37, 19 (8 Jan 1927) 292-5.
Speaks out against child marriage and *pardā* and for a legal minimum age of consent of 16 years, more widespread female education (advocates coeducation, attention to physical culture and compulsory primary education), improved inheritance and property rights for women and improved circumstances for Indian princesses.

937 MAJUMDAR, R.C. Social reform. *In* R.C. Majumdar, ed. British paramountcy and Indian renaissance, part II. Bombay: Bharatiya Vidya Bhavan, 1965. pp.256-94. (History and Culture of the Indian People, 10).
Addresses the general point that "almost all the important social reforms of the nineteenth century . . . centre around women" and discusses the particular issues of *satīs*, infanticide, widow marriage and female education.

938 MAZUMDAR, VINA. The social reform movement in India: from Ranade to Nehru. *In* B.R. Nanda, ed. Indian women: from purdah to modernity. New Delhi: Vikas, 1976. pp.41-66.
Considers continuities and breaks with tradition relating to women in a major segment of the social reform movement.

939 MIR AMIRUDDIN, BEGAM. Women and social reform. *In* Indian Social Reformer 52, 17 (27 Dec 1941) 198-9.
Proposes particular social reform tasks relating to Muslim women.

940 MÜLLER, F. MAX. Rukhmabai and Ramabai. *In* Nineteenth Century Studies 10 (Apr 1975) 235-44. [*Reprint from* Indian Magazine 201 (Sep 1887)].
Letter to the editor of a major newspaper on the plight of Indian women who choose not to fulfill their pre-arranged marriage contract because of incompatability. Also treats the difficulties of widowhood. Argues that British law should take no part in enforcing "conjugal rights," and suggests that the British help in the establishment of a home and school for child-widows.

941 MURDOCH, JOHN. The women of India and what can be done for them. Madras: Christian Vernacular Education Society, 1888. 150p.
Survey essay that concludes with "remedies which are in the power of the people," the aim being "to urge the reader to adopt certain measures in his own family for which the sanction of government is not required." Topics addressed include education issues, marriage issues, family life, female seclusion, widows and *satīs*. A brief section on literature for women lists various regional language books and periodicals for women.

942 NATARAJAN, S. A century of social reform in India, 2d rev. and enl. ed. Bombay: Asia Publishing House, 1962. 223p. [*1st ed.* 1954].
A history of the social reform movement by a participant, the former editor of the *Indian Social Reformer*.

943 NIHAL SINGH, SAINT. The submerged half in India. *In* Nineteenth Century 67,399 (1910) 817-33.
"The women of Hindostan have seriously retarded the progress of their people" as shown in "the feminine attitude toward early marriage and enforced widowhood — two of the most noxious institutions that afflict the Indian polity." Asserts that Indian women suffer but want to go on doing so and are therefore at cross-purposes with the male social reformers. Educated men and uneducated women are poorly matched. The religiosity of Indian women is cold and stereotyped. Reformers can take heart in the small but significant number of admirable women in Indian history and in the slow but steady advances under the influence of social reform efforts.

943a OMAN, JOHN CAMPBELL. Theism in Bengal: a study in Brahmaism. *And* Hindu social reformers. *In his* The brahmans, theists and Muslims of India: studies of goddess-worship in Bengal, caste, Brahmaism and social reform, with descriptive sketches of curious festivals, ceremonies, and faquirs. Delhi: Indological Book House, 1973? pp.99-237. [*Reprint of* 1907 ed.].
Includes sections on the Brahmo Samaj and marriage reform, widowhood, temple dancers, female education and other reform issues in North and East India.

944 ROY, RAMMOHUN. Modern encroachments on the ancient rights of Hindoo females. *In* Oriental Herald 10,32 (1826) 251-8. [*Reprint in his* Translation of several principal books, passages and texts of the Veds, and of some controversial works on Brahmunical theology, 2d ed. London: Parbury, Allen, and Company, 1832. *And in his* The English works of Raja Rammohun Roy, v1. Ed. by Jogendra Chunder Ghose. Calcutta: Srikanta Roy, 1901].
Argues that contemporary Hindu practices have forsaken the honor and esteem accorded women by ancient lawgivers. "The native community places greater confidence in the honest judgement . . . of European gentlemen than in that of their own countrymen. But should the Natives receive the same advantages of education that Europeans enjoy . . . they will, I trust, be found, equally with Europeans, worthy of the confidence of their countrymen and the respect of all men." From a treatise originally printed and distributed privately in Bengal.

945 ROYAL EMPIRE SOCIETY, LONDON. LIBRARY. India: women. *In its* Subject catalogue of the library of the Royal Empire Society, formerly Royal Empire Institute, v4: the Mediterranean colonies, the Middle East, Indian Empire, Burma, Ceylon, British Malaya, East Indian Islands, and the Far East. Comp. by Evans Lewin. London: the Society, 1937. pp.413-5.
List of over one hundred works on women in British India in the holdings of the Royal Empire Society. Bibliography of British involvement in India in the period 1875 to 1936. Much of the material documents the British concern with social reform. Cross-referenced to relevant sections in the catalog.

946 SARKAR, SUMIT. Bibliographical survey of social reform movements in the eighteenth and nineteenth centuries. New Delhi: Indian Council of Historical Research, 1975. 54p.
Bibliographic essay dealing with all-India, Islamic and regional reform efforts.

947 SESHADRI, P., ed. Har Bilas Sarda commemoration volume: presented on the occasion of his completing seventy years. Ajmer: Vedic Yantralaya, 1937. 554p.
Festschrift to the author of the Child Marriage Restraint Act of 1929 contains nearly 200 brief articles. Many concern social reform issues relating to women (e.g., widows, education, inheritance, child marriage). Many are by prominent women.

948 SHORE, JOHN. On some extraordinary facts, customs, and practices of the Hindus. *In* Asiatic Researches 4,22 (1807) 329-48.
Paper presented in 1794. Urges Europeans to become more familiar with Indian social customs. Reviews a number of "extraordinary" practices including matricide, widow immolation and infanticide.

949 SORABJI, CORNELIA. The position of Hindu women fifty years ago. *In* Shyam Kumari Nehru, ed. Our cause: a symposium by Indian women. Allahabad: Kitabistan, 1938? pp.3-21.
Recounts 19th century social reforms for women through 1886.

950 SRINIVASA SASTRI, V.S. Rights and status of women in India. Madras: S. Viswanathan, 1956? 74p.
Lectures delivered in 1928 and 1940 urge reform regarding numerous women's issues and a general equality of opportunity of the sexes.

951 STEEL, F.A. [FLORA ANNIE (WEBSTER) STEEL]. East Indian women. *In* North American Review 169,517 (1899) 846-54.
Argues that "nine-tenths of the English women who manifest that somewhat over-sentimental interest in their Indian sisters" erroneously believe that no widow may marry, all girls are married at a very early age and all women are secluded. Attempts to draw a more accurate picture of these issues.

952 SUKTANKAR, SUNDARABAI. Three social evils. *In* Shyam Kumari Nehru, ed. Our cause: a symposium by Indian women. Allahabad: Kitabistan, 1938? pp.212-20.
Describes history and ill effects of and solutions to the evils of child marriage, *pardā* and prostitution.

953 The suttee and the widow. *In* Asiatic Journal n.s. 23,90 (1837) 112-23.
Didactic tale about the trials of a young Hindu girl. Implicitly criticizes widow burning, treatment of widows, Hindu family patterns, female seclusion and early age of female marriage.

954 YOUNGHUSBAND, FRANCIS. Dawn in India: British purpose and Indian aspiration. London: J. Murray, 1930. 331p.
Major sections are "Political" and "Spiritual." Contains material on Indian women. [Unexamined. MRL].

i) *Satī*, "a woman who is true," versus suttee, "widow-burning"

955 Abolition of suttees: 1829, Regulation 17. *In* Asiatic Journal n.s. 2,5 (1830) 38-9.
Text of Sati Regulation passed in 1829 by the Governor-General in Council declaring *satī* illegal in Bengal.

956 AITKEN, R.H. Suttee. Bombay, 1872. [Unexamined].

957 BANERJI, BRAJENDRANATH. Raja Radhakanta Deb's services to the Company. *In* Bengal: Past and Present 33 (Jan/Jun 1927) 130-3.
Selections from favorable statements about Rammohun Roy's opponent in anti-*satī* movement. [Unexamined].

958 A BENGALI CIVILIAN. On the practice of suttee. *In* Asiatic Journal 27,157 (1829) 57-63.
Based on 22 years of experience in India, the author takes the position that, "the opposing of even religious errors by violence is at all times to be deprecated . . ." Reacting to East-India House debates of 1827, he urges that widow immolation be permitted in strict accordance with religious law. Speculates about motives for mounting the pyre.

959 BOSE, PRAMATHA NATH. Sati. *In his*

History of Hindu civilisation during British rule, v2. Calcutta: W. Newman, 1894. pp.65-83. [*Reprint* Asian Publication Services, 1978].
Brief history of the practice of widow immolation. Reproduces Sleeman's firsthand account and details of another. Provides statistics for recorded incidents in various cities of eastern India and discusses East India Company policy and measures.

960 BOULGER, DEMETRIUS C. The abolition of widow-burning. *In his* Lord William Bentinck. Oxford: Clarendon Press, 1892. pp.77-111. (Rulers of India).
Discusses in detail events leading up to Bentinck's Minute of 1829, which precipitated anti-*satī* legislation throughout British India. Author considers this to be the most memorable event of his Governor-Generalship. With text of Minute.

961 Burning of Hindoo widows. *In* Oriental Herald 1,4 (1824) 551-60. *And* J. of General Literature 2,6 (1824) 173-86.
Paper designed to call greater public attention to the information contained in papers on widow burning, which had recently been presented to the House of Commons. To allow the custom to continue is a "foul stain on our national reputation, which cannot be too speedily wiped away."

962 Burning of widows in India. *In* Wesleyan Methodist Magazine, 3d series 6 (Mar-Apr 1827) 187-90, 261-5.
Extracts (resolutions, speeches and an adopted petition) from the proceedings of a meeting held in New York City in 1827 to petition Parliament on the subject of the immolation of Hindu widows.

963 CHAINA MALL. Tombs of satis. *In* Punjab Notes and Queries 3,30 (1886) 92.
Brief note concerning reverence orthodox Hindus have toward monuments to ***satīs***.

964 COLLET, SOPHIA DOBSON. Dilip Kumar Biswas and Prabhat Chandra Ganguli, eds. The life and letters of Raja Rammohun Roy, 3d ed. Calcutta: Sadharan Brahmo Samaj, 1962. 562p. [*1st ed.* London, 1900].
Called by the editors the "standard biography in English" of Rammohun Roy, this detailed work includes the following related to the anti-*satī* campaign: account of Roy's witnessing his elder brother's wife jump onto her husband's funeral pyre; a chapter, "Spiritual Theism versus Idolatry and Suttee," which discusses Roy's earlier reform efforts up to 1920; a chapter on "The Abolition of Suttee," 1828-1830; and copies of Roy's congratulatory letter to Lord Bentinck and the latter's reply.

965 DAVIDSON, CHARLES JAMES C. Tara, the Suttee: an Indian drama in five acts; with copious notes, explanatory, original and selected. London: the author, 1851 178p.
[Unexamined. NUC].

966 English version of a song or hymn sung by a Hindoo woman, on the point of being burned on the pile with her husband's body. *In* Oriental Herald (Aug 1828).
[Unexamined].

967 GANGULY, NARENDRANATH. A note on sati. *In* Bengal: Past and Present 70,133 (1951) 55-7.
Account of a woman who became a ***satī*** in Howrah in 1828. Portrays a widow determined to immolate herself, despite the protests of English observers. Argues, based on the ***śāstras,*** that a widow's death is not mandatory. With table of reported incidences in the Bengal Divisions, 1815-28.

968 GRIFFITHS, PERCIVAL. Suttee. *In his* The British impact on India. London: Macdonald, 1952. pp.216-25.
Describes widow immolation as a central social reform issue with respect to British policy: "In deciding whether to suppress ***suttee*** or not the British Government were in effect deciding whether to accept Hindu standards of value for India or to denounce them, at least in this respect, as barbarous." Reproduces some firsthand accounts and briefly reviews the history of British policy.

969 LOVETT, VERNEY H. Suttee. *In* Asiatic Review n.s. 24,78 (1928) 314-20.
Comments on Thompson's investigation of ***satīs.***

970 NAG, JAMUNA. Crusade against suttee. *In author's* Raja Rammohun Roy: India's great social reformer. New Delhi: Sterling Publishers, 1972. pp.44-65.
Discusses the "Conferences" and various historical details of Rammohun Roy's anti-*satī* campaign. Considers Roy to have provided the systematic propaganda that enabled the government to abolish widow sacrifices.

971 NANDY, ASHIS. Sati: a nineteenth century tale of women, violence and protest. *In* V.C. Joshi, ed. Rammohun Roy and the process of modernization in India. New Delhi: Vikas, 1975. pp.168-94.
Offers historical and psychological analyses of widow immolation and shows how this issue embodied the confrontation of traditional and modern values in 19th century India. States that Rammohun Roy was able to offer his society "alternate symbols of authority" that were "more compatible with large-scale industrial, social and economic changes then taking place." Includes important bibliographic references.

972 AN OLD INHABITANT OF BENGAL. Plan for abolishing human sacrifices in India. *In* Oriental Herald 8,27 (1826) 479-88.
A European writes that women in India are "playthings and breeders. . . . debased and sunk" and that they must become ***satīs*** if their relatives so desire. The plan includes gain-

ing the support of influential brahmans; making compulsion, aiding and abetting illegal; using government "frowns" to influence involved parties; and clogging the ceremony of burning "with sundry petty forms and difficulties." Asserts that references to "suttees" and "cremations" are too indirect; in this "diabolical cookery of women," they are being "'FRIED' alive over a slow fire!"

973 On the burning of Hindoo widows. *In* Oriental Herald 8,25 (1826) 1-20.
Reviews various accounts of *satīs*, the anti-*satī* movement and resistance to this movement. Describes the attitudes and actions of various British administrators in India. "If we allow [their bloody rites] to be practised under the sanction of our supreme authority, do we not incur a deeper share of responsibility than even the deluded wretches themselves. . . ?"

974 On the burning of widows. *And* The subject continued. *And* Review of a pamphlet. *And* On female immolation. *In* Essays relative to the habits, character, and moral improvement of the Hindoos. London: Kingsbury, Parbury and Allen, 1823. pp.1-86.
Presents anecdotes, opinions of textual authorities and details of Hindu practices in severely critical tone. Originally published in the *Friend of India*, a periodical of the Serampore missionaries.

975 PEGGS, J. Meeting for the abolition of the burning of widows in India. *In* Oriental Herald 20,63 (1829) 539-45.
Proceedings of the meeting preceded by a lament that the East India Company only assumes social responsibility in India under pressure. Meeting proceedings include various statistics, discussion of previous efforts against widow sacrifices, resolutions to castigate and abolish them, a petition to be presented to the House of Commons and House of Lords and future plans of the group for preventing "suttee and other cruel customs in India."

976 ________. Suttees. *In his* India's cries to British humanity, relative to infanticide, British connection with idolatry, ghaut murders, suttee, slavery, and colonization in India; to which are added, humane hints for the melioration of the state of society in British India, 3d rev. ed. London: Simpkin and Marshall, 1832. pp.213-78. [*Revision of his* The Suttees' cry to Britain: showing from essays published in India and official documents that the custom of burning Hindoo widows is not an integral part of Hindoism, and may be abolished with ease and safety, 2d ed. London: Seely and Son, 1828. 97p. *Abridged version* Appeal to Britain on the burning of Hindoo widows. *In* Oriental Herald 21,65 (1829) 292-308].
Compendium of firsthand accounts, statistics, statements of various persons in support of and opposed to the practice and details of British policy and the vicissitudes of the practice in the early 19th century. From many private and official sources. Author was a missionary.

977 ROY, RAMMOHUN. Translation of a conference between an advocate and an opponent of the practice of burning widows alive from the original Bungla. [Calcutta], 1818. 28p. [*Reprint in his* Translation of several principal books, passages and texts of the Veds, and of some controversial works on Brahmunical theology, 2d ed. London: Parbury, Allen, and Company, 1832. *And in his* The English works of Raja Rammohun Roy, v1. Ed. by Jogendra Chunder Ghose. Calcutta: Srikanta Roy, 1901].
Dialogue presents both sides of the issue, each citing textual authorities. Roy's essential point is that mounting the pyre is an optional and voluntary matter according to the *śāstras*; penances can be performed to compensate for not doing so and widows can lead noble lives.

978 ________. A second conference between an advocate and an opponent of the practice of burning widows alive. Tr. from Bengali. Calcutta: printed at the Baptist Mission Press, 1820. 50p. [*Reprint in his* Translation of several principal books, passages and texts of the Veds, and of some controversial works on Brahmunical theology, 2d ed. London: Parbury, Allen, and Company, 1832. *And in his* The English works of Raja Rammohun Roy, v1. Ed. by Jogendra Chunder Ghose. Calcutta: Srikanta Roy, 1901].
Continuation of the debate. The opponent refutes additional arguments of the "advocate," as had been expressed in a response to the first dialogue drawn up by some brahman authorities of Calcutta.

979 ________. Abstract of arguments regarding the burning of widows, considered as a religious rite. *In his* Translation of several principal books, passages and texts of the Veds, and of some controversial works on Brahmunical theology, 2d ed. London: Parbury, Allen, and Company, 1832. *And in his* The English works of Raja Rammohun Roy, v1. Ed. by Jogendra Chunder Ghose. Calcutta: Srikanta Roy, 1901].
First written ca. 1816 to 1820. [Unexamined. Books in NUC].

980 ________. Some remarks in vindication of the resolution passed by the Government of Bengal in 1829 abolishing the practice of female sacrifices in India. *In* Modern Review 55,3 (1934) 272-6.
Reproduction of a rediscovered tract originally published in England in 1832. Replies to the agitation to rescind the 1829 Sati Regulation. Has appendix with names of various British officials and their opinions on the *satī* issue.

981 STEIN, DOROTHY K. Women to burn: suttee as a normative institution. *In* Signs: J. of Women in Culture and Society 4,2 (1978) 253-68.
Discusses practice of widow sacrifice in the context of general Hindu values and reviews the movement to suppress it and resistance encountered. Considers the related movements for widow marriage and increasing the age of consent that arose later in the 19th century. Points to parallels in 19th century British and Indian conceptions of womanhood in general and widowhood in particular. Both "divided women into exalted and degraded classes" with respect to behavior and its supervision. "Respectable society in both places maintained a posture of exaggerated sentimentalism over the one class, exaggerated horror over the other. Both societies shared assumptions about the fragility and irreparability of the line between the two."

982 Suttee. *In* Calcutta Review 46,92 (1868) 221-61.
Reviews the history of the British effort to abolish *satīs* in India, using House of Commons papers, 1821-25. Includes British actions, court cases, accounts of *satīs*, statistics, etc. Authors note that the practice "recalls to us the sort of abominations which may spring up when the natives are left practically to their own guidance and choice, and which it is the glory of British administrators to have abolished."

983 The Suttee Regulation. *In* Asiatic Journal n.s. 2,7 (1830) 134-40.
Contains several items: 1) petition to W.C. Bentinck, Governor-General of India, from 800 Hindus protesting a resolution to abolish widow sacrifices; 2) Bentinck's reply defending British policy; 3) paper citing support in the *śāstras* for *satīs* and signed by 120 brahman authorities; 4) translation of Bengali address expressing gratitude to Bentinck for the Sati Regulation of 1829; 5) Bentinck's reply; 6) Bentinck's reply to another address from the Christian community of Calcutta; and 7) report of a meeting held by petitioners (no. 1) following Bentinck's reply (no. 2).

984 Suttees. *In* Asiatic Journal 24,141-2 (1827) 277-84, 405-10.
First part contains statistics of reported *satīs* in the various presidencies during 1923 and 1924 and accounts of successful and unsuccessful attempts by officials to suppress them. Second part discusses policy and the alternatives of immediate, forceful abolition or gradual abolition through education and social amelioration.

985 THOMPSON, EDWARD. The prohibition of widow-burning in India. *In* London Quarterly Review 148 (Jul 1927) 57-66.
Reviews prior local efforts of native rulers and various colonial powers to prohibit women from becoming *satīs* and the British campaign, which culminated in the 1829 Sati Regulation.

986 ________. The suppression of suttee in native states. *In* Edinburgh Review 245,500 (1927) 274-86.
British officers' activities regarding *satīs* in non-British India, from 1829, when they were prohibited in British India, until they were eliminated in the native states. Bound by instructions not to go beyond verbal and diplomatic protest of the practice (said to have been only rarely exceeded), these officers gradually persuaded princes to abolish it themselves.

ii) Female infanticide

987 EDWARDES, S.M. Infanticide and child-murder. *In his* Crime in India: a brief review of the more important offences included in the Annual Criminal Returns, with chapters on prostitution & miscellaneous matters. London: Humphrey Milford, Oxford University Press, 1924. pp.29-33.
Considers prevalence and causes of female infanticide and measures taken to end it in India. ". . . although wholesale female infanticide no longer exists, much carelessness in respect of female life still prevails."

988 Female infanticide in central and western India. *In* Calcutta Review 1 (Aug 1844) 372-448.
Observes that the Rajput "towering pride" of family descent is the root of the "horrid crime" of female infanticide. Considers the only effective solution to be the moral education provided by Christianity. Contains observations by British authorities, a history of the problem, attempted solutions and various census data. Based on official papers on infanticide in India from 1824, 1828 and 1843.

989 MOOR, EDWARD, ed. Hindu infanticide: an account of the measures adopted for suppressing the practice of the systematic murder by their parents of female infants, with incidental remarks on other customs peculiar to the natives of India. London: J. Johnson and Company, 1811. 312p.
[Unexamined. NUC].

990 PAKRASI, KANTI. On female infanticide in India. *In* Bulletin of the Cultural Research Institute 7,3/4 (1968) 33-48.
Discusses 19th and early 20th century practices, legislation and census data. Focuses on variations among different castes and communities in an effort to understand the causes and effects of female infanticide.

991 ________. The genesis of female infanticide. *In* Humanist Review 2,7 (1970) 255-81.

Reviews a variety of theoretical explanations for female infanticide and discusses these in the context of South Asian ethnographic data. In India "war or want" can generally explain the practice among "primitive" peoples while status consciousness in marriage alliances governs the practice among caste groups.

992 PANIGRAHI, LALITA. British social policy and female infanticide in India. New Delhi: Munshiram Manoharlal, 1972. 204p.
Discusses the British discovery of the practice of female infanticide in India; East India Company social policy in Bombay, Rajputana, the North-Western Provinces and the Punjab; and the development and consequences of the Prevention of Female Infanticide Act of 1870. Bibliography of many official and private sources.

993 PEGGS, JAMES. Infanticide. *In his* India's cries to British humanity, relative to infanticide, British connection with idolatry, ghaut murders, suttee, slavery, and colonization in India; to which are added, humane hints for the melioration of the state of society in British India, 3d rev. ed. London: Simpkin and Marshall, 1832. pp.1-76.
Compendium of anecdotes, attitudes, statistics and British intervention experiences from many early private and official sources.

994 ________. The infanticide's cry to Britain: the present state of infanticide in India, chiefly extracted from Parliamentary Papers, 4th ed. London, 1844.
[Unexamined. BMG].

995 VAIDYA, NARAYANA KESHAVA. Om! the sin of infanticide exhibited, and means for its prevention suggested. Bombay: Nirnaya-Sagar Press, 1887.
[Unexamined. BMG].

iii) Family and marriage patterns attacked and defended

996 BOSE, PRAMATHA NATH. Marriage customs. *In his* History of Hindu civilisation during British rule, v2. Calcutta: W. Newman, 1894. pp.36-64. [*Reprint* New Delhi: Asian Publication Services, 1978].
Regarding widow marriage, child marriage and polygamy, and related legislative and other efforts at reform in the 19th century.

997 A BRAHMIN OFFICIAL. Child marriage and enforced widowhood in India. *In* Asiatic Quarterly Review 10,20 (1890) 421-33.
Bengali author argues that administrative policy concerning child marriage and enforced widowhood should be based upon "all the upper-caste Hindus, who are not educated in English, from every part of India." He is indignant with the arrogance of the reform-minded, particularly those who have never been to India.

998 ________. The family life of the Hindus. *In* Imperial and Asiatic Quarterly Review n.s. 1,2 (1891) 398-409.
Defends Hindu family life and particularly the position of women within the family. Cultural relativist position.

999 CATON, A.R. Home and marriage. *In* A.R. Caton, ed. The key of progress: a survey of the status and conditions of women in India. London: Humphrey Milford, Oxford University Press, 1930. pp.101-14, 123-30.
Critical view of marriage and family life of Indian women. Focuses on child marriage and treatment of widows.

1000 FORBES, JEHANGIR CURSETJI. Law and practice of divorce in India: being a commentary on the Indian Divorce Act (iv. of 1869) (as amended up to date) and the Indian and Colonial Divorce Jurisdiction Act, 1926. Bombay: N.M. Tripathi and Company, 1938. 476p.
[Unexamined. NUC].

1001 ________. The Muslim divorce law: being a commentary on the Dissolution of Muslim Marriages Act (viii of 1939) . . . Bombay: New Book Company, 1939. 53p.
[Unexamined. NUC].

1002 INDIA. HOME DEPARTMENT. Papers relating to infant marriage and enforced widowhood in India. Calcutta: Home Department, Government of India, 1886. 303p. (Selections from the Records of the Government of India in the Home Department, 223, Home Department Serial, 3). [*Also* Behramji M. Malabari, comp. Infant marriage and enforced widowhood in India: being a collection of opinions, for and against, received by Mr. Behramji M. Malabari, from representative Hindu gentlemen and official and other authorities. Bombay: printed at the Voice of India Printing Press, 1887. 109p.].
Contains B.M. Malabari's "Notes on Infant Marriage in India and Enforced Widowhood" in which he assesses and proposes solutions to the two related social problems. He proposes that no student with a child-wife be eligible for a university degree, that the government favor unmarried applicants for public service jobs and that widows be given specific legal rights. Includes opinions on the various propositions solicited by the government from over 150 local officials and others. Respondents generally agree that solutions are in order but oppose state intervention. Many

responses also appear in Dayaram Gidumal's ***The Status of Women in India: or, a Handbook for Social Reformers*** (entry 899).

1003 Indian Social Reformer. v1-63 (1894?-1952). Founded in Madras, moved to Bombay. Weekly.
This journal fostered extensive discussion of marriage reform and particularly the age of consent and widow marriage issues.

1004 JAYAKAR, M.R. The rights of women in joint Indian families. *In* Indian Institute of Bankers Journal (Jan 1930) 38-49.
[Unexamined].

1005 KIDWAI, MUSHIR HOSAIN. Polygamy. Lahore, 1920. 24p.
Defense of polygyny? [Unexamined. IOL].

1006 LAM, M. TATA. Divorce in India. *In* Shyam Kumari Nehru, ed. Our cause: a symposium by Indian women. Allahabad: Kitabistan, 1938? pp.287-305.
Outlines important features of Islamic, Hindu, Parsi and Christian divorce laws, citing particular cases.

1007 MAYO, KATHERINE. The women and children of India. New York: Child Welfare Committee of America, Inc., 1928? 13p. (*Its* Publication 68, Series 1928).
Indian marriage patterns. Likely a critique of child marriage and enforced widowhood. [Unexamined. NUC].

1008 MEHTA, HANSA MANUBHAI. The woman under the Hindu law of marriage and succession. Bombay: Pratibha Publications, 1943? 52p. (Pratibha Publications, 2).
[Unexamined. NUC].

1009 MITAL, H.C. The statute law of marriage in India: being a complete commentary on acts relating to marriage and cognate subjects. Calcutta: Eastern Law House, 1936. 134p.
[Unexamined. NUC].

1010 MUDHOLKAR, R.N. Marriage reform among the Hindus. *In* C. Yajneswara Chintamani, ed. Indian social reform: being a collection of essays, addresses, speeches, etc., with an appendix. Madras: printed at the Minerva Press, 1901. First part, pp.166-87.
Critique of child marriage, compulsory marriage and enforced widowhood. Discusses various reform efforts and impediments to progress.

1011 NEHRU, SHYAM KUMARI. Legal forms of marriage in India. *In* Shyam Kumari Nehru, ed. Our cause: a symposium by Indian women. Allahabad: Kitabistan, 1938? pp.223-55.
Outlines Hindu and Muslim religious marriage law as observed in India; British-induced law relating to Europeans, Christians, Parsis, some Malabar communities and inter-marriage between communities; and the customary law of certain communities.

1012 NILIMA DEVI. House decoration and furnishing. *In* Shyam Kumari Nehru, ed. Our cause: a symposium by Indian women. Allahabad: Kitabistan, 1938? pp.29-35.
Argues that homemakers should resist modern European tastes and decorate their homes in an Indian fashion.

1013 SHOME, JOY GOBINDO. Hindu marriage customs. *In* Nineteenth Century Studies 10 (Apr 1975) 217-34. [*Reprint from* The speeches of eminent Indian gentlemen on "Hindu marriage customs." Calcutta: Prabhakar Press, 1887. pp.4-34].
Address by a Christian focuses on age at marriage and consent and choice of spouses. Originally written as advice to Christian missionaries, the essay consists of tempered criticism both of traditional Hindu marriage customs and of extreme reformist propositions.

1014 SORABJI, CORNELIA. Stray thoughts of an Indian girl. *In* Nineteenth Century 30 (Oct 1891) 638-42.
Opposes marriage reform. Asserts that most child marriages are happy ones and most women are content with them. Proponents of widow marriage must not overlook the spiritual position of widows.

1015 The speeches of eminent Indian gentlemen on "Hindu marriage customs." Calcutta: Prabhakar Press, 1887.
[Unexamined].

1016 SUBRAMANIA IYER, G. The Hindu joint family system. *In* C. Yajneswara Chintamani, ed. Indian social reform: being a collection of essays, addresses, speeches, etc., with an appendix. Madras: printed at the Minerva Press, 1901. First part, pp.107-43.
Discusses the "evils of the Hindu joint family system," assuming that "the progress of the Western nations, more especially of the Anglo-Saxon race, marks the lines on which the progress of our own country should be directed." Argues that the joint family system is oppressive and degrading to women. Some comments about *pardā*.

1017 TAGORE, RABINDRANATH. The Indian ideal of marriage. *In* Hermann Keyserling, ed. The book of marriage: a new interpretation by twenty-four leaders of contemporary thought. New York: Harcourt, Brace and Company, 1926. pp.98-122. [*Also in* Visna-Bharati Quarterly 3,2 (1925) 89-108].
Compares marriage in the Hindu and Judeo-Christian traditions. With particular comments about the nature of women and their place in marriage and family systems.

1018 THOMAS, P. Women and marriage in India. London: George Allen and Unwin Ltd., 1939. 224p.

Critical look at marriage and family patterns in India and the place accorded women within them. Main sections discuss women's traditional subjection, trends of emancipation and the need for new values. Concludes: "We cannot expect healthy, virile men and women [who will be needed in independent India] to be born of child-wives, slave-mothers, and anaemic Purdahnashins . . . . Above all, we must insist upon the physical and mental fitness of women for motherhood. It is in the womb of woman that great victories are won."

iv) The "age of consent" issue: minimum legal age of females at marriage consummation

1019 BALDWIN, OLIVIA A. Sita: a story of child-marriage fetters. New York: Fleming H. Revell Company, 1911? 353p.
Physician's contribution to the child marriage controversy. [Unexamined. MRL].

1020 FAWCETT, MILLICENT GARRETT. Infant marriage in India. *In* Contemporary Review 58 (Oct 1890) 712-20.
Argues that legislation prohibiting child marriage is needed. Supports position with material from books and articles written by Hindu women, conversations with them, statements of female doctors with experience in India and newspaper accounts of cases of murder, mutilation and suicide of child-wives.

1021 HEIMSATH, CHARLES H. The origin and enactment of the Indian Age of Consent Bill, 1891. *In* J. of Asian Studies 21, 4 (1962) 491-504.
Describes reform of age of consent as one social reform issue upon which all English-educated Indians could agree. Traces the issue from Malabari's publications in 1884 to the passing of the Age of Consent Bill in 1891. With attention to particular responses of various regions and the connection of age of consent to widow issues.

1022 INDIA. AGE OF CONSENT COMMITTEE. Age of Consent Committee evidence, 1928-1929. Calcutta: Central Publication Branch, Government of India, 1929. 9v. [*Chair* Moropant Vishwanath Joshi].
Each volume is composed of "oral evidence and written statements of witnesses" from a particular area of the country.

1023 ________. Report, 1928-1929. Calcutta: Central Publication Branch, Government of India, 1929. 353p. [*Chair* Moropant Vishwanath Joshi].
Report recommends "that the age of consent within the marital relation be raised to 15 years." With chapters on the formation of the committee, history of age of consent legislation, provincial conditions, objections to reform, recommendations and remedies. Numerous appendixes with statistical and other information.

1024 KULKARNI, G.V. Child Marriage Restraint Act no. 19 of 1929, with amendments up to date by Act no. 41 of 1949, Act no. 48 of 1952. Ahmednagar: K. Prakashan, 1953. 180p.
[Unexamined. NUC].

1025 MAYO, KATHERINE. Volume two. New York: Harcourt, Brace, 1931. 301p.
Critique of child marriage that appeared shortly after the Age of Consent Committee report. Appendixes discuss medical evidence supporting an increased age of consent and reproduce the testimonies of Kamaladevi Chattopadhyaya and Sir Tej Bahadur Sapru and the text of the 1928 Child Marriage Restraint Act ("Sarda Bill").

1026 NEHRU, RAMESHWARI. Early marriage. *In* Shyam Kumari Nehru, ed. Our cause: a symposium by Indian women. Allahabad: Kitabistan, 1938? pp.256-67.
Evaluates contemporary practices, attitudes and governmental solutions, including the Child Marriage Restraint Act and the recommendations of the Age of Consent Committee.

1027 RANADE, MAHADEVA GOVIND. The sutra and smriti texts on the age of Hindu marriage. *In his* Religious and social reform: a collection of essays and speeches. Comp. by M.B. Kolasker. Bombay: Gopal Narayen, 1902, pp.26-52
"It is hoped that, after the present reaction subsides, men will come to see that, in clinging to the existing order of things, they are really setting at naught the traditions of their own best days and the injunctions of their own Shastras." Supports reform of female age at marriage.

1028 RATHBONE, ELEANOR F. Child marriage: the Indian minotaur; an object lesson from the past to the future. London: Allen and Unwin, 1934. 138p.
". . . the main facts concerning child marriage — its effects, the efforts made to end it, and their results." Based upon the opinions of various authorities and Rathbone's own conception of "the most hopeful means of remedy."

1029 REES, J.D. Meddling with Hindu marriages. *In* Nineteenth Century 28 (Oct 1890) 660-76.
Unimpassioned and relatively rational discussion of the ethics of British and legal intervention with female age at marriage in India. Cites many statistics and opinions of prominent persons.

1030 RYDER, EMILY BRAINERD. The little wives of India. Philadelphia: Allen, Lane and Scott, 1903. 134p.
Condemnatory essay on child marriage with

many anecdotes and opinions excerpted from contemporary sources. Discusses progress made in reform of child marriage. Eight photographs.

1031 SIRCAR, MAHENDRA LAL. Letter to the chief secretary to the government of Bengal on the Age of Consent Bill. *In* C. Yajneswara Chintamani, ed. Indian social reform: being a collection of essays, addresses, speeches, etc., with an appendix. Madras: printed at the Minerva Press, 1901. Fourth part, pp.247-54.
Compilation of excerpts from author's previous statements opposing child marriage in reply to chief secretary's request for his opinion. He states that he has now come to the conclusion that "legislative interference" is required in this matter.

1032 ________ et al. On the earliest marriageable age. *In* C. Yajneswara Chintamani, ed. Indian social reform: being a collection of essays, addresses, speeches, etc., with an appendix. Madras: printed at the Minerva Press, 1901. Fourth part, pp.255-91.
Article reprinted from the *Calcutta Journal of Medicine* and numerous letters from doctors propose advisable minimum female age at marriage.

1033 SORABJI, CORNELIA. Shubala: a child mother. Calcutta: Baptist Mission Press, 1920. 27p.
[Unexamined. IOL].

1034 A terrible memorial: fifty-five lady-doctors, missionary and otherwise, petition the Indian government on the subject of child-marriage. *In* Medical Missionary Record 6,12 (1891) 271-2.
These doctors attest to the physical damage sometimes done to young brides by their adult husbands during sexual intercourse. [Unexamined].

v) The unfavorable position of widows and prohibitions against widow marriage

1035 BANERJI, PORESH NATH. The remarriage of Hindu widows. *In* Calcutta Review 115 (Jul 1902) 101-10.
Reviews and refutes arguments that have been put forth in opposition to widow marriage — population pressure, neglect of children of a woman's first marriage, unfairness to "old maids," natural sexual inequality and the surrender of individuality in Hindu society.

1036 HUNTER, WILLIAM WILSON. The Hindu child-widow. *In* Asiatic Quarterly Review 2,4 (1886) 241-82. [*Reprint* The Hindu child-widow. Bombay: Voice of India, 1887. 48p.].
Reviews interest in the reform of the position of Hindu widows in the late 19th century. Focuses on legislation; proposes some legislative changes. Presents some anecdotes, comments on the changing position of widows in contemporary literature and notes position of widows in early texts. Considers Brahmanic orthodoxy to be chief obstacle.

1037 K., V.V. The problem of widow remarriage. *In* Indian Social Reformer 37, 45 (9 Jul 1927) 708-9.
Implies that traditional treatment of Hindu widows provides support for idea that Indians are not fit for self-rule. Urges reform.

1038 LAKHANPAL, CHANDRAVATI. The Hindu widow. *In* Shyam Kumari Nehru, ed. Our cause: a symposium by Indian women. Allahabad: Kitabistan, 1938? pp.268-86.
Discusses *satīs* and the anti-*satī* movement in the early 19th century, the Hindu Widow's Remarriage Act of 1856 (reproduces text), Behramji Malabari's 1884 note to the government on the problem of enforced widowhood (reproduces excerpts) and the condition of Indian widows in the 1930s.

1039 NAIDU, MUTHYALAYYA. Beginnings of widow remarriage movement in India. *In* Modern Review 118,6 (1965) 490-2.
Brief survey of the early widow marriage reform efforts of Vidyasagar and others in Bengal and of similar efforts in Bombay, Madras, Punjab, Bihar, United Provinces and Central Provinces. Also considers government legislative efforts.

1040 RAGOONATH, R. [R. RAGHUNATH RAO]. The Hindu widow. *In* Asiatic Quarterly Review 5,9 (1888) 43-53.
Friendly but critical response to Hunter who has "treated the subject as fairly as a foreigner wishing to do good to this country and its people could have done." Author was Prime Minister of Indore.

1041 RANADE, MAHADEVA GOVIND. Vedic authorities for widow marriage. *In his* Religious and social reform. Comp. by M.B. Kolaskar. Bombay: Gopal Narayen, 1902. pp.53-91.
Argues that marriage of high-caste widows is sanctioned by *śruti* and *smṛti* texts. Article was originally written in about 1870 as a contribution to the widow marriage controversy of the time.

1042 SUBRAMANYAM, M. The tonsure of Hindu widows: an essay. Madras: G.A. Natesan and Company, 1909? 69p.
Pamphlet prepared "under the authority of the Madras Hindu Association." [Unexamined. MRL].

1043 VAIDYA, NARAYAN KESHAB, ed. A collection containing the proceedings which led to the passing of Act XV of 1856, an act to remove all legal obstacles to the marriage of widows. Bombay, 1885.
[Unexamined].

vi) Female education

1044 ALL-INDIA FEDERATION OF EDUCATIONAL ASSOCIATIONS. Women sectional conference proceedings. *In* M.S. Sabhesan, ed. Report of the proceedings of the XXI All-India Education Conference, Madras, December, 1945. Madras: South Indian Teacher, 1946.
[Unexamined. Report in MRL].

1045 ALL-INDIA WOMEN'S CONFERENCE. CULTURAL SECTION. Education of women in modern India. Aundh: Aundh Publishing Trust, 1946. 87p.
Symposium of programmatic papers by various leaders of the Indian women's movement. Topics include aims and ideals of women's education, children's education, basic education, physical education, home science, art education, college curriculum, professional education, training for citizenship and spiritual and moral education.

1046 ALL-INDIA WOMEN'S CONFERENCE EDUCATIONAL REFORM. Proceedings. 1-4 (1927-1930?) Mangalore, etc.
[Unexamined. ULS].

1047 ASHWORTH, M. The education of women in India. *In* Asiatic Review 11 (15 May 1917) 388-98. *With* Discussion on the foregoing paper, pp.399-406.
Paper presented at a meeting of the East India Association reviews 19th and early 20th century programs for female education in various parts of India and recommends their continued facilitation.

1048 BASU, A.N. Women's education in India in the 19th and 20th centuries. *In* Calcutta Review 3d series 60,1 (1936) 67-80.
Denotes and details four periods: 1)1820-50, government inaction, lack of policy, minor private efforts, 2) 1850-82, beginning of state initiative and policy, 3) 1882-1900, tremendous influence of religious, social and political movements and 4) 1900-, the modern period, in which influence by the various movements continues, along with an increase in both popular demand and government acknowledgement of the extent of the task. Focuses on persons and institutions active in promotion of female education.

1049 BASU, B.D. Female education was not encouraged by the East India Company. *In his* History of education in India under the rule of the East India Company. Calcutta: Modern Review Office, 1922. pp.174-85.
Regarding the Educational Dispatch of 1854, said to include the first considerations for female education by the Indian government.

1050 BHOWNAGGREE, MANCHERJEE M. The present condition and future prospects of female education in India. *In* J. of the Society of Arts 33,1687 (1885) 452-62. *With* Discussion, pp.462-7.
Reviews main historical trends of female education in India over the centuries and the variety of 19th century regional efforts. Addresses the question of appropriateness of government involvement. Discusses and endorses the expanded training of native and European female teachers and zenana education. Notes favorable effect of medical missions on educational aims.

1051 BISWAS, USHA. The training of teachers for village girls' schools and community service: planning for the future. *In* Modern Review 55,6 (1934) 621-5.
Stresses many ways that village schools are vital for rural uplift. Urges recruitment of village women as teachers and presents some guidelines for their training. Encourages a curriculum that would teach rural girls "how to make better homes and better villages."

1052 Bombay ladies' conference. *In* Indian Social Reformer 37,14 (4 Dec 1926) 213-5.
Regarding a conference on women's education held in Bombay in 1926. Contains presidential address by Sarojini Naidu and resolutions adopted.

1053 BOSE, KHEROTH M. The ideal of womanhood as a factor in missionary work, IV: Indian women in the past and to-day. *In* International Review of Missions 3,2 (1914) 255-65.
Considers balance of native and Christian ideals appropriate for female education in India as it outgrows its tie to mission work.

1054 BOSE, MONI MOHAN. Female education in India. Cawnpore: B.D. Gupta, 1921. 17p.
Historical survey. [Unexamined].

1055 BOSE, PRAMATHA NATH. Education under British rule: female education. *In his* A history of Hindu civilisation during British rule, v3. New Delhi: Asian Publication Services, 1978. pp.205-16. [*Reprint of* 1894 ed.].
Briefly considers missionary efforts in the early 19th century; the establishment of the Bethune School in 1849; progress in Bengal, 1859-93; progress in Bombay, 1824-92; progress in Madras, 1841-92; progress in the Northwest, 1855-92; and progress in the Punjab, 1855-92.

1056 BUTLER, MARGARET L. Women's views on

women's education. Bangalore: Bangalore Press.
[Unexamined].

1057 CARPENTER, MARY. On female education in India. *In* Great Britain. Parliament. House of Commons. . . . British sessional papers, v63 (1877). Ed. by Edgar L. Erickson. New York: Readex Microprint Corporation, n.d. pp.436-46.
Copy of an English social worker's report to the Marquis of Salisbury on a tour of many teacher training schools throughout India. Includes recommendations for teacher training programs.

1058 CENTRAL PROVINCES AND BERAR. FEMALE EDUCATION COMMITTEE. Report. Nagpur: Education Department, Government of the Central Provinces and Berar, 1927. 52p. [*Chair* R.H. Beckett].
[Unexamined].

1059 CHATTERJEE, BANKIM CHUNDER. The education of women in India: a plea for breaking the *purdah* system. Tr. from Bengali by P.N. Bose and H.W.B. Morens. *In* Hindustan Review 38,228 (1918) 126-7.
Prominent Bengali writer/reformer (1838-1894) speaks out against the lack of female education and a chief obstacle, the early marriage age.

1060 CHIPLUNKAR, G.M. S.B. Hudlikar, ed. The scientific basis of woman's education. Poona: the editor, 1930. 333p.
[Unexamined. NUC].

1061 CHOKSI, MRS. [MITHAN CHOKSI]. Some impressions of Indian women's colleges. *In* Evelyn C. Gedge and Mithan Choksi, eds. Women in modern India: fifteen papers by Indian women writers. Bombay: D.B. Taraporewala Sons and Company, 1929. pp.63-77. [*Reprint* Westport, Connecticut: Hyperion Press, 1976. (Pioneers of the Women's Movement)].
Reviews movement for female higher education in late 19th and early 20th centuries. Considers establishment and programs of various colleges and debate about medium of instruction and curriculum. Describes benefits of college education for women.

1062 COWAN, MINNA G. The education of the women of India. Edinburgh: Oliphant, Anderson and Ferrier, 1912. 256p. [*Also* New York: Fleming H. Revell Company].
Discusses progress of female education in various parts of India and considers contributing factors of "the Government, the missionary, and spontaneous Indian effort." Historically surveys female education in India and includes chapters on university education and the religious element in education. Photographs.

1063 DASGUPTA, JYOTIPROVA. Girls' education in India in the secondary and collegiate stages. Calcutta: University of Calcutta, 1938. 269p.
Discusses the progress of women's education in various states and provinces. Proposes a reorganization at postprimary levels. Various statistics. [Unexamined. IOL].

1064 Draft scheme for the establishment of a *zanana* school for orthodox Hindu girls submitted to the Calcutta University Commission by the lady principal of the Diocesan College, Calcutta. *In* India. Calcutta University Commission, 1917-19. Report, v6: appendices and index. Calcutta: Superintendent of Government Printing, Government of India, 1920. pp.86-90.
Letter from the "Lady Principal" of the Diocesan College, Calcutta, outlines proposed aims, staff, curriculum and funding. Dated 1919.

1065 DUFF, ALEXANDER. Missionary addresses delivered before the general assembly of the Church of Scotland, in the years 1835, 1837, 1839; with additional papers on female education, and the Danish, or earliest protestant mission to India. Edinburgh: Johnstone and Hunter, 1850. 370p. [*Also* London: J. Nisbet and Company].
[Unexamined. NUC].

1066 DURRANI, F.K. KHAN. Female education. *In his* A plan of Muslim educational reform. Lahore: Sheikh Ghulam Ali, 194_. pp.132-41.
Islamic modernist arguments for female education, which "should fit woman for her higher function of building a better humanity . . . . of training the citizenship of Islam." Supports coeducation only at primary level. Encourages a curriculum including domestic topics, Urdu and Arabic, Islamic teachings, geography, mathematics and English.

1067 Education in India. *In* Frances E. Warwick, ed. Progress in women's education in the British Empire, being the report of the Education Section, Victorian Era Exhibition, 1897. London: Longmans, Green and Company, 1898. pp.238-85.
Series of brief papers dealing with programmatic aspects of female education, progress made during the 19th century and British responsibility in this area. Some Indian participants.

1068 The education of girls and women. *In* India. Calcutta University Commission, 1917-19. Report, v2, part I: analysis of present conditions. Calcutta: Superintendent of Government Printing, Government of India, 1919. pp.1-36.
Main sections are: "The Social Importance of Women's Education," "The Obstacles in the Way of Women's Education," "Secondary Education for Girls," "The Arts Colleges for Women," "Professional Training for Women," "Proposal for Reform" and "The Need for a Special Organisation."

1069 The education of women. *In* India.

Calcutta University Commission, 1917-19. Report, v4, part 2: recommendations of the commission. Calcutta: Superintendent of Government Printing, Government of India, 1919. pp.364-73.
Recommendations of the Calcutta University Commission for the improvement of higher education for women.

1070 ESQUER, A. L'éducation des femmes de l'Inde [The education of Indian women]. *In his* Essai sur les castes dans l'Inde. Pondichéry: A. Saligny, 1870. pp.455-78.
[Unexamined. Book in NUC].

1071 FLEMING, DANIEL JOHNSON. The family system. *In his* Schools with a message in India. London: Oxford University Press, 1921. pp.63-76.
Details of four schools for girls in various parts of India operating according to the "family system." The curriculum includes housekeeping, sanitation and hygiene, child care, thrift and so forth.

1072 GOKHALE, G.K. Appendix C: female education in India. *In his* Speeches. Madras: Natesan, n.d. pp.133-42. [*Also in* Frances E. Warwick, ed. Progress in women's education in the British Empire, being the reports of the Education Section, Victorian Era Exhibition, 1897. London: Longmans, Green and Company, 1898. pp.254-69].
Paper read at the Education Congress held in connection with the Women's Section (Education) of the Victorian Era Exhibition, 1897. Gokhale notes the educational opportunities offered females in ancient India and discusses 19th century efforts to promote widespread female education in various parts of India.

1073 GOWAN, EDNA et al. Indian women's education. *In* Asiatic Review n.s. 33, 113 (1937) 33-45.
Discusses the need for educating India's women and describes the establishment of the Central College for the women of Nagpur. Includes data on disparity of men's and women's education. States that education is needed to make women better wives, better mothers of future generations and "to make them realize how they can best help their country to rid itself of its own social evils and to take its proper part in international affairs."

1074 GRAY, H. Education. *In* A.R. Caton, ed. The key of progress: a survey of the status and conditions of women in India. London: Humphrey Milford, Oxford University Press, 1930. pp.1-44.
Surveys problems and prospects of formal education for females in India in the 1920s. Includes a review of the major institutions, by presidency and province.

1075 GREAT BRITAIN. INDIAN STATUTORY COMMISSION. Education of girls and women. *In its* Interim report of the Indian statutory Commission (review of growth of education in British India by the Auxiliary Committee appointed by the commission). London: His Majesty's Stationery Office, 1929. pp.145-83.
Major sections on statistical data and disparity between boys' and girls' education, importance of girls' education, obstacles to progress, varying conditions in different provinces, organization and control, colleges and schools, curriculum and training, teachers and signs of progress.

1076 HARTOG, LADY [MABEL HÉLÈNE (KISCH) HARTOG]. The education of girls in India. *In* J. of the Royal Society of Arts 84,4348 (20 Mar 1936) 499-514. *With* Discussion, pp.514-7.
Briefly summarizes the progress of formal education for girls in India at all levels in 1936. Main topics are recent influx of girls into schools, primary level, secondary level, higher level, funding, teacher training and prospects for the future. Paper read before the Royal Society of Arts.

1077 HARTOG, PHILIP. Special problem of the education of girls and women. *In his* Some aspects of Indian education past and present. London: Oxford University Press, 1939. pp.52-8. (University of London, Institute of Education, Studies and Reports, 7).
Some efforts and problems in expanding female education at all levels.

1078 History of the Society For Promoting Female Education in the East (established in the year 1834). London, 1847. 288p.
[Unexamined].

1079 INDIA. BUREAU OF EDUCATION. The beginning of female education. *In* J.A. Richey, ed. Selections from Educational Records, part 2 (1840-1859). Delhi: Manager of Publications, Government of India, 1965. pp.32-63.
Extracts from minutes, reports, addresses and so forth regarding female education in mid-19th century India. Much information on the founding of particular institutions.

1080 INDIA. CENTRAL ADVISORY BOARD OF EDUCATION. WOMEN'S EDUCATION COMMITTEE. Report to consider the curriculum of girls' primary schools in India. Simla: printed by the Manager, Government of India Press, 1937. 20p. [*Chair* Gertrude C. Grigg].
[Unexamined. NUC].

1081 Indian Social Reformer. v1-63 (1894?-1952). Founded in Madras, moved to Bombay. Weekly.
During its years of publication, this journal fostered extensive discussion about education for women and girls. Scattered throughout are many brief articles about educational conferences, relevant speeches, newspaper excerpts and so forth.

1082 Indian women's education. *In* Asiatic Review n.s. 33 (Jan 1937) 33-45.
Proceedings of a meeting of the East India Association held at Bedford College in 1936 to discuss women's education. The distinguished participants discuss details of institutions being established in India and prominent South Asians involved.

1083 Indian women's education association: general meeting and report for two years ending October 20, 1932. *In* Asiatic Review n.s. 29 (1933) 361-6.
Primarily about scholarships given by this group to female Indian students. General assessment is that the group is small and has limited means but does steady, solid and laudable work.

1084 KARVE, D.K. Education of women in India. *In* Asiatic Review n.s. 25,84 (Oct 1929) 664-73. *With* Discussion on the foregoing paper, pp.674-81.
Paper read before the East India Association. Noted women's educationist Karve grimly notes the lack of education of the majority of Indian women and briefly notes his own ideas about and experiences with female education. He urges mass support by government and private agencies.

1085 KESHAWAJI, HARI and TIRMAL RAO. Essays on the promotion of female education in India. Edinburgh: Alexander Coeston, 1839.
[Unexamined].

1086 KRISHNASWAMI AIYAR, C.V. Education of Hindu girls. *In* Modern World 5 (1913) 125-38.
[Unexamined].

1087 LAW, NARENDRA NATH. Promotion of learning in India by early European settlers (up to about 1800 A.D.). Bombay: Longmans, Green and Company, 1915. 159p.
Material on early female education efforts dispersed throughout.

1088 MC DOUGALL, ELEANOR. A tour of enquiry into the education of women and girls in India, 1912-1913. *In* International Review of Missions 3 (1914) 107-20.
Cites the need for and superiority of Christian mission schools for the education and social reform of Indian women. By contrast, government schools cannot adequately deal with the problems of Indian girls.

1089 _______. Some problems of the higher education of Indian women. *In* International Review of Missions 29,68 (1940) 441-51.
Regarding rapid growth of university education for Indian women in the early 20th century and problems, prospects and mission involvement.

1090 MAYHEW, ARTHUR. Education and the home. *In his* The education of India: a study of British educational policy in India, 1835-1920, and of its bearing on national life and problems in India today. London: Faber and Gwyer, 1926. pp.264-80.
From summary of chapter: "Bearing of women's education on national life — Present system deplorable — . . . All obstacles ultimately due to Indian view of women — Radical changes in marriage system required — And new attitudes toward professional women — Zenana work — Possibilities and restrictions."

1091 MEHTA, V.N. An all-India women's university. *In* Hindustan Review 34,203 (1916) 11-8.
Argues against an all-India women's university because "you require different types of universities for her geographically and ethnologically differentiated provinces." Feels coeducation is essential only for women planning careers. Widespread high school education is a priority over university considerations. High school education should facilitate the national ideal of womanhood, which includes self-abnegation and a focus on motherhood.

1092 MUKHERJEE, H.B. Tagore on women's education. *In* Education Quarterly 13,50 (1961) 123-7.
Tagore's views regarding education and the development of women's unique nature and abilities.

1093 MUTHULAKSHMI REDDI. Note on women's education. *In* Great Britain. Indian Statutory Commission. Interim Report of the Indian Statutory Commission (review of growth of education in British India by the Auxiliary Committee appointed by the commission). London: His Majesty's Stationery Office, 1929. pp.369-78.
Statement in support of female education consonant with the philosophy that "no education can be complete if it is dissociated from the daily life of the people and if it takes the pupil away from the cherished thoughts and ideals of his ancestors; and no education can fulfil its chief purpose if it is not going to train patriotic, useful and selfless citizens to serve humanity."

1094 NILAM, MRS. A.R.M. Education: the birthright of every Muslim girl. Lahore: Muhammad Ashraf, 1946. 157p.
[Unexamined. NUC].

1095 NORONHA, GEORGE E. Background in the education of Indian girls. Washington, D.C.: Catholic University Press, 1939. 237p.
"In this [revised] dissertation are surveyed the conditions of which cognizance must be taken in the formulation of principles and plans for girls' education." Major sections discuss political, economic, physical, social and religious factors of education in India, factors relating to Indian women, development of "new forces in Indian life to which

the educator must turn for support," and recommendations of broad principles for female education in India.

1096 Question 23: women's education. *In* India. Calcutta University Commission, 1917-19. Report, v12: evidence and documents; classified replies to the commissioners' questions 17-23. Calcutta: Superintendant Government Printing, India. 1919. pp.401-61.
Responses of prominent persons and organizations to commission's query about distinctive nature of women's higher educational needs.

1097 SCINDIA, MAHARANI OF GWALIOR. Thoughts on women's education in India. *In* Asiatic Review n.s. 26 (Apr 1930) 212-7.
Address given by the Maharani of Gwalior on women's education. She endorses among other things: having some subjects suitable to the disposition of each sex, coeducation, the place of physical well-being in the education of females.

1098 SEN, HANNAH. Education of women and girls. *In* Shyam Kumari Nehru, ed. Our cause: a symposium by Indian women. Allahabad: Kitabistan, 1938? pp.93-110.
On various dimensions of female education: major government policies, limited scope of existing institutions, financial demands, literacy, coeducation, the place of domestic studies in the curriculum, other suitable subjects, teacher training, unsuitability of communal schools, significance of adult education, vocational training and overall structure of education system.

1099 SHAH, GUNVANT B. Genesis of women's education in India. *In* NIE [National Institute of Education] Journal 9,3 (1975) 1-9.
Reviews history of female education in India from 18th through early 20th centuries. Discusses efforts of missionaries, social reformers and the government.

1100 Special ladies number containing specially written articles by eminent lady educationalists and leaders of thought, both Indian and foreign, on the aims and methods of women's education and other useful information on the subject. *In* Vedic Magazine 11 (1918) 395-458.
[Unexamined].

1101 SPEER, ROBERT E. Some aspects of the present economic and religious environment of the church in India. *In* Robert E. Speer and Russell Carter. Report on India and Persia of the deputation sent by the Board of Foreign Missions of the Presbyterian Church in the U.S.A. to visit these fields in 1921-22. New York: the Board, 1922. pp.135-70.
Contains material on women's education. [Unexamined. Report in NUC].

1102 SUBRAMANIA IYER, P.A. Female education in India. *In* Educational Review 22, 10-11 (1916) 622-8, 734-43.
Second part deals with Madras. [Unexamined].

1103 WASI, MURIEL. Education. *In* Tara Ali Baig, ed. Women of India. Delhi: Publications Division, Ministry of Information and Broadcasting, Government of India, 1958. pp.153-60.
History of the changing educational opportunities for Indian women in the 19th and 20th centuries. Photographs.

1104 WYCKOFF, CHARLOTTE C. The boarding school girl. Ajmer: Christian Education, n.d. 52p.
[Unexamined. MRL].

vii) Adequate health care and its obstacles: funds, female seclusion and "superstition"

See also medical mission material within "(e) Christian missions. . .," entries 1556-1643

1105 BADLEY, MRS. M.A. The National Association for Supplying Female Medical Aid to the Women of India. *In* Calcutta Review 85,170 (1887) 229-46.
Considers medical work done prior to existence of the National Association and the organization of, need for, work accomplished by and securing of funds of the Association. [Unexamined].

1106 BALFOUR, MARGARET IDA and RUTH YOUNG. The work of medical women in India. London: Oxford University Press, 1929. 201p.
Comprehensively surveys medical problems of Indian women and the history of the effort of British and American women to solve these problems. Includes map showing distribution of hospitals staffed by women. Reflects a sympathetic acceptance of the custom of *pardā*.

1107 BEALS, ROSE F. The woman doctor in India. *In* Medical Woman's Journal 33,7 (1926) 204-7.
Dr. Beals notes that the female doctor who works in India experiences great rewards as well as great hardships. She describes amenities available there and some of her experiences in the town of Wai. [Unexamined].

1108 BHATIA, S. The Association of Medical Women in India. *In* World Medical Journal 11,1 (1964) 31-3.
Reviews history of 19th century interest in medical care for Indian women, establishment of Association of Medical Women in India in 1907 and aims and activities of the Association.

1109 BROWN, EDITH M. Women's medical education in India. *In* J. of Sociologic

Medicine 16 (Apr 1915) 79-82.
Argues for need for female medical personnel in India. [Unexamined].

1110 _______. Indian women and the village: the time for action. *In* Asiatic Review n.s. 35,121 (1939) 1-9. *With* Discussion on the foregoing paper, pp.10-6.
Paper read after tea at a social meeting of the East India Association. "I refer to questions of health, sanitation, rural uplift and medical aid, matters which . . . must largely be dealt with by women." Reviews some earlier (late 19th century) efforts of medical work among Indian women and discusses problems involved. Proposes a scheme whereby a colony of female health workers and a teacher would live in a compound in a central village and offer a variety of services to women of the surrounding villages.

1111 DENGAL, ANNA. The work of medical women in India. *In* Medical Woman's Journal 37,5 (1930) 132-5.
Discusses need for female medical personnel in India given widespread patterns of female seclusion. Reviews work of medical missionaries among secluded women and the small group of female physicians. Notes inadequacy of care by indigenous midwives. [Unexamined].

1112 DUFFERIN, HARRIOT [. . . MARCHIONESS OF DUFFERIN AND AVA]. The National Association for Supplying Female Medical Aid to the Women of India. *In* Asiatic Review 1,2 (1886) 257-74.
Report of the formation, financial support, aims and policies of the National Association for Supplying Female Medical Aid to the Women of India by its founder.

1113 _______. A record of three years' work of the National Association for Supplying Female Medical Aid to the Women of India, August, 1885, to August, 1888. Calcutta: Thacker, Spink, and Company, 1888. 102p.
[Unexamined. NUC].

1114 FRANKS, H.G. Better dais. Bombay: Government Central Press, 1928.
Program for improved midwifery. Author was honorary publicist of Lady Wilson Village Maternity Association. [Unexamined].

1115 HAMID ALI, MRS. Maternity and welfare work in India. *In* Evelyn C. Gedge and Mithan Choksi, eds. Women in modern India: fifteen papers by Indian women writers. Bombay: D.B. Taraporewala Sons and Company, 1929. pp.138-43. [*Reprint* Westport, Connecticut: Hyperion Press, 1976 (Pioneers of the Women's Movement)].
Programmatic paper about ways to improve health of women and children.

1116 HEHIR, PATRICK. Medical work of women in India. *In his* The medical profession in India. London: Henry Frowde and Hodder and Stoughton, 1923. pp.121-31. (Oxford Medical Publications).
Description, problems and prospects of medical care for women in India. Deals with training of doctors, training of midwives and infant mortality.

1117 HOGGAN, FRANCES ELIZABETH. Medical women for India. *In* Contemporary Review 42 (Aug 1882) 267-75.
Discusses the Indian Medical Service, the small percentage of native men who utilize it and the far smaller percentage of native women. Attributes this to the lack of women skilled in medicine. Urges separate medical facilities for women throughout the system and the establishment of a Medical Department "managed by women and responsible only to some high officer of state, working in harmony with the existing Medical Service, but co-ordinate and not subordinate to it. Women alone, highly trained, efficient, with the ready sympathies of their sex, can rightly inaugurate and carry out such a beneficent reform."

1118 HUNTER, W.W. A female medical profession for India. *In* Contemporary Review 56 (Aug 1889) 207-15.
Brief history of the 1885 establishment and early activities of Lady Dufferin's National Association for Supplying Female Medical Aid to the Women of India.

1119 JEX-BLAKE, SOPHIA. Medical women. *In* Nineteenth Century 22,129 (1887) 692-707.
Regarding discrimination against female doctors in England's medical profession. "It is, however, of course in India and other parts of the East that the ***necessity*** for medical women is most apparent and their usefulness most indisputable . . . . the immense size of the field now open in India, and the enormous numbers of medical women that would be required adequately to meet its needs." Briefly discusses activities of medical women in India. Author was herself a doctor.

1120 JHIRAD, J. Some aspects of medico-social work in India. *In* Evelyn C. Gedge and Mithan Choksi, eds. Women in modern India: fifteen papers by Indian women writers. Bombay: D.B. Taraporewala Sons and Company, 1929. pp.133-7. [*Reprint* Westport, Connecticut: Hyperion Press, 1976. (Pioneers of the Women's Movement)].
Doctor describes the work of the maternity and child welfare movement. Among problems it faces are high mortality rates, female conservatism and poorly trained local midwives.

1121 _______. Pioneer work by and for medical women. *In* J. of the Association of Medical Women in India 39,2 (1951) 29-34.
Reviews early physicians and medical missionaries, educational facilities and associations by and for women in India. [Unexamined].

1122 LAZARUS, HILDA. The sphere of Indian women in medical work. *In* Evelyn C. Gedge and Mithan Choksi, eds. Women

in modern India: fifteen papers by Indian women writers. Bombay: D.B. Taraporewala Sons and Company, 1929. pp.51-62. [*Reprint* Westport, Connecticut: Hyperion Press, 1976. (Pioneers of the Women's Movement)].
Doctor reviews the first 50 years of medical work by Indian women, including establishment and programs of training institutions, medical facilities and philanthropic associations.

1123 MC KIBBIN-HARPER, MARY [MARY (MC KIBBIN) HARPER]. Medical women in India. *In* Medical Woman's Journal 33, 10 (1926) 287-9.
Reviews some of the organizations, institutions and personnel at work in India and the obstacles they face. [Unexamined].

1124 ________. A medical woman looks at Mother India. *In* Medical Review of Reviews 35,9 (1929) 457-76.
Based on her travels in the 1920s, Dr. McKibbin-Harper describes various impressions of India and the work done by western and Indian female medical personnel. [Unexamined].

1125 ________. The doctor takes a holiday: an autobiographical fragment. Cedar Rapids, Iowa: Torch Press, A Bookfellow Book, 1941. 349p.
Account of travels throughout the Middle and Far East in the 1920s, supplemented with other materials. Focuses on India and China. Many topics covered including descriptions of local medical practices and the work of medical women. Photographs. [Unexamined. NUC].

1126 Medical colleges. *In* J. of the Association of Medical Women in India 24,2 (1936) 68, 70-6.
Reviews programs, fees and other details of particular medical colleges. [Unexamined].

1127 MUIR-MACKENZIE, LADY. Indian women and national well being. *In* Asiatic Review n.s. 8,22 (1916) 198-202. *With* Discussion, pp.203-11.
Regarding problems of health care for Indian women.

1128 NATARAJAN, BHAVANI. Child welfare. *In* Shyam Kumari Nehru, ed. Our cause: a symposium by Indian women. Allahabad: Kitabistan, 1938? pp.68-72.
Some guidelines for the operation of a child welfare center including the education of mothers in the health needs of children.

1129 NATIONAL ASSOCIATION FOR SUPPLYING FEMALE MEDICAL AID TO THE WOMEN OF INDIA. Report. 1st-? (1886-?). Annually.
[Unexamined. MRL].

1130 PLATT, K.A. Health and sanitation. *In* A.R. Caton, ed. The key of progress: a survey of the status and conditions of women in India. London: Humphrey Milford, Oxford University Press, 1930. pp.45-79.
Reviews the health problems facing Indian women and some of the educational and financial programs created to solve them.

1131 RAJWADE, LAXMIBAI. The Indian mother and her problems. *In* Shyam Kumari Nehru, ed. Our cause: a symposium by Indian women. Allahabad: Kitabistan, 1938? pp.73-89.
Discusses high maternal mortality as a result of "premature maternity, frequent maternity and primitive obstetrics." Present statistics relating to maternal mortality and offers a "plan of action."

1132 REES, J.D. Medical women in India. *In* Asiatic Quarterly Review 6,11 (1888) 374-81.
Response to criticisms of the National Association for Supplying Female Medical Aid to the Women of India in Jex-Blake's "Medical Women" article.

1133 ROBERTSON, JOHN. On Hindu midwifery. *In* Edinburgh Medical and Surgical Journal 65,167 (1846) 308-19.
Argues that "Hindu midwifery . . . is destructive to life in a degree never paralleled, according to the information we possess, in any other quarter of the world, rude or refined." Quotes a Hindu and a European doctor, both practicing in Calcutta, on lying-in conditions there. The former estimates that three to five women of every twenty die in parturition. Points to general unavailability of information on Hindu "domestic constitution" to Europeans and to the commonly held but mistaken notion that simpler peoples have satisfactory simpler techniques for handling childbirth. Encourages midwifery education for native women.

1134 SCHARLIEB, MARY. A woman's words to women on the care of their health in England and in India. London: S. Sonnenschein and Company, 1895. 240p.
[Unexamined. NUC].

1135 SIRCAR, MAHENDRA LAL. On female medical aid to the women of India. *In* C. Yajneswara Chintamani, ed. Indian social reform: being a collection of essays, addresses, speeches, etc., with an appendix. Madras: printed at the Minerva Press, 1901. Fourth part, pp.240-7.
Statements reproduced from the third and sixth annual meetings of the National Association for Supplying Female Medical Aid to the Women of India. The former speaks to the need for the association and praises its work. The latter documents its growth and discusses the traditional neglect of women that must be ended.

1136 STEWART, DUNCAN. Statistical record of the duration of diseases in 13,019 fatal cases in Hindoos — extraordinary mortality among lying-in women. *In* J. of the Asiatic Society of Bengal 1st series 8,88 (1839) 316-8.
Table of police mortality records of Hindus

compiled from various places. Examination of problems associated with childbirth reveals "the existence of many unhappily fatal habits and prejudices on the part of the people [and the] most barbarous, perhaps sinful, obstetricy on the part of the practitioners. The mortality in child-bed is *one-tenth* of the whole; that is, equal to one-fifth of all the deaths among females."

1137 THOMSON, BERTHA M. Opportunities for medical women in India. *In* Medical Woman's Journal 39,10 (1932) 251-4.
Argues that secluded upper-class Hindu and Muslim women in India require female medical personnel and that a priority is the training of native women physicians. Describes services available at time of publication.
[Unexamined].

1138 VAUGHAN, KATHLEEN. Educated Indians and Indian women. *In* Hindustan Review 35,212 (1917) 275-7.
Plea for the government of India to take greater responsibility for providing health services for Indian women and children. Says that private efforts are inadequate and discusses some of the difficulties involved.

1139 WATNEY, DANIEL. The Countess of Dufferin's fund. *In* Asiatic Quarterly Review 3 (Apr 1887) 284-91.
Plea for support of the National Association for Supplying Female Medical Aid to the Women of India. The author discusses the need for this organization and its aims and needs.

viii) Dancing ("nautch") girls, *devadāsīs* and prostitution

1140 ANDERSON, LILY STRICKLAND. Nautch-girls and old rhythms of India. *In* Asia 25,8 (1925) 676-81, 700-1.
Miscellaneous descriptive material and accounts of various performances witnessed by the author. Six photographs.

1141 Indian Social Reformer v1-63 (1894?-1952). Founded in Madras, moved to Bombay. Weekly.
The pages of this journal have fostered discussion and general condemnation of the *devadāsī* institution. With excerpts of speeches, details of legislation and so forth.

1142 LEAGUE OF NATIONS. COMMISSION OF ENQUIRY INTO TRAFFIC IN WOMEN AND CHILDREN IN THE EAST. Report to the Council. Geneva: League of Nations, 1932. 556p. (League of Nations Publication, C.849.M.393.1932.IV [C.T.F.E./Orient 39,1]) [*Chair* Regnault].
Has sections "Studies of Laws and Conditions Relating to International Traffic by Countries Visited: India" (pp.329-75) and "Ceylon" (pp.376-87) that review prostitution legislation and mention details of the social organization of prostitution.

1143 MENON, LAKSHMI NANDAN. Traffic in women and children. *In* Shyam Kumari Nehru, ed. Our cause: a symposium by Indian women. Allahabad: Kitabistan, 1938? pp.183-98.
Outlines various causes of prostitution in India, international efforts against it and existing social welfare agencies, along with solutions proposed for India and other countries.

1144 MUTHULAKSHMI REDDI, S. and JERBANOO MISTRI. Two social evils. *In* A.R. Caton, ed. The key of progress: a survey of the status and conditions of women in India. London: Humphrey Milford, Oxford University Press, 1930. pp.177-98.
"The Devadasis, or Religious Prostitution" and "Commercial Prostitution" are the evils described. Presents proposals for their amelioration, including prohibitive legislation and social work attention.

1145 ROTHFELD, OTTO. The dancing girl. *In his* Women of India. London: Simpkin, Marshall, Hamilton, Kent and Company, 1920? pp.151-74.
States that the only profession open to Indian women that has traditionally been both remunerative and honorable is that of the dancing girl. Author points out the misnomer of this appellation, saying that dancing is an adjunct to singing. Discusses the institution of the dancing girl in various localities and argues against social reformers: "To stifle a class of women, living their own lives in independence, graceful, accomplished, often clever, to degrade them, to make them outcastes and force them into shameful by-ways, is not merely to sin against charity; it is also a blunder against life."

1146 STRICKLAND, LILY. The real nautch girl. *In* Dance Magazine 13 (Dec 1939) 21, 55-6.
[Unexamined].

1147 VENKATARATNAM NAIDU, R. Social purity and anti-Nautch movement. *In* C. Yajneswara Chintamani, ed. Indian social reform: being a collection of essays, addresses, speeches, etc., with an appendix. Madras: printed at the Minerva Press, 1901. First part, pp.249-81.
"Secret vice and veneered inchastity are to be found all the world over; but immorality as a heredity and acknowledged profession, living in peace . . . amidst other avocations, fortified against the attacks of time and change, and endowed with the privileges of social sanction, is peculiar to this land."

ix) Female seclusion — *pardā* / "purdah" — and zenana life

See also zenana mission material within "(e) Christian missions. . .," entries 1556-1643

1148 CATTELL, MILLY. Behind the purdah: or, the lives and legends of our Hindu sisters. Calcutta: Thacker, Spink and Company, 1916. 92p.
Describes the "inside," the lives of women who observe *pardā*. ". . . the wonderful, living, warm, palpitating India is still an unread book. It lies hidden, inside, behind the Purdah of the Purdah." The author was a governess in Indian families.

1149 COOPER, ELIZABETH. My lady of the Indian purdah. New York: Frederick A. Stokes Company, 1927. 205p.
Illustrated. [Unexamined. NUC].

1150 HABIBULLAH, ATTIA. Seclusion of women. *In* Shyam Kumari Nehru, ed. Our cause: a symposium by Indian women. Allahabad: Kitabistan, 1938? pp.205-11.
Argues that while *pardā* was consonant with the social conditions of "medieval" society, it is not appropriate in a modern democracy. *Pardā* has "deprived women of any significance in political and economic spheres." Criticizes double standards of men toward wives, mothers and daughters on the one hand and courtesans and prostitutes on the other.

1151 KIDWAI, MUSHIR HOSAIN. Harem, purdah or seclusion. Lahore: Muslim Book Society, 1920. 29p.
Defends *pardā* and traditional Islamic views of women's roles. [Unexamined. IOL].

1152 MARTELLI, E. Purdah. *In* A.R. Caton, ed. The key of progress: a survey of the status and conditions of women in India. London: Humphrey Milford, Oxford University Press, 1930. pp.115-23.
Reviews various adverse effects of *pardā* observance on women and some solutions, proposed and in effect.

1153 MAUDOODI, ABUL 'ALA. al-Ash'ari, ed. Purdah and the status of women in Islam. Tr. by the editor. Lahore: Islamic Publications, 1972. 231p.
Translator mentions the extreme popularity of the book and says "This book, more than any other has in recent years helped people to understand clearly the nature of the correct relationship between man and woman in the social life, and appreciate the great design that Nature wills to fulfil through them on the earth." Text supports *pardā* and offers a detailed interpretation of Islamic social theory and comparisons with the West. First published as a book in 1939.

1154 MUKHERJEE, JOGENDRA NATH and NARA NATH MUKHERJEE. The law relating to pardanashins in British India: civil and criminal. Calcutta: R. Cambray and Company, 1906. 199p.
[Unexamined. BMG].

1155 NIAZ HUSSAIN, R. The purdah (veil) system amongst the Muslims of India. *In* Islamic Review 17,9 (1929).
[Unexamined].

1156 ROLLESTON, CHARLES J. Behind the purdā. *In* Nineteenth Century and After 72,428 (1912) 811-21.
Review and affirmation of statements arguing for a more systematic protection of the legal and health rights of *pardā*-observing women.

1157 RUSTOMJI, HILLA. Purdah. *In* Shyam Kumari Nehru, ed. Our cause: a symposium by Indian women. Allahabad: Kitabistan, 1938? pp.201-4.
Indictment of the *pardā* system as "one of the main causes of the present deplorable conditions in India." Problems induced by *pardā* include poor health and a limitation of women's economic productivity. Compulsory education is the proposed solution.

1158 RUKHMABAI, DR. Purdah: the need for its abolition. *In* Evelyn C. Gedge and Mithan Choksi, eds. Women in modern India: fifteen papers by Indian women writers. Bombay: D.B. Taraporewala Sons and Company, 1929. pp.144-8. [*Reprint* Westport, Connecticut: Hyperion Press, 1976. (Pioneers of the Women's Movement)].
Reviews variations in *pardā* observance according to region and class, and community and social welfare activities that have adapted to its limitations. The author favors abolishment rather than accommodation to "this deplorable custom, which by causing unhealthy conditions for mothers drains the national vigour, and which degrades India in the eyes of the world."

1159 SHEONARAIN, PANDIT. The purdah system. *In* Muslim Review 4,4 (1930) 35-9.
Pros and cons of *pardā* reform. Urges a moderate form that provides for modesty but does not impair health.

1160 SORABJI, CORNELIA. Love and life behind the purdah . . . London: Freemantle and Company, 1901. 239p.
[Unexamined. BMG].

1161 ________. The purdahnashin. Calcutta: Thacker, Spink, 1917. 80p.
Describes "the woman as she is in orthodox Hindu zenanas of Bengal, Bihar, Orissa and Assam" and how her needs can best be met. Based upon 23 years' experience in zenanas. Sorabji recommends that the zenana worker have a great knowledge of and sensitivity to the ways of life of these women. Includes appendixes regarding the health care and education of *pardānaśīns*.

1162 SULTAN JAHAN BEGAM, NAWAB OF BHOPAL. Al-hijab: or, why purdah is necessary. Calcutta: printed by Thacker, Spink and Company, 1922. 212p.
The woman who ruled Bhopal state writes in support of *pardā*. [Unexamined. BMG].

1163 VAUGHAN, KATHLEEN OLGA. The purdah system and its effect on motherhood:

osteomalacia caused by absence of light in India. Cambridge: W. Heffer and Sons, 1928. 48p.
Doctor argues that the *pardā* system has a serious detrimental effect on health. [Unexamined. MRL].

x) Economic position of women: property rights and employment opportunities

1164 BELL, EVA MARY. Appendix I: The dependents of Indian soldiers. *In* A.R. Caton, ed. The key of progress: a survey of the status and conditions of women in India. London: Humphrey Milford, Oxford University Press, 1930. pp.207-17.
Outlines features of the Indian Army pension plan for soldiers' dependents. Benefits include "a scheme of social welfare admirably adapted to the needs and sentiments of those illiterate, ignorant, and lovable women and children it seeks to aid."

1165 CHATTERJEE, KAMALA. Women in industry. *In* Shyam Kumari Nehru, ed. Our cause: a symposium by Indian women. Allahabad: Kitabistan, 1938? pp.129-57.
Includes data on women working in factories, mines, plantations and other industries. Examines working conditions, unemployment, low wages, housing and related problems. Tables.

1166 DAS, RAJANI KANTA. Woman labour in India. *In* International Labour Review 24,4-5 (1931) 376-409, 536-72.
Reviews growth, employment conditions, aspects of health and safety, hours, efficiency, wages, standard of living and associated welfare services of women in Indian plantations, factories and mines. Surveys labor legislation from the mid-19th century. Concludes with recommendations.

1167 Hindu women's property rights: report of the committee appointed by His Highness the Maharaja Gaekwad. Baroda: printed at the Government Press, 1930. 213p.
"Having noticed . . . that the differences in the rights of inheritance enjoined in Hindu Law between males and females requires to be harmonised with the improved status of females . . . His Highness was pleased to direct that [several persons] should form themselves into a committee, (a) to examine the question of the property rights of women under Hindu law, and (b) to suggest amendments, if any, called for under modern conditions for removing defects in the existing Law." Evidence from religious law and numerous contemporary sources, including a specially prepared questionnaire.

1168 INDIA. LAWS, STATUTES, ETC. Hindu Women's Rights to Property Act (act no. XVIII of 1937) as amended by Act no. XI of 1938, 3d ed. By Kumud Ṅath Bhaumik. Calcutta: Eastern Law House, Ltd., 1946. 122p.
[Unexamined. NUC].

1169 _______. Hindu Women's Rights to Property Act, Acts XVIII of 1937 and XI of 1938 Central, and acts of Assam, Bengal (bill), Bihar, Bombay, Central Provinces, Madras (nil), North-West Frontier (nil), Orissa, the Punjab (nil), Sind and United Provinces, 2d ed. By Rishindra Nath Sarkar. Calcutta: S.C. Sarkar, 1944. 117p.
[Unexamined. NUC].

1170 _______. Legislation affecting Hindu women: containing Hindu Women's Right to Property Act . . . . With annotations by Rishindra Nath Sarkar. Calcutta: S.C. Sarkar, 1947. 217p. [*2d ed.* India (Republic). Laws, Statutes, etc. Legislation affecting Hindu women. By Rishindra Nath Sarkar. Calcutta: Calcutta Weekly Notes, 1951. 201p.].
[Unexamined. NUC].

1171 KELMAN, JANET HARVEY. Labour in India: a study of the conditions of Indian women in modern industry. London: George Allen and Unwin, 1923. 281p. (Selly Oak Colleges, Central Council Publications, 5).
Inquires into the conditions of Indian women working in textile mills, along with general labor conditions. Treats cotton and jute industries, industrial migration, wages, mill conditions, housing, unions, labor and management, health and living standards and legislation. Based on an investigation conducted in 1920-21.

1172 KUMARAPPA, J.M. The woman as wage earner. *In* Indian J. of Social Work 1,2 (1940) 162-78.
Observes that though the employment of women may help solve family financial situations it endangers their biological and social functions as wife and mother, inducing a "pathological relationship which is a menace to the family in particular and to society in general." With tables showing participation rates.

1173 MARTELLI, E. Women in industry. *In* A.R. Caton, ed. The key of progress: a survey of the status and conditions of women in India. London: Humphrey Milford, Oxford University Press, 1930. pp.155-76.
Distribution of women in industrial occupations and various associated labor and family problems.

1174 NARANG, SHARADA. Women and property. *In* Shyam Kumari Nehru, ed. Our cause: a symposium by Indian women. Allahabad: Kitabistan, 1938? pp.309-11.
Summarizes Hindu, Islamic, Parsi and Christian personal laws of inheritance for women. Finds the Hindu law "the most archaic" and inequitable. The Islamic and Christian laws, on the other hand, "leave little to be desired."

1175 RAY, RENUKA. Women in mines. Aundh: Aundh Publishing Trust, 1945. 20p. (All-India Women's Conference, Tract 2). [Unexamined. NUC].

1176 TILAK, TARA. Possibilities of social work in India. *In* Evelyn C. Gedge and Mithan Choksi, eds. Women in modern India: fifteen papers by Indian women writers. Bombay: D.B. Taraporewala Sons and Company, 1929. pp.149-61. [*Reprint* Westport, Connecticut: Hyperion Press, 1976. (Pioneers of the Women's Movement)].
Avenues of social welfare work among women and children suitable for "women who have had the privilege of a good education." Focuses on problems of female urban industrial workers.

xi) Conditions among rural women

1177 CATON, A.R. Women in rural life. *In* A.R. Caton, ed. The key of progress: a survey of the status and conditions of women in India. London: Humphrey Milford, Oxford University Press, 1930. pp.131-54.
Life of rural women, their problems and their place in rural welfare schemes. "So far the rural scene has been practically untouched by the new movement for the advancement of women."

1178 HAMID ALI, SHAREEFAH. Village reconstruction. *In* Shyam Kumari Nehru, ed. Our cause: a symposium by Indian women. Allahabad: Kitabistan, 1938? pp.172-9.
Various ideas regarding 'village uplift'. "In every village improvement scheme, the lessening of the burden from the shoulders of the woman should be a first consideration."

1179 PILLAY, A.P. Welfare problems in rural India. Bombay: D.B. Taraporevala Sons and Company, 1931. 195p.
Guide book and almanac of the needs of women and children in the work of rural uplift; a view of what is being done and what might be done. Includes check lists, statistics, comparisons with foreign programs, photographs. Has information on obstetrics and infant care. A companion volume to Pillay and Subramanyam, 1928.

1180 ________ and M. SUBRAMANYAM. Maternity and child welfare: a hand-book for public health and welfare workers in India. Sholapur: Maternity and Infant Welfare Association, 1928. 94, 43p.
Companion to previous volume. Includes contributions by M.I. Balfour, Miss R. Piggott, H.V. Tilak, A. DaGama. [Unexamined. NUC].

xii) Origins of the birth control movement in the subcontinent

1181 AIYAR, S. KRISHNAMURTHI. Population and birth-control in India. Madras, 1930?
[Unexamined. NUC].

1182 MANGUDKAR, M.P., ed. Dr. Ambedkar and family planning. Poona: Suvarna Mangudkar, 1976. 68p.
Articles and speech to the Bombay Legislative Assembly by Ambedkar and others favoring mechanical birth control measures. From the 1930s, a period when the Gandhian solution, abstinence, was favored by most political leaders.

1183 MAUDUDI, ABUL 'ALA. Khurshid Ahmad and Misbahul Islam Faruqi, eds. Birth control: its social, political, economic, moral and religious aspects. Tr. by the editors. Lahore: Islamic Publications Ltd., 1968. 186p. [Originally serialized in 1930s. *1st book ed.* 1943].
As an Islamic state Pakistan requires Islamic sanction for its policies. Argues that "There is no justification . . . to claim that Islam approves a popular movement of birth control." Birth control interferes with the plan of God.

1184 PHADKE, N.S. Sex problems in India: a scientific exposition of sex life and some curious marriage customs prevailing in India from time immemorial to the present day, 2d ed. Bombay: D.B. Taraporevala Sons, 1929. 322p.
Views the condition of India as "extremely pitiful from a Eugenic viewpoint." Seeks to remedy this condition by bringing eugenics into the practical politics of the country. Proposes variety of solutions to the problems of overpopulation, unfit parenthood, sexual disease and vice based on the integration of modern medicine and technology with ancient Indian wisdom. Advocates numerous reforms (see especially chapter entitled "The Mother of the Race"). Foreword by Margaret Sanger.

1185 SANGER, MARGARET. Who can take a dream for truth? *And* Depth but not tumult. *In her* Margaret Sanger: an autobiography. New York: W.W. Norton and Company, 1938. pp.461-92.
Mrs. Sanger describes her travels throughout India in 1936-37 promoting the birth control movement. She was invited by Margaret Cousins to speak before the All-India Women's Conference, which had passed a resolution in support of birth control at the previous meeting. She reports a futile conversation with Mahatma Gandhi who would only support continence as a birth control method and a more favorable meeting with Rabindranath Tagore. "There was considerable heat" at the All-India Women's Conference. "No Indian women were against it, only converted Eurasians; all mothers were for it and all those against it were unmarried."

1186 WATTAL, PYARE KISHEN. The population problem in India: a census study. Bombay: Bennett, Coleman and Company, 1916. 83p.
Argues that findings of India's 1911 census portend problems of population control; from a time when population control in India received little attention. [Unexamined. BMG].

xiii) Legal rights: legislation and accessibility

Legislative material on particular topics (e.g., widowhood) is located according to topic

1187 AMRIT KAUR. Women under the new constitution. *In* Shyam Kumari Nehru, ed. Our cause: a symposium by Indian women. Allahabad: Kitabistan, 1938? pp.366-81.
Reviews the provisions for women under the Government of India Act of 1935 and describes the unsuccessful efforts of major women's organizations to secure the removal of all disqualifications on the basis of gender, universal adult suffrage and absence of reserved legislative and administrative seats.

1188 APPA RAO. Law of maintenance and alimony. Madras: Madras Law Journal, 1939. 183p.
[Unexamined].

1189 APPASAMY, PAUL. Status of women. *In his* Legal aspects of social reform. Madras: Christian Literature Society for India, 1929. pp.1-110.
Regarding 20th century reform of Hindu religious laws and traditions. Organized according to 13 topics (child marriage, education, monogamy, etc.).

1190 BURWAY, R.G. The present position of Hindu women and the means of ameliorating their lot. Bombay: D.B. Taraporevala Sons and Company, 1941. 29p.
Regarding the legal status of Hindu women. First appeared in *Bombay Law Journal*, February and March, 1944. [Unexamined. NUC].

1191 DERRETT, J. DUNCAN M. Essays in classical and modern Hindu law, v3: Anglo-Hindu legal problems. Leiden: E.J. Brill, 1977. 414p.
Volume of collected articles includes material on adoption by women, illegitimacy, female property rights and birth control.

1192 GAJENDRAGADKAR, K.B. Legal rights of Hindu women: discussion of some necessary urgent reforms. Bombay: Indian Institute of Sociology, 1942. 27p.
[Unexamined. NUC].

1193 GHARPURE, JAGANNATH RAGHUNATH. Rights of women under the Hindu law. Bombay: University of Bombay, 1943. 165p. (*Its* Sir Lallubhai A. Shah Lectures, 1939).
[Unexamined. NUC].

1194 INDIA. LAWS, STATUTES, ETC. The unrepealed general acts of the Governor General in Council: with chronological table of all unrepealed acts passed by the Governor General in Council and an index, 4th ed. Calcutta: Superintendent Government Printing, India, 1909. 6v.
Collection of texts of "such of the Acts passed by the Governor General in Council as are still in force and which extend to the whole of British India, or . . . to the greater portion of British India [with provision for] extension to the rest of British India or which apply to the three Presidency-towns." The six volumes cover 1834 through 1908.

1195 MAIR, J.H. P. Brookes-Smith, ed. Behind the curtain: India's first woman lawyer. Madras: Christian Literature Society, 1961. 93p. [*Also* P. Brookes-Smith, ed. Behind the purdah: selfless social service by India's woman lawyer. Madras: Christian Literature Society, 1963. 94p.].
Autobiography? Biography by the woman's husband? About Cornelia Sorabji? [Unexamined. IBP].

1196 MEHTA, RAMANLAL V. A thesis on the legal rights of women under the different communal laws in vogue in India. Bombay: G.G. Bhat, 1933. 93p.
Prize-winning essay written for the Civil Marriage Association of Bombay. From publisher's foreword: "This thesis . . . is nearly an exhaustive and complete survey of [Indian women's legal rights and liabilities] and so it is calculated to present in a non-technical and lucid style a vivid picture, to the Indian women, of the numerous disabilities and obstacles that baulk their way to progress and social independence."

1197 NAGARKAR, MRS. K.C., ed. Statutes for the protection of women and children in British India. Bombay: National Council of Women in India, 1934. 25p.
[Unexamined. IOL].

1198 NATIONAL COUNCIL OF WOMEN IN INDIA. Report. 6th biennial. Bombay, 1943.
Report of a conference sponsored by the Council on the "Legal Status of Indian Women." [Unexamined].

1199 RATHBONE, ELEANOR. The political status of Indian women. *In* Asiatic Review n.s. 29,98 (1933) 303-14.
From an address to the East India Association in anticipation of the new constitution and the Government of India Act, 1935: "In view

of all that we know of the conditions of women in India . . . are we content to renounce our trusteeship without at least putting into the hands of women the means, the constitutional means, of securing for themselves that release from cruel laws and customs which we ourselves have so unquestionably failed to effect for them?"

1200 RAY, RENUKA. Legal disabilities of Indian women: a plea for a commission of enquiry. *In* The Modern Review 56,5 (1934) 529-32.
"In Hindu law a wholesale revision is absolutely necessary as regards inheritance and marriage, if we are to remove the disabilities under which women suffer." Islamic law seen as better but in need of alteration as well.

1201 SANKARAN NAIR, C. Indian law and English legislation. *In* Contemporary Review 100 (Aug-Sep 1911) 213-26, 349-64.
Regarding legislative "interference with the Hindu religion in the service of humanity." Discusses ***satīs*** and various marriage issues.

1202 SORABJI, CORNELIA. The legal status of women in India. *In* Nineteenth Century 44,261 (1898) 854-66.
Notes prevalent misconception that the Indian woman has minimal "affairs" and is not in need of help in managing them; rather "she needs protection for her life as well as her goods." Reviews major legal provisions for Hindu and Muslim women. Proposes a specific program for the legal assistance of Indian women, including female personnel.

1203 ________. Safeguards for purdanashins. *In* Asiatic Quarterly, 3d series, 15, 29 (1903) 69-78.
Describes problems that ***pardā*** observing women have in securing their legal rights. Reviews relevant court cases and presents opinions of various judges regarding their disabilities. Urges intervention and the organization of programs.

1204 TATA, MITHAN. Women and the law. *In* Evelyn C. Gedge and Mithan Choksi, eds. Women in modern India: fifteen papers by Indian women writers. Bombay: D.B. Taraporewala Sons and Company, 1929. pp.124-32. [*Reprint* Westport, Connecticut: Hyperion Press, 1976. (Pioneers of the Women's Movement)].
Lawyer describes both the movement of women into legal profession in India during the late 19th and early 20th centuries and the main legal provisions for Hindu and Muslim women in effect in the 1920s.

xiv) Hindu Code Bill, 1937-1956: whether to codify, how to codify, women's legal rights

1205 BANNINGAN, JOHN A. The Hindu code bill: the proposed bill, backed by Nehru but opposed by Hindu traditionalists, would codify and modernize Hindu law, giving greater rights to women. *In* Far Eastern Survey 21,17 (3 Dec 1952) 173-6.
Includes review of the legal benefits for Hindu women under the (then) proposed Hindu Code Bill. "These concessions to the Hindu woman represent only a small, though vital, part of the draft code. There is reason to think that the property provisions [in this part], although they are not emphasized by the opposition, are the sections which opponents of the bill are really most interested in killing."

1206 DERRETT, J. DUNCAN M. Hindu law past and present: being an account of the controversy which preceded the enactment of the Hindu Code, the text of the Code as enacted, and some comments thereon. Calcutta: A. Mukherjee and Company, 1957. 408p.
About one half of this book considers the Code, topic by topic, and assesses the implications of the codification. Remaining materials discuss the problems of codification, the arguments for and against it, the history of the Hindu Code (1937-1956) and its likely effects. Appendixes give notes and references and the various texts that compose the Code.

1207 GAJENDRAGADKAR, P.B. The Hindu Code Bill. Dharwar: Karnatak University, 1951? 52p. (Karnatak University Extension Lectures Series, 2).
Two lectures on the Hindu Code Bill by a progressive judge addressed to students while the bill was before Parliament. Urges uniform Hindu code for all, "irrespective of caste, creed, Varna or sex."

1208 GOUR, HARI SINGH. The Hindu Code: being a codified statement of Hindu law with a commentary thereon and relevant acts annotated, 5th ed. Rev. by B. Malik et al. Allahabad: Law Publishers, 1974-78. 4v. [*4th ed.* 1938].
Vast synthesis of Hindu Law as it currently functions. Topical chapters present relevant legislation and cases. Much on women.

1209 INDIA. HINDU LAW COMMITTEE. Report. New Delhi: Manager of Publications, Government of India, 1947. 183p.
Report of the committee appointed in 1944 to formulate a detailed standardized code of Hindu Law, following the widespread circulation of the recommendations. Includes background of the committee and its procedures, the proposed Code itself, discussion of points found most objectionable to the public (all concern women) and lists of those consulted and their opinions on various issues.

1210 Oral evidence tendered to the Hindu Law

Committee, 1945. Madras: printed by the Superintendent, Government Press, 1947. 74p.
Transcripts of meetings and interviews sponsored in various cities in 1945 by the Hindu Law Committee in order to ascertain public opinion regarding aspects of Hindu law and its standardization.

1211 OVERSTREET, GENE D. The Hindu Code Bill. *In* Lucien W. Pye, ed. Cases in comparative politics: Asia. Boston: Little, Brown and Company, 1970. pp.161-219.
Concise history of the Hindu Code Bill from the 1941 Rau Committee to the final enactment in 1955. Suggests profound involvement — conservative to liberal — of the country's leaders in issues relating to women.

1212 RAY, RENUKA. The background of the Hindu Code Bill. *In* Pacific Affairs 25,3 (1952) 268-77.
Argument in support of the Hindu Code Bill and its provisions for women in the face of unexpectedly strong opposition from within the Indian National Congress.

1213 SARKAR, LOTIKA. Jawaharlal Nehru and the Hindu Code Bill. *In* B.R. Nanda, ed. Indian woman: from purdah to modernity. New Delhi: Vikas, 1976. pp.87-98.
Brief history of the Hindu Code Bill and identification of its provisions for women. Considers Nehru's key role in its later stages.

1214 Written statement submitted to the Hindu Law Committee, 1945. Madras: Printed by the Superintendent, Government Press, 1947. 2v.
Statements from hundreds of organizations and individuals (many prominent) solicited by the Hindu Law Committee following circulation of their proposed Code of Hindu Law. Matters related to woman and family predominate.

xv) Christian "women's work" and conversions

See also "(e) Christian missions. . .," entries 1556-1643

1215 BATLEY, D. SIBELLA. With A.M. ROBINSON. Devotees of Christ; some women pioneers of the Indian church. London: Church of England Zenana Missionary Society, 1937. 147p.
Collection of 14 chapter-length biographies of Indian women. "Its aim is to introduce a few representative pioneers, forerunners of the splendid band of Christian women of the second, third and even fourth generation, who are to-day seizing the opportunities of service presented to them in religious, social and national circles." Sixteen photographs.

1216 BRITTAN, HARRIETTE G. Shoshie, the Hindoo zenana teacher. New York: T. Whittaker, 1873? 222p.
On zenana missions. [Unexamined. NUC].

1217 Heathen sacrifices: the Hindoo girl and little George. Philadelphia: Presbyterian Board of Publication, 184_. 36p.
Account of a young Christian convert? [Unexamined. NUC].

1218 KARN, N.E. Indian women and the religious life. *In* International Review of Missions 24,2 (1935) 248-55.
Regarding the establishment of Christian religious orders for Indian women. "We must desire to have no desires of our own . . . . we need little centres of devotion, whose anchorites will lead . . . lives of attractive power."

1219 MAC MINN, EDWIN. Nemorama, the nautchnee: a story of India. New York: Hunt and Eaton, 1891. 291p.
On zenana missions? The story of a convert? [Unexamined. MRL].

1220 MIZLAFF, EUGENIA VON. [EUGENIA VON MITZLAFF]. Promadeni: a biographical sketch connected with the Indian mission among women. Tr. from German. London: S.P.C.K., 1871 160p.
A convert? Illustrated. [Unexamined. MRL].

1221 SATTHIANADHAN, KRUPABAI. Saguna: a story of native Christian life. Madras: Srinivasa, 1895. 247p. [*Also* Saguna: aus dem Leben einer indischen Christin. Leipzig: H.G. Wallmann, 1900. 335p.].
Autobiography of early years of the daughter of Bombay's first brahman converts to Christianity. Contains ethnographic details of brahman and Christian communities in second half of 19th century. First printed in *Christian College Magazine*. [Unexamined. NUC].

1222 The story of Noni Chatterji: a tale of zenana life in Simla. London: Society for Promoting Christian Knowledge, 1924? 127p.
Fictional account of the meeting in Simla of a young Bengali girl and a missionary and her subsequent conversion.

1223 THOMÄ, HEDWIG. Sarah Chakko: eine grosse Inderin [Sarah Chakko: a great Indian woman]. Stuttgart: Evang. Missionsverlag, 1955. 91p. (Weltweite Reihe, 4).
A "churchwoman" of India. [Unexamined. MRL].

1224 WEITBRECHT, MRS. [MARTHA (EDWARDS) WEITBRECHT]. An Indian blossom which bore fruit: a memory of Rabee . . . London: E. Suter, 1849. 24p.
A convert? [Unexamined. BMG].

b) Nationalist movements

i) The Indian freedom movement

1225 BAGAL, JOGESH C. Women in India's freedom movement. *In* Modern Review 93,6 and 94,1 (1953) 467-73, 53-61.
Regarding the participation of particular women in various events and facets of the nationalist movement. Focuses, though not exclusively, on Bengal. Numerous photographs.

1226 BASU, APARNA. The role of women in the Indian struggle for freedom. *In* B.R. Nanda, ed. Indian women: from purdah to modernity. New Delhi: Vikas, 1976. pp.16-40.
Detailed account, drawn largely from personal interviews, newspapers and other primary sources.

1227 CHATTOPADHYAYA, KAMALADEVI. Women reform India. *In* Living Age 357,4480 (1940) 418-22.
Women's participation in the freedom struggle is "true to the *Shakti* tradition of warding evil away from man." Reviews variety of contributions women have made. Author is "Madame Kamaladevi."

1228 ________. The struggle for freedom. *In* Tara Ali Baig, ed. Women of India. Delhi: Publications Division, Ministry of Information and Broadcasting, Government of India, 1958. pp.14-31.
Describes the context in which women emerged to take part in the freedom movement, along with key events and personalities. Photographs.

1229 GHOSH, SATYAVRATA. Women terrorists of India. *In* Illustrated Weekly of India 94,4 (28 Jan 1973) 34-8.
From editor's introduction: "They lived underground, made and threw bombs, shot British Governors and spent the best years of their youth in prison . . . . Who were these brave and reckless women who thought nothing of giving their lives for the Cause? What was their contribution to the Independence movement? Has an ungrateful nation forgotten their sacrifices?" Discusses numerous events and personalities. Photographs.

1230 JHAVERI, VITHALBHAI K. and SOLI S. BATLIVALA, eds. Jai-Hind: the diary of a rebel daughter of India with the Rani of Jhansi Regiment. Bombay: Janmabhoomi Prakashan Mandir, 1945. 130p.
Diary of an anonymous Indian woman who joined the Rani of Jhansi Regiment of Subhas Chandra Bose's anti-British Azad Hind government in Southeast Asia in 1943.

1231 KRISHNA, GOPAL. The development of the Indian National Congress as a mass organization: 1918-1923. *In* J. of Asian Studies 25,3 (1966) 413-30. [*Reprint in* Thomas Metcalf, ed. Modern India: an interpretive anthology. London: Macmillan Company, 1971. pp.257-72].
Includes figures on growth of female participation in annual sessions of the Indian National Congress and as members of the All-India Congress Committee. Mentions meeting of Marwari women in Calcutta at which Gandhi collected Rs. 10,000 in cash and ornaments.

1232 MANMOHAN KAUR. Role of women in the freedom movement, 1857-1947. New Delhi: Sterling Publishers, 1968. 287p.
Well-documented history, from the Mutiny to independence, based upon published and unpublished government records, correspondence, newspapers, Indian National Congress records, books and articles. Extensive bibliography.

1233 ________. Great women of India. New Delhi: Sterling, 1970. 2v.
Brief sketches of notable women and their involvement in the freedom struggle: the Rani of Jhansi, Annie Besant, Kasturba Gandhi, Sarojini Naidu, Rajkumari Amrit Kaur, Vijaya Lakshmi Pandit and Indira Gandhi. [Unexamined. IBP].

1234 MENON, LAKSHMI N. Women and the national movement. *In* Devaki Jain, ed. Indian women. New Delhi: Publications Division, Ministry of Information and Broadcasting, Government of India, 1975. pp.17-25.
Highlights of women's involvement in the nationalist movement.

1235 MINAULT, GAIL. Parda politics: the role of Muslim women in Indian nationalism, 1911-1924. *In* Hanna Papanek, ed. Purdah in South Asia: the segregation of women. Princeton, New Jersey: Princeton University Press?, forthcoming.
Examines the participation of Indian Muslim women in political activity from 1911 to 1924, particularly with respect to the Khilafat movement. Describes 1917 public appearance of *burqa'*-clad Bi Ammon on behalf of her imprisoned son, Muhammad Ali, who had been elected president of the Muslim League. Reviews political activities of other Muslim women at this time and assesses their ideas. With some speech excerpts. Considers male response. [Unexamined. Verified with editor].

1236 MOUNTBATTEN, LADY. Lady Mountbatten on the women of India. *In* Asiatic Review n.s. 45, 161 (1949) 439-48.
Text of a talk by Lady Mountbatten on the important part played by women in India's independence movement and in the relief measures for refugees at partition. Considers the emancipation of Indian women to be the result of their own efforts, aided by the encouragement of Mahatma Gandhi and Sarojini Naidu.

1237 PANDIT, VIJAYA LAKSHMI. Prison days. Calcutta: Signet Press, 1945? 129p.

Excerpts from the author's diary, August 1942 to June 1943, written while serving a prison sentence on political charges. [Unexamined. NUC].

1238 PARULEKAR, N.B. Indian women as non-cooperators. *In* Asia 31,1 (1931) 22-7.
Gives examples of various noncooperative women's activities throughout India, including singing protest songs (two translated), boycotting foreign goods and picketing. Five photographs.

1238a ROY CHOWDHURY, BULU. Madame Cama: a short life-sketch. New Delhi: People's Publishing House, 1977. 34p.
Reviews Bhikaji Rustom Cama's revolutionary activist work in Europe for the Indian freedom struggle, 1902 to 1935. Appendixes and photographs reproduce various documents.

Portrait.

1239 SAHA, PANCHANAN. Madame Cama (Bhikaji Rustom K.R.): "Mother of Indian Revolution." Calcutta: Manisha, 1975. 47p. (International Women's Year, 1).
Brief biography of a woman who worked extensively abroad for the Indian freedom movement.

1239a SAINSARA, GURCHARAN SINGH. A Sikh heroine of the Ghadar Party: Gulab Kaur. *In* J. of Sikh Studies 4,2 (1977) 93-8.
Discusses ro/e of Gulab Kaur in the Ghadar movement of the second and third decades of the 20th century. This "great lioness," along with thousands of other Panjabi emigrants, primarily Sikhs, returned to India to take an activist role in the freedom movement. Based on accounts of her associates.

ii) The Pakistan Muslim separatist movement and Hindu-Muslim communalism

1240 BERKELEY-HILL, OWEN. Hindu-Muslim unity. *In* International Journal of Psycho-Analysis 6,3 (1925) 282-7.
Argues that positive Hindu associations with mother goddesses, the mother land and [mother] cows have been related to Hindu-Muslim tensions in India, for Muslim attitudes and invasions have been viewed as exceptionally irreverent.

1241 HARTOG, LADY [MABEL HÉLÈNE (KISCH) HARTOG]. The Indian situation: the woman's point of view. *In* Asiatic Review n.s. 37,130 (1941) 250-60. *With* Discussion on the foregoing paper, pp.261-70.
Address to the East India Association argues that the "deplorable disunity" between the Indian National Congress and the Muslim League can be bridged with the help of the All-India Women's Conference, which stands for non-violence, equality of race and individual freedom. States that Indian women have a long tradition of service and self-sacrifice and realize the necessity of unity.

1242 MIRZA, SARFARAZ HUSSAIN. Muslim's women's role in the Pakistan movement. Lahore: Research Society of Pakistan, University of the Punjab, 1969. 166p. (Research Society of Pakistan, 14).
Concerns activities of Muslim women in the struggles against British imperialism and Hindu dominance in Muslim majority areas of the subcontinent, 1937 to 1947. Based on contemporary sources and interviews with participants. Reviews history of Muslim women in the subcontinent during the 19th and early 20th centuries. Appendix gives brief biographical sketches of numerous women.

1243 NEHRU, RAMESHWARI. Recovery of abducted women. *In* Indian J. of Social Work 9,4 (1949) 303-9.
Account of various measures adopted by the Dominion of India to recover women and girls who were abducted and raped in the partition struggles. Gives procedures and statistics by province/state. Concludes: "Considering the large number of women who are abducted on both sides, the number 14,094 which has been recovered is very small. Recovery figures are dwindling very fast."

(c) The Indian women's movement

See also "Political participation" sections, entries 1270-86 and 2546-79

1244 AMRIT KAUR, RAJKUMARI. The woman's movement in India. *In* Modern Review 53,4 (1933) 400-3.
Brief discussion of the early history and issues of the Indian women's movement.

1245 BAHADURJI, G.J. Women and political struggle. *In* Shyam Kumari Nehru, ed. Our cause: a symposium by Indian women. Allahabad: Kitabistan, 1938? pp.321-38.
". . . I shall attempt to lay out briefly the true nature of [Indian women's struggle for equality], some of its inevitable concomitants and characteristics, and its undeniable ultimate goal and purpose." The author takes a progressive position in the name of women's basic rights and the advancement of the country.

1246 CHAKRAVARTTY, RENU. The women's movement in India. *In* Vimla Farooqi and Renu Chakravartty. Communism and women. New Delhi: Communist Party of India, 1973. pp.27-48.
Surveys trends in the Indian women's movement before and after independence; focuses on its intimate connection with broader political events.

1247 CHATTOPADHYAYA, KAMALADEVI. Future of Indian women's movement. *In* Shyam Kumari Nehru, ed. Our cause: a symposium by Indian women. Allahabad: Kitabistan, 1938? pp.385-402.
Socialist perspective. Considers Russia, where women are "establishing complete equality," to foreshadow the worldwide future of womankind. The author describes various aspects of ideal future social conditions. The feminist movement "is a symptom of Capitalist society and has no place or reality in a mass class struggle such as one visualises India to be heading for."

1248 _______. The women's movement — then and now. *In* Devaki Jain, ed. Indian women. New Delhi: Publications Division, Ministry of Information and Broadcasting, Government of India, 1975. pp.27-36.
Considers the once vigorous women's movement to be now in a state of "decline and extinction." Discusses factors involved in this decline.

1249 CHOUDHRANI, SARALA DEVI. A women's movement. *In* Modern Review 10,4 (1911) 344-50.
Describes the founding, organization, goals and activities of the Bharat Stree Mahamandal. This organization, established in 1910 by and for women, offered programs in zenana home education, handiwork marketing and medical aid and promoted vernacular literature.

1250 COUSINS, MARGARET E. The awakening of Asian womanhood. Madras: Ganesh and Company, 1922. 160p.
Articles relating to the Indian women's movement by a prominent figure in women's movements, both East and West. Includes an opening chapter by the same name as the book; two status survey papers; papers dealing with the topics of women as a national resource, marriage, freedom and franchise; and papers on Ramabai Ranade, Sarojini Naidu and Abala Bose.

1251 EVERETT, JANA GENEVIEVE MATSON. The Indian women's movement in comparative perspective. Ph.D. dissertation, Department of Political Science, University of Michigan, Ann Arbor, Michigan, 1976. 369p. [University Microfilms 76-19,128].
Thesis assumes that "much can be learned about improving the status of women from an examination of the strengths and limitations of the Indian women's movement," and examines the question: "To what extent can the origins, ideology, and success of the Indian women's movement be explained by the same conditions which explain these aspects of Western women's movements and to what extent by conditions specific to the Indian experience[?]"

1252 _______. Women and social change in India. New Delhi: Heritage, 1979. 233p. [*Also* New York: St. Martin's Press, 1979].
Examines Indian women's movement and, to a lesser extent, those in England and the United States to investigate conditions under which they emerged, types of justification for demands and conditions under which they were successful. Considers Indian campaigns for political representation and Hindu law reform in depth. Based on various primary and secondary documents. Appendix provides biographical notes concerning numerous participants in the Indian women's movement.

1253 A FEMINIST. The woman's movement in India. *In* Hindustan Review 86,541 (1950) 75-82.
Reviews progress of this movement. "From where to where are women moving? The noble pioneers were moving very definitely on the path of self-sacrifice, from ignorance to knowledge; from slavery to freedom; from injustice to justice; from impurity to purity; from sickness to health — and drawing with them others from the wretchedness of darkness to a beneficent light."

1254 FORBES, GERALDINE H. "Awakenings" and "Golden Ages": historical writings on Indian women. *In* Neera Desai, ed. The trends of change: studies on media response to the women's movement. Bombay: Allied Publishers, forthcoming. (SNDT Women's University, Bombay; Women in a Changing Society).
Points to problems and gaps in current understanding of the Indian women's movement and analyzes historical writings about this movement in terms of four theories of what inspired women's "awakening": western impact, nationalism, social reform and "Golden Age." Concludes with discussion of various problems relating to women's place in Indian historiography. [Manuscript examined].

1255 _______. Women's movements in India: traditional symbols and new roles. *In* M.S.A. Rao, ed. Social movements in India, v2. New Delhi: Manohar, forthcoming.
Examines life work of two leaders of the Indian women's movement. Discusses Saroj Nalini Dutt as an example of a person who worked in one state (Bengal), used the regional language and worked exclusively for women's uplift. Discusses Sarojini Naidu as an example of a person who worked on an all-India scale, used English and worked for social and political issues. Concludes with observations about the nature and influence of the women's movement. [Manuscript examined].

1256 Hind Mahila/The Indian Woman. v1-? (1920-?). Bombay.
Early English-language magazine for Indian women. [Unexamined. BUP].

1257 Indian Ladies' Magazine. v1-? (1901-1918, 1927-1938). Madras.
First English language magazine published by a woman for Indian women. Helped to promote social reform and spread new ideas. It aimed to reach, among others, women in orthodox homes. Kamala Satthianadhan was editor. [Unexamined. BUP].

1258 Indian Social Reformer. vl-63. (1894?-1952). Founded in Madras, moved to Bombay. Weekly.
The editors of this journal were sympathetic to and provided good coverage of the Indian women's movement. See numerous brief articles that report on meetings of women's organizations and progress of relevant pieces of legislation, excerpt statements from speeches and newspapers and so forth.

1259 MAYHEW, ARTHUR INNES. The women's movement in India and what we can learn from it. *In* Overseas Education (Jan 1942) 274-80.
[Unexamined. MRL].

1260 MIR AMIRUDDIN, BEGAM. The women [*sic*] movement in India. *In* Indian Social Reformer 52,16 (20 Dec 1941) 186-7.
Aims and ideals of the women's movement. Discusses problems of following western model too closely, suggests that mothers as teachers have great part to play in fostering understanding among the castes and creeds. Proposes that women are not the same as men and that they have special contributions to make.

1261 OLIVER, B.C. An onlooker at the All-India Women's Conference. *In* National Christian Council Review n.s. 50,3 (1930) 132-40.
Summary of the proceedings of the fourth annual conference. "After twenty-eight years in India one does not expect many more thrills at new sights, but I can neither describe nor analyse the deep emotion I experienced at the sight of the hundreds of women, from all over India, drawn together by the one purpose of service for their fellow countrywomen."

1262 RAY, RENUKA. Impressions of the tenth session of the All-India Women's Conference. *In* Modern Review 59,2 (1936) 209-12.
Highlights of the tenth session of the AIWC held at Travancore: the hospitality of Maharani Setu Parvati Bayi of Travancore, the practical nature of the resolutions, Margaret Sanger's appearance as a special visitor promoting birth control, structural expansion of the conference organization, patterns of support for government legislation, financial needs and ongoing aims.

1263 SHAH NAWAZ, BEGAM [JAHAN ARA SHAH NAWAZ]. Women's movement in India, Indian Paper no. 5. *In* Conference of the Institute of Pacific Relations 8th, December 1942. New York: International Secretariat, Institute of Pacific Relations, n.d. 12p.
Reviews the major provincial, state and all-India women's organizations and some of the more powerful women associated with them. Summarizes the female suffrage movement in India. Describes progress of education and major social and legislative reforms.

1264 Stri Dharma. vl-19 (1918-1936). Madras: Women's Indian Association.
[Unexamined. ULS, BUP].

1265 SWAMINATHAN, V.S. Women's movement in India. *In* Contemporary Review 174,991 (1948) 26-30.
Presents three reasons for the success and effectiveness of the Indian women's movement, both in general and vis à vis the women's movement in England: the dominant religions, Hinduism and Islam, venerate women and motherhood; women were prominent in political agitations; and struggles of women in the West paved the way. Reviews activities of the women's movement in the 1940s.

1266 VAN DOREN, ALICE B. Modern movements among women in India. *In* International Review of Missions 17,66 (1928) 291-305.
Surveys changes that took place in Indian society due to the women's and social reform movements. Offers some comparisons with western women's movements.

1267 WOMEN'S INDIAN ASSOCIATION. Report. 1-? (1917/18-1945/46?). Madras? Annually.
[Unexamined. MRL].

1268 YOUNG WOMEN'S CHRISTIAN ASSOCIATION OF INDIA, BURMA AND CEYLON. Conference reports. vl-? (1893?-?). Triennially or quadrennially.
[Unexamined. MRL].

1269 YOUNG WOMEN'S CHRISTIAN ASSOCIATION OF INDIA, BURMA AND CEYLON. NATIONAL COMMITTEE. Report. vl-? (1897?-?). Annually.
[Unexamined. MRL].

(3) Political participation: rapid strides within limited sectors

1270 ASAF ALI, ARUNA. Women's suffrage in India. *In* Shyam Kumari Nehru, ed. Our cause: a symposium by Indian women. Allahabad: Kitabistan, 1938? pp.345-65.
Discusses the history of the women's suffrage movements in India and England and the obstacles that remain to women's political participation. "The gaining of the vote will prove meaningless if it does not open up to women new opportunities of services and of self and national development."

1271 BONDURANT, JOAN V. India's stateswomen. *In* Independent Woman 27,10 (1948) 282-4.
Regarding several of the most prominent, politically active women in India upon its independence.

1272 BOSE, MRS. P.K. Women's franchise. *In* Indian Social Reformer 43,47 (15 Jul 1933) 729-30. [*Reprint from* Modern Review 54,1 (1933) 88-90].

Urges broadening of categories of women who are eligible to vote. Suggests potential range of inclusion and special provisions, as for women observing ***pardā***.

1273 DATTA, JATINDRA MOHAN. Vote for women: how they use it. *In* Quarterly J. of the Local Self-Government Institute 9 (Jan 1939) 243-50.
Analyzes voting figures. [Unexamined].

1274 FORBES, GERALDINE H. "Votes for women": the demand for women's franchise in India, 1917-1937. *In* Vina Mazumdar, ed. Symbols of power: studies on the political status of women in India. Bombay: Allied Publishers, 1979. pp.3-23. (SNDT Women's University, Bombay; Women in a Changing Society).
Traces franchise issue from first franchise delegation in 1917 until first elections held under 1935 Government of India Act in 1937. Refutes popular notion that the struggle was easy and argues that major impetus for demand for vote came from influence of British women and nationalist movement rather than ideas concerning needs of Indian women. Extensive use of historical sources. [Manuscript examined].

1275 GRAY, MRS. R.M. Women in Indian politics. *In* John Cumming, ed. Political India, 1832-1932. London: Oxford University Press, 1932. pp.156-65.
Primarily details the movement for women's franchise in India from the Montagu-Chelmsford Reforms of 1921, which allowed provincial legislative councils the prerogative to enfranchise women, to the Indian Franchise Committee's recommendations of 1932.

1276 GREAT BRITAIN. INDIAN FRANCHISE COMMITTEE. Report. Calcutta: Government of India Central Publication Branch, 1932. 5v.
Volumes two through five contain oral and written evidence, by province, collected by the Indian Franchise Committee. This committee was charged with ascertaining public opinion on franchise reforms in anticipation of a new constitution. The first volume reproduces the committee's subsequent report. Material on women interspersed throughout.

1277 HAJRAH BEGAM. Women in the party in the early years. *In* New Age 23,50 (14 Dec 1975) 11-2.
Anecdotes and reminiscences by a woman who joined the Communist Party of India in 1937. Discusses women's reasons for joining and activities in the years 1936 to 1946.

1278 KATZENSTEIN, MARY FAINSOD. Towards equality? Cause and consequence of the political prominence of women in India. *In* Asian Survey 18,5 (1978) 473-86.
Examines three issues: 1) extent to which women hold elite political positions, 2) possible explanations for prominence of women at elite political levels and 3) impact of female political participation on position of women in society at large. Argues that a small number of women have been highly visible due to historical circumstances of nationalist movement. Benefits for women as a whole have been "insubstantial."

1279 KHERA, P.N. History of female franchise in India. *In* Indian History Congress 5, 1941, Hyderabad. Proceedings 5. Hyderabad: printed at Osmania University Press and Azam Steam Press, 1943. pp.543-5.
Summary of the paper. Surveys political participation of Indian women in the nationalist movement and in wartime activities. Describes the movement for the vote from the 1917 deputation to Lord Montagu to provisions for franchise under the Government of India Act of 1935. Includes several criticisms of the provisions.

1280 MEHTA, HANSA. Political status of the Indian woman. *In* Shyam Kumari Nehru, ed. Our cause: a symposium by Indian women. Allahabad: Kitabistan, 1938? pp.339-44.
Briefly describes "the political status of the Indian woman as it was, as it is and as it should be."

1281 MORAES, FRANK. In political life. *In* Tara Ali Baig, ed. Women of India. Delhi: Publications Division, Ministry of Information and Broadcasting, Government of India, 1958. pp.90-104.
Traces important political activity by women in India beginning with the fight for women's enfranchisement, 1917-26, and including participation in Gandhi's ***satyāgraha*** movement and election and appointment to government positions. Focuses on notable women as well as general trends. Photographs.

1282 ONE WHO KNOWS, comp. Mrs. Margaret Cousins and her work in India, with a brief life sketch of her colleagues and comrades. Adyar, Madras: Avvai Home, 1956. 84p.
Collection of many documents (newspaper articles, letters, speeches, photographs and so forth) relating to the movement for women's suffrage in India. The title is misleading; while Mrs. Cousins' work for suffrage was very important, the documents reflect the work and involvement of many.

1283 SHAH NAWAZ, BEGAM [JAHAN ARA SHAH NAWAZ]. Indian women and the new constitution. *In* Asiatic Review n.s. 29, 99 (Jul 1933) 435-45. ***With*** Discussion, pp.446-58.
Text of a speech read to a distinguished audience of the East India Association. Criticizes the size of the female electorate proposed by the Indian Franchise Committee and the White Paper. Urges maximum enfranchisement. Text of the Association's discussion of the speech follows.

1284 STOCKS, MARY D. Eleanor Rathbone: a biography. London: Victor Gollancz, 1949. 376p.
Includes an account of Rathbone's trip to

India "to make contact with politically articulate Indian women for the purpose of achieving a better understanding of their point of view and of helping them to face the political and technical realities of the franchise problem." Appendix includes relevant correspondence.

1285 SUBBARAYAN, P. The political status of women under the new Indian constitution. Madras, n.d.
Pamphlet by a woman who was centrally involved in the women's franchise campaign. [Unexamined].

1286 TATA, HERABAI A. A short sketch of Indian women's franchise work. London: Pelican Press, n.d.
[Unexamined].

(4) Prominent personalities of the period: autobiographies, biographies and writings

Consult author index for additional writings that relate to women's issues, which are located according to topic

(a) Collected biographies, directories

1287 CHAPMAN, MRS. E.F. [GEORGIANA CHARLOTTE CLIVE BAYLEY CHAPMAN]. Sketches of some distinguished Indian women. London: W.H. Allen and Company, 1891. 139p.
The lives and work of Pandita Ramabai Sarasvati; Anandibai Joshi; Suniti Devi, Maharani of Cooch Behar; Toru Dutt; and Cornelia Sorabji.

1288 HUMPHREY, MRS. E.J. Gems of India: or, sketches of distinguished Hindoo and Mahomedan women. New York: Nelson and Phillips, 1875. 206p. [*Also* Cincinnati: Hitchcock and Walden].
Missionary's biographical sketches. Portraits.
[Unexamined. NUC].

1289 MUKERJEE, RADHAKAMAL et al. Great Indian women of the nineteenth century. *In* Swami Madhavananda and Ramesh Chandra Majumdar, eds. Great women of India. Mayavati, Almora: Advaita Ashrama, 1953. pp.395-413.
Biographical sketches of several queens, writers and social reformers.

1290 SEN, ELA. Wives of famous men. Bombay: Thacker and Company, Ltd., 1942. 122p.
Wives of statesmen and other prominent men from various countries. Includes sketches of Kamala Nehru and Kasturba Gandhi. [Unexamined. NUC].

1291 SEN, S.P., ed. Dictionary of national biography. Calcutta: Institute of Historical Studies, 1972-74. 4v.
Alphabetical arrangement of biographical sketches of prominent 19th and 20th century figures in India.

1292 SENGUPTA, PADMINI. Pioneer women of India. Bombay: Thacker, 1944. 195p.
Brief biographical sketches of 25 prominent and accomplished women of 19th and 20th century India. Illustrated.

1293 Women in India: who's who? Bombay: printed at the British India Press for the National Council of Women, India, 1935. 91p.
Biographical sketches of Indian women and western women in India of wide-ranging talents, interests and experiences during the 19th and 20th centuries. Major sections are "Members of Ruling States," deceased "Pioneers" and "Who's Who" of living persons. Planned as the first volume in a series, this may be the only one to have been released.

1294 WOODSMALL, RUTH FRANCES. Biographical sketches: Pakistan. *And* Biographical sketches: India. *In her* Women and the new East. Washington, D.C.: Middle East Institute, 1960. pp.391-5, 400-6.
Biographical sketches of 18 prominent contemporary women.

(b) Particular persons

i) The Sorabji family — Franscina and Kharsedji and their daughters, Susie and Cornelia

1295 SORABJI, CORNELIA. "Therefore": an impression of Sorabji Kharsedji and his wife Franscina. [London]: Oxford University Press, 1924. 87p.
Cornelia Sorabji's memoir of her parents. Parsis converted to Christianity, they became quite involved in the social reform movement, including women's issues, and fostered talented, pioneering daughters. Illustrated.
[Unexamined. MRL].

1296 ________. Susie Sorabji, Christian-Parsee educationist of western India: a memoir. London: Oxford University Press, 1932. 71p.
Memoir about the founder of St. Helena's High School in Poona (now Pune). The school fostered coeducational, interracial and intercultural education. By her sister. Photos.

1297 ________. India calling: the memories of Cornelia Sorabji. London: Nisbet and Company, 1934. 308p.
Cornelia Sorabji recounts her youth in a prominent Parsi Christian family, her educational successes in India and England, her success-

ful representation of an accused woman in court and her subsequent decision to become a lawyer to assist secluded women. Also describes involvement in Calcutta in the implementation of the Court of Wards Act, subsequent cases (many relating to princely families), her work for the establishment of the League of Social Service for Women and other work with secluded women. Much regarding the changing social and political climate of the early 20th century. Photographs.

ii) Mohandas Karamchand Gandhi, the Mahatma, 1869-1948

1298 AMRIT KAUR, RAJKUMARI. Gandhiji and women. *In* Visva-Bharati Quarterly, Gandhi Memorial Peace Number (1949) 166-71.
By an intimate female associate. Summarizes Gandhi's support of and expectations for women as, in his words, "the economic and moral solution of India."

1299 BOSE, ANIMA. Women in Gandhi's India. *In* India International Centre Quarterly 2,4 (1975) 280-91.
Discusses Gandhi's faith in ***strī śakti***, the power of women, and his favorable attitudes toward them.

1300 DASTUR, ALOO J. Gandhiji and the status of Indian women. *In* Indian J. of Social Work 30,3 (1969) 217-20.
Discusses Gandhi's efforts for the social and political equality of Indian women and their contributions to his ***satyāgraha*** campaigns.

1301 ________ and USHA MEHTA, eds. Gandhi and the emancipation of women. Bombay: SNDT Women's University, 1969?
Proceedings from the seminar, "Relevance of Gandhi to our Time," held in Bombay in September 1969. Has articles on Gandhi and women. [Unexamined].

1302 DIWAKER, R.R. Gandhi and the uplift of women. *In* Gandhi Marg 8,2 (1964) 120-6.
Gandhi's concern for women as part of his effort to raise humanity to "higher levels of existence." By the chairman of the Gandhi Smarak Nidhi. "There are one or two books which speak of 'Women in Gandhi's Life' or 'Women Behind Gandhi'. But it is high time that we had a book on 'Gandhi in Women's Lives' so that we may know how, when, to what extent and in what respect Gandhi influenced the innumerable eminent women of his time."

1303 GANDHI, MANUBEHN. Bapu, my mother. Tr. from Gujarati by Chitra Desai. Ahmedabad: Navajivan Publishing House, 1949. 56p.
Vignettes from Gandhi's last years by his grandniece and constant companion of this period. The title refers to the maternal aspects of Gandhi's personality that Manubehn experienced in her relationship with him.

1304 ________. Last glimpses of Bapu. Tr. from Gujarati by Moti Lal Jain. Delhi: Shiva Lal Agarwala, 1962. 348p.
Daily record of the last month of Gandhi's life, kept by his young grandniece and constant associate. Includes speeches and letters. Photos.

1305 GANDHI, MOHANDAS KARAMCHAND [MAHATMA GANDHI]. Anand T. Hingorani, ed. To the women. Karachi: the editor, 1941. 247p. (Gandhi Series, 2). [*Abridged ed.* The role of women. Bombay: Bharatiya Vidya Bhavan, 1964. 120p. (Pocket Gandhi Series, 9)].
Gandhi's collected writings and speeches on numerous topics relating to women, 1918 to 1940. Indexed.

1306 ________. Bapu's letters to Mira, 1924-1948. Ahmedabad: Navajivan Publishing House, 1949. 387p. [***Also*** Gandhi's letters to a disciple. London: V. Gollancz, 1951. 234p. ***And*** New York: Harper, 1950. 234p.].
Letters to Mirabehn (Madeleine Slade). [Unexamined. NUC].

1307 ________. Kaka Kalelkar, ed. Bapu's letters to ashram sisters from 6-12-1926 to 30-12-1929. Tr. from Gujarati by Arvindlal L. Mazmudar. Ahmedabad: Navajivan Publishing House, 1952. 115p.
To Sabarmati Ashram sisters. [Unexamined. NUC].

1308 ________. Women and social injustice, 4th enl. ed. Ahmedabad: Navajivan Publishing House, 1954. 207p. [*1st ed.* 1942].
Collected writings and speeches updated in the fourth edition to include all such material relating to women. Indexed.

1309 ________. Letters to Rajkumari Amrit Kaur. Ahmedabad: Navajivan Publishing House, 1961. 248p.
Nearly 300 letters selected from Gandhi's correspondence with Rajkumari Amrit Kaur document his brotherly relationship with his co-worker. Her work for Gandhi's movement in the villages and as a liaison with the public is also documented.

1310 KAMALADEVI [KAMALADEVI CHATTOPADHYAYA]. Woman the comrade. *In* D.G. Tendulkar et al., eds. Gandhiji: his life and work. Bombay: Karnatak Publishing House, 1944. pp.166-75. [***Also*** Bombay: Keshav Bhikaji Dhawale, 1944. pp.132-41].
Tribute to Gandhi's thought concerning and work for the betterment of Indian women as part of his service to all humanity. By a devoted female associate.

1311 KRIPALANI, KRISHNA. Gandhi and womanhood. *In* Indian Horizons 24,4 (1975) 25-9.
"Gandhi's concept of womanhood was universal

. . . . If Gandhi saw the divine in man, he saw even more of the divine in woman . . . . Gandhi had both tenderness and admiration for women and a high ideal of their role in human society . . . . Gandhi was at once revolutionary and conservative."

1312 MAZUMDAR, AMMU MENON. Women's welfare. *In her* Social welfare in India: Mahatma Gandhi's contributions. Bombay: Asia Publishing House, 1964. pp.86-120.
Considers the "new urgency" and action in women's social reform and welfare cause that Gandhi inspired. Women played an essential part in his nonviolent campaigns; he believed wholeheartedly in their equality. Views his influence vital to changes in attitudes of and toward women in India.

1313 MIRABEHN [MADELEINE SLADE]. The spirit's pilgrimage. New York: Coward-McCann, 1960. 318p. [*Also* London: Longman's].
Autobiography of a devoted disciple of Gandhi. As Madeleine Slade, the daughter of an admiral of the British navy, she read a book about Gandhi and knew she "was to go to Mahatma Gandhi, who served the cause of oppressed India through fearless truth and non-violence, a cause which, though focused in India, was for the whole of humanity. . . . The call was absolute." The following year, 1925, she went to India.

1314 MORTON, ELEANOR [ELISABETH GERTRUDE STERN]. Women behind Mahatma Gandhi. London: Max Reinhardt, 1954. 271p. [*Also* Bombay: Jaico, 1961. 311p. *And* The women in Gandhi's life. New York: Dodd, Mead, 1953. 304p.].
Considers Kasturba Gandhi, Putlibai Gandhi, Sarojini Naidu, Vijaya Lakshmi Pandit and Mirabehn, among many others. From personal letters, conversations, interviews, clippings, books.

1315 PATEL, M.S. Gandhiji on women and their education. *In his* Educational philosophy of Mahatma Gandhi. Ahmedabad: Navajivan Publishing House, 1953. pp.233-42.
General statement about Gandhi's attitudes toward women and discussion of their place in his ideas about education. Topics include: female education and national development, women as teachers, basic education and co-education.

1316 RUDOLPH, LLOYD I. and SUSANNE HOEBER RUDOLPH. The traditional roots of charisma: Gandhi. *In their* The modernity of tradition: political development in India. Chicago: University of Chicago Press, 1967. pp.155-249.
This account includes comments about Gandhi's preferred feminine identification. Women, he felt, embodied *ahiṃsā* ("non-harming"), self-suffering, caretaking and other desired qualities. Suggests that these qualities were a part of his successful appeal. Discusses British accusations of the "femininity" of non-martial groups in India and Gandhi's conflicts in this respect.

1317 RYLAND, SHANE. The theory and impact of Gandhi's feminism. *In* Feminine sensibility and characterization in South Asian Literature. Guest ed: Fritz Blackwell. 12,3/4 (1977) 131-44.
Reassesses Gandhi's views on women in light of many highly subjective sources that tend to eulogize this aspect of his work. Argues that in spite of complexities, which are often oversimplified, Gandhi was a "dedicated feminist" and was able to dramatically involve women in public life. Numerous references.

1318 SHRIDEVI, S. Gandhi and the emancipation of Indian women. Hyderabad, India: Gandhi Sahithya and Prachuranalayam, 1969. 132p.
Much regarding the women's movement. [Unexamined. ALI].

1319 Special number on Gandhi centenary. Women's Forum 3,3 (1969). 23p. [Unexamined].

iii) Kasturba Gandhi, "Ba," 1869-1944

For work of Kasturba Trust see "Social welfare" section, entries 2454-64

1320 BRIGHT, J.S. Woman behind Gandhi. Lahore: Paramount Publications, 1944? 160p.
Biography of Kasturba Gandhi. Describes her early married life, her experiences with Gandhi in Africa and London, her work for the Indian freedom struggle and her death and the response to it throughout India. Portrays her as an embodiment of the ideal Hindu woman. Concludes with description of establishment of the Kasturba Gandhi National Memorial Trust and selected quotes from Mahatma Gandhi relating to women, marriage and sexuality.

1321 GANDHI, M.K. Kasturba. *In* D.G. Tendulkar et al., eds. Gandhiji: his life and work. Bombay: Keshav Bhikaji Dhawale, 1944, pp.5-13.
Gandhi reflects upon his wife and marriage. Photographs from the later years.

1322 Kasturba — life and reminiscences. *And* Kasturba work — vision and view. *In* Kasturba memorial. Indore: Kasturba Gandhi National Memorial Trust, 1962. pp.121-42, 143-90.
Biographical details by relatives, coworkers and others.

1323 NAYYAR, SUSHILA. Kasturba: wife of Gandhi. Tr. from Hindi by the author. Wallingford, Pennsylvania: Pendle Hill, 1948. 71p. [*Also published as* Kasturba: a personal reminiscence.

Ahmedabad: Navajivan Publishing House, 1960. 102p.].
Biography written at request of M.K. Gandhi. Contains his brief introduction about his relationship with his wife. The author had a long relationship with both husband and wife and was involved in the Kasturba Gandhi National Memorial Trust after Kasturba's death.

1324 PRABHU, R.K., ed. Sati Kasturba: a life sketch, with tributes in memoriam. Bombay: Hind Kitabs, 1944. 87p.
Brief biography, from her birth to the national mourning of her death. Appendix of collected personal and press tributes upon her death.

1325 RAI, GANPAT. Gandhi and Kasturba: the story of their life. Lahore: Kasturba Memorial Publications, 1945? 156p.
[Unexamined. NUC].

iv) Sarojini Naidu, 1879-1949

Regarding Sarojini Naidu's poetry see entries 2722-42

1326 BAIG, TARA ALI. Sarojini Naidu. New Delhi: Publications Division, Ministry of Information and Broadcasting, Government of India, 1974. 175p. (Builders of Modern India).
Biography that benefits from the willing participation of many friends, relatives and co-workers. Focuses on her political life.

1327 BHATTACHARYA, K.K. Sarojini Naidu, the greatest woman of our time. *In* Modern Review 85,4 (1949) 289-91.
Tribute written shortly after Sarojini's death.

1328 NAIDU, SAROJINI. Speeches and writings of Sarojini Naidu, 3d ed. Madras: G.A. Natesan, 1925. 444p.
Speeches and writings to 1925 on diverse topics. Introduction provides brief biographical sketch.

1329 RAMASWAMI AIYAR, C.P. Srimati Sarojini Naidu. *In his* Biographical vistas: sketches of some eminent Indians. Bombay: Asia Publishing House, 1968. pp.107-11.
Biographical sketch by a long-time acquaintance. Discusses her early work as a poet and the later period when she "plunged into the struggle for women's emancipation and for self-rule for India."

1330 SARANGAPANI, M.P. Mrs. Sarojini Naidu. *In* Modern Review 39,1 (1926) 98-107.
Biographical sketch with family photographs.

1331 SEN, ELA. Sarojini Naidu. *In her* Testament on India. London: George Allen and Unwin Ltd., 1939. pp.109-21.
Biographical sketch of the "greatest woman of the present age." Focuses on her character and demeanor and her activities connected with the freedom struggle.

1332 SENGUPTA, PADMINI. Sarojini Naidu: a biography. Bombay: Asia Publishing House, 1966. 359p.
Includes much regarding her youth and poetry and her later political involvement in the Indian freedom and women's movements. With poems, letters, photographs.

1333 SUBRAHMANYA AYYAR, P.A. Sarojini Devi. Madras: Swathanthra Press, 1956? 124p.
[Unexamined].

1334 WISER, CHARLOTTE VIALL. "Madam President" in the chair in India: a woman's hands and her fiery words guiding the Indian National Congress. *In* Asia 26,7 (1926) 634-42.
Review of the 40th Indian National Congress gives prominence to Sarojini Naidu's activities and style as its president. Includes excerpts of a speech on Indian womanhood. Photograph.

v) S. Muthulakshmi Reddy, 1886-1968

1335 MUTHULAKSHMI REDDY, S. My experience as a legislator. Madras: Current Thought Press, 1930. 246p.
Author writes with two aims: to demonstrate to other Indian women how women's natural activities can be extended to concern for the nation as one's larger family, and to demonstrate to non-Indians the honor and respect Indian men have for their female colleagues. She discusses the various reforms she has advocated, including women's and children's health care and the abolition of the ***devadāsī*** and child marriage institutions. Appendixes reproduce legislative texts.

1336 ________. Autobiography of Dr. (Mrs.) S. Muthulakshmi Reddy. Mylapore: printed at M.K.J. Press, 1964? 175p.
Includes accounts of author's childhood, education and work for women's and children's social reform issues (particularly ***devadāsī***, age of consent and health care). Numerous appendixes reproduce key documents from her life. Photographs.

1337 REDDI, T.S. The story of a dedicated life. Madras: Shakti Karyalayam, 1949.
Biography of S. Muthulakshmi Reddy. [Unexamined].

vi) Kamaladevi Chattopadhyaya, 1903-

1338 BRIJ BHUSHAN, JAMILA. Kamaladevi Chattopadhyaya: portrait of a rebel. New Delhi: Abhinav Publications, 1976. 187p.
Biography by a long-time acquaintance based upon lengthy interviews with Kamaladevi, contemporary newspaper articles and other materials. Photographs.

1339 COBB, BETSEY. Kamaladevi Chattopadhaya. *In* Special issue: Asian women. Guest ed: Phyllis Andors. Bulletin of Concerned Asian Scholars 7,1 (1975) 67-72.
Biographical sketch.

1340 KAMALADEVI [KAMALADEVI CHATTOPADHYAYA]. Yusuf Meherally, ed. At the crossroads. Bombay: National Information and Publications, Ltd., 1947. 226p.
Collected speeches and writings, with a brief introductory biographical sketch by the editor. Among the papers are "Women's Movement in Perspective," originally written in 1944, and biographical sketches of Sarojini Naidu and Kasturba Gandhi.

vii) Jawaharlal Nehru, 1889-1964

1341 LUTHRA, BIMLA. Nehru and the place of women in Indian society. *In* B.R. Nanda, ed. Indian women: from purdah to modernity. New Delhi: Vikas, 1976. pp.1-15.
Gathers material from letters, newspapers, biographies and other sources to demonstrate Jawaharlal Nehru's progressive attitudes toward women.

1342 NEHRU, JAWAHARLAL. Foreword. *To* Tara Ali Baig, ed. Women of India. Delhi: Publications Division, Ministry of Information and Broadcasting, Government of India, 1958. pp.v-viii.
Nehru, then prime minister, pays tribute to the women of India for their important contributions to Indian civilization. He notes the progress women have made and hopes for the continued improvement of their status. Succinct statement of his view of Indian women.

1343 ________. Krishna Nehru Hutheesing, ed. Nehru's letters to his sister. London: Faber and Faber, 1963. 191p.
Ninety-three letters written from 1930 to 1955. Includes material on women's issues and his attitude toward his sister as a woman. Introduction by the editor.

viii) Vijaya Lakshmi (Nehru) Pandit, 1900-

1344 ANDREWS, ROBERT HARDY. A lamp for India: the story of Madame Pandit. Englewood Cliffs, New Jersey: Prentice-Hall, 1967. 406p. [*Also* London: Arthur Barker].
Adoring political biography. Photographs.

1345 BRITTAIN, VERA. Envoy extraordinary: a study of Vijaya Lakshmi Pandit and her contribution to modern India. London: Allen and Unwin, 1965. 178p.
Biography based, in part, on interviews with Vijaya Lakshmi Pandit and her three daughters. "Authorized" by her brother, Jawaharlal Nehru. Focuses on "her diplomatic achievements [especially after independence] against their international background."

1346 GUTHRIE, ANNE. Madame Ambassador: the life of Vijaya Lakshmi Pandit. New York: Harcourt, Brace and World, 1962. 192p.
Admiring biography that focuses on Madame Pandit's family, her involvement in the nationalist movement and her diplomatic career. Numerous photographs.

1347 JENSEN, IRENE KHIN KHIN. The men behind the woman: a case study of the political career of Madame Vijaya Lakshmi Pandit. *In* Contributions to Asian Studies 10 (1977) 76-93.
Attributes Madame Pandit's accomplished political career to personal qualifications and the support of four men: her father, her brother, her husband and Mahatma Gandhi.

1348 KHAN, ABDUL MAJID. Great daughter of India: an appreciative study of Mrs. Vijaya Lakshmi Pandit and her ideas in the background of Nehru family's heroic struggle for the political emancipation of India. Lahore: Indian Printing Works, 1946. 266p.
Essentially political biography stresses Mrs. Pandit's commitment to Gandhian ideals. Includes excerpts from her writings and speeches and some poorly reproduced photographs.

1349 KHIPPLE, R.L. The woman who swayed America: Vijaya Lakshmi Pandit. Lahore: Lion Press, 1946. 171p.
[Unexamined. MRL].

1350 PANDIT, VIJAYA LAKSHMI. So I became a minister. Allahabad: Kitabistan, 1939? 154p.
Collected essays and addresses, some autobiographical. Reveals author's increasing sense of personal freedom. [Unexamined. NUC].

1351 ________. The scope of happiness: a personal memoir. New York: Crown Publishers, Inc., 1979. 333p.
Mrs. Pandit reviews her life of great personal

fulfillment and public service. Details her participation in the changing social order of 20th century India. Main topics are her childhood and Nehru family background, the nationalist movement, her diplomatic career and the political "Emergency" of her niece, Indira Gandhi. Photographs (100).

1352 SAHGAL, NAYANTARA, CHANDRALEKHA MEHTA and RITA DAR, eds. Sunlight surround you. New Delhi: Nayantara Sahgal, 1970. 176p.
Selected tributes, edited by Mrs. Pandit's three daughters, which were published as a "birthday bouquet" for her 70th birthday.

ix) Indira (Nehru) Gandhi, 1917-

1353 ABBAS, KHWAJA AHMAD. Indira Gandhi: return of the red rose. Bombay: Popular Prakashan, 1966. 189p.
"I have sought to present . . . the story of Indira Gandhi . . . in the context of the series of revolutionary developments in India and the world, the events that influenced her, educated her, moulded her personality and her thinking." Up to her 1966 election as prime minister. Includes photographs and an interview with John Kenneth Galbraith.

1354 ALEXANDER, MITHRAPURAM K. Indira Gandhi: an illustrated biography. New Delhi: New Light Publishers, 1968? 204p. [*Also* Madame Gandhi: a political biography. North Quincy, Massachusetts: Christopher Publishing House, 1969. 226p.].
Short account focuses on her public life. Indian edition has photographs; American edition does not.

1355 ARORA, JAGDISH. Indira Gandhi, harbinger of peace. Lucknow: Puri Publishers, 1976. 174p.
"This book . . . presents . . . the quality and substance of her day-to-day life, statesmanship, dynamic leadership, democratic approach, national unity, national integration, self-reliance, education and youth, social welfare, mass media and arts, India and the world, emergency and 20-point economic programme and its implementation." Photographs.

1356 BHATIA, KRISHAN. Indira: a biography of Prime Minister Gandhi. New York: Praeger, 1974. 290p.
Author is a journalist. "In collecting material for it, I met Mrs. Gandhi's opponents as well as her supporters. In assessing the material I endeavored consciously to try to see that her successes — and they have been many — did not influence my judgement about her failures." Up to the 1971 war for Bangladesh. Photographs.

1357 CHOKSI, M. India's Indira. Bombay: Orient Longman, 1975. 180p.
Portrait of Indira as a courageous, dedicated but power-seeking leader. From her childhood to 1974. Photographs.

1358 DESAI, BHADRA. Indira Gandhi: call to greatness. Bombay: Popular Prakashan, 1966. 117p.
Life story of Indira Gandhi until her election as leader of the Congress Parliamentary Party, by a journalist who covered her career for many years. Aimed at youth, the book includes an interview Indira gave to *Kriti*, a publication of the Indian Youth Congress.

1359 DRIEBERG, TREVOR. Indira Gandhi. New York: Drake Publishers, 1973. 221p.
". . . a political study of the Prime Minister, timed for release at the start of the general election" in March 1972. Focuses on the 1960s and early 1970s. Photographs, selections from speeches and political documents.

1360 GANDHI, INDIRA. Half the world: thoughts of Indira Gandhi on women. New Delhi: Directorate of Advertising and Visual Publicity, 1975. 38p.
[Unexamined].

1361 ________. India: the speeches and reminiscences of Indira Gandhi, prime minister of India. Calcutta: Rupa and Company, 1975. 221p.
Includes memories of her childhood, her father and Mahatma Gandhi; some pieces on family life and 26 political speeches and articles dating from 1966 to 1972.

1362 HUTHEESING, KRISHNA NEHRU. Dear to behold: an intimate portrait of Indira Gandhi. London: Macmillan Company, 1969. 221p.
Affectionate and admiring biography by her aunt. Through Indira's 1967 re-election.

1363 Indira Gandhi: a heritage of power. Produced and directed by Paul Saltzman. 1976. 21 min. Color. 16mm. [*Distributed by* Eccentric Circle Cinema Workshop, Greenwich, Connecticut].
Film of interviews with Mrs. Gandhi in her home and at work. Focuses on her accomplishments and policies as India's prime minister. [Unexamined].

1364 Indira Gandhi of India. 1967. 52 min. Color. 16mm. [*Distributed by* Time-Life Multimedia Distribution Center, 100 Eisenhower Drive, Paramus, New Jersey 07652. *And* University of Washington, Audio Visual Services, B-54 Administration Building AC-30, Seattle, Washington 98195].
In this film Mrs. Gandhi discusses her Allahabad childhood, the influences of Mahatma Gandhi and Jawaharlal Nehru on her life, her participation in the nationalist movement and her attitudes about independent India and its government. [Unexamined].

1365 KARANJIA, R.K. and K.A. ABBAS. Face to face with Indira Gandhi. New Delhi: Chetana Publications, 1974. 127p.

Interviews with Indira Gandhi by authors and journalists. From her 1966 election as prime minister to the early 1970s.

1366 KHOSLA, G.D. T.S. Nagarajan and P.D. Chandwadkar, picture eds. Indira Gandhi. Delhi: Thomson Press, Publication Division, 1974. 152p.
Photograph album with a biographical sketch and a chronology.

1367 MASANI, ZAREER. Indira Gandhi: a biography. New York: T.Y. Crowell, 1976. 341p.
Political biography; from her early years up to the first months of the "Emergency" in 1975.

1368 MOHAN, ANAND. Indira Gandhi: a personal and political biography. New York: Meredith Press, 1967. 303p.
Based on extensive interviews with relatives, teachers, friends, coworkers, colleagues in government, members of her official and household staffs and critics. Up to her 1966 election as prime minister.

1369 MOODGAL, H.M.K., S. MAJUMDAR and R.K. SHARMA, eds. and comps. Indira Gandhi: a select bibliography. New Delhi: Gitanjali Prakashan, 1976. 275p.
Numerous sources (2,889) relating to or by Indira Gandhi, organized by topic. Reproduces chapter titles of books. Includes lengthy chronology of her life.

1370 Our Indira. Produced by Pramod Pati. Directed by S.N.S. Sastry. 1973. 15 min. Black and white. 35 mm. [*Distributed by* Films Division, Ministry of Information and Broadcasting, 24 G. Deshmukh Marg, Bombay 400 026].
Collection of film clips showing some of Mrs. Gandhi's activities and speeches as prime minister. [Unexamined].

1371 RAU, M. CHALAPATHI et al. Indira Priyadarshini. New Delhi: Popular Book Services, 1966. 116p.
Contains five essays (on Indira's life as a whole, her early years and as a politician), some of her "Significant Thoughts," a chronology of her life, political cartoons by Ranga and photographs.

1372 SEN, ELA. Indira Gandhi: a biography. London: Peter Owen, 1973. 198p. [*Also* Calcutta: Rupa and Company].
By a Nehru family acquaintance who focuses on the trials and difficulties Indira has faced and her development into a more secure and self-confident leader. With photos.

1373 SHARMA, P.L. World's greatest woman. Delhi: Indian School Supply Depot, Publication Division, 1972. 407p.
"To me, Mrs. Indira Gandhi is a Cosmic Mind. I have tried my best to present her real psychography." Primarily a political biography. Photographs.

1374 VASUDEV, UMA. Indira Gandhi: revolution in restraint. Delhi: Vikas Publishing House, 1974. 582p.
Major sections are "Life," "Power," "Leadership" and "Image." Up to her March 1971 reelection as prime minister. With a 1973 interview as epilogue. Based on interviews, unpublished correspondence and published material. Many photographs.

1375 ________. Two faces of Indira Gandhi. New Delhi: Vikas Publishing House, 1977. 208p.
Personal and political transformation of Indira Gandhi in the years 1971 to 1977, by a journalist.

x) Other Nehrus — Kamala Nehru, Krishna (Nehru) Hutheesing, Nayantara (Pandit) Sahgal

Regarding Nayantara Sahgal's creative writing see entries 2790-2801

1376 HUTHEESING, KRISHNA NEHRU. With no regrets: an autobiography. New York: Asia Press, John Day, 1945. 160p. [*Also* Toronto: Longmans, Green].
Biography written during a period of loneliness and isolation in 1942 when author's husband and other family members were imprisoned. Recounts her extraordinary childhood in the Nehru family and the turmoil of involvement in the nationalist movement. Name on title page is Krishna Nehru.

1377 ________. We Nehrus. Bombay: Pearl Publications, 1967. 343p. [*Also* New York: Holt, Rinehart and Winston].
Krishna Nehru writes of her exceptional family. Focuses on political involvement. Photographs.

1378 KALHAN, PROMILLA. Kamala Nehru: an intimate biography. Delhi: Vikas Publishing House, 1973. 145p.
Considers Kamala Nehru's marriage with Jawaharlal Nehru, her role in the freedom movement, her relationship with daughter Indira, her struggle with poor health and other topics. Includes many letters and photographs.

1379 SAHGAL, NAYANTARA. Prison and chocolate cake. New York: Knopf, 1954. 236p.
"We grew up . . . when India was the stage for a great political drama, and we shall always remain a little dazzled . . . . This is the story of its influence on our lives . . . . Much of the atmosphere we knew as children is fast vanishing . . . . So I have tried to recapture a little of that fading atmosphere." Growing up in Nehru family through college in America. Theme of individual and national freedom predominates.

1380 ________. From fear set free. New

York: W.W. Norton, 1963. 240p. [*Also* London: Victor Gollancz, 1962].
Author's perspectives on independent India and her place in it. Considers her marriage and motherhood, the prime ministership of her uncle, Jawaharlal Nehru, and other topics. A sequel to ***Prison and Chocolate Cake.***

xi) Other participants in the Indian freedom movement, women's movement and much else

1381 BAIG, TARA ALI. Durgabai Deshmukh. *In* B.N. Ganguli, ed. Social development: essays in honour of Smt. Durgabai Deshmukh. New Delhi: Sterling Publishers, 1977. pp.3-25.
Fond and detailed life sketch of this woman who has been freedom fighter, political scientist, lawyer, co-founder of the Andhra Mahila Sabha, educationalist, social worker (organizer of the Central Social Welfare Board) and legislator.

1382 COUSINS, MARGARET E. Mrs. Rukmini Lakshmipathi, first Congress Woman M.L.C. *In* Modern Review 57,6 (1935) 644-6.
Biographical sketch of a Telugu brahman woman known for her imprisonment (one year's hard labor) for making salt as part of the civil disobedience campaigns and her later election to the Madras Legislative Council in April 1935.

1383 DONGERKERY, KAMALA S. On the wings of time: an autobiography. Bombay: Bharatiya Vidya Bhavan, 1968. 246p.
Autobiography combined with her husband's biography. Includes details of her childhood in a middle-class Karnataka family, marriage, increasing influences of freedom movement, her participation in various women's organizations, worldwide travels, household staff and the various circumstances of her ten siblings and cousins. Photographs.

1384 DUTT, G.S. A woman of India: being the life of Saroj Nalini, 3d ed. London: Oxford University Press, 1941. 143p. [*1st ed.* London: Leonard and Virginia Woolf, 1929].
A husband's fond personal biography of his wife written shortly after her death. Considers her women's welfare work and particular Bengali associations that she influenced.

1385 KRIPALANI, SUCHETA. An unfinished autobiography. *In* Illustrated Weekly of India 96,1-2 and 9-10 (5-12 Jan and 2-9 Mar 1975) 22-7, 24-6, 29-31, 32-5.
Four installments from an autobiography interrupted by author's death. Primarily details her political participation in the freedom struggle and the events surrounding independence and partition. Kripalani became the first female chief minister of a state (U.P.) and was married to the freedom fighter Acharya Kripalani.

1386 ________. K.N. Vaswani, ed. Sucheta: an unfinished autobiography. Ahmedabad: Navajivan Publishing House, 1978. 265p.
Contains brief record of Kripalani's public activities, selections from her writings and speeches and tributes. Plates. [Unexamined. ALI].

1387 Lady Tata: a book of remembrance. Bombay: printed at the Commercial Printing Press, 1932. 159p.
Tribute to a prominent Parsi woman of Bombay who served the cause of female uplift. Contains life sketch; "appreciations;" accounts of memorial meetings, resolutions, tributes and press notices following her death; her collected speeches and letters; and photographs.

1388 MEHTA, USHA. I travelled west. Achalpur City: Sarwajanik Vachanalaya, 1966. 162p.
Autobiography of a woman who has been freedom fighter, political science professor and writer. [Unexamined. IBP].

1389 NATARAJAN, K. Lady Tata. *In* Indian Social Reformer 43,43 (17 Jun 1933) 661-2.
Admiring sketch of Lady Tata's philanthropical work that focused on women's issues.

1390 NAYER, SUSHILLA [SUSHILA NAYYAR]. Our changing life in India. *In* Barbara E. Ward, ed. Women in the new Asia: the changing social roles of men and women in South and South-east Asia. Paris: UNESCO, 1963. pp204-15.
Frank autobiographical account by an accomplished woman who was a physician for Gandhi, a member of Indian Parliament and a minister of health.

1391 NEHRU, RAMESHWARI. Gandhi is my star. Patna: Pustak Bhandar, 1950. 201p.
Collected writings and speeches. Major sections: "Women's Movement in India," "The Home and Women in India," "The Harijan Movement in India," "Thoughts on Education in India" and "Extracts from Addresses." Introductory matter gives some biographical background. Photographs.

1392 RAMA RAU, DHANVANTHI. An inheritance: the memoirs of Dhanvanthi Rama Rau. New York: Harper and Row, 1977. 305p.
Lady Rama Rau discusses a century of her family's history and her place in it, including her life as wife of a government official and her work with the women's and family planning movements.

1393 SEN, SUSHAMA. Memoirs of an octogenarian. New Delhi: Hilly Chatterjee and Jai Pradeep Sen, 1971. 706p.
Her childhood background in a family of scholars and reformers, her marriage to the Brahmo Samaj member P.K. Sen, her work for women's welfare and in politics, her family life and

much more. Includes many letters and photographs.

1394 SENGUPTA, PADMINI. The portrait of an Indian woman. Calcutta: YMCA Publishing House, 1956? 200p.
An admiring biography of Kamala Satthianadhan by her daughter. Mrs. Satthianadhan was a highly educated South Indian Christian woman who, among other things, edited the *Indian Ladies' Magazine* and tutored a local rani, both after being widowed. Much detail concerning middle-class lifestyles in transition.

xii) Participants in the Muslim League, Pakistan movement and Pakistani women's movement

1395 DWARKADAS, KANJI. Ruttie Jinnah: the story of a great friendship. Bombay: the author, 1963? 63p.
Biography of the Parsi wife of Mohammad Ali Jinnah with many anecdotes, letters and impressions. By a family friend.

1396 HUSAIN, M. ARSHAD. Miss Mumtaz Shah Nawaz. *In* Pakistan Quarterly 1,2 (1949) 24-5.
Tribute to this Pakistani poet, known affectionately as "Tazi," who died in a 1948 plane crash. Summarizes major stages of her work and briefly discusses her involvement in socialist and nationalist politics of Pakistan. Contains poetry selections.

1397 IKRAMULLAH, SHAISTA S. From purdah to Parliament. London: Cresset Press, 1963. 168p.
Autobiography of a prominent Muslim woman. [Unexamined. NUC].

1398 MAC BETH, MADGE. With faith and an ideal. *In* Independent Woman 30,8 (1951) 222-4, 247.
Biographical sketch of Ra'ana Liaquat Ali Khan, including her efforts for the emancipation of Pakistani women.

1399 MILES, KAY. The dynamo in silk: a brief biographical sketch of Begum Ra'ana Liaquat Ali Khan, 2d ed. Karachi: Educational Press, 1974. [*1st ed.* Rome, 1963].
Much on her social service work, including the founding of the All-Pakistan Women's Association. [Unexamined].

1400 Modern woman from the world's newest state. *In* Independent Woman 29,6 (1950) 173.
Brief biographical sketch of Ra'ana Liaquat Ali Khan, wife of Pakistan's former prime minister, Liaquat Ali Khan. Details her work for women's welfare in Pakistan.

1401 Quaid-i-Azam and Muslim women. Islamabad: National Committee for Birth Centenary Celebrations of Quaid-i-Azam Mohammad Ali Jinnah, Ministry of Education, Government of Pakistan, 1976. 73p.
Contents: "The Quaid as I knew him" by Jahan Ara Shah Nawaz, "Saviour of Muslim Women" by Salma Tasadduque Hussain, "Women and Politics" by Shaista Ikramullah, "Emancipation of Women" by Khudeja G.A. Khan, "Women and Independence" by Khurshid Ara Begam and "Muslim Women's Liberation Movement" by Parveen Shaukat Ali.

1402 SHAH NAWAZ, JAHAN ARA. Father and daughter: a political autobiography. Lahore: Nigarishat, 1971. 304p.
The author describes her background in a Panjabi Muslim family in which women were told, "Become worthy daughters of today and develop into women who could be the leaders of tomorrow." The family organized a women's society and was highly progressive in many respects. She tells how her father groomed her to be active in political life from the age of twelve. The account follows her family life (her daughter was Mumtaz Shah Nawaz) and her involvement with the women's movement and Muslim politics throughout the first half of the 20th century.

1403 Unveiled ambassadress. *In* Newsweek 43, 25 (21 Jun 1954) 38-40.
Short biographical sketch of Ra'ana Liaquat Ali Khan, the feminist widow of Pakistan's first prime minister. Appeared on the occasion of her appointment as Pakistani ambassador to the Netherlands, making her the first female ambassador from any Muslim nation.

(5) The myriad roles and activities of western women in colonial South Asia

See also entries 787-99 and sections on western women within "2. History and culture of the regions of South Asia. . ."

(a) Assessments of their lifestyle: primarily a dreary picture

1404 Anglo-Indian life: marriages, elopements, and disappointments. *In* Asiatic Journal n.s. 29,113 (1839) 12-23.
Circumstances and difficulties of marital arrangements among Europeans in India. Anecdotal.

1405 BILLINGTON, MARY FRANCES. Anglo-Indian society. *And* Notes on travelling and outfit. *In her* Woman in India. London: Chapman and Hall, 1895.

pp.271-93, 293-342.
View of a journalist who toured India to write a series on Indian women for the ***Daily Graphic***. Her assessment of Anglo-Indian life is rather critical. Biographical details of some highly placed women in the first chapter. Second chapter details her travel experiences.

1406 DAWSON, J.E. Woman in India: her influence and position. *And* The Englishwoman in India: her influence and responsibilities. *In* Calcutta Review 83 (Oct 1886) 347-57, 358-70.
Describes "the trials, the drawbacks, the difficulties that beset the path of the Englishwoman in India," including those who are native born, those who come as young brides and who arrive "at a maturer age." Instead of being engulfed in "the waters of fashionable life," Englishwomen must share their husbands' deep responsibility for improving the natives' conditions and for setting a high and honorable moral example for them to follow. Encourages the study of native languages, customs and history.

1407 DIVER, MAUD. The Englishwoman in India. London: William Blackwood and Sons, 1909. 259p.
Articles that originally appeared in ***Womanhood***. Contains "The Englishwoman in India" and "Pioneer Women of India." [Unexamined. NUC].

1408 AN ENGLISH-WOMAN IN INDIA. English women in India. *In* Calcutta Review 80, 159 (1885) 137-52.
Details problems faced by Englishwomen and their families in India including climate, health, servants, housekeeping, marriage, idleness, "gossip and scandal," economics and child rearing. "That English-women suffer greatly in India is certain, and the life that they are to a certain extent bound to lead, does not tend to lessen the evil."

1409 English women in Hindustan. *In* Calcutta Review 4 (1845) 96-127.
Attempts "to consider the position of our fellow-countrywomen in this land, and to note its particular advantages and disadvantages." Includes observations on domestic life, being the proper wife of a soldier, problems of "selfishness and inanity," remedies for boredom, opportunities for social service, etc.

1410 GANGULI, J.M. Englishwomen in India. *In* Indian Social Reformer 50,1 (2 Sep 1939) 9-10.
Diatribe against the frivolous lifestyles of Englishwomen in India. "By leading such life they make people wonder if the race which they represent is really deserving of the world possessions, which some intrepid, adventurous heroes of yore have secured and left for it."

1411 KINCAID, DENNIS. British social life in India, 1608-1937. London: George Routledge and Sons, 1938. 312p.
General survey with many anecdotes about particular personalities and events. Numerous plates and a substantial index.

1412 Married life in India. *In* Calcutta Review 4,8 (1845) 394-417.
Attempts to remove the common prejudices concerning British married life in India. Includes advice to Englishwomen on opportunities for self-cultivation and relations with the "natives."

1413 MARRYAT, FLORENCE (MRS. ROSS CHURCH) [FLORENCE (MARRYAT) CHURCH LEAN]. "Gup": sketches of Anglo-Indian life and character. London: Richard Bentley, 1868. 284p.
"Gossip," a series of recollections of British social life in India reprinted from ***Temple Bar***. [Unexamined. NUC].

1414 ROBERTS, EMMA. Scenes and characteristics of Hindostan, with sketches of Anglo-Indian society. London: W.H. Allen and Company, 1835. 3v.
Series of sketches on both "native" and "Anglo-Indian" society in India, originally published in serial form in ***Asiatic Journal***.

1415 STANFORD, J.K. Ladies in the sun: the memsahibs' India, 1790-1860. London: Galley Press, 1962. 145p.
Addresses two questions: "what was life like for a woman on board an east-bound sailing vessel in the nineteenth century, and what sort of life was she coming to when her vessel at last reached India?" Based primarily on diaries and letters. Photographs.

1416 TURKHUD, ALICE M. A visit to a zenana. *In* Indian Magazine 16,187 (1886) 371-3. *And* M.A.T. Observations. pp.373-5.
Englishwoman recounts her visit to a dark, prison-like zenana in western India. M.A.T. notes the corresponding wasteful monotony of the life of the typical Englishwoman in India and calls upon "***every Englishwoman*** out there" to undertake some form of social service work "and thus, while saving herself from herself, do the noble work of elevating her Native sisters."

[No entry 1417].

(b) Guides for domestic arrangements: cookery, servants, health, travels, etc.

1418 Dainty dishes for Indian tables, 2d ed. Calcutta: W. Newman and Company, 1881. 448p.
Complete manual of cookery "for the Anglo-Indian household." [Unexamined. NUC].

1419 DENNING, MARGARET B. Dainty cookery for the home: triple cookery containing English, American and Indian dishes. Madras: Methodist Publishing House, 1917. 236p.
[Unexamined. BMG].

1420 A LADY RESIDENT. The Englishwoman in

India: containing information for the use of ladies proceeding to, or residing in, the East Indies, on the subjects of their outfit, furniture, housekeeping, the rearing of children, duties and wages of servants, management of the stables, and arrangements for travelling; to which are added receipts for Indian cookery. London: Smith, Elder and Company, 1865. 211p.
[Unexamined. NUC].

1421 MACLEOD, ANNE C. [ANNE CAMPBELL (MACLEOD) WILSON]. Hints for the first years of residence in India. Oxford: Clarendon Press, 1904. 70p.
[Unexamined. BMG].

1422 PLATT, KATE. The home and health in India and the tropical colonies. London: Baillière, Tindall and Cox, 1923. 216p.
From preface: "This little book has been written in the hope that it may be of use to the woman who is making her home in India or in one of the tropical colonies of our empire." Considers domestic life, health, hygiene, child care and social and moral questions. [Unexamined. NUC].

1423 S., A.C. The Mem Sahibs' book of cookery, 2d ed. Calcutta? 1894. 283p.
[Unexamined. NUC].

1424 STEEL, F.A. and G. GARDINER. The complete Indian housekeeper and cook: giving the duties of mistress and servants, the general management of the house, and practical recipes for cooking in all its branches. London: W. Heinemann, 1898. 373p.
[Unexamined. NUC].

(c) Personalities: autobiographies, biographies, writings

See also entries 1503-1643 and 2075-93 and sections on western women within "2. History and culture of the regions of South Asia. . .," entries 2994-4629

1425 BARR, PAT. The memsahibs: the women of Victorian India. London: Secker and Warburg, 1976. 210p.
Detailed biographical accounts of several 19th century Englishwomen and briefer accounts of many others. Aims to portray the lifestyles of wives, mothers, sisters, teachers and other European women in British India.

1426 DYSON, KETAKI KUSHARI. A various universe: a study of the journals and memoirs of British men and women in the Indian subcontinent, 1765-1856. Delhi: Oxford University Press, 1978. 406p.
[Unexamined. ALI].

i) Emily Eden: travels in India as Lord Auckland's sister

1427 EDEN, EMILY. Portraits of the people and princes of India. London: J. Dickinson and Son, 1844. 24p., 24 plates.
Travel and description. [Unexamined. NUC].

1428 ________. 'Up the country': letters written to her sister from the upper provinces of India. London: R. Bentley, 1866. 2v. [*Also* With an introduction and notes by Edward Thompson. London: Oxford University Press, 1930. 410p.].
Travel and description. [Unexamined. NUC].

1429 ________. Her niece, ed. Letters from India. London: Bentley, 1872. 2v.
Travel and description. [Unexamined. NUC].

1430 ________. Violet Dickinson, ed. Miss Eden's letters. London: Macmillan, 1919. 414p.
Includes letters from India, beginning in 1835, when she went there upon the appointment of her brother, Lord Auckland, as governor-general.

ii) The Kinnairds: aristocratic Scottish family dedicated to social service

1431 FRASER, DONALD. Mary Jane Kinnaird. London: J. Nisbet and Company, 1890. 160p.
[Unexamined. NUC].

1432 KINNAIRD, EMILY. Reminiscences. London: J. Murray, 1925. 199p.
On YWCAs. [Unexamined. NUC].

1433 ________. My adopted country, 1889 to 1944. Lucknow, 1944. 124p.
On Indian civilization and the British in India. [Unexamined. NUC].

iii) Mary Carpenter: an English social worker promoting female education

1434 CARPENTER, JOSEPH ESTLIN. The life and work of Mary Carpenter. London: MacMillan and Company, 1879. 495p.
[Unexamined. NUC].

1435 CARPENTER, MARY. Six months in India. London: Longmans, Green and Company, 1861. 2v in 1.
On social life, women and education in India. The author, a well-known social worker from England, became involved with India in her later years. [Unexamined. NUC].

1436 ________. Addresses to the Hindoos, delivered in India. London: Longmans, 1867. 92p.
[Unexamined. NUC].

1437 M., S. Miss Mary Carpenter's first visit in Calcutta. *In* Calcutta Review 129 (Jul 1909) 257-66.
Describes the activities of the social reformer in Calcutta during her visit of 1866, including visits to women's schools, meetings and addresses concerning women's education and efforts to establish an Indian society for social science.

1438 MANTON, JO. India's daughters: 1866-1870. *In her* Mary Carpenter and the children of the streets. London: Heinemann, 1976. pp.194-210.
Account of Carpenter's visits to India late in life following a lifelong interest in the country. Discusses the circumstances and activities of her first trip, including her work for female education; her subsequent narrative, *Six Months in India*, and the acclaim it brought; her attempts to induce the Viceroy's Council to take a substantial responsibility for women's education; and her subsequent efforts for female education in India, at home and abroad.

iv) Annie Besant: interpreter of India to the West, theosophist, nationalist leader

1439 Annie Besant. Madras: Theosophical Publishing House, 1939. 155p. (Besant Spirit Series, 3).
[Unexamined].

1440 Annie Besant: builder of new India. Madras: Theosophical Publishing House, 1942? 156p.
[Unexamined].

1441 Annie Besant, warrior: a woman world-honoured. Madras: Theosophical Publishing House, 1943. 128p. (Besant Spirit Series, 11).
[Unexamined].

1442 BESANT, ANNIE. Annie Besant: an autobiography, 2d ed. London: T. Fisher Unwin, 1908. 368p. [*Also* Madras: Theosophical Publishing House, 1939. 653p. *1st ed.* 1893].
Besant's first 44 years, up to joining the Theosophical Society and before her "India work." Photographs. The Madras edition contains a biography by George S. Arundale, President of the Theosophical Society (pp.11-99), and a section of "Biographical Notes" (pp.469-653) compiled chiefly from Besant's own writings.

1443 ________. India bond or free? A world problem. London: G.P. Putnam's Sons, 1926. 216p.
"I propose to prove in the following pages that British Rule in India is inefficient in the matters that concern the Nation's life; that India is slowly wasting away and will inevitably perish, unless she regains her right to rule herself."

1444 ________. India, a nation: a plea for Indian self government, 4th ed. Madras: Theosophical Publishing House, 1930. 226p. [*1st ed.* London: T.C. and E.C. Jack *and* New York: Dodge Publishing Company, 1916. 94p. (The People's Books, 127)].
[Unexamined. NUC].

1445 BESTERMAN, THEODORE. Mrs. Annie Besant: a modern prophet. London: K. Paul, Trench, Trubner and Company, 1934. 273p.
[Unexamined. NUC].

1446 COUSINS, JAMES H., ed. The Annie Besant centenary book, 1847-1947. Madras: Besant Centenary Celebrations Committee, 1947. 264p.
[Unexamined. NUC].

1447 GUPTA, SUBODH BHUSHAN. Annie Besant: a political sketch. *In* Political Science Review 3,1 (1964) 89-100.
Brief account of Besant's efforts to help India achieve self-government.

1448 JINARAJADASA, CURUPPUMULLAGE. Biography of Annie Besant. Madras: Theosophical Publishing House, 1971. 73p. [*Also* Wheaton, Illinois: Theosophical Publishing House. *1st ed.* 1932].
[Unexamined. NUC].

1449 MANMOHAN KAUR. Annie Besant: a descriptive bibliography. Chandigarh: Panjab University, 1962. 75p.
[Unexamined].

1450 NETHERCOT, ARTHUR H. The first five lives of Annie Besant. Chicago: University of Chicago Press, 1960. 419p.
The lives of her "English phase": "Christian Wife," "Atheist Mother," "Martyr of Science," "Socialist Labor Agitator" and "Chela of the Mahatmas." Takes her up to her Theosophy involvement and details her growing interest in India.

1451 ________. The last four lives of Annie Besant. Chicago: University of Chicago Press, 1963. 483p.
These later lives are "Indian Educator, Propagandist, and Mystic," "President of the

Indian National Congress," "Deserted Leader" and "Life in Death." Numerous photographs.

1452 NIHAL SINGH, ST. Annie Besant: a personal impression. *In* Modern Review 54,5 (1933) 489-96.
Recollections of a contributor to Besant's *New India* newspaper.

1453 OWEN, HUGH F. Towards nation-wide agitation and organisation: the Home Rule Leagues, 1915-18. *In* D.A. Low, ed. Soundings in modern South Asian history. Berkeley: University of California Press, 1969. pp.159-95.
". . . aims to describe how [Annie Besant and Bal Gangadhar Tilak] took control of the Indian National Congress and committed it to the agitation which they had initiated on a nation-wide scale; how they drew increasing numbers into it and how . . . they helped to mould this movement and set it on the path that it was to follow for the next thirty years."

1454 _______. Mrs. Annie Besant and the rise of political activity in South India, 1914-1919. *In* R.E. Asher, ed. International Conference Seminar of Tamil Studies 2, 1968, Madras. Proceedings 2. Madras: International Association of Tamil Research, 1971. pp.257-66.
Regarding Besant's organization of the home rule movement in the Madras Presidency, her involvement in the movement for a separate Andhra province and her involvement in the South Indian non-brahman movement. Discusses her unique qualifications for these activities stemming from her "East meets West" theosophist concerns.

1455 PAL, BEPIN CHANDRA [BIPIN CHANDRA PAL]. Mrs. Annie Besant: a psychological study. Madras: Ganesh, 1917. 725p.
[Unexamined. NUC].

1456 PRAKASA, SRI. Annie Besant: as woman and as leader, 3d ed. Bombay: Bharatiya Vidya Bhavan, 1962. 225p. [*1st ed.* 1940].
Biography by the son of a Theosophical Society colleague of Besant. A personal and anecdotal account.

1457 RAMASWAMI AIYAR, CHETPAT PATTABHIRAMA. Annie Besant. Delhi: Publications Division, Ministry of Information and Broadcasting, Government of India, 1963. 152p. (Builders of Modern India).
[Unexamined].

1458 _______. Dr. Annie Besant. *In his* Biographical vistas: sketches of some eminent Indians. Bombay: Asia Publishing House, 1968. pp.90-106.
Brief life-sketch. Discusses Besant's unhappy marriage, politicization during a Parliament campaign in England, move to socialism and work for labor reform, conversion to Theosophy, efforts to increase the self-respect of Indians and involvement in the Indian freedom movement.

1459 RANGASWAMI AIYER, A. Dr. Annie Besant: her work for swaraj. Madras, 1955.
[Unexamined].

1460 ROBB, PETER. The government of India and Annie Besant. *In* Modern Asian Studies 10,1 (1976) 107-30.
Regarding Annie Besant's influence upon the shift from a governmental policy dominated by repression to one dominated by conciliation. Close documentation of political events in India from 1916 to 1920.

1461 STEAD, WILLIAM THOMAS. Annie Besant: a character sketch. Madras: Theosophical Publishing House, 1946. 100p.
[Unexamined. NUC].

1462 WEST, GEOFFREY. The life of Annie Besant. London: Gerald Howe, 1929. 295p.
[Unexamined. MRL].

v) Sister Nivedita: disciple of Swami Vivekananda, educator, nationalist sympathizer

1463 ATMAPRANA, PRAVRAJIKA. Sister Nivedita. Madras: Ramakrishna Math, 1967. 311p.
[Unexamined. IBP].

1464 BAGCHEE, MONI. Sister Nivedita. Calcutta: Presidency Library, 1956. 315p.
Considers the life and work of Sister Nivedita: her dedication to Swami Vivekananda, her pioneering work in educating Indian women, her part in the swadeshi movement and her writings. Concludes with brief statements about Nivedita by ten Indians and non-Indians.

1465 CHAKRAVARTY, BASUDHA. Sister Nivedita. New Delhi: National Book Trust, 1975. 84p. (National Biography).
Contribution to the National Biography Series in commemoration of International Women's Year.

1466 DASGUPTA, N.K. Biplab Sadhanay Nivedita. Calcutta: Debendra Granthalaya, 1970. 225p.
Biography of Nivedita. [Unexamined. IBP].

1467 FOXE, BARBARA. Long journey home: a biography of Margaret Noble (Nivedita). London: Rider and Company, 1975. 239p.
Biography based extensively on primary sources, many of which are cited in the text. Describes Nivedita's early life in England, her experiences with Swami Vivekananda and their consequences, her departure from the Ramakrishna Order for political work, her work for female education and famine relief,

her writings and her final days.

1468 MAJUMDAR, R.C. Sister Nivedita. *In* Bulletin of the Ramakrishna Mission. Institute of Culture 21,2 (1970) 29-33.
Biographical sketch given at the inauguration of the Sister Nivedita centenary celebration (1965-67).

1469 MAZUMDAR, AMIYA KUMAR, ed. Nivedita commemoration volume. Calcutta: Vivekananda Janmotsava Samiti, 1968. 321p.
Twenty-six commemorative essays on Nivedita's life, thought and work. Includes photos and manuscript facsimiles.

1470 NIVEDITA, SISTER [MARGARET ELIZABETH NOBLE]. Select essays of Sister Nivedita. Madras: Ganesh, 1911? 264p.
[Unexamined. NUC].

1471 ________. Studies from an eastern home. London: Longmans, Green and Company, 1913. 213p.
Continuing interpretations of woman, family, religion and other aspects of life in India for westerners. Preceded by a memorial statement and tributes to Nivedita.

1472 ________. The complete works of Sister Nivedita: birth centenary publication. Calcutta: Ramakrishna Sarada Mission, Sister Nivedita Girls' School, 1967-68. 4v.
From editor's preface: "In this edition of her works will be found all her original writings which we know to have been published by Nivedita herself or those posthumous publications which, we are convinced, are authentic." Photographs.

1473 ________. Pravrajika Atmaprana, ed. Sister Nivedita's lectures and writings: hitherto unpublished collection of lectures and writings of Sister Nivedita on education, Hindu life, thought and so on. Calcutta: Ramakrishna Sarada Mission, Sister Nivedita Girls' School, 1975. 427p.
Major sections are: "On Education" (including five pieces relating to women), "On Hindu Life, Thought and Religion," "On Political, Economic and Social Problems," "Biographical Sketches and Reviews," "Newspaper Reports of Speeches and Interviews" and "Miscellaneous Articles Written Before Meeting Swami Vivekananda" (including six pieces on women's rights).

1474 REYMOND, LIZELLE. The dedicated: a biography of Nivedita. Tr. from French. New York: John Day Company, 1953. 374p. [*French ed.* Nivédita: fille de l'Inde. Paris: V. Attinger, 1945. 350p.].
Biography based largely upon correspondence and interviews with Nivedita's relatives, friends, disciples and admirers.

1475 ROY, BHUPENDRANATH. Nivedita. Golamara, Purulia: Sraban Mahato, 1975? 163p.
Biography based primarily on Nivedita's writings. Discusses her early life and search, training under Swami Vivekananda, *gurubhakti*, concept of nationality and educational philosophy.

1476 SARKAR, JADUNATH. Sister Nivedita. *In* Bulletin of the Ramakrishna Mission Institute of Culture 21,11/12 (1970) 249-55.
Sketch of Nivedita's life from a talk originally given in 1952 by an admiring acquaintance.

vi) Margaret Cousins: champion of Indian women's advancement

1477 COUSINS, JAMES H. and MARGARET E. COUSINS. We two together. Madras: Ganesh, 1950. 784p.
Margaret Cousins was centrally involved in the Indian women's movement. [Unexamined. NUC].

1478 RAJWADE, LAKSHMIBAI. A tribute to Margaret Cousins. Madras, 1956.
[Unexamined].

vii) Wives of officials and civil servants

1479 BUTLER, IRIS. The viceroy's wife: letters of Alice, Countess of Reading, from India, 1921-25. London: Hodder and Stoughton, 1969. 190p.
Account of five-year residence in India as the wife of Rufus Isaacs, first Earl of Reading, sent to administer the Montagu-Chelmsford Reforms. From letters to her family. Photographs.

1480 DIVER, MAUD. Honoria Lawrence in 1843. *In* Cornhill Magazine 153,917 (1936) 513-26.
Account of Lady Lawrence's 900-mile trip across North India to join her husband, Sir Henry Lawrence, "first and best-loved ruler of the Punjab and the famous defender of Lucknow," who was to be the British resident at Nepal. Primarily selections from her journals and letters.

1481 DUFFERIN, MARCHIONESS OF [HARIOT GEORGINA (HAMILTON) HAMILTON-TEMPLE-BLACKWOOD, MARCHIONESS OF DUFFERIN AND AVA]. Our viceregal life in India: selections from my journal, 1884-1888. London: John Murray, 1890. 2v.
Collection of "journal-letters" written by the wife of the viceroy of India during his term of office. Includes accounts of social activ-

ities and travels.

1482 ELWOOD, COLONEL, MRS. [ANNE KATHERINE (CURTEIS) ELWOOD]. Narrative of a journey overland from England: by the continent of Europe, Egypt, and the Red Sea to India; including a residence there, and voyage home, in the years 1825, 26, 27, and 28. London: H. Colburn and R. Bentley, 1830. 2v.
[Unexamined. NUC].

1483 FITZROY, YVONNE. Courts and camps in India: impressions of viceregal tours, 1921-1924. London: Methuen and Company, 1926. 243p.
Account of a tour with Lord and Lady Reading. The author reports that her "indifference to [India] which seems the characteristic of the majority of men and women at home" was soon dispelled. It is "too challenging for indifference . . . . There is no high road to understanding, no single impression that is not tangled by half a hundred contradictions." Diary selections and recollections describe the tour and people, monuments and landscape encountered. Photographs (27).

1484 HARE, AUGUSTUS JOHN CUTHBERT. The story of two noble lives, being memorials of Charlotte, Countess Canning, and Louisa, Marchioness of Waterford. London: George Allen, 1895. 3v.
Text is extensively edited correspondence to, from and relating to these two sisters. The first volume is a family history. The second includes much material on Charlotte Canning's life in India, beginning in 1855 with her husband's appointment as governor-general. Includes details of the Mutiny of 1857-58. Volume three takes Lady Canning to her death in Calcutta in 1861 and is primarily concerned with her sister's widowhood in Europe.

1485 KING, MRS. ROBERT MOSS [E. AUGUSTA KING]. The diary of a civilian's wife in India, 1877-1882. London: R. Bentley and Son, 1884. 2v.
Includes impressions of Indian social life. [Unexamined. NUC].

1486 LAWRENCE, LADY [ROSAMOND NAPIER LAWRENCE]. Indian embers. Oxford: George Ronald, n.d. 397p.
Picture of the pleasures and trials of colonial life in India from 1914 to 1920 by the wife of a British commissioner of Belgaum and, later, Sind.

1487 LEONOWENS, ANNA HARRIETTE. Life and travel in India: being recollections of a journey before the days of railroads. Philadelphia: Porter and Coates, 1884? 325p.
She is Anna, of the "Anna and the King of Siam" story. [Unexamined. NUC].

1488 LOGIN, E. DALHOUSIE, ed. Lady Login's recollections: court life and camp life, 1820-1904, [*2d ed.* Patiala]: Languages Department, Punjab, 1970. 345p. [*Reprint of* 2d ed.].
Editor (Login's daughter) tells of "the strangely varied scenes through which my mother had passed in the course of a long life, and [of] how closely, on occasion, she had been brought into contact with the men and women who made the history of the nineteenth century." Based on letters, documents, notes and memories of Lady Lena Campbell Login's anecdotes regarding her experiences as the wife of a prominant civil servant in Lucknow and Lahore. With details of the royal families of these two cities, and Queen Victoria's involvement in Indian affairs. Photographs.

1489 Mrs. Chisholm. *In* Colonial and Asiatic Review 10 (Apr 1853) 284-90.
Mrs. Chisholm, the wife of an East India Company officer, had social service interests. [Unexamined].

1490 NICOLSON, NIGEL. Mary Curzon. New York: Harper and Row, 1977. 277p. [*Also* London: Weidenfeld and Nicolson, 1977].
Biography of Mary Leiter Curzon, born in Chicago, who married an English politician, George Curzon and later became vicereine of India. About one-half of the book deals with her life in India. Based on letters, diaries and other documents. Photographs.

1491 SURTEES, VIRGINIA. Charlotte Canning: lady-in-waiting to Queen Victoria and wife of the first viceroy of India, 1817-1861. London: John Murray, 1975. 319p.
Substantial portion of this book is devoted to Lady Canning's experiences in the upper echelons of English society in India as the wife of the governor-general who became the first viceroy of India.

1492 WOOD, MARIA LYDIA BLANE. Jane Vansittart, ed. From Minnie with love: the letters of a Victorian lady, 1849-1861. London: P. Davies, 1974. 188p.
Includes her years in India as wife of an officer during the last days of the East India Company, 1856-60. Discusses day-to-day management, childbirth, illnesses, the Mutiny, her unhappy marriage and other topics.

viii) Various travelers and a theosophist

1493 BECHER, AUGUSTA. H.G. Rawlinson, ed. Personal reminiscences in India and Europe, 1830-1888. London: Constable and Company, Ltd., 1930. 230p.
Travel and description. [Unexamined. NUC].

1494 COOK, NILLA CRAM. My road to India. New York: Lee Furman, Inc., 1939? 462p.
Account of travels and social life in India. [Unexamined. NUC].

1495 GOLLOCK, GEORGINA A. A winter's mails from Ceylon, India and Egypt: being journal letters written home. London: Church Missionary Society, 1895. 189p.
Impressions of life in the various countries. [Unexamined. NUC].

1496 LUTYENS, EMILY. Candles in the sun. London: Rupert Hart-Davis, 1957. 196p.
"This is the story of a spiritual ferment. It tells of my joining the Theosophical Society in 1910 and of how I came to leave it twenty years later; of the difficulties which my new faith caused in my domestic life and of the slow dissolution of that faith." Lady Lutyens describes her long involvement with the Theosophical Society and its political factions and her relationship with Krishnamurti. Photographs.

1497 M., C.M. [CLARA M. MINER]. Stray bits from the orient: experiences of an American in Hindostan — what she saw, heard and learned. Buffalo: Courier Company, 1892. 183p.
[Unexamined. NUC].

1498 MITCHELL, MRS. MURRAY. [MARIA HAY (FLYTER) MITCHELL]. In India: sketches of Indian life and travel from letters and journals. London: T. Nelson and Sons, 1876. 319p.
The wife of a missionary in Bengal and Madras. [Unexamined. NUC].

1499 SAVORY, ISABEL. A sportswoman in India: personal adventures and experiences of travel in known and unknown India. London: Hutchinson and Company, 1900. 408p. [*Also* Philadelphia: J.B. Lippincott Company].
Description of hunting and travel adventures. Numerous illustrations. [Unexamined. NUC].

1500 SETON, GRACE THOMPSON. "Yes, Lady Saheb": a woman's adventurings with mysterious India. London: Hodder and Stoughton, 1925. 366p. [*Also* New York: Harper and Brothers].
Lively account of author's travels throughout India and Ceylon in the early 1920s. Meetings with many notable persons of the day. Much on Indian women. Numerous photographs.

ix) Women in India as relatives of Indians

1501 HAUSWIRTH, FRIEDA [FRIEDA MATHILDA (HAUSWIRTH) DAS]. A marriage to India. New York: Vanguard Press, 1930. 303p.
American woman writes of her encounter with colonial India as the wife of an Indian. Portrays a difference in values that, in spite of her increasing interest in and acceptance of Indian life, could not ultimately be bridged.

1502 WERNHER, HILDA. My Indian family. New York: John Day Company, 1943? 298p.
European woman tells of her experiences in India in the 1930s as companion to her daughter who married a Muslim man. Among other things, life in India served as the inspiration for several novels.

(d) Writing inspired by the experience of India

1503 SMITH, D.J. The mem-sahib in her books. *In* Literary Criterion 9,4 (1971) 42-50.
Concerns the image of Englishwomen in India during the British Raj in the fiction of English men and women. It is on the whole not favorable although the female writers have been more sympathetic. Discusses stereotypes, ideals and quality of interaction with Indian women.

i) Flora Annie Steel and her works

See also entry 735

1504 PATWARDHAN, DAYA. A star of India, Flora Annie Steel: her works and times. Bombay: the author, 1963. 219p.
"This is a tribute, long overdue, to the memory of a simple, charming and colourful British author who through her novels, short stories and miscellaneous writings reveals India with love and understanding. Thus I pay, at least partially, the debt which my country owes to this remarkable woman." Treats her novels of British life in India, novel of the Mutiny, short stories, historical fiction relating to Mughals, portrayal of contemporary social life in India and role as ambassador of India to the West. Detailed bibliography includes Mrs. Steel's works and contemporary reviews.

1505 STEEL, FLORA ANNIE. From the five rivers. London: W. Heinemann, 1893. 212p. [*Also* New York: D. Appleton and Company].
Short stories. Contents: "Gunesh Chund," "The Blue Monkey," "Shah Sujah's Mouse," "Suttee," "At a Girls' School," "In a Citron Garden," "Mir Jehan," "Shurfee the Zaildar" and "Songs of the People." [Unexamined. NUC].

1506 ________. Miss Stuart's legacy. New York: Macmillan Company, 1893. 460p. [*Also* London: W. Heinemann, 1900].
Novel. British life in India.

1507 ________. The flower of forgiveness and other stories. New York: Macmillan

Company, 1894. 355p.
Short stories. From a contemporary review: "There is found here as intimate knowledge of the subject as that of Mr. Kipling, together with a vastly greater sympathy with native feeling and native suffering. The stories are intense, often tragic, with the tragedy of humble sacrifice and pain, and yet with glimpses of Anglo-Indian fun."

1508 _______. The potter's thumb: a novel. New York: Harper and Brothers, 1894. 351p. [*Also* London: Heinemann, 1898. 318p.].
Novel. Anglo-Indian life. [Unexamined. NUC].

1509 _______. On the face of the waters: a tale of the Mutiny. London: W. Heinemann, 1897. 475p. [*Also* New York: Macmillan].
Novel based upon events surrounding the Mutiny.

1510 _______. In the permanent way. New York: Macmillan Company, 1897. 400p. [*Also* In the permanent way and other stories. London: W. Heinemann, 1898. 306p.].
Short stories. Topics include Indian spirituality, problems of the childless wife, female seclusion, Indian social life and the Mutiny. [Unexamined. NUC].

1511 _______. The hosts of the Lord. London: W. Heinemann, 1900. 344p. [*Also* New York: Macmillan Company].
Novel. British life in India. [Unexamined. NUC].

1512 _______. Voices in the night. London: W. Heinemann, 1900. 365p. [*Also* New York: Macmillan Company. 418p.].
Novel. Anglo-Indian life. [Unexamined. NUC].

1513 _______. In the guardianship of God. London: W. Heinemann, 1903. 310p. [*Also* Leipzig: B. Tauchnitz. 269p. *And* New York: Macmillan Company. 357p.].
Short stories. Topics include Indian spirituality, servants in British households in India, Indian social life, the Mutiny and British social life in India. [Unexamined. NUC].

1514 _______. The mercy of the Lord. London: W. Heinemann, 1914. 311p. [*Also* New York: George H. Doran Company].
Short stories. Topics include Indian spirituality, servants in British households in India, problems of childless women, female seclusion, Indian social life, the Mutiny and British social life in India. [Unexamined. NUC].

1515 _______. The law of the threshold. London: W. Heinemann, 1924. 310p. [*Also* New York: Macmillan Company].
Novel. Anglo-Indian life. [Unexamined. NUC].

1516 _______. The garden of fidelity, being the autobiography of Flora Annie Steel, 1847-1929. London: Macmillan, 1930. 293p.
Written at age 82, this retrospective volume includes coverage of author's 30 years in India as the wife of a civil servant. Many observations about women and an account of her writing career.

1517 _______. Indian scene: collected short stories of Flora Annie Steel. London: Edward Arnold, 1933. 638p.
Short stories (37). [Unexamined. NUC].

ii) The fiction of Fanny Emily Penny

1518 PENNY, FANNY EMILY. The romance of a nautch girl. London: S. Sonnenschein, 1898. 359p.
Novel. [Unexamined. NUC].

1519 _______. The Sanyasi. London: Chatto, 1911. 328p. [*Also* London: P. Allen, 1936?].
Fiction. [Unexamined. NUC].

1520 _______. The Malabar magician. London: Chatto and Windus, 1912. 344p.
Fiction. [Unexamined. NUC].

1521 _______. The outcaste. London: Chatto and Windus, 1912. 426p.
Fiction. [Unexamined. NUC].

1522 _______. The swami's curse. London: Hodder and Stoughton, 1922? 319p.
Fiction. [Unexamined. NUC].

iii) The fiction of Maud Diver

1523 DIVER, MAUD [KATHERINE HELEN MAUD (MARSHALL) DIVER]. Candles in the wind. New York: John Lane Company, 1909. 392p. [*Also* Edinburgh: W. Blackwood and Sons, 1911. *And* New York: Dodd, Mead and Company, 1923].
Fiction. Life in India. [Unexamined. NUC].

1524 _______. Lonely furrow. Boston: Houghton Mifflin Company, 1913. 433p.
Fiction. Life in India. [Unexamined. NUC].

1525 _______. Sunia and other stories. Edinburgh: W. Blackwood and Sons, 1913. 345p. [*Also* Sunia: a Himalayan idyll, and other stories. New York: G.P. Putnam's Sons, 1913. 362p.].
Short stories (13). Some reprinted from various periodicals. [Unexamined. NUC].

1526 ________. Far to seek: a romance of England and India. Boston: Houghton Mifflin Company, 1921. 458p.
Novel. Colonial life. [Unexamined. NUC].

1527 ________. Ships of youth: a study of marriage in modern India. Boston: Houghton Mifflin Company, 1931. 496p. [*Also* Edinburgh: W. Blackwood and Sons, Ltd., 1931. 563p.].
Fiction. [Unexamined. NUC].

1528 ________. The singer passes: an Indian tapestry. Edinburgh: W. Blackwood, 1934? 582p. [*Also* New York: Dodd, Mead and Company].
Fiction. [Unexamined. NUC].

1529 ________. The dream prevails: a story of India. Boston: Houghton Mifflin Company, 1938. 431p.
Fiction. [Unexamined. NUC].

iv) The novels of Rumer Godden

1530 GODDEN, JON and RUMER GODDEN. Two under the Indian sun. New York: Alfred A. Knopf, 1966. 240p.
The Godden sisters fondly recall their childhood and youth in what is now Bangladesh as daughters of a steamer company employee stationed there.

1531 GODDEN, RUMER. Black narcissus. Boston: Little, Brown and Company, 1939. 294p. [*Also* London: P. Davies, 1939. 319p.].
Novel. The transformations of five Anglican sisters sent to establish a convent in a remote Himalayan community. [Unexamined. NUC].

1532 ________. Breakfast with the Nikolides. Boston: Little, Brown and Company, 1942. 291p. [*Also* London: P. Davies, 1942. 257p.].
Novel. Set in a government farm and school in East Bengal. Much on the conflicts between the European director's wife and older daughter. [Unexamined. NUC].

1533 ________. The river. Boston: Little, Brown and Company, 1946. 176p.
Novel. Children growing up in a European family in Bengal.

1534 ________. Rungli-rungliot means in Paharia: thus far and no further. Boston: Little, Brown and Company, 1946. 196p.
Account of an introspective year spent in a small settlement in Darjeeling District with her two children during World War II.

1535 ________. Mooltiki: stories and poems from India. New York: Viking Press, 1957. 151p. [*Also* London: Macmillan and Company, 1957. 135p.].
Poetry and short stories. A series of works set in Bengal, the Himalayas, Kashmir and the jungle.

1536 ________. Kingfishers catch fire, a novel. London: Macmillan, 1965. 293p.
Novel. A European widow with two children lives and identifies with peasants of Kashmir. [Unexamined. NUC].

1537 HARTLEY, LOIS. The Indian novels of Rumer Godden. *In* Mahfil 3,2/3 (1966) 65-75.
Traces development of literary skill and sensitivity to India in four novels set in India. Points to some features of Godden's autobiographical writings that illuminate literary concerns.

1538 SIMPSON, HASSELL A. Rumer Godden. New York: Twayne Publishers, Inc., 1973. 160p.
". . . an attempt to provide both a general estimate and a detailed analysis of her novels." Chapters on biographical background, her first three novels, various themes and *In This House of Brede* as a culmination of her distinctive style. Bibliography of primary and secondary sources.

v) Fiction by other western women

1539 DAS, FRIEDA HAUSWIRTH. Leap-home and gentlebrawn. London: J.M. Dent and Sons, 1932. 260p.
Short stories. Based on author's experience in India as the wife of an Indian. "The 'mysterious East' turns very humanly confiding eyes to anyone seeking it in simple, direct, kindly contact free from religious, race, or imperial bias." With author's illustrations.

1540 ________. Into the sun. London: J.M. Dent and Sons, Ltd., 1933. 311p.
Novel. Theme of the emancipation of Indian women based upon Gandhian ideals. [Unexamined. NUC].

1541 DUNCAN, SARA JEANETTE [SARA JEANETTE (DUNCAN) COTES]. The simple adventures of a memsahib. London: Chatto and Windus, 1893. 311p.
Novel. Englishwoman marries a tea and indigo clerk stationed in Calcutta and goes there to live. Illustrated.

1542 AN ELDERLY SPINSTER [MARGARET WILSON?]. Tales of a polygamous city. *In* Atlantic Monthly 120,6 (1917) 721-30; 121,1 and 5 (1918) 43-9, 601-14; and 122,4 (1918) 467-74.
Fiction? Experiences of a western woman in colonial North India among other westerners and natives.

1543 GRAY, MAXWELL [MARY GLEED TUTTIETT].

In the heart of the storm: a tale of modern chivalry. London: Kegan Paul, 1891. 339p. [*Also* New York: United States Book Company].
Novel. Young British couple in India during the Mutiny; focuses on poor position of women in Anglo-Indian society.

1544 A LADY. The East India sketch-book, 2d series. London: R. Bentley, 1833. 2v in 1. [*Also* The East India sketch-book: comprising an account of the present state of society in Calcutta, Bombay &c. . . New York: T. Foster, 1836. 250p.].
Fiction. Anglo-Indian social life. [Unexamined. NUC].

[No entries 1545-46].

1547 PERRIN, ALICE. East of Suez. London: Chatto and Windus, 1909. 311p.
Short stories. Set in India. [Unexamined. NUC].

1548 ________. The Anglo-Indians. London: Methuen and Company, Ltd., 1912. 312p.
Fiction. [Unexamined. NUC].

1549 ROSE, ISABEL BROWN. The measure of Margaret: a tale of India. New York: Fleming H. Revell Company, 1927? 256p.
Fiction. [Unexamined. MRL].

1550 ________. Diana's Indian diary. New York: R.R. Smith, Inc., 1930. 248p.
Fiction? Account of mission and social life in India. [Unexamined. MRL].

1551 UNDERHILL, BARBARA. The excellent way: a novel of Indian life. London: Highway Press, 1935. 170p.
Novel. [Unexamined. MRL].

1552 WERNHER, HILDA. The land and the well. New York: John Day Company, 1946. 243p.
Fiction. About a Jat family in Rajasthan. [Unexamined. MRL].

1553 ________. The story of Induraja: a novel. Garden City, New York: Doubleday, 1948. 251p.
Novel. [Unexamined. MRL].

1554 WILSON, MARGARET. Daughters of India. New York: Harper and Brothers Publishers, 1928. 369p.
Novel. Mission work in colonial Bengal.

1555 ________. Trousers of taffeta: a tale of a polygamous city. London: J. Cape, 1929. 285p. [*Also* Trousers of Taffeta: a novel of the child mothers of India. New York: Harper and Brothers, 1929].
Fiction? [Unexamined. MRL].

(e) Christian missions: "women's work" and other tasks

i) On women as missionaries, women as missionaries' wives and work among women

1556 BRYCE, L. WINIFRED. Life and work of women in the church in India. *In* National Christian Council Review n.s. 27,10 (1949) 429-31.
Regarding policy reformulation of working women in the Church and the Church's work for women. "India is now winning international fame from the quality of women who are serving the State . . . . Are Christian women not competent to make a comparable contribution in the service of the Church? The contrast is more poignant when one remembers that the modern advancement of Indian women has been made on the foundation of Christian education."

1557 CHRISTIAN MEDICAL ASSOCIATION OF INDIA. Women's hospitals. *In its* Tales from the inns of healing of Christian medical service in India, Burma and Ceylon. Nagpur, 1942. [*Also* Toronto: Committee on Missionary Education, United Church of Canada, 1944?].
History of medical mission work for Indian women. Photographs. [Unexamined. Book in NUC].

1558 FULLER, MRS. MARCUS B. [JENNY FROW FULLER]. The wrongs of Indian womanhood. New York: Revell, 1900? 302p.
Problems of women and social life in India; with Christianity as solution. Originally published in *Bombay Guardian*. With introduction by Pandita Ramabai Sarasvati. [Unexamined. NUC].

1559 HARRIS, E.F. and A.M. ROBINSON. About India. London: Church of England Zenana Missionary Society, 1933. 53p.
Has material concerning Indian women. Plates. [Unexamined. BMG].

1560 LEITH, M.L. Women's part in Indian mass movements. *In* International Review of Missions 27,3 (1938) 479-85.
Call for female European missionaries to work for the Church in India so as to advance the cause and prevent regression "until more young Indian women are available as leaders."

1561 LOVETT, RICHARD. Work among Hindu women. *In his* History of the London Missionary Society, 1795-1895, v2. London: Oxford University Press, 1899. pp.237-56.
Discusses schools, zenana work and female medical missions.

1562 LOWE, JOHN. Zenana medical missions: the qualifications, training, and position of the female medical missionary. *In his* Medical missions: their place and power, 3d ed. New York: Fleming H.

Revell Company, n.d. pp.177-98. [*1st ed.* 1886].
Argues the need for zenana medical missions and describes desired qualifications for various types of workers.

1563 MORELAND, ELIZABETH, ed. The life and work of women in the church: a research project by the Women's Work Committee of the Christian Council of India and Pakistan. Indore: Sat-Prachar, 1949. 142p.
[Unexamined. MRL].

1564 MURDOCH, JOHN, comp. Women's work for women. *In his* Indian missionary manual: hints to young missionaries in India, 3d ed., rev. and enl. London: James Nisbet and Company, 1889. pp.526-51.
Extracts and compiler's comments regarding the missionary wife, female education, zenana missions, literary work, voluntary English workers, voluntary native workers and social meetings. "No branch of missionary labour has developed more rapidly or is more promising."

1565 PHILLIPS, MRS. E.G. The work for missionaries' wives. *In* The Assam Mission of the American Baptist Missionary Union: papers and discussions of the jubilee conference held in Nowgong, December 18-29, 1886. Calcutta: the mission, 1887. pp.203-10.
The wife of a missionary stationed in Assam reexamines the purported drawbacks of marriage for male missionaries. Discusses the position of women as helpers and counterparts of men, the duties of wives as assigned by God and the Christian model of a devoted wife. Concludes that a wife who performs her God-given duties cannot be a hindrance to her missionary husband.

1566 PITMAN, EMMA RAYMOND. Indian zenana missions: their need, origin, objects, agents, modes of working, and results. London: J. Snow, 1903? 48p. (Outline Missionary Series).
Considers social conditions among Indian women and establishment, aims, personnel and results of zenana missions.

1567 VAN DOREN, ALICE B. Lighted to lighten the hope in India: a study of conditions among women in India. West Medford, Massachusetts: Central Committee on the United Study of Foreign Missions, 1922. 160p.
Indian women and mission work in their midst.

[Unexamined. MRL].

1568 ________. The women of India. *In* John McKenzie, ed. The Christian task in India. London: Macmillan, 1929. pp.43-65.
"Among the sixty millions of India's depressed classes, one-half are of course women and girls, and it is to them, perhaps, above all others, that the hearts of Christian women must turn in love and pity . . . . The special burden . . . is her responsibility toward her lowly sisters of the Christian community." Reflects upon the relationship of the message of Christ to the particularities of the socio-historical setting of 20th century India.

1569 VINCENT, SHELOMITH I. The kingdom of God and the rise of womanhood in India. *In* Message of the kingdom of God: Sat Tal Ashram essays, 1932. Calcutta: YMCA Publishing House, 1933. pp.287-310.
[Unexamined. Book in NUC].

1570 WEITBRECHT, MRS. [MARTHA (EDWARDS) WEITBRECHT]. The Christian woman's ministry to her heathen sisters in India. London, 1874.
[Unexamined. BMG].

1571 ________. The women of India and Christian work in the zenana. London: Nisbet and Company, 1875. 232p.
[Unexamined. BMG].

1572 WILSON, JOHN. Evangelization of India: considered with reference to the duties of the Christian church at home and of its missionary agents abroad; in a brief series of discourses, addresses, &c. . . Edinburgh: Whyte, 1849. 489p.
Considers duties toward Indian women. [Unexamined. MRL].

1573 WOODSMALL, RUTH FRANCES. Eastern women: today and tomorrow. Boston: Central Committee on the United Study of Foreign Missions, 1933. 221p.
First part discusses changing conditions of women in India, Burma, China and Japan. Considers education, health, religion, women's associations and rural life; also considers problems created by the changes. Second part discusses role and contributions of Christian missions in the development of eastern women. Photographs.

ii) Mission organizations devoted to women's work: histories and programs

1574 BAPTIST MISSIONARY SOCIETY. WOMEN'S MISSIONARY ASSOCIATION. Jubilee, 1867-1917: fifty years' work among women in the Far East. London: Carey Press, 1917? 51p.
Reviews the establishment of the then Ladies' Association for the Support of Zenana Work and Bible Women in India in 1867 and the subsequent growth of activities and organizations up to 1917. Lists mission stations (regular and medical), personnel connected with them and missionaries connected with the society over the years (great majority worked in India and Ceylon). Photographs.

1575 BARNES, IRENE H. Behind the pardah:

the story of the C.E.Z.M.S. work in India. New York: F.Y. Crowell and Company, 1897. 264p. [*Also* London: Marshall Brothers, 1899. 268p.].
On Church of England Zenana Missionary Society work from 1880 to 1897. Gives names of various female missionaries and quotes diaries and journals. Shows their perceptions of the problems of Indian women. Mostly on education; some attention to medical work. Illustrated. [Unexamined. NUC].

1576 _______. Between life and death: the story of C.E.Z.M.S. missions in India, China, and Ceylon. London: Marshall Brothers and Church of England Zenana Missionary Society, 1901. 302p.
Includes medical missions. Illustrated. [Unexamined. NUC].

1577 CHAMBERLAIN, MRS. W.I. Fifty years in foreign fields: . . . a history of five decades of the Woman's Board of Foreign Missions Reformed Church in America . . . 1875-1925. New York: the board, 1925. 292p.
Includes consideration of the India mission field. Plates, portraits. [Unexamined. MRL].

1578 CHURCH MISSIONARY SOCIETY. The awakening of India's womanhood: a sketch of C.M.S. educational opportunities in India and Ceylon. London: the society, 1912. 32p.
[Unexamined. MRL].

1579 CHURCH OF ENGLAND ZENANA MISSIONARY SOCIETY. Report. v1-? (1880/81-?). London. Annually.
[Unexamined. BUP].

1580 _______. Lamps of hope: glimpses of medical work among the women and girls of India and China in the hospitals and dispensaries of the C.E.Z.M.S. London: the society, 1919? 70p.
[Unexamined. MRL].

1581 _______. Jubilee souvenir, 1880-1930. London: the society? 1930? 36p.
Surveys work of 713 missionaries to India, Ceylon, China and Singapore. Contains a series of "Jubilee Greetings," a jubilee hymn, portraits of numerous workers with brief identifications, historical review, selected missionary and native statements ("Voices from the Past"), greetings from missionaries and "Voices from the Home Side."

1582 DAGGETT, MRS. L.H., ed. Historical sketches of women's missionary societies in America and England. Boston: the author. 1879. 142p.
[Unexamined. NUC].

1583 Daybreak. v1-88 (1886-1914). London?: Church of England Zenana Missionary Society.
[Unexamined. BUP].

1584 GRACEY, MRS. J.T. [ANNIE RYDER GRACEY]. Medical work of the Woman's Foreign Missionary Society, Methodist Episcopal Church. Dansville, New York: printed by A.O. Bunnell, 1881. 191p. [*Also* Boston: Woman's Foreign Missionary Society, Methodist Episcopal Church, 1888. 191p. *With* Supplement. 48p.].
Details the first, pioneering decade of work by this society in India and China, 1870 to 1880. Includes summaries of the contributions of various individuals. Illustrated. [Unexamined. NUC].

1585 [Heathen Woman's Friend. v1-? (1869-1896). Boston: Woman's Foreign Missionary Society, Methodist Episcopal Church. *Became* Woman's Missionary Friend. v?-73 (1896-1940).], [Woman's Missionary Record. v1-40 (1885-1924). Greensboro, New Jersey etc: Board of Missions, Methodist Protestant Church. *Became* Missionary Record. v41-53 (1924-1940)] *and* [Woman's Home Missions of the Methodist Episcopal Church. v1-57 (1884-1940). New York and Cincinnati]. *Became* Methodist Woman. v1-29 (1940-1968). Cincinnati: Board of Missions, Methodist Protestant Church. *Which, with* World Evangel. v1-87 (1882-1968). Dayton, Ohio: Women's Society of World Service, Evangelical United Brethren Church. *Became* Response. v1- (1969-). Cincinnati, Ohio: United Methodist Women.
[Unexamined. ULS, BUP].

1586 India's Women. v1-15 (1881-1895). London?: Church of England Zenana Missionary Society. *Became* India's Women and China's Daughters. v16-59 (1896-1939). *Absorbed* Zenana: or, Woman's Work in India. v1-42 (1893-1935). London: Zenana Bible and Medical Mission. Monthly. *Previously* The Indian Female Evangelist. v1-13 (1872-1893). London: Nisbet and Company. Quarterly. *Became* Looking East at India's Women and China's Daughters. v60-77? (1940-1957?).
[Unexamined. BUP, ULS].

1587 Missionary Herald. n.s. v1-93 (1857-1911). London?: Baptist Missionary Society. *Absorbed* Zenana Missionary Herald (1893-1895). London?: [1] Ladies' Association for the Support of Zenana Work and [2] Bible-Women in India and China, in connection with [3] Baptist Missionary Society. *Became* The Herald: The United Monthly Magazine of the [1] Baptist Missionary Society, [2] Zenana Mission and [3] Medical Auxiliary. v94-100 (1912-1918). *Became* Missionary Herald. v100- (1918-).
[Unexamined. BUP].

1588 MONTGOMERY, HELEN BARRETT. Western women in eastern lands: an outline study of fifty years of woman's work in foreign missions. New York: Macmillan Company, 1910. 286p.

Describes origin and growth of various mission organizations, conditions of women in non-Christian lands, the life story of several prominent female missionaries, changing conditions of women of the orient and financial, organizational and other needs. Much on work in South Asia. Photographs.

1589 News of Female Missions in Connection with the Church of Scotland. 1-?, n.s. 1-51 (1859-1869, 1876-1897). Edinburgn: Church of Scotland.
Previous to 1883 the Church of Scotland had a Scottish Ladies' Association for the Advancement of Female Education in India, which became the Ladies' Association for Foreign Missions and later the Church of Scotland Women's Association for Foreign Missions. [Unexamined. BUP].

1590 POLLOCK, J.C. Shadows fall apart: the story of the Zenana Bible and Medical Mission. London: Hodder and Stoughton, 1958. 221p.
Author has "sought to feature the most significant events, capture the spirit of the Mission's work and ideals, and portray the outstanding personalities down the years." From mid-19th century to 1958.

1591 SHERRING, M.A. Edward Storrow, ed. The history of protestant missions in India, rev. ed. London: Religious Tract Society, 1884. 463p.
Interspersed references to women's work; shows its place amidst early protestant mission efforts in India.

1592 WASSERZUG-TRAEDER, GERTRUD. Deutsche evangelische Frauenmissionsarbeit: ein Blick in ihr Werden und Wirken [The work of German evangelical women's missions: a look at their advent and activity]. München: Chr. Kaiser Verlag, 1927. 168p.
Has material on their work in India. Plates. [Unexamined. MRL].

1593 WIGRAM, E.F.E. The C.M.S. delegation in India and Ceylon. *In* Church Missionary Review (Jun 1922) 114-26.
Includes material on the Church Missionary Society's activities relating to South Asian women. [Unexamined].

1594 Woman's Work for Women. v1-15 (1872-1885). New York: Woman's Foreign Missionary Societies, Presbyterian Church. *And* Our Mission Field. v1-15 (1871-1885). New York: Ladies Board of Missions, Presbyterian Church. *Became* Woman's Work for Women and Our Mission Field. v1-4 (1886-1889). New York: Woman's Foreign Missionary Societies, Presbyterian Church. *Became* Woman's Work for Woman. v5-19 (1890-1904). *Became* Woman's Work. v20-39 (1905-1924). *Which, with* Home Mission Monthly. v1-38 (1886-1924). New York: Woman's Executive Committee of Home Missions, Presbyterian Church. *Became* Women and Missions. v1-23 (1924-1946). *Became* Outreach. v1-12 (1947-1958). New York: Board of National Missions, Presbyterian Church in the U.S.A.
[Unexamined. ULS, BUP].

1595 ZENANA BIBLE AND MEDICAL MISSION. Report. 1-? (1852-?). London? Annually.
[Unexamined. BUP].

iii) Firsthand accounts and contemporaneous biographies: rich sources for social history

1596 ARMSTRONG-HOPKINS, S. [SALENI (ARMSTRONG) HOPKINS]. Within the purdah, also, in the zenana homes of Indian princes, and heroes and heroines of Zion; being the personal observations of a medical missionary in India. New York: Eaton and Mains, 1898? 248p. [*Also* Cincinnati: Curts and Jennings].
Author was a doctor. [Unexamined. NUC].

1597 ________. Khetwadi castle: sequel to "Pork and mustard," v2. Syracuse: C.W. Bardeen, 1900. 401p.
Missions in India, medical missions and Indian customs. [Unexamined. NUC].

1598 BLACKWELL, M.L. Loving service: extracts from the diary and letters of Mary Lilian Blackwell. London: Partridge, n.d. 128p.
From 19th century India. A missionary? [Unexamined. MRL].

1599 BOOTH, MARY WARBURTON. "Take this child." London: Marshall, Morgan and Scott, 1926. 152p.
Zenana missions. Plates. [Unexamined. MRL].

1600 ________. "Whosoever shall receive. . ." London: Marshall, Morgan and Scott, 1929. 152p.
Zenana mission work. Plates. [Unexamined. MRL].

1601 ________. "They that sow." London: Pickering and Inglis, 1935? 199p.
Has material on Indian women and mission work. Plates. [Unexamined. NUC].

1602 ________. "These things I have seen." London: Pickering and Inglis, 1939. 186p.
Account of work in Indian missions. [Unexamined. NUC].

1603 ________. "Them also." London: Pickering and Inglis, n.d. 254p
Illustrated. [Unexamined. MRL].

1604 BRITTAN, HARRIETTE G. A woman's talks about India: or, the domestic habits and customs of the people. Philadelphia: American Sunday School Union, 1880? 214p.
By a missionary of Calcutta. [Unexamined. NUC].

1605 BROWN, JAMES H. Frances E. Brockway: memoirs . . . London: Unwin Brothers, Ltd., n.d. 140p.
Memoirs of a woman connected with India in the 19th century. A missionary? [Unexamined. MRL].

1606 BUTLER, CLEMENTINA. Mrs. William Butler: two empires and the kingdom. New York: Methodist Book Concern, 1929? 202p.
Daughter's recollections of a woman who served as a missionary in India. Plates. [Unexamined. MRL].

1607 CLARKE, FLORA. Sisters: Canada and India. Moncton, New Brunswick: Maritime Press, 1939. 682p.
Canadian women's missionary work among Indian women? Illustrated. [Unexamined. MRL].

1608 CLARKE, MAUREEN. Letters from India. London: Zenana Bible and Medical Mission, 1954. 68p.
[Unexamined. BMG].

1609 DAVIDSON, C.I. Up against odds. London: Church of England Zenana Missionary Society, n.d. 140p.
Mission work with Indian women. [Unexamined. MRL].

1610 DAWSON, E.C. Missionary heroines in India: true stories of the wonderful bravery of patient endurance of missionaries in India. London: Seeley, Service and Company, Ltd., 1924. 152p.
[Unexamined. MRL].

[No entry 1611].

1612 DEWAR, PHEBE RUTHERFORD. Janet S. Dey, ed. From India's burning plains: letters . . . Edinburgh: U.F.S. Women's Foreign Mission, 1924. 110p.
Letters of a missionary. Plates. [Unexamined. MRL].

1613 EVANGELICAL NATIONAL SOCIETY IN SWEDEN. Från Indiens kvinnovärld: en 20-årsskrift, utgifven af vänner till zenanamissionen [From the world of Indian women: a book of twenty years, edited by friends of zenana missions]. Stockholm: Evang. Fosterlands-stiftelsens förlags-exp., 1913. 83p.
Zenana missions. [Unexamined. MRL].

1614 FALLON, L. "Maika": the mother's home . . . London: Zenana Bible and Medical Mission, 1911? 118p.
Illustrated. [Unexamined. NUC].

1615 GRACEY, MRS. J.T. [ANNIE RYDER GRACEY]. Eminent missionary women. Chicago: Missionary Campaign Library, 1898. 208p.
Brief biographical sketches of 29 women. Those connected with mission work in South Asia are Mrs. T.C. Doremus, Hannah Catherine Mullens, Mary Reed, Fanny Jane Butler, Hannah Marshman, Harriet Brittan, Louisa Anstey, Eliza Agnew and Clara Swain.

1616 GRÜNDLER, O. Frauenelend und Frauenmission in Indien . . . [Women's poverty and women's missions in India . . .]. Basel: Missionsbuchhandlung, 1899. 84p.
Illustrated. [Unexamined. MRL].

1617 GUINNESS, LUCY E. . . . across India at the dawn of the 20th century. London: Religious Tract Society, 1898. 260p. [*Also* New York: F.H. Revell Company].
Mission life and impressions of India. Many illustrations, diagrams, maps. [Unexamined. MRL].

1618 HARVARD, WILLIAM MARTIN. Memoirs of Mrs. Elizabeth Harvard, late of the Wesleyan mission to Ceylon and India: with extracts from her diary and correspondence. London: John Mason, 1833. 130p.
[Unexamined. NUC].

1619 HIGGINBOTTOM, ETHEL CODY. Through teakwood windows: close-up views of India's womanhood. New York: Fleming H. Revell Company, 1926? 129p.
Missions and women in India. [Unexamined. NUC].

1620 _______. Bells of India: stories of life in the great peninsula. New York: Fleming H. Revell Company, 1931? 172p.
Indian social life and missions. [Unexamined. NUC].

1621 HUGHES-HALLETT, FLORENCE. Breaking fetters of Indian custom. *In her* Awakening of womanhood. London: Church Missionary Society, 1927. pp.39-54.
[Unexamined. Book in NUC].

1622 HUMPHREY, MRS. E.J. Six years in India: or, sketches of India and its people, as seen by a lady missionary. New York: Carlton and Porter, 1866. 286p.
Local life and missions. [Unexamined. NUC].

1623 KNIGHT, F.M. The shout of a king: a true story of the Zenana Bible and Medical Mission. London: Hodder and Stoughton, 1938. 256p.
Fictional account? [Unexamined. MRL].

1624 LATHAM, S.F. Memories of zenana mission life. London: Religious Tract Society, n.d. 96p.

Zenana missions in India. [Unexamined. MRL].

1625 LOWE, CLARA M.S. Punrooty: or, the gospel winning its way among the women of India. London: Morgan and Scott, 188_. 142p.
[Unexamined. NUC].

1626 Memoirs of Sister Elza Thronburg Antrim who gave her life in the mission fields of India. n.p., n.d. 111p.
Photographs. [Unexamined].

1627 MILLER, BASIL. Mother Eaton of India. Los Angeles: Bedrock Press, 1951? 132p. [*Also* 3d ed. Pasadena: International Gospel League, 1953. 172p.].
On Emma G. Eaton (b.1869), a missionary of the Church of the Nazarene. [Unexamined. NUC].

1628 MORLING, OLIVE M. Light in Hindu homes. London: Strict Baptist Mission, Ladies' Zenana Auxiliary, 1946. 67p.
Illustrated. [Unexamined. NUC].

1629 OTTMAN, NINA. The stolen god, and other experiences of Indian palace life, 2d ed. London: Carey Press, 1915. 85p.
Includes material on Indian women. Author was a medical missionary. Illustrated. [Unexamined. NUC].

1630 RAINY, CHRISTINA. A visit to our Indian mission field . . . Paisley: Parlane, 1887? 358p.
Contains material on Indian women. [Unexamined. NUC].

1631 ROTERBERG, H., ed. Was unsere Missionarsfrauen erzählen [What our missionary women relate]. Berlin-Friedenau: Gossnersche Mission, n.d. 94p.
Female missionaries in India. [Unexamined. MRL].

1632 SEAMANDS, RUTH. Missionary mama: the lighter side of the labors of those who serve the Lord in strange, exotic vineyards, revealed in delightfully realistic letters from India. New York: Greenwich Book Publishers, 1957. 128p.
[Unexamined. MRL].

1633 SOME OF THE MISSIONARIES OF THE ZENANA BIBLE AND MEDICAL MISSION. Bright gems for His crown. London: Z.B.M., n.d. 91p.
[Unexamined. MRL].

1634 TEMPLE, HELEN F. Branch of my planting: missionary stories from the heart of India. Kansas City, Missouri: Beacon Hill Press, 1954. 79p.
[Unexamined. MRL].

1635 THOBURN, J.M. Life of Isabella Thoburn. Cincinnati: Jennings, [1903]. 373p.
Isabella Thoburn spent 31 years in India as a Methodist missionary. [Unexamined. MRL].

1636 THOMPSON, JEMIMA. Memoirs of British female missionaries: with a survey of the condition of women in heathen countries and also a preliminary essay on the importance of female agency in evangelizing pagan nations . . . London: Smith, 1841. 251p.
Includes several women who worked in India: Mrs. Elizabeth P. Harvard, Mrs. Martha C. Mundy, Mrs. Margaret M. Clough, Miss Bird and Mary A. Smith. [Unexamined. MRL].

1637 UNDERHILL, BARBARA. Doctor Joan: of Australia and India. London: Church of England Zenana Missionary Society, 1941?
[Unexamined. NUC].

1638 WARNE, FRANCIS WESLEY. A tribute to the triumphant. New York: Methodist Book Concern, 1926. 95p.
Life of Mrs. Lois Stiles (Lee) Parker, 1834-1925, who worked in India. [Unexamined. MRL].

1639 WEATHERLEY, ELLA M. From West to East: being the story of a recent visit to Indian missions . . . London: Zenana Bible and Medical Mission, 1910. 128p.
On work with Indian women. Illustrations, portraits. [Unexamined. MRL].

1640 WEITBRECHT, MRS. [MARTHA (EDWARDS) WEITBRECHT]. Female missionaries in India: letters from a missionary's wife abroad to a friend in England. London: Nisbet, 1843. 151p.
[Unexamined. MRL].

1641 WHITE, ROSE. Daughters from afar. London: Partridge, n.d. 192p.
Mission work in India. Plates. [Unexamined. MRL].

1642 WILLIAMS, EDITH A. Heroines of India: for senior girls. London: United Council for Missionary Education, 1919. 64p.
Missionary heroines? [Unexamined. BMG].

1643 WILLIAMS, NANCY. Dawn of a new day: letters from India. London: Zenana Bible and Medical Mission, 1949. 62p.
Illustrated. [Unexamined. BMG].

b. Continuity and change in contemporary South Asia

For corresponding developments within cultural regions and areas of South Asia see "2. History and culture of the regions of South Asia. . .," entries 2994-4629

(1) The interest persists: studying women and women's studies

1644 AGNEW, VIJAY. A review of the literature on women. *In* J. of Indian History 55,1/2 (1977) 307-24.
Bibliographic essay surveys the history of interpreting Indian women in the 19th and 20th centuries. Most material reviewed relates to exceptional and/or urban women. Includes some unpublished papers. Somewhat analytical approach.

1645 BETEILLE, ANDRE. Position of women in Indian society. *In* Devaki Jain, ed. Indian women. New Delhi: Publications Division, Ministry of Information and Broadcasting, Government of India, 1975. pp.59-68.
Argues that while many have discussed the position of women in India, few have done so within an adequately sociological framework. This means that 1) women must be examined at the level of basic structural divisions (religion, region, social stratum), 2) behavioral facts must be compared with behavioral facts and behavioral ideals with ideals and 3) women of a particular segment of society must be evaluated in terms of that segment's norms.

1646 DUBE, LEELA. Woman's worlds: three encounters. *In* Andre Beteille and T.N. Madan, eds. Encounter and experience: personal accounts of fieldwork. Delhi: Vikas Publishing House, 1975. pp.157-77.
Author discusses her fieldwork among Gond women of Chhattisgarh, among women of a Rajput village in U.P. and on the island of Kalpeni in the Laccadive Islands of the present Lakshadweep Union Territory. She relates her experiences as a female fieldworker, noting how these varied with different contexts.

1647 INDIA (REPUBLIC). COMMITTEE ON THE STATUS OF WOMEN IN INDIA. Approach to the study of status of women in India. *In its* Towards equality: report of the Committee on the Status of Women in India. New Delhi: Department of Social Welfare, Ministry of Education and Social Welfare, Government of India, 1975. pp.1-8. [*Chair* Phulrenu Guha].
Discusses the complex issues involved in studying contemporary Indian women, the sources of data used by the Committee on the Status of Women in India and the constitutional and ethical framework within which the committee worked.

1648 INDIAN COUNCIL OF SOCIAL SCIENCE RESEARCH. Programme of women's studies. New Delhi: Indian Council of Social Science Research, 1977. 26p. (*Its* Publication 104).
ICSSR's women's studies program in the context of 1) *United Nations World Plan of Action* for women, 1975-85, and 2) *Towards Equality*, report of the government sponsored Committee on the Status of Women in India (entry 1704). Details completed and ongoing research sponsored by the ICSSR and the council's objectives, priorities and research funding program for women; provides names and addresses of members of the ICSSR Advisory Committee on Women's Studies and of persons directing its various research projects.

1649 Indian women: recent Indian publications. News and Reviews from ERC 8 (Dec 1975) 8-44.
Brief reviews of 14 books on Indian women published from 1970 to 1975 and a select bibliography of additional materials. Most concern 20th century events and personalities.

1650 JAIN, DEVAKI. Indian women: some reflections on a two-sector analysis. *In* Social Change 5,1/2 (1975) 17-20.
Discusses various models of the status of women in India. While none are totally incorrect, "much of the suspense as well as the differences can be resolved if women in India are divided into two classes — the rich and the poor." Paper elaborates upon this idea.

1651 MAZUMDAR, VINA and KUMUD SHARMA. Women's studies: new perceptions and challenges. *In* Economic and Political Weekly 14,3 (20 Jan 1979) 113-20.
Sketches the changing approaches and perspectives to studying Indian women over the 19th and 20th centuries. Poses various questions about transitions and discontinuities. Reviews and assesses contemporary programs, policies, trends and findings. Much on women's studies program sponsored by the Indian Council of Social Science Research.

1652 MUKHERJEE, BISHWA NATH. A multidimensional conceptualisation of status of women. *In* Social Change 5,1/2 (1975) 27-44.
Attempts both to adequately define and provide a means for quantifying the concept of the "status of women." Tests model using

rural and urban sample data from Haryana, Tamil Nadu and Meghalaya.

1653 PAPANEK, HANNA. The woman field worker in a purdah society. *In* Human Organization 23,2 (1964) 160-3.
Supports contention that ". . . the foreign woman working in a *purdah* society has certain unusual advantages in contributing to her own role definition in varying circumstances, whereas a man's role is much more rigidly defined."

1654 ________. Women in South and Southeast Asia: issues and research. *In* Signs: J. of Women in Culture and Society 1,1 (1975) 193-214. [*Reprint in* Social Change 7,2 (1977)].
Discusses research issues relating to immediate empirical problem-solving in Bangladesh, India, Pakistan and Indonesia. Asserts that poverty, overpopulation and employment are the overriding concerns within the social context of South and Southeast Asia. Also considers law and women's associations. Reflects upon sociology and psychology of scholarship and policy relating to women. Includes bibliographic review of research trends by country.

1655 SINGH, ANDREA MENEFEE. The study of women in India: some problems in methodology. *In* Social Action 25,4 (1975) 341-64. [*Reprint in* Alfred de Souza, ed. Women in contemporary India: traditional images and changing roles. Delhi: Manohar Book Service, 1975. pp.189-218. *Also in* Satish Saberwal, ed. Towards a cultural policy. Delhi: Vikas, 1975].
Examines problems and advantages associated with the particular gender of a researcher; women as a category; and the need to take dimensions of region, religion, family structure and kinship and marriage system into account in the study of Indian women.

1656 THAPAR, ROMILA. Looking back in history. *In* Devaki Jain, ed. Indian women. New Delhi: Publications Division, Ministry of Information and Broadcasting, Government of India, 1975. pp.3-16.
Argues that neither women's liberation nor any simplified scheme for change are especially appropriate to the complexities of women in the Indian subcontinent. Even when texts assign an unequivocal status to all women, contemporaneous historical evidence of diversity can be found. Discusses some important contextual variables that affect women (e.g., urban/rural, caste, heterodox/orthodox dimensions).

(2) Biography: dictionaries, directories, sketches of contemporary women

Directories relating to particular fields are located according to those fields

1657 Part 3: biographies. *In* B.K. Vashishta, ed. Encyclopaedia of women in India, 1976. New Delhi: Praveen Encyclopaedia Publications, 1976. Third part, pp.1-276.
Contains biographical sketches and addresses of several hundred contemporary Indian women. Many entries include photograph.

1658 Part 4: women recipients of national awards and honours. *In* B.K. Vashishta, ed. Encyclopaedia of women in India, 1976. New Delhi: Praveen Encyclopaedia Publications, 1976. Fourth part, pp.1-20.
Lists female recipients of various national awards. Provides year of award and mailing address.

1659 Who's who: contemporary Indian women. *In* Ajeet Cour and Arpana Cour, eds. Directory of Indian women today, 1976. New Delhi: India International Publications, 1976. pp.13-659.
Brief biographical sketches and mailing addresses of hundreds of living Indian women, arranged by profession. Many accompanied by photograph.

1660 Who's who of Indian women, international, v1. Amal, editor-in-chief. Madras: National Biographical Centre, 1977. 109p.
Biographical directory with several hundred entries, some accompanied by photograph. Prepared in Madras and influenced by South Indian naming patterns, the book is alphabetized according to first names. South Indians and Bengalis are well represented. The compilers attempted both to present well known women and to "discover talents." A supplement is planned.

(3) "Status of Women": many contemporary statements

(a) Women of particular nations — statements by South Asians

1661 AGARWALA, S.N., ed. Women and social change in Asia. Berlin: Maharashtra State Women's Council and German Foundation for Developing Countries, 1970. [Unexamined].

1662 ANURADHA and S.D. MUNI. Tradition vs modernity: women in Nepal and Sri Lanka. *In* Urmila Phadnis and Indira Malani, eds. Women of the world: illusion and reality. New Delhi: Vikas

Publishing House Pvt. Ltd., 1978. pp.30-54.
Briefly reviews social, economic and political status and future prospects of women in Nepal and Sri Lanka, respectively.

i) Indian women

1663 ASAF ALI, ARUNA. Women's role in a just world order. *In* Link 17,27 (16 Feb 1975) 9-26.
Various topics. Has brief sections on India's International Women's Year program, legal rights of Indian women, employment and unemployment, prostitution, education, sports, western influence and health problems, as well as brief statements about women's problems and activities in other countries, including Pakistan and Bangladesh.

1664 BAIG, TARA ALI. India's woman power. New Delhi: S. Chand, 1976. 301p.
Three parts. The first examines the changing position of women in India in the context of Asian social systems and values and contemporary worldwide trends. The second discusses the life cycle of the Hindu woman. Part three examines the changing position of Indian women, how these changes have affected society as a whole and what women have gained and lost in the process. This section includes a chapter on recent biological developments as they might influence Asian women and families.

1665 CHATTOPADHYAYA, KAMALADEVI. The place of women in the new society. *In* Modern Review 80,1 (1946) 21-4.
Argues for the elimination of double economic, legal, educational and moral standards and rights for men and women. Places status of Indian women in context of recent historical change.

1666 CHAUDHURI, NIRAD C. Women in social life. *In his* To live or not to live! An essay on living happily with others. Delhi: Hind Pocket Books, 1970? pp.67-86.
Light and anecdotal sketch of the position of women in contemporary India by a well-known journalist and author.

1667 DAS, VEENA. Indian women: work, power, and status. *In* B.R. Nanda, ed. Indian women: from purdah to modernity. New Delhi: Vikas, 1976. pp.129-45.
Critically reassesses notions of position of and attitudes toward Indian women by examining several issues: women as communications facilitators in kin networks, power and fear of women, the relation between work and the status of women and women's position in India as compared with women's position in the West.

1668 A daughter is as good as a son. Produced and directed by K.T. John. 1971. 13 min. Black and white. 16 and 35 mm. [*Distributed by* Films Division, Ministry of Information and Broadcasting, 24 G. Deshmukh Marg, Bombay 400 026].
Film about the changing position of women in India in recent decades. Suggests that women were exploited in the preindustrial and early industrial phases of India's history and that recently, with education and new employment opportunities, things are changing. Uses folk dance, classical dance and interviews to tell the story. Implicity encourages viewers to not bear children solely for the sake of having a son. [Unexamined. CF].

1669 DE SOUZA, ALFRED. Women in India: fertility and occupational patterns in a sex-segregated less developed society. *In* Social Action 26,1 (1976) 66-79. [*Expanded version* Introduction. *To* Alfred de Souza, ed. Women in contemporary India: traditional images and changing roles. New Delhi: Manohar, 1975. pp.ix-xxvi].
Argues that most Indian women experience discrimination more acutely than their sisters in developed countries due to sex segregation patterns, widespread poverty and traditional values. Discusses effects of these factors on fertility, health, education, marriage and occupations.

1670 DUBE, S.C. Men's and women's roles in India: a sociological review. *In* Barbara E. Ward, ed. Women in the new Asia: the changing social roles of men and women in South and South-east Asia. Paris: UNESCO, 1963. pp.174-203.
Provides a historical perspective, discusses contemporary attitudes and considers male and female roles in three types of families: tribal and lower strata rural and urban, upper strata rural and traditional upper strata urban and, lastly, progressive urban families.

1671 GUPTA, L.N. and KALYANI SHANKAR. "Men won't willingly give up a pampered status": an interview with Indo-Anglian novelist Nayantara Sahgal. *In* Eve's Weekly 29,27 (5 Jul 1975) 15.
Comments concerning the position of modern Indian women.

1672 INDIA (REPUBLIC). COMMITTEE ON THE STATUS OF WOMEN IN INDIA. Socio-cultural setting of women's status: changing milieu and roles of women. *In its* Towards equality: report of the Committee on the Status of Women in India. New Delhi: Department of Social Welfare, Ministry of Education and Social Welfare, Government of India, 1975. pp.83-91. [*Chair* Phulrenu Guha].
Discusses idea that although men and women are legally equal, "Indian society implicitly accepts a sharp distinction between men's spheres and women's spheres and between masculine roles and feminine roles." While women are generally associated with the home and men with the outside world, concepts of fem-

ininity and masculinity vary by region and community. Notes some patterns of division of labor and authority and some problems in combining home activities and outside work.

1673 Indian women. 1969. 20 min. Black and white. 16 and 35 mm. [*Distributed by* Films Division, Ministry of Information and Broadcasting, 24 G. Deshmukh Marg, Bombay 400 026].
Interviews with women about their lives. Considers influence of Gandhi and Kasturba. [Unexamined. CF].

1674 JANAH, SUNIL. The second creature. Calcutta: Signet Press, 1949. 13p.
Photographs of Indian women. [Unexamined. IBP].

1675 KALHAN, PROMILLA. Women. *In* S.C. Dube, ed. India since independence: social report on India 1947-1972. New Delhi: Vikas Publishing House, 1977. pp.215-39.
Survey article deals with education, work, legislation, politics and other topics in the context of recent reform movements. Also predicts future trends.

1676 KAPUR, PROMILLA. The changing role and status of women. *In* The Indian family in the change and challenge of the seventies: selected papers of a seminar organised by the Family Life Centre of the Indian Social Institute, New Delhi. New Delhi: Sterling Publishers, 1972. pp.46-59.
Contrasts the classical Brahmanic view of women as dependent and limited with the empirical view based upon changing evidence of women's capabilities in the 19th and 20th centuries. Discusses changing values and relationships, middle-class employed wives and their problems and changing expectations.

1677 KARVE, IRAWATI. The Indian women in 1975. *In* Perspectives, supplement to the Indian J. of Public Administration 12,1 (1966) 103-35.
Prominent female anthropologist predicts what the next ten years will bring to Indian women. Concentrates on trends and prospects for women in education and employment. Includes tables of male/female ratios in these areas.

1678 KHANNA, GIRIJA and MARIAMMA A. VARGHESE. Indian women today. New Delhi: Vikas Publishing House Pvt. Ltd., 1978. 212p.
Report of open-ended questionnaire given to 1,000 women from various parts of India and upper, middle and lower socio-economic groups. Chapters discuss their attitudes and practices regarding marriage, sex and family planning, the generation gap, "socio-economic and cultural aspects," fashion, social issues, employment and roles and ideals.

1679 KHOSLA, G.D. Status of Indian woman. *In his* A taste of India. Bombay: Jaico Publishing House, 1970. pp.69-85.
Former judge of the Punjab High Court argues that to assess the status of women they themselves must be asked whether they feel of inferior status, subservient to men and under the burden of disabilities. He points to the extensive legal provisions recently enacted on women's behalf and their limited effectiveness. The perplexing contemporary questions about the relations between the sexes "must be answered by men and women working together as a research team with equal, but not identical status."

1680 MAJUMDAR, LILA. Position of women in modern India. *In* Swami Madhavananda and Ramesh Chandra Majumdar, eds. Great women of India. Mayavati, Almora: Advaita Ashrama, 1953. pp.112-28.
Survey paper, with the author's attitudes and aspirations openly expressed.

1681 MANKEKAR, KAMALA. Women in India. New Delhi: Central Institute of Research and Training in Public Cooperation, 1975. 76p.
Booklet, issued in conjunction with International Women's Year activities in India, designed to "enlighten the public regarding various constitutional and legal provisions for the benefits of women and to provide talking points for generating debate and discussion" (from P.N. Luthra's Foreword). Includes historical survey from Vedas to present, summary of post-independence legislative reforms, discussion of opportunities in education and public life and various documents relevant to women's rights.

1682 MAZUMDAR, VINA. Towards equality? Status of women in India. *In* Urmila Phadnis and Indira Malani, eds. Women of the world: illusion and reality. New Delhi: Vikas Publishing House Pvt. Ltd., 1978. pp.17-29.
Discusses complexity of concept of status of Indian women. Considers Indian women's status from politico-legal and demographic perspectives. Asserts that the gap between noble ideals and dim realities for Indian women has not decreased since independence.

1683 MEHTA, RAMA. The status and role of women. *In* Ved Dan Sudhir, ed. The crisis of changing India. Delhi: National Publishing House, 1974. pp.195-200.
Optimistic statement about the remarkable changes that have occurred in the 20th century. "Today, in modern India the status of woman is one of equality and of dignity."

1684 MENON, LAKSHMI N. Indian women since independence. *In* Indian and Foreign Review 10,20 (15 Aug 1973) 27-9.
Briefly reviews the changing circumstances for women in India.

1685 MITRA, ASOK. The status of women. *In* Frontier 9,46 (1977) 6-9.
Assesses status of contemporary Indian women as quite low. Contains an outline of a program to bring about the most basis and essential changes.

1686 MUKERJI, D.P. The status of Indian women. *In* International Social Science Bulletin 3,4 (1951) 793-801.
Describes "the vague, pervasive unrest among modern Indian women," some of its causes and its effect on the family and marriage.

1687 MUKHERJEE, BISHWA NATH. The status of married women in Haryana, Tamil Nadu and Meghalaya. *In* Social Change 4,1 (1974) 4-17.
Survey of 1,872 women reveals that among obstacles to their higher status are low standard of living, illiteracy, traditional role beliefs and ignorance of their own fundamental rights. Discusses variations among the three sample areas. Includes tables.

1688 NARAIN, VATSALA. India. *In* Raphael Patai, ed. Women in the modern world. New York: Free Press, 1967. pp.21-41.
Broad survey concerned primarily with present circumstances. Topics include Vedic and post-Vedic society, property rights, legal status, marriage reforms, women's education, occupations, marriage patterns, family roles, political rights, women's organizations and needed improvements.

1689 Position of women: from bad to worse. *In* Economic and Political Weekly 13, 30 (29 Jul 1978) 1195-6.
Report of a recent study conducted by the Indian Council of Social Science Research that "has revealed an alarming trend of continued, and indeed accelerated, deterioration in the material conditions and status of women." Reviews some findings on life expectancy, employment, education and health.

1690 ROY, BINA. The status and role of women in our changing society. *In* B.N. Ganguli, ed. Social development: essays in honour of Smt. Durgabai Deshmukh. New Delhi: Sterling Publishers, 1977. pp.57-84.
Reviews problems Indian women face today in areas of employment, health, education, family life and psychological integration. Proposes solutions and priorities for solving these problems.

1691 SARMA, N.A. Woman and society. Baroda: Padmaja Publications, 1947. 120p.
Social and moral questions relating to Indian women. Has foreword by Kamaladevi Chattopadhyaya. [Unexamined. NUC].

1692 SEN, MRINALINI. Knocking at the door: lectures and other writings. Calcutta: Living Age Press, 1954. 208p.
On women in India. Author was a proponent of women's enfranchisement in Bengal. [Unexamined. NUC].

1693 SEN GUPTA, ANIMA K. The role of women in Indian public life in modern times. Ph.D. dissertation, Department of Sociology?, American University, 1958. 426p. [University Microfilms 58-2819].
Places recent trends of women's involvement in family life, religion, economic life, education, politics and women's organizations in context of social structural changes of modern Indian society. [Unexamined. DAI].

1694 ________. Indian woman: her position and problems in modern times. *In* J. of Family Welfare 10,4 (1964) 51-9.
Compares contemporary changes in the position of women in India with those of women in Europe and the United States.

1695 SENGUPTA, PADMINI. Women in India. New Delhi: Information Service of India, Ministry of External Affairs, Government of India, 1964. 58p.
Surveys historical transitions and contemporary circumstances. Illustrated. [Unexamined. IBP].

1696 SINGH, MALA. Women of India: the old order changeth, but only for a few. *In* Illustrated Weekly of India 91,31 (9 Aug 1970) 6-11.
Surveys the changing position of Indian women today. Photographs.

1697 SINGHI, NARENDRA KUMAR. Women in society: victims of institutionalized myths. *In* Ved Dan Sudhir, ed. The crisis of changing India. Delhi: National Publishing House, 1974. pp.201-13.
Argues, citing Simone de Beauvoir and other western authorities, that ideas about the nature of women are essentially culturally constituted. Urges "radical transformation of the value-structure, cultural ethos and social system, which have created myths of sexes and their discriminatory potentialities, leading to submissiveness and lack of full personal development of women."

1698 SRIVASTAVA, K.K. and J.N. LAL. Status of women in India. *In* Modern Review 138,4 (1975) 257-64.
Describes changes in the position of women in 19th and 20th century India. Briefly describes historical periodization of Indian women.

1699 TRIPATHI, HARSHA J. Changing attitudes of woman in post independent India. *In* J. of the Gujarat Research Society 29,2 (1967) 92-7.
Survey paper deals with many topics.

1700 VINOBA [VINOBA BHAVE]. Women's power. Varanasi: Sarva Seva Sangh Prakashan, 1975. 130p.
Recent lectures and essays on a variety of topics.

1701 WADIA, AVABAI B. Women's role in new India. *In* Asiatic Review n.s. 48,176 (1952) 248-56. *With* [Discussion], pp.256-65.
Lecture given at a joint meeting of the East India Association and the Over-Seas League. Summarizes the legal and social welfare position of women in the Republic of India. Summary of the discussion follows.

1702 WICKRAMANAYAKE, D. Plight of the

Indian women. *In* Plural Societies 6,4 (1975) 67-70.
Presents a completely negative picture of Indian women. Briefly contrasts India with Sri Lanka, which "has a different story to tell about her women."

1703 Women in India: a handbook. Bombay: Research Unit on Women's Studies, Shreemati Nathibai Damodar Thackersey Women's University, 1975. 84p. (*Its* Publication 1).
Briefly reviews various aspects of women's lives: education, work participation, political participation, legal position and women's organizations. From demographic and other perspectives.

ii) In depth investigation by the Committee on the Status of Women in India

1704 INDIA (REPUBLIC). COMMITTEE ON THE STATUS OF WOMEN IN INDIA. Towards equality: report of the Committee on the Status of Women in India. New Delhi: Department of Social Welfare, Ministry of Education and Social Welfare, Government of India, 1975. 480p. [*Chair* Phulrenu Guha].
Report of a committee constituted in 1971 by a Ministry of Education and Social Welfare resolution in order to obtain guidelines for social policy formation. The committee was charged with assessing the impact of legal and administrative provisions and educational and economic participation in the post-independent decades, comprehensively examining the social position of women and making recommendations. Data was gathered from personal tours, seminars, commissioned studies, consultation with experts and other means. The concise and multifaceted report treats the topics of studying women, demographic dimentions, socio-cultural contexts, legal position, economic opportunities, education, political position, welfare and development policies and programs, and influence of mass media. For descriptions of the various topical sections see entries 1647, 1672, 1760, 1977, 2168, 2251, 2316a, 2409, 2448, 2532, 2547 and 2658.

1705 KALHAN, PROMILLA. Do we underrate our women? *In* Eve's Weekly 29,15 (12 Apr 1975) 10-1.
Briefly considers composition and organizational problems of the Committee on the Status of Women in India and some of its major findings and recommendations. Identifies some of the 75 or so experts who contributed specialized reports.

1706 MASANI, MEHRA. Indian women: second-class citizens. *In* Illustrated Weekly of India 96,9 (2 Mar 1975) 4-13.
Brief report of the findings of the Committee on the Status of Women in India, with author's commentary.

1707 MASANI, SHAKUNTALA. Indian women: equal in law, unequal in fact. *In* Illustrated Weekly of India 94,22 (3 Jun 1973) 30-3.
Experiences, findings and recommendations of the Committee on the Status of Women in India after its first year and a half of investigation.

1708 MAZUMDAR, VINA. Status of women in India. *In* Demography India 4,2 (1975) 258-64.
Discussion of some demographic problems and considerations that emerged while the Committee on the Status of Women in India was preparing its report. Author was committee's Member-Secretary.

1709 Status of women in India: a synopsis of the report of the national Committee on the Status of Women, 1971-74. New Delhi: Indian Council of Social Science Research, 1975? 188p.
Synopsis prepared in order to make the committee's work more widely available. Seven chapters review findings and present recommendations: "Demographic Perspective," "The Socio-cultural Setting," "Women and the Law," "Roles, Rights and Opportunities for Economic Participation," "Educational Development," "Political Status" and "Policies and Programmes for Women's Welfare and Development." Opening chapter discusses approach of committee and appendix lists its members and provides 40 statistical tables and 12 graphs.

1710 SWAMINATHAN, MEENA. And miles to go. *In* Social Change 5,1/2 (1975) 21-6.
Review of the committee's report. "Ultimately, the Committee is betrayed by its own terms of reference for the complete social transformation that it seeks, based on the principles of equality and justice, is surely not a world *of* women or *for* women alone, but a new social order which can provide a better life for all, and the achievement which needs a social revolution in which both men and women must play a part."

iii) Pakistani women

See also entries 3845-58 and 4417-28

1711 AHMED, SHEREEN AZIZ. Pakistan. *In* Raphael Patai, ed. Women in the modern world. New York: Free Press, 1967. pp.42-58.
Briefly reviews Muslim political history in South Asia and effects of partition and independence upon Pakistani women. Reviews contemporary trends with respect to education, female seclusion, legal rights, marriage and divorce, employment, political participation, home life, jewelry and dress. Concludes with statement concerning the "Responsibility of

Educated Women."

1712 ALL-PAKISTAN WOMEN'S ASSOCIATION. Pakistani women look to the future. Rawalpindi: Ferozsons, 1960. [Unexamined].

1713 AMJAD ALI, ZAHIDA. The status of women in Pakistan. *In* Pakistan Quarterly 6,4 (1956) 46-53. Views changing opportunities for Pakistani women as an important consequence of partition. Reviews women's organizations, committees and a conference; women's political rights, employment opportunities and marital rights; and the recommendations of the Commission on Marriage and Family Laws established in 1955 as a response to public controversy about women's rights.

1714 BONDREY, RAZIA. Women of Pakistan. *In* Illustrated Weekly of India 91,3 (6 Sep 1970) 16-9. Discusses educational and career opportunities for contemporary Pakistani women. Numerous photographs.

1715 BURNEY, NAUSHABA. The new woman of Pakistan. *In* Perspective 1,12 (1968) 49-56. Describes changing opportunities for and activities of Pakistani women in recent decades. Photographs.

1716 FARIDI, TAZEEN. The changing role of women in Pakistan. Karachi: Department of Advertising, Films and Publication, Government of Pakistan, 1961? 30p. Illustrated. [Unexamined. NUC].

1717 HYDER, QURRATULAIN. Women of Pakistan. *In* Eastern World 7,7 (1953) 13. Highlights women's participation in the creation of Pakistan and in social reform.

1718 IKRAMULLAH, SHAISTA SUHRAWARDY. Pakistani women. *In* African Women 2,4 (1958) 89-92. Discusses traditional position of Pakistani women, difficulties westerners have had in correctly understanding these women and factors that have dramatically changed their lives. From address to Royal Society of Arts.

1719 ________. Behind the veil. Karachi: Pakistan Publications, 195_. 112p. Concerns Pakistani women. Illustrated. [Unexamined. NUC].

1720 KAMAL, MEHR. Women of Pakistan. *In* Perspective 3,12 (1970) 17-24. Profile of the improving status of Pakistani women and their increasing participation in government, education, professional careers and social welfare programs. Photographs.

1721 LIAQUAT ALI KHAN, BEGAM [RA'ANA LIAQUAT ALI KHAN]. The women of Pakistan. *In* Asiatic Review n.s. 45, 163 (1949) 726-8. Excerpts from an address given to the Advising Council of Women in Indian and Pakistan Affairs, London. Briefly discusses problems of partition, the Pakistan Women's National Guard and the Women's Muslim League.

1722 PARVEEN SHAUKAT ALI. Status of women in the Muslim world: a study in the feminist movements in Turkey, Egypt, Iran, and Pakistan. Lahore: Aziz Publishers, 1975. 248p. Regarding the status of women in these four countries with respect to education, family, social life, legal status and political rights. Separate chapters address position of woman in Islamic thought, women's movements in the various countries (including Muslim women in British India) and changing trends.

1723 Women of Pakistan, 3d ed. Karachi: Pakistan Publications, 1955. 86p. Reviews Pakistani women's participation in various spheres in the early years following independence. Illustrated. [Unexamined. NUC].

1724 ZEB-UN-NISA HAMIDULLAH [ZAIB-UN-NISSA HAMIDULLAH]. The progressive role of women in Pakistan. *In* Public Administration Review (Apr 1964) 12-22. Considers women as wives and mothers, educated and employed women and women in the public sphere. The author, a writer, states that the most important role that a woman must play, if she is to fulfill her destiny, is that of wife and mother: before she can succeed in any other sphere, she must succeed at home. Text of an address to an apparently all-male audience at the National Institute of Public Administration.

(b) Women of particular nations — statements by westerners

1725 FALLACI, ORIANA. The useless sex. Tr. from Italian by Pamela Swinglehurst. New York: Horizon Press Publishers, 1964. 183p. Journalist's view of the status of women in Asia. First two chapters discuss women in Pakistan and India, respectively. Includes a discussion of a Pakistani wedding and *pardā*, and interviews with Begam Tazeen Faridi (at the time head of the All-Pakistan Women's Association in Karachi), Rajkumari Amrit Kaur and Gayatri Devi, the Maharani of Jaipur. Overall tone is condescending.

1726 WARD, BARBARA E. [BARBARA (WARD) JACKSON]. Men, women and change: an essay in understanding social roles in South and South-east Asia. *In* Barbara E. Ward, ed. Women in the new Asia: the changing social roles of men and women in South and South-east Asia. Paris: UNESCO, 1963. pp.25-99. Compares the impact of general trends in medicine, communication, urbanization, family, education, employment and political awareness on women's and men's roles in South and Southeast Asian countries.

i) Indian women

1727 FRANDA, MARCUS F. Of women, men, and families in India. Hanover, New Hampshire: American Universities Field Staff, 1975. 14p. (*Its* Letters and Reports on Current Developments in World Affairs, South Asia Series, 19,14).
Broad view of the issues and problems facing Indian women today. Considers classical Hindu thought, demography, family, education, employment, reforms, etc. Photographs.

1728 FRAZER, HEATHER T. Female power in changing India: myth or reality. *In* Michael V. Belok, ed. Women: an international perspective. Meerut: Anu Prakashan, 1977? pp.108-18.
Argues that while both regressive and progressive changes are taking place, the image of profound social change in lives of women is illusory. Surveys 20th century historical events and trends.

1729 HARTOG, LADY [MABEL HÉLÈNE (KISCH) HARTOG]. Social life and social change. *In her* India: new pattern. London: George Allen and Unwin, 1955. pp.74-83.
Lady Hartog describes changes in the lives of women that took place in India in the course of a 20 year absence, during which the country gained independence.

1730 KAUL, INGE. Zur Diskussion der gesellschaftlichen Position der Frau in Indien: ein Literaturbericht [A discussion of the social position of the woman in India: a report on the literature]. *In* Internationales Asienforum 4,4 (1973) 599-614.
Reviews recent portrayal of Indian women in social scientific literature with respect to family life, educational opportunities and labor force participation.

1731 LEONARD, KAREN. Women in India: some recent perspectives; research note. *In* Pacific Affairs 52,1 (1979) 95-107.
Reviews problems facing Indian women today; draws heavily on the report of the Committee on the Status of Women in India, ***Towards Equality***, "the best single research and advocacy work available." Discusses current research trends, "pointing to areas where scholarly debate is vigorous or where further research and clarification is needed," and assesses "current thinking in India about the nature of the problems for women and the solutions sought for those problems."

1732 MOUNTBATTEN, LADY [EDWINA ASHLEY MOUNTBATTEN]. On the women of India. *In* Asiatic Review n.s. 45,161 (1949) 439-46.
Text of address to joint meeting of East India Association, Over-Seas League and Women's Council on Indian Affairs detailing the changing position of Indian women, their part in the troubles of partition and the author's own experiences in India.

1733 WOODSMALL, RUTH FRANCES. Women in India. *In her* Women and the new East. Washington, D.C.: Middle East Institute, 1960. pp.243-332.
Assesses the changing status of women in India in the first decade after independence. While based upon western values, this review article is less judgemental and more balanced in its viewpoints than many others of its kind. Covers many topics. Includes photographs; tables on education, health personnel and employment; and lists of women's colleges and organizations.

ii) Pakistani women

1734 WILBUR, DONALD N. Pakistan: its people, its society, its culture. New Haven: HRAF Press, 1964.
Has two chapters (pp.117-53) on various aspects of women's lives. [Unexamined].

1735 WOODSMALL, RUTH FRANCES. Women in Pakistan. *In her* Women and the new East. Washington, D.C.: Middle East Institute, 1960. pp.99-148.
Assesses the changing conditions of Pakistani women in the decade following independence and partition. While based upon western values, the paper is less judgemental and less polar in its viewpoints than many others of its kind. Covers many topics. Includes photographs, an appendix listing women's organizations and key information about them and tables of educational and employment statistics.

(c) Women of particular nations — collected papers

1736 APPADORAI, A., ed. Status of women in South Asia. Bombay: Orient Longmans, 1954. 171p.
Summary of proceedings and selected papers from the UNESCO-sponsored "Seminar on the Status of Women in South Asia" held in Delhi in 1952-53. Main topics considered are general social status, legal position, political participation and methodology. For partial contents see entries 2549, 2557 and 3115.

1737 BAIG, TARA ALI, ed. Women of India. Delhi: Publications Division, Ministry of Information and Broadcasting, Gov-

ernment of India, 1958. 276p.
Articles, mostly by various Indian professional women, concerning the historical position; creative, political and professional achievements; education; family life; etc. of Indian women. Numerous photos, many of historical interest. For contents, see entries 54, 78, 329, 345, 559, 807, 906, 1103, 1227, 1281, 1342, 1803, 1984, 2016, 2186, 2296, 2311, 2315 and 2641.

1738 BHASIN, KAMLA, ed. The position of women in India: proceedings of a seminar held in Srinagar, September 1972. Bombay: Arvind A. Deshpande, 1973. 131p.
Series of brief papers on many topics from a seminar organized by the Leslie Sawhny Programme of Training for Democracy and the Friedrich-Naumann-Stiftung.

1739 DE SOUZA, ALFRED, ed. Women in contemporary India: traditional images and changing roles. Delhi: Manohar Book Service, 1975. 264p.
Introduction and eleven articles on various contemporary topics, most reprinted from special International Women's Year issue of ***Social Change*** [25,3 (1975)]. For contents see: 1655, 1669, 1761, 2142, 2380, 2541, 3194, 3199, 3544, 4071, 4162 and 4618.

1740 Education of women for involvement in national development: report of regional seminar, S.E. Asia, held at the Sri Lanka Foundation Institute, Colombo, November 6-11, 1975. Colombo: Sri Lanka Foundation Institute, 1975. 152p.
Seminar proceedings include material on the Sri Lanka Women's Conference; events and activities in Sri Lanka in association with International Women's Year; patterns of female education and development in Indonesia, Nepal, Pakistan and Sri Lanka; and various general papers on international peace, family and community responsibilities, advancement of women, equality between the sexes, mass media, prostitution and women's associations. Lists of recommendations and participants.

1741 Facts and views. Shanta Serbjeet Singh, co-editor. *In* Ajeet Cour and Arpana Cour, eds. Directory of Indian women today, 1976. New Delhi: India International Publications, 1976. pp.A-F, I-XLVIII.
Fourteen brief articles on contemporary Indian women. Various topics.

1742 INDIAN NATIONAL CONGRESS. ALL INDIA CONGRESS COMMITTEE. ALL INDIA CONGRESS WOMEN'S CONVENTION, 1960. Souvenir, Trivandrum: Reception Committee, All India Congress Women's Convention, 1960. 172p.
Forty-four brief articles on many topics, most relating to women.

1743 The Indian woman. *In* Yojana 19,13/14 (15 Aug 1975) 6-48.
Numerous articles on the changing position of Indian women. Topics include legal reform, employment, unwed mothers, mythological images and the feminist movement. Numerous photographs.

1744 The Indian woman: a symposium on the changing conditions of our women in the developing urban society. Seminar 52,12 (1963) 57p.
Issue contains articles entitled "The Problem," "Through the Ages," "The Social Image," "Marriage," "Motherhood," "The Acceptance of Equality," "Working Woman" and "Legal Status." Reviews books on women and includes a bibliography for further reading.

1745 International Women's Year 1975. Social Welfare 22,6/7 (1975) 124p.
Contains many brief articles by various authors grouped under topics of mothers and daughters, employment, marriage and family, single women, tribal women, contemporary social change and national development. Includes a photo essay.

1746 International Women's Year, special number. Social Action 25,3 (1975) 320p.
Includes eight articles on contemporary Indian women, one of which also considers women of Pakistan and Bangladesh. For contents see entries 1761, 2142, 2380, 2541, 3194, 3199, 3544 and 4618.

1747 IWY [International Women's Year] supplement. *In* Social Welfare 22,8 (1975) 20-32.
Five brief articles on women's banks, change in rural areas, rural industries, IWY and female literacy.

1748 Kasturba memorial. Indore: Kasturba Gandhi National Memorial Trust, 1962. 250p.
Collection of numerous brief articles. About one half of the book is devoted to various topics relating to women. The second half details Kasturba Gandhi's life and work and the work of the Kasturba Gandhi National Memorial Trust established to promote the welfare of village women and children.

1749 KINIKAR, ROY, ed. Priyadarshini: international women's year book. Bombay: Yashodhara Publications, 1975. 332p.
Collection of about 50 articles covering a wide range of topics relating to contemporary women. Many distinguished authors. Includes a section of brief biographical sketches (pp.275-326).

1750 NANDA, B.R., ed. Indian women: from purdah to modernity. New Delhi: Vikas Publishing House, 1976. 187p.
Collection of essays about Indian women in the 20th century. Diverse topics. Includes brief biographical sketches of about 80 women prominent in recent decades. For contents, see entries 43, 938, 1213, 1226, 1341, 1667, 1774, 1988 and 4217.

1751 NAYAK, SHARADA, ed. Profiles of Indian women. New Delhi: Educational Resources Center, University of the State of New York, State Education Department, 1977? 56p.
Fifteen brief biographical vignettes suggest the variety of roles, activities and attitudes of Indian women today. Each is accompanied by a photograph. Appended section contains suggestions for use of these profiles in the classroom, a list of further resources and a glossary.

1752 Role and status of women in Indian society. Calcutta: Firma KLM, 1978. 167p.
Contents: "Introduction" by Renuka Ray, "Status and Role of Women: Great Indian Women Through the Ages" by Roma Chaudhury, "Movement for Emancipation of Women in the Nineteenth Century" by Krishna Basu, "Changing Role of Women Towards Emancipation: 1947 to the Present Day" by Chitra Ghosh, "New Women in Old Society" by Manashi Dasgupta, "The New Woman: Problems and Challenges" by Leena Nandi, "Sex-Socio-Economic Developments" by Kalyani Karlekar, "The Cry of Liberation: Is it Viable?" by Sipra Mookerjee, "Status of Women and Education" by Aleyamma George, "Status of Women and Education" by Gita Mukharji, "Attitude Towards Women Writers and Woman's Self-Image" by Nabaneeta Dev Sen, "Family Planning and Women" by Sushila Singhi, "Tribal Women: A Study of Modern Conditions and Future Prospects" by Bharati Debi and "Themes of Consciousness among some Educated Working Women of Bangladesh" by Joanna Kirkpatrick.

1753 SHINTRI, SAROJINI, C.R. YARAVINTELIMATH and S.L. SHANTAKUMARI, eds. Woman: her problems and her achievements. Dharwar: Karnatak University, 1977. 128p.
Proceedings of a symposium at Karnatak University inspired by International Women's Year. Topics include family planning, dowry, employment, political rights and exploitation of women.

1754 Special issue: International Women's Year. Eve's Weekly 29,19 (10 May 1975) 70p.
Includes articles on legal rights, education, rural women, health and family planning, status of single women, influence of mass media on women's position, divorced women, male domination, employment, history of women's status, their innate abilities, women's liberation, housework, solving women's problems, film industry, "it's a man's world," attitudes of Indian men, social welfare and women in other countries. Includes an interview with Indira Gandhi on women.

1755 Status of women: a symposium on the discriminated section of society. *In* Seminar 165 (May 1973) 9-46.
Contents: "The Problem" by Zarina Bhatty, "In Law" by Lotika Sarkar, "In Education" by Kamla Bhasin-Kapur, "In Employment" by Bina Agarwal, "In Attitudes" by Uma Vasudev and "In a Community" by Shahida Lateef. With book reviews, a selected bibliography and report of a seminar.

1756 WARD, BARBARA E. [BARBARA (WARD) JACKSON], ed. Women in the new Asia: the changing social roles of men and women in South and South-east Asia. Paris: UNESCO, 1963. 529p.
Papers presented at a meeting of social scientists in Calcutta in 1958 to further the objectives of UNESCO's major project for the mutual appreciation of eastern and western cultural values. Includes autobiographical accounts as well as sociological and anthropological papers concerning India, Sri Lanka, Pakistan and Bangladesh as well as Southeast Asian countries. Photographs. For South Asia contents, see entries 915, 1390, 1670, 1726, 3020, 3744, 3880 and 4468.

1757 Women in the struggle for a new humanism. *In* Religion and Society 23,1 (1976) 1-75.
Entire issue devoted to various aspects of womanhood in contemporary India. Several articles relate to women in Christianity.

1758 Women of India. Guest ed: Shyla Boga. Onlooker, annual number (1977) 77p.
Prominent and exceptional Indian women speak out informally about their experiences. Prominent Indian men speak out about women.

1759 A world of difference. New Delhi: Educational Resources Center, University of the State of New York, State Education Department, 1977? 52p.
Extracts from writings of Indians and foreigners on Indian women. [Unexamined. ALI].

(d) Women of the subcontinent's major religious traditions

1760 INDIA (REPUBLIC). COMMITTEE ON THE STATUS OF WOMEN IN INDIA. Socio-cultural setting of women's status: images of women in religious traditions. *In its* Towards equality: report of the Committee on the Status of Women in India. New Delhi: Department of Social Welfare, Ministry of Education and Social Welfare, Government of India, 1975. pp.38-54. [*Chair* Phulrenu Guha].
Surveys main practices and beliefs relating to women in eight organized religious traditions and in tribal communities along with major reform movements and associations (Brahmo Samaj, Prarthna Samaj, Arya Samaj) of the 19th and 20th centuries. Considers these efforts to have been "elitist in character and limited in approach."

1761 KING, URSULA. Women and religion: image and status of women in some major religious traditions. *In* Social Action

25,3 (1975) 277-91. [*Reprint in* Alfred de Souza, ed. Women in contemporary India: traditional images and changing roles. Delhi: Manohar Book Service, 1975. pp.110-28].
Discusses the challenge that the changing position of women throughout the world presents to the understanding of women in various religious traditions. Primarily considers Hindu and Christian traditions. Argues that ideals of asceticism entail low female status, no religion appears to have a model consistent with the self-image of many contemporary women and an adequate theology must be developed by both men and women.

i) The Hindu tradition — encompassing about 68% of the South Asian population

1762 AGRAWAL, CHANDRA. Need for the resurgence of the Vedic woman. *In* Hindu Vishwa 4,8 (1978) 1-5.
Discusses two prevalent notions of Indian womanhood: 1) the negative downtrodden image of social scientists and 2) the noble idealized image of cultural revivalists. Argues that "the heritage of the strong, independent female householder, that is of the Vedic patni, has been forgotten. To reinstate the place of the Indian woman as householder . . . what is sorely needed is the knowledge and understanding of the roles of the Vedic woman, man and home."

1763 GUPTA, A.R. Women in Hindu society: a study of tradition and transition. New Delhi: Jyotsna Prakashan, 1976. 264p.
General status survey. Most material deals with the past century and most deals with topics of kinship, family, marriage and sexuality. Author does, however, discuss historical background and a wide variety of other topics.

1764 HATE, CHANDRAKALA A. Hindu woman and her future. Bombay: New Book Company, 1948. 293p.
Report of a sociological investigation of the social and economic situation of Indian women. Supplements data from Bombay with that from Poona (now Pune) and some cities in North India. Includes short life histories, a history of the women's movement and recommendations for the future. Provides appendixes on central pieces of legislation and important resolutions regarding women passed by the Indian National Social Conference and the All-India Women's Conference.

1765 JHA, AKHILESHWAR. Man-woman relationship in Hindu society. *In his* Modernization and the Hindu socio-culture. New Delhi: B.R. Publishing Corporation, 1978. pp.91-100.
Essentially a status of women paper. Suggests that Hindu women are entirely subordinate to men and are viewed as sex objects.

1766 SRINIVAS, M.N. The changing position of Indian women. *In* Man n.s. 12,2 (1977) 221-38. (Huxley Memorial Lecture, 1976). [*Also* Delhi: Oxford University Press, 1978. 30p.].
Approaches the admittedly complex topic by considering social processes of Sanskritization and urbanization, rural agricultural classes and caste position and the effects of reform and freedom struggle movements. With prefacing remarks on the recent interest in studying women. Essentially relates to Hindu women.

ii) The Islamic tradition — encompassing about 25% of the South Asian population

1767 Advice to daughter. Karachi: Peermahomed Ebrahim Trust, 1976. 78p.
Shī'ah interpretation of duties and responsibilities of a woman according to Islamic principles. Encourages daughters to avoid modern trends. Describes what young girls should be taught, ideal transition to married life and ideal qualities of mothers, wives, sisters-in-law and women in general.

1768 ALI, AMEER. The real status of women in Islam. *In* Nineteenth Century 30, 175 (1891) 387-99. [*Reprint in* Razi Wasti, ed. Syed Ameer Ali on Islamic history and culture. Lahore: People's Publishing House, 1968. pp.1-15].
Defense in response to an article written by a Christian woman criticizing the position of women in Islam. Argues that there are many admirable features of the position of women in Islam and if they "are not so advanced as their Christian sisters in the West, their backwardness is not due to the Quranic teachings, but to the general extinction among the Muslims of culture and progress under the avalanche of savagery which issued from the wilds of Tartary in the thirteenth century."

1769 _______. Woman in Islam: with the addition of the three articles from the Mussulman of India on the same subject. Lahore: Islamia Press, 1893. 41p.
[Unexamined. NUC].

1770 _______. The legal position of women in Islam. London: University of London Press, 1912. 47p.
[Unexamined. NUC].

1771 ANSARI, UMER. Women in Islamic society. Lahore: Islamic Publications, 1967.

[Unexamined].

1772 ANWAR, SHAMIM. Women recreated. Lahore: Zareen Art Press, 1964. [Unexamined].

1773 AZIZ AHMAD. Islamic modernism in India and Pakistan, 1857-1964. London: Oxford University Press, 1967. 294p.
contains various references to Islamic modernist conceptions of womanhood, including a summary of Mumtaz Ali's 1898 treatise on the rights of women.

1774 BHATTY, ZARINA. Status of Muslim women and social change. *In* B.R. Nanda, ed. Indian women: from purdah to modernity. New Delhi: Vikas, 1976. pp.99-112.
Examines status of Muslim women in India "in the context of the ideals of equality and social justice." Critical view.

1775 HIMA AKHLAQ HUSAIN. Bhooli hooi baten, 2d ed. Karachi: Peer Mahomed Ebrahim Trust, 1969. 163p.
Guide for Muslim women on the conduct of their lives. [Unexamined. NUC].

1776 HYDER, QURRATULAIN. Muslim women of India. *In* Devaki Jain, ed. Indian women. New Delhi: Publications Division, Ministry of Information and Broadcasting, Government of India, 1975. pp.187-202.
History of major educational, literary, legislative and other events involving Muslim women in India in the past century. Placed in the context of the history and character of Islam.

1777 JAMEELAH, MARYAM [MARGARET MARCUS]. Islam and the Muslim woman today. Lahore: Mohammad Yusuf Khan, 1976. 51p.
Extols the positive values in the orthodox Islamic view of women and contrasts this view with contemporary emancipation movements. By an American who converted to Islam, migrated to Lahore and married a member of the Jamā'at-i-Islamī movement.

1778 JONES, VIOLET STANFORD and L. BEVAN JONES. Woman in Islam: a manual with special reference to conditions in India. Lucknow: Lucknow Publishing House, 1941. 455p.
Survey prepared for women of the Church of Christ in India with the hope that "it will quicken in them an intelligent interest in, and genuine sympathy for, the Muslim women of this country." Based primarily on Islamic texts and contemporary publications. An ethnographic and textual compendium with major sections on social and religious life. Bibliography includes many British-period documents regarding Muslim women.

1779 Lessons to learn by married couples. Tr. from Urdu and Gujarati. Karachi: Peermahomed Ebrahim Trust, 1976. 175p.
Collection of articles on proper conduct in and noble values of marriage. Previously published in various Gujarati magazines. Directed primarily toward women, they discuss the dangers of western influence and immodest behavior, "Hints for Avoiding Dangers that Living in a City Poses for Women," the importance of being a loving and attentive wife and Islamic teachings as a safeguard against evil influence.

1780 LICHTENSTADTER, ILSE. The Muslim woman in transition: based on observations in Egypt and Pakistan. *In* Sociologus n.s. 7,1 (1957) 23-38.
Assessment of the changing circumstances for women in these two countries based upon a broad range of personal experiences. Considers *pardā*, education, Islamic law and other topics. While Pakistan is considered to be quite conservative, the author concludes that "the goal must not be destruction of valid religiosity, only deliverance from superstitious interpretations and ignorance of the real religious values of Islam."

1781 Man and woman. Karachi: Peermahomed Ebrahim Trust, 1976. 80p.
Collection of reprinted pieces: "The Rights of Man on Woman," "Rights of Women on Men," "Woman and Islam," "Woman the Complement of Man," "Status of Women in Islam," "Role of Woman," "Gift to Woman," "On Women's Lib," "Women in America Equalling Men in all Fields," "Woman's Equality with Man — A Critical Analysis," "Women's Qualities," "Character Building" and "Duty and Obligation." Most ideas are not linked to particular traditional Islamic authorities.

1782 NAJI, GHULAMALI ISMAIL. A guidance for women. Tr. from Urdu and Gujarati. Karachi: Peermahomed Ebrahim Trust, 1973. 260p.
The "Affairs of Women." An almanac of sorts offering advice and information on a wide variety of topics, e.g., husband-wife relations, child care, health, proper conduct. Illustrates many issues anecdotally. Authorities are the *Qor'ān*, the *Ḥadīs̤* and various individual specialists. With appendixes on menstruation and leucorrhoea. The author is an interpreter of Islamic thought to Khojas.

1783 OMAR, KAMAL. Social status of women. Karachi: available at S.M. Mir, Fazleesons Ltd., 1965. 28p.
On Muslim women. [Unexamined. NUC].

1784 RALLIA RAM, MAYAVANTHI. New facets of Muslim women. *And* Emerging attitudes of Muslim women in Delhi. *In* Mainstream 11,19-20 (6-13 Jan 1973) 29-34 and 40,34-5 and 40.
Excerpts from interviews with professional Muslim women concerning their family backgrounds, educations, careers and views about Muslim law and family planning.

1785 ________. Muslim women in India: dilemma of change. *In* Mainstream 11,27 (3 Mar 1973) 19-22.
Focuses on problems of the reform of Muslim

personal and family laws and the views of women concerning these changes.

1786 ________. Modernisation and Muslim women. *In* Mainstream 14,48 (31 Jul 1976) 22-3.
Summarizes findings of a survey of 785 urban Muslim women from U.P., Delhi and Srinagar concerning their attitudes toward education, social freedom and sex education. In general, "It was the women in the professional field who struck a balance between the orthodoxy of the housewife and the liberalism of the student."

1787 SIDDIQI, MOHAMMAD MAZHERUDDIN. Women in Islam. Lahore: Institute of Islamic Culture, 1971. 182p. [*1st ed.* 1952].
"What the Muslim women in Pakistan and other Muslim countries lack is not any rights but the consciousness of their rights. They . . . have been placed under many fetters of custom and artificial tradition not sanctioned by Islam. If they receive proper Islamic education . . . they can easily break their chains." Includes chapters on marriage, divorce, social restrictions, *pardā*, polygamy, coeducation, birth control and deviations from Islam.

1788 SMITH, WILFRED CANTWELL. Modern Islām in India: a social analysis, 2d rev. ed. London: Victor Gollancz Ltd., 1946. 344p.
Study of the Muslim community of India passing through a "turbulent" period, late-19th through mid-20th centuries. Numerous interspersed references to women-related issues, including a critical section (pp.72-81) arguing that there has been a general refusal to admit that "the traditional Islamic position could be improved."

1789 THANVI, ASHRAF ALI. Syed Akhtural Islam, ed. Bahishti zewar: requisites of Islam. Tr. from Urdu by Rahm Ali al-Hasmi. Delhi: Dini Book Depot, 1973. 548, 187p.
Apparently written in Urdu in the 19th century for the Islamic education of young women who lacked Arabic language skills, this book contains major sections on cleanliness and pollution, prayer, funeral and burial, fasting, charity, pilgrimage, conjugal relations and business. Discusses numerous other topics, including festivals and rites, in appendixes.

1790 WOODSMALL, RUTH FRANCES. Moslem women enter a new world. New York: Round Table, 1936. 432p.
Surveys changing conditions of Muslim women in the Middle East and South Asia. Based on extensive residence in Turkey and Syria and extended travel elsewhere. Photographs.

(e) Women of rural and urban areas

i) The rural majority: about 82% of the South Asian population

1791 DHINDSA, RAGWINDER KAUR. Changing status of women in rural India. Ph.D. dissertation, Department of Sociology?, University of Illinois, 1968. 250p. [University Microfilms 69-10,682].
Study of relationship between women's status on the one hand and both physical isolation and mass media on the other. Based on census materials from 65 villages in Tamil Nadu, Karnataka, Rajasthan and Uttar Pradesh. Concludes that role of mass media in fostering change is substantial. [Unexamined. DAI].

1792 The farmer's wife. 1972. 30 min. Color. 16 and 35 mm. [*Distributed by* Films Division, Ministry of Information and Broadcasting, 24 G. Deshmukh Marg, Bombay 400 026].
Film showing importance of work of the "farmer's wife" in various stages of agricultural production and as a homemaker. [Unexamined. CF].

1793 HAQ, ISAR-UL. Status of village women in Pakistan society. *In* Haider Ali Chaudhari et al., eds. Pakistan sociological perspectives: collected papers of the Pakistan Sociological Association's II, III, and IV conferences. Lahore: University of the Punjab, 1968. pp.198-205.
Asserts that while contributions of village women are substantial, their general status is quite low. [Unexamined. Book in NUC].

1794 LOOMIS, CHARLES P. Change in rural India as related to social power and sex. *In* Behavioural Sciences and Community Development 1,1 (1967) 1-27.
Study of modernization in rural India. Based on interviews with 5,810 adults in various localities. "Randomly chosen males are . . . more rational, realistic and effectively linked to governmental services than the randomly chosen females but less so than the village influentials, most of whom are males." Women were "more tradition-bound and less oriented toward modernity than males." Specific data on attitudes and practices regarding disease, education, media contact, agricultural improvements, village level workers, community development officials, untouchability and urban contact.

1795 Uski roti. Directed by Mani Kaul. (Hindi dialogue/French subtitles). 1970. 130 min. Black and white. [*Distributed by* Film Finance Corporation, White House, Walkeshwar Road, Bombay 400 006].
Film explores the culturally patterned silent suffering of a village wife. [Unexamined].

1796 Who seek the light. Produced through G.R. Sethi, Bombay. 1964. 19 min. Black and white. 16 and 35 mm. [*Distributed by* Films Division, Ministry of Information and Broadcasting, 24 G. Deshmukh Marg, Bombay 400 026].

Portrayal of the experiences of a village girl to demonstrate the changing opportunities for rural women, the obstacles they must face and the benefits to be gained. Shows some social welfare activities that facilitate the transition. [Unexamined. CF].

ii) Women in towns and cities: about 18% of the South Asian population

1797 DURGA, S.A. Traditional ideas in the life of modern women. *In* Bulletin of the Institute of Traditional Cultures, Madras (Jul 1975) 238-44.
Describes various traditional ideals and practices of middle- and upper-class educated women. Supports the thesis that the modern woman acts in the role of mediator between the forces of social change and cultural stability.

1798 KAPUR, PROMILLA. Studies of urban women in India. *In* Giri Raj Gupta, ed. Family and Social Change in modern India. New Delhi: Vikas, 1976. pp.65-102. (Main Currents in Indian Sociology, 2).
Reviews literature concerning urban Indian women, pointing to gaps.

1799 KAPUR, VEENA. Social character of women in the changing Indian society. Ph.D. dissertation, Department of Psychology?, Catholic University of America, 1973. 235p. [University Microfilms 73-21,633].
Negative assessment of the effects of modernization on middle- and upper-middle-class women. Result of interviews with and psychological tests of 20 educated Hindu women. [Unexamined. DAI].

1800 KHOSLA, G.D. The modern young lady. *In his* A taste of India. Bombay: Jaico Publishing House, 1970. pp.185-90.
Argues that young, educated, middle-class urban women, in spite of westernized appearances, have essentially Indian values and aspirations.

1801 MIES, MARIA. Indische Frauen zwischen Patriarchat und Chancengleichheit: Rollenkonflikte studierender und berufstätiger Frauen [Indian women between patriarchy and equal opportunity: role conflicts of studying and professional women]. Meisenheim am Glan: Hain, 1973. 266p.
Reviews earlier and recent history of Indian womanhood to show that the modern Indian woman must operate within a society in which ideology and reality conflict. Investigates attitudes toward women as students and as professionals and women's motivations for participating in such activities. Seeks means by which role conflicts are solved. With case studies. Data from various major Indian cities.

(f) Women of other communities and groups

i) India's tribal women: *ādivāsīs*, the "original dwellers"

1802 EHRENFELS, U.R. Aboriginal womanhood and culture contact. *In* Eastern Anthropologist 3,1 (1949) 48-54.
"The still palpable independence of Indian aboriginal womanhood can in part be ascribed to the effects, on social habits, of their original economic system, [the] food gathering method." Asserts that culture contact with non-aboriginals, including matrilineal peoples, has tended to lower status of tribal women, within their own groups. With specific examples from Tamil Nadu and Kerala to illustrate the process of change. Recommends appropriate welfare aims concerning tribal women.

1803 ELWIN, VERRIER. Tribal women. *In* Devaki Jain, ed. Indian women. New Delhi: Publications Division, Ministry of Information and Broadcasting, Government of India, 1975. pp.203-13. [*Reprint from* Tara Ali Baig, ed. Women of India. Delhi: Publications Division, Ministry of Information and Broadcasting, Government of India, 1958. pp.200-7].
Sympathetic overview of tribal women's difficult lifestyles, personal qualities, relations with men as expressed in folk traditions and important religious roles. "They have an important role in festivity and funeral; they can more than hold their own with their men; they are free and self-reliant, respected and loved by their menfolk and adored by their children. Their life is full, interesting and satisfied." Photographs.

1804 GARG, B.M. Status of women in tribal communities in India. *In* Indian J. of Social Work 21,2 (1960) 191-7.
Presents data from various tribal communities regarding domestic, economic, social and religious spheres. No general conclusions.

1805 MOHAN, BRIJ. Status of women in tribal communities in India. *In* Vanyajati 10,2 (1962) 60-6.
[Unexamined].

1806 SACHCHIDANANDA. Social structure, status and mobility patterns: the case of tribal women. *In* Man in India 58,1 (1978) 1-12.
Distinguishes and briefly characterizes three tribal zones in India — across the middle from Gujarat to West Bengal, the northeastern Himalayan area and small portions of Tamil Nadu and Kerala — and contrasts patrilineal

and matrilineal social structure. Contrasts tribal women with nontribal women (on the whole, status of the former is "better"). Tribal women's status is determined by socio-structural principle rather than economic role. Reviews contemporary trends of change.

1807 SARKAR, R.M. Women in tribal India through customs and traditions. *In* Folklore [Calcutta] 9,12 (1968) 458-67. [*Reprint in* Sankar Sen Gupta, ed. Women in Indian folklore. Calcutta: Indian Publications, 1969. pp.201-10. (*Its* Folklore Series, 15)].
Position of women in tribal communities based on various anthropological parameters — matriliny/patriliny, polyandry/polygyny, etc.

1808 SHASHI, S.S. The tribal women of India. Delhi: Sundeep Prakashan, 1978. 163p.
Eleven chapters review the position of women in various tribal communities. Remaining material surveys tribal women of particular regions and general topics, including change and acculturation. Photographs.

1809 Tribal women in India. Calcutta: Indian Anthropological Society, 1978. 199p.
Twenty-five brief articles on various communities and topics. Photos. [Unexamined. ALI].

ii) India's scheduled caste women: former "untouchable" communities

1810 TRIVEDI, HARSHAD R. Scheduled caste women: studies in exploitation with reference to superstition, ignorance and poverty. Delhi: Concept Publishing Company, 1977. 256p.
Major sections are: profile of scheduled caste women from census and other relevant literature; study of exploitation of scheduled caste women for "immoral traffic in human flesh" in Bijapur District, Karnataka, Raipur District, M.P. and Uttarkashi District, U.P.; case studies of prostitutes and *devadāsīs*; survey results and conclusions. Appendixes list research assistants and facilitators, reproduce census tables, provide genealogies for the case studies and detail survey results.

iii) Sanskritizing and westernizing groups

1811 SRINIVAS, M.N. A note on Sanskritization and westernization. *In his* Caste in modern India, and other essays. Bombay: Asia Publishing House, 1962. pp.42-62. [*Reprint from* Far Eastern Quarterly 15,4 (1956) 481-96].
Gives examples of how Sanskritization (. . . "the adoption of new customs and habits, but also the exposure to new ideas and values which have found frequent expression in the vast body of Sanskrit literature . . ."), motivated by desire for upward mobility, "results in harshness towards women." Argues that the westernization process results in relative freedom for women.

(4) The life cycle

1812 KHANNA, GIRIJA. Woman: sixteen to sixty. Delhi: Vikas Publishing House, 1974. 141p.
[Unexamined].

(a) Growing up female: socialization, ideals, self-images, roles

1813 CORMACK, MARGARET LAWSON. Traditional patterns in the interiorization of the ideals of womanhood by Hindu girls: with special reference to urban, educated women. Ph.D. dissertation, Department of Sociology, Columbia University, 1951. 261, 88p. [University Microfilms 2802].
Regarding values enjoined upon Hindu girls as they grow up. Considers various life cycle rites and self-images. [Unexamined. NUC].

1814 ________. The Hindu woman. New York: Bureau of Publications, Teachers College, Columbia University, 1953. 207p. (Teachers College Studies in Education).
Based on segments of author's dissertation. [Unexamined. NUC].

1815 DIXIT, RAMESH C. Sex role consciousness among village children of upper and lower caste groups. *In* J. of the Indian Academy of Applied Psychology 5 (1968) 32-6.
Study of three- to five-year-olds. Greater sex role consciousness was shown by upper-caste children and five-year-old boys as compared to lower-caste children and three-year-old boys, respectively. Upper-caste girls were more "feminine" than lower-caste girls. [Unexamined].

1816 KALAKDINA, MARGARET. The upbringing of a girl. *In* Devaki Jain, ed. Indian women. New Delhi: Publica-

tions Division, Ministry of Information and Broadcasting, Government of India, 1975. pp.87-97.
Contrasts experiences and personal qualities of boys and girls. Comments on problems and prospects of these issues in modernization process.

1817 KENNEDY, BETH C. On being a woman, Indian and American: a comparative study. *In* Asian Survey 13,9 (1973) 833-52.
American and Indian women from various places (mostly middle-class professionals) were asked to 1) draw how they felt about being a woman, 2) describe their drawing and the colors used and 3) write the first ten words associated with the word "woman." The author, a marriage, family and child counselor, compares the responses.

1818 MANDELBAUM, DAVID G. Family roles: girl and woman. *In his* Society in India, v1: continuity and change. Berkeley: University of California Press, 1972. pp.82-94.
Reviews pertinent ethnographic and autobiographical material organized according to the life cycle. Discusses myth and reality of quarreling women.

1819 MITTAL, V.K. Personality differences among conservative and progressive ladies. *In* Research J. of Philosophy and Social Sciences 2,1 (1965) 125-8.
Questionnaire survey of 50 women found a positive correlation between conservativism and neurosis and a negative correlation between conservativism and self-sufficiency and introversion. [Unexamined].

1820 RAMA DEVI, B. Indian woman and her attitude toward traditional values. *In* J. of Psychological Research 7,1 (1963) 72-8.
Attitudes toward glorification of womanhood in texts of the Hindu tradition. [Unexamined].

1821 SCHERMERHORN, R.A. Socio-cultural history and sex roles in an urban minority of India. *In* Sociological Focus 8,2 (1975) 173-80.
Considers qualities and stereotypes of Anglo-Indian men and women. Reviews history of Anglo-Indian community and circumstances that have "tended to skew the sex roles . . . away from the traditional male dominance pattern . . . . women became competent, efficient breadwinners while men engaged in a life of leisure."

1822 VENKATARAYAPPA, K.N. Feminine roles. Bombay: Popular Prakashan, 1966. 139p.
Attempts to present "the essential facts of feminine roles" by examining morphology, psyche and social roles. Concludes that "sex is a pervasive fact of our lives and penetrates every aspect of our thought and striving." Views inherently feminine qualities as highly admirable. Rejects notions of inferiority of women. Worldwide examples but mainly with reference to India.

(b) Marriage

1823 DUMONT, LOUIS. Dowry in Hindu marriage: as a social scientist sees it. *In* Economic Weekly 11,15 (11 Apr 1959) 519-20.
Brief comments on traditional Hindu marriages in the light of reformist trends.

1824 KANNAN, C.T. Inter-caste and inter-community marriages in India. Bombay: Allied Publishers, 1963. 236p.
Study of 250 couples from various communities and localities throughout India. Investigates informants' modes of meeting, courting experiences and adjustments relating to language and religion. Also examines the reactions of conjugal and natal families and provides a review of the literature on inter-community marriages.

1825 KRISHNAMURTI, K.S. Marriage, married life and children (stellar astrology). Madras: the author, 1971. 276p. (Reader 4).
Guide to the use of astrology in securing a proper mate and in answering marital questions. "What kind of a personality we have brought over as the karmaic inheritance of our activities in previous lives, ***we may learn only from a study of astrology***."

1826 Marriage: Indian styles. 30 min. Black and white. 16 and 35 mm. [*Available from* University of Michigan Television Center, 310 Maynard Street, Ann Arbor, Michigan 48108].
Film about variety of marriage patterns in India. Shows four ceremonies: Muslim, Sikh, South Indian Hindu and North Indian Hindu. Discusses inter-community marriages and divorce. [Unexamined].

1827 SWAMINATHA, K. Bridal duty: a tax proposal. Mysore: Rao and Raghavan, 1967. 35p.
Various proposals regarding the gathering of marriage statistics. Suggests compulsory marriage registration and providing incentive to register in the form of a prize. Proposes a tax on marriage contracts (and details its implementation) as well as a tax and ceiling on marriage expenditures.

1828 THANKAPPAN NAIR, P. Marriage and dowry in India. Calcutta: Minerva, 1978. 205p.
Informal catalog of "the curious marriage practices of the people of India." Has chapters on economic aspects of marriage, marriage by lot and by choice, marriage according to various rules, mock marriages, couvade and defloration.

i) Arrangements: matrimonial advertisements, advantageous unions, love marriages

1829 ANAND, K. An analysis of matrimonial advertisements. *In* Sociological Bulletin 14,1 (1965) 59-71.
Analysis of 1,000 matrimonial ads from the North Indian *Hindustan Times* and *Tribune* newspapers. Discusses patterns relating to caste, education, occupation and personal appearance in the ads. Concludes that although the "secular section" is represented, the majority of advertisers continue to value traditional matchmaking considerations.

1829a BHATIA, PRATIMA. Change in matrimonial values: a study through matrimonial advertisements. *In* Eastern Anthropologist 26,3 (1973) 271-7.
Study of advertisements in English newspapers from Delhi and Lucknow. Suggests that marital standards for women tend to reflect traditional values while standards for men show greater western influence.

1830 DAS, VEENA. The structure of marriage preferences: an account from Pakistani fiction. *In* Man 8,1 (1973) 30-45.
"My purpose . . . is to describe the various strategies which are used in arranging marriages between cousins in the popular Urdu fiction of West Pakistan . . . . preference for marriage with patrilateral parallel cousin is associated with . . . regions in which Islam is the predominant religion. However . . . it operates along with a number of other rules which may either support or contradict it." Shows strategies to be dependent upon the "right to bestow a woman" and "claims over a woman." With structural implications and seven cases of alliance and romantic intrigue from Urdu novels.

1831 DERRETT, J. DUNCAN M. Sociology and family law in India: the problem of Hindu marriage. *In* Giri Raj Gupta, ed. Family and social change in modern India. New Delhi: Vikas, 1976. pp. 47-61. (Main Currents in Indian Sociology, 2).
Argues that many marriage negotiations are undertaken with reference to family feuds and for other reasons that do not regard the best interests of the couple. Stresses the need for further studies of betrothals (including relatives' expectations) and litigation procedures.

1832 GIST, NOEL P. Mate selection and mass communication in India. *In* Public Opinion Quarterly 17,4 (1953) 481-95.
Content analysis of a series of matrimonial advertisements from four leading Indian English-language newspapers.

1833 KHANNA, P.N. Choosing your mate for marriage. New Delhi: Social Publications, 1970? lv.
Observations and advice on how to select a proper spouse and have a happy marriage. The last section "In search of a husband" is addressed specifically to women. Clearly directed to westernized, urban people.

1834 Maya darpan. Directed by Kumar Shahani. (Hindi dialogue/French subtitles). 1972. 100 min. Color. [*Distributed by* Film Finance Corporation, White House, Walkeshwar Road, Bombay 400 006].
Film. A young woman remains single and locked into a conservative household because her father cannot find a bridegroom of sufficiently high status. She attempts to break out of these traditional bonds when she meets an architect. [Unexamined].

1835 NIEHOFF, ARTHUR. A study of matrimonial advertisements in North India. *In* Eastern Anthropologist 12,2 (1958/59) 73-86.
Analysis of 213 matrimonial advertisements from four North Indian English newspapers, 1953-54. Discusses contrasting male and female patterns and ranks desirable qualities.

1836 REYES-HOCKINGS, AMELIA. The newspaper as surrogate marriage broker in India. *In* Sociological Bulletin 15,1 (1966) 25-39.
Compares changing patterns in matrimonial advertisements from *The Hindu*, a Madras newspaper, 1936-61, with attitudes of 75 Indian students in the U.S. toward these "matrimonials."

1837 THEODORSON, GOERGE A. Romanticism and motivation to marry in the United States, Singapore, Burma, and India. *In* Social Forces 44,1 (1965) 17-26. [*Reprint in* Frank D. Cox, ed. American marriage: a changing scene? Dubuque, Iowa: William C. Brown Company Publishers, 1972. pp.96-107].
When studied in several student populations, the romantic value complex proved to be of least importance among Indians. The complex is measured by importance of physical attraction, confidence, equality of sacrifice and trust.

1838 UPRETI, H.C. Matrimonial advertisements: a brief sociological analysis. *In* J. of Family Welfare 14,1 (1967) 33-43.
Analyzes 200 ads from the *Hindustan Times* in Delhi by categories of age, caste, education, income of advertisers and qualities desired in a spouse.

1839 VREEDE-DE STUERS, CORA. Huwelijkadvertenties in India [Matrimonial advertisements in India]. *In* Mens en Maatschappij 37,1 (1962) 11-23 and 41,5 (1966) 378-85.
Analysis of matrimonial advertisements placed in *The Hindu* and the *Hindustan Times Weekly* in the late 1950s.

1840 _______. The relevance of matrimonial advertisements for the study of

mate selection in India. *In* Bijdragen: Tot de Taal-, Land- en Volkenkunde 125 (1969) 103-17.
Analyzes 569 matrimonial ads from the *Hindustan Times Weekly*, February 1964. Compares material with similar such studies as well as the author's study of female students of Jaipur.

1841 WIEBE, PAUL D. and G.N. RAMU. Marriage in India: a content analysis of matrimonial advertisements. *In* Man in India 51,2 (1971) 111-20.
Using a sample of marriage advertisements from English newspapers of Delhi and Madras, the authors contrast North and South Indian advertisers on the basis of their self-descriptions and criteria for mate selection. Subcaste and *gotra* stipulations in arrangement of marriages are found to be less important than general *varṇa* identifications. Individual preferences in the process of mate selection seem to be increasingly important. These changes are most typical of northern males.

ii) Rites

1842 BHATTACHARJEE, SUROVI. The bridal costume in different parts of India. *In* Times of India Annual (1963) 19-26.
Photographs and descriptions of variations in bridal clothing, jewelry and adornment among the regions of India.

1843 HUSAIN, YUSUF JAMAL. The story of a wedding in Pakistan. *In* Asian Folklore Studies 26,1 (1967) 119-27.
Presents essential elements of a Muslim wedding in South Asia, from marriage proposal to the return of the bride to her natal home. Notes regional variations.

1844 IKRAMULLAH, SHAISTA SUHRAWARDY. Wedding. *In* Pakistan Quarterly 1,5 (1951?) 55-7.
Describes ceremonies and procedures for an orthodox Muslim wedding, although such an elaborated version is rarely performed. Drawings.

1845 Invitation to an Indian wedding. Produced by Ezra Mir. Directed and written by Ramesh Gupta. 1961. 19 min. Color. 16 and 35 mm. [*Distributed by* Films Division, Ministry of Information and Broadcasting, 24 G. Deshmukh Marg, Bombay 400 026. *And* Information Service of India, 975 National Press Building, 529 14th Street NW, Washington, D.C. 20004].
Film of images of elaborate weddings from North and western India. The former includes a glittering bride, groom on horseback and *śahanāī* music. The latter includes scenes of the inspection of the bride, horoscope consultation, wedding band and fireworks. A three minute version, *An Indian Wedding*, depicting the western Indian wedding with narration, is available. [Unexamined. NUC].

iii) Economics of marriage: dowry and inheritance

1846 Dowry custom. Vivekananda Kendra Patrika 2,2 (1973) 256p.
Sixty-three brief articles, many excerpted and reprinted from other sources. Includes essays, skits, short stories, the text of the Dowry Prohibition Act of 1961 and survey results. The editorial position is to oppose dowry in any form.

1847 Dry leaves. Produced through Cine Co-operatives Limited, Bombay. 1961. 19 min. Black and white. 16 and 35 mm. [*Distributed by* Films Division, Ministry of Information and Broadcasting, 24 G. Deshmukh Marg, Bombay 400 026].
Film concerning problems created by the dowry system. [Unexamined. CF].

1848 HINCHCLIFFE, DOREEN. The widow's dower-debt in India. *In* Islam and the Modern Age 4,3 (1973) 5-22.
Summarizes important court cases concerning this aspect of Muslim widows' inheritance in India.

1849 INDIA (REPUBLIC). LAWS, STATUTES, ETC. Dowry Prohibition Act: containing an illuminating commentary on the act and states' notifications. By M.R. Achar and T. Venkanna. Allahabad: Law Book Company, 1962. 80p.
[Unexamined. NUC].

1850 ________. The prohibition of dowry act (act 28 of 1961). By R.L. Anand and Gargi Sethi. Allahabad: Law Publishers, 1962. 136p.
[Unexamined. NUC].

iv) The increasing female age at marriage: its causes and effects

Regarding age at marriage as fertility variable see entries 1901-24

1851 AGARWALA, S.N. Age at marriage in India. Allahabad: Kitab Mahal, 1962. 296p.
Study applying statistical techniques to census data from 1891 to 1951. Findings include a gradual increase in mean marriage age of women from approximately 13 to 15. Mean age for males has remained at approximately 20.

Much data analyzed by state, religion, caste, sex, age and year. With many tables and graphs.

1852 AHMED, FEROZ. Age at marriage in Pakistan. *In* J. of Marriage and the Family 31,4 (1969) 799-807.
Attempts to correct errors in previous estimates based on inaccurate census data. Also examines inter-regional and rural/urban differences. Tables.

1853 ALAM, SYED IQBAL. Age at marriage in Pakistan. *In* Pakistan Development Review 8,3 (1968) 489-98.
Estimates mean age at marriage, by sex, for the then Pakistan, East Pakistan and West Pakistan and the cities of Dacca, Karachi and Lahore, 1962-65.

1854 DANDEKAR, KUMUDINI. Age at marriage of women. *In* Economic and Political Weekly 9,22 (1 Jun 1974) 867-74.
Considers changing age at marriage patterns in India by state and rural/urban dimensions; compares overall patterns to those of several other countries, including Pakistan and Sri Lanka. Discusses reasons why age at marriage legislation has been ineffective in raising the actual marital age and factors that are effective in doing so.

1855 GOYAL, R.P. Shifts in age at marriage in India between 1961 and 1971. *In* Demography India 4,2 (1975) 336-44.
Concludes that age at marriage for males and females, urban and rural populations and all regions rose in the decade 1961-71. For women the mean age rose from 16.1 to 17.2 years and for men, from 21.4 to 22.2 years. "Kerala continues to hold the first position and Madhya Pradesh the last position in regard to mean age at marriage of both males and females."

1856 GULATI, SUBHASH CHANDER. Impact of literacy, urbanization and sex-ratio on age at marriage in India. *In* Artha Vijñana 11,4 (1969) 685-97.
Concludes, from 1961 census data, that, "for India as a whole it is literacy level which is most effective for a rise in age of marriage; this holds true for both sexes."

1857 Implications of raising the female age at marriage in India. Bombay: Demographic Training and Research Centre, 1968.
Proceedings of a seminar. [Unexamined].

1858 INDIA (DOMINION). LAWS, STATUTES, ETC. The Child Marriage Restraint Act, as amended up-to-date by Act XLI of 1949. Ed. by L.S. Sastry. Allahabad: Law Book Company, 1949. 114p.
[Unexamined. NUC].

1859 INDIA (REPUBLIC). LAWS, STATUTES, ETC. The Child Marriage Restraint Act: being an exhaustive, critical and up to date commentary on the Child Marriage Restraint Act, XIX of 1929, as amended by the Child Marriage Restraint (Amendment) Act, VII of 1938, the Child Marriage Restraint (Second Amendment) Act, XIX of 1938 and the Child Marriage Restraint (Amendment) Act, XLI of 1949. By Tek Chand and H.L. Saran, 2d ed. Calcutta: Eastern Law House, 1951. 128p.
[Unexamined. NUC].

1860 ________. The Child Marriage Restraint Act (as amended up to date). By L.S. Sastri . . . 2d ed., rev by R.B. Sethi . . . Allahabad: Law Book Company, 1956. 121p. [*1st ed.* India (Dominion). Laws, Statutes, etc. L.S. Shastry, ed. The Child Marriage Restraint Act, as amended up-to-date by Act XLI of 1949. Allahabad: Law Book Company, 1949. 106p.].
[Unexamined. NUC].

1861 JAIN, P.K. Marriage age patterns in India. *In* Artha Vijñana 11,4 (1969) 662-84.
Tabulates marriage age by sex, state and urban/rural residence using 1961 census data. Tables.

1862 KALE, B.D. Education and age at marriage of females in India. *In* J. of the Institute of Economic Research 4,1 (1969) 59-74.
Concludes that expanded female education would indirectly work toward raising female age at marriage. Examines urban/rural and regional differences in marriage age. Based on 1961 census data.

1863 KARKAL, MALINI. Annotated bibliography of studies on age at marriage in India. Bombay: International Institute for Population Studies, 1971. 25p.
References to 170 books, articles and unpublished papers.

1864 MALAKER, C.R. Socio-economic and demographic correlates of marriage patterns in India. *In* Demography India 4,2 (1975) 323-35.
Study determines that female age at marriage can be accurately predicted, with the aid of some socio-economic and demographic variables: female literacy rate; size of the female work force (15-35), ratio of single males (15-45) to single females (10-40) and size of urban population. "Male nuptuality, however, cannot be predicted so satisfactorily . . . . Female literacy plays a very crucial role in the determination of age at marriage and marriage rate for the female population."

1865 PATHAK, K.B. Marriage pattern of females in India during the decade 1951-61. *In* Artha Vijñana 14 (Jun 1972) 196-202.
Regarding the generation of female marriage probability statistics for studying changes in the level of fertility in the absence of a compulsory marriage registration system.

1866 SADIQ, NASIM MAHMOOD. The economic effects of postponement of marriage for

Pakistan. Ph.D. dissertation, American University, 1964. 204p. [University Microfilms 64-6769].
Estimates expected rise in age at marriage and its demographic and economic consequences. Focuses on women and their fertility. Compares East and West Pakistans. [Unexamined. DAI].

1867 SARKAR, B.N. Studies on age at first marriage in India. Calcutta?: Indian Statistical Institute, 1971. (Technical Report, Demo/6/71).
Reviews various studies and attempts to isolate factors affecting age of females and males at marriage. Notes that legislation has not had desired impact. [Unexamined].

1868 YADAV, S.S. Trends in marriage age of girls in India. *In* Artha Vijñāna 13,1 (1971) 119-37.
Concludes that the main trend in recent decades "has been a decline in marriages at ages 10-14 in 1941 and thereafter. Marriages so deferred took place at 15-19 and in some instances at 20-24 . . . . There has been little change in the proportion marrying after 25 . . . . trends in marriage patterns in individual states closely followed those observed for all India."

v) Polygamous marriages

1869 INDIA (REPUBLIC). OFFICE OF THE REGISTRAR GENERAL. Polygynous marriages in India: a survey. New Delhi: Office of the Registrar General and Census Commissioner, Government of India, 1975? 269p. (Census of India, 1971; Series 1: India, Miscellaneous Studies; Monograph 4 (1961 Series)).
Statistical tables of "State and village-wise incidence of polygynous marriages according to caste/tribe/community and religion" in different census decades.

1870 PETER, H.R.H. PRINCE OF GREECE AND DENMARK. A study of polyandry. The Hague: Mouton, 1963. 601p.
Section on the theory of polyandry considers questions of its existence, its distribution, its function and its correlates and reviews literature on the topic. Ethnographic section discusses polyandrous systems in Sri Lanka, South India and Tibet. The final section concludes with the "proposed Anthropological Theory of Polyandry."

1871 _______ et al. A study of polyandry. *In* Current Anthropology 6,1 (1965) 88. *With* Reviews, pp.88-104.
A *Current Anthropology* review of Prince Peter's *A Study of Polyandry*: following a short précis by the author, 16 scholars discuss and criticize the book; finally, the author responds to the various reviewers.

vi) Marriage legislation

1872 AGARWALA, RAJ KUMARI. Restitution of conjugal rights under Hindu law: a plea for the abolition of the remedy. *In* J. of the Indian Law Institute 12,2 (1970) 257-68.
Argues that this provision in the Hindu Marriage Act, 1955, which enables a court to compel a spouse to resume cohabitation, is insufficient for effecting a reconciliation and should be abolished. Legal interference in this matter of private morality is said to be unjust. Urges, instead, provisions for facilitating reconciliation by way of a counseling procedure.

1873 BAGGA, V., ed. Studies in the Hindu Marriage and Special Marriage Acts; under the auspices of the Indian Law Institute, New Delhi. Bombay: N.M. Tripathi, 1978. 352p.
Selected papers from the Seminar on the Hindu Marriage Act, 1956, and the Special Marriage Act, 1954, New Delhi, 1975. The papers critically examine various provisions of these laws and recommend improvements.

1874 DESAI, KUMUD. Hindu Marriage Act, 1955. Bombay: Popular Prakashan, 1965. 75p.
[Unexamined. IBP].

1875 _______. Special Marriage Act, 1954. Bombay: Popular Prakashan, 1965. 57p.
[Unexamined. IBP].

1876 INDIA (REPUBLIC) LAWS, STATUTES, ETC. The Special Marriage Act: act no. 43 of 1954. By L.S. Sastry. Allahabad: Law Book Company, 1955. 81p.
[Unexamined. NUC].

1877 _______. The Special Marriage Act, 1954 (act no. 43 of 1954): with an exhaustive commentary, explanatory and critical notes, case-law, High Court and state government rules, table of cases, index, etc. By D.H. Chaudhari, 2d ed. Calcutta: Eastern Law House, 1958. 340p.
Text and detailed interpretation of this act permitting civil marriages across caste and religious lines.

1878 _______. The commentaries on Hindu Marriage Act, 1955 (act no. XXV of 1955). By Kashi Prasad Saksena. Lucknow: Eastern Book Company, 1955. 234p.
[Unexamined. NUC].

1879 _______. The Hindu Marriage Act, 1955: act no. 25 of 1955: with an exhaustive commentary, explanatory and critical notes, case law, other mar-

riage and divorce acts, High Court rules, table of cases, index, etc. By D.H. Chaudhari, 2d ed. Calcutta: Eastern Law House, 1957. 413p.
Text and detailed interpretation of a key section of the Hindu Code. Appendixes contain texts of numerous previous pieces of marriage legislation.

1880 _______. Hindu marriage law: containing exhaustive commentaries on the Hindu Marriage Act (25 of 1955) and a detailed exposition of Hindu marriage law from earliest times to date, with useful appendices. By T.P. Gopalakrishnan. Allahabad: Law Book Company, 1957. 274p. [*2d ed.* Allahabad: Law Book Company, 1959. 352p.].
[Unexamined. NUC].

1881 _______. Hindu Marriage Act, act no. 25 of 1955. By Rishindra Nath Sarkar. Calcutta: S.C. Sarkar, 1956. 131p.
[Unexamined. NUC].

1882 _______. The Hindu Marriage Act: act no. 25 of 1955, as amended up to date. By P.V. Deolalkar, 2d ed. Allahabad: Law Book Company, 1964. 347p.
Contains text of act, commentary, High Court cases, and rulings and texts of numerous other pieces of marriage legislation.

1883 _______. The Hindu Marriage Act: act no. XXV of 1955. By P.S. Bindra, 2d ed., rev. and enl. Delhi: Metropolitan Book Company, 1965. 605p.
[Unexamined. NUC].

1884 _______. Indian law of marriage and divorce. By Kumud Desai, 3d ed. Bombay: N.M. Tripathi, 1978. 576p.
Includes provisions, amendments and relevant case law of Special Marriage Act, 1954; Hindu Marriage Act, 1955; Parsi Marriage and Divorce Act, 1936; Indian Christian Marriage Act, 1872; Indian Divorce Act, 1869; and, in less detail, a variety of other enactments. Discusses Muslin personal law.

1885 JAI LAL. Law of marriage and divorce in India. Delhi: Metropolitan Book Company, 1956. 262p.
[Unexamined. NUC].

1886 LATIFI, DANIAL. Indian marriage laws and the rights of women. *In* Enquiry n.s. 2,3 (1965) 103-18.
Briefly summarizes civil and religious marriage codes in India. Gives historical background and stresses need for reforms.

1887 MADHAVA, ANAND and MIRZA KAZIM HUSAIN. Marriage and the dissolution of marriage in Muslim law: with a commentary of the Dissolution of Muslim Marriages Act. Lucknow: Eastern Book Company, 1950. 127p.
Sections on marriage, divorce and maintenance according to the Muslim law of India. Reproduces text of Dissolution of Muslim Marriages Act, 1939.

1888 QURESHI, M.A. Marriage and matrimonial remedies: a uniform civil code for India. Delhi: Concept Publishing Company, 1978. 484p.
"All the existing matrimonial laws of India . . . have been discussed and compared to reach the right conclusion." Critically examines "form, content, nature, and potential" of the personal marriage laws and remedies for marriage problems of the various religious communities in India. Argues for need for a uniform code applying to all.

1889 SILVA, S. Christian marriage legislation. *In* New Review 30 (Feb 1950) 69-76.
Discusses provisions of the Indian Christian Marriage Act of 1872, a consolidation of Christian marriage enactments from 1852 to 1872, which, slightly amended, continued to be in effect in 1950 when this article was written.

1890 VERMA, B.R. Muslim marriage and dissolution. Allahabad: Law Book Company, 1971. 358p.
Study of the relationship between pure Muslim personal law relating to marriage and Muslim marriage law as enacted and administered in India in the 19th and 20th centuries. Much on women, directly and indirectly.

1891 ZAFAR, EMMANUEL. Law relating to Christian marriages in Pakistan, India and Bangladesh. Lahore: Eastern Law House, 1976. 122p.
This handbook was not designed to be a "detailed and full commentary" on Christian marriage law, but rather a "reliable and comprehensive guide" in a "handy form" for the use of clergymen, judicial officials and lawyers. Consists mainly of an annotated text of the Indian Christian Marriage Act, 1872, along with appendixes of ecclesiastical laws.

(c) Reproductive patterns

Regarding family planning see entries 2477-2529

1892 KABIRAJ, SHIBNARAYAN. Women in the domestic rites and beliefs of the Hindus and the Muslims. *In* Folklore [Calcutta] 10,2 (1969) 38-54. [*Also in* Sankar Sen Gupta, ed. Women in Indian folklore. Calcutta: Indian Publications, 1969. pp.259-76. (*Its* Folklore Series, 15)].
Discusses rites associated with aspects of women's reproductive life: menstruation, pregnancy, newborn children and barrenness. Based on fieldwork in Muzaffarpur and neigh-

boring areas of Bihar, Nadia District in West Bengal and Bakerganj District of the then East Pakistan.

1893 SEN, TULIKA. Reproductive life of Indian women. *In* Man in India 33,1 (1953) 31-54.
Compares data from Calcutta, a nearby village and Travancore with respect to age at menarche, interval between menarche and conception, age of mother at first birth, sex ratios of children, number of children, birth intervals, interval between last birth and menopause and age at menopause.

i) Onset of menstruation

1894 CHAKRAVARTTI, R. and Y. RENUKA. The trend of age at menarche in India. *In* J. of Social Research 13,2 (1970) 82-94.
Compares data from various caste levels, religious communities and geographical areas. The most striking variations found were with respect to the urban/rural variable: onset of menstruation tended to be earlier in rural areas.

1895 CHATTOPADHYAY, P.K. and S. KHULLAR. The age at menarche in Indian girls. *In* Kanti B. Pakrasi, Amulya R. Banerjee and Amal K. Das, eds. Biosocial studies in India: a reading in collected papers, 1961-70. Calcutta: Editions Indian, 1976. pp.54-8.
Assesses evidence presented in 19 published local studies regarding regional variation in mean age at menarche. Suggests numerous socio-economic factors that might be more influential than environmental ones. Urges further study.

1896 ROBERTSON, JOHN. On the period of puberty in Hindu women. *In* Edinburgh Medical and Surgical Journal 64,164 (1845) 156-69. *And* Supplement, pp.257-64. *With* Modusoodun Gupta. On menstruation among Hindu females, pp.257-61.
A segment of Robertson's "inquiries concerning the alleged influence of climate in different regions of the earth in determining the earlier or later occurrence of female puberty." He reviews information solicited from Europeans in India, including a list of 90 cases with an average menarche age of twelve years and four months, and compares this to figures from other parts of the world. Modusoodun Gupta supplies opinions of Hindu tradition textual authorities on the subject and observations from his medical practice in Calcutta and environs. He provides data from 149 women, the average menarche age of which is twelve years and seven months. The articles contain cultural as well as statistical information.

ii) Fertility studies

1897 BEBARTA, PRAFULLA CHANDRA. Recent studies in fertility. *In* Sociological Bulletin 10,2 (1961) 27-41.
Review article with 57 references. Compares studies from India and elsewhere to examine relationship of demographic patterns to research trends.

1898 DANDEKAR, KUMUDINI. Trends of fertility behaviour reflecting the status of women. *In* Social Change 4,3/4 (1974) 36-41.
Considers the relationship between Indian women's overall low status and their lack of control over their fertility. Reflects upon the consequence of this situation for the nation as a whole.

1899 MANDELBAUM, DAVID G. Human fertility in India: social components and policy perspectives. Berkeley: University of California Press, 1974. 132p. [*Expanded version of* Social components of Indian fertility. *In* Economic and Political Weekly 8,4/6 (1973) 151-72].
Surveys Indian family planning program, considers traditional reasons for large families and for limiting fertility, along with traditional methods of birth control. "Finally, suggestions are proposed for applying our knowledge of the social and cultural components of fertility behavior to family planning programs, both in the immediate future and in the longer time perspective."

1900 PATANKAR, TARA. A bibliography of fertility studies in India. Bombay: Demographic Training and Research Centre, 1969. 38p.
Annotated bibliography of 200 books, articles and unpublished papers relating to fertility studies in India in the first 18 years after independence.

iii) Fertility differentials and correlates

1901 AGARWALA, S.N. Social and cultural factors affecting fertility in India. *In* Population Review 8,1 (1964) 73-8.
Discusses three factors: age at marriage, age at widowhood and family-building patterns.

1902 BASAVARAJAPPA, K.G. and M.I. BELVALGIDAD. Changes in age at marriage of females and their effect on the birth rate in India. *In* Eugenics Quarterly 14,1 (1967) 14-26. *With*

Prem P. Talwar. A note on changes in age at marriage of females and their effect on the birthrate in India. 14,4 (1967) 291-5. *And* K.G. Basavarajappa. Changes in age at marriage of females and their effect on the birth rate in India: a reply. 15,4 (1968) 293-5.
Calculates effect of hypothetical situation of an average female age at marriage of over 20 years on birth rate, other demographic features remaining constant. Concludes: "The ultimate decline in the birthrate . . . may not exceed 10 per cent." Therefore such efforts by themselves are insufficient for controlling India's population. Ensuing discussion concerns methodological problems.

1903 DUBEY, D. and AMITA BARDHAN. Status of women and fertility in India. New Delhi: National Institute of Family Planning, 1972. 49p. (*Its* Monograph Series, 18).
Briefly reviews fertility ideals for Indian women and relates various socio-economic features (urban/rural, educational level, etc.) to fertility patterns.

1904 DUZA, MOHAMMED BADRUD. Differential fertility in Pakistan. *In* Warren C. Robinson, ed. Studies in the demography of Pakistan. Karachi: Pakistan Institute of Development Economics, 1967. pp.93-137.
Considers differential fertility rates by region, urban/rural, city size, marital behavior, religion and other parameters. Data from 1961 census. Includes 104 references, most to demography and fertility in Pakistan.

1905 HUSAIN, I.Z. Mean age at marriage and natality: state and divisional estimates; report. Lucknow: Demographic Research Centre, University of Lucknow, 196_. 68p.
[Unexamined. ALI].

1906 INAYATULLAH, ATTIYA. Impact of culture on fertility in Pakistan. *In* International Planned Parenthood Federation Conference 7th, Singapore, 1963. pp.111-5.
Reviews values and practices that encourage high fertility in Pakistan. [Unexamined].

1907 INDIA (REPUBLIC). DIRECTORATE OF THE NATIONAL SAMPLE SURVEY. Tables with notes on couple fertility. Delhi: Manager of Publications, Government of India, 1970. 180p. (National Sample Survey, 154).
Presents extensive statistical documentation of fertility patterns. Data from 1961-62.

1908 INDIA (REPUBLIC). VITAL STATISTICS DIVISION. Fertility differentials in India: results of the fertility survey in a sub-sample of SRS, 1972. New Delhi: Vital Statistics Division, Office of the Registrar General and Census Commissioner, Ministry of Home Affairs, Government of India, 1976. 106p.
Fertility figures from the Sample Registration System (SRS), initiated in India in 1964-65, with respect to many socio-economic variables.

1909 JAIN, S.P. Certain statistics on fertility of Indian women to show the effect of age at marriage. New Delhi: Office of the Registrar General, Government of India, 1964.
Associates later age at marriage with decreased fertility. [Unexamined].

1910 ________. Indian fertility: our knowledge and gaps. *In* J. of Family Welfare 10,4 and 11,1 (1964) 16-32, 6-19.
Describes fertility patterns and discusses physiological and social factors behind them. Based upon a sample survey rather than a review of the literature.

1911 KHAN, MASIHUR RAHMAN and LEE L. BEAN. Interrelationships of some fertility measures in Pakistan. *In* Pakistan Development Review 7,4 (1967) 504-18.
Data from the early 1960s. "The corollary of a high fertility is a *young population* with a high burden of children . . . . A high dependency burden exerts a continued pressure for consumption at the cost of savings. High fertility also reduces the number of women available for both household work and gainful employment." Concludes that family planning program expansion will have a greater impact than efforts to increase age at marriage.

1912 KLEINMAN, DAVID S. Fertility variation and resources in rural India, 1961. *In* Economic Development and Cultural Change 21,4, part 1 (1973) 679-96.
Attempts to show that rational, economic decisions are related to the fertility patterns reflected in the 1961 census, in contrast to frequent arguments in the literature for the exclusive sway of cultural factors.

1913 KOSAMBI, D.D. and S. RAGHAVACHARI. Seasonal variation in the Indian birth-rate. *In* Annals of Eugenics 16, 2 (1951) 165-92.
Reviews various data concerning seasonal birth variation in India and presents it on polar coordinate graphs, which have the advantage of clarity and precision. Attributes urban variation directly to changes in weather and rural variation to weather changes and ensuing demands for agricultural labor.

1914 KURUP, R.S., ed. Studies on fertility in India. Gandhigram: Gandhigram Institute of Rural Health and Family Planning, 1975. 510p. (*Its* Monograph Series, 7).
Thirty-one papers address fertility differentials, regional trends, family planning programs and other topics.

1915 MANDELBAUM, DAVID G. Fertility of early years of marriage in India. *In* K.M. Kapadia, ed. Professor Ghurye felicitation volume. Bombay: Popular Book Depot, 1954? pp.150-68.

Census-based study argues that raising the minimal legal age at marriage by a few years would have little effect on the birth rate because of a period of relative infecundity following menarche. Discusses psychosocial strain that expectation of pregnancy brings to young brides.

1916 NAG, MONI. Factors affecting human fertility in nonindustrial societies: a cross-cultural study. New Haven, Connecticut: Department of Anthropology, Yale University, 1962. 227p. (Yale University Publications in Anthropology, 66).
Essay (a revised dissertation) considers the relationship of postpartum abstinence, frequency of coitus, lactation period, extent of polygyny, menstrual taboos on intercourse, age at marriage, absence of males, celibacy, divorce, widow marriage and other factors to fertility in nonindustrial societies. Examines five societies in detail, including rural Sinhalese and rural Bengali Hindus and Muslims. Appendix C coordinates ethnographic and statistical data.

1917 _______. Sex, culture and human fertility: India and the United States. *In* Current Anthropology 13,2 (1972) 231-7.
Study of "average frequency of complete coitus within regular sexual union" as a fertility variable. Refutes assumption of high frequency of coitus in India, which is often linked to poverty and lack of alternate recreation: "The average frequency of coitus among Indian women of various age groups is found to be less than that among American white women of corresponding age groups."

1918 _______. Tribal — non-tribal fertility differential in India. *In* Demography India 2,1 (1973) 104-20.
Asserts that the general acceptance of widow marriage in tribal communities is a significant variable in the higher fertility rates of tribal women. Urges further research in this area.

1919 PAKRASI, KANTI. Fertility and population problems in India: a biosocial study. *In* J. of the Indian Anthropological Society 10,2 (1975) 181-94.
Study of "some important factors which are thought to have significant impact on fertility vis-a-vis population increase in Indian society at large." Discusses 1961-71 growth rate, female age at marriage, female age at effective marriage, proportion of women married, age at menarche and average number of live births per couple. Stresses need for a sophisticated understanding of interrelationship of variables.

1920 PRABHU, JOHN COELHO. Social and cultural determinants of fertility in India: a codification of research findings. Ph.D. dissertation, Department of Sociology?, University of Massachusetts, 1970. 174p. [University Microfilms 70-23,039].
Assesses scientific merit of 168 fertility surveys. Isolates 68 cultural variables said to determine fertility in the studies and relates them to a series of 40 hypotheses. [Unexamined. DAI].

1921 PUNEKAR, VIJAYA. Fertility, education and social change. *In* Sociological Bulletin 23,1 (1974) 99-111.
Review article regarding the relationship between female education and fertility level in India.

1922 SAMUEL, T.J. Culture and human fertility in India. *In* J. of Family Welfare 9,4 (1963) 45-53.
Examines ways in which Hindu culture has influenced reproductive patterns through its emphasis on "social stability." Discusses the joint family, the householder stage of life, virginity and early marriage, caste endogamy, ban on widow marriage, sexual abstinence during festivals, abortion.

1923 SINGHA, P. Infant mortality and the level of fertility in India: a review. *In* Demography India 4,2 (1975) 457-76.
Suggests that a lower rate of infant mortality would reduce fertility rates because parents would feel secure with a fewer number of children. Bibliography of 96 relevant works.

1924 SRINIVAS, M.N. and E.A. RAMASWAMY. Culture and human fertility in India. Delhi: Oxford University Press, 1977. 32p.
Relates domestic, economic and political factors to rural fertility in India as revealed in the ethnographic literature. Argues that fundamentals of Indian fertility have not been grasped because fertility has not been treated as an aspect of culture.

iv) Maternity data

1925 CHANDRASEKHAR, S. Infant mortality, population growth and family planning in India. London: George Allen and Unwin, 1972. 399p. [*Also* Chapel Hill: University of North Carolina Press].
". . . an attempt to survey the level, causes, and course of infant mortality in India during the last seventy years, 1901-71." Also "examines the various implications of high and low infant mortality on the country's major problem of population growth and the current population policy designed to reduce the birth rate through family planning."

1926 INDIA (REPUBLIC). CENSUS COMMISSION. Maternity data: 1951 census. Delhi: Manager of Publications, Government of India, 1953. 95p. (Census of India, 1951, Papers, 5).
Compilation of 1951 census data from

Travancore-Cochin and Madhya Pradesh on various maternity patterns: average number of children born and surviving according to age of mother, mother's age at first birth and so forth. Excerpts from 1921 and 1931 censuses show parallel all-India figures from an earlier period.

1927 SEN GUPTA, S.K. and P.N. KAPOOR. Maternal mortality in India. New Delhi: Central Bureau of Health Intelligence, Directorate General of Health Services, Ministry of Health and Family Planning, Government of India, 1972. 1v. (*Its* Technical Studies, I-15).
Attempts to describe the rates and trends of maternal mortality in India and its major causes. Uses data from the registration system, the medical certification of cause of death program of several cities, the model registration program of certain primary centers and the records of medical institutions. Consists primarily of numerous tables.

1928 SURJIT KAUR. Wastage of children. New Delhi: Sterling Publishers Pvt. Ltd., 1978. 282p.
Presents and assesses data on child wastage (abortion, miscarriage, stillbirth and infant mortality) from three field surveys. Includes material on maternal health problems, social pressure to bear children (especially male children), male/female infant mortality, relationship of child mortality to parity and other issues, by region. Reviews many studies and presents statistical material in tables (pp.151-278). Recommendations focus on improved female education and health services for women.

v) Midwifery

1929 BREY, KATHLEEN HEALY. The missing midwife: why a training programme failed. *In* South Asian Review 5,1 (1971) 41-52.
Study of midwives and the midwife training program officially sponsored by the government of India since 1956. Based on project files and reports in New Delhi and ethnographic reports. Stresses absence of available information on midwives.

1930 DAMLE, Y.B. Auxiliary nurse midwife: a study in institutionalized change. *In* Bulletin of the Deccan College Research Institute 19,3/4 (1959) 237-79.
Study of a training institution for women specializing in midwifery. Focuses on three aspects: institutional organization, attitudes and socio-economic background of trainees and social organization of the institutional community. Location unspecified.

vi) Birth rites and "female horoscopy"

1931 BHATNAGAR, MANJU. Singing away the in-law blues. *In* Eve's Weekly 30,29 (17 Jul 1976) 28.
"Jachcha songs, sung during pregnancy rituals [in many parts of India], give women an opportunity to mock at the in-laws." English translations of three such songs.

1932 GHURYE, G.S. "Disposal of human placenta": with special reference to India. *In his* Anthropo-sociological papers. Bombay: Popular Prakashan, 1963. pp.95-173. [*Reprint from* J. of the University of Bombay 6, part I (1937/38) 1-65].
Reviews customs regarding the use and disposal of the placenta and afterbirth in South Asian and other communities.

1933 SRIVASTAVA, SAHAB LAL. Birth-rites: a comparative study. *In* Eastern Anthropologist 24,2 (1971) 181-96.
Compares data obtained from older women on pregnancy and birth rites in a village from Rajasthan's Jaipur District and a village in Gorakhpur District, U.P. Considers villages to be socio-economically "more or less comparable" and notes many similarities.

1934 SURYANARAYAN RAO, BENGAKURU. Strijataka or female horoscopy, 7th ed? Bangalore: Raman Publications, 1970. 149p.
[Unexamined. IBP].

1935 THANKAPPAN NAIR, P. Couvade: a vanishing custom in India. *In* Quarterly J. of the Mythic Society, Bangalore 61, 1/4 (1970) 81-91.
Reviews taboos and rituals observed by new fathers among various tribal and peasant groups. Rarely performed today, "relics of its practice" are, however, widespread. Speculates about its distant history.

vii) Abortion, infanticide

1936 CHANDRASEKHAR, S. Should we legalize abortion in India? *In* Population Review 10,2 (1966) 17-22.
Proposes that, while conventional scientific contraceptive measures are desirable, legalized abortions should be available when these measures fail. Time of abortion is opportune for encouraging sterilization or providing information on reliable contraceptive methods.

1937 ________. Abortion in a crowded world: the problem of abortion with special reference to India. London: George Allen and Unwin, 1974. 184p. [*Also* Seattle: University of Washington Press. (John Danz Lecture Series)].
Three lectures delivered at the University of Washington regarding: 1) views of abortion in India and elsewhere, 2) India's population problem and 3) India's liberalization of her abortion law. Appendixes include: 1971 legal status of abortion in selected countries; medical indications for pregnancy termination; questionnaire of Committee to Study the Question of the Legalization of Abortion, India; anonymous report of illegal abortions done in an Indian clinic; selected population figures from 1951, 1961 and 1971 censuses of India; religious composition in these three censuses; selected editorial opinions on abortion from Indian press and some US Supreme Court decisions on abortion.

1938 CHATTERJI, SARAL KUMAR, ed. Legalisation of abortion. Madras: Christian Literature Society, 1971. 71p. (Studies on National Legislation, 3).
Papers presented at a seminar on the Medical Termination of Pregnancy Bill in 1970. [Unexamined. NUC].

1939 GOUR, HARI SINGH. Law of hurt and homicide: along with causing of miscarriage, injuries to unborn children, of the exposure of infants, etc., and Medical Termination of Pregnancy Act, 1971. Rev. by M.C. Desai et al. Allahabad: Delhi Law House, 1974. 743p.
Sections consider law relating to abortion and infanticide (pp.430-54).

1940 INDIA (REPUBLIC). COMMITTEE TO STUDY THE QUESTION OF LEGALISATION OF ABORTION. Report. New Delhi: Department of Family Planning, Ministry of Health and Family Planning, Government of India, 1967. 143p.
Recommends a liberalization of the Indian legal code to permit an abortion when the mother's physical or mental health is in danger, when the child will likely be handicapped, when the pregnancy is a result of rape or when the mother is under 16 and unmarried or mentally defective, along with other policy considerations. Appendixes give resolution that established the committee, questionnaire sent to numerous state and other agencies throughout India and summary of results and a summary of abortion laws in other countries (including Nepal).

1941 KARKAL, MALINI. A bibliography of abortion studies in India. Bombay: International Institute for Population Studies, 1970. 10p.
Briefly annotated references to 108 sources.

1942 MOHANTY, S.P. A review of some selected studies on abortion in India. *In* J. of Family Welfare 14,4 (1968) 39-48.
Reviews studies on abortion in rural and urban areas of India. Emphasizes difficulties involved in obtaining reliable information on this topic.

1942a Seminar on medical and socio-economic aspects of abortion, Calcutta, November 25-27, 1972. Calcutta: Family Planning Association of India, 1973? 172p.
Seminar designed to help develop an educational program that would make the Medical Termination of Pregnancy Act of 1971 effective. Contains various inaugural addresses and 20 papers from sessions on medical and socio-economic aspects of abortion. Appendix reproduces text of act.

1943 SINGH, K.S. and R.K. RAIZADA. Abortion law in India: past and present. Chandigarh: Family Planning Association of India, Haryana Branch, 1976. 171p. [Unexamined. ALI].

1944 TEMPLE, RICHARD CARNAC. Folk medicine: abortion. *In* Panjab Notes and Queries 2,15 (1884) 42-3.
One strong and three standard strength recipes for medicines to induce abortion. Source not given.

viii) Menopause

1945 TALUKDAR, SUMITA. On age at menopause in India. *In* Man in India 57,4 (1977) 345-50.
Reviews 14 studies of age at menopause from West Bengal, Arunachal Pradesh, Assam, Delhi and Maharashtra. Concludes: "1. Caste hierarchy or social status seem to have no relation with mean age at menopause. 2. Mean menopausal age seems to be low where the mean menarcheal age is high. 3. Parity seems to have no relation with the mean menopausal age."

(d) Motherhood and child rearing

1946 ARYA, SUBHASH C. Infant and child care for the Indian mother. Delhi: Vikas, 1972. 195p.
Illustrated. [Unexamined. IBP].

1947 DEVADAS, RAJAMMAL P. Mother and child care. *In* B.N. Ganguli, ed. Social development: essays in honour of Smt. Durgabai Deshmukh. New Delhi: Sterling

Publishers, 1977. pp.206-13.
"The care of the mother and child needs attention in three major areas: health, nutrition, and personality development." Reviews the aims, principles and programs of the Integrated Child Development Scheme (ICDS), the "main thrust of the social welfare sector in the Fifth Plan."

1948 Four families. Produced by National Film Board of Canada. Directed by Ian McNeill. 1965. 2 parts: 30 and 30 min. Black and white. 16 mm. [*Distributed by* New York University Film Library, 43 Press Annex, Washington Square, New York, New York 10003. *And* Contemporary/McGraw-Hill Films, Department BF, 1221 Avenue of the Americas, New York, New York 10020].
First part of this film examines families in India and France, including details of child rearing and religious activities. Margaret Mead narrates, describing the relation between child rearing and national character. Families in Canada and Japan are compared in the second part. [Unexamined. NUC].

1949 GHOSH, SHANTI. The feeding and care of infants and young children, 2d ed. New Delhi: Voluntary Health Association of India, 1977. 114p.
Expansion and adaptation to Indian conditions of a United Nations manual on feeding infants and young children. Both descriptive and programmatic, the report considers many aspects of maternal and child nutrition and health.

1950 GOKULANANTHAN, K.S. and K.S. VERGHESE. Child care in a developing community: a preliminary survey. Ernakulam: printed at Anand Press, 1967. 72p.
Descriptive and prescriptive material on nutrition, immunization, clothing and hygiene by two pediatricians.

1951 GUPTA, BIMALENDU. Upbringing of an Indian child. *In* Baidya Nath Varma, ed. Contemporary India. Bombay: Asia Publishing House, 1964. pp.187-200.
Considers prenatal environment and childbirth, postnatal care, childhood and adolescent experiences and, briefly, non-Hindu upbringing. Stresses socialization and psychological development. Based on studies of high-caste and middle-class families made by the B.M. Institute of Psychology and Child Development, Ahmedabad, and others.

1952 KAKAR, SUDHIR. Mothers and infants. *In his* The inner world: a psycho-analytic study of childhood and society in India. Delhi: Oxford University Press, 1978. pp.52-112.
An "exploration of the intra-psychic, social and cultural forces that shape Indian motherhood" in order to understand the "initial crystallization of the infant's inner world." Examines feminine identity patterns in order to understand the developmental experiences of the upper-caste Hindu male.

1953 LAHIRI, SUBRATA. Preference for sons and ideal family in urban India. *In* Indian J. of Social Work 34,4 (1974) 323-36.
Calculates intensity of preference for sons and correlations with various socio-economic factors, using data from twelve urban areas. Contains interstate comparisons.

1954 ________. Sex preference in relation to desire for additional children in urban India. *In* Demography India 4,1 (1975) 86-107.
Suggests which circumstances favor the desire for children of a particular gender, using National Sample Survey data, 1960-61, from 16,000 husbands from many cities and towns.

1955 LEBOYER, FREDERICK. Loving hands. New York: Alfred A. Knopf, 1976. 139p.
Photo-documentation of a Calcutta mother practicing "the traditional Indian art of baby massage" with her two small children.

1956 Maa. Produced through Art Films of Asia Private Limited, Bombay. 1956. 23 min. Black and white. 16 and 35 mm. [*Distributed by* Films Division, Ministry of Information and Broadcasting, 24 G. Deshmukh Marg, Bombay 400 026].
Film. Portrays the problems of unmarried mothers and their children in India. [Unexamined. CF].

1957 PANDIT, VIJAYA LAKSHMI. Children and their upbringing. *In* Shyam Kumari Nehru, ed. Our cause: a symposium by Indian women. Allahabad: Kitabistan, 1938? pp.36-47.
Advice for parents encouraging respect, restraint, appreciation, gentle guidance and acceptance of individual differences. Also encourages sex education.

1958 Special issue: your baby. Eve's Weekly 30,51 (18 Dec 1976) 73p.
Includes articles on child development, early education, parenting, readers' views of motherhood, fathers' role, pets, toys, health, etc. Photographs.

1959 TIRUMALA RAO, P. Infant upbringing habits in India. *In* P. Tirumala Rao, ed. Pediatric problems in developing countries: Dr. S.T. Achar commemoration volume. Madras: Orient Longmans, 1970. [Unexamined. ALI].

1960 Training of children. Karachi: Peermahomed Ebrahim Trust, 1976. 193p.
Numerous topics covered briefly in this guide to the proper upbringing of children for *Shī'ah* Muslims.

1961 VAKIL, JAFAR ALI M. At mother's feet. Tr. from Urdu and Gujarati. Karachi: Peermahomed Ebrahim Trust, 1975. 130p.
Shī'ah interpretation of the status of mother in Islam. Parables, sayings, advice and in-

junctions about the proper behavior and attitudes of children for mothers and vice versa. Includes an address, "To Community Mothers," given by Mahomedalibhoy C. Bhojani on the occasion of International Women's Year.

(e) Adult and unmarried: a small minority with unique problems

1962 DESAI, ARVINDRAI N. The spinster has a world to win. *In* Social Welfare 18, 11 (1972) 15,22.
Argues that, with a positive attitude, an older unmarried woman can lead a fulfilling life.

(f) Widowhood: status, rates, remarriage

1963 AGARWAL, S.N. Widow remarriages in some rural areas of northern India. *In* Demography 4,1 (1967) 126-34.
Study of 1% of the rural households in Mathura and Saharanpur Districts, U.P., and Rohtak District, Punjab, reveals that 19, 34 and 25 percent, respectively, of the ever-widowed females remarried. Associates higher remarriage rates with lower age groups, Muslims and low castes.

1964 BHATE, VAIJAYANTI. Decline in mortality and change in age at marriage as factors affecting incidence of widowhood. *In* Artha Vijñāna 6,2 (1964) 92-105.
Relates decline in mortality and change in age at marriage to a decline in incidence of widowhood in India, using data from 1951, 1961 and 1971.

1965 HAAS, V. and R. MUKHERJI. Hindu widows. *In* Aryan Path 9 (1941) 396-405. [Unexamined].

1966 KAMAT, A.R. The decline in death rate and its effect on the extent of widowhood. *In* Sociological Bulletin 12,1 (1963) 18-31.
Uses data from a Maharashtrian village, all-India census data and international demographic statistics to investigate the hypothesis that a decline in mortality in a population will reduce the extent of widowhood, but as the process continues the extent of widowhood in the older age group is likely to increase.

1967 Kanku. Directed by Kantilal Rathod. (Gujarati dialogue/English subtitles). 1970. 100 min. Black and white. [*Distributed by* Film Finance Corporation, White House, Walkeshwar Road, Bombay 400 006].
Film portrays events in the life of a village widow. Kanku runs her own farm and arranges her son's wedding. When she becomes pregnant and refuses to identify the child's father, the village women arrange for a substitute candidate. [Unexamined].

1968 PAKRASI, KANTI. A study on widowhood in India, 1951. *In* Bulletin of the Cultural Research Institute, Calcutta 5,1/2 (1966) 67-74. [*Reprint in* Kanti B. Pakrasi, Amulya R. Banerjee and Amal K. Das, comps. Biosocial studies in India: a reading in collected papers, 1961-70. Calcutta: Editions Indian, 1976. pp.370-81].
Demographical geography of Indian women from "disrupted" marriages. Does not statistically distinguish widowed women from the proportionally small group of divorced women. Finds greater marriage instability among women from urban areas of southern, western and central regions.

1969 SHETH, JYOTSNA. Widows. *In* Eve's Weekly 26,9 (26 Feb 1972) 10-1.
Criticizes traditional attitudes toward and expectations of widows.

1970 [Special section on widowhood]. *In* Eve's Weekly 32,32 (12 Aug 1978) 33-42.
A series of articles review and criticize traditional and contemporary position of Indian widows, describe the mourning and adjustment experiences of several widows and offer advice to recent widows.

(5) The "inner" world: home and family life, often considered women's sphere par excellence

1971 Centre calling. v1- (1966-). New Delhi: printed at Department of Social Welfare, Government of India. Monthly.
"'Centre Calling' is devoted to the cause of family welfare but does not restrict itself to the official point of view alone." Brief articles, often with photographs. Much on women.

1972 DAS, VEENA. The status of women in relation to the institutions of kinship and marriage. *In* Veena Das, ed. The social fabric: studies on family and kinship. Bombay: Allied Publishers, forthcoming. (SNDT Women's University, Bombay; Women in a Changing Society).
Examines rules of 1) descent, inheritance and

succession, 2) residence and 3) marriage in India as they affect the status of Hindu and, to a lesser extent, Muslim women. [Manuscript examined].

1973 ________, ed. The social fabric: studies on family and kinship systems. Bombay: Allied Publishers, forthcoming. (SNDT Women's University, Bombay; Women in a changing society).
Papers sponsored jointly by the Indian Council of Social Science Research and the SNDT Women's University. [Unexamined].

1974 DEVANANDAN, P.D. and M.M. THOMAS, eds. The changing pattern of family in India, enl. and rev. ed. Revised by R.W. Taylor. Bangalore: Christian Institute for the Study of Religion and Society, 1966. 228p.
Describes traditional joint family relationships and contemporary changes. Considers consequences of these changes, including mental health risks, population growth and modern ideals. Concludes with a Christian perspective on the family.

1975 DUBE, LEELA. Sociology of kinship: a trend report. *In* A survey of research in sociology and social anthropology, v2. Bombay: Popular Prakashan, 1974. pp.233-366. [*Reprinted as* Sociology of kinship: an analytical survey of literature. Bombay: Popular Prakashan, 1974. 154p.].
Extensive bibliographic essay sponsored by the Indian Council of Social Science Research. Lists and discusses (descriptively and critically) hundreds of books, articles, theses and unpublished papers. Concludes with a discussion of needed research. Many materials are indirectly rather than directly related to women.

1976 DUMONT, LOUIS. Marriage in India: the present state of the question, 1: marriage alliance in South-east India and Ceylon. *And* Postscript to Part 1. *And* 2: marriage and status, Nayar and Newar. *And* 3: North India in relation to South India. *In* Contributions to Indian Sociology 5 (1961) 75-95, 7 (1964) 77-80, 80-98 and 9 (1966) 90-114. *With* Christoph von Fürer-Haimendorf. Comment 7 (1964) 99-102.
Reviews South Asian kinship studies of the 1950s and early 1960s and assesses their conclusions with respect to structural-alliance theory. The papers offer much on the place of women in South Asian kinship systems and in structural theory.

1977 INDIA (REPUBLIC). COMMITTEE ON THE STATUS OF WOMEN IN INDIA. Socio-cultural setting of women's status: descent, marriage and family. *In its* Towards equality: report of the Committee on the Status of Women in India. New Delhi: Department of Social Welfare, Ministry of Education and Social Welfare, Government of India, 1975. pp.54-83. [*Chair* Phulrenu Guha].
Concise survey of contemporary kinship patterns that "provide the major contours of the socio-cultural setting in which women are born, brought up, and live their lives." Main topics treated are matrilineal and patrilineal descent, family organization, marriage, bride-price and dowry, widowhood, age at marriage and customary marriages. Addresses variations by religion, region, class, community and so forth.

1978 KAPUR, PROMILLA. Women in modern India. *In* Man Singh Das and Panos D. Bardis, eds. The family in Asia. New Delhi: Vikas, 1978? pp.108-47.
"An attempt is being made to present a general and broad all-India picture of women in relation to the family." Reviews history of womanhood in India and contemporary status in various spheres (political, educational, legal, employment). Describes patterns of marriage and family relationships and changing trends. In the process, reviews numerous studies.

1979 KOLENDA, PAULINE M. Region, caste, and family structure: a comparative study of the Indian "joint" family. *In* Milton Singer and Bernard S. Cohn, eds. Structure and change in Indian society. Chicago: Aldine Publishing Company, 1966. pp.339-96.
A "comparison of 26 sociological and anthropological studies, all carried out in India since 1949, which include quantitative data on the frequency of various types of families." Does not focus upon women in particular.

1980 ________. Regional differences in Indian family structure. *In* Robert I. Crane, ed. Regions and regionalism in South Asian studies: an exploratory study. Durham, North Carolina: Duke University Press, 1967. pp.147-226. (Monograph and Occasional Paper Series, Monograph 5).
Comparative study of data from six localities. Concludes that "nuclear families develop where the wife has high bargaining power institutionalized in such cultural practices as a wife's right to a legal divorce, bride-price negotiation of marriage, economic and social support to a couple from the wife's natal family or lineage .... where [such factors] do not appear, there is a high proportion of joint families."

1981 KURIAN, GEORGE, ed. The family in India: a regional view. The Hague: Mouton, 1974. 391p. (Studies in the Social Sciences, 12).
Collection of essays emphasizing regional marriage and family systems. A wide range of social settings is represented: from tribals to overseas immigrants, from Nepal to Kerala, in both rural and urban areas. For those papers containing material explicitly on women, see entries 211, 499, 2038, 3216-7, 3240, 3272, 3523, 3528, 4119, 4201 and 4627.

1982 ________. The Indian family in transition: some regional variations. *In* Giri Raj Gupta, ed. Family and social change in modern India. New Delhi: Vikas, 1976. pp.3-18. (Main Currents in Indian Sociology, 2).
Discusses need to consider regional variations when discussing family in India. Reviews recent local studies of the family, pointing out variations.

1983 MAJUMDAR, D.N. Status of woman in patrilocal societies in South Asia. *In* Eastern Anthropologist, 7,2 (1953/54) 99-115.
General statement of women's role in such marriage and family systems. Reviews tribal and peasant ethnographic findings.

(a) Overviews: the Hindu family

1984 BAIG, TARA ALI. The family and the home. *In* Tara Ali Baig, ed. Women of India. Delhi: Publications Division, Ministry of Information and Broadcasting, Government of India, 1958. pp.105-30.
Surveys women and family life in Hindu India. Considers life cycle events, marriage expectations, the nature of the joint family, rural and urban patterns, role of festivals and trends of change. Briefly discusses other religious communities. Photographs of domestic life.

1985 DAS, VEENA. Marriage among the Hindus. *In* Devaki Jain, ed. Indian women. New Delhi: Publications Division, Ministry of Information and Broadcasting, Government of India, 1975. pp.69-86.
Discusses correlations between various Hindu "norms of marriage and kinship" and the position of women.

1986 FRUZZETTI, LINA, ÁKOS ÖSTÖR and STEVE BARNETT. The cultural construction of the person in Bengal and Tamil Nadu. *In* Contributions to Indian Sociology n.s. 10,1 (1976) 157-82.
Comparison of informants' conceptions of various aspects of "kinship" relations. The authors note similarities in "what is passed from parent to child, . . . what each parent contributes to the child and how this affects the child's place within family and caste." Contrasting notions of blood in the two systems, however, entail different notions of a woman's place in them.

1987 GORE, M.S. The traditional Indian family. *In* M.F. Nimkoff, ed. Comparative family systems. Boston: Houghton Mifflin Company, 1965. pp.209-31.
Overview of basic characteristics of the Hindu family. Topics include family structure, patterns of authority, marriage rules, the position of women, religion, family sentiments and pressures for change.

1988 MADAN, T.N. The Hindu woman at home. *In* B.R. Nanda, ed. Indian women: from purdah to modernity. New Delhi: Vikas, 1976. pp.67-86.
General assessment of the familial position of Hindu women. ". . . her position at home in the family is a very onerous and difficult one."

1989 NARAIN, D. Growing up in India. *In* Family Process 3,1 (1964) 127-54.
Review of the literature. Primarily concerns Hindu community. Discusses various dyadic family relationships, sex preferences for offspring and childcare patterns.

(b) Overviews: the Muslim family

1990 AHMAD, IMTIAZ, ed. Family, kinship and marriage among the Muslims of India. New Delhi: Manohar, 1976. 367p.
Collection of twelve papers, each discussing the kinship system of Muslims in a particular locality of India. With an introduction by the editor. For contents pertinent to the position of women, see entries 3237, 3256, 3494, 3522, 3524, 3734, 4165, 4212 and 4443.

1991 Family life in Pakistan: a report of the proceedings and recommendations of three-day seminar on "Family Life in Pakistan" organized by the Social Services Coordinating Council, Karachi, during May 17/19, 1963. Karachi: Social Services Coordinating Council, 1963? 57p.
Papers, reports and recommendations address topics of changing and future family patterns, marriage problems, economic problems, the family in society and family relationships.

1992 Husband and wife. Tr. from Urdu and Gujarati. Karachi: Peermahomed Ebrahim Trust, 1976. 202p.
Contemporary trends and recommendations of appropriate, Islam-sanctioned behavior with respect to wide variety of marital topics.

1993 NAJI, GHULAMALI ISMAIL. Family life in Islam. Tr. from Urdu and Gujarati. Karachi: Peermahomed Ebrahim Trust, 1973. 643p.
Collection of brief statements on various aspects of marriage and divorce, sexual union, pregnancy and childbirth. Substantial appendixes, including: "Family Planning," "Adultery," "Sodomy and Homosexuality," "The Truth about Polygamy," "Why not Polyandry?," "Taharatunnisa" (concerns menstruation, vag-

inal secretions and bleeding that follows giving birth), "Leucorrhoea," "Islamic Family System," "Law of Inheritance," "Generation Gap" and "Islamic Law of Inheritance (Economics)."

1994 Rana. 1977. 19 min. 16? mm. [*Distributed by* Wombat Productions Inc., Little Lake, Glendale Road, Ossining, New York 10562].
Twenty-one year old Muslim university student from India discusses her family and community. Considers family life, *pardā* and courtship. [Unexamined].

(c) Relationships within the family

1995 AIYAPPAN, A. Sociology of avoidance. *In* Dhirendra Narain, ed. Explorations in the family and other essays: Professor K.M. Kapadia commemoration volume. Bombay: Thacker and Company, 1975. pp.193-205.
Compares kinship avoidance behavior between a man and his younger brother's wife in Orissa and between a man and his elder brother's wife in Kerala. Notes differences in the structures of marriage and family systems in the two regions to explain the differing avoidance emphases.

1996 CHAUBE, RAMGHALIB. The taboo against the husband or wife naming each other. *In* North Indian Notes and Queries 5,2 (1895/96) 28-9.
Concerns belief that saying spouse's name shortens his or her life. Briefly mentions three ceremonies in which women do mention their husbands' names.

1997 The householder. Directed by James Ivory. Story and screenplay by Ruth Prawer Jhabvala. 1963. 100 min. Black and white. 16 mm. [*Distributed by* Film Images, 17 W. 60th Street, New York, New York 10023].
First year of marriage of a quiet young Delhi school teacher and his wife. Portrays their shy, early period of acquaintance. [Unexamined].

1998 Kamala's letters to her husband. Mylapore, Madras: English Publishing House, 1902. 223p.
Anonymous letters offered by husband of "Kamala" for publication. The letters are preoccupied with fantasies of the husband's adultery but include material on many other topics as well. Area not stated.

1999 NARAIN, DHIRENDRA. Interpersonal relationships in the Hindu family. *In* Reuben Hill and René König, eds. Families in East and West: socialization process and kinship ties. Paris: Mouton, 1970. pp.454-80.
Describes, for each of 20 dyadic intrafamilial relationships, traditional norm and contemporary behavior and explains discrepancies between the two. Cites various ethnographic reports.

2000 NIVEDITA, SISTER [MARGARET E. NOBLE]. The cycle of Indian wifehood. *In her* Cradle tales of Hinduism. London: Longmans, Green, 1907. pp.33-99.
Contemporary versions of classical legends of Satī, Umā, Sāvitrī and Nala and Damayantī. Told by a prominent interpreter of Hinduism to the West.

2001 WIESINGER, RITA. The parent-daughter relationship among the Hindus. *In* Sociologus n.s. 15,2 (1965) 143-61.
Report of questionnaires from 700 Hindu high school and college girls, aged 15 to 21 years, from Bombay, Indore and Khandwa. Characterizes parents' attitudes towards daughters as simultaneously indulgent and dominating. The subjugation of daughters is seen as creating a "lack of initiative and high degree of dependence on parents even when they are adults." Tables.

(d) Domestic problems: family and marriage disorganization, divorce

2002 AGRAWALA, RAJ KUMARI. Matrimonial remedies under Hindu law. Bombay: N.M. Tripathi, 1974. 332p.
"This book attempts to survey and evaluate form, content and potential of the law of marital reliefs available to Hindus in India." Considers restitution of conjugal rights, judicial separation, nullity, divorce, maintenance and alimony, desertion, cruelty, adultery, impotence and other grounds for claiming reliefs, procedure and other issues.

2003 AHMAD, BASHIR. Status of women and settlement of family disputes under Islamic law. *In* Tahir Mahmood, ed. Islamic law in modern India. Bombay: N.M. Tripathi Private Ltd., 1972. pp.186-91.
"The purpose of this paper is, first, to explain the true nature of certain legal institutions in Islam affecting the status and rights of Muslim women and, secondly, to suggest the enactment of a law providing to Muslim women better facilities of redressing grievances against their husbands." Includes draft of a proposed "Muslim Family Disputes Settlement Act," which is legitimated by a verse from the *Qor'ān*.

2004 AHMED, K.N. The Muslim law of divorce. Islamabad: Islamic Research Institute, 1972. 1107p.
Detailed discussion of *Ḥanafī* religious law of divorce with details of laws of other

Muslim sects and Anglo-Muslim law where they differ. ". . . I have relied in my discussion on authoritative books on Muslim Law. I have also endeavored to give and discuss the basic ideas underlying the rules laid down by the Imams and other Muslim Jurists."

2005 FONSECA, MABEL B. All about your intimate sex and married life. New Delhi: Bell Books, Vikas Publishing House, 1976. 231p.
"This book is not a sociological treatise on the subject of marriage and family problems, but only a collection of answers to problems experienced by people in our society today." Structured around responses by a social worker and family sociologist to letters to advice columns in the magazines ***Femina*** and ***Eve's Weekly***.

2006 HINCHCLIFFE, D. Divorce in Pakistan: judicial reform. *In* J. of Islamic and Comparative Law 2 (1968) 13-25. [Unexamined].

2007 KHANNA, P.N. Why marriages fail in India: is it judgement or destiny? New Delhi: Social Publications, 1970? 586p.
Popular approach that "represents the work of hundreds of experts." Contains observations and advice, a mixture of common sense, witty sayings, literary quotes and "excerpts from actual life dramas." Chapters include "Personality Factors," "The Honeymoon," "Wives Who Wreck Homes," "How to be an Ideal Wife," "Understanding Women" and so forth.

2008 MALIK, IJAZ ILAHI. Our marriage problems. *In* Pakistan Review 17,10 (1969) 21-6.
Reflections on various aspects of arranging marriages among Pakistani Muslims. Author suggests that practice of examining suitable girls at their homes is humiliating and should be stopped. Also discussed are problems regarding educated women, economic aspects of marriage and the practice of abducting girls for prostitution on the premise of marriage.

2009 MEHTA, RAMA. Divorced Hindu woman. Delhi: Vikas Publishing House, 1975. 173p.
An analysis of interviews with 50 lower- and upper-middle-class western-educated divorced or separated women from Delhi, Bombay and Udaipur. Chapters on background of respondents, causes of divorce, life after divorce and conclusions.

2010 NARAIN, DHIRENDRA. Family disorganization in India. *In* Dhirendra Narain, ed. Explorations in the family and other essays: Professor K.M. Kapadia commemoration volume. Bombay: Thacker and Company, 1975. pp.81-106.
Report of a nationwide demographic study of widowed, divorced, disabled, homeless, institutionalized and unemployed men and women as indicators of family disorganization. Data is organized by sex, state and rural or urban location. Based on 1961 census. Tables.

2011 Sara akash. Directed by Basu Chatterji. (Hindi dialogue/English subtitles). 1970. 100 min. Black and white. [*Distributed by* Film Finance Corporation, White House, Walkeshwar Road, Bombay 400 006].
Adapted from Rajendra Yadava's novel of the same name, this film portrays tensions of a young married couple. Although the husband is unable to adjust, it is the wife who is blamed for the difficulties. [Unexamined].

2012 TIKKER, KHEMA. Specific marriage problems for women in India. *In* Social Action 14,11 (1964) 554-62. [Unexamined].

(e) Legislation concerning family life

Legislative material on particular topics (e.g., divorce) is located according to topic

2013 AHMAD, KHURSHID, ed. Marriage Commission Report x-rayed: a study of the family law of Islam and a critical appraisal of the modernist attempts to 'reform' it. Karachi: Chiragh-e-Rah, 1959. 315p.
Among contributors is Islamic fundamentalist leader Abul 'Ala Maudoodi. Includes Pakistan Marriage Commission questionnaire and report in full. [Unexamined. NUC].

2014 AKRAM, MUHAMMAD. The Muslim family laws. Lahore: Pakistan Legal Publications, 1973. 112p. [Unexamined. NUC].

2015 ANWARI, KHAWAJA ARSHAD MUBEEN. The manual of family laws. Lahore: Kyber Law Publishers, 1976. 416p.
Series of texts and interpretations of civil family laws pertaining to Pakistan in 1976, with reference to Muslims, Hindus, Christians, Buddhists and Parsis. Includes relevant laws enacted in British India.

2016 CHAKRAVARTY, RENU. The law as it affects women. *In* Tara Ali Baig, ed. Women of India. Delhi: Publications Division, Ministry of Information and Broadcasting, Government of India, 1958. pp.72-89.
Outlines the development and major features of key family and marriage laws, including the Special Marriage Act of 1954, the Hindu Marriage Act of 1955, the Hindu Succession Act of 1956 and the Hindu Adoptions and Main-

tenance Act of 1956 ("forming the core of the Hindu Code"), as well as other important laws relating to Christians, Parsis, Muslims and Hindus.

2017 CHAUDHARY, MUHAMMAD ANWAR. Muslim family laws: containing Muslim Family Laws Ordinance and rules; with Child Marriage Restraint Act, Dowry (Prohibition of Display Act), Dissolution of Muslim Marriages Act, Family Courts Act and rules; and thirty years' digest of Muslim Family Law cases reported during 1941-1971. Lahore: Lahore Law Times Publications, 1971. 159p.
Texts and rules of the various acts, with interpretive comments and chronological summary of courts' interpretations of the laws.

2018 CHAUDHARY, ZAFAR H. and ZIA-UL-ISLAM JANJUA. The Muslim Family Laws. Lahore: National Law Publications, 1975.
Text of Muslim Family Laws Ordinance, 1961, and related pieces of legislation. [Unexamined].

2019 COULSON, N.J. Reform of family law in Pakistan. *In* Studia Islamica 7 (1957) 135-55.
Characterizes the recommendations of the 1955 commission of family law reform in Pakistan (the basis of the 1961 Muslim Family Laws Ordinance) as "a sudden and total break with past tradition by the re-opening of the door of *ijtihād* [speculation]." Compares and contrasts Pakistan reforms with reforms in other Muslim countries, which nominally recognized the authority of established religious law and its principles as applied by the four legal schools. Refers to several of the women's issues involved.

2020 ________. Islamic family law: progress in Pakistan. *In* J.N.D. Anderson, ed. Changing law in developing countries. New York: Frederick A. Praeger, 1963. pp.240-57. (Studies on Modern Asia and Africa, 2). [*Also* London: George Allen and Unwin, 1963].
Discusses progress toward sexual equality in Pakistan with respect to the reformulation of traditional Islamic law. Details provisions of the Muslim Family Laws Ordinance of 1961 as a compromise between modernist and traditionalist approaches to integrating Islamic law into the civil law of a modern nation.

2021 FARUKI, KEMAL A. Islamic family law in Pakistan. Karachi: produced for the Ministry of Information and Broadcasting, by the Department of Films and Publications, 1964. 18p.
[Unexamined. NUC].

2022 GANDHI, AMBALAL BHIKHABHAI. The law of maintenance of wives, children and parents in India. Bombay: Milan Law Publishers, 1975. 135p.
Concerns legislation relating to Hindus, Muslims and Parsis. Cites critical and recent court cases.

2023 GUPTE, S.V. Hindu law of adoption, maintenance, minority and guardianship. Bombay: N.M. Tripathi, 1970. 39, 438p.
[Unexamined. NUC].

2024 LEVY, HAROLD. Hindu family law and social change. *In* David C. Buxbaum, ed. Chinese family law and social change in historical and comparative perspective. Seattle: University of Washington Press, 1978. (Asian Law Series, 3).
[Unexamined. Book in BP].

2025 MAHMOOD, SHAUKAT. Commentary on Muslim Family Laws Ordinance, VIII of 1961, with West Pakistan and East Pakistan rules and forms. Lahore: Pakistan Law Times, 1961? 33p.
[Unexamined. NUC].

2026 MAHMOOD, TAHIR. South and Southeast Asia. *In his* Family law reform in the Muslim world. Bombay: N.M. Tripathi, 1972. pp.167-262.
A "survey of the various substantive and regulatory reforms introduced into the Muslim family laws" in countries that have reformed Islamic family law. Has chapters on India, Ceylon and Pakistan with texts of legislation reproduced in appendixes. Conclusion discusses family law reform in all such countries.

2027 PAKISTAN. LAWS, STATUTES, ETC. A brief commentary on the Muslim Family Laws Ordinance, Child Marriage Restraint Act, Dissolution of Muslim Marriages Act. [By M. Noorani] . . . Karachi: Pakistan Publishing House, 1961. 58p.
Pakistan's Muslim Family Laws Ordinance, 1961, includes amendment provisions for the Child Marriage Restraint Act, 1929, and the Dissolution of Muslim Marriages Act, 1939, legislation from prepartition India. [Unexamined. NUC].

2028 ________. Family laws in Pakistan: as amended up-to-date with exhaustive commentary. By Muhammad Ashraf. Lahore: Premier Book House, 1969. 246p. *And* Supplement. Lahore: Premier Book House, 1974. 19p.
Texts of and commentary on 19 pieces of legislation relating to families in Pakistan enacted from 1875 to 1969.

(f) Home science, family life education

2029 DEVADAS, RAJAMMAL P. Teaching of home science in India. *In* Education Quarterly 13,50 (1961) 128-37.
Assesses the objectives and effectiveness of home science programs of various levels and in various contexts.

2030 Home Science. vl- (1963-). New Delhi: Farm Information Unit; Directorate of Extension; Ministry of Food, Agriculture, Community Development, and Cooperation. Monthly.
Supercedes *Home Science Bulletin*. [Unexamined. ALI].

2031 INDIA (REPUBLIC). CENTRAL SOCIAL WELFARE BOARD. Family life education for ladies and marriageable girls: course outline. Lucknow: Family Life Institute, 1969.
[Unexamined].

2032 PATTISON, MATTIE and SHAKTI CHHAYA, comps. Annotated bibliography of research related to home science in India. Baroda: Faculty of Home Science, Maharaja Sayajirao University of Baroda, 1967. 262p.
Includes entries on marriage, family, child development, family planning, nutrition, home management and education. Most items are Master's theses from Indian universities. Also reviews some published and some unpublished nondegree research papers and some Ph.D. dissertations.

(g) Matrilineal systems and matriarchal tendencies

2033 BHATTACHARYA, N.N. Matrilineal inheritance in India. *In* D.C. Sircar, ed. Social life in ancient India. Calcutta: University of Calcutta, 1971. pp.63-71. (*Its* Centre of Advanced Study in Ancient Indian History and Culture, Lectures and Seminars, VI-B (Seminars), part 2).
Considers matrilineal inheritance patterns in southwestern and northeastern India. Notes its presence or "survivals" of it in other areas. Cites myth from *Mahābhārata* that explains its origin.

2034 D'SOUZA, VICTOR S. Mother-right in transition. *In* Sociological Bulletin 2,2 (1953) 135-42.
Considers some elements of "mother-right" in the social systems of various Muslim groups along the western coast of India that demonstrate "different stages of transition of mother-right under different influences."

2035 EHRENFELS, U.R. VON. The dual system and mother-right in India. *In* Anthropos 35/36,4/6 (1940/41) 655-681.
[Unexamined].

2036 ________. The comparative study of matrilineal civilizations in India. *In* J. of the University of Gauhati 4? (1953).
[Unexamined].

2037 ________. Matrilineal social systems in India. *In* Cultural Department of the Embassy of the Federal Republic of Germany, New Delhi, ed. German scholars on India: contributions to Indian studies, vl. Varanasi: Chowkhamba Sanskrit Series Office, 1973. pp.50ff.
Volume is festschrift to memory of Friedrich Max Müller. [Unexamined. Book in ALI].

2038 ________. Matrilineal joint family patterns in India. *In* George Kurian, ed. The family in India: a regional view. The Hague: Mouton, 1974. pp.91-106. (Studies in the Social Sciences, 12).
Contrasts family patterns of patrilineal and matrilineal groups in South Asia. Matrilineal groups considered are Kerala communities, Khasi and Garo. Notes effects of some contemporary social change processes (e.g., westernization) on the matrilineal family and suggests that worldwide feminist movements could encourage "a certain revival of matrifocal trends in the Indian family."

2039 ________ and P.V. VELAYUDHAN. Legislation against matriliny. *In* Anthropologist 3,1/2 (1956) 35-47.
Compares matrilineal and patrilineal systems in context of Hindu Succession Act, 1956, and inheritance law. "Women of the patrilineal parts of the country . . . may regard the passing of this act as a panacea to their evils, but women of the matrilineal societies of India may at the same time regard it as an intrusion into their rights." The matrilineal system offers "greater advantages for women, and through them, for the entire society."

(6) Women's power and sexuality, women's danger to others and seclusion

(a) Women inspiring reverence and fear

2040 ABBOTT, J. The keys of power: a study of Indian ritual and belief. Secaucus, New Jersey: University Books, 1974. 560p. [*Reprint of* 1932 ed.].
Encyclopedia of manifestations of power (*Śakti, barakat*) in day-to-day life. Author was a British civil servant with experience in western and northwestern India. Much on women; see especially third chapter, 'The power of Woman." "The mystery of woman . . . finds some solution if she be regarded as a manifestation of creative *śakti*."

2041 COCKBURN, W. Nazar: women not subjects. *In* Panjab Notes and Queries 1,5 (1884) 51.

Notes that females are not subject to the effects of evil eye after puberty, except insofar as it affects their children, who are susceptible. Their own *naẓar*, however, is powerful.

(b) Aspects of sexuality

2042 BALSE, MAYAH. The Indian female: attitude towards sex. New Delhi: Chetana Publications, 1976. 124p.
Report of informal interviews with students, wives, prostitutes and other women (primarily from the urban middle class) concerning marriage, sex education, sexual freedom, courtship, prostitution, promiscuity, divorce and other topics.

2043 The causes and consequences of debauchery. Karachi: Peermahomed Ebrahim Trust, 1973. 164p.
Extensive series of examples in which the moral laxity of western civilization is contrasted with the noble principles of Islam. Recurring material on women and sexuality.

2044 CHANDRA, SUDHIR. The married woman and our sex morality. *In* Quest 81 (Mar 1973) 41-5.
Notes that while extramarital sexual relations have long been acceptable for men, they continue to be unacceptable for women. Argues that neither prohibition nor divorce offer satisfactory solutions and recommends "implementation of a sex ethic based on the acceptance of extra-marital intimacy" as the "least objectionable and most rational and practicable alternative at the moment."

2045 CHITRE, DILIP. Marriage and morals: updating the pativrata prostitute. *In* Quest 82 (May 1973) 81-3.
Reply to Chandra stressing that his discussion ignores the fundamental fact of men's domination and exploitation of women. The Hindu male "needs a slave and a prostitute" in addition to "a mother to feed him." Thus no modern sex morality will be acceptable to him.

2046 RAMPAL, S.N. Indian women and sex. New Delhi: Printox, 1978. 192p.
Compilation of admiring personal observations, data from a questionnaire returned by Delhi doctors, citations from studies and other sources. Primarily concerns the contemporary urban middle class. Includes a tribute to Indian women and chapters on problems of relationships between the sexes in India, Vātsyāyana's approach to sexuality in the *Kāmasūtra*, attitudes of Indian men, attitudes and practices of Indian women (from questionnaire), prostitution, opinions of western authorities, position of major religions and potential for equality between the sexes.

2047 TULI, JITENDRA. The Indian male: attitude towards sex. New Delhi: Chetana Publications, 1976. 136p.
Observations and case study material on sexual attitudes and practices of Indian men and the social circumstances that foster them. Largely relates to middle-class urban society. Companion volume to entry 2042.

2048 VERMA, DAYANAND. Ramesh Chander, ed. An intimate study of sex behaviour. Tr. from Hindi by Sudarshan Sharma. New Delhi: Star Publications, 1971. 108p.
Illustrated. [Unexamined. ALI].

2049 YALMAN, NUR. On the purity of women in the castes of Ceylon and Malabar. *In* J. of the Royal Anthropological Institute 93,1 (1963) 25-58.
Examines a series of rites concerning puberty and other aspects of female sexuality as they relate to the structure of caste and to various local kinship systems. Attempts to explain "the concern centering around female sexuality when male sexuality is not necessarily ritualized. I hope to show that filiation through the mother, and the protection of female purity is fundamental to the caste system of Ceylon and Malabar and that these principles may have structural implications in other Hindu castes." Refutes Gough's explanations of unconscious motivations (entry 3209), arguing that collective rituals are to be explained by collective facts. In the locality under consideration, wherever one finds the caste phenomenon one may also expect to find a concern with "dangers" to pure women.

(c) Female seclusion

2050 HAMID, S.M. ABDUL. Islạmi purdah. Karachi: Hamid, 1978. 64p.
[Unexamined. ALP].

2050a KHAN, MAZHAR UL HAQ. Social pathology of the Muslim society. Delhi: Amar Prakashan, 1978. 196p. [*Also* Purdah and polygamy: a study in the social pathology of the Muslim society. Peshawar Cantonment: Nashiran-e-Ilm-o-Taraqiyet, 1972. 232p.].
Attributes decay and downfall of Muslim peoples in recent times to *pardā* and polygamy. Describes origins of *pardā* system and its theoretical operation. States that in practice the system results in women who are indolent, timid, ill-tempered, ignorant and without strength of character (the "purdah syndrome"). Consequently there is a severe adverse effect on children and society as a whole.

2051 PAPANEK, HANNA. Purdah: separate worlds and symbolic shelter. *In* Comparative Studies in Society and History

15,3 (1973) 289-325.
Reviews scholarly and literary materials on *pardā* in South Asia. Explores the relation of female seclusion to the broader social setting in three main sections: 1) the multiple facets of *pardā* observance and religious and regional variation, 2) types of work done by women and by men and 3) dynamics of impulse control, status, family honor and marital arrangements.

2052 ________. Sex, status and segregation: a theoretical introduction and survey of the literature on purdah. *In* Hanna Papanek, ed. Purdah in South Asia: the segregation of women. Forthcoming.
Suggests general principles by which *pardā* can be compared to other ways in which societies define women's place and specifically indicates how various *pardā* practices implement values concerning sexuality and family status. The social context of individual behavior is seen as a crucial determinant of variations in *pardā* observance. Review of literature on *pardā* complements earlier published survey articles (see entries 2051 and 2209). [Unexamined. Information supplied by author].

2053 ________. Breaking my purdah: Hamida Khala remembers. *In* Hanna Papanek, ed. Purdah in South Asia: the segregation of women. Forthcoming.
Life history of a Muslim woman now in her sixties. Focuses on her great conflicts about following her husband's request to give up the *pardā* observances she had followed in her father's house. Vividly describes her struggles to reconcile her religious beliefs with changes in her appearance and behavior, along with the details of her early life in strictly segregated circumstances. Includes a written autobiographical statement by "Hamida Khala" and excerpts from taped interviews, as well as the author's interpretive introduction and detailed discussion of these materials. [Unexamined. Information supplied by author].

2054 ________, ed, Purdah in South Asia: the segregation of women. Forthcoming.
Papers from two conferences on *pardā* in South Asia and additional chapters requested from specific writers are included in this volume. They provide a rounded view of the segregation of women among both Muslims and Hindus from the perspective of Asian and non-Asian authors in several academic disciplines. A general theoretical introduction and overview of the existing literature on *pardā* links the various contributions and also suggests principles for comparing the phenomenon of *pardā* to the means by which other societies define women's place. For contents, see entries 1235, 2052-3, 2056, 2058, 2339, 3730, 3811, 3887, 3945, 4214, 4218 and 4455. [Unexamined. Information supplied by editor].

2055 PRABHA, pseud. Purdah woman abode. Bombay: Popular Book Depot, 1962. 100p.
Fictionalized polemic against the evils of *pardā*. Depicts the personal suffering of a South Indian girl, "Kalpana," and her family when she marries into a *pardā*-observing family in Rajasthan.

2056 RAHMAN, FAZLUR. A modernist interpretation of the position of women in Islam. *In* Hanna Papanek, ed. Purdah in South Asia: the segregation of women. Forthcoming.
Discusses Islamic views of female seclusion with respect to changes within the *Qor'ān* as it developed over two decades at the advent of Islam and with respect to the change in social context between the time the *Qor'ān* was written and the present day. Considers the question of social context to be crucial to the interpretation of the original prescriptions. Author describes himself as a "Muslim Modernist." [Unexamined. Verified with author].

2057 RALLIA RAM, MAYAVANTI. Purdah and social stratification of Muslim society. *In* Mainstream 14,19 (10 Jan 1976) 21-2.
Some observations about patterns of *burqa'* wearing by Muslim women in Indian cities.

2058 VATUK, SYLVIA. Parda revisited: shelter, segregation and family harmony. *In* Hanna Papanek, ed. Purdah in South Asia: the segregation of women. Forthcoming.
Argues that differences between Hindu and Muslim "systems" of *pardā* have been unduly exaggerated. Female veiling and seclusion are, for both communities, ways to protect women (especially regarding sexual matters) and to promote harmony among family members. Supports argument with ethnographic data from both communities. [Unexamined. Verified with editor].

(7) The spiritual life and religious observances

2059 GOONEWARDENE, E.T. Are women spiritually inferior? *In* J. of the Maha Bodhi Society 56 (1948).
[Unexamined].

2060 An Indian pilgrimage: Ramdevra. Produced by South Asian Area Center, University of Wisconsin. Directed by Joseph W. Elder. Mira Reym Binford and Michael Camerini, filmmakers. 1975. 25 min. Color. 16 mm. [*Distributed by* South Asia Area Center, University of Wisconsin, 1242 Van Hise Hall, Madison, Wisconsin 53706].

Follows a group of Gujaratis on a pilgrimage from Bombay to the Rajasthani desert temple of the 15th century saint Rāmadeva. Most of the pilgrims are women and four are introduced at the onset. They go in search of their own or a family member's welfare. Scenes include the possession of one woman by the saint and a visit to the shrine of an orphaned untouchable female disciple who Rāmedeva adopted. Teachers' guide accompanies film. [Unexamined].

2061 Sectarian Hinduism: the Goddess and her worship. By David Knipe. 1975. 30 min. Color. 3/4 in. videocassette. (Exploring the Religions of South India). [*Distributed by* South Asian Area Center, 1242 Van Hise Hall, University of Wisconsin, Madison, Wisconsin 53706].
The Goddess and *Śakti* as all-pervasive general concepts and in various manifestations. Manifestations portrayed include various goddesses of the Hindu pantheon and the living figures, Sarada Devi and Anandamayi Ma. [Unexamined].

2062 SIVANANDA, SWAMI. Sthree dharma: or, ideal womanhood, 2d ed. Sivanandanagar (via Rishikesh), Himalayas: Yoga-Vedanta Forest Academy, 1960. 115p.
Guide to spiritual success. Considers worldly life and ideal women from the Indian past. Illustrated. [Unexamined. NUC].

(a) Spiritual leaders: Sarada Devi, The Mother, Anandamayi Ma and others

See also section on Sister Nivedita, entries 1463-76

i) Sarada Devi / Sri Ma / the Holy Mother: spiritual consort of Sri Ramakrishna

2063 APURVANANDA, SWAMI. Sri Ramakrishna and Sarada Devi. Tr. from Bengali. Madras: Sri Ramakrishna Math, 1961. 245p.
". . . the first attempt to depict the lives of this divine couple in one book. We cannot get the complete picture of the life of the one without reading side by side the life of the other." Popular biography, compiled primarily from various Bengali sources.

2063a GAMBHIRANANDA, SWAMI. The Holy Mother: Shri Sarada Devi, 2d ed. Tr. from Bengali by the author. Madras: Sri Ramakrishna Math, 1969. 540p.
Detailed biography written in commemoration of Sarada Devi's birth centenary. Photographs of people and places.

2064 GHANANANDA, SWAMI. Śrī Sāradā Devī: the Holy Mother. *In* Ramakrishna Vedanta Centre. Women saints of East and West: Śrī Sāradā Devī (The Holy Mother) birth centenary memorial. London: Ramakrishna Vedanta Centre, 1955. pp.94-121.
Detailed biographical information and 34 aphorisms.

2065 HER DIRECT DISCIPLES. At Holy Mother's feet: teachings of Shri Sarada Devi. Tr. from Bengali by Lila Majumdar and Swami Gambhirananda. Calcutta: Advaita Ashrama, 1963. 383p.
Conversations with and anecdotes regarding the Holy Mother. With an introductory biographical sketch.

2066 JUNNARKAR, P.B. Sri Sri Sarada Devi. Calcutta: Presidency Library, 1959. 395p.
[Unexamined. IBP].

2067 MOOKERJEE, NANDA, ed. Sri Sarada Devi: consort of Sri Ramakrishna. Calcutta: Firma KLM, 1978. 135p.
Tributes, reminiscences, biographical data and other articles on the life and teachings of Sri Sarada Devi by "great monks, eminent scholars and thinkers of international repute and . . . common men and women." Reprinted from various sources.

2068 NIKHILANANDA, SWAMI. Holy Mother: being the life of Sri Sarada Devi, wife of Sri Ramakrishna and helpmate in his mission. Madras: Ramakrishna Math, 1962. 334p. [*Also* New York: Ramakrishna Vivekananda Center. *And* London: George Allen and Unwin].
[Unexamined. IBP, BP].

2069 NIRVEDANANDA, SWAMI. The Holy Mother. *In* Swami Madhavananda and Ramesh Chandra Majumdar, eds. Great women of India. Almora: Advaita Ashrama, 1953. pp.464-539.
Detailed biography of Sarada Devi, known as the "Holy Mother." As a child she was married to the man who, as Sri Ramakrishna, soon renounced worldly life. She remained his spiritual consort until his death and became a central figure to their followers until her own death.

2070 PAVITRANANDA, SWAMI. A short life of the Holy Mother. Calcutta: Advaita Ashrama, 1942? 80p.
Concise biography with a series of the Holy Mother's aphorisms.

2071 RANGANATHANANDA, SWAMI. The Indian ideal of womanhood. Calcutta: Ramakrishna Mission Institute of Culture, 1966. 63p. (Institute Booklets, 18).
Four lectures by a senior monk of the Ramakrishna order: "The Indian Ideal of Womanhood," "Women in Indian Culture," "Swami Vivekananda's

Message to our Women" and "Sarada Devi, the Holy Mother."

2072 REYMOND, LIZELLE. Shrī Sāradā Dévī et Shrī Rāmakrishna dans leurs villages [Sri Sarada Devi and Sri Ramakrishna in their villages]. Lyon: Derain, 1950. 30p.
Report of brief visits to Jayrambali and Kamarpukar, the natal Bengali villages of Sri Sarada Devi and Sri Ramakrishna, and to Bagh Bazar in Calcutta where Sarada Devi spent much of her last ten years. The author describes these places and the people she met there. Most material relates to Sarada Devi, including the recollections of old village women and the author.

2073 Sri Sarada Devi: the Holy Mother, 5th rev. ed. Madras: Sri Ramakrishna Math, 1977. 395p. [*1st ed.* 1940].
In two parts. The first, "Life," is a biography written by Swami Tapasyananda. The second, "Her Conversations," is a series of selections from diaries and reports of her disciples translated from the Bengali by Swami Nikhilananda. With a chronology, the Holy Mother's horoscope and a glossary. Photographs.

2074 Vedanta Kesari. v1- (1914-). Madras: Sri Ramakrishna Math. Monthly.
Has numerous articles on Sarada Devi throughout.

ii) La Mère / The Mother: spiritual consort of Sri Aurobindo

2075 AUROBINDO, SRI [AUROBINDO GHOSE]. The Mother: with letters on The Mother and translations of prayers and meditations. Pondicherry: Sri Aurobindo Ashram, 1972. 495p.
[Unexamined. NUC].

2076 GUPTA, NOLINI KANTA. Sweet Mother. *In his* Collected works of Nolini Kanta Gupta, v5. Pondicherry: Sri Aurobindo International Centre of Education, 1974. pp.83-112.
Collected writings and addresses that attempt to interpret the ongoing meaning and describe the ongoing presence of The Mother following her departure from her material body.

2077 KAPALI SASTRI, T.V. Flame of white light. Pondicherry: Aurobindo Ashram, 1960. 59p.
On The Mother. [Unexamined. IBP].

2078 KAUL, H.K. The Mother. *In his* Sri Aurobindo: a descriptive bibliography. New Delhi: Munshiram Manoharlal, 1972. pp.122-33.
Lists 125 bibliographic entries, some with brief annotations.

2079 THE MOTHER [LA MÈRE]. Questions and answers, 1956. Pondicherry: Sri Aurobindo Ashram, 1973. 375p.
Translation of taped conversations of The Mother with disciples of the Sri Aurobindo Ashram.

2080 ________. Collected works, centenary edition. Pondicherry: Sri Aurobindo Ashram, 1976?-. v1-.
Centenary edition is to be complete in 15 volumes.

2081 ________. Douce Mère: notes de lumière [Sweet Mother: marks of enlightenment]. Comp. by Mona Sarkar. Pondichéry: Sri Aurobindo Ashram, 1978. 41p.
Conversations with The Mother in which she expounds on Aurobindo's philosophy using her signature, her photographs and other means. Photographs.

2082 NANDAKUMAR, PREMA. Our Mother. Pondicherry: Sri Aurobindo Society, 1977? 40p.
Three essays concisely discuss life-story of The Mother, growth of Sri Aurobindo Ashram and the establishment of Auroville. Numerous photographs and a select bibliography.

2083 ________. The Mother (of Srī Aurobindo Ashrama). New Delhi: National Book Trust, 1977. 136p. (National Biography).
Her life and teachings.

2084 NIRODBARAN. The Mother: sweetness and light. Pondicherry: Éditions Auropress, 1978. 212p.
A disciple reminisces about his relationship with The Mother, which spanned more than four decades. Details his spiritual experiences, his work in the ashrama dispensary, numerous conversations, anecdotes and so forth. Photographs.

2085 PANDIT, M.P. Lamps of light. Pondicherry: printed at Sri Aurobindo Ashram Press, 1963. 77p.
Teachings of and anecdotes concerning The Mother by a devotee.

2086 ________. The Mother of love. Pondicherry: Sri Aurobindo Ashram, 1965-69. 4v.
Contains brief introductory interpretation of the meaning of The Mother's life; numerous studies of her writings, prayers and meditations arranged by topic; numerous succinct "gems" from The Mother; recollections and anecdotes; and floral, New Year's and Christmas messages from her.

2087 ________. Under The Mother's banner. Pondicherry: Dipti Publications, 1975. 167p.
Collected speeches and other statements about Aurobindo and The Mother by a devotee.

2088 _______, ed. Memorable moments with The Mother. Pondicherry: Dipti Publications, 1975. 42p.
Devotees respond to the question, "What was your most memorable moment with the Mother?"

2089 PASUPATI [PASUPATI BHATTACHARYA]. On The Mother divine. Prafullanagar, 24 Parganas: Phanibhusan Nath, 1968. 97p.
The author, whose life was made peaceful through contact with Aurobindo and The Mother, discusses her life, philosophy, personality, identity, grace and so forth. With selected teachings.

2090 RAVINDRA. The white lotus: at the feet of The Mother. New Delhi: S. Chand, 1978. 214p.
Life and teachings of The Mother. Includes photographs and a chapter "Mother and Women" (pp.179-93).

2091 RISHABHCHAND. The Mother's work for peace on earth. Pondicherry: Sri Aurobindo Society, 1936. 40p.
". . . I have attempted to show by a string of quotations from the Mother's writings . . . how she has been toiling almost all of her life for the establishment of peace on earth by employing the only radical means, which are capable of accomplishing it." Photograph.

2092 SAT PREM. Mère ou le matérialisme divin [Mother or divine manifestation]. *And* Mère ou l'espèce nouvelle [Mother or the new type]. *And* Mère ou la mutation de la mort [Mother or death's transformation]. Madras: printed at Macmillan India Press, 1976. 483, 568, 343p.
Teachings of The Mother based on the author's 19 years of living as an ascetic in her service. With numerous anecdotes and conversations.

2093 SRINIVASA IYENGAR, K.R. On The Mother: the chronicle of a manifestation and ministry, 2d rev. and enl. ed. Pondicherry: Sri Aurobindo International Centre of Education, 1978. 2v.
[Unexamined. ALI].

iii) Anandamayi Ma, a saint fully realized from birth

2094 ANANDAMAYI MA. Aux sources de la joie [Sources of bliss], 5th ed. Tr. [from Bengali?] by Jean Herbert. Lyon: Paul Derain, 1963. 75p.
Translation of 100 brief statements of Anandamayi Ma on various topics.

2095 _______. Words of Sri Anandamayi Ma. Tr. [from Bengali?] and comp. by Atmananda, 2d ed. Varanasi: Shree Shree Anandamayee Sangha, 1971. 242p. [*1st ed.* 1961].
Illustrated. [Unexamined. NUC].

2096 _______. L'enseignement de Mā Ananda Moyī [The teachings of Anandamayi Ma]. Tr. from Bengali by Josette Herbert. Paris: Albin Michel, 1974. 378p. (Spiritualités Vivantes, Série Hindouisme).
[Unexamined. NUC].

2097 Ānanda Vārtā. v1- (1952-). Varanasi: Shree Shree Anandamayee Sangha. Quarterly.
"A quarterly presenting the divine life and teaching of Sri Anandamayi Ma and various aspects of universal dharma." Published in Bengali and English, and in Hindi and English. [Unexamined. IPP].

2098 BANERJEE, SHYAMANANDA. A mystic sage: Ma Anandamayi. Calcutta: the author, 1973. 217p.
Portrait based largely on anecdotal accounts of devotees. Emphasizes her extraordinary powers and explains how she manifests characteristics of sages extolled in the *upaniṣads*.

2099 BHAIJI. Mother as reavealed to me, 4th ed. Tr. from Bengali by G. Das Gupta. Benares: Shree Shree Anandamayee Sangha, 1972.
[Unexamined].

2100 DESJARDINS, ARNAUD. Ma Anandamayi. *And* Retour auprès de Ma [Return to the side of Ma]. *In his* Ashrams: les yogis et les sages. Paris: La Palatine, 1962? pp.63-108, 199-240.
Account of the author's visits to Anandamayi's principal ashram in Varanasi. Describes the physical site, some activities there and, especially, Anandamayi, her teachings and her spiritual effect on the author and others.

2101 DEVOTEES. Ma Anandamayi. Benares: Ma Anandamayi Asram, 1946. 253p.
A relatively earlier English source about Anandamayi Ma, this book contains devotees' tributes, recollections, anecdotes and so forth. It was presented as an offering on her 51st birthday.

2102 GURUPRIYA DEVI. Matrivani, 4th ed. Tr. from Bengali by Brahmacarini Atmananda. Benares: Shree Shree Anandamayee Sangha, 1977. [*1st ed.* 1959?].
[Unexamined].

2103 JOSHI, HARI RAM. Mā Ānandamayī līlā: memoirs of Hari Ram Joshi. Varanasi: Shree Shree Anandamayee Sangha?, 1974.
[Unexamined].

2104 LIPSKI, ALEXANDER. Some aspects of the life and teachings of the East Bengal saint Ānandamayī Mā. *In* History of Religions 9,1 (1969) 59-77. [*Also in* Alexander Lipski, ed. Conference on Bengal Studies 4th, 1968?, Hamilton,

New York. East Lansing: Asian Studies Center, Michigan State University, 1969? pp.19-35. (*Its* South Asia Series, Occasional Paper 13)].
Discusses Anandamayi's rural East Bengali background, the development of her spiritual self and the growth of her following through all of India and beyond. Considers her teachings, which "appear fully formulated from the beginning," and comments on their sophistication despite her simple, illiterate background.

2105 ________. Life and teachings of Śrī Ānandamayī Mā. Delhi: Motilal Banarsidass, 1977. 74p.
Chapters on her *līlā* and her personality and teachings. Appendixes reproduce selected sayings, advice for daily living and selected poems and songs offered by her devotees and discuss her conception of the seven *cakras* along the spinal column. Includes a brief bibliographic essay. The author spent some time with Anandamayi Ma. Based on his article in *History of Religions*.

2106 MASCHMANN, MELITA. Der Tiger singt Kirtana: Indienfahrt mit einer Hinduheiligen [The tiger sings a *kīrtana*: Indian journey with a Hindu saint]. Weilheim: Otto Wilhelm Barth-Verlag, 1967. 251p.
Account of five months of travel in North India in 1962-63 with Anandamayi Ma. A travelogue, a documentation of portions of Ma's life and a reflection on various elements of Indian spirituality and their relevance for the West.

2107 Mother as seen by her devotees, 3d ed. Benares: Shree Shree Anandamayee Sangha, 1976.
[Unexamined].

2108 MUKERJI, BITHIKA. From the life of Sri Anandamayi Ma. Varanasi: Shree Shree Anandamayee Sangha, 1970-.
Illustrated. [Unexamined. NUC].

2109 SURYANANDA LAKSHMI. Six mois de visions divines [Six months of divine insight]. Tr. [from Bengali?] by Jean Herbert. Lyon: Derain, 1949. 23p. (Les Dieux Hindous, 4).
[Unexamined. IOL].

iv) Various other female spiritual leaders

2110 Correspondence between Maulana Maudoodi and Maryam Jameelah. Lahore: Mohammad Yusuf Khan, 1969. 88p.
Correspondence, beginning in 1960, between the former Margaret Marcus and a prominent Pakistani Islamic revivalist leader. Miss Marcus, an American, describes her interest in Islamic religion and disenchantment with her own society. The correspondence discusses women's, East versus West and other issues. Reveals Maryam Jameelah's spiritual development and presents the background to her migration to Pakistan.

2111 LEE, ADA. An Indian priestess: the life of Chundra Lela, expanded ed. London: Fleming H. Revell, 1903. 111p. [*1st ed?* Chundra Lela: the converted fakir. Cincinnati: printed for the author by Curts and Jennings, 1898. 93p.].
Biography of a woman widowed as a child, who, in the course of undertaking a pilgrimage to the great shrines at the four cardinal points of India practiced severe asceticism and gained a following. She went to Calcutta, disappointed with the ineffectuality of her ascetism, converted to Christianity and then traveled throughout India and Nepal preaching about Christianity.

2112 SAHUKAR, MANI. Sweetness and light: an exposition of Sati Godavari Mataji's philosophy and way of life. Bombay: Bharatiya Vidya Bhavan, 1966. 136p.
Illustrated. [Unexamined. ALI].

2113 SHAM RAO, D.P. Shri Kanya Kumari Sati Godavari Mataji. *In his* Five contemporary gurus in the Shirdi (Sai Baba) tradition. Madras: Christian Institute for the Study of Religion and Society, 1972. pp.19-27.
Brief comments on her life, teachings, self-conception and meaning for devotees.

2114 VASWANI, J.P. A child of God: glimpses of the life of Sister Shanti T. Vaswani. Poona: Gita Publishing House, 1970? 48p.
Biography about a woman who was spiritual and "different" as a child and came to be devoted to Beloved Dada, Sadhu T.L. Vaswani.

2115 ________. Shanti speaks. Poona: Gita Publishing House, 1972. 32p. (East and West Series, 172).
Collection of 34 "conversations which dear Shanti [Shanti T. Vaswani] had with her devoted friends and others who came to her for guidance." Author recalls interchanges from memory.

v) Sri Ramakrishna: his femininity, female devotees and attitudes toward women

2116 GAURI MA. Visions de pureté [Visions of clarity]. [Tr. from Bengali?]. Lyon: Derain.
Spiritually-minded from childhood, Gauri Ma or Gaurimani Devi refused to marry and spent much of her life in pilgrimage and worship. She was a disciple of Sri Ramakrishna, who encouraged her to work in the world in the ser-

vice of women. She had many devotees of her own. [Unexamined].

2117 GHANANANDA, SWAMI. Some holy women figuring in the life of Śrī Rāmakṛishṇa. *In* Ramakrishna Vedanta Centre. Women saints of East and West: Śrī Sāradā Devī (The Holy Mother) birth centenary memorial. London: Ramakrishna Vedanta Centre, 1955. pp.122-35.
Discusses his guru, Yogeshwari Bhairavi Brahmani, along with Aghormani Devi ("Gopaler Ma"), Lakshmimani Devi (Lakshmi Didi"), Yogindra Mohini Bishwas ("Yogin Ma"), Golap Sundari Devi ("Golap Ma") and Gaurimani Devi ("Gauri Ma").

2118 SARADANANDA, SWAMI. Sri Ramakrishna, the great master, 3d ed. Tr. [from Bengali?] by Swami Jagadananda. Madras: Sri Ramakrishna Math, 1963. 960p.
This biography contains descriptions of Ramakrishna's childhood feminine identifications and his adult ***madhura bhāva***, sweet devotion to Kṛṣṇa as Rādhā herself. [Unexamined. NUC].

2119 SHARMA, ARVIND. Rāmakṛṣṇa Paramahaṁsa: a study in a mystic's attitudes towards women. *In* Rita M. Gross, ed. Beyond androcentrism: new essays on women and religion. Missoula, Montana: Scholars Press, 1977. pp.115-24. (American Academy of Religion, Aids for the Study of Religion, 6).
Discusses Ramakrisha's attitudes toward women; he is one of the few mystics whose attitudes are well-documented. Concludes that his attitude was positive towards women if their actions were consonant with "God-realization" and negative if they were not.

2120 TAPASYANANDA, SWAMI. Motherhood of God as revealed by Sri Ramakrishna. *In* Prabuddha Bharata 75,3-4 (1970) 93-100, 144-6.
Ramakrishna taught that "Brahman and Śakti are identical." The author states that "Mother signifies to the child trust, protectiveness, sweetness, forbearance and wisdom. He feels the mother to be his very own and can even press his demands on her. One who invokes the Deity as Mother [experiences] intimacy with regard to the supreme." Discribes Kālī symbolism, Ramakrishna's contribution to the cult and "aberrations" of the Mother cult. Second part contains selections from Ramakrishna's writings on the topic.

2121 TEJASANANDA, SWAMI. Great women devotees of Shrī Rāmakṛiṣhṇa. *In* Swami Madhavananda and Ramesh Chandra Majumdar, eds. Great women of India. Almora: Advaita Ashrama, 1953. pp.414-63.
Brief biographical sketches of Rani Rasmani, Yogeshwari Bhairavi Brahmani, Aghormani Devi ("Gopaler Ma"), Yogindra Mohini Bishwas ("Yogin Ma"), Golap Sundari Devi ("Golap Ma"), Gauri Ma and Lakshmimani Devi.

(b) Worship of the Goddess, Devī, and her manifestations in contemporary South Asia

2122 CHAINA MALL. Devi-worship of little girls. *In* Panjab Notes and Queries 3,30 (1886) 92.
Brief note about feasts and worship of young girls under ten as incarnations of the goddess Devī.

2123 CHAUDHURI, NANI MADHAB. Some cure deities. *In* Indian Culture 7,4 (1941) 417-32.
Much of this article on the "divine agency of cure" in the Hindu tradition is devoted to the association of various local contemporary goddesses with the cause and cure of disease. Has numerous references to various related ethnographic materials.

2124 CROOKE, WILLIAM. The cults of the mother goddesses in India. *In* Folklore [London] 30 (1919) 282-308.
Based primarily on contemporary ethnographic data. Goddess worship as an ancient rite to ensure well-being, life and power. [Unexamined].

2125 God as Mother. *In* Indian Social Reformer 46,7 (19 Oct 1935) 104-6.
A brief article on *Śākta* philosophy and practices. Argues that it is important for the "cultural Renaissance in India" to revive the "true Shakta ideal" in order to bring dignity to *Śākta* religion and the women of India.

2126 The goddess comes home. 30 min. Black and white. 16 and 35 mm. [*Distributed by* Films Division, Ministry of Information and Broadcasting, 24 G. Deshmukh Marg, Bombay 400 026].
Young married woman returns to her natal home for *Durgā pūjā*. [Unexamined].

2127 Journal of the Anthropological Society of Bombay. v1-n.s. 14. (1886-1972). Bombay. Irregularly.
Old series (discontinued in 1936) contains numerous descriptions of the worship of particular goddesses in various parts of South Asia.

2128 Mata. v1- (1949-). Ghaziabad: Sri Matri Kendar. Monthly.
Devoted to Mother Goddess worship. Has both English and Hindi editions. [Unexamined. IPP].

2129 Matri Bani. v1- (1967-). Allahabad: Matri Sangha. Bimonthly.
Devoted to Mother Goddess worship. Has Bengali, Hindi and English editions. [Unexamined. IPP].

2130 Matru Sri. v1- (1966-). Guntur.

Monthly.
Periodical published in Telugu and English devoted to Mother Goddess worship. [Unexamined. IPP].

2131 MISRA, BABAGRAHI. Sitala: the smallpox goddess of India. *In* Asian Folklore Studies 28,2 (1969) 133-42.
Reviews Śītalā legends and worship in various areas of India. Based on ethnographic reports.

2132 MITRA, SARAT CHANDRA. The worship of the Earth-Mother. *In* Hindustan Review 34,203 (1916) 47-55.
Worship of the earth as a mother goddess in various areas of contemporary India. Examples from other civilizations as well.

(8) The "outer" world and issues and patterns of female employment

(a) Should women work outside the home? Some opinions

2133 CHAUDHURI, NIRAD C. Working women. *In his* To live or not to live!: an essay on living happily with others. Delhi: Hind Pocket Books, 1970? pp.133-51.
Critical and anecdotal assessment of the causes and effects of women's employment in contemporary India. "I regard the emergence of the working woman, unmarried as well as married, as the greatest threat to the family in every country and society, and as even a greater threat in India and Indian society." Author is a well-known writer and journalist.

2134 D'SOUZA, ANTHONY A. Should wives work? *In* Social Action 18,1 (1968) 15-24.
Concludes that "the home and the family must come first in the thinking and planning of every married woman who has a job." However, a husband and wife may agree on mutually acceptable arrangements for the wife to successfully play the "dual role of job-holder and homemaker."

2135 For the family. Produced and directed by Ama Pvt. Ltd. 1959. 22 min. Black and white. 16 and 35 mm. [*Distributed by* Films Division, Ministry of Information and Broadcasting, 24 G. Deshmukh Marg, Bombay 400 026. *Also* 11 min. version].
Film. Although her husband objects, the wife of a primary school teacher finds employment to supplement their inadequate income. She is assisted by a program of the government's Central Social Welfare Board. Set in a small town. [Unexamined. CF].

2136 MANORAMA BAI, H. Educated women: marriage or career? *In* Social Welfare 13,2 (1966) 4-5.
Argues that a woman has inherent maternal instincts that should not be thwarted by the novel glamour of a career.

2137 On women working to earn a living. *In* Monthly Public Opinion Surveys of the Indian Institute of Public Opinion 13, 3 (1967) 22-6.
Tables present attitudes of 472 informants (by education level, household income and occupation) toward "women working outside their homes to earn their living." Considers unmarried women, married women without children and married women with children. Also investigates attitudes toward employment "in offices along with men." No information on source, sex distribution and other features of sample.

(b) Labor force participation, occupational distribution

2138 AMBANNAVAR, JAIPAL P. Changes in economic activity of males and females in India: 1911-61. *In* Demography India 4,2 (1975) 345-64.
Asserts that while the socio-economic status of female agriculturists likely did not change in the period 1911-61, "women's share in the non-agricultural sector has declined because of the destruction of rural industry in competition with new technology." Notes the likelihood that members of this displaced group would have had lower fertility levels had they been employed. Education, child care facilities and other modern provisions tend to encourage female labor force participation but employment opportunities for the country as a whole are limited.

2139 BEAN, LEE L. Utilisation of human resources: the case of women in Pakistan. *In* International Labour Review 97,4 (1968) 391-410.
Compares utilization of female labor force in Pakistan with that of other countries. Considers effects of Islam on female employment and the structure of the rural, urban and total female labor force in Pakistan. Based on census figures.

2140 BOSERUP, ESTER. Women in the labour market. *In* Devaki Jain, ed. Indian women. New Delhi: Publications Division, Ministry of Information and Broadcasting, Government of India, 1975. pp.99-111.
Considers worldwide trends of female participation in the labor market, with comments relating to India.

2141 D'SOUZA, VICTOR S. Changing socio-economic conditions and employment of women in India. *In* M.K. Chaudhuri, ed.

Trends of socio-economic change in India, 1871-1961: proceedings of a seminar. Simla: Institute of Advanced Study, 1969. pp.443-57. (*Its* Transactions, 7).
Attempts to explain regional variation in the female employment rates of different communities. "In regions where the rate of employment of women is already relatively high, with the improvement in the socio-economic conditions in the community there would be a decline in this rate . . . if the rate of employment of women in the region as a whole is relatively low, with the improvement in the socio-economic conditions in a community, the rate would tend to increase." Presents data to support these hypotheses.

2142 _______. Family status and female work participation: an empirical analysis. *In* Social Action 25,3 (1975) 267-76. [*Reprint in* Alfred de Souza, ed. Women in contemporary India: traditional images and changing roles. Delhi: Manohar Book Service, 1975. pp.129-41].
Presents a variety of hypotheses regarding social-structural factors underlying female employment rates as they vary according to time and place in India.

2143 EHRENFELS, U.R. Women's work. *In* Women's Welfare Journal 7? (1951) 1-5.
Distinguishes two main classes of female employment, manual and "intellectual." Overt discrimination regarding wages is said to characterize the former and not the latter. Like prestige-bringing brides supported by their conjugal families, women in the intellectual sector are often paid for their presence rather than their work. Contrasts the circumstances of these two groups unfavorably with tribal and particularly matrilineal tribal women among whom the author has done research.

2144 GULATI, LEELA. Female work participation: a study of inter-state differences. *In* Economic and Political Weekly 10,1/2 (11 Jan 1975) 35-42. *With* J.N. Sinha. A Comment. 10,16 (19 Apr 1975) 672-4. *And* D. Narasimha Reddy. A Comment. 10,23 (7 Jun 1975) 902-5. *And* Leela Gulati. A Reply. 10,32 (9 Aug 1975) 1215-8.
Gulati's paper examines the relationship between female employment and various economic and demographic factors (i.e., per capita income, cropping pattern, literacy levels, male employment rates, scheduled caste and tribal proportion in population, sex ratio), by Indian state. She finds that these factors are not significant. Sinha criticizes the validity of her data and methods. Narasimha Reddy argues that "inter-regional variations in female activity rates are firmly rooted in differences in agricultural factors." In her reply, Gulati considers Sinha's criticisms, reevaluates her results and reaffirms her conclusions.

2145 _______. Occupational distribution of working women: an inter-state comparison. *In* Economic and Political Weekly 10,43 (25 Oct 1975) 1692-1704.
Census-based study considers both primary or "main activity" work and secondary or part-time work performed by women. Discusses ways in which census categories are problematic. Tables.

2146 INDIA (REPUBLIC). PLANNING COMMISSION. Some characteristics of women job seekers on the live register of employment exchanges. New Delhi: Government of India, 1966.
[Unexamined].

2147 JORAPUR, P.B. A comparative picture of the demographic characteristics of working and non-working women. *In* Indian J. of Social Work 29,2 (1968) 183-91.
Describes various socio-economic characteristics of employed and nonemployed women in rural and urban areas. [Unexamined].

2148 MITRA, ASOK, ADHIR K. SRIMANY and LALIT P. PATHAK. The status of women: household and nonhousehold economic activity. Bombay: Allied Publishers, 1979. 78p. (ICSSR Programme of Women's Studies, 3).
Brief essay (pp.1-17) considers trends in the relative participation of men and women in household and nonhousehold economic activities in rural and urban areas of India as reflected in the 1961 census. Related statistical tables compose rest of book. The work is a part of a joint project of the Indian Council of Social Science Research and Jawaharlal Nehru University to analyze trends of 1872 through 1971 censuses and related data. [Unexamined].

2149 NATH, KAMLA. Women in the working force in India. *In* Economic and Political Weekly 3,31 (Aug 1968) 1205-13.
Notes prominent trends. The great majority of employed women are engaged in agriculture, traditional village industries and service occupations. Rural women have a higher participation rate than urban women; illiterate women have a higher participation rate than literate women. Overall, women's employment rate is on the decline. "Unless countervailing forces come into play, economic development with its accompanying urbanisation, spread of education and growth of modern industries will be accompanied by a progressive decline in the participation rate for women."

2150 _______. Female work participation and economic development: a regional analysis. *In* Economic and Political Weekly 5,21 (23 May 1970) 846-9.
Investigates hypothesis that female employment rate declines with increase in economic development. The hypothesis is substantiated at the district level in India but not at the state level. Findings of study suggest a decline in family work participation in coming decades. Urges further research in

this area. Uses data from 1961 census.

2151 PAKISTAN. NATIONAL MANPOWER COUNCIL. RESEARCH AND STATISTICS BRANCH. A report on the characteristics of the female labour force in Pakistan. Karachi: Government of Pakistan, 1964. [Unexamined].

2152 PANDEY, R.N. Women: status, employment and wage disparity. *In* Indian Labour Journal 17,1 (1976) 1-18.
Presents data showing a glaring and growing disparity between male and female employment opportunities. Tables.

2153 SINGH, BIRENDRA, H.C. AGARWAL and N.I. KIM. Female labour force participation in some ECAFE countries. Bombay: Demographic Training and Research Centre, 1969. 51p.
Participation rates for members of the former Economic Commission for Asia and the Far East. [Unexamined].

2154 YOUSSEF, NADIA H. Social structure and the female labor force: the case of women workers in Muslim middle eastern countries. *In* Demography 8,4 (1971) 427-39.
Examines data from Pakistan, Morocco, Egypt, Chile and Mexico. Argues that the systematically low female participation rate in economic activities outside of agriculture in the Middle East can be attributed to "the interplay between the volitional avoidance by women of certain occupational sectors because of the social stigmatizing aspect and the prohibition of occupational opportunities imposed by males."

i) In villages

2155 MEHTA, SWARNJIT. India's rural female working force and its occupational structure, 1961: a geographical analysis. *In* Indian Geographer 12,1/2 (1967) 49-68.
Description and analysis of regional patterns in rural female employment. Considers rate of participation and occupational distribution.

2156 Women workers. 1960. 24 min. Black and white. 16 and 35 mm. [*Distributed by* Films Division, Ministry of Information and Broadcasting, 24 G. Deshmukh Marg, Bombay 400 026].
Film about recent positive changes among rural Indian women. Shows handicraft activities and contributions of gramsevikas, community development workers. [Unexamined. CF].

ii) In towns and cities

2157 The Indian working woman's new horizons. Monthly Public Opinion Surveys of the Indian Institute of Public Opinion 13, 11/12 (1968) 62p.
Statistical tables present results of survey of 500 middle-class working women from Bombay, Calcutta and Delhi. The women were asked about economic motivations to work outside the home, attitudes of family members, satisfactions and frustrations, interest in changing jobs, ideal employment circumstances, relationship of employment and marriage and attitudes toward religion, morals and politics.

2158 JOSHI, HEATHER. Prospects and case for employment of women in Indian cities. *In* Economic and Political Weekly 11,31/33 (1976) 1303-8.
Argues that conditions of urban centers in India make female employment there important and essential. States that women have been essentially neglected in urban employment policy; urges explicit incorporation of this group into such policy as mere maintenance of an already low participation rate will be difficult.

2159 KAPUR, PROMILLA. The changing status of the working woman in India. Delhi: Vikas Publishing House, 1974. 178p.
Reviews and assesses studies of educated working women in India. First part considers trends in marital relationships of this group including changing attitudes and problems. Second part presents author's contributions to report of Committee on the Status of Women in India and to Indian Council of Social Science Research programs, in revised form. This section describes patterns and problems of educated women in various occupations (office and "unusual") and recommends means by which their status can be improved.

2160 ________. Problems of urban working women. *In* B.N. Ganguli, ed. Social development: essays in honour of Smt. Durgabai Deshmukh. New Delhi: Sterling Publishers, 1977. pp.107-39.
Treats the various problems faced by two broad groups: poor, poorly educated and unskilled women and educated middle- and upper-class women. Urges further research, attitude change and situational change, including a series of supportive facilities. Includes about 75 references relating to employment problems.

2161 NATH, KAMLA. Urban women workers: a preliminary study. *In* Economic Weekly 17,37 (11 Sep 1965) 1405-12.
Preliminary study of the diversified urban occupational structure for females. Details variation in participation rate, by state and education level, and distribution of women in various occupations (based on 1961 census), along with changes in the female work participation rates from 1901 to 1961 in 15 major cities.

2162 RANADE, S.N. and P. RAMACHANDRAN. Women and employment: reports of pilot studies conducted in Delhi and Bombay by the Delhi School of Social Work, Delhi, and Tata Institute of Social Sciences, Bombay, on behalf of the Ministry of Education, Government of India, New Delhi. Bombay: Tata Institute of Social Sciences, 1970. lv. (*Its* Series, 20).
Studies conducted in an attempt to ascertain whether the government should actively facilitate part-time employment opportunities for women and, if so, what the guidelines might be. A total of 920 women were interviewed. A significant proportion were found to desire full or more than full time work due to financial needs and another group was found to desire part-time employment. The former tended to be unmarried and the latter married.

(c) Surveys of employment patterns and problems

2163 ADYANTHAYA, N.K. Women's employment in India. *In* International Labour Review 70,1 (1954) 44-66.
"The purpose of this article is to discuss briefly the extent and trends of women's employment in India, their wages and working conditions, the legislative measures adopted by the central and state governments for the protection of women workers and their effect on women's employment and other connected problems." Author was director of the Labour Bureau of India.

2164 AHLUWALIA, KAMLA. Trends in the employment of women. *In* Indian J. of Economics 39,3 (1959) 329-35.
Assesses female employment trends in India in the first half of the 20th century, using census data. Compares these patterns with those of leading industrial nations. Recommendations.

2165 Economic rights. *In* K.T. Shah, ed. Woman's role in planned economy: report of the sub-committee. Bombay: Vora and Company, 1947. pp.45-117. (National Planning Committee, 6).
Reviews the circumstances of employed women in India, focusing on problems and recommendations. From report of Subcommittee on a Woman's Role in Planned Economy of the National Planning Commission.

2166 GADGIL, D.R. Women in the working force in India. Bombay: Asia Publishing House, 1965. 33p. (Kunda Datar Memorial Lectures, 1964).
From the foreword: "Professor Gadgil has brought together . . . all the available information in a compact form and indicated a few tentative but important conclusions on the nature and extent of women's participation in economic activity in India and the impact of development on them."

2167 GIRI, V.V. Economic and social conditions of women workers. *In his* Labour problems in Indian industry, 2d ed., rev. and enl. Bombay: Asia Publishing House, 1959. pp.374-408.
Main sections consider employment patterns (overall and in agriculture, factories, mines, plantations and other industries), the light and unskilled nature of most women's jobs, recruitment and training, wages, working conditions, workers' social backgrounds, trade union participation and problems of health and welfare.

2168 INDIA (REPUBLIC). COMMITTEE ON THE STATUS OF WOMEN IN INDIA. Roles, rights and opportunities for economic participation. *In its* Towards equality: report of the Committee on the Status of Women in India. New Delhi: Department of Social Welfare, Ministry of Education and Social Welfare, Government of India, 1975. pp.148-233. [*Chair* Phulrenu Guha].
States that the problem of women's participation in employment in India has focused upon three sets of issues: 1) human rights and social justice, 2) utilization of human resources and 3) implications of social change. Reviews problems in assessing and dominant trends of women's economic participation in India. Details trends for two major and very different groups, the organized sector (only a small percentage of female workers) and the unorganized sector. Concludes with wide-ranging recommendations.

2169 INDIA (REPUBLIC). LABOUR BUREAU. Economic and social status of women workers in India. Simla: Ministry of Labour, Government of India, 1953? 97p. (*Its* Publication 15).
[Unexamined. NUC].

2170 _______. Women in employment, 1901-1956: a joint study by Labour Bureau, Simla, and Labour and Employment Division, Planning Commission. New Delhi, 1958. 41p.
[Unexamined. NUC].

2171 _______. Women in employment. Simla: Labour Bureau, Ministry of Labour and Employment, Government of India, 1964. 146p. (*Its* Pamphlet Series, 8).
Surveys trends "in women's employment in different sectors of the economy in India, the laws and regulations governing the employment of women, their wages and earnings, the factors affecting the employment prospects for women workers, the extent to which women workers have been attracted to trade unionism and related topics." Mostly tables from census and other government sponsored data.

2172 JAI PRAKASH. Women in industry. *In* Indian Labour Journal 16,8 (1975) 1145-62.
Reviews the employment problems faced by women in India. Discusses training, wages, working conditions, trade unions, occupational distribution, etc.

2173 JOSHI, DINA NATH. The problem of the welfare of women workers. *In* Indian J. of Social Work 22,3 (1961) 179-88.
Considers discrimination against female workers, the problem of who has responsibility for their welfare, objectives of a welfare program for female workers, means to these ends, legislative provisions in India and their effectiveness, the negative effects of modernization and rationalization and the kinds of welfare services available and needed.

2174 RANADIVE, VIMAL. Women workers of India. Calcutta: National Book Agency, 1976. 100p.
A socialist perspective. Chapters consider dwindling job opportunities, wage discrimination, maternity benefits and needs, effectiveness of protective legislation, trade unions, female workers in capitalist versus socialist countries and the need for a united struggle.

2175 SAIBABA, G. and N. SATYANARAYANA RAJU. Problems of working women in India. *In* Southern Economist 14,16 (15 Dec 1975) 17, 19-20.
Focuses on problems of training, wages, housing and role conflict.

2176 Seminar on part time employment of women. Report. Coimbatore: University Women's Association of Coimbatore, 1964. 42p.
Addresses and papers from a 1964 seminar recommending increased opportunities for women's part-time employment and calling for government support.

2177 SHARMA, J.N. and JAI PRAKASH. Woman workers in India. *In* J.N. Mongia, ed. Readings in Indian labour and social welfare. Delhi: Atma Ram and Sons, 1976. pp.701-39.
Summary of employment patterns of women in India. Considers participation rates, rural versus urban sectors, patterns in several selected industries, factors affecting female employment, operation of the National Employment Service, vocational training opportunities, organized versus unorganized sectors, working conditions, wages, trade unions and India's response to International Labour Organisation's International Labour Code.

2178 SINGH, ANDREA MENEFEE. Women in the unorganised sector: the need for minimum wage, hiring and promotional guidelines. *In* Law and Society Quarterly 6, 1/4 (1976) 19-25.
[Unexamined].

2179 Women in working force. Social Change 2,1 (1972) 71p.
Contents include: "Law and Women in India" by Durgabai Deshmukh, "Participation in National Politics" by Shipra Sen, "Typist or Executive?" by Aileen D. Ross, "Success or Failure in Executive Positions" by Usha Rai and "National Development and Women Workers" by Maniben Kara.

2180 Working women in changing India. New Delhi: International Labour Organization, India Branch, 1963. 109p.
[Unexamined].

2181 Working women in India, their problems: a symposium. *In* Weekly Round Table 1, 16 (21 May 1972) 26-35.
[Unexamined].

2182 YOUSSEF, NADIA H. Women and work in developing countries. Westport, Connecticut: Greenwood Press, 1976. [*Also* Berkeley: Institute of International Studies, University of California, 1974. (*Its* Population Monograph Series, 15)].
[Unexamined. BP].

(d) Employment patterns in various occupations and professions

2183 CHETTUR, USHA. The woman invades man's world. *In* Yojana 11,1 (26 Jan 1967) 32-6.
Brief article about the variety of occupations women have entered in recent years. Photographs.

2184 KAPUR, PROMILLA. The new Indian woman. *In* Onlooker 37,6 (1 May 1975) 8-11.
Concerns changing employment opportunities for women.

2185 MAPPILAPARAMBIL, ANNIE. Die indische Frau zwischen traditioneller Familienbindung und moderner Arbeitswelt [The Indian woman between traditional family ties and the modern working world]. *In* Jahrbuch des Instituts für Christliche Sozialwissenschaften der Westfälischen Wilhelms-Universität, Münster 5 (1964) 141-64.
First part, a general statement of the position of woman in Indian society, considers historical development, religious influences and family roles. The second part considers women's employment in industry, on plantations, in agriculture, as social workers, as domestic helpers and in the professions. Third section describes conflicts between new opportunities and traditional ideals.

2186 SENGUPTA, PADMINI. In trades and professions. *In* Tara Ali Baig, ed. Women of India. Delhi: Publications Division, Ministry of Information and Broadcasting, Government of India, 1958. pp.236-60.
Observes progress in the employment of women in the fields of agriculture, industry, domestic service, education, medicine, journal-

ism, business, broadcasting, government administration and other occupations. Tables and photographs.

2187 _______. Women workers of India. Bombay: Asia Publishing House, 1960. 296p.
Survey encompassing wide range of occupations.

i) Agriculturalists: the majority of female workers

2188 GULATI, LEELA. Unemployment among female agricultural labourers. *In* Economic and Political Weekly 11,13 (27 Mar 1976) 31-9.
Analyzes the report of the Rural Labour Enquiry (1964-65). Concludes that the level of unemployment of female agricultural workers is twice that of their male counterparts, when measured in terms of number of days work is desired versus number of days work is obtained. Also notes a tendency for the female unemployment level to be high when the male level is high. Includes tables showing rural/urban and statewide figures.

2189 SHARMA, KRISHAN DATT. Female participation in rural agricultural labour in northern India: a spatial interpretation, 1971. *In* Manpower Journal 8,4 (1973) 52-67.
Delineates three broad regions from the expanse of North India (Punjab to Mizoram) having varying rates of female participation in the agricultural labor force. Proposes that four sets of economic/cultural factors are primarily responsible for the variation: 1) supply of male laborers, male migration, landholding, population pressure, 2) presence or absence of social taboo against female participation in economic activities, 3) agronomic practices, including presence or absence of labor-intensive crops and level of mechanization and 4) amount of diversification in economy and non-agricultural employment opportunities.

2190 Women in agriculture. Indian Farming 25,8 (1975) 5-71.
Special issue containing articles on various rural development programs for women and the position of women in various areas of India. Stresses need to train women in modern techniques; proposes programs. [Unexamined].

ii) Women in village industries

2191 BHARATIA, L.K. The socio-cultural effects on the women working in village industries. *In* J. of the Anthropological Society of Bombay n.s. 14,2 (1972) 16-28.
Summarizes women's employment trends in various sectors of India's rural economy. Assesses threefold way in which women benefit from rural industrial schemes: economic, social and cultural. Tables present participation rates and earnings for various industries.

2192 DHAMIJA, JASLEEN. Handicrafts: a source of employment for women in developing rural economies. *In* International Labour Review 112,6 (1975) 459-65.
Argues that handicrafts are an ideal form of employment for women in many developing economies. Some examples from Indian women's experiences with handicrafts.

2193 DIXON, RUTH B. The roles of rural women: female seclusion, economic production, and reproductive choice. *In* Ronald G. Ridker, ed. Population and development: the search for selective interventions. Baltimore: Johns Hopkins University Press, 1976. pp.290-321. (Resources for the Future).
Argues that "female seclusion, by depriving girls and women of direct access to material and social resources in the community at large, creates in them a condition of extreme economic and social dependence that not only compels their early marriage but also militates against the effective practice of birth control within the marital union." Discusses both Hindu and Muslim women in South Asia and Muslim women elsewhere and proposes a program of small-scale, labor-intensive light industry cooperatives employing only women as a solution that would offer substantial opportunities for women while minimally challenging the social system.

2194 _______. Rural women at work: strategies for development in South Asia. Baltimore: Johns Hopkins University Press, 1978. (Resources for the Future).
Drawing on her experiences in Bangladesh, India, Nepal and Pakistan, the author outlines a proposed program for small rural cooperative industries. The plan includes considerations of education, regular peer contact, consciousness raising through functional literacy, access to family planning knowledge and exercise of group decision making in family and community. [Unexamined. BP].

2195 OZA, GHANSHYAMBHAI. Role of women in rural industries. *In* Khadi Gramodyog 22,1 (1975) 9-14.
Address outlining trends of women's participation in various rural industries (including spinning, weaving, leather working, pottery, cereal and pulse processing). Tables show relative participation rates.

iii) Women in factories and mines

2196 AGNIHOTRI, V. Women in industry. *In* Indian Labour Journal 4,9 (1963) 895-917.
Briefly discusses the history and trends of women's participation in industry on a world-wide basis. Assesses female industrial participation in India. Numerous tables.

2197 Asian seminar on conditions of workers, especially women workers in textile industries; Bombay, 23-26 November, 1975. New Delhi: T.N. Siddhanta for All-India Trade Union Congress, 1976? 114p.
Addresses, speeches, papers and reports from this seminar include miscellaneous materials on women in the various South Asian countries, in comparative perspective with other Asian women.

2198 DESHMUKH, DURGABAI. The new dimensions of woman's life in India. *In* His Royal Highness the Duke of Edinburgh's study conference on the human problems of industrial communities within the Commonwealth and Empire, v2: background papers, appendixes and index. London: Oxford University Press, 1957. pp.11-9.
Focuses on employment in industry (where "we come to . . . realize what immense strides have been made since Independence") and its impact on families and women's consciousness.

2199 GROVER, ANIL. The woman coal miner: are some careers still beyond our reach? *In* Eve's Weekly 30,32 (7 Aug 1976) 8-10.
Examines the prospects for underground female employment in the coal mining industry. Includes interviews with coal officials and female coal workers and photographs.

2200 INDIA (REPUBLIC). LABOUR BUREAU. Women in industry. Simla: Labour Bureau, Ministry of Labour, Government of India, 1975. 241p.
An "exhaustive statistical profile of women in industry" from various sources. Prepared for International Women's Year. Considers employment, training, wages, working conditions, etc. Numerous tables.

2201 INDIAN COUNCIL OF MEDICAL RESEARCH. Proceedings of the seminar on women in industry, held in New Delhi from 6th to 8th July, 1968. New Delhi: Indian Council of Medical Research, 1969. 71p.
Includes synopses of papers presented, summary of seminar, recommendations and statistical tables. Topics of paper were: health; legislation; university research; mutual attitudes of female workers, management and trade unions; problems in textile industry; problems in jute industry; and employment in pharmaceutical industry.

2202 MONGIA, J.N. Some special problems of women in industry. *In* J.N. Mongia, ed. Readings in Indian labour and social welfare. Delhi: Atma Ram and Sons, 1976. pp.762-70.
Discusses attitudes toward female workers, special problems of female factory workers, their economic position and future trends.

2203 MUKERJEE, RADHAKAMAL. Woman and child labour. *In his* The Indian working class, 3d rev. and enl. ed. Bombay: Hind Kitabs, 1951. pp.91-105.
Describes numbers, wages and working conditions of female laborers in plantations, factories, mica mines and shellac, bidi and rice-milling industries. Tables.

2204 SHAH, M.S. Wages and employment of women in India. *In* Indian Labour Journal 16,2 (1975) 167-84.
Details continuing wage and employment discrimination against women in various industries. Tables.

2205 Women in industry. 1962. 9 min. Black and white. 16 and 35 mm. [*Distributed by* Films Division, Ministry of Information and Broadcasting, 24 G. Deshmukh Marg, Bombay 400 026].
Film concerning special accommodations for female industrial workers, including provisions for their children and improved working conditions. [Unexamined. CF].

iv) Women in service and professional occupations

See also particular fields (e.g., "Health care") within "b. Continuity and change in contemporary South Asia"

2206 Crossfield directory of women executives in India, 1977. New Delhi: Crossfield, 1977. 321, 86p.
[Unexamined. IBP].

2206a DAFTARY, SHARAYU. Women managers. *In* Indian Management 15,5 (1976) 4-8.
Argues that qualities instilled in Indian women by virtue of their social position — capacities to adjust, bargain, endure and suffer — "are essential and required in administration and business management." Reviews problems of professional women, offers advice for combining family and career and discusses a variety of other aspects of the lives of employed women.

2207 NATH, KAMLA. Women in service occupations. *In* Economic and Political Weekly 2,1 (7 Jan 1967) 25-30.
Considers changes in female participation in service occupations from the 1951 to 1961 censuses. Projects a future need for women employed in education field. "The work participation rate of educated women is very low and this low rate imposes a severe limitation on

the speed at which the number of women workers can be increased in the modern service occupations."

2208 Our World. v1- (1967-). New Delhi: Delhi Polytechnic for Women. Monthly. [Unexamined. IPP].

2209 PAPANEK, HANNA. Purdah in Pakistan: seclusion and modern occupations for women. *In* J. of Marriage and the Family 33,3 (1971) 517-30.
Precursor to author's *pardā* review article (entry 2051). Discusses general features of *pardā* in South Asia and the influence of female seclusion and associated values on women's participation in contemporary occupations. Due to the need for female personnel in a sex-segregated system, medicine and teaching are important, prestigious occupations for educated women.

2210 ROSS, AILEEN D. Changing aspirations and roles: middle and upper class Indian women enter the business world. *In* Giri Raj Gupta, ed. Family and social change in modern India. New Delhi: Vikas, 1976. pp.103-32. (Main Currents in Indian Sociology, 2).
Describes four phases in the movement of upper- and middle-class Indian, Australian and Canadian women into the business labor force. Indian women may best be located in the third phase, and Australian and Canadian women in the fourth.

2211 Saris and careers. 30 min. Black and white. 16 and 35 mm? [*Available from* University of Michigan Television Center, 310 Maynard Street, Ann Arbor, Michigan 48108].
Film. Includes interviews with three professional women: a physicist, a physician and a microbiologist. Considers lifestyles of contemporary women in India, including issues of marriage and employment. [Unexamined].

2212 WASI, MURIEL. The professional women in India: dangerous corners. *In* Monthly Public Opinion Surveys of the Indian Institute of Public Opinion 18, 1 (1972) 17-20.
Discusses some problems of the Indian woman who pursues a professional career.

2213 Women employees in Indian railways. *In* Indian Railways 20,5 (1975) 57-64. [Unexamined].

2214 Women in business and industry (Who's who: industry and business). *In* Ajeet Cour and Arpana Cour, eds. Directory of Indian women today, 1976. New Delhi: India International Publications, 1976. pp.53-63, 544-7.
Series of brief biographical sketches. Includes mailing address and, in many cases, photograph.

2215 Women in government services (Who's who: government services). *In* Ajeet Cour and Arpana Cour, eds. Directory of Indian women today, 1976. New Delhi: India International Publications, 1976. pp.188-213, 566-70.
Series of brief biographical sketches. Includes mailing address and, in many cases, photograph.

2216 Women in other professions (Who's who: other professions). *In* Ajeet Cour and Arpana Cour, eds. Directory of Indian women today, 1976. New Delhi: India International Publications, 1976. pp.520-32, 617-21.
Series of brief biographical sketches. Includes mailing address and, in many cases, photograph.

2217 Women in sciences and applied sciences. (Who's who: scientists). *In* Ajeet Cour and Arpana Cour, eds. Directory of Indian women today, 1976. New Delhi: India International Publications, 1976. pp.278-324, 577-81.
Series of brief biographical sketches. Includes mailing address and, in many cases, photograph.

2218 Women's Polytechnic Annual. v1- (1966-). Trichur. Annually. [Unexamined. IPP].

2219 YOUNG WOMEN'S CHRISTIAN ASSOCIATION, INDIA. The educated woman in Indian society today. Bombay: Tata McGraw-Hill Publishing Company, 1971. 287p.
Regarding the Indian woman with higher education and "how to use her education most profitably." Many articles are relevant to work and employment topics: "Demographic Portrait of Professional Women Employed in India" by Idrak Bhatty and Zarina Bhatty; "Investment and Employment" by Zarina Bhatty; Women in Four Important Professions and Consolidation of Achievement in Four Important Professions: "Teaching" by Eva I. Shipstone, "Social Work" by Sita Basu, "Medicine and Surgery" by Perviz Heera and "Nursing" by Madhavi D. Sharma; "The Beginnings and Growth of Professionalism Among Women" by L.S. Chandrakant and Muriel Wasi; "Established and New Professions: Untapped Capacities" by Vidyut Khandwala; "New Directions: Openings in Mass Media of Communication" by C.R. Ekambaram and "Vocational Guidance, Personnel Counselling and Placement Services" by Perin H. Mehta.

(e) Participation in cooperatives and trade unions, legislative protection

2220 Annual review of the working of the Maternity Benefit Acts (central as well as states) during 1972. *In* Indian Labour Journal 16,3 (1975) 365-74.

Text presents main provisions and administration and operation of the Maternity Benefit Act, 1961. Tables give figures concerning its operation in 1972. Annual reports for other years appear in other volumes of this journal.

2221 INDIAN COOPERATIVE UNION. Women's employment: some viable projects. New Delhi: Indian Cooperative Union, AIFACS, Rafi Marg, 1978.
[Unexamined].

2222 MATHUR, MANORAMA. Women and Indian trade union movement. *In* Asian Labour 23,121 (1975) 8-13.
Presents and discusses data on women's trade union participation. In pre-independent India, participation rose from 1.1% of the total membership in 1927-28 to 4.9% in 1946-47. In post-independent India the rate has fluctuated from a high of 11.8% in 1956-57 to a low of 5.9% in 1956-66. Notes that the agricultural sector, with the largest group of female workers, is unorganized. Reviews the accomplishment of eminent female leaders in the trade union movement.

2223 MOHINDER KAUR. Women and the cooperative movement in India. *In* Women Today 6,2 (1964) 28-30.
Brief survey of women's participation in industrial and crafts cooperatives in India.

2224 Regional Conference on the Role of Women in Cooperative Development, Kuala Lumpur, Malaysia, July 1975. New Delhi: International Cooperative Alliance, 1976.
[Unexamined].

2225 RUIKAR, MALATHI. Women in trade unions. *In* Indian J. of Social Work 13,4 (1953) 250-6.
Observes that women have not taken an active part in India's trade union movement due to lack of time, education and experience in union organization and leadership. Tables show extent of female participation in factories and mines and growth of male and female trade union participation in India, 1927 to 1949.

(f) Vocational guidance for women

2226 AZIZ, WAHIDA. Careers. Allahabad: Kitab Mahal, 1945. 75p. (Kitab Mahal Women's Series, 1).
Vocational guidance for Indian women. [Unexamined. NUC].

2227 BORGES, B.C. Careers for women. Bombay: Institute of Vocational Guidance and Selection, 1963. (Guidance Series, 8).
[Unexamined].

2228 GULATI, J.S. Careers for women. Calcutta: YMCA Publishing House, 1956.
[Unexamined].

2229 MOHAN, M.C. Guide to careers for girls. Lahore: Students' Popular Depot, n.d. 343p.
[Unexamined].

2230 WADIA, AVABAI B. Some careers for women. Bombay: Thacker and Company, 1947. 39p.
[Unexamined].

(g) Employment and other roles: conflicts and compatabilities

2231 NARULA, UMA. Career failure among women. *In* Social Welfare 14,2 (1967) 4-5.
Presents results of an attitude survey made by a social psychologist, noting aspects that frustrate women's careers.

2231a NATIONAL INSTITUTE OF PUBLIC COOPERATION AND CHILD DEVELOPMENT. Working mother and early childhood education: report of a research sponsored by UNESCO. New Delhi: National Institute of Public Cooperation and Child Development, 1978. 120p.
Report of study conducted in India. [Unexamined. ALI].

2232 PAPANEK, HANNA. Men, women, and work: reflections on the two-person career. *In* American J. of Sociology 78,4 (1973) 852-72. [*Also in* Joan Huber, ed. Changing women in a changing society. Chicago: University of Chicago Press, 1973. pp.90-110].
Observes tendencies promoting the "two-person career" in the United States, whereby middle-class wives achieve vicariously through their husbands' work. This "two-person career" is generally absent in South Asia due to such factors as widespread separation of men's and women's spheres, ideas about the complementarity of the sexes and family ideals.

2233 SARWAL, AMITA et al. Will the creche replace the mother-in-law? *In* Eve's Weekly 30,51 (18 Dec 1976) 24-7, 53.
Interviews with nine urban professional working mothers concerning their views on child care. Photographs.

2234 SINGH, MRS. K.P. Career and family, women's two roles: a study in role conflict. *In* Indian J. of Social Work 33, 3 (1972) 277-81.
An attitude survey of 171 married working women. Concludes that those who work by choice

do not perceive their work as interfering with child-care responsibilities; those who work out of economic necessity do perceive a conflict. Locality not specified.

(9) The "outer" world and issues and patterns of female education

(a) The merits of female education, some opinions

2235 AZAM, IKRAM. Woman and home. *In* Pakistan Review 17,12 (1969) 13-4, 32.
Argues that the central issue involved in whether women should receive an education or not is how the home would be affected because "a woman who fails in her essential functions as a wife, mother and sister, is a misfit. . . . she is no woman. Her products will . . . be misfits; and the whole society . . . abnormal . . . . Woman! Stay home — where you can . . . rule subtly by your heart, affection, and tact [and not] with your tongue and temper!"

2236 Education and veil. Karachi: Peermahomed Ebrahim Trust, 1975. 164p.
Describes Islamic views of female seclusion. Argues that female education is very important and that it should be done in accordance with the nature of women and their place in society: "She should learn . . . so that she might be a chaste wife and a sincere caretaker of her children."

2237 NAMJOSHI, A.N. Educated woman: a great power. *In* Lok Rajya 28,12 (16 Oct 1972) 2-5, 14.
Convocation address from Shreemati Nathibai Damodar Thackersey Women's University. Briefly mentions SNDT's phases of development and a philosophy of women's education.

(b) Comprehensive surveys, reports, collected papers and a bibliography

2238 AGGARWAL, J.C. Indian women: education and status; including major recommendations of the report of the national Committee on the Status of Women in India, 1971-74. New Delhi: Arya Book Depot, 1976. 106p.
Includes miscellaneous materials: recommendations of various committees and commissions (most predominantly, the recent Committee on the Status of Women in India) on various aspects of female education, historical review of female education in India, demographic tables, constitutional rights of Indian women and so forth.

2239 ASSOCIATION OF THE ALL-CEYLON WOMEN'S CONFERENCE, COLOMBO. Inaugural regional conference on the 'Education of Women in a Changing East', 23rd-25th July, 1954, Colombo. Report. Colombo, 1954. 87p.
[Unexamined].

2240 KHANDWALA, VIDYUT, ed. Bibliography: women's education in India, 1850-1967. *In* G.B. Sardar, Shakuntala Mehta and Neera Desai, eds. Golden jubilee commemoration volume, 1916-1966. Bombay: Shreemati Nathibai Damodar Thackersey Women's University, 1968. Fourth part, 115p.
Nine hundred seventy-six English, Gujarati, Hindi and Marathi references arranged by topic. Many have brief annotations.

2241 MAZUMDAR, VINA, ed. The challenge of education: studies on issues in women's education. Bombay: Allied Publishers, forthcoming. SNDT Women's University, Bombay; Women in a Changing Society).
Papers sponsored jointly by the Indian Council of Social Science Research and Shreemati Nathibai Damodar Thackersey Women's University. [Unexamined].

2242 MEHTA, HANSA MANUBHAI. Post-war educational reconstruction: with special reference to women's education in India. Bombay: Pratibha Publications, 1945? 23p. (Pratibha Publication 4).
[Unexamined. NUC].

2243 The role of women in education in India: a report of the National Seminar on the Role of Women in Education in India held from October 3 to 5, 1975, at the Lady Willingdon Training College, Madras-5, under the chairmanship of Dr. Mrs. Rajammal P. Devadass. [Madras]: Society for the Promotion of Education in India, 1976. 62p.
Summary of proceedings, papers on "Role of Women in Education in India" and "The Challenges in Education for Women" and reports of discussions and committees. Considers all levels of formal and informal education.

2244 SARDAR, G.B., SHAKUNTALA MEHTA and NEERA DESAI, eds. Golden jubilee commemoration volume, 1916-1966. Bombay: Shreemati Nathibai Damodar Thackersey Women's University, 1968. lv.
See "Part II: Articles and Speeches" for a collection of materials on various aspects of women's education in contemporary India and abroad and "India" section of Part III for a demographic profile of formal female education in India.

2245 SEN, N.B., ed. Progress of women's education in free India: being a symposium on women's education by nearly sixty experienced and distinguished lady educationists of modern India; together with glorious, inspiring and invaluable thoughts and views on women, expressed by eminent educationists, scholars, poets, writers, philosophers and reformers of the East and the West. New Delhi: New Book Society of India, 1969. 331p.
Numerous brief articles concerning general and specific aspects of female education in India.

2246 _______. Development of women's education in new India: containing contributions from many distinguished educationists and eminent ladies in different walks of life, on various aspects of women's education and its progress since Independence; together with several thousand invaluable, inspiring and glorious thoughts of eminent philosophers, poets, scholars, writers, thinkers and social reformers of the East and the West, on affection, love, romance, courtship and marriage. New Delhi: New Book Society of India, 1969. 304p.
Companion to the above volume, similar in scope and format.

2247 SENGUPTA, PADMINI. Women's education in India. New Delhi: Ministry of Education, Government of India, 1960. 30p.
[Unexamined. IBP].

2247a THACKERSEY, PREMLILA V. Education of women: a key to progress. [New Delhi]: Ministry of Education and Youth Services, Government of India, 1970. 96p. ([*Its*] Publication 879).
Reviews history of women's education in India from 1813 through the post-independent period. Also considers access to higher education and presents problems and future aims. Appendixes compare female education trends in India with those of other major nations of the world, reproduce recommendations of the 1964-66 Education Commission, provide recommended readings and present major educational trends in graphic form.

i) Histories of female education in 19th and 20th century India

2248 MATHUR, Y.B. Women's education in India, 1813-1966. Bombay: Asia Publishing House, 1973. 208p.
Well-documented survey with a basic bibliography. Key documents reproduced in appendixes.

2249 MISRA, LAKSHMI. Democratic India and women's education. *In* Education Quarterly 13,50 (1961) 119-22.
Historical view of 19th and 20th century efforts to promote female education. Highlights government programs.

2250 _______. Education of women in India, 1921-1966. Bombay: Macmillan and Company, 1966. 225p.
Extensively documented study of formal education, organized chronologically: the background (1700-1921), 1921-1937, 1937-1947, independence through First Five Year Plan and Second and Third Five Year Plans. Considers legislation and missionary, governmental and women's organizational activities.

ii) Official reports

2251 INDIA (REPUBLIC). COMMITTEE ON THE STATUS OF WOMEN IN INDIA. Educational development. *In its* Towards equality: report of the Committee on the Status of Women in India. New Delhi: Department of Social Welfare, Ministry of Education and Social Welfare, Government of India, 1975. pp.234-82. [*Chair* Phulrenu Guha].
Notes discrepancy between 19th century reformist and post-independent views of the value of education for women. The former argued that education enhances women's abilities to play their traditional roles as wives and mothers while the latter find education important for women as "citizens, house-wives, mothers, contributors to the family income and builders of the new society." Surveys progress of formal female education before and since independence, literacy rates and the widespread "imbalance in the distribution of educational effort and resources among different sections of the population." Offers a series of wide-ranging recommendations.

2252 INDIA (REPUBLIC). COMMITTEE TO LOOK INTO THE CAUSES FOR LACK OF PUBLIC SUPPORT PARTICULARLY IN RURAL AREAS FOR GIRLS' EDUCATION AND TO ENLIST PUBLIC CO-OPERATION. Report. New Delhi: National Council of Women's Education, Ministry of Education, Government of India, 1965. 98p.
Multifaceted report concentrates on "educationally backward" states. Assesses 19th and 20th century programs and progress in these states and compares enrollment rates with all-India figures. Considers explanations and suggestions of local personnel. Offers recommendations. Appendixes provide various educational statistics for all Indian states.

2253 INDIA (REPUBLIC). EDUCATION COMMISSION. Recommendations on women's education: a compilation prepared by the Education Commission. New Delhi: Edu-

cation Commission, Government of India, 1965. 112p.
Digest of the recommendations made by various Indian councils and committees from 1949 to 1965, grouped by topic.

2254 INDIA (REPUBLIC). MINISTRY OF EDUCATION. NATIONAL COMMITTEE ON WOMEN'S EDUCATION. Report, May 1958 to January 1959. Delhi: Manager of Publications, Government of India, 1959. 335p. (Publication no. 408). [*Chair* Durgabai Deshmukh].
Report of committee established upon the 1957 recommendation of the Education Panel of the Planning Commission to investigate all levels of public and private educational opportunities for Indian women and make recommendations for improvements. Based upon interviews with government officials, educationists and social workers; questionnaires completed by various officials; local tours; state documents on particular local problems; the women-power requirements of the Second and Third Plans; and several special studies by members of the Committee.

2255 NATIONAL COUNCIL FOR WOMEN'S EDUCATION. Report. 1- (1960/61-). Coimbatore. Annually.
The council was established in 1959 to advise the government on issues relating to all levels of female education, to propose policies and programs, to seek ways to utilize volunteer efforts in female education, to suggest methods of public education concerning female education, to evaluate the progress of the various efforts and to recommend particular areas for study.

(c) Formal education

2256 BHANDARI, ARVIND. Ethnicity, women and education. Meerut: Anu Prakashan, 1978. [Unexamined].

2257 INDIA (REPUBLIC). COMMITTEE ON DIFFERENTIATION OF CURRICULA FOR BOYS AND GIRLS. Report. New Delhi: Ministry of Education, Government of India, 1964. 86p.
Report prepared under auspices of National Council for Women's Education. [Unexamined].

2257a KAMAT, A.R. Women's education and social change in India. *In* Social Scientist 5,1 (1976) 3-27.
Concerns various aspects of formal education since independence. Major sections describe trends, assess achievements and shortcomings and consider effects upon employment and in other areas.

2258 KUREISHI, M. Women's education in Pakistan. *In* Pakistan Quarterly 7,3 (1957) 18-21.
Reviews progress made in women's education in Pakistan and careers that have correspondingly become available to women. Briefly notes obstacles to widespread female education. Photographs.

2259 NISCHOL, K. The invisible woman: images of women and girls in school textbooks. *In* Social Action 26,3 (1976) 267-81.
Report of a study of selected English language textbooks used in Indian schools. Examines images of women and girls in textual material and illustrations. Females portrayed were found to be "invisible," having no names and playing few (largely familial) roles. Girls are portrayed as relatively passive and are mentioned less frequently than boys. They lack intellectual interests and resourcefulness. Sexes are usually separated.

2260 PHADKE, SINDHU. Special problems of the education of women. *In* M.S. Gore, I.P. Desai and Suma Chitnis, eds. Papers in the sociology of education in India: papers prepared as part of a project in the sociology of education in India, sponsored by the Education Commission and the National Council of Educational Research and Training, New Delhi. New Delhi: National Council of Educational Research and Training, 1967. pp.173-200.
Regarding formal education. Reviews 19th and 20th century changes that affected female education, problems associated with contemporary female education and the relationship of female education to other socio-economic factors.

i) Secondary education

2261 DESHMUKH, DURGABAI et al. Curriculum for girls at the secondary stage. *In* Secondary Education 6,4 (1962) 1-11.
Four authors offer differing opinions regarding whether a separate curriculum for female students would better fulfill their needs.

ii) Higher education

2262 ANANT, SANTOKH SINGH. Segregation of sexes in Indian universities. *In* G.S. Mansukhani, ed. Crises in Indian universities. New Delhi: Oxford and IBH Publishing Company, 1972. pp.150-61. (Studies in Indian Education, 1).
Argues that sex segregation in universities and elsewhere throughout Indian society impedes social development and mature adult relationships.

2263 BHASIN, KAMALA. Role of educated young women in changing India. *In* Ved Dan Sudhir, ed. The crisis of changing India. Delhi: National Publishing House, 1974. pp.214-23.
Criticizes the small proportion of Indian women receiving vocational, college or university educations; the quality of the education they are receiving; and the extent to which their educations are wasted. Argues that the potential role of educated Indian women in the future of their country is great.

2264 CORMACK, MARGARET. She who rides a peacock: Indian students and social change. Bombay: Asia Publishing House, 1961. 264p. [*Also* New York: Praeger, 1962].
Report of questionnaire given to 500 college students throughout India concerning attitudes toward family, marriage, women's roles, education, politics and other topics. Results are tabulated by sex.

2265 FISHER, MARGUERITE J. Higher education of women and national development in Asia. *In* Asian Survey 8,4 (1968) 263-9.
Report on higher educational aspects of a 1966 seminar on Asian women and development sponsored by the United Nations. Includes table of statistics on female students and staff in the various Asian countries for the years 1955, 1958 and 1963.

2265a GIDWANI, N.N. and K. NAVALANI, comps. and eds. College magazines. *In their* Current Indian periodicals in English: an annotated guide, 2d rev. and enl. ed. Jaipur: Saraswati Publications, 1978. pp.67-87.
List of hundreds of college magazines includes numerous publications of women's schools. Notes title, first year of publication, frequency of publication, price, editor, publisher, place and language(s).

2266 INDIA (DOMINION). UNIVERSITY EDUCATION COMMISSION. Women's education. *In its* Report, December 1948-August 1949, v1. Delhi: Manager of Publications, Government of India, 1949? pp.392-402. (Report of the University Education Commission, 1).
Argues that it is essential for women to be well-educated in order to be good mothers, that women and men are equally competent academically and that university curricula should expand to offer specializations appropriate "to the education of women as women." Discusses four such fields: home economics, nursing, teaching and fine arts.

2267 MEHTA, RAMA. The western educated Hindu woman. Bombay: Asia Publishing House, 1970. 216p.
Study of 50 women from various areas of India who were educated in convent schools and Indian universities. Documents their attitudes toward a variety of topics. Concludes that these women generally do not maintain a commitment to or transmit Hindu traditions.

2268 MEHTA, SUSHILA. Women in Indian universities. *In* G.S. Mansukhani, ed. Crises in Indian universities. New Delhi: Oxford and IBH Publishing Company, 1972. pp.162-180. (Studies in Indian Education, 1).
Stresses the rapidly increasing numbers and proportion of women in Indian universities and its impact upon these women in terms of age at marriage, individualistic values and career opportunities.

2269 ORR, INGE C. The educated woman in modern India. *In* United Asia 14,4 (1962) 239-49.
Includes views of educated women concerning career and family, along with a summary of educational opportunities for women at all levels. Tables.

2270 SHAH, MADHURI R. Status and education of women in India. *In* J. of the Gujarat Research Society 38/39,4/1 (1976/77) 15-24.
Briefly reviews formal educational trends in India since independence, by sex. Considers goals and objectives of women's education and argues that higher education is not wasted when married women do not work outside the home. Education for women must, however, become more oriented toward employment skills.

2271 SHRIDEVI, SRIPATI. The development of women's higher education in India. Ph.D. dissertation, Department of Education?, Columbia University, 1954. 407p. [University Microfilms 10,184].
Traces growth of women's higher education from influences of 19th and early 20th century social, religious and political movements to mid-20th century. [Unexamined. DAI].

2272 ________. Women's higher education since independence. *In* N.B. Sen, ed. Development of education in new India: containing contributions from many experienced and outstanding educationists of India on various aspects of education and its development since independence. New Delhi: New Book Society of India, 1966. pp.205-10.
Discusses effects of higher education on women's economic freedom and use of leisure time, family and children.

2273 WASI, MURIEL. The quiet revolution. *In* Indo Asian Culture 12,2 (1963) 69-73.
Discusses repercussions throughout Indian society of increasing numbers of educated women.

2274 Women and education. 1957. 14 min. Black and white. 16 and 35 mm. [*Distributed by* Films Division, Ministry of Information and Broadcasting, 24 G. Deshmukh Marg, Bombay 400 026].
Life of a young college girl demonstrates changing educational opportunities for Indian women. [Unexamined. CF].

2275 YOUNG WOMEN'S CHRISTIAN ASSOCIATION,

INDIA. The educated woman in Indian society today. Bombay: Tata McGraw-Hill Publishing Company, 1971. 287p.
Regarding the Indian woman with higher education and "how to use her education most profitably." Many articles concern employment. Those related directly to education are: "Who is the Educated Woman of India Today?" by Muriel Wasi, "Perspective: The Educational System and the Educated Woman of India" by Muriel Wasi, "Development of the Infrastructure for Life-Long Education" by Dorthea E. Woods, "Development of Resourcefulness: Education for Self-Reliance" by K. Rangachari, "Training for Leadership" by Muriel Wasi, "Wanted: Clearing House of Information" by Vidyut Khandwala, "Planning for Tomorrow" by Lakshmi N. Menon and "Summing Up" by Muriel Wasi.

(d) Adult / nonformal education

2276 ADALENE, M. From theory to practice: Grihini schools, an experiment in adult education. *In* Social Action 18, 1 (1968) 56-64.
Argues for the education of tribal women and girls as an important aspect of preparing tribal people for life in modern India. Offers suggestions regarding the priorities and structure of such an education based on the experience of missionary workers in Grihini schools for home and family life education.

2277 Adult education of women in the changing pattern of society; report of the national seminar, New Delhi, October 27-30, 1978. New Delhi: Indian Adult Education Association, 1973. 96p. (*Its* Series, 95).
Papers, resolutions, reports and recommendations concerning programs and goals for adult female literacy.

2278 INDIA (REPUBLIC). COMMITTEE FOR REVIEW AND EVALUATION OF THE PROGRAMME OF "CONDENSED COURSES OF EDUCATION OF ADULT WOMEN." Report. New Delhi: Ministry of Education, 1964.
Report prepared under the auspices of the Central Social Welfare Board. [Unexamined].

2279 INDIA (REPUBLIC). COMMITTEE ON ADULT EDUCATION PROGRAMMES FOR WOMEN. Adult education programmes for women: report of the committee appointed by the Ministry of Education and Social Welfare. New Delhi: Ministry of Education and Social Welfare, Government of India, 1978. 15p.
Argues that traditional social patterns and traditional policy of planners and administrators have limited the progress of adult education programs for Indian women. Proposes revised goals and the operational means to reach them.

2280 INDIA (REPUBLIC). DIRECTORATE OF NON-FORMAL (ADULT) EDUCATION. Misconceptions influencing nonformal education for women. New Delhi: Directorate of Nonformal (Adult) Education, Ministry of Education and Social Welfare, 1975. 8p. (*Its* Question Series, 5).
Discusses misconceptions about development, illusions about education and prejudices about women. "The problem of women's education. . . . is, therefore, an inseparable component of fundamental, general and deep-rooted socio-economic, socio-political and socio-cultural aspirations, needs and trends."

2281 JUMUNABAI, J. Women's education: the role and content of adult education in the changing social pattern with special reference to women's education. *In* Indian J. of Adult Education, 23,2 (1962) 15-6.
Outlines some community development education programs designed for women.

2282 NIMBKAR, KRISHNABAI. Voluntary organization and women's education. *In* Indian J. of Adult Education 22 (Mar 1961) 5-7.
Adult education programs? [Unexamined].

(e) Reaching rural girls and women

2283 DORAISWAMI, S. Educational advancements and socio-economic participation of women in India. *In* Design of educational programmes for the promotion of rural women. Teheran: International Institute for Adult Literacy Methods, 1975.
Evaluates various efforts to educate rural Indian women and describes literacy and nonformal programs in operation at the time of writing. [Unexamined].

2284 KABIR, HUMAYUN. Women's education in rural areas. *In* Kurukshetra: a symposium on community development. Delhi: Publications Division, Ministry of Information and Broadcasting, Government of India, 1961. pp.253-7.
Programmatic statement.

2285 LAL, MOHAN. Problems of girls' education in rural areas. *In* Education Quarterly 13,50 (1961) 167-9.
Details economic and social problems affecting rural women's education and suggests remedial steps.

2286 SARAN, RAKSHA. Education of girls and

women in rural areas, India. New Delhi: Ministry of Education, Government of India, 1962.
[Unexamined].

2287 SRIVASTAVA, K.N. Women's education in rural communities. *In* Education Quarterly 13,50 (1961) 170-4.
Considers three features essential to successful rural female education: motivation, presence of leisure time and appropriate institutional arrangements. Includes a series of recommendations.

(f) Literacy rates

2288 KALE, B.D. Contours of female education and age at marriage in urban India: a district level study. *In* J. of the Institute of Economic Research 4,2 (1969) 34-49.
Presents mean female literacy and age at marriage rates by districts of India in tabular and map forms. With discussion. Based on 1961 census data.

(g) Sex education

2289 JILANI, GHULAM. Pakistan. *In* Susan Burke, ed. Responsible parenthood and sex education: proceedings of a working group held in Tunisia, November 1969. London: International Planned Parenthood Federation, 1970. pp.126-31.
Summary of a paper. Outlines a series of objectives for a sex education program, the place of sex education in Islamic thought and some key facets of a proposed program.

2290 MUKERJI, RENUKA. Programme in sex education for college girls. *In* J. of Family Welfare 5,4 (1959) 37-42.
[Unexamined].

2291 RUHELA, S.P. Sociology of sex education in India. Delhi: Dhanpat Rai and Sons, 1969. 45p.
Discusses "the various aspects of sex education in theoretical perspectives of sociology as well as from a practical point of view, keeping in view the demands made by the Indian situation in particular." The topic was given no attention by three major education commissions in India.

(h) Physical education and sports participation

2292 BUCK, H.C. A programme of physical education for girls' schools in India. Madras: Oxford University Press, 1938. 377p.
[Unexamined].

2293 HAMID, T. Sports among women in Pakistan. *In* Pakistan Review 3 (May 1955).
[Unexamined].

2294 INDIA (REPUBLIC). MINISTRY OF EDUCATION. A suggested syllabus of physical education for girls. Delhi: Manager of Publications, Government of India, 1956. 30p. [*Reprint of* A national plan of physical education and recreation].
[Unexamined].

2295 KAMAL, SHOUKAT. Women on the sports field. *In* Perspective 3,8/9 (1970) 73-6.
Considers physical education and sports participation of Pakistani women and girls. Chiefly a review of prominent athletes and their sports.

2296 MALIK, AMITA. Women in sport. *In* Tara Ali Baig, ed. Women of India. Delhi: Publications Division, Ministry of Information and Broadcasting, Government of India, 1958. pp.193-9.
Profiles the growing field of women's athletics. Mentions historical background and notable athletes. Photographs.

2297 Women's World. v1- (1939-). Calcutta: Women Inter College Sports Association. Monthly.
[Unexamined. IPP].

(i) Education as a profession for women

2298 SEN GUPTA, ROSHANI et al. Women are learning to teach. *In* Eve's Weekly 30, 28 (10 Jul 1976) 8-12.
Profiles four women in government- and UNICEF-sponsored teacher training programs in Delhi, Bangladesh, Bhutan and Nepal.

2299 Women in education (Who's who: educationists). *In* Ajeet Cour and Arpana Cour, eds. Directory of Indian women today, 1976. New Delhi: India International Publications, 1976. pp.100-87, 556-65.
Series of brief biographical sketches. Includes mailing address and, in many cases, photograph.

(10) Hand in hand: women as agents in the development process and beneficiaries of social welfare measures

2300 AGENCY FOR INTERNATIONAL DEVELOPMENT. Franziska P. Hosken, ed. International directory of women's development organizations. Washington: US Agency for International Development, 1977. 311p.
International directory of women's organizations "contributing . . . to the social and economic development process." Based on responses to questionnaires. Provides detailed information (activities, size, publications, etc.) on 31 such organizations in South Asia and lists an additional 14.

2301 ALAUDDIN, TALAT K. Status of women and socio-economic development: a selected and annotated bibliography. Islamabad: Pakistan Institute of Development Economics, 1977. 125p. (*Its* Bibliography (New) Series, 1).
First 200 entries specifically relate to Pakistan. The remaining 969 entries concern other countries (in many cases, India) and general, theoretical topics. A small portion is annotated. Includes English-language books, articles, theses, unpublished papers, pamphlets, government reports and UN publications.

2302 ASSOCIATED COUNTRY WOMEN OF THE WORLD. The place of rural women's organisations in their country's development: past, present and future. London, 1957.
Report of an international seminar held in Ceylon in 1957. [Unexamined].

2303 JAHAN, ROUNAQ and HANNA PAPANEK, eds. Women and development: perspectives from South and Southeast Asia. Dacca: University Press, forthcoming.
Papers presented at a 1977 regional seminar sponsored by the Bangladesh Institute of Law and International Affairs. Authors and topics relevant to South Asia are: Hanna Papanek, introduction; Rounaq Jahan, summary of conference and its policy recommendations; Vina Mazumdar on development and public policy; Rounaq Jahan on public policy; Durga Ghimire on development in Nepal; Ashish Bose, Devaki Jain, Nalini Singh and Malini Chand on methodological issues in work participation analysis; Hanna Papanek on work and development; A. Farouk on rural Bangladesh women as a disadvantaged class; Sarfaraz Khan Qureshi on determinants of paid employment for Pakistani women; Obaidullah Khan on rural women of Bangladesh; Sharifa Khatun on women's education in a rural community of Bangladesh; Nasra M. Shah on employed/unemployed women's fertility differentials in Pakistan, 1973; Rafiqul Huda Chaudhury on female status and fertility in a metropolitan area of Bangladesh; Florence McCarthy, Taherunnessa Abdullah and Sondra Zeidenstein on women's programs as viewed by action workers; Satnam Mahmud on nonformal education in Pakistan; Shamima Islam on nonformal education in Bangladesh; and Ela R. Bhatt on organizing self-employed women in India. [Unexamined. Information supplied by coeditor].

2304 MAZUMDAR, VINA, ed. Role of rural women in development: report of an international study seminar held at the Institute of Development Studies, University of Sussex, U.K., 5th January to 10th February 1977. Bombay: Allied Publishers, 1978. 125p.
Among seminar participants were women from Bangladesh, India, Pakistan and Sri Lanka. The participants prepared a series of task force reports, which are reproduced in the volume: "Family, Marriage and Law," "Access to Rural Services" and "Mobilization and Self Reliance." Also includes a series of case studies (none from South Asia) and appendixes giving guidelines for planners, researchers and field personnel. [Unexamined. ALI].

2305 NELSON, NICI. Why has development neglected rural women?: a review of the South Asian literature. Oxford: Pergamon Press, Ltd., 1979. 106p. (Women in Development, 1).
Critically evaluates over 300 sources and the programs to which they refer. Attempts to account for paucity of material and attention and makes recommendations directed toward researchers, planners and administrators. [Unexamined. Information supplied by publisher.].

2306 RIHANI, MAY. Development as if women mattered: an annotated bibliography with a third world focus. Washington, D.C.: New TransCentury Foundation, 1978. 137p. (Overseas Development Council Occasional Paper Series, 10).
While coverage of potential materials is limited (there are 287 total entries), this bibliography provides thorough annotations and includes many unpublished papers and reports, some of which may be ordered directly from the New TransCentury Foundation.

2307 TINKER, IRENE, MICHÈLE BO BRAMSEN and MAYRA BUVINIĆ, eds. Women and world development: with an annotated bibliography. New York: Praeger Publishers, 1976. 382p.
Includes: twelve essays prepared for and proceedings of the seminar on Women and Development held in Mexico City, 15-18 June 1975, in connection with the World Conference of International Women's Year; well-annotated bibliography arranged by development topics and geographical areas; list of special journal issues relating to women and development; and a bibliography of appropriate bibliographies.

(a) India: accomplishments, tasks and facilities

2308 AGARWAL, R.C. Role of women in economic development. *In* The Economic Studies 15,7-8 (1975) 269-79, 319-28.
Programmatic paper dealing briefly with many topics: "The improvement of the status of women depends, among other things, on the development of educational opportunities and vocational guidance programmes for women, on increased possibilities of employment and better working conditions, and on schemes aimed at the improvement of physical and mental health."

2309 AMRIT KAUR. To women, 2d ed. Ahmedabad: Navajivan Publishing House, 1948. 31p. [*Reprint in her* Selected speeches and writings. Ed. by G. Borkar. New Delhi: Archer Publications, 1961? pp.150-77].
Plan for various aspects of women's uplift in India written during imprisonment for political activities. The booklet is aimed at instructing "women of the educated and well-to-do classes as to how best they can serve their less fortunate sisters."

2310 ________. On women and their role in life. *In her* Selected speeches and writings. Ed. by G. Borkar. New Delhi: Archer Publications, 1961? pp.149-95.
Contains her "To Women," a program for women's welfare, and several brief pieces: "The Place of Women in a Gandhian Society," "Ideal Education for Women," "The Educated Woman in Indian Life" and "Women and Military Training." Author was freedom fighter and disciple of Mahatma Gandhi.

2311 BEDI, FREDA. Voluntary social service. *In* Tara Ali Baig, ed. Women of India. Delhi: Publications Division, Ministry of Information and Broadcasting, Government of India, 1958. pp.217-35.
Chronicles the major contributions of women to social service and social reform and institutions and organizations with which they have worked, both before and after independence. Photographs.

2312 BILIMORIA, NAJOO. Women and the Five Year Plan. *In* Asian Review 49,180 (1953) 272-4.
Brief statement about place accorded to women in India's First Five Year Plan, 1951-56.

2313 CHATTOPADHYAYA, KAMALADEVI. Welfare of women in India. *In* India (Republic). Planning Commission. Social Welfare in India. Ed. by Durgabai Deshmukh. New Delhi: Publications Division, Ministry of Information and Broadcasting, Government of India, 1955. pp.149-72.
Presents key demographic figures from the 1951 census and discusses various aspects of health, employment, rehabilitation and education programs. Photographs.

2314 DESAI, M.M. Women's welfare. *In* A.R. Wadia, ed. History and philosophy of social work in India: a souvenir volume of the silver jubilee celebrations of the Tata Institute of Social Sciences. Bombay: Allied Publishers, 1961. pp.177-92.
Reviews welfare activities and needs of women. Assesses the periodization of women's history in South Asia: they generally led happy and contented lives in the "ancient" and "middle" periods; while the disintegration of the rural economy under British rule adversely affected many women, "ideals of Rationalism, Liberty, and Equality" stimulated "social rejuvenation."

2315 DESHMUKH, DURGABAI. Women in planning. *In* Tara Ali Baig, ed. Women of India. Delhi: Publications Division, Ministry of Information and Broadcasting, Government of India, 1958. pp.261-8.
Details the involvement of women in the planning and implementation of the government's social welfare and training programs aimed at women's needs. Photographs.

2315a DORAISWAMI, S. Educational advancement and socio-economic participation of women in India: perspectives, problems, impediments, concerns. New Delhi: Directorate of Nonformal (Adult) Education, Ministry of Education and Social Welfare, Government of India, 1975? 33p.
[Unexamined. ALI].

2316 ERLBECK, RUTH. Frauen in Indien [Women in India]. Münster: Verlag Frauenpolitik, 1978. 160p. (Frauen in der Dritten Welt, 2).
Argues that "development" processes and capitalization in India are adversely affecting lower-class women. Traces changes in mode of production and their effects on women from pre-British society to the present. Considers recent women's activist movements. Argues that true liberation for women will occur when they gain control of their reproductive lives rather than through work, as many Marxist theories presuppose. Photographs and statistical tables. [Unexamined].

2316a INDIA (REPUBLIC). COMMITTEE ON THE STATUS OF WOMEN IN INDIA. Policies and programmes for women's welfare and development. *In its* Toward equality: report of the Committee on the Status of Women in India. New Delhi: Department of Social Welfare, Ministry of Education and Social Welfare, Government of India, 1975. pp.306-46. [*Chair* Phulrenu Guha].
Reviews provisions for women's welfare and development in India's Five Year Plans and in government programs and agencies. Discusses three aspects in detail: health, family planning and welfare (e.g., mother-child, nutri-

tion, adult education). Concludes with a series of recommendations that include reorganization of government structures.

2317 INDIAN COUNCIL OF SOCIAL SCIENCE RESEARCH. ADVISORY COMMITTEE ON WOMEN'S STUDIES. Critical issues on the status of women: suggested priorities for action. New Delhi: Indian Council of Social Science Research, 1977. 32p. (*Its* Publication 107). [*Chair* B.N. Ganguli].
Describes "national neglect of women" in areas of health, education and employment and proposes priorities for reversal of present trends. Statistical tables.

2318 JACOBSON, DORANNE. Indian women in processes of development. *In* J. of International Affairs 30,2 (1976/77) 211-42.
". . . a general overview of women's roles in the ongoing processes of Indian national development is presented, especially as these relate to the traditional roles of women in South Asian society. Particular attention is paid to the relevance of male-female relations and sex segregation to women's activities in modernizing India." Author draws upon her own research in Central India and other scholarly work and reviews selected solutions that have been proposed.

2319 Journal of Family Welfare. v1- (1954?-). Bombay: Family Planning Association of India. Quarterly.
"This journal is devoted to discussing views and providing information on all aspects of family planning, including social, cultural, and demographic factors, medical problems and methods of fertility control, and questions pertaining to education for marriage and family living . . . . in a non-technical manner [for] the lay public as well as social workers."

2320 LALITHA, N.V. Voluntary work in India: a study of volunteers in welfare agencies. New Delhi: National Institute of Public Cooperation and Child Development, 1975. 344p.
Study of approximately one-third of the welfare agencies from nine Indian cities to ascertain policy toward volunteers, scope of voluntary work, contributions of volunteers, motivation and satisfaction of volunteers, problems relating to voluntary workers and potential improvements to be made. Considers agencies according to eleven types, two of which are "women welfare" and "moral and social hygiene work."

2321 National plan of action for women. Delhi: Institute of Applied Manpower Research, 1975?
[Unexamined].

2322 Optimum utilisation of woman power for development. *In* Social Change 5,3/4 (1975) 34-7.
Summary of a seminar by the same name held in New Delhi in 1975. Includes brief statements reviewing the inaugural address and the 17 papers presented. Papers were grouped under four topics: "Factors Impeding Legal and Constitutional Rights of Women," "Female Work Participation," "Education and Employment of Women" and "Problems in the Utilisation of Educated Women Power."

2323 RUNGANADHAN. Indian Christian women and nation building. *In* Asiatic Review n.s. 43,153 (1947) 22-4.
Notes contributions of some Indian Christian women and describes potential for further contributions by women of this community given their freedom from *pardā* and other social constraints.

2324 SARAN, RAKSHA. Welfare of women in India. *In* India (Republic). Planning Commission. Social welfare in India, rev. and abr. ed. New Delhi: Director, Publications Division, Government of India, 1960. pp.48-54.
Reviews miscellaneous factors and agencies that affect women's welfare, including various organizations, legislation, education, family planning, employment, the Central Social Welfare Board and the All-India Handicrafts Board.

2325 SHAH, K.T., ed. Woman's role in planned economy: report of the subcommittee. Bombay: Vora and Company, 1947. 265p. (National Planning Committee, 6).
Report of a subcommittee of the National Planning Committee established in India in 1938. ". . . the Sub-Committee has reviewed every field in which woman operates, or should operate, to contribute her share of the nation's wealth and the people's well-being. While considering principally the material aspect . . ., the cultural or spiritual position of woman under a National Plan . . . is by no means ignored." Large section (pp.45-117) devoted to employment.

2326 Social Welfare. v1- (1954-). New Delhi: Publications Division, Central Social Welfare Board. Monthly.
Most issues of this journal contain one or more brief articles relating to women's welfare — particular programs, particular needs, etc.

2327 TALEYARKHAN, HOMI J.H. Kamaladevi Chattopadhyaya's post-war plan for the women of India. *In his* They told me so. Bombay: Thacker and Company, 1947. pp.69-74.
Summary of interview with Kamaladevi Chattopadhyaya about women's welfare programs. Author begins "The air is thick these days with every variety of post-war plan — except perhaps one for women." Focuses on employment, health services and uplift work.

2328 WADIA, AVABAI. Women's role in the new India. *In* Asiatic Review n.s. 48, 176 (1952) 248-65.
Reviews constitutional and legislative rights, participation in public life, work of women's

organizations and welfare activities benefitting women. "Surely . . . one can now begin with the proposition that women have an equal status with men, assured by solemn constitutional guarantee."

2329 Wives and wives. Produced by Ezra Mir. Directed by Pramod Pati. Animation by G.K. Gokhale. 1962. 4 min. Color. 16 and 35 mm. [*Distributed by* Films Division, Ministry of Information and Broadcasting, 24 G. Deshmukh Marg, Bombay 400 026].
Brief animated film showing the role of housewives in India's national development. A bachelor visits a marriage bureau to select a woman who will make a good wife. [Unexamined. NUC].

2330 Women and development. *In* Economic and Political Weekly 10,49 (6 Dec 1975) 1864.
Report of Seminar on Optimum Utilisation of Women Power for Development sponsored by the Council for Social Development, New Delhi, in late 1975.

2331 Women: creating an awareness. *In* Link 18,1 (15 Aug 1975) 89, 91, 93, 95.
Briefly explores roles women can play in India's development. Includes opinions of some prominent women.

2331a Women's development: some critical issues; report of a seminar of women legislators sponsored by Gandhi Peace Foundation in collaboration with Indian Council of Social Science Research, Department of Social Welfare, Government of India, and UNICEF. New Delhi: Marwah, 1978. 93p.
Seminar proceedings. [Unexamined. ALI].

2332 Women's Welfare Journal. v1-? (194_?-?). Madras.
[Unexamined].

i) Women's and girls' organizations

2333 ALL-INDIA WOMEN'S CONFERENCE. Proceedings. 1st session- (1927-). Various places: various publishers. Annually.
Sample volume, that of the ninth session, contains lists of sponsors, officers, committee members and delegates; the conference schedule; various addresses given; messages from well-wishers; the annual report and various committee reports; resolutions and discussions on variety of topics; selection of important resolutions passed at previous sessions; AIWC "lines of work," constitution, by-laws and regulations, rules for starting new constituencies and registration statement; budgets; schedule for coming year; statement on women's rights made jointly with other national organizations; local branch conference and officer lists, maps and proposed redistribution; details of All-India Women's Education Fund Association; history of AIWC; and photos of the ninth session.

2334 ________. Tract. no. 1-? (1945-?). Swantrapur, etc.
[Unexamined. NUC].

2335 ________. Roshni. v1- (1946-). Bombay. Monthly (irregular).
Official journal of the All-India Women's Conference. IPP implies a new series began in 1970. [Unexamined. ULS, IPP].

2336 CHAKRAVARTTY, RENU. New perspectives for women's movement: after 25 years of drift. *In* Link 15,1 (15 Aug 1972) 177-81.
Historical overview of some significant women's organizations, including the All-India Women's Conference, the Mahila Atmaraksha Samiti in Bengal, the National Federation of Indian Women and trade unions.

2337 Delhi Commonwealth Women's Association Magazine. v1- (1969-). New Delhi. Monthly.
[Unexamined. IPP].

2338 Every Member. v1-? (19__-?). Calcutta: Young Women's Christian Association of India, Burma and Ceylon. *Became* Today. v1- (1962-). New Delhi: Young Women's Christian Association of India. Quarterly.
[Unexamined. BUP, NST].

2339 FORBES, GERALDINE. From purdah to politics: the social feminism of the all-India women's organizations. *In* Hanna Papanek, ed. Purdah in South Asia: the segregation of women. Forthcoming.
Discusses the ideology, structure and work of the Women's Indian Association, the National Council of Women in India and the All-India Women's Conference with respect to the segregation of the sexes. Argues that these nationwide women's organizations tended to sanction *pardā* as a "separate world" for women while rejecting it as "symbolic shelter," thus enabling the support and participation of women from conservative households and the support of men. By enlarging the concept of "separate worlds" from the local to the national level they were able to create an arena of public activity considered particularly appropriate for women. [Unexamined. Verified with editor].

2340 Girl Guides of India. Produced through Rustom P. Master, Bombay. 1964. 11 min. Black and white. 16 and 35 mm. [*Distributed by* Films Division, Ministry of Information and Broadcasting, 24 G. Deshmukh Marg, Bombay 400 026].
Film. Considers growth and activities of Girl Guides in India. [Unexamined. CF].

2341 The Indian Social Reformer v1-63. 1894?-1952. Founded in Madras, moved to Bombay. Weekly.

This journal gave extensive coverage and editorial support to the various national and local women's organizations in India during its years of publication. See numerous scattered and largely brief articles, especially reports of annual meetings.

2342 KHAN, IVY. Voluntary organisations: their role and relevance. *In* Young Women's Christian Association, India. The educated woman in Indian society today. Bombay: Tata McGraw-Hill Publishing Company, 1971. pp.226-40.
Assesses place of voluntary organizations in Indian society, in general and with respect to women. Lists 74 all-India and 11 state/regional non-governmental agencies (not limited to work by or for women).

2343 LANKESTER, GRACE, LADY PARES and DORTHEA LANKESTER. The woman of India today: 1. a general survey; 2. the conference at Akola; 3. the younger generation. *In* Asiatic Review n.s. 43,155 (1947) 202-9.
Addresses the effects of the women's movement on Indian women, reviews the history of the All-India Women's Conference and the proceedings of its 1947 meeting at Akola and comments on the character of the post-nationalist generation of women met at Akola.

2344 MACLAY, SUSAN RUTH. Women's organizations in India: voluntary associations in a developing society. Ph.D. dissertation, Department of Government and Foreign Affairs, University of Virginia, 1969. 231p. [University Microfilms 70-4811].
Examines voluntary associations as contributors to economic and social development. Primarily deals with Women's Indian Association, All-India Women's Conference, YWCA of India and Kasturba Gandhi National Memorial Trust. Also considers National Council of Women in India, Andhra Mahila Sabha and Bharatiya Grameen Mahila Sangh. Considers historical background and post-independent circumstances.

2345 MAZUMDAR, LAKSHMI. The Girl Guide movement in India. *In* India (Republic). Planning Commission. Social Welfare in India. Ed. by Durgabai Deshmukh. New Delhi: Publications Division, Ministry of Information and Broadcasting, Government of India, 1955. pp.119-32.
History (from 1911 establishment), organization and aims of the Girl Guide movement in India.

2346 NATIONAL COUNCIL OF WOMEN IN INDIA. Report. (1926/27?-). Bombay. Biennially.
The NCWI was established in 1925 to "promote sympathy of thought and purpose among Women in India," to unite women of all communities for the promotion of women's and children's welfare, to coordinate national and local organizations to this end, to work for the removal of women's disabilities, to "assure to every child an opportunity for full and free development" and to serve as a link with the International Council of Women. The only report examined, that of 1928/29, contains lists of officers, the council's constitution, copy of the organization's registration memorandum, The Maharani of Baroda's presidential address, general and provincial reports, report of delegates to the International Council of Women meeting, report of a London advisory committee to the NCWI and biennial budget.

2347 _______. Bulletin. v1-? (1932-?). Calcutta? *Became* N.C.W.I. Bulletin. v1- (1958-). Nagpur, etc. Bimonthly.
[Unexamined. BUP, NUC].

2348 WOMEN'S INDIAN ASSOCIATION. Golden jubilee celebration. Madras, 1967.
[Unexamined].

2349 Young Women. v1- (1968-). Delhi: National Young Women's Organisation. Quarterly.
[Unexamined. IPP].

2350 YOUNG WOMEN'S CHRISTIAN ASSOCIATION. News and Notes. v1- (1946-). Madras. Monthly.
[Unexamined. IPP].

2351 _______. Association News. v1- (1966-). Calcutta. Monthly.
[Unexamined. IPP].

2352 YOUNG WOMEN'S CHRISTIAN ASSOCIATION OF INDIA. Programme Bulletin. v1- (1970-). New Delhi. Irregularly.
[Unexamined. IPP].

2353 Yuvak. v1- (1968-). Delhi: National Council of Young Women's Christian Association of India. Bimonthly.
[Unexamined. IPP].

ii) Social welfare policy, programs and organizations

2354 BHATT, NEELA. The Kasturba Gandhi National Memorial Trust. *In* Indian J. of Social Work 10,2 (1949) 94-101.
Discusses establishment, development and program of Kasturba Trust, dedicated to uplift of village women and children.

2355 Encyclopaedia of social work in India. Delhi: Publications Division, Ministry of Information and Broadcasting, Government of India, 1968. 3v.
Many of the 133 major articles and 212 statistical tables give information relevant to women. Many of the biographical sketches discuss persons concerned with women's issues. Also includes directory of agencies, list of central and state legislative acts significant to social welfare and numerous appendixes.

2356 INDIA (REPUBLIC). WOMEN'S WELFARE DIVISION. Women in India: a compen-

dium of programmes. New Delhi: Women's Welfare Division, Department of Social Welfare, Government of India, 1975. 118p.
Descriptive survey of government and voluntary services and programs for women in education, health, family planning, employment, training, welfare and rehabilitation. Includes materials on provisions of the Fourth and Fifth Five Year Plans. Tables, charts, photos. "Issued on the occasion of the International Women's Year."

2357 Kasturba Gandhi National Memorial Trust: saga of 16 years service. *In* Kasturba memorial. Indore: Kasturba Gandhi National Memorial Trust, 1962. pp.191-250.
Details the organization and programs of the trust.

2358 Part 2: women's welfare organisations. *In* B.K. Vashishta, ed. Encyclopedia of women in India, 1976. New Delhi: Praveen Encyclopedia Publications, 1976. Second part, pp.1-17.
Concise information about 13 nation-wide welfare associations. Includes circumstances of founding, central activities, address and publications.

2359 SARAN, RAKSHA. Twenty years of women's welfare activities in India. *In* Social Welfare 17,2 (1970) 22.
Briefly reviews national and state programs for women's welfare in India, beginning with the 1953 establishment of the Central Social Welfare Board. Includes recommendations for future priorities.

2360 SHYAMLAL. Thakkar Bapa and the Kasturba Trust. *In* T.N. Jagadisan and Shyamlal, eds. Thakkar Bapa: eightieth birthday commemoration volume. Madras: printed at Diocesan Press, 1949. pp.245-52.
Brief account of the founding of the Kasturba Trust and the role of Thakkar Bapa (A.V. Thakkar) in particular. Summarizes services provided by the trust.

2361 Social welfare organisations. *In* Ajeet Cour and Arpana Cour, eds. Directory of Indian women today, 1976. New Delhi: India International Publications, 1976. pp.i-liv.
Lists hundreds of Indian social welfare organizations serving women, by state. Includes addresses.

2362 Sunrise on mud walls. 1960. 26 min. Black and white. 16 and 35 mm. [*Distributed by* Films Division, Ministry of Information and Broadcasting, 24 G. Deshmukh Marg, Bombay 400 026].
Activities of Samaj Kalyan Kendras, centers for women's and children's welfare established by the Central Social Welfare Board. [Unexamined. CF].

2363 TELLIS-NAYAK, J. Women's welfare services. *In* The Indian family in the change and challenge of the seventies: selected papers of a seminar organised by the Family Life Centre of the Indian Social Institute, New Delhi. New Delhi: Sterling Publishers, 1972. pp.211-24.
"This paper will discuss the movements in India which have contributed towards the improvement of the status of women and it will also touch upon problems and programmes in education, social welfare, health and employment meant specifically for women."

2364 Women in social welfare (Who's who: social workers). *In* Ajeet Cour and Arpana Cour, eds. Directory of Indian women today, 1976. New Delhi: India International Publications, 1976. pp.325-488, 581-602.
Series of brief biographical sketches. Includes mailing address and, in many cases, photograph.

iii) Reaching the rural sector

2365 AMRIT KAUR, RAJKUMARI. Women and community projects. *In* Kurukshetra: a symposium on community development. Delhi: Publications Division, Ministry of Information and Broadcasting, Government of India, 1961. pp.245-8.
Programmatic statement about ideal goals of India's Community Development Programme with respect to rural women.

2366 CHAKRAVORTY, SHANTI. Women extension functionaries: their problems and opportunities. *In* B.N. Ganguli, ed. Social development: essays in honour of Smt. Durgabai Deshmukh. New Delhi: Sterling Publishers, 1977. pp.140-52.
Regarding the gramsevika and mukhyasevika workers of India's Community Development Programme, women trained to impart social education and skills to rural women and children. Reviews background of program, qualifications and job expectations, training programs and pay scale. Problems include absence of local facilities (housing, health services, schools for their children, etc.), assignment of unreasonably large territories, outmoded administration, lack of promotion opportunities, inadequate resources and inadequate evaluation of women's role in rural development.

2367 DAS, PARIMAL. Women under India's Community Development Programme. *In* International Labour Review 80,1 (1959) 26-45.
Discusses absence of special consideration for women in early years of Community Development Programme, organization of subsequently established women's program and aims and future of the program. Author was director of Women's Programme, Ministry of Community Development.

2368 DEVADAS, RAJAMAL P. Our gram sevikas. *In* Kurukshetra: a symposium on commu-

nity development. Delhi: Publications Division, Ministry of Information and Broadcasting, Government of India, 1961. pp.87-90.
Discusses training, accommodations and areas of work for female village workers in India's Community Development Programme. "The Gram Sevika by her example and work in the village should stimulate in rural women an awareness of the part they can play in making their villages better places to live, and strive to attain happier and healthier homes."

2369 GEORGE, M. Women's role in social education under the community projects. *In* Indian J. of Adult Education 15,1 (1954) 17-22.
Discusses types of work for which female workers are particularly suited. [Unexamined].

2370 INDIA (REPUBLIC). MINISTRY OF COMMUNITY DEVELOPMENT AND COOPERATION. A guide to gram sevikas and mukhya sevikas. New Delhi: Ministry of Community Development and Cooperation, Government of India, 1960. 71p.
[Unexamined. IBP].

2371 JAYAMANI, KUMARI N. Indian national extension service workers. *In* African Women 4,2 (1961) 41-3.
On the establishment (in 1955-56) and operations of the gramsevika program of female development workers at the village level. Discusses training, aims and activities.

2372 MEHTA, B.H. Training of women for rural work. *In* Indian J. of Social Work 7,1 (1946) 11-8.
Describes urgent task of participants in Indian women's movement as rural welfare work. Outlines appropriate rural programs: with children, women, education, family case work and sanitation.

2373 NAIDU, P.P. Women's welfare in development projects. *In* Kurukshetra 3,5 (1955).
[Unexamined].

2374 NIMBKAR, KRISHNABAI. Rural women and development work. *In* Kurukshetra 3,1 (1954) 39-41, 45.
Describes potential benefits of widespread incorporation of female workers and programs for women in Community Development Programme. Recommends particular foci. [Unexamined].

2375 ________. Development work among rural women: a guidebook. Delhi: Indian Adult Education Association, 1958. 45p.
[Unexamined. IBP].

2376 ________. Women and development work. *In* Kurukshetra: a symposium on community development. Delhi: Publications Division, Ministry of Information and Broadcasting, Government of India, 1961. pp.248-53.
Notes that previous community development projects have largely ignored rural women. "I would now place before the readers a few salient points on what I consider to be a total approach to the education and awakening of rural women, which could lead to their active association with nation-building activities." Stresses their unique needs.

2377 PRASAD, AMBA. Women in the villages. *In* Kurukshetra 2,6 (1954) 24.
Stresses importance of programs to improve skills and awareness of village women. [Unexamined].

2378 The village and I. Produced through H.D. Sethna, Bombay. 1958. 20 min. Black and white. 16 and 35 mm. [*Distributed by* Films Division, Ministry of Information and Broadcasting, 24 G. Deshmukh Marg, Bombay 400 026].
Shows training of a young widow for social welfare work among rural women at a Kasturba Gram Sevika Vidyalaya. [Unexamined. CF].

2379 Village and women. 1955. 24 min. Black and white. 16 and 35 mm. [*Distributed by* Films Division, Ministry of Information and Broadcasting, 24 G. Deshmukh Marg, Bombay 400 026. *Shorter version* 1956. 13 min. Black and white. 16 and 35 mm.].
Portrays significant role of women in the success of the Community Development Programme. [Unexamined. CF].

iv) International Women's Year (IWY) and India

2380 CHITNIS, SUMA. International Women's Year: its significance for women in India. *In* Social Action 25,3 (1975) 203-20. [*Also in* Alfred de Souza, ed. Women in contemporary India: traditional images and changing roles. Delhi: Manohar Book Service, 1975. pp.1-24].
Considers significance of objectives set for the International Women's Year by the United Nations — equality, development and peace — for Indian women. "The first two sections [discuss] the problems and opportunities of integrating women more effectively in the process of national development. The third section discusses the complex issue of the redefinition of sex-typed roles in the family and society and the concluding section outlines some concrete action programmes . . . for integral human development in India."

2381 DAMODARA MENON, LEELA. India and the International Women's Year. *In* Indian Quarterly 31,3 (1975) 276-81.
[Unexamined].

2382 International Women's Year Newsletter. no. 1-10 (Mar-Dec 1975). New Delhi: Women's Welfare Division, Department of Social Welfare, Government of India. Monthly.
[Unexamined. ALI].

2383 International Women's Year: special issue. Stree Vimukti (Aug 1975).
Special issue in honor of IWY. The journal, "Women's Liberation," is the organ of the Progressive Organization of Women (POW) established in June 1974. [Unexamined].

2384 IWY: the Indian woman speaks. *In* Eve's Weekly 29,37 (13 Sep 1975) 14-5, 18-9, 27.
Interviews with 16 urban homemakers and career women concerning the impact of IWY and the women's movement on their lives and on the lives of Indian women in general.

2385 JAHAN, ROUNAQ. International Women's Year Conference in Mexico City: the impressions of an observer. *In* International and Comparative Public Policy 1,1 (1976) 61-6.
Prominent woman from Bangladesh discusses her overall very positive feelings about the conference, the contrast between issues raised by women from developed and third world countries and her sense of the significance of the conference.

2386 KAPUR, PROMILLA. News and information regarding the measures taken in India during IWY. *In* Canadian Newsletter of Research on Women 5,3 (1976) 104-5.
List of 14 items — legislation, programs, facilities, activities — adopted or organized in India during IWY.

2387 MUKHERJEE, KANAK. International Women's Year and ourselves. Calcutta: Eksathe, 1976. 31p.
Argument, substantiated with Indian data, that IWY is only a charade by the feudal-capitalist bosses to "create false hope among the masses of women." Proposes that the only real solution to the problems of women is revolutionary socialism.

2388 RAMACHANDRAN, PADMA. International Women's Year: India's role. *In* Southern Economist 14,16 (15 Dec 1975) 13,16.
Discusses various events in India in connection with IWY. Perceives it as a catalyst for social change in India.

(b) Pakistan: accomplishments, tasks and facilities

2389 ALL-PAKISTAN WOMEN'S ASSOCIATION. Participation of women in public life in Pakistan: report of the seminar, Lahore, November 21, 1960. Karachi: Information and Research Bureau, Government of Pakistan, 1961.
[Unexamined].

2390 ________. Ra'ana Liaquat Ali Khan, ed. Role of women in the developing economy of Pakistan. Karachi, 1961. 81p.
Papers from an All-Pakistan Women's Association triennial conference on contributions of homemakers, programs and organizations for women, educational opportunities, employment and so forth. [Unexamined].

2391 ________ in cooperation with UNESCO. Seminar on "The Role of Women in the Preservation and Development of Cultures in the Community." Karachi: printed at Iqbal Printing Press Ltd., 1958? 189p.
Proceedings of seminar held in Karachi in 1958 and attended by delegates from South and Southeast Asia and Iran. Contains lists of participants, opening and closing addresses and summaries and recommendations from plenary sessions. Topics of the sessions were "The Role of Women in the Family in the Preservation of Culture in the Community," "Effects of Socio-Economic Changes on Family Life," "Women's Role in Education," "The Role of Handicrafts and Arts" and "The Contribution of Women's Organizations in the Preservation of Culture in the Community."

2392 ANSARI, KHURSHEED A. SALAM. Women and national reconstruction. *In* Pakistan Review 11,3 (1963) 21-3, 41.
Describes role of women in various spheres of national reconstruction (education, medical and health services, cottage industries, cooperation, social work) and contributions of various women's organizations to Pakistan's development.

2393 FARIDI, TAZEEN. Pakistan. *In* International Institute of Differing Civilizations. Women's rôle in the development of tropical and subtropical countries: report of the XXXIth [sic] meeting, held in Brussels on 17th, 18th, 19th and 20th September 1958. Brussels, 1959. pp.255-77.
[Unexamined. Book in NUC].

2394 HYMER, ESTHER W. Soldiers in saris. *In* Independent Woman 34,3 (1955) 92-4.
American visitor's impressions of the "remarkable contributions the women of Pakistan, only yesterday veiled and secluded in ***purdah***, are making to the building of their new nation." Photographs.

2395 JINNAH, FATIMA. Salahuddin Khan, ed. and comp. Speeches, messages and statements of Madar-i-Millat Mohtarama Fatima Jinnah, 1948-1967. Lahore: Research Society of Pakistan, 1976. 505p. (*Its* Publications, 36).
Addresses, etc., from 1948 to 1967. Most focus on nationalism and national development of Pakistan in the spirit of author's brother, Mohammad Ali Jinnah.

2396 KHAN, AKHTER HAMEED. The role of women in a country's development. Comilla: Pakistan Academy for Rural Development, 1963. 5p.
On the role of Pakistani women. [Unexamined. NUC].

2397 PAKISTAN COUNCIL FOR NATIONAL INTEGRATION, LAHORE BRANCH. Women's role

in Pakistan's future. *In* Pakistan Review 16,3 (1968) 23.
Summary of remarks of four speakers at a symposium on "The Role of Women for Future of Pakistan."

i) Women's and girls' organizations

2398 AHMED, ZEENAT RASHID. APWA. *In* Pakistan Quarterly 2,2 (1952) 39-43.
Discusses establishment, organization, early achievements and activities of the All-Pakistan Women's Association. Describes a conference held at Lahore and attended by women from throughout the Muslim world. Photographs.

2399 ALL PAKISTAN WOMEN'S ASSOCIATION. Report. v1- (1959/60?-). Karachi. Annually.
Reviews the activities of the central and various local branches in such areas as education, home extension, rural development and youth work. Discusses activities of several affiliated organizations. Presents budget. Sometimes published biennially.

2400 ________. Women's movement in Pakistan. Karachi: Publicity Section and Information and Research Bureau, All Pakistan Women's Association, 1963. 60p.
Contains profiles of 44 national, regional and local Pakistani women's organizations and institutions and lists 47 others. Photographs.

2401 CHIPP, SYLVIA A. The role of women elites in a modernizing country: the All Pakistan Women's Association. Ph.D. dissertation, Department of Political Science?, Syracuse University, 1970. 430p. [University Microfilms 71-21,516].
Examines APWA as an organization with aspirations for effecting change within the terms of Islamic values. Focuses on leadership. Based in large part on archival materials and interviews with participants. [Unexamined. DAI].

2402 ________. Tradition vs. change: the All Pakistan Women's Association. *In* Islam and the Modern Age, 1,3 (1970) 69-90.
Details the history, current goals and activities of APWA as a progressive organization working within traditional Islamic principles.

2403 Muslim womanhood on the march: the annual conference of the All-Pakistan Women's Association held at Lahore, Pakistan (29th March, 1952-2nd April, 1952) which was attended by 500 women delegates from various parts of Pakistan, Iran, Iraq, Egypt, Turkey, Indonesia, the Lebanon and England. *In* Islamic Review 40,6 (1952) 20-9.
"For the first time in Muslim History, Muslim women from many Muslim countries have met to confer about the importance of their role." Contains the address of Ghulam Muhammad, Governor-General of Pakistan, criticizing the backwardness of women in Muslim countries as "un-Islamic," and the address of Begam Liaquat Ali Khan on the rights guaranteed to women by Islamic law. Photographs.

2404 SHERAZEE, M.H. Girl guiding in West Pakistan. Lahore?: West Pakistan Bureau of Education, 1960? 22p. (*Its* Educational Pamphlets Series, 2).
[Unexamined. NUC].

2405 WOODSMALL, RUTH FRANCES. Women's organizations in Pakistan. *In her* Women and the new East. Washington, D.C.: Middle East Institute, 1960. pp.141-4.
Brief list of about 20 women's associations. Identifies year of establishment, aims and activities.

ii) Participation in military services

2406 HAMADANI, NASEEM. Sea maidens: Pakistan Women's Naval Reserve. *In* Pakistan Quarterly 2,4 (1952) 26-9.
Presents the work and lifestyle of members of the Pakistan Women's Naval Reserve through the story of one recruit. Photographs.

2407 NAZIR AHMAD, RAZIA. Pakistan Women's National Guard. *In* Pakistan Quarterly 1,6 (1951) 35-9.
Photo essay illustrating the work, training, ceremonies and other activities of the Pakistan Women's National Guard. Praises the success of the organization as "a symbol of the increasing awareness of the women of Pakistan of their duties to the State."

2408 WAHEED, BUSHRA. Role of women during September War. *In* Perspective 3,4/5 (1969) 47-51.
Regarding the participation and support of women during the 1965 war with India. "This moment of crisis brought out some dormant qualities, latent strength in us women." Photographs.

(c) Social welfare issues

2409 INDIA (REPUBLIC). COMMITTEE ON THE STATUS OF WOMEN IN INDIA. Sociocultural setting of women's status: some special problems. *In its* Towards equality: report of the Committee on the Status of Women in India. New Delhi: Department of Social Welfare, Ministry of Education and Social Welfare, Government of India, 1975. pp.91-101. [*Chair* Phulrenu Guha]. Briefly reviews selected social problems relating to women: prostitution, prisoners, unmarried mothers, aging women and destitute women. Notes the decline in concern for women's problems since the momentum of the Freedom Movement and urges joint responsibility from community (especially women's) organizations, legislators and the government.

i) Problems of poverty

2410 Life begins anew. 1969. 18 min. Black and white. 16 and 35 mm. [*Distributed by* Films Division, Ministry of Information and Broadcasting, 24 G. Deshmukh Marg, Bombay 400 026]. Film on social policy and programs for destitute women. [Unexamined. CF].

ii) Health care and problems, participation in the medical profession

2411 ADRANWALA, T.K. Nursing profession in India. *In* India (Republic). Planning Commission. Social welfare in India. Ed. by Durgabai Deshmukh. New Delhi: Publications Division, Ministry of Information and Broadcasting, Government of India, 1955. pp.383-95. [*Also in* Rev. and abr. ed., 1960. pp.188-95]. Presents statistical and other information on this profession that is "mainly for women" in India: training courses, Indian Nursing Council, role of nurse, employment opportunities and numerical strength of profession according to kinds of schools and kinds of personnel.

2412 ASSOCIATION OF MEDICAL WOMEN IN INDIA. Journal. v1- (1909-). Bombay, etc. Recent sample issue [67,2 (1977)] contains: articles on iron deficiency, use of a particular abortifacient and hysterotomy for second trimester pregnancy termination and hysterectomy complications; biographical sketch of newly-elected association president; international news; and proceedings of the annual Council Meeting of the Association of Medical Women in India.

2413 CHAUDURI, S. All-India Women's Reserve Medical Unit. *In* J. of the Association of Medical Women in India 37,3 (1949) 53-4, 56. Regarding a group of graduates of Lady Hardinge Medical College organized in 1942 to assist air-raid victims. Urges establishment of more permanent women's medical reserve for variety of emergency situations. [Unexamined].

2414 Health. Karachi: Peermahomed Ebrahim Trust, 1976. 181p. Islamic perspectives on pregnancy, birth, postnatal care, obesity, exercise, beauty, relaxation, nutrition, stimulants, fasting, effects and requirements of seasons, life stages and various other matters. Much explicitly concerns women.

2415 INDIA (REPUBLIC). MATERNAL AND CHILD HEALTH ADVISORY COMMITTEE, 1968. TARGETS FOR MATERNAL AND CHILD HEALTH SERVICES IN COMMUNITY HEALTH PROGRAMMES SUB-COMMITTEE, 1969. Report. New Delhi: National Institute of Health Administration and Education, 1969. 88p. [Unexamined].

2415a Journal of Obstetrics and Gynaecology of India. v1- (1951?-). Bombay: Federation of Obstetrics and Gynaecology of India. Bimonthly. Contains technical articles on wide variety of health problems and physiological circumstances. Issued quarterly through December 1964.

2416 KAPOOR, INDIRA. Women in the health sector: past and present. *In* J. of Family Welfare 22,2 (1975) 67-74. Briefly reviews history of 19th and 20th century medical care for and by Indian women and discusses fields of nursing, health work and social work today. Reports high rate of unutilized medical talent among married women and urges them to consider part-time employment.

2417 KATONA-APTE, JUDIT. The relevance of nourishment to the reproductive cycle of the female in India. *In* Dana Raphael, ed. Being female: reproduction, power and change. The Hague: Mouton, 1975. pp.43-8. (World Anthropology). Brief but wide-ranging observations and comments on problems associated with inadequately met nutritional needs of females and the strenuous demands of reproduction on women's health.

2418 MUKTANANDA SARASWATI, SWAMI. Nawa yogini tantra: for every woman who seeks health, happiness, and self-realization. Monghyr: Bihar School of Yoga, 1977. 363p. From publisher's introduction: "The scientific application of yogic principles to the specific needs of women is the aim of this book, which has been created as a tool for bringing every woman health, happiness and self-realization." The first section is a discussion, in essentially western scientific terms, of the female body, gender identification and so forth. The second section discusses yoga techniques relating to physical and mental problems of women.

2419 National Conference on Women Doctors in India, New Delhi, September 19-20, 1975. Proceedings. New Delhi: Indian Medical Association, 1975? 96p. [Unexamined. ALI].

2420 Women in the medical profession (Who's who: doctors and nurses). *In* Ajeet Cour and Arpana Cour, eds. Directory of Indian women today, 1976. New Delhi: India International Publications, 1976. pp.64-99, 548-56.
Series of brief biographical sketches. Includes mailing address and, in many cases, photograph.

2421 Women in white. 1951. 11 min. Black and white. 16 and 35 mm. [*Distributed by* Films Division, Ministry of Information and Broadcasting, 24 G. Deshmukh Marg, Bombay 400 026].
Film of the life of a nurse demonstrates the training and devotion required for the nursing profession in India. [Unexamined. CF].

2422 Women medicos: a triumph of determination over hostility. *In* Femina 19,16 (8 Sep 1978) 13, 15, 17, 19, 57, 59.
Series of reports on female doctors in various cities. Based on interviews.

iii) Issues relating to sexuality: prositution, rape, VD and moral danger

2423 BULLOUGH, VERN et al., eds. Area studies: India. *In their* A bibliography of prostitution. New York: Garland Publishing, Incorporated, 1977. pp.40-2. (Garland Reference Library of Social Science, 30).
Forty-four references.

2424 CHANDRAN, RAMESH. Should prostitution be banned? *In* Illustrated Weekly of India 93,48 (26 Nov 1972) 8-15.
Reviews various definitions of prostitution and thoughts on its psychology. Points to number of commercial prostitutes today who were ***devadāsīs*** earlier in the century. Notes several historical circumstances that have fostered prostitution in South Asia. Discusses venereal disease, legislation and its bias against women, pros and cons of legal regulation and problems faced by prostitutes. Photographs.

2425 COSTA, BENEDICT. How to prevent sex crimes. *In* Illustrated Weekly of India 93,20 (14 May 1972) 6-11, 13.
Regarding the incidence of rape in India and the corresponding effectiveness of the judicial system, various treatments of offenders, the rise of VD, harrassment of women in public and related difficulties.

2426 Deserted women. Produced through Fact Films, Bombay. 1956. 18 min. Black and white. 16 and 35 mm. [*Distributed by* Films Division, Ministry of Information and Broadcasting, 24 G. Deshmukh Marg, Bombay 400 026].
On the problems of women's vulnerability to wayward lives due to difficult home circumstances. Shows work of rescue homes in rehabilitation. [Unexamined. CF].

2427 HUSAIN, MAZHAR. Mazhar Husain's The Suppression of Immoral Traffic in Women and Girls Act, 1956: with critical commentary, case law and states' rules, 3d ed. Rev. and enl. by Vijay Malik. Lucknow: Eastern Book Company, 1978. 210p. [*1st ed.* 1958].
Text of the law interspersed with detailed interpretation and references to relevant cases. Appendixes give texts of several state- and province-level suppression laws and that of the Women's and Children's Institutions (Licensing) Act, 1956.

2428 INDIA (REPUBLIC). CENTRAL BUREAU OF CORRECTIONAL SERVICES. Women and girls in moral and social danger. New Delhi: Central Bureau of Correctional Services, Department of Social Welfare, Government of India, 1971. 127p.
Reviews institutional and noninstitutional "rescue" services initiated under India's first three Five Year Plans at official and nonofficial levels in the various states. Recommends improvements. Data is from questionnaires (appended to report) and on site inspections by the Social and Moral Hygiene Advisory Committee.

2429 INDIA (REPUBLIC). SOCIAL AND MORAL HYGIENE ADVISORY COMMITTEE. Report. New Delhi: Central Social Welfare Board, Government of India, 1956. 175p. [*Chair* Dhanvanthi Rama Rau].
[Unexamined].

2430 JAYAKAR, R.B.K. Prostitution and immoral traffic in India. *In* India (Republic). Planning Commission. Social Welfare in India. Ed. by Durgabai Deshmukh. New Delhi: Publications Division, Ministry of Information and Broadcasting, Government of India, 1955. pp.353-71. [*Also in* Rev. and abr. ed., 1960. pp.160-73].
Reviews prostitution legislation of various states and proposes need for an all-India act. Criticizes policy of tolerating but regulating prostitution. Discusses rescue homes and rehabilitation, the importance of sex education and problems associated with venereal disease.

2431 KAPUR, PROMILLA. The life and world of call-girls in India: a socio-psychological study of the aristocratic prostitute. New Delhi: Vikas, 1973. 368p.
Study of "clandestine prostitutes," women who secretly practice while "maintaining a semblance of respectability and social place," said to be a phenomenon in India of the last three decades. The author wanted to investigate "why they started, continued or left their lives as call-girls, whether they were happy in their chosen lives and what their ambitions and aspirations, attitudes and values were . . . . their socio-economic as well as socio-psychological situations, their satisfactions and problems . . . " Based on "guided case-study" interviews with 150 women from Delhi, Bombay and Calcutta.

2432 The land of Kamasutra. *In* Far Eastern Economic Review 91,2 (9 Jan 1976) 22-4.
Brief comments on prostitution in contemporary India. Includes references to remnants of the *devadāsī* system.

2433 Problems of social vice and social diseases: a report of the proceedings and recommendations of a 3-day Seminar on Social and Moral Hygiene. Karachi: Social Services Coordinating Council, 1961. 74p.
Problems and recommendations, relating to prostitution in Pakistan. Includes papers on venereal disease, rehabilitation of destitute girls, health education, role of family and economic circumstances and other related topics.

2434 SHARMA, PIARE LAL. World famous trials of rape and murder. New Delhi: Pankaj Publications, 1978. 116p.
Reviews legal and ethical considerations relating to rape in India and presents material from three rape cases in this country. One of the murder cases considered is that of the actress Meena Kumari.

2435 TRIBHUWAN, JYOTSNA. Suppression of Immoral Traffic in Women and Girls Act, 1956: a critical study. Ahmednagar: the author, 1966. 26p.
Reviews provisions of act, certain related cases and possible effects of act in its early years. Includes suggestions for amendment.

2436 We want to live. Produced by P. Pati. Directed by B.N. Mehra. 1970. 18 min. Black and white. 16 and 35 mm. [*Distributed by* Films Division, Ministry of Information and Broadcasting, 24 G. Deshmukh Marg, Bombay 400 026].
Film explores the roots of prostitution and the need for social welfare attention. Includes interviews with prostitutes, essentially in Hindi, and opinions of social scientists and social workers. Stresses need to incorporate prostitutes into society. [Unexamined. CF].

iv) Crime and imprisonment

2437 AHUJA, RAM. Female murderers in India: a sociological study. *In* Indian J. of Social Work 31,3 (1970) 271-84.
Report of study of 136 female murderers from Rajasthan, Punjab and M.P. to ascertain motivation for murder, role of family and family's adjustment following female imprisonment. Concludes that these murders are due to family maladjustment and not criminal tendencies (all were first offenders) and that sentences must be related to the particular social circumstances in order to be ethical and effective.

2438 NEHRU, KRISHNA [KRISHNA (NEHRU) HUTHEESING]. Shadows on the wall. New York: Asia Books, John Day, 1948. 116p. [*Also* Bombay: Kutub Publishers, 1946. 150p.].
Twelve stories about various women the author met while serving a year-long prison term for her involvement in the nationalist movement. ". . . I got to know my fellow 'politicals' better . . . . I also got to know many of the so-called 'criminals,' and hearing of the sad experiences that had brought them into prison, I was able to get a picture of the travails through which the less fortunate women were expected to learn dignity and self-respect."

2439 SOHONI, NEERA KUCHREJA. Women prisoners. *In* Indian J. of Social Work 35, 2 (1974) 137-48. [*Also in* Interdiscipline 11,2 (1974) 31-52].
Stresses lack of information on female prisoners in India and general insensitivity to problems of this group. Includes a socio-economic profile of convicted women by region, age, education, type of offence, ratio of repetition as compared with men, etc., from the limited data available. Discusses policy and its economics and urges policy improvement based on particular characteristics of female prisoners.

v) Alcoholism

2440 RAMANATHAN, JAYA. The woman alcoholic. *In* Eve's Weekly 30,34 (21 Aug 1976) 8-9.
Brief article estimates that women constitute three to four percent of the alcoholics in the Indian population. They tend to come from the highest and lowest strata. Suggests that most female drinkers in India are from the Christian community. With very brief case studies.

vi) Housing needs

2441 YOUNG WOMEN'S CHRISTIAN ASSOCIATION, INDIA. A place to live: a study on housing for women. Bombay: Allied Publishers, [1975]. 136p.
Study of housing needs of students, employed women and the aged in India who live apart from their families. Various contributors discuss the three groups, review world and Indian housing patterns and problems, describe voluntary agencies at work in India and recommend solutions to some problems elucidated. Numerous tables.

(11) The demographic perspective

2442 AGARWALA, S.N. Some problems of India's population. Bombay: Vora and Company Publishers Private Ltd., 1966. 151p.
Overall review of demographic situation in India. Chapters explicitly concerned with women consider age at marriage, age at widowhood, widow marriage, fertility and sterility.

2443 BHENDE, ASHA A., TARA KANITKAR and G. RAMA RAO. Teaching and research in population studies: seventeen years of IIPS. Bombay: International Institute for Population Studies, 1976. 294p.
Reviews work of International Institute for Population Studies from 1956 to 1974. Major sections concern genesis and organization of the institute and development of the teaching program and present curricula and research activities (with bibliographies, including many unpublished papers) and conferences and seminars sponsored by the institute. Appendixes name students who have attended the institute and indicate their research foci.

2444 BOSE, ASHISH. A demographic profile of Indian women. *In* Devaki Jain, ed. Indian women. New Delhi: Publications Division, Ministry of Information and Broadcasting, Government of India, 1975. pp.125-84.
Brief comments on declining sex ratio, literacy and education rates, age at marriage rates, fertility rates, employment rates and political participation and substantial appendix of 39 tables relating to above-mentioned topics.

2445 BOULDING, ELISE et al., eds. Handbook of international data on women. New York: Sage Publications, Halsted Press, John Wiley, 1976. 468p.
Demographic data includes South Asian countries. Main divisions (most feature many subdivisions) are: general economic activity; economic activity by status, by industry and by occupation; literacy and education; migration; marital status; life, death and reproduction; political and civic participation; and world overview. Appendix A explains procedures and definitions used in compiling tables and appendix B surveys UN data on women.

2446 HASHMI, SULTAN S. and IQBAL ALAM. The problem of obtaining age data in Pakistan: a study of age reporting of a panel of ever married females in yearly enumerations, 1962-1965. Karachi: Pakistan Institute of Development Economics, 1969. 18p. (*Its* Research Report 83).
Examines patterns in age reporting of 4,117 women over four consecutive years. Correlates trends with age group, numerical patterns (odd/even, multiples of five) and parity. "The net effect of over and under statement of ages on the age structure of females inspite of cancellation of errors is not negligible."

2447 HUSAIN, I.Z., ed. State and status of demographic research in the country: seminar papers. Lucknow: Demographic Research Centre, Department of Economics, Lucknow University, 1970. 326p.
Seminar papers and lengthy bibliography of primarily unpublished works review various aspects of demographic research in India.

2448 INDIA (REPUBLIC). COMMITTEE ON THE STATUS OF WOMEN IN INDIA. Demographic perspective. *In its* Towards equality: report of the Committee on the Status of Women in India. New Delhi: Department of Social Welfare, Ministry of Education and Social Welfare, Government of India, 1975. pp.9-36. [*Chair* Phulrenu Guha].
Presents, in concise and primarily tabular form, key aspects of 20th century patterns of sex ratio, mortality, age distribution, age at marriage, female marital status, fertility and family planning, education, work and migration.

2449 INDIA (REPUBLIC). DIRECTORATE OF NATIONAL SAMPLE SURVEY. The National Sample Survey. No. 1- (1952-). Calcutta, etc. Irregularly.
These reports organize demographic data concerning a wide range of topics. Over 200 published to date. A list of titles appears at the end of each report.

2450 ________. Tables with notes on differential fertility and mortality rates in India. Delhi: Manager of Publications, Government of India, 1969? 84p. (National Sample Survey, 175).
Correlates fertility and mortality data of various populations in India with numerous socio-economic variables.

2451 ________. Tables with notes on the fertility and mortality rates in urban areas of India. Delhi: Manager of Publications, Government of India, 1971? 72p. (National Sample Survey, 180).
Key demographic statistics, 1960-61.

2452 INDIA (REPUBLIC). OFFICE OF THE REGISTRAR GENERAL. Bibliography of census publications in India. Comp. by C.G. Jadhav. With assistance of Charan Singh and Anand Prakash. Ed. by B.K. Roy Burman. Delhi: Manager of Publications, Government of India, 1972. 520p. (Census Centenary Publication, 5).
Guide to publications of the national census, 1872 through 1961, and of the various provincial censuses from their inception through 1961. Includes sections on areas now composing Pakistan and Bangladesh.

2453 INDIA (REPUBLIC). PLANNING, RESEARCH, EVALUATION AND MONITORING DIVISION.

The Indian woman: a statistical profile. New Delhi: Planning, Research, Evaluation and Monitoring Division, Department of Social Welfare, Ministry of Education and Social Welfare, Government of India, 1975. 57p.
Presents data on sex ratio, vital statistics, family planning, literacy, education, employment, political participation, etc., according to such dimensions as rural/urban, various decades, religion, age group, marital status and region. Issued for International Women's Year, 1975.

2454 MITRA, ASOK. The status of women. *In his* India's population: aspects of quality and control, v1. New Delhi: Abhinav Publications, 1978. pp.287-496.
In the work author seeks "to identify the minimum number of areas of policy action that can improve our quality of life." Considers status of women to be "the crux of quality of life in the Indian situation." The section contains chapters on general status, age at marriage, sex ratio, literacy and employment and over 100 tables.

2455 ________. The status of women: literacy and employment. Bombay: Allied Publishers, 1979? 74p. (ICSSR Programme of Women's Studies, 2).
Separate sections discuss trends in female literacy and employment. Numerous tables. The book is a part of a joint project of the Indian Council of Social Science Research and Jawaharlal Nehru University to analyze trends of 1872 to 1971 censuses and related data. [Unexamined ALI].

2456 NATARAJAN, DANDAPANI. Age and marital status. New Delhi: Office of the Registrar General, Government of India, 1972. 170p. (Census Centenary Monograph 8).
Compilation of relevant excerpts from the 1872 through 1951 all-India census reports with supplementary interpretive information.

2457 ROY BURMAN, B.K. Social demography in India: a trend report. *In* A survey of research in sociology and social anthropology. Bombay: Popular Prakashan, 1974. pp.1-81.
Extensive bibliographic essay, sponsored by the Indian Council of Social Science Research. Lists and discusses hundreds of books, articles, theses and unpublished papers. Also provides a brief review of the history of demography in India and recommends research priorities.

2458 A status study on population research in India. New Delhi: Tata McGraw-Hill Publishing Company, 1974-75. 3v.
Project to assess demographic research on India. Extensive concern with women. Individual volumes are ***Behavioural Sciences*** by Udai Pareek and T. Venkateswara Rao, ***Demography*** by S.P. Jain and ***Biomedical Aspects*** compiled by G.P. Talwar.

(a) The sex ratio issue — why do women constitute only 48% of South Asia's population? — and differentials

2459 DANDEKAR, KUMUDINI. Why has the proportion of women in India's population been declining? *In* Economic and Political Weekly 10,42 (18 Oct 1975) 1663-7.
Considers social factors underlying high female mortality and thus declining proportion of females in India's population. These include unpopularity of female children, low status of women, low levels of education and employability and excessive childbearing. Includes cross-national comparisons of demographic data.

2460 DESAI, P.B. Variation in population sex ratios in India, 1901-61. *In* Ashish Bose, ed. Patterns in population change in India, 1951-61. Bombay: Allied Publishers, 1967. pp.372-88.
States that the reoccurrence of the decline in the proportion of females in the population in the 1961 Indian census has yet to be understood. Presents a selected series of available sex ratios, along with some ratios computed from census figures "with a view to broadly indicating how the phenomenon of declining sex ratios has affected populations in the different States of the Indian Union."

2461 ________. Size and sex composition of population in India, 1901-1961. Bombay: Asia Publishing House, 1969. 263p. (Census Studies, 1).
[Unexamined. ALI].

2462 GOSAL, GURDEV SINGH. The regionalism of sex composition of India's population. *In* Rural Sociology 26,2 (1961) 122-37.
Considers sex ratio trends in India during the first half of the 20th century by region and in rural/urban context. Attempts to account for variations.

2463 GULATI, S.C. Component analysis of the change in the sex ratio: 1951-61. *In* Demography India 4,2 (1975) 289-304.
Seeks to understand the factors behind regional variations in sex ratio in order to understand the cause of the decline in the ratio of females to males during the period covered by the 1961 census. Concludes that sex differentials in mortality predominate as factors in some states and internal migration predominates in certain others.

2464 INDIA (REPUBLIC). OFFICE OF THE REGISTRAR GENERAL. The sex ratio of the population of India. By Pravin M. Visaria. New Delhi: Office of the Registrar General, India; Ministry of Home Affairs, 1971? 83p. (Census of India,

1971, vI, part IIE, Monograph 10).
Text, tables and charts describe sex ratio trends over the past century of area now comprising India, Pakistan, Bangladesh and Sri Lanka.

2465 LALL, AMRIT. Age and sex structures of cities of India. *In* Geographical Review of India 24,1 (1962) 7-29.
Considers a range of factors involved in the observed variation of age and sex ratios of cities having a population of over 100,000. Based on 1951 census data.

2466 MITRA, ASOK. Implications of declining sex ratio in India's population. Bombay: Allied Publishers, 1979. 85p. (ICSSR Programme of Women's Studies, I).
Briefly discusses the nature and causes of the "steadily deteriorating" proportion of women in India's population. Numerous tables (pp.1-30), followed by appended tables presenting sex ratios according to district — total, urban and rural — from the 1901 through 1971 censuses. [Unexamined].

2467 NATARAJAN, DANDAPANI. Changes in sex ratio. New Delhi: Office of the Registrar General, Government of India, 1972. 105p. (Census Centenary Monograph 6).
Reviews and excerpts sex ratio material from Indian censuses, 1871 to present. Includes material on female infanticide and other factors to which low proportion of females has been attributed.

2468 PAKRASI, KANTI and AJIT HALDER. Sex ratios and sex sequences of births in India. *In* J. of Biosocial Science 3,4 (1971) 377-87.
Regarding interralationship of sex ratio, birth order and gender, including the unusually high ratio of male to female first births reported in India. Suggests this is due to "recall relapse": tendency not to report a first female child who died and a tendency to report a first son as older than a first daughter.

2469 RUKANUDDIN, ABDUL RAZZAQUE. A study of the sex ratio in Pakistan. *In* Warren C. Robinson, ed. Studies in the demography of Pakistan. Karachi: Pakistan Institute of Development Economics, 1967. pp.139-225.
Attempts to explain high rate of males to females in Pakistan's population. Considers several hypotheses: disproportionate ratio of the sexes at birth, greater female mortality and underenumeration of females. Argues that higher female mortality is most significant factor. Data from 1901-61 decennial censuses.

2470 RAMACHANDRAN, K.V. and VINAYAK A. DESHPANDE. The sex ratio at birth in India by regions. *In* Milbank Memorial Fund Quarterly 42,2, part I (1964) 84-95.
Study using data collected in hospitals and health centers throughout India, which is considered to be more reliable than census, survey or vital statistics enumerations. "Its findings do not support the popular notion that the sex ratio at birth varies widely by region, for which regional differences in diet, climate, and health conditions are usually held responsible."

2471 REITH, DAVID JEROME. Structural and regional bases of sex ratios in the population of India. Ph.D. dissertation, Department of Geography?, University of Illinois at Urbana-Champaign, 1975. 250p. [University Microfilms 75-24,390].
Delineates six regions within India on the basis of forty-six variables relating to sex ratio. Describes unique population dynamics of the six regions and their effect on sex ratio. [Unexamined. DAI].

2472 SEN, J.C. The sex composition of India's towns with 20,000-50,000 inhabitants, 1961. *In* Indian Geographical Journal 38,3/4 (1963) 90-9. [*Also* Sex-structure of India's urban centres with more than 20,000 inhabitants. *In* Research Bulletin of the Panjab University n.s. 14 (Jul 1963) 153-9].
Finds migration for economic reasons to be the major factor in producing female to male ratios in urban India that are lower than those of the population as a whole. Discusses the differentials among urban centers.

2473 VISARIA, PRAVIN M. The sex ratio of the population of India and Pakistan and regional variations during 1901-61. *In* Ashish Bose, ed. Patterns of population change in India, 1951-61. Bombay: Allied Publishers, 1967. pp.334-71.
Attempts to examine "the facts and the explanatory hypotheses" of the sex ratio figures of India and Pakistan based on the decennial censuses, 1901-61. Considers possible effects of spatial mobility (within India and between the two countries) and the evidence for hypotheses attempting to explain the excess of males. Predicts future trends.

(b) Female mortality rates

2474 ASLAM, MUHAMMAD, SULTAN S. HASHMI and WILLIAM SELTZER. Abridged life tables of Pakistan and provinces by sex, 1962. *In* Pakistan Development Review 7,1 (1967) 66-106.
Longevity tables based on data from the Population Growth Estimation experiment. Among the conclusions: "Males in Pakistan have longer duration of life than females . . . . The sex differences in longevity become more pronounced in the reproductive ages showing that the incidence of maternal mortality in Pakistan is quite high."

2475 GUPTA, B.R. Future trends in sex-differential of expectation of life at birth in India. *In* Artha Vijñāna 14 (Jun 1972) 152-76.
Argues that female expectation of life at birth should surpass that of males in India by 1991 due to "improvement in health conditions, old age care, decline in fertility and maternal mortality, improved care of female children, and other social and economic factors."

2476 RUKANUDDIN, ABDUL RAZZAQUE. The effect of mortality on the sex ratio in Pakistan. Karachi: Pakistan Institute of Development Economics, 1967. 12p.
[Unexamined. ALP].

(12) Problems of family planning and population control

2477 AGARWALA, S.N. Population control in India: progress and prospects. *In* Law and Contemporary Problems 25,3 (1960) 577-92.
An early review article with a substantial bibliography.

2478 Asia. *In* Special issue: progress and problems of fertility control around the world. Demography 5,2 (1968) 642-784.
About half of the articles in this section are concerned with South Asian countries (India, Pakistan, Sri Lanka).

2479 BARDIS, PANOS D. Social change and family planning in India: a suggestion for attitude research. *In* J. of Social Research 13,2 (1970) 64-9.
Considers miscellaneous aspects of family planning in India. Includes a brief chronology of highlights in the family planning movement, 1916 to 1960.

2480 Bibliography of cost benefit studies on family planning in India and IUCD studies in India. Bombay: Demographic Training and Research Centre, 1970. 21p.
Fifty three annotated cost benefit studies by Kul Bhushan Suri and S.P. Mohanty and 84 annotated intrauterine contraceptive device (IUCD) studies by Asha Bhende. Includes references to unpublished papers.

2481 Family Planning News. v1- (1960-). New Delhi: National Institute of Family Planning. Monthly.
Brief articles on various programs, contraceptive methods, conferences, officials, etc.

2482 GOYAL, M.M.L., comp. Studies on intrauterine contraceptive devices in India. New Delhi: Central Family Planning Institute, 1970. 21p.
[Unexamined. NUC].

2483 KRISHNAMURTHY, K.G. Research in family planning in India. Delhi: Sterling Publishers, 1968. 108p.
Bibliographic essay with major sections on attitudes (by geographical area), fertility, contraception and communication of information. Includes many unpublished papers. Lists relevant Indian journals.

2484 NATIONAL RESEARCH INSTITUTE OF FAMILY PLANNING. Inventory of family planning research in Pakistan. Karachi: the institute, 1969.
Lists 237 studies. [Unexamined].

2485 Pakistan Journal of Family Planning. v1-3? (1967-1969?). Karachi: National Research Institute of Family Planning. Biannually.
Primarily contains reports of knowledge/attitudes/practices (KAP) studies, fertility differential studies and investigations of the success of various contraceptive methods.

2486 RAO, KAMALA GOPAL. Studies in family planning in India: a review for programme implications. New Delhi: Central Family Planning Institute, 1968. 489p.
Summaries of studies organized by various categories. [Unexamined. NUC].

2487 ________. Studies in family planning: India. New Delhi: Abhinav Publications, 1974. 863p.
Extensively annotated bibliography of over 550 studies conducted from 1951 to 1974. Annotations discuss objectives, method, sample and findings.

2488 SANYAL, R.K., A.K. NANDA and A.D. TRIPATHI, eds. Demographic situation in India. New Delhi: National Institutde of Family Planning, 1975. 130p. (*Its* Report Series, 15).
Concisely summarizes data relevant to family planning, by state and territory. Compiled for National Population Conference, New Delhi, 1974.

2489 THAPAR, SAVITRI. Family planning in India. *In* Population Studies 17,1 (1963) 4-19.
Reviews the history of family planning efforts in India from the publication of Pyare Kishen Wattal's ***The Population Problem in India*** in 1916 to the family planning policies of the Third Five Year Plan, begun in 1961.

(a) Relationship between status of women and fertility control

2490 BHATNAGAR, N.K. Status of women and family planning in India. *In* J. of Family Welfare 18,3 (1972) 21-9.
Argues that improving the status of women through education (especially) and other means has a positive effect on their interest in

adoption of family planning measures.

2491 CHAHIL, RENU. The status of women, work, and fertility in India. *In* Stanley Kupinsky, ed. The fertility of working women: a synthesis of international research. New York: Praeger Publishers, 1977. pp.146-71. (Praeger Special Studies in International Economics and Development).
Following brief surveys of general 20th century demographic trends, family planning programs and demographic and socio-economic factors relating to population growth in India, the author, reviewing selected studies, discusses the relationship of labor force participation, education and fertility. One conclusion is that "The status of women may possibly be one of the critical factors in influencing fertility." Another is that the frequently found correlation between employment and low fertility does not seem to hold for Indian women as most available occupations do not interfere with child care. Various recommendations.

2492 CHANDRASEKHAR, S. Emancipation of women and family planning. *In* Swasth Hind 12,5 (1968) 167-72 and 192.
Convocation address to SNDT Women's University graduates. Summarizes history of Indian womanhood and urges need for "biological emancipation," the right to select marriage partners and plan births.

2493 DHILLON, H.S. Status of women in India and implications for the family planning programme. New Delhi: Central Health Education Bureau, 1970. (Technical Series, 9; Reference 45).
[Unexamined].

2494 Family planning and the status of women in India: report of a seminar held on August 10-14, 1969, in New Delhi. New Delhi: Central Institute of Research and Training in Public Cooperation, 1972? 207p. (*Its* Publications, 17).
Contents: "Changing Status of Women: a Historical Perspective" by Lakshmi N. Menon, "Cultural Factors Affecting Family Planning in India" by Kamala Gopala Rao, "Social Reform Movements and Legislation for Women" by Chandrakala K. Hate, "Social Reform and Legislation for Women in India" by G.D. Khosla, "Status of Women in India" by S. Chandrasekhar, "Population Growth and Socio-Economic Development" by S.N. Agarwala, "Discussion: Crux of the Problem, Social Change," "Fertility Status of Indian Women" by B.L. Raina, "Discussion: Factors to Enhance Status of Women," "Family Size and Status of Women" by Krishna Puri, "Discussion: Exercise of Rights and Responsibilities," "Status and Factors Affecting Change in Status" by H.S. Dhillon, "Discussion: the Worker and his Clients," "Women's Role in Promoting their Cause" by Premlata Gupta, "Discussion: the Distinct Role of Women," "Problems for a Woman's Status" by Lakshmi N. Menon, "Suggestions and Recommendations" and miscellaneous appendixes.

2495 GEORGE, ALEYAMMA. Population growth, status and role of women in India. *In* Demography India 4,1 (1975) 108-27.
Factors involved in low status of women are said to include "low standard of living, low level of literacy and education among women, economic dependence of women, ignorance of their own fundamental rights, low inter-spousal communication, the stronghold of tradition and so on." Control of family size will be more successful as these constraints are mitigated. India's family planning program "has not so far been guided by an understanding of the status and role of women."

2496 MUKHERJEE, B.N. Status of women as related to family planning: an empirical study in Haryana, Tamil Nadu and Meghalaya. *In* J. of Population Research 2 (1975).
[Unexamined].

2497 One man's family. 1975. 27 min. Color. 16 mm. [*Distributed by* Asterisk Productions, Toronto, Canada. *Also released as* 3900 million and one. 52 min.].
Film. Examines population problems in India with particular reference to women's social situation. Deals with the relationship between bearing sons and high female status, fear of barren women and so forth. [Unexamined].

(b) Government programs and policies

i) India

2498 The arithmetic of people. 30 min. Black and white. 16 and 35 mm.? [*Distributed by* University of Michigan Television Center, 310 Maynard Street, Ann Arbor, Michigan 48108].
Film. Considers the birth control programs of the Indian government, particularly those directed toward women. [Unexamined].

2499 BHOURASKAR, D.M. On "improvident maternity." *In* Indian Economic Journal 7,2 (1959) 175-91.
A response to a census commissioner's recommendation that improvident maternity, "a child-birth occurring to a mother who has already given birth to three or more children of whom at least one is alive," be reduced. Examines proposal in quantitative and practical terms. Concludes that it is "impracticable and, if implemented, likely to end in failure."

2500 BOGUE, DONALD J. Some tentative recommendations for a "sociologically

correct" family planning communication and motivation program in India. *In* Clyde V. Kiser, ed. Research in family planning. Princeton, New Jersey: Princeton University Press, 1962. pp.503-38.
Briefly discusses 27 recommendations. Based on fertility studies, communication-motivation literature and discussions with family planning workers.

2501 DANDEKAR, KUMUDINI. Vital rates and the efforts at family planning in the various states of India. *In* Artha Vijñāna 6,4 (1964) 290-300.
Relates interstate fertility differentials for the period 1951-61 to the range and depth of family planning programs in the various states.

2502 Family planning and maternity and child health at Primary Health Centre: a manual for health and family planning staff. [New Delhi: Ministry of Health and Family Planning, 1972]. 58, 65p.
Guide prepared for the primary health agency at the local, block level. Treats objectives of National Family Planning Programme, structure of the program, job descriptions, program operations, records and reports, special purpose mobile service camps, training programs for local leaders and health staff, educational activities and basic equipment.

2503 INDIA (REPUBLIC). MINISTRY OF HEALTH AND FAMILY PLANNING. DEPARTMENT OF FAMILY PLANNING. Trends in sterilisation of women. *In its* Studies in family planning. New Delhi: Directorate General of Health Services, 1960. pp.91-6.
[Unexamined].

2504 MUKHERJEE, RAMKRISHNA. Family and planning in India. Bombay: Orient Longman, 1976? 88p.
Evaluates family planning programs in India with reference to socio-economic factors.

ii) Pakistan

2505 ADIL, ENVER. The use of statistical guides and measures of effectiveness in determining government policy for influencing fertility: Pakistan. *In* World Population Conference, 1965, Belgrade. Proceedings, v2: selected papers and summaries: fertility, family planning, mortality. New York: Department of Economic and Social Affairs, United Nations, 1967. pp.63-7.
Discusses various guides and indexes for establishing goals of and approaches to Pakistan's family planning program. "Most of them are tried and widely used methods that need no elaboration. However, the paper focuses on several techniques which are perhaps not as familiar and are being used or will be used in Pakistan. Data derived by these techniques or formulas prepared for them are used as illustrations."

2506 BEAN, LEE L. and A.D. BHATTI. Three years of Pakistan's new national Family-Planning Programme. *In* Pakistan Development Review 9,1 (1969) 35-57.
Assesses the early years of "Phase IV" of family planning in Pakistan, 1965-68, in which the first comprehensive government-administered family planning program began to operate. "The programme appears to be strikingly successful . . . . [and] has proved to be both flexible and imaginative." Main areas of progress are considered to be program organization, personnel training and contraception adoption. Authors call for studies evaluating impact on fertility and staff efficiency.

2507 CHOUDHURI, A.S. Role of para-medical personnel in the family-planning program in Pakistan. *In* Gerald I. Zatuchni, ed. Post-partum family planning: a report on the international program. New York: McGraw-Hill, 1970. pp.185-9.
Report of program of intrauterine contraceptive device insertion for married women. Favorable results were obtained through the use of paramedical personnel.

2508 JAFAREY, S.A., J. GILBERT HARDEE and A.P. SATTERTHWAITE. Use of medical-paramedical personnel and traditional midwives in the Pakistan Family Planning Program. *In* Demography 5,2 (1968) 666-78.
"The purpose of this paper is to examine the utilization of medical-paramedical personnel [Lady Health Visitors, Lady Family Planning Visitors and Lady Organizers] and local midwives (dais) in the national program in order to give a provisional assessment of their effectiveness at this stage of the program." Considers the use of paramedicals to have substantially affected the reproductive life of villagers. Considers midwives to be important to the family planning program.

2509 ROBINSON, WARREN C. Family planning in Pakistan's Third Five Year Plan. *In* Pakistan Development Review 6,2 (1966) 255-81.
"This article will review the population policy contained in the plan and its supporting documents. Our analysis is sometimes critical but never unsympathetic. The planners in Pakistan have recognized the importance of population control and the present Plan devotes considerable resources to this goal."

2510 ________. Family planning in Pakistan, 1955-1977: a review. *In* Pakistan Development Review 17,2 (1978) 233-47.
"The present article reviews family planning . . . to see what has been learned which can be of value to future planning . . . . we focus on the main assumptions, strategies and organizational changes through which the programme has passed."

(c) Practice of family planning: motivations and obstacles

i) Family dynamics: communication channels, desire for sons, etc.

2511 CHANDRASEKARAN, C. Cultural factors and the propagation of family planning in the Indian setting. *In* J. of Family Welfare 5,3 (1959) 43-51.
[Unexamined].

2512 Couples in India. Directed by David Ruskin. 197_. 30 min. Color. 16 mm. [*Distributed by* Martha Stuart Communications, 66 Bank Street, New York, New York 10014].
Film made for World Population Year, 1974. Young couples discuss birth control and parenting. [Unexamined].

2513 DUBEY, D.C. and A.K. DEVGAN. Family planning communications studies in India: a review of findings and implications of studies on communications. New Delhi: Central Family Planning Institute, 1969. 96p. (Monograph Series, 8).
Survey with an annotated bibliography of 66 references.

2514 GANGRADE, K.D. Social values and family planning. *In his* Dimensions of social work in India: case studies. New Delhi: Marwah Publications, 1976. pp.45-52.
Case study of a 32-year-old village woman who bore eleven children but had no living sons. She and her husband secretly used a diaphragm as she has no desire for additional children. Her mother-in-law found out and became enraged.

2515 KHARE, R.S. A study of intra-family problems of motivation in relation to family planning in India. *In* Eastern Anthropologist 18,2 (1965) 73-9.
Examines attitudes of other household members and various joint family circumstances as factors influencing couples' attitudes toward and motivation for family planning. Suggests that family planning programs should direct communication toward couples' key relatives as well as couples themselves as a way of sustaining strong motivation.

2516 MASCARENHAS, MARIE M. The Indian woman's ancient maternal role must shape approach to family planning. *In* World Education Reports 9 (Jun 1975) 2p.
Argues that women's primary positive identity in India is through motherhood, and this has been an obstacle to effective family planning. Proposes that family planning campaigns should stress the benefits children of planned families receive. [Unexamined].

ii) KAP (Knowledge, Attitudes, Practices) studies

2517 INDIA (REPUBLIC). DIRECTORATE OF NATIONAL SAMPLE SURVEY. Tables with notes on family planning. Delhi: Manager of Publications, Government of India, 1967. 164p. (National Sample Survey, 116).
Presents numerous KAP statistics compiled in 1960-61.

2518 JAHINA, MEHRU B. Discrepancies in the responses of husbands and wives regarding the couples' practice of family planning. *In* Demographic Training and Research Centre. Five years of research in family planning. Bombay: the centre, 1968.
[Unexamined].

2519 KAPIL, KRISHAN K. and DEVENDRA N. SAKSENA. A bibliography of family planning knowledge, attitude, and practice studies in India, 1951-68. *In* Demographic Training and Research Centre Newsletter 26 (1968) 19-38.
[Unexamined].

2520 MALIK, M. Attitude of women towards use of contraceptives. Bombay: Tata Institute of Social Sciences, 1963.
[Unexamined].

2521 MUKHERJEE, BISHWA NATH. Family planning in Haryana and Tamil Nadu. *In* Social Change 3,1/2 (1973) 33-45.
General evaluation of the results of KAP surveys made in 1971-72 in Haryana and Tamil Nadu and designed to help evaluate family planning programs. Tables.

2522 _______. A comparison of the results of family planning KAP surveys in Haryana and Tamil Nadu, India. *In* Studies in Family Planning 5,7 (1974) 224-31.
Reports various knowledge/attitudes/practices findings. Attributes "KAP gap," the lag of practice behind knowledge and attitudes, to social factors and urges broader, social perspectives. Survey found that while Haryana informants tended to know more about contraception and practice it at higher rates than Tamil informants, Tamil attitudes were more favorable.

2523 RAMACHANDRA SASTRY, K. Female work participation and work-motivated contraception. Gandhigram, Madurai District: Gandhigram Institute of Rural Health and Family Planning, 1976. 119p. (*Its* Monograph Series, 8).
[Unexamined. ALI].

2524 RAMAN, M.V. Knowledge and practice of contraception in India: a survey of

some recent studies. *In* Artha Vijñāna 5,2 (1963) 81-96.
Reviews a series of studies and summarizes the trends.

2525 Urban attitudes toward family planning: a survey in eleven cities, October 1967. *In* Monthly Public Opinion Surveys of the Indian Institute of Public Opinion 13,1 (1967) 3-30.
Survey of 1,000 literate urban adults. Results are tabulated by sex, age, education, income, and number of children. Indicates a wide awareness of family planning but a lesser degree of actual practice. Tables.

iii) Programs of women's organizations

2526 BRUCE, JUDITH. Women's organizations: a resource for family planning and development. *In* Family Planning Perspectives 8,6 (1976) 291-7.
Reviews family planning activities of various women's organizations. Considers the following South Asian groups: Nepal Women's Organization, Social Welfare Society of Pakistan, Concerned Women (Bangladesh) and the Integrated Rural Development Program (Bangladesh).

iv) Religious principles: Islam

2527 Islam and family planning. Dacca: Directorate of Population Control and Family Planning, Government of the People's Republic of Bangladesh, 1977. 43p.
"In this booklet Fatwas and articles of some eminent Muslim jurists and religious thinkers have been published with the hope that better understanding of the Islamic point of view on family planning will help resolve population problem." All contributors feel that family planning is compatible with Islam.

2528 KHAN, AKHTER HAMEED. Islamic opinions on contraception. Dacca: East Pakistan Government Press, 1963. 12p.
[Unexamined. NUC].

2529 MAHMOOD, TAHIR. Family planning: the Muslim viewpoint. New Delhi: Vikas Publishing House, 1977. 152p.
The author, a specialist in Islamic comparative law, argues, citing the *Qor'an*, that Muslims are enjoined to practice family planning to limit family size. Compares contemporary attitudes in India to those elsewhere in the Muslim world, including Pakistan and Bangladesh.

(13) Legal rights and the legal profession

(a) Legislative provisions for women

2530 DERRETT, J. DUNCAN M. Essays in classical and modern Hindu law, v4: current problems and the legacy of the past. Leiden: E.J. Brill, 1978. 454p.
Fourth and final volume of collected papers. Articles relating explicitly to women include "Section 488 of the Criminal Procedure Code and the Rights of Women: an Unruly Horse," "If a Christian Woman Marries a Hindu solely in a Hindu Ceremony of Marriage is She Entitled to an Order for Maintenance Under 488 of the Criminal Procedure Code?", "The Deserted Wife's 'Equity' and Modern Indian Law," "A Coparcener's Wife's Jeopardy," "An Intestate's Daughter's Marriage Expenses," "The Testamentary Capacity of a Sole Surviving Coparcener and the Rights of Widows" and "May a Hindu Woman be the Manager of a Joint Family at Mitakshara Law?"

2531 GANGRADE, K.D., ed. Social legislation in India. Delhi: Concept Publishing Company, 1978. 2v.
Presents basic aspects of social legislation in India in terms easily understood by lay people, points to deficiencies and offers solutions. Although none of the topical chapters concern women per se, many are relevant; considers law relating to family and marriage, medical termination of pregnancy, maternity benefits and immoral traffic in women and girls.

2532 INDIA (REPUBLIC). COMMITTEE ON THE STATUS OF WOMEN IN INDIA. Women and the law. *In its* Towards equality: report of the Committee on the Status of Women in India. New Delhi: Department of Social Welfare, Ministry of Education and Social Welfare, Government of India, 1975. pp.102-47. [*Chair* Phulrenu Guha].
Reviews major legislative provisions for women in the Republic of India by topic and, within topics, by religious community. Main topics are polygamy, age at marriage, dowry, divorce, adoption, guardianship, maintenance and inheritance. Criticizes British policy of non-intervention with religious law. Concludes with a series of recommendations.

2533 INDIA (REPUBLIC). PLANNING COMMISSION. Social legislation: its role in social welfare. New Delhi: Planning Commission, Government of India, 1956. 418p.
Summarizes social welfare legislation with the aim of educating the lay public. Sections include "Woman and the Law" (pp.13-136), "Immoral Traffic" (pp.255-79) and summaries of present conditions and suggested improvements with respect to these topics (pp.355-64, pp.382-8). Book was inspired by aims of

India's First Five Year Plan.

2534 PEARL, DAVID. The legal rights of Muslim women in India, Pakistan and Bangladesh. *In* New Community 5,1/2 (1976) 68-74.
Reviews major legislative provisions.

2535 SARKAR, LOTIKA. Law and the status of women in India. *In* Law and the status of women: an international symposium. New York: Centre for Social Development and Humanitarian Affairs, United Nations, 1977? pp.95-122. [*Reprint from* Columbia Human Rights Law Review 8,1 (1977) 95-122].
Reviews constitutional and legislative provisions for Indian women. Considers health, employment, inheritance and other topics. States that the Preamble and Fundamental Rights section of the constitution provide for equal status and opportunity, which had been lost in the economic changes of the British period. Modern judicial and executive powers, however, have not always been able to give effect to this policy and sections of various pieces of legislation are not consonant with it.

2536 ________, ed. The invisible gap: studies on the legal status of Indian women. Bombay: Allied Publishers, forthcoming. SNDT Women's University, Bombay; Women in a Changing Society).
Papers sponsored jointly by the Indian Council of Social Science Research and the Shreemati Nathibai Damodar Thackersey Women's University. [Unexamined].

2537 SIVARAMAYYA, B. Equality of sexes as a human and constitutional right and the Muslim law. *In* Tahir Mahmood, ed. Islamic law in modern India. Bombay: N.M. Tripathi Private Ltd., 1972. pp.69-79.
"Equality of sexes is now recognized as a human right. In India equality before law is also a right protected under the Constitution. The purpose of this paper is to advocate implementation of the principle of equality of sexes under the Muslim personal law, as applicable in India." Argues that adherence to secular principles is appropriate for Muslims in a country where there are multiple faiths.

2538 SMITH, DONALD EUGENE. Religion, law, and secularism. *In his* India as a secular state. Princeton, New Jersey: Princeton University Press, 1963. pp.265-91.
Discusses the problems involved in India's commitment to becoming a "secular state in the liberal democratic tradition" while fostering freedom of religion and having two major religious communities whose laws continue to regulate many civil matters. Includes specific examples of numerous legislative issues relating to women.

2539 Women and law in India. Social Change 2,1 (1972) 71p.
Special issue. [Unexamined].

(b) The effectiveness of legislative provisions

2540 ALMENAS-LIPOWSKY, ANGELES J. The position of Indian women in the light of legal reform: a socio-legal study of the legal position of Indian women as interpreted and enforced by the law courts compared and related to their position in the family and at work. Wiesbaden: Franz Steiner Verlag, 1975. 217p. (Beiträge zur Südasienforschung, Südasien Institut, Universität Heidelberg, 11).
Considers relative influence of legal provisions and other factors on position of women at home and at work, effectiveness of law based upon western ideas of equality between the sexes and role of court system in legislative effectiveness. "A comparison between the legal and actual position of Indian women at work and in the family brings to light some of the problems left unsolved after women are granted equal civil rights to men, special protection at work, and an increase of rights in the family."

2541 MINATTUR, JOSEPH. Women and the law: constitutional rights and continuing inequalities. *In* Social Action 25,3 (1975) 292-301. [*Also in* Alfred de Souza, ed. Women in contemporary India: traditional images and changing roles. Delhi: Manohar Book Service, 1975. pp.96-109].
Reviews major legislation regarding women enacted by the central legislature of India throughout the 20th century. Points to its minimal impact.

2542 PAPPU, SHYAMALA. Legal provisions: an assessment. *In* Devaki Jain, ed. Indian women. New Delhi: Publications Division, Ministry of Information and Broadcasting, Government of India, 1975. pp.113-24.
Observes that legislation regarding women in India in recent decades has been largely ineffective in promoting change. Criticizes aspects of existing legislation and recommends future alterations.

(c) Law as a profession for women

2543 CHAUDHARY, PAWAN. Women lawyers in a man's world. *In* Social Welfare 19,12 (1973) 2-3, 26-7.
Interviews seven female attorneys about their professional experiences.

2544 MANOHAR, SUJITA. Women lawyers. *In* Illustrated Weekly of India 91,31 (9

Aug 1970) 12-3, 56.
Brief history of women's participation in the legal profession in India; assesses some problems involved and current situation. Photographs.

2545 Women in legal profession (Who's who: law and judiciary). *In* Ajeet Cour and Arpana Cour, eds. Directory of Indian women today, 1976. New Delhi: India International Publications, 1976. pp.214-28, 570-3.
Series of brief biographical sketches. Includes mailing address and, in many cases, photograph.

(14) Political participation

2546 BERREMAN, GERALD D. On the role of women. *In* Bulletin of the Atomic Scientists 22,9 (1966) 26-8.
Anthropologist approaches the problem of why women have occupied the highest political positions in India and Sri Lanka and not in the West despite its older democratic traditions. One conclusion: India and Sri Lanka surpass the West in their regard for the dignity of women as persons.

2547 INDIA (REPUBLIC). COMMITTEE ON THE STATUS OF WOMEN IN INDIA. Political status. *In its* Towards equality: report of the Committee on the Status of Women in India. New Delhi: Department of Social Welfare, Ministry of Education and Social Welfare, Government of India, 1975. pp.283-305. [*Chair* Phulrenu Guha].
Briefly reviews trends in women's political participation in India from the 19th century through independence. Reviews participation trends of female voters and candidates, as gleaned from committee's investigations. Describes trends in political attitudes of women, policies of major political parties in relation to women, role of women in political elite and effectiveness of campaigns to mobilize women. Recommendations include opposition to a policy of reserved seats for women in state assemblies and Parliament.

2548 MAZUMDAR, VINA, ed. Symbols of power: studies on the political status of women in India. Bombay: Allied Publishers, 1979. 373p. SNDT women's University, Bombay; Women in a Changing Society).
Papers are divided into three sections; 1) women and national politics, 2) study of the politicization of women in Gujarat, Maharashtra and West Bengal and 3) profiles of women in state politics. The book is an outcome of a joint research project of the Indian Council of Social Science Research and the Shreemati Nathibai Damodar Thackersey Women's University. [Unexamined].

2549 MENON, LAKSHMI N. Political rights of women in India. *In* A. Appadorai, ed. The status of women in South Asia. Bombay: Orient Longmans, 1954. pp.85-103.
Discusses the rapid and widespread politicization of Indian women in connection with the social reform and nationalist movements and their participation in early post-independent years.

2550 MIES, MARIA. Indian women and leadership. *In* Special issue: Asian women. Guest ed: Phyllis Andors. Bulletin of Concerned Asian Scholars 7,1 (1975) 56-66.
Contrasts two kinds of female leaders: The well-to-do and educated leaders of the nationalist movement emphasized voluntary service and self-sacrifice in keeping with traditional roles. Gandhi was instrumental in glorifying the "ascetic, puritan, brahmanical tradition." Female leaders of and participants in recent peasant revolts, like most women of India, belong to its "little tradition." They suffer economic problems, strive for self-interests and lack the bourgeois ideal exemplified by Sītā. The quality of their activities reflects these characteristics.

2551 Women in politics (Who's who: politicians and statesmen. *In* Ajeet Cour and Arpana Cour, eds. Directory of Indian women today, 1976. New Delhi: India International Publications, 1976. pp.229-77, 573-7.
Series of brief biographical sketches. Includes mailing address and, in many cases, photograph.

(a) National and state levels

2552 AGNEW, VIJAY. Elite women in Indian politics. New Delhi: Vikas, 1979? 163p.
Revision of author's 1976 thesis from the University of Toronto. [Unexamined. ALI].

2552a AHMED, IMTIAZ. Women in politics. *In* Devaki Jain, ed. Indian women. New Delhi: Publications Division, Ministry of Information and Broadcasting, Government of India, 1975. pp.299-312.
Twelve brief case studies from various political levels and areas of India illustrate factors relating to women's political involvement. Numerous conclusions suggest that women generally have a "passive political orientation."

2553 CHANDER, PARKASH. Women members in Lok Sabha. *In* J. of Parliamentary Information 19,1 (1973) 52-74.
"This paper seeks to analyse (i) the causes

for the low representation of women in the Lok Sabha; (ii) the socio-economic background of the women members of the Lok Sabha to determine the strata of society from which they come; and (iii) the experience of public life which they bring with them." Based on biographies, who's whos and other published sources.

2554 DESAI, PADMA and JAGDISH N. BHAGWATI. Women in Indian elections. *In* Jagdish N. Bhagwati et al. Electoral politics in the Indian states: three disadvantaged sectors. Delhi: Manohar Book Service, 1975. pp.165-99. (Studies in Electoral Politics in the Indian States, 2).
Report of exploratory study of female candidates and winners in the 1962 Lok Sabha and 1967 Lok Sabha and Legislative Assembly elections. Considers interstate and interparty differences. Poses numerous provocative questions. Tables present election results. Tribal and postprincely constituencies are the other disadvantaged groups considered in this book.

2555 INDIA (REPUBLIC). INFORMATION SERVICES. Women legislators of India. New Delhi, 1953. 30p. Illustrated. [Unexamined. IOL].

2556 INDIAN NATIONAL CONGRESS. ALL INDIA CONGRESS COMMITTEE. WOMEN'S DEPARTMENT. Women and the elections. New Delhi, 1956. 11p.
[Unexamined. NUC].

2557 KOGEKAR, S.V. Role of women in the general elections in India, 1951-52. *In* A. Appadorai, ed. The status of women in South Asia. Bombay: Orient Longmans, 1954. pp.104-14.
Discusses absence of women's issues in party platforms, apathy of women's organizations in electoral matters following independence, high urban participation rate, small number of female candidates and voting patterns.

2558 MEHTA, USHA. Women and the elections. *In* Indian J. of Political Science 23,4 (1962) 371-9.
Summarizes the history of Indian women's franchise and candidates and voting behavior in the 1957 and 1962 elections.

2559 NIMBKAR, KRISHNABAI. A political dissenter's diary, 1970-1978. Pune: International Book Service, 1978-79. 2v.
[Unexamined. ALI].

i) Indian National Congress

2560 INDIAN NATIONAL CONGRESS. ALL INDIA CONGRESS COMMITTEE. WOMEN'S DEPARTMENT. Constructive programme for women: a handbook. New Delhi, 1956. 60p.
[Unexamined. NUC].

2561 ________. Women's wing of the Congress. New Delhi, 1958. 12p.
[Unexamined. NUC].

2562 Women on the March. v1- (1957-). New Delhi: Women's Department, All India Congress Committee, Indian National Congress. Monthly.
Miscellaneous Indian National Congress news items, along with other political and social welfare topics. Not entirely regarding women.

ii) Communist Party of India

2563 CHAKRABORTY, RENU. Communist Party and status of women. *In* New Age 22, 39 (29 Sep 1974) 11.
[Unexamined].

(b) Women's movements and women's liberation: socialist and other perspectives

2564 ALL-INDIA CONFERENCE ON WOMEN, 1975, TRIVANDRUM. Women of India. *In* Social Scientist 4,7 (1976) 57-69.
Conclusions from the conference about economic and social exploitation and the women's movement, with a set of immediate demands. Conference was organized by the Indian School of Social Sciences.

2565 BELOK, MICHAEL V., ed. Women: an international perspective. Meerut; Anu Prakashan, 1977? 118p.
Articles on feminism in India, Canada, Russia and the United States. [Unexamined. ALI].

2566 CHANDRAN, VICTORIA M. In Christ no male or female. *In* Ecumenical Review 27,2 (1975) 134-8.
Indian Christian woman argues that "it cannot be said that the Church continues to take a pioneering role in women's liberation" in India and elsewhere.

2567 CHATTOPADHYAYA, KAMALADEVI. Social disabilities of women. *In* B.N. Ganguli, ed. Social development: essays in honour of Smt. Durgabai Deshmukh. New Delhi: Sterling Publishers, 1977. pp.85-90.
Veteran of the Indian women's movement reflects upon trends of the worldwide women's movement of today. She criticizes women's anger at men (for women themselves have often been the strongest supporters of the status quo), women's willingness to compete and concern themselves with quantitative issues and their adoption of male mannerisms, appearance, etc. A central task before India is to make

women of the masses aware of "their own identity, the significance of their special role in the family and society, the rights they enjoy under the prevailing laws of the land."

2568 A CORRESPONDENT. Marxist cobwebs. *In* Economic and Political Weekly 11,8 (21 Feb 1976) 304-6.
Report of the Communist Part of India's All-India Conference on Women sponsored by the Indian School of Social Sciences and held at Trivandrum in December 1975. Reviews papers and evaluates proceedings from political point of view. Considers the oppression of women and potential for action.

2569 DESHPANDE, DINKAR YASHWANT. Women, family, and socialism. Bombay: Hind Kitabs, 1948. 65p.
Social and moral questions relating to women. [Unexamined. NUC].

2570 LATEEF, SHAHIDA. Whither Indian women's movement? *In* Economic and Political Weekly 12,47 (19 Nov 1977) 1948-51.
Briefly examines the history of the Indian women's movement; argues that the gains in public life enjoyed by Indian women were fought for and won by women themselves. Asserts that Indian women in more recent decades have too readily yielded responsibility for preservation of their rights to institutions of state and society.

2571 MAHINDRA, INDIRA. Is this liberation? *In* Eve's Weekly 30,31-2 and 34-7 (31 Jul-7 Aug and 21 Aug-11 Sep 1976) 16-7, 11-3, 20-1, 20ff, 11-3, 14-5ff.
Six-part series on problems faced by contemporary women. Titles are: "Marriage or Bonded Labour?" "A Woman's Right over Her own Body," "Women are Willing Victims," "Divided and Ruled," "The Ma-Bahen Syndrome" and "The American Woman and her Cross."

2572 Manushi. Issue 1- (1979-). New Delhi: [Manushi Trust?] Bimonthly.
New journal of a feminist collective in New Delhi. The title awkwardly translates as "Female Person." The collective aims to present a variety of perspectives on sex roles, primarily in India. Features include short stories and poems as well as nonfiction. A simultaneous Hindi edition is published with minor variations (e.g., book reviews). [Unexamined].

2573 OMVEDT, GAIL. Caste, class and women's liberation in India. *In* Bulletin of Concerned Asian Scholars 7,1 (1975) 43-8. [*Reprint in* Manorama Barnabas, S.K. Hulbe and P.S. Jacob, eds. Challenges of societies in transition. Delhi: Macmillan Company of India, 1978. pp.238-52].
Argues that: 1) Indian women have greatly benefitted from the nationalist and social reform movements, 2) the tradition of independence among low-caste women is important to their liberation, 3) the greatest barriers to the full liberation of women lie in socioeconomic inequalities and 4) western impact has been neutral at best.

2574 ________. College girls. *In* Frontier 8,26/27 (8/15 Nov 1975) 11-5.
Addresses problem of why militant middle-class women have not emerged as leaders to organize rural women workers in India. In general, students and teachers have "no innate emotional identification with women for whom work is a necessity. But . . . large numbers of middle class women are beginning to feel that a life which revolves around rituals and vows and cooking . . . is not really a full human life . . . . And in this discontent and questioning lie the seeds of broader unity."

2575 ________. Women and rural revolt in India. *In* South Asia Papers 1,4/5 (1977) 1-59. [*Also* Irvine, California: Program in Comparative Culture, University of California, Irvine, 1978. 65p. (Occasional Papers, 6)].
Discusses a recent, developing militant women's movement involving working-class and poor peasant women and middle-class and peasant students. Examines factors underlying women's work participation and changing modes of agricultural production.

2576 ________. On the participant study of women's movements: methodological, definitional and action considerations. *In* Gerritt Huizen, ed. The politics of anthropology. The Hague: Mouton, forthcoming.
Numerous observations and propositions about the understanding of women's movements in general and particular observations relating to the author's experiences in India. She asserts that, contrary to the common picture, many Indian women feel they are oppressed: "I found . . . occasional outbursts of outrage against the continuous bondage to housework; expressions of hardly concealed pride among lowcaste women about their ability to 'break' orthodox norms about remarriage and affairs with men; nearly universal hostility to the dowry system but an almost equally universal sense of helplessness." [Manuscript examined].

2577 ________ and CHAYA DATAR. Women in India. *In* Black Struggle 2,1 (1977). [Unexamined].

2578 Special number on women. Social Scientist 4,4/5 (1975) 160p.
Contents: "Perspective of the Women's Movement" by E.M.S. Namboodiripad, "Women's Liberation and Productive Activity" by Manorama Savur, "Patriarchal Capitalism and the Female-headed Family" by Carol A. Brown, "Rural Origins of Women's Liberation in India" by Gail Omvedt, "Women Office Workers: Petty-bourgeoisie or New Proletarians?" by Martin Oppenheimer, "Towards Emancipation" by Mythily Shivaraman, "Employment, Incomes and Equality" by Kumaresh Chakravarty, "Status of Women in India: A Historical Perspective" by Sophie M. Tharakan and Michael Tharakan, "Problems of Working Women in Urban Areas" by Wandana

Sonalkar, "Literacy: Doorway to Liberation" by Aleyamma George, "Working-class Women" by Vimla Randive and "Sex Discrimination in Work and Wages" by Leela Gulati.

2579 Stree Vimukti. vl- (1974?-). Hyderabad?: Progressive Organization of Women.
The Progressive Organization of Women (POW) has fought against dowry, price increases, "eve-teasing" and other matters of concern to women. Established in June 1974, their headquarters are in Hyderabad-Secunderabad. The title of their journal means "Women's Liberation." [Unexamined].

(15) Fine, folk and performing arts

2580 APPASAMY, JAYA. Modern Indian women and the visual arts. *In* Indian Horizons 24,4 (1975) 30-4.
Considers problems of contemporary artists. Names some prominent female artists and their media. Several plates.

2581 Kala Jyoti. vl- (1962-). Patiala: Government Art and Craft Teachers Training Institute for Women. Annually.
[Unexamined. IPP].

2582 KHOSLA, G.D. Pornography and censorship in India. New Delhi: Indian Book Company, 1976. 168p.
Examines criteria for obscenity in art and literature in the context of erotic themes in classical Indian thought, literature and art. Discusses findings of social science, legal and other considerations.

2583 KOHLI, SURESH, ed. Sex and violence in literature and arts. New Delhi: Sterling Publishers, 1973. 110p.
Contents: "The Perspective" by Suresh Kohli, "Thoughts on Controversial Books" by Prabhakar Machwe, "Obscenity and Literature" by Kamala Das, "Sex in Indian Cinema" (with photographs) by K.L. Arora, "Violence in Indian Cinema" by Jag Mohan, "Towards a Mood in Bengali Literature" by Aditya Sen, "One Man's Cry in Hindi Literature" by Shrikant Verma, "Sex and Violence in Punjabi and Urdu Literatures" by K.S. Duggal, "Tradition and Change in South Indian Languages" by K.P.R. Pillai and "Sensuousness in Indian Artistic Tradition" by Kapila Vatsyayan.

2584 MARWAH, MALA. Women as practioner of art. *In* Link 18,1 (15 Aug 1975) 95-7.
Notes some relatively rare references to female artists in texts such as the ***Arthaśāstra*** and the ***Mahābhārata***. Mentions some contemporary notable female artists in India, their media, their styles and the problems they have faced.

2585 RAIZADA, R.K. Khajuraho in dollar market: socio-legal appraisal of obscenity. *In* J. of the Indian Law Institute 13,2 (1971) 208-19.
Argues that erotic sculpture, literature and cults of ancient and medieval India, if understood in their social contexts, are not obscene and have been misrepresented in contemporary commercial enterprises. Argues, citing the Enquiry Committee on Film Censorship, that young minds are particularly apt to be influenced by films. Urges legal regulation. Compares media exploitation of women as sex objects to prostitution. "In judging the quality of any object we may ask: has the author, painter, carver or sculptor worked for *the love of his art* or with commercial objectives?"

2586 RUKMINI DEVI [RUKMINI DEVI ARUNDALE]. "Woman as artist." *In* Shyam Kumari Nehru, ed. Our cause: a symposium by Indian women. Allahabad: Kitabistan, 1938? pp.113-20.
Considers woman's unique grace, compassion and refinement to be creative, liberating powers. ". . . only as women regain their power as artists and inspirers, only as women express all that is truest and most beautiful in womanhood, will men themselves regain their own manhood and nobility, and all the world emerge from darkness and unhappiness."

2587 TYABJI, RAIHANA. Music or Brahmanāda. *In* Evelyn C. Gedge and Mithan Choksi, eds. Women in modern India: fifteen papers by Indian women writers. Bombay: D.B. Taraporewala Sons and Company, 1929. pp.116-23. [*Reprint* Westport, Connecticut: Hyperion Press, 1976. (Pioneers of the Women's Movement)].
Speculates that women must have been involved in music traditions of the past and reviews their participation in a "musical revival" following a period of stagnation under western influence. Urges widespread music education for girls and acceptance of music as a legitimate means of livelihood for women.

2588 Women in the fine arts (Who's who: artists). *In* Ajeet Cour and Arpana Cour, eds. Directory of Indian women today, 1976. New Delhi: India International Publications, 1976. pp.13-52, 533-44.
Series of brief biographical sketches. Includes mailing address and, in many cases, photograph.

(a) Classical dance forms and performers

i) Forms

2589 AMBROSE, KAY. Classical dances and costumes of India. London: Adam and Charles Block, 1950. 95p.
Includes discussion of the ***bhārata nāṭyam*** ren-

aissance. Describes the elements of ***bhārata nāṭyam*** and has material on other classical dance forms relating to India. Photos and drawings.

2590 Bharata natyam. 1951. 11 min. Black and white. 16 mm. [***Distributed by*** University of California, Extension Media Center, Berkeley, California 94720].
Two dance segments by leading performers, with explanation of chief elements. [Unexamined. NUC].

2591 Bharata natyam. Mārg 10,4 (1957) 58p.
Issue devoted to the ***bhārata nāṭyam*** dance form. Articles discuss spiritual and historical background, guru genealogies, particular performers, musical accompaniment, "dance-units," related dance forms and dance representations in sculpture. Many drawings and photographs.

2592 Bharat Natyam. 1956. 13 min. Color. 16 and 35 mm. [***Distributed by*** Films Division, Ministry of Information and Broadcasting, 24 G. Deshmukh Marg, Bombay 400 026].
Narration of this film explains the chief characteristics of ***bhārata nāṭyam*** and dancer Kamala demonstrates. [Unexamined. CF].

2593 Classical Indian dances. ***In*** Illustrated Weekly of India 84,46-50 and 52; 85,1 (17-24 Nov and 1-15 and 29 Dec 1963 and 5 Jan 1964) 40-51, 8-13, 36-43, 40-3, 32-5, 44-9, 12-3.
Series reviews classical dance forms. Has interviews with and photographs of numerous female performers and considers the temple dancing tradition.

2594 RAGINI DEVI. Dance dialects of India. Delhi: Vikas Publications, 1972. 227p.
Surveys classical and folk dance forms. The author, who was central to the revival of ***kathakalī*** and ***bhārata nāṭyam,*** includes some autobiographical material. Of special note are two chapters: "The Devadasis of South India" and "Bharata Natya: the Dance of the Devadasis." Illustrated.

ii) Life and work of performers

2595 AGRAWAL, CHANDRA P. Sitara in Kathak. ***In*** New Quest 2 (Aug 1977) 47-9.
Briefly discusses Sitara's ***kathak*** style and its roots. Relates her incorporation of energetic themes and movements into her style as opposed to delicate ones to family influence and place of origin, particularly to her mother's worship of ***Śākta*** images and to the cultural traditions of Nepal and Calcutta.

2596 ASMI, SALEEM. Memoirs of a dancing queen. ***In*** The Herald [Karachi] 9,7 (1978) 37-41.
Madam Auzurie recalls her passion for dancing despite the disapproval of the general public and her father. She describes her career in films, her marriage to a Muslim man (her father was German Catholic and her mother South Indian brahman). Comments negatively on the state of dance in today's Pakistani films. Photographs.

2597 Balasaraswathi. By John Frazier. 1963. 20 min. Color. 16 mm. [***Distributed by*** Center for Arts, Wesleyan University, Middletown, Connecticut 06457].
Film of an early 1960s performance by one of India's leading ***bhārata nāṭyam*** artists. [Unexamined].

2598 BEDI, FREDA. Rukmini Devi Arundale. ***In*** March of India 8,9 (1956) 8-12.
Biographical sketch. Illustrated. [Unexamined].

2599 BOWERS, FAUBION. Shanta Rao: "India's mysterious dancer-genius." ***In*** Vogue 152,10 (1968) 218-25, 281-2.
Provides details of Shanta Rao's biography, her attitudes toward her work and South Indian dance forms. Text is preceded by a color photo essay by Arnaud de Rosnay.

2600 CHANDRASEKHARAN, K. Studies and sketches. Madras: S. Viswanathan, 1950? 94p.
Includes biographical sketches of dancers Balasaraswati and Rukmini Devi Arundale. [Unexamined. Book in NUC].

2601 DE KLEEN, TYRA. Menaka and Indian dancing. ***In*** Ethnos 2,2 (1937) 47-55.
Regarding the first "genuine Indian danseuse" to give "an exhibition of genuine Indian dancing" in Europe. Discusses Menaka's (Leilavati Sokhey's) style and interest in promoting a dance renaissance in India. Includes her photograph and a survey of some basic hand and body movements.

2602 DE ZOETE, BERYL. Bharata natyam, part II: Balasaraswati. ***And*** Bharata natyam, part III: Shanta. ***In her*** The other mind: a study of dance in South India. New York: Theatre Art Books, 1960. pp.180-211.
Portraits of two famous ***bhārata nāṭyam*** dancers, the second of which includes an autobiographical account of the strenuous training required.

2603 HALL, FERNAU. Close-up of Shanta Rao. ***In*** Dance Magazine 29,6 (1955) 26-33, 76-9.
Comments on classical dance and reviews Shanta Rao's US performance in April 1955. Illustrated. [Unexamined].

2604 Heartbeat. Produced by Shanti Varma. Directed by K. Vishwanath. 1973. 30 min. Black and white. 16 mm. [***Distributed by*** Films Division, Ministry of Information and Broadcasting, 24 G. Deshmukh Marg, Bombay 400 026].
Film. Depicts a European modern dancer, Vija Vetra, in ***bhārata nāṭyam*** performances, both traditional and with music of Vivaldi and Bach. Miss Vetra studied under the renowned Chowkalingam Pillai. [Unexamined].

2605 NARAYAN, SHOVANA. Sadhona Bose: end of a long quest. *In* Lipika 2,3/4 (1973) 29-35, 56.
Memorial tribute to the life and work of a great classical dancer from Bengal. With photographs. "Sadhonaji had a vast knowledge of all the classical dances, namely, Bharatnatyam, Kathakali, Manipuri and Kathak. She had also experimented and adapted steps and techniques of the western dance to Indian classical style. Her significant achievement was in choreographing all the styles together."

2606 NARAYANA MENON. Balasaraswati. New Delhi: Inter-national Cultural Centre, 1963? 23p.
Brief descriptions of the ***bhārata nāṭyam*** dance tradition and Balasaraswati's life and work. Includes her genealogy and photographs of her in performance.

2607 Sitara Devi, Nritya Samrajnee, kathak dance of India. Gramophone Company of India EALP 1260.
Recording of Sitara Devi dancing. Choube Maharaj plays ***tablā***. [Unexamined].

2608 VENKATACHALAM, GOVINDRAJ. Srimati Shanta, Bharata Natyam: Srimati Shanta and her art. Bangalore: Hosali Press, 1944. 102p.
On the great ***bhārata nāṭyam*** dancer, her medium and related dance forms. Includes a list of her repertoire and a letter of praise from her teacher. Illustrated. [Unexamined. BMG].

2609 ________. Dance in India. Bombay: Nalanda Publications, 194_. 131p.
Brief sketches and photographs of performers, including Balasaraswati, Rukmini Devi, Shanta Rao, Menaka, Shrimati Hutheesing and Sadhona Bose. Brief historical sketches of several dance forms.

(b) Classical vocalists

i) Life and work of performers

2610 ASMI, SALEEM. Roshan Ara Begum talks of her visit to India. *In* The Herald [Karachi] 9,5 (1978) 39-42.
Interview with Roshan Ara Begam about her first trip to India since leaving to live with her husband's family in Pakistan 30 years before. She speaks of her life and work at home in Lala Musa. Photographs.

2611 Begum Akhtar. Produced through Issar Films, Bombay. 1971. 17 min. Black and white. 16 and 35 mm. [***Distributed by*** Films Division, Ministry of Information and Broadcasting, 24 G. Deshmukh Marg, Bombay 400 026].
Scenes from the life of the "Ghazal and Thumri Queen." Shows her at home and in performance. [Unexamined. CF].

2612 CHITRE, DILIP. The loss of Kesarbai. *In* New Quest 5 (Dec 1977) 62-4.
Memorial tribute to Kesarbai Kerkar, the last classical vocalist from the North Indian Antrauli school. Characterizes her as a woman who "sang on her own terms [and] ridiculed her critics and detractors." She rarely performed for a "public she considered mediocre" and perhaps did not have disciples to carry on her tradition as she "terrified" them.

2613 GANAPATI, R. M.S. and her world of music. *In* Bhavan's Journal 22,7 (26 Oct 1975) 146-57.
Interview with M.S. Subbulakshmi about her background, training, film career, conception of art, achievements and other topics: Photographs and paintings.

2614 HYDER, QURRATULAIN. Sheila Dhar. *In* Illustrated Weekly of India 97,5 (1 Feb 1976) 21, 23.
Brief biographical sketch of a vocalist renowned for her performance of classical Hindustani *ghazals*.

2615 JAGANNATHAN, MATHILY. Mathily Jagannathan talks to Siddeshwari Devi, the queen of "thumri." *In* Lipika 2,1 (1973) 16-19, 32.
Interview with Siddeshwari Devi, an accomplished singer of classical and light classical song forms and 1966 recipient of the Sangeet Natak Akademi award. About her life and her art.

2616 MALHOTRA, L.K. Begum Akhtar: random thoughts and personal reminiscences. *In* Sangeet Natak 37 (Jul 1975) 16-20.
Author, an acquaintance of nearly three decades, recalls Begam Akhtar's five-year break from performance following her marriage and his involvement in her reemergence as a performer. He describes her attachment to home and family in spite of fame and travels and recounts anecdotes.

2617 SURYA, REKHA. 'The Living Legend' becomes a legend: a tribute. *In* Sangeet Natak 37 (Jul 1975) 21-4.
Discusses Begam Akhtar's style, technique and repertoire. Photographs.

ii) Selected recordings

2618 Begum Akhtar. Gramophone Company of India ECSD 2374.
Begam Akhtar sings four selections with ***tablā*** accompaniment. [Unexamined].

2619 Begum Akhtar: in memorium. Gramophone Company of India ECSD 2741. [***Distributed by*** Peters International, Inc., 619 West 54th Street, New York, New

York 10019]. [Unexamined. Verified with distributor].

2620 Begum Akhtar sings Ghalib, Urdu. Gramophone Company of India ECSD 2399.
Eight Urdu ***ghazals***. [Unexamined].

2621 In concert from her American tour, M.S. Subbulakshmi. World-Pacific Records WPS 21463.
Accompanied by violin, ***mṛdaṅga*** and ***ghaṭa***. [Unexamined].

2622 Lata Mangeshkar sings Ghalib, Urdu. Gramophone Company of India ECSD 2426. [***Distributed by*** Peters International, Inc., 619 West 54th Street, New York, New York 10019].
Ghazals? [Unexamined. Verified with distributor].

2623 Nirmala Devi and Lakshmi Shankar. Gramophone Company of India ECLP 2350.
Thumarī selections: two duets and two solos. ***Tablā*** accompaniment. [Unexamined].

2624 Nirmala Devi and Lakshmi Shankar, Sawan Beeta Jaye. Gramophone Company of India ECLP 2317.
Thumarī selections: two duets and two solos. ***Tablā*** accompaniment. [Unexamined].

2625 Roshan Ara Begum sings. Gramophone Company of India CLP 1530.
Roshan Ara Begam sings two ***rāgas***. [Unexamined].

2626 Sanskrit recitation, devotional: M.S. Subbulakshmi. Gramophone Company of India ECLP 2293.
M.S. Subbulakshmi sings devotional music accompanied by ***mṛdaṅga*** and violin. [Unexamined].

2627 Smt. M.S. Subbulakshmi: Bhaja Govindam, Vishnu Sahasranamam. 8-track tape, no. 8P.F.I.-6166. [***Distributed by*** Peters International, Inc., 619 West 54th Street, New York, New York 10019].
M.S. Subbulakshmi sings two ***Vaiṣṇava*** devotional songs. [Unexamined. Verified with distributor].

2628 The sounds of Subbulakshmi, recorded in concert at Vasanta Vihar, Madras, 30 December 1965. World-Pacific Records WPS 21440/WS 21440.
M.S. Subbulakshmi sings five Karnatak devotional compositions accompanied by ***mṛdaṅga***. [Unexamined].

2629 A tribute to Ustad Abdul Karim Khan. Gramophone Company of India CLP 1514.
Roshan Ara Begam sings two ***rāgas***. [Unexamined].

2630 The voice of Lakshmi Shankar. World-Pacific Records WPS 21461. ***And*** Gramophone Company of India ECSD 2391.
Lakshmi Shankar sings Hindustani ***rāgas***. Accompanied by ***tablā*** and ***tāraśahanāī***. [Unexamined].

2631 With Smt. Radha Viswanathan: music recital by M.S. Subbulakshmi at the United Nations on Sunday, 23 October 1966. Gramophone Company of India MOAE 5001-3. 3 disc set.
These two accomplished female vocalists sing selections primarily from the South Indian musical tradition. They are accompanied by South Indian instruments: ***mṛdaṅga***, violin and ***ghaṭa***. A booklet included with the set describes the selections and instruments and gives biographies and photographs of the performers. [Unexamined].

(c) Life and work of painters

2632 ALI, S. AMJAD. Women artists of Pakistan. ***In*** Pakistan Quarterly 10,1 (1960) 49-56.
Comments on major exhibitions by female painters of Pakistan in 1960. Gives short biographical sketches and notes on works of Anna Molka Ahmed, Zakia Mallick, Anwar Afzal, Razia Feroz, Zubeida Agha, Naz Ikramullah, Abbasi Akhtar, Begam Noon and Atiya Hasan. Photographs of artists and selected works.

2633 THAKUR SINGH, S.G. Paintings of Indian womanhood. Amritsar: Thakur Singh School of Arts, [1971]. 22 plates.
Mounted color plates of single female figures or, in several cases, a pair of women. They are shown in the course of everyday activities — bathing, daydreaming, worshipping, adorning themselves and so forth. They were done in the 1920s and early 1930s.

i) Zubeida Agha

2634 IKRAM AZAM, R.M. Zubaida Agha: radio talk. ***In*** Pakistan Review 11,4 (1963) 24-7.
A short overview of her life and work, stressing her belief that "the distinction between life and art does not exist." Demonstrates how the world view of this "rebel" artist is reflected in her work. Reproduces four of her works.

2635 TASEER, CHRISTABLE. Zubeida Agha. ***In*** Pakistan Quarterly 2,2 (1952) 56-9, 61.
Short treatment of the life and work of Pakistani painter and sculptor Zubeida Agha. She is compared to the post-impressionists, seeing beauty in line, color and form. Photographs of her works.

ii) Amrita Sher-Gil

2636 Amrita Sher Gil. Produced and directed by B.D. Garga. 1969. 19 min. Color. 16 and 35 mm. [*Distributed by* Films Division, Ministry of Information and Broadcasting, 24 G. Deshmukh Marg, Bombay 400 026].
Examines the work, somber in tone, of an early modern painter of India. Sher-Gil was the daughter of an Indian mother and a Hungarian father. [Unexamined. CF].

2637 Amrita Sher-Gil. Guest eds: Geeta Kapur, Vivan Sundaram and Gulam Mohammad Sheikh. Mārg 25,2 (1972) 72p. [*Also* Vivan Sundaram et al. Amrita Sher-Gil. Bombay: Marg Publications, 1972? 144p.].
Both the special *Mārg* issue and the book contain "Introduction" by Geeta Kapur, "Amrita Sher-Gil: Life and Work" by Vivan Sundaram, "The Evolution of Content in Amrita Sher-Gil's Paintings" by Geeta Kapur, a chronology of the artist's life, "Amrita Sher-Gil: Dialectics of Academicism and Pictorial Situation of Traditional Indian Art" by Gulam Mohammed Sheikh, "Amrita Sher-Gil and the East-West Dilemma" by K.G. Subramanyan and 71 photographs and reproductions. In addition, the book contains a list of Sher-Gil's paintings, selected statements by various persons on her life and work, selections from her correspondence and several brief articles by Sher-Gil on art, Indian art and her art.

2638 HYDER, QURRATULAIN. A portrait of the artist as a young woman: Amrita Sher-Gil, her life and times. *In* Illustrated Weekly of India 93,47 (19 Nov 1972) 21-5.
Variety of details suggesting the complexity of Sher-Gil's life: her family background, personality, career as an artist, artistic inspirations, etc. With two photographs of her and reproductions of six paintings and a drawing.

2639 KHANDALAVALA, KARL J. Amrita Sher-Gil. Bombay: New Book Company, 1944. 71p.
Concerns artist's life and work. With 28 plates of works done in Hungary and India. [Unexamined. NUC].

2639a Sher-Gil. [New Delhi]: Lalik Kalā Akademi, [1965]. 25 plates. (Contemporary Series of Indian Art).
Reproductions of 25 paintings in black and white and color. Brief anecdotal introduction by a childhood playmate who became reacquainted with the artist in adulthood.

(d) Folk art forms

2640 Helping the human hand. *In* Eve's Weekly 32,33 (19 Aug 1978) 8-11.
Reviews contributions of twelve women who have been instrumental in preserving, promoting and reviving Indian handicraft traditions. Photographs.

2641 JAYAKAR, PUPUL. Handicrafts. *In* Tara Ali Baig, ed. Women of India. Delhi: Publications Division, Ministry of Information and Broadcasting, Government of India, 1958. pp.208-16.
Surveys the handicrafts practiced by rural Indian women. With brief statements on the place of handicrafts in Indian civilization and contemporary patterns of change. Photographs.

2642 KRAMRISCH, STELLA. The art ritual of women. *In her* Unknown India: ritual art in tribe and village. Philadelphia: Falcon Press, 1968. pp.65-70.
Catalog from a 1968 exhibit. Discusses ritual diagrams, *kānthā* embroidered cloths (primarily from area that is now Bangladesh) and wall paintings from Mithila, northern Bihar. Includes black and white and color plates.

i) Domestic ritual designs

2643 BONNERJEA, BIREN. India, ritual designs: note on geometrical ritual designs in India. *In* Man 33,168 (1933) 163-4.
Short article suggests the broad geographical range of domestic ritual designs in India and proposes some questions for future investigators.

2644 Rangoli. Produced by Mushir Ahmad. Directed by Dilip Jamdar. 1968. 16 min. Color. 16 and 35 mm. [*Distributed by* Films Division, Ministry of Information and Broadcasting, 24 G. Deshmukh Marg, Bombay 400 026].
Documents technique and forms of auspicious floor and ground designs created by women in various areas of India. Shows aspects of women's ritual activities but gives little interpretation of ethnographic and symbolic significance. [Unexamined. CF].

2645 SAKSENA, JOGENDRA. Mandana: the heritage of the Rajasthani woman. *And* Mandana art: a case for preservation and revival. *In* Shakti 1 (Jan and Mar 1965) 24-7, 31-5.
Regarding the ritual designs created by rural women. First article discusses various contexts for creating such figures, certain motifs used and various factors associated with the decline of the art. Provides two examples and lists names of comparable figures in other areas of India. Second article discusses the decline of rural women's folk arts in general and proposes various programs designed to reverse the trend.

ii) Henna hand and foot designs

2646 BHANAWAT, MAHENDRA. Menhadi rang rachi: folkloric study of colourful myrtle. Udaipur: Bhartiya Lok-Kala Mandal, 1976. 64p. (*Its* Granthawali, 35).
The ethnography of ***meṃhadī***, designs dyed on women's hands and feet with henna in conjunction with festive occasions. Topics include history, cultivation of the plant, paste-making procedure, styles and designs, application, ***meṃhadī*** use by Muslims and related proverbs and folk songs. With numerous drawings of ***meṃhadī*** designs.

2647 VINEŚA, M.B. Meṃhadī race mere hātha: beautiful palm paintings. Jayapura: Pramukha Vikretā Vāṇī Mandira, 19__-. vI-.
Collection of palm and sole designs, which women paint in connection with festive occasions. Hindi introduction discusses historical significance. Apparently at least three volumes are available. [Unexamined. ALI].

iii) Embroidery traditions

2648 CHANDRA, JAGDISH, comp. Embroidery. *In his* Bibliography of Indian art, history and archaeology, vI: Indian art. Delhi: Delhi Printers Prakashan, 1978. pp.246-8.
Sixty-eight references to survey materials and those relating to several particular embroidery traditions.

2649 CHATTOPADHYAYA, KAMALADEVI. Indian embroidery. New Delhi: Wiley Eastern Limited, 1977. 76p.
Illustrations (some in color) and brief discussions of distinctive technical and stylistic features of embroidery traditions in various regions of India. Except in Kashmir, these traditions are almost exclusively practiced by women.

2650 DONGERKERY, KAMALA S. The Romance of Indian embroidery. Bombay: Thacker and Company, 1951. 62p.
Elsewhere the author states that this book "deals with the cultural, aesthetic and traditional aspects of Indian embroidery." Plates. [Unexamined. MRL].

2651 ________. Traditional embroidery of India. New Delhi: Ministry of Commerce and Industry, Government of India, 1961-63. 2 parts.
Companions to her ***Romance of Indian Embroidery***, these volumes deal with practical aspects of instructing embroiderers in essentials of various embroidery traditions (stitches, materials, motifs, etc.) in order to preserve these traditions. Illustrative sketches and color photographs of finished works.

2652 Painting with the needle. Guest eds: Kamaladevi Chattopadhyaya and Jasleen Dhamija. Mārg 17,2 (1964) 72p.
Embroidery issue. See: "Origin and Development of Embroidery in our Land" by Kamaladevi Chattopadhyaya, "The Survey of Embroidery Traditions" edited by Jasleen Dhamija and "Place of Embroidery in Indian Crafts" by Kamala Dongerkery. Texts focus upon the feminine nature of the craft. Extensively illustrated.

iv) Folk dance traditions

2653 BANERJI, PROJESH. The folk-dance of India. Allahabad: Kitabistan, 1944. 129p.
Surveys male and female folk dance genres and events, by province, in prepartition India.

2654 VATSYAYAN, KAPILA. Traditions of Indian folk dance. New Delhi: Indian Book Company, 1976? 280p.
Inventory of folk dance forms, by region. Discusses context, musical accompaniment, gender of performers and other topics. Five-page bibliography of ethnographic and other sources for folk dance material. Photos.

v) Folk literature

2655 BALOCH, N.A. Folk-literature of West Pakistan. *In* Perspective 1,5 (1967) 49-56.
Compares (primarily women's) folk traditions from East and West Pakistan, showing their great similarity due to the common Islamic cultural heritage. Lists names of numerous folk forms and their regions. With some examples, translated into English.

2656 SEN GUPTA, SANKAR, ed. Women in Indian folklore: a short survey of their social status and position: linguistic and religious study. Calcutta: Indian Publications, 1969. 327p. (*Its* Folklore Series, 15).
Twenty-six brief articles on the portrayal of women in various regional folklore traditions and religious communities. Originally published in the journal ***Folklore*** from Calcutta. For contents see entries 39, 99, 111, 427, 1807, 1892, 3339, 3341-2, 3345, 3531, 3592, 3737, 3740, 3751, 3793-5, 3797, 3947, 4192-3, 4195, 4323, 4333 and 4337.

(16) Mass media and literary arts

2657 DESAI, NEERA, ed. The trends of change: studies on media response to the women's movement. Bombay: Allied Publishers, forthcoming. SNDT Women's University, Bombay; Women in a Changing Society).
Papers sponsored jointly by the Indian Council of Social Science Research and Shreemati Nathibai Damodar Thackersey Women's University. [Unexamined].

2658 INDIA (REPUBLIC). COMMITTEE ON THE STATUS OF WOMEN IN INDIA. The role and influence of the mass media on the status of women. *In its* Toward equality: report of the Committee on the Status of Women in India. New Delhi: Department of Social Welfare, Ministry of Education and Social Welfare, Government of India, 1975. pp.347-53. [*Chair* Phulrenu Guha].
Examines various media — the press, radio, television, literature, youth magazines and films — with respect to images of women, influence on audience as whole and influence on women. Proposes creation of an autonomous commission to gather and evaluate relevant information and recommend and implement policy.

2659 PAKISTAN. INFORMATION AND BROADCASTING DIVISION. Women writers and artists. *In its* Women of Pakistan. Islamabad: Information and Broadcasting Division, Directorate of Research, Reference and Publications, Government of Pakistan, 1975. pp.63-88.
Photo essay. Text notes the accomplishments of numerous Mughal women and the subsequent decline in the scholarship of Muslim women of the subcontinent. "Only the rise of Muslim nationalism stirred, once again, the talent that had remained dormant behind the veil." Mentions Muslim women's educational efforts and journalistic activities associated with this renaissance. Notes prominent writers of novels, short stories, poetry and plays. Discusses prominent painters, actresses, producers, directors, singers and television and radio personalities.

2660 Women and the reluctant media. *In* Vidura 13,1 (1976) 1-64.
Partial contents: "Women, Development and the Press" by Vina Mazumdar, "Where is the Communication Gap?" by Rami Chhabra, "Woman Reporter" by Prabha Dutt, "How newsworthy are Women? A Study of Sunday Newspapers, 1975" by Shibani Dasgupta, "Women's Magazines and Social Purpose" by Vidya Bal, "What are Women's Magazines About?" by Malavika Karlekar, "Change at A.I.R.?" by Rosalind Wilson, "Advertising and Women" by K.S. Srinivasan, "Women in Indian Films" by Vijaya Mulay, "Textbooks and Sexist Messages" (no author given) and "Source List for Reporters: Information about Women." Other papers discuss similar issues as they relate to the US and France. From a 1976 seminar on the role of media in changing attitudes and practices relating to women.

2661 Writers and journalists (Who's who: writers and journalists). *In* Ajeet Cour and Arpana Cour, eds. Directory of Indian women today, 1976. New Delhi: India International Publications, 1976. pp.489-519, 602-17.
Series of brief biographical sketches. Includes mailing address and, in many cases, photograph.

(a) Women and the film industry

i) Opportunities and problems for actresses and others

2662 Helen: queen of the nautch girls. Produced by Ismail Merchant. Directed by Anthony Kramer. 1972. 30 min. Color. 35 mm. [*Distributed by* New Yorker Films, 43 West 61st St., New York, New York 10023].
Documentary film about Helen and her career as a prominent dancer in Bombay's film industry (over 500 films). She is the daughter of a Burmese mother and an English father. [Unexamined].

2663 MEHTA, VINOD. Meena Kumari. Bombay: Jaico Publishing House, 1972. 187p.
From the jacket: ". . . first serious biography of a great film star . . . . In search of material [Mehta] visited the dingy chawl where she grew up, the flats and mansions where she lived, the studios where she acted, the hospital where she died, the cemetery where she was buried. He talked to everyone close to her."

2664 MUNSHI, LILAVATI. Women and film industry. *In* Shyam Kumari Nehru, ed. Our cause: a symposium by Indian women. Allahabad: Kitabistan, 1938? pp.158-64.
Stresses the opportunities for women in the early years of the Indian film industry. Describes numerous associated problems: securing gobs, "the sordity which prevails in many studios," disrespectability, technical and personal inadequacies, stereotypic plots and the need to remain youthful and attractive.

2665 Special issue: women behind the screen. Filmfare 24,26 (26 Dec 1975) 54p.
Issue in honor of International Women's Year. Primarily consists of brief articles about actresses. Other material includes an editorial urging fuller participation of women in all aspects of the film industry, a survey of women who have directed Indian films, a notice about a documentary film about Sarojini Naidu and brief mention of some Indian women who have worked in direction, script and musical aspects of the industry.

ii) Images: issues of exploitation, sexuality and censorship

2666 ABBAS, KHWAJA AHMAD. Kamasutra via Hollywood. *In* Illustrated Weekly of India 94,15 (15 Apr 1973) 48-51.
Brief article on portrayal of sexuality in Indian films. "The uninhibited artistic approach must take Love and Sex and relate them to the totality of our contemporary life with its changing social and ethical values . . . . Kamasutra, unfortunately, had to come back to India via Hollywood and the porno films of Western Europe."

2667 BAGCHI, JOSODHARA. Two women. *In* Frontier 9,2 (1976) 9-11.
Comments on the presentation of sexual exploitation of women in two films, Satyajit Ray's *Jana Araṇya* and Shyam Benegal's *Niśānta.*

2668 MAHMOOD, HAMEEDUDDIN. The kaleidoscope of Indian cinema. New Delhi: Affiliated East-West Press, 1974. 219p.
Collection of previously published articles. "Sex + Violence = Cinema," "Eroticism No More" and "The Dilemma of Censorship" concern issues of sexuality and censorship in films. Contains a tribute to actress Meena Kumari.

2669 RAZDAN, C.K., ed. Bare breasts and bare bottoms: anatomy of film censorship in India. Bombay: Jaico Publishing House, 1975. 158p.
Editor defines central problem: "On what criteria do the Film Censors act, when they cut, chop, maul or even ban a film [?] . . . . The original code as framed under the Cinematograph Act of 1952 has become completely outdated. "The censors' main attentions have been "to the bouncing breasts, shapely shanks and luscious legs of our actresses."

2670 SHANTARAM, V. "New wave," "nude wave" and all that. *In* Illustrated Weekly of India 93,40 (1 Oct 1972) 48-9.
Author's opinions about sexuality in films based upon 50 years in cinema. Believes that good and innovative aspects will remain and bad elements will fall aside: the "nude wave" is a passing phase.

(b) Journalism

i) Selected popular English language magazines for women

2671 Adam and Eve. v1-10? (1968-1977?). Madras. Monthly.
Popular journal, which considered itself to be "the complete magazine for the family." Included such materials as romantic fiction, gossip columns, health articles, interviews with movie stars, fashion photos and recipes.

2672 Beads and Bangles. v1- (1969-). Bombay. Quarterly.
Women's magazine. [Unexamined. IPP].

2673 Elegant. v1- (1964-). Bombay. Monthly.
Women's magazine. [Unexamined. IPP].

2674 Elegant. v1- (1965-). Bombay. Annually.
[Unexamined. IPP].

2675 Eve's Annual. v1- (1953-). Bombay. Annually.
[Unexamined. IPP].

2676 Eve's Weekly. v1- (1947-). Bombay. Weekly.
Popular, cosmopolitan English-language weekly. Features include articles about prominent women (e.g., in public service, film stars), romantic and other fiction, recipes, fashions, jokes, health column and advice column.

2677 Femina. v1- (1959-). Bombay. Fortnightly.
Magazine directed toward middle-class women. Has fashion and child care articles, medical notes, recipes, fiction, book reviews, etc.

2678 Home Life. v1- (1975-). Bombay: Bombay St. Paul Society. Monthly.
"An illustrated magazine for the family." Includes features on fashion and interior decoration, recipes, fiction and material of interest to children. [Unexamined. ALI].

2679 Journal of the Indian Housewife. v1- (1977-). Madras. Monthly.
Features, as described in advertisement, "regular information and expert advise on good grooming, beauty care, better health, child care, physical fitness programmes . . . and numerous other topics that are taboo and not covered by other magazines." [Unexamined].

2680 Kumari. v1- (1967-). Beawer. Monthly.
Popular magazine for young women. [Unexamined. IPP].

2681 Rasvanti. v1- (1968-). Ahmedabad: Rasvanti Prakashan. Monthly.
Has English and Gujarati editions. [Unexamined. IPP].

2682 Sreemati. v1- (1949-). Rajahmundry. Fortnightly.
Magazine for women, published in English, Hindi and Telugu. [Unexamined. IPP].

2683 Sthree. v1- (1964-). Cochin. Monthly.
Magazine for women in English and Malayalam. [Unexamined. IPP].

2684 Trend: the National Pictorial. v1-5 (1945-1949). Bombay. *Became* Indian Woman's Trend. v1-3 (1952-1954). Bombay. Monthly. *Became* Trend: the Magazine for Indian Women. v3-14

(1954-1965). *Became* Star and Style. v14- (1965-). Bombay. Fortnightly.
Women's magazine. [Unexamined. IPP, ULS, NST].

2685 Women's Era. v1- (1973-). New Delhi. Fortnightly.
English counterpart to the older Hindi *Saritā* (1964-). Directed toward middle-class women. Articles on social problems, handicrafts, recipes, personalities, etc. [Unexamined].

2686 Women's Forum. v1- (1966-). Ahmednagar. Fortnightly.
English and Marathi editions published. [Unexamined. IPP].

2687 Women's Own Weekly. v1-? (1960-?). Bombay. Weekly.
[Unexamined].

2688 Women's Voice. v1- (1969-). New Delhi. Fortnightly.
Women's magazine published in English, Sindhi and Hindi. [Unexamined. IPP].

ii) Images of women in popular magazine fiction

2689 RICHTER, LINDA K. Roles of women in Indian magazine fiction. *In* Feminine sensibility and characterization in South Asian literature. Guest ed: Fritz Blackwell. J. of South Asian Literature 12,3/4 (1977) 81-94.
Report of content analysis of 192 stories from *Eve's Weekly*, *Femina* and *Illustrated Weekly of India* (English) and *Saritā* and *Dharmayuga* (Hindi). Compares female role images and attitudes from 1970-71 with those from the early 1960s. Concludes that "women may continue to retreat from the political and social activism of the nationalist era. Exposure to western female images may have a negative effect on the sense of efficacy in Indian women."

(c) Women and literature

See also entries 344-66 and regional literature traditions within "2. History and culture of the regions of South Asia"

2690 BANDYOPADHYAY, PRANAB, ed. Women poets of India: an anthology of Indian poetry. Calcutta: United Writers, 1977. 78p.
Anthology of the work of 18 major female poets in English and in translation from various languages. The works date from the late 19th century to the present.

2691 DESAI, ANITA. Women writers. *In* Quest 65 (Apr 1970) 39-43.
Reflects upon aspects of writing, aspects of the lives of Indian women and on problems and strengths of the interface.

2692 KAMLESHWAR. Rama Jain and the Jnanpith award. *In* Illustrated Weekly of India 97,9 (29 Feb 1976) 10-2, *And* Teji Bachchan and Phulmani Varma. The Ramaji I knew, p.13.
Memorial tributes to a woman who, influenced by Gandhi's vision of Hindustani as a language of the people, became a patron of Hindi and other South Asian literatures. She instituted the prestigious Jnanpith Award for literature.

2693 LAL, LAKSHMI NARAIN. Woman in the literary context: a note. *In* Feminine sensibility and characterization in South Asian literature. Guest ed: Fritz Blackwell. J. of South Asian Literature 12,3/4 (1977) 151-2.
Brief comments by a noted male Hindi writer on the difficulties of knowing women in general and as characters and fellow writers in particular.

2694 MACHWE, PRABHAKAR. Prominent women writers in Indian literature after independence. *In* Feminine sensibility and characterization in South Asian literature. Guest ed: Fritz Blackwell. J. of South Asian Literature 12,3/4 (1977) 145-9.
Briefly mentions many writers: lists ten women who have won Sahitya Akademi Awards (for the best book published in a given year in each of the fifteen official languages), lists women serving on Sahitya Akademi advisory panels and names outstanding female writers of poetry, novels, short stories and essays in post-independence India.

2695 RAO, C. VIMALA. Women and fiction. *In* Literary Criterion 7,3 (1966) 42-51.
Discusses the part women have played in the development of fiction. Author offers "a few comments on why women have taken to the writing of fiction more than any other form of literature and how women have contributed to the popularising of this form of writing." Discusses sociological as well as artistic reasons for the use of novel form by women. Assesses the influence of female readers on fiction. Illustrations of Indian writers.

2696 Seminar of All India Women Writers: souvenir. Hyderabad: Andhra Pradesh Sahitya Akademi, 1965? lv.
Reproduces the opening addresses, a series of 13 papers on current trends in the literature of various South Asian languages (writing by men and women, but the latter is often prominent), a paper on the heroine in Urdu fiction and a summary. Includes photographs of the seminar, which was held in Hyderabad in April 1965.

(d) English literature by South Asians

2697 ASNANI, SHYAM M. Contribution of women in Indo-English novel. *In* Triveni 44,2 (1975) 45-52.
Surveys works and dominant themes of leading female Indian novelists writing in English.

2698 BELLIAPPA, N. MEENA. East-West encounter: Indian women writers of fiction in English. *In* Literary Criterion 7,3 (1966) 18-27.
Considers theme of the problems in "harmonious relations between diverse races and cultures" in the writings of Kamala Markandaya, Santha Rama Rau and Ruth Prawer Jhabwala. "The search for an optimum point of contact . . . seems to have yielded only negative results. A fruitful union at a significant depth is not treated by any of the three writers. It is the point of separation that stands underlined in their works."

2699 BLACKWELL, FRITZ. Krishna motifs in the poetry of Sarojini Naidu and Kamala Das. *In* J. of South Asian Literature 13,1/4 (1977/78) 9-14.
Analyzes two poems by each poet. Asserts that the primary distinction between their respective approaches is that Naidu's Rādhā is a devotee of Kṛṣṇa while Das' is his lover; Naidu's work is "flowing" and "spiritual" while Das' is "heavy" and "psycho-sexual." Considers each to be representative of her respective generation of Indian poets.

2700 CHADDAH, R.P. Women Indo-English poets. *In* Thought 27,26 (28 Jun 1975) 15-8.
Briefly discusses outstanding female Indian poets writing in English from the late 19th century to the present.

2701 DASGUPTA, MARY ANN, ed. Hers, Indian perspectives: an anthology of poetry in English by Indian women. Calcutta: Writers Workshop, 1978? 106p.
Poetry of 30 women of the 20th century. Includes work of both little- and well-known artists. Biographical/bibliographical notes.

2702 KIRKPATRICK, JOANNA. Women in Indian-English literature: the question of individuation. *In* Feminine sensibility and characterization in South Asian literature. Guest ed: Fritz Blackwell. J. of South Asian Literature 12,3/4 (1977) 121-9.
Contrasts female aspirations in autobiographies of Ishvani and Savitri Devi Nanda and in two of Kamala Markandaya's novels with a female character of R.K. Narayan. In contrast to Narayan's portrayal and to traditional conceptions of Indian women, the writing of the women demonstrates a concern with female individuation.

2703 LAL, P., ed. New English poetry by Indian women. Calcutta: Writers Workshop, 1976. 96p.
Poetry. [Unexamined. IBP].

2704 MUKHERJEE, MEENAKSHI. The theme of displacement in Anita Desai and Kamala Markandaya. *In* World Literature Written in English 17,1 (1978) 225-33.
Examines several novels about exile from India. Notes that this theme of displacement seems to interest English language writers in India. Neither this theme nor other features of these novels seems to be related to the authors as women.

2705 NAMBIAR, K.C. Indian women novelists writing in English. *In* J. of the School of Languages, Jawaharlal Nehru University 2,1 (1974) 75-84.
Observations about the work of female novelists and the Indian experience of womanhood.

2706 RAHEEM, RYHANA and SIROMI FERNANDO. Women writers of Sri Lanka. *In* World Literature Written in English 17,1 (1978) 268-78.
Considers themes, technical ability, output, characters, etc., of two Sri Lanka writers in English: Yasmine Gooneratne, poet, and Punyakante Wijenaike, novelist. Gooneratne is characterized by competence and technical perfection and Wijenaike by sensitive portrayal of rural women of Sri Lanka.

2707 SARADHI, K.P. Three Indo-Anglian women poets: Gauri Deshpande, Roshen Alkazi and Kamala Das. *In* J. of Indian Writing in English 2,1 (1974) 29-35.
Illustrates the "vision of life" manifested in the work of these three poets. Suggests the "range of their poetic landscape," their rich expressive abilities and their sensitivity to life's problems.

2708 SRINIVASA IYENGAR, K.R. The women novelists. *In his* Indian Writing in English, 2d rev. ed. New York: Asia Publishing House, 1973. pp.435-77. [*1st ed.* 1962].
Reviews prominent themes in works of major 19th and 20th century female writers in English.

2709 SRIVASTAVA, NARSINGH. Some Indian women writers in English. *In* Indian Literature 18,4 (1975) 63-72.
Brief appraisal of writers of English poetry from Toru Dutt to the present.

2710 Sunbird library of cassettes. Calcutta: Writers Workshop. [*Distributed by* Writers Workshop, 162/92 Lake Gardens, Calcutta 700 045].
Series of professionally recorded cassettes of Indian writing in English. In most cases authors read their own works. Female poets represented include: Meena Alexander, Anjana Basu, Margaret Chatterjee, Mary Ann Dasgupta, Ketaki Kushari Dyson, Lakshmi Kannan, Tapati Mookerji, Shreela Ray and Monika Varma reading their own poems; P. Lal reading English poetry by various Indian women; and Priyadarshini Lal

reading poems of Toru Dutt. [Unexamined].

2711 VARMA, MONIKA. Facing four: Indo-Anglian poetesses. Calcutta: Writers Workshop, 1972. 54p.
Criticism. [Unexamined. IBP].

i) Toru Dutt, 1856-1877

2712 DAS, HARIHAR. Life and letters of Toru Dutt. London: Humphrey Milford, Oxford University Press, 1921. 364p.
Short biography written largely from the reminiscences of Toru Dutt's English friend, Mary Martin. With 53 of Toru's letters to Miss Martin, an analysis of her personality as revealed in the letters and interpretive pieces about some of her writings. Photographs.

2713 ________. Classical tradition in Toru Dutt's poetry. *In* Asiatic Review n.s. 27,92 (1931) 695-715.
Analysis of poems from her ***Ancient Ballads and Legends of Hindustan***. In spite of her European exposure and Christian background, "her passionate love for Indian classical literature and its themes" is striking in "her best work in English."

2714 DUTT, TORU. Bianca or the young Spanish maiden. *In* Bengal Magazine 6 (Jan-Apr 1878) 264-75, 279-94, 325-31, 371-81.
Novel. Unfinished melodramatic romance set in England. An editorial note indicates that this was probably a sketch for a later novel in French. The volume also contains selections of her poetry.

2715 ________. A sheaf gleaned in French fields, new ed. London: C.K. Paul and Company, 1880. 374p.
Poetry. Translations of French works. With a "prefatory memoir" by Govin Chunder Dutt, pp.vii-xxvi. [Unexamined. NUC].

2716 ________. Ancient ballads and legends of Hindustan. London: Kegan Paul, Trench and Company, 1882. 139p.
Poetry. Main section, "Ancient Ballads of Hindustan," contains long poems about ancient ideal figures, including Sītā and Sāvitrī. The "Miscellaneous Poems" were inspired by experiences of the poet in Europe. Includes Edmund W. Gosse's admiring "Introductory Memoir."

2717 ________. Marguerite. Tr. from French by Prithwindra Mukherjee. *In* Illustrated Weekly of India 84,42-45 and 47-50 and 52 (20-7 Oct and 3-10, 24 Nov and 1-15, 29 Dec 1963) 30-3, 42-5, 48-51, 42-5, 34-7, 54-7, 46-9, 42-7, 22-7. [*1st French ed.* Le journal de Mademoiselle d'Arvers. Paris: Didier, 1879].
Novel. A Frenchwoman returns from convent school and becomes attached to a neighbor although her parents wish her to marry another. After much tragedy she agrees to marry her parents' choice and comes to love this man.

2718 DWIVEDI, A.N. Toru Dutt. New Delhi: Arnold-Heinemann, 1977. 168p. (Indian Writers, 15).
Evaluates Dutt's "total contribution to the development of Indo-Anglian literature" as a writer of poems, essays, novels and letters and as a translator.

2719 SENGUPTA, PADMINI. Toru Dutt. New Delhi: Sahitya Akademi, 1968. 94p. (Makers of Indian Literature).
Literary biography. Discusses the international environment that shaped the author's mind during her childhood and the productive years she spent with her family in England and France. Describes her intense and lonely young womanhood, her friendship with Clarisse Bader and her early death. Also critically evaluates her poems and novels.

2720 SRINIVASA IYENGAR, K.R. Toru Dutt. *In his* Indian writing in English, 2d rev. ed. New York: Asia Publishing House, 1973. pp.55-73. [*1st ed.* 1962].
Considers her writing, in biographical context.

2721 VIJAYALAKSHMI, P. Toru Dutt. *In* D.V.K. Raghavacharyulu, ed. The two-fold voice: essays on Indian writing in English. Guntur: Navodaya Publishers, 1971. pp.1-6.
Considers Toru Dutt's intellectual background and the influence of Christian thought on her Hindu background. Compares her poetic visions to those of Romesh Chander Dutt and Sri Aurobindo and evaluates her achievements as a poet.

ii) Sarojini Naidu, 1879-1949

See also entries 1326-34

2722 BHATNAGAR, RAM RATAN. Sarojini Naidu: the poet of a nation. Allahabad: Kitab Mahal, 1946. 67p.
[Unexamined. NUC].

2723 BOSE, A. Sarojini Naidu. *In* Literary Criterion 2,3 (1955) 1-8.
Author remarks that Sarojini was a powerful speaker and laments her decision to write in English. He discusses the main characteristics of her style.

2724 COUSINS, JAMES H. The poetry of Sarojini Naidu. *In his* The renaissance in India. Madras: Ganesh and Company, 1918? pp.247-77.
The author, himself a poet who resided in India, offers a generally critical assessment of Sarojini's third poetry volume, ***The Broken Wing***, and an appreciative assessment of her

two earlier volumes. He argues that her portrayal of women unfortunately perpetuates the Indian "door-mat" attitude toward them and notes that although she has led an unconventional life, "she reflects in her poetry the derivative and dependent habit of womanhood that masculine domination has sentimentalised into a virtue: in her life she is feminist up to a point, but in her poetry she remains incorrigibly feminine."

2725 DUSTOOR, P.E. Sarojini Naidu. Mysore: Rao and Raghavan, 1961. 54p. (Indian Writers and Their Work).
Biography focusing on Sarojini Naidu as poet, an aspect of her life that essentially ended in 1914 when she met Gandhi and became passionately involved in the nationalist movement.

2726 GUPTA, A.N. and SATISH GUPTA. Sarojini Naidu's select poems: with an introduction, notes and bibliography for further study. Bareilly: Prakash Book Depot, 1976. 230p.
Annotated selection of Sarojini Naidu's poems. Discusses in detail her life — her career as a poet, as an orator, as a nationalist leader — and analyzes her craft of poetry, her place in English literature, various themes of her poetry and the literary criticism available concerning her poetry.

2727 GUPTA, RAMESHWAR. Sarojini, the poetess. Delhi: Doaba House, 1975. 142p.
Critical evaluation of Sarojini Naidu's poetry along with some biographical comments. Presents her "as seen both by the neo-modernists and the non-modernists." Examines poems thematically.

2728 Den gyldne terskel: et festskrift til Morten Ringard på 60-arsdagen, 18 Mai 1968 [The golden threshold and festschrift to Morten Ringard on his 60th birthday, 18 May 1968]. Oslo: H. Aschehoug and Company, 1968. 146p.
Includes a life-sketch of Sarojini Naidu as poet and politician by Morten Ringard (pp.17-58) and selected poems translated into Norwegian (pp.61-121).

2729 JHA, AMARNATH. The poetry of Sarojini Naidu. *In* Indian Review 50? (Mar 1949). [Unexamined].

2730 MALHOTRA, M.L. An Indo-Anglian woman poet: Sarojini Naidu. *In his* Bridges of literature: 23 critical essays in literature. Ajmer: Sunanda Publications, 1971. pp.156-65.
Compares and contrasts Sarojini's biographical data with those of Toru Dutt and Rabindranath Tagore. Offers a brief critical evaluation of her works. Despite "emotion being often in excess of the occasion or situation," the author considers her to be one of the "eternal" poets.

2731 MOKASHI-PUNEKAR, SHANKAR. A note on Sarojini Naidu. *In* M.K. Naik, S.K. Desai and G.S. Amur, eds. Critical essays on Indian writing in English. Dharwar: Karnatak University, 1968. pp.181-91.
Attempts to describe Sarojini's poetic genius as it actually was rather than as it came to be portrayed in the myth in which it was surrounded. Argues that her works reveal the Hyderabad landscape more prominently than Bengali *Vaiṣṇava* lyricism, that she has been neglected because of the subtlety and simplicity of her work, that this neglect "is a symptom of the infancy of Indo-English poetry" and that the New Criticism is not by its nature able to appreciate various aspects of Sarojini's work.

2732 NAIDU, SAROJINI. The bird of time: songs of life, death and the spring. London: William Heinemann, 1914. 102p. [*Also* New York: John Lane].
Poetry. With Edmund Gosse's introduction discussing Sarojini's personality and work. The present collection differs from her earlier ones, says Gosse, in that a "graver music" has replaced "girlish ecstasy."

2733 _______. The golden threshold. New York: John Lane Company, 1916. 98p. [*Also* London: W. Heinemann, 1916].
Poetry. Her first anthology with an introduction by Arthur Symons.

2734 _______. The broken wing: songs of love, death and destiny, 1915-1916. London: W. Heinemann, 1917. 107p. [*Also* New York: John Lane Company].
Poetry. [Unexamined. NUC].

2735 _______. The sceptred flute: songs of India. New York: Dodd, Mead and Company, 1917. 231p. [*Also* Allahabad: Kitabistan, 1958].
Poetry. With an introduction by Joseph Auslander: the "lyrical graces" of the poet who "sings from the heart" express "true India" in this volume. First American edition of her poetry. Contents were originally published as ***The Broken Wing, The Bird of Time*** and ***The Golden Threshold***.

2736 _______. H.G. Dalway Turnbull, ed. Select poems. Bombay: Oxford University Press, 1930. 241p.
Poetry. [Unexamined. NUC].

2737 NARASIMHAIAH, C.D. Indian writers of English: Sarojini Naidu. *In* Literary Criterion 2,2 (1955) 35-42.
Reviews Sarojini's background and discusses selected verses.

2738 RAJYALAKSHMI, P.V. A note on nature in Sarojini Naidu's poetry. *In* D.V.K. Raghavacharyulu, ed. The two-fold voice: essays on Indian writing in English. Guntur: Navodaya Publishers, 1971. pp.15-23.
Sarojini Naidu as a poet who "unfolds the beauties, the transformations and the significances of our natural world." Discusses her depiction of nature in its human context and of humanity in its natural context.

2739 ________. The lyric spring: a study of the poetry of Sarojini Naidu. New Delhi: Abhinav Publications, 1977. 221p.
Discusses the major themes in Sarojini Naidu's poetry — nature, love, life, the folk — that reveal "an inner consistency of vision as well as an extraordinary grasp of the reality of human emotion and aspiration." Bibliography of numerous critical works.

2740 SRINIVASA IYENGAR, K.R. Sarojini Naidu. *In his* Indian writing in English, 2d rev. ed. New York: Asia Publishing House, 1973. pp.207-25. [*1st ed.* 1962].
Discusses her poetry, in biographical context.

2741 SUNDARAMAIAH, R. Sarojini Naidu: an appreciation. *In* D.V.K. Raghavacharyulu, ed. The two-fold voice: essays on Indian writing in English. Guntur: Navodaya Publishers, 1971. pp.7-14.
Depicts Sarojini Naidu as a poet who is successful in the expression of Indian sensibilities in English medium. Discussion and examples of life and love as portrayed in her poetry.

2742 VISWANATHAN, K. The nightingale and the naughty gal. *In* Banasthali Patrika 12 (Jan 1969).
[Unexamined].

iii) Lila Ray, 1910-

2743 RAY, LILA. Alive and dying. Calcutta: United Writers, 1976. 38p.
Poetry. Themes of death predominate in this collection.

2744 ________. The days between and other poems. Calcutta: United Writers, 1976. 37p.
Poetry. Somber themes: war, death, pain and so forth.

2745 ________. Songs of mourning. Calcutta: United Writers, 1976. 29p.
Poetry. Theme of death predominates in the collection.

iv) Bharati Sarabhai, 1912-

2746 NANDAKUMAR, PREMA. Bharati Sarabhai's English plays. *In* M.K. Naik, S.K. Desai and G.S. Amur, eds. Critical essays on Indian writing in English. Dharwar: Karnatak University, 1968. pp.249-69.
Critical analysis of the two plays of the only Indian woman writing in English who "has attempted drama with some considerable measure of success." Includes summaries and excerpts; considers themes and techniques.

2747 SARABHAI, BHARATI. The well of the people. Calcutta: Visva-bharati, 1943. 54p.
Play. Addresses the Gandhian conception of social order. The work was inspired by the true story of a poor old lady who spent her savings to have a well dug for the benefit of the poor. [Unexamined. NUC].

2748 ________. Two women. Bombay: Hind Kitabs, 1952. 121p.
Play. Deals with the complex social and political situation of pre-independent Gandhian India. A wealthy family in a princely state is caught between tradition and modernization. Conceives of confusion and complexity as a series of dualities.

v) Attia Hosain, 1913-

2749 HOSAIN, ATTIA. Phoenix fled and other stories. London: Chatto and Windus, 1953. 203p.
Short stories. Most stories in this collection are about women: young and old, rural and urban, traditional and contemporary.

2750 ________. Sunlight on a broken column. London: Chatto and Windus, 1961. 318p.
Novel (autobiographical). The life of a Muslim girl of an influential North Indian family during the freedom movement of the 1930s and 1940s. Depicts individual and national struggles for independence.

vi) Monika Varma, 1916-

2751 VARMA, MONIKA. Green leaves and gold. Calcutta: Writers Workshop, 1970. 38p.
Poetry.

2752 ________. Quartered questions and queries. Calcutta: Writers Workshop, 1971. 41p.
Poetry. Many poems in this collection concern the poetic process itself.

2753 ________. Past imperative: a collection of poems, 1953-1964. Calcutta: Writers Workshop, 1972. 47p.
Poetry. Various themes.

vii) Nergis Dalal, 1920-

2754 DALAL, NERGIS. Minari. Bombay: Pearl Publications, 1967. 236p.
Novel. Love and politics set in a hill station of present-day India. [Unexamined. NUC].

2755 ________. Never a dull moment. Bombay: Orient Longmans, 1970. 120p.
Essays. Previously published as "middles" in *Times of India, The Statesman* and *Indian Express* under the pseudonym "Aries."

2756 ________. The sisters. Delhi: Hind Pocket Books, 1973. 149p.
Novel. Domestic intrigue and conflict between twin sisters of an English mother and Parsi father.

2757 ________. The inner door. New Delhi: Orient Paperbacks, 1975. 144p.
Novel. Experiences of an Indian boy who is lured into a money making scheme, "yoga for sex," conducted by foreigners in an ashram in Hardwar.

2758 ________. The nude. New Delhi: Orient Paperbacks, 1977. 158p.
Short stories (16). [Unexamined. ALI].

viii) Zaib-un-Nissa Hamidullah

2759 ZAIB-UN-NISSA HAMIDULLAH. Lotus leaves. Calcutta: Gulistan Publishing House, 1946. 73p.
Poetry. [Unexamined. NUC].

2760 ________. The flute of memory. Karachi: Mirror Publications, 1964? 115p.
Poetry. [Unexamined. NUC].

2761 ________. No music before mosque. *In* Under the green canopy: selections from contemporary creative writings of Pakistan. Lahore: Afro-Asian Book Club, 1966. pp.146-56.
Short story. Depicts the highly empathic and giving qualities of a six-year-old girl in a rural Muslim extended family and her ability to mediate family tensions in her mind although lacking the authority to effect change.

2762 ________. The young wife and other stories, 2d ed. Karachi: Mirror Press, 1971. 114p. [*1st ed.* 1958].
Short stories. Most have prominent female characters. Set in East and West Pakistan.

2763 ________. Poems. Karachi: Mirror Press, n.d. 130p.
Poetry. "I have striven to serve society, and particularly Pakistan, as a writer of Prose. In my Poetry it is emotions that hold sway, and feelings that find utterance." Preface discusses various aspects of author's creative experiences.

ix) Rama Mehta, d.1978

2764 MEHTA, RAMA. The life of Keshav: a family story from India. New York: McGraw-Hill Book Company, 1969. 223p.
Novel. Depicts family life in a Rajasthani village. Centers around the character of a boy who industriously rises above the lower middle class and brings joy to the village community. Portrays well-knit structure of Indian village life and nature of filial relationship.

2765 ________. Inside the haveli. New Delhi: Arnold-Heinemann Publishers, 1977. 208p.
Novel. Life within a *havelī*, a large household with divided inner courtyards, in the city of Udaipur. Focuses upon the lives of *pardā* observing women.

x) Santha Rama Rau, 1923-

2766 DESAI, S.K. Santha Rama Rau. New Delhi: Arnold-Heinemann Publishers, 1976. 96p.
Critical evaluation of Rau's autobiographies, travelogues, novels and drama. Considers her primary identity to be Indian despite extensive residence abroad.

2767 RAMACHANDRA, RAGINI. Santha Rama Rau: the imagination of fact. *In* Literary Criterion 12,2/3 (1976) 98-114.
Discusses Santha Rama Rau's writing as a "search for identity . . . self-realization . . . . a quest . . ." in the context of her extensive residences and travels throughout the world. "If all good literature is imaginative recreation of life, then Santha Rama Rau's writing certainly occupies a fair place in it."

2768 RAU, SANTHA RAMA. Home to India. New York: Harper, 1945. 236p.
Author's experiences in and impressions of India after ten years of schooling in England.

2769 ________. Remember the house. New York: Harper, 1956. 241p.
Novel. Contrasts life among westernized Indians of Bombay in the years preceding independence with traditional life in Malabar. Addresses East-West encounter and problems of identity.

2770 _______. Gifts of passage. New York: Harper and Row, 1961. 223p.
Collected and reprinted autobiographical essays concerning international travel. Essays are arranged in chronological order and prefaced with supplementary commentary.

2771 _______. Who cares? *In* K. Natwar-Singh, ed. Tales from modern India. New York: Macmillan Company, 1966. pp.248-74.
Short story. Develops themes of contrasting western individualistic and Indian communal styles and identifications. A young woman and a young man, both recently returned to Bombay from the United States, commiserate about Bombay social life and scheme about the traditional-minded distant cousin the man's family invites to visit as his future bride.

xi) Kamala Markandaya, 1924-

2772 ABIDI, S.Z.H. Kamala Markandaya's Nectar in a Sieve: a critical study. Bareilly: Prakash Book Depot, 1976. 127p.
Briefly touches on many aspects of the novel and novelist, e.g., themes, characters, realism, plot and language. Based in large part on critical works of others.

2773 CHANDRASEKHARAN, K.R. East and West in the novels of Kamala Markandaya. *In* M.K. Naik, S.K. Desai and G.S. Amur, eds. Critical essays on Indian writing in English. Dharwar: Karnatak University 1968. pp.62-85.
Contrasts portrayal of India and Indians with portrayal of England and the English in Markandaya's first four novels. "The implied message . . . is that India should confidently pursue her own path holding fast to her traditional values and using methods appropriate to her culture."

2774 CHAUHAN, P.S. Kamala Markandaya: sense and sensibility. *In* Literary Criterion 12,2/3 (1976) 134-47.
Asserts that Markandaya, the "brightest" of the Indo-Anglian writers, has been ignored or misunderstood at home and abroad. Characterizes her writing as idea oriented and appealing for the ironic and sympathetic story it tells. She skillfully writes of politics and East-West confrontation using mythical elements. With detailed illustration from her "finest portrayal of cultural contrasts," *The Coffer Dams*.

2775 HARREX, S.C. A sense of identity: the early novels of Kamala Markandaya. *In his* The fire and the offering: the English-language novel of India, 1935-1970, vl. Calcutta: Writers Workshop, 1977. pp.245-61.
Addresses prominence of the theme of the "dispossessed personality's quest for identity" in artist's writings, which are said to crystalize two contemporary concerns of the English novel in India, the philosophical and the socio-political. Provides detailed examples of these points.

2776 JAIN, JASBIR. The novels of Kamala Markandaya. *In* Indian Literature 18,2 (1975) 36-43.
Addresses the juxtaposition of two different world views and value systems in Markandaya's novels.

2777 MARKANDAYA, KAMALA [KAMALA (PURNAIYA) TAYLOR]. Nectar in a sieve. New York: John Day, 1954. 255p.
Novel. Depicts the negative impact of modern economy and technology on peasant life. A woman narrates the sadness that befalls her happy family, including their work as urban laborers and the death of her husband.

2778 _______. Some inner fury. London: Putnam, 1955. 286p.
Novel. Details a woman's personal tragedy amidst the confusion of the Quit India movement in the early 1940s.

2779 _______. A silence of desire. New York: John Day Company, 1960. 253p.
Novel. Examines a middle-class husband and wife and their struggles with illness, emotional attachments and discrepant conceptions of spirituality.

2780 _______. Possession. New York: John Day, 1963. 249p.
Novel. Examines the clash between eastern spirituality and western materialism. Illustrates supremacy of art over worldly possessions through the presentation of an artist.

2781 _______. A handful of rice. New York: John Day Company, 1966. 297p. [*Also* London: H. Hamilton, 1966. 233p.].
Novel. Examines a marriage in the throes of urban life. [Unexamined. NUC].

2782 _______. The coffer dams. New York: John Day, 1969. 256p.
Novel. English company of dam builders profoundly affects a tribal community in South India. Work is a protest against the onslaught of modern technology on the simplicity of earlier traditional life.

2783 _______. The nowhere man. New York: John Day Company, 1972. 312p.
Novel. Indian immigrant to England in the 1920s and 1930s loses himself in another culture and a changing world and suffers psychological stress.

2784 _______. Two virgins. New York: John Day, 1973. 250p.
Novel. Illustrates theme of decay of traditional culture in urban context. Portrays the lives of two sisters of different temperament. The elder, depicted as a victim of

urban life, loses her virginity and brings pain to her family.

2785 NARAYANA RAO, KOLAR SURYA. The new harvest: the Indian novel in English in the post-independence era; women at work: Kamala Markandaya. Ph.D. dissertation, Pennsylvania State University, 1968. 356p. [University Microfilms 69-14,559].
Study of themes, characterization and other aspects of Markandaya's first five novels. [Unexamined. DAI].

2786 _______. Kamala Markandaya: the novelist as craftsman. *In* Indian Writing Today 3,2 (1969) 32-40.
Reviews Markandaya's first five novels with an emphasis on her female characters. Suggests that much other writing is explicitly autobiographical.

2787 _______. Some notes on the plots of Kamala Markandaya's novels. *In* Indian Literature 13,1 (1970) 102-12.
Portrays Markandaya as a documentary novelist who writes primarily about India's poor. Relates chronology of her novels to chronology of world and subcontinental events. Argues that female characters are more prominent than male characters and are depicted as trapped and struggling against the environment. Provides illustrations from the novels.

2788 SINGH, R.S. Soulful East and ratiocinative West: Kamala Markandaya. *In his* Indian novel in English: a critical study. New Delhi: Arnold-Heinemann Publishers, 1977. pp.136-49.
Theme of clash of East and West and painful process of modernization in seven novels of Kamala Markandaya.

2789 VENKATESWARAN, SHYAMALA. The language of Kamala Markandaya's novels. *In* Literary Criterion 9,3 (1970) 57-67.
Discusses Markandaya's inadequate use of the English language and inadequate presentation of life. Argues that she does not express "the sensibility of her characters." Illustrations.

xii) Nayantara Sahgal, 1927-

See also entries 1377-80

2790 ASNANI, SHYAM M. The novels of Nayantara Sahgal. *In* Indian Literature 16,1/2 (1973) 36-69.
Discusses four novels in depth with considerable attention to issues of male-female relationships and women amidst contemporary social change.

2791 JAIN, JASBIR. Nayantara Sahgal. New Delhi: Arnold-Heinemann, 1978. 176p. (Indian Writers Series, 16).
Suggests that Sahgal is the only modern Indian writer who integrates both journalism and creative writing, "the only political novelist on the Indo-English scene . . . . The struggle is not between the old and the new but between dedication and power . . . . a genuine concern for human values and human beings." The book traces the influence of Gandhian philosophy and the nationalist movement, Hinduism and women's issues on Sahgal's work. Other chapters discuss her portrayal of men, consciousness of history, political philosophy, ideals and world view. Select bibliography includes many of her journalistic writings and interviews as well as critical works.

2792 KRISHNA RAO, A.V. Nayantara Sahgal: a study of her fiction and non-fiction, 1954-1974. Madras: M. Seshachalam, 1976. 98p.
First "full-length" critical evaluation of the work of Nayantara Sahgal. Examines her first four novels in chronological order, discusses her nonfiction and offers an overall assessment of her work.

2793 MALHOTRA, M.L. Nayantara Sahgal: the angry young woman. *In his* Bridges of literature: 23 critical essays in literature. Ajmer: Sunanda Publications, 1971. pp.212-36.
Examines Sahgal as a political novelist, providing biographical details and illustrations from her first four novels. Discusses her concern with the theme of personal relationships against the backgrop of political situations in a "world of separations, betrayals, broken relations and promiscuity."

2794 PATNAIK, BIBUDHENDHRA NARAYAN. Nayantara Sahgal's novels. *In* Sambalpur University Journal 4 (Dec 1971) 38-43.
[Unexamined].

2795 SAHGAL, NAYANTARA. A time to be happy. New York: Alfred Knopf, 1958. 277p. [*Also* London: Victor Gollancz].
Novel. Concerns the adjustment of young upper-middle-class urban Indians to the political turbulence in the years preceding independence. Sahgal's first novel. [Unexamined. NUC].

2796 _______. Storm in Chandigarh. New York: Norton, 1969. 251p.
Novel. Details problems in upper-class marital relationships and politics in post-partition Chandigarh, Punjab.

2797 _______. This time of morning. Delhi: Hind Pocket Books, 1969. 224p.
Novel. Depicts personal and public lives of members of the diplomatic service in post-independent India. A polemic about politics, bureaucracy and ideals. [Unexamined. IBP].

2798 _______. The day in shadow. Delhi: Vikas Publications, 1971. 236p.
Novel (autobiographical). Deals with problems related to divorce in traditional Indian society. Depicts problems of delayed legal

proceedings and financial hardship imposed by a husband on his wife. The latter seeks to realize herself as an independent human being. Comments on the decaying political situation in India after 1947.

2799 _______. A situation in New Delhi. London: Magazine Editions, 1977.
Novel. Portrays a disintegrating political situation. [Unexamined].

2800 _______. A voice for freedom. Delhi: Hind Pocket Books, 1977.
Articles and interviews on political topics. [Unexamined. IBP].

2801 SARMA, M.N. Nayantara Sahgal's novels. *In* J. of Indian Writing in English 4,1 (1976) 35-44.
Argues that Sahgal's literary skill and effectiveness grew significantly from her first to her fourth novel. Considers development of presentation of socio-political issues and personal relationships in her first four novels.

xiii) Mrinalini Sarabhai, 1928-

2802 SARABHAI, MRINALINI. Captive soil. Bombay: International Book House, 1945. 47p.
Play. Poetic work symbolizing freedom struggle. [Unexamined. NUC].

2803 _______. This alone is true. Delhi: Hind Pocket Books, 1977. 192p.
Novel. An upper-class Indian girl participates in the revival of classical temple dance forms despite its disrespectability in the eyes of her mother and others. Author is an award-winning dancer.

2804 _______. Kān. New Delhi: Mayfair Paperbacks, Arnold-Heinemann, 1978. 63p.
Prose and poetry. Themes of yearning for and mystical union with one's beloved based on the Rādhā-Kṛṣṇa legend.

xiv) Punyakante Wijenaike, 1933-

2805 WIJENAIKE, PUNYAKANTE. The third woman and other stories. Colombo: the author, 1963. 205p.
Short stories. ". . . my impressions of the life I have observed around me here in the city and out in the countryside of Ceylon. The simple unsophisticated life of the men and women who move about in these pages calls for very little invention on the part of a writer." Much on lives of rural women.

2806 _______. The waiting earth. Colombo: Colombo Apothecaries' Company, 1966. 325p.
Novel. A village woman suffers from her husband's obsession with obtaining a plot of his ancestral land. Details the tragedy of a daughter's pregnancy out of wedlock, effects of gossip on villagers' lives and other aspects of rural life.

2807 _______. How I write a story. *In* Leisure 1,2 (1971) 14-5.
[Unexamined].

xv) Kamala Das, 1934-

See also entries 3356-57

2808 DAS, KAMALA. Summer in Calcutta: fifty poems. New Delhi: Rajinder Paul, 1965. 64p.
Poetry. Author's first volume.

2809 _______. The descendants. Calcutta: Writers Workshop, 1967. 35p.
Poetry. Themes of love and death predominate.

2810 _______. The old playhouse and other poems. Delhi: Orient Longman, 1973. 54p.
Poetry. [Unexamined. IBP].

2811 _______. Alphabet of lust. New Delhi: Orient Paperbacks, 1976. 147p.
Novel. A middle-aged female poet in a simple and unrewarding marriage becomes involved with high-level politicians. A story of ambition, political patronage and affairs.

2812 _______. My story. Jullundur: Sterling Publishers, 1976. 195p.
Autobiography written as a diversion and to pay debts during a serious illness. Includes much material on author's unhappy marriage and her sexuality, for which she has been ostracized by her family. "This book has cost me many things that I held dear, but I do not for a moment regret having written it."

2813 _______. A doll for the child prostitute. New Delhi: India Paperbacks, 1977. 104p.
Short stories. Title story is a tragic tale about a young prostitute.

2814 KOHLI, DEVINDRA. Virgin whiteness: the poetry of Kamala Das. Calcutta: Writer's Workshop, 1968. 28p. (Indian Writers in English, 3). [*Also in* Literary Criterion 7,4 (1967) 64-79].
Describes confrontation with the "luridness and complexity" of human relationships in the modern world in the work of a personal poet. Compares the extent and quality of her confrontation to that of her contemporaries. Characterizes her poetic images as sexual,

impulsive and situational. Analyzes her feminine images in two chapters on her poetry, "Virgin Whiteness" and "The Descendants."

2815 ________. Kamala Das. New Delhi: Arnold-Heinemann, 1975. 128p. (Indian Writers Series, 10).
Critical and biographical interpretation of artist's poetry. Provides extensive bibliography of her writings and criticism about them.

2816 ________. Kamala Das. *In* Literary Criterion 12,2/3 (1976) 173-86.
Characterizes Das as a frank "poet of the modern Indian woman's ambivalence." Her favorite theme is "the shadowy borderline between fulfillment and unfulfilment of love" and she is compelled "to articulate and understand the workings of the feminine consciousness." Extensive examples from her poetry.

2817 RAM, ATMA. An interview with Kamala Das. *In* New Quest 2 (Aug 1977) 41-2.
The author briefly describes Das' background, her English and Malayalam writings, her activities, the influence of a serious illness, her experience of writing poetry, favorate writers, attitudes toward Indo-Anglian literature and more.

xvi) Anita Desai, 1937-

2818 BELLIAPPA, MEENA. Anita Desai: a study of her fiction. Calcutta: Writer's Workshop, 1971. 52p. (Indian Writers in English).
Examines Desai's early short stories and first two novels. Emphasizes her concern with subjective reality, state of mind and nuance, as opposed to social documentation. Examples from her prose.

2819 DESAI, ANITA. Cry, the peacock. London: Peter Owen, 1963. 188p.
Novel. Details the inner life and sensibilities of a lonely woman who is ill at ease with her surroundings, particularly her marriage. Set in Delhi.

2820 ________. Voices in the city: a novel. London: Peter Owen, 1965. 265p.
Novel. Tragedy of a married woman lost in the urban maze of Calcutta and unhappy in her relationship with her husband. [Unexamined. NUC].

2821 ________. Bye-bye blackbird. Delhi: Hind Pocket Books, 1971? 266p.
Novel. Examines lives of "coloured" Indian immigrants in England.

2822 ________. Where shall we go this summer? New York: International Book Distributors, 1975.
Novel. [Unexamined. BP].

2823 ________. Fire on the mountain. New York: Harper and Row, 1977? 145p.
Novel. An elderly woman, fatigued, withdraws from life and brings tragedy to her great granddaughter and her friend. [Unexamined. NUC].

2824 MALHOTRA, M.L. A writer of promise: Anita Desai. *In his* Bridges of literature: 23 critical essays in literature. Ajmer: Sunanda Publications, 1971. pp.205-11.
Concentrates on Desai's "total proccupation with the individual," the "inner turmoil, the chaos inside the mind," and contrasts the introspective nature of her fiction with other novelists' interest in socio-political issues.

2825 RAM, ATMA. An interview with Anita Desai. *In* World Literature Written in English 16,1 (1977) 95-103.
Mrs. Desai answers questions about her background and daily routine, her process of writing novels, favorite and inspirational writers, the contribution of women as novelists, her various novels and other topics.

2826 RAMACHANDRA RAO, B. The novels of Mrs. Anita Desai: a study. New Delhi: Kalyani Publishers, 1977? 65p.
Considers problems of Indian writing in English. Discusses content and merits of four of Desai's novels from a literary point of view and assesses her place among Indo-Anglian fiction writers. [Unexamined. ALI].

2827 SINGH, R.S. Aloneness alone: Anita Desai and Arun Joshi. *In his* Indian novel in English: a critical study. New Delhi: Arnold-Heinemann Publishers, 1977. pp.164-78.
Explores "the lone individual" and inner psychic states in Desai's novels.

xvii) Bharati Mukherjee

2828 BLAISE, CLARK and BHARATI MUKHERJEE. Days and nights in Calcutta. New York: Doubleday and Company, 1977.
Journal of a trip to India written by Mukherjee and her Canadian husband. Her section considers problems Indian women have with personal fulfillment and identity. [Unexamined. BP].

2829 MUKHERJEE, BHARATI. Bless this day. *In* P. Lal, ed. The first Workshop story anthology. Calcutta: Writers Workshop, 1967. pp.21-30.
Short story. Depicts tensions between a young Indian couple living in the United States. Focuses on emotions and subtle communication that characterizes their interaction.

2830 ________. The tiger's daughter. Boston: Houghton Mifflin Company, 1972.

210p.
Novel. Details a Bengali woman's capacity for living with disappointment and alienation. [Unexamined. NUC].

2831 _______. Wife. Boston: Houghton Mifflin Company, 1975. 213p.
Novel. Depicts the conflicts of a young middle-class Calcutta woman, whose romantic aspirations are not realized in her marriage.

xviii) Meena Alexander, 1951-

2832 ALEXANDER, MEENA. The bird's bright ring. Calcutta: Writers Workshop, 1976. 31p.
Poetry. Long poem in English and French.

2833 _______. I root my name. Calcutta: United Writers, 1977? 29p.
Poetry. [Unexamined. ALI].

2834 _______. Without place. Calcutta: Writers Workshop, 1978. 39p.
Poetry. Themes of exile and alienation, with an introduction that discusses the relationship of Indian writing in English to this theme. By a woman who was raised and educated in Khartoum, Sudan.

xix) Various other female writers

2835 AHMAD, SHAHRAN. "Hush, hush winter's coming." *In* Pakistan Review 16,1 (1968) 24-5.
Short story. Female teacher envies a gardener's pregnant wife and feels lonely and unfulfilled without a child and family life.

2836 BALSE, MAYAH. The singer. Bombay: Jaico Publishing House, 1975. 178p.
Novel. A crippled woman finds fame as a popular singer but experiences loneliness and hollow relationships in the modern and elite world of popular music.

2837 BHARUCHA, PERIN. The fire worshippers. Bombay: Strand Book Club, 1968. 216p.
Novel. A relatively rare fictionalized view of life in the Parsi community. The middle-class wife of a Bombay merchant, discontent with her marriage, becomes involved with a more sophisticated young man from a prominent family.

2838 BHISE, SAROJ. My only friend: a book of poems. [Bombay: Crown Stationers and Printers], 1973. 56p.
Poetry. Author's "maiden effort in the field of letters."

2839 CHITALE, VENU. In transit. Bombay: Hind Kitabs, 1950. 504p.
Novel. Chronicle of a brahman joint family of Poona (now Pune) and their experience of the socio-political upheaval of 1915 to 1935. Portrays various social reform issues, financial difficulties and the decreasing elaborateness of religious observances.

2840 DANIELS, SHOURI. The salt doll. New Delhi: Bell Books, Vikas Publishing House, 1978. 191p.
Novel. A woman recounts scenes from her life — her youth in a Syrian Christian family and her young adulthood with friends, acquaintances and husband in India and abroad.

2841 DESHPANDE, GAURI. Lost love. Calcutta: Writers Workshop, 1970. 38p.
Poetry.

2842 DIMMITT, MARJORIE A., ed. When the tom-tom beats and other stories by students of Isabella Thoburn College. Lucknow, 1932. 221p.
Short stories. [Unexamined. IOL].

2843 FUTEHALLY, ZEENUTH. Zohra. Bombay: Hind Kitabs, 1951. 325p.
Novel. A Muslim girl from an aristocratic Hyderabad family is married to an efficient, westernized man. She falls in love with her husband's younger brother, an active participant in the Gandhian movement. Examines Gandhian versus industrial options for India's economic development and the romanticism of Indian women.

2844 GOONERATNE, YASMINE. Word, bird, motif. Kandy: Sithumina Press, 1971. 71p.
Poetry. Collection of poems with literary, personal, social and traditional themes, treated intellectually. With some translations from the French and the Sinhala.

2845 GUPTA, SHAKTI M. Women on men. New Delhi: Sterling Publishers, 1976? 201p.
Novel. Portrays the hollow life — cocktails, extramarital affairs, etc. — of the wealthy, westernized upper class of metropolitan India through the exploits of one woman.

2846 HABIBOLLAH, ATTIA. The parrot in a cage. *In* Mulk Raj Anand and Iqbal Singh, eds. Indian short stories. London: New India Publishing Company, 1946. pp.133-7.
Short story. Muslim girl is "caged" within the four walls of a household as is the family parrot that she inadvertently sets free. Portrays existence of women in Indian Muslim society as constrained.

2847 HUSSAIN, IQBALUNNISA. Purdah and polygamy: life in an Indian Muslim household. Bangalore: printed by D.N. Hosali at the Hosali Press, 1944. 310p.
Novel. Illustrates trials and tribulations of female seclusion and polygamy. A man marries four women and his mother is harsh with her daughters-in-law. His son reacts against these customs. [Unexamined. NUC].

2848 JAIN, SUNITA. Man of my desires: poems. Calcutta: Writers Workshop, 1978. 31p.
Poetry. Jain's first volume of English poems, some reprinted.

2849 KHAN, RAZIA. Cruel April. Dacca: Lutfur Rahman, 1977. 58p.
Poetry. [Unexamined. ALB].

2850 NARASIMHAN, RAJI. The marriage of Bela. Calcutta: Writers Workshop, 1978? 102p.
Short stories. Some reprinted.

2851 NIMBKAR, JAI. Temporary answers. New Delhi: Orient Longman, 1974. 221p.
Novel. A young widow attempts to free herself from the traditional values of a middle-class Marathi Hindu family.

2852 PAINTAL, VEENA. An autumn leaf. Delhi: Hind Pocket Books, 1976. 160p.
Novel. Depicts the marriage of a middle-class Delhi woman, its disintegration and divorce and her ensuing affair.

2853 PURI, MEENAKSHI. Pay on the first. Delhi: Siddhartha Publications, 1968? 95p.
Novel. Details the lives of government workers of Delhi.

2854 RAINA, VIMALA. Indian love legends. New Delhi: Popular Book Services, 1967. 215p.
Poetry. Critical of modern artistic trends, the author has "tried to write poetry in an age which derides and scoffs at softness of music and rhythm, clarity of vision and thought, simplicity of diction and emotion in verse." The collection includes two "full-length love stories," one about a *devadāsī* and a yogi and the other inspired by a popular legend of Manipur, and six shorter pieces. Illustrations by author's daughter. (See also her historical novel, entry 450).

2855 RAJ, HILDA. The house of Ramiah. Lucknow: Lucknow Publishing House, 1967. 260p.
Novel. Follows the domestic life of a South Indian Christian family over four generations.

2856 RAMESHWAR RAO, SHANTA. Children of God. Bombay: Sangam, Orient Longmans, 1976. 157p.
Novel. Portrays the difficulties that continue to be present for untouchables in India. Told in the first person by a woman who tragically loses her son. Author's first novel.

2857 SATTHIANADHAN, MRS. S. [KRUPABAI SATTHIANADHAN]. Kamala: a story of Hindu life. Madras: Srinivasa, Varadachari and Company, 1894. 208p. [*Also* Bombay: Mrs. R.A. Sagoon. *And* Kamala: eine Geschichte aus dem Hinduleben. Leipzig: Wallmann, 1898. 287p. *And* Kamala: en fortaelling om Hinduliv. Tr. by L.P. Larsen. København, 1921. 265p.].
Novel. Account of a woman's difficulties in her husband's home. Set in 19th century Nasik District. [Unexamined. NUC].

2858 SENGUPTA, PADMINI. Red hibiscus. Bombay: Asia Publishing House, 1962. 165p.
Novel. A college student, at home in her village for *Durgā pūjā*, becomes romantically involved with a young soldier just as her family plans to arrange a traditional marriage with a local man. She marries the latter and finds adjustment to life in his household difficult.

2859 SHAH NAWAZ, MUMTAZ. The heart divided. Lahore: Mumtaz Publications, 1957. 507p. [*Excerpted in* Perspective 1,9 (1968) 67-96].
Novel (autobiographical). Depicts the experiences of a Muslim girl in Punjab during the turbulent social change of the 1930s. Examines effects of freedom movement on women's lives.

2860 SHRINAGESH, SHAKUNTALA. The little black box. London: Secker and Warburg, 1955. 202p.
Novel. [Unexamined. NUC].

2861 SORABJI, CORNELIA. Love and life behind the purdah. London: Freemantle and Company, 1901. 239p.
Short stories (11). Some reprinted. [Unexamined. NUC].

2862 SUSHILA, pseud. No, I am not ashamed. New Delhi: Capital Book Company, n.d.
Novel. First person narrative tracing a woman's life from happy marriage to widowhood to seduction and, finally, to a Calcutta brothel. [Unexamined].

xx) Men writing about women

2863 ANAND, MULK RAJ. The old woman and the cow. Bombay: Kutub-Popular, 1960. 287p.
Novel. Portrays the difficult life of a young Panjabi village woman. Due to economic pressures and family conflicts neither her mother nor her new husband can support her emotionally or physically.

2864 BAHADUR, UMRAO. The curse of society. Delhi: Printing and Stationery Depot, n.d. 121p.
Novel. Examines a woman's life as a widow and her subsequent marriage. [Unexamined].

2865 BHATTACHARYA, BHABANI. Women in my stories. *In* Feminine sensibility and characterization in South Asian literature. Guest ed: Fritz Blackwell. J. of South Asian Literature 12,3/4 (1977) 115-20.
Briefly discusses two images in Bhattacharya's

work: a variety of grandmothers and a young girl in ***So Many Hungers!*** who displays her body to soldiers during a famine in order to buy and distribute bread to people who call her "The Mother."

2866 DAYANANDA, JAMES Y. The image of women in Manohar Malgonkar's novels. ***In*** Feminine sensibility and characterization in South Asian literature. Guest ed: Fritz Blackwell. J. of South Asian Literature 12,3/4 (1977) 109-13.
Considers three distinct categories of female characters in the essentially male worlds of Malgonkar's novels: submissive wives, sex objects/concubines and sensual women.

2867 FISHER, MARLENE. The women in Bhattacharya's novels. ***In*** World Literature Written in English 11,1 (1972) 95-108.
Regarding the prominent, sensitive and sympathetic portrayal of female characters in Bhabani Bhattacharya's novels. Examples.

2868 GOSWAMI, KEWAL. The woman. ***In*** Social Welfare 16,6 (1969) 20-1.
Short story. Examines the sufferings of a young childless village woman deserted by her husband. The maternal recompense she gains in caring for a young puppy is shattered when it is killed.

2869 JHA, AKHILESHWAR. The Janpath kiss. New Delhi: Sterling Publishers, 1976. 167p.
Novel. Examines a disjointed marriage with conflicting individualistic versus traditional values in North India. An engineer resents his traditional, dutiful wife and the economic terms under which his marriage was arranged. He rebels by kissing a stranger in public. His wife, who accepted his years of extended absences and inattention, is outraged and hurt by this socially inappropriate act.

2870 KAKAR, V.N. Women. ***In his*** How to 'kill' a wife and other thoughts. Delhi: New Asian Publishers, 1977. pp.9-53.
Collection of eleven humorous and satirical "middles" about women reprinted from several Indian newspapers and ***Eve's Weekly***.

2871 KHAN, MIR ALIM. The Begum. ***In*** Pakistan Review 15,2 (1967) 14-7.
Short story. An unflattering portrait of a woman from a Pakistani family that became wealthy in the circumstances surrounding partition. She is arrogant, miserly, superficial, flamboyant and more, qualities that bring tragedy to her life.

2872 KHOSLA, G.D. The awakening. ***In his*** The price of a wife. Bombay: Jaico Publishing House, 1958. pp.153-61.
Short story. An extramarital sexual encounter brings life to a woman who is ill-matched in her marriage.

2873 KURMANADHAM, K. Women characters in Dr. Mulk Raj Anand's novels. ***In*** Contemporary Indian Literature 6,6/7 (1966) 11-2, 26-7.
Discusses numerous characters, stressing their variety. Although they directly influence the male heroes, they are subordinate to them.

2874 KUSIKA [APPAV-AIYA MADHAV-AIYA]. Short stories. Madras: Methodist Publishing House, 1916. 1v.
Fiction relating to marriage reform and related topics among high-caste Hindus of South India. First published in ***The Hindu*** and ***Social Reform Advocate***. [Unexamined. NUC].

2875 MENON MARATH, S. The wound of spring. London: Dennis Dobson, 1960. 223p.
Novel. A large matriarchal Nayar family in Kerala of the 1920s is affected by contemporary political stirrings and the heresy of a son who marries an untouchable.

2876 MUKHERJEA, CHARULAL. The witch: a short story based on Santhal witchcraft. ***In*** Modern Review 59,6 (1936) 628-31.
Short story depicts the tragedies that the institution of witchcraft can bring to a village.

2877 NARAIN, RAM. The tigress of the harem. New York: Macaulay Company, 1930? 388p.
Novel? [Unexamined. NUC].

2878 PANCHAPEKESA AYYAR, A.S. Sense in sex, and other stories of Indian women. Bombay: D.B. Taraporevala Sons and Company, 1929. 288p. [***2d ed.*** Madras: Teachers' Publishing House, 1948. 284p.].
Short stories. Twelve romantic stories, set in South India. Subjects not limited to the contemporary period. [Unexamined. NUC].

2879 RAJAN, BALACHANDRA. Too long in the West. Bombay: Jaico, 1961. 192p. [***Also*** Thompson, Connecticut: Inter-Culture Associates, 1961].
Novel. Young South Indian woman returns from abroad to find many suitors. [Unexamined. IBP, BP].

2880 RAJA RAO. Kanthapura. London: Allen and Unwin, 1938. 269p.
Novel. Portrays women's changing roles in village and family as they become involved in the nationalist movement.

2881 RAUF, ABDUR. Mother. ***In*** Pakistan Review 15,3 (1967) 19-20.
Short story. A lonely old woman, who neither married not bore children, finds comfort and solace in "motherhood" in her final moments with two young men on a train.

2882 SHARMA, SOM P. Raja Rao's search for the feminine. ***In*** Feminine sensibility and characterization in South Asian literature. Guest ed: Fritz Blackwell. J. of South Asian Literature 12,3/4 (1977) 95-102.

Regarding the ***tāntrika*** search for fusion with the feminine by protagonists in Raja Rao's autobiographical novels, ***The Serpent and the Rope*** and ***The Cat and Shakespeare***.

2883 SREENIVASAN, KASTHURI. Devadaasi. Madras: Christian Literature Society, 1976. 120p.
Novel. Considers the changing temple dancing tradition in South India in the late 19th century. A ***devadāsī*** breaks her marriage with God to marry a common man.

2884 SRINIVASA IYENGAR, K.R. The first canto of Sri Aurobindo's 'Savitri'. *In* M.K. Naik, S.K. Desai and G.S. Amur, eds. Critical essays on Indian writing in English. Dharwar: Karnatak University, 1968. pp.133-46.
On the first canto of a nearly 24,000-line spiritual poem. "Savitri . . . is more than the loving and sorrowing wife that fights for her husband's life and beats back death; she is also a saviour spirit, a pathfinder, a redeemer."

2885 TANTIA, RAMESHWAR. Aunt to the world. *In* Triveni 44,4 (1976) 55-8.
Short story. A poor old Rajasthani village woman, widowed as a child, insists on spending her security and life-savings to build a well for her husband's village.

2886 VERMA, K.D. Myth and symbol in Aurobindo's ***Savitri***: a revaluation. *In* Feminine sensibility and characterization in South Asian literature. Guest ed: Fritz Blackwell. J. of South Asian Literature 12,3/4 (1977) 67-72.
Argues for a multiplicity of meaning in Aurobindo's epic poem and his use of the traditional ideal figure of Sāvitrī.

(e) Urdu literature: criticism and in translation

2887 CHUGTAI, ISMAT. The heroine in Urdu fiction. *In* Asian Horizon I (Sum 1948) 36-43.
[Unexamined].

2888 HASHIMI, NASIRUDDIN. Muslim women story writers of India and Pakistan. *In* Islamic Review 39,1 (1951) 32-6.
Life and work, in brief, of 22 female Muslim writers of Urdu short stories.

2889 HUSAIN, SALIHA ABID. Women writers and Urdu literature. Tr. from Urdu by Mohammed Zakir. *In* Indian Horizons 23, 2/3 (1974) 5-14.
Surveys the roughly 90-year history of Urdu prose writing by women. Discusses prominent figures, their media and major works, the rise of women's magazines and the context and nature of their writings.

2890 IKRAMULLAH, SHAISTA AKHTAR BANU. Women novelists. *In her* A critical survey of the development of the Urdu novel and short story. London: Longmans, Green and Company, 1945. pp.123-65.
Discusses foremost Urdu novelists, their works and prominent themes, 1901-25. These novels were more popular and have "a higher tone and language much more polished and literary" than those written by male contemporaries. Asserts that the didactic social novel with a reform message predominated in this period.

2891 ________. Women short-story writers. *In her* A critical survey of the development of the Urdu novel and short story. London: Longmans, Green and Company, 1945. pp.233-41.
Brief survey of the works, themes and characters of major writers.

2892 ________. The role of women in the life and literature of Pakistan. *In* Islamic Review 47,4 (1959) 15-9, 22. [*Also in* Asian Review 55,201 (1959) 14-26]. (George Birdwood Memorial Lecture).
The author states that Pakistani women, in the roles of daughter, wife and mother, have always held a position of privilege and honor and have been as conversant with literature as men since Mughal times. She reviews female Urdu writers of the 20th century and their works.

2893 KEEBLE, U. Magazines for women. *In* Pakistan Review I (Jun 1953) 33-7.
[Unexamined].

2894 RASHID, S. Our women novelists: A.R. Khatoon. *In* Pakistan Review 6 (1958).
[Unexamined].

i) Ismat Chugtai, 1915-

2895 CHUGTAI, ISMAT. Little mother. Tr. from Urdu. *In* Mulk Raj Anand and Iqbal Singh, eds. Indian short stories. London: New India Publishing Company, 1946. pp.103-14.
Short story. A child-widow becomes the mother of an illegitimate child and suffers at the hands of traditional Hindu society. Negative comment on child marriage system in India.

2896 ________. Tiny's Granny. Tr. from Urdu by Ralph Russell. *In* Contemporary Indian short stories, series I. New Delhi: Sahitya Akademi, 1959. pp.117-29.
Short story. Portrays the bleak existence of a lonely old woman in an urban neighborhood.

2897 ________. Sleep. Tr. from Urdu by Hardev Singh. *In* Thought 21,14 (5 Apr 1969) VIII-X.
Short story. Depicts the loneliness of a modern urban woman within the bonds of mar-

riage: the double life that husband and wife lead, dried-up emotions and various empty sexual encounters.

2898 ________. The quilt. Tr. from Urdu by Surjit Singh Dulai and Carlo Coppola. *In* Mahfil 8,2/3 (1972) 195-202.
Short story. Depicts lesbian relationships in the segregated women's quarters of a well-to-do Muslim household.

2899 ________. Wedding clothes. Tr. from Urdu by Suzanne Schwartz. *In* Mahfil 8, 2/3 (1972) 203-14.
Short story. Details dowry and other marriage preparations in a Muslim family.

2900 ________. Housewife. Tr. from Urdu by Fatima Ahmad. *In* K.S. Duggal, ed. Modern Indian short stories, vl. New Delhi: Indian Council for Cultural Relations, 1975. pp.144-53. [*Also in* Indian Horizons 22,1 (1973) 84-95].
Short story. Street urchin becomes mistress in the house of a grocer. Contrasts women as wives and as lovers. Examines nature of mutual attachment of men and women. [*Indian Horizons* issue unexamined].

2901 Interview with Ismat Chugtai. *In* Mahfil 8,2/3 (1972) 169-88.
Regarding her life and work.

2902 LATIF, KHALID. Ismat Chugtai: a personality sketch. *In* Mahfil 8,2/3 (1972) 189-94.
Anecdotes, reminiscences and impressions.

ii) Razia Sajjad Zaheer, 1918-

2903 ZAHEER, RAZIA SAJJAD. Know her? Tr. from Urdu by Firaq Gorakhpuri. *In* Illustrated Weekly of India 85,22 (31 May 1964) 19-20.
Short story. Tale of an artist who despises a neighborhood beggar woman and is later filled with remorse when faced with her generosity for an emergency national defense fund.

2904 ________. The story of a story. Tr. from Urdu by the author. *In* K.S. Duggal, ed. Modern Indian short stories, vl. New Delhi: Indian Council for Cultural Relations, 1975. pp.154-9.
Short story. A woman buys a coat and reflects on the creative process of writing.

iii) Qurratulain Hyder, 1927-

2905 HYDER, QURRATULAIN. Moored on the other banks. Tr. from Urdu. *In* Nasir Ahmad Farooki, ed. and tr. A selection of contemporary Pakistani short stories. Lahore: Ferozsons, 1955. pp.235-46.
Short story. Following an unhappy marriage a young Muslim woman marries the Englishman whom she had previously loved.

2906 ________. Dervish. Tr. from Urdu by the author. *In* Suresh Kohli, ed. Modern Indian short stories. New Delhi: Arnold Heinemann, 1974. pp.123-31.
Short story. Presents a woman's reactions over many years to a man who falsely assumes numerous opportunistic roles.

2907 ________. I Tiresias. Tr. from Urdu by the author. *In* Khushwant Singh and Qurratulain Hyder, eds. Stories from India. New Delhi: Sterling Publishers, 1974. pp.161-72. [*Also in* Illustrated Weekly of India 90,28 (13 Jul 1969) 25-9].
Short story. Indian tourists in Egypt confront the country's past and present.

2908 ________. Memories of an Indian childhood. Tr. from Urdu by the author. *In* K.S. Duggal, ed. Modern Indian short stories, vl. New Delhi: Indian Council for Cultural Relations, 1975. pp.160-73. [*Also in* Illustrated Weekly of India 91,12 (22 Mar 1970) 29-33].
Short story. Memories of social life within the upper middle class of colonial Bengal.

iv) Mumtaz Shirin

2909 SHIRIN, MUMTAZ. Awakening. Tr. from Urdu. *In* Nasir Ahmad Farooki, ed. and tr. A selection of contemporary Pakistani short stories. Lahore: Ferozsons, 1955. pp.167-87. [*Also* Tr. by the author. *In* Pakistan Quarterly 1,5 (1951?) 29-31ff.].
Short story. A woman looks back on her college days, her intense love for her female professor there and her eventual happy relationship with her husband. Suggests that female seclusion system fosters lesbianism.

2910 ________. Defeat. Tr. from Urdu by S. Amjad Ali. *In* Pakistan Quarterly 6,4 (1956) 59-65.
Short story. An aging man struggles to remain independent from his grown daughters and their families.

2911 ________. Passing clouds. Tr. from Urdu by Shahnaz Hashmi. *In* Pakistan Quarterly 11,2 (1962) 54-9.
Short story. A woman, longing for her husband who is immersed in a law career, becomes vindictive.

2912 ________. Descent. Tr. from Urdu by the author. *In* Under the green canopy: selections from contemporary creative writings of Pakistan. Lahore: Afro-Asian Book Club, 1966. pp.247-55.

Short story. A poor young woman descends into death following a hard life and the strain of bearing many children.

2913 ________. The atonement. *In* Perspective 1,4 (1967) 17-24.

Short story. A first person narrative of a woman's illness from the strain of childbirth and her overwhelming sorrow for her child who died shortly thereafter. Originally written in English, this short story was later translated into Urdu.

v) Other female writers

2914 AGRAWAL, CHANDRA P. Dreams, schemes and rebellion in the fiction of Begum Tabassum. *In* Feminine sensibility and characterization in South Asian literature. Guest ed: Fritz Blackwell. J. of South Asian Literature 12,3/4 (1977) 45-54.
Examines social criticism in the Urdu short stories of Vazida Tabassum, whose female characters are powerless in the face of social constrainsts.

2915 AHMED, RAZIA FASIH. Mama's coup-de-grace. Tr. from Urdu by Anwar Husain. *In* Pakistan Quarterly 13,1 (1965) 60-3.
Short story. Concerning arranging marriages. Adamjee Prize winner of 1964.

2916 AMIN, RAFIA MANZURUL. Crossroad. Tr. from Urdu. *In* Agha Iqbal Mirza, ed. and tr. Modern Urdu stories. Calcutta: Writers Workshop, 1975. pp.26-34.
Short story. Two young friends take in a feisty old beggar woman and an abandoned baby girl out of pity.

2917 NAQVI, S.A.H. An early woman novelist of Urdu. *In* Perspective 3,12 (1970) 59-60.
Briefly discusses Muhammadi Begam's brief career as an editor of a women's paper, the feminist approach in her social novels and her concern with contemporary problems in three novels.

vi) Men writing about women

2918 AKHTER, SALEEM. Miss Ahmed, B.A., B.T. Tr. from Urdu. *In* Agha Iqbal Mirza, ed. and tr. Modern Urdu stories. Calcutta: Writers Workshop, 1975. pp.9-25.
Short story. A Muslim teacher fights a battle against loneliness. Poignantly portrays her strong emotional attachment to various women and refusal to marry in a society where this is almost unthinkable. Portrays women's unhappiness with unsympathetic men.

2919 AZEEM, ANWER. Cinderella. Tr. from Urdu by Iqbal Akhtar. *In* Indian Literature 19,6 (1976) 62-86.
Short story. Depicts the empty, lonely life of a single, educated, westernized woman employed in Delhi.

2920 BEDI, RAJINDER SINGH. I take this woman. Tr. from Urdu by Khushwant Singh. Delhi: Hind Pocket Books, 1967. 103p.
Novel. The life of a Panjabi peasant woman and her trials with her husband, mother-in-law, poverty, social conventions, etc. Winner of a Sahitya Akademi Award.

2921 ________. Sculptress and the antique dealer. Tr. from Urdu by Kuldip Singh. *In* Illustrated Weekly of India 90,47 (23 Nov 1969) 48-9.
Short story. Details the callous, insensitive and exploitative attitudes of an "antique" dealer toward a female artist.

2922 MANTO, SAADAT HASAN. A mother's craving. Tr. from Urdu by Nusrat Ali. *In* Pakistan Review 14,5 (1966) 34-5.
Short story. Presents the intense psychological strains of an apparently barren Muslim woman whose husband is immersed in business matters.

2923 ________. These women! Tr. from Urdu by Hardev Singh. *In* Thought 20,40 (5 Oct 1968) X-XII.
Short story. Concerns the conflicts of Indian men and women regarding nudity and sexuality. A husband and then his wife overcome shock at frank portrayal in an imported film. Contrasts public denial of interest in and acceptability of such matters with personal fascination.

2924 MUFTI, MUMTAZ. Sister. Tr. from Urdu. *In* Nasir Ahmad Farooki, ed. and tr. A selection of contemporary Pakistani short stories. Lahore: Ferozsons, 1955. pp.37-51.
Short story. Character study of a Muslim girl who is self-effacing to the point of spoiling her own prospects for marriage and happiness. Editor's introduction suggests that such silence and submissiveness are not atypical and result in many emotional difficulties.

2925 NAZIR AHMAD. The bride's mirror: a tale of domestic life in Delhi forty years ago. Tr. from Hindustani by G.E. Ward. London: H. Frowde, Oxford University Press, 1903. 187p.
Novel. Didactic tale originally written for author's daughter. The translator has also edited a transliterated version of this novel "intended as a text-book for students in Hindustani." [Unexamined. NUC].

2926 QASIMI, AHMAD NADEEM. The wild woman. Tr. from Urdu by Abul Khair Kashfi and Janet Powers. *In* Mahfil 2,2 (1965)

43-8.
Short story. A proud, uncompromising old peasant woman clashes with urban bourgeois manners, values and experiences during a bus ride.

2927 RUSWA, MIRZA MUHAMMAD HADI. The courtesan of Lucknow. Tr. from Urdu by Khushwant Singh and M.A. Husaini. Delhi: Hind Pocket Books, 1970? 240p. (UNESCO Collection of Representative Works, Indian Series).
Novel. The social life of 19th century aristocratic Muslim Lucknow as filtered through the life of a courtesan. Based on an actual life history narrated to the author.

2928 SAEED DEHLVI, MOHAMMED. Izabella: a unique book of its kind for comparative study of Islam and Christianity. Tr. from Urdu by Rahm Ali al-Hashmi. Delhi: Dini Book Depot, 1974. 188p.
Novel (historical). The daughter of the chief Christian priest of Cordova becomes disillusioned with Christianity and converts to Islam. She devotes her life to the service of Islam and becomes a saint.

2929 SULTANA, FARRUKH. Status of woman in Iqbal's thought. *In* Pakistan Review 16,5 (1968) 35-6, 45. [*Also in* Islamic Literature 17,1 (1971) 49-54].
Notes the honor accorded to women in Iqbal's writings and in Islamic thought and his negative views of western womanhood. Selected passages in Urdu and translation.

(17) Clothing, adornment, beauty

2930 CROOKE, W. The head-dress of Banjara women. *In* J. of the Bihar and Orissa Research Society 4,3 (1918) 247-56.
Considers the origin, distribution and significance of the high-peaked headdress of the Banjara women of North and Central India. With comparative data from other areas of India. Photographs.

2931 DONGERKERY, KAMALA S. Jewelry and personal adornment in India. New Delhi: Indian Council for Cultural Relations, 1970. 77p.
Illustrated. [Unexamined. NUC].

2932 FAROOKI, NAZRATUN NAEEM. At the altar of beauty. *In* Pakistan Quarterly 2,1 (1952) 53-7, 68.
Cosmetic and jewelry patterns of the various regions of Pakistan. Briefly mentions comparable materials found in Indus valley civilization excavations. Photographs.

2933 Feminine fashions. 1953. 11 min. Black and white. 16 and 35 mm. [*Distributed by* Films Division, Ministry of Information and Broadcasting, 24 G. Deshmukh Marg, Bombay 400 026].
Film showing panorama of clothing and adornment styles in various parts of India. [Unexamined. CF].

2934 MEHRA, PRAMILA. Beauty care. Delhi: Hind Pocket Books, 1977. 103p.
[Unexamined].

2935 PAL, CORA. A dictionary of fashion and beauty for Indian women. Bombay: Jaico Publishing House, 1968. 176p.
Guide for the modern Indian woman. Discusses make-up, diet, clothes, exercises, behavior, etc.

2936 REEJHSINGHANI, AROONA. Woman's world. Bombay: Jaico Publishing House, 1972. 501p.
"This book is a comprehensive guide to cookery, beauty, health and housekeeping which every woman could profitably consult on all occasions." An almanac of recipes, remedies, beauty tips, male and female names and their meanings and so forth, with a contemporary, cosmopolitan orientation.

2937 Special issue: fashion and beauty. Eve's Weekly 29,33 (16 Aug 1975) 74p.
Entire issue of this popular magazine for urban middle-class women is devoted to fashion and beauty. Articles include: "Your Skin," "Beauty for your Teenager," "Loveliness Comes from Within!" and "Has the Saree Become Outmoded?"

(a) Clothing: communicator of levels of modesty and modernity and other kinds of identity

2938 BURNEY, NAUSHABA. Women's costumes. *In* Pakistan Quarterly 13,2/3 (1965) 71-81.
Descriptions, drawings and photographs of women's clothing in Muslim areas of South Asia, including various regions in the former East and West Pakistans and Bhopal.

2939 DONGERKERY, KAMALA S. The Indian sari. New Delhi: All India Handicrafts Board, Ministry of Commerce and Industry, Government of India, 1959? 99p.
Surveys the broad regional and local ethnic variants in saris (names, fabrics, draping techniques, etc.). Introductory section traces historical development of the garment. Numerous photographs of historical garment styles in art works and contemporary fabrics and styles.

2940 IMTIAZ ALI, SURRAYA. Un-Islamic school uniform for girl students. *In* Islamic Literature 17,3 (1971) 185-8.
"By replacing dupatta with a V-shaped band, much damage has been done to the Islamic concept of decency and decorum in dress . . . .

A well-covered head . . . . shields feminine charms from the male eye, thereby applying a brake right at the set off."

2941 RAJALAKSHMI, C.R. Women's dress. *In* Nirmal Kumar Bose, ed. Peasant life in India: a study in Indian unity and diversity, 2d ed. Delhi: Manager of Publications, Government of India, 1967. pp.41-9. (Anthropological Survey of India, Memoir 8).
Classifies and describes regional, tribal and caste variations in types of garments and in styles of wearing them. Illustrations and maps.

2942 RAJPUT, A.B. How she dresses. *In* Perspective 1,1 (1967) 73-80.
Describes various contemporary clothing styles of the then East and West Pakistans. Considers individual and regional variations.

2943 RASHID AHMAD, ZINAT. Women's costumes in Pakistan. *In* Pakistan Quarterly 1,1 (1949) 14-8.
Reviews recent fashion trends and preferences in Pakistan. Discusses three main styles, the Pakistani *gharāra* dress, the Panjabi *shalvār-dupaṭṭā* and the sari, and briefly mentions variety of other traditional ethnic clothing found there. Photographs.

2944 SINGH, JUSTINA ARJUN. "Modern" draped sari replaces traditional costumes of educated Indian women and the relation of this change to the development of education and communication in India. Ph.D. dissertation, Department of Home Economics?, Pennsylvania State University, 1966. 444p. [University Microfilms 66-10,475].
Report of questionnaire survey of 150 educated Indian women to ascertain changes in sari wearing between their grandmothers' and mothers' generations and their own. Attributes changes such as movement away from traditional clothing and knowledge of related symbolism and movement toward greater clothing diversity and interest in fashion to contemporary education and communication patterns. [Unexamined. DAI].

(b) Jewelry: important source of status and wealth for women

2945 GHULAM ALI, ANIS. The necklace. *In* Pakistan Quarterly 1,5 (1951?) 39-44.
Describes various types of Pakistani necklaces and their relative popularity. Photographs.

2946 JOHNSON, RANI. Bangles. *In* Pakistan Quarterly 1,6 (1951) 83-6.
Photographs and descriptions of the various types of wrist ornaments worn by Pakistani women with notes about their history and relative popularity.

2947 SEN, JYOTI and PRANAB KUMAR DAS GUPTA. Ornaments in India: a study in culture trait distribution. Calcutta: Anthropological survey of India, Government of India, 1973. 74p. (*Its* Memoir 22).
Discusses regional styles of (primarily women's) jewelry, according to part of body on which it is worn. Line drawings.

2948 SENGUPTA, PADMINI. Working women's bank. *In* Illustrated Weekly of India 91,31 (9 Aug 1970) 16-7.
On the tendency of employed women to invest savings in jewelry, "which serves the double purpose of satisfying their vanity and holding their savings close to their persons." Photographs.

2949 ZAIB-UN-NISSA HAMIDULLAH. Pakistani ornaments and jewellery. *In* Pakistan Quarterly 1,2 (1949) 41-6.
Summarizes recent jewelry styles and modes of wearing them. Notes the urban trend toward wearing less jewelry and toward coordinating it with clothing. Also briefly discusses urban/rural differences and the role of jewelry in social life. Photographs.

2950 ________. Earrings. *In* Pakistan Quarterly 1,3 (1950?) 33-6.
Describes varieties of the two major types of ear adornment used in Pakistan: the traditional heavy jewel-studded variety and the more modern delicate designs. Notes that fashion has gone full-circle and returned to a preference for traditional styles. Mentions change of ear-piercing from a matter of great ceremony to a casual affair. Photos.

(18) Western women in postcolonial South Asia

(a) Writers

i) Ruth Prawer Jhabvala, 1927-

2951 ASNANI, SHYAM M. Jhabvala's novels: a thematic study. *In* J. of Indian Writing in English 2,1 (1974) 38-47.
Favorable assessment of Jhabvala's work. Discusses the unique western sensibility through which she presents Indian characters, "undulating between tradition and modernity." Examples from her works through *Esmond in India*.

2952 BELLIAPPA, MEENA. A study of Jhabvala's fiction. *In* Banasthali Patrika 4 (1969) 70-82.
[Unexamined].

2953 DE SOUZA, EUNICE. The blinds drawn and the air conditioner on: the novels of Ruth Prawer Jhabvala. *In* World Literature Written in English 17,1

(1978) 219-24.
Examines Jhabvala's autobiographical *An Experience of India* and maintains that her novels do not reflect the distinct phases through which she claims to have passed: "there is a monotonous sameness in the writing." Characters are said to be stereotypic, language threadbare and sociological perception faulty.

2954 HARTLEY, LOIS. R. Prawer Jhabvala: novelist of urban India. *In* Literature East and West 9,3 (1965) 265-73.
Jhabvala as a "master of characterization and of gentle satire of [urban North] Indian manners." Discusses an interview with the novelist R.K. Narayan regarding Jhabvala and the themes of her various novels.

2955 JHABVALA, R. PRAWER. Amrita. New York: W.W. Norton, 1956. 283p. [*Also published as* To whom she will. London: George Allen, 1955].
Novel. Concerns Panjabi refugees in Delhi following events of independence and partition and the miracle of their self-rehabilitation in a new environment. Study of resourceful, practical people and confused human relationships during a period of great social change.

2956 ________. The nature of passion. London: G. Allen and Unwin, 1956. 261p.
Novel. A social commentary regarding the nature of the nouveau riche of India in the 1950s. Satire of the dealings between two men to close a business deal and a marriage contract.

2957 ________. Esmond in India. London: George Allen and Unwin, 1958. 256p.
Novel. Delineates shallowness of East-West encounter through the life of an Englishman who becomes disillusioned with things Indian.

2958 ________. Get ready for battle. London: John Murray, 1963? 224p.
Novel. A husband and wife attempt to break loose from traditional mores and live separate lives. A portrait of a woman learning to be assertive.

2959 ________. Like birds, like fishes, and other stories. New York: W.W. Norton, 1964. 224p.
Short stories. Depicts the confrontation between subcultural groups — young and old, male and female and Indian and English.

2960 ________. A backward place. New York: W.W. Norton, 1965. 255p.
Novel. Explores the theme of emptiness in human relationships, exemplified by an Indian husband and his English wife.

2961 ________. The householder: a screenplay. Delhi: Ramlochan Books, 1965? 168p.
Screenplay, based on Jhabvala's novel by same name. Comedy based on the marital disharmony of a newly married couple. With 60 stills from the film (entry 1997).

2962 ________. A stronger climate: nine stories. London: John Murray, 1968. 214p.
Short stories. Concerns the various circumstances of foreigners in India and difficulties in adjusting to cultural differences, i.e., "the stronger climate."

2963 ________. An experience of India. New York: W.W. Norton, 1972. 220p.
Short stories (autobiographical). Various aspects of women's changing roles in changing India.

2964 ________. A new dominion. London: J. Murray, 1972. 218p.
[Unexamined. NUC].

2965 ________. Travelers. New York: Harper and Row, 1973. 247p.
Novel. A group of westerners in India search for greater meaning in life. [Unexamined. NUC].

2966 ________. Heat and dust. New York: Harper and Row, 1976. 181p.
Novel. Presents oddities of British social life in India. Draws parallels between princely and modern India.

2967 ________. How I became a holy mother, and other stories. New York: Harper and Row, 1976? 218p.
Short stories. Collection portrays the world of the westernized, wealthy Indian. Title story is a tale of a woman who seduces a young swami about to go abroad as the "Holy Father," thus becoming the "Holy Mother."

2968 KRISHNA SASTRY, L.S.R. The alien consciousness in Jhabvala's short stories. *In* D.V.K. Raghavacharyulu, ed. The two-fold voice: essays on Indian writing in English. Guntur: Navodaya Publishers, 1971. pp.164-73.
Argues that the alien consciousness of Jhabvala affords her the benefit of a double vision as both sympathetic spectator and interested participant in the India situation. Deals with the theme of East-West encounter.

2969 SHAHANE, VASANT A. An artist's experience of India: Ruth Prawer Jhabvala's fiction. *In* Literary Criterion 12, 2/3 (1976) 47-62.
Argues that Jhabvala should not be classed with Indian writers of English, that her European perspective on her subject matter is unique. "Jhabvala's great merit as an artist is that she has eminently succeeded in giving artistic expression to this sense of mild alienation in her awareness of man and society in India."

2970 ________. Ruth Prawer Jhabvala. New Delhi: Arnold-Heinemann Publishers, 1976. 198p. (Indian Writers Series, 11).
Critical introduction to Jhabvala's exploration of her experience of India through the

medium of fiction. Provides a positive appraisal, in contrast to usual criticism of her work as "rather thin and sometimes desultory."

2971 ________. Ruth Prawer Jhabvala's 'A New Dominion'. *In* G.V.L.N. Sharma, ed. Essays and studies: festscrift in honour of Prof. K. Viswanatham. Machilipatnam: Triveni Publishers, 1977. pp.19-29.
Asserts that this novel, characterized by Jhabvala in a 1974 interview as her best, reflects a new transition in her work, portraying India as a "promised land" rather than a "backward" country. While she has made a "bold attempt at grasping contemporary Indian society," it "comes off rather badly."

2972 SINGH, R.S. Ironic vision of a social realist: Ruth Prawer Jhabvala. *In his* Indian novel in English: a critical study. New Delhi: Arnold-Heinemann Publishers, 1977. pp.149-63.
Concerns "clash between the real and the romantic, the mundane and the mystical, and the existential and the spiritual" in Jhabvala's novels.

2973 VARMA, P.N. A note on the novels of R. Prawer Jhabvala. *In* University of Rajasthan Studies 5 (1971) 87-96. [Unexamined].

2974 WILLIAMS, HAYDN MOORE. The yogi and the Babbitt: themes and characters of the new India in the novels of R. Prawer Jhabvala. *In* Twentieth Century Literature 15,2 (1969) 81-90.
Examines Jhabvala's novels from the point of view of themes and characterization. Considers Jhabwala to be a novelist of manners rather than ideas, a novelist whose major concern is to depict family life, marriage and expatriation rather than notions of class and economic conflict. Discusses lack of communication between the yogis and the bourgeois.

2975 ________. The fiction of Ruth Prawer Jhabvala. Calcutta: Writers Workshop, 1973. 60p.
Novel-by-novel analysis of Jhabvala's work. Discusses plots, themes, characters.

ii) Others

2976 DASGUPTA, MARY ANN. The peacock smiles. Calcutta: Writers Workshop, 1970. 27p.
Poetry. First published volume of work by the American-born wife of the Bengali poet Pranabendu Dasgupta. Many poems are reprinted from other sources.

2977 ________. The circus of love. Calcutta: Writers Workshop, 1975. 26p.
Poetry.

2978 RUBENSTEIN, CAROL. The third meaning of apricot, concerning its light: poems in August 1976, India and Nepal. Calcutta: Writers Workshop, 1977? 38p.
Poetry. Written in North India and Nepal by an American woman who has been an editor, choreographer and dancer as well as a poet.

(b) Women in social service: missionaries and a Peace Corps volunteer

2979 CARTER, LILLIAN and GLORIA CARTER SPANN. Away from home: letters to my family. New York: Simon and Schuster, 1977. 155p.
Letters from Chicago and Maharashtra of US President Carter's mother, "Miss Lillian," while serving as a Peace Corps nurse, 1966-68.

2979a CLAPP, ESTELLE BARNES. One woman's India: experiment in living. DeLand, Florida: Everett/Edwards, Inc., 1966. 268p.
Account of author's two-year assignment in India in the early 1960s with the Experiment in International Living. Photographs.

2980 D'CUNHA, S. Mother of the motherless: a short sketch of the life and work of Mother Teresa. Bangalore: Society of St. Paul Dasarahalli, 1975. 80p.
Mother Teresa's life and work in brief, with an emphasis on her Christian philosophy. Based largely on Muggeridge's account. Appendix lists awards bestowed upon Mother Teresa.

2981 DOIG, DESMOND Mother Teresa: her people and her work. New York: Harper and Row, 1976. 175p.
The work of Mother Teresa and her Missionaries of Charity in Calcutta. With selected statements of Mother Teresa, extraordinary color and black and white photographs and a chronology of her life.

2982 FISHER, WELTHY. Handbook for minister's wives. New York: Woman's Press, 1950? 136p. [*Also* New York: W. Morrow].
Guidebook based upon Mrs. Fisher's mission experiences in China and India. [Unexamined. NUC].

2983 ________. To light a candle. New York: McGraw-Hill Book Company, 1962. 279p.
Autobiography of an American Methodist missionary who founded Literacy Village near Lucknow in 1956 with the goal of training teachers for schoolless Indian villages. Discusses her early work in China and her work in India against illiteracy, which was still going on when she wrote this book at age

eighty. Photographs.

2984 India Calling Youth. v1-? (1948-?). London: Zenana Bible and Medical Mission.
[Unexamined. BUP].

2985 MUGGERIDGE, MALCOLM. Something beautiful for God: Mother Teresa of Calcutta London: William Collins and Sons, 1971. 156p.
"What we are expressly concerned with here is the work she and her Missionaries of Charity — an order she founded — do together, and the life they live together, in the service of Christ, in Calcutta and elsewhere. Their dedication is to the poorest of the poor; a wide field indeed." Describes their work and presents thoughts of Mother Teresa, a conversation with her, a chronology and numerous photographs.

2986 Welthy Fisher. 1967. 30 min. Black and white. 16 mm. [*Distributed by* Indiana University, Audio-visual Center, Bloomington, Indiana 47401].
Film about Mrs. Fisher's philosophy of education and her educational activities in India. [Unexamined].

(c) Wives of South Asians

2987 COTTRELL, ANN BAKER. Outsiders' inside view: western wives' experience in Indian joint families. *In* J. of Marriage and the Family 37,2 (1975) 400-7.
Experiences of western women who have lived in their Indian husbands' joint families. Their reports focus upon issues relating to the priority of collective over individual concerns and hierarchical authority patterns.

2988 SINGH, JACQUELIN. "Dear Mrs. Jhabvala." *In* Illustrated Weekly of India 93,36 (3 Sep 1972) 22-3.
Response to article by Ruth Prawer Jhabvala who described the difficulty of her encounter with India. Mrs. Singh, also a western woman married to an Indian and settled in India, describes her favorable response to life there. Photo.

(d) Travelers, a student and others

2989 ARMSTRONG, RUTH GALLUP. Sisters under the sari. Ames: Iowa State University Press, 1964. 498p.
An American widow describes her relationship with an Indian widow and their travels together throughout India (circa 1960).

2990 DE VIRI, ANNE. Indrani and I. New York: Red Dust, 1965. 127p.
A young woman from New York tells of her experiences while studying at an Indian university. Much on problems of friendships with young Indian women.

2991 News Circle. v1- (1957-). New Delhi: American Women's Club of Delhi. Monthly.
[Unexamined. IPP].

2992 RICHARDSON, JANE [JANE (RICHARDSON) HANKS]. Tender hearts of India. Delhi: Vikas Publications, 1970. 255p.
An American woman, who traveled throughout India as a guest of the Indian government, recounts her experiences. Her attitude is generally exuberant.

2993 TYLER, MARY. My years in an Indian prison. Middlesex: Penguin Books, 1978. 218p. [*Also* London: Victor Gollancz Ltd., 1977].
Englishwoman's account of more than five years in Bihar prisons on political charges, beginning in May 1970. Includes much material on fellow female prisoners she came to know.

2. History and culture of the regions of South Asia and South Asian immigrants in other countries

a. Indic cultural region

(1) Sri Lanka: area of Sinhala and island-Tamil languages

(a) The colonial experience: social reform issues

i) Education

2994 COOMARASWAMY, ETHEL. The education of girls in Ceylon. *In* J. of the Ceylon University Association 1,2 (1906) 210-2. [Unexamined].

2995 HARRISON, MINNIE. Uduvil, 1824-1924: being the history of one of the oldest girls' schools in Asia. Tellipalai: American Ceylon Mission Press, 1925. 167p.
First century of Uduvil Girls' College in Uduvil near Jaffna, the first girls' boarding school in Asia. The school currently enrolls students from first grade to advanced (arts and science) levels and is managed by the Jaffna Diocese of the Church of South India. [Unexamined. NUC].

2996 HITCHCOCK, OLIVE, ed. This is the victory, even our faith: a history of C.M.S. Ladies' College, Colombo, 1900-1955. Colombo, 1957. 115p.
The Ladies' College, Colombo, was founded by the Church Missionary Society and is now managed by the Church of Ceylon. The institution currently enrolls students from nursery school through advanced levels. Illustrated. [Unexamined. MRL].

2997 KIRTHISINGHE, BUDDHADASA P. Marie Musaeus Higgins: American mother of Ceylon's Buddhist womanhood. *In* Maha Bodhi 76,11/12 (1968) 327-32. [*Also* German-American mother of Ceylon's Buddhist womanhood. *In* Modern Review 124,12 (1969) 897-901].
Sketch of Mrs. Higgins' 35 years of work for the education of Buddhist girls in Sri Lanka, including her founding of the Musaeus College in 1893.

2998 LANGDON, SAMUEL. Punchi Nona: a story of female education and village life in Ceylon. London: T. Woolmer, 1884. 156p.
Illustrated. [Unexamined. NUC].

ii) Health

2999 MARSHALL, HENRY. Prevailing diseases among the inhabitants, female complaints, notes respecting the practice of medicine among the Kandyans. *In his* Notes on the medical topography of the interior of Ceylon and on the health of the troops employed in the Kandyan provinces during the years 1815, 1816, 1817, 1818, 1819, and 1820 with brief remarks on the prevailing diseases. London: Burgess and Hill, 1821. pp.39-73.
[Unexamined. Book in NUC].

iii) Prostitution

3000 HUMAN, GRACE. Brothels and young girls: a letter to Ceylonese parents. *In* National Monthly of Ceylon 1,8 (1912) 335-6.
Colombo brothels. [Unexamined].

iv) Enfranchisement

3001 WOMEN'S FRANCHISE UNION OF CEYLON. Women and the vote. Colombo: W.E. Bastian and Company, 1928. 16p.
[Unexamined].

(b) The colonial experience: western women in Ceylon

i) Missionaries

3002 CLOUGH, MARGARET MORLEY. Extracts from the journal and correspondence of the late Mrs. M.M. Clough, wife of the Rev. Benjamin Clough, missionary in

Ceylon. London: J. Mason, 1829. 174p.
[Unexamined. NUC].

3003 COORAY, G.L., ed. Evelyn Karney: pioneer missionary. Talawa, Ceylon: House of Joy, 1966. 73p.
[Unexamined].

3004 GREGSON, FANNY [FANNY (GREGSON) LIESCHING]. Letters from Ceylon. London: Marshall Brothers, 1893? 208p.
On mission work. [Unexamined. NUC].

3005 KARNEY, E.S. and W.W.S. MALDEN. Shining land: the story of CEZMS work in Ceylon . . . London: Church of England Zenana Missionary Society, n.d. 96p.
[Unexamined. MRL].

3006 LEITCH, MARY and MARGARET W. LEITCH. Seven years in Ceylon: stories of mission life. New York: American Tract Society, 1890. 170p.
Two missionaries describe their experiences in letters and essays. Work is an effort to enlighten the public about mission work and suggest "what we women can do in the foreign field." Etchings and photographs.

3007 WINSLOW, MYRON. Memoir of Mrs. Harriet L. Winslow, combining a sketch of the Ceylon mission. New York: Leavitt, Lord and Company, 1835. 408p. [*Also* Memoir of Mrs. Harriet L. Winslow, thirteen years a member of the American mission in Ceylon. New York: A.T.S., 1840? 479p.].
[Unexamined. MRL].

ii) Travelers and others

3008 CORNER, CAROLINE [CAROLINE CORNER-OHLMUS]. Ceylon, the paradise of Adam: the record of seven years' residence in the island. London: John Lane, 1908. 323p.
[Unexamined].

3009 FRERE, ALICE M. [ALICE M. (FRERE) CLERK]. The antipodes and around the world: or, travels in Australia, New Zealand, Ceylon, China, Japan and California. London: Hatchards, 1870. 633p.
Twelfth chapter (pp.144-91) details author's travels in Ceylon. [Unexamined. Book in NUC].

3010 GORDON-CUMMING, C.F. Two happy years in Ceylon. Edinburgh: Williams Blackwood and Sons, 1892. 2v. [*Also* New York: C. Scribner's Sons].
Nearly 900 pages describe travel and life in Ceylon. Illustrated by author. [Unexamined. NUC].

3011 P, F.E.F. [FANNY EMILY (FARR) PENNY]. Fickle fortune in Ceylon. Madras: Addison and Company, 1887. 69p.
Local description and experiences of tea cultivation. [Unexamined. NUC].

(c) General statements: ethnographic and other

3012 BLAZÉ, RAY. Women of Ceylon. *In* Geographical Magazine 34,1 (1961) 55-62. [*Also in* Ceylon Today 10,6 (1961) 6-13].
Survey article. Briefly describes the historical background since the coming of Buddhism in the third century B.C.E. and discusses the changing opportunities for women in the 19th and 20th centuries. Photographs. [*Ceylon Today* issue unexamined].

3013 CASTILLO, GELIA T. The women of Ceylon: some vital statistics. *In* Asia 24 (Win 1971/72) 67-100.
[Unexamined].

3014 CRAWFORD, E.A. Ceylon. *In* T. Athol Joyce and N.W. Thomas, eds. Women of all nations: a record of their characteristics, habits, manners, customs and influence, v4. London: Cassel and Company, 1915? pp.626-32. [*Also* New York: Funk and Wagnalls Company, 1915].
Surveys "races," marriage customs, dress, "Sinhalese grace," occupations, etc. Photographs.

3015 GOONETILLEKE, WILLIAM. Sinhalese women. *In* Orientalist 4 (1890) 92-4.
Translation of an excerpt from ***Das Frauenleben der Erde*** of Amand freiherr v. Schweiger-Lerchenfeld, with original German. Primarily describes marriage ceremonies with several footnoted corrections by the editor. Also describes physical features and disposition of the women.

3016 GUNAWARDHANA, THEJA. Freedom and woman. *In* New Lanka 5,2 (1954) 65-71.
[Unexamined].

3017 HUSTON, PERDITA. Sri Lanka. *In* Message from the village. New York: Epoch B Foundation, 1978. pp.62-82.
This book is the result of an invitation to some poor, uneducated women of Sri Lanka, Kenya, Egypt, Sudan, Tunisia and Mexico to speak, ultimately anonymously, about their concerns and interests and their ideas about changing conditions for women. The various sections contain background material about the particular country and women's circumstances there, excerpts from conversations

held and comments about the conversations.

3018 ______. Third world women speak out: interviews in six developing countries. Washington, D.C.: Overseas Development Council, 1978?
Analyzes approximately 150 conversations the author had with poor, uneducated women in Sri Lanka, Kenya, Sudan, Egypt, Mexico and Tunisia. Although primarily concerned with family planning and development, she had informal conversations through interpreters about a variety of the concerns and interests of these women. [Unexamined].

3019 JAYAWEERA, SWARNA. Aspects of the role and position of women. *In* Tissa Fernando and Robert N. Kearney, eds. Modern Sri Lanka: a society in transition. Syracuse: Maxwell School of Citizenship and Public Affairs, Syracuse University, 1979. (*Its* Foreign and Comparative Studies Program, South Asian Series, 4).
Volume emphasizes contemporary Sri Lanka. [Unexamined].

3020 SIRIWARDENA, B.S. The life of Ceylon women. *In* Barbara E. Ward, ed. Women in the new Asia: the changing social roles of men and women in South and South-east Asia. Paris: UNESCO, 1963. pp.150-72.
Contrasts women's roles in traditional and modern Ceylon with respect to education, socialization from infancy to adolescence, marriage and division of labor in the home. Includes a brief autobiographical statement.

3021 WIJESEKERA, N.D. The people of Ceylon, 2d ed. Colombo: M.D. Gunasena and Company, 1965. 311p. [*1st ed.* 1949].
Ethnographic survey of social life in rural Sinhalese society based on travels throughout the island. Much on women.

3022 Womanpower: a woman's place is . . . Produced by United Nations. 30 min. Color. [*Distributed by* FMS Films, P.O. Box 7316, Alexandria, Virginia 22307].
Film about women in Sri Lanka and Sweden. Describes Madame Bandaranaike's efforts to involve women in Sri Lanka's mechanized agricultural program and ways that women of Sri Lanka are encouraged to pursue agricultural studies and participate in cooperatives. Argues that pervasive change of women's roles requires change in social conditioning at home and at school as is occurring in Sweden. [Unexamined].

(d) The life cycle

3023 NEVILL, HUGH. Social rites of the Sinhalese. *In* Taprobanian 2,2 (1887) 47-52.
Considers pregnancy, birth, puberty, marriage and death rites. [Unexamined].

3024 SCARPA, ANTONIO. Observations of the sexual cycle of the Sinhalese and Tamil women on the island of Ceylon. *In* Medical Digest 22,3 (1954).
[Unexamined].

3025 WOODWARD, FRANK LEE. Girls, wives and mothers. *In* Ceylon National Review 1,1 (1906) 15-9.
[Unexamined].

i) Puberty rites, menstruation

3026 ALLAHAKOON, H.W. Ceremonies observed by low country Sinhalese: a girl attaining the age of puberty and maidenhood. *In* Monthly Literary Register and Notes and Queries for Ceylon 1,7 (1893) 153-5.
[Unexamined].

3027 GOONETILLEKE, WILLIAM. Women during the period of catamenia. *In* Orientalist 3 (1888/89) 201-3.
Comparative discussion of menstrual taboos with examples from Sri Lanka, ancient Greece, North India, Africa and Canada. Includes a description of a Sinhalese puberty ritual.

3028 LEACH, EDMUND R. A critique of Yalman's interpretation of Sinhalese girls' puberty ceremonial. *In* Jean Pouillon and Pierre Maranda, eds. Échanges et communications: mélanges offert à Claude Lévi-Strauss à l'occasion de son 60ème anniversaire. The Hague: Mouton, 1970. pp.819-28. (Studies in General Anthropology, 5).
See Sinhalese date presented in Yalman's "On the Purity of Women in the Castes of Ceylon and Malabar" (entry 2049). [Unexamined. Book in NUC].

ii) Marriage age and arrangements

3029 DIXON, RUTH BRONSON. The social and demographic determinants of marital postponement and celibacy: a comparative study. Ph.D. dissertation, Department of Sociology?, University of California, Berkeley, 1970. 390p. [University Microfilms 71-15,754].
Examines factors influencing rate and timing of nuptiality in Sri Lanka and France. Finds major variables to be marriage desirability, marriage feasibility and mate availability. [Unexamined. DAI].

3030 FERNANDO, DALLAS F.S. Changing nupti-

ality patterns in Sri Lanka, 1901-1971. *In* Population Studies 29,2 (1975) 179-90.
Examines census data to show steady increase in male and female age at marriage throughout 20th century. The current shortage of males for marriageable females, which is aggravated by economic constraints, should move the mean age at marriage still higher. These trends have "considerable significance for fertility reduction."

3031 FERNANDO, P.T.M. Factors affecting marital selection: a study of matrimonial advertisements by middle-class Sinhalese. *In* Ceylon J. of Historical and Social Studies 7,2 (1964) 171-88.
Discusses relative importance of numerous qualifications sought in ads by Sinhalese. Notes differences between ads placed in English and Sinhala newspapers. Compares findings to those of similar studies of matrimonial ads in India.

3032 MAHAWALATENNE, S.D. A few facts regarding the unions of Kandyan men with low-country women and low-country men with Kandyan women in *diga* and *binna*. *In* Kandyan 1,3/4 (1918) 115-22.
[Unexamined].

3033 PERERA, S.G. A priest's letters to a niece on love, courtship and marriage. Colombo, 1948.
[Unexamined].

iii) Marriage ceremonies

3034 BAWA, AHAMADU. The marriage customs of the Moors of Ceylon. *In* J. of the Royal Asiatic Society, Ceylon Branch 10,36 (1888) 219-33.
Describes a hypothetical marriage arrangement and ceremony: ". . . it may be remarked with perfect truth that matrimony among the Moors of Ceylon is merely a 'matter of money', — love and courtship playing no parts as factors in the great social institution."

3035 A brief sketch of the marriage ceremony of the Tamil Catholics. *In* Ceylon Literary Register 5,29 (1891) 227-8.
[Unexamined].

3036 DE ALWIS, JAMES. Marriage customs of the Sinhalese. *In* Ceylon Magazine 1,7 (1841) 278-83.
[Unexamined].

3037 DE SILVA, C.M. AUSTIN. The *magul tahanciya*: an ancient Sinhalese marriage custom. *In* Sir Paul Pieris felicitation volume presented by his friends and admirers. Colombo: Sir Paul Pieris Felicitation Volume Committee, 1956. pp.29-37.
[Unexamined. Book in NUC].

3038 ________. The magul poruva or customary form of Sinhala marriage. *In* Spolia Zeylanica 30,1 (1963) 173-81.
Provides details of this and related marriage rites, historical references and drawings of various stages in the ritual. Considers rite to be associated with fertility.

3039 ________. Marriage customs of the Sinhalese. *In* Ceylon Folklore 1 (Dec 1969) 1-8.
Marriage rites. [Unexamined].

3040 GALPIN, C.A. Notes on marriage and its attendant customs, particularly among the low-country Sinhalese. *In* Ceylon Antiquary and Literary Register 2,2 (1916) 100-7.
Describes puberty rites and marriage arrangements, ceremonies and consummation. Includes appendix on "up-country" Kandyan marriage ceremonies.

3041 MILN, LOUISE JORDAN. Some stray thoughts in Ceylon. *And* Among the Buddists of Ceylon. *In her* Wooings and weddings in many climes. London: C.A. Pearson, 1901. pp.160-70, 171-86. [*Also* Chicago: H.S. Stone and Company].
Illustrated. [Unexamined. Book in NUC].

3042 PEIRIS, EDMUND. Marriage customs and ceremonies of Ceylon. *In* J. of the Royal Asiatic Society, Ceylon Branch n.s. 8,1 (1962) 1-28.
[Unexamined. BAS].

3043 RAGHAVAN, M.D. A Sinhalese wedding. *In his* Ceylon: a pictorial survey of the peoples and arts. Colombo: M.D. Gunasena and Company, 1962. pp.44-52.
Describes ceremonies of the more common marriage form in which the wife lives in her husband's home and the less common form in which the husband lives in his wife's home.

iv) Polyandrous marriages

3044 IEVERS, R.W. The custom of polyandry in Ceylon. *In* J. of the Royal Asiatic Society, Ceylon Branch 16,50 (1899) 3-6.
Remarks of a district administrator on the history and function of polyandry in Sri Lanka.

3045 LEACH, E.R. Polyandry, inheritance and the definition of marriage: with particular reference to Sinhalese customary law. *In* Man 55,199 (1955) 182-6. [*Reprint in his* Rethinking anthropology. London: Athlone Press, 1961. pp.105-13].
Uses Sinhalese data to show that no single definition of marriage has universal applicability. Concludes: "Polyandry exists in Ceylon because, in a society where both men and

women inherit property, polyandrous arrangements serve, both in theory and practice, to reduce the potential hostility between sibling brothers."

3046 TAMBIAH, S.J. Polyandry in Ceylon, with special reference to the Laggala region. *In* Christoph von Fürer-Haimendorf, ed. Caste and kin in Nepal, India and Ceylon: anthropological studies in Hindu-Buddhist contact zones. Bombay: Asia Publishing House, 1966. pp.264-358.
Includes historical references to Sinhalese polyandry, a detailed ethnographic study of polyandry in Laggala, interpretations of its significance and case studies of polyandrous families. Charts and tables.

v) Marriage law

3047 BEVEN, EDWIN. Kandyan marriages. *In* Ceylon Antiquary and Literary Register 3,2 (1917) 131-7.
Problems of civil versus customary Kandyan marriage law.

3048 DABRERA, A.L.J. CROOS. Rights and status of married women. *In* Ceylon Law Students Magazine 1 (1925) 33-6.
[Unexamined].

3049 GOONESEKERE, R.K.W. A married woman's right to maintenance. *In* University of Ceylon Review 18,3/4 (1960) 177-93.
". . . we will first examine the provisions of the Roman-Dutch Law, which is our Common Law, and then consider statutory provisions modelled on English Law."

3050 ________. A review of the Marriage and Divorce Commission report. *In* Ceylon Law College Review (1960/61) 15-23.
[Unexamined].

3051 HALANGODA, JOHN ASHFIELD. A plea for the reform of the Kandyan marriage laws. *In* J. of the Kandyan Association 1,2 (1916) 35-44.
[Unexamined].

3052 JAYAWARDENA, H.A. Husband and wife in Ceylon. *In* Ceylon Law Review 5 (1906) 125-33.
[Unexamined].

3053 JAYAWARDENA, J.R. Kandyan marriages. *In* Ceylon Law Students Magazine n.s. 1,6 (1930) 19-25.
[Unexamined].

3054 RAJAH, R.S. Development of the law relating to married women. *In* Ceylon Law College Review (1955/56) 77-84.
[Unexamined].

3055 WILLE, G.A. Marriage and majority of Mohamedan women. *In* Ceylon Law Review 7 (Oct 1910) 223-8.
[Unexamined].

3056 ________. Movable property of married women under Ordinance 15 of 1876. *In* Ceylon Law Review 7 (1910) 277-82.
[Unexamined].

vi) Fertility patterns

3057 ABHAYARATNE, O.E.R. and C.H.S. JAYEWARDENE. Fertility trends in Ceylon. *In* Ceylon J. of Historical and Social Studies 7,2 (1964) 99-111.
Reviews fertility trends from 1871 to 1963 using censuses and other documents. Numerous tables.

3058 ________. Fertility trends in Ceylon. *In* Ceylon J. of Medical Science 13 (1964) 1-77.
[Unexamined].

3059 ________. Fertility trends in Ceylon. Colombo: Colombo Apothecaries' Company, 1967. 421p.
First part presents population and fertility trends from 1900 to 1960. The second part reports the results of a survey of 8,043 villagers, undertaken just before the implementation of the nation-wide family planning program. The survey represents six demographic regions and considers socio-economic factors influencing family planning and fertility. Numerous tables.

3060 CEYLON. DEPARTMENT OF CENSUS AND STATISTICS. Fertility trends in Ceylon. Colombo: Government Press, 1954. 5p. (Department of Census and Statistics, Monograph 3).
[Unexamined. NUC].

3061 CHINNATAMBY, SIVA. Fertility trends in Ceylonese women. *In* J. of Reproduction and Fertility 3,3 (1962) 342-55.
Data on reproductive lives of 5,223 women. Reports average ages at menarche, marriage and menopause for various socio-economic groups.

3062 RYAN, BRYCE. Institutional factors in Sinhalese fertility. *In* Milbank Memorial Fund Quarterly 30,4 (1952) 359-81.
Presents a framework for considering social context of fertility and its control. Considers certain aspects of the Sinhalese marriage system and discusses attitudes toward sex and fertility in a particular peasant village. Compares attitudes of men and women toward family size and birth control. Concludes that "educational and public relations techniques cannot easily surmount the conjoined effects of male sex dominance and distinctive male rewards for numerous progeny."

3063 SAMARAKKODY, AMARA. Woman's status and fertility rates in Sri Lanka. Ph.D. dissertation, Department of Anthropology, State University of New York at Buffalo, 1976. 140p. [University Microfilms 77-3578].
Documents the decline of women's status brought about by industrialization and westernization in Sri Lanka. Refutes common assumption that fertility decline in developing countries requires industrialization. Asserts that women's status is more dependent upon economic control than upon employment itself and effective family planning programs can be implemented without industrialization where female status is high. [Unexamined. DAI].

vii) Pregnancy and childbirth

3064 DISSANAIKE, A. Some Sinhalese customs relating to maternity, child-birth and children. *In* National Monthly of Ceylon 2,10 (1913) 236-8.
[Unexamined].

3065 GOONETILLEKE, WILLIAM. Doladuk (dohada). *In* Orientalist 2 (1885/86) 81-2.
Briefly discusses the craving for certain foods, especially clay, by pregnant Sinhalese women. Also discusses Sinhalese practice of "kissing" with the nose. With Sanskrit quotations from Kālidāsa and other sources.

3066 HILDBURGH, W.L. Notes on Sinhalese magic. *In* J. of the Royal Anthropological Institute 38 (1908) 148-87.
Includes material on controlling gender of forthcoming child, along with cures for barrenness, lack of breast milk and pregnancy and parturition complications.

3067 JOSEF, BYRON. The demon of puerperal sepsis in wild Ceylon. *In* Man 35,109 (1935) 100-1.
Describes ceremony performed in the eighth month of pregnancy in the "belief that puerperal fever is due to the 'devil' of puerperal sepsis having intercourse with the pregnant woman just before childbirth."

3068 OBEYESEKERE, G. Pregnancy cravings (dola-duka) in relation to social structure and personality in a Sinhalese village. *In* American Anthropologist 65,2 (1963) 323-42.
Relates the patterns of the regression-nausea-vomiting-craving complex in Rambadeniya village, Central Province, to problems that the social system creates for women. Considers this complex to be a culturally constituted defense.

3069 SHAMSUDEEN, A.T. Ceremonies relating to childbirth observed by the Moors of Ceylon. *In* Orientalist 3 (1888/89) 17-20.
Describes customs and rituals pertaining to pregnancy, childbirth and early infancy including the general treatment, diet and birth impurity of the mother and the infant's naming, tonsure and feeding ceremonies.

viii) Motherhood and child rearing

3070 DE SILVA, KINGSLEY. Trends in maternal mortality. *In* J. of Obstetrics and Gynaecology of the Association of Obstetricians and Gynaecologists of Ceylon 1 (1969) 14-25.
Part one considers Ceylon trends from 1900 to 1965. The second part presents data from De Soysa Hospital for Women, Colombo, 1957-67. Tables and graphs. [Unexamined].

3071 THWAITES, JEANNE. Mother and child. South Brunswick, New Jersey: A.S. Barnes, 1967. 136p. [*Also* London: Thomas Yoseloff].
Photo essay devoted primarily to women and children of traditional backgrounds, e.g., peasants and fisherfolk. [Unexamined. BAS].

ix) Rebirth accounts

3072 STEVENSON, IAN. The case of Gnanatilleka. *In his* Twenty cases suggestive of reincarnation. New York: American Society for Psychical Research, 1966. pp.118-34.
Case study of a young girl from Central Ceylon who, from her first year onward, made references to her previous life as a particular boy. Data from various interviews suggest that the girl possesses paranormal knowledge.

3073 ________ and FRANCIS STORY. A case of the reincarnation type in Ceylon: the case of Disna Samarasinghe. *In* J. of Asian and African Studies 5,4 (1970) 241-55.
Case study of a Sinhalese girl from Udobagawa village near Kandy. Attempts to explain her reincarnation story. Reports her statements about persons, places and objects from her previous life, which were substantiated, and her behavior, which was consonant with that of the previous personality. Makes a clear distinction between possession and reincarnation as explanations for the case.

(e) Domestic sphere and family life

3074 GREEN, THOMAS LESLIE. Evolution de la famille à Ceylan sous l'influence de l'instruction et des contacts sociaux [Development of the Ceylon family under the influence of education and cross-cultural contact]. *In* Familles Dans le Monde 9,4 (1956) 283-98.
[Unexamined].

3075 RYAN, BRYCE. The Sinhalese family system. *In* Eastern Anthropologist 6,3/4 (1953) 143-63.
Describes Sinhalese family and marriage patterns.

3076 TAMBIAH, S.J. Kinship fact and fiction in relation to the Kandyan Sinhalese. *In* J. of the Royal Anthropological Institute 95,2 (1965) 131-73.
Lengthy article concerned with many aspects of Sinhalese kinship. Includes a major section on land rights of women.

3077 YALMAN, NUR. Under the Bo tree: studies in caste, kinship and marriage in the interior of Ceylon. Berkeley: University of California Press, 1967. 406p.
Major sections discuss Sri Lanka background as relevant to a highland village, describe kinship and marriage systems of several Sri Lanka villages and compare Sri Lanka kinship structure to that found in South India. Interspersed material on women.

(f) Women's sexuality, seclusion, spirit possession

3078 OBEYESEKERE, GANANATH. The idiom of demonic possession: a case study. *In* Social Science and Medicine 4,1 (1970) 97-111.
Attempts to "illustrate some of the interconnections between cultural idiom and mental illness "with the case history of a village woman from the Western Province. Her symptoms are seen to reflect conflicts with the role of women as inferior, unclean, submissive and so forth. Spirit possession, in this woman's case, is a medium of expression of hostile and repressed feelings "transformed into a publicly intelligible cultural idiom" that "facilitates communication between patient, ritual specialist, the family and the larger community."

3079 _______. Psychocultural exegesis of a case of spirit possession in Sri Lanka. *In* Vincent Crapanzano and Vivian Garrison, eds. Case studies in spirit possession. New York: John Wiley and Sons, 1977. pp.235-94. [*Adapted from* Contributions to Asian Studies 8 (1975) 41-89].
Detailed case study of "Somavati," a 29-year-old Buddhist woman of a cultivator caste living in an urban village near Colombo. "These tendencies [sexual puritanism and inhibition of aggression] are widespread among the general female population, and cannot be considered the cause of spirit possession . . . . But if some of the modal psychological problems are intensified, or new stresses have to be coped with, then I believe conditions favorable to spirit possession may arise." Views most ecstatic religious experiences as predicated upon individual experiences but expressed in culturally constructed ways.

3080 YALMAN, NUR. On the meaning of food offerings in Ceylon. *In* Robert F. Spencer, ed. Forms of symbolic action: proceedings of the 1969 annual spring meeting of the American Ethnological Society. Seattle: University of Washington Press, 1969. pp.81-96. [*Also in* Social Compass 20,2 (1973) 287-302].
Section entitled "Cooking" contains brief comments on relations between women, men, food and sex in Sinhalese culture. "Cooking for a man implies sexual intercourse in this culture."

3081 YOOSOOF, P.M. Is "purdah" a hindrance to Muslim women's progress in Ceylon? *In* Islamica Zeylanica 3 (1952/53) 23-5.
[Unexamined].

(g) The spiritual life and religious observances

i) Goddess Pattini and her cult

3082 GOMBRICH, R. Food for seven grandmothers: stages in the universalisation of a Sinhalese ritual. *In* Man n.s. 6,1 (1971) 5-17.
Describes the stages of transformation of the ritual of providing a meal for seven grandmothers from its existence as a local-level practice to its integration into the main body of Buddhist worship, or "the assimilation of a ceremony associated with Pattinī to a ceremony congenial to Theravāda Buddhist ideology." Includes material on mothers, grandmothers, goddesses and breast feeding.

3083 HIATT, LESTER R. The Pattini cult of Ceylon: a Tamil perspective. *In* Social Compass 20,2 (1973) 231-49.
Analyzes the role of the Pattini cult and particularly the "horn play" rite in the social structure and psychological fantasy world of Sri Lanka Tamils. Data from the eastern coastal village of Thambiluvil.

3084 KANAPATHIPILLAI, KANDASAMY. The story of Kannaki: a Ceylon version. *In* Hindu Organ, Diamond Jubilee Number (Apr 1950) 11-6.

[Unexamined].

3085 LE MESURIER, C.J.R. Aṇ-keḷiya. *In* J. of the Royal Asiatic Society, Ceylon Branch 8,29 (1884) 368-94.
Describes "horn play" game associated with worship of Pattini. Also relates accounts by previous observers and provides Sinhala excerpts and English translation of a poem concerning episodes from Pattini's life and the origins of the game.

3086 MANJUSRI, L.T.P. The goddess Pattini. *In* Ceylon Today 5,8 (1956) 23-6.
[Unexamined].

3087 OBEYESEKERE, GANANATH. The goddess Pattini and the Lord Buddha: notes on the myth and the birth of the deity. *In* Social Compass 20,2 (1973) 217-29.
Asserts that Pattini and Lord Buddha are "born in the human world in order to help or redeem mankind." In order to remain pure, Pattini is "conceived and born outside of the normal manner, unmediated by impure sexual intercourse and semen emission." She is born from a mango pierced by an arrow, itself symbolic of sexual intercourse. Some myths further portray her as a virgin and as incapable of menstruating.

3088 PERTOLD, OTAKAR. Die ceylonische Göttin Pattinī [The Ceylon goddess Pattini]. *In* Archiv Orientální 13 (1942) 201-24.
Major sections consider general characteristics of Pattini cult, Pattini in Sinhala folk songs, the relationship of the Sinhala Pattini legend to the Tamil Kaṇṇaki legend, forms of the Pattini cult in Sri Lanka, the similarity of Pattini and the Kiri Ammās and the origin of the Pattini myth.

3089 RAGHAVAN, M.D. The Pattini cult as a socio-religious institution. *In* Spolia Zeylanica 26,2 (1951) 251-61. (Ethnological Survey of Ceylon, 3).
Presents details of two popular aspects of Pattini propitiation as observed in a village near Colombo, the "horn play" and the "village hall" rites. Thirteen photographs.

3090 WIJESEKERA, N.D. Pūnāva clay vessels with symbolic snakes used in the cult of Pattini in Ceylon. *In* Man 40,60 (1940) 49-50.
Describes ceremonial vessels and supplies a short version of Pattini's birth story. Photographs.

3091 YALMAN, NUR. Dual organization in Central Ceylon? Or, the goddess on the tree-top. *In* J. of Asian Studies 24,3 (1965) 441-57. [*Revised reprint in* Manning Nash, ed. Anthropological studies in Theravada Buddhism. New Haven, Yale University Press, 1966. pp.197-223].
Analyzes "horn play" ritual from Pattini cult (with myth summary), reviews central features of rite and discusses its relation to village social organization and sexual divisions. The rite concerns sexual relations and the male-female dichotomy. It "counteracts unions 'against the grain' (*pratiloma*), and thereby protects the purity of the castes and the community. The purity of the community enhances its luck, fertility, health, wealth, and the general well being of the inhabitants."

ii) Sītā in Lanka

3092 RAGHAVAN, M.D. Sita Eliya and its legends. *In his* Ceylon: a pictorial survey of the peoples and arts. Colombo: M.D. Gunasena and Company, 1962. pp.212-7.
Regarding contemporary legends and sites of Sri Lanka relating to Sītā's sojourn there as described in the *Rāmāyaṇa*.

iii) Images of women in Sinhalese Buddhism

3093 AMARASINGHAM, LORNA RHODES. The misery of the embodied: representations of women in Sinhalese myth. *In* Judith Hoch-Smith and Anita Spring, eds. Women in ritual and symbolic roles. New York: Plenum Press, 1978. pp.101-26.
Regarding the depiction of women as metaphors for wordly impermanence and sorrow in Sinhalese Buddhism. Explores two aspects, the embodiment of sensual pleasure and the act of giving birth. Analyzes a series of "little tradition" demon myths thematically to show that "women play a central role not only in actually giving birth to the demon but also in expressing, activating, or encouraging the desires that are the essence of his demonic character." Proposes that this is consistent with portrayal in "great tradition" texts.

3094 DHAMMADINNA, SISTER. Bhikkhuni Samgha must be revived. *In* J. of the Maha Bodhi Society 58 (1950).
[Unexamined].

iv) Our Lady of Lanka

3095 ANTHONY, D.J. Our Lady of Lanka. Tr. by John M. Senaveratne. Colombo: Colombo Catholic Press, 1945. 44p.
Considers Catholicism in Ceylon, with special reference to the distinctive worship of the Holy Mother. In honor of 400th year of Catholicism in the country. Plates. [Unexamined].

(h) Employment

i) Patterns and opportunities

3096 ABEYESOORIYA, SAMSON. Ceylon's women workers and the war. Colombo: St. Gerard's Press, 1918. 21p.
[Unexamined. BMG].

3097 FERNANDO, E.C. [SYLVIA E.C. FERNANDO?]. Entry of women into the ranks of the gainfully employed. *In* Industrial Ceylon: J. of the Ceylon National Chamber of Industries 1,1 (1961) 27-31.
[Unexamined].

3098 FERNANDO, SYLVIA. Patterns of female employment in Ceylon. *In* Independent Ceylon: the first year, Feb. 4, 1948-Feb. 4, 1949. Colombo: Department of Information, 1949. pp.47-50.
[Unexamined].

3099 KANNANGARA, IMOGEN. Women's employment in Ceylon. *In* International Labour Review 93,2 (1966) 117-26.
Discusses changing patterns of female employment in Sri Lanka and some of the variables involved.

3100 SENEVIRATNE, MAUREEN, ed. A handbook of careers for women in Ceylon. Colombo: Good Shepherd Convent, 1969. 149p.
Reviews requirements and job descriptions in nearly 50 fields, with opening remarks on choosing a career. Issued to commemorate the Careers for Women Exhibition held at the Good Shepherd Convent, Kotahena, in 1969.

ii) Particular occupations

3101 Lady law students. *In* Ceylon Law Recorder 10 (Oct 1928).
[Unexamined].

3102 Lady law students: editorial notes. *In* Ceylon Law Students' Magazine 1 (1925) 38.
[Unexamined].

3103 RYAN, BRYCE and SYLVIA FERNANDO. The female factory worker in Colombo. *In* International Labour Review 64,5/6 (1951) 438-61. [*Reprint* Geneva: International Labour Organization, 1952. 24p.].
Interpretation of interviews with 238 women employed in various industries. Describes "the economic distress and socially abnormal background of the women forced into the role of wage-earner .... The prevalence of desertion, widowhood and conglomerate family compositions, as well as the frequency of unsupervised children, speak eloquently of the need for various forms of social service."

3104 WIJAYARATNE, C.M., A.M.T. GUNAWARDANA and SAMIR ASMAR. Study of income generating activities for farm women. Colombo: Agrarian Research and Training Institute, 1978. 73p. (*Its* Research Study Series, 25).
Study conducted by Agrarian Research and Training Institute in collaboration with the Farm Women's Agricultural Extension Project, Department of Agriculture. [Unexamined. ALS].

3105 Women and legal education. *In* Ceylon Law Students' Magazine (1927) 52-3.
[Unexamined].

(i) Education

3106 Agricultural education for women in Ceylon. *In* African Women 5,1 (1962) 22-3.
Discusses agricultural education opportunities for women at the School of Agriculture at Kundasale, at the Practical Farm Schools and in Young Farmer's Clubs.

3107 FERNANDO, G.P.S. and T.A.C. SIRIWARDENA. The outlook for certified school girls: a prognostic study. *In* Probation and Child Care Journal 7,1 (1969) 19-24.
[Unexamined].

3108 MOTWANI, CLARA. Education of women in Ceylon. *In* Education Quarterly 13, 50 (1961) 175-7.
Reviews the recent rapid growth in educational opportunities and, consequently, in career participation of Sri Lanka women.

(j) Development and social welfare

i) Women's associations

3109 ASSOCIATION OF WOMEN'S INSTITUTES IN CEYLON. Report. 1- (1929/30?-). [Colombo]. Annually.
[Unexamined. NUC].

3109a ________. Lanka Mahila Samiti (affiliated to the Associated Country Women of the World) 1930-1955. [Colombo, 1955?]. 157p.

Illustrated. [Unexamined. NUC].

3110 HUNTSWORTH, C. ELIZABETH. Lanka Mahila Samiti: women against the jungle. *In* Free World (Mar 1952). [Unexamined].

3110a MARGA INSTITUTE. The Lanka Mahila Samiti (the Sri Lanka Women's Association). ***And*** The Girl Guides' Association of Sri Lanka. ***And*** The Young Women's Christian Association. ***In its*** Nonformal education in Sri Lanka: a study. Colombo: Marga Institute, 1974. pp.125-32, 139-40, 145-9, 218-20.
Briefly outlines the establishment, organization, membership, objectives and activities of these women's and girls' organizations.

ii) Family planning

3111 ABHAYARATNE, O.E.R. and C.H.S. JAYEWARDENE. Family planning in Ceylon. Colombo: Colombo Apothecaries' Company, 1968. 188p.
Study designed to evaluate effectiveness of the government family planning program, socio-economic background of patrons of Family Planning Association clinics of greater Colombo and relative efficacy of male- and female-oriented propaganda. Briefly reviews history of family planning movement in Sri Lanka and discusses the nation's population policy.

3112 KINCH, ARNE. A preliminary report from the Sweden-Ceylon family planning pilot project. *In* Clyde V. Kiser, ed. Research in Family Planning. Princeton, New Jersey: Princeton University Press, 1962. pp.85-102.
Summary of the early years of a rural family planning project in Sri Lanka sponsored jointly by the governments of Sweden and, then, Ceylon. The program was designed to assess local family planning attitudes, to investigate family planning potentials and to provide family planning instruction and was established in a village area among Sinhalese Buddhists and on a tea estate among Tamil Hindus.

3113 RYAN, BRYCE. Hinayana Buddhism and family planning in Ceylon. *In* . . . the interrelations of demographic, economic, and social problems in selected underdeveloped areas: proceedings of a round table at the 1953 annual conference of the Milbank Memorial Fund. New York: the Fund, 1954. pp.90-102.
Briefly discusses the "textual and metaphysical bearing of Buddhism upon family planning" and reports upon a survey of 86 Buddhist monks regarding contraception. While Buddhist texts are concerned with rebirth and nonharming, they do not deal specifically with contraception. However, villagers "generally" find conscious family planning attempts to be in opposition to these principles. Well-educated monks tended to view family planning as ethically good. Poorly educated ones tended to concur with villagers.

(k) Political participation

i) Leadership and elections

3114 JAYAWARDENA, KUMARI. The participation of women in the social reform, political and labour movements of Sri Lanka. *In* Logos 13,2 (1974) 17-25.
Briefly reviews many female leaders of Sri Lanka, primarily of the 20th century.

3115 WEERAWARDANA, I.D.S. Role of women in the Ceylon general election of 1952. *In* A. Appadorai, ed. The status of women in South Asia. Bombay: Orient Longmans, 1954. pp.115-124.
General survey. Concludes that political participation of all classes and groups of women in Sri Lanka is low. Volume is proceedings of a UNESCO seminar held in December 1958 and January 1959.

ii) Sirimavo Bandaranaike, prime minister 1960-65, 1970-77

3116 DHANAPALA, D.B. Madam Premier. Colombo: M.D. Gunasena, 1960. 40p. Illustrated. [Unexamined].

3117 MUKERJI, KRISHNA PRASANNA. Madame Prime Minister Sirimavo Bandaranaike. Colombo: M.D. Gunasena, 1960. 75p. Illustrated. [Unexamined].

3118 SENEVIRATNE, MAUREEN. Sirimavo Bandaranaike, the world's first woman Prime Minister: a biography. Colombo: Hansa Publishers, 1975. 209p.
Reviews Mrs. Bandaranaike's life story to 1960 when she assumed the position of prime minister of Ceylon. Discusses her birth into a royal Kandyan family, her work with the Lanka Mahila Samiti and her marriage with S.W.R.D. Bandaranaike, assassinated prime minister of Ceylon. Numerous photographs.

(l) Popular magazines for women

For creative writing in English by women of Sri Lanka see entries 2706, 2805-07 and 2844

3119 Ceylon Housewife. vl- (1956-). Colombo.
[Unexamined. BMG].

3120 Ceylon Woman. vl- (1953-). Colombo.
[Unexamined. BMG].

3121 Fair Ceylon . . . the Premier Journal of Women in Ceylon. vl- (1951?-). Colombo. Monthly.
[Unexamined. BMG].

3122 Fashion Panorama. vl- (1957-). Colombo. Monthly.
[Unexamined].

(m) Jewelry

3123 JAYAWARDANA, SITA. Ceylon's traditional jewelry. *In* Times of Ceylon Annual (1951).
[Unexamined].

3124 SHAMSIDIN, A.T. Ornaments worn by the Moorish women of Ceylon. *In* Orientalist 2 (1885/86) 152-5.
Catalogs and describes 39 ornaments worn on the head, nose, ears, neck, arms, wrists, waist and feet.

(n) Western women in independent Sri Lanka

3125 BLAZÉ, RAY. A great social worker: Dr. Mary Rutnam. *In* Ceylon Today 7,9 (1958) 15-8.
[Unexamined].

3126 NESIAH, LANKA. Sister Elizabeth of Navajeevanam. *In* Ceylon Methodist Church Record 116,4 (1972) 15-8.
Her mission work in Paranthan, Northern Province. A western woman? [Unexamined].

3127 RANASINGHE, ANNE. Poems. Colombo: Lake House Investments, 1971. 53p.
Themes in this first published collection reflect poet's German background and her more recent experiences as a resident of Sri Lanka.

3128 ________. With words we write our lives: past, present, future. Colombo: Hansa Publishers, 1972. 162p.
Short stories and poetry reprinted from various sources. Somber themes predominate, reflecting the author's experiences in Germany, England and Sri Lanka.

3129 ________. Plead mercy. n.p., 1975. 38p.
Poetry. [Unexamined. BAS].

(2) South India: area of mainland-Tamil, Malayalam, Kannada and Telugu languages

(a) The colonial experience: social reform issues

3130 DUFF, MRS, GRANT. Speeches, 1884-5-6. Madras: Higginbotham and Company, 1886. 89p.
Reproduces a series of addresses given by Mrs. Duff in connection with the establishment and ongoing operations of schools, hospitals and other institutions in South India, many exclusively serving women.

3130a KESAVANARAYANA, B. Progress of women. *In his* Political and social factors in Andhra, 1900-1956. Vijayawada: Navodaya, 1976. pp.193-265.
History of women's movement in Andhra in the first half of the 20th century. Considers impetus given by freedom movement and influence of Annie Besant and Mahatma Gandhi. Considers social reform issues and particularly details widow marriage, ***devadāsī*** reform and female education movements. Documented with numerous contemporary sources.

3131 Women's work in Madras: reminiscences. Madras: Women's Indian Association. [Unexamined].

i) Widow marriage

3132 LEONARD, JOHN G. Kandukuri Viresalingam, 1949-1919: a biography of an Indian social reformer. Ph.D. dissertation, Department of History, University of Wisconsin, Madison, 1970. 420p. [University Microfilms 70-20, 853].
Discusses his pioneering efforts in Madras and Rajahmundry, with a detailed account (pp.146-98) of his work for the promotion of widow marriage. He himself performed numerous widows' marriage ceremonies, established two girls' schools, began two widows' homes for the destitute and edited a journal publicizing these and other activities.

ii) Education

3133 BROCKWAY, K. NORA. A larger way for women: aspects of Christian education for girls in South India, 1712-1948. Madras: Oxford University Press, 1949. 189p.
"This book traces the development of education for Indian girls carried on in South India by non-Roman missions and churches from the year 1712 until 1948." Discusses nascent efforts at the Tranquebar Mission; the Vepery Mission; the consequences of the Charter Act of 1813, which included education in the duties of the East India Company and facilitated the arrival of many missionaries and their wives; the role of the government in 19th century mission education; the increasing involvement of Indians as their own leaders; and the rising social reform movement. Concludes with "Thoughts on Christian Education." Photographs.

3134 ________ and GETSIE R. SAMUEL. A new day for Indian women: the story of St. Christopher's Training College, Madras, 1923-1963. Madras: Christian Literature Society, 1963. 226p.
Brockway, who wrote the larger section of the book, was closely connected with the college from its founding in 1923 until her retirement. Considers establishment of school and growth of curriculum, facilities and personnel. Photographs.

3135 BROCKWAY, K.N. and MARJORIE SYKES. Unfinished pilgrimage: the story of some South Indian schools, 1823-1923, 1923-1973. Madras: Christian Literature Society, 1973. 114p. (St. Christopher's Training College, Golden Jubilee Volume, 1923-1973).
History of St. Christopher's Training College and related institutions in the broader context of South Indian educational movements. Uses material from ***A Larger Way for Women*** and ***A New Day for Indian Women***, supplemented and updated.

3136 KINGSCOTE, GEORGIANA. A brahmin school-girl. *In* Nineteenth Century 25 (Jan 1889) 133-9.
Describes the Maharani's Girls' School (precursor to Maharani's College for Women) at Mysore, "established by a Hindu for [high-caste] Hindus on strictly Hindu lines." Includes a summary of the curriculum and a letter from a student to the author describing her school life.

3137 MC DOUGALL, ELEANOR. Women's Christian College, Madras, 1915-1925. Madras: Women's Christian College, 1926. 36p.
Plates. [Unexamined. BMG].

3138 ________. Lamps in the wind: South Indian college women and their problems. London: Cargate Press, 1940. 165p.
Events, personalities and problems of the first quarter century of Women's Christian College, Madras. Work was written to demonstrate to sympathetic westerners the growing needs of Indian women's higher education, which could no longer be accommodated by missionaries.

3139 MALHARI RAO, S. Female education in India: H.H. the Maharani's Girls' School, Mysore. *In* Educational Review 2, (Jan-Feb, Apr, Jul 1896) 15-9, 63-7, 172-6, 321-3.
[Unexamined].

3140 MILLER, WILLIAM. Female education in southern India. Edinburgh, 1878.
[Unexamined].

3141 Queen Mary's College: the first two decades. Madras: Queen Mary's College, 1936.
[Unexamined].

3142 ROSENTHAL, E. Some aspects of women's education in Hyderabad. *In* Asiatic Review n.s. 32,112 (1936) 763-8.
Considers the Nizam of Hyderabad's most significant civic achievements to be in the area of women's education. Reviews the establishment and programs of various institutions and organizations associated with women's education there, most notably the Osmania University College for Women (formerly Zenana College).

3143 Women pioneers in education: Tamil Nadu. Prepared by the National Seminar on the Role of Women in Education in India, International Women's Year, 1975. Madras: Society for the Promotion of Education in India, 1975. 69p.
Sketches of the lives and achievements of five women who pioneered in founding educational and welfare institutions in the late 19th and early 20th centuries: Sister R.S. Subbalakshmi, Mrs. E.S. Appasamy, Annie Besant, Mary Clubwala Jadhav, and Dr. Muthulakshmi Reddy.

3144 WOMEN'S CHRISTIAN COLLEGE. Report of the council. (1915/16-). Madras. Annually.
These reports exist from 1915/16 through at least 1965/66. [Unexamined. MRL].

3145 Women's College Magazine. v1- (1938-). Trivandrum. Annually.
Published in English, Hindi, Malayalam, Sanskrit and Tamil. [Unexamined. IPP].

iii) Health

3146 KUGLER, ANNA S. Guntur Mission Hospital, Guntur, India . . . Philadelphia: Women's Missionary Society, United Lutheran Church in America, 1928. 135p.
Documents work and growth of Guntur Mission Hospital in the first quarter of the 20th century. The author details her own participation and that of other women, programs, budgets and so forth. Photographs.
[Unexamined. NUC].

3146a SCHARLIEB, MARY. Reminiscences. London: Williams and Norgate, 1924. 239p.
Memoirs based on diaries. Dr. Scharlieb became determined to become a doctor when she realized that many Hindu and Muslim women could not be treated by male doctors. Recounts her struggles to overcome prejudice against female doctors during training and practice. Her Indian work included the founding of the Royal Victoria Hospital for Caste and Gosha Women, Madras. [Unexamined].

iv) *Devadāsīs, basavis* and "nautch girls"

3147 ANANTHA KRISHNA IYER, L.K. Devadasis in South India: their traditional origin and development. *In* Man in India 7,1 (1927) 47-52.
Devadāsīs as one of eight classes of *dāsīs* enumerated in Sanskrit texts. Provides some ethnographic details of South Indian *devadāsīs* and compares them with *basavis* of Kurnool and Bellary Districts. The latter are a class of women who, through a simple temple ceremony, acquire the right to act as sons in inheritance and other family matters.

3148 CHATTERJEE, SANTOSH. Devadasi: temple dancer. Calcutta: Book House, 1945. 128p.
Regarding the *devadāsīs* and *basavis* of South India. Discusses recruitment, training, social organization. anti-*devadāsī* movement and legislation, recent changes and South India dance forms related to the tradition. Opposes complete abolition of the institution. Reviews South Asian antecedents and cross-cultural similarities. With drawings of dancers and hand gestures and excerpts from various accounts.

3149 DE ZOETE, BERYL. Bharata natya, part I: the devadasis and their role in mediaeval Hindu society. *In her* The other mind: a study of dance in South India. New York: Theatre Art Books, 1960. pp.160-79.
Discussion focuses on *devadāsīs* in the 19th century (drawing from several published accounts) and the *bhārata nāṭyam* dance form, which evolved from their tradition.

3150 FAWCETT, FRED. On basavis: women who, through dedication to a deity, assume masculine privileges. *In* J. of the Anthropological Society of Bombay 2 (1889) 322-45. *With* W. Dymock. A note on the same subject, pp.345-5. *And* Appendix: extracts from works on Hindu law on the "appointed daughter," pp.346-53.
"In the western part of the Bellary district, . . . and . . . portions of Dharwar and the Mysore Province . . . women of the lower Sudra castes . . . take a son's place in performance of funeral rites of parents and in inheritance of property . . . . 'Basavis. . . . live in their father's house; they do not marry, yet they bear children, the father of whom they may choose at pleasure, who inherit the family name." An ethnographic report on this practice employed primarily by sonless families.

3151 KARKHANIS, G.G. Devadasi: a burning problem of Karnataka. Bijapur: Radha Printing Works, 1959.
[Unexamined].

3152 Manifesto to Madras Government by members of the Devadasi Association. Madras: Aurora Press, 1927.
[Unexamined].

3153 Mukti. Directed by N. Laxminarayan. (Kannada dialogue/English subtitles). 100 min. Black and white. [*Distributed by* Navodaya Chitra, 87a 2nd Main Road, Palace Guttahalli, Bangalore 3].
Daughter of an aging *devadāsī* struggles between her mother's attempts to secure her as a "keep" for her mother's patron and her own interests in studying and the man of her choosing. [Unexamined].

3154 NADKARNI, VITHAL C. Devadasis: married to God and Mammon. *In* Illustrated Weekly of India 96,50 (14 Dec 1975) 8-15.
Primarily an interview with a Kannada woman who was betrothed to the goddess Ellamma by her parents on the day of her birth so that they could go to heaven. She describes the *jōgati* community of which she is thus a member, her marriage rite, a myth associated with the group and public attitudes toward members of the group. The article also discusses the identity of Ellamma and the origin of *devadāsīs*. Photographs.

3155 PARASURAMA, supposed author. La devadassi (bayadère): comédie en quatre parties [The temple dancer: a comedy in four acts]. Tr. from Tamil by Louis Jacolliot. Paris: Librarie Internationale, 1868. 46p.
Play. [Unexamined. NUC].

3156 SARANGAPANI AYYANGAR, P.S. The devadasi system. *In* South Indian Natyakala Conference 8, December 27 1955-January 3 1956. Proceedings. 1956? pp.22-31.
General discussion. Argues that *devadāsīs* are not prostitutes. [Unexamined].

3157 SHORTT, JOHN. The bayadère or dancing girls of southern India. *In* Memoirs Read Before the Anthropological Society of London 3 (1867/69) 182-94.
Ethnography of temple dancers based on data from various parts of South India. Considers recruitment and training, daily life, dress, details of performance (instruments, dance styles) and place in larger society.

3158 SRINIVAS, M.N. The basavis (religious prostitutes) of Mysore. *In his* Marriage and family in Mysore. Bombay: New Book Company, 1942. pp.177-84.
Ethnographic details of the *basavi* institution in Karnataka. Discusses various motives for dedicating girls to deities; the dedication procedure; sexuality of *basavis*; distinctions among *basavis*, *devadāsīs* and other groups of women with unconventional life styles; and the auspiciousness of these women.

3159 THURSTON, EDGAR. Dēva-dāsi. *In his* Castes and tribes of southern India, v2. Madras: Government Press, 1909. pp.125-53.
Compilation of official and nonofficial statements about *devadāsīs*. Considers origin, various historical aspects, social organization, variant regional patterns, dancing girls as entertainment, *basavis*, recruitment, legal disputes and proverbs.

3160 TIRUMALAYYA NAIDU, C. Music and the anti-nautch movement. Madras, 1906.
[Unexamined].

v) Christian conversion

3161 FLEMING, DANIEL JOHNSON. An industrial institution for women. *In his* Schools with a message in India. London: Oxford University Press, 1921. pp.97-106.
Regarding the programs of the Lucy Perry Noble Bible School, Madurai, among "the oldest and most successful" of institutions designed to meet the needs of Christian women rejected from orthodox homes and traditional support systems in years before marriage. Based on reports, other documents and interviews with the principal.

3162 HARBAND, BEATRICE M. Jaya: which means victory; this is the story of a Hindu girl of high degree, telling of her life's struggles as a maiden, wife and widow. London: Marshall Brothers, 1914? 302p.
Story of a South Indian woman who embraces Christianity and her struggles with traditional society. Comments on reform issues of child marriage and dancing girls.

3163 PICKEN, W.H. JACKSON. From an India zenana: the story of Lydia Muttulakshmi . . . London: C.H. Kelly, 1892. 64p.
A convert to Christianity? [Unexamined. BMG].

(b) The colonial experience: western women in South India

i) Dr. Ida and the Scudder family

3164 BEATTY, JEROME. So that mothers may live. *In* Reader's Digest 43,259 (1943) 101-4.
Reviews Dr. Ida Scudder's background and the medical work she has done over the years in the Vellore area.

3165 JEFFERY, MARY PAULINE. Dr. Ida, India: the life story of Ida S. Scudder. New York: Fleming H. Revell Company, 1938. 212p.
Dr. Ida Scudder's youth and early years of medical work in Vellore.

3166 ________. Ida S. Scudder of Vellore: the life story of Ida Sophia Scudder. Mysore: Wesley Press, 1951? 273p.
Revised and enlarged jubilee biography. Numerous photographs document Dr. Scudder's life and the growth of her medical facilities at Vellore.

3167 SCUDDER, DOROTHY JEALOUS. A thousand years in thy sight: the story of the Scudders of India. Shelter Island, New York: the author, 1970. 418p.
Account of four generations of medical mission work in India. Much concerns the well-known Dr. Ida Sophia Scudder and her niece, Dr. Ida Belle Scudder, and their work for India's women and children. [Unexamined].

3168 WILSON, DOROTHY CLARKE. Dr. Ida: the story of Dr. Ida Scudder of Vellore. New York: McGraw-Hill, 1959. 358p. [*Also* London: Hodder and Stoughton, 1960. 350p.].
Dr. Ida's medical mission work. Illustrated. [Unexamined. NUC].

ii) Amy Wilson-Carmichael's mission work

3169 HOUGHTON, FRANK. Amy Carmichael of Dohnavur: the story of a lover and her beloved. London: S.P.C.K., 1953. 390p.
Her work for child welfare. Illustrated. Portraits. [Unexamined. MRL].

3170 WILSON-CARMICHAEL, AMY [AMY (WILSON) CARMICHAEL]. Things as they are: mission work in southern India. London: Morgan and Scott Ltd., 1903. 304p.
Hindu life in South India and the work of missionaries there. Much on women. "The book is a battle-book, written from a battle-field where the fighting is not pretty play but stern reality." Photographs.

3171 ________. Overweights of joy. London: Morgan and Scott, 1906. 300p.
Mission life and work in South India by a Keswick missionary of the Church of England Zenana Missionary Society. Sequel to her *Things as They Are.* Thirty-four photographs.

3172 ________. Lotus buds. London: Morgan and Scott Ltd., 1910. 341p.
Describes incidents from mission work for children in South India and provides biographical and character sketches of workers and children. Fifty striking black and white photographs.

3173 ________. Gold cord: the story of a fellowship. London: S.P.C.K., 1932. 375p.
Work with Indian children. Plates. [Unexamined. MRL].

iii) Other missionary and social service work

3174 BOOTH, WINIFRED. Pictures from a missionary's album. London: Marshall Brothers, Limited, 1923. 76p.
From cover: "Evangelistic incidents among Indian women." Concerns Madras missions. Plates. [Unexamined. NUC].

3175 CHRISTLIEB, M.L. Uphill steps in India. Boston: Houghton Mifflin Company, 1931. 254p. [*Also* London: George Allen and Unwin, 1930].
A woman recalls her mission experiences in South India and relates her impressions of India.

3176 CHURCHILL, MRS. GEORGE [MATILDA (FAULKNER) CHURCHILL]. Grace McLeod Rogers, ed. Letters from my home in India: being the correspondence of Mrs. George Churchill, 1871-1916. New York: George H. Doran Company, 1916? 305p.
Mission work in South India. Illustrated. [Unexamined. MRL].

3177 HARBAND, BEATRICE M. Daughters of darkness in sunny India. New York: Fleming H. Revell Company, 1903. 302p.
"This little volume is sent forth in the hope that the true story of some of the sufferings of India's daughters may appeal to the sympathetic hearts of the more favoured daughters of lands where Jesus, the light of the world rules and reigns." A fictionalized account of mission work in South India by a female mission-

ary who worked there among women and children.

3178 HER MOTHER [ANNIE HERSHEY DOWNIE]. Young missionary: the story of the life of Annie Kennard Downie. Philadelphia: American Baptist Publication Society, 1904. 106p.
A missionary of turn-of-the-century South India. [Unexamined. MRL].

3179 HINKLEY, EDYTH and MARIE L. CHRISTLIEB. A struggle for a soul, and other stories of life and work in South India. London: Religious Tract Society, 1906. 190p.
[Unexamined. NUC].

3180 JACKSON, ELVA. Never a dull moment. London: Highway Press, 1956. 144p.
Mission work in South India. [Unexamined. MRL].

3181 A LADY [JULIA CHARLOTTE MAITLAND]. Letters from Madras during the years 1836-1839. London: John Murray, 1861. 145p. [*Also* 1843 ed. 300p.].
Observations of colonial and native life by "a young married lady, who had accompanied her husband to Madras for the first time." Includes "some description of the Author's intercourse with the natives of Hindostan, and of the endeavours in which she shared to improve their condition," (from introduction).

3182 MITCHELL, MRS. MURRAY [MARIA HAY (FLYTER) MITCHELL]. In southern India: a visit to some of the chief mission stations in the Madras Presidency. London: Religious Tract Society, 1885. 383p.
Account of a tour by husband and wife missionaries. Includes discussion of "female work" and observations of women's lives. Engravings.

3183 MUNSON, ARLEY. Jungle days: being the experiences of an American woman doctor in India. New York: D. Appleton and Company, 1913. 297p.
Travel and Wesleyan medical mission work in Medak. Photographs. [Unexamined. NUC].

3184 WILSON, DOROTHY CLARKE. Granny Brand: her story. Chappaqua, New York: Christian Herald Books, 1976? 222p.
Story of the life and achievements of Evelyn Brand, missionary and mother of a pioneer in surgery and rehabilitation for leprosy, who worked among the hill peoples of Tamil Nadu for 60 years. Photographs.

3185 Women's work in heathen lands. Paisley: Parlane, 1885-87.
Includes: "Gospel in Central India," "Home Jottings" and "Scraps from my Indian Diary" by Mrs. Fordyce; "After Many Days" by John Fordyce; "Girls' School and Zenana Work in Madras" by William Stevenson; "Our Jubilee" by C. Rainy; "Rajahgopaul" by A. Alexander; and "Memorial Sketch of Mrs. Anderson of Madras" by Susan Rajahgopaul. [Unexamined. Book in MRL].

iv) Impressions of a resident and a traveler

3186 PENNY, F.E. On the Coromandel Coast. London: Smith, Elder and Company, 1908. 358p.
Personal experiences and impressions of native and European life in southeast India of the late 19th century by the wife of a chaplain stationed there.

3187 QUIN, EVA WYNDHAM. A trip to Travancore. *In* Nineteenth Century, 31,180 (1892) 255-62.
Account of a six-week camping and hunting tour. "I do not think we shall ever regret having penetrated to the backwaters of Western India and explored the forest-clad hills and lonely jungles of Travancore." Itinerary, arrangements, scenery.

(c) General statements: ethnographic and other

3188 ANDHRA PRADESH. COMMITTEE FOR INTERNATIONAL WOMEN'S YEAR and WOMEN'S WELFARE DEPARTMENT. Women of Andhra Pradesh at a glance. 1974.
[Unexamined].

3189 BEALS, ALAN R. Gopalpur: a South Indian village. New York: Holt, Rinehart and Winston, 1962. 99p. (Case Studies in Cultural Anthropology).
This ethnography of a village in northern Karnataka tends to focus upon the political, economic and other activities of men. Nevertheless, the second and third chapters and various comments and incidents recounted throughout offer much information about women's lives.

3190 BECK, BRENDA E.F. Peasant society in Koṅku: a study of right and left subcastes in South India. Vancouver: University of British Columbia Press, 1972. 334p.
Ethnographic account relating territorial and social organizations in the Konku region of Tamil Nadu. Has much interspersed material on goddesses, particularly Māriyammaṉ, and on women's place within the kinship structure.

3191 DUBE, S.C. Indian village. Ithaca, New York: Cornell University Press, 1955. 248p.
Anthropological account of social life in the village of Shamirpet in the Telangana area of Hyderabad State. Considers child rearing,

festivals, goddesses, dyadic relations within the family, marriage and other life cycle rites, *pardā* observance among Muslims, witchcraft, sexuality and other topics.

3192 In southern India. *In* Annie Van Summer and Samuel M. Zwemer, eds. Our Muslim sisters: a cry of need from lands of darkness interpreted by those who heard it. New York: Fleming H. Revell Company, 1907. pp.253-62.
Various impressions and anecdotes regarding Muslim women in South India. Describes problems of female seclusion and the ameliorating effects of the gospel, the policy of the royal family of Hyderabad regarding women and the particularly conservative nature of many women. Based on mission experience.

3192a KERALA. BUREAU OF ECONOMICS AND STATISTICS. Women in Kerala. [Trivandrum: Bureau of Economics and Statistics, 1978?]. 85p.
Primarily tables. [Unexamined. ALI].

3193 MAC FARLANE, EILEEN W. EARLANSON. Notes on the comparative anthropology of the Christian Mukkuvan women of Travancore. *In* J. of the Indian Anthropological Institute 2,3/4 (1939/40) 19-30.
[Unexamined].

3194 MURICKAN, J. Women in Kerala: changing social status, attitudes and self-image. *In* Social Action 25,3 (1975) 249-66. [*Reprint in* Alfred de Souza, ed. Women in contemporary India: traditional images and changing roles. Delhi: Manohar Book Service, 1975. pp.73-95].
General review of the status of contemporary women in Kerala. Highlights significant contrasts with women in other areas of India, including a higher ratio of women to men, many nationally and internationally prominent women, low female infant and maternal mortality rates and high female literacy. Makes extensive use of unpublished studies.

3195 NITYANANDA, SARASVATHI. Women in Tamil Nadu. *In* Bulletin: Madras Development Seminar Series 5,10 (1975) 552-69.
[Unexamined. BAS].

3196 PADFIELD, J.E. The Hindu at home: being sketches of Hindu daily life, 2d ed. Madras: S.P.C.K. Depository 1908. 298p. [*Also* London: Simpkin, Marshall, Hamilton, Kent and Company. *1st ed.* 1896].
Domestic life in South India. See chapters on women's religion, marriage and ornaments. Appendix relates resolutions of the 1907 Social Reform Conference for South India, Vizagapatam.

3197 PENNY, F.E. South India. *In* T. Athol Joyce and N.W. Thomas, eds. Women of all nations: a record of their characteristics, habits, manners, customs and influence, v4. London: Cassel and Company, 1915? pp.605-25. [*Also* New York: Funk and Wagnalls Company, 1915].
Describes the status, roles and marriage and other customs of Muslim, Hindu and tribal women. Numerous photographs.

3198 SWAMINATHAN, MINA. Chellamma: an illustration of the multiple roles of traditional women. *In* Devaki Jain, ed. Indian women. New Delhi: Publications Division, Ministry of Information and Broadcasting, Government of India, 1975. pp.269-80.
A day in the life of "Chellamma," an elderly brahman woman of Thanjavur District, Tamil Nadu. Composite portrait based upon the lives of several such women known to the author.

3199 ULLRICH, HELEN E. Etiquette among women in Karnataka: forms of address in the village and the family. *In* Social Action 25,3 (1975) 235-48. [*Reprint in* Alfred de Souza, ed. Women in contemporary India: traditional images and changing roles. Delhi: Manohar Book Service, 1975. pp.54-72].
Forms of address among women in "Totagadde" village in the Western Ghats of Karnataka State reflect women's place in village and family structures. Changes in usage at the village level indicate a trend toward egalitarian relationships.

(d) Autobiography, biographies

3200 FELTON, MONICA. A child widow's story. New York: Harcourt, Brace and World, 1966. 192p.
Life story of a Tamil brahman woman as narrated to the author. Sister Subbalakshmi (b.1886), widowed in childhood, was educated and spent the rest of her life promoting female education in South India. Contains much information about political and social reform events of the 20th century.

3201 RATHNAMAL, SITA. Beyond the jungle: a tale of South India. London: William Blackwood, 1968. 253p.
Autobiography of a tribal woman from the Nilgiri hills who went to an English-language school and later received training as a nurse in Madras. Topics include her relationship with a doctor and fond recollections of tribal life. Illustrated. [Unexamined. NUC].

3202 WILSON, DOROTHY CLARKE. Take my hands: the remarkable story of Dr. Mary Verghese. New York: McGraw-Hill, 1963. 216p. [*Also* London: Hodder and Stoughton].
Biography of a leader in the field of physi-

cal rehabilitation. Dr. Verghese, a Padma Shri winner, is currently associated with the Christian Medical College, Vellore. [Unexamined. MRL].

(e) The life cycle

3203 EICHINGER FERRO-LUZZI, GABRIELLA. Women's pollution periods in Tamilnad (India). *In* Anthropos 69,1/2 (1974) 113-61.
Summary of data from interviews with over 1,200 Hindu, Christian, Muslim, Jain and tribal women from various parts of Tamil Nadu regarding beliefs and practices associated with women's pollution. Treats occasions of pollution (puberty, regular menstruation, birth), factors influencing length and strength of pollution, associated symbolism and reasons for persistence or change of beliefs.

3204 ________. Temporary female food avoidances in Tamilnad: interpretations and parallels. *In* East and West n.s. 25, 3/4 (1975) 471-85.
Attempts to understand the principles behind the categorization of foods as hot or cold, pure or impure and health- or disease-promoting (the three sets are not necessary mutually exclusive) and the relationship of particular food taboos to the life cycle events of puberty, menstruation, pregnancy, the puerperium and lactation. Examines cross-cultural parallels.

3205 JA'FAR SHARIF. William Crooke, ed. Islam in India, or the Qānūn-i-Islām: the customs of the Musalmāns of India, comprising a full and exact account of their various rites and ceremonies from the moment of birth to the hour of death. Tr. from Urdu by G.A. Herklots. New Delhi: Oriental Books Reprint Corporation, 1972. 374p. [*1st ed.* Qanoon-i-Islam or the customs of the Moosulmans of India. 1832].
Muslim social life of the early 19th century in the area of present day Thanjavur District. Relevant to women's lives is material on pregnancy, birth, birth rites, puberty, marriage, festivals, magic, dress.

3206 SRINIVAS, M.N. Marriage and family in Mysore. Bombay: New Book Company, 1942. 218p.
Discusses marriage restrictions and choices, marriage rites, widow marriage, divorce, birth rites, the desire for children, the family as reflected in folklore and fiction and the position of women. Based on author's master's thesis.

i) Puberty and menstruation

3207 DUMONT, LOUIS. Les mariages Nayar comme faits Indiens [Nayar marriages as facts of Indian society]. *In* L'Homme 1,1 (1961) 11-36.
Responding to Gough's paper, which explains Nayar marriage-initiation rites from a psychoanalytic point of view (entry 3209), Dumont argues that the Nayar system can be understood in the context of general South Asian social conceptions and institutions, and attempts to do so. Compares Nayar women to *basavis*.

3208 EICHINGER FERRO-LUZZI, GABRIELLA. Food avoidances at puberty and menstruation in Tamilnad. *In* Ecology of Food and Nutrition 2 (1973) 165-72.
[Unexamined].

3209 GOUGH, E. KATHLEEN. Female initiation rites on the Malabar Coast. *In* J. of the Royal Anthropological Institute 85,1/2 (1955) 45-80.
Social and psychoanalytic analyses of the "tali-tying marriage" rite, a symbolic pre-puberty defloration, among two Nayar and two Tiyyar communities. Author argues that the social structure encourages the common male fantasy that it is "both necessary to give away the sexual rights in natal kinswomen (who are identified with the mother as desirable but forbidden sexual objects) before they are in danger of becoming mature [and] dangerous to deflower the virgins of other lineages who . . . are also unconsciously likened to the mother."

3210 JAMES, V. First menstruation ceremonies among the Parayans of a Nilgiri village. *In* Man in India 54,2 (1974) 161-72.
Details the particularly elaborate menarche rites of a scheduled caste from Boby village, Kunnoor District.

3211 MADHAVAN, SHANTHA. Age at menarche of South Indian girls belonging to the states of Madras and Kerala. *In* Indian J. of Medical Research 53,7 (1965) 669-73.
Rural/urban and Tamil Nadu/Kerala comparisons of mean age at menarche.

3212 UČIDA, NORIHIKO. Folk songs and the observance of puberty ceremony in South India, I and II. *In* J. of Intercultural Studies 3-4 (1976-77) 12-22, 51-4.
First part contains a brief introduction to Telugu puberty ceremonies and transliterations and translations of six puberty song texts. Second part contains a brief introduction to girls' puberty rites among the Saurashtra weaver community of Tamil Nadu. Includes two examples of "erotic songs (*cālugītu*) to impart sex education to the girl," transliterated and translated. The songs and ceremonies have recently declined in popularity, probably due to changing standards of morality.

ii) Marriage rules, age and arrangements

3213 Courtship. Produced by Guy Glover. 1961. 2 parts: 30 and 30 min. Black and white. 16 mm. [*Distributed by* National Film Board of Canada, 1251 Avenue of the Americas, New York, New York 10020].
Film about marital arrangements and courtship. Contrasts eastern arranged marriages with western marriages of individual choice. First part shows a Kerala family in the process of arranging their eldest son's marriage and comparable material from Italy. Second part shows scenes from Iran and Canada. [Unexamined. NUC].

3214 GOUGH, E. KATHLEEN. A comparison of incest prohibitions and the rules of exogamy in three matrilineal groups of the Malabar Coast. *In* International Archives of Ethnography 46 (1952) 82-105.
Demonstrates, using data from two Nayar groups and the Muslim Mappillas, the hypothesis that "incest prohibitions and the rules of exogamy form an integral part of the total configuration of kinship relations, and may therefore be expected to vary in accordance with local and institutional variations within the same basic kinship system."

3215 GULATI, LEELA. Age of marriage of women and population growth: the Kerala experience. *In* Economic and Political Weekly 11,31/33 (Aug 1976) 1225-34.
Notes that in Kerala an increase in age at marriage alone did not reduce fecundity. The reduction of infant mortality rate, due in part to increased age at marriage and in part to improved health care (pre- and post-natal), seems to have influenced the number of children women want to have. The Kerala experience "cautions us against relying only on higher age of marriage to reduce the rate of growth of population because . . . higher age of marriage alone might well lead to higher rates of growth of population, at least in the immediate future."

3216 KURIAN, GEORGE. Modern trends in mate selection and marriage with special reference to Kerala. *In* George Kurian, ed. The family in India: a regional view. The Hague: Mouton, 1974. pp.351-67. (Studies in the Social Sciences, 12).
Contrasts arranged marriages with self-choice marriages with respect to mate selection procedure, dowry payments and postmarital adjustment. Points to the "advantages of a modified form of arranged marriage."

3217 ________. Child marriage: a case study in Kerala. *In* Dhirendra Narain, ed. Explorations in the family and other essays: Professor K.M. Kapadia commemoration volume. Bombay: Thacker and Company, 1975. pp.206-17. [*Also* Comments on the experiences of couples who married before the age of fourteen in Kerala state. *In* George Kurian, ed. The family in India: a regional view. The Hague: Mouton, 1974. pp.277-89. (Studies in the Social Sciences, 12)].
Survey of 20 Christian couples from the Keezhillam area in Kerala who had been married as children. Includes attitudes about child marriage as well as personal statistics. All but five couples deemed their marriages successful.

3218 MATHEW, ANNA. Expectations of college students regarding their marriage partner. *In* J. of Family Welfare 12,3 (1966) 46-52.
Survey of 75 male and 25 female students of two Tirupati colleges. Women favored higher marriage age for both sexes than men and both sexes preferred traditional parental choice of spouse, subject to the approval of the son or daughter. Tables.

3219 NATESA SASTRI, S.M. Madras — choice of wife — marriage customs — orthodox Hindus. *In* Indian Notes and Queries 4,43-7 (1887) 127-9, 144-6, 161-2, 178-80, 198-9.
Describes proper matching of brides' and grooms' horoscopes.

3219a SUKUMARAN NAIR, P.K. Intercaste marriage and status of women. *In* J. of Kerala Studies 4,2/3 (1977) 251-60.
Study of 36 women from Trivandrum and environs who married out of their castes. Examines socio-economic backgrounds; attitudes of natal and conjugal families, coworkers and neighbors; and social participation. Concludes that such women have no major adjustment problems.

iii) Marriage ceremonies and definitions

3220 GOUGH, E. KATHLEEN. The Nayars and the definition of marriage. *In* J. of the Royal Anthropological Institute 89,1/2 (1959) 23-34.
Response to a paper by E.R. Leach who argued, using the data of Gough and others, that no single definition is appropriate for the various arrangements that ethnographers call "marriage." Gough's paper "will begin by analyzing traditional Nayar marital institutions [and] will in general clarify what has always proved a crucial but difficult borderline case for theorists of kinship. The paper will conclude with a new definition of marriage . . . . The aim is to show that there *is* a common element [in the more typical and more atypical circumstances of marriage encountered by ethnographers]."

3221 NAYAR, K. KANNAN. The matrimonial customs of the Nayars. *In* Malabar Quarterly Review 7,3 (1908).

[Unexamined].

3222 ROCHE, PAUL. The marriage ceremonies of the Christian Paraiyans of the Kumbakonam area, India. *In* Asian Folklore Studies 36,1 (1977) 83-95.
Hindu and Christian elements in engagement and other marriage rites of Catholic Paraiyans of Tamil Nadu.

iv) Fertility patterns

3223 DAS, NITAI CHANDRA. A note on the effect of postponement of marriage on fertility. *In* World Population Conference, 1965, Belgrade. Proceedings, v2: selected papers and summaries — fertility, family planning, mortality. New York: Department of Economic and Social Affairs, United Nations, 1967. pp.128-31.
Argues that a limited rise in the age at marriage does not necessarily cause a reduction in fertility as is often assumed. Uses National Sample Survey data, 1951-59, from Kerala and the former Mysore and Madras States.

3224 GEORGE, MOLLY KUTTY. Tradition and fertility in a rural community. *In* Indian J. of Social Work 34,1 (1973) 1-9.
Reviews a study, which sought to elucidate the fertility patterns of traditional and nontraditional women in three villages near the city of Trivandrum.

3225 KANBARGI, RAMESH. Induced abortions in Bangalore City, 1972-1974. Bombay: Allied Publishers, 1977? 57p. (Institute for Social and Economic Change, Staff Paper Series, 7).
Study of 996 cases of hospital-performed abortions. Describes 1) socio-economic and demographic characteristics of women who have had an abortion, 2) age, marital status, number of living children and the length of pregnancy before termination, 3) grounds for performing the abortion and 4) the relationship between abortion and contraception.

3226 RAMAKUMAR, R. and Y.S. GOPAL. Husband-wife communication and fertility in a suburban community exposed to family planning. *In* J. of Family Welfare 18,3 (1972) 30-6.
Statistical study, conducted near Trivandrum. Correlates husband-wife communication about contraception with fertility, socio-economic level, attitudes toward family planning and family size preference.

3227 SRINIVASAN, K. A prospective study of the fertility behaviour of a group of married women in rural India: design and findings of the first round of enquiry. *In* Population Review 11,2 (1967) 46-60.
Fertility trends and differentials of a sample of 2,093 married women in rural Tamil Nadu.

v) Pregnancy, childbirth and motherhood

3228 BEAN, SUSAN S. Referential and indexical meanings of *amma* in Kannada: mother, woman, goddess, pox, and help! *In* J. of Anthropological Research 31,4 (1975) 313-30.
Analyzes various meanings of the Kannada term *amma*. Related to its primary or literal meaning, "mother," are metaphoric meanings, "woman politely" and "goddess," the metonymic meaning "pox" and its nonreferential, indexical use as an interjection. Argues that such an approach is of ethnographic and linguistic relevance.

3229 EICHINGER FERRO-LUZZI, GABRIELLA. Food avoidances of pregnant women in Tamilnad. *In* Ecology of Food and Nutrition 2 (1973) 259-66.
[Unexamined].

3230 ________. Food avoidances during the puerperium and lactation in Tamilnad. *In* Ecology of Food and Nutrition 3 (1974) 7-15.
[Unexamined].

3231 GHOSH, B.N. An exploratory study on midwifery practice of the local indigenous dais in Pondicherry and utilisation of domiciliary midwifery services of a health centre by a semi-urban slum community. *In* Indian J. of Public Health 12,3 (1968) 159-64.
Results of interviews with mothers regarding their preferences for childbirth services. Gives reasons for preference for hospital care, health center midwife or barber woman (*dāī*). Interviews with barber midwives yielded data on their ages, fees, delivery practices and recommended diets for postnatal mothers. Discusses mothers' methods of bathing and feeding babies.

3232 NICHOLSON, SYDNEY. Birth customs of the Telugus. *In* J. of the Anthropological Society of Bombay 10,4 (1914) 297-302.
Recounts birth rituals and "superstitions." No source of data is mentioned.

vi) Widowhood and aging

3233 JAMBAGI, SADANAND and SULOCHANA JAMBAGI. Life and activities of Lingayat widows in Mysore State. *In* Social Welfare 17,2 (1970) 11-2, 28.

Briefly reviews a study of 65 urban widows. Describes socio-economic profile; economic, leisure and religious activities; and relationship with spouses before marriage.

3234 MARULASIDDAIAH, H.M. Old people of Makunti. Dharwar: Karnatak University, 1969. 223p.
Ethnography of aging men and women in a village near Dharwar. Their role and problems "against the total life of the community. . . as a vital part of the social structure of the village."

vii) Rebirth account

3235 STEVENSON, IAN. The case of Mallika. *In his* Twenty cases suggestive of reincarnation. New York: American Society for Psychical Research, 1966. pp.93-6. (*Its* Proceedings, 26).
Presents the case of a Tamil girl who claimed to have been a particular woman in a previous life and produced numerous details about the woman's life. Although the author was not able to verify and supplement certain details, he presents evidence that suggests her paranormal knowledge.

(f) Domestic sphere and family life

3236 ANANTHA KRISHNA IYER, K.K. Anthropology of the Syrian Christians. Ernakulam: Cochin Government Press, 1926. 338p.
Ethnography of the Syrian Christian community of the Malabar coast area. Most material relating to women is contained in the kinship chapters.

3237 D'SOUZA, VICTOR S. Kinship organization and marriage customs among the Moplahs on the south-west coast of India. *In* Imtiaz Ahmad, ed. Family, kinship and marriage among Muslims in India. New Delhi: Manohar, 1976. pp.141-68. [*Reprint from* Anthropos 54 (1959) 487-516].
Presents kinship system of a heterogeneous Muslim community. The kinship system of the Mappillas/Moplahs includes Arabic Islamic, local matrilineal and local patrilineal elements.

3238 GOUGH, E. KATHLEEN. Brahman kinship in a Tamil village. *In* American Anthropologist 58,5 (1956) 826-53.
Describes brahman kinship in the Tanjore village of Kumbapettai and compares it with kinship system of local nonbrahman groups. Considerable attention to contrasting circumstances of women within the higher and lower systems.

3239 KURIAN, GEORGE and MARIAM JOHN. Women and social customs within the family: a case study of attitudes in Kerala, India. *In* Dana Raphael, ed. Being female: reproduction, power, and change. The Hague: Mouton Publishers, 1975. pp.255-65. (World Anthropology).
Study of attitudes of rural Malayali women, by generation and religious community, toward marriage rites, dowry system, children's education and occupation and children's decision making.

3240 MENCHER, JOAN P. and HELEN GOLDBERG. Kinship and marriage regulations among the Namboodiri brahmans of Kerala. *In* George Kurian, ed. The family in India: a regional view. The Hague: Mouton, 1974. pp.291-316. (Studies in the Social Sciences, 12). [*Reprint from* Man n.s. 2,1 (1967) 87-107].
Kinship and marriage among "an extremely atypical Dravidian society" in the context of larger Kerala society and as a complement to Nayar data. Features include extreme patrilineality, large dowries, absence of affinal terms for male speakers and "total amalgamation of the female with her husband."

i) Family relationships

3241 BECK, BRENDA E.F. The kin nucleus in Tamil folklore. *In* Thomas R. Trautmann, ed. Kinship and history in South Asia: four lectures. Ann Arbor: Center for South and Southeast Asian Studies, University of Michigan, 1974. pp.1-27. (Michigan Papers on South and Southeast Asia, 7).
Emphasizes the central position of women in Tamil kinship: ". . . the female is quite explicitly surrounded and constrained by four male relatives: her father, brother, husband and son. These four males must guard her in order to direct her energies to constructive ends . . ." Uses Tamil myths to support kin nucleus hypothesis.

3242 KUMARA GURU [CHANDRASEKHAR SUBRAHMANYA AYYAR]. Life's shadows. Bombay: D.B. Taraporevala Sons (v1) and Madras: the author (v2), 1938-43. 2v.
Regarding the relationships of an educated Tamil brahman with various persons. The first volume includes "Wife" and the second includes "A Daughter's Shadow." [Unexamined. Books in NUC].

3243 SRINIVAS, M.N. A joint family dispute in a Mysore village. *In* J. of the Maharaja Sayajirao University 1,1 (1952) 7-31.
Detailed account of a dispute that resulted

in a family partition in Rampura village. "The conventional explanation that the women who come into the family ultimately break it may be regarded as a convenient myth the function of which is to protect another myth which is that of the solidarity of the brothers."

3244 _______. The remembered village. Berkeley: University of California Press, 1976. 356p.
Ethnography of Rampura village in Mysore District. Depicts women in the context of village life among numerous other topics. See especially the fifth chapter, "The Sexes and the Household," (pp. 137-63).

ii) Domestic rites

3245 BALASUBRAHMANYAM, K. Some women's rites in South India. *In* Man in India 8,1 (1928) 63-6.
Brief comments on various rites performed for the welfare of one's family.

3246 DURAI, MRS. H. GNANA. Preliminary note on geometrical diagrams (kolam) from the Madras Presidency. *In* Man 29, 60 (1929) 77.
Ethnographic details of ritual designs constructed with white powder by women. With a plate of 11 examples.

3247 FAWCETT, FRED. On the Berulu Kodo, a sub-sect of the Moras Vokaligaru of the Mysore Province. *In* J. of the Anthropological Society of Bombay 1 (1886) 449-74.
Concerning the custom among women of this community of amputating the last phalanges of the third and fourth fingers, right hand, previous to the ear- and nose-piercing of their children. Considers history, ritual, reputed origin and changes that occurred when the practice was made illegal.

3248 LAYARD, JOHN. Labyrinth ritual in South India: threshold and tatoo designs. *In* Folklore [London] 48,2 (1937) 115-82.
Context, technique and, particularly, design of threshold patterns "drawn by women only in the unlucky Tamil month of Margali" to counteract negative influences. Compares designs to material from the Melanesian island of Malekula and motifs used by tatooers of the Korava community in South India.

3249 Rādhā's day: Hindu family life. Directed and written by H. Daniel Smith. 1969. 17 min. Color. 16 mm. (Image India: the Hindu Way). [*Distributed by* Film Rental Center, Syracuse University, 1455 E. Colvin St., Syracuse, New York 13210].
Day in the life of a teenaged daughter in a middle-class brahman household of Madras city. Includes worship of ***Lakṣmī*** and ***Gaṇeśa*** and construction of threshold designs. [Unexamined. NUC].

3250 REYNOLDS, HOLLY BAKER. "To keep the tāli strong": women's rituals in Tamilnad, India. Ph.D. dissertation, Department of South Asian Studies, University of Wisconsin, 1978. 527p. [University Microfilms 78-22,269].
Study of the five ***nōṉpu*** calendrical rituals performed by women of Madurai District, Tamil Nadu, to ensure family welfare, their husbands' long lives and their own auspiciousness. "This study explores the ritual structure, the intent, and the meaning of these five rites against a background of female status possibilities exemplified in life cycle rites; cultural evaluations of status possibilities; and notions of female power." [Unexamined. Information supplied by author].

3251 Threshold designs. *In* Folklore [London] 49,2 (1938) 181.
Two brief contributions, undoubtedly in response to Layard's article, concerning technique, context and categories of threshold designs.

iii) Inheritance

3252 DERRETT, J. DUNCAN M. "Mother-in-law v. daughter-in-law": a translation of the anonymous Svaśrū-snuṣā-dhana-saṁvāda. *In* B.R. Saksena, ed. Umesha Mishra commemoration volume. Allahabad: Ganganatha Jha Research Institute, 1970. pp.261-77. [*Also in* J. of the Ganganatha Jha Research Institute 24 (1968) 261-77. ***Also in his*** Essays in classical and modern Hindu law, v2: consequences of the intellectual exchange with the foreign powers. Leiden: E.J. Brill, 1977. pp.323-39].
Legal treatise of an early 19th century court ***śāstrī*** argues that the mother and wife of a man who dies without a son should share equally in his estate.

3253 _______. 'Mother-in-law v. daughter-in-law': a Hindu lawyer's opinion of the early nineteenth century. ***In his*** Essays in classical and modern Hindu law, v2: consequences of the intellectual exchange with the foreign powers. Leiden: E.J. Brill, 1977. pp.299-322. [***Reprint from*** Adyar Library Bulletin 31/32 (1967/68) 531-53].

3254 _______. The rights of inheritance of women: another opinion of a Hindu lawyer of the early nineteenth century. ***In his*** Essays in classical and modern
Regarding a South Indian manuscript of about 1815, the ***Śvaśrū-Snuṣā Dhanasaṃvāda,*** that argues for the equal inheritance of property by a man's widow and mother. Provides statement of its significance and summary and transliteration of text.

Hindu law, v2: consequences of the intellectual exchange with the foreign powers. Leiden: E.J. Brill, 1977. pp.340-87. [*Reprint from* Adyar Library Bulletin 33,1/4 (1969) 135-81].
On a South Indian manuscript of about 1830 to 1850, the *Devara-Suta-Sapatnī-Sutā Dhanavivāda*, that "deals with the very general question of the estate which a widow takes in the property left by her (divided) husband and the connected question, who shall take it on her death (her intestacy is taken for granted)." Discusses sources and structure of the argument. Includes transliteration of the text and extract from a report of a case to which the opinion is tentatively assigned. Takes position that an opinion at law must be based on custom of high castes as well as traditional texts. "The wheel has come full circle, and the proposition of the *Mitākṣarā*, upheld in our present remarkable little treatise, has at length prevailed." Attributes text to the author of the *Śvaśrū-Snuṣā Dhanasaṃvāda*.

iv) Continuity and change

3255 CONKLIN, GEORGE H. Urbanization, cross-cousin marriage, and power for women: a sample from Dharwar. *In* Contributions to Indian Sociology n.s. 7 (1973) 53-63.
Discusses the relationship of relative decision making power of men and women to cross-cousin marriage. Finds limited support for the proposition that marriage to a cross cousin results in a household with more freedom for women. Urbanization and employment of women outside the household are found to be related to women's relative power within the household.

3256 ________. Muslim family life and secularization in Dharwar, Karnataka. *In* Imtiaz Ahmad, ed. Family, kinship and marriage among Muslims in India. New Delhi: Manohar, 1976. pp.127-40.
Investigates attitudes and practices with respect to family life in Dharwar. Compares rural and urban Muslims with rural and urban non-Muslims. Includes some material on the husband-wife relationship. One conclusion is that "both Muslims and non-Muslims in the sample are being very much influenced by the effects of urbanization and education, especially the women."

3257 KURIAN, GEORGE. The Indian family in transition: a case study of Kerala Syrian Christians. 's Gravenhage: Mouton, 1961. 142p. (Publications of the Institute of Social Studies, Series Maior, 6).
Reviews a questionnaire-based study of rural Syrian Christians in Kerala and migrants in Bombay to assess changing family and marriage patterns. Apparently all informants were men. Includes variety of data on kinship and a section on attitudes toward freedom for women.

3258 LEONARD, KAREN. Women and social change in modern India. *In* Feminist Studies 3,3/4 (1976) 117-30.
Presents changing family and caste patterns of Kayastha women in 19th and 20th century Hyderabad against a discussion of the Indian social reform movement. Examines several variables to assess extent of change — naming patterns, age at marriage, extent and type of education, employment outside home, ratio of never-married women to all women, marriage across caste and subcaste lines and marriage in or out of birth order.

3259 ROSS, AILEEN D. Hindu family in its urban setting. Toronto: University of Toronto Press, 1961. 325p.
Considers traditional urban joint family in Bangalore and changes brought by industrialization and urbanization with respect to authority, sentiments, work, education, friendships and marriage. Much on women.

3260 WOODRUFF, GERTRUDE M. Family migration into Bangalore. *In* Economic Weekly 12, 4/6 (Jan 1960) 163-72.
Research in a "hutment" slum neighborhood of Bangalore suggests a whole-family pattern of migration into the city, which contrasts with the single-man pattern often found in North India and has considerable consequences for urban adjustment and the character of a city.

v) Nayars of Kerala and other matrilineal communities

3261 DUBE, LEELA. Matriliny and Islam: religion and society in the Laccadives. Delhi: National Publishing House, 1969. 125p. (University of Saugar Monographs in Anthropology and Sociology).
Ethnography of social structure and religious life. Discusses interaction of a matrilineal social system transported to Laccadive Islands from Kerala with Islam, which "assumes and emphasizes a patrilineal social structure."

3262 EHRENFELS, U.R. Towards understanding of South Indian social structure. *In* L.K. Bala Ratnam, ed. Anthropology on the march: recent studies of Indian beliefs, attitudes and social institutions. Madras: Book Centre and Social Sciences Association, 1963. pp.155-64.
Compares North and South Indian social structure in an attempt to trace the origins of "mother-right" and explain the prevalence of matriliny in South India. Discusses succession in the matriline, the prominent position of the mother's brother, worship of female deities and celebration of first menstruation in South India.

3263 FULLER, C.J. The Nayars today. London: Cambridge University Press, 1976. 173p. (Changing Cultures).

Considers contemporary data on the Nayar kinship and marriage system in "Ramankara" village, central Travancore, in the context of the history of the area and the general ethnographic setting of the village. Discusses the "traditional" Nayar marriage system and 19th and 20th century changes, including the disintegration of the matrilineal joint family.

3264 KUTTY, A.R. Marriage and kinship in an island society. Delhi: National Publishing House, 1972. 227p. (University of Saugar Monographs in Anthropology and Sociology).
Describes matrilineal social structure of Kalpeni, a Laccadive island. Considers kinship and marriage and life cycle in the broader ethnographic and historical context.

3265 KUTTY, KRISHNA. Female domination in Kerala. *In* AICC [All India Congress Committee] Economic Review 11,10 (15 Sep 1959) 23-6.
Argues that Kerala's women have contributed to its predisposition to Communism: the "permission" given to Nayar women "to dominate over men in society is badly used," and although Namboodiri women are uneducated, they are highly influential.

3266 LAWRENCE, JAMES H. The empire of the Nairs (1811). Delmar, New York. Scholars' Facsimiles and Reprints, 1976. 4v in 1. [*Reprint of* The empire of the Nairs or, the rights of women: an utopian romance in twelve books, 2d ed. London: printed by F. Vigurs, 1811. 4v].
Novel concerning Nayars and their matrilineal system. The author states in his introduction that the Nayar system offers substantial benefits to women, "is favorable to population . . . and . . . would augment the happiness and liberty of mankind." Makes references to contemporary feminist literature and criticizes contemporary western marital arrangements.

3267 MENCHER, JOAN P. Changing familial roles among South Malabar Nayars. *In* Southwestern J. of Anthropology 18,3 (1962) 230-45.
Discusses effects of the dissolution of large Nayar matrilineal kin groups in the past century upon interpersonal relationships within the family. Finds that female roles have been more continuous than male roles.

3268 ________. The Nayars of South Malabar. *In* M.F. Nimkoff, ed. Comparative family systems. Boston: Houghton Mifflin Company, 1965. pp.163-91.
Reviews traditional and contemporary forms of Nayar kinship system. Much on women, including rites and relationships with various family members.

3269 NAKANE, CHIE. The Nayar family in a disintegrating matrilineal system. *In* John Mogey, ed. Family and marriage. Leiden: E.J. Brill, 1963. pp.17-28. (International Studies in Sociology and Social Anthropology, 1). [*Also in* International J. of Comparative Sociology 3,1 (1962) 17-28].
Presents the case history of the disintegration of the Marayil kin group in Ernakulam from the 19th century to the present and describes remaining matrilineal elements.

3270 PUTHENKALAM, J. Marriage and the family in Kerala: with special reference to matrilineal castes. Calgary, Alberta: Journal of Comparative Family Studies, 1977. 246p. (*Its* Monograph Series).
Examines changing marriage and family patterns in Kerala. Based upon autobiography, literature and interviews and questionnaires with persons representing a wide cross-section of matrilineal castes throughout the state.

3271 RAMAN UNNI, K. Visiting husbands in Malabar. *In* J. of the Maharaja Sayajirao University of Baroda 5,1 (1956) 37-56.
Examines the Nayar "visiting husbands" custom in two villages of South Malabar and suggests a much less dramatic change in Nayar social structure than that reported by other observers.

3272 UNNITHAN, T.K.N. Contemporary Nayar family in Kerala. *In* George Kurian, ed. The family in India: a regional view. The Hague: Mouton, 1974. pp.191-203. (Studies in the Social Sciences, 12).
States that although the Nayar family has long been an "anthropologists' paradise," it has not been adequately understood. Attempts to describe recent changes and the present Nayar family system. Concludes that the Nayar family of today is not nearly as "primitive and exotic" as one might suppose from the academic attention it has received; it is "unique at present only in superficial respects."

(g) Women's power, sexuality, dangers

3273 EPSTEIN, SCARLETT. A sociological analysis of witch beliefs in a Mysore village. *In* K.S. Mathur and B.C. Agrawal, eds. Tribe, caste and peasantry. Lucknow: Ethnographic and Folk Culture Society, 1974. pp.361-74. [*Reprint from* Eastern Anthropologist 12,4 (1959) 234-51].
Data from "Wangala" village in Mandya District. "I shall argue that the tensions created by women having become moneylenders are projected into witchcraft accusations because they can find no other medium of expression in Wangala's present-day social organization." Witchcraft in this village is said to act as a moralizing agent by condemning undesirable behavior, maintaining social equilibrium (by accusing the spirit in a woman rather than the woman

herself) and upholding traditional social structure in which women were not moneylenders.

3274 FAWCETT, FRED. "On a mode of obsession" which deals with the belief in a part of Bangalore, in the possession of women by the spirits of drowned persons. *In* J. of the Anthropological Society of Bombay I (1886) 533-5.
Regarding circumstances under which such women are possessed, manifested behavior and mode of exorcism.

3275 HARPER, EDWARD B. Spirit possession and social structure. *In* L.K. Bala Ratnam, ed. Anthropology on the march: recent studies of Indian beliefs, attitudes and social institutions. Madras: Book Centre and Social Sciences Association, 1963. pp.165-77.
Presents data from the Havik brahman community to demonstrate the relationship between the dominated position of women within the local authority structure and their use of spirit possession as a means of stress reduction.

3276 ________. Fear and the status of women. *In* Southwestern J. of Anthropology 25 (1969) 81-95.
Attempts to explain why Havik brahman widows and women in general are considered to be defiling, dangerous and disruptive. Discusses a "poison" widows are believed to cause people to ingest. Argues that guilt may be experienced concerning the low position of women, particularly widows, in the social structure and may in turn create unrealistic fears. Data from Sagar in the Malnad region.

3277 MATHUR, P.R.G. Smārtavicāram among the Nampūtiri brahmans of Kerala. *In* J. of Kerala Studies 2,3 (1975) 353-63.
Defines custom as "procedure or the court of enquiry of the traditional caste council of the Nampūtiris in respect of a woman's conjugal infidelity." Considers structure and function of traditional caste council, great authority of elders, trial proceedings and penalty of excommunication imposed upon transgressors.

3278 The serpent deities: art and ritual in South India. By Clifford Jones. 1976. 18 min. Color. 16 mm. (Traditional Art and Ritual in South India). [*Distributed by* Bullfrog Films, Inc., Box 114, Milford Square, Pennsylvania 18935].
Serpent worship among the women of the Pulluvan community of Kerala. Young girls serve as spiritual mediums while dancing entranced over *maṇḍalas* constructed for the occasion. [Unexamined].

3279 SHANMUGAM, T.E. Sex delinquency and emotional instability in women. *In* Indian J. of Social Work 17,1 (1956) 30-43.
Regarding a study comparing a group of sexually "delinquent" women from the Rescue Home and Vigilance Home, Madras, with a "normal" group of comparable socio-economic background. The women were interviewed and given a questionnaire. "The Syndrome of '*Hypersensitivity*' and '*Excitability*' were common to both the groups; whereas, '*Paranoid*', and '*Neuresthenic tendencies*' and '*Sleep disorders*' were important in the sex delinquent group."

3280 SINGH, T.R. Some aspects of ritual purity and pollution. *In* Eastern Anthropologist 19,2 (1966) 131-42.
Interprets data from an Andhra village in an attempt "to understand how the notions of ritual purity and impurity regulate relations between individuals, and also between individuals on the one hand and animate and inanimate objects on the other." Presents scale of relative degrees of pollution states and of auspicious states. Among the pollution states are: secong degree — sexual intercourse, third degree — postparturition and menstruation, fourth degree — intercourse with a low-caste woman and fifth degree — intercourse with a low-caste man.

(h) The spiritual life and religious observances

3281 HIEBERT, PAUL G. Konduru: structure and integration in a South Indian village. Minneapolis: University of Minnesota Press, 1971. 192p.
Women are prominent in the numerous incidents recounted in this ethnography of a village in Andhra Pradesh. The chapter, "Rituals," particularly rich in material, considers women's rites and powers, goddesses and Śakti demons.

i) Spiritual leaders

3282 BHARADWAJA, E. Life and teachings of The Mother. Bapatla: Matrusri Publications, 1968? 110p.
Regarding Anasuyadevi, the holy Mother of Jillellamudi, Guntur District. The Mother, a married householder, was fully realized at birth. Provides a life sketch, a description of her "House of All" at Jillellamudi, a description of her personality, anecdotes from her devotees, sample conversations between Anasuyadevi and devotees, sayings and photographs.

3283 CHIRANTANANANDA, SWAMI. Tarigoṇḍa Veṅkamāmbā. *In* Ramakrishna Vedanta Centre. Women saints of East and West: Śrī Sāradā Devī (The Holy Mother) birth centenary memorial. London: Ramakrishna Vedanta Centre, 1955. pp.86-93.
Biographical details of the 19th century saint

Venkamma, as she is popularly known. Discusses her devotion to the god Veṅkaṭēśvara at Tirupati and her writing.

3284 The divine descent: the life and mission of Her Holiness Sadguru Swami Sri Gnanananda Sarasvathi. Madras: Sri Gnana Advaitha Peetam, 1976. 73p.
Life and teachings of a South Indian woman who has been able to combine life as a mother, wife and householder with pursuit of spirituality and liberation. Details the development of her spiritual interests and powers. Numerous photographs.

3285 ROYAL, C.S. A divine child of India. *In* Open Court 25,11 (1911) 701-3.
Brief account of the first 15 years of Sri Gyanamamba, a Telugu girl born in 1895 and considered to be an incarnation of a goddess. Includes a drawing of her.

ii) Goddesses

3286 CLAUS, PETER J. The Siri myth and ritual: a mass possession cult of South India. *In* Ethnology 14,1 (1975) 47-58.
Regarding the annual worship of a local deity at six temples in South Kanara District, Karnataka. "Hundreds, and at the larger temples thousands of people, mostly women, gather to propitiate the *bhūta*, Siri, to sing her legend, and to become possessed." Discusses her legend and its relation to Tuluva matriliny and women's place within it: "it establishes a justification for matrilineality [yet] it reveals the system's pitfalls." Also addresses rituals and cult distinctiveness.

3287 ELMORE, WILBUR THEODORE. Dravidian gods in modern Hinduism: a study of the local and village deities of southern India. *In* University Studies of the University of Nebraska 15,1 (1915) 1-149. [*Reprint* Hamilton, New York: the author, 1915. 157p.].
Notes that local deities in South India tend to be female. Discusses iconography and worship of numerous local goddesses, the worship of a married woman whose husband is alive, worship of female Śakti demons, female diviners and demon possession, origin legends and events, other legends and general conceptions and characteristics. Based on author's local investigations over many years. Photographs.

3288 FAWCETT, F. On some festivals to village goddesses. *In* J. of the Anthropological Society of Bombay 2 (1889) 261-82.
Describes village goddess festivals in Bellary District of the present Karnataka State.

3289 The goddess Bhagavati: art and ritual in South India. By Clifford Jones. 1976. 15 min. Color. 16 mm. (Traditional Art and Ritual in South India). [*Distributed by* Bullfrog Films, Inc., Box 114, Milford Square, Pennsylvania 18935].
Documents the ritual construction of the goddess Bhagavatī in the Ambalavasi community of Kerala. Installed on a large *maṇḍala* drawn on the floor, she is completed with various ritually significant colors and awakened. Shows a Nayar priest who enters a trance in her presence. With musical accompaniment. [Unexamined].

3290 JACOB-PANDIAN, E.T. The goddess of chastity and the politics of ethnicity in the Tamil society of South Asia. *In* Contributions to Asian Studies 10 (1977) 52-63.
Describes Kaṇṇaki, the Tamil goddess of chastity, as a "master symbol" of the Tamil ethos that functions "as a vehicle for synthesizing the Hindu world view and the Tamil ethos."

3291 MENON, C. ACHYUTHA. Kāḷi worship in Kēraḷa, 2d ed. Madras: University of Madras, 1959. 2v. (*Its* Malayalam Series, 8). [*1st ed.* 1943?].
First volume, in Malayalam, discusses various aspects of Kerala's Kāḷi cult. The second volume [unexamined] "fully" discusses "the evolution of the Kāḷi temple, the influence of the cult on the political evolution of Kēraḷa and its martial traditions, its primitive outlook, Aryan influence on the indigenous cult, different concepts of the Mother, the merging of Kaṇṇaki into Kāḷi, the ritualistic literature . . . it has developed."

3292 RAMANAN, V.V. Small-pox goddess. *In* Siddhanta Deepika 4 (1901) and 5 (1902).
Cult of Māriyammaṉ. [Unexamined].

3293 Wedding of the goddess. By Mira Reym Binford, Michael Camerini and Joseph Elder. 1975? 2 parts: 36 and 40 min. Color. 16 mm. (Contemporary South Asia Film Series). [*Distributed by* South Asian Area Center, 1242 Van Hise Hall, University of Wisconsin, Madison, Wisconsin 53706].
Film about the annual *Cittirai* (April-May) festival at Madurai celebrating the marriage of goddess Mīnākṣī to Sundareśvara. The first part presents background material on the history of the temple and festival, legends of the goddess and the strong influence of the temple complex on local religion. The second part presents vivid scenes from the festival itself.

3294 WHITEHEAD, HENRY. The village gods of South India, 2d ed. Calcutta: Association Press, 1921. 175p. (Religious Life of India). [*Reprint of 2d ed.* Delhi: Sumit Publications, 1976].
Describes numerous village deities (which are almost exclusively female), shrines and modes of worship. Based largely on personal observation. Photographs and drawings.

(i) Employment

i) Patterns and problems

3295 GARZA, JOSEPH M. and NANDINI RAO. Attitudes toward employment and employment status of mothers in Hyderabad, India. *In* J. of Marriage and the Family 34,1 (1972) 153-5.
Study of 40 pairs of sisters, one employed as a teacher and the other exclusively a homemaker, matched on various variables, to assess attitudes toward husbands' income, material comfort, aspirations for children's education, social contact and images of working mothers. The two groups showed differing trends in all five categories.

3296 JORAPUR, P.B. Working women in Dharwar Taluka. *In* J. of the Institute of Economic Research, Dharwar 1,2 (1966) 20-5.
Contrasts certain socio-economic features of employed and nonemployed women of rural and urban areas of Dharwar Taluka.

3297 MADRAS SCHOOL OF SOCIAL WORK. Working mothers in white collar occupations. Madras, 1970.
Employed and nonemployed wives and their husbands were interviewed about attitudes and practices. [Unexamined].

3298 RAO, VELAGAPUDI NANDINI PRAKASA. Role conflict of employed mothers in Hyderabad, India. Ph.D. dissertation, Department of Sociology?, Mississippi State University, 1971. 124p. [University Microfilms 71-27,025].
Study of pairs of sisters, one employed and one nonemployed, to determine consequences of employment on family life. Reports variety of correlations, including findings of increased "role conflict" with employment. [Unexamined. DAI].

3299 SAVITHRI, T.S. Structural changes in female employment: in the non-agricultural sector in South India. *In* AICC [All India Congress Committee] Economic Review 21,14 (1970) 13-21.
Analyzes changing patterns of nonagricultural employment in the four southern states of India using 20th century census data. Describes numerous trends, yet "it is questionable whether female employment has undergone any radical changes in South India in the course of half a century."

3300 ULLRICH, HELEN E. Caste differences between brahmin and non-brahmin women in a South Indian village. *In* Alice Schlegel, ed. Sexual stratification: a cross-cultural view. New York: Columbia University Press, 1977. pp.94-108.
Data from women of the Havik brahman and Divaru agriculturalist communities of "Totagadde" village in the Malnad region illustrates a positive relationship between importance of women's economic contribution and their power. Although the Havik community dominates the village economically, politically and ritually, Divaru women are more powerful than Havik women: "The independence and experience gained from being a part of the work force extends to the recognition of their competence in positions of authority and a more nearly equal role in ritual."

ii) Particular occupations

3301 ARAVAMUDAN, GITA. Nurses and nuns of Kerala. *In* Devaki Jain, ed. Indian women. New Delhi: Publications Division, Ministry of Information and Broadcasting, Government of India, 1975. pp.251-9.
Presents material from interviews with Malayali nurses and nuns, most of whom are from Christian families, and attempts to explain their disproportionate numbers in these vocations in India and elsewhere in the world.

3302 GULATI, LEELA. Profile of a female agricultural labourer. *In* Economic and Political Weekly 13,12 (25 Mar 1978) A27-A35.
Profiles "Kalyani," a 35-year-old female agricultural laborer of a scheduled caste who lives in a squatter settlement in Trivandrum. ". . . her children, despite whatever 'education' they have been able to receive, will continue in the same occupation; hunger, disease and indebtedness are an integral part of their life; . . . there is little prospect of anyone in the family breaking out of this vicious circle."

3303 INDIA (REPUBLIC). ALL INDIA HANDICRAFTS BOARD. Report on embroidery craft in southern India (Tamil Nadu, Kerala, Karnataka and Goa). New Delhi: All India Handicrafts Board, Planning and Research Section, Ministry of Commerce, Government of India, 1975. 76p.
Concerns organization and economics of hand embroidery production. Attempts to identify production centers and population involved, value of sales and wages and marketing channels. Includes addresses of 55 sites of production visited for the survey.

3304 MUKHERJI, A.B. Female participation in rural agricultural labour in Andhra Pradesh: a study in population geography. *In* Deccan Geographer 12,1 (1974) 1-25.
Attempts to identify factors involved in high proportion of female workers in agricultural labor force and to describe spatial patterns. Maps and tables. [Unexamined].

3305 TALPALLIKAR, M.B. Life and labour of women workers in the Bellampalli mines.

In Indian J. of Social Work 9,3 (1948) 208-17.
Study of a group of female mine workers from the former Hyderabad State. Considers method of recruitment, work and home conditions, economic level, trade union activities and existing and recommended welfare and benefits.

(j) Education

3306 ANDHRA PRADESH. STATE EVALUATION COMMITTEE. Working of the Andhra Pradesh State Council for education of women and girls. Hyderabad: Directorate of Printing and Stationery, Government Secretariat Press, Government of Andhra Pradesh, 1968. 55p. (*Its* Evaluation Studies, 34).
[Unexamined. NUC].

3307 ROSS, AILEEN D. Education and family change. *In* Sociological Bulletin 8,2 (1959) 39-44.
Discusses ambitions of a sample of 150 middle- and upper-class Hindus in Bangalore regarding education of their children. Considers different attitudes toward education of sons and daughters and the eventual effect of children's education on relationships with the family.

i) Adult/nonformal education

3308 ANDHRA PRADESH. STATE EVALUATION COMMITTEE. Study on the working of the special schools for adult women. Hyderabad: Directorate of Printing and Stationery, Government Secretariat Press, Government of Andhra Pradesh, 1968. 22p. (*Its* Evaluation Studies, 6).
[Unexamined. NUC].

ii) Higher education

3309 GOLDSTEIN, RHODA L. Students in saris: college education in the lives of young Indian women. *In* J. of Asian and African Studies 5,3 (1970) 193-201.
Study of Bangalore college graduates for whom a college degree is a mark of status, an economic asset and an asset or a liability in the marriage system. Discusses effects of college education upon marital choice.

3310 ________. Indian women in transition: a Bangalore case study. Metuchen, New Jersey: Scarecrow Press, Inc., 1972. 172p.
Report of questionnaire survey of graduates from Bangalore University to learn about their place in a changing society. Chapters discuss the study itself, socio-economic background of the sample, significance of education, attitudes toward marriage, attitudes toward employment and conclusions.

3311 ________. Tradition and change in the roles of educated Indian women. *In* Dhirendra Narain, ed. Explorations in the family and other essays: Professor K.M. Kapadia commemoration volume. Bombay: Thacker and Company, 1975. pp.268-87.
Attitude survey of 97 female graduates of Bangalore University concerning the importance of marriage; the effects of education and employment on marriage choices, marital roles and adjustments; and preferred marriage age.

3312 NATARAJ, P. Mental pictures of college girls of Hindus, Muslims and Christians. *In* Indian J. of Social Work 26,3 (1965) 287-92.
Study of 120 students from Maharani's College for Women, Mysore. Examines attitudes about personal qualities of members of three religious groups. Concludes: own group images are highly favorable; Muslims and Christians view Hindus in slightly unfavorable light as do Christians and Hindus view Muslims, while Hindus and Muslims have quite favorable views of Christians.

3313 ________. Social distance within and between castes and religious groups of college girls. *In* J. of Social Psychology 65,1 (1965) 135-40.
Investigates social distance as measured by a series of hypothetical questions about marriage, food, worship, friendship, residential propinquity and citizenship. Students are probably from Maharani's College for Women, Mysore.

(k) Development and social welfare

i) Associations, programs, agencies

3314 ANDHRA MAHILA SABHA. Mahila Bulletin. v1- (1970-). Madras. Irregularly.
[Unexamined. IPP].

3315 Andhra Mahilā Sabhā silver jubilee souvenir. Madras, 1962.
[Unexamined].

3316 KARNATAKA. WOMEN AND CHILDREN'S WELFARE DEPARTMENT. A Note on the Department of Women and Children's Welfare in Karnataka. 1- (1975/76-). Bangalore. Annually.
[Unexamined. ALI].

3317 RAMA, K.G. Women's welfare in Tamil Nadu. Madras: Sangam Publishers, 1974. 55p.
Report of survey conducted to evaluate effectiveness of state Women's Welfare Programme. Includes demographic figures; data on use and effectiveness of crafts, child care and family planning programs; and assessment of participants' attitudes and evaluations of the programs.

3318 Voluntary effort for women's welfare. *In* Andhra Pradesh special number. Social Welfare 21,5 (1974) 39-51.
Contains articles on institutions and organizations concerned with women's welfare in Andhra Pradesh, the state's Women and Child Welfare Department, activities of the local branch of Association for Moral and Social Hygiene in India (concerning prostitution and VD) and Hyderabad's Mother and Child Care Society.

ii) Health

3319 Gynaecological survey in Ramanagaram. *In* Family Planning News 7,2 (1966) 16-7.
Concerns range and type of gynecological disorders found in a random sample from the town of Ramanagaram, Bangalore District, and surrounding villages. Sample consisted of 150 oral history cases and 100 oral history and physical examination cases. Discusses difficulties encountered in executing the study.

iii) Prostitution

3320 AIYAPPAN, PARVATHI. Prostitutes: notes from a rescue home. *In* Devaki Jain, ed. Indian women. New Delhi: Publications Division, Ministry of Information and Broadcasting, Government of India, 1975. pp.261-8.
Brief case studies of four young women from Ernakulam. The rescue home in which they live was established under the provisions of the Suppression of Immoral Traffic in Women and Girls Act.

3321 RANGA RAO, M. and J.V. RAGHAVENDER RAO. The prostitutes of Hyderabad: a study of the socio-cultural conditions of the prostitutes of Hyderabad. Hyderabad: Association for Moral and Social Hygiene in India, Andhra Pradesh Branch, 1970? 79p.
Report of a study of 70 prostitutes and 30 "singing and dancing girls." Considers demography, education, income and attitudes toward the profession. Includes recommendations, tables and an appendix of ten short life histories.

iv) Housing

3322 ANDHRA PRADESH. STATE EVALUATION COMMITTEE. Study on the working of the district shelters for women in Andhra Pradesh. Hyderabad: Directorate of Printing and Stationery, Government Secretariat Press, Government of Andhra Pradesh, 1968. 19p. (*Its* Evaluation Studies, 15).
Almshouses. [Unexamined. NUC].

3323 _______. Study on the working of the state after-care homes for women. Hyderabad: Directorate of Printing and Stationery, Government Secretariat Press, Government of Andhra Pradesh, 1968. 47p. (*Its* Evaluation Studies, 19).
Rehabilitation centers. [Unexamined. NUC].

3324 SARADA, K. Some aspects of the housing problem of women teachers in Hyderabad. *In* Asian Economic Review 2,3 (1960) 398-406.
[Unexamined].

v) Mother-child welfare program of Mahbubnagar District, Andhra Pradesh

3325 An experimental non-formal education project for rural women to promote the development of the young child: an action-cum-research project integrating maternal and child health, nutrition, child care, and family planning through functional literacy and mother child centres, August 1972-August 1975, draft, final report submitted to UNICEF, India. New Delhi: Council for Social Development, 1975? 435p.
Collection of papers concerned with mother-child welfare-research project in Mahbubnagar District. [Unexamined. ALI].

3326 Experimental project begins in Indian villages. *In* World Education Reports 2,2 (1973) 6p.
Discusses establishment of mother and child welfare program in villages of Mahbubnagar District. The multifaceted program includes research and development aspects and considers health, education and family planning needs. [Unexamined].

3327 KOSHY, T.A. Integrated non-formal education for mothers. *In* Social Change 3,1/2 (1973) 28-32.
Report of a plan for an "action-cum-research

project integrating maternal and child health, nutrition, child care and family planning education and services" that would establish guidelines for a program to "help to decrease infant mortality and morbidity, improve the physical health and nutritional status of young children, increase the ability of rural women to acquire . . . more useful knowledge . . . and to foster their family's health and well-being . . ." The project was to be conducted with pregnant mothers and mothers of infants in villages of Mahbubnagar District.

vi) Family planning

3328 BALAKRISHNA, S. Family planning: knowledge, attitude and practice — a sample survey in Andhra Pradesh. Hyderabad: National Institute of Community Development, 1971. 139p.
Study of 350 men from rural Rajendranagar Block near Hyderabad to ascertain their family planning knowledge, attitudes and practices; to correlate these findings with selected socio-economic variables; and to ascertain their reproductive ideals (e.g., family size, age at marriage, interval between pregnancies). Points to paucity of information on knowledge, attitudes and practices of men.

3329 BASKARA RAO, N. [N. BHASKARA RAO]. Family planning in India: a case study of Karnataka. New Delhi: Vikas Publishing House, 1976. 72p.
Examines structure and evolution of family planning program in Karnataka, trends in adoption of family planning methods, socio-economic background of adopters, etc. Compares districts within Karnataka and compares Karnataka with other Indian states.

3330 CHANDRASEKHAR, SRIPATI. Report on a survey of attitudes of married couples toward family planning in the Pudupakkam area of the city of Madras, 1958. Madras: printed by the Controller of Stationery and Printing, 1959. 35p.
[Unexamined. NUC].

3331 KATTI, A.P. and R.L. PATIL. A study on the relative performance of male and female investigators in collecting data on fertility and family planning, etc., in Karnataka (Mysore) State. Dharwar: Demographic Research Centre, Institute of Economic Research, 1975? 144p.
Examines whether a same-sex investigator can gather better data on various demographic topics than a cross-sex investigator. Determines that proficiency and experience have more influence on the quality of information than gender of investigator.

3332 KRISHNA RAO, H., R.A. SATYANARAYANACHAR and AMEENA BEGAM. The attitude of Muslim women towards family planning in Bangalore. *In* J. of the Institute of Economic Research 7,2 (1972) 1-22.
Study of family planning knowledge, attitudes and practices. Concludes that Muslims do not differ from other religious communities with respect to practice of family planning.

3333 [Special issue devoted to family planning in Karnataka]. J. of Institute of Economic Research, Dharwar 5,2 (1970) 63p.
Includes articles on the progress of the state Family Planning Programme, the socio-economic background of a sample of sterilized women, intrauterine device acceptors in two districts, surgical methods for family planning among women and registration techniques.

(l) Political participation and issues

3334 HARDGRAVE, ROBERT L. The breast-cloth controversy: caste consciousness and social change in southern Travancore. *In* Indian Economic and Social History Review 5,2 (1968) 171-87.
Account of political struggle in 19th century Kerala for female modesty and other privileges denied to the Nadar community. "By tradition in Travancore, the breast was bared in deference to those of higher status as a symbol of respect . . . the Nairs . . . bared their breasts before the Nambudiri Brahmins, and the Brahmins did so only before the deity. The Nadars, like all of the lower castes, were categorically forbidden to cover their breasts at any time."

3335 SUNDARAYYA, P. The women in the Telangana movement. *In* Telangana people's struggle and its lessons. Calcutta: Communist Party of India, 1972. pp.328-53.
Considers role of women in a communist peasant revolt against landlords of Hyderabad State in the 1940s and early 1950s. Gives heroic examples of land defense, fights for wage increase and defense against police repression and attacks, including rape. Discusses various individual participants.

3336 YESUDAS, R.N. A people's revolt in Travancore: a backward class movement for social freedom. Trivandrum: Manju Publishing House, 1975. 281p.
Considers the revolt of the Nadar/Shanar Christian community in Travancore against the upper castes during the early and mid-19th century. A central issue was the insistence by the upper castes that Nadar women keep their upper bodies unclothed as a gesture of deference.

(m) Arts

3337 LAKSHMI, C.S. Notes from a monograph on Tamil women: Savithri is anxious to please. *In* Femina (27 Aug 1976) 40-1.
Argues that the images of women in popular Tamil films and magazines demonstrate that attitudes concerning the role of women in Tamil society have not changed in recent years.

i) Folk literatures

3338 RADHA KRISHNA MURTY, K. Folk-lore and the woman of Andhra. *In* Bulletin of the Cultural Research Institute, Calcutta 8,1/2 (1969) 116-21.
Examines images of women in Telugu folk songs. With excerpts in translation.

3339 ________. Telugu women in the folk-sayings. *In* Folklore [Calcutta] 10,4 (1969) 129-35. [*Reprint in* Sankar Sen Gupta, ed. Women in Indian folklore. Calcutta: Indian Publications, 1969. pp.223-30. (*Its* Folklore Series, 15)].
Presents numerous sayings and a song in transliteration and translation. Various topics.

3340 SHUNMUGA SUNDARAM, S. Image of women in Tamil folklore. *In* Bulletin of the Institute of Traditional Cultures, Madras (Jul 1975) 244-58.
Discusses female images in folk songs, proverbs, tales, ballads and folk beliefs. With extracts in transliteration and translation.

3341 SUBRAMANIAM, K. Women in the folk sayings of Tamilnad. *In* Folklore [Calcutta] 9,5 (1968) 155-60. [*Reprint in* Sankar Sen Gupta, ed. Women in Indian folklore. Calcutta: Indian Publications, 1969. pp.109-15. (*Its* Folklore Series, 15)].
Transliteration, translation and interpretation of 17 folk sayings.

3342 THANKAPPAN NAIR, P. Malayalam women: their past and present. *In* Folklore [Calcutta] 10,5 (1969) 157-77. [*Reprint in* Sankar Sen Gupta, ed. Women in Indian Folklore. Calcutta: Indian Publications, 1969. pp.236-56. (*Its* Folklore Series, 15)].
Folk life of Nayar women in proverbs, rituals, dances, games and pastimes.

3343 ________. Nair women in Malayalam proverbs. *In* J. of the Anthropological Society of Bombay, n.s. 14,1 (1969) 1-14.
Describes qualities attributed to Nayar women, in various familial roles and in general. Selected proverbs in transliteration and translation.

3344 ULLRICH, HELEN E. Women in selected Kannada folk-tales. *In* Giri Raj Gupta, ed. Family and social change in modern India. New Delhi: Vikas, 1976. pp.184-206. (Main Currents in Indian Sociology, 2).
Examines portrayal of women in four Kannada folk tales. Considers surface and underlying meanings and relationship to ethnographic context. Based on fieldwork among Havik brahmans of "Totagadde" village, northwestern Karnataka.

3345 VANAMAMALAI, N. Women in Tamil folklore. *In* Folklore [Calcutta] 9,8 (1968) 285-301. [*Reprint in* Sankar Sen Gupta, ed. Women in Indian folklore. Calcutta: Indian Publications, 1969. pp.1-19. (*Its* Folklore Series, 15)].
Discusses romantic, familial and agricultural themes in various genres of Tamil folklore. With examples in translation.

3346 VERGHESE, J. An evaluation of the position of Badaga woman of the Nilgiri Hills through proverbs. *In* Folklore [Calcutta] 4,12 (1963) 418-25.
Transliterates, translates and explicates a series of proverbs. Topics are general status, birth, position before marriage, wife and mother. Includes brief comments on Badaga community.

ii) Tamil literature

3347 CHATFIELD, JEAN. Some women in modern Tamil short stories: a study in irony. *In* Feminine sensibility and characterization in South Asian literature. Guest ed: Fritz Blackwell. J. of South Asian Literature 12,3/4 (1977) 19-24.
Examines female characterization by contemporary Tamil social critics and realists, all of whom are male. Female Tamil writers, the author comments, tend to provide female characters with romantic and happy resolutions. The social critics, however, portray women in difficult and powerless situations, "as though they are caught up, perhaps in the wheel of dharma."

3348 JANAKIRAMAN, T. The sins of Appu's mother. Tr. from Tamil by M. Krishnan. Delhi: Hind Pocket Books, 1972. 168p.
Novel. Focuses upon mothers and sons and feminine virtue. An adulterous woman sends her son to study the Vedas so that she may die peacefully at his feet.

3349 JAYAKANTHAN. The recoil. Tr. from Tamil by Ashokamitran. *In* K.N. Subramanyam, ed. Modern Indian short stories, v3. New Delhi: Indian Council for Cultural Relations, 1977. pp.84-90.
Short story. Portrays the bitter jealousy of an old woman at the end of a long and satis-

fying marriage.

3350 JOHN SAMUEL, GNANA SIROMONI. The cult of revolutionary womanhood in Bharati and Shelley. *In his* Studies in comparative literature: Tamil, Malayalam and English. Madras: Mani Pathippakam, 1977. pp.54-80.
Compares ideals of revolutionary womanhood in the romantic poets Percy Bysshe Shelley and Subrahmanya Bharati. Traces their respective backgrounds and influences. For Bharati this included Shelley himself, the nationalist movement, the revival of the *Śākta* cult, the identification of the Mother Goddess with Mother India and the influence of Sister Nivedita. Compares two sets of characters and discusses their respective concepts of women's liberation and free love.

3351 LAKSHMI, C.S. Tradition and modernity of Tamil women writers. *In* Social Scientist 5,9 (1976) 37-45.
Discusses themes and values with respect to women in contemporary Tamil fiction by men and women.

3352 MADHAVIAH, A. Muthumeenakshi: the autobiography of a brahmin girl. Tr. from Tamil by one of author's daughters. Madras: Law Printing House, 1915. 121p.
Novel? Didactic work about plight of women as widows, as daughters-in-law and in other roles. [Unexamined].

3353 PADMANABHAN, NEELA. The generations. Tr. from Tamil by Ka Naa Subramanyam. Delhi: Orient Paperbacks, Hind Pocket Books, 1972. 192p.
Novel. A young husband mistreats his wife, blaming her for his own shortcomings. Her brother is sensitive to the largely socially constructed injustice and intercedes.

3354 RAMAMRITHAM, L.S. Paarkadal. Tr. from Tamil by Ashokamitran. *In* K.N. Subramanyam, ed. Modern Indian short stories, v3. New Delhi: Indian Council for Cultural Relations, 1977. pp.73-83.
Short story. A new wife reflects upon various sweet and bitter aspects of family life in a letter to her husband.

3355 SANJEEVI, KRISHNA. Women in the works of Bhārathi and Bhārathidāsan. *In* Bulletin of the Institute of Traditional Cultures, Madras (Jul 1975) 232-7.
Compares images of the emancipated woman in the works of these two Tamil writers and social reformers.

iii) Malayalam literature

3356 DAS, KAMALA. The guest. Tr. from Malayalam by K. Nicholson. *In* Suresh Kohli, ed. Modern Indian short stories. New Delhi: Arnold Heinemann, 1974. pp.61-3.
Short story. A friendly young visitor evokes past memories in an aging woman.

3357 ________. The scent of the bird. Tr. from Malayalam by R. Nandakumar. *In* K.N. Subramanyam, ed. Modern Indian short stories, v3. New Delhi: Indian Council for Cultural Relations, 1977. pp.56-60.
Short story. Young woman faces a multitude of fears, among which are seeking employment and death. Set in Calcutta.

3358 PADMANABHAN, T. A woman of Kadayanellore. Tr. from Malayalam by A.N. Nambiar. *In* K.N. Subramanyam, ed. Modern Indian short stories, v3. New Delhi: Indian Council for Cultural Relations, 1977. pp.30-42.
Short story. Traces the development of friendship and passion between a young, unhappily married village woman and a senior inspector stationed there.

3359 SIVASANKARA PILLAI, THAKAZHI. Forever virgin. Tr. from Malayalam by C. Paul Verghese. *In* Indian Literature 13,2 (1970) 109-18.
Short story. Portrays an elder unmarried sister's sadness due to her younger sister's wedding and married life. The elder sister agrees to care for a bedridden mother and yearns for the status and satisfactions her sister enjoys as mistress of a household, mother and wife. She finally has a confusing sexual encounter in middle age.

3360 ________. The unchaste. Tr. from Malayalam by M.K. Bhaskaran. Delhi: Orient Paperbacks, Hind Pocket Books, 1971. 112p.
Novel. Concerns the family life of a woman and the man who married her after she was seduced and impregnated by another.

iv) Kannada literature

3361 KARANTH, K.S. The whispering earth. Tr. from Kannada by A.N. Murthy Rao. Delhi: Vikas Publishing House, 1974. 206p.
Novel. A Karnataka peasant family through several generations. Much on women's lives and family relationships.

3362 TRIVENI [ANASUYA SHANKAR]. The "mad woman." Tr. from Kannada by Meera Narvekar. Bombay: Jaico Publishing House, 1975. 156p.
Novel. A young Kannada woman returns home following two years in a mental hospital to find that her husband has a mistress. Flash-

backs detail her psychic conflicts and contrast her previous conjugal and maternal happiness with her present romantic and maternal disappointments. Those around her perceive her response to these disappointments as madness.

v) Telugu literature: male writer P. Padmaraju

3363 PADMARAJU, PALAGUMMI. On the boat. Tr. from Telugu by the author. *In* K. Natwar-Singh, ed. Tales from modern India. New York: Macmillan Company, 1966. pp.236-46.
Short story. A man recounts an encounter with a village woman. The woman repeatedly suffers at the hands of and takes risks for a man who physically and psychologically abuses her. The narrator marvels at her tie to this man.

3364 ________. Granny is dead. Tr. from Telugu by the author. *In* K.N. Subramanyam, ed. Modern Indian short stories, v3. New Delhi: Indian Council for Cultural Relations, 1977. pp.166-77. [*Also in* Suresh Kohli, ed. Modern Indian short stories. New Delhi: Arnold Heinemann, 1974. pp.105-17].
Short story. Portrays an old Telugu widow and her significant place within her family.

vi) Dance forms

3365 KALYANIKUTTY AMMA, KALAMANDALAM. Mohiniattam. Tr. from Malayalam by K.B. Nair. *In* Durgadas Mukhopadhyay, ed. Lesser known forms of performing arts in India. New Delhi: Sterling Publishers, 1978. pp.64-9.
Discusses a dance form from Kerala and compares it to the similar *bhārata nāṭyam*. Describes efforts of artists to revive its popularity and retain its purity.

3366 RAGHAVAN, V. The veethi bhagavatam of Andhra. *In* Durgadas Mukhopadhyay, ed. Lesser known forms of performing arts in India. New Delhi: Sterling Publishers, 1978. pp.34-7.
"When Kuchupudi Bhagavata attained its high water-mark, it gave birth to a derivative solo performance called the *Veethi Bhagavata* or *Gollakalapa*. The masters of Kuchupudi themselves thought of this new type and it evolved through women-artistes of courtesan families (*Kalavantula*) who were proficient in the solo dance-art of *Nautch*."

(n) Adornment: saris and personal names

3367 NICHOLSON, S. Women's cloths in the Cuddapa District, South India. *In* Man 20,72 (1920) 149-52.
Brief ethnography of saris. Discusses purchase, first wearing and significance of various patterns woven into the inner, concealed end of the cloth. The patterns are associated with particular deities and particular social circumstances in which one honors these deities. Includes drawings of various patterns, the significance of which "is rapidly being forgotten."

3368 RAMASUBRAMANIAN, N. Personal name study: Madras Hindu female names. *In* Shrinivas Ritti and B.R. Gopal, eds. Studies in Indian history and culture: volume presented to Dr. P.B. Desai. Dharwar: Prof. P.B. Desai Felicitation Committee, Karnatak University, 1971. pp.519-30.
Regarding structure of feminine names, patterns of naming after ancestors, other classes of names, variation by caste and sect, pet names, pen names, names applicable to both sexes, modern names, names of twins, double names, initials and feminine markers.

(3) West India: area of Marathi and Gujarati languages

(a) The colonial experience: social reform issues

3369 BOMBAY (PRESIDENCY). WOMEN'S COUNCIL. Handbook of women's work, 1928-1929, 2d ed. Bombay: Women's Council, Government of Bombay, 1929. 87p. [*1st ed.* 1920].
Directory of women's welfare agencies in the Bombay Presidency. Provides aims, sponsorship, officers, founding information, programs, etc., where available or relevant. Categories include "Charity, Relief, Medical Relief," "Co-operative Societies," "Clubs, Playgrounds, Etc.," "Crêches," "Classes — Adult Education," "Employment Bureau," "Hostels," "Industrial Classes & Workrooms," "Libraries," "Magazines," "Maternity & Health," "Orphanages & Shelters for Children," "Rescue Work & Rescue Homes," "Scholarships," "Special Schools," "Social Gatherings & Lectures &c.," "Social Training," "Temperance Work," "Work Amongst Widows, Remarriage, Homes, Education" and "General and Miscellaneous."

3370 CHITALIA, K.J. Directory of women's institutions, Bombay Presidency . . ., v1. Bombay: Servants of India Society, 1936. 71p.
Additional volumes were apparently planned. [Unexamined. BMG]

3371 DADACHANJI, FAREDUN K., comp. List of Hindu charities in Bombay. Bombay: Social Service League, 1919. 91p.
Lists 759 charities in Bombay City and environs, many relating to women's welfare. Includes such information as addresses, associated personnel, assets and services provided.

3372 DESAI, NEERA. Ideas which influenced the movement for changing the status of women in India in the 19th century: with special reference to the Gujarati society. *In* Bisheshwar Prasad, ed. Ideas in history: proceedings of a seminar on ideas motivating social and religious movements and political and economic policies during the eighteenth and nineteenth centuries in India. Bombay: Asia Publishing House, 1968. pp.110-24.
Discusses personalities, ideas, events and changing social circumstances. Argues that liberal ideas were applied 1) only to problems of certain urban upper-caste women, 2) in an inconsistent way and 3) in advance of a supportive social structure.

3373 ENGINEER, MISS and MRS. CHOKSI [MITHAN CHOKSI]. Seva Sadan and other social work in Bombay. *In* Evelyn C. Gedge and Mithan Choksi, eds. Women in modern India: fifteen papers by Indian women writers. Bombay: D.B. Taraporewala Sons and Company, 1929. pp.43-50. [*Reprint* Westport, Connecticut: Hyperion Press, 1976. (Pioneers of the Women's Movement)].
Reviews establishment and work of Seva Sadan, Bombay Presidency Women's Council, Maharastra Women's Co-operative Credit Society and various other women's organizations and social service associations for women's welfare in western India.

3374 GOKHALE, A.R., ed. Seva Sadan speaks: golden jubilee, Poona Seva Sadan Society, Nagpur branch, Nagpur. Nagpur: Poona Seva Sadan Society, Nagpur Branch, 1977? 13, 106, 114p.
Brief articles in English and Marathi review various aspects of the work for women performed by the Seva Sadan's Nagpur branch from 1927 to 1976. Articles consider funds, facilities, visitors, celebrations, workers and so forth.

3375 NILKANTH, LADY RAMANBHAI. Recollections of social progress in Gujarat. *In* Evelyn C. Gedge and Mithan Choksi, eds. Women in modern India: fifteen papers by Indian women writers. Bombay: D.B. Taraporewala Sons and Company, 1929. pp.38-42. [*Reprint* Westport, Connecticut: Hyperion Press, 1976. (Pioneers of the Women's Movement)].
Briefly mentions social reform progress in Gujarat and elsewhere in the Bombay Presidency with respect to female seclusion, education, women's organizations and widows' opportunities.

i) *Satī*/suttee

3376 BALLHATCHET, KENNETH. Social policy and social change in western India, 1817-1830. London: Oxford University Press, 1957. 335p. (London Oriental Series, 5).
Concluding chapters contain an account of the government's anti-*satī* campaign in western India (pp.275-91, 298-305). Based on official records.

3377 Human sacrifice — self-immolation — vows. *In* Panjab Notes and Queries 2,23

(1885) 197.
Discusses site where sons give their lives in fulfillment of vows made by their mothers who had believed themselves to be barren.

3378 KENNEDY, RICHARD HARTLEY. The sutti, as witnessed at Baroda, November 29th, 1825. London, 1855.
Booklet includes an eyewitness description. [Unexamined. BMG].

3379 Suttees. *In* Asiatic Review n.s. 2,8 (Aug 1830) 205-6.
Account of a ***satī*** in Ratnagiri in 1830 and notice of policy dictated by the Governor in Council at Bombay to civil authorities of the presidency with respect to ***satīs***.

ii) Female infanticide

3380 BOMBAY (PRESIDENCY). Reports of the measures, commencing with the year 1805, adopted, in concert with the government, by the late Colonel Alexander Walker; and subsequently by Mr. J.P. Willoughby, Political Agent in Kattywar, and by his successors, for the suppression of female infanticide in that province. By Alexander Walker et al. Bombay: printed at Bombay Education Society's Press, 1856. pp.317-721. (Selections from the Records of the Bombay Government, n.s. 39, part 2).
Official correspondence, reports and other government documents organized chronologically from 1805 to 1855. Includes speculations about the origin and history of female infanticide, observations about contemporary practices, demographic data, details of government efforts and policy and other information. Focuses on Jhareja, Jethva and Soomra communities of Kathiawar.

3381 ________. Repression of female infanticide in the Bombay Presidency: a compilation report setting out briefly all the measures taken to repress the crime in Gujarat and some of the neighbouring native states, and the result of these measures. By H.R. Cooke. Bombay, 1875. 102p. (Selections from the Records of the Bombay Government, n.s. 147).
Covers 1836 to 1872. [Unexamined].

3382 BURNES, ALEXANDER. On female infanticide in Cutch. *In* J. of the Royal Asiatic Society 1 (1834) 193-9, 285-8.
Report and letter from a lieutenant, based upon "a residence in Cutch for nearly four years, and a minute inquiry into the population of that country." In the report he argues, presenting statistics, that the East India Company has been premature in believing its attempts to abolish female infanticide to have been successful. Includes comments on the problems its abolition would entail in the Jhareja Rajput community and how British policy must take this into account. In the letter, he discusses conversations with Jhareja chieftains on the topic, who pointed out "that it was most difficult for them to support their character (lāj) as Rājapūts and to fulfil their engagements towards [British officials]" and explained its importance to their social system.

3383 CAVE BROWNE, JOHN. Indian infanticide: its origin, progress, and suppression. London: W.H. Allen and Company, 1857. 234p.
In western India. [Unexamined. NUC].

3384 CORMACK, JOHN. Account of the abolition of female infanticide in Guzerat: with considerations on the question of promoting the gospel in India. London: Black, Parry, and Company, 1815. 412p.
[Unexamined. NUC].

3385 Female infanticide. *In* Asiatic Journal n.s. 19,76 (1836) 250-2.
Reviews efforts of Colonel Pottinger to repress female infanticide in early 19th century Cutch.

3386 Human sacrifices and infanticide in India. *In* Edinburgh Review 119,244 (1864) 389-412.
Reviews John Wilson's book on female infanticide in western India and urges harsher government measures against the practice.

3387 LE GRAND, JACOB. Infanticide in Kattyar. *In* Transactions of the Bombay Geographical Society 7 (1842) 1-96.
[Unexamined].

3388 MEHTA, MAKRAND J. A study of the practice of female infanticide among the Kanbis of Gujarat. *In* J. of the Gujarat Research Society 28,1/4 (1966) 57-66.
Considers British efforts to end female infanticide among the Kanbis, statistics and various techniques of killing infants. Cites hypergamy and the dowry system as the chief causes. Appendix reproduces a questionnaire about dowry and responses given by members of the Kanbi community in 1848.

3389 MODY, COOVERJEE RUSTOMJEE. An essay on female infanticide, to which the prize offered by the Bombay government, for the second best essay against female infanticide among the Jadajas and other Rajpoot tribes of Guzerat, was awarded. Bombay, 1849. 50p.
[Unexamined. NUC].

3390 NATH, VISWA. Female infanticide and the Lewa Kanbis of Gujarat in the nineteenth century. *In* Indian Economic and Social History Review 10,4 (1973) 386-404.
Considers form and prevalence of female infanticide in this peasant caste and its relation-

ship to "hypergamy, polygyny, lineage system, and other social institutions." Based primarily on records of the Bombay government.

3391 PAKRASI, KANTI B. Female infanticide in India: a century ago. *In* Bulletin of the Socio-economic Research Institute, Calcutta 2,2 (1968) 21-30.
"In this paper some facts and figures have been presented to expose the prevalence, extent, causes and modes of female infanticide" among the Jhareja Rajputs of Kathiawar, 1805-55.

3392 _______. 'Benevolent crusade' to suppress infanticides in India: an observation. *In* Calcutta Review n.s. 2,2 (1970) 195-205.
Argues that the "benevolent crusade" was actually a justification for British military intervention and expansion of political authority over the "high-spirited" Rajputs. Focuses on events in peninsular Gujarat around 1800.

3393 _______. Female infanticide in India. Calcutta: Editions Indian, 1970. 304p.
Closely documented history of female infanticide and its suppression among Jhareja and other Rajput groups of Kathiawar, 1808-55. Considers demographic and social structural factors. Based on original documents.

3394 WILSON, JOHN. History of the suppression of infanticide in western India under the government of Bombay, including notices of the provinces and tribes in which the practice has prevailed. Bombay: Smith, Taylor, 1855. 457p. [*Also* London: Smith, Elder].
Considers the late 18th century British discovery of female infanticide in areas of the present Gujarat and Rajasthan and subsequent efforts to suppress it. Based primarily on records of the Bombay government.

iii) Widow marriage, age of consent

3395 BHATE, G.C. Permitting widow-marriages. Poona: Widow Marriage Association, 1907. [Unexamined].

3396 GIDUMAL, DAYARAM [DAYARAM GIDUMAL SHAHANI]. Malabari réformateur social [Malabari, the social reformer]. *In his* Un réformateur Parsi dans l'histoire contemporaine de l'Inde: Behramji M. Malabari. Tr. from English [by D. Menant?]. Paris: Ernest Flammarion, 1898. pp.143-88. [*English ed.* The life and life-work of Behramji M. Malabari, with selections from his writings and speeches on infant marriage and enforced widowhood and also his "Rambles of a Pilgrim Reformer." Bombay: printed at the Education Society's Press, Byculla, 1888. 329p. *Rev. ed.* Behramji M. Malabari: a biographical sketch. London: T.F. Unwin, 1892. 254p.].
Regarding Malabari's work for the cause of marriage reform, i.e., in opposition to child marriage and in support of widow marriage. Includes lengthy excerpts from Malabari's writings. The original edition [1888, unexamined] is said to contain 132 of Malabari's *Indian Spectator* articles, 1884-87.

3397 KOLHATKAR, WAMANRAO M. Widow remarriage. *In* C. Yajneswara Chintamani, ed. Indian social reform: being a collection of essays, addresses, speeches, etc., with an appendix. Madras: printed at the Minerva Press, 1901. First part, pp.282-311.
Criticizes prohibitions against widow marriage. With an extended discussion of the early widow marriage movement in western India.

3398 MALABARI, B. Appendice I: Appel des filles de l'Inde [An appeal from the daughters of India]. *In* Gidumal Dayaram [Gidumal Dayaram Shahani]. Un réformateur Parsi dans l'histoire contemporaine de l'Inde: Behramji M. Malabari. Tr. from English [by D. Menant?]. Paris: Ernest Flammarion, 1898. pp.189-206. [*Originally* An appeal from the daughters of India. London: Farmer and Sons, 1890. 20p.].
Appeals to the women of England to become active in the marriage reform movement in India: "Infant-Marriage, Baby-Wife, Girl-Mother, Virgin-Widow. Ce langage est-il celui des hommes ou des démons?" [Is this the language of men or demons?].

3399 PATHARE REFORM ASSOCIATION. Marriage of Hindu widows, advocated by the Pathare Reform Association of Bombay; with an epitome of the history of Bim Raja, founder of the race of Pathare Prabhus. Bombay, 1863? [*2d ed.* Bombay: "Indu-Prakash" Press, 1869. 29p.].
In English and Marathi. [Unexamined. BMG].

3400 RUGNATHDAS, MADHOWDAS. Story of a widow remarriage: being the experiences of Madhowdas Rugnathdas. Bombay: S.K. Khambata, 1890. 118p.
Personal testimony of a Bombay merchant who, after losing three wives, married a widow in 1871 to help improve the circumstances of widows. A tale of "ceaseless torment and persecution" aimed at securing legislative reform.

3401 SINGH, JOGENDRA. B.M. Malabari: rambles with the pilgrim reformer. London: G. Bell and Sons, 1914. 202p. [Unexamined. NUC].

3402 TELANG, K.T. Reply to Malabari's note on infant marriage and enforced widowhood in India. *In his* Selected writings and speeches. Bombay: K.R. Mitra, Manoranjan Press, 1916? pp.239-58.

Letter of 1884 expressing gratitude for Malabari's interest in marriage reform issues but dissent with respect to most of the specific remedies suggested. Offers counterproposals that are more conservative. The author, who was a justice, scholar and politician, classifies himself as one of the "letaloneists."

iv) Education

3403 Alexandra Girls' English Institution centenary souvenir, 1863-1963. Bombay, 1963. 45p.
[Unexamined].

3404 BOMBAY (PRESIDENCY). EDUCATIONAL DEPARTMENT. Compilation of opinions on the subject of the education of girls and women called for by the government order number 1268 dated May 15th, 1916. Bombay: Government Central Press, 1916. 473p.
[Unexamined].

3405 BRUCE, C.H. Pioneers of secondary education in the Bombay Presidency: American Mission Girls' High School founded in 1838. *In* Progress of Education 15,1 (1938) 13-26.
School in Ahmednagar. Later became American Marathi Mission Girls' Boarding School. [Unexamined].

3406 Canda Ramji Girls' High School golden jubilee, 1960-61: souvenir. Bombay, n.d. 40, 55p.
Collected articles on female education. [Unexamined].

3407 GRAY, HESTER. Missionary settlements for university women. *In* International Review of Missions 34,136 (1945) 400-5.
Presents a general philosophy of social reform in context of the twilight of the colonial relationship. Details the 1895 establishment and subsequent work of the Missionary Settlement for University Women in Bombay and environs, devoted to manifold support of university educated women.

3408 Higher education of native girls. *In* Bombay Educational Record 20 (1884) 253-72.
Proceedings of an 1884 meeting in Poona (now Pune) to discuss the establishment of a girls' school. [Unexamined].

3409 JASBHAI, MANIBHAI. A memorandum on Hindu female education in the Bombay Presidency. Bombay: Bombay Gazette, 1896. 162p.
[Unexamined. MRL].

3410 KARVE, D.K. Higher education of women. *In* Progress of Education 1,2 (1924) 34-8.
Discusses Indian Women's University. [Unexamined].

3411 MAHALAKSMIVALA, CAVASJI DHANJIBHAI. A note on the education of Parsee children with suggestions for reform in accordance with modern educational ideals and principles. Bombay, 1921. 248p.
Has section on education of Parsi girls (pp.367-73). [Unexamined].

3412 MISSIONARY SETTLEMENT FOR UNIVERSITY WOMEN. Report. 1-? (1895/96-?). London? Annually.
Sample report, the 33rd (1928/29), contains lists of past western female residents in western India and present officeholders, reports by various staff members, details of branch activities, notice of contributions from the British Isles and Australia and budgets. The stated aim of the MSUW is to "carry the teaching and standards of Christianity to (1) University Women Students in Bombay, (2) Parsi and other educated Indian women."

3413 NIHAL SINGH, SAINT. Recent educational progress in India. *In* Contemporary Review 113 (Jan 1918) 63-9.
Regarding higher education advancements in India in the second decade of the 20th century. One section discusses the establishment of the Indian Women's University in Poona (now Pune) by Professor D.K. Karve and others and their conception of an appropriate curriculum.

3414 ________. Forcing the pace of women's literacy. *In* Modern Review 53,2 (1933) 170-9.
Regarding the progress of female education in Gondal State, Kathiawar, due to the support of the Maharaja Bhagvat Sinhjee and his wife, Nandkunverba. Photographs.

3415 NIKAMBE, SHEVANTIBAI M. Ratanbai: a sketch of a Bombay high caste young wife. London: Marshall Brothers, 1895. 88p.
A didactic fictional account of the merits of education for high-caste Hindu women interwoven through material on brahman social life. The author devoted much of her life to the education of such girls and women. Includes photographs of her pupils and others.

3416 PARANJPE, M.R. Sreemati Nathibai Damodar Thackersey Women's University, Poona, 1916-1931. *In* Progress of Education 8,9 (1931) 2-15.
[Unexamined].

3417 SHAH, K.K. and S.N. NANAVATI, eds. The Sophia College case. Bombay: the editors, 1944? 136p.
Collected documents relating to the dispute that occurred when the Sophia College for Women, Bombay, sought affiliation with the University of Bombay in 1940. The chief issue was an objection to the proselytizing of the students by the nuns operating the school.

v) Health

3418 BODLEY, RACHEL L. Introduction. *To* The high caste Hindu woman. By Pandita Ramabai Sarasvati. London: Bell and Sons, 1890. pp.1-28.
Includes details of the life of Anandibai Joshi, a Maharashtrian brahman woman who earned an M.D. in the United States in 1886.

3419 DALL, CAROLINE HEALEY. The life of Dr. Anandabai Joshee: a kinswoman of the Pundita Ramabai. Boston: Roberts Brothers, 1888. 187p.
Biography of the first Hindu woman to become a doctor. Following medical education at the Women's Medical College of Pennsylvania, Anandibai Joshi returned to practice in Kolhapur. Based in large part on her correspondence, with many letters reproduced. Portrait.

3420 Dr. Rukhmabai: a pioneer medical woman of India. *In* World Medical Journal 11, 1 (1964) 35-6.
Sketch of Dr. Rukhmabai who received her M.D. from the London School of Medicine for Women in 1894. British women of Bombay arranged for her medical education following her involvement in a widely publicized court case: she successfully defended against her husband's charge for restitution of conjugal rights. Describes her medical work. Portrait.

3421 JEHANGIR, LADY COWASJI. Maternal welfare work in Bombay. *In* Asiatic Review 33 n.s. (Oct 1937) 759-67.
Regarding four organizations established in the 1920s and 1930s for the promotion of maternal and infant welfare and public health in the Bombay Presidency: 1) Bombay Presidency Infant Welfare Society, 2) Bombay Presidency Baby and Health Week Association, 3) Society for the Study and Promotion of Family Hygiene and 4) Bombay Mofussil Maternity and Child Welfare and Health Council.

vi) Prostitution and dancing girls

3422 BOMBAY (PRESIDENCY). PROSTITUTION COMMITTEE. Report. Bombay: Home Department, Government of Bombay, 1922? 16p. [*Chair* Jamsetji Jejeebhoy].
[Unexamined. BMG].

3423 CORREIA, A.C.G. DA SILVA. Bayaderes and other courtesans of Portuguese India: anthropometry, sexology, ethnography, sociology, venereology and prophylaxis. *In* Arquivos da Escola Médico-Cirúgica de Goa, Ser. A. (1939) 61-384.
[Unexamined].

3424 RAGHUNATHJI, K. Bombay dancing girls. *In* Indian Antiquary 13 (Jun 1884) 165-78.
Social organization of *kalāvatīs*, women versed in the arts (of dancing), in the Bombay Presidency. Describes recruitment, marriage, categories of performance and the particularities of four "sects." Makes comparisons with dancing girls of Madras.

3425 RODRIGUES, LUCIO. The dakni: "the songs of the dancing girl." *In* Folklore [Calcutta] 4,11 (1963) 361-8.
Uses translated excerpts from songs of Goan dancing girls to discuss aspects of the lives of the dancers. In addition, the poetic qualities of the songs are evaluated. The dancers, descended from the temple dancing tradition, are said to live near temples as singers, dancers and prostitutes of a secular nature.

vii) Female seclusion

3426 TYABJI, F.B. Social life in 1804 and 1929 amongst Muslims in Bombay. *In* J. of the Royal Asiatic Society, Bombay Branch, n.s. 6 (1930) 286-300.
Author discusses *pardā* from the perspective of his own experience within the Khoja family and community. "In Bombay no man who wishes the ladies of his family to come out of strict pardah will meet with any insuperable difficulties."

viii) Property rights

3427 BARODA. COMMITTEE ON HINDU WOMEN'S PROPERTY RIGHTS. Report. Baroda: printed at the Government Press, 1930. 213p.
Reviews law relating to Hindu women's property rights as explained in traditional texts . and as in effect in Baroda State at the time of enquiry. With recommendations for improvements. The Maharaja of Baroda appointed the committee, having noticed "that the difference in the rights of inheritance . . . between males and females requires to be harmonised with the improved status of females."

ix) Christian conversion and missions

3428 STAELIN, CHARLOTTE DENNETT. The influence of missions on women's education in India: the American Marathi Mission in Ahmadnagar, 1830-1930. Ph.D. dissertation, Department of History, University of Michigan, 1977.

349p. [University Microfilms 77-18, 125].
Detailed case study of a single mission based largely on primary sources. Discusses establishment of American Marathi Mission and its subsidiary institutions, its policies and its effects. Shows that mission schools were significant as chief 19th century female education agencies yet they also caused problems for the women they served. Considers various problems. [Unexamined. DAI].

3429 STORRIE, KATE. Soonderbai Powar: for 45 years an earnest worker for God in India, friend of Pandita Ramabai. London: Pickering and Inglis, n.d. 110p.
Mission work. [Unexamined. MRL].

x) Pandita Ramabai Sarasvati's work for women

3430 BUTLER, CLEMENTINA. Pandita Ramabai and her work. Boston: American Ramabai Association, 1910. 24p.
[Unexamined. NUC].

3431 _______. Pandita Ramabai Sarasvati: pioneer in the movement for the education of the child-widow of India. New York: Fleming H. Revell Company, 1922? 96p.
With plates. [Unexamined. NUC].

3432 CHAPPELL, JENNIE. Pandita Ramabai: a great life in Indian missions. London: Pickering and Inglis, 1938? 95p. (Memoir Series of Mighty Men and Noble Women, 11).
Illustrations, portraits. [Unexamined. NUC].

3433 CLARK, MURIEL. Pandita Ramabai. London: Morgan and Scott, 1920? 62p.
On her mission work for women. [Unexamined. NUC].

3434 DONGRE, RAJAS KRISHNARAO and JOSEPHINE E. PATTERSON. Pandita Ramabai: a life of faith and prayer. Madras: Christian Literature Society, 1963. 112p.
Biography by two women involved in carrying out Pandita Ramabai's work (Miss Dongre is her grandniece). Includes Ramabai's autobiographical "Testimony," memoirs by a coworker and a relative (Miss Dongre?), photographs and a brief statement about the Mukti Mission today.

3435 DYER, HELEN S. Pandita Ramabai: the story of her life. New York: Fleming H. Revell, 1911. 197p. [*Also* London: Morgan and Scott, 1900?, 94p.].
Story of Ramabai's life and work by a woman who established the Sisters of India Prayer Union in England in support of this work.

3436 _______. Pandita Ramabai: her vision, her mission and triumph of faith. London: Pickering and Inglis, 1920? 173p.
[Unexamined. NUC].

3437 FULLER, MARY LUCIA BIERCE. The triumph of an Indian widow: the life of Pandita Ramabai. New York: Christian Alliance Publishing Company, 1928. 72p.
Biography by an "intimate acquaintance" who spent several years at the Ramabai Mukti Mission during Ramabai's lifetime and whose mother was regarded by Ramabai as a "spiritual mentor." Photographs of Ramabai, her family and the Mukti Mission.

3438 HASTIE, M. LISSA. A daughter of the East: or sweet incense unto God. Ajmer: Scottish Mission Industries Company.
Biography of Ramabai's daughter and coworker, Manoramabai. [Unexamined].

3439 MACNICOL, NICOL. Pandita Ramabai. Calcutta: Association Press, 1926. 147p. (Builders of Modern India). [*Also* London: Student Christian Movement].
"I have made an attempt . . . to grasp and to present the idea of her life, when in her person the Indian soul meets Christ and is transformed. Further, my desire has been to make this woman better known to those in India who, like her, call themselves Christians." Six photographs.

3440 MILLER, BASIL. Pandita Ramabai: India's Christian pilgrim. Grand Rapids, Michigan: Zondervan Publishing House, 1949? 121p.
[Unexamined. NUC].

3441 Mukti Prayer-Bell. v1-6 (1903-1916)? Khedgaon: Ramabai Mukti Mission. Quarterly?
Pandita Ramabai Sarasvati edited this periodical about her mission's work. [Unexamined. ULS].

3442 NIKAMBE, MRS. [SHEVANTIBAI M. NIKAMBE?]. Pandita Ramabai and the problem of India's married women and widows. *In* Evelyn C. Gedge and Mithan Choksi, eds. Women in modern India: fifteen papers by Indian women writers. Bombay: D.B. Taraporewala Sons and Company, 1929. pp.14-24. [*Reprint* Westport, Connecticut: Hyperion Press, 1976. (Pioneers of the Women's Movement)].
A coworker reviews Ramabai's life and work and describes her own Married Women's School in Bombay and the special educational needs and problems of married women.

3443 RAMABAI ASSOCIATION. Report. 1-10. (1888-1898). Boston. *Became* American Ramabai Association. Report. 1-? (1899-?). Boston.
[Unexamined. ULS, NUC].

3444 RAMABAI MUKTI MISSION. Report. 1- (189_-). Khedgaon. Annually.
[Unexamined. MRL].

3445 Ramabai Mukti Mission Praise and Prayer. vl-? Philadelphia: American Council of the Ramabai Mukti Mission. Monthly.
[Unexamined. MRL].

3446 RAMABAI SARASVATI, PANDITA. A testimony, 9th ed? Kedgaon: Ramabai Mukti Mission, 1968? 66p. [*1st ed.* 1907? *Also* J.J. Lucas, ed. Pandita Ramabai: a wonderful life, being "A Testimony." Condensed by the editor. Allahabad, 1919. 18p.].
Ramabai's autobiographical statement about her life, including her family background and conversion to Christianity. Illustrated. Reprinted in entry 3434. [Unexamined. NUC, BMG].

3447 _______. Sister Geraldine, comp. A.B. Shah, ed. The letters and correspondence of Pandita Ramabai. Bombay: Maharashtra State Board for Literature and Culture, 1977. 36, 435p.
Correspondence, 1883-1917. [Unexamined. ALI].

3447a SENGUPTA, PADMINI. Pandita Ramabai Saraswati: her life and work. Bombay: Asia Publishing House, 1970. 364p.
Detailed biography written at request of Pandita Ramabai Centenary Memorial Committee.

3448 SHAH, A.B. Pandita Ramabai. *In* New Quest 2 (Aug 1977) 11-26.
Prepared as an introduction to Ramabai's published correspondence, this article reviews her life and work, drawing on her letters and other contemporary sources.

3449 VICKERY, K.C. Ramabai: the Hindu widow's friend. *In* Missionary Review 45 (Sep 1922) 696-703.
[Unexamined].

3450 Women who ventured: Pandita Ramabai, the Indian orphans' friend; Ann H. Judson, missionary heroine of Burma. London: Pickering and Inglis, 1935? 93p.
Illustrations, portraits. [Unexamined. MRL].

xi) Dhondo Keshav Karve's work for women

3451 CHANDAVARKAR, G.L. Dhondo Keshav Karve. New Delhi: Publications Division, Ministry of Information and Broadcasting, Government of India, 1970. 248p. (Builders of Modern India). [*Also* Maharshi Karve. Bombay: Popular Book Depot, 1958. 233p.].
Biography focuses on Maharshi Karve's work for women in western India. Based primarily on his autobiographical writings.

3452 HINGNE STREE-SHIKSHAN SAMSTHA. Report. 1- (1896/97-). Poona. Annually.
[Unexamined].

3453 _______. Maharshi Karve: his 105 years. Poona: Hingne Stree-Shikshan Samstha, 1963. 108p.
Drawings, historic photographs and captions and a chronology tell the story of Maharshi Karve's life and work.

3454 KARVE, ANANDIBAI. Autobiography. Tr. from Marathi. *In* D.D. Karve, ed. and tr. The new brahmans: five Maharashtrian families. Berkeley: University of California Press, 1963. pp.58-79.
Translation of selections from Anandibai Karve's 1944 Marathi autobiography, "My Story." She discusses her family background, her widowhood at the age of eight, her life in her parents-in-law's house, her experiences as the first student in Pandita Ramabai's school for widows, her second unorthodox marriage to D.K. Karve and the subsequent supportive role she played in her husband's work for widows and women in general.

3455 KARVE, DHONDO KESHAV. My twenty years in the cause of Indian women. *In* Indian Interpreter (Oct 1913) 103-13.
[Unexamined].

3456 _______. My twenty years in the cause of Indian women: or, a short history of the origin and growth of the Hindu Widow's Home and cognate institutions. Poona, 1915. 50p.
[Unexamined. NUC].

3457 _______. Professor Karve's work in the cause of Indian women as described by himself. *In* Modern Review 18,5 (1915) 537-46.
D.K. Karve discusses his work for the Widow Marriage Association, the Hindu Widows' Home, the Mahila Vidyalaya and the Nishkama Karma Matha in Poona (now Pune) during the late 19th and early 20th centuries. He describes his bold marriage to a widow in 1893 and his subsequent interest in women's welfare.

3458 _______. Looking back. Poona: Hindu Widows' Home Association, 1936. 199p.
Autobiography. Author describes his childhood and educational background, his marriage to a widow and his involvement with numerous institutions and associations for widows and female education in western India. With appendixes on propaganda and subscription tours.

3459 _______. My life story. Tr. from Marathi. *In* D.D. Karve, ed. and tr. The new brahmans: five Maharashtrian families. Berkeley: University of California Press, 1963. pp.17-57.
Contains portions from D.K. Karve's Marathi autobiography, first published in 1915, and a conclusion from his 1936 English memoirs, ***Looking Back***. In the selections, Professor Karve discusses his family background and education; his first marriage and wife's premature death; his unorthodox, second marriage to a brahman widow and the public's

response (includes newspaper excerpts); and his work on behalf of widows.

3460 KARVE, IRAWATI. Grandfather. Tr. from Marathi. *In* D.D. Karve, ed. and tr. The new brahmans: five Maharashtrian families. Berkeley: University of California Press, 1963. pp.80-104.
Well-known anthropologist writes of her experiences with and impressions of her father-in-law, the social reformer Maharshi Karve, in his 100th year.

3461 PARANJPE, R.P. A sketch of D.K. Karve's life and work. Madras, 1918. [Unexamined].

3462 The story of Dr. Karve. Produced by Ezra Mir. Directed by Neil Gokhale and Ram Gokhale. 1958. 21 min. Black and white. 16 and 35 mm. [*Distributed by* Films Division, Ministry of Information and Broadcasting, 24 G. Deshmukh Marg, Bombay 400 026].
Dramatization of the life of Maharshi Karve and his work for the causes of women's education and widow emancipation. Includes footage of Dr. Karve himself, at age 100. [Unexamined. NUC].

xii) Behramji M. Malabari's and Karsondas Mulji's work for women

3463 KARKARIA, R.P. India, forty years of progress and reform: a sketch of the life and times of Behramji M. Malabari. London: Henry Frowde, 1896. 151p.
Includes material on Malabari's reform work relating to marriage issues and female education amongst his own Parsi community and to marriage issues among Hindus.

3464 MOTIWALA, B.N. The pioneer Gujarati Hindu reformer. *In his* Karsondas Mulji: a biographical study. Bombay: Karsondas Mulji Centenary Celebration Committee, 1935? pp.163-288.
Biography of a man who promoted numerous causes, including reforms concerning high-caste Hindu women. Considers influences of western ideas during student days and student activities in Bombay, his insistence upon his own simplified marriage ceremony, his mild and straightforward means of effecting reform, a trip to England, his involvement in the first and subsequent Bania widow marriages and the various successes and obstacles that came his way. Has excerpts from his writings on women, sexual morality and female education.

(b) The colonial experience: autobiographies documenting social history

3465 ATHAVALE, PARVATI. My story: the autobiography of a Hindu widow. Tr. from Marathi by Justin E. Abbott. New York: G.P. Putnam's Sons, 1930. 149p.
Life story of the sister of D.K. Karve's second wife. Tells of her family background, early widowhood, lifelong work in the service of Indian widows (including work at Professor Karve's Widows' Home), casting off signs of widowhood and travels in America and Europe. Photographs.

3465a ISHVANI. The brocaded sari. New York: John Day, 1946. 205p. [*Also published as* Girl in Bombay. London: Pilot Press, 1947. 199p.].
Tender reminiscences of author's childhood and youth in a well-to-do Khoja Muslim family of Bombay. Concludes with her unhappy marriage, divorce and departure for England.

3466 JUSSAWALA, D.C. Story of my life. Bombay: Alavi Book Depot, 1911. 500p.
An orthodox Hindu woman of Bombay recounts her life story. [Unexamined].

3467 KARVE, IRAWATI. A family through six generations. *In* L.K. Bala Ratnam, ed. Anthropology on the march: recent studies of Indian beliefs, attitudes and social institutions. Madras: Book Centre and Social Sciences Association, 1963. pp.241-62.
Presents an elderly widow's account of the transition of a brahman family of western Maharashtra from a rural landed family to an urban family with no agricultural revenues over six generations. Includes material on the changing roles of men and women.

3468 PATWARDHAN, LILABAI. Our eleven years. Tr. from Marathi. *In* D.D. Karve, ed. and tr. The new brahmans: five Maharashtrian families. Berkeley: University of California Press, 1963. pp.289-300.
Selection from author's 1945 Marathi autobiography. She discusses her marriage to the Marathi scholar, and poet, V. Madhav Trimbak Patwardhan, from 1928 to 1939. The account includes references to changing patterns of education and marriage for upper-caste women of the day.

3469 RANADE, RAMABAI. Himself: the autobiography of a Hindu lady. Tr. from Marathi and adapted by Katherine Van Akin Gates. New York: Longmans, Green and Company, 1938. 253p. [*Also* Ranade: his wife's reminiscences. Tr. from Marathi by Kusumavati Deshpande. Faridabad: Publications Division, Ministry of Information and Broadcasting, Government of India, 1963. 232p.].
Wife of Justice Mahadeo Govind Ranade discusses her childhood background, their married life and her social service work for women's education and other causes following her husband's death. Presents details of founding and early history of Seva Sadan institution

for women's education in Bombay and Poona (now Pune). A picture of upper-caste life during a time of tremendous social change.

3470 SORABJI, S. Shrimati Ramabai Ranade. *In* Evelyn C. Gedge and Mithan Choksi, eds. Women in modern India: fifteen papers by Indian women writers. Bombay: D.B. Taraporewala Sons and Company, 1929. pp.25-37. [*Reprint* Westport, Connecticut: Hyperion Press, 1976. (Pioneers of the Women's Movement)].
Stresses the conflicts Ramabai Ranade endured when her progressive husband, Justice Ranade, insisted on educating her and she was ostracized by the conservative women of his family. Describes her establishment of the Seva Sadan for women's uplift in Poona (now Pune), its aims and its early growth. Includes several anecdotes and a description of public response to her death.

3471 TILAK, LAKSHMIBAI. I follow after: an autobiography. Tr. from Marathi by E. Josephine Inkster. Bombay: Oxford University Press, 1950. 353p.
Lakshmibai Tilak discusses her childhood and that of her husband, Narayan Waman Tilak; their marriage in her eleventh year; quarrels, deaths, marriages and other aspects of family life; her husband's peculiar temperament; his conversion to Christianity and the trials that resulted for her; and the couple's commitment to social service.

3472 ________. From Brahma to Christ: the story of Narayan Vaman Tilak and Lakshmibai, his wife. Tr. from Marathi by E. Josephine Inkster. London: United Society for Christian Literature, Lutterworth Press, 1956. 95p. (World Christian Books, 9). [*Also* New York: Association Press, 1956. 93p.].
Selections from Lakshmibai Tilak's *I Follow After* that focus on her husband's conversion to Christianity, her eventual conversion, the effects of conversion on their lives and Hindu-Christian contrasts.

(c) The colonial experience: mission and medical work by western women

3473 AMENT, G. Babyland: stories of the Harvey Babies' Home at Nasik. London: Zenana Bible and Medical Mission, 1932. 35p.
Work of Rosalie Harvey? Plates. [Unexamined. BMG].

3474 CARTER, THOMAS. Rose Harvey, friend of the leper. London: "Z" [Zenana] Press, 1933. 159p.
Plates. [Unexamined. BMG].

3475 CRAWFORD, C.W. Women's work in the Maratha country. *In* Our church's work in India: the story of the missions of the United Free Church of Scotland in Bengal, Santalia, Bombay, Rajputana and Madras. [Edinburgh]: Oliphant, n.d.
[Unexamined. MRL].

3476 DYER, HELEN S. A life for God in India: memorials of Mrs. Jennie Fuller of Akola and Bombay. New York: F.H. Revell, 1903? 109p.
[Unexamined. NUC].

3477 HESTON, WINIFRED. A bluestocking in India: her medical wards and messages home. New York: Fleming H. Revell Company, 1910? 226p.
Account by a doctor who worked in western India. [Unexamined. MRL].

3478 HINTON, MRS. W.H., comp. Ethel Ambrose: pioneer medical missionary, Poona, and Indian village missionary, Bombay Presidency, India. London: Marshall, Morgan and Scott, Ltd., n.d. 255p.
Illustrated. [Unexamined. MRL].

3479 LUTZKER, EDYTHE. Edith Pechey-Phipson, M.D.: the story of England's foremost pioneering woman doctor. New York: Exposition Press, 1973. 259p.
Biography of one of the first five women to work for medical education for women in England. Dr. Pechey-Phipson worked in India from 1883 to 1905. There she worked at the Cama Hospital in Bombay, set up a private practice and, with her husband, established a sanitarium for women and children near Nasik. Photos. [Unexamined].

3480 MILLER, ALFRED DONALD. 'Aayi' ('Mother'): glimpses of Rosalie Harvey of Nasik and her friends, the lepers. London: The Mission to Lepers, 1929? 45p.
[Unexamined. NUC].

3481 UNITED FREE CHURCH OF SCOTLAND. FOREIGN MISSION COMMITTEE. Dr. Agnes Henderson of Nagpur: a story of medical pioneer work. Edinburgh: United Free Church of Scotland, Women's Foreign Mission Publication Department, 1927. 64p.
[Unexamined. MRL].

3482 WILSON, JOHN. Memoir of Mrs. Margaret Wilson, of the Scottish mission, Bombay: including extracts from her letters and journals. Edinburgh: Johnstone, 1838. 636p.
[Unexamined. MRL].

(d) General statements: ethnographic and other

3483 BEDEKAR, MALATIBAI. Women in Maharashtra. Tr. from Marathi by Sitaram Raikar. *In* Achyut Keshav Bhagwat, ed. Maharashtra, a profile: Vishnu Sakharam Khandekar felicitation volume. Kolhapur: V.S. Khandekar Amrit Mahotsava Satkar Samiti, 1977. pp.537-79.
Reviews problems of and changing opportunities for Maharashtrian women in the 19th and 20th centuries. Considers circumstances of village women, urban middle-class women and employed women in detail.

3483a FULLER, MARY LUCIA BIERCE. Infinitude of things. *In* Atlantic Monthly 136 (Sep 1925) 334-42.
A missionary's description of a train trip in the women's compartment from Bombay to southern Maharashtra. Recounts details of Indian female passengers, their reasons for traveling and conversations with them about marriage, evil eye, vows and religion.

3484 GHURYE, G.S. The Mahadev Kolis. Bombay: Popular Book Depot, 1957. 267p.
Ethnography of Mahadev Koli communities in Nimgiri village, Poona (now Pune) District; Manik Ozar village, Ahmednagar District; and Devargaon village, Nasik District. Considers goddesses, food preparations, witchcraft, menstruation, pregnancy, birth, marriage patterns and ceremonies, fasts and festivals and other topics.

3485 GISBERT, P. The Warli woman. *In* J. of the Anthropological Society of Bombay n.s. 9,1 (1955) 1-24.
Presents material on women of this tribal community in Thana District from published ethnographic reports and a brief 1953 visit. Discusses birth practices, childhood, menstruation, marriage, priestesses and witchcraft.

3486 HATÉ, CHANDRAKALA A. Changing status of woman in post-independence India. Bombay: Allied Publishers, 1969. 284p.
Analyzes the responses of 1,793 women from four Maharashtrian cities (chiefly Bombay) to questions concerning marriage, family, family planning, education, career and other topics. Supplements data with various statistics. Concludes that today's woman "has the status of equality but in day-to-day life, she is still far away from this ideal to a lesser extent on the world stage but to a greater extent on the Indian scene, especially in the lower middle and lower social strata."

3487 KARKARIA, BACHI J. Parsi women: are they really more liberated? *In* Illustrated Weekly of India 96,36 (7 Sep 1975) 30-3.
". . . from the most ancient times, the girls of this community have been conscious of equal rights — have demanded them and got them." Profiles factors accounting for the more "liberated" status of Parsi women including education and marriage laws. Photographs.

(e) The life cycle

3488 GHURYE, G.S. Marriage and widowhood in India: a study of a middle class sample of 3,400 marriages. *In his* Anthroposociological papers. Bombay: Popular Prakashan, 1963. pp.69-79. [*1st published* 1936?].
Report of the statistics of 3,400 Vadnagar Nagar brahman marriages in Kathiawar towns, considered to be more reliable than census data for the study of demographic features. Considers age at marriage, wife's age at birth of first and last child, number of children, duration of marriage, demographic aspects of widowhood, etc.

3489 RAKSHIT, SIPRA. Reproductive life of some Maharashtrian brahman women. *In* Man in India 42,2 (1962) 139-59.
Reports "complete" reproductive histories of 103 brahman women from Nagpur. Tables present statistical trends of major reproductive events from menarche to menopause. Compares findings with similar data from Bengal and Assam.

i) The natal home

3490 FULLER, MARY. Maher. *In* Man in India 23,2 (1943) 111-22.
Provides translations and interpretations of Maharashtrian women's songs expressing fond feelings for a woman's natal home, *māhera*.

ii) Puberty rites, adolescence

3491 BHAGWAT, DURGA. Premarital puberty-rites of girls in western Maharashtra. *In* Man in India 23,2 (1943) 123-6.
Considers songs and rites of Marathas and Kunbis of Ratnagiri District.

3492 PATEL, HARIBHAI G. Problems of adolescent girls in an Indian village. *In* J. of the Gujarat Research Society 26,1 (1964) 57-64.
Reports responses of 30 girls from a village near Baroda to a questionnaire about their problems. Correlates categories of problems with age and caste. Briefly compares findings with results of other studies of adolescent girls.

iii) Marriage: social structure and demography

3493 KARKAL, MALINI. Marriage among Parsis. *In* Demography India 4,1 (1975) 128-45.
Demographic account of Parsi marriage patterns in Bombay. Statistical analysis of 7,430 marriages using government data generated by the Bombay Registration of Marriages Act, 1954. Describes the spouses' previous marital history, age at marriage, education, rural or urban residence and intermarriage by either caste or religion. Tables.

3494 LAMBAT, ISMAIL A. Marriage among the Sunni Surati Vohras of South Gujarat. *In* Imtiaz Ahmad, ed. Family, kinship and marriage among Muslims in India. New Delhi: Manohar, 1976. pp.49-82.
Surveys marriage patterns of the Muslim Vohra community of Gujarat known as Sunni Surati. Based on fieldwork in numerous villages of Bulsar and Surat Districts.

3495 MOKASHI, P.R. Some social aspects of marriages in Poona District, 1955-56. Poona: Deccan College Postgraduate and Research Institute, 1968. 184p. (Deccan College Monograph Series, 33).

3496 VEEN, KLAAS W. VAN DER. I give thee my daughter: a study of marriage and hierarchy among the Anavil brahmans of South Gujarat. Assen: Van Gorcum, 1972. 297p. (Studies of Developing Countries, 13).
Ethnographic study that relates marriage practices to socio-economic and ideological factors. Considers women's roles in hypergamous marriage networks and familial status aspirations.

iv) Marriage ceremonies

3497 ATHALYE, YASAVANT VASUDEV. On betrothal among the Mahārāshtra brāmanas. *In* J. of the Anthropological Society of Bombay 1 (1886) 51-75. *With* Discussion, pp.75-6.
Paper presented to the society includes: "1) Description of the ceremony, as laid down in works on ritual. 2) Observations on the symbolical portion of the ceremony. 3) Modern deviations from the enjoined ritual, together with their causes and effects. 4) The nature and legal consequences of the ceremony."

3498 GUPTE, B.A. A Prabhu marriage: customary and religious ceremonies performed in the marriage of a member of the Chāndraseni Kāyasth Prabhus of Bombay, with a chapter on some curiosities of marriage customs in India. Calcutta: Superintendent Government Printing, 1911. 76p.
Report of the Ethnographic Survey of India. Detailed description of proceedings from betrothal until the bride returns to her parents' house to await her first menstruation.

3499 MEGHANI, J.K. Marriage songs of Kathiawad. *In* J. of the Gujarat Research Society 6,3-4 (1944) 127ff., 197-203 and 7,1 (1945) 12-6.
Three-part article on marriage songs from various communities. With Gujarati texts, English translations and brief contextual comments. [First part unexamined].

3500 MEHTA, S.S. Some customary rites as a preliminary to the marriage festivity amongst the Hindus. *In* J. of the Anthropological Society of Bombay 10,4 (1914) 272-82.
Describes the worship of the goddess Gaurī in Gujarat.

3501 ________. Marriage songs: what light they can throw on ancient customs. *In* J. of the Anthropological Society of Bombay 14,1 (1928) 32-46.
Describes a wedding ceremony. Includes Gujarati song texts.

3502 MODI, JIVANJI JAMSHEDJI. A few marriage songs of the Parsees of Nargol. *In* J. of the Anthropological Society of Bombay 13,6 (1926) 629-38 and 14,2 (1928) 244-56.
Provides four Gujarati song texts, translations and some contextual comments.

3503 NATHUBHAI, TRIBHOVANDAS MANGULDAS. Betrothal among the Kupole Baniās. *In* J. of the Anthropological Society of Bombay 5,7 (1900) 406-17.
Discusses betrothal and marriage ceremonies and suggests legal reform measures to facilitate widow marriage and inheritance among the Kupole Banias of Gujarat.

3504 TRIPATHI, GOVARDHANRAM M. On betrothal among the Vadnagarā Nāgar brāhmans at Nadiad. *In* J. of the Anthropological Society of Bombay 1 (1887?) 139-49.
Describes marriage choice, negotiations, ceremonies and revocation.

v) Marriage compatibilities and conflicts

3505 BAROT, JYOTI. Modern trends in marital relations. *In* The Indian family in the change and challenge of the seventies: selected papers of a seminar organized by the Family Life Centre of the Indian Social Institute, New Delhi. New Delhi: Sterling Publishers, 1972. pp.60-8.
Report of study of couple adjustment in arranged marriages. Based upon data from 300 couples of Ahmedabad, Baroda and Surat. Describes spouses' ratings of degree of happiness of marriage and sources of happiness. Finds

slight trend toward preference for personal happiness and satisfaction over duty and self-sacrifice. Describes sources of marital tension.

3506 DESHPANDE, C.G. On intercaste marriage: an empirical research. Poona: Uma Publication, 1972. 164p.
Report of survey of 75 Maharashtrian couples who married across caste lines. Examines personality, attitudes, mate choice, adjustment and other topics. Compares group's responses with those of a control group, which generally showed better adjustment and less conflict both within and outside of marriage.

3507 FONSECA, MABEL. Counselling for marital happiness. Bombay: Manaktalas, 1966. 291p.
First section analyzes data from records of 894 court cases of divorced couples and from a Bombay social service agency. The second section presents results from a questionnaire administered to 304 young people from Bombay about attitudes concerning marriage and family life. Most results are presented according to sex of the respondent. The third section deals with marital counseling. Tables.

3508 KELKAR, M.P. When marriages are in a turmoil. Nagpur: Vishwa Bharati Prakashan, 1976. 140p.
A Nagpur attorney who specializes in matrimonial cases presents twelve cases of divorce proceedings from his experiences.

vi) Fertility patterns

3509 BISWAS, SUDDHENDU. Abstinence, post-partum amenorrhoea and inter-pregnancy interval. *In* Demography India 2,2 (1973) 203-11.
Assesses effect of conventional postpartum abstinence upon interpregnancy interval. Data from 1,535 women of Bombay.

3510 DESHMUKH, RAJGURU. The Manwat murders. Bombay: Lalvani Publishing House, 1977. 142p.
True story of two lovers from the small town of Manwat, Parbhani District. The woman was unable to conceive but desired a child. They learned from an oracle that the wrath of god could be appeased with the sacrificed blood of a virgin and ten women were consequently murdered. The author describes his local investigations and the court case. Numerous photos.

3511 DRIVER, EDWIN D. Differential fertility in Central India. Princeton: Princeton University Press, 1963. 152p.
Report of interviews with about one percent of heads of households in Nagpur District to ascertain population dynamics. "It presents the patterns of fertility and mortality prevailing among various social strata and seeks to isolate the physical and cultural factors which account for fertility differentials. It also delineates the attitudes of couples toward birth control techniques and family limitation."

3512 EL-BADRY, M.A. A study of differential fertility in Bombay. *In* Demography 4,2 (1967) 626-40.
Describes differential fertility patterns of a sample of 50 percent of the registered births in Bombay in 1960. Factors considered include mother's age, locality, religion, father's state of birth and duration of stay in Bombay.

3513 KARKAL, MALINI. Cultural factors influencing fertility: postpartum abstention from sexual intercourse. *In* Man in India 51,1 (1971) 15-26.
Considers interrelationships of religion, observance and duration of customary postpartum sexual abstinence and educational level. Data from Bombay.

3514 SHAH, M.H. and J.S. AGARWAL. Medical termination of pregnancy programme, Gujarat, 1973-74: an overview. Ahmedabad: Demographic and Evaluation Cell, State Family Planning Bureau, Directorate of Health Services (HS), Gujarat, 1974? 10p.
Describes progress of program established under Medical Termination of Pregnancy Act of 1971, reasons for abortions and socio-economic backgrounds of participants in the program.

3515 SOVANI, N.V. The fertility survey. *In his* The social survey of Kolhapur City, part I: population and fertility. Poona: Gokhale Institute of Politics and Economics, 1948. pp.35-68. (*Its* Publications, 18).
Report of results of questionnaire administered to 1,659 women regarding numerous dimensions of fertility patterns.

vii) Pregnancy, childbirth, gender preference

3516 KHATRI, A.A. and B.B. SIDDIQUI. "A boy or a girl?": preferences of parents for sex of offspring as perceived by East Indian and American children, a cross-cultural study. *In* J. of Marriage and the Family 31,2 (1969) 388-92.
Report of study of 148 Ahmedabad children who were asked to complete an adoption story, indicating a husband's and a wife's preferences for gender of the child. As in a similar study of American children, a majority indicated that the father would prefer a boy and the mother a girl. Authors attempt to explain results of the two studies.

3517 KIRTIKAR, K.R. On the ceremonies observed among Hindus during pregnancy and parturition. *In* J. of the Anthropological Society of Bombay I (1887?) 394-402. *With* Discussion, pp.403-4.
A surgeon describes ceremonies observed in the Prabhu community of western India.

viii) Widow marriage

3518 DANDEKAR, KUMUDINI. Widow remarriage in six rural communities in western India. *In* Medical Digest 30 (1962) 69-78. [*Also in* International Population Conference 2d, 1961, New York. Proceedings 2. pp.191-207].
[Unexamined].

(f) Domestic sphere and family life

3519 FONSECA, MABEL B. Family disorganisation and divorce in Indian communities. *And* 'Marital separations' — disorganisation as seen through an agency. *In* Sociological Bulletin 12,2 (1963) 14-33 and 13,1 (1964) 47-60.
The first paper examines court records of 894 persons seeking matrimonial redress in the Bombay City Civil Court since 1954. Describes various socio-economic features of the sample: education, occupation, age and age differentials, length of marriage, number of children and cause of dissatisfaction. Tables. The second paper discusses desertion resulting from domestic discord and presents a socio-economic profile of cases handled by a (Bombay?) agency.

3520 MERCHANT, K.T. Changing views on marriage and family: Hindu youth. Madras: B.G. Paul and Company, 1935. 292p.
Report of questionnaire survey of young educated adults in various cities of the Bombay Presidency. Presents data on attitudes and practices relating to betrothal, marriage age, qualities desired in a spouse, function of woman in society, economic transactions at marriage, marriage reforms, joint family system and so forth. Discusses discrepancies between men's and women's responses and provides extensive quotes, identifying gender of the sources.

3521 NAIK, T.B. Family in Gujarat. *In* J. of the Gujarat Research Society 15, 3/4 (1953) 117-37.
Survey paper covers many topics: composition, kin terms and relations, status of various members, sexuality, child rearing, economics, social functions and areas of tension.

3522 SAIYED, A.R. and PATHAN MIRKHAN. Purdah, family structure and the status of women: a note on a deviant case. *In* Imtiaz Ahmad, ed. Family, kinship and marriage among Muslims in India. New Delhi: Manohar, 1976. pp.239-64.
Considers the striking absence of veiling and associated attitudes and behavior in the Jamaati Muslim community of Ratnagiri District in the context of Jamaati family patterns.

3523 SHAHANI, SAVITRI. Kinship in an Indian village. *In* George Kurian, ed. The family in India: a regional view. The Hague: Mouton, 1974. pp.139-50. (Studies in the Social Sciences, 12).
Data from the village of Lonikhand near Pune compares kinship features of two Maratha groups. Includes material on marriage networks, dowry and brideprice, divorce and remarriage of women.

3524 WRIGHT, THEODORE P., JR. Muslim kinship and modernization: the Tyabji clan of Bombay. *In* Imtiaz Ahmad, ed. Family, kinship and marriage among Muslims in India. New Delhi: Manohar, 1976. pp.217-38.
Account of the recent history of changes in marriage and family patterns of the Tyabji merchants of Bombay, pioneers in westernization and modernization among Muslims of South Asia. Details central role of women in these processes.

i) Family roles and relationships

3525 GANDHI, RAJ S. Kin and caste interactions among the women of an urban sub-caste. *In* International Congress of Human Sciences 30. Proceedings. Leiden: E.J. Brill, forthcoming.
Details maintenance of kin and caste relations by Jaina women in the city of Jamnagar. Based on interviews and questionnaires. [Unexamined].

3526 NAIK, T.B. Joking relationships. *In* Man in India 27,3 (1947) 250-66.
Examines joking relationship dyads with special reference to Gujarat and attempts to explain the social basis of the pattern. Emphasizes the privileged familiarity of cross-sex relations.

3527 STRAUS, JACQUELINE H. and MURRAY A. STRAUS. Family roles and sex differences in creativity of children in Bombay and Minneapolis. *In* J. of Marriage and the Family 30,1 (1968) 46-53.
Report of experiments testing "conformity, inhibition" theory that persons whose social positions require greater conformity will be less creative. Girls' scores were lower than boys' in both Minneapolis and Bombay. The sex difference was greatest in the latter case, suggesting high conformity demands upon the

Bombay women.

3528 STRAUS, MURRAY A. Some social class differences in family patterns in Bombay. *In* George Kurian, ed. The family in India: a regional view. The Hague: Mouton, 1974. pp.233-48. (Studies in the Social Sciences, 12).
A survey of 1,165 seventh standard Bombay schoolchildren suggests that, in contrast to middle-class families, working-class families are characterized by 1) a higher proportion of incomplete nuclear household units and non-normative types of joint households, 2) less sharing of decision power between spouses, 3) lower interpersonal support and 4) greater conflict between spouses and between parents and children.

3529 _______. Husband-wife interaction in nuclear and joint households. *In* Dhirendra Narain, ed. Explorations in the family and other essays: Professor K.M. Kapadia commemoration volume. Bombay: Thacker and Company, 1975. pp.134-50.
Study of 64 husband-wife-child groups from Bombay. Compares representatives of joint and nuclear households and middle and lower classes in the performance of a manual laboratory task to determine variation in family power structure and husband-wife solidarity. Joint households tended to have more powerful husbands and lower husband-wife support scores than nuclear households. Middle-class families tended to have more powerful husbands but higher husband-wife support scores than lower-class families.

3530 _______ and DORETHEA WINKELMANN. Social class, fertility, and authority in nuclear and joint households in Bombay. *In* J. of Asian and African Studies 4,1 (1969) 61-74.
Explores the extent, causes and consequences of joint versus nuclear residence. Considers respective consequences for fertility rates and relative power of husband and wife. Based on data from students in four Marathi-language Bombay schools.

ii) Family in folk literature, domestic rites

3531 BABAR, SAROJINI. Women in Marathi folklore. *In* Folklore [Calcutta] 9,1 (1968) 7-16. [*Reprint in* Sankar Sen Gupta, ed. Women in Indian folklore. Calcutta: Indian Publications, 1969. pp.48-58. (*Its* Folklore Series, 15)].
Considers family life as portrayed in Marathi folklore, particularly songs. Includes Marathi song texts and author's interpretations of them.

3532 FULLER, MARY. Nag-panchami. *In* Man in India 24,2 (1944) 75-81.
Describes rites, games and songs of a calendrical festival observed by women and girls in Maharashtra.

2533 GOPALAN, GOPALAN V. Vrat: ceremonial vows of women in Gujarat, India. *In* Asian Folklore Studies 37,1 (1978) 101-29.
Catalog of annual and weekly ***vratas***, their occasion, purpose and participants. Discusses ***vrata*** tales in detail and provides examples. Considers trends of contemporary change.

3534 KARVE, IRAWATI. Appendix 2: some Marathi folk-songs. *In her* Kinship organization in India, 2d rev. ed. Bombay: Asia Publishing House, 1965. pp.205-10.
Presents translations of 43 grinding mill song texts and succinct comments about the kinship dynamics expressed. The songs were collected in Ahmednagar District.

(g) The spiritual life and religious observances

3535 CHANDARVAKER, PUSHKER. Vaduchi Ma (goddess Vaduchi). *In* Folklore [Calcutta] 2,4 (1961) 217-21.
Discusses worship and legends of Vaḍucī near Cambay.

3536 ERIKSON, JOAN. Mata ni pachedi: a book on the temple cloth of the Mother Goddess. Ahmedabad: National Institute of Design, 1968. 74p.
Discusses manufacture, sale and use of ***pacheḍī*** cloths in Ahmedabad. These cloths are printed with goddess motifs and used in goddess worship.

3537 JUNGHARE, INDIRA Y. Songs of the goddess Shitala: religio-cultural and linguistic features. *In* Man in India 55,4 (1975) 298-316.
Translation and analysis of texts of songs honoring the smallpox goddess in Nagpur District. Discusses religious and cultural function of songs and some linguistic features.

3538 KIRTANE, SUMATI. Educated women and the cult of gurubhakti. *In* Bulletin of the Deccan College Research Institute 31/2 (1970/72) 353-9.
Study of 408 educated women of Poona (now Pune) examines attitudes toward devotion to a guru as a measure of religiosity. Makes no comparison with lesser-educated women.

3539 MODI, JIVANJI JAMSHEDJEE. On the chariot of the goddess, a supposed remedy for driving out an epidemic. *In* J. of the Anthropological Society of Bombay 4,8 (1899) 419-26.
Describes processions of a goddess chariot in an effort to appease the village goddesses at Tithal, Jalalpore and Mahabaleshwar.

3540 POCOCK, D.F. Goddess cults: status and

change. *In his* Mind, body and wealth: a study of belief and practice in an Indian village. Totowa, New Jersey: Rowman and Littlefield, 1973. pp.41-80.
Considers "beliefs and actions about *mātā* which are the most prominent spirit beings of the village pantheon . . . . how beliefs and rituals vary with the social aspirations of the villagers." Describes three goddess ceremonies performed by the Patidar community of Sundarana village, Kaira District.

3541 VETSCHERA, TRAUDE. Laxmiai: a mother-goddess of the Deccan. *In* Anthropos 71,3/4 (1976) 452-65.
Regarding Lakṣmīāī, chief goddess of the Mang "untouchable" community in Ahmednagar District. Discusses her identity and various forms and the duties origin story, costumes and installation of the *potarāja* priests who attend to her.

(h) Employment

i) Employment patterns

3542 BRAHME, SULABHA. Earnings in different occupations in relation to age and sex. *In* Artha Vijñāna 1,4 (1959) 282-97.
Results of a survey made in Poona (now Pune) show earnings of females to be about one-third that of males due to their predominant employment in unskilled manual jobs. Notes that wages for this type of work do not increase with time. Tables.

3543 DABHOLKAR, VENU. Life and labor of employed women in Poona. *In* Artha Vijñāna 3,3 (1961) 181-94.
Study of women representing a series of blue-collar and a series of white-collar occupations. Compares age group proportions; family types, heads and sizes; earnings and economic level of family; dependency load carried by worker; and correlations among these factors.

3544 WOOD, M.R. Employment and family change: a study of middle class women in urban Gujarat. *In* Social Action 25,3 (1975) 221-34. [*Reprint in* Alfred de Souza, ed. Women in contemporary India: traditional images and changing roles. Delhi: Manohar Book Service, 1975. pp.37-53].
Intensive study of twelve employed middle-class women of Ahmedabad focuses on contrasts between behavior and attitudes with respect to natal and conjugal families. A central finding is a striking similarity in present lifestyles despite diverse natal family backgrounds.

ii) Particular occupations

3545 BAL, SHARAYU. A psycho-economic survey of married women-teachers (secondary schools) with children (age group 1-15 years). *In* J. of the S.N.D.T. Women's University 2 (1969) 34-68.
Presents results of a questionnaire survey of 75 high school teachers from Poona (now Pune). Describes their attitudes and activities and the consequences of simultaneously being mothers, homemakers and teachers.

3546 DWARKADAS, KANJI. Women and children in industry. *In* Indian J. of Social Work 9,1 (1948) 43-51.
Study of Bombay mill workers describes working and living conditions and various problems. Urges a comprehensive creche system for child care and a separate bureau in the government labor department that would look after interests of women and children.

3547 JAMES, RALPH C. Discrimination against women in Bombay textiles. *In* Industrial and Labor Relations Review 15,2 (1962) 209-20.
"This article documents statistically the decline in female employment in Bombay textiles, analyzes it as a partial function of hiring discrimination motivated by prior female aggression, and presents a socio-psychological explanation for this militancy of women workers." Based on surveys conducted by the Bombay Millowners' Association, discussions with various Bombay management officials and observations of women in six Bombay mills.

3548 MAHARASHTRA. COMMITTEE TO EXAMINE THE PROBLEMS FACING WOMEN EMPLOYEES IN GOVERNMENT SERVICE. Report. Bombay: Government Central Press, 1972. 172p. [*Chair* V.P. Naik].
Report motivated by increasing incidence of harrassment and assault of women working for the Community Development Scheme in rural areas. Based on questionnaire responses of government officials, prominent and interested individuals and institutional administrators and material gathered at four public hearings. Discusses the variety of problems such workers face and presents recommendations. Numerous appendixes present related documents and various statistics and list respondents.

3548a MEHTA, ABAN B. The domestic servant class. Bombay: Popular Book Depot, 1960. 324p.
Surveys the demographic, economic, housing, family, education and leisure circumstances of Bombay servants from the Christian, Marathi and Gujarati communities. The sample of 500 includes 260 women. Many tables; most differentiate data by sex.

(i) Education

3549 DESAI, CHITRA. Girls' school education and social change. Bombay: A.R. Sheth and Company, 1976. 293p.
Relates changing social circumstances in 19th and 20th century Gujarat to changing patterns of primary and secondary education for girls. Considers, to lesser extent, pre-British developments and reviews relevant literature. Based on secondary sources, interviews with parents and educators and author's survey.

i) Attitudes of educated women

3550 BAL, SHARAYU and S.J. VANARASE. Attitude of college girls towards marriage: a study. *In* J. of S.N.D.T. Women's University 1 (1966) 19-31.
Results of a survey of 48 students of the college in Poona (now Pune) affiliated with the SNDT Women's University. "On the whole . . . the young college girls of today are still in line with the traditional ideas about marriage and married life, even though they are fully acquainted with the western ideas of sex pleasure and individual freedom." Tables, graphs.

3551 HATE, C.A. The economic conditions of educated women in Bombay City. *In* J. of the University of Bombay 3,4 (1935) 1-43.
Survey of 267 female college students and employed and nonemployed college graduates. Considers personal, family and educational background and present attitudes, career goals and income. Results suggest that the "educated woman is no longer satisfied with her former status of a lifelong dependence."

ii) SNDT Women's University

3552 BOMBAY (PROVINCE). EDUCATION AND INDUSTRIES DEPARTMENT. Report of the committee regarding statutory recognition of the Shreemati Nathibai Damodar Thackersey Indian Women's University. Bombay: Education and Industries Department, Government of Bombay, 1948. 40p.
[Unexamined].

3553 DOCTOR, GEETA. Sixty years of SNDT. *In* Illustrated Weekly of India 97,35 (29 Aug 1976) 25-9.
Discusses the founding and current circumstances and programs of SNDT Women's University. Photographs.

3554 PANANDIKAR, SULABHA, NEERA DESAI and KAMALINI BHANSALI, eds. Future trends in women's higher education and the role of the S.N.D.T. Women's University: report of the round table discussion. Bombay: Shreemati Nathibai Damodar Thackersey Women's University, 1975. 170p.
Includes history of SNDT, description of its recent programs, results of survey of students (primarily with respect to socio-economic backgrounds), paper on "The Role and Relevance of the University in Changing Times," a working paper highlighting women's higher educational issues, discussion highlights and recommendations of the editorial committee.

3555 SHREEMATI NATHIBAI DAMODAR THACKERSEY WOMEN'S UNIVERSITY. Report. 1- (1916/17-). Bombay. Annually.
[Unexamined. ALI].

3556 SHREEMATI NATHIBAI DAMODAR THACKERSEY WOMEN'S UNIVERSITY. RESEARCH UNIT ON WOMEN'S STUDIES. Newsletter. v1- (197_-). Bombay?
[Unexamined].

3557 S.N.D.T. Women's University: retrospect and prospect. *And* S.N.D.T. Women's University, Bombay. *In* G.B. Sardar, Shakuntala Mehta and Neera Desai, eds. Golden jubilee commemoration volume, 1916-1966. Bombay: Shreemati Nathibai Damodar Thackersey Women's University, 1968. First part, pp.173-88; third part, pp.12-32.
The first selection includes a brief history of SNDT Women's University with an assessment of its position in Indian women's education, numerous statistics relating to its organization and programs and a chronology. The second selection is a series of charts, tables and diagrams providing a demographic profile of the university.

3558 THACKERSEY, PREMLILA V. As I look back: my fifty years' association with the S.N.D.T. Women's University. *In* G.B. Sardar, Shakuntala Mehta and Neera Desai, eds. Golden jubilee commemoration volume. Bombay: Shreemati Nathibai Damodar Thackersey Women's University, 1968. pp.1-6.
Reminiscences by the then Vice-Chancellor of SNDT and wife of its principal benefactor.

(j) Development and social welfare

i) SEWA of Ahmedabad and other organizations

3559 JAIN, DEVAKI. From dissociation to rehabilitation: report on an experiment to promote self-employment in an urban area. Bombay: Allied Publishers, [1975]. 39p. (Women in a Developing Economy, 1).
Describes the work of the successful Self-Employed Women's Association in Ahmedabad. SEWA ("service") provides credit, promotes low-level technological improvements and offers other benefits to poor and illiterate women. Illustrated.

3560 WITLIN, RAY. Sisters of misery and

hope in Ahmedabad: the spirit of Gandhi lives on in India's first association of self-employed women. *In* Asia 2,1 (1979) 8-15.
Describes the involvement of founder Ela Bhatt, the problems faced by uneducated female workers and their experiences with the services provided by SEWA. SEWA has provided day care for children, vocational and domestic skills training, legal assistance and a cooperative bank. Photographs.

3561 Women's welfare. *In* Maharashtra special number. Social Welfare 21,3/4 (1974) 53-60, 77.
Articles describe several Maharashtrian institutions for women's welfare: "Maharashtra State Women's Council" by Nibha Walawalkar, "Matru Sewa Sangh" by D.M. Thergaonkar, "New Programmes of Shraddhanand Mahilashram" by R.S. Tatke and "Hingne Stree-Shikshan Sanstha: Poona" by B.D. Karve.

ii) Poverty

3562 MODY, SUSAN N. and SHARAYU MHATRE. Sexual class in India. *In* Bulletin of Concerned Asian Scholars 7,1 (1975) 49-55.
Report of interviews with three women who live in a Bombay slum. Considers how their stories "reflect the various ways in which social and economic conditions and the attitudes they engender perpetuate sexual class." Photographs.

3563 ________. Slum women of Bombay. *In* Devaki Jain, ed. Indian women. New Delhi: Publications Division, Ministry of Education and Broadcasting, Government of India, 1975. pp.237-50.
Presents five brief case studies of slum-dwelling women from various communities. Concludes with discussion of problems particular to such an urban existence.

iii) Prostitution and crime

3564 MISRA, PRASHANTA. What's wrong with prostitution? *In* Surya India 1,4 (1977) 53-7.
Excerpts from interviews with Bombay prostitutes emphasize the need for their improved living and working conditions. "Banning prostitution will only drive it underground and increase the diseases accompanying it. Why not treat our prostitutes like human beings instead of animals and turn the profession into an art as our forefathers did?" Photographs.

3565 PUNEKAR, S.D. and KAMALA RAO. A study of prostitutes in Bombay: with reference to family background. Bombay: Allied Publishers, 1962. 242p. [*2d rev. ed.* Bombay: Lalvani Publishing House, 1967. 244p.].
Report of interviews with 370 "common prostitutes" and 75 mistresses/concubines ("keeps") regarding their socio-economic backgrounds, lifestyles and reasons for participating in prostitution. Includes reflections upon the relationship of this kind of prostitution to dancing girl and ***devadāsī*** systems.

3566 TSOLINAS, GEORGE. Women in cages. New York: Vantage Press, 1970. 213p.
On "moral conditions" (prostitution?) and criminals in Bombay. [Unexamined. NUC].

iv) Family planning

3567 CHANDRASEKARAN, C. and KATHERINE KUDER. Family planning through clinics: report of a survey of family planning clinics in greater Bombay. Bombay: Allied Publishers, 1965. 272p. (Research Monograph Series, 2).
Presents results of interviews with selected female clients of twelve Bombay clinics to ascertain why they came to the clinic, impressions of the clinic, previous visits, effectiveness of services and clinic's role in their family planning knowledge. Summarizes the operations of the clinics and makes recommendations.

3568 CHANDRASEKHAR, S. Attitudes of Baroda mothers towards family planning. *In* International Conference on Planned Parenthood 3, 24-29 Nov. 1952, Bombay. Proceedings. Bombay: Family Planning Association of India, 1952. pp.68-72.
Presents statistical results of a questionnaire given to 500 mothers. Compares Gujarati, Marathi and "other" speakers and income levels regarding family planning attitudes.

3569 DANDEKAR, KUMUDINI. Communication in family planning: report on an experiment. Bombay: Asia Publishing House, 1967. 109p. (Gokhale Institute Studies, 49).
Report of an experiment in Manchar, a small town in Poona (now Pune) District, to determine receptiveness of female patients of a small dispensary and hospital to freely offered family planning information and services.

3570 ________ and VAIJAYANTI BHATE. Prospects of population control: evaluation of contraception activity, 1951-1964. Bombay: Orient Longman, 1971. 253p. (Gokhale Institute Studies, 58).
Discusses family planning movement and its possible impact on the birthrate in Poona (now Pune), a city that had been determined to be a favorable ground for promotion of

family planning. Although the 1961 census indicated that for India as a whole "the two five-year plans had made no dint on birth rate," the birthrate in Poona declined by about 20 percent from 1951 to 1964.

3571 MEHTA, H.S. Attitude of Gujarati couples towards family planning. Bombay: Tata Institute of Social Sciences, 1968.
[Unexamined].

3572 MORRISON, WILLIAM A. Attitudes of males toward family planning in a western Indian village. *In* Milbank Memorial Fund Quarterly 34,3 (1956) 262-86.
Data from Badlapur village, (Thana District?). "The number of living children, number of living male offspring, years married, age, and education were significantly associated with the desire for additional offspring and the four variables of education, number of living children, number of living male offspring, and caste were similarly associated with willingness to use contraceptives."

3573 ________. Attitudes of females toward family planning in a Maharashtrian village. *In* Milbank Memorial Fund Quarterly 35,1 (1957) 67-81.
Data from 126 women of Badlapur village in the Konkan. Relates desire to limit number of offspring to various factors, discusses attitudes toward family planning and compares data gathered from men and women. While education and total number of offspring relate to both men's and women's willingness to use contraception, the latter was particularly important for men and is considered to be an "ego-involving" factor.

3574 POFFENBERGER, SHIRLEY B. and THOMAS POFFENBERGER. Interview report of fifty-six sterilization cases performed at a rural camp. *In* J. of Family Welfare 9,1 (1962) 1-7.
Account of interviews made at a mobile sterilization camp near Nadiad, Gujarat, with 50 women and three men. Topics pursued include reasons for having the operation, attitudes about it and why wives rather than husbands tended to have it.

3575 POFFENBERGER, THOMAS. Fertility and family life in an Indian village. Ann Arbor: Center for South and Southeast Asian Studies, University of Michigan, 1975. 114p. (Michigan Papers on South and Southeast Asia, 10). [*Revision of* Thomas Poffenberger et al. Husband-wife communication and motivational aspects of population control in an Indian village. New Delhi: Central Family Planning Instutute, 1969. 117p. (CPFI Monograph Series, 10)].
Study of "Rajpur" village near Baroda to clarify relation of family patterns to fertility. Briefly considers historical and ethnographic background. Reports in greater detail findings about fertility control: roles and communication of husband and wife, desired family size, advantages and disadvantages of particular family sizes, relationship of desire for a son and fertility behavior, relationship of caste and acceptance of sterilization and other topics.

3576 ________ and SHIRLEY B. POFFENBERGER. The social psychology of fertility in a village in India. *In* James T. Fawcett, ed. Psychological perspectives on population. New York: Basic Books, 1973. pp.135-62.
Fertility data from "Rajpur" village near Baroda. Discusses potential for lowering birthrate by exploiting traditional attitudes and patterns.

(k) Political participation

i) Organizing rural women

3577 Missing link. *In* Economic and Political Weekly 10,44/45 (1 Nov 1975) 1720-1.
Report of a women's conference held in Pune in October 1975 to discuss common concerns. Describes participants (including many agricultural laborers and other workers), their activities and experiences and the major issues of the conference.

3578 OMVEDT, GAIL. Little women. *In* Frontier 8,5-7 (7-21 Jun 1975) 3-6, 4-7, 4-7.
Discusses employment- and economic-related dissatisfactions of rural Maharashtrian women and their organizational activities (with accounts of various local meetings). The three parts are subtitled: "The Unorganised," "The Organizers" and "Organizational Defeat."

3579 ________. Working women: toward a democratic front. *In* Frontier 8,25 (1 Nov 1975) 2-5.
Considers meetings and incipient movements of poor peasant and tribal women of Maharashtra. Focuses on economic/employment dissatisfactions.

3580 ________. 'From the masses, to the masses'. *In* Economic and Political Weekly 10,51 (20 Dec 1975) 1943-5.
Discusses women's movements in Maharashtra in 1975. Describes a meeting of about 2,000 agricultural laborers and working women and 1,000 men in a village in Ahmednagar District. The meeting was a medium for a strong and explicit expression of women's dissatisfactions and demands.

3581 ________. The downtrodden among the downtrodden: an interview with a Dalit agricultural laborer. *In* Signs: J. of Women in Culture and Society 4,4 (1979) 763-74.
First part is interview with Kaminibai, an

"untouchable" agricultural laborer. Focuses on male and female work patterns and Kaminibai's frustrations with her oppressed condition. Second part is author's commentary. She points to lack of material concerning lower-class and lower-caste Indian women and argues against the common notion that this group is traditional-minded and generally accepts the status quo. Notes Kaminibai's double sense of oppression as a woman and as a member of a Dalit ("oppressed," "downtrodden") group. Discusses emerging Dalit consciousness in western India and Dalit views of women as the "downtrodden among the downtrodden." Criticizes Dalit view of women as passive victims.

3582 PARULEKAR, GODAVARI. Adivasis revolt: the story of Warli peasants in struggle. Calcutta: National Book Agency, 1975. 188p.
Personal account of events in Thana District by a female activist. [Unexamined. BAS].

3583 Towards a women's movement. *In* Economic and Political Weekly 14,9 (3 Mar 1979) 503-4.
Report of a women's conference in Pune on 10-11 February 1979 sponsored by the Stree Mukti Sangathan. Describes proceedings and related activities and range of participants' backgrounds. Lists seven demands formulated by the group. The unidentified correspondent concludes with some reflections on the grievances and solutions.

ii) Candidates and elections

3584 BILLIMORIA, MRS. R.N. Women and the Bombay municipal elections, 1973. *In* J. of the Gujarat Research Society 37, 4 (1975) 20-31.
Study of the 38 female candidates in the 1973 Bombay municipal elections. Presents data on their party distribution, political experiences, campaign experiences and financial arrangements. Describes circumstances under which they became candidates, their attitudes toward polling arrangements and various other topics and voters' attitudes toward them. Considers question of special representation for women.

3585 KINI, N.G.S. Modernization in India: women voting behaviour as index. *In* Political Science Review 8,1 (1969) 12-22.
Study of voting behavior in the 1967 general elections in Nagpur West (the most modernized constituency of Nagpur City) in an effort to distinguish being truly modern from "being enclosed in the trappings of modernization." Results concerning motivation, party affiliation and participation in voluntary associations were not as anticipated.

3586 SIRSIKAR, V.M. Role of women in the campaign. *In his* Political Behaviour in India: a case study of the 1962 general elections. Bombay: P.C. Manaktala and Sons, 1965. pp.93-5.
Brief section suggests the general lack of interest of political parties in women and vice versa in the 1962 general elections in Poona (now Pune).

(l) Arts

i) Folk literatures

3587 BACHMAN DE MELLO, HEDWIG. Von der Seele der indischen Frau: im Spiegel der Volkssprüche des Konkan. Bastora: Tipografia Rangel, 1941. 467p. [*Also* On the soul of the Indian woman as reflected in the folk-lore of the Konkan. Tr. from German by Shilavati Ketkar. Bastora: Tip Rangel, 1942-43. 2v].
Author contrasts the relative freedom of women as expressed in Konkani proverbs and folk sayings with the constraints imposed upon women in much of the Hindu textual tradition.

3588 BHAGVAT, A.R. Maharashtrian folk songs on the grind-mill. *In* J. of the University of Bombay n.s. 10,1 and 4 (1942/43) 134-86, 137-74.
Marathi transliterations and English translations of 507 songs sung while grinding grain. The songs are organized according to various family relationships, relations with neighbors and various aspects of womanhood.

3589 FULLER, MARY LUCIA BIERCE. Marathi grinding songs. *In* New Review 11 (1940) 382-92, 508-20.
[Unexamined].

3590 ________. Sixteen Marathi grinding songs. *In* Man in India 23,1 (1943) 19-20.
List of 16 song texts in English translation.

3591 JUNGHARE, INDIRA Y. and JUDY FRATER. The Ramayana in Maharashtrian women's folk songs. *In* Man in India 56,4 (1976) 285-305.
Examines "the importance of the *Ramayana* in embodying values and ideals essentially supportive of the socio-cultural structure of Indian society, and of folk songs as part of the oral tradition conveying these values and ideals to village people." Examples of numerous work songs from Nagpur District in English translation.

3592 MAJMUDAR, M.R. Women in Gujarati folklore. *In* Folklore [Calcutta] 9;8 (1968) 267-84. [*Reprint in* Sankar Sen Gupta, ed. Women in Indian folklore. Calcutta: Indian Publications, 1969. pp.138-56. (*Its* Folklore Series, 15)].

Discusses women's roles in the family and in religious life, including role relations and conflicts, village "godlings" and miscellaneous aspects of women's folklife.

3593 SATYARTHI, DEVENDRA. The Marathi ovi. *In his* Meet my people: Indian folk poetry. Hydrabad: Chetana, 1951. pp.219-25.
Briefly discusses the Marathi *ovī*, a song sung to the rhythm of work at the grinding stone. Examples of 32 *ovīs* in English translation.

ii) Popular magazines for women

3594 PARIKH, R.D. Social content in women's magazines: a study of two women's weeklies in Gujarati. *In* J. of the Maharaja Sayajirao University of Baroda 19,2 (1970) 35-7.
Compares Gujarati magazines *Śrī* and *Strī* with respect to types of materials and prominent themes (e.g., "harmony," "amity," "peace"). Considers circulation and readership and compares these magazines with English-language magazines for women.

iii) Marathi literature

3595 DESHPANDE, KUSUMAVATI. Wet and shine. Tr. from Marathi by Rameshchandra Sirkar. *In* Bhabani Bhattacharya, ed. Contemporary Indian short stories, series II. New Delhi: Sahitya Akademi, 1967. pp.147-55.
Short story. A young female teacher feels despondent about her work and her life in general.

3596 GADGIL, GANGADHAR. The rough and the smooth. *In* Ian Raeside, tr. The rough and the smooth: short stories translated from Marathi. Bombay: Asia Publishing House, 1966. pp.1-10.
Short story. Portrays subtleties of conflict and harmony in joint family life through the eyes of a wife/daughter-in-law/sister-in-law.

3597 GOKHALE, ARAVIND. The unmarried widow and other stories. Tr. from Marathi by Snehprabha Pradhan. Bombay: Jaico Publishing House, 1957. 121p.
Short stories. Predominantly about women's lives. Themes include pregnancy out of wedlock, the depth of an apparently ordinary woman, selling of a girl child, barrenness and cowives, marital discord of an urban employed woman and a mother's longing for a child and attempt to have one via the friend of her seemingly sterile husband.

3598 MANE, VASUDHA. Psychedelic shadow. Tr. from Marathi by Meenakshi Puri. *In* Sarala Jag Mohan, ed. Modern Indian short stories, v2. New Delhi: Indian Council for Cultural Relations, 1977. pp.80-5.
Short story. Fragments from a woman's mental life reflect upon social, political and economic events of contemporary India.

3598a ______. The purple haze. Tr. from Marathi by the author. *In* Ka Naa Subramanyam, ed. Contemporary Indian short stories. New Delhi: Vikas Publishing House, 1977. pp.25-32.
Short story. Examines the hardships of a Marathi family during the freedom struggle. The girl who tells the story experiences agony over not being able to afford cloth for the school embroidery lessons. Her father is in jail and her mother supports the family as a teacher.

3599 PATWARDHAN, VASUNDHARA. Fair customer. Tr. from Marathi by Asha Bhalekar. *In* Illustrated Weekly of India 85,44 (1 Nov 1964) 25, 27, 59.
Short story. A cultured and mysterious woman causes a shopkeeper confusion.

iv) Gujarati literature

3600 KAPADIA, KUNDANIKA. Paper-boat. Tr. from Gujarati by Usha R. Sheth. *In* Sarala Jag Mohan, ed. Modern Indian short stories, v2. New Delhi: Indian Council for Cultural Relations, 1976. pp.22-7.
Short story. Portrays the companionship of two small village boys and their reactions when one is bitten by a snake.

3601 PATHAK, SAROJ. The changing scene. Tr. from Gujarati by Sarala Jag Mohan. *In* Sarala Jag Mohan, ed. Modern Indian short stories, v2. New Delhi: Indian Council for Cultural Relations, 1976. pp.43-50.
Short story. Examines the mental life of a woman who struggles to understand where her husband's life leaves off and her own begins. Also considers issue of social propriety versus meaningful human relationships.

(4) Lowland East India: area of Oriya, Assamese and western Bengali languages

(a) The colonial experience: social reform issues

3602 BOSE, NEMAI SADHAN. The Indian awakening and Bengal, 2d ed. Calcutta: Firma K.L. Mukhopadhyay, 1969. 342p.
Discusses religious and social reform movements in 19th century Bengal. Treats *satīs*, widow marriage and female education. Appendixes list and describe public organizations and newspapers and journals.

3603 CHAKRABORTY, USHA. Condition of Bengali women around the 2nd half of the 19th century. Calcutta: the author, 1963. 232p.
Contains chapters on domestic life, women outside the home (beggars, prostitutes, etc.), female education, mission work, economic life, women's associations and political participation, along with biographical sketches of 16 prominent Bengali women. Appendixes list books written by 194 women (1856-1910), 26 female editors and their periodicals (1860-1910), journals for women edited by men, and graduates from Calcutta University (1883-1910).

3604 ________. Women in Bengali society. *In* Bulletin of the Ramakrishna Mission Institute of Culture 15,11 (1964) 372-80.
Discusses the changing circumstances for Bengali women in the 19th and 20th centuries with a brief review of earlier times.

3605 DEB, MAHESH CHUNDRA. A sketch of the condition of the Hindoo women. *In* Goutam Chattopadhyay, ed. Awakening in Bengal in early nineteenth century: selected documents, v1. Calcutta: Progressive Publishers, 1965. pp.89-105.
Paper read to Society for the Acquisition of General Knowledge, Calcutta, in 1839. Attributes the "truly deplorable" state of Hindu women to Muslim invasions and injunctions of *śāstras*. With reference to local conditions of Bengal.

3606 DUTT, SAROJNALINI. Women's welfare organisations in Bengal. *In* Modern Review 37,3 (1925) 318-20.
Describes the organization and activities of a proposed central Mahila Samiti that would guide local groups. Author briefly notes her experiences in establishing several such local groups.

3607 LUSHINGTON, CHARLES. The history, design and present state of the religious, benevolent and charitable institutions founded by the British in Calcutta and its vicinity. Calcutta, 1824.
[Unexamined. NUC].

3608 MAHTAB, B.C. Studies. Calcutta: W. Newman and Company, 1904. 91p.
"I have endeavored in this little book to describe the effect of the British Rule on certain classes of people in Bengal, and the results of present-day education; and above all to point out certain religious and social defects which are found more or less everywhere in Bengal, and which, unless checked, will bring her people to a pretty pass." Includes chapters on early marriage, widow marriage, prostitution and female education.

3609 MUKHERJEE, AMITABHA. Early social reforms. *In his* Reform and regeneration in Bengal, 1774-1823. Calcutta: Rabindra Bharati University, 1968. pp.203-311.
Deals extensively with agitation against *satīs* and slavery and promotion of female education.

3610 MUKHERJI, SASHIBHUSHAN. Social reform in Bengal. *In* Calcutta Review (1910) 145-63.
[Unexamined].

3611 RATTÉ, MARY LOU. The lotus and the violet: attitudes toward women in Bengal, 1792-1854. Ph.D. dissertation, Department of History?, University of Massachusetts, 1977. 242p. [University Microfilms 77-15,112].
Relates late 18th and early 19th century British interest in Bengali women to the social order in England of the same period. Considers image of Hindu women as victims in context of anti-*satī* movement and image of Hindu women as moral heroines in context of female education movement. [Unexamined. DAI].

3612 STORROW, E. The eastern lily gathered: a memoir of Bala Shoondaree Tagore; with observations on the position and prospects of Hindu female society. London, 1852. [*2d enl. ed.* London: John Snow and Company?, 1856].
Bala Shoondaree Tagore was a Hindu woman who converted to Christianity. [Unexamined. BMG].

3613 TATTVABHUSHAN, SITANATH. Social reform in Bengal: a side sketch. Calcutta: City Book Society, 1904. 98p.
Includes several essays devoted to the female education and widow marriage movements. "I discuss the general principles of reform and try to prove, by references to our ancient

records, that the present reform movement is, in a true sense, a revival movement, our reformed ideas being mostly revivals of those which are sanctioned in the Shashtras and which actually guided the conduct of our ancestors in ancient India."

i) *Satī* / suttee

See also entries 955-86

3614 ANDERSON, J.D. The legend of Sati. *In* Asiatic Quarterly Review n.s. 1,2 (1913) 277-92.
Summary with commentary of Dinesh Chandra Sen's English translation of his contemporary Bengali version of the Satī legend. "His purpose is . . . to explain how it is that, in the minds of a race not more callous or cruel than our own, voluntary submission to a painful end is regarded as an act of virtue in the widows of Bengal."

3615 MITTRA, KALIPADA. Suppression of the suttee in the Garhjat State of Orissa. *In* Bengal: Past and Present 43 (Jan/Jun 1932) 133-6.
[Unexamined].

3616 ________. Suppression of suttee in the province of Cuttack. *In* Bengal: Past and Present 46 (Jul/Dec 1933) 125-31.
[Unexamined].

3617 MUKHOPADHYAY, AMITABHA. Sati as a social institution in Bengal. *In* Bengal: Past and Present 76,1 (1957) 99-115.
Examines the history and geographical distribution of *satīs*. Attempts to explain the practice in social and psychological terms and the exceptionally high rates in Bengal.

3618 ________. Movement for the abolition of sati in Bengal. *In* Bengal: Past and Present 77,143 (1958) 20-41.
Discusses the circumstances that gave birth to the anti-*satī* movement and the series of events that led to its success. Considers governmental policy, Rammohun Roy's campaign against *satīs*, Lord William Bentinck's role and the Indian reaction.

3619 NANDY, ASHIS. Sati: a nineteenth century tale of women, violence and protest. *In* V.C. Joshi, ed. Rammohun Roy and the process of modernization in India. New Delhi: Vikas Publishing House, 1975. pp.168-94.
"The [first] section analyses the culture of sati in historical and psychological terms and shows how this ritual became a battleground between the old and the new, the indigenous and the imported, and the Brahmanic and the folk. The remainder . . . is an attempt to show how . . . Rammohun Roy, subverted this ritual by introducing his society to alternative symbols of authority . . ." In the context of the Bengali social setting.

3620 SEED, GEOFFREY. The abolition of suttee in Bengal. *In* History n.s. 40, 140 (1955) 286-99.
Regarding Lord William Bentinck and the question of whether *satī* could be abolished without danger to the government.

3621 SEN, DINESH CHANDRA. Sati: a mythological story. Tr. from Bengali by the author. Calcutta: A.C. Chakraverti and N.K. Roy, 1916. 31, 107p.
Preface by J.D. Anderson. [Unexamined. NUC].

ii) Female infanticide and human sacrifice

3622 DAS, MANMATHA NATH. Female infanticide among the Khonds of Orissa. *In* Man in India 40,1 (1960) 30-5.
Summarizes enquiries made by British authorities into the nature of the custom and their attempts to discourage its practice in the mid-19th century. Includes some data on the relation of the custom to the Khond social system.

3623 The first series of government measures for the abolition of human sacrifices among the Khonds. *In* Calcutta Review 6 (1846) 45-108.
Detailed review of the British efforts towards "the abolition of the horrid practices of human sacrifice and infanticide among the Khonds, and the introducing of these wild and barbarous tribes within the pale of civilization."

3624 INDIA. HOME DEPARTMENT. History of the rise and progress of the operations for the suppression of human sacrifice and female infanticide in the hill tracts of Orissa. Calcutta: F. Carbury, Bengal Military Orphan Press, 1854. 146p. (Selections from the Records of the Government of India, Home Department, 5).
On Orissa and Bengal, 1836-54. Considers causes of female infanticide, describes British policy and gives figures of lives saved. [Unexamined. NUC].

3625 The Khonds: abolition of human sacrifice and female infanticide. *In* Calcutta Review 10,20 (1848) 273-341.
Containues discussion of British campaign against these practices from entry 3623.

3626 MITRA, SARAT CHANDRA. On a case of human sacrifice and cannibalism from the district of Nadiyā, Bengal. *And* Further notes on a case . . . *In* J. of Anthropological Society of Bombay 11,1 and 4 (1917-18) 40-7, 376-82.
Account of a mother who murdered her two children at the instigation of her spiritual preceptor, who then consumed part of their flesh

in an apparent goddess sacrifice. "Further Notes . . ." gives a report of the court trial. The papers focus upon the ethnographic interest of the case.

iii) Widow marriage

3627 RISLEY, H.H. Widow and infant marriage in Bengal. *In* Asiatic Quarterly Review 4,8 (1887) 367-92.
Discusses widow and infant marriage customs among tribes and castes of Bengal in the 19th century. Predicts future tendencies and proposes reform measures based upon textual authorities.

3628 SEN, ASOK. Iswar Chandra Vidyasagar and his elusive milestones. Calcutta: Riddhi-India, 1977. 194p.
Biography with interspersed references to Vidyasagar's efforts for the reform of laws and attitudes regarding widowhood and widow marriage.

3629 VIDYASAGARA, ISVARACHANDRA. Marriage of Hindu widows. Tr. from Bengali. Calcutta: K.P. Bagchi, 1976. 144p. [*1st Bengali ed.* 1855].
Extracts from two Bengali tracts in support of widow marriage, the second being a well-documented reply to critics of the first. Introduction by Arabinda Podder provides historical and biographical contexts. Two articles on Vidyasagar and his work are appended.

iv) Education

3630 ADAM, WILLIAM. Adam's reports on vernacular education in Bengal and Behar, submitted to government in 1835, 1836 and 1838; with a brief view of its past and present condition by the Rev. J. Long. Calcutta: printed at the Home Secretariat Press, 1868. 46, 342p.
Statistical and other information concerning female education in East India through the 1860s is dispersed throughout.

3631 BAGAL, JOGESH CHANDRA. Female education movement in mid-nineteenth century: origin of the Bethune School. *In* Modern Review 74,1 (1943) 65-9.
Describes establishment of the Bethune School in the context of the social climate of the time. Notes other efforts for female education in mid-19th century Bengal. Based on many original sources.

3632 _______. The Bethune School: first phase. *In* Modern Review 85,6 (1949) 468-72.
Regarding the establishment of the Bethune School. Includes contemporary addresses, notices, portraits and descriptions.

3633 _______. Steering through the storm, 1928-35. *In* Modern Review 88,3 (1950) 227-31.
History of the Bethune Vidyalaya set in the context of the increasingly volatile political situation of the period.

3634 _______. Women's education in eastern India, the first phase: mainly based on contemporary records. Calcutta: World Press, 1956. 132p. [*Also* Calcutta: Ranjan Publishing House, 1944].
[Unexamined. ALI].

3635 BANERJEA, KRISHNA MOHAN. A prize essay on native female education, 2d ed. Calcutta: R.C. Lepage and Company, etc., etc., 1848. 156p. [*1st ed.* Calcutta: Bishop's College Press, 1841. 154p.].
Reverend Banerjea's essay on the education of Bengali women was influential in bringing the issue to the attention of Europeans. [Unexamined. NUC].

3636 BANERJI, BRAJENDRANATH. Ishwarchandra Vidyasagar as a promoter of female education in Bengal: based on unpublished state records. *In* J. of the Asiatic Society of Bengal n.s. 23 (1927) 381-97.
Examines problems Vidyasagar had in securing governmental financial support for the female educational institutions he established. Considers Bethune School and other institutions. Based on original sources.

3637 BETHUNE SOCIETY. Proceedings. (Nov 1859-Apr 1869). Calcutta.
May have been published in Calcutta in 1870 with the transactions of the Bethune Society. [Unexamined. BUP].

3638 BOSE, KOYLASCHUNDER. On the education of Hindoo females. *In* Nineteenth Century Studies 10 (Apr 1975) 193-216. [*Reprint of* A lecture on the education of Hindu females: how best achieved under the present circumstances of Hindu society. *In* Selections from the Bethune Society Papers, 3. Calcutta: P.S. D'Rozario and Company, 1857. pp.141-60].
Impassioned plea for the cause of women's education. Discusses its power to transform Hindu society and the reasons why it has not become wide spread. With special reference to conditions in Bengal.

3639 CHAPMAN, PRISCILLA. Hindoo female education. London: R.B. Seeley and W. Burnside, 1839. 175p.
Primarily regarding the Ladies' Association for Native Female Education in and around Calcutta and Mary Anne Cooke (Mrs. Wilson). [Unexamined. NUC].

3640 CHOWDHURY, SUPROVA, ed. Victoria Institution centenary memorial volume,

1871-1971. Calcutta, 1971.
Collected articles in English and Bengali. Includes English reminiscences of students and teachers. [Unexamined].

3641 DE, S.K. Women's education in Bengal from the battle of Plassy to sepoy Mutiny. *In* Calcutta Review 161,3 (1961) 255-65.
Describes efforts of Christian missionaries and Bengali merchants and zamindars to foster women's education during a period when the government assumed no responsibility, 1757-1857.

3642 East Indian education and the Doveton Colleges. *In* Calcutta Review 24 (1855) 288-330.
Includes some information on Andrew Morgan and the establishment of the Calcutta Young Ladies' Institution in 1855.

3643 GIBSON, B.D. The Calcutta University report and the education of women. *In* International Review of Missions 9,34 (1920) 260-73.
Summarizes a report on women's education in Bengal. Deals with the importance of women's education, obstacles (customary, religious, financial) to women's education, educational institutions for women in Bengal and the need to preserve the fine qualities of Bengali girls while training them for performance of household duties or for professions.

3644 LONG, JAMES. Educational institutions. *In his* Hand-book of Bengal missions in connexion with the Church of England, together with an account of general educational efforts in North India. London: John Farquhar Shaw, 1848. pp.399-497.
The educational efforts of the Bengal missions. Describes the establishment and work of the European Female Orphan Asylum, the Ladies' Society for Native Female Education and the Ladies' Association for Native Female Education, all in Calcutta.

3645 MARTIN, MARY E.R. A chapter on the education of Indian women in early times. *In* Asiatic Review n.s. 28,94 (1932) 283-90.
Reviews K.M. Banerjea's ***A Prize Essay on Native Female Education.***

3646 MITTRA, PEARY CHAND. Chapter II. *In his* David Hare. Calcutta: Basumati Sähitya Mandir, 1949. pp.51-74. [*Reprint of* A biographical sketch of David Hare. Calcutta: W. Newman and Company, 1877].
Chapter includes an account of this Scottish educationist's efforts regarding female education in Bengal in the first half of the 19th century.

3647 NAG, KALIDAS and LOTIKA GHOSH, eds. Bethune School and College centenary volume, 1849-1949. Calcutta: Bethune College, 1950? 237p.
Includes material in English and Bengali on the history of the Bethune School and College and the development of social and educational movements for women in India. [Unexamined. NUC].

3648 NIVEDITA, SISTER [MARGARET ELIZABETH NOBLE]. The project of the Ramakrishna School for Girls, Calcutta, India. [New York], 1900. 29p.
Concerning the Sister Nivedita Girls' School? [Unexamined. NUC].

3649 ________. The Ramakrishna Famine-School for Girls, Kishengarh, India. [London, 1900]. 8p.
[Unexamined. NUC].

3650 ________. Report upon the House of the Sisters, Calcutta, India. Calcutta? [1904]. 14p.
A letter to Sara C. Bull that describes work of the Ramakrishna order for Hindu women. [Unexamined. NUC].

3651 SEN, KESHAB CHUNDRA. The improvement of Indian women. *In* Bela Dutt Gupta, ed. Sociology in India: an enquiry into sociological thinking & empirical social research in the nineteenth century, with special reference to Bengal. Calcutta: Centre for Sociological Research, 1972. Second part, pp.205-20.
Paper read before the Bengal Social Science Association in 1871. Argues for blending of Oriental and Occidental civilizations. Reviews progress of female education and women's literary activities in Bengal. Urges establishment of Normal Schools, establishment of position of "Inspectress" to oversee public and private educational efforts, adult classes, secular zenana teachers, "visits to interesting places" and periodical examinations and prize distributions. Urges conservative fellow countrymen to consider the general merits in and benefits of the education of women.

3652 WILSON, JAMES. Female education in Bengal. Calcutta: H.C. Gangooly, 1890. [Unexamined].

v) Enfranchisement

3653 COUSINS, MARGARET E. When will Bengal give woman suffrage? *In* Modern Review 30,3 (1921) 328-30.
Argues that Bengal should follow the examples of the Bombay and Madras Legislative Councils in granting women the right to vote. Reasons include the facilitation of social reform, the restoration of social equality and the enhancement of both national honor and international prestige.

vi) Work

3654 CURJEL, DAGMAR F. Women's labour in Bengal industries. Calcutta: Superintendent Government Printing, 1923. 40p.
A doctor reviews women's employment patterns in Bengali industries and discusses effect of working conditions on their health.

3655 GHOSE, GRISH CHUNDER. Female occupations in Bengal. *In* Manmathanath Ghosh, ed. Selections from the writings of Grish Chunder Ghose, the founder and first editor of "The Hindoo Patriot" and "The Bengalee." Calcutta: Indian Daily News Press, 1912. pp.44-53. [*Also in* Bela Dutt Gupta, ed. Sociology in India: an enquiry into sociological thinking & empirical social research in the nineteenth century, with special reference to Bengal. Calcutta: Centre for Social Research, 1972. Second part, pp.52-63.
Read before the Bengal Social Science Association in 1868, this paper was meant to demonstrate that Hindu Bengali women are not distinguished "by a large vacuity of mind as well as of occupation" and to urge the promotion of female teachers. Describes the work that rural and urban Hindu women do within the household and outside. Distinguishes work of rich, middle station and poor women.

vii) Contributions of various reformers

See also work of Rammohun Roy and Iswar Chandra Vidyasagar on all-India level within entries 920-1043

3656 BANERJI, ALBION RAJKUMAR. An Indian pathfinder: being the memoirs of Sevabrata Sasipada Banerji, 1840-1924. Oxford: Kemp Hall Press, 192_? 143p.
Biography of a Bengali social reformer by his son. Relates, among other things, his work for the emancipation of women. Banerji established homes and schools for girls, founded a journal for the benefit of secluded women and set up a home for Hindu widows that imparted vocational training and domestic science. Bibliography lists several other English biographies.

3657 MAJUMDAR, LILA. The world of women. *In* Atulchandra Gupta, ed. Studies in the Bengal renaissance: in commemoration of the birth centenary of Bipinchandra Pal. Jadavpur: National Council of Education, Bengal, 1958. pp.509-16.
The work of 19th century social reformers of Bengal with respect to women.

3658 MITRA, SUBAL CHANDRA. Isvar Chandra Vidyasagar: a story of his life and work. Delhi: Ashish Publishing House, 1975. 675p. [*Reprint of* Calcutta: Sarat Chandra Mitra, 1902].
Biography of a 19th century Bengali educationist and social reformer. Discusses his work for the promotion of widow marriage and female education.

3659 TRIPATHI, AMALES. Vidyasagar, the traditional moderniser. Bombay: Orient Longman, 1974. 112p.
Iswar Chandra Vidyasagar as a reformer who perceived creative possibilities for social change within the Indian context if some correctives were applied from the western experience. Discusses his support of female education, widow marriage and abolishment of *kulīna* polygamy in Bengal. Extensive use of historical documents.

viii) Contributions of Brahmo Samaj

3660 KOPF, DAVID. The Brahmo idea of social reform and the problem of female emancipation in Bengal. *In* John R. McLane, ed. Bengal in the nineteenth and twentieth centuries. East Lansing: Asian Studies Center, Michigan State University, 1975. pp.35-58. (*Its* Occasional Papers, South Asia Series, 25).
Considers background to 1878 Brahmo Samaj revolt against Keshub Chandra Sen's leadership over issue of women's education and emancipation. Focuses on life of progressive reformer Sivanath Sastri and influence of Unitarian social activists and thus western women's movements in Bengal. Extensive historical documentation. Paper from ninth conference on Bengal studies.

3661 ________. The Brahmo Samaj and the shaping of the modern Indian mind. Princeton, New Jersey: Princeton University Press, 1979. 399p.
History of Brahmo Samaj from establishment of the Calcutta Unitarian Committee in 1823 to the death of Rabindranath Tagore in 1941. Contains interspersed material on its pioneering position on women and on early Indian (primarily Bengali) and western women involved in reform issues. In latter categories are Kasambini Bose, Mukhi Bose, Mary Carpenter and Annette Akroyd Beveridge.

3662 SASTRI, SIVANATH [SIBNATH SASTRI]. History of the Brahmo Samaj. Calcutta: R. Chatterji, 1911-12. 2v.
Includes miscellaneous references throughout to the work of and for women associated with the Brahmo Samaj.

ix) Christian conversion

3663 BRITTAN, HARRIETTE G. Kardoo, the Hindoo girl, 2d ed. New York: William B. Bodge, 1869. 183p.
Fictionalized account of "Kardoo," a Bengali girl who converts to Christianity, and the author's impressions of the "manners, habits, and modes of life of these poor heathen sisters . . . . who are living lives of hopeless degradation" in zenanas. Author was a missionary sent to Calcutta by the Woman's Union Missionary Society of America for Heathen Lands.

3663a LESLIE, MARY E. Eastern blossoms: sketches of native Christian life and work in India. London: John Snow and Company, 1975. 141p.
Includes "Beedoo: the Story of a Native Female Evangelist." Author was a missionary in Calcutta. [Unexamined. Book in NUC].

3664 VICKLAND, ELLEN ELIZABETH. Daughter of Brahma: a tale of the Brahmaputra country. New York: Revell, 1935. 64p.
Story of a convert? [Unexamined. MRL].

(b) The colonial experience: ruling families of native / princely states

3665 SUNITY DEVEE, MAHARANI OF COOCH BEHAR [SUNITI DEVI, MAHARANI OF COOCH BEHAR]. The autobiography of an Indian princess. London: John Murray, 1921. 251p.
Suniti Devi discusses her childhood and family background (she was the daughter of Brahmo Samaj leader Keshub Chundra Sen), her marriage at the age of 13 to the maharaja of Cooch Behar and the distress this caused both to orthodox Hindu members of the royal family and reformist Brahmos, her happy married life, the growth of her family, a trip to England in 1887 for Queen Victoria's jubilee, her children's educations and marriages, King Edward's coronation, the maharaja's illness and death, her eldest son's accession to the Cooch Behar throne and death shortly thereafter, experiences with British officials and travels and trials of her later years.

3666 VINCENT, GLADYS. Behind the purdah. *In* Asia 28,10-12 (1928) 773-9, 899-903, 974-9, 1032-4.
Born in India and fluent in Hindustani, the author worked as a governess for a young prince in Orissa. In this series of articles she discusses the routine of the household. Includes various details of zenana life, confidential conversations with the rani, palace concubines and life in their quarters, a visit of the women and prince to the Jagannātha temple at Puri to secure the prince's well-being, visitors, dancing girl entertainment, and the rani's transition to widowhood and death. Photographs.

(c) The colonial experience: freedom movement and World War II

3667 BOSE, KRISHNA. Important women in Netaji's life. *In* Illustrated Weekly of India 93,33-34 (13-20 Aug 1972) 34-5, 48-9.
Discusses the women who most influenced Subhas Chandra Bose — his mother, C.R. Das's wife, his brother Sarat's wife and his own wife. The author states that most of the women who had an influence on Netaji appear to be of the mother type and that Netaji admired courageous and independent women. The important women in his life are portrayed as women of strong will and determination. Photographs.

3668 DUTT, KALPANA. Chittagong armoury raiders: reminiscences. Tr. from Bengali by Arun Bose and Nikhil Chakravarty. Bombay: People's Publishing House, 1945. 101p.
Account of a 1930 terrorist attack on behalf of the freedom movement. The author, a female revolutionary who participated in the attack, spent eight years in jail and later worked for the Communist Party. She writes of the ideals that inspired them and the comradeship that nurtured them.

3669 FORBES, GERALDINE. The ideals of Indian womanhood: six Bengali women during the independence movement. *In* John R. McLane, ed. Bengal in the nineteenth and twentieth centuries. East Lansing: Asian Studies Center, Michigan State University, 1975. pp.59-74. (*Its* Occasional Papers, South Asia Series, 25).
Argues that the evocation of ancient ideals of "true Indian women" was more effective in bringing women into public life in the early decades of the 20th century than "rational" or "scientific" arguments. Revivalist views of women successfully merged with reformist aspirations for women to become active in public life: "These women . . . never became involved in a cultural revolt . . . . They continued to personify the ideals of Indian womanhood — compassion, sacrifice and saintliness." Considers lives of Sarojini Naidu, Basanti Das, Bina Das, Saroj Nalini Dutt, Shudha Mazumdar and Renu Chakravartty. Paper from ninth Conference on Bengal Studies.

3670 GODDEN, RUMER. Bengal journey: a story of the part played by women in the province, 1939-1945. Calcutta: Longmans, Green and Company, 1945. 132p.
Concerns the war work of British and Indian women in Bengal. Contains brief descriptions of the activities of a wide range of women's organizations. Photographs.

3670a SORABJI, CORNELIA. A Bengali woman revolutionary. *In* Nineteenth Century 114,681 (1933) 604-11.
The story of an unnamed female agent of the Extremists, a revolutionary group that, inflamed by the partition of Bengal, aimed to capture the government on the 50th anniversary of the 1857 Mutiny. The author knew this woman personally.

(d) The colonial experience: autobiography documenting social history

3671 MAZUMDAR, SHUDHA. Geraldine H. Forbes, ed. A pattern of life: the memoirs of an Indian woman. Columbia, Missouri: South Asia Books, 1977. 246p.
Autobiographical account of the first 30 years in the life of a Bengali Hindu woman. Mrs. Mazumdar, through such influences as a westernized father, marriage to a member of the Bengal Civil Service and meeting and working with Saroj Nalini Dutt in various women's organizations, represents a striking but integrated break with the past. Editor's introduction puts Mrs. Mazumdar's life in the context of broader historical patterns and reviews the course of her life following the period of the memoirs.

(e) The colonial experience: western women in lowland East India

3672 Anglo-Indian domestic life: 'a letter from an artist in India to his mother in England, 2d ed., rev. and enl. Calcutta: Thacker Spink and Company, 1862. 181p.
Elaborate details of British domestic life in mid-19th century Calcutta. Describes residence construction, methods of coping with heat and insects, cooking patterns and provisions available, conveyance, servants, communications with natives, daily routine and other topics. Profusely illustrated.

3672a Sketches of Indian society, 1: Bengal bridals and bridal candidates. *In* Asiatic Journal n.s. 10,37 (1833) 21-31.
Regarding European marriages in India.

3673 Sketches of Indian society, 2: feminine employments, amusements, and domestic economy. *In* Asiatic Journal n.s. 10,38 (1833) 105-16.
Discusses social life and domestic arrangements of British women in Bengal.

i) Missionaries

3674 BLEAKLEY, ETHEL. A country doctor in Bengal. London: Church of England Zenana Missionary Society, 1928. 72p.
Includes material on Indian women. Plates. [Unexamined. NUC].

3675 ________. Meet the Indian nurse. London: Zenith Press, 1948? 72p. Illustrated. [Unexamined. MRL].

3676 ________. Meet the Indian villager. London: Zenith Press, 1950. 88p.
From Church of England (Zenana Missionary Society?) mission experience. Illustrated. [Unexamined. NUC].

3677 BOND, E.C. The two Mrs. Masons. *In* The Assam mission of the American Baptist Missionary Union: papers and discussions of the jubilee conference held in Nowgong, December 18-29, 1886. Calcutta: the mission, 1887. pp.256-62.
Describes the first and second wives of a missionary of Assam as devoted wives and mothers who set an example of Christian living before those who were non-Christian.

3678 BURDETTE, MIRIAM R. Work for Garo women. *In* The Assam mission of the American Baptist Missionary Union: papers and discussions of the jubilee conference held in Nowgong, December 18-29, 1886. Calcutta: the mission, 1887. pp.192-202.
Considers missionary use of prayer meetings and schools to teach Garo and Bengali languages and sewing, as well as Christian scriptures. The freedom of the Garo woman is found to differ from that of the *pardā* woman of the plains in kind rather than in degree.

3679 CLARK, MARY MEAD. A corner in India. Philadelphia: American Baptist Publication Society, 1907. 168p.
Mission life in Assam and local description. [Unexamined. MRL].

3680 HER HUSBAND [GEORGE HENRY ROUSE]. Work while it is day: a memoir of Lydia Miriam Rouse. Calcutta: Thomas, [1885]. 160p.
A missionary who worked in Bengal. [Unexamined. MRL].

3681 JOHNSON, LEWIS. Hilda Johnson: a memoir . . . London: London Missionary Society, 1920. 118p.
A missionary in turn-of-the-century Bengal. Plates. [Unexamined. MRL].

3682 KEELER, ORRELL. Woman's work among the Assamese. *And* Discussion. *In* The Assam mission of the American Baptist Missionary Union: papers and discussions of the jubilee conference held in Nowgong, December 18-29, 1886. Calcutta: the mission, 1887. pp.184-91, 200-2.
History of the work of Baptist missionary wom-

en discusses the founding of schools and orphanages, zenana work and conversion efforts. Stresses the need for native Bible workers and suggests the possibility of training Hindu widows for this purpose.

3682a LESLIE, MARY E. The dawn of light: a story of the zenana mission. London: John Snow and Company, 1868. 157p.
Concerns conditions of upper-class Hindu women and work among them. Author was a missionary in Calcutta. [Unexamined. NUC].

3683 MITCHELL, MRS. MURRAY [MARIA HAY (FLYTER) MITCHELL]. A missionary's wife among the wild tribes of South Bengal: extracts from the journal of Mrs. Murray Mitchell. Edinburgh: John MacLaren, 1871. 70p.
[Unexamined. NUC].

3684 MOORE, MRS. P.H. [JESSIE FREMONT MOORE]. Twenty years in Assam: or, leaves from my journal. Nowgong: the author, 1901. 222p.
[Unexamined. NUC].

3685 ________. Further leaves from Assam: a continuation of my journal "Twenty Years in Assam." Nowgong: the author, 1907. 191p.
Account of the activities of the Moores and other missionaries in Nowgong, Assam, and their contacts and concerns with friends, relatives and colleagues elsewhere, from 1900 through 1907.

3686 ________. Autumn leaves from Assam: a continuation of my journal "Twenty Years in Assam" and "Further Leaves from Assam." Nowgong: the author, 1910. 96p.
[Unexamined. NUC].

3687 ________. Stray leaves from Assam: a continuation of my journal "Twenty Years in Assam," "Further Leaves from Assam," and "Autumn Leaves from Assam." Rochester: the author, 1916. 128p.
[Unexamined. NUC].

3688 MULLENS, MRS. [HANNAH CATHERINE (LACROIS) MULLENS]. Faith and victory: a story of the progress of Christianity in Bengal. London: J. Nisbet, 1865. 248p.
[Unexamined. NUC].

3689 ________. Life by the Ganges: or, faith and victory. Philadelphia: Presbyterian Publication Committee, 1867? 288p.
Female education work in school and zenana. [Unexamined. NUC].

3690 MULLENS, JOSEPH. Brief memorials of the Rev. Alphonse François Lacrois, missionary of the London Missionary Society in Calcutta, by his son-in-law; with brief memorials of Mrs. Mullens, by her sister. London: James Nisbet, 1872. 483p.
Includes material about Hannah Catherine Lacrois Mullens. [Unexamined. NUC].

3691 THE WIFE OF A MISSIONARY IN BENGAL. Scenes among which we labour. London: Stock, 1868. 93p.
Mission and social life in Bengal. [Unexamined. MRL].

3692 WILSON, ELIZABETH. Through an Indian counting glass. New York: Woman's Press, 1926. 116p.
Account of a YWCA-sponsored class for female weaving teachers in Serampore. Plates. [Unexamined. MRL].

ii) Mary Frazer Campbell / Mrs. Monkland

3693 MONKLAND, MRS. [MARY FRAZER CAMPBELL]. Life in India: or, the English at Calcutta . . . London: H. Colburn, 1828. 3v.
[Unexamined. NUC].

3694 ________. The nabob's wife. London: R. Bentley, 1837. 3v.
Fiction. [Unexamined. NUC].

3695 ________. The nabob at home: or, the return to England. London: H. Colburn, 1842. 3v. [*Also* New York: Harper, 1842. 132p. (Harper's Novels, 6)].
Fiction. [Unexamined. NUC].

3696 PIPPING, ELLA. Indien bortom haven: bilder ur ett släktarkiv [India across the seas: portrait from a family archives]. [Helsingfors:] Schildt, 1972. 215 p.
On the experiences of Mary Frazer Campbell who lived in Calcutta in the early 19th century.

(f) General statements: ethnographic and other

3697 BOSE, SHIB CHUNDER. The Hindoos as they are: a description of the manners, customs and inner life of Hindoo society in Bengal. Calcutta: W. Newman and Company, 1881. 305p.
Describes for Europeans various aspects of Hindu life in Calcutta as it is "passing from a condition of almost impenetrable darkness to that of marvellous light." Relating to women are chapters describing the household; birth of a Hindu; *vrata* performance; the story of the *Sāvitrī vrata*; marriage ceremonies; "brother festival"; "son-in-law festival"; *Durgā, Kālī* and *Sarasvatī pūjās*; females in general; polygamy; widows; and *satīs*.

3698 ROY, MANISHA. The concepts of "femininity" and "liberation" in the context of changing sex-roles: women in modern India and America. *In* Dana Raphael, ed.

Being female: reproduction, power, and change. The Hague: Mouton Publishers, 1975. pp.219-30. (World Anthropology).
"The two concepts — 'femininity' and 'liberation' (or freedom) — were used as a heuristic device to contrast differences and effects in the socialization process of women in these two cultures, and to show the deep-seated and far-reaching implications in various sociological, economic and psychological aspects of women's roles." Concludes that for Bengali women self-images tend to coincide with socially prescribed roles. American women tend to experience greater conflict between the two.

3699 SUR, A.K. Folk elements in Bengali life. Calcutta: Indian Publications, 1975. 112p. (*Its* Folklore Series, 24).
Examines the varieties of folk belief and practice among Hindus in West Bengal. Covers such topics as marriage arrangement and astrology, life cycle rites, ***pūjās, vratas,*** magic. References to women occur throughout.

3700 VICKLAND, E. ELIZABETH. Women of Assam. Philadelphia: Judson Press, 1928. 179p.
Reflections on Assamese womanhood by a Baptist missionary who worked in Assam. Considers general position, daily life and religious practices of Hindu and Muslim women. Briefly describes tribal and Christian women. Photographs.

(g) The life cycle

3701 ALBERS, A. CHRISTINA. A daughter of the zenana. *In* Open Court 25,11 (1911) 667-84.
Sketch of the major life experiences of a brahman girl/woman in Nadia District, West Bengal. Discusses her childhood, education, marriage, life in her husband's home, motherhood and death.

3701a ROY, MANISHA. Ideal and compensatory roles in the life cycle of upper-class Bengali women. Ph.D. dissertation, Department of Anthropology, University of California, San Diego, 1972. 259p. [University Microfilms 72-25,736].
Discusses expectations for and experiences of upper-middle- and upper-class Bengali women at various stages in the life cycle. Argues that many personality needs are generated and subsequently frustrated, and describes various means of compensation. [Unexamined. DAI].

3702 ________. Bengali women. Chicago: University of Chicago Press, 1975. 205p.
Examines developmental expectations for and experiences of upper-middle- and upper-class urbanized Bengali Hindu women. A central thesis is that heightened romantic expectations regarding the conjugal relationship and unfulfilled realities lead to frustrations and attempts to find compensatory relationships with such figures as a guru or other family members. Photographs.

i) Puberty and menstruation

3703 BANERJEE, D. and S.P. MUKHERJEE. The menarche in Bengali Hindu girls. *In* J. of the Indian Medical Association 37 (1961) 261-76.
Presents data from a sample of 1,047 Bengali women from rural and urban areas with mean menarche age of 13.6 years. [Unexamined].

3704 DAS, PRIYA BALA and BHUBAN M. DAS. Age at menarche of Kalita girls in Assam. *In* Kanti B. Pakrasi, Amulya R. Banerjee and Amal K. Das, eds. Biosocial studies in India: a reading in collected papers, 1961-70. Calcutta: Editions Indian, 1976. pp.66-9. [*Reprint from* Man in India 47,2 (1967) 113-7].
Finds no significant variation in mean age of menarche in four caste communities of Assam. Compares survey results with those of similar studies conducted in various areas of India.

3705 DATTA, NALINEE. Influence of marital life on the reproductive cycles in women. *In* J. of Family Welfare 5,4 (1959) 8-14.
Comments on methodology and compares the menstrual cycles of 51 married and 59 unmarried women of Calcutta. [Unexamined].

3706 ________. Influence of seasonal variations on the reproductive cycles in women. *In* Population Review 4,1 (1960) 46-55.
Statistical analyses of menstrual cycles (frequency of cycle and days of flow) of women in Calcutta, which takes into account both biological and environmental factors.

3707 FOLL, C.V. The age at menarche in Assam and Burma. *In* Archives of Disease in Childhood 36,187 (1961) 302-4.
Compares onset of menstruation of 1,150 girls of Digboi, Assam and 704 girls of Chauk, Burma. Socio-economic factors, including nutrition are said to be relevant to variation in age at menarche, while climate and race are considered to be substantially negligible.

3708 GUPTA, A.M. On menstruation of Hindu females. *In* The anatomy of Indian diseases. London: Thacker and Company, 1848.
Presents mean menarche age of sample of Bengali girls. [Unexamined].

3709 PATTNAIK, BIJOYLAKSHMI. Age at menarche among urban upper caste women of Orissa. *In* Man in India 51,3 (1971)

217-22.
Compares age at menarche by caste and generation. Finds increase in the mean menarcheal age of daughters. Summarizes studies of age at menarche conducted elsewhere in India. Based on data from three towns of Orissa.

3710 SARKAR, S.S. and JAYA RAY (CHOUDHURY). The secular trend of menarcheal age in the city girls of Calcutta. *In* Kanti B. Pakrasi, Amulya R. Banerjee and Amal K. Das, eds. Biosocial studies in India: a reading in collected papers, 1961-70. Calcutta: Editions Indian, 1976. pp.59-65. [*Reprint from* Man in India 48,4 (1968) 349-56].
Authors conclude from previous studies and their own recent sample that the average age at menarche of Bengali Hindu girls of Calcutta is decreasing at the annual rate of five to seven days. Reviews findings of studies conducted elsewhere in India.

3711 SEN, TULIKA. A study on the age at menarche of the urban Bengalee girls: a search for its secular trend. *In* J. of the Indian Anthropological Society 10,2 (1975) 173-9.
Discusses the findings from a 1966-67 sample and compares these with previous studies of age at menarche in Bengal going back over a century. Differences in results are suggested to be due to methods of studies. Concludes that it is not possible to ascertain whether there is a changing trend or not.

3712 SRIVASTAVA, R.P. and M. GOSWAMI. Menarcheal age of Assamese girls. *In* Anthropologist 15,1/2 (1968) 57-60.
Presents data from town of Dibrugarh on age at menarche, by community. Compares findings with studies from Bengal, U.P., Maharashtra and Kerala. The mean age of this sample, 11.71 years, is said to be the lowest reported for an Indian population.

ii) Marriage ceremonies

3713 ROY, SATINDRA NARAYAN. Stree-achar in West Bengal. *In* Man in India 8,2/3 (1928) 181-90.
Brief account of the women's portion of customary marriage rites among upper-caste Hindus.

iii) Fertility patterns

3714 BASU, M.N., ATRAYEE BHOWMIK and K.K. CHAUDHURI. Relation of family type to fertility of Muslim women. *In* Society and Culture 2,2 (1971) 141-4.
Data from Padmerat Bangla, Twenty-four Parganas District, suggests that fertility levels of rural Muslim women are higher in extended families than in nuclear ones. Makes no attempt to explain this finding.

3715 BASU, M.N., ATRAYEE BHOWMIK and P. DAS. Relation of community participation to fertility performance of Muslim women. *In* Society and Culture 2,1 (1971) 3-9.
[Unexamined].

3716 BHOWMIK, K.L. et al. Fertility of Muslim women in lower Bengal. Calcutta: Publication Division, Institute of Social Studies, 1974. 175p.
Statistically describes rural fertility rates and trends and attempts to relate fertility differentials to various socio-economic variables.

3717 CHANDRASEKARAN, C. and M.V. GEORGE. Mechanisms underlying the differences in fertility patterns of Bengalee women from three socio-economic groups. *In* Milbank Memorial Fund Quarterly 40,1 (1962) 59-89.
Statistically examines differential fertility of Hindu women in the Calcutta area to obtain a picture of reproductive patterns and assess their relationship to socio-economic factors.

3718 CHANDRASEKARAN, C. et al. Enquiry into the reproductive patterns of Bengalee women. Calcutta: All-India Institute of Hygiene and Public Health, 1951.
[Unexamined].

3719 MUKHERJEE, S.P. Studies on fertility rates in Calcutta: based on the socio-economic survey, 1954-55 to 1957-58. Calcutta: Bookland Pvt. Ltd., 1961. 153p.
[Unexamined. IBP].

3720 NAG, MONI. Family type and fertility. *In* World Population Conference 2d, 1965, Belgrade. Proceedings, v2: selected papers and summaries — fertility, family planning, mortality. New York: Department of Economic and Social Affairs, United Nations, 1967. pp. 160-3.
Concludes that women in joint families have lower fertility rates than women in nuclear families due to circumstances that limit sexual relations in joint families.

3721 PAKRASI, KANTI and CHITTARANJAN MALAKAR. The relationship between family type and fertility. *In* Milbank Memorial Fund Quarterly 45,4 (1967) 451-60.
Study of fertility rates of joint and nuclear families in Calcutta. Compares samples from Three socio-economic groups (determined by husbands' employment) — professionals and service workers; clerks, supervisors and retail traders; and manual laborers. As has been found in a rural population of Bengal, women of nuclear families tended to have higher fertility

rates. Rates were lowest for the professional extended family group.

3722 SENGUPTA, A. IUCD from personal and impersonal angles: opinions of women in a Calcutta city project. *In* J. of Family Welfare 17,1 (1970) 18-30.
Statistically investigates the nature, source and communication process of rumors concerning the intrauterine contraceptive device that caused a drop in the number of users.

iv) Pregnancy and childbirth

3723 MAITY, P.K. Dharma Thakur of Bengal and his association with human fertility. *In* Folklore [Calcutta] 12,3 (1971) 81-94.
Regarding the worship of Dharma Ṭhākura, a fertility god. Focuses on the rites of barren women.

3724 MITRA, KALIPADA. Customs and taboos observed by a West Bengal woman from pregnancy to childbirth. *In* Man in India 4,3/4 (1924) 174-92.
Observations about practices of Hindu women in Burdwan and Hooghly Districts.

3725 SINHA, S.M. Maternity statistics from Gauhati. *In* Man in India 35,2 (1955) 101-9.
Statistically analyzes 1,133 cases from obstetric registers of American Baptist Mission Hospital, Gauhati, 1940-49. Considers monthly distribution of confinements, maternal deaths, male and female stillbirths, abortions, sex ratios and correlation of first and subsequent births with others factors.

v) Abortion

3726 BANERJEE, D. and S.P. MUKHERJEE. Abortions. *In* Calcutta Medical Journal 59 (1962?) 162-77.
Study of hospital abortion cases. One finding is a seasonal variation, March and May being peak months. [Unexamined].

3727 BARDIS, PANOS D. Abortion attitudes among university students in India. *In* Man Singh Das and Panos D. Bardis, eds. The family in Asia. New Delhi: Vikas, 1978? pp.148-68.
Reviews birth control situation in India (13.3 percent of couples in the reproductive years are "protected in some way"), attitudes toward abortion in texts of the Hindu tradition, modern legal position of abortion in India and selected studies. Reports on a study of abortion attitudes of 75 male and 75 female college students in Calcutta. Among conclusions: education has a liberalizing influence and women and Muslims are more conservative than men and Hindus.

vi) Rebirth account

3728 PAL, P. A case suggestive of reïncarnation in Bengal. *In* Indian J. of Parapsychology 3 (1961/62) 5-21.
Case of Sukla on whom Stevenson reports. [Unexamined].

3729 STEVENSON, IAN. The case of Sukla. *In his* Twenty cases suggestive of reincarnation. New York: American Society for Psychical Research, 1966. pp.50-63. (*Its* Proceedings, 26).
Case study of a Bengali girl who, from early childhood, recounted information from a previous life. Using interviews and geographical data, the author attempts to show the evidence for her paranormal knowledge.

(h) Domestic sphere and family life

3730 BEECH, MARY HIGDON. The domestic realm in the lives of Hindu women in Calcutta. *In* Hanna Papanek, ed. Purdah in South Asia: the segregation of women. Forthcoming.
Describes household geography and other symbolic means by which women are associated with the domestic realm. Considers ways that women identify with this realm while not remaining physically in it. Describes conditions that encourage an intensification of concern with the domestic realm. Considers reasons for increasing rate of employment of urban middle-class women and justifications women give for leaving the domestic realm. [Manuscript examined].

3731 FRUZZETTI, LINA MARIA. Conch-shell bangles, iron bangles: an analysis of women, marriage and ritual in Bengali society. Ph.D. dissertation, Department of Anthropology?, University of Minnesota, 1975. 398p. [University Microfilms 76-14,888].
Considers concepts, categories and symbols of the domain of Bengali Hindu women's social relations and the relation of the women's subculture to the larger society. Examines marriage and ***strī ācāra***, women's rituals, in detail.

3732 ________ and ÁKOS ÖSTÖR. Seed and earth: a cultural analysis of kinship in a Bengali town. *In* Contributions to Indian Sociology n.s. 10,1 (1976) 97-132.

"This essay is a preliminary attempt to define some of the symbols, categories and concepts which differentiate, express and explain the Bengali domain of kinship . . . . Bengali categories and constructs expressing relationships among persons in terms of Bengali culture." Presents data from Hindus of the town of Bishnupur on conceptions of person, kinsperson, marriage, blood, birth, maleness and femaleness, and contributions of mothers and fathers to procreation and child rearing.

3733 INDEN, RONALD B. and RALPH W. NICHOLAS. Kinship in Bengali culture. Chicago: University of Chicago Press, 1977, 139p.
Attempts to describe Bengali kinship as a system of meaningful symbols used by Bengalis themselves to define their relationships. Considers qualities of the "female genus" (*strījāti*), a woman as transformed into the "half-body" of her husband (*ardhāṅginī*) and a member of his *jñāti* at marriage, "popular" women's rites of a marriage ceremony, concepts of conception, birth rites and birth and death impurity.

3734 IRSHAD ALI, A.N.M. Kinship and marriage among the Assamese Muslims. *In* Imtiaz Ahmad, ed. Family, kinship and marriage among Muslims in India. New Delhi: Manohar, 1976. pp.1-25.
Surveys kinship system of Assamese Muslims based on field research in Singimari village, Darrang District; Gauhati City; and Uttar Jalukbari, a community near Gauhati. With summary of history of Islam in Assam.

3735 URQUHART, MARGARET M. Women of Bengal: a study of the Hindu pardanasins of Calcutta, 2d ed. Calcutta: Association Press, 1926. 165p. [*Also* London: Student Christian Movement, 1926].
Argues that Indian women have been misunderstood because they have been compared with western ideals. Compares the domestic life of secluded Hindu women of Calcutta with their own traditional ideals. Chapters describe houses and furnishings; family life; manners, dress and activities; religious life; and changing conditions. Illustrations.

i) Family relationships

3736 Charulata. Directed by Satyajit Ray. (Bengali dialogue/English or French subtitles). 1965. 115 min. Black and white. 16 and 35 mm. [*Distributed by* Contemporary Films, McGraw-Hill, 330 West 42nd Street, New York, New York 10020].
A lonely, educated woman, whose husband is preoccupied with politics and writing, becomes attached to his young cousin. The cousin feels compelled to leave to avert disaster. Based on Tagore's novel by the same name. [Unexamined].

3737 DAS, KUNJA BIHARI. Women in the folk-sayings of Orissa. *In* Folklore [Calcutta] 10,3 (1969) 96-100. [*Reprint in* Sankar Sen Gupta, ed. Women in Indian folklore. Calcutta: Indian Publications, 1969. pp.231-5. (*Its* Folklore Series, 15)].
Discusses extended family relations as portrayed in Oriya folklore. With several examples in English translation.

3738 DAS, SISIR KUMAR. Forms of address and terms of reference in Bengali. *In* Anthropological Linguistics 10,4 (1968) 19-31.
Describes "a special group of lexical items and their relation to the cultural pattern of Bengali society." Includes a section on terminological usage by and with respect to women.

3739 Kanchenjungha. Directed by Satyajit Ray. 1962. 102 min. Color. 16 and 35 mm. [*Available from* Audio Film Center, 34 MacQuesten Parkway South, Mount Vernon, New York 10550].
Two daughters from a well-to-do Bengali family refuse to acquiesce to the traditional expectations of their father and others. [Unexamined].

3740 MAITY, PRADYOT KUMAR. Co-wives in Bengali folklore. *In* Folklore [Calcutta] 10,3 (1969) 86-95. [*Reprint in* Sankar Sen Gupta, ed. Women in Indian folklore. Calcutta: Indian Publications, 1969. pp.295-305. (*Its* Folklore Series, 15)].
Verses and proverbs in Bengali and English reveal negative attitudes of women toward co-wives.

3741 ROY, MANISHA. The oedipus complex and the Bengali family in India: a study of father-daughter relations in Bengal. *In* Thomas R. Williams, ed. Psychological anthropology. The Hague: Mouton, 1975. pp.123-34. (World Anthropology).
Regarding resolution of the oedipus complex among upper- and upper-middle-class urban Bengali Hindu women. Concludes that 1) the composite element of the father's role (encompassing numerous roles of male relatives) becomes the crucial factor in prolonging the complex, 2) resolution may take place only outside the joint family structure in a dyadic relation with a guru who replaces the father and 3) religious ideology may be supportive of the oedipus complex by offering a cultural superego (e.g., a goddess).

3742 SAHA, NIRMAL KANTI. Husband, wife and children in a Santal village: a study on role analysis. *In* Bulletin of the Research Institute, Calcutta 8,3/4 (1969) 97-102.
Discusses Santal expectations regarding the various dyads and the way they change with

the ongoing family cycle. Data from Midnapur District.

3743 SARMA, JYOTIRMOYEE. Formal and informal relations in the Hindu joint household of Bengal. *In* Man in India 31,2 (1951) 51-71.
Discusses expected attitudes and behavior between generations and elder and younger family members and within particular dyads. Considers terminology and joking relationships.

3744 ________. Three generations in my Calcutta family. *In* Barbara E. Ward, ed. Women in the new Asia: the changing social roles of men and women in South and South-east Asia. Paris: UNESCO, 1963. pp.216-28.
Traces changes in an urban brahman family from the time of the author's grandmother to the present.

3745 SEYMOUR, SUSAN. Some determinants of sex roles in a changing Indian town. *In* American Ethnologist 2,4 (1975) 757-69.
While investigating family roles and child rearing practices in Bhubaneswar, Orissa, "some variations in sex role behavior were observed. These are described for a more traditional and a more modern sector of the town, and social network theory is used to explain some of the differences found. In addition certain variations in the organization of sex roles among lower socioeconomic households are attributed to economic factors."

3745a SHASMAL, KARTICK CHANDRA. Divorce and its causes among the Bauris of West Bengal. *In* Bulletin of the Cultural Research Institute, Calcutta 6,1/2 (1967) 73-7.
Survey of 286 marriages of this scheduled caste in Hooghly District found that 102 of the women and 90 of the men were married for a second time. Almost half of the divorces were due to the "tender age" of the bride and her unwillingness to live with her husband. Also discusses seven other factors.

ii) Domestic rites / arts

3746 Alpana. New Delhi: Publications Division, Ministry of Information and Broadcasting, Government of India, 1960. 40p. [*Reprint* 1976].
Brief text speculates about historical development of *ālipanā* ritual designs and discusses decline of the art, its development at Santiniketan (now Visva Bharati University), the potential for its revival through the Community Development Programme and change in the art that might accompany a revival. Considers technique and style and reproduces village and Santiniketan designs.

3747 BAGCHI, PROBODH CHANDRA. Female folk-rites in Bengal: the suvachani-vrata puja. *In* Man in India 2,1/2 (1922) 62-8.
Discusses this *vrata* performed by a married woman for the welfare of designated relatives. Provides invocative *mantra* in Bengali and English. Considers essential features of the associated story and rites.

3748 BHOWMICK, PRABODH KUMAR. Tusu festival of Midnapur. *In* Indian Folklore 1,2 (1958) 17-31.
Regarding a "feminine festival." Presents 88 Bengali songs that are primarily concerned with family relationships, translating and explicating several of them.

3749 CHATTERJI, TAPAN MOHAN. Alpona: ritual decoration in Bengal. Bombay: Orient Longmans, 1948. 62p. [*Excerpts in* Mārg 3,4 (1949) 66-7].
Illustrations by Abanindranath Tagore and notes by Tarak Chandra Das. [Unexamined. NUC].

3750 DAS, S.R. Kumārī vrata-chaḍās of Bengal. *In* All-India Oriental Conference 12, 1943/44, Benares. Proceedings and transactions 12, v2. Benares: Benares Hindu University, 1946. pp.575-86.
Concerns vows made by unmarried girls to facilitate such desires as gaining a good husband, an immortal son or freedom from widowhood.

3751 GHOSAL, SAMIR. Women in folk-rites and beliefs. *In* Folklore [Calcutta] 10,4 (1969) 115-28. [*Reprint in* Sankar Sen Gupta, ed. Women in Indian folklore. Calcutta: Indian Publications, 1969. pp.306-20. (*Its* Folklore Series, 15)].
Discusses *strī ācāra*, women's domestic rites, in West Bengal and Orissa.

3752 MUKHERJEA, CHARULAL. Bratas in Bengal. *In* Man in India 26,3/4 (1946) 202-6. [*Also in* Man in India 30,2/3 (1950) 66-72].
Describes two *vratas* for the attainment of physical beauty and discusses their magical significance.

3753 RAY, SUDHANSU KUMAR. The ritual art of the bratas of Bengal. Calcutta: Firma K.L. Mukhopadhyay, 1961. 68p., 24 plates.
Examines art as an indispensable means of communication between the devotees and the gods in the *vrata* rites. Cites Abanindranath Tagore's conception of *vrata* components: "First the desire, then the art (*alpana*), next the spell (*chhada*) and in the end, the story (*katha*) or history — all these complete a *brata*." Drawings, photographs and references to Bengali works on *vratas*.

3754 SARKAR, JAYANTA. Village girls as portrayed in Tusu songs. *In* Folklore [Calcutta] 12,6 (1971) 229-35.

Examines songs sung by unmarried girls in West Bengal on the occasion of *Ṭusu vrata*. The songs reflect the love of parents for their daughters and the aspirations of marriageable girls. Includes Bengali texts and free translations of seven songs.

3755 SEN, GOPINATH. Rituals of women-folk of Bengal. *In* Indian Folklore 2,2 (1959) 107-11.
On the conjoining of *ālipanā* arts, folk tales, and folk songs with *vratas*. Distinguishes the ritual life of women from that of men.

3756 TAGORE, ABANINDRANATH. L'alpona: ou, les décorations rituelles au Bengale [*Ālipanā*: ritual designs of Bengal]. Tr. from Bengali by Andrée Karpelès and Tapanmohan Chatterji. Paris: Bossard, 1921. 87p.
With 50 figures. [Unexamined. NUC].

(i) Witchcraft

3757 CHAUDHURI, BUDDHADEB. An analytical study of witchcraft among the Mundas of Midnapur. *In* Bulletin of the Cultural Research Institute, Calcutta 8,1/2 (1969) 87-92.
Discusses Munda witchcraft beliefs, presenting two case studies. Widows living alone and without male issue are seen to be especially vulnerable to witchcraft accusations. Suggests that such persons are vulnerable in a patrilineal social system.

3758 ROY, SATINDRA NARAYAN. The witches of Orissa. *In* J. of the Anthropological Society of Bombay 14,2 (1928) 185-200.
Discusses history, popular beliefs and practice of witchcraft throughout Orissa. Concludes with examples of similar beliefs in England.

(j) The spiritual life and religious observances

i) Spiritual leaders

3759 ELWIN, VERRIER. The Saora priestess. *In* Bulletin of the Department of Anthropology, Government of India 1,1 (1952) 59-85.
Deals with priestess' recruitment by marriage to a spirit-helper from the underworld as a result of a dream experience, her powers of divination and healing and her duties on ceremonial occasions. Based on field work among the Saora tribal community in Orissa. With photographs, personal accounts and descriptions.

3760 KANAN DEVI, MA MAHAJNANA SHRI GURU. On the quest. Kharagpur: Ma-Mahajnana Shriguru Kanan Devir Mandir, 1977. 151p.
Spiritual and philosophical teachings of Kanan Devi directed to westerners. She is said to combine worldly life and spirituality in a uniquely harmonious way. Includes her portrait and a bibliography of Bengali materials relating to her life and teachings.

ii) *Devadāsīs*

See also entry 3791

3761 DAS GUPTA, RAJATANANDA. The institution of devadasis in Assam. *In* J. of Indian History 43,2 (1965) 565-76.
[Unexamined].

3762 KHOKAR, MOHAN. Devadasis of Orissa. *In* South Indian Natyakala Conference 12th, 27 December 1958-2 January 1959. Proceedings. 1959? pp.27-9.
Historical account. Illustrated. [Unexamined].

3763 MARGLIN, FRÉDÉRIQUE APFFEL. The auspicious women: a study of the rituals of the devadāsīs. Ph.D. dissertation, Department of Anthropology, Brandeis University, forthcoming, 1979. [*Also* University Microfilms, forthcoming].
Report of a field study of the community of the ten remaining and final *devadāsīs* at the Jagannātha temple, Puri. Focuses on the social organization and rituals of these women who consider themselves to be married to Lord Jagannātha. Considers the cultural constructs of auspiciousness and inauspiciousness and kingship. [Unexamined. Information supplied by author].

3764 SHARMA, SADASHIV RATHA. The mahari. *In* Durgadas Mukhopadhyay, ed. Lesser known forms of performing arts in India. New Delhi: Sterling Publishers, 1978. pp.104-7.
Regarding the *devadāsī* tradition at the Lord Jagannātha temple at Puri. Describes the history and dancing gestures.

iii) Goddesses

3765 BANG, B.G. Current concepts of the smallpox goddess Sitala in parts of West Bengal. *In* Man in India 53,1 (1973) 79-104.
Based on visits to shrines and talks with devotees in rural and urban areas, this essay examines concepts of Śītalā's origin and power and of the cause and cure of smallpox. Ex-

amines current indigenous and immigrant practices and concepts. Compares them with those described in literary sources from the early 19th century to the present.

3766 BHATTACHARYYA, ASUTOSH. The cult of Sasthi in Bengal. *In* Man in India 28,3 (1948) 152-62.
On the folk nature, characteristics, worship and legends of a goddess associated with childbirth.

3767 ________. The rites of the serpent-goddess. *In* Folklore [Calcutta] 1,4 (1960) 233-40 and 2,1 (1961) 41-8.
Ethnographic details of Manasā worship in various parts of Bengal.

3768 BHOWMICK, PRABODH KUMAR. Four temples in Midnapur, West Bengal. *In* Man in India 40,2 (1960) 81-108.
Regarding four goddess temples. Priests were paid to keep a record of who came, why they came, mode of worship, etc., over a six-month period. This paper reports results of these surveys and discusses iconography and priest and servant groups.

3769 CHAKRAVARTI, CHINTAHARAN. The worship of the goddess Durga. *In* Bulletin of the Ramakrishna Mission Institute of Culture 9,4 (1958) 81-7.
Describes Durgā *pūjā* in Bengal and summarizes references to Durgā and her worship in *purāṇas* and *tantras*.

3770 CHATTOPADHYAY, TUSHAR. Bhadu: a folk godling. *In* Bulletin of the Cultural Research Institute, Calcutta 7,3/4 (1968) 58-61.
Describes worship of Bhādu, particularly her annual festival. She is associated with licentiousness and fertility and is predominantly worshipped by young women.

3771 Devi. Produced, directed and written by Satyajit Ray. (Bengali dialogue/English subtitles). 1960? 96 min. Black and white. 16 and 35 mm. [*Distributed by* Audio Film Center, 34 MacQuesten Parkway South, Mount Vernon, New York 10550].
Film. A man dreams that his new daughter-in-law is a reincarnation of the goddess Kālī. He installs her as such and peasants stream to worship her. The stress becomes too great for her: she becomes mentally disorganized and commits suicide. Set in late 19th century Bengal. Music by Ali Akbar Khan.

3772 FRIEDLANDER, EVA. The mundane and prosaic in Bengali folk songs. *In* J. of South Asian Literature 11,1/2 (1975) 131-46.
Includes discussion and examples of songs sung at the *Bhadū pūjā* by young unmarried cultivator girls.

3773 GANAI, AMARENDRA. Short notes on the cult of Meleni: a folk goddess. *In* Indian Folklore 1,2 (1958) 46-8, 81.
Concerning a goddess of skin diseases and her origin in the folk tradition of Bengal.

3774 GHOSHA, PRATAPACHANDRA. Durga puja. Calcutta: Hindoo Patriot Press, 1871. lv.
A detailed examination of Durgā *pūjā*, the "chief national festival of the Hindus of Bengal" (according to ***Hindoo Patriot*** editor), this volume addresses the construction and painting of images, ***mantras***, prayers, ritual and sacrifice. Introduction discusses Durgā in relation to astrology, in the context of the Hindu pantheon and as assuming different forms.

3775 NEOG, MAHESHWAR. Ai, the small-pox goddess of Assam. *In* Man in India 31,2 (1951) 72-83.
Surveys names and modes of worship of small-pox goddesses in various parts of India. Includes details of Āī worship in Assam.

3776 NICHOLAS, RALPH W. *Śītalā* and the art of printing: the transmission and propagation of the myth of the goddess of small-pox in rural West Bengal. *In* Mahadev L. Apte, ed. Mass culture, language and arts in India: papers presented at a symposium at Duke University, Durham, North Carolina. Bombay: Popular Prakashan, 1978.
Contrasts printed and oral myth propagation. Summarizes a printed version of the *Śītalā maṅgala*, two discrepant versions of an orally transmitted myth of Olābibi and the dramatization of the Śītalā story by a group of traveling performers. Data from the Kelomal villages of Midnapur District. [Manuscript examined].

3777 ________ and ADITI NATH SARKAR. The fever demon and the census commissioner: Śītalā mythology in eighteenth and nineteenth century Bengal. *In* Marvin Devis, ed. Bengal: Studies in literature, society and history. East Lansing: Asian Studies Center, Michigan State University, 1976. pp.3-68. (*Its* Occasional Papers, South Asian Series, 27).
Examines worship of Śītalā in Bengal in the context of 18th and 19th century social, epidemiological and ecological events. Appendix contains translations of two ***Śītalā maṅgala*** texts describing the accomplishments of the goddess, her character and the events surrounding her coming to be worshipped on earth. Paper from Conference on Bengal Studies.

3778 NIVEDITA, SISTER [MARGARET ELIZABETH NOBLE]. Kali the mother. Mayavati, Almora: Advaita Ashrama, 1950. 110p. [*Also* London: Sonnenschein, 1900. 114p.].
Interpretation of the motherhood of God in the form of Kālī. Directed toward westerners.

3778a RAMESHWAR RAO, SHANTA. The legend of Manasa Devi. Bombay: Orient Longman, 1977. 41p. (Indian Myths and Legends).
Story of how Manasā, goddess of snakes, came to be recognized and worshipped.

3779 The Shaktas: their characteristics and practical influence in society. *In* Calcutta Review 24,47 (1855) 31-67.
Describes religious practices of the worshippers of Śakti in Bengal. Concludes that the "abominable" and "impure" public rituals, which include "bloody sacrifices" and "obscene" and "indecent" gestures and expressions, are "highly injurious to the life and character of men."

3780 THIERRY, SOLANGE. Présentation de la déesse indienne Manasā [Portrait of the Indian goddess Manasā]. *In* Objets et Mondes 5,1 (1965) 3-20.
Regarding an image of Manasā obtained in Goalpura District and accompanying objects relating to her cult gathered in and around the same area. Photographs, descriptions and background material to Manasā worship based chiefly on the Dimock and Ramanujan articles (entries 647-8).

(k) Employment

3781 ASSAM. DIRECTORATE OF EMPLOYMENT AND CRAFTSMAN TRAINING. STATE EMPLOYMENT MARKET INFORMATION UNIT. Report on special study of woman applicants in the live register of employment exchanges in Assam, as on 31st December, 1975. Gauhati: issued by Directorate of Employment and Craftsman Training, Assam, 1977. 26p.
Demographic and socio-economic assessment of female job applicants.

i) Problems and solutions

3782 BEECH, MARY J.H. Factors influencing the recent increase in middle class female labor force participation. *In* Richard L. Park, ed. Bengal: the American Connection. East Lansing: Asian Studies Center, Michigan State University, forthcoming. (*Its* Occasional Papers, South Asia Series).
Examines why urban middle-class female labor force participation has been increasing in India despite a steady overall female participation decline for several decades. Investigates the Bengali Hindu cultural definition of women's roles and discrepant conceptions of employed and nonemployed women. Employed women are able to resolve the conflict of operating "outside" in the men's sphere by "the rationale of exceptional circumstances, the rationale of expandable walls, and the rationale of essential humanity." Based on interviews with middle-class married employed women of Calcutta. Paper from twelfth Conference on Bengal Studies. [Manuscript examined].

3783 CHAKRABORTTY, KRISHNA. Maternal employment and its effects on the mother. *In* Socialist Perspective 3,3 (1975) 22-33.
Report of survey of 161 professional and nonprofessional working mothers (of Calcutta?). Compares the job-related attitudes of those working solely for economic gain, those working solely for personal fulfillment and those working for both reasons. Results revealed differences in self-satisfaction and role conflict among the three groups.

3784 ________. The conflicting worlds of working mothers: a sociological inquiry. Calcutta: Progressive Publishers, 1978. 305p.
Report of study of role conflict of middle-class educated married women of Calcutta who are employed and mothers. Based on a questionnaire survey. Gives both statistical and case study data.

3785 Mahanagar. Directed by Satyajit Ray. (Bengali language/English subtitles). 1963? 122 min. Black and white. 16 and 35 mm. [*Distributed by* Audio Film Center, 35 MacQuesten Parkway South, Mount Vernon, New York 10550].
Film. A young wife in a middle-class family in Calcutta takes a job when her husband's salary can barely support his numerous dependents. The tension created by the unseemliness of her employment and independence are increased when her husband loses his own bank job. She finds enjoyment in her work.

3786 ORISSA. LABOUR DEPARTMENT. Annual report and returns on the administration of the Maternity Benefit Act, 1961, in the state of Orissa. 1- (19__-).
[Unexamined. ALI].

3787 WEST BENGAL. DEPARTMENT OF LABOUR. Unemployment among women in West Bengal. Calcutta: the department, 1959.
[Unexamined].

ii) The jute industry

3788 NARASIMHA RAO, MANTHRIPRAGADA and H.C. GANGULY. Women labour in the jute industry of Bengal: a medico-social study. *In* Indian J. of Social Work 11,2 (1950) 181-91. [*Also* Women labourers in jute industry of Bengal. Calcutta: All-India Institute of Hygiene and Public Health, 1956].
Argues that female health and personnel problems require particular attention apart from those of men. Three hundred forty-seven women working in a jute mill in Howrah District and a group of comparable but nonemployed women were interviewed to determine their social background, home conditions and any negative effects of work on their health. Gives socio-

economic profiles and considers posture, fatigue, maternity benefits, menstruation, pregnancy and vital losses (abortions, miscarriages, stillbirths, neonatal deaths). Industrial employment is stated to be significantly related to vital losses.

(l) Sex ratio

3789 DATTA, JATINDRA MOHAN. Variation in the sex-ratio in Bengal during 150 years. *In* Man in India 37,2 (1957) 133-48.
A statistical profile, based on 1872 to 1941 census materials. Discusses the enumeration of women and possible reasons for the diminishing proportion of women in the population. With districtwise data.

(m) Arts

i) Dance traditions

3790 BANERJEE, GOPA. A note on the dancing girl (nachni) of Purulia. *In* Man in India 53,3 (1973) 279-93.
Study of dancing girls in Purulia District based on case studies. Considers socio-economic background, motivations for joining profession, categories of dancers, dance forms, relationships with male partners and relationship to family and caste. Considers the institution to be a manifestation of low-caste vulnerability to and domination by upper castes.

3791 DEVI, RITHA. Five tragic heroines of Orissi dance-drama: the *pancha-kanya* theme in mahari *nritya*. *In* Feminine sensibility and characterization in South Asian literature. Guest ed: Fritz Blackwell. J. of South Asian Literature 12,3/4 (1977) 25-30.
Briefly discusses the vicissitudes of the *nṛtya* dance of *devadāsīs* in Orissa. Although social reform efforts have destroyed the temple dancing tradition, the dance form has been revised for the contemporary stage. Discusses the "five maidens," principle dance characters.

3792 KOTHARI, SUNIL. Gotipua dancers of Orissa. *In* Durgadas Mukhopadhyay, ed. Lesser known forms of performing arts in India. New Delhi: Sterling Publishers, 1978. pp.93-8.
About "a class of young male dancers in Orissa who, dressed as girls, perform the traditional classical Odissi dance." Considers history (they evolved out of the *Vaiṣṇava* devotional tradition of identifying with the consort of God), religious association, training, costume and performance.

ii) Folk literatures

3793 BHOWMICK, P.K. Women in nursery rhymes of border Bengal. *In* Folklore [Calcutta] 9,12 (1968) 443-50. [*Reprint in* Sankar Sen Gupta, ed. Women in Indian folklore. Calcutta: Indian Publications, 1969. pp.157-66. (*Its* Folklore Series, 15)].
Nursery rhymes from Midnapur District. Most themes express the concerns of married women.

3794 GOSWAMI, PRAPHULLADATTA. Women in Assam's folklore. *In* Folklore [Calcutta] 9,2 (1968) 39-45. [*Reprint in* Sankar Sen Gupta, ed. Women in Indian folklore. Calcutta: Indian Publications, 1969. pp.41-7. (*Its* Folklore Series, 15)].
Discusses various images of women in songs, sayings and tales, with examples in English translation. Briefly raises questions about the representativeness and distinctiveness of folklore from a particular regional tradition and about folklore as representative of female points of view.

3795 KAYAL, AKSHAY KUMAR. Women in folk elements of Bengal. *In* Folklore [Calcutta] 10,1 (1969) 1-25. [*Reprint in* Sankar Sen Gupta, ed. Women in Indian folklore. Calcutta: Indian Publications, 1969. pp.177-200. (*Its* Folklore Series, 15)].
Concerns images of Hindu women in Bengali folklore, primarily proverbs and sayings. Bengali selections and English translations.

3796 LONG, JAMES. Three thousand Bengali proverbs and proverbial sayings illustrating native life and feeling among ryots and women. Calcutta, 1872. 174p.
Women's folk sayings specifically designated? [Unexamined. NUC].

3797 MISHRA, GOPAL CHANDRA. Women in Oriya folklore. *In* Folklore [Calcutta] 10,3 (1969) 75-85. [*Reprint in* Sankar Sen Gupta, ed. Women in Indian folklore. Calcutta: Indian Publications, 1969. pp.211-22. (*Its* Folklore Series, 15)].
Discusses the Oriya folk song as primarily a genre of women. Includes several examples, translated and transliterated, on a variety of topics.

3798 Prabad mala: or, the wit and wisdom of Bengali ryots and women as shewn in their proverbs and proverbial sayings. Calcutta: printed at the Englishman Press, 1869. 70p.
Reprinted from the *Englishman's Weekly Journal*. Folk sayings of women noted as such? [Unexamined. NUC].

3799 ROY, SATINDRA NARAYAN. Select proverbs and popular sayings of the housewives of Orissa. *In* J. of the Anthropological Society of Bombay 14,3 (1929) 319-33.
[Unexamined].

iii) Oriya literature: Nandini Satpathy

3800 SATPATHY, NANDINI. The future of Babli. Tr. from Oriya by Kishen Chander. *In* Ganeswar Misra, ed. Modern short stories from Indian authors. Cuttack: Cuttack Students' Store, 1974. pp.56-60.
Short story. A young boy is constrained by his mother's expectations.

3801 ________. The homecoming. Tr. from Oriya by Suresh Kohli. *In* Suresh Kohli, ed. Modern Indian short stories. New Delhi: Arnold Heinemann, 1974. pp.99-103.
Short story. A woman who gives up her teaching job to be a dutiful wife finds herself preparing to resume teaching many years later.

3802 ________. Song of the evening and other stories. Tr. from Oriya by J.B. Mohanty. New Delhi: Orient Paperbacks, 1975. 110p.
Short stories. From the publisher's introduction: "As character after character makes [sic] their appearance, the book becomes a living fresco of women, suffering their rise and fall, their good luck and misfortune, but always with the irrepressible pulse of life .... Intense drama, double-standard morality and tragedy are [tightly] woven to make this book an extraordinary work of contemporary fiction."

iv) Bengali literature: female writers

3803 ASHAPURNA DEVI. A bouquet of modern short stories. Tr. from Bengali by Anima Bose. New Delhi: Pankaj Publications, 1978. 72p.
Short stories. In a brief introductory note, "The Creative Artist Ashapurna Devi," the translator discusses Ashapurna Devi's original interest in writing, her spontaneous and rebellious style and her various literary awards.

3804 BOSE, ANIMA. Ashapurna Devi: perspective on a Bengali novelist. *In* Indian Literature 19,3 (1976) 80-95.
"When it comes to women Ashapurna Devi's short stories and novels have indeed a lot of uncommon information to give away — specially about the women of Bengal." Discusses the main character in her novel ***Subarṇalatā*** and reports on a series of 1976 interviews with the author.

3805 CHATTERJEE, SITA and SANTA CHATTERJEE. Tales of Bengal. Tr. from Bengali. London: Humphrey Milford, Oxford University Press, 1922. 110p. (An Eastern Library, 1).
Short stories. Two sisters, daughters of a prominent Bengali Brahmo and editor, write about Bengali social life and particularly the changing relationship between the sexes.

3806 GHOSAL, MRS. [SVARNA KUMARI DEVI GHOSAL]. To whom?: or, an Indian lovestory. Tr. from Bengali by Sovona Devi. Calcutta: S.K. Lahiri and Company, 1910? 207p.
[Unexamined. NUC].

3807 ________. An unfinished song. New York: Macmillan, 1913. 219p.
Novel. Romance told in the first person by an educated woman from a westernizing, turn-of-the-century Hindu family near Dacca. Introduction discusses author's background. English original?

3808 ________. Short stories. Tr. from Bengali. Madras: Ganesh and Company, 1919? 242p.
Short stories (14). Collection translated in an attempt to help the western reader understand "a little of the life that pulsates in the quiet East." The stories primarily concern women's lives. Illustrated.

3809 ________. Princess Kalyani: a play in three acts. Madras: Ganesh and Company, 1930. 223p.
Play (historical drama). English original? [Unexamined. NUC].

3810 ________. The fatal garland. Tr. from Bengali by A. Christina Albers. Calcutta: S.K. Lahiri and Company, n.d. 172p. [*Also* New York: Macmillan Company, 1915? 224p. *And* London: T.W. Laurie, 1915. 224p.].
Novel (historical romance). Portrays upper-class life in 14th century Bengal. Illustrated.

3811 JAHAN, ROUSHAN. The dreamer and the dream: the writings of Rokeya Sakhawat Hossain, 1880-1932. *In* Hanna Papanek, ed. Purdah in South Asia: the segregation of women. Forthcoming.
Examines the strongly feminist, anti-***pardā*** writings of Begam Rokeya in the context of her life and the condition of women in her time. Many illustrations from her fiction and essays are translated from Bengali and discussed. In addition, the text of Begam Rokeya's first short story (written in 1905 [1908?] in English is reproduced. This story, "Sultana's Dream," depicts a utopia in which men are secluded; women, with the help of advanced science and technology, run an idyllic society without poverty, illiteracy or violence. [Unexamined. Information supplied by editor].

3812 MAITREYI DEVI. It does not die: a romance. Tr. from the Bengali by Shyamasree Devi. Calcutta: Writer's Workshop, 1976. 274p.
Novel (autobiographical). A Bengali Hindu woman recalls her romance of four decades past at age sixteen with a young European student of her father, the philosopher Surendranath Das Gupta.

3813 MILLER, BARBARA STOLER, NABANEETA DEV SEN and AGUEDA PIZARRO DE RAYO. Splitting the mother tongue: Bengali and Spanish poems in English translations. *In* Signs: J. of Women in Culture and Society 3,3 (1978) 608-21.
A unique project in three parts: 1) Miller's comments on conveying diverse layers of meaning in the translation of Sanskrit religious-erotic poetry and the work of contemporary female poets, 2) Sen's autobiographical comments and two poems translated by Miller and 3) Pizzaro de Rayo's autobiographical comments and two poems translated with Miller. Sen discusses differences in the public reception of male and female writers; the experiences of her mother, the poet Radharani Debi (pseudonym, Aparajita Debi); differences in her Bengali and English writing; and problems of female writers in India.

3814 MUKHERJEE, MEENAKSHI. 'Desh' and 'Amrit': two special numbers. *In* Indian Writing Today 3,4 (1969) 19-23.
Concerning special numbers of two Bengali weeklies. Includes some brief comments about the tendency to select female writers to write about a featured female writer. In some cases, gender is the only common feature of the two: "If a woman writer is important enough for discussion, surely she can be treated as a writer rather than as a woman, and not relegated to a compartment labelled 'Ladies Only'."

3815 RAJLUKSHMI DEBEE. The owl and other poems. Tr. from Bengali by the author and others. Calcutta: Writers Workshop, 1972. 36p.
Poetry. Author's first collection of poems in translation.

3816 RAY, LILA. Some women writers. *And* More women writers. *And* Women writers again. *In her* A challenging decade: Bengali literature in the forties. Calcutta: D.M. Library, 1953. pp.22-3, 58-9, 116-7.
Briefly reviews the work of various female Bengali writers from the mid-19th to mid-20th centuries.

3817 SĀKHĀOYĀTA HOSENA, ROKEYĀ [BEGAM ROKEYA/ROKEYA SAKHAWAT HOSSAIN]. Sultana's dream. *In her* Rokeyā racanābalī. Dacca: Bangla Academy, 1973. pp.573-88. [*Reprint in* Hanna Papanek, ed. Purdah in South Asia: the segregation of women. Princeton, New Jersey: Princeton University Press?, forthcoming].
Short story. Fantasy of a utopian land: women, unsecluded, rule peacefully and intelligently while men are secluded, their shortcomings having been clearly demonstrated. Only English work of a Bengali writer, feminist and educationist of the late 19th and early 20th centuries.

3818 SEN, SNEHALATA. Nehal the musician and other tales. Tr. from Bengali. Madras: S. Ganesan, 1923. 143p.
Short stories. [Unexamined. NUC].

v) Bengali literature: male writers

3819 BASU, MANOJE. The beauty: the Bengali novel "Rupavati." Tr. from Bengali by Sachindra Lal Ghosh. Bombay: Jaico Publishing House, 1969. 179p.
Novel. Story of the tragic response of a village when a beautiful young woman is raped. Set in Bengal of the 1930s.

3820 BASU, TARAPADA. La société Bengalie du vingtième siècle dans l'oeuvre de Sarat Chandra Chatterji [Twentieth century Bengali society in the work of Sarat Chandra Chatterji]. Paris: Imprimerie Artistique Moderne, A. Lapied, 1940. 174p.
Has several references to female characterization and influences and summaries of Chatterji's many works.

3821 CHATTERJEE, BANKIM CHANDRA. Kopalkundala: a tale of Bengali life. Tr. from Bengali by H.A.D. Phillips. London: Trübner and Company, 1885. 208p.
Novel. A tale of romantic love written at a time when this concept had little meaning for Bengalis. The author identifies the heroine's beauty and other qualities with the natural beauties of Bengal and places the novel in a semi-wild, semi-fantastic setting.

3822 ________. Rajmohan's wife. Tr. from Bengali by Brajendra Nath Banerji. Calcutta: Bangiya Sahitya Parishad, 1940. 100p.
Novel. A traditional peasant wife foils her husband's plans to rob a zamindari family and suffers for it. Parts of this work were originally written in English.

3823 ________. Krishnakanta's will. Tr. from Bengali by J.C. Gosh. Norfolk, Connecticut: New Directions Books, 1962. 172p. (UNESCO Collection of Representative Works, Indian Series).
Novel. Didactic in spirit, this work relates the unhappy consequences when a Bengali husband takes a young widow as mistress. His wife, says the translator "is held up for admiration throughout and deified at the end" while the mistress "is disliked throughout and degraded at the end."

3824 CHATTERJI, SARAT CHANDRA [SARATCHANDRA

CHATTOPADHYAYA]. The eldest sister and other stories. Tr. from Bengali. Allahabad: Central Book Depot, 1950. 125p.
Short stories. Three tales of romance. One is a love story of a Hindu widow; another relates the unorthodox love between a high-caste Hindu man and a snake charmer's daughter; remaining story is set in historical Burma. [Unexamined. NUC].

3825 ________. The fire. Tr. from Bengali by Sachindra Lal Ghosh. Calcutta: Silpee Sangstha Prakasani, 1964. 276p.
Novel. A middle-class urban woman, the English-educated daughter of a Brahmo Samaj father, is torn between her passionate extramarital love affair and anxiety to maintain marital decorum with a quiet, stable husband. Psychological portrayal of conflicts of a modern Bengali woman of the early 20th century.

3826 ________. Mothers and sons: two novelettes — Deliverance and The Compliant Prodigal. Tr. from Bengali by Dilip Kumar Roy. Bombay: Pearl Publications, 1968. 177p.
Novels. Much material regarding the place of women in the joint family of the newly British-educated Bengali middle class.

3827 ________. Chandranath: queen's gambit. Tr. from Bengali by Sachindralal Ghosh. Bombay: Jaico Publishing House, 1969. 101p.
Novel. Examines the problems of a young girl in late 19th century Bengal whose widowed mother leaves home with her childhood lover. Has humanistic interest in the social circumstances of women.

3827a DIMOCK, EDWARD C., JR. The symbol of the motherland in Tagore's patriotic songs. *In* Warren M. Gunderson, ed. Studies on Bengal. East Lansing: Asian Studies Center, Michigan State University, 1975. pp.1-5. (*Its* Occasional Papers, South Asia Series, 26).
English translations of selected songs and brief commentary. "His land as mother was no metaphor, no abstraction." Paper presented to seventh Conference on Bengal Studies.

3828 GANGULI, T.N. Svarnalata: scenes from Hindu village life in Bengal. Tr. from Bengali by Dakshinacharan Roy. London: Macmillan and Company, 1914. 281p.
Novel. Portrays rural domestic life and the development of a romance.

3829 GUPTA, NAGENDRANATH. Rabindranath Tagore: the man and the poet. *In* Modern Review 42,1 (1927) 1-12.
Contains Tagore's Bengali poem, ***Urvaśī***, and a translation and discussion of it. Recalling this legendary ***apsaras***, referred to as early as the ***Ṛgveda***, Tagore portrays an eternally sexual and seductive woman, unencumbered with the social roles of wife and mother.

3830 LAGO, MARY M. Tagore's liberated women. *In* Feminine sensibility and characterization in South Asian literature. Guest ed: Fritz Blackwell. J. of South Asian Literature 12,3/4 (1977) 103-7.
Contrasts Tagore's view of women in a lecture delivered during a US tour in 1916 entitled "Woman" with his fictional images. The former stresses the natural nurturing tendencies of women as homemakers that are essential for public peace and prosperity and encourages female subordination of self to community. The fiction, however, portrays women "struggling toward liberation of the mind."

3831 MAJUMDAR, BIMANBEHARI. Heroines of Tagore: a study in the transformation of Indian society, 1875-1941. Calcutta: Firma K.L. Mukhopadhyay, 1968. 345p. (Yogendramohini Lectures, 1967).
Examines the development of female characterization in Tagore's work as a reflection of the transition from the "predominantly agricultural semi-feudal society of 1875" to the "industrialised urban community of 1941." Discusses Tagore's socio-political context; his maidens, married women and widows; his use of characters from the Hindu-Buddhist tradition; and the changing quality of his heroines. Appendixes list heroines and the works in which they appear.

3832 MUKHOPADHYAYA, DAMODAR. Mother and daughter: or, a true picture of Hindu life in Bengal. Tr. from Bengali by R.P. De. Calcutta: Oriental Publishing Company, n.d. 185p.
Novel. Portrays the difficult existence of a poor brahman widow and her daughter in a 19th century Bengali village. "Our main object has been to depict the triumph of virtue over the discomfiture of vice."

3833 RAY, ANNADA SANKAR. Woman and other stories. Tr. from Bengali by Lila Ray. Calcutta: United Writers, 1977. 108p.
Short stories (8). Themes relating to women predominate.

3834 SEN GUPTA, NARES CHANDRA. The idiot's wife: a stirring story of domestic and social life in Bengal, 2d ed. Tr. from Bengali by the author. Madras: G.A. Natesan, 1944. 59p.
Novel. [Unexamined. NUC].

3835 TAGORE, RABINDRANATH. Vision. Tr. from Bengali by C.F. Andrews. *In his* The hungry stones and other stories. New York: Macmillan Company, 1916. pp.133-69.
Short story. A woman who goes blind derives some satisfaction from being an ideal wife and encouraging her husband to remarry. Later, when he attempts to do so, she is distraught.

3836 ________. The home and the world. Tr. from Bengali by Surendranath Tagore. New York: Macmillan Company, 1919. 293p.
Novel. A husband is concerned to know if his

traditional, dutiful Hindu wife treats him so out of love or ritualism. He encourages her to leave the home for the freedom of the world, first via education and later with actual physical mobility. Tale depicts her ensuing conflicts. Set in early 20th century Bengal, the work reflects the freedom and women's emancipation movements of the period.

3837 ________. The wreck. Tr. from Bengali. New York: Macmillan Company, 1921. 347p.
Novel. The mistaken exchange of two brides during a storm provides a means of examining the theme of a woman's intense loyalty to her husband.

3838 ________. Malini. Tr. from Bengali. *In his* Collected poems and plays. London: Macmillan and Company, 1936. pp.483-500.
Play. The heroine, a princess, seeks to escape her happy home in order to give of herself and help to ameliorate the sorrows of the world. Depicts woman as all-sacrificing and all-forgiving. Inspired by a Buddhist legend.

3839 ________. "Why deprive me, my Fate, of my woman's right." Tr. from Bengali. *In* Modern Review 59,6 (1936) 603.
Poetry. Portrays a woman's desire to experience love without concern for conventional standards of womanliness, as exemplified by the coy bride patiently awaiting her husband.

3840 ________. Two sisters. Tr. from Bengali by Krishna Kripalani. Calcutta: Visva Bharati, 1964. 103p.
Novel. Examines the conflicts that arise for a man when a woman does not embody qualities of both the mother and the beloved. Two sisters in early 20th century Bengal each embody qualities of a single and opposed relationship.

3841 Two daughters. Directed by Satyajit Ray. (Bengali dialogue/English subtitles). 1961. 114 min. Black and white. 16 mm. [*Distributed by* James Films, 745 Fifth Avenue, New York, New York 10022].
Film based on stories by Tagore. The first part, "The Postmaster," portrays the relationship between a student who serves as postmaster of a village and a young girl who looks after him. When he is to leave, they realize their mutual attachment. In the second part, "The Conclusion," a bride flees the groom arranged for her only to return with genuine love. [Unexamined].

3842 VAN METER, RACHEL R. Women's rights. *In her* Bankimchandra Chatterji and the Bengali renaissance. Ph.D. dissertation, Department of South Asia Regional Studies, University of Pennsylvania, 1964. pp.68-86. [University Microfilms 65-1396].
Discusses views of female education, treatment of widows, widow marriage, polygamy, ***kulīna*** practices, and ***satī*** in the essays and, particularly, novels of Bankim Chandra Chatterjee. His ideal Hindu woman is "basically educated, deeply religious, married at an early age, modest in behavior, showing deep respect and devotion for her husband in the traditional Hindu ways."

3843 VIJAYALAKSHMI, C. The heroines of Tagore: ***Chitra*** and ***Home and the World***. *In* D.V.K. Raghavacharyulu, ed. The two-fold voice: essays on Indian writing in English. Guntur: Navodaya Publishers, 1971. pp.37-46.
Classifies and illustrates two types of women in Tagore's work: the sensual and charming Urvaśī and the serene and graceful Lakṣmī.

(n) Women's language: Bengali dialect

3844 SEN, SUKUMAR. Women's dialect in Bengali. *In* J. of the Department of Letters, University of Calcutta 18 (1929) 1-83.
Women's speech is said to be characterized by greater conservativism, many intensive words and expletive particles, euphemism, superstitious avoidance, limited vocabulary and perjorative terms and expressions. Following discussions about women's dialect in Old and Middle Indo-Aryan, the author presents idioms from the "standard colloquial of Western Bengal," according to parts of speech, the above-named characteristics and other categories. Provides idioms in Bengali and in English translation. Interpretation is minimal.

5. Bangladesh: Islamic area of eastern Bengali language

For colonial period see entries 2602-64

(a) General statements: ethnographic and other

3845 ABDULLAH, TAHRUNNESSA AHMED. Village women as I saw them. Dacca: Ford Foundation, 1974. 32p.
"The purpose of this survey was to learn about the life cycle, customs and culture that are associated with the day-to-day activities of rural women. This will bring into focus the fundamental problems of village women, particularly those of Bangali Muslim society." Based on open-ended discussions and observations with women in twenty villages in Comilla District and with personnel of the Women's Education and Home Development Programme of the Bangladesh Academy for Rural Development, Comilla.

3846 ________ and SONDRA A. ZEIDENSTEIN. Finding ways to learn about rural women: experiences from a pilot project in Bangladesh. Dacca: Ford Foundation, 1976. 32p. (Report 44).
Five sections discuss: an unidentified Women's Programme established in 1974 to integrate rural women into the development process in Bangladesh, misinformation about rural women, lack of information about rural women, difficulties in obtaining such information and the Women's Programme as a source of such information.

3847 ALAMGIR, SUSAN FULLER. Profile of Bangladeshi women: selected aspects of women's roles and status in Bangladesh. Dacca: prepared for USAID Mission to Bangladesh, 1977. 82p.
First part focuses on women's legal and social status, particularly on civil and personal laws as they apply to women's property, marriage and divorce rights. Although emphasis is on Muslim women, Hindu and Christian women are also discussed. Second part deals with rural women, particularly with division of labor, sex roles, decision making and authority.

3848 ELLICKSON, JEAN. Rural women: a field survey. *In* Women for women: Bangladesh 1975. Dacca: University Press Limited, 1975. pp.81-9.
Some observations from fieldwork in "Kolaidanga" village. Argues that policy and action should encourage women to be self-sufficient rather than more skillful at being dependent as they now are.

3849 JAHAN, ROUNAQ. Women in Bangladesh. *In* Ruby Rohrlich-Leavitt, ed. Women cross-culturally: change and challenge. The Hague: Mouton, 1975. pp.5-30. (World Anthropology). [*Also* Dacca: Ford Foundation, 1974. 45p. *And in* Women for women: Bangladesh 1975. Dacca: University Press Limited, 1975. pp.1-30].
Survey paper reviews the divergent life styles of women in Bangladesh; their legal, economic, political and social status; and women's organizations and movements. Focuses on advantages men have over women and elite women have over the masses of rural and traditional women.

3850 KABIR, KHUSHI, AYESHA ABED and MARTY CHEN. Rural women in Bangladesh: exploding some myths. Dacca: Ford Foundation, 1976. iv. (Report 42).
Discusses nine myths about rural women and work, development and conservativism. Presents relevant experiences of the Bangladesh Rural Advancement Committee of which the authors are staff members.

3850a KIRKPATRICK, JOANNA. Themes of consciousness among some educated working women of Bangladesh. *In* Richard L. Park, ed. Bengal: the American connection. East Lansing: Asian Studies Center, Michigan State University, forthcoming. (*Its* Occasional Papers, South Asia Series).
Report of interviews with educated middle- and upper-class women associated with Rajshahi University and a small college in Rajshahi. Considers students' heros and heroines, compares these to ideal figures of male students and concludes that women tend to have a national as opposed to sectarian identification. Examines attitudes toward self-sacrifice and its effects on health and psychological patterns. Discusses informants' responses to the traditional suppression of female individuality and their conceptions of social change processes. Concludes that "whereas the fundamental existential problem for middle class women in the United States is the question of identity, for middle class women in Bangladesh..., the fundamental problem is the question of autonomy." Revision of paper presented to twelfth Conference on Bengal Studies. [Manuscript examined].

3851 LINDENBAUM, SHIRLEY. Woman and the left hand: social status and symbolism in East Pakistan. *In* Mankind 6,11 (1968) 537-44.
"A number of classifications, both symbolic and real, are aligned with the biological distinction between the sexes, and serve to define and emphasize the position of women in the community." The right/left dichotomy denotes not only male/female but also authority/submission, good/bad, purity/impurity and other paired opposites.

3852 _______. Forms of consciousness among middle class Bangladeshi women. Dacca: Ford Foundation, 1975.
[Unexamined].

3852a MC CARTHY, FLORENCE E. The status and condition of rural women in Bangladesh. Dacca: Women's Section, Planning and Evaluation Cell, Ministry of Agriculture and Forests, 1978. 34p.
[Unexamined. ALB].

3853 _______, SALEH SABBAH and ROUSHAN AKHTER. Bibliography and selected references regarding rural women in Bangladesh. Dacca: Women's Section, Planning and Development Division, Ministry of Agriculture, 1978. 44p.
Two hundred seven references, published and unpublished. Includes some material on urban women and general social conditions in Bangladesh.

3854 Problems in field work with village women. *In* Survey and Research Bulletin, Pakistan Academy for Rural Development, Comilla 12 (Nov 1964).
[Unexamined].

3855 SATTAR, ELLEN. Women in Bangladesh: a village study. Dacca: Ford Foundation, 1974. 60p.
Study based on interviews with all the women of a Muslim and Hindu village in Comilla District. Major sections describe the village and the household as spatial and social units, lives of the women who were interviewed (education level, family and marriage patterns, *pardā* observance and attitudes toward these topics) and their daily and annual work cycles.

3856 SCHOUSTRA-VAN BEUKERING, E.J.E. Sketch of the daily life of a Bengali village woman. *In* Plural Societies 6,4 (1975) 51-66.
Reviews life cycle stages, daily work schedules, spatial mobility and temporal perspectives of women in a "more or less modern" village of Khulna District.

3857 SMOCK, AUDREY CHAPMAN. Bangladesh: a struggle with tradition and poverty. *In* Janet Zollinger Giele and Audrey Chapman Smock, eds. Women: roles and status in eight countries. New York: John Wiley and Sons, 1977. pp.81-126.
Summarizes the historical background of Bangladesh and recent research on her women with respect to family, education, economy and employment, fertility and family planning and politics. Bibliography lists numerous published and unpublished sources. Author's conclusion to the volume (pp.383-421) puts some of this material in comparative perspective.

3858 Women for women: Bangladesh 1975. Dacca: University Press Limited, 1975. 248p.
Articles by members of the Women for Women collective, a group of professionals organized in 1973 to investigate problems faced by women of Bangladesh. For contents, see entries 355, 3848-9, 3873, 3890, 3892, 3896, 3899, 3918 and 3946.

(b) The life cycle

3859 LINDENBAUM, SHIRLEY. The value of women. *In* John R. McLane, ed. Bengal in the nineteenth and twentieth centuries. East Lansing: Asian Studies Center, Michigan State University, 1975. pp.75-83. (*Its* Occasional Papers, South Asia Series, 25).
Equates low female "consumption value" with three life-cycle phases of relatively high mortality: birth to five years, early childbearing years and from about the fifty-ninth year. Discusses shifting tendency from brideprice to dowry and reflects upon demographic patterns of Bangladesh as a whole. Data from Shaitnal village, Comilla District, 1963-65. Paper from ninth Conference on Bengal Studies.

i) Fertility

3860 AFZAL, MOHAMMAD. The fertility of East Pakistan married women. *In* Warren C. Robinson, ed. Studies in the demography of Pakistan. Karachi: Pakistan Institute of Development Economics, 1967. pp.51-91.
Provides estimates of "age-specific fertility rates, total fertility rates and gross-reproduction rates for total as well as rural and urban married women" and "mean age at marriage for rural and urban women" from 1961 census data. Numerous tables.

3861 CHAUDHURY, RAFIQUL HUDA. Differential fertility by religious group in East Pakistan. *In* Social Biology 18,2 (1971) 188-91.
Compares the fertility levels of Muslims, caste Hindus and scheduled caste Hindus in the former East Pakistan. Relates Muslim fertility rate, the highest, to lengthy conjugal life, high infant mortality, less ritual abstinence and unfavorable attitudes to family planning. Scheduled caste Hindus had lowest fertility rates. Based on district-level data of 1961 census.

3862 _______. Labour force status and fertility. *In* Bangladesh Development Studies 2,4 (1974) 819-38.
[Unexamined].

3863 CHEN, LINCOLN C. et al. A prospective study of birth interval dynamics in rural Bangladesh. Dacca: Ford Foundation, 1974. 55p.

Report of study of 193 noncontracepting married fecund women who were regularly interviewed about menstruation, pregnancy, lactation and husband's occupational absences and given urine tests for pregnancy. Results suggest a "seasonal trend in fecundability" associated with coolest months. Lactation amenorrhea was prolonged and there was a seasonal trend of first postpartum ovulation. Average birth interval was 33 months.

3864 CHOWDHURY, NUIMUDDIN and RAFIQUL HUDA CHAUDHURY. Socio-biological factors affecting fertility behaviour in a rural area of Bangladesh. Dacca: Bangladesh Institute of Development Studies, 1978. 44p. (*Its* Discussion Paper Series, 1).
Report of survey conducted in Mithakhali village, Barisal District. [Unexamined. ALB].

3865 SIRAGELDIN, ISMAIL, DOUGLAS NORRIS and MAHBUBUDDIN AHMAD. Fertility in Bangladesh: facts and fancies. *In* Population Studies 29,2 (1975) 207-15.
Reviews findings from 1969 fertility survey of several thousand women and comments upon conclusions of other such studies. Previous studies tended to be based on small local samples; the present one provides "for the first time data on current fertility levels and recent fertility trends in Bangladesh on a national basis and examines its structures and prospects."

3866 STOECKEL, JOHN and A.K.M. CHOUDHURY. Seasonal variation in births in rural East Pakistan. *In* J. of Biosocial Science 4,1 (1972) 107-16.
Data from Matlab Thana, former East Pakistan, suggests: mean minimum air temperature nine months previous to birth is inversely related to birth rate; all occupations have differential seasonal birth rate patterns; and all birth orders have similar seasonal patterning.

ii) Pregnancy, childbirth and motherhood

3867 CHEN, LINCOLN C. et al. Maternal mortality in rural Bangladesh. *In* Studies in Family Planning 5,11 (1974) 334-41. [*Also* Dacca: Ford Foundation, 1974. lv].
Data from a vital registration system in rural Comilla District. "Levels of maternal mortality are presented; probable causes of death are identified; and the relationship of maternal mortality to selected demographic variables is examined." Concludes with programmatic implications.

3868 CROLEY, H.T., et al. Characteristics and utilization of midwives in a selected rural area of East Pakistan. *In* Demography 3,2 (1966) 578-80.
Report of interviews with 632 married women of two villages near Dacca and the 21 midwives who have assisted in their deliveries. Six percent of the women were found to use midwives for deliveries. Reports findings about age, marital status, training, clientele, competence, knowledge, etc., of the midwife group.

3869 GHAFFAR, SAYEDA. Studies on attitude towards breast-feeding among the women of urban areas in Bangladesh (Dacca City). Dacca: Institute of Nutrition and Food Science, University of Dacca, 1977? 40p.
Report of study to determine correlation of socio-economic features with attitudes toward and practice of breast feeding. Based on interviews with 200 Dacca mothers of diverse backgrounds. Most favored breast feeding in contrast to effects of urbanization reported for other countries. Text and tables describe socio-economic structure of sample, awareness of significance of breast feeding and practice of breast feeding.

3870 MAJUMDER, DHIRENDRA NATH. Customs and taboos observed by an East Bengal woman from pregnancy to childbirth. *In* Man in India 3,3/4 (1923) 232-42.
Describes customary observances of Hindu women.

3871 RIZVI, NAJMA. Food avoidances during post-partum period among Muslim women in Bangladesh. *In* Shishu Diganta: a Child's Horizon 1 (Dec 1976).
[Unexamined].

3872 UNIVERSITY OF DACCA. INSTITUTE OF STATISTICAL RESEARCH AND TRAINING. Statistical profile of children and mothers in Bangladesh. Dacca: the institute, 1977. 80p.
Collection of statistical tables on numerous topics relating to mothers and children. Main sections are "Population and Demography," "Health," "Nutrition," "Housing and Physical Environment," "Education," "Social Development" and "Water Uses."

iii) Widowhood

3873 KHATUN, SHARIFA and KAMRUNNESSA BEGAM. Life of urban middle class widows. *In* Women for women: Bangladesh 1975. Dacca: University Press Limited, 1975. pp.180-203.
Report of interviews with 50 widows (from Dacca?). Considers socio-economic profile of the group, changes that occurred at husband's death (i.e., in dress, residence, expenditures, participation in functions and ceremonies, education, employment, household activities, attitudes and assistance of relatives and neighbors and relationship to children), pastimes, religious activities, feelings about husbands' death, attitudes about remarriage and major problems.

(c) Domestic sphere and family life

3874 DAS, S.R. A note on votive clay figurines used in a folk-rite of Bengal. *In* Man in India 32,2 (1952) 105-15.
Describes clay figurines that are worshipped in some *vrata* rites observed by unmarried girls in areas of present-day Bangladesh. The figures are associated with fertility and procreation. Compares figures to those found at Indus valley sites. Photograph.

3875 ______. A study of the vrata rites of Bengal. *In* Man in India 32,4 (1952) 207-45. [*Also* A study of the vrata-rites. Calcutta: S.C. Kar, 1953. 49p. (Folk Religion of Bengal, part 1,1)].
Discusses historical references to and various categories of *vratas* with details of the *Lakṣmī pūjā vrata*, the *Suvacanī vrata* and others observed in areas of present-da; Bangladesh. Author is concerned with the origin, Aryan or pre-Aryan, of elements in these rites.

3876 GANGULI, KALYAN KUMAR. Kantha: the enchanted wrap. *In* Indian Folklore 1,2 (1958) 3-10.
Discusses technique and motifs of women's patchwork-embroidery wrap making work. Desire for the well-being of a loved one is expressed in design symbolism and it is believed that the desire is fulfilled through performance-construction.

3877 KRAMRISCH, STELLA. Kanthas of Bengal. *In* Mārg 3,2 (1949) 18-29.
Describes and interprets the craft of embroidered wrap or spread making. *Kānthās* are made only by women and are presented to close relatives on festive occasions as offerings of love. The symbolism of the making and giving of the *kānthā* is reinforced by that of the embroidered design. Photographs.

3878 MITRA, SARAT CHANDRA. Note on a taboo forbidding the son-in-law to meet or touch his mother-in-law. *In* Man in India 6,4 (1926) 308-11.
Discusses Hindu taboo found in Chittagong District that involves the notion of the mother-in-law's shadow as a source of dangerous influence.

3879 MOOKERJEE, AJIT. Kanthas: embroidered works. *In* Modern Review 74,4 (1943) 277-9.
Describes technique, types (according to function) and various other details of this embroidery craft done primarily by women of the former East Bengal.

3880 NAZMUL KARIM, A.K. Changing patterns of an East Pakistan family. *In* Barbara E. Ward, ed. Women in the new Asia: the changing social roles of men and women in South and South-east Asia. Paris: UNESCO, 1963. pp.296-322.
Male author's perspective on changing patterns in his traditional teacher-class Muslim family. Considers structure, relationships, marriage arrangements, dress and daily life.

3881 ROY, BARNIK. A Natai Chandi brata of East Bengal. *In* Indian Folklore 2,2 (1959) 112-7.
Presents the *kathā*, story, of a calendrical rite for the purpose of gaining a husband as told by the author's mother. With some general comments about *vrata* rites.

(d) Work: as employment and without remuneration

3882 GERARD, RENEE et al. Report of a feasibility survey of productive/income generating activities for women in Bangladesh. Dacca: Women's Development Programme, UNICEF, 1977. 1v.
Surveys women's programs in Bangladesh that relate to productive/income generating activities and other basic social services. Assesses the social position of women in Bangladesh and discusses women's work, existing programs, cottage industries and intermediate technology. Bibliography includes much unpublished material. Photographs.

3883 Women's work. Dacca: Bangladesh Co-operative Book Society Ltd., 1974.
Prepared under auspices of Women's Rehabilitation division of National Board of Bangladesh? [Unexamined].

i) Rural women

3884 HASSAN, MD. NAZMUL. Spare time of rural women: a case study of 508 women of five selected villages of Baidyer Bazar, Bangladesh. Dacca: Institute of Nutrition and Food Science, University of Dacca, 1978. 45p.
Study conducted to ascertain the availability of rural women for educational and, ultimately, economically productive activities such as food preservation, kitchen gardening and poultry raising. Women's daily schedules were recorded and they were interviewed. Gives socioeconomic profile of respondents and considers seasonal variation in work patterns. Describes women's spare-time activities and willingness to attend to various proposed alternatives. The respondents were assessed to have four to five spare-time hours per day (although this includes sewing, paddy husking and sleeping). Most were willing to receive vocational training if provided and do certain income-generating tasks.

3885 ISLAM, MEHERUNNESA. Food preservation in Bangladesh: a manual for instructors. Dacca: Women's Development Programme,

UNICEF, 1977. 51p.
Food preservation as an income-generating activity for rural women. Includes history of the National Food Preservation Programme, methods of teaching the subject and detailed recipes and instructions for making and bottling preserves.

3886 KHATUN, SALEHA and GITA RANI. T. Abdullah and S. Zeidenstein, eds. Bari-based post harvest operations and livestock care: some observations and case studies. Dacca: Ford Foundation, 1977. 24p. (Report 48).
Describes women's household activities relating to postharvest work requirements and suggests related research problems and policy implications. Presents detailed case studies of single day's activities of two women during rice processing period and observations from activities of others. Brief observations on seed and livestock care.

3887 MC CARTHY, FLORENCE and SHELLEY FELDMAN. Purdah, social class and Bengali women. *In* Hanna Papanek, ed. Purdah in South Asia: the segregation of women. Forthcoming.
Data from rural Bangladesh is used to support the thesis that the need for women's labor in a given social setting will affect the pattern of ***pardā*** observance. The authors distinguish "internal" ***pardā***, modesty in deportment, from "external" ***pardā***, ***burqa'*** wearing, and stress the flexibility and mobility that ***burqa'*** wearing enable. [Unexamined. Verified with editor].

3888 MC CARTHY, FLORENCE E., SALEH SABBAH and ROUSHAN AKHTER. A working paper on rural women workers in Bangladesh: problems and prospects. Dacca: Women's Section, Planning and Development Division, Ministry of Agriculture, 1978. 57p.
Argues that while much information on general status of rural women of Bangladesh has now accumulated, empirical data on specific processes and issues has yet to be gathered. Summarizes six sets of data on rural women, including two collected by the recently formed Women's Section within the Planning and Development Division of the Ministry of Agriculture. Aims to show heterogeneous conditions of the women, the problems they face and their responses to them and areas where further further research is needed. Considers marital status, age, education, economic condition, family size, husband's occupation and wages.

3889 MARTIUS-VON HARDER, GUDRUN. Participation of women in rural development: a field study in four villages of Comilla Kotwali Thana. Comilla: Bangladesh Academy for Rural Development, 1975. 16p.
Report of study to ascertain conditions under which rural women work outside the homestead and the work patterns of women who do. Generally, economic activities of women occur in the homestead. Suggests types of work that can be done there and means of effecting change. [Manuscript examined].

3890 ________. Women's role in rice processing. *In* Women for women: Bangladesh 1975. Dacca: University Press Limited, 1975. pp.66-80.
Describes various postharvest rice processing activities done by women secluded within the homestead in Kotwali Thana, Comilla District. Includes statistics on rates of participation in various aspects of rice processing.

3891 O'KELLY, ELIZABETH. Simple technologies for rural women in Bangladesh, 2d ed. Dacca: Women's Development Programme, UNICEF, 1978. 70p.
Examines the work, division of time and labor and existing technology of rural women. Discusses the need for time and labor saving technologies that do not conflict with local custom. Examines the Intermediate Technology of Dr. Schumacher, author of ***Small is Beautiful***, in the context of lives of rural women in Bangladesh. Photographs and diagrams, with descriptions and instructions, illustrate some technological proposals. Lists manufacturers' addresses.

3892 SATTAR, ELLEN. Village women's work. *In* Women for women: Bangladesh 1975. Dacca: University Press Limited, 1975. pp.33-65. [*Adapted from her* Women in Bangladesh: a village study. Dacca: Ford Foundation, 1974. 60p.].
Study of women's lives in a Comilla District village. Briefly considers attitudes and practices regarding education, marriage, health, family planning, ***pardā*** and skills and describes daily and annual work cycles.

3893 The socio-economic implications of introducing HYV in Bangladesh: proceedings of the international seminar held in April, 1975. Kotbari, Comilla: Bangladesh Academy for Rural Development, 1975. 88p.
Reviews proceedings of seminar to assess implications of introducing high-yielding varieties (HYVs) of grain. One of the four sessions was devoted to rural women. Describes seminar organization; reviews sessions, discussions and recommendations; and provides lists of participants and papers and annotations of selected papers.

3894 TAHERA, SAYEDA. Rural industrialisation and role of women. *In* Arthanīti Jārnāla 1,1 (1976) 197-200.
Attempts "to analyse how the womenfolk gain from rural industrialisation and contribute to it," with reference to Bangladesh. Briefly considers various aspects, with recommendations.

3895 Women and agriculture. Guest ed: Marty Chen. ADAB [Agricultural Development Agencies in Bangladesh] News 4,6 (1977) 36p.
Brief articles describe various aspects of women's participation in agriculture and associated problems, particular programs that facilitate this participation and proposals for further facilitation.

ii) Urban women

3896 ALAM, BILQUIS A. Women in nursing: a study of the nurses of Dacca Medical College Hospital. *In* Women for women: Bangladesh 1975. Dacca: University Press Limited, 1975. pp.121-53.
Study of 63 nurses to ascertain socio-economic background, factors related to occupational choice and some problems they face.

3897 CHAUDHURY, RAFIQUL HUDA. Married women in urban occupations of Bangladesh: some problems and issues. Dacca: Bangladesh Institute of Development Studies, 1976. 92p. (*Its* Research Report Series, n.s. 22). [*Rev. version* Marriage, urban women, and the labor force: the Bangladesh case. *In* Signs: J. of Women in Culture and Society 5,1 (1979) 154-63.
Report of survey conducted in Dacca. Considers socio-economic background of employed women, their motivations for seeking employment, contributions they make to incomes of husbands' and fathers' families, consequences of employment for the discharge of traditional domestic duties and job satisfaction.

3898 HUSAIN, A.F.A. Employment of middle class Muslim women in Dacca. Dacca: Socio-Economic Research Board, Dacca University, 1958. 165p.
[Unexamined. NUC].

3899 ISLAM, MAHMUDA. Women at work in Bangladesh: a sample survey of working women. *In* Women for women: Bangladesh 1975. Dacca: University Press Limited, 1975. pp.93-120.
Study of 200 women working in remunerative occupations outside the home in metropolitan Dacca. Reports occupational distribution, marital status, age distribution, education, socio-economic background, husbands' occupation, parents' education and occupation, motivation to work, attitudes toward work and effects on home life.

(e) Education

3900 ASHRAF, ASIA. Women of East Pakistan since independence. *In* Pakistan Quarterly 15,3 (1967) 55-8.
Cites education as the feature that most distinguishes types of women and their activities in the former East Pakistan. Reviews trends in female education and opportunities subsequent to education. Provides statistics of male and female participation rates at various levels, 1947-48 and 1965-66.

3901 BAWANY, ZEB. Problems of female education in East Pakistan. *In* Pakistan Review 16,6 (1968) 24-6, 29.
Problems faced by female students in colleges and universities.

3902 ISLAM, SHAMIMA. Women's education in Bangladesh: needs and issues. Dacca: Foundation for Research on Educational Planning and Development (FREPD), 1977. 145p.
". . . an overview on the existing status of women's education in Bangladesh. An attempt . . . to identify vital needs and issues relating to the improvement of women's education in the country." Based on secondary sources. Main sections consider literacy, primary education, secondary education, post-secondary education and nonformal education. Points out that educational profile of women is largely unavailable from the various statistical and research investigations conducted in Bangladesh.

3903 KRIPPENDORFF, SULTANA. Women's education in Bangladesh: needs and issues, content analysis. Dacca: Foundation for Research on Educational Planning and Development (FREPD), 1977. 58p.
Report of a content analysis of the ***Bangla Reader*** textbooks for levels two through ten to "ascertain what ideas and attitudes about women are currently being taught to children." Found that women are underrepresented and relegated to lesser roles than men. The real and important contributions they make to the society are not adequately portrayed.

3904 MC KENZIE, ALINE. Pioneering home economics in East Pakistan. *In* National Business Woman 37,10 (1958) 12-3.
Report of the establishment and structure of home economics programs at the Women's Training College, Mymensingh, and the Eden Girls' College, Dacca. Includes details of the plans in progress for a Home Economics College in Dacca. Author is the American woman who organized these programs.

3905 Women and education: Bangladesh, 1978. Dacca: Women for Women, Research and Study Group, 1978. 174p.
Collected papers from the Women for Women collective, Dacca. Contents: "Women's Education and Emancipation in a Purdah Society: The Co-eds of the 50s" by Roushan Jahan, "Data on Attitudes towards Urban Girls Education" by Noorunnahar Fyzunnessa, "Mother's Attitudes toward Freedom of Children and Academic Achievement of the Child" by Hamida Akhtar, "Female Primary Education in Bangladesh" by Mahmuda Islam, "The Position of Women in Secondary School Education in Bangladesh: A Case Study of Dacca Division" by Ellen Sattar, "Married Female Students in Higher Education" by Khurshid Jalal and Ishrat Shamim, "Women in Education Administration" by Jahanara Huq, "Non-formal Education in Bangladesh: Some Selected Lessons and Choices of Strategy" by Shamima Islam and "Rural Women's Education: A Case for Realistic Policy Making" by Perveen Ahmad and Nazmunnessa Mahtab.

(f) Development and social welfare, legal provisions

3906 ADNAN, SHAPAN and RUSHIDAN ISLAM. Social change and rural women: posibilities of participation. *In* Business Studies 1,1 (1976).
[Unexamined].

3907 EPSTEIN, SCARLETT. Rural social science development and the role of women in rural development. Dacca: Ford Foundation, 1975?
Criticizes nature and organization of social science research relating to rural Bangladesh Recommendations. [Unexamined].

3908 GERMAIN, ADRIENNE. Women's roles in Bangladesh development: a program assessment. Dacca: Ford Foundation, 1976. lv.
Highlights significant features of the lives of (especially rural and poor) women of Bangladesh, "raises central program and policy issues and gives examples of the kinds of planning and analysis that might be undertaken."

3909 HOSSAIN, MONOWAR, RAIHAN SHARIF and JAHANARA HUQ, eds. Role of women in socio-economic development in Bangladesh: proceedings of a seminar held in Dacca, May 9-10, 1976. Dacca: Bangladesh Economic Association, 1977. 197p.
Reproduces various addresses, fifteen English and seven Bengali papers and reports of the various panels. Main topics are productive activities, rural women and development, education and population planning. Jahanara Huq says in her introduction, "For the first time in the history of Bangladesh women from diverse walks of life [about 300] submitted the fruits of their wide experience, deep insight and painstaking research, and . . . were able to articulate their views on various social and economic issues confronting members of their sex."

3910 SERAJUL HAQUE, ALAUDDIN TALUKDER and MOHAMMAD SHAMSUL ISLAM KHAN. Bangladesh demography: a select bibliography. Dacca: Bangladesh Institute of Development Studies, 1976. 44p. (BIDS Library Bibliography Series, 11).
References to 518 books, articles and unpublished papers. The 18 categories include "Family Planning," "Fertility and Mortality," "Marriage and Family" and others relevant to women.

3911 Shishu Diganta: A Child's Horizon. Issue 1- (Dec 1976-). Dacca: Communication-Information Section, UNICEF.
Social service journal with a special focus on women's and children's welfare in Bangladesh. Articles in English and Bengali. A sample issue, the fourth (May 1978), contains English articles on a windmill made of bamboo poles and jute mats, a village school under a mango tree, rural UNICEF programs in Bangladesh, a women's cultivation program, a bank for children and the headmaster who developed it, a school for street boys, Bangladesh plans for International Year of the Child and peanut cultivation.

3912 TAHERA, B.S. Rural women and development. *In* Grindlays Bangladesh (Dec 1976) 44-7.
Various comments on activities and largely unrecognized contributions of rural women of Bangladesh. Describes hindrances to their still greater contributions and programs that would facilitate change.

3913 ZEIDENSTEIN, SONDRA and LAURA ZEIDENSTEIN. Observations on the status of women in Bangladesh. *In* World Education Issues 2 (Jul 1974) 24p.
Major sections discuss issues of women and development; the difficult conditions for women of Bangladesh; major groups, projects and services in operation to support them; and recommendations for central and local government, private institutions, higher educational institutions, political organizations, women's associations, individuals and consciousness-raising groups. Photographs.

i) Associations, programs, agencies

3914 ABDULLAH, TAHERUNNESSA A. and SONDRA A. ZEIDENSTEIN. Village women of Bangladesh: prospects for change. London: Pergamon Press, forthcoming 1979.
Describes various aspects of the lives of rural women and details the early years of a project that is directing resources to them. Considers how change has been initiated in order to foster change in the future. [Unexamined].

3915 BANGLADESH ACADEMY FOR RURAL DEVELOPMENT. WOMEN'S EDUCATION AND HOME DEVELOPMENT PROGRAMME. Report. 1- (1963-). Comilla.
Reports of a program that promotes the health, education and skills of rural women. Specific concerns include child care, family planning, home sanitation, kitchen gardening, spinning, midwifery and literacy. Reports trace establishment and growth of the program and review major events, state of ongoing programs, past directions, future goals and budgets. Originally issued by Pakistan Academy for Rural Development.

3916 GÉRARD, RENÉE, MEHERUNNESSA ISLAM and MEHRAJ JAHAN. Training for women in Bangladesh: an inventory and sample survey of training programmes. Dacca: Women's Development Programme, UNICEF, 1977. 100p.
Study of 196 governmental and nongovernmental, formal and informal training programs for poor women in Bangladesh. Reviews goals and operations of the various programs, evaluates them and attempts to determine which women are be-

ing reached and identify areas in which training programs are needed.

3917 HOQUE, NASEEM. Informal education for women in Bangladesh: with emphasis on agency and organizational programs serving economically disadvantaged women. East Lansing: Agency for International Development and Institute for International Studies in Education, Michigan State University, n.d. 63p. (Program of Studies in Non-formal Education, Supplementary Paper 5).
Report of study of voluntary and nongovernmental organizations assisting semiliterate and illiterate, poor, young and old unskilled women. Assesses such programs as a group and examines four in detail. The study, conducted in 1974-75, examines the programs in the context of the history of Bangladesh.

3918 ISLAM, SHAMIMA. Women drop-outs in nonformal education: a case study. *In* Women for women: Bangladesh 1975. Dacca: University Press Limited, 1975. pp.154-79.
"The present study attempts to develop a descriptive profile of participant drop-outs in . . . the Bangladesh Women's Rehabilitation Programme, uncovering some thematic problems and some relevant socio-economic information." Covers trainees and production workers who dropped out in 1973-74 after one month or more of participation.

3919 LINDENBAUM, SHIRLEY. The social and economic status of women in Bangladesh. Dacca: Ford Foundation, 1974. 32p.
Surveys numerous pilot women's welfare organizations in Bangladesh, most of which were established to assist women affected by the 1971 war. Discusses the future of these programs and makes recommendations, in part based upon experience gained from field trips to a village in Comilla District.

3920 MC CARTHY, FLORENCE E. The women's programme at Comilla, Pakistan. *In* Women Today 6,2 (1964) 25-8.
A report on the Women's Education and Home Development Programme of the Pakistan (now Bangladesh) Academy for Rural Development. Discusses health, family planning, spinning, gardening, paddy loans and literacy.

3921 ________. Bengali village women as mediators of social change. *In* Human Organization 36,4 (1977) 363-70.
Study of 57 village women who were trained in the 1960s at the Pakistan Academy for Rural Development, Comilla, to teach practical skills and impart knowledge to the women of their respective villages. The attempt to mobilize women in this society is especially complicated as men are "gatekeepers for knowledge" and women are "relegated to nonvisible roles." The first step to women's involvement includes maximizing their own unique contributions."

3922 NELSON, J.A. et al. Characteristics and job practices associated with successful female village organizers in Joydebpur, Dacca. *In* Pakistan J. of Family Planning 3,2 (1969) 113-6. [Unexamined].

3923 RAPER, ARTHUR F. The women's and family planning programs. *In his* Rural development in action: the comprehensive experiment at Comilla. Ithaca, New York: Cornell University Press, 1970. pp.157-85.
Notes that village women have been simultaneously indispensable and overlooked. Describes establishment of the Women's Programme of the Pakistan Academy for Rural Development in the early 1960s and its subsequent growth during the decade. Discusses program for training village women to impart skills and knowledge in their respective villages, various other specialized programs and family planning endeavors.

ii) Development and welfare through the law

3924 RAHMAN, ZEBUN NESSA, ed. The status of women in the eye of the law in Bangladesh. Dacca: Bangladesh Mohila Samity, 1977.
Contains survey papers and papers specifically relating to inheritance, marriage and divorce, economic transactions associated with marriage, work, political rights and aims and activities of Bangladesh Mahila Samiti. [Unexamined].

3925 SOBHAN, SALMA. Legal status of women in Bangladesh. Dacca: Bangladesh Institute of Law and International Affairs, 1978. 53p.
Broad survey of legal provisions for women and relevant cases in Bangladesh, in nonspecialist's terms. Considers common legal heritage shared by Bangladesh, Pakistan and India. Five sections: introduction, survey of legislative provisions by area (civil, labor, penal, etc.), survey of personal law of various religious communities, legal status of women in tribal areas and conclusions and policy recommendations. [Unexamined. ALB].

iii) Family planning

3926 AHMED, MOHIUDDIN and FATEMA AHMED. Male attitudes toward family limitation in East Pakistan. *In* Eugenics Quarterly 12,4 (1965) 209-26.
Interviews with 195 married men (from Rajshahi?) revealed a close association between the desire for children and factors such as "the number of ever-born children, the num-

ber of living children, the number of living sons, the age and the number of years married." Factors such as income, education level and occupation were found to have a limited association. "The attitude toward birth control indicated close association with education and occupation . . . and limited association with the number of living children and the number of living sons."

3927 AITKEN, ANNIE and JOHN STOECKEL. Muslim-Hindu differentials in family planning knowledge and attitude in rural East Pakistan. *In* J. of Comparative Family Studies 2,1 (1971) 75-87.
Investigates the relationship between religious affiliation and knowledge of and attitudes toward family planning. "Hindus have significantly higher proportions with knowledge and approval of family planning than Muslims." Proposes that as there are no substantial doctrinal differences with respect to family planning, the constraints of Muslim *pardā* observance help to explain the findings. Based on interviews with 2,000 rural women near Comilla.

3928 BANGLADESH ACADEMY FOR RURAL DEVELOPMENT. PILOT PROJECT IN FAMILY PLANNING. Progress report. 1- (1961/62-). Comilla. Annually.
Program is devoted to establishing local social factors relating to fertility, developing a nonmedical family planning program and training local women to promote family planning. Originally issued by Pakistan Academy for Rural Development. [Unexamined. NST].

3929 BAYBASTHAPANA SHANGSAD LIMITED. A desk research report on family planning activities in Bangladesh, 1952-1974. Dacca: the Shangsad, 1974. 133p. [*Cover title* Review of family planning activities of Bangladesh, 1952-74].
Reviews the development of family planning programs and policies and their effects. With recommendations and a large bibliography of primarily unpublished papers.

3930 ________. Study report on knowledge, attitude, and practice of family planning. Dacca: the Shangsad, 1975. 142p.
Study of rural, urban and industrial/semi-urban samples in selected areas of Bangladesh in anticipation of a contraceptive marketing campaign. Chapters on knowledge, attitudes, practices, contraceptive sources and family planning communication media.

3931 CARLAW, RAYMOND W. et al. Underlying sources of agreement and communication between husbands and wives in Dacca, East Pakistan. *In* J. of Marriage and the Family 33,3 (1971) 571-83.
Finds such factors as age of spouses, age of marriage and education to have limited relation to husband-wife communication patterns. Urges inclusion of husbands in family planning programs, development of a more sophisticated communication model and further research regarding husband-wife communication.

3932 HOSSAIN, T. et al., eds. Proceedings of Seminar in Family Planning. Dacca: Ministry of Health and Family Planning, 1973?
Proceedings of seminar held in November 1972. Includes papers on law and family planning, various contraceptive methods, fertility differentials, family planning programs and other topics. Over 800 pages? [Unexamined].

3933 KHAN, A.M. and H.M. CHOLDIN. New "family planners" in rural East Pakistan. *In* Demography 2 (1965) 1-7.
Report of a fertility survey in five villages in the former East Pakistan. Examines the social characteristics of adopters of family planning in order to suggest which segments of the rural population are most ready to adopt family planning after an educational program.

3934 KHAN, ATIQUR R., DOUGLAS H. HUBER and MAKHLISUR RAHMAN. Household distribution of contraceptives in Bangladesh: the rural experience. Dacca: Cholera Research Laboratory, 1977. 16p. (Scientific Report 5).
Compares levels of contraceptive practice in control and oral contraception distribution areas of rural Comilla District. In one year, 1975-76, contraceptive practice rose from about one percent to about fifteen percent in distribution area.

3935 KHAN, ATIQUR RAHMAN, S.M. D'SOUZA and HALIDA HANUM AKHTAR. Menstrual regulation (M.R.) service: a preliminary report. Dacca: Johns Hopkins University Fertility Research Project, 1975. 11p. (FRP Report 2).
Report of a survey made at a model clinic in Dacca that performs menstrual extraction as a birth control technique.

3936 KHAN, ATIQUR RAHMAN et al., comps. A preliminary bibliography of demographic and family planning literature on Bangladesh. Dacca: Johns Hopkins University Fertility Research Project, 1975. 37p. (FRP Report 3).
References to published and unpublished articles and some monographs. No subdivisions, index, annotations.

3937 KHAN, ATIQUR RAHMAN et al. A study of oral pill acceptors of the Bangladesh Postpartum Family Planning Program. Dacca: Ford Foundation, 1975. Iv.
Analysis of national statistics of pill acceptors, 1971-73, who accounted for over two-thirds of all postpartum contraception acceptors. With recommendations and tables.

3938 MANNAN, M.A. Intensive family planning information and service delivery campaign: a short evaluation in Comilla. Comilla: Bangladesh Academy for Rural Development, 1976. 23p.
[Unexamined. NUC].

3939 MOSENA, PATRICIA WIMBERLEY and JOHN STOECKEL. Impact of desired family size upon family planning practices in rural

East Pakistan. *In* J. of Marriage and the Family 33,3 (1971) 567-70.
Study of 1,600 rural women near Comilla found that significantly more women whose actual family size equaled or exceeded desired family size practiced family planning than those who had not yet attained desired family size. Suggests that family planning programs should attempt to influence norms of family size and related factors.

3940 ROBERTS, BERYL J. et al. Family planning survey in Dacca, East Pakistan. *In* Demography 2 (1965) 74-96.
Presents the results of the first family planning survey in an urban setting (Dacca) in East Pakistan. Statistical picture of the correlation between various socio-economic factors and fertility, patterns of knowledge and use of family planning methods and attitudes toward family planning.

3941 STOECKEL, JOHN. Social and demographic correlates of contraceptive adoption in a rural area of East Pakistan. *In* Demography 5,1 (1968) 45-54.
Study of women who purchased contraceptives from "village organizers" of selected villages near Comilla over a five-year period. Long-term adoption (13 months or more) was found to be associated with membership in cooperatives, Hinduism, the 30 or over age group, being married at age 15 or over and six or more parities. Consistent correlations were not found with respect to occupation, education and landholding.

3942 _______ and MOQBUL A. CHOUDHURY. Fertility, infant mortality and family planning in rural Bangladesh. Dacca: Oxford University Press, 1973. 154p.
Study of 1,600 rural women near Comilla that aimed to 1) evaluate impact of current family planning programs on pregnancy and fertility, 2) describe trends in pregnancy, fertility and infant mortality rates, 3) describe prevailing knowledge, attitudes and practices (KAP) relating to family planning, 4) assess methods for obtaining KAP data, 5) identify socio-economic factors relating to KAP and 6) assess norms about family size and their impact on family planning.

3943 YAUKEY, DAVID, WILLIAM GRIFFITHS and BERYL J. ROBERTS. Couple concurrence and empathy on birth control motivation in Dacca, East Pakistan. *In* American Sociological Review 32,5 (1967) 716-27.
Study of 547 Dacca couples found a high rate of husband-wife concurrence regarding family size goals. Attributes concurrence to coincidentally shared views as opposed to husband-wife communication.

3944 YAUKEY, D. et al. Husbands' versus wives' responses to a fertility survey. *In* Population Studies 19 (1965) 29-43. [Unexamined].

(g) Political participation

3945 JAHAN, ROUNAQ. Purdah and participation: women in the politics of Bangladesh. *In* Hanna Papanek, ed. Purdah in South Asia: the segregation of women. Forthcoming.
Assesses role of *pardā* in political participation of women of Bangladesh by examining data on voting behavior in the 1973 elections and on female legislators. Considers the norms of *pardā* to segregate and limit women's public political participation. One striking example relates to the importance of having a senior political patron in Bangladesh politics: aspersions would be cast upon a woman who emphasized such a relationship with a male patron. [Unexamined. Verified with editor].

3946 JALAL, KHURSHID. Women in politics. *In* Women for women: Bangladesh 1975. Dacca: University Press Limited, 1975. pp.204-14.
Reports of interviews with women who entered East Pakistani politics in the 1950s and remained active in politics of Bangladesh in the 1970s to ascertain their socio-economic backgrounds, attitudes toward various social and political issues relating to women and problems as politically active women. Concludes that they are not "political in the real sense of the term," but "basically housewives, with better education and free time at their disposal, pursuing a career that fed their ego and vanity."

(h) Arts

For creative writing in Bengali see entries 3803-43

i) Folk literature

3947 ALAMGIR, JALIL. Women in folklore of East Pakistan. *In* Folklore [Calcutta] 9,10 (1968) 390-400. [*Reprint in* Sankar Sen Gupta, ed. Women in Indian folklore. Calcutta: Indian Publications, 1969. pp.20-32. (*Its* Folklore Series, 15)].
Images of women in various folk forms. Familial topics predominate. Provides examples in Bengali transliteration with English translation or summary.

3948 MITRA, SARAT CHANDRA. On some lullabies and nursery-rhymes from the district of Pābnā in eastern Bengal. *In* J. of the Anthropological Society of

Bombay 12,1 (1920) 129-46.
Texts and commentary. In the lullabies babies are likened to beautiful flowers and birds and exhorted to sleep. The nursery rhymes contain ethnographic data on child care, marriage and aspirations and affections of women.

3949 ________. On some nursery-rhymes from the district of Chittagong in eastern Bengal. *In* J. of the Anthropological Society of Bombay 12,5 (1922?) 564-93.
Collection of nursery rhymes in Bengali and translation, with commentary. The rhymes contain material on marriage ceremonies, the Hindu homestead, behavior of the new bride, personification of the givers of sleep and sunshine as feminine forces and other topics.

3950 SEN, DINESCHANDRA, comp. and ed. Eastern Bengal ballads. Calcutta: University of Calcutta, 1923-32. 4v in 8 parts.
"The female characters in these ballads are by far the most prominent deserving a full analytical criticism." The first part of each volume includes a substantial general introduction, translations of numerous ballads (each with own preface) and illustrations. Second part consists of Bengali texts. Female characters include the "gipsy girl," "true wife," "saintly daughter," "betrothed maiden" and "forsaken lady."

ii) Reading interests

3951 BENGALI ACADEMY. What women read in East Pakistan: a survey. Karachi: National Book Centre of Pakistan, 1964. 60p. (Reading Habits in Pakistan, 3).
Statistically analyzes the results of a survey conducted to elucidate women's interests in Bengali reading materials. Considers books, *pũthi* literature, magazines, newspapers, juvenile literature and materials written or edited by women. Issuing agency is now called Bangla Academy.

(i) Experiences of 1971 Bangladesh war of liberation

3952 Cimmeria. Produced and directed by Robin Dharmaraj. 1972. 9 min. Black and white. 16 mm. [*Distributed by* Robin Dharmaraj, 37 New Marine Lines, Bombay 400 020].
Examines psyche of a young woman of Bangladesh who was raped and subsequently abandoned by her husband in the course of that country's freedom struggle. [Unexamined].

3953 KARKARIA, BACHI J. Raped women of Bangladesh. *In* Illustrated Weekly of India 93,25 (18 Jun 1972) 14-7.
On the problems faced by women who were raped during the Bangladesh freedom struggle and social welfare efforts that emerged to assist them. With photographs, biographical details and an account of a violent attack on a Dacca University dormitory.

(6) North / Central India: area of Hindi-Urdu, Central Pahari and eastern Panjabi languages

(a) The colonial experience: social reform issues

3954 SAXENA, R.K. Social reforms: infanticide and sati. New Delhi: Trimurti Publications, 1975. 155p.
Examines social systems fostering and movements opposing female infanticide and widow immolation in Rajasthan during the first half of the 19th century.

3955 _______. Education and social amelioration of women: a study of Rajasthan. Jaipur: Sanghi Prakashan, 1978. 244p.
Traces movements to extend female education, eliminate *satīs*, permit widow marriage and end child marriage in Rajasthan, from 1818 to 1935.

i) *Satī* / suttee

3956 Attempt to be a sati. *In* Indian Social Reformer 43,2 (10 Sep 1932) 27-8.
Report of a controversy regarding a *satī* in a village of Agra District, United Provinces, that occurred over a century after widow immolation was made illegal in British India.

3957 BUSHBY, HENRY JEFFREYS. Widow burning: a narrative. London: Longman, Brown, Green, and Longmans, 1855? 62p.
Mainly an account of Major Ludlow's campaign to eliminate *satīs* during the 1840s in Rajputana. Includes accounts of *satīs*, observations on the nature of the custom and plans for "teaching the Hindoo a higher and truer civilization." A postscript adds that recent Sanskrit scholarship by Müller and Wilson confirms the "glaring discrepancies" between beliefs and customs such as widow immolation and the scriptures that are purported to support them.

3958 D'GRUYTHER, W.J. Panjab — Rajputana — Pataudi — Jesalmer — burning with dead by men and women — sati — satu. *In* Indian Notes and Queries 4,39 (1886) 44-5.
Account of *mā satī* stones, marking the immolation of mothers upon their sons' deaths. Notes custom of male and female slaves or servants burning with the men or women they have served.

3959 SLEEMAN, W.H. Rambles and recollections of an Indian official, 2d ed., rev. and annotated. Karachi: Oxford University Press, 1973. 667p. (Oxford in Asia Historical Reprints). [*1st ed.* 1844].
Includes a firsthand account of a *satī* in 1829 in Jabalpur District of present-day Madhya Pradesh (pp.18-31).

3960 TEMPLE, RICHARD CARNAC. Panjab — Bashahr — song of a sati — Himalayan dialect. *In* Indian Notes and Queries 4,37 (1886) 17-8.
Transliteration and translation of a song about a woman who became a *satī* in Bashahr in 1800.

ii) Female infanticide

3961 DAS, MANMATHA NATH. Female infanticide among the Bedees and Chauhans: motives and modes. *In* Man in India 36,4 (1956) 261-6.
Report based upon observations by British administrators in northwestern India of the mid-19th century. Identifies various motives and techniques of the two groups.

3962 _______. Movement to suppress the custom of female infanticide in the Punjab and Kashmir. *In* Man in India 37,4 (1957) 280-93.
Native and British efforts in the 1850s. Based on primary sources.

3963 DE LA VALETTE, JOHN. Civic uplift and women's welfare in Kashmir. *In* Asiatic Review n.s. 28,95 (1932) 470-3.
Briefly reviews educational and other reform and welfare efforts with respect to Kashmiri women in the early decades of the 20th century.

3964 Female infanticide. *In* Asiatic Journal n.s. 3,10 (1830) 164-7.
Argues that the abstract statements of zealous reformers are a hindrance to actual reform: "No practical scheme of dealing with the deep-rooted prejudices of superstition or policy from whence these customs have originated, is pointed out." Argues that female infanticide chiefly prevails among Rajput communities for sociologically comprehensible reasons and that these people are British allies and not subjects. Gives some ethnographic data.

3965 L., M. Female infanticide in the Punjab. *In* Calcutta Review 104 (Jan 1897) 145-76.
Covers the history, causes, past ineffective

British solutions and recommended solutions. Causes include "pride of race," "disgrace of having a son-in-law" and the economic burdens of providing a dowry and maintaining relations with the son-in-law. Proposed remedies include "subjecting the whole population of a particular class to punishment" in a village where the offender is sheltered by the sympathy of other villagers and female education and technical training.

3966 NORTH-WESTERN PROVINCES. Reports on measures adopted in the district of Mynpoory for the future prevention of female infanticide. [Agra: Secundra Orphan Press, 1855]. 10p. (Selections from the Records of Government, North-Western Provinces 3, no. 12, article 1).
Covers 1844-51 period. Discusses causes of infanticide and government opposition to it. [Unexamined. NUC].

3967 ________. Female infanticide. [Allahabad: Government Press, 1866]. 90p. (Selections from the Records of Government, North-Western Provinces n.s. 2, no. 2].
During the years 1848-54. [Unexamined. NUC].

3968 ________. Female infanticide in the Jounpore District. By E.T. Atkinson. [Allahabad: Government Press, 1870]. pp.139-48. (Selections from the Records of the Government of the North-Western Provinces, 2d series 3, no. 2, article 9).
In the year 1866. [Unexamined. NUC].

3969 ________. Female infanticide in Agra District. By R. Benson. [Allahabad: Government Press, 1870]. pp.273-96. (Selections from the Records of Government, North-Western Provinces, 2d series 3, no. 3, article 17).
Discusses causes of female infanticide and government's policy and actions. Gives sex ratio figures. Covers 1854-69. [Unexamined. NUC].

3970 ________. Female infanticide in Pergunnah Bara, Zillah Allahabad. By T.W. Rawlins. [Allahabad: Government Press, 1870]. pp.297-305. (Selections from the Records of Government, North-Western Provinces, 2d series 3, no. 3, article 18).
In the year 1869. [Unexamined. NUC].

3971 ________. Female infanticide in the N.-W.P. By R. Simson. 1871? 112p. (Selections from the Records of Government, North-Western Provinces, 2d series, article 1).
[Unexamined. NUC].

3972 NORTH-WESTERN PROVINCES. INFANTICIDE COMMITTEE. Report of the proceedings. Allahabad, 1870. 33p. [*Chair* J.D. Inglis].
[Unexamined].

3973 O'BRIAN, A.J. Female infanticide in the Punjab. *In* Folklore [London] 19 (1908) 261-75.
Examines relationship of female infanticide to importance of female chastity for family honor, hypergamous marriages and obligation to marry females. Provides ethnographic examples.

3974 PUNJAB. Minute on infanticide in the Punjab. By R. Montgomery. Lahore: Chronicle Press, 1853. (Selections from the Public Correspondence of the Punjab Administration, 16).
Concerns the period 1851-53. [Unexamined].

3975 VASHISHTHA, V.K. Abolition of female infanticide in Rajputana. *In* J. of the Rajasthan Institute of Historical Research 11,4 (1974) 29-34.
"The purpose of this study is to trace the British policy in abolishing female infanticide in the States of Rajputana and to examine the methods by which it succeeded." Based on contemporary documents.

iii) Education and health

3976 AGHA, SHARKESHWARI. Some aspects of the education of women in U.P. Allahabad, 1933.
[Unexamined].

3977 BROWN, EDITH. Indian women and the village: the time for action. *In* Asiatic Review n.s. 35,121 (1939) 1-9. *With* Discussion, pp.10-6.
"I refer to questions of health, sanitation, rural uplift and medical aid, matters with which I have been closely in touch for forty-seven years, and matters which must largely be dealt with by women." Discusses Women's Christian Medical College, Ludhiana, and proposes a village health scheme.

3978 ________. Training Indian women doctors: Ludhiana Women's Christian Medical College. *In* Missionary Review of the World 62 (Sep 1939) 405-8.
Illustrated. [Unexamined].

3979 CONDICT, ALICE B. Just what they need: the story of the North India school of medicine for Christian women . . . London: Morgan, n.d. 32p.
Illustrated pamphlet concerning the Women's Christian Medical College, Ludhiana. [Unexamined. MRL].

3980 FLEMING, DANIEL JOHNSON. A commonwealth of girls. *In his* Schools with a message in India. London: Oxford University Press, 1929. pp.77-96.
Account of the Industrial Settlement, Baptist Zenana Mission, at Salamatpur near Delhi, based upon annual reports and correspondence. Includes details of its various programs (e.g., Montessori education, industrial work, "fam-

ily system" home life training) and of the organization of the community and particular problems it has faced.

3981 FRENCH, FRANCESCA. Miss Brown's hospital: the story of the Ludhiana Medical College and Dame Edith Brown, D.B.E., its founder. London: Hodder and Stoughton, 1954. 120p.
Following medical training in Edinburgh, Dr. Brown established the Women's Christian Medical College, Ludhiana, where she served for nearly 50 years. Describes growth of facilities and services of the college. Illustrated. [Unexamined. NUC].

3982 TINLING, CHRISTINE I. India's womanhood: forty years' work at Ludhiana. London: Lutterworth Press, 1935. 119p.
On the Women's Christian Medical College, Ludhiana. Illustrated. [Unexamined. NUC].

3983 WOMEN'S CHRISTIAN MEDICAL COLLEGE. Report. 1- (1894/95-). Ludhiana. Annually.
[Unexamined. MRL].

iv) Village uplift

3984 BRAYNE, F.L. The remaking of village India: being the second edition of 'Village Uplift in India'. London: Humphrey Milford, Oxford University Press, 1929. 262p.
Report of a rural uplift program in Gurgaon District. The second edition incorporates material on female and infant uplift. See chapter entitled "Women's Welfare Work" (pp.84-99) and interspersed material throughout. Describes efforts made and offers recommendations in numerous areas.

(b) The colonial experience: autobiography documenting social history

3985 NANDA, SAVITRI DEVI. The city of two gateways: the autobiography of an Indian girl. London: Allen and Unwin, 1950. 278p.
The author recalls growing up in an aristocratic Hindu family of the Punjab, her education at the urging of her father, her resistance to marriage and her preparations to continue studies in England. Covers her first 19 years.

(c) The colonial experience: ruling families of native/princely states

See also entries 768-70

i) Royal women of Oudh

3986 KNIGHTON, WILLIAM. The private life of an eastern king. New York: J.S. Redfield, 1855? 246p.
A narrative "compiled from the notes I took of passing events during the three and a half years that I lived in the court of Lucknow." The chapter "The King's Harem" (pp.152-72) contains secondary information on life in the royal harem. Discussions of dancing girls, female attendants, a wedding and other topics are found elsewhere. Author was "a member of the household of His . . . Majesty, Nussir-u-Deen, King of Oude."

3987 _______. Elihu Jan's story: or, the private life of an eastern queen. London: Longman, Green, Longman, Roberts, Green, 1865. 210p.
The "life of Janáb Aulia, wife of Amjad 'Ali, and mother of Wajid 'Ali, Kings of Oudh, as told by one of her attendants." [Unexamined. NUC].

ii) Bhopal Begam-Nawabs

3988 KNOWLES-FOSTER, FRANCES G. One of India's most interesting queens and authoresses, Her Highness the Begum of Bhopal: a few historical notes upon her state and personality. *In* Asiatic Review n.s. 3,6 (1914) 275-8.
Briefly discusses Sultan Jahan Begam who, while observing *pardā*, assumed rule of Bhopal in 1901. Notes some of her female predecessors.

3989 SULTAN JAHAN BEGAM, NAWAB OF BHOPAL. An account of my life. Tr. from Urdu by C.H. Payne (v1, v3) and Abdus Samad Khan (v2). London: John Murray (v1) and Bombay: Times Press (v2-3), 1910-27. 3v.
Lengthy autobiography of the woman who, following her grandmother and mother, ruled Bhopal from 1901 to 1926. She writes, she tells us, to share the experiences of herself and her family and the history of Bhopal with future family members, Bhopal subjects and fellow rulers in India. Sultan Jahan Begam discusses family life, travels, state functions, social and administrative reforms, female education, Bhopal history, pilgrimage, etc. Numerous photographs.

3990 _______. Hayat-i-Qudsi: life of the Nawab Gauhar Begum alias the Nawab Begum Qudsia, of Bhopal. Tr. from Urdu by W.S. Davis. London: K. Paul, Trench, Trubner, 1918. 160p. [*Also* New York:

E.P. Dutton].
Sultan Jahan Begam's biography of her great-grandmother, also a regent of Bhopal. Plates. [Unexamined. NUC].

3991 ________. Hayat-i-Shahjehani: life of her highness the late Nawab Shahjehan Begum of Bhopal, C.I., G.C.S.I. Tr. from Urdu by B. Ghosal. Bombay: Times Press, 1926. 301p.
Biography of author's mother and predecessor as ruler of Bhopal. Discusses Shah Jahan Begam's childhood; accession to Bhopal rule; marriage arrangements; administrative structure, personnel and reforms; involvement in various all-India political matters; good relationship with British; ceremonial events; travels; writings (including the first "Women's Encyclopedia" printed in India); and death. With photographs and 25 appendixes that reproduce various documents.

3992 VADIVELU, A. Her Highness the Nawab Sultan Jahan Begum, G.C.S.I., G.C.I.E., C.I., Begum of Bhopal. *In his* The ruling chiefs, nobles and zamindars of India, v1. Madras: G.C. Loganadham Brothers, 1915. pp.84-94.
Reviews interests, experiences and activities of Sultan Jahan Begam. With a brief history of Bhopal State.

iii) Rajputana princesses

3993 H.H. THE DOWAGER MAHARANI OF COOCH BEHAR [SUNITI DEVI, MAHARANI OF COOCH BEHAR]. The Rajput princesses. London: W. Straker, 19__. 1v.
[Unexamined. NUC].

3994 PLUNKETT, FRANCES TAFT. Royal marriages in Rajasthan. *In* Contributions to Indian Sociology n.s. 7 (1973) 64-80.
Presents data on marriage among the ruling houses of Rajasthan as examples of dynastic marriages in Hindu North India. Considers the interrelationship of polygyny, alliance and exchange and hypergamy, focusing on the 19th and 20th centuries. One finding is that Mewar, generally considered to be the chief state, neither killed its daughters nor prohibited them from marrying as might be expected: "While rulers married girls from non-royal houses on a hypergamous basis, among themselves the States functioned more importantly as receivers of each other's girls in a generally reciprocal pattern [than] as bride-takers in a strictly hypergamous sense."

iv) Sikh princesses of the Punjab

3995 AHLUWALIA, M. Mai Chand Kaur's rule in the Punjab: an estimate. *In* India (Republic). Indian Historical Records Commission 31, 1955, Mysore. Proceedings 31. Delhi: Albion Press, 1955? Second part, pp.65-74.
Reviews political life of Chand Kaur: her birth to the leader of Kanhaya ***misal***, her marriage to Ranjit Singh's heir, the death of her husband and only son, squabbling and maneuvering at the 1840 Lahore Durbar and problems of her month-long rule ("how a lady behind the pardah could manage to govern the nation of warriors and how far she could succeed in suppressing those very evil forces which she had herself allowed to develop at the Court with a view to gain her own end").

3996 NIJJAR, BAKHSHISH SINGH. Maharani Jind Kaur: the queen-mother of Maharaja Dalip Singh. New Delhi: K.B. Publications, 1975. 72p.
Detailed study of the life of the youngest wife of Maharaja Ranjit Singh to assess her role and responsibility in the loss of the Sikh kingdom of the Punjab in the mid-19th century. Based largely on official British records. Appendixes reproduce letters and other documents in translation and transliteration.

3997 SINGH, GANDA. Maharani Jind Kaur of Lahore. *In* Illustrated Weekly of India 60? (22 Jan 1939).
[Unexamined].

3998 ________. Three letters of Maharani Jind Kaur. *In* Indian History Congress 13, 1950, Nagpur. Proceedings 13. pp.304-13. [*Also in* J. of Indian History 42,1 (1964) 265-80].
Translations of and background to three letters written in 1847 by Jind Kaur to John Lawrence regarding East India Company imperialism in the Punjab and her incarceration.

(d) The colonial experience: women and the Mutiny of 1857-58

i) The Rani of Jhansi

3999 BURN, R. and PATRICK CADELL. Rani Lakshmi Bai of Jhansi. *In* J. of the Royal Asiatic Society (1944) 76-8.
Takes issue with Kincaid who sought to exonerate Lakshmibai from any part in the massacre of the English at Jhansi during the Mutiny. She was, says the author, quoting Sir Evelyn Wood, "the bravest and most implacable of our foes."

4000 KINCAID, CHARLES AUGUSTUS. Lakshmibai Rani of Jhansi. *In* J. of the Royal Asiatic Society (1943) 100-4.
Account of Lakshmibai's role in the Mutiny and her political activities shortly thereafter. Argues that she cannot be considered to be a mutineer or a rebel and that her good character and gallantry must be recognized. Cites Hugh Rose's epitaph of her: "The best

man on the side of the enemy was the Rani of Jhansi."

4001 ________. Lakshmibai, Rani of Jhansi. *In his* Lakshmibai, Rani of Jhansi and other essays. London, 194_.
Defends Lakshmibai's involvement in Mutiny. Presents background of her efforts for the succession of Jhansi from the Dalhousie administration and proposes that she was not responsible for the massacre of English prisoners by Jhansi mutineers. [Unexamined. NUC].

4002 KULKARNI, V.B. Rani Lakshmibai. *In his* Heroes who made history. Bombay: Bharatiya Vidya Bhavan, 1965. pp.197-204.
Brief sketch of Lakshmibai's part in the events surrounding the Mutiny.

4003 LANG, JOHN. Wanderings in India: and other sketches of life in Hindostan. London: Routledge, Warne, and Routledge, 1859. 415p.
Contains account of a visit to the Rani of Jhansi before the Mutiny. [Unexamined. Book in NUC].

4004 MAJUMDAR, R.C., ed. Some unpublished documents regarding the Mutiny of 1857. *In* Bengal: Past and Present 76,142 (1957) 45-70.
Newly found papers that raise doubts about participation of Rani Lakshmibai of Jhansi in the Mutiny of 1857. They reveal that at the time of the Mutiny, the rani was engaged in fighting against her own people, not against the British. Later, having learned the British held her responsible for the Mutiny, she joined the fight against them and displayed heroic courage and military skill in the campaigns.

4004a SMYTH, JOHN. The rebellious rani. London: Frederick Muller Ltd., 1966. 223p.
"I have started this book by briefly setting the scene of the Mutiny as a whole and then, in that context, have told the story of the Rani and the Central India Field Force .... two brilliant and forceful personalities emerge — the Rani and Sir Hugh Rose." Based on documents from the India Office Library. Illustrated.

4005 TAHMANKAR, D.V. The Ranee of Jhansi. London: MacGibbon and Kee, 1958. 178p. [*Also* Bombay: Jaico Publishing House, 1961. 166p.].
By citing evidence overlooked or unavailable to British historians, the author tries to show that the rani of Jhansi was not the originator of the 1857 Mutiny and only participated in its leadership in a late phase. Portrays the rani as a courageous and patriotic woman whose fight to regain sovereignty over her state became a fight against the British. Photographs and illustrations.

4006 TAIMURI, M.H.R. Some unpublished documents on the death of the rani of Jhansi and the Mutiny in Central India. *In* India (Republic). Indian Historical Records Commission 29, 1953, Bhopal. Proceedings 29. n.p., n.d. Second part, pp.157-9.
Reviews contents of six letters to Sikandar Begam, Nawab of Bhopal, from her representative to the political agent to the governor-general in Central India concerning political events of 1858. Provides translation of letter about Lakshmibai's death in battle.

4007 VAIDYA, G.M. Rani Lakshmibai. Poona: Vidarbha Marathwada, 1965. 34p. (Makers of India, 10).
[Unexamined. IBP].

4008 VERMA, S.K. Women warriors of 1857. *In* Illustrated Weekly of India 78 (18 Aug 1957).
[Unexamined].

4009 Women warriors in India. *In* United Service Magazine 175 (1916).
[Unexamined].

ii) Accounts by and of westerners

4010 [BARTRUM, KATHERINE MARY]. A widow's reminiscences of the siege of Lucknow. London: J. Nisbet and Company, 1858. 102p.
[Unexamined. NUC].

4011 BENNETT, AMELIA. Ten months' captivity after the massacre at Cawnpore. *In* Nineteenth Century and After 73,436 and 74,437 (1913) 1212-34, 78-91.
A 74-year-old Englishwoman's recollections of her experiences as an 18-year-old girl during the Indian Mutiny. She describes burning of the barracks, a massacre at the ghat, her capture by a sepoy, her forced conversion to Islam, marching with rebels, ten months of captivity and her advocacy for pardon of her sepoy captor in return for her freedom.

4012 CASE, MRS. [ADELAIDE TEAGUE CASE]. Day by day at Lucknow: a journal of the siege of Lucknow. London: R. Bentley, 1858. 348p.
[Unexamined. NUC].

4013 COOPLAND, MRS. R.M. A lady's escape from Gwalior and life in the fort of Agra during the Mutinies of 1857. London: Smith, Elder and Company, 1859. 316p.
[Unexamined. NUC].

4014 DUBERLY, MRS. HENRY [FRANCES ISABELLA (LOCKE) DUBERLY]. Campaigning experiences in Rajpootana and Central India during the suppression of the Mutiny, 1857-1858. London: Smith, Elder, 1859. 254p.
[Unexamined].

4015 GERMON, MARIA. Michael Edwardes, ed. Journal of the siege of Lucknow: an

episode of the Indian Mutiny. London: Constable Publishers, [1958]. 136p.
Vivid eyewitness account of the Mutiny in Lucknow by the wife of an English officer.

4016 HALDANE, JULIA. The story of our escape from Delhi in 1857. Agra: S. Brown and Sons, 1888. 26p.
[Unexamined. BMG].

4017 HARRIS, KATHERINE. A lady's diary of the siege of Lucknow. London: John Murray, 1858. 208p.
[Unexamined].

4018 HUMPHREY, MRS. E.J. Heerah: a story of the sepoy Mutiny. Boston: Long and Putnam, 1878? 192p.
Author was a missionary. [Unexamined. NUC].

4019 INGLIS, JULIA SELINA. The siege of Lucknow: a diary. London: James R. Osgood, McIlvaine and Company, 1893. 224p. [*Also* Leipzig: B. Tauchnitz, 1892. 255p. *And* New York: C. Scribner's Sons, 1892. 240p.].
[Unexamined. NUC].

4020 JACKSON, ALICE F. A brave girl: a true story of the Indian Mutiny. London: Christian Knowledge Society, 1899. 127p.
Tale for children? [Unexamined. BMG].

4021 [MAC KENZIE, HELEN DOUGLAS]. Englishwomen in the rebellion. *In* Calcutta Review 33 (Sep 1859) 108-26.
Relates incidents of feminine bravery and fortitude bolstered by unflinching faith: "So long as we have Christian Officers as well as Christian women we do not fear for India." Drawn from various firsthand accounts.

4022 MAC MUNN, GEORGE. Mees Dolly: an untold tragedy of '57. *In* Cornhill Magazine n.s. 63 (Sep 1927) 327-31.
Investigates accuracy of a statement from a letter by Field-Marshal Sir Henry Norman that a European woman was involved in the 1857 uprising at Meerut and subsequently hanged for it. Offers various bits of information that support the statement and fill in some of the background.

4023 MOORE, KATE. At Meerut during the Mutiny: a lady's narrative of her experiences during the outbreak. *In* Nineteenth Century and After 54,321 (1903) 826-38.
Narrative of the events relating to the Mutiny in Meerut in the eyes of a young woman of 18. Originally written as private account to author's nephew.

4024 MUTER, MRS. D.D. [ELIZABETH MC MULLIN MUTER]. Travels and adventures of an officer's wife in India, China, and New Zealand. London: Hurst and Blackett, 1864. 2v.
[Unexamined. NUC].

4025 ________. My recollections of the sepoy revolt, 1857-1858. London: John Long, 1911. 266p.
Account of events at Meerut by the wife of a military officer. [Unexamined. NUC].

4026 OUVRY, M.H. A lady's diary before and during the Indian Mutiny. Lymington: printed by C.T. King, 1892. 166p.
Author was an officer's wife. Much on her personal life. [Unexamined. NUC].

4027 PAGET, MRS. LEOPOLD [GEORGIANA THEODOSIA (FITZMOOR-HALSEY) PAGET]. Camp and cantonment: a journal of life in India in 1857-1859, with some account of the way thither; to which is added a short account of the pursuit of the rebels in Central India by Major Paget. London: Longman, Green, Longman, Roberts, and Green, 1865. 469p.
Diary of an officer's wife. [Unexamined. NUC].

4028 SOPPITT, MRS. Diary of an officer's wife. *In* W.H. Fitchett. The tale of the great Mutiny, 2d ed., enl. London: J. Murray, 1912.
[Unexamined. Book in NUC].

4029 TAYLOR, MEADOWS [PHILIP MEADOWS TAYLOR]. Seeta, 5th ed. London: Kegan Paul, Trench and Company, 1887. 442p.
Novel. Portrays the love of a noble Hindu widow and an English officer during the Mutiny.

4030 TISDALL, E.E.P. Mrs. Duberly's campaigns: an Englishwoman's experiences in the Crimean War and Indian Mutiny. Chicago: Rand McNally, 1963. 224p.
In India, Fanny Duberly traveled through Rajputana with her husband whose troops pursued Tantia Topee. Based on her published journals and letters to her sister.

4031 TYTLER, HARRIET C. Through the Sepoy Mutiny and the siege of Delhi: a personal narrative. *In* Chamber's Journal 21 (1931) 1-4, 21-3, 46-8, 55-8, 72-5, 86-8, 101-4, 119-21, 135-7, 155-8, 172-4, 187-90, 200-1.
Recollections of events from May 1857 to May 1858 made in 1894 by a woman who was wife and daughter of British officials. "As the *only* lady who went through the whole siege, I have been led to believe that a simple narrative from myself might interest others."

(e) The colonial experience: western women in other capacities

i) Missionaries

4032 ANDERSON, EMMA DEAN and MARY JANE CAMPBELL. In the shadow of the Himalayas: a historical narrative of the missions of the United Presbyterian Church of North America as conducted in the Punjab, India, 1855-1940.

Pittsburgh: Women's General Missionary Society, 1942.
[Unexamined. NUC].

4033 CAMPBELL, MARY JANE. One hundred girls of India . . . an account of incidents occurring during Miss Campbell's connection with the girls' boarding school at Sialkot, in the Punjab, India. Columbus, Ohio: Hann and Adair, 1900. 95p.
Illustrated. [Unexamined. NUC].

4034 _______. The power-house at Pathankot: what some girls of India wrought by prayer. Philadelphia: Board of Foreign Missions of the United Presbyterian Church of North America, 1918? 192p.
On missions and temperance. With plates and portraits. [Unexamined. NUC].

4035 CAVALIER, A.R. In northern India: a story of mission work in zenanas, hospitals, schools, and villages. London: S.W. Partridge, 1899. 174p.
Introduction by Lord Kinnaird. [Unexamined. NUC].

4036 EMERY, G.W. and M.W. ANDERSON. Things touching the king: the story of the Duchess of Teck Hospital. London: Marshall, Morgan and Scott, 1952? 125p.
Concerning a hospital in Patna. Apparently a project of the Zenana Bible and Medical Mission. [Unexamined. MRL].

4037 GREENFIELD, M. ROSE. Five years in Ludhiana: or, work amongst our Indian sisters. London: Partridge, 1886. 128p.
Work in zenana missions. [Unexamined. MRL].

4038 HAYES, MARIE ELIZABETH. Her mother, ed. At work: letters of Marie Elizabeth Hayes, M.B., missionary doctor, Delhi, 1905-8. London: Marshall Brothers, 1909. 263p.
Letters of Dr. Hayes and her coworkers, edited by her mother. She received special training in tropical medicine and was director of a mission hospital in Rewari at the time of her premature death. Photographs. [Unexamined. NUC].

4039 HOLCOMB, HELEN H. Mabel's summer in the Himalayas. Philadelphia: Presbyterian Board of Publication, 1886. 192p.
Author was a missionary in Bundelkhand. [Unexamined. NUC].

4040 _______. Bits about India. Philadelphia: Presbyterian Board of Publication, 1888? 272p.
A missionary writes about social life and customs in India. Illustrated. [Unexamined. NUC].

4041 _______. King's daughter and other sketches: or, women as seen and taught in Indian zenanas. Philadelphia: Westminster Press, n.d. 143p.
[Unexamined. MRL].

4042 HOLCOMB, JAMES F. and HELEN H. HOLCOMB. In the heart of India: or, beginnings of missionary work in Bundela Land; with a short chapter on the characteristics of Bundelkhand and its people, and four chapters of Jhansi history. Philadelphia: Westminster Press, 1905. 251p.
[Unexamined. NUC].

4043 HOSKINS, MRS. ROBERT [CHARLOTTE LEWIS (ROUNDEY) HOSKINS]. Clara A. Swain, M.D.: first medical missionary to the women of the orient. Boston: Woman's Foreign Missionary Society, Methodist Episcopal Church, 1912? 31p.
Following medical training at the Woman's Medical College of Pennsylvania, Dr. Swain went to India. In Bareilly she opened a women's hospital and taught medical skills to Indian women. In Khetri she served as physician to a maharani. Photographs. [Unexamined. NUC].

4044 MAC KENZIE, MRS. COLIN [HELEN (DOUGLAS) MAC KENZIE]. Life in the mission, the camp, and the zenana: or, six years in India. London: R. Bentley, 1853. 3v. [*Also* New York: Redfield, 1853. 2v. *Also published as* Six years in India; Delhi: the city of the great Mogul; with an account of the various tribes in Hindostan: Hindoos, Sikhs, Affghans, etc. London: R. Bentley, 1857. 288p.].
[Unexamined. NUC].

4045 [_______]. Journal of six years in India. *In* Calcutta Review 21,42 (1853) 524-44.
[Unexamined].

4046 MACLEOD, ANNE C. [ANNE CAMPBELL (MACLEOD) WILSON]. Five years in India: or, life and work in a Punjaub district. London: Blackie and Son, 1895. 312p.
[Unexamined. BMG].

4047 _______. Letters from India, 1889-1909. Edinburgh: William Blackwood and Sons, 1911. 417p.
On life in India. [Unexamined. BMG].

4048 RICHARDS, E.J. Memoirs of Mrs. Anna Maria Morrison, of the North India mission. New York: M.W. Dodd, 1843. 176p.
Mrs. Anna Maria (Ward) Morrison, 1814-1838, worked in Punjab. [Unexamined. NUC].

4049 The story of the Delhi mission. Westminster: Society for the Propagation of the Gospel in Foreign Parts, 1908. 171p.
See chapters on "The Women of Delhi" and "The Medical Mission" by Mabel Stevenson and on "Zenana Work," "Girls' Schools" and "St. Mary's Home" by Deaconess Julia. Photographs.

4050 SWAIN, CLARA A. A glimpse of India: being a collection of extracts from the letters of Dr. Clara A. Swain, first medical missionary to India of

the Woman's Foreign Missionary Society of the Methodist Episcopal Church in America. New York: J. Pott and Company, 1909. 366p.
Edited letters, primarily written to author's sister, on mission life and impressions of India. One major section relates to her work in Bareilly where she established a women's hospital and taught medical skills to Indian women. Another section details her work in Khetri as a maharani's physician. [Unexamined. MRL].

4051 WILSON, DOROTHY CLARKE. Palace of healing: the story of Dr. Clara Swain, first woman missionary doctor, and the hospital she founded. New York: McGraw-Hill Book Company, 1968. 245p.
Story of Dr. Swain and the establishment and growth of the first hospital for women in India, now the Clara Swain Hospital, at Bareilly. [Unexamined].

4052 YOUNG, MIRIAM. Among the women of the Punjab: a camping record. London: Carey Press, 1916. 139p.
Account of a three-month "camping tour" through Panjabi villages by an English missionary. Though written in the third person, it seems to be an autobiographical account. Photographs.

4053 ________. Seen and heard in a Punjab village. London: Student Christian Movement Press, 1931. 228p.
Report of an experiment. An Englishwoman established a household with a companion in the village of "Khera." They lived there for three years, attempting to learn as much about village life as possible. Later in their stay they made cautious and largely unsuccessful efforts at Christian conversion. Much of the account centers around a brahman widow, their "guide, philosopher and friend."

ii) Relatives of civil servants

4054 ASHBY, LILLIAN LUKER. My India: recollections of fifty years. Boston: Little, Brown and Company, 1937. 287p. [*Also* London: Michael Joseph Ltd., 1938. 352p.].
The life story of Lillian Ashby, an Englishwoman who lived in India for more than 50 years as the daughter (third generation to be born in India) and then the wife of police officers. Her autobiography covers her life through later years and includes daily life sketches, memorable experiences and anecdotes, observations and reflections on life in India. Photographs.

4055 ASHMORE, HARRIETTE. Narrative of a three months' march in India, and a residence in the Dooab; by the wife of an officer in the 16th foot . . . London: R. Hastings, 1841. 354p.
Travel and description. [Unexamined. NUC].

4055a PARKS, FANNY [FANNY (PARKS) PARLBY]. Wanderings of a pilgrim in search of the picturesque. Karachi: Oxford University Press, 1975. 2v. (Oxford in Asia Historical Reprints). [*Reprint of* Wanderings of a pilgrim, in search of the picturesque, during four-and-twenty years in the East: with revelations of life in the zenāna. London: Pelham Richardson, 1850. 2v].
The wife of an East India Company employee stationed primarily at Allahabad, Fanny Parks spent the second quarter of the 19th century in North India. Her lengthy diary recounts her experiences there — extensive travels, adventures, hobbies, acquaintances and so forth. Includes much on British social life in India of the period and extensive observations about upper-class women in and out of zenanas. Illustrated, primarily by the author. Reprint edition includes introduction and notes by Esther Chawner.

4056 TWO SISTERS [MADELINE ANNE WALLACE-DUNLOP and ROSALIND HARRIET MARIA (WALLACE-DUNLOP) INVERARITY]. The timely retreat: or, a year in Bengal before the Mutinies. London: Richard Bentley, 1858. 2v.
Two sisters recount their travels and residence in Meerut as guests of their brother, a company official stationed there. Upon arriving they quickly "started on the sea of Indian life, receiving visitors, &c." Much on social life and sea and overland travel conditions.

4056a Wanderings of a pilgrim in the East. *In* Calcutta Review 15,30 (1851) 475-500.
Reviews ***Wanderings of a Pilgrim in Search of the Picturesque*** by Fanny Parks. Includes lengthy excerpts and observations. The reviewer laments her unrefined attitude as evidenced by her invocation to the Hindu deity Gaṇeśa, the "levity . . . with which she refers to her own faith" and her lack of philanthropic zeal.

(f) General statements
i) Ethnographic contexts

4057 AGNIHOTRI, HARENDRA KUMAR. Status of women in Jaganpur village. *In* Agra University J. of Research, Letters 22, 2 (1974) 49-56.
[Unexamined].

4058 BERREMAN, GERALD D. Hindus of the Himalayas: ethnography and change, 2d ed., rev. and enl. Berkeley: University of California Press, 1972. 440p. [*1st ed.* 1963].
Ethnography of "Sirkanda" village of the lower Himalayas in western U.P. contains various details of lives and social position of women.

"The nature of Pahari economic organization has ramifications in the position of women, which is one of unusual freedom compared to that of high-caste plains women. Like low-caste women of the plains, hill women participate in the economy in a way incompatible with seclusion . . ."

4059 JACOBSON, DORANNE. The women of North and Central India: goddesses and wives. *In* Carolyn J. Matthiasson, ed. Many sisters: women in cross-cultural perspective. New York: Free Press, 1974. pp.99-175. [*Reprint in* Doranne Jacobson and Susan S. Wadley. Women in India: two perspectives. Columbia, Missouri: South Asia Books, 1977. pp.17-111].
Reviews diversity of life patterns of contemporary, primarily rural, women residing north of the Narmada River in India. Numerous illustrations.

4060 Looking behind mud walls, 1925-1975. Narrated by Charlotte V. Wiser. 1975. 167 frames. Black and white and color. [*Distributed by* Asian Studies Curriculum Center, 735 East Building, Washington Square, New York University, New York, New York 10003].
Filmstrip of life in "Karimpur" village as it was during the Wisers' first residence there and when Mrs. Wiser returned several decades later. Includes material on life in the village's courtyards. Portrays families discussed in Charlotte Wiser's ***Four Families of Karimpur***. [Unexamined].

4061 LUSCHINSKY, MILDRED STROOP. The life of women in a village of North India: a study of role and status. Ph.D. dissertation, Cornell University, 1962. 767p. [University Microfilms 63-749].
Comprehensive description of attitudes and activities of women in a U.P. village. Considers child rearing, socialization, education, life cycle, marriage, family life, kin relations, domestic and remunerative work, divorce, widowhood, political activity, religious activity and other topics. Includes many informants' statements. Discusses outsiders' images of Indian women.

4062 MEER HASSAN ALI, MRS. Observations on the Mussulmauns of India: descriptive of their manners, customs, habits, and religious opinions made during a twelve years' residence in their immediate society. Delhi: Oxford University Press, 1974. 442p. [*Reprint of* 2d ed. W. Crooke. ed. London: Humphrey Milford, Oxford University Press, 1917. *1st ed.* London: Parbury, Allen, 1832].
Record of the impressions and observations of an Englishwoman who married a Lucknow official and lived in India for twelve years in the early 19th century. Although the author tells us little about herself, she provides much information on such topics as the five pillars of Islām, calendrical festivals, wedding ceremonies, seclusion of women and zenana life, plurality of wives and birth and management of children among Muslims of the Lucknow area.

4063 MINTURN, LEIGH and JOHN T. HITCHCOCK. The Rājpūts of Khalapur, India. New York: John Wiley and Sons, 1966. 158p. (Six Cultures Series, 3). [*Also in* Beatrice B. Whiting, ed. Six cultures: studies of child rearing. New York: John Wiley and Sons, 1963. pp.203-361].
First part is an ethnographic survey of the Rajput community of Khalapur village, Saharanpur District; second part focuses on Rajput child rearing patterns. Both sections contain much material about women's lives. The volume edited by Beatrice Whiting includes reports of five other comparable studies conducted elsewhere in the world.

4064 North Indian village. Produced by Patricia J. Hitchcock, John T. Hitchcock and Morris L. Opler. 1955. 32 min. Color. 16 mm. [*Distributed by* International Film Bureau, 332 S. Michigan Avenue, Chicago, Illinois 60604. *And* School of Education, Boston University, 765 Commonwealth Avenue, Boston, Massachusetts 02215].
Some footage from this film portrays male-female relationships, within the family and in other settings. From a Cornell University anthropology project. Khalapur village in U.P. [Unexamined. NUC].

4065 SINGH, INDERA P. A Sikh village. *In* J. of American Folklore 71 (1958) 479-503. [*Also in* Milton Singer, ed. Traditional India: structure and change. Philadelphia: American Folklore Society, 1959. pp.273-97].
Survey of the various communities, major festivals and aspects of Sikh values and social life in Daleke village, Amritsar District. Has brief section, "Women of Daleke," which briefly discusses work, widows, family position, political influence, female infanticide and other topics.

4066 TOD, JAMES. Chapter 23. *And* Chapter 24. *In his* Annals and antiquities of Rajasthan, or the central and western Rajput states of India, v2. Ed. by William Crooke. London: Humphrey Milford, Oxford University Press, 1920. pp.707-59. [*1st ed.* 1830?].
These two chapters in particular in Tod's account of the history and social life of and his own experiences in Rajputana contain much material on women. Topics include ***satīs***, ***jauhar***, Rajput treatment of women, seclusion, devotion and courage of Rajput women (with anecdotal examples), infanticide, influence of women on society and dress and domestic life.

4066a UPRETI, H.C. The position of women among Khasas of Kumaon. *In* J. of Social Research 10,1 (1967) 37-45.
Describes various aspects of the "pitiable" position of the women of this community and discusses recent influences that are having an ameliorating effect.

4067 WISER, CHARLOTTE V. Four families of

Karimpur. Syracuse, New York: Maxwell School of Citizenship and Public Affairs, Syracuse University, 1978. 229p. (Foreign and Comparative Studies, South Asia Series, 4).
Discusses changes that have come to four families of "Karimpur" village over several generations. The author, who has lived there intermittently over 50 years, writes of agriculturalist, oil-presser, carpenter and brahman families. Mrs. Wiser has had access to and interest in women's lives, details of which are prominent in the book.

4068 WISER, WILLIAM and CHARLOTTE WISER. Behind mud walls, 1930-1960, 2d rev. ed. Berkeley: University of California Press, 1963. [*1st ed.* 1930].
The chapter "In Family Courtyards" of this early village study by two American missionaries focuses on women's lives. Such matters as the conflict between the hereditary village midwife and the government-trained midwife, changing clothing styles and anecdotes about young girls are discussed elsewhere in the volume. "Karimpur" village is in Mainpuri District, U.P.

ii) Collected papers

4069 DANDIYA, C.K. Women in Rajasthan: proceedings of a seminar on 'Women: the Untapped Potential of Rajasthan'. Jaipur: Department of Adult Education (Extension), University of Rajasthan, 1975. 231p.
Seminar proceedings include opening addresses and papers and summaries of discussions from sessions entitled "Women in Society," "Women and Education," "Women and Employment," "Rural and Tribal Women" and "New Challenges: Political, Social and Community Work."

4070 DEEPAK, ANWANT KAUR, ed. Souvenir in commemoration of International Woman Year, 1975. Amritsar: Punjab Yuvak Kala Kendra, 1976? 226p.
Contains more general articles and specific ones focusing on the Punjab and the Sikhs, e.g., "Giani Zail Singh: Maker of Modern Punjab and an Indefatigable Crusader for the Cause of Woman Uplift" and "Women in Punjabi Proverbs." Most articles are in Panjabi.

iii) Patterns of social change

4071 BHATTY, ZARINA. Muslim women in Uttar Pradesh: social mobility and directions of change. *In* Social Action 25,4 (1975) 365-74. [*Reprint in* Alfred de Souza, ed. Women in contemporary India: traditional images and changing roles. Delhi: Manohar Book Service, 1975. pp.25-36].
Compares patterns of marriage, education and work of Ashraf (descendants of distinguished non-Indian ancestors) and non-Ashraf women of a village near Lucknow, U.P., and different patterns of social change within the two groups. "Largely because of education and urbanisation, Ashraf women are coming out of purdah and seeking employment outside the home; . . . upwardly mobile non-Ashraf families, for whom the traditional Ashrafs function as reference models, are withdrawing their women from the family work force and putting them back in purdah."

4072 MANN, R.S. Acculturation and woman's standing. *In* Indian J. of Social Work 22,2 (1961) 77-80.
Concludes that recent social changes in Alipur village several miles north of Delhi have had a positive effect on the status of women, which is to say that western values (relating, for example, to widow marriage and female education) have been incorporated to a certain extent.

4073 NATH, KAMALA. Women in the new village. *In* Economic Weekly 17,20 (15 May 1965) 813-6.
Considers effects of technological and economic change on Jat cultivator women near "Jitpur" village, Ludhiana District. Discusses work patterns, household life, medical practices and attitudes toward female education.

4074 ROY, SHIBANI. Status of Muslim women in North India. Delhi: B.R. Publishing Corporation, 1979. 250p.
Empirical study of Muslim women assesses changing circumstances in various areas: education, employment, marriage, *pardā* observance and so forth. Believes influence of Islamic tenets to be slowly waning due to progressive social forces in post-independent India. [Unexamined].

4075 SETHI, RAJ MOHINI. Modernization of working women in developing societies. New Delhi: National Publishing House, 1976. 168p.
Comparative study of women and modernization in Chandigarh, India, and Ankara, Turkey. "Part one concerns . . . the definition of the problem and the concepts used, devising a measure of modernity and finding out the level of modernity of women and showing how attitudinal modernity is associated with socio-demographic characteristics. Part two analyses the attitudes toward the position of women in the two societies." Lengthy bibliography.

iv) Case studies of Delhi and Bihari women

4076 CHHABRA, RAMI. Six faces of India. *In* Ms. 3,6 (1974) 23-6.

Brief glimpse into the lives of six Delhi women of various backgrounds and economic means to illustrate the variety of satisfactions and problems of Indian women. Photographs.

4077 STOKES, OLIVIA. Women of rural Bihar. *In* Devaki Jain, ed. Indian women. New Delhi: Publications Division, Ministry of Information and Broadcasting, Government of India, 1975. pp.215-28.
Brief case studies of six scheduled caste women from the village of Guriama in Bihar.

v) Santal and Bhil tribal women

4078 BODDING, P.O. Some remarks on the position of women among the Santals. *In* J. of the Bihar and Orissa Research Society 2,3 (1916) 239-49.
Discusses the position of Santal women living in the Santal Parganas with respect to marriage, property ownership, household authority, inheritance and adoption.

4079 VYAS, N.N. Women in tribal society. *In* Cultural Forum 11,1/2 (1968/69) 67-71.
Brief assessment of status of women among the Bhils of Rajasthan in the form of a list of customs.

(g) The life cycle

4080 AGARWALA, S.N. A demographic study of six urbanising villages. Bombay: Asia Publishing House, 1970. 195p.
Compilation of data from 944 rural households near Delhi. Focuses particularly upon relationship of caste and occupational class to the various demographic aspects investigated — villages; households; marriage; widowhood, separation and remarriage; fertility; child mortality; birth and death rates.

4081 BRYCE, L. WINIFRED, comp. and ed. Women's folk-songs of Rajputana. Delhi: Publications Division, Ministry of Information and Broadcasting, Government of India, 1964. 187p.
Translations of 121 women's songs, discussed and arranged in a sequence "intended to let the songs tell . . . the story of a woman's life and picture her in the setting of her family relationships. It reveals the life of women who would otherwise be inarticulate . . . . [they] themselves draw aside for us, as it were, the veil that covers the expressive face of the *Rajputni*."

4081a DAS, VEENA. Reflections on the social construction of adulthood. *In* Sudhir Kakar, ed. Identity and adulthood. Delhi: Oxford University Press, 1979. pp.89-104.
Reflects upon life cycle of Panjabi Hindu females. Based upon fieldwork in North Indian cities, folk literature and fiction. Briefly points to male life cycle contrasts.

4082 ELWIN, VERRIER. Primitive ideas of menstruation and the climacteric in the East Central Provinces of India. *In* J.P. Mills et al., eds. Essays in anthropology presented to Rai Bahadur Sarat Chandra Roy. Lucknow: Maxwell Company, 1942? pp.141-68.
Discusses various practices and views relating to menstruation among tribal communities of the Maikala Hills — references to menstruating women, theory of procreation, mythological origin of menstruation, menarche, taboos and avoidances and their sanctions, husband during menstruation, menstrual disorders, magical use of menstrual blood and menopause.

4083 FLINT, MARCHA PROTTAS. Menarche and menopause of Rajput women. Ph.D. dissertation, Department of Anthropology?, City University of New York, 1974. 210p. [University Microfilms 74-13,441].
Study of Rajput women in Himachal Pradesh and Rajasthan. Attributes later menarcheal ages and earlier onset of menopause of Himachal Pradesh women to altitude. Discusses familial patterns relating to menarche, menstruation and menopause. [Unexamined. DAI].

4084 GILL, HARJEET SINGH. A phulkari from Bhatinda. Patiala: Department of Anthropological Linguistics, Punjabi University, 1977? 44p., 36 plates.
Examines use of *phulakari* embroidered cloths in the Punjab at the key junctures in a woman's life — marriage, birth of a son and death. Text consists of a fictional case study of "Preeto" and two essays, "Preeto's Cultural Heritage: the Legends of the Medieval Punjab" and "Preeto's Phulkari: Signs and Significance." Color photographs.

4085 PRASAD, B.G., AMLA R. RAO and S.B. NAYAR. A study on beliefs and customs in a Lucknow village in relation to certain diseases, menstruation, child birth and family planning. *In* Indian J. of Social Work 30,1 (1969) 45-54.
Various kinds of information obtained primarily from chief male earner and eldest female of 68 households. Concludes with recommendations.

4086 SINGH, RAJENDRA. Reproductive life of Birhor women. *In* Bulletin of the Bihar Tribal Research Institute 5,1 (1963) 124-42.
Report of a survey among three Birhor colonies near Ranchi. Presents data on age at menarche, menarche-conception interval, birth and birth interval, mother's age at birth, sex ratio, infant mortality and menopause

4087 TRIVEDI, G.M. Women in the folklore of Awadh. *In* Sangeet Natak 37 (Jul 1975) 29-41.
Life cycle of Hindu women as depicted in

Avadhi dialect folk songs from Unnao, Rai Bareli and Fatehpur Districts. The songs emphasize home life and traditional values. Provides transliterations and translations of 28 selections.

i) Youth and adolescence

4088 BHATNAGAR, VATSALA. Attitude of teen-age girls toward sex. *In* Eastern Anthropologist 26,4 (1973) 339-42.
Report of interviews with Lucknow girls on views of sexuality and morality, free mixing and boy-girl relationships. Argues that the young have not been able to reconcile old moral views with the permissiveness of the modern social system.

4089 DUBE, S.C. Token pre-puberty marriage in Middle India. *In* Man 53,25 (1953) 18-9.
"Arrow marriage" as an important rite of passage among various tribal and caste groups of the Chattisgarh highlands whose females marry at a relatively late age. Considers this rite to be a precaution against the permanent defilement that would result from "any sexual act or serious social lapse."

4090 GHOSH, MOLINA. Fantasy life of girls at the pre-adolescent and adolescent stages. *In* University of Rajasthan Studies, Education, 3 (1958) 54-82.
Based on author's dissertation. [Unexamined].

ii) Marriage systems

4091 ANSARI, GHAUS. Muslim marriage in India. *In* Wiener Völkerkundliche Mitteilungen 3,2 (1955) 191-206.
Examines rituals, rules and prohibitions associated with Muslim marriages in the Avadh region of U.P. Considers broader context of Islamic history.

4092 CHOWDHURY, UMA. Marriage customs of the Santals. *In* Bulletin of the Department of Anthropology, Government of India 1,1 (1952) 86-116.
Describes marriage rites and various forms of marriage and divorce in Santal villages of Hazaribagh District.

4093 GUPTA, SHIVA KUMAR. Marriage among the Anglo-Indians. Lucknow: Ethnographic and Folk Culture Society, 1968. 86p.
Discusses marriage patterns — rules, restrictions and ceremonies — among Anglo-Indians of the city of Lucknow. Asserts that European influences predominate, including the concept of romantic love and the period of courtship and dating. The husband-wife relationship takes precedence over all others. No cases of divorce were found. Premarital sex is discouraged. There are no traditions of dowry or bride price. Photographs.

4094 HUSAIN, SHEIKH ABRAR. Marriage customs among Muslims in India: a sociological study of the Shia marriage customs. New Delhi: Sterling Publishers, 1976. 226p.
Report of survey of 450 male and 50 female *Shī'ah* Muslims from several cities of Uttar Pradesh. Discusses marriage choices, marriage rites, dowry, divorce, widow marriage and other topics.

4095 SRIVASTAVA, RAM P. Marriage and divorce among the eastern Bhotias. *In* Anthropologist 4,1/2 (1957) 34-43.
Focuses on traditional rules and practices of a seminomadic community living in the districts of Almora and Garhwal in U.P.

iii) Marriage rules and types

4096 BERREMAN, GERALD D. Village exogamy in northernmost India. *In* Southwestern J. of Anthropology 18,1 (1962) 55-9.
Relates absence of village exogamy in the Central Pahari area, which is unusual in North India, to the relatively high status of women there.

4097 CAMPBELL, A. Santal marriage customs. *In* J. of the Bihar and Orissa Research Society 2,3 (1916) 304-37.
Examines the various types of regular and irregular Santal marriages: bride "purchase," marriage of widows and divorcées, elopement, daughter exchange, intrusion marriage and others.

4098 CHAMBARD, JEAN-LUC. Les mariages secondaires et l'acquisition des femmes dans l'Inde centrale [Remarriage and acquisition of wives in Central India]. *In* Congrès International des Sciences Anthropologiques et Ethnologiques VIe, 30 Jul-6 Aug 1960, Paris. Proceedings. Paris: Musée de l'Homme, 1963. pp.33-7. *With* Discussion pp.37-8.
Outlines characteristics distinguishing both first and additional marriages in northern Madhya Pradesh. Discusses reasons for female remarriage and describes characteristic bride-price transactions.

4099 DUMONT, LOUIS. Le mariage secondaire dans l'Inde du Nord [Remarriage in North India]. *In* Congrès International des Sciences Anthropologiques et Ethnologiques VIe, 30 Jul-6 Aug 1960, Paris. Proceedings. Paris: Musée de l'Homme, 1963. pp.53-5. *With* Discussion, p.55.
Describes general characteristics of remarriages in eastern U.P. Notes differences between ceremonies of first and additional marriages and the way the two types of marriages

affect and reflect the status of men and women. Briefly contrasts North and South Indian remarriage patterns.

4100 VREEDE-DE STUERS, CORA. Mariage préférentiel chez les Musulmans de l'Inde du Nord [Preferential marriage among Muslims of North India]. *In* Revue du Sud-est Asiatique 2 (1962) 141-52. [Unexamined. BAS].

iv) Marriage age and arrangements

4101 RAJAGOPALAN, C. and JASPAL SINGH. Changing trends in Sikh marriages. *In* J. of Family Welfare 14,2 (1967) 24-32. Report of interviews with Chandigarh residents about their own and their parents' marriages to ascertain changing patterns of range in choice of spouse, criteria in selection of spouse and procedure for spouse selection. With the exception of a more rigorous religious endogomy, all trends observed were away from tradition.

4102 SINGH, J. Sikh marriage in transition. *In* Social Action 18,3 (1968) 224-30. Report of interviews with 51 Sikhs from an urban area (Chandigarh?) to ascertain changing marriage patterns. Compares experiences of men with their reports of the marriages of their sons or sons-in-law and women's experiences with those reported for their daughters or daughters-in-law.

4103 SINGH, MRS. K.P. Women's age at marriage. *In* Sociological Bulletin 23,2 (1974) 236-44. Attempts "to observe the trends in age at marriage in three generations [and] to study the attitudes of women towards women's age at marriage in general and the actual age at which they married their daughters . . . . to ascertain whether there is any discrepancy between . . . attitudes and . . . actual behaviour and, if it is so, . . . the reasons . . ." Found that although age at marriage is increasing, it remains below desired age at marriage.

v) Marriage ceremonies

4104 CROOKE, W. Marriage songs in northern India. *In* Indian Antiquary 55 (May-Aug and Oct 1926) 81-8, 104-7, 129-33, 153-8, 196-9. Collection of 27 Hindu and 3 Muslim marriage song texts in transliteration and translation, with brief explanatory notes. From Mirzapur, Mathura, Etawa and other places located in present-day Uttar Pradesh.

4105 HENRY, EDWARD O. North Indian wedding songs. *In* J. of South Asian Literature 11,1/2 (1975) 61-93. Considers women's wedding songs from "Indrapur" village near Varanasi in eastern U.P. Focuses on ways that songs reflect the social order and inform actors of significance of the rites that they accompany. Presents a series of translations of song texts with commentary. Briefly discusses ethnography of the women's songfest.

4106 REDDY, N.S. Rites and customs associated with marriage in an Indian village. *In* Eastern Anthropologist 9,2 and 3/4 (1955/56) 77-91, 178-90. Describes in detail marriage ceremonies from betrothal to bride's arrival at husband's home in the village of "Senapur," Jaunpur District. Based on observances of Thakur, Ahir and Lohar castes.

4107 ROSE, H.A. Hindu betrothal observances in the Punjab. *In* J. of the Royal Anthropological Institute 38 (1908) 409-18. Describes three types of Panjabi Hindu betrothals and prebetrothal observances. Discusses age at betrothal. Provides, for comparative purposes, description of orthodox Hindu betrothal furnished to the author by a pandit. Data from various areas of prepartition Punjab.

4108 ROSNER, VICTOR. The marriage ceremonies of the Telia Nagesia of Jashpur, India. *In* Anthropos 59,3/4 (1964) 400-26. Describes in detail the marriage rites of a scheduled tribe in Raigarh District. Photographs.

4109 VETSCHER, TRANDE [TRAUDE VETSCHERA]. Betrothal and marriage among the Minas of South Rajasthan. *In* Man in India 53,4 (1973) 387-413. Ethnographic details of marriage arrangements and ceremonies of the Mina tribal community of Chitorgarh District.

4110 VREEDE-DE STUERS, CORA. Le mariage chez les Musulmans de condition "Ashraf" dans l'Inde du Nord: coutumes et cérémonies [Marriage of Ashraf Muslims in North India: clothing and ceremonies]. *In* Orient 7,1 (1963) 35-71. Describes Ashraf Muslim wedding ceremonies. Composite based upon statements of informants and observations in Delhi and Uttar Pradesh. Emphasizes similarity of Muslim and Hindu customs. Includes examples of wedding transactions and a glossary of important terms.

4111 ________. Chansons de mariage chez les Musulmans de l'Inde du Nord [Marriage songs of Muslims in North India]. *In* Orient 7,4 (1963) 125-39. Describes marriage songs that both idealize and ridicule marital relations in their social and ceremonial contexts. Considers those that ridicule to be safety valves, enabling a harmless expression of underlying tension. With song texts in French translation.

vi) Dowry

4112 HOOJA, SWARN L. Dowry system among Hindus in North India: a case study. *In* Indian J. of Social Work 28,4 (1968) 411-26.
Report of questionnaire survey of 498 Delhi families regarding attitudes toward dowry. Correlates results by caste level, age, sex, marital status, education and income.

4113 ________. Dowry system in India: a case study. Delhi: Asia Press, 1969. 236p.
Four hundred ninety-eight Delhi families were surveyed "to understand more correctly the reasons why people believe in this custom and the practical difficulties they confront in following it." Presents findings according to caste, sex, marital status, education, income and age. Final chapter discusses "remedies to remove this evil." Photographs.

vii) Polyandrous and polygynous marriages

4114 BERREMAN, GERALD D. Pahari polyandry: a comparison. *In* American Anthropologist 64,1 (1962) 60-75.
Seeks economic, demographic or social-structural differences that correlate with presence of polyandry in Jaunsar-Bawar area and its absence in neighboring Garhwal. The only difference identified is in the sex ratio. Argues that polyandry and monandry can often function in similar ways. Author's data refutes hypotheses that economic uselessness of women, dowry or property rights held by women and shortage of women are universal correlates of polyandry.

4115 HAQQI, S.A.H. Polygamy among Indian Muslims: a case study. *In* Indian J. of Politics 8,1/2 (1974) 143-52.
Report of study conducted in Aligarh to determine extent of polygamous (i.e., polygynous) marriage, circumstances in which additional wives are taken, whether "bigamy" is not more descriptive of local practices and whether legislation is required to "'control' this problem."

4116 MAJUMDAR, D.N. Family and marriage in a polyandrous society. *In* Eastern Anthropologist 8,2 (1954/55) 85-110.
Describes family and marriage patterns among various castes of Jaunsar-Bawar in Dehra Dun District. Much on women's lives.

4117 ________. Himalayan polyandry: structure, functioning and culture change, a field-study of Jaunsar-Bawar. Bombay: Asia Publishing House, 1962. 389p.
An anthropological account of the caste communities of the Jaunsar-Bawar region of Dehra Dun District, U.P. Considerations include division of labor in the home, dyadic role relationships, polyandrous conjugal relation and its social and economic bases, the principle of female inferiority, women as economic dependents and socio-ritual inferiors and double standards of sexual conduct for women at their fathers' and husbands' houses. Photographs.

4118 PARMAR, Y.S. Polyandry in the Himalayas. Delhi: Vikas Publishing House, [1975]. 191p.
The ethnography of polyandry among various castes of Himachal Pradesh by an observer of 30 years. Much on women, including the chapter "Economic Importance of Women."

4119 SAKSENA, R.N. Marriage and family in the polyandrous Khasa tribe of Jaunsar-Bawar. *In* George Kurian, ed. The family in India: a regional view. The Hague: Mouton, 1974. pp.107-17. (Studies in the Social Sciences, 12).
Considers the history of the Khasas, the origin of Aryan polyandry, economic factors and marriage. Argues that "the hardships of economic life have completely influenced the social life and customs of the people, who have been forced to adopt a system of family life in keeping with the demand for joint labor within a village. The practice of polyandry is the outcome of this demand." Describes certain dynamics involved in a group of Khasa brothers sharing one or more wives.

viii) Fertility patterns

4120 ANAND, K. An analysis of intergenerational fertility. *In* Indian J. of Social Work 27,4 (1967) 361-6.
Study of 100 women of Chandigarh investigated their own, their mothers' and their daughters' fertility. Attributes decrease in average family size over these generations from 6.84 to 2.65 persons to increasing age at marriage and trends toward higher education and employment of women.

4121 DUBEY, D.C., A. BARDHAN and S. GARG. Fertility behaviour of working and non-working women. New Delhi: National Institute of Family Planning, 1975. 55p. (*Its* Monograph Series, 24).
Brief report of a survey conducted among Delhi women to compare fertility preferences and performances and family planning knowledge of those who are and are not employed outside the home.

4122 FREED, STANLEY A. and RUTH S. FREED. The relationship of fertility and selected social factors in a North Indian village. *In* Man in India 51,4 (1971) 274-89.
Examines the relationship of fertility and literacy, urbanization, landownership, caste level and family type in "Shanti Nagar" village near Delhi. High caste level, landownership, literacy of household head and urban orientations were associated with lower fertility rates.

4123 MINKLER, MEREDITH. Fertility and female labour force participation in India: a survey of workers in Old Delhi area. *In* J. of Family Welfare 17,1 (1970) 31-43.
Report of study conducted to investigate whether commonly reported inverse relationship between fertility and female employment is limited to educated women alone. Compares a group of educated employed women from Delhi with an uneducated employed group with respect to family planning attitudes and practices and family-size ideals. Fertility attitudes and practices were also compared to income levels and work attitudes and practices. The uneducated employed sample had an average number of children very similar to a comparable group of nonemployed women. However, uneducated women whose place of work provided family planning information and materials showed a strong receptivity to such services.

4124 MITRA, SARAT CHANDRA. On a women's folk-rite from the district of Monghyr in South Bihar. *In* J. of the Anthropological Society of Bombay 15,6 (1935/36) 613-7.
Describes women's fertility rites, which include worship of the spirit of the pipal tree, the moon, the goddess Ṣaṣṭhī and the god Śiva by those who desire children.

4125 POTTER, ROBERT G. et al. Applications of field studies to research on the physiology of human reproduction: lactation and its effects upon birth intervals in eleven Punjab villages, India. *In* Mindel C. Sheps and Jeanne Clare Ridley, eds. Public health and population change: current research issues. Pittsburgh: University of Pittsburgh Press, 1965. pp.577-99.
Results of investigation of effects of lactation upon birth intervals in rural Ludhiana District. Found that lactation substantially prolonged postpartum amenorrhea, thus increasing birth intervals. Results suggest why effects of contraception and abortion may be limited. Data from Khanna rural population study.

4126 _______. A fertility differential in eleven Punjab villages. *In* Milbank Memorial Fund Quarterly 43,2 (part 1) (1965) 185-201.
Compares fertility rates among Jats and Chamars. A tentatively inferred induced abortion, rather than the more widespread use of contraceptives or other factors, is proposed to account for the greater reduction of births among the Jats.

4127 SAKSENA, D.N. Differential urban fertility, Lucknow: report of the Intensive Fertility Survey of Lucknow City. Lucknow: Demographic Research Centre, Department of Economics, Lucknow University, 1973. 157p.
Report of questionnaire survey of 1,423 ever-married women regarding fertility and mortality differentials, attitudes toward and use of contraception, family size values and attitudes toward abortion.

4128 SAXENA, G.B. Differential fertility in rural Hindu community: a sample survey of the rural Uttar Pradesh. *In* Eugenics Quarterly 12,3 (1965) 137-45.
Examination of relationship of caste level ("upper," "intermediate," "low") and occupation ("service," "business and artisan," "agriculture," "labor") to fertility. Found inverse relation between caste level and fertility and no significant relationship between occupational category and fertility.

4129 SEN, D.K. Some notes on the fertility of Jaunsari women. *In* Eastern Anthropologist 10,1 (1956) 60-7.
Survey of women of polyandrous Jaunsar area of Dehra Dun District revealed an exceptionally low fertility rate. Refutes idea that polyandry itself is cause of this low rate.

4130 SINHA, UMESH P. A study of fertility of the Santal and the Paharias of Santal Parganas. *In* Bulletin of the Bihar Tribal Research Institute 5,1 (1963) 82-123.
Compares fertility rates and related demographic features of two tribes of the Santal Parganas District.

4131 VERMA, K.K. Socio-cultural dimensions of fertility: a case study of the Santal. *In* J. of Social Research 13,2 (1970) 70-81.
Discusses incidence of marriage, age at marriage, fertility rites, origin myth, concept of procreation, sex and sex taboos and opinions about birth control. Finds the Santals to be culturally oriented toward high fertility. Concludes that the idea of limiting family size is not in conformity with the orientation of this community. Data from three villages in Hazaribagh District.

4132 WYON, JOHN B. et al. Delayed marriage and prospects for fewer births in Punjab villages. *In* Demography 3,1 (1966) 209-17.
Found that although age at marriage of women in seven Panjabi villages rose between 1924 and 1945, start of cohabitation was not correspondingly delayed. The further rise in age of marriage between 1945 and 1959 did effect a change in cohabitation age and, in addition, expectations for number of children had dropped.

ix) Pregnancy and childbirth

4133 BAJPAI, P.C. et al. Observations on perinatal mortality. *In* Indian Pediatrics 3,3 (1966) 83-98.
". . . an attempt has been made to assess the incidence of perinatal mortality at the Queen Mary's Hospital, Lucknow, and to analyse the causative factors in perinatal deaths." Higher perinatal loss was associated with mother's age not in 20 to 25 year range; first, third and later pregnancies; low birth weights; and low

socio-economic status. Gives various statistics and cites other similar, hospital-based studies conducted in India.

4134 DUBE, LEELA. Pregnancy and child birth among the Amat Gonds. *In* Eastern Anthropologist 2,3 (1949) 153-9. [*Also in* Man in India 28,4 (1948) 222-9]. Reviews beliefs and rites of Gonds of Raipur District associated with menstruation, pregnancy, childbirth and child care and barrenness.

4135 ELWIN, VERRIER. Conception, pregnancy and birth among the tribesmen of the Maikal Hills. *In* J. of the Royal Asiatic Society of Bengal, Letters 9,1 (1943) 99-148. Ethnographic account of native views and practices relating to wide range of topics. Based upon fieldwork among Gonds, Agarias, Baigas and other communities.

4136 GIDEON, HELEN. A baby is born in the Punjab. *In* American Anthropologist 64,6 (1962) 1220-34. Presents data on pregnancy, childbirth and obstetrical practices among rural Sikhs through the medium of a story of a young woman who marries and has her first child. Composite portrait is based upon hundreds of cases considered during the Khanna rural population study.

4137 GORDON, JOHN E., HELEN GIDEON and JOHN B. WYON. Childbirth in rural Punjab, India. *In* American J. of the Medical Sciences n.s. 247,3 (1964) 344-62. Discusses rates and various causes of maternal and neonatal mortality and describes at length obstetric practices in rural Punjab. Focuses on the success rates of various types of attendants and factors involved in choice of attendant. From Khanna rural population study.

4138 ________. Complications of childbirth and illnesses during the puerperium in 862 Punjab village women: a field study. *In* J. of Obstetrics and Gynaecology of India 15,2 (1965) 159-67. [Unexamined].

4139 ________. A field study of illnesses during pregnancy, their management and prenatal care in Punjab villages. *In* Indian Pediatrics 2 (Sep 1965) 330-5. From Khanna study. [Unexamined].

4140 ________. La obstetricia tradicional en las regiones rurales [Traditional obstetrics in rural areas]. *In* Boletín de la Oficina Sanitaria Panamericana 59 (1965) 313-24. [Unexamined].

4141 ________. Midwifery practices in rural Punjab, India. *In* American J. of Obstetrics and Gynecology 93,5 (1965) 734-42. Associates high perinatal and neonatal death rates observed in rural Ludhiana District during Khanna rural population study with obstetrical practices, child care deficiencies and an "unfavorable environment" (primarily infection and malnutrition). Urges midwife training programs and public health education programs. Tables and text describe labor duration, stillborn and liveborn death patterns, placenta delivery, treatment of umbilical cord and maternal death rates.

4142 MUNDRI, LAL SINGH. A Munda birth. *In* Man in India 36,1 (1956) 56-72. Describes in detail events observed in 1953 in association with the birth of a Munda couple's first child in Katowa village, Singhbhum District.

4143 PRASAD, TAREKESWAR. Folk songs relating to dream-issues in 'doḥada' stage. *In* Indian Folklore 1,2 (1958) 40-1. Translations of three Bhojpuri folk songs concerning dreams of pregnant women.

4144 RAZA, MAULVI HASAN. Customs at and before birth, at circumcision and at betrothal — Mahomedans, Upper Ganges — Jamnah Duabah. *In* North Indian Notes and Queries 3,11 (1894) 186-93. Includes details of rites and customs of pregnancy, birth and breastfeeding; and transliterations and translations of ten songs sung at the *rasma* ceremony during pregnancy and three *lorī* lullabies.

4145 ROSE, H.A. Hindu pregnancy observances in the Punjab. *In* J. of the Royal Anthropological Institute 35 (1905) 271-8. Discusses rites, taboos, gifts, worship, bathing, dressing and eating during pregnancy. Data from various areas of prepartition Punjab.

4146 ________. Hindu birth observances in the Punjab. *In* J. of the Royal Anthropological Institute 37 (1907) 220-36. Encyclopedic account of various events relating to birth and childhood. Data from areas of prepartition Punjab.

4147 ROY, SARAT CHANDRA. Birth, childhood and puberty ceremonies among the Birhōrs. *In* J. of the Bihar and Orissa Research Society 4,2 (1918) 214-31. Regarding the danger that is present in the transition between life stages and the rites and precautions undertaken to counteract harmful influences. Special emphasis on rites of pregnant and parturient women.

4148 SARKAR, ARATI, NIREN CHOUDHURI and GAUTAM SANKAR RAY. Birth and pregnancy rites among the Oraons. *In* Man in India 35,1 (1955) 46-51. Describes beliefs and practices associated with conception, pregnancy and birth. Makes comparisons with earlier Oraon ethnography. Based on observations and case histories from the village of Chaha in Ranchi District.

4149 SATYARTHI, DEVENDRA. The village gives birth in pain. *In* Rural India 6,6 (1943) 240-5. Songs from Punjab. [Unexamined].

4150 SINGH, SIRDAR GURDYAL. Memorandum on the superstitions connected with childbirth, and precautions taken and rites performed on the occasion of the birth of a child among the Jāṭs of Hoshiyārpur in the Panjāb. *In* J. of the Asiatic Society of Bengal 52, part 1,3/4 (1883) 205-10.
Describes techniques of preventing abortion, avoiding evil eye, securing the health of mother and child and so forth.

x) Motherhood and child rearing

4151 ARCHER, W.G. The illegitimate child in Santal society. *In* Man in India 24,3 (1944) 154-69.
Examines views of illegitimacy and methods by which children of Santal mothers become Santals.

4152 CARSTAIRS, G. MORRIS. The twice-born: a study of a community of high-caste Hindus. Bloomington, Indiana: Indiana University Press, 1958. 343p.
Examines male personality formation in three communities of "Deoli" village near Udaipur. The chapter "Family Relationships" discusses qualities of various dyads. The chapter "Hindu Personality Formation: Unconscious Processes" discusses mother-child and especially mother-son relations in depth. Similar material can be obtained from the three lengthy life histories included in the book.

4153 _______. Customs and beliefs in relation to infant and maternal welfare. *In* Pacific Forum (1959) 37-43.
[Unexamined].

4154 MATHUR, SHANTA and INDIRA SHAHI. Mothers' attitudes towards child rearing practices in two cultures. *In* J. of Family Welfare 10,1 (1963) 64-8.
Compares attitudes of 25 tribal women from Ranchi and 25 nontribal women from Patna toward child rearing using a modified Likert scale. "On the whole the results are not significant."

4155 MINTURN, LEIGH and WILLIAM W. LAMBERT. Mothers of six cultures: antecedents of child rearing. New York: John Wiley, 1964. 351p.
Report of cross-cultural study of child rearing in six communities, one of which is Khalapur village, Saharanpur District, U.P. First part describes mothers' culturally patterned differences of opinion and practice with respect to child rearing and proposes explanations. Second part presents quantitative and other descriptive data for the respective communities and concludes with some intracultural hypotheses. Third section, appendixes, contains statistical material and selections from interviews with the mothers. See also entry 4063.

xi) Barrenness

4156 PANDEY, INDU PRAKASH. Desire for a son. *In* Folklore [Calcutta] 1,5 (1960) 299-304.
On Avadhi songs that "narrate the woes and worries, disgust and despair of a barren woman."

4157 PRASAD, TARKESHWAR. Fate of a barren woman in Hindu society. *In* Indian Folklore 2,1 (1959) 15-9.
Presents original text, transliteration and interpretation of five Bhojpuri folk songs depicting the "woes in the lives of sterile women."

xii) Widowhood, aging, menopause

4158 BOSE, A.B. and M.L.A. SEN. Some characteristics of the widows in rural society. *In* Man in India 46,3 (1966) 226-32. [*Reprint in* Kanti B. Pakrasi, Amulya R. Banerjee and Amal K. Das, comps. Biosocial Studies in India: a reading in collected papers, 1961-70. Calcutta: Editions Indian, 1976. pp.382-8].
Statistically examines the age, sex, living arrangements and economic status of widows and widowers of Jalore, Barmer, and Sirohi Districts.

4159 DUBEY, BHAGWANT RAO. Widow remarriage in Madhya Pradesh. *In* Man in India 45, 1 (1965) 50-6. [*Reprint in* Kanti B. Pakrasi, Amulya R. Banerjee and Amal K. Das, comps. Biosocial studies in India: a reading in collected papers, 1961-70. Calcutta: Editions Indian, 1976. pp.389-94].
Refutes prevailing belief that Indian widows may not remarry. Survey of widows from three villages in the Narmada valley found that 45 percent remarried. Argues that this tolerance is an aspect of traditional rural social organization rather than influence of modern ideas.

4160 Re-marriage of widows. *In* Panjab Notes and Queries 2,16 (1885) 58.
Notes castes in the eastern districts of the former North-Western Provinces that do and do not allow widows to marry.

4161 SINGH, T.R. Widow remarriage among brahmans: a sociological study. *In* Eastern Anthropologist 22,1 (1969) 75-87.
Presents data from rural Madhya Pradesh to illustrate how "a caste whose social and ritual superiority was taken for granted . . . . deviates from the caste norms" in allowing mar-

riage of widows and separated women. Describes processes by which subsequently incurred decline of rank is recovered over several generations.

4162 VATUK, SYLVIA. The aging woman in India: self-perceptions and changing roles. *In* Alfred de Souza, ed. Women in contemporary India: traditional images and changing roles. Delhi: Manohar Book Service, 1975. pp.142-63.
Examines aging women of Raya Rajput community in "Rayapur," an urbanized village in Delhi State. Considers indigenous definitions of old age, residence patterns of the elderly, work, religious concerns, sexuality, conceptions of female life cycle stages and other topics.

4163 WYON, JOHN B., STEPHEN L. FINNER and JOHN E. GORDON. Differential age at menopause in the rural Punjab, India. *In* Population Index 32,3 (1966) 328.
Abstract of paper presented at 1966 meeting of the Population Association. Khanna rural population study investigations found median age at menopause to be 44 years and a positive correlation between late birth of last child and late attainment of menopause. Notes importance of gathering menopause data and of prospective studies of women's reproductive lives as opposed to retrospective studies.

xiii) Rebirth account

4164 STEVENSON, IAN. The case of Swarnlata. *In his* Twenty cases suggestive of reincarnation. New York: American Society for Psychical Research, 1966. pp.63-79. (*Its* Proceedings, 26).
Case study of a young girl from northern Madhya Pradesh who related much information about a previous life. Examines evidence for her paranormal knowledge given facts of geography and likelihood of communications.

(h) Domestic sphere and family life

4165 AGGARWAL, PARTAP C. Kinship and marriage among the Meos of Rajasthan. *In* Imtiaz Ahmad, ed. Family, kinship and marriage among Muslims in India. New Delhi: Manohar, 1976. pp.265-96. [*1st published as* The Meos of Rajasthan and Haryana. *In* Imtiaz Ahmad, ed. Caste and social stratification among the Muslims. Delhi: Manohar Book Service, 1973. pp.21-44].
Reviews kinship system of the Meo community of Chavandi Kalan village, Alwar District.

4166 DAS, VEENA. Masks and faces: an essay on Punjabi kinship. *In* Contributions to Indian Sociology n.s. 10,1 (1976) 1-30.
Presents data from Panjabi families of various urban centers, primarily Delhi. Considers informants' conceptions of mother-child, husband-wife and brother-sister relationships; sexuality; daughters and family honor; alliance and prestation networks; and other topics.

4167 FUCHS, STEPHEN. The Korku family. *In* Dhirendra Narain, ed. Explorations in the family and other essays: Professor K.M. Kapadia commemoration volume. Bombay: Thacker and Company, 1975. pp.163-92.
Concise ethnographic summary of marriage, sexual behavior, child rearing and family roles and relationships of this tribal group of Central India.

4168 GUPTA, GIRI RAJ. Marriage, religion and society: pattern of change in an Indian village. Delhi: Vikas Publishing House, 1974? 187p.
Ethnography of the Rajasthani village of Awan in Kota District. Contains much material relating to marriage ceremonies, family relationships and castes and their interrelationships. Details of women's lives interspersed throughout.

4169 KHARE, R.S. 'Embedded' affinity and consanguineal 'ethos': two properties of the northern kinship system. *In* Contributions to Indian Sociology n.s. 9,2 (1975) 245-61.
Contrasts male and female perspectives of kin terms, consanguinity and affinity in high-caste communities of the town of Rai Bareli and surrounding villages. The consanguinity of father and son differs from that of father and daughter. A son's marriage evokes one notion of affinity while a daughter's evokes another. Argues that two meanings of consanguinity and affinity comprise the primary set of distinctions around which the system is consistently organized.

4170 NEWELL, WILLIAM H. The submerged descent line among the Gaddi people of North India. *In* J. of the Royal Anthropological Institute 92,1 (1962) 13-22.
Examines rights retained or obtained by women of the extremely patriarchal Gaddi community near Brahmaur in the present-day Himachal Pradesh. Argues that the ambiguity of a married woman's maintenance of membership in both her natal and her husband's clans offers her a certain amount of power and resources to act according to her interests within the extremely patriarchal social system. Stresses importance of the relationship of a married woman and her brother.

4171 SAHAI, INDU. Family structure and partition: a study of the Rastogi community of Lucknow. Lucknow: Ethnographic and Folk Culture Society, 1973. 117p. (*Its* Monograph Series, 5).
Examines family organization and change in an urban business community. Considers household composition, income management and expenditure, domestic division of labor, authority, family relationships and strains and household partition.

i) Marriage networks, kin groups, prestations

4172 GOULD, HAROLD A. The micro-demography of marriages in a North Indian area. *In* Southwestern J. of Anthropology 16,4 (1960) 476-91.
Examines marriage network of "Sherupur" village, Faizabad District. Explains finding that marital villages of village daughters tended to be closer to Sherupur than natal villages of in-marrying women by 1) higher ratio of men to women and the ability to have greater control over a daughter's marriage, 2) desire for frequent visiting on the part of parents and daughters, 3) greater importance of marrying a daughter to a good and appropriate person than a son and 4) need to make clear that a daughter has no defects.

4173 JACOBSON, DORANNE. Songs of social distance. *In* J. of South Asian Literature 11,1/2 (1975) 45-59.
Discusses ethnography of the songfest in "Nimkhera" village of the Bhopal region of Madhya Pradesh, focusing on songs that accent tension between and opposition of a woman's natal and conjugal kin. Considers the abusive *gālī*, a song sung during weddings by bride's natal kinswomen to groom's kinsmen and directed by groom's natal kinswomen toward bride's kinswomen, and childbirth songs. Includes translations of eight songs.

4174 ________. Flexibility in Central Indian kinship and residence. *In* Kenneth David, ed. The new wind: changing identities in South Asia. The Hague: Mouton, 1978. pp.263-83. [*Also published as* You have given us a daughter: flexibility in Central Indian kinship. *In* S. Devadas Pillai, ed. Changing India: Studies in honour of Prof. G.S. Ghurye. Bombay: Popular Prakashan, 1976. pp.315-26].
Examines women's relationship to natal and conjugal families in "Nimkhera" village of the Bhopal region. Argues that a woman's relationship to each group is quite different, that the transfer of a woman to her husband's group is only partial and that women's travels back and forth between the two groups constitute an important regional communication system.

4175 MAHAR, JAMES MICHAEL. Marriage networks in the northern Gangetic plain. Ph.D. dissertation, Department of Anthropology, Cornell University, 1966. 300p. [University Microfilms 67-1477].
Study of scope and operations of marriage network of three generations of Rankhandi village, Saharanpur District. Although the report is not presented to elucidate the meaning of these networks for women's lives, many of the questions addressed are clearly relevant to women.

4176 ROWE, WILLIAM L. The marriage network and structural change in a North Indian community. *In* Southwestern J. of Anthropology 16,3 (1960) 299-311.
Investigates the scope and operations of and recent changes in the network of natal villages of women who married into the Noniya community of "Senapur" village in eastern Uttar Pradesh.

4177 VATUK, SYLVIA. Gifts and affines in North India. *In* Contributions to Indian Sociology n.s. 9,2 (1975) 155-96.
Detailed ethnographic documentation of "the tendency for kinship-related gift-giving to express the perpetual donor-recipient relationship held to properly exist between givers of brides and those who take them in marriage" within the Gaur brahman community of western U.P.

4178 VATUK, VED PRAKASH and SYLVIA VATUK. Social context of gift exchange in North India. *In* Giri Raj Gupta, ed. Family and social change in modern India. New Delhi: Vikas, 1976. pp.207-32. (Main Currents in Indian Sociology, 2).
Analyzes Hindi terms for gift transactions using an exchange model. Considers role of women in kin networks. Based upon fieldwork in rural Meerut District.

ii) Family relationships: social science perspectives

4179 AGARWAL, A.K. Patterns of marital disharmonies. *In* Indian J. of Psychiatry 13,3 (1971) 185-93.
Examines interaction patterns of couples in dysfunctional marital relationships and considers causes. Based largely on observations made during psychotherapy with 40 couples at a clinic in New Delhi.

4180 BOKIL, KAMALA. Mothers' perception of the parent-child relationships of adolescent girls in urban Indian families. Ph.D. dissertation, Department of Education?, University of Florida, 1966. 161p. [University Microfilms 67-12,-913].
Report of study based upon interviews with 100 middle-class Hindu mothers of adolescent daughters in Benares (now Varanasi) to determine their conceptions about their relationships with their daughters. Reports scaled scores relating to harmony and conflict, coercion and permissiveness and warmth and coolness. [Unexamined. DAI].

4181 CHATTERJEE, MARY. Conjugal roles and social networks in an Indian urban sweeper locality. *In* J. of Marriage and the Family 39,1 (1977) 193-202.
Discusses theories relating patterns of conjugal roles to the structure of social networks and proposes modifications based upon observations of a sweeper community in Varanasi.

4182 GANGRADE, K.D. Conflicting value system and social work. *In his* Dimensions of

social work in India: case studies. New Delhi: Marwah Publications, 1976. pp.16-31.
Presents the case study of a Jat woman of Rampur village (in Uttar Pradesh?) whose husband works away from home, whose younger brother-in-law makes advances and whose mother-in-law tolerates the situation. Includes interview material.

4183 ________. Family centered approach and social work. *In his* Dimensions of social work in India: case studies. New Delhi: Marwah Publications, 1976. pp.32-44.
Presents the case study of a young Jat woman from Shantipur village (in Uttar Pradesh?) who is caught between the modern expectations of her husband and the traditional expectations of her mother-in-law.

4184 GORE, M.S. The husband-wife and mother-son relationships. *In* Sociological Bulletin 11,1/2 (1962) 91-102.
Compares attitudes of members of the Agarwal community from joint and nuclear families and rural and urban backgrounds regarding the husband-wife and mother-son relationships. Considers male and female views of these relationships. Discusses precedence of filial and fraternal over conjugal relationships in the joint family. Conducted in Delhi area.

4185 HIVALE, SHAMRAO. The dewar-bhauji relationship. *In* Man in India 23,2 (1943) 157-67.
Considers relationship of a woman and her husband's younger brother among the Gonds and Pardhans of eastern Mandla District. Presents examples of folklore that refer to this relationship. One older woman told the author, "The word dewar is poetry to us."

4186 KHARE, R.S. The Hindu hearth and home. New Delhi: Vikas Publishing House, 1976. 315p.
Ethnography of normal and ceremonial cooking, serving and eating patterns within families of the urban centers of Lucknow, Kanpur and Gosainganj and in Gopalpur village near Lucknow. Focuses on subtle chronological and spatial distinctions. In urban extended twiceborn families without cooks, "on an average the womenfolk spent three to four hours in the morning cycle and four to five hours in the evening one." A woman and a hearth "are considered to be inseparable natural companions." Women were said to impart "sweetness" and "taste" to foods.

4187 OPLER, MORRIS E. Family, anxiety, and religion in a community of North India. *In* M.K. Opler, ed. Culture and mental health: cross-cultural studies. New York: Macmillan, 1959. pp.273-89.
Discusses a series of calendrical festivals as performed in "Senapur" village, Jaunpur District. "A large part of the religious system is an elaborate aparatus for putting family members and family interests under the protection of benign supernaturals, and for defending the family from unfriendly supernatural attacks. Such ceremonies obviously assuage anxiety throughout a given calendrical year." Conclusions focus on the reasons why women rather than men are primarily concerned with these festivals.

4188 PAREEK, UDAI and ADARSH KHANNA. An investigation into the ideal image of husband and its relationship with other images. *In* Indian J. of Social Work 20,2 (1959) 119-24.
Examines the ideal image of the husband and its relationship with ideal and actual images of the father, mother and hero. Based upon a survey of views of Delhi college girls. Results are largely inconclusive.

4189 RUDOLPH, SUSANNE HOEBER and LLOYD I. RUDOLPH. Rajput adulthood: reflections on the Amar Singh diary. *In* Daedalus 105,2 (1976) 145-67.
Discusses dynamics of Rajput joint family life as reflected in an extensive diary. Contains various observations relating to women, e.g., "A large part of Indian family literature stresses the dominance of the affective tie between mother and son. In the diary, that tie was less important than Amar Singh's mother's authority over him, which to a considerable extent she exercised indirectly through control of her daughter-in-law."

4190 VATUK, SYLVIA. Reference, address, and fictive kinship in urban North India. *In* Ethnology 8,3 (1969) 255-72.
Relates use of kinship terminology to social interaction and interpersonal relationships. Considers distinctions between male and female speakers and subjects of speech. Data from two upper- and middle-caste neighborhoods of a city in western Uttar Pradesh.

4191 WADLEY, SUSAN S. Brothers, husbands, and sometimes sons: kinsmen in North India ritual. *In* Eastern Anthropologist 29,2 (1976) 149-70.
Examines calendrical rites of women and girls in "Karimpur" village, Mainpuri District, that reiterate and emphasize the qualities of their ties with brothers, husbands and sons.

iii) Family relationships: in folk literature

4192 BHATNAGAR, MANJU. The position of women as depicted in Rajasthani folklore. *In* Folklore [Calcutta] 9,1 (1968) 17-36. [*Reprint in* Sankar Sen Gupta, ed. Women in Indian folklore. Calcutta: Indian Publications, 1969. pp.59-78. (*Its* Folklore Series, 15)].
Considers songs and proverbs about women as daughters, sisters, wives, cowives, daughters-in-law, mothers and mothers-in-law. Includes selections in translation and transliteration.

4193 MISHRA, S.D. Importance of women in Hindi folksongs. Tr. from Hindi by

Maya Srivastava. *In* Folklore [Calcutta] 9,4 (1968) 140-5. [*Reprint in* Sankar Sen Gupta, ed. Women in Indian folklore. Calcutta: Indian Publications, 1969. pp.90-6. (*Its* Folklore Series, 15)].
Discusses images of women's family life in Hindi folk songs. Includes Hindi song texts.

4194 NATH, KIDAR. Daughter in Kangra folk songs. *In* March of India 10 (1958). [Unexamined].

4195 SHARMA, N. Women in Magahi folklore. *In* Folklore [Calcutta] 9,3 (1968) 86-96. [*Reprint in* Sankar Sen Gupta, ed. Women in Indian folklore. Calcutta: Indian Publications, 1969. pp.79-89. (*Its* Folklore Series, 15)].
Considers images of women in familial contexts in Magahi folk songs. Contains examples in transliteration and English translation.

4196 TIWARI, UDAI NARAIN. Piriya: a curious folk-festival of the Bhojpuri women. *In* Man in India 29,3/4 (1949) 175-84.
Briefly describes a festival of Bihar and Uttar Pradesh in which women curse their loved ones. Includes transliterations and translations of Bhojpuri songs and stories. Does not discuss social significance of rite.

4197 UPADHYAYA, HARI S. The joint family structure and familial relationship patterns in the Bhojpuri folksongs. Ph.D. dissertation, Department of Folklore, Indiana University, 1967. 400p. [University Microfilms 68-7244].
Analysis of 500 Bhojpuri folksongs collected from a single female informant in Ballia District. Includes informant's life history, tables showing frequency of particular dyadic relationships and relative emotional intensities and discussion of the quality of the various relationships.

4198 _______. Familial patterns of behavior between brother and sister in the Hindu joint family structure: a study based upon the analysis of Bhojpuri folksongs of India. *In* Indian Sociological Bulletin 6,3 (1969) 197-206.
Reviews a variety of writings on the Hindu family and the content of Bhojpuri folk songs that suggest the exceptional affection within the brother-sister relationship and the threat of the brother's wife to this relationship.

4199 _______. Patterns of mother-son behavior in the Hindu family as depicted in the Bhojpuri folksongs of India. *In* Anthropologica 11,2 (1969) 203-14.
Discusses aspects of Hindu family system that contribute to the intensity of the mother-son relationship. Illustrates qualities of this relationship with translated excerpts from Bhojpuri folk songs.

4200 VATUK, VED PRAKASH and SYLVIA VATUK. The lustful stepmother in the folklore of northwestern India. *In* J. of South Asian Literature 11,1/2 (1975) 19-43.
Considers "what the study of the Lustful Stepmother motif in its variant expressions in the folklore of northwestern India reveals specifically about the nature of relations within the family and between the sexes in this society and about some underlying assumptions and inherent cultural contradictions pertaining to the nature of human sexuality and its social control." Focuses on the ideal constructs of a mother and a virtuous son and the significance of a woman's character.

iv) Continuity and change

4201 AHMAD, ZEYAUDDIN. Marriage and family among the Muslims of Bihar. *In* George Kurian, ed. The family in India: a regional view. The Hague: Mouton, 1974. pp.317-33. (Studies in the Social Sciences, 12).
Describes marriage customs and family life of Bihari Muslims as "a curious blend of Hindu traditions and Islamic laws." Considers women's roles and how they are affected by the simultaneous forces of Islamization and westernization. Various issues discussed pertain to women.

4202 GORE, M.S. Urbanization and family change in India. Bombay: Popular Prakashan, 1968. 273p.
Study of families from the Agarwal business community in and around Delhi to assess impact of urbanization and industrialization. Considers women's familial roles. [Unexamined. NUC].

4203 KAUL, INGE. Equality or emancipation? The changing social position of women. *In* S. Devadas Pillai, ed. Aspects of changing India: studies in honour of Prof. G.S. Ghurye. Bombay: Popular Prakashan, 1976. pp.347-61.
Investigates and verifies hypothesis "that the formal adjustment of women's social chances in India today results from changes in the socio-economic structures of society necessitating women's participation in extra-familial spheres but not allowing or calling for a factual equality of the sexes." Based on interviews with married educated employed women of urban Dhanbad District. Found that informants held employment roles to be supplementary to the primary and natural roles of mother and wife. Social equality was evoked to justify women's labor force participation, which is used to maintain and stabilize the social status of urban middle-class families.

4204 LUSCHINSKY, MILDRED STROOP. The impact of some recent Indian government legislation on the women of an Indian village. *In* Asian Survey 3,12 (1963) 573-83.
Attempts to understand cultural obstacles to influence of provisions of Hindu Marriage

Act, 1955, and Hindu Succession Act, 1956, in "Madhopur" village near Benares (now Varanasi). Considers why high-caste women do not utilize divorce rights, why low-caste families violate age of consent provisions, why all families deviate from inheritance provisions and status of widow marriage.

4205 VATUK, SYLVIA J. Trends in North Indian urban kinship: the "matrilateral asymmetry" hypothesis. *In* Southwestern J. of Anthropology 27,3 (1971) 287-307.
Compares kinship patterns found in rural western U.P. to those of two neighborhoods in the city of Meerut to test the "matrilateral asymmetry" hypothesis: with industrialization and the separation of men's instrumental from familial roles, the solidarity of matrilateral relationships will come to predominate. Concludes that while Meerut kinship patterns are not characterized by "matrilateral asymmetry," the trend is toward increasing emphasis on matrilateral relationships.

4206 ________. Kinship and urbanization: white collar migrants in North India. Berkeley: University of California Press, 1972. 219p.
Anthropological account of the impact of urbanization on kinship and the significance of the urban neighborhood in a changing society. Based on fieldwork in a Hindu white-collar middle-class community of Meerut. Contains much material about women's lives.

4207 VREEDE-DE STUERS, CORA. De Hindoese vrouw en moeder: traditie en nieuwe denkbeelden [The Hindu wife and mother: tradition and new ideas]. Amsterdam: Voor het Koninklijk instituut voor de tropen uitg. door Arbeiderspers, 1962. 104p.
Illustrated. [Unexamined. BAS].

(i) Women's sexuality, seclusion, dangers

i) Ideals of chastity

4208 HERSHMAN, PAUL. Virgin and mother. *In* Ioan Lewis, ed. Symbols and sentiments: cross-cultural studies in symbolism. London: Academic Press, 1977. pp.269-92.
Examines ideals of womanhood among Hindus and Sikhs of the Jullundur Doaba region. The contradiction between socially positive values of female fertility and motherhood and socially negative values of female sexuality and birth is "resolved through two dominant ritual symbols both anomalous in character: 'the Mother goddess who is also a virgin' and 'Mother Cow' . . . . As in so much of Punjabi ritual, 'that which is most dirty' is identical with 'that which is most powerful.'"

4209 JACOBSON, DORANNE. The chaste wife: cultural norm and individual experience. *In* Sylvia Vatuk, ed. American Studies in the Anthropology of India. New Delhi: Manohar Publications, 1978. pp.95-138.
Examines the prominent theme of wifely fidelity and the forms it has taken in the life of an older woman from "Nimkhera" village in the Bhopal region. "The paper discusses the development of her feelings about chastity from her childhood to her old age, how she dealt with threats to her chastity and to her image as a woman of high morals, and the relationship of her chastity to her security and well-being." Includes relevant excerpts from a lengthy life history.

ii) Seclusion

4210 GUHA, U. Attitude of U.P. village women to purdah and divorce. *In* Bulletin of the Department of Anthropology, Government of India 3,2 (1954) 1-7.
Report of interviews with Hindu and Muslim women in 13 villages of Jaunpur District. Enumerates informants' various stated reasons in support of and against *pardā* and divorce. Most women continued to be in support of *pardā*. Those opposed gave reasons of employment or equality. Very few favored divorce.

4211 JACOBSON, DOROTHY ANN [DORANNE JACOBSON]. Hidden faces: Hindu and Muslim purdah in a Central Indian village. Ph.D. dissertation, Department of Anthropology, Columbia University, 1970. 554p. [University Microfilms 73-16,209].
Considers numerous aspects of *pardā* observance in "Nimkhera" village, Raisen District. Sections discuss the ethnographic setting, distinctions between Hindu and Muslim *pardā* observance and the basis for these, function of *pardā*, its operation in daily life and through the life and calendrical festival cycles and women's physical mobility. Appendixes consider traditional criticisms of *pardā* in light of Nimkhera data and review published accounts of *pardā* observance elsewhere in India. Photographs.

4212 ________. The veil of virtue: purdah and the Muslim family in the Bhopal region of Central India. *In* Imtiaz Ahmad, ed. Family, kinship and marriage among Muslims in India. New Delhi: Manohar, 1976. pp.169-216.
Relates patterns of female seclusion to changing kinship patterns of Pathan and non-Pathan Muslims of the Bhopal region of Madhya Pradesh.

4213 ________. Purdah in India: life behind the veil. *In* National Geographic Magazine 152,2 (1977) 270-86.
Reviews traditional and changing forms of *pardā* observance in "Nimkhera" village, Raisen

District. Color photographs.

4214 _______. Purdah and the Hindu family in Central India. *In* Hanna Papanek, ed. Purdah in South Asia: the segregation of women. Forthcoming.
Contrasts ***pardā*** observance of Hindus and Muslims in the Bhopal region and argues that Hindu ***pardā*** observance must be understood as an integral part of the local Hindu subculture rather than an offshoot of a Muslim ***pardā*** system. Describes rules of Hindu ***pardā*** as they relate to caste, position in life cycle, daily routine and family interaction and the functions they serve. [Unexamined. Verified with editor].

4215 JEFFERY, PATRICIA M. Frogs in a well: Indian women in purdah. London: Zed Press, 1979. 187p. (Women in the Third World, 1).
Anthropological account of the strictly secluded lives of Pirzada women, whose menfolk are custodians of a ***ṣūfī*** shrine several miles south of Old Delhi. Chapters discuss seclusion systems of the Middle East and South Asia, world of Pirzada men and place of their womenfolk in it, domestic life of Pirzada women, values and subtleties of behavior relating to female seclusion in this community, dissatisfactions of Pirzada women, physical mobility and conclusions. The study includes numerous quotations of informants and considers questions of male control of economic resources and reproduction, women's acceptance or rejection of various aspects of Islamic ideology and aspects of the community's social structure that are devisive to women.

4216 KHWAJA, B.A. Attitude towards purdah among Muslim girl students of Kanpur. *In* Man in India 45,3 (1965) 223-7.
Finds that observance of ***pardā*** is inversely proportional to education and father's income. Education and increasing political consciousness are considered to be the main factors in the gradual disappearance of ***pardā***.

4217 MEHTA, RAMA. From purdah to modernity. *In* B.R. Nanda, ed. Indian women: from purdah to modernity. New Delhi: Vikas, 1976. pp.113-28.
Discusses striking changes ("a near revolution") that have occurred in female seclusion patterns of the Oswal community of former Mewar State in recent decades. Relates these changes to the broader social setting.

4218 _______. Purdah among the Oswals of Mewar. *In* Hanna Papanek, ed. Purdah in South Asia: the segregation of women. Forthcoming.
Examines ***pardā*** nuances at the local level. Considers ways it affects women's relationships with men and with other women. Discusses changes in ***pardā*** observance over recent decades as they relate to socio-political factors. Considers ***pardā*** observance among the Oswal community to promote an undivided patriarchal family by minimizing certain social interactions and encouraging self-control. Is accompanied by descriptive passages from the author's novel, ***Inside the Haveli*** (entry 2765), about the same community. [Unexamined. Verified with editor].

4219 PRABHA, pseud. Hope for Rajasthan and abolition of purdah. Bombay: Popular Book Depot, 1959. 16p.
Details evils of female seclusion as observed in Rajasthan. A polemic that encourages government officials to abolish the ***pardā*** system.

4220 RAZA, S. MUSI. Changing purdah-system in Muslim society: a survey study in Patna. *In* Islam and the Modern Age 6,4 (1975) 40-56 and 7,1 (1976) 57-78.
Discusses ***pardā*** as an Islamic ideal, as traditionally observed among Indian Muslims and as it exists in theory and practice in the city of Patna today. Second part contains a copy of the questionnaire used and a tabulation of results. Concludes that ***pardā*** observance is dimishing and that it was only briefly observed according to actual Islamic principles and has been more commonly observed with greater rigidity than Islamic law requires.

4221 SHARMA, URSULA M. Women and their affines: the veil as a symbol of separation. *In* Man n.s. 13,2 (1978) 218-33.
Describes practice of veiling from male affines senior to one's husband in Ghanyari village, Una District. Argues that female seclusion must be "considered as a feature of the social and political structure of the wider village community" rather than as merely a domestic practice as some have suggested. Stresses that this behavior is a symbolic response to a social demand rather than an absolute insurance of the control of women. In fact, women of Ghanyari play a covertly active role in village political life.

4222 VREEDE-DE STUERS, CORA. Pardah. *In* Revue des Études Islamiques 30,1 (1962) 151-212.
Consists of casual personal observations of ***pardā*** phenomena in urban and rural settings of Delhi and U.P.; an analysis of variation according to age, economic circumstances, urbanization and other factors; and a review of the literature on ***pardā***. Distinguishes and describes four degrees of ***pardā*** observance: strict, partial, intermittent and absent. Discusses social reform efforts and problems of education.

4223 _______. Parda: a study of Muslim women's life in northern India. Assen: Van Gorcum, 1968. 128p. (Samenlevingen Buiten Europa/Non-European Societies, 8).
Major sections discuss kinship and ***pardā*** observance of Muslims in Delhi and environs and in Aligarh. From interviews and personal observations. Photographs. Based mainly on several articles published in French (see entries 4100, 4110-1 and 4222).

iii) Witchcraft

4224 ARCHER, W.G. The Santal treatment of witchcraft. *In* Man in India 27,2 (1947) 103-21.
Ethnography of Santal witchcraft. Considers characteristics of witches, initiation of girls, witch gathering rite, methods of causing physical harm, diagnosis and cure of witch-induced maladies and punishment of witches.

4225 ISRAIL, MD. Witchcraft in an Oraon village. *In* Bulletin of the Bihar Tribal Research Institute 5,1 (1963) 38-52.
Examines female practice of witchcraft in the Oraon community of Anjan village in Chota Nagpur. Argues that its origin lies in jealousy, hatred and greed; that it operates where there is stress or strain between persons in close social interaction; and that it provides an effective means of social control.

4226 SARAN, A.B. Witchcraft in tribal and non-tribal societies. *In his* Tribal studies. Ranchi: Ranchi Offset Printers, 1978. pp.97-111.
Discusses witchcraft beliefs in nontribal villages and among the Munda and Oraon tribal communities of Bihar.

iv) Women's response to social constraints

4227 ARCHER, W.G. The women's hunt. *In* J.P. Mills et al., eds. Essays in anthropology presented to Rai Bahadur Sarat Chandra Roy. Lucknow: Maxwell Company, 1942? pp.187-93.
Describes the women's hunt that occurred among the tribes and castes of Ranchi District in 1940 and the Oraon myth that explains it. Involving role reversal and transvestism, the hunt and myth are said to relieve the tension between the formal structure of these communities, particularly the principle of male dominance, and the actual relation of equality between men and women.

4228 CARSTAIRS, G. MORRIS. Village women of Rajasthan. *In* Devaki Jain, ed. Indian women. New Delhi: Publications Division, Ministry of Information and Broadcasting, Government of India, 1975. pp.229-35.
Account of event witnessed by author during fieldwork in the hamlet of Sujarupa in the former Mewar State. While most males of the Rawat community were away in a wedding party, the women, unmarried girls to grandmothers, engaged in a mock wedding with vigorous dancing and free expression of resentments and hostilities. Author contrasts such a display with their more typical demure behavior and notes the unified solidarity and shared feelings of the women.

4229 FREED, STANLEY A. and RUTH S. FREED. Spirit possession as illness in a North Indian village. *In* Ethnology 3,2 (1964) 152-71.
Describes the case of Daya, a 15-year-old Chamar girl from a village near Delhi, along with cases of three other women and one man from the same village. Proposes psychological and cultural interpretations. Concludes that "spirit possession seems to fit contemporary descriptions of hysteria," involving an underlying intrapsychic tension and a precipitating condition involving difficulties with family members. Married women are most susceptible to spirit possession.

4230 MODI, JIVANJI JAMSHEDJI. A note on "the women's hunt" (jani-sikār) among the Orāons of Chota Nagpur. *In* J. of the Anthropological Society of Bombay 10,7 (1916) 543-7.
Describes examples of the ritual transfer of calamity from village to village, including the "women's hunt."

4231 RAO, SHARADAMBA. Sex distribution of mental disorders: a study in India. *In* Indian J. of Psychiatry 9,4 (1967) 264-71.
Compares male and female admissions (4,039 total) to a Ranchi public mental health hospital with regard to dimensions of education, marital status, rural/urban background, diagnosis, socio-economic group and particular situation precipitating breakdown.

(j) Ceremonial friendship

4232 BANDOPADHYAY, BISWANATH. Ceremonial friendship among the Bhumij of Manbhum. *In* Man in India 35,4 (1955) 274-86.
Describes and analyzes the institution of ceremonial friendship between two married women or widows of the Bhumij community of Manbhum District. Considers reasons friendship is undertaken, means of establishment and associated ceremonies. Case histories and census data illustrate predominant features of the custom.

(k) The spiritual life and religious observances

4233 GOPAL, K. Religiosity among Hindu women. *In* Ram Nath Sharma, ed. Research in religion. Meerut: Anu Prakashan, 1977. pp.34-43.
Results of survey of female students from Meerut College, high school and college teachers in Meerut and residents of a Meerut neighborhood. Presents informants' ideas about God and incarnation, use of sacred texts, belief in "idolatry," daily religious

routine, fast observances, group worship (*kathā-kīrtana*), particular occasions for worship and reactions to encounter of a deity while traveling.

4234 WADLEY, SUSAN SNOW. Shakti: power in the conceptual structure of Karimpur religion. Chicago: Department of Anthropology, University of Chicago, 1975. 222p. (University of Chicago Studies in Anthropology, 2).
Study of village religion in "Karimpur," Mainpuri District. Discusses "The Women's World," including the significance of *pardā* and the physical structure of houses (pp.26-32). Analyzes in detail annual cycle of rites, most of which are performed by women and directly express their concerns. Gives transliterations and translations of texts of numerous Hindi songs that accompany the rites. Discusses the Goddess, *Devī*, and relates her to other classes of deities. Photographs.

4235 WIESINGER, RITA. The woman's part in the religious life of the Bhil. *In* Anthropos 62,3/4 (1967) 497-508.
Examines religious attitudes, roles and beliefs of women in a community in which religion is primarily the concern of men. Data from Jhabua District.

i) Spiritual leaders

4236 KAPOOR, JYOTSANA. "Krishna speaks directly to me." *In* Eve's Weekly 30,30 (24 Jul 1976) 11.
Portrait of Sanyasini Lalibai, a guru of Delhi with many female followers, "who claims to be in direct communication with Lord Krishna" and "has all her difficulties solved by Him."

4237 MITRA, SARAT CHANDRA. A modern saint of northern India. *In* Hindustan Review 34, 206/207 (1916) 299-305.
The life and thought of Rupakala Bhagbanprasad who "worships Sitaram in the light of a lover or husband . . . . He has, therefore, assumed the feminine name Rupakala . . . . Just as a woman, who is in love, devotes her whole life, youth and charms to the service of her beloved, so Bhagbanprasad has consecrated his whole life to the service of his beloved Sitaram."

4238 _______. A note on the rise of a new Hindu sect in Bihar. *In* J. of the Anthropological Society of Bombay 11,1 (1917) 48-52.
Discusses the life and followers of Rupakala Bhagbanprasad who, as female consort, worships Sītārāma. Compares this devotional style to that of Rādhā-Kṛṣṇa cults and particularly the Sakhibhavikas. The saint "exercises a great influence for good on the moral well-being of Bihar." With portrait. Sections of this article are excerpted from ***Hindustan Review*** article above.

ii) Goddesses

4239 BABB, LAWRENCE A. Marriage and malevolence: the uses of sexual opposition in a Hindu pantheon. *In* Ethnology 9,2 (1970) 137-48.
Argues that goddesses who dominate or lack consorts in the Chhattisgarh region of M.P. are considered malevolent, while goddesses who are dominated by their consorts are benign/restrained. The former are generally non-Sanskritic, while the latter are generally Sanskritic.

4240 _______. Heat and control in Chhattisgarhi ritual. *In* Eastern Anthropologist 26,1 (1973) 11-28.
Describes *javārā* goddess worship ceremony in detail, including cooling rituals. Views these rites as an occasion for controlled human encounter with a heat that is dangerous and responsible for disease. Considers principle of thermal balance to occupy a particularly prominent place in Chhattisgarhi and other South Asian encounters with the female divinity.

4241 CHANDOLA, SUDHA. Some goddess rituals in non-narrative folk song of India. *In* Asian Folklore Studies 36,1 (1977) 57-68.
Classifies and discusses songs associated with the Goddess according to context. Includes English translations of 13 Hindi song texts. Source of material not specified.

4242 CHAUBAY, GANESH. Folk gods of Bihar. *In* L.P. Vidyarthi and Ganesh Chaubay, eds. Bihar in folklore study: an anthology. Calcutta: Indian Publications, 1971. pp.115-33. (*Its* Folklore Series, 18).
Includes material on local goddesses and related rituals. [Unexamined. Book in IBP].

4243 FREED, RUTH S. and STANLEY A. FREED. Two mother goddess ceremonies of Delhi State in the great and little traditions. *In* Southwestern J. of Anthropology 18,3 (1962) 246-77.
Describes and compares the "Durgā Eighth" and "Cold Seventh" goddess ceremonies as representatives of the "great" and "little" traditions, respectively. The two differ with respect to the way religious behavior is learned and participants. They share underlying concepts of paths of religious behavior, one deity with many aspects and omnipresence of the deity.

4244 MITRA, SARAT CHANDRA. The cult of the goddessling Dowār Devī. ***And*** The cult of the goddessling Sapahī Devī. *In* J. of the Bihar and Orissa Research Society 10,1/2 (1924) 114-27.
Examines worship of two village goddesses in Champaran District.

4245 PRIDEAUX, EDWIN. Mother Kosi songs.

In Man in India 23,1 (1943) 61-8. Collection of 19 songs dedicated to the goddess of Bihar's Kosi River. Provides English translations.

iii) The Rādhā-Kṛṣṇa legend

4246 HEIN, NORVIN. Mathurā's own Rāslīlā. *In his* The miracle plays of Mathurā. New Haven, Connecticut: Yale University Press, 1972. pp.127-271.
Regarding the performance of episodes from the life of Kṛṣṇa in Mathura. ". . . all who have love for Kṛishṇa in their hearts are gopīs, regardless of their sex. Kṛishṇa is . . . their real 'husband' . . . . Like the gopīs of old, we should express our affection and longing for Kṛishṇa by performing and seeing the imitation of his līlās." The most prominent sentiment portrayed, the *mādhurya rasa,* is the adoring of the Lord as one's beloved.

4247 SWANN, DARIUS. The Braj Rās Līlā. *In* Mahfil 10,2/4 (1975) 21-44.
Transcription, with notes, of a performance about the divine love of Rādhā and Kṛṣṇa.

(l) Work and economic position

i) Jewelry and other resources

4248 JACOBSON, DORANNE. Women and jewelry in rural India. *In* Giri Raj Gupta, ed. Family and social change in modern India. New Delhi: Vikas, 1976. pp.135-83. (Main currents in Indian Sociology, 2).
"This paper analyzes the importance to individual women, to couples, and to joint families, of jewelry ownership and conversions of wealth over which a woman has little control to jewelry over which a woman has complete control." Considers role of jewelry in economic power within community and kin groups and in relative economic power of men and women. Based on data from "Nimkhera" village, Raisen District.

4249 JAFFER, MEHRU. The Lucknow all-woman bank. *In* Eve's Weekly 30,38 (18 Sep 1976) 37.
Briefly describes aims and inaugural day transactions of the first women's bank in Lucknow, which was established to serve poor, backward and secluded women.

4250 VATUK, VED PRAKASH and SYLVIA VATUK. On a system of private savings among North Indian village women. *In* J. of Asian and African Studies 6,3/4 (1971) 179-90.
Discusses a system of acquisition, saving and expenditure of cash and goods by women in a western U.P. village. Over a period of about forty years "seven women secretly deposited cash, new clothing, and occasionally other valuables with a Brahman woman of the ***mohalla*** for the purpose of retaining a private store of property for their personal use, outside of the joint account of the household. Several of these women also borrowed money from her periodically." Describes family circumstances of the eight women, bank operations and resource sources and uses. The primary informant was the brahman banker. Such a system is said to be a common occurrence in village India.

ii) Participation in agriculture and other occupations

4251 BHARADWAJ, ARUNA. Police modernisation in India: a study of women police in Delhi. *In* Indian J. of Social Work 37,1 (1976) 39-48.
Describes range of situations in which presence of a female police officer is definitely advisable and required qualifications and training. Reports results of questionnaires received from 45 female Delhi officers of assistant sub-inspector rank and above on their socio-economic backgrounds, motivations for police profession, experiences in securing the job, attitudes toward various aspects of police work and recommended improvements. Various statistical tables.

4252 BILLINGS, MARTIN H. and ARJUN SINGH. Mechanisation and the wheat revolution: effects on female labour in Punjab. *In* Economic and Political Weekly 5,52 (26 Dec 1970) A:169-74.
Argues that the following three factors, in descending order, are primarily responsible for interregional variation in female agricultural participation rates in the Punjab: proportion of agriculturists in work force, female literacy rate and gross value product per worker. Shows that women's agricultural participation rate has declined in areas of "economic development" in the Punjab.

4253 CHAKRAVORTY, SHANTI. Farm women labour: waste and exploitation. *In* Social Change 5,1/2 (1975) 9-16.
Intensive study of several families in Rohtak District during the peak of the wheat harvest to "understand the role played by a woman in the rural economy and the social and economic values attached to her role performance." Urges greater appreciation for the significance of women's agricultural labor and greater access of available skills and technology to women.

4254 CHANDNA, R.C. Female working force in rural Punjab: 1961. *In* Manpower Jour-

nal 2,4 (1967) 47-62.
Examines interdistrict variation in the proportion of females employed in the rural Indian Punjab in 1961. Finds inverse correlation between female participation and urbanization. Notes that spatial patterns correspond closely with linguistic divisions.

4255 CHAWDHARI, T.P.S. and B.M. SHARMA. Female labour of the farm family in agriculture. *In* Agricultural Situation in India 16,6 (1961) 643-50.
Assesses contributions of adult female members of agriculturist families to their families' total agricultural work. Based on interviews with women of 68 farm families in a village near Delhi and cost account studies on employment of family labor in selected families from nearby villages. "The data gathered reveal elements of exploitation to which the females in families belonging even to the upper rungs of the agricultural ladder are victims. This exploitation takes the form of longer working hours, more numerous working days and feminisation of socially degrading jobs."

4256 DANG, SATYAPAL. Plight of women sweepers. *In* Mainstream 12,50 (10 Aug 1974) 20,22.
Briefly considers working conditions and wages of female sweepers in various cities of the Indian Punjab. Urges regularization and amelioration through legislation at the state level.

4257 MUKHERJI, A.B. Female participation in agricultural labour in Uttar Pradesh: spatial variations, 1961. *In* National Geographer 6 (1971) 13-8.
[Unexamined].

4258 RANADE, S.N. and G.P. SINHA. Women construction workers: reports of two surveys. Bombay: Allied Publishers, 1975? 79p. (Women in a Developing Economy, 2).
Report of studies of female construction workers in Delhi (mainly private projects) and in Bihar government projects to ascertain socio-economic backgrounds, recruitment routes, work conditions, types of work, wages, welfare facilities and standard of living. The ultimate aim was to assess the problems of women in this largely unexplored industry.

iii) Attitudes, activities and conflicts of women at work

4259 DIXIT, ASHA. A survey of leisure time activities of working women in Jaipur. *In* Indian J. of Adult Education 37,1 (1976) 11-4.
[Unexamined].

4260 KALA RANI. Performance of job role by working women. *In* Indian J. of Social Work 37,3 (1976) 281-92.
Report of study of 150 married Patna women who were educated and employed to assess their attitudes toward employment and factors relating to self-perception of job performance.

4261 ________. Role conflict in working women. New Delhi: Chetana Publications, 1976. 242p.
Report of interviews with married mothers in Patna who were educated and employed. Examines their conflicts between domestic and employment roles. Chapters discuss literature on employed women; role theory; socio-economic background of informants; their motivations for being employed; their attitudes and activities at home and at work; circumstances of employed women who are widowed, separated or divorced; chief conflicts and resolutions and conclusions and recommendations. Includes ten brief life histories.

4262 KAPUR, PROMILLA. Marriage and the working woman in India. Delhi: Vikas Publications, 1970. 528p.
Examines marital adjustment and maladjustment of middle-class Delhi women who are employed outside the home. Based upon interviews with 300 teachers, doctors and office workers. Presents extensive case study material.

4263 KAPUR, RAMA. Role conflict among employed housewives. *In* Indian J. of Industrial Relations 5,1 (1969) 39-67.
Examination of role conflict of women employed as nurses, social workers and research workers in Delhi. Considers role of independent variables such as traditional or modern values, economic or noneconomic motivation to work, job satisfaction, coping facilities, job tenure age, family income, family dependency load, duration of marriage and availability of household help.

4264 SRIVASTAVA, VINITA. Employment of educated married women in India: its causes and consequences. New Delhi: National Publishing House, 1978. 192p.
Report of questionnaire interviews with employed and nonemployed women in Chandigarh. Reviews literature and research problem and discusses methodology, socio-economic correlates with the two groups, relative prestige of husband's and wife's occupation, effects of employment on fertility, family composition and domestic arrangements, employed women as homemakers and mothers, social interaction patterns of the two groups and effects of employment on attitudes.

4265 VERMA, MALKA. Study of the middle class working women in Kanpur. *In* Indian J. of Social Work 24,4 (1964) 305-13.
Attempts to understand why increasing numbers of middle-class women are employed outside the home and whether their attitudes to family planning and marriage are changing. Based on questionnaires from 500 women in various professions. [Unexamined].

4266 WADHERA, KIRON. The new bread winners: a study on the situation of young working women. New Delhi: Vishwa Yuvak Kendra, 1976. 377p.

Report of interviews with 1,000 employed women of Delhi who were between 20 and 30 years of age and possessed at least the matriculate. Examines attitudes toward employment and numerous other aspects of their lives.

(m) Education

i) Attitudes of educated women toward family life, *pardā* and other topics

4267 AHMAD, SHADBANO. Education and purdah nuances: a note on Muslim women in Aligarh. *In* Social Action 27,1 (1977) 45-52.
Studies the relationship between education and observance of *pardā* among middle-class Muslim women in Aligarh City. Despite completing a secondary education, over one-fourth continued to observe *pardā* to some extent. Suggests that while the community values secular education for women, it is valued for the most traditional of reasons — enhancement on the marriage market.

4268 GORWANEY, NAINTARA. Self-image and social change: a study of female students. New Delhi: Sterling Publishers, 1977? 276p.
Study of female students at the University of Rajasthan, Jaipur, explores educated women as agents of modernization. Focuses on the relationship of one's family background to level of self-esteem and level of self-esteem to attitudes toward and performance of other roles. Includes extensive theoretical and methodological considerations.

4269 JHABVALA, RENANA and PRATIMA SINHA. Girl students: between school and marriage — a Delhi sample. *In* Devaki Jain, ed. Indian women. New Delhi: Publications Division, Ministry of Information and Broadcasting, Government of India, 1975. pp.281-7.
Case study material from questionnaires and interviews with female students at Delhi University. Concludes that for most, college "is just a means of spending the time till they get married. Those girls to whom college means more than a period of waiting are definitely the exceptions."

4270 KAPUR, PROMILLA. Love, marriage, and sex. Delhi: Vikas Publishing House, 1973. 302p.
Compares two statistically matched surveys of the attitudes of educated married middle- and upper-class Hindu women from Delhi and Agra conducted in 1959 and 1969, respectively. Analyzes material and presents case studies.

4271 MAHAJAN, AMARJIT. A study of attitudes of women students towards mate-selection. *In* J. of Family Welfare 12,1 (1965) 36-9.
Survey of 237 unmarried women at Panjab University, Chandigarh, found that "educated girls no longer wish to play a passive role in their marriage." A majority "thought that knowing the future partners well in advance contributes towards a happy married life." However, most would yield to parental objection to a potential spouse.

4272 SRIVASTAVA, VINITA. Professional education and attitudes to female employment: a study of married working women in Chandigarh. *In* Social Action 27,1 (1977) 19-32.
Survey found that length of education, particularly exposure to a college education, and work experience have a greater effect upon job satisfaction than does type of education.

4273 VREEDE-DE STUERS, CORA. Girl students in Jaipur: a study in attitudes towards family life, marriage, and career. Tr. from Dutch by Marly Peek-Ter Marsch. Assen: Van Gorcum, 1970. 141p. (Studies of Developing Countries, 9). [*Dutch ed.* Meisjesstudenten in Jaipur: haar houding tegenover sommige aspecten van het veranderende Hindoese familieleven. Amsterdam: Universiteit van Amsterdam, 1968. 126p.].
Attempts to ascertain social factors determining the attitudes and aspirations of female students at Rajasthan University. Based on interviews with 128 undergraduate and 75 graduate students. Examines attitudes toward various facets of traditional Indian family life and female employment.

4274 ________. Attitudes of Jaipur girl students towards family life. *In* Dhirendra Narain, ed. Explorations in the family and other essays: Professor K.M. Kapadia commemoration volume. Bombay: Thacker and Company, 1975. pp.151-62.
Results of interviews and participant observation with 203 university students concerning their attitudes toward the joint family. Although overall attitudes varied considerably, low-income students were more likely to favor and high-income students to dislike joint family life. Notes a degree of ambivalence in students' responses.

ii) Attitudes toward female education

4275 PANDEY, RAJENDRA. Youth's aspirations for women's education and some correlates. *In* J. of Social and Economic Studies 2,1 (1974) 57-77.
Attitude survey of rural and urban male college students in Varanasi District. Correlates results with socio-economic factors.

4276 PARASHAR, OM DATT. Parents' attitude to girls' education. *In* Educational Review 72,7 (1966) 145-9.
Study of the attitudes of 200 villagers of the Delhi area concerning female education. Factors such as higher socio-economic status, higher education and employment of women of the family tended to be associated with a favorable attitude.

iii) Educational institutions and programs

4277 Banasthali. Produced by Mohan N. Wadhwan. Directed by Dilip Jamdar. 1966. 10 min. Black and white. 16 and 35 mm. [*Distributed by* Films Division, Ministry of Information and Broadcasting, 24 G. Deshmukh Marg, Bombay 400 026].
Film of life in Rajasthan's Banasthali Vidyapeeth, a free girls' school for primary through higher educational levels. Focuses on its liberal arts education and creative atmosphere. [Unexamined. CF].

4278 DIMMITT, MARJORIE. Isabella Thoburn College. Cincinnati: World Outlook Press, 1961.
Volume undoubtedly published in conjunction with the 75th anniversary year of this Lucknow women's college. [Unexamined].

4279 HANS, PUSHPA. St. Stephen's opens its doors to girls. *In* Eve's Weekly 29,35 (30 Aug 1975) 10-11, 16.
Reactions of male and female students to the opening of a Delhi college to women.

4280 KUNDU, C.L. Women's education in India, retrospect and prospect: silver jubilee issue. Dayalbagh, Agra: Women's Training College, 1971.
[Unexamined].

4280a TRIVEDI, SHEELA. Nonformal education for women officers, Education Department, U.P.: report of the state level orientation seminars on nonformal education. Lucknow: Literacy House, 1977. 119p.
Report of 1976 seminars organized by the Family Life Centre of Literacy House for selected administrators of girls' schools and teacher training institutions. Main objective was to assess concept and programs of nonformal education for girls and women. Includes reports, statistics, discussion sheets, list of participants and so forth. In English and Hindi.

(n) Development and social welfare

i) Understanding sex ratio differentials

4281 DANGE, A.S. An analysis of sex-ratio differentials by regions of Madhya Pradesh. *In* Artha Vijñāna 14 (Sep 1972) 273-86.
Census data reveals a lower male/female ratio in rice and rice-wheat producing regions and a higher ratio in wheat and wheat-jowar regions. Considers census inaccuracy, sex ratio at birth and migration to be related to this pattern. Relatively low sex ratios are said to be found in rice-growing regions of India and Asia as a whole.

4282 KASHYAP, S.S. The changing pattern of sex ratio in the Punjab. *In* Demography India 4,2 (1975) 316-22.
Cites four key factors in the low ratio of females to males in Punjab State, India: 1) influence of spatial mobility, 2) sex-selective omissions in census, 3) higher birth rate for males and 4) mortality differentials adverse to females.

ii) Programs and institutions for women

4283 CHATTERJEE, BISHWA BANDHU. A candle in woodland: Kasturba Kanya Ashram, Niwali: past, present, and future. Bombay: Allied, 1977. 234p.
Evaluation of a Gandhian ashram for tribal women in Indore District sponsored by the Kasturba Gandhi National Memorial Trust. Includes a history of the center and the development of its activities, which include health care, Mahila Mandals, camps, peace marches, conferences, a seed store, a farm and a People's Court. Critically evaluates the impact of the programs in various areas based on interviews with participants. Offers recommendations. Photographs and tables.

4284 KAUL, T.N. Women's education and rural development. *In* M.S. Randhawa, ed. Developing village India: studies in village problems, rev. ed. Bombay: Orient Longmans, 1951. pp.252-4.
Assesses experiments in rural education for women established by the author in Faizabad (1940) and Farrukhabad (1945) Districts of the former United Provinces. With recommendations for future programs.

4285 Women's programmes: draft report of the baseline survey. Lucknow: Government of Uttar Pradesh, 1960. 129p.
On the Ajit Mal pilot project for female uplift. Conducted by the Planning, Research and Action Institute, Lucknow? [Unexamined. IBP].

iii) Khanna rural population study, 1953-60 and 1969, Ludhiana District, Punjab

See also entries 4125-26, 4132, 4136-41 and 4163

4286 WYON, JOHN B. and JOHN E. GORDON. The Khanna study: population problems in the rural Punjab. Cambridge, Massachusetts: Harvard University Press, 1971. 437p.
Report of an intensive eight-year study of population dynamics in a predominantly Sikh area of rural Ludhiana District and a follow up investigation a decade later. Using a community-wide "epidemiology of health" approach, the team observed population dynamics of villagers exposed and not exposed to a family planning program. Includes much material on women's reproductive lives, much attention to methodology and many photographs.

iv) Family planning knowledge, attitudes and practices

4287 AGARWAL, S.K. Attitude of females towards family planning in Barwala. *In* Medical Digest 29,11 (1961) 649-54.
[Unexamined].

4288 ANAND, K. Opinion and attitude towards family planning in Chandigarh. *In* J. of Family Welfare 10,4 (1964) 60-5.
Study of 100 Chandigarh women "of completed fertility" to assess attitudes and practices regarding family size, artificial contraceptive intervention and appropriate age of girls at marriage.

4289 BEBARTA, PRAFULLA C. Attitude of women toward family planning: a study in differences by family type in six villages of Delhi. *In* Quarterly J. of Indian Studies in Social Sciences 1,1 (1967) 78-84.
Interviews with 729 rural women in the Delhi area revealed striking differences in family planning attitudes between members of joint and nuclear families. Women of nuclear families were as a group more willing to learn about family planning, less desirous of further children and more aware of family planning practices.

4290 BHARDWAJ, K.S. and SAROJ MULLICK. Attitudes of Indian women towards abortion. *In* Indian J. of Social Work 33, 4 (1973) 317-22.
Correlates attitudes of 615 Delhi women toward abortion with various socio-economic features: age group, number of living children, number of pregnancies, income, occupation, education, family type, contraceptive method, expected number of children and ideal number of children.

4291 BHATIA, J.C. Abortionists and abortion seekers. *In* Indian J. of Social Work 34,3 (1973) 275-85.
Report of study of 36 male practitioners of indigenous medicine in Ludhiana District who perform abortions. Investigates socio-economic characteristics of those who perform abortions as opposed to those who do not, number performed, abortion as a source of income, marital status of clients, stage of pregnancy of clients, age of clients and assistance from female workers.

4292 ________ and ALFRED K. NEUMANN. Practitioners of indigenous medicine and India's family planning programme. *In* Indian J. of Social Work 34,1 (1973) 27-35.
Report of a study of 62 male indigenous medical practitioners (IMPs) in Ludhiana District to ascertain their knowledge, attitudes and practices relating to family planning. Results suggest that IMPs have great potential for enhancing the government family planning efforts.

4293 CHADDHA, PROMILA. Comparative study of the opinion of wives whose husbands have undergone vasectomy and those whose husbands have not undergone vasectomy in three villages of Mehrauli Block. Delhi: Delhi University, 1968.
[Unexamined].

4294 DUBEY, DINESH CHANDRA and HARVEY M. CHOLDIN. Communication and diffusion of the IUCD: a case study in urban India. *In* Demography 4,2 (1967) 601-14.
Compares communication patterns of New Delhi spouses regarding the intrauterine contraceptive device. While husbands tended to get their first information about the IUCD from impersonal sources (e.g., newspapers) and discuss the information with friends, women tended to get initial information from personal sources (e.g., clinic staff) and discuss it with neighbors. Considers couples' decisions to adopt IUCD.

4295 GOULD, KETAYUN H. Sex and contraception in Sherupur: family planning in a North Indian village. *In* Economic and Political Weekly 4,49 (6 Dec 1969) 1887-92.
Study of cultural obstacles to effective contraceptive practice in "Sherupur" village, Faizabad District. Author found that, contrary to the prevailing myth, village women were willing to freely discuss intimate matters. Discusses frequency of intercourse in terms of a woman's life cycle stage, precoital practices that limit certain potential contraceptive techniques, menstrual attitudes and beliefs and indigenous contraceptive practices.

4296 GUHA, UMA. Attitude of U.P. village woman on planned parenthood. *In* Bulletin of the Department of Anthropology, Government of India 4,1 (1955) 41-50.
Report of interviews with Hindu and Muslim wom-

en of 13 villages in Jaunpur District. Abortion appeared to be the most popular way these women avoided pregnancy while some practiced abstinence; few knew of contraceptive methods. Asserts that while "not always articulate, the idea and wish to plan family is there." Also provides brief socio-economic profile of the group and discusses attitudes toward related topics.

4297 GUHARAJ, AYSHA and S.C. GUPTA. Attitude survey of married women regarding family planning at urban health centre, Alambagh, Lucknow. *In* Indian J. of Public Health 12,3 (1968) 165-71.
Ninety-four married women were interviewed regarding income, education, husband's occupation, family type, number of children and awareness and use of contraceptive methods. Although 83% of the group knew of family planning, only 29.8% had ever used any birth control method. Does not correlate socio-economic factors with birth control use or attitudes.

4298 KHAN, LILIAN. The dai: an essential member of the family planning organisation. *In* J. of Family Welfare 9,1 (1962) 8-10.
Brief report of a study of village midwives near Najafgarh made prior to the establishment of a local training program for them and the changes in their knowledge and attitudes brought about by participating in the program.

4299 MAJUMDAR, D.N. Report on the enquiry into fertility and family planning among a section of married women in Kanpur. Lucknow: Department of Anthropology, Lucknow University, 1955?
[Unexamined].

4300 MALHOTRA, PRABHA and LILIAN KHAN. Factors favoring acceptance of family planning among women attending some New Delhi M.C.W. Centers. *In* J. of Family Welfare 8,2 (1961) 1-18.
Reviews results of interviews with 101 female patrons of New Delhi Maternity and Child Welfare Centers. Findings suggest need for greater emphasis on contraceptive use for spacing and limitation, on education regarding decreasing infant mortality rates and on the relationship of standard of living to family size. Considers reasons why informants desired additional children.

4301 ________. Family planning knowledge and practices among women attending some New Delhi M.C.W. centres: a pilot study. *In* Indian J. of Public Health 6,3 (1962) 121-32.
Report of interviews with 101 female clients of several New Delhi Maternity and Child Welfare Centers regarding various aspects of their knowledge of family planning and interests in limiting their own families. Considers implications of findings for policy and planning.

4302 MAMDANI, MAHMOOD. The myth of population control: family, caste and class in an Indian village. New York: Monthly Review Press, 1973. 173p.
Considers relationship of the social system to fertility in a Panjabi village. [Unexamined. BAS].

4303 MARSHALL, JOHN F. Some "meanings" of family planning to an Indian villager. *In* Research Previews 19,1 (1972) 24-9.
Based on field research in a village of western U.P., this report identifies some of the local meanings of family planning and describes the cultural context in which they occur. Considers native views of government officers as family planning agents, pregnancy, limitation of village population growth and infant mortality. Discusses implications for policy development and program implementation.

4304 PHATAK, L.V., ANRUDH K. JAIN and R. CHHABRA. Post insertion contraceptive and fertility behaviour of IUCD acceptors. New Delhi: National Institute of Family Planning, 1973. 30p. (NIFP Technical Paper 18).
Report of study of about 2,000 IUCD acceptors from a clinic in New Delhi.

4305 RAINA, B.L., ROBERT R. BLAKE and EUGENE M. WEISS. A study in family planning communication: Meerut District. New Delhi: Central Family Planning Institute, 1967. 82p. (*Its* Monograph Series, 3).
Illustrated. [Unexamined. NUC].

4306 RASTOGI, SITA RAM. Role of managements and trade unions in family planning programme: a study of industrial undertakings at Kanpur. Lucknow: Demographic Research Centre, Department of Economics, Lucknow University, 1977. 53p. (*Its* Series B, Survey Report 6).
[Unexamined. ALI].

4307 SINHA, UMESH PRASAD. Attitude towards family planning of Santal and Paharias of Santal Parganas. *In* Bulletin of the Bihar Tribal Research Institute 5,2 (1963) 301-10.
Report of interviews with Santals, Sauria Paharias and Mal Paharias of Santal Parganas District. Discusses interest in family planning, additional number of sons and daughters desired and reasons given, preferred family planning method and medicinal contraceptives. Compares responses of men and women. Photographs of tribal women and children.

4308 SURJIT KAUR. Family planning in two industrial units: a study. Delhi: Sterling Publishers, 1976. 256p.
"The overall objective of this study is to determine the feasibility of extending family planning services to the factory employees in the industrial settings. An attempt is also made to determine the types of services and family planning communication media approaches which are most effective in increasing adoption of family planning." Based on interviews with male workers in the Escorts Ltd. and Bata Shoe Company factories in Faridabad.

v) Poverty

4309 SINGH, ANDREA MENEFEE. Women and the family: coping with poverty in the *bastis* of Delhi. *In* Social Action 27, 3 (1977) 241-65. [*Also in* Alfred de Souza, ed. The Indian city: poverty, ecology and urban development. New Delhi: Manohar, 1978. pp.61-94].
Study of women in four unauthorized squatter settlements of New Delhi, which "focuses on the consequences for them of rural-urban migration and urban settlement, role allocation and decision making within the family, the economic dimension of family life, the links of women and the family to the wider urban environment, and the kinds of dreams women hold for the future." Stresses urgent need for consideration of this sector in development policy.

vi) Prostitution

4310 AGNIHOTRI, VIDYADHAR. Fallen women: a study with special reference to Kanpur. Kanpur: printed at Maharaja Printers, 1954? 99p.
Study of 400 Kanpur prostitutes. Considers recruitment to profession, economics, socio-economic backgrounds and standards of living. Suggests "measures for minimising the evils of prostitution." With photographs, tables and some case history materials.

4311 GUPTA, RABINDRA NATH. From the green hills of Purola to the brothels of Delhi and Meerut: a study of the immoral trafficking in women from the Purola Block of Uttarkashi District (U.P.). *In* Bonded labour in India: a shocking tale of slave labour in rural India. Calcutta: Indian School of Social Sciences, 1974? pp.37-52.
Investigation of prostitution in Purola and Delhi reveals how prostitution in the Purola region "is inextricably linked up with the problem of bonded labour and rural indebtedness among the Harijan Community." With life histories. Volume is proceedings of the 1974 Seminar on Cultural Action for Social Change.

4312 KUMAR, PRAMOD. Prostitution: a socio-psychological analysis. *In* Indian J. of Social Work 21,4 (1961) 425-30.
Study of 136 prostitutes from two prostitute villages in Agra District. They tend to have small incomes, be poorly educated, be single or widowed and have little "health consciousness." Presents three brief case studies showing how the women came to prostitution. Comments on poor mental health of the group, makes policy recommendations and presents survey results.

4313 MATHUR, A.S. and B.L. GUPTA. Prostitutes and prostitution. Agra: Ram Prasad and Sons, 1965. 255p.
Ethnography of prostitution based upon interviews with women from a Protective Home in U.P. and from the streets of Agra, verified and supplemented by interviews with doctors, "accompanists" and others. Appendixes contain life histories of the main informants.

4314 RAINA, BHUSHAN. Delhi's singing girls. *In* Illustrated Weekly of India 93,48 (26 Nov 1972) 16-7.
Regarding a small community of dancing and singing girls in Delhi, some of whom claim historical ties to dancers of courts of former Indian states. Indirectly suggests they are involved with prostitution and discusses various aspects of prostitution in Delhi. Photographs.

vii) Crime and imprisonment

4315 AHUJA, RAM. Female offenders in India. Meerut: Meenakshi Prakashan, 1969. 131p.
Report of study of convicts and probationers from the Female Reformatory of Jaipur's Central Jail. Study sought to discover shared behavior traits, examine nature and pattern of crime, ascertain role of family, assess family adjustment to absent women, evaluate corrective system and review policy.

4316 PUNJAB (INDIA). BOARD OF ECONOMIC INQUIRY. Report on socio-economic background of women prisoners in Ludhiana Jail. Chandigarh: Economic and Statistical Organisation, Government of the Punjab, 1964. 41p. (*Its* Publication 98).
[Unexamined].

4317 SANYAL, SHUBHRA. An empirical study of certain personality characteristics and attitudes of 25 female convicts of Nari Bandi Niketan. *In* Social Defence 11,41 (1975) 31-43, 30.
A group of predominantly illiterate rural women from a (New Delhi?) jail was found to have generally good physical health but emotional instability. Most had committed murders (of these 56% murdered husbands, 20% murdered mothers-in-law and 12% murdered lovers). Investigates attitudes toward parents, religion, authorities, fellow inmates and neighbors.

viii) Health

4318 BANERJEE, SACHCHIDANANDA, SANTOSH KUMARI MAHINDRA and ASOK BANDYOPADHYAY. Food intake of adolescent college girls of Rajasthan. *In* Indian J. of

Medical Research 51,3 (1963) 494-501.
A nutritional analysis of the food consumed by twelve college women on three alternate days. Primarily presents individuals' and group's average daily consumption of various nutrients.

4318a GORDON, JOHN E., SOHAN SINGH and JOHN B. WYON. Causes of death at different ages, by sex, and by season, in a rural population of the Punjab, 1957-59: a field study. *In* Indian J. of Medical Research 53,9 (1965) 906-17.
Report of physicians' investigation of 615 deaths. "The excess beyond the desirable and potentially obtainable rates of about 10 per 1,000 per year [they found approximately 17 per 1,000 per year] was identified as due primarily to high death rates among infants, preschool children and the elderly; among females as a class; and among persons of low social and economic status." Primary recommendation is increased maternal and child health services.

4319 KIRKPATRICK, JOANNA. Primary and secondary institutions in the delivery of hospital services in South Asia: a case study and model. *In* J. of the Institute of Bangladesh Studies 1,1 (1976) 169-90.
Study based on observations in and around Christian Medical College and Hospital, Ludhiana. Discusses ways that female patients and staff members in gynecology ward mutually dealt with "discrepancies or conflicts between modern cultural definitions of [hospital] services and Indian definitions of themselves as clients." Among topics discussed are reluctance to seek hospital treatment, pattern of being accompanied by a family member escort, conceptions of illness etiology, diet problems, ritual status hierarchies and pollution management. Concludes with client-institution interaction model.

(o) Political participation

4320 AERY, RAJ RANI. Women legislative elite in Rajasthan (1962-65): an analysis of intra-legislative performance. *In* Political Science Review 6,1 (1967) 39-57.
Socio-economic profiles and legislative performance of the 15 female legislators in Rajasthan's three legislative assemblies, 1962-65. Regarding their performance, the author concludes that a few "more vocal ones more than compensated for the comparative passivity of others."

4321 ROTHERMUND, INDIRA. Women in a coalmining district. *In* Economic and Political Weekly 10,31 (2 Aug 1975) 1160-5.
Examines rural-urban differences in female political participation in Dhanbad District. Urban women in the sample, most of whom were homemakers, were assessed as having greater political awareness than quasi-urban or rural women, many of whom were working in industry or agriculture. Both groups tended to be rather apolitical.

4322 SAYEED, S.M. Woman's participation in U.P. politics: a study of political attitudes and performance of the woman members of the U.P. Assembly. *In* Indian J. of Political Science 32,2 (1971) 213-31.
Study of the 18 women who successfully campaigned in the 1969 midterm poll for the U.P. Assembly, based largely on interviews. Gives socio-economic profile and discusses informants' entry into politics, pre-Assembly social and political activities, views of reasons for success or failure, financial sources, views of role as legislators and political attitudes.

(p) Arts

For Urdu literature see entries 2887-2929

i) Folk literatures and oral traditions

4323 BEDI, SOHINDER SINGH. Women in folksayings of Panjab. *In* Folklore [Calcutta] 9,10 (1968) 381-9. [*Reprint in* Sankar Sen Gupta, ed. Women in Indian folklore. Calcutta: Indian Publications, 1969. pp.167-76. (*Its* Folklore Series, 15)].
Images of women in Sikh and Hindu folklore of various genres. Primarily familial topics. Includes examples in English translation.

4324 Folk music of India: Uttar Pradesh. Recording and notes by Laxmi G. Tewari. New York: Lyrichord Discs Inc. LLST 7271. Stereo.
Recording includes a swinging song that describes a married woman's relations with members of her natal household, a childbirth song and songs about Rādhā-Kṛṣṇa and Sītā-Rāma *bhakti*. Translations of most selections are printed on the jacket.

4325 HENRY, EDWARD OSCAR. Women's music. *In his* The meanings of music in a North Indian village. Ph.D. dissertation, Department of Anthropology, Michigan State University, 1973. pp.31-118, 251-66. [University Microfilms 74-13,904].
Ethnography of women's music in "Indrapur" village near Varanasi. Categorizes songs and discusses the characteristic ritual symbolism, language and structure of women's songs. Text includes numerous translations of song texts; appendix provides Hindi transliterations.

4326 JORDAN-HORSTMANN, MONIKA. Social aspects of Sadani oral literature. *In*

Asian Folklore Studies 36,1 (1977) 69-81.
Discusses family relationships as portrayed in folk songs sung in a Bhojpuri dialect by tribals and low-caste Hindus of Chota Nagpur. Focuses on a festival to promote crop fertility. The dominant position of women in this festival is said to contrast with their more typically subordinate position. Songs they sing at this time are often rebellious and critical.

4327 KHOSLA, G.D. The rani's sacrifice. *In his* The price of a wife. Bombay: Jaico Publishing House, 1958. pp.172-9.
The legend of Nenna Devi, first queen of Chamba, and her heroic offering of her life for the welfare of the kind and kingdom. "Sahil Varma [her husband] and his tribe are gone but Nenna Devi lives. In commemoration of her sacrifice, a fair, called the Suhi Mela, is held in Chamba every year in the first fortnight of April. Women and children dress themselves in their gayest attire and climb up to the shrine erected by Sahil Varma. They sing the Rani's praises."

4328 SATYARTHI, DEVENDRA. Thus sing the countrywomen in the Punjab. *In* Modern Review 59,1-2 (1936) 47-55, 140-7.
Discusses Panjabi women's folk song themes — nature, rivers, love, days of chivalry — and occasions — spinning, weddings, births of sons, rainy season, death. Includes English translations of numerous excerpts.

4329 ________. Punjabi songs of soldiers' wives. *In* Modern Review 72,1 (1942) 41-5.
English translations of song texts illustrate the difficulties faced by soldiers' wives. "These women have always suffered and their songs have sprung from the good earth of their time-honoured traditions and living emotions." Photographs.

4330 ________. Spin, Girl, spin. *In* Rural India 6,9 (1943) 374-8.
Translations of and commentary on Panjabi spinning songs.

4331 ________. Sisters of the spinning wheel. *In* Modern Review 80,1 (1946) 36-41. [*Abridged in his* Meet my people: Indian folk poetry. Hydrabad, India: Chetana, 1951. pp.89-104].
Describes Panjabi "spinning-bees" and songs that accompany them. "Through their songs the sisters of the spinning-wheel express their joy and sorrow, hope and despair, anger and fear." With photos, translations and transliterations.

4332 SHARMA, SHAKTI. Women in Dogri folk songs. *In* Folklore [Calcutta] 12,9 (1971) 320-7.
Analyzes songs concerned with the social behavior and emotions of women, focusing on the theme of love and separation in the husband-wife relationship. With transliterated and translated examples.

4333 SINGH, K. JAGJIT. Women in Punjabi folksongs. *In* Folklore [Calcutta] 9,4 (1968) 122-31. [*Reprint in* Sankar Sen Gupta, ed. Women in Indian folklore. Calcutta: Indian Publications, 1969. pp.97-108. (*Its* Folklore Series, 15)].
Interprets, transliterates and translates selected lines. "Punjab is thus a land where a woman is looked at with respect by one and all."

4334 SINHA, SURAJIT. Expression of sentiments in the songs associated with the Karam festival of rural Manbhum (Bihar, India). *In* Man in India 37,1 (1957) 34-48.
Describes this festival as observed in the former Manbhum District. Provides translations of 43 songs, grouped according to topic. States that major themes are positive associations with a woman's natal home (particularly the brother-sister relationship) and negative associations with her conjugal home, women's fertility and crop fertility.

4335 PRASAD, BAIJNATH. The legend of the origin of dancing girls. *In* North Indian Notes and Queries 5,10 (1895) 169-70.
Short legend collected in Bara Banki District that depicts the first dancing girls as offspring of a holy man and the woman directed by Satan to temp him. Raised and educated by the disguised Satan under the patronage of a king, they were ultimately taught the singing and dancing arts and became the king's consorts.

4336 UPADHYAYA, KRISHNA DEVA. Some aspects of Indian folk-culture as depicted in Bhojpuri folksongs and folk-tales. *In* Folklore [Calcutta] 7,9 (1966) 330-49.
Focuses on images of women in Bhojpuri folk literature — through the life cycle, chastity and ordeals to prove their virtue, relations vis à vis other family members, early marriage, polygamy and *pardā*.

4337 ________. The position of women in Bhojpuri folklore. *In* Folklore [Calcutta] 9,7 (1968) 243-50. [*Reprint in* Sankar Sen Gupta, ed. Women in Indian folklore. Calcutta: Indian Publications, 1969. pp.129-37. (*Its* Folklore Series, 15)].
Considers themes relating to Hindu women in Bhojpuri folk tales. "Woman has been relegated to a very humble status."

4338 ________. On the position of women in Indian folk culture. *In* Asian Folklore Studies 27,1 (1968) 81-100.
Reviews themes relating to various life cycle stages and other topics (e.g., *satīs*, chastity, children's marriage, *pardā*) in Bhojpuri folk literature.

4339 WADLEY, SUSAN S. Folk literature in Karimpur. *In* J. of South Asian Literature 11,1/2 (1975) 7-18.
Reviews oral folk traditions in "Karimpur" village, Mainpuri District. Considers categories and characteristics of men's and women's songs, respectively.

ii) Domestic folk arts of Mithila: printed sources

4340 ARCHER, W.G. Maithil painting. *In* Mārg 3,3 (1949) 24-33.
Considers preparation of wall, materials, inspiration, division of labor, transmission of skills, caste styles, occasions for production, motifs, lines, color, stylization and function. Photographs.

4341 JAYAKAR, PUPUL. Paintings of Mithila. *In* Times of India Annual (1971) 29-36.
Text and 17 color and black and white photographs of Mithila paintings. Describes development of paper painting as a drought relief program in 1968 and the subsequent revival of an art that had been disappearing. Discusses the dignity this gave to local female painters and various details of motifs, themes (predominantly fertility), styles, colors and materials.

4342 JHA, RATNADHAR. Mithila paintings. *In* Durgadas Mukhopadhyay, ed. Lesser known forms of performing arts in India. New Delhi: Sterling Publishers, 1978. pp.38-44.
Discusses rise of Mithila paintings to popularity in the late 1960s, predominant motifs and styles, place of the paintings in the lives of local women and work of several artists.

4343 MATHUR, J.C. and MILDRED ARCHER. Domestic arts of Mithila. *In* Mārg 20,1 (1966) 43-51.
Briefly discusses four categories of domestic arts: line drawings on ground, wall paintings, figurines and dolls of terra cotta and other materials and "utility articles." Black and white photographs of wall paintings.

4344 RAI, RAGHU. The colour of Madhubani. *In* New Delhi 1,1 (4 Sep 1978) 56-9.
Photo essay about Madhubani wall and paper paintings and painters.

4345 THAKUR, UPENDRA. Painting. *In his* History of Mithila: circa 3000 B.C.-1556 A.D. Darbhanga: Mithila Institute, 1956. pp.386-90.
Includes brief section on the contemporary domestic wall-painting tradition. Considers materials, motifs, color and style.

4346 UPADHYAYA, DAYA SHANKAR. The folk-paintings of Mithilā. *In* J. of the Bihar Research Society 54,1/4 (1968) 306-18.
Ethnography of wall-painting and floor/earth line-drawing traditions in Mithila. Considers artists, contexts, content, colors and materials. Reproduces six paintings.

4347 _______. Folk-arts of Bihar. *In* L.P. Vidyarthi and Ganesh Chaubay, eds. Bihar in folklore study: an anthology. Calcutta: Indian Publications, 1971. pp.81-106. (*Its* Folklore Series, 18).
Contains some notes on the history of the region and a survey of wall-painting, line-drawing, henna hand design, doll and tattooing traditions and related rituals. [Unexamined. Book in IBP].

4348 VEQUAUD, YVES. The women painters of Mithila. Tr. from French by George Robinson. London: Thames and Hudson, 1977. 112p. [*French ed.* L'art du Mithila. Paris: Presses de la Connaissance, 1976].
Introduction briefly discusses historical background of Mithila, *tāntrika* and Vedic elements of the paintings, ritual contexts for painting, deities portrayed, painters and technique. Contains several photographs and 88 illustrations, most in color, with brief commentary. Discusses and illustrates both wall paintings and floor/earth line drawings.

iii) Domestic folk arts of Mithila: film sources

4349 Madhubani paintings. Produced by Miniature Films. Directed by Debabrata Roy. 1971. 15 min. Color. 16 and 35 mm. [*Distributed by* Films Division, Ministry of Information and Broadcasting, 24 G. Deshmukh Marg, Bombay 400 026].
Scenes of Bihar village life, the female painters and their work. [Unexamined. CF].

4350 Mithila: Bodenzeichnung der Kayastha-Frauen in Jitvarpur [Mithila: ground drawings of Kayastha women of Jitvarpur]. Erika Moser-Schmitt, filmmaker. (Silent). 1973? 12 min. Color. 16 mm. [*Distributed by* Pennsylvania State University Audio-visual Services, 17 Willard Building, University Park, Pennsylvania 16802. *And* Institut für den Wissenschaftlichen Film, Nonnenstieg, 3400 Göttingen, Federal Republic of Germany. *Order number* E 2295].
Film of execution of two octagonal ground drawings in a courtyard. A deity is installed and supplementary motifs are drawn with rice-flour paste and colored powder in preparation for an impending rite. A printed text is planned as an accompaniment to the film. [Unexamined. Information supplied by filmmaker].

4351 Mithila: Bodenzeichnung für die Satyanarayan-Zeremonie durch Brahmanen-Frauen in Jitvarpur [Mithila: ground drawing for the Satyanārāyaṇa ceremony by brahman women of Jitvarpur]. Erika Moser-Schmitt, filmmaker. (Silent). 1973? 12 min. Color. 16 mm. [*For distributor see entry 4350. Order number* E 2294].
Film portrays the preparation of ground drawings that serve as an altar for life cycle and calendrical rites. Using rice-flour

paste and colored powder, the women install a diety. The accompanying rite is to be performed later in the day. A printed text is planned as an accompaniment to the film. [Unexamined. Information supplied by filmmaker].

4352 Mithila: Handbemalung der Kayastha-Frauen in Jitvarpur [Mithila: hand painting of Kayastha women of Jitvarpur]. Erika Moser-Schmitt, filmmaker. (Silent). 1973? 8-1/2 min. Black and white. 16 mm. [*For distributor see entry 4350. Order number* E 2297].
Film of the 16-year-old Durga Kumari decorating her hand with henna paste. Her mother prepares the paste and Durga Kumari draws a stylized lotus on her left palm. She decorates her fingers and nails as well but leaves her middle finger undecorated in order that harm not be brought to her brother. After several hours the dried paste is removed. The reddish brown stain will remain for several weeks. A printed text is planned as an accompaniment to the film. [Unexamined. Information supplied by filmmaker].

4353 Mithila: Herstellen von Blumengirlanden durch Angehörige der Mali-Kaste in Jitvarpur [Mithila: manufacture of flower garlands by members of the Mali community of Jitvarpur]. Erika Moser-Schmitt, filmmaker. (Silent). 1973? 10-1/2 min. Black and white. 16mm. [*For distributor see entry 4350. Order number* E 2300].
Film shows division of labor in a Mali gardener family. A husband prepares threads from banana fibers. The following day his wife strings flowers on the dried threads and wraps them in leaves to keep them fresh. Her son distributes them to village households for use in daily domestic rites. The husband, assisted by his wife, demonstrates how the flowers are used in domestic rites. A printed text is planned as an accompaniment to the film. [Unexamined. Information supplied by filmmaker].

4354 Mithila: Herstellen von Lehm-Reliefs und Wandmalerei durch Harijan-Frauen in Jitvarpur [Mithila: manufacture of mud reliefs and wall painting by harijan women of Jitvarpur]. Erika Moser-Schmitt, filmmaker. (Silent). 1973? 17-1/2 min. Color. 16 mm. [*For distributor see entry 4350. Order number* E 2370].
Film depicts harijan women sculpting clay reliefs on one end of an unfinished home. A young woman who will live in the house is soon joined by friends and relatives. The women form elephants, cows, buffaloes, birds and other figures. Stimulated by the presence of the camera, they spontaneously cover all available space. When the clay has dried for one week, it is reinforced with a coating of cow dung paste. Several days later the future inhabitant adds several paintings to the other side of the house. A printed text is planned as an accompaniment to the film. [Unexamined. Information supplied by filmmaker].

4355 Mithila: Malen eines Krishna-Bildes auf Papier durch Brahmanen-Frauen in Jitvarpur [Mithila: brahman women of Jitvarpur painting a Kṛṣṇa figure on paper]. Erika Moser-Schmitt, filmmaker. (Silent). 1973? 12 min. Color. 16 mm. [*For distributor see entry 4350. Order number* E 2368].
The gifted young painter, Bauadevi, paints a picture of her favorite deity, Kṛṣṇa, for the film. Paper painting is a contemporary commercial variant of the traditional wall-painting and earth-drawing traditions of Mithila. Bauadevi's sequence follows that of traditional murals, from the initial border to the affixing of the deity's eye. A printed text is planned as an accompaniment to the film. [Unexamined. Information supplied by filmmaker].

4356 Mithila: Malen eines Sarasvati-Bildes auf Papier durch Brahmanen-Frauen in Jitvarpur [Mithila: brahman women of Jitvarpur painting a Sarasvatī figure on paper]. Erika Moser-Schmitt, filmmaker. (Silent). 1973? 10-1/2 min. Color. 16 mm. [*For distributor see entry 4350. Order number* E 2369].
Film of the painter Sitadevi in her courtyard painting a Sarasvatī image on handmade paper with dried grass and natural fibers wound on a stick. Her signature indicates an artistic consciousness. Sitadevi, the best known of the Mithila painters, was awarded the All-India Handicrafts Board's National Award for Mastercraftsmen in 1975. In recent years, she has participated in international folklore meetings in Europe and the United States. Her son serves as her assistant, traveling companion and manager. A printed text is planned as an accompaniment to the film. [Unexamined. Information supplied by filmmaker].

4357 Mithila: Malerei auf Papier durch Harijan-Frauen in Jitvarpur [Mithila: paper painting by harijan women of Jitvarpur]. Erika Moser-Schmitt, filmmaker. (Silent). 1973? 13 min. Color. 16mm. [*For distributor see entry 4350. Order number* E 2296].
Film of two harijan women drawing and painting on paper. Unlike high-caste women, these women do not regularly paint on paper as a commercial activity and the paintings, done for the film, are therefore spontaneously created. The first woman paints an open air meeting of men and women with motifs indicative of a feast. The second woman paints the performance of a traditional dance of her community. Colors are applied without regard to outlines in a style reminiscent of primitive-inspired western art. A printed text is planned as an accompaniment to the film. [Unexamined. Information supplied by filmmaker].

4358 Mithila: Wandbemalung für kultzwecke durch Brahmanen-Frauen in Jitvarpur

[Mithila: wall painting for religious purposes by brahman women of Jitvarpur]. Erika Moser-Schmitt, filmmaker. (Silent). 1973? 18 min. Color. 16 mm. [*For distributor see entry 4350. Order number* E 2371].
Film of a young brahman painter, Bauadevi, painting images of Durgā, Kālī Gaṇeśa and Hanumān. The execution occurs in a fixed sequence. A printed text is planned as an accompaniment to the film. [Unexamined. Information supplied by filmmaker].

4359 Soziale grundlagen der traditionellen und kommerziellen Bildkunst der Brahmanen und Harijan-Frauen [The social background of traditional and commercial art of brahman and harijan women]. Erika Moser-Schmitt, filmmaker. (German commentary). 1973? 13 min. Color. 16mm. [*For distributor see entry 4350. Order number* D 1196].
Film of excerpts from the Jitvarpur village film series depicts a succession of contrasting scenes of the daily life of high- and low-caste communities and the artistic activities of brahman and harijan women. A printed text is planned as an accompaniment to the film. [Unexamined. Information supplied by filmmaker].

iv) Rajasthani literature: work of Rani Laxmi Kumari Chundawat

4360 SOLANKI, M.S. Rani Laxmi Kumari Chundawat. *In* Contemporary Indian Literature 6,9/10 (1966) 7-9.
Reviews the literary contributions of this bilingual (Rajasthani, Hindi) writer from a royal family of Rajasthan. "Leaving aside the half-a-dozen works in Hindi prose, her entire production in over two dozen volumes, consists of folklore in prose and poetry. She has arduously [collected] folk-songs and Rajasthani poetry . . . . the editing of songs and poetry is beautifully done . . . her genius is . . . in the prose rendering of old stories of facts and fiction."

v) Hindi literature: images of women

4361 AGRAWAL, CHANDRA P. The dynamic heroine of modern Hindi novel. *In her* Studies in Indian literature and culture. Lucknow: Lucknow Publishing House, 1977. pp.69-78.
Brief discussion of the development of feminine characterization in the Hindi novel, followed by an examination of heroines of three novels written by women (K.L. Sabbarwal, Shanti Joshi and Usha Priamvada) from 1965 to 1971. Projects the trends of the near future. Makes "two underlying assumptions: one, that the enrichment of the heroine is integrally related to the development of female status in the society; and two, that the consciousness of women writers affects the female status significantly."

4362 ANSARI, DAGMAR. Die Frau im modernen Hindi-Roman nach 1947 [Woman in the modern Hindi novel since 1947]. Berlin: Akademie Verlag, 1970. 238p. (Deutsche Akademie der Wissenschaften zu Berlin Institut für Orientforschung, 68).
Surveys the position of women in 34 Hindi novels by 18 authors from 1947 to 1964. The women are portrayed as "living human beings . . . who have been deprived of the right to be complete human beings by the traditions of thousands of years. Most Hindi writers regard the question of how far Indian women have asserted their right to independent feelings, thoughts and action as an essential aspect of life." Has English summary, "Women's Problems in the Hindi Novel after 1947."

4363 DELL, DAVID. The sati theme. *In* Feminine sensibility and characterization in South Asian literature. Guest ed: Fritz Blackwell. J. of South Asian Literature 12,3/4 (1977) 55-66.
Examines ideal of the virtuous woman who is willing to die rather than act against her principles in 20th century Hindi literature. This theme, popular with the Chayavad writers of the 1920s and 1930s, later lost its appeal for more realistic and antiromantic readers and writers.

4364 NILSSON, USHA SAKSENA. A woman's experience: three novels of Hindi. *In* Feminine sensibility and characterization in South Asian literature. Guest ed: Fritz Blackwell. J. of South Asian Literature 12,3/4 (1977) 11-8.
Reviews trends of female characterization in the 20th century Hindi novel. Contrasts a series of novels depicting stereotypic objectified, deified, idealized or victimized women with three recent novels by women (Krishna Sobti, Mannu Bhandari and Usha Priyamvada). The recent works depict autonomous, individualistic female characters.

vi) Hindi literature: female writers

4365 AGRAWAL, CHANDRA P. Stories of Mansfield and Bhandari: a comparison. *In* Indian Literature 21,1 (1978) 45-56.
Compares the English stories of Katherine Mansfield and the Hindi stories of Mannu Bhandari, a pioneer of the "new story" movement. They are alike in their sympathy for pain, suffering and the victimized. They differ with respect to their respective uses of Chekhovian techniques and conceptions of good and evil.

4366 CHAUHAN, VIJAY. Women writers in Hindi. *In* Contemporary Indian Literature 6,4 (1966) 5-7.
Brief essay traces the thematic concerns of various female writers in Hindi throughout the 20th century. Asserts that "it is in fiction that a woman writer finds her natural medium." With some reference to female writers in other South Asian languages. Author herself writes in Hindi.

4367 MAHADEVAN, MEERA. Shulamith. Tr. from Hindi. Delhi: Arnold-Heinemann, 1975. 208p. (Indian Novels, 7).
Novel. Focuses on the life of an Indian Jewish family in Bombay. Portrays a woman's roles as wife, daughter-in-law, mother and general philanthropic mistress of the household. She sacrifices her own happiness by refusing to go to Israel with her husband and prefers to stay in India where she feels she belongs. Depicts impact of Hindu cultural values on Jewish family life.

4368 SCHOMER, KARINE. Mahadevi Varma's Allahabad: an exploration of the modern Hindi literary community. *In* Berkeley Working Papers on South and Southeast Asia 1 (1975/76) 201-59. *With* Commentary. By Kathryn Hansen. pp.260-5.
Examines "the Hindi literary community as it developed in the first half of the twentieth century, particularly in the city of Allahabad . . . . approaches the subject through the experiences of Mahadevi Varma, one of the major poets of the Chayavad movement in Hindi poetry, and one of the few women writers of her time." Details a community with strong identity and close interaction.

4369 VARMA, MAHADEVI. A pilgrimage to the Himalayas: and other silhouettes from memory. Tr. from Hindi by Radhika Prasad Srivastava and Lillian Srivastava. London: Peter Owen, 1975. 127p. (UNESCO Collection of Representative Works, Indian Series).
Collection of memoirs, essays and sketches describing India of the 1930s and 1940s, along with the author's comments and evaluations, which, say the translators, "serve as poetic asides." "My memoirs are not meant to be mere detached descriptions of incidents, nor reportage of my own life story or the life stories of others. Rather they are emotional journeys begun with the purpose of recreating those moments in which I shared and lived the feelings and experiences of others."

vii) Hindi literature: male writers

4370 BLACKWELL, FREDERICK WARN. Characterization of women in three contemporary Hindi playwrights: Jai Shankar Prasad, Lakshmi Narain Lal, and Mohan Rakesh. Ph.D. dissertation, Department of South Asian Studies, University of Wisconsin, 1973. 222p. [University Microfilms 74-8992].
Considers feminine characterization in the major dramatic works of three playwrights, one by one, with a brief conclusion. Although female characters of all three are "subordinated in the relationship with man, it is the woman who time after time emerges the stronger character." Although she is present by virtue of her relationship to a man, "she emerges as carrier and support for the man and of the dramatic situation, *if* she possesses an inner-strength: *śakti* for Prasad, adherence to dharma for Lal, and in Rakesh's Sundarī her *svābhimān*."

4371 CHANDAR, KRISHAN. The four-anna aunt. Tr. from Hindi by Jai Ratan. *In* Thought 16,26 (27 Jun 1964) 11-4. [*Also* Tai Eesree. Tr. from Panjabi by Khushwant Singh. *In* Khushwant Singh and Jaya Thadani, eds. Land of the five rivers: stories from the Punjab. Bombay: Jaico Publishing House, 1965. pp.85-101].
Short story. Portrays an aging Hindu aunt who displays qualities of generosity, acceptance, forgiveness and self-sacrifice.

4372 ________. All-India heroines' conference. Tr. from Hindi. *In* Thought 20, 40 (5 Oct 1968) III-VII.
Short story. Mocks lifestyle of female film stars.

4373 DIVYA, AMBIKA PRASAD. The woman of Khajuraha. Tr. from Hindi. Ajaigarh: Sahitya Sadan, 1964. 111p.
Poetry. Apparently inspired by erotic temple sculpture at Khajuraho. Illustrated. [Unexamined. ALI].

4374 KUMAR, JAINENDRA. The resignation: a novel. Tr. from Hindi by S.H. Vatsyayan. Delhi: Siddhartha Publications, n.d. 106p.
Novel. Examines life of a woman through the eyes of her brother's son. Recounts their relationship from childhood, her extramarital affair and pregnancy, the dissolution of her marriage and her subsequent sufferings.

4375 KUMAR, PREM. Four figures in love: Anna Karenin, Emma Bovary, Constance Chatterly, and Chitralekha. *In* Feminine sensibility and characterization in South Asian literature. Guest ed: Fritz Blackwell. J. of South Asian Literature 12,3/4 (1977) 73-80.
Contrasts Anna Karenin's "totality in love," Emma Bovary's "escape in love," Lady Chatterly's "sensuality in love" and Chitralekha's "maturity in love." The latter is the chief character in Bhagwati Charan Verma's Hindi novel by the same name.

4376 ORR, INGE C. Premchand's use of folklore in his short stories. *In* Asian Folklore Studies 36,1 (1977) 31-56.
Argues that Premchand considered Indian folk customs and beliefs to be inconsistent with both ancient and abstractly humanitarian

ideals. In reformist spirit he portrayed the sway of folk traditions over his female characters. His male characters are ambivalent in this respect and reflect the tension between old and new values.

4377 PREMCHAND, pseud. [DHANPAT RAI SRIVASTAVA]. Daughter of a noble family. Tr. from Hindi by B.A. Bhandarkar. *In* Thought 8,5 (4 Feb 1956) 9-11.
Short story. An aristocratic girl marries into a poor village family. Portrays her problems of adjustment and her precarious yet pivotal position in joint family life as a woman.

4378 _______. Miss Malti. Tr. from Hindi by Jai Ratan and P. Lal. *In* Daniel L. Milton and William Clifford, eds. A treasury of modern Asian stories. New York: New American Library, 1961. pp.48-60.
Excerpt from Premchand's last complete novel, *Godān* ("The Gift of a Cow"). Illustrates his characterization of the striking contemporary figure, Miss Malti. [Unexamined. Book in NUC].

4379 _______. Subhagi. Tr. from Hindi by Madan Gopal. *In* Illustrated Weekly of India 84,7 (17 Feb 1963) 19-21.
Short story. A poor child-widow remains cheerful, hardworking, self-sacrificing and devoted to her parents.

4380 _______. Step-mother. Tr. from Hindi by Madan Gupta. *In* Thought 15,11 (16 Mar 1963) 11-2.
Short story. A kind-hearted and giving stepmother attempts to compensate for a young boy's loss of his mother. Suggests psychological problems from loss of mother and wife and offers an untraditional view of the stepmother.

4381 SHARMA, RATAN LAL. The blunt arrows. Tr. from Hindi by Paresh Sharma. *In* Social Welfare 16,1 (1969) 20-1.
Short story. A lonely old woman bitterly complains about lack of affection and concern from her grown sons.

4382 VAID, KRISHNA BALDEV. The old woman and her bundle. Tr. from Hindi by the author. *In* New Quest 2 (Aug 1977) 5-9.
Short story. Examines the attitudes of various persons toward an elderly woman who has retreated from worldly concerns and involvement.

4383 VERMA, BHAGWATI CHARAN. Chitralekha. Tr. from Hindi by Chandra B. Karki. Bombay: Jaico Publishing House, 1956. 159p.
Novel (historical). Depicts the renunciation/participation conflict perennial to the Hindu-Buddhist tradition. A consort and dancer of the Mauryan court joins a yogi's hermitage.

4384 _______. And she did not return. Tr. from Hindi by D.P. Pandey. New Delhi: Arnold-Heinemann, 1976. 103p.
Novel. Depicts the mysterious attraction and relationship between a complex woman and a businessman, as told by the latter. Portrays the complexities of contemporary urban life — legal entanglements, financial difficulties, unstable relationships.

viii) Panjabi literature: work of Amrita Pritam

4385 AMRITA PRITAM. The skeleton. Tr. from Panjabi by Khushwant Singh. *In* Illustrated Weekly of India 84,32-8 and 40-1. (11-25 Aug and 1-22 Sep and 6-13 Oct 1963) 18-20, 29-33, 25-7, 49-51, 29-33, 25-9, 29-31, 29-31, 29-31 and 59.
Novel. A Panjabi Hindu peasant girl, abducted by a young Muslim to avenge a family feud, is rejected by her family. She comes to love her abductor and they become involved in assisting victims of Hindu-Muslim communalism surrounding partition.

4386 _______. Black rose. Tr. from Panjabi by Charles Brasch in collaboration with the author. [New Delhi: Nagmani, 1967]. 31p.
Poetry.

4387 _______. Existence and other poems. Tr. from Panjabi by Mahendra Kulasrestha in collaboration with the author. New Delhi: Nagmani, 1968. 33p.
Poetry. Introspective and political themes predominate.

4388 _______. Pritish Nandy, ed. Selected poems of Amrita Pritam. Tr. from Panjabi by various persons. Calcutta: Dialogue Calcutta Publications, [1970]. lv.
Poetry. Most poems in this small volume are reprinted from other anthologies in English translation.

4389 _______. Two faces of Eve. Tr. from Panjabi by G.S.P. Suri and Prabhakar Machwe. Delhi: Hind Pocket Books, [1971]. 160p.
Novel and short story. Both *Two Faces of Eve* and "Aerial" depict heroines who grapple with complications of marital relations and extramarital affairs.

4390 _______. Flirting with youth. Tr. from Panjabi by Raj Gill. New Delhi: Sterling Publishers, 1973. 144p.
Novel. [Unexamined. ALI].

4391 _______. That man. Tr. from Panjabi by Krishna Gorowara. New Delhi: Sterling Publishers Pvt. Ltd., 1974. 106p.
Novel. Examines the problematic existence of a man whose mother dedicated him to the lifelong service of Śiva in exchange for the god's granting her a son.

4392 _______. A line in water. Tr. from

Panjabi by Krishna Gorowara. New Delhi: Arnold-Heinemann Publishers, 1975. 141p. (Indian Novels, 4).
Novel. A young painter with a studio in the Kangra valley is tormented by his feelings for the young woman who comes to be his student.

4393 ________. Time and again and other poems. Tr. from Panjabi. Calcutta: United Writers, 1975. 40p.
Poetry. [Unexamined. ALI].

4394 ________. Death of a city. Tr. from Panjabi by various persons. New Delhi: Arnold-Heinemann Publishers, 1976. 223p.
Short stories. Most have prominent female characters. Death and despair, romance and sexuality are prominent among the themes represented.

4395 ________. Nobody Knows and Time and Beyond: two short novels. Tr. from Panjabi by Krishna Gorowara. New Delhi: Himalaya Books, 1977. 112p.
Novels. ***Nobody Knows*** depicts the ill-fated love of a young couple. In ***Time and Beyond,*** a woman's brother and lover attempt to resolve her strange disappearance and restore her honor.

4396 ________. The revenue stamp: an autobiography. Tr. from Panjabi by Krishna Gorowara. New Delhi: Vikas Publishing House, 1977? 130p.
Autobiography. Discusses author's family background and the context in which some of her works were written. Contains miscellaneous excerpts from diaries and photographs. Title alludes to the dubious worth of an autobiographical project.

4396a ________. The aerial and other stories. Tr. from Panjabi by various persons. Calcutta: United Writers, 1978. 154p.
Short stories. Eleven selections. Also includes Revti Saran Sharma's examination of the author's portrayal of women's lives, "The Search for Feminine Integrity (the Course of Amrita Pritam's Fiction)" (pp.130-54).

4397 ________. Doctor Dev. Tr. from Panjabi by Krishan Gujral. Delhi: Hind Pocket Books, n.d. 94p.
Novel. Follows a love affair ruined by the couple's vulnerability to the "clutches of society."

4398 Amrita Pritam number. Mahfil 5,3 (1968/69) 134p.
Contains lengthy interview with Amrita Pritam about her life and work, a selection of her poetry, an article about her poetry by Surjit Singh Dulai, a selection of her short stories, Revti Saran Sharma's "The Search for Feminine Integrity" about female characterization in her fiction and a bibliography of original Panjabi editions of author's novels and short stories.

ix) Panjabi literature: male writers

4399 ASHK, UPENDRA NATH. The nuptial bed. Tr. from Panjabi by Khushwant Singh. ***In*** Khushwant Singh and Jaya Thadani, eds. Land of the five rivers: stories from the Punjab. Bombay: Jaico Publishing House, 1965. pp.149-63.
Short story. A young man, tormented by attachments to his mother, is miserable during his wedding and on the evening of the consummation of his marriage.

4400 BEDI, RAJINDER SINGH. Lajwanti. Tr. from Panjabi by Khushwant Singh. ***In*** Khushwant Singh and Jaya Thadani, eds. Land of the five rivers: stories from the Punjab. Bombay: Jaico Publishing House, 1965. pp.120-31.
Short story. Examines the feelings of a Panjabi couple for one another before, during and after their separation during the events of partition. The husband, who formerly abused his wife, comes to appreciate her after she is abducted; his wife reacts negatively.

4401 SINGH, SATINDRA. The outcaste. ***In his*** Dreams in debris: a collection of Punjabi short stories. Tr. by Khushwant Singh. Bombay: Jaico Publishing House, 1972. pp.69-75.
Short story. A young Hindu widow is treated like an outcaste by her own family but loved warmly by a Muslim who protects her during the partition riots. Depicts callousness of Hindu society with respect to widows and inappropriate stereotypes that inflame communalism.

4402 YASHPAL. Saadat. Tr. from Panjabi by Arvind Kumar. ***In*** Khushwant Singh and Jaya Thadani, eds. Land of the five rivers: stories from the Punjab. Bombay: Jaico Publishing House, 1965. pp.107-13.
Short story. A young man, educated, employed and in search of a wife, is compelled to make a visit to the beautiful, sweet-tempered woman who cared for him in his childhood. He learns that "the beauty of a woman is not mortal like her human form. It is something as eternal as truth itself."

b. Northwestern Islamic cultural region: area of western Panjabi, Sindhi, Baluchi, Pushto, Urdu and Kashmiri languages

(1) The colonial experience: western women in Northwest India

For other material relating to colonial period see entries 3945-85

(a) Missionaries

4403 CARUS-WILSON, MRS. ASHLEY [MARY LOUISA GEORGIANA (PETRIE) CARUS-WILSON]. A woman's life for Kashmir: Irene Petrie, a biography. Chicago: Fleming H. Revell Company, 1901. 343p. [*Also* Irene Petrie: missionary to Kashmir. London: Hodder and Stoughton, 1900].
An appreciative memorial biography of the first woman to serve the Church Missionary Society in Kashmir. She died there prematurely several years after her arrival. Based upon letters, journals, mission records and recollections of friends and coworkers.

4404 CLARK, ROBERT. Robert Maconachie, ed. Missions of the Church Missionary Society and the Church of England Zenana Missionary Society in the Punjab and Sindh. London: Church Missionary Society, 1904. 280p.
[Unexamined. MRL].

4405 DAVIDSON, FLORA MARION. Hidden highways: experiences on the Northwest Frontier of India. New York: F.H. Revell Company, 1948. 191p.
On mission life in the North-West Frontier Province. [Unexamined. NUC].

4406 Dr. Fanny Jane Butler. *In* Medical Missionary Record 5,3 (1890) 57-62.
Biographical sketch of a woman considered to be the first well-prepared English medical missionary to India. [Unexamined].

4407 HANBURY, C. Under canvas: C.E.Z.M.S. work in the Punjab . . . London: Church of England Zenana Missionary Society, n.d. 63p.
Medical missions. [Unexamined. MRL].

4408 HULL, E.G. Vignettes of Kashmir . . . London: Church of England Zenana Missionary Society, 1903. 96p.
Zenana mission life. [Unexamined. MRL].

4409 STUART, E. GERTRUDE. An Austin Twelve on the frontier: medical relief in and around Quetta. London: Church of England Zenana Missionary Society, 1938? 47p.
Illustrated. [Unexamined. MRL].

4410 TONGE, E.M. Fanny Jane Butler: pioneer medical missionary. London: Church of England Zenana Missionary Society, n.d. 54p.
Life story of a woman who operated a medical mission branch of the Church of England Zenana Missionary Society in Srinagar.

4411 VINES, CHARLOTTE S. In and out of hospital: sketches of medical work in an Indian village mission . . . London: Church of England Zenana Missionary Society, 1905. 192p.
[Unexamined. MRL].

4412 _______. Indian medical sketches. London: Church of England Zenana Missionary Society, [1908]. 127p.
[Unexamined. MRL].

4413 _______. A woman doctor on the frontier. London: Church of England Zenana Missionary Society, 1925. 78p.
[Unexamined. MRL].

(b) Others

4414 DIVER, MAUD. Honoria Lawrence: a fragment of Indian history. Boston: Houghton Mifflin, 1936. 524p.
Biography of the wife of Sir Henry Lawrence, the first British ruler of the Punjab. Details their adventures, romance and mutual support and devotion. Illustrated.

4415 PRIOR, L.F. LOVEDAY. Punjab prelude. London: John Murray, 1952. 218p.
"This book is purely a description of personal experiences, personal observation and personal opinion . . . . What I saw . . . is probably as relevant or significant as what anyone else saw." The author spent her childhood in India and returned in 1945 to teach at Aitchison College, Lahore. Considers many topics with interspersed material on women.

4416 STRATTON, ALFRED WILLIAM. Letters from India, with a memoir by his wife Anne Booth Stratton. London: Archibald Constable and Company, 1908. 368p.
Letters of an Orientalist and philologist,

edited and supplemented by his wife. The final third of the book details her arrival in India in 1900 and their married life in northwestern India until his death in 1902.

(2) General statements

(a) Ethnographic contexts

4417 BURTON, RICHARD F. The Sindi woman: especially her person and dress. *In his* Sind revisited: with notices of the Anglo-Indian Army; railroads; past, present and future, etc., v1. London: Richard Bentley and Son, 1877. pp.317-43.
"I must request you to be present at the unpacking of a Sindi gentlewoman of high degree; during which operation I shall lecture upon the points most likely to interest you, Sir." So begins an exposition of her dress, education, marriage and family life.

4418 The condition of Mohammedan women in Baluchistan. *In* Annie Van Summer and Samuel M. Zwemer, eds. Our Moslem sisters: a cry of need from lands of darkness interpreted by those who heard it. New York: Fleming H. Revell Company, 1907. pp.249-52.
Describes the "dark picture" of sale of daughters, extensive household labor burdens, polygyny, concubinage and widespread health problems.

4419 DARLING, MALCOLM LYALL. Rusticus loquitur: or, the old light and the new in the Punjab village. London: H. Milford, Oxford University Press, 1930. 400p.
[Unexamined. NUC].

4420 ________. Wisdom and waste in the Punjab village. London: H. Milford, Oxford University Press, 1934. 368p.
An early village study with much on women. Considers work patterns, dress, seclusion, infanticide, education and other topics. Plates. [Unexamined. NUC].

4421 EGLAR, ZEKIYE. A Punjabi village in Pakistan. New York: Columbia University Press, 1960. 240p.
A village ethnography in which women are exceptionally visible. As a woman and a Muslim the author had considerable access to the women's world of Mohla village in Gujrat District. She lived in Pakistan from 1949 to 1955 and documents social change in the early postpartition years. Ethnography focuses on a system of gift and service exchange and the central role of women in it.

4422 HONIGMANN, JOHN J. Woman in West Pakistan. *In* Stanley Maron, ed. Pakistan: society and culture. New Haven: Human Relations Area Files, 1957. pp.154-76.
Briefly considers diverse aspects of women's lives in the former West Pakistan.

4423 ________. Three Pakistan villages. Chapel Hill, North Carolina: Institute for Research in Social Science, University of North Carolina, 1958. 95p.
Ethnographic surveys of Chiho village in Sind, Tordher village in the North-West Frontier Province and Chak 41 MB village in Punjab. Includes information concerning women's work, general status, family roles, birth experiences, dress, seclusion patterns and other topics.

4424 MATHESON, SYLVIA. The tigers of Baluchistan. London: Arthur Barker Limited, 1967. 213p.
A journalist-archeologist describes her experiences with the Bugti tribe in the late 1950s. Although her report focuses on Bugti men, it contains interspersed comments on the women, including the events surrounding several weddings.

4425 PEHRSON, ROBERT N. The social organization of the Marri Baluch. New York: Wenner Gren Foundation for Anthropological Research, 1966. 127p. (Viking Fund Publications in Anthropology, 43). [*Also* Chicago: Aldine Publishing Company, 1966].
Ethnography of a nomadic tribal people of northeastern Baluchistan. Has material on women throughout but especially in chapters on "Kinship" and "Marriage and the Relation between Man and Woman."

4426 RAI, JAMIAT. Denys Bray, ed. The domiciled Hindus. Delhi: B.R. Publishing Corporation, 1964. 98p. [*First published as* Ethnographic survey of Balūchistān, v2. 1913].
Ethnographic survey of Hindus in the predominantly Muslim Baluchistan. Considers various topics relating to women, e.g., dress and ornament, goddess worship and numerous domestic ceremonies.

4427 SLOCUM, W.L., JAMILA AKHTAR and ABRAR FATIMA SAHI. Village life in Lahore District: a study of selected sociological aspects. Lahore: Social Sciences Research Centre, University of the Panjab, 1960. 50p.
Brief report of an ethnographic survey from six villages in Lahore District. Interspersed material on women.

4428 WESTERN, R.H. Some women of Sindh: in home and hospital. London: Church of England Zenana Missionary Society, 1930? 155p.
Observations and experiences of an English medical missionary who worked at CEZMS hospitals for women and children at Sukkur and Larkana. With drawings.

(b) Collected papers and a bibliography

4429 Books and theses on women in Dr. Mahmud Husain Library (Karachi University Library): exhibition during the Women's Week in Pakistan, 22nd October 1976 to 28th October 1976. Karachi: University of Karachi, 1976. 27p.
Lists 72 English books on Pakistani and other women in Karachi University's collection and 83 English and Urdu master's theses from the university's departments of sociology, social work and library science. Also lists published Urdu holdings.

4430 JAFRI, ROQUYYA, ed? A Pakistan souvenir: International Women's Year, 1975. Lahore: Istiqlal Press, 1976.
Collection of papers on legal and political status of Pakistani women. [Unexamined].

4431 PAKISTAN. INFORMATION AND BROADCASTING DIVISION. Women of Pakistan. Islamabad: Information and Broadcasting Division, Directorate of Research, Reference and Publications, Government of Pakistan, 1975. 119p.
Issued in celebration of International Women's Year, this book records, chiefly in photographs, some of the more modern achievements of the women of Pakistan. Both exceptional and more typical women are documented in sections on careers, social services, defense services, Girl Guides, writers and artists, sports and costumes and cosmetics. For contents, see entries 2659, 4465, 4484, 4490-2 and 4514.

4432 Special report: the state of womankind in 1975. *In* Pakistan Economist (3 May 1975) 14-26.
Report and selected papers from an International Women's Year symposium on the future role of women in Pakistan sponsored by the Pakistan Institute of International Affairs. Papers address general status questions, the major socio-economic features of Pakistani women, issues of sexual inequality, rural women and other topics.

(3) The life cycle

(a) Marriage

4433 AFZAL, MOHAMMAD, LEE L. BEAN and IMTIAZUDDIN HUSAIN. Muslim marriages: age, mehr, and social status. *In* Pakistan Development Review 12,1 (1973) 48-61.
Examines rate of marriage, age at first marriage and relationship of age at first marriage to amount of dower (*mahr*) paid by groom to bride. Based upon marriage registration data from Karachi in 1962 and 1965, as required by the Muslim Family Laws Ordinance, 1961.

4434 AFZAL, MOHAMMAD, M. IQBAL HASHMI and N.H. NIZAMI. Marriage patterns in a rural agglomeration. *In* Pakistan Development Review 12,3 (1973) 273-82.
Examines marriages registered under the Muslim Family Laws Ordinance of 1961 in a group of villages in Sheikhupura District, 1964 and 1969. Considers age distribution and average age of males and females at first marriage; relationship of age at first marriage to amount of dower, groom's payment to bride; and migration of bride at marriage to groom's residence.

4435 BALOCH, S.K. Marriage customs: old and new. *In* Pakistan Review 15,2 (1967) 18-20.
Reviews contemporary marriage ceremonies, presumably in the former West Pakistan. Characterizes modern marriages by the avarice of bridegrooms: the demand for dowry payment indicates that even today the woman is placed in a position of disadvantage in the marital relationship.

4436 MC NAIR, JOHN FREDERICK and THOMAS LAMBERT BARLOW. Customs and ceremonies observed at a betrothal and at a wedding by Mohammedans of the farmer class in the district near Ghazi in the Punjab. *In* Folklore [London] 9 (1898) 136-56.
[Unexamined].

4437 MATHESON, SYLVIA. Bugti wedding. *In* Geographical Magazine 35,5 (1962) 280-92.
Details of a Baluchi tribal wedding with photographs of the bride and her attendants, enabled because the groom and his uncle were trusted friends of the author. Describes events of the women's and men's camps, respectively.

4437a ROSE, H.A. Mohammadan betrothal observances in the Punjab. *In* Man 17,45 and 66 (1917) 58-62, 91-7.
Describes the lexicon and rites of Muslim betrothals as practiced in various areas of prepartition Punjab.

(b) Fertility

4438 AFZAL, MOHAMMAD, MOHAMMAD AZHAR and TARIQ SAJJAD JAN. Estimation of net currently married life within the reproductive period for females in Pakistan. *In* Pakistan Development Review 14,1 (1975) 85-99.
Estimates "net currently married life of females in Pakistan by allowing for the effects of widowhood, divorce and mortality till the end of the reproductive period." Considers

variation with respect to age, age at marriage cohorts and duration of marriage.

4439 KARIM, MEHTAB S. and IQBAL ALAM. Age reporting in Pakistan and its implications for fertility analysis. *In* Pakistan Development Review 14,1 (1975) 100-19.
"An attempt is made to compare the age reporting patterns of female population in the [Population Growth Estimation Project] (1963-65) and the [Population Growth Survey] (1968, 1969 and 1971) and to assess their possible effect on estimates of [total fertility rates] and [age-specific fertility rates]." Argues that correcting for age misrepresentation in population surveys of Pakistan "is both economical and feasible." Reviews previous studies of age misrepresentation in Pakistani population surveys.

4439a SYED, SABIHA HASSAN. Female status and fertility in Pakistan. *In* Pakistan Development Review 17,4 (1978) 408-30.
Assuming opportunities for education and for employment to be indexes of female status, the author presents data from the 1975 Pakistan Fertility Survey showing relationship of education and employment to reproductive lives of Pakistani women and discusses implications for population policy. Briefly reviews other studies relating to education, employment and fertility in Pakistan.

(c) Pregnancy and childbirth

4440 ROSE, H.A. Muhammadan pregnancy observances in the Punjab. *In* J. of the Royal Anthropological Institute 35 (1905) 279-82.
Describes rites, charms to prevent miscarriage, gifts and feasting, food cravings, taboos and determination of child's sex. Data from various areas of prepartition Punjab.

4441 ________. Muhammadan birth observances in the Punjab. *In* J. of the Royal Anthropological Institute 37 (1907) 237-60.
Describes birth and childhood rites as observed in various areas of prepartition Punjab. With numerous song texts, transliterated and translated.

(4) Domestic sphere and family life

(a) The family and social change

4442 BAQAI, M. SABIHUDDIN. Role structure in the middle class families of Pakistan. *In* University Studies, Karachi University 7,1 (1970) 49-63.
Report of study of 80 Lahore families to ascertain changes that have occurred from preceding to present generations. Considers changing roles of wives and daughters.

4443 KHATANA, R.P. Marriage and kinship among the Gujar Bakarwals of Jammu and Kashmir. *In* Imtiaz Ahmad, ed. Family, kinship and marriage among Muslims in India. New Delhi: Manohar, 1976. pp.83-127.
Reviews kinship system of a community of Muslims pastoral nomads of Jammu and Kashmir. Includes details of the position of women in this system.

4444 KORSON, J. HENRY. Dower and social class in an urban Muslim community. *In* J. of Marriage and the Family 29,3 (1967) 527-33.
Examines role of the money a groom pays to a bride among upper-, middle- and lower-class samples from Karachi. Considers role of dower in marriage stability and women's financial security and discusses changing opportunities for Pakistani women.

4445 ________. The roles of dower and dowry as indicators of social change in Pakistan. *In* J. of Marriage and the Family 30,4 (1968) 696-707.
Report of a survey of male and female middle- and upper-class university students in Karachi and Lahore. Explores attitudes toward various aspects of dower and dowry as an index of social change. Attitudes reflecting "modernity" were frequently found in conjunction with traditional normative practice. Male and female responses were strikingly similar.

4446 ________. Some aspects of social change in the Muslim family in West Pakistan. *In* Dhirendra Narain, ed. Explorations in the family and other essays: Professor K.M. Kapadia commemoration volume. Bombay: Thacker and Company, 1975. pp.324-43. [*Also in* Contributions to Asian Studies 3 (1973) 138-55].
Asserts that relatively slight changes have occurred in recent decades in a family that is "highly patriarchal, patrilineal, patrilocal, and ideally of the extended type." Considers *pardā*, dower, dowry, mate selection, legislation, family planning and status of women.

4447 ________. Modernization and social change: the family in Pakistan. *In* Man Singh Das and Panos D. Bardis, eds. The family in Asia. New Delhi: Vikas, 1978? pp.169-207.
Survey paper explicitly considers changes in women's lives. Discusses female seclusion patterns, education and labor force participation and the role of legislation and the All-Pakistan Women's Association as agents of change.

4448 MADAN, T.N. Family and kinship: a study of the Pandits of rural Kashmir. Bombay:

Asia Publishing Company, 1965. 259p. Detailed examination of the kinship system of the Pandit brahman community in Utrassu-Umanagari village, Anantnag District. Contains much on women in the context of material on family relationships, marriages and other life cycle events, family disputes and partitions and other topics. Photographs.

(b) Legislation

See also entries 2013-28

4449 FARANI, M. Family laws manual. Lahore: Lahore Law Times Publications, 1977. 354p.
Presents texts of and commentary on legislation relating to marriage and divorce of members of various religious communities, adultery, inheritance, *sharī'at*, guardians and wards, dower, maintenance, restitution of conjugal rights and parents and children. Lists cases and rulings relating to family law in Pakistan from 1975 to 1977.

4450 PATEL, RASHIDA. Women and the law in Pakistan. Karachi: Faiza Publishers, 1979. 194p.
First two chapters review the status of women in Pakistan, and argue that Muslim law should be reformed according to contemporary conditions, citing examples relating to women. Remaining chapters examine the law with respect to various social institutions: "A Girl Child is Born," "Marriage-Nikah," "Husband and Wife," "Polygamy," "Talaq, Talaq, Talaq," "Divorce by Wife," "Inheritance" and "Matrimonial and Family Law Courts." These chapters consider the opinions of various sources of Islamic law on the institutions, relevant legal acts and case law, and their relation to social conditions in Pakistan. The author, a prominent lawyer and the Vice-Chairman of the All Pakistan Women's Association, plans to address additional topics in a second volume.

4451 PEARL, DAVID. The impact of the Muslim Family Laws Ordinance, 1961, in Quetta (Baluchistan) Pakistan. *In* J. of the Indian Law Institute 13,4 (1971) 561-9.
"The limited object of this paper is to illustrate that in one town of Pakistan, Quetta, the Ordinance has had a very minimal effect." Considers various provisions of the Muslim Family Laws Ordinance — minimum female age at marriage, polygamy, divorce and maintenance — and shows, using local records, its general ineffectiveness.

(5) Sexuality, honor/shame and seclusion

4452 PASTNER, CARROLL MC CLURE. Sexual dichotomization in society and culture: the women of Panjgur, Baluchistan. Ph.D. dissertation, Department of Anthropology, Brandeis University, 1971. 277p. [University Microfilms 71-30,143].
"Based upon a study of the oasis of Panjgur . . ., this thesis is concerned with the structural and ideological variables of a cultural configuration founded on the dichotomization of the sexes," as opposed to the great majority of Middle East ethnographic investigations, which consider only the "male view of social organization." Other dichotomies considered are "great" and "little" traditions, synchrony and diachrony, public and private domains and honor and shame.

4453 _______. A social structural and historical analysis of honor, shame and purdah. *In* Anthropological Quarterly 45,4 (1972) 248-61.
Aims "(1) to describe a specific code of honor and shame; (2) to relate this ideological focus to social organization — kinship and stratification in particular; (3) to document historically the elaboration of an ideology based on honor and shame into the ritual of purdah as an example of the interaction between a 'great' and a 'little' tradition." Data from oasis of Panjgur, Makran District.

4454 _______. Accommodations to purdah: the female perspective. *In* J. of Marriage and the Family 36,2 (1974) 408-14.
Relates *pardā* observance on the Panjgur oasis, Makran District, to various contexts in which values of honor and shame are invoked. Describes certain common behavioral and structural "accommodations" to the system that "influence decision making on the part of males." These are "deviant from the male point of view since they are supposedly nonsanctioned and contradict ideal notions of proper feminine behavior. For women, of course, they are not deviant since they are regularly utilized and fully institutionalized means of coping with domestic life."

4455 _______. Gradations of purdah and the creation of social boundaries on a Baluchistan oasis. *In* Hanna Papanek, ed. Purdah in South Asia: the segregation of women. Forthcoming.
Examines the assumption that *pardā* observance marks boundaries and differentiates individuals and groups of varying hierarchical statuses using ethnographic and historical data from the Panjgur oasis in Makran. Considers gradations among Baluchis and between Baluchis and non-Baluchis and ways that women manipulate the system for their own advantage. [Unexamined. Verified with editor].

4456 WHITE, ELIZABETH HERRICK. Women's status in an Islamic society: the problem of purdah. Ph.D. dissertation, Graduate School of International Studies, University of Denver, 1975. 262p.

[University Microfilms 76-8185]. Examines *pardā* and other Islamic restrictions relating to women as obstacles to female education and family size limitation. Based upon interviews with rural and urban women of various economic classes in the North-West Frontier Province. Informants were asked about their own and the preceding generation and the expected circumstances of the following generation.

(6) Work and economic position

(a) Property

4457 PASTNER, CARROLL MC C. The status of women and property on a Baluchistan oasis in Pakistan. *In* Lois Beck and Nikki Keddie, eds. Women in the Muslim world. Cambridge: Harvard University Press, 1978. pp.434-50.
Concludes that "in their capacity as daughters and wives, Muslim women can and do have access to several kinds of property," both movable and immovable. However, as "protected persons" they are "forced to play out their economic roles largely through men." *Pardā* is seen as a major factor in the "degree to which women have economically meaningful control over their own property." Also discusses factors of Islamic law, marriage, inheritance and dowry.

(b) Labor force participation

4458 ANWAR, SEEMIN and FAIZ BILQUEES. The attitudes, environment and activities of rural women: a case study of Jhok Sayal. Islamabad: Pakistan Institute of Development Economics, 1976. 70p. (Research Report Series, 98).
Attempts "to outline the different dimensions of economic activity of rural women and to describe the attitudinal and environmental factors which influence village women's participation in the rural economy." Based on brief period of participant observation in "Jhok Sayal" village, Lyallpur District. Sections decribe the village, its women and their daily and annual work activities.

4459 SAEED, KISHWAR. Rural women's participation in farm operations. Lyallpur: West Pakistan Agricultural University, 1966. 75p.
Examines correlations between female labor force participation and patterns of "community" (i.e., "Junglees," "Settlers," or "Refugees"), caste, education, landholding and tenancy status. The first two variables were found to be most significant. Tables present survey results. Data from four villages in Lyallpur District.

4460 SHAH, KHALIDA. Womanpower and employment promotion in Pakistan. *In* Manpower Review 1,1 (1975) 7-20.
Reviews changing trends in female employment and considers related factors. [Unexamined].

4461 SHAH, NASRA M. Female labour force participation and fertility desires in Pakistan: an empirical investigation. *In* Pakistan Development Review 14,2 (1975) 185-206.
Reviews relevant literature and examines data from the National Impact Survey, 1968-69, regarding married women whose ideal family size exceeds real family size. Considers relationship between female employment and fertility desires both by controlling for selected variables that have a significant effect on fertility desires and by a multivariate analysis of relative effect of several variables. The latter "showed the 'net' effect of wife's employment on wanting another child to be negligible."

4462 ________. Work participation of currently married women in Pakistan: influence of socio-economic and demographic factors. *In* Pakistan Development Review 14,4 (1975) 469-92.
Considers influence of demographic factors (e.g., age, number of living children), socioeconomic factors (e.g., education, family structure, observance of *pardā*) and aspects of modernization on labor force participation in rural and urban areas.

4463 ________, NASREEN ABBASI and IQBAL ALAM. Interdistrict and interprovincial differentials in correlates of female labour force participation, 1961. *In* Pakistan Development Review 15,4 (1976) 424-45.
Describes demographic and socio-economic correlates with labor force participation and nonagricultural labor force participation at district, provincial and metropolitan center levels. Tables.

(c) Job opportunities

4464 KAZI, KHAWAR, comp. A general guide to job opportunities for qualified women in Lahore. Lahore: Pakistan Women's Institute, 1977? 146p.
Presents results of a survey prepared to inform new students at Kinnaird College and their parents about professional job opportunities for female college graduates. Describes, for each of ten fields, categories of jobs (including part-time positions), qualifications, pay scales and benefits.

4465 PAKISTAN. INFORMATION AND BROADCASTING DIVISION. Career women. *In its* Women of Pakistan. Islamabad: Information and Broadcasting Division, Directorate

of Research, Reference and Publications, Government of Pakistan, 1975. pp.19-38.
Photo essay. Text reviews increasing enrollment of females at higher educational level, increasing participation of urban women in professions and trades and the traditional role of rural women as helpmates of their menfolk.

(d) Attitudes and problems of employed women

4466 BAQAI, M. SABIHUDDIN. Constraint in employment of women. Islamabad: Pakistan Institute of Development Economics, 1976. 10p. (Research Report Series, 99).
Survey of "career" and "domestic" women in Karachi metropolitan area to determine extent to which following constraints were felt: discouragement by relatives, attitudes of male coworkers, hesitation to work in sex-integrated environment, perception of male superiority, traditional values and perception of woman's place as in the home. Marriage was "found to act as a restraint on women's participation in the labour force," and "as education and income increased, perception of constraints in employment decreased."

4467 BIRJIS, ZAHIDA. Women at work: study of values and attitudes of officials about employment of women in West Pakistan. Lahore: National Institute of Public Administration, 1964? 52p.
Report of survey of 181 West Pakistani government officials to ascertain their attitudes toward female employment.

4468 GANI, AMNA. Combining marriage and career in Karachi. *In* Barbara E. Ward, ed. Women in the new Asia: the changing social roles of men and women in South and South-east Asia. Paris: UNESCO, 1963. pp.323-39.
Personal narrative of an educated Muslim woman from the Memon community who married into a conservative family but was later able to move out of seclusion to a social work career.

4469 It's not a woman's world. *In* The Herald [Karachi] 9,10 (1978) 15-24.
Series of brief articles on employment experiences of Pakistani women. Considers general employment problems, reactions of men, employment in a match factory, the case of a woman who is illtreated by her husband, exploitation and problems of Islamic societies in the 20th century.

4470 KORSON, J. HENRY. Career constraints among women graduate students in a developing society: West Pakistan. *In* J. of Comparative Family Studies 1,1 (1970) 82-100.
Data from interviews with female graduate students from Karachi and Lahore. Presents socio-economic profile of this group, family attitudes toward daughter's employment and a discussion of the developmental drain of educated but nonemployed women. With comparisons between the two cities.

4471 SHAFI, M. West Pakistan Maternity Benefit Ordinance, 1958: with commentary. Karachi: Bureau of Labour Publications, 1967. 14p.
Texts of West Pakistan Maternity Benefit Ordinance, 1958, and West Pakistan Maternity Benefit Rules, 1961, legislation providing maternity benefits to employed women.

4472 SHAH, KHALIDA. Problems of Pakistani women seeking employment. *In* Contemporary Affairs 2,7 (1970) 45-62.
Reports difficulties faced by a group of Lahore women. [Unexamined].

4473 ZAIDI, S.M. HAFEEZ. Changing role and status of professional women in Pakistan. *In* Pakistan J. of Psychology 4,1/2 (1971) 47-61.
[Unexamined].

(7) Education

(a) Overviews, problems, statistics

4474 HASHMI, SALIMA. Education of rural women in West Pakistan. Lyallpur: West Pakistan Agricultural University Press, 1968. 142p.
Argues for widespread rural female education. Chapters on primary, secondary and higher education briefly review 19th and 20th century history in India and Pakistan, discuss contemporary circumstances, describe programs in other countries and present recommendations regarding the levels. Also considers education for the gifted, vocational and technical education, religious education, adult education, role of youth organizations and views of various Pakistani educationists.

4475 NUZHAT QURESHI, K. Role of female education in development planning of N.-W.F.P. Peshawar: Board of Economic Enquiry, North-West Frontier Province, University of Peshawar, 1972. 73p. (*Its* Publication 74).
Interviews with educated and uneducated women of Peshawar District document the substantial positive effects of education on what are generally considered their primary duties to family and household and on their secondary duties to community. Briefly reviews the history of Muslim education in the subcontinent and surveys contemporary female education and professional employment patterns in N.W.F.P. With recommendations and numerous tables.

4476 PAKISTAN. CENTRAL BUREAU OF EDUCATION. Pakistan education statistics, 1947-48 to 1972-73. Islamabad: Bureau of Educational Planning and Management and Central Bureau of Education, Ministry of Education. 1974? 1v.
Presents many types of educational statistics at provincial and administered area levels. Numerous tables give breakdown by sex.

4477 QURASHI, SALMA MUSTAFA. Female education in the Peshawar District, West Pakistan. Peshawar: Board of Economic Enquiry, N-W.F., Peshawar University, 1960. 135p. (*Its* Publication 7).
Reviews types of institutions, financial support, curricula, family influences and details of teachers. Considers all levels of formal education. Includes numerous statistics, recommendations and photographs. Based upon interviews with heads of institutions, teachers, parents and students.

4478 SAEED, S.A. Problems of female education in rural areas. *In* Pakistan Review 16,12 (1968) 23-4.
Briefly reviews and assesses various aspects of rural female primary education.

(b) Attitudes and experiences of educated women

4479 HUSSAIN, ASAF. The educated Pakistani girl: a sociological study. Karachi: Ima Printers, 1963. 181p.
Presents a generalized picture of various types of educated females and their attitudes. Discusses conservative and modern women, love, marriage, career women versus homemakers, sex consciousness and leisure activities. Author states that he undertook the study out of concern for the clash between modern educated women and the inability of most men to accept them. Based on questionnaires, diaries, personal observations, etc., which are liberally quoted. Probably conducted in Karachi.

4480 SHAH, KHALIDA. Attitudes of Pakistani students toward family life. *In* Marriage and Family Living 22,2 (1960) 156-61.
Assesses differences in attitudes toward family life of male and female college students in Lahore. Female students favored larger families; were more orthodox regarding religious practices, dower and dowry, parental authority, sex education for children and female employment; and were more liberal about female education and the husband's role in the home. Men considered themselves more intelligent while women stressed equality in intelligence. Based on questionnaires.

4481 SHAMIM, MOHAMMAD and RAKHSHINDA REHMAN. A study of marital preference of educated Pakistani women. *In* Pakistan J. of Psychology 5,1/2 (1972) 61-9.
Examines all marriage advertisements from daily and weekly Urdu and English newspapers in 1970 in the then West Pakistan in which educated females sought partners of particular professions. Compares rate of preference of the nine professions most preferred in newspaper ads to personal and postulated parental preferences for profession of spouse elicited from group of 90 single educated women of Karachi.

4482 Zarina goes to college. *In* Pakistan Quarterly 1,4 (1950) 82-4.
Experiences of a middle-class Pakistani girl at college. Photos.

(c) Physical education and sports

4483 MC CANDLESS, BOYD R. and FAHMIDA ALI. Relations among physical skills and personal social variables in three cultures of adolescent girls. *In* J. of Educational Psychology 57,6 (1966) 366-72.
Examines the hypothesis that physical skills are evaluated differently by girls in coeducated and sex-segregated school systems. Presents data from ninth grade girls from an American coeducational public school, an American Catholic private girls school and a Pakistani Muslim girls school (Urdu speaking, location unidentified). Various findings.

4484 PAKISTAN. INFORMATION AND BROADCASTING DIVISION. Women in sports. *In its* Women of Pakistan. Islamabad: Information and Broadcasting Division, Directorate of Research, Reference and Publications, Government of Pakistan, 1975. pp.89-98.
Photo essay. Text discusses resistance in Pakistan to female sports participation and changing attitudes and opportunities of recent years.

4485 SABRA AZAM. Physical education for girls in West Pakistan. Lahore: West Pakistan Bureau of Education, 1964. 78p.
Evaluates growth of physical education programs for West Pakistani girls, isolates obstacles and makes recommendations for improvements. Argues that "physical education is an essential subject in the school curriculum" and presents a concrete program. With diagrams.

(8) Development and social welfare

4486 CHAUDHARY, MRS. A.R. Role of women in economic development: a case study of Pakistan. *In* Economic Journal [Lahore] 8,2 (1975) 107-22.

Compares worldwide and Pakistani women's training opportunities, employment opportunities and employment patterns. Various conclusions, recommendations and tables.

4487 Mother and Child. vl- (19__-). Lahore: Maternity and Child Welfare Association of Pakistan. Quarterly.
Contents from sample issue [13,4 (1976)]: "Editorial: Reaching the Unreached," "UNICEF in Pakistan: its Achievements," "Report of International Union of Family Organisations' Meeting, June 21-25, 1976," "Barefoot Doctors Cover China's Countryside," "Traditional Birth Attendants in Pakistan: a Sociological Perspective," "Treatment and Prevention of Dehydration in Diarrhoeal Diseases: a Guide for Use at Primary Level," "Habitat: Improving the World in which Children Live," "Twelve Facts about the State of Children in Developing Countries Today" and "News from Branches of MCWAP."

4488 PAKISTAN. PAKISTAN WOMEN'S RIGHTS COMMITTEE. Report, part I. Karachi?: Ministry of Law and Parliamentary Affairs, 1976.
Much of this report is devoted to a summary of relevant legistlation. [Unexamined].

(a) Associations, programs and agencies

4489 ADULT EDUCATION DEVELOPMENT BOARD. Adult education workshop. Lahore: Adult Education Development Board, 1973. 97p.
Topics include maternal and child health, home life and nutrition awareness. [Unexamined].

4490 PAKISTAN. INFORMATION AND BROADCASTING DIVISION. Women in social service. *In its* Women of Pakistan. Islamabad: Information and Broadcasting Division, Directorate of Research, Reference and Publications, Government of Pakistan, 1975. pp.39-46.
Photo essay. Text discusses background and activities of All-Pakistan Women's Association and briefly mentions other social service organizations operated for and by women.

4491 ________. Women in defence services. *In its* Women of Pakistan. Islamabad: Information and Broadcasting Division, Directorate of Research, Reference and Publications, Government of Pakistan, 1975. pp.47-52.
Photo essay. Text briefly discusses women's participation in the Pakistan Army Medical Corps, the Armed Forces Nursing Services and the National Guards.

4492 ________. The Girl Guides movement. *In its* Women of Pakistan. Islamabad: Information and Broadcasting Division, Directorate of Research, Reference and Publications, Government of Pakistan, 1975. pp.53-62.
Photo essay. Text reviews activities of the Pakistan Girl Guides Association, which has been important in developing character, instilling initiative and discipline and orienting its participants toward community service.

4493 PAKISTAN WOMEN'S INSTITUTE. News Letter. vl- (1975?-). Lahore. Quarterly.
Sample issue [2,1 (1976)] contains an editorial on Pakistani women's need for better public transportation, notice of a book on communism by a Pakistani woman, an American student's statement about her research in Lahore, institute news and other local and national news relating to women. The *News Letter* is "issued from Kinnaird College for Women."

4494 Seminar: "Role of Industrial Homes in Promoting Women's Socio-economic Welfare"; proceedings and recommendations. Lahore, Director General, Social Welfare, Government of the Punjab, 1971? 52p.
Texts of speeches and discussion, summary and recommendations of a seminar investigating the problems and prospects of centers for women's vocational training in industry and crafts in the Pakistan Punjab.

(b) Family planning

4495 BEAN, LEE L. and A.D. BHATTI. Pakistan's population in the 1970's: problems and prospects. *In* J. Henry Korson, ed. Contemporary problems of Pakistan. Leiden: E.J. Brill, 1974. pp.99-118. (International Studies in Sociology and Social Anthropology, 15).
Examines Pakistan's family planning program in the context of recent historical developments and the country's ethnic diversity.

4496 CHAUDHRY, MOHAMMAD IQBAL. Family planning in Hazara District. Peshawar: Board of Economic Enquiry, University of Peshawar, 1967. (*Its* Publication 33).
Survey found high rate of approval and low rate of practice of family planning at village level. [Unexamined].

4497 GARDEZI, HASSAN NAWAZ. Midwife as a local functionary and her role in family planning: some research findings. *In* Haider Ali Chaudhari et al., eds. Pakistan sociological perspectives: collected papers of the Pakistan Sociological Association's II, III, and IV conferences. Lahore: University of the Punjab, 1968.
Survey of Lahore midwives to assess their attitudes toward participating in structured training and client service programs. Favorable results. [Unexamined. Book in NUC].

4498 _______ and ATTIYA INAYATULLAH. The dai study: the dai, midwife, a local functionary and her role in family planning. Lahore: West Pakistan Family Planning Association, 1969. 106p.
Presents results in statistical form, of a survey of 72 midwives in Lahore. Examines family planning role the midwife, as local functionary can play by communicating new information through established channels.

4499 HARDEE, J. GILBERT and MOHAMMAD AZHAR. Change and differentials in women's knowledge of, attitude towards and practice of family planning in Pakistan during the 1960s. *In* Pakistan Development Review 14,3 (1975) 334-63.
Examines 1) evidence for change in Pakistani women's family planning knowledge, attitudes and practices (KAP) from the inception of the government family planning program in the early 1960s to the late 1960s, 2) KAP differentials, 3) effects of knowledge and attitudes on behavior, 4) program and policy implications of findings and 5) areas in need of further research.

4500 KHAN, W.A. Family planning: a survey on knowledge of, attitude towards, and practice of contraceptive methods in twenty-three districts of West Pakistan. *In* Seminar on Research in Family Planning 3d biennial. Proceedings. Karachi: National Research Institute of Family Planning, 1967. pp.86-107.
Although female informants tended to have little objection to family planning, few were found to be practicing it. [Unexamined. Book in NUC].

4501 SHAH, NASRA M. The role of interspousal communication in adoption of family planning methods: a couple approach. *In* Pakistan Development Review 13,4 (1974) 452-69.
Presents data on relationship of interspousal communication and fertility attitudes and behavior from West Pakistan section of 1968-69 National Impact Survey. Finds strong positive relationship between interspousal communication and family planning use. Urges couple-oriented family planning policy.

4502 TAJ, KOKAB. A comparative study of the attitudes of married women and college students toward family planning in a selected community of Hyderabad, West Pakistan. Ph.D. dissertation, Southern Illinois University, 1969. 117p. [University Microfilms 70-7320].
Discusses results of interviews with 300 married women and questionnaire survey of 200 college students. Found no major differences in attitudes of the two groups. [Unexamined. DAI].

4503 YOUSUF, FARHAT [FARHAT YUSUF]. Attitudes of a sample of married women in Lahore towards family planning and some aspects of family formation. *In* Seminar on Research in Family Planning 2d biennial. Proceedings. Karachi: National Research Institute of Family Planning, 1966. pp.121-34.
Correlates family planning attitudes with socio-economic variables. [Unexamined. Series in NUC].

4504 ZURAYK, HUDA C. Demand for contraception in Pakistan: dialogue between data and theory. Ph.D. dissertation, Johns Hopkins University, 1974. 178p. [University Microfilms 74-29,030].
Develops a methodology for determining factors involved in motivation to contracept at the family level and applies it to data from Pakistan's 1968 National Impact Survey. [Unexamined. DAI].

(c) Various problems: the poor, the infirm, runaways

4505 BOS-KUNST, EMMY. Women of Azam Basti: a social study among women of a slum area in Karachi, Pakistan. Karachi: Foundation for Scientific Research in Tropical Countries, 1970.
Study of socio-economic composition and lifestyle of women in this slum. General assessment is that they are oppressed and their lives are very difficult. [Unexamined].

4506 NALLAZARILLI, GULSHAN as told to CAROL MUSKE. Kashmir: some call it paradise. *In* Ms. 3,1 (1974) 12-4.
A Muslim physician from Kashmir briefly discusses several topics: the identity of Kashmir, the depressed state of its womanhood, some of the health problems of Kashmiri women and her own background. Her father encouraged her to study medicine abroad and return to treat Kashmiris. She describes the difficulty she had in setting up a practice. The major health problems of Kashmiri women are gynecological but they consider the female body "unclean and an 'improper' subject for discussion."

4507 The runaway women speak. *In* The Herald [Karachi] 9,7 (1978) 16-9.
Three brief articles on runaway women in Pakistan and a home, Darul Aman, in Karachi that cares for runaways and other underprivileged women. Many flee family problems, particularly ill treatment, or come to join a lover.

(9) Political participation: Sindhi nationalist movement

4508 BALUCH, AKHTAR. 'Sister, are you still here?': the diary of a Sindhi woman prisoner. *And* Preface to Akhtar Baluch's prison diary. Introduction and notes by Mary Tyler. *In* Race and Class 18,3-4 (1977) 219-45, 389-95.
Background to and excerpts from the diary of an 18-year-old Hyderabad college student ar-

rested in 1970 for protesting the detention of Sindhi nationalist and peasant leaders. Both preface and excerpts consider her prison experiences in light of a feudal social system, including its effects on the relations between the sexes.

(10) Arts

Regarding Urdu and Panjabi literatures see entries 2887-2929 and 4385-4402, respectively

(a) Painters

4509 AHMED, ANNA MOLKA. The coming women artists of Pakistan. *In* Pakistan Quarterly 3,3 (1953) 36-41.
Briefly discusses the work of several emergent painters and of the Department of Fine Arts at University of the Punjab, Lahore. Includes photographs of students, artists and their work.

(b) Reading interests

4510 SALAHUDDIN, AHMAD. Reading habits of women in West Pakistan. Karachi: National Book Centre of Pakistan, 1964. 55p. (Reading Habits in Pakistan, 1).
Results of a survey of reading interests of women of the then West Pakistan. Examines reading preferences of young, middle-aged and widowed women, as well as rural women. Reviews response patterns to questionnaires and interviews and reproduces examples of both modes of investigation.

(c) Sindhi literature: work of Popti Hiranandani

4511 HIRANANDANI, POPTI. The dark-brown stain. Tr. from Sindhi by Rajika Kripalani. *In* Sarala Jag Mohan, ed. Modern Indian short stories, v2. New Delhi: Indian Council for Cultural Relations, 1976. pp.115-20.
Short story. Examines the loneliness and stigma of childlessness that a woman experiences, whether her inability to conceive is her own or her husband's fault, and the joys of a longed-for pregnancy and child.

4512 ________. The wailing laughter. Tr. from Sindhi by Hashoo Kewal Ramani. *In* Hashoo Kewal Ramani, ed. Sindhi short stories, 2d ed. New Delhi: Hashmat Publications, n.d. pp.50-8.
Short story. Portrays the frustrations of poverty in a middle-class family.

(11) Clothing, adornment, beauty

4513 BONDREY, RAZIA. Beauty business is booming. *In* Perspective 4,1 (1970) 41-4.
Examines the contemporary phenomenon of beauty salons in Karachi.

4514 PAKISTAN. INFORMATION AND BROADCASTING DIVISION. Costumes and cosmetics. *In its* Women of Pakistan. Islamabad: Information and Broadcasting Division, Directorate of Research, Reference and Publications, Government of Pakistan, 1975. pp.99-112.
Photo essay. Text notes urban and regional clothing and hair styles and types of indigenous cosmetics and jewelry.

c. Nepal/high Himalayan cultural region: area of Nepali and northern Tibeto-Burman languages

(1) General statements

(a) Ethnographic contexts

4515 BENNETT, LYNN. Mother's milk and mother's blood: the social and symbolic roles of women among the Brahmans and Chetris of Nepal. Ph.D. dissertation, Department of Anthropology, Columbia University, 1977. 565p. [University Microfilms 77-24,321].
Discusses fundamental Hindu views of women and the forms they take in Brahman-Chetri society of Nepal. Analyzes women's rituals and goddess worship as they relate to the kinship system. Considers symbolism associated with women in this culture and the idea of separate realities for men and women. [Unexamined. DAI].

4516 FÜRER-HAIMENDORF, CHRISTOPH VON. Elements of Newar social structure. *In* J. of the Royal Anthropological Institute 86,2 (1956) 15-38.
Points to aspects of Newar social structure relating to women, which contrast significantly with more orthodox Hindu viewpoints. Caste endogamy rules are relaxed. Sexual intercourse has a lesser effect upon caste status than ritually relevant foods. Social status is transmittable through male and female lines. Marriages are relatively easily dissolved and "a woman's sexual relations with a man . . . do not permanently alter her ritual and social status."

4517 ________. The Sherpas of Nepal: Buddhist Highlanders. London: John Murray, 1964. 298p.
Ethnography based upon fieldwork in numerous Sherpa communities. Contains interspersed material on women as family members, lovers, nuns, witches, widows. Photographs.

4518 MISHRA, INDRA RAJ. The women of Nepal. *In* Women on the March 15,1 (1971) 27-8.
Reviews changing circumstances for Nepali women in recent decades.

4519 NEPALI, GOPAL SINGH. The Newars: an ethno-sociological study of a Himalayan community. Bombay: United Asia Publications, 1965. 476p.
Anthropological account based upon fieldwork in Kathmandu and Pangra village. Considers pregnancy, childbirth, initiation ceremonies for girls and boys, marriage ceremonies, death ceremonies, kinship terms, dyadic relationships, male and female deities and their worship and festivals.

(b) Collected papers and a photo essay

4520 In commemoration of International Women's Year, 1975. *In* Vasudha 15,10 (1976) 9-56.
Partial contents: "A Summary of Report of the International Women's Year Committee Nepal 1975" by Shanti Mishra (reviews IWY programs in Nepal), "Promotion of Equality Between Men and Women" by Mohan Lohani (reviews changing circumstances of Nepali women since 1951 and proposes means for further change), "A Revealing Look at our Women and at What They Say" (photographs and opinions of 22 prominent, employed women on women's issues), "The Practice of Suttee in Nepal" by Prakash A. Raj (reviews references from dynastic and recent history) and "Women in Nepal in Pictures" (photo essay showing women of nine ethnic groups).

4521 NEPAL. INTERNATIONAL WOMEN'S YEAR COMMITTEE. Women in Nepal. Kathmandu: Gorkhapatra Samsthan's Press, 1976. [Unexamined].

4522 Nepal: complicated, magical. Text by Mary Roblee Henry. Photographs by Irving Penn. *In* Vogue 152,10 (1968) 230-9, 286.
Brief text with miscellaneous comments on Nepali women. The well-known photographer's work is striking, but far from candid. Photographs are in color and, with one exception, of women.

(2) The life cycle

(a) *Rodī*, Gurung youth association

4523 ANDORS, ELLEN. The *rodighar* and its role in Gurung society. *In* Contributions to Nepalese Society 1,2 (1974) 10-24.
Ethnography of the Gurung youth association. Girls' *rodīs*, unlike those of boys, involve permanent sleeping arrangements and gathering places. Discusses life cycle of such

groups; functions, activities and ceremonies; patterns of change; and other topics.

4523a _______. The rodi: female associations among the Gurung of Nepal. Ph.D. dissertation, Department of Anthropology?, Columbia University, 1976. 260p. [University Microfilms 76-29,575].
Examines the social organization of the *rodī*, youth association for girls of the Gurung community. Describes functions of this group for its members and for the community as a whole. Considers female life cycle and socialization. [Unexamined. DAI].

(b) Courtship and marriage

4524 ADAM, LEONHARD. Nepal, marriage ceremony: a marriage ceremony of the Pun-clan (Magar) at Rigah (Nepal). *In* Man 34,23 (1934) 17-21.
Marriage ceremonies in the Magar community. Based on a narrative given by a soldier of this western Nepal community temporarily interned in a prisoner-of-war camp in Rumania in 1918.

4525 BAJRACHARYA, PURNA HARSHA. Newar marriage customs and festivals. *In* Southwestern J. of Anthropology 15,4 (1959) 418-28.
Regarding the various rites associated with marriage in this Kathmandu valley community. Also describes two festivals associated with the deceased.

4526 JONES, REX L. Courtship in an eastern Nepal community. *In* Anthropos 72,1/2 (1977) 288-99.
Describes the Limbu "rice dance," which enables men and women to contract and break their own marriages. It is an especially important option for women, who are generally expected to be "passive" in marriage. This aspect of courtship appears to be unique to the Limbu among Nepali hill communities.

4527 SAGANT, PHILIPPE. Mariage par enlèvement chez les Limbu (Népal) [Marriage by abduction among the Limbu of Nepal]. *In* Cahiers Internationaux de Sociologie 48 (1970) 71-98.
Describes the effects of an alternate and less standard Limbu marriage form on a potential bride, a potential groom and their respective fathers. This form, which the author translates as the marriage "de la fille," offers a certain margin of liberty, individuality and resolution of conflict.

(c) Fertility and motherhood

4528 BENNETT, LYNN. Sex and motherhood among the Brahmins and Chhetris of East-Central Nepal. *In* Contributions to Nepalese Studies 3, special issue (1976) 1-52.
Regarding the lives of mothers and young children in a rural community of predominantly Brahmans and Chetris on the periphery of the Kathmandu valley. Topics include: positive Hindu attitudes to fertility and child bearing and contradictions to these; cultural beliefs about barrenness, fertility, miscarriage and abortion and the effects of sorcery; local experience of conception, pregnancy and childbirth and related rituals; concepts of early childhood development; and interpretation and treatment of common childhood diseases. Photographs.

4529 GOLDSTEIN, MELVYN C. Fraternal polyandry and fertility in a high Himalayan valley in Northwest Nepal. *In* Human Ecology 4,3 (1976) 223-33.
Study of effect of polyandrous social structure on fertility among Tibetan peoples of the Limi valley. Concludes that "fraternal polyandry (of the Tibetan type) clearly operates to depress population growth by producing a residue of females who are only marginally involved in reproduction . . . . fraternal polyandry in Limi is part of a negative feedback process which operates to adjust, to a degree at least, population size to resources."

(3) Domestic sphere and family life

(a) Overviews, marriage stability, family relationships

4530 BENNETT, LYNN. *Maiti-ghar*: the dual role of high caste women in Nepal. *In* James F. Fisher, ed. Himalayan anthropology: the Indo-Tibetan interface. The Hague: Mouton Publishers, 1978. pp. 121-40.
Contrasts in detail women as consanguines and as affines in Brahman-Chetri society.

4530a _______. Dangerous wives and sacred sisters: the social and symbolic roles of women among the Brahmans and Chetris of Nepal. New York: Columbia University Press, forthcoming.
Revision of "*Maiti-ghar*" paper. [Unexamined].

4531 JONES, REX LEE. Kinship and marriage among the Limbu of eastern Nepal: a study of marriage stability. Ph.D. dissertation, Department of Anthropology, University of California, Los Angeles, 1973. 305p. [University Microfilms 73-13,148].
Presents data from genealogies and 23 case histories of Limbu marriages. Argues that economic independence of Limbu and marriage stability are inversely related. [Unexamined. DAI].

4532 _______ and SHIRLEY KURZ JONES. The Himalayan woman: a study of Limbu women

in marriage and divorce. Palo Alto, California: Mayfield Publishing Company, 1976. 155p. (Explorations in World Ethnology).
Ethnographic study of Limbu women of eastern Nepal, who are shown to have important roles in domestic and public spheres. Links control over marriage and divorce to the options Limbu culture provides these women. Stresses the need to examine women's lives and reevaluate traditional western conceptions of the family in South Asia. Photographs.

4533 JONES, SHIRLEY KURZ and REX JONES. Limbu women, divorce, and the domestic cycle. *In* Kailash 4,2 (1976) 169-84.
Examines "the problem of Limbu marital stability from a woman's perspective . . . . the decision making powers of a Limbu woman in marriage are powers that she holds by virtue of her status as a socially productive adult . . . . the economic role of women is extremely important in marriage."

4534 LALL, KESAR. Women of Kathmandu. *In* Vasudha 13,8 (1970) 21-4.
Presents transliterations and translations of four Newar songs that illustrate women's relationship to various family members.

(b) Property rights

4535 JOSHI, ANGUR BABA. Property rights of unmarried daughters. *In* Regmi Research Series 8,2 (1976).
[Unexamined].

4536 Property rights of widows. *In* Regmi Research Series 2,6 (1970) 127-34.
Since 1866. [Unexamined].

(4) Sexuality, witchcraft

4537 GLOVER, JESSIE R. The role of the witch in Gurung society. *In* Eastern Anthropologist 25,3 (1972) 221-6.
Presents details of the institution of witchcraft, which is rarely a male practice, among the Gurungs of Central Nepal. Discusses characteristics of witches, curses and their cures and a theoretical proposition about the conditions that foster witchcraft.

4538 A healthy earthiness in Nepal. *In* Far Eastern Economic Review 91,2 (9 Jan 1976) 25.
Brief comments on prostitution, sexuality and marriage in Nepal.

(5) The spiritual life and religious observances

(a) Ascetic communities

4539 CAPLAN, PATRICIA. Ascetics in western Nepal. *In* Eastern Anthropologist 26,2 (1973) 173-82.
Describes the beliefs, practices, monastery organization and lifestyles of female *Śaiva* ascetics. Discusses reasons why women become ascetics and attempts to explain the preponderance of female ascetics in Nepal.

4540 FÜRER-HAIMENDORF, CHRISTOPH VON. A nunnery in Nepal. *In* Kailash 4,2 (1976) 121-54.
Report of field study of the "Pleasure Garden of Deathless Good Fortune" nunnery in Bigu village, Dolakha District. Details its history, economic base, community structure and relationship to surrounding lay community. With photographs and biographical sketches of members.

(b) A women's festival: *Tīja / Ṛṣi Pañcamī*

4541 BENNETT, LYNN. The wives of the Rishis: an analysis of the Tij-Rishi Panchami women's festival. *In* Kailash 4,2 (1976) 185-207.
Analyzes two associated festivals celebrated by women of the Brahman-Chetri cultural community of Nepal. Relates associated myths, rituals and their symbolism (including that of menstrual blood) to the patrilineal kin structure and related attitudes about women's sexuality. Photographs.

4542 BISTA, KHEM BAHADUR. Tīj ou la fête des femmes [Tīja, the women's festival]. *In* Objets et Mondes 9,1 (1969) 7-18.
Regarding a festival celebrated by women of the Kathmandu valley. While interpretors have asserted that the purpose of the festival is to obtain a good husband or to ensure the long life and prosperity of one's husband, author argues that it is a time when women purify themselves from faults committed during the previous year and a time for leisure and recreation. Describes stages of the ritual and material objects used, as well as the accompanying myth. Photographs.

(c) *Kumārī* worship, *devīkī* tradition

4543 ALLEN, MICHAEL. The cult of Kumari: virgin worship in Nepal. Kathmandu: Institute of Nepal and Asian Studies, Tribhuvan University, 1975. 67p.

Reviews historical references to Kumārī worship in South Asia, lists eleven places and communities in Nepal that install living forms of Kumārī. Describes selection, duties of attendant, worship and other details of major and minor Kumārīs. Concludes with symbolic interpretation, focusing on Kumārīs' dual identity as young virgin and sexually mature mother goddess. Photographs and diagrams.

4544 ________. Kumari or 'virgin' worship in Kathmandu valley. *In* Contributions to Indian Sociology n.s. 10,2 (1976) 293-316.
Presents data to illustrate the recurrent theme of dangerous sexuality associated with the installation and subsequent worship of two- to three-year-old girls as living forms of the goddess Kumārī in the Newar community. Discusses cult in relation to caste and notions of relative purity. Argues that a Kumārī is ambiguously both a virgin and an erotic female. Blood is feared as a polluting substance but venerated as a source of life. The Kumārī cult is informed by the notion of the danger of sexual maturity in an unmarried girl. Photographs.

4545 Daughters of the temple. *In* Far Eastern Economic Review 91,2 (9 Jan 1976) 24.
Briefly discusses ***devīkī*** tradition of devoting a daughter to the service of a deity in northwestern Nepal.

4546 Living goddesses. *In* Asia Magazine (21 May 1971) 16-7.
Color photographs. [Unexamined].

4547 MOAVEN, NILOUFAR. Enquête des Kumari [Investigation of Kumārīs]. *In* Kailash 2,3 (1974) 167-88.
[Unexamined].

4548 Sad fate of little girls in Nepal who happen to be goddesses. *In* Atlas 18,5 (1969) 30-1.
Describes ***Durgā pūjā*** celebrations and various other practices and beliefs associated with Kumārī worship in Nepal. Photograph.

4549 SAYAMI, DHOOSWAN. Kumari: the cult of mother goddess. *In* Nepalese Perspective 5,52 (27 Sep 1969) 12-4.
On the worship of young girls as Kumārī goddesses in Nepal. Discusses the origin, history, selection, installation, worship, deposition and subsequent life of these girls.

(d) Goddesses, Newar *tāntrika* tradition

4550 SLUSSER, MARY. Jogini of the sword: a visit to her shrine. *In* Vasudha 15,2 (1974) 20-7. [*Also in her* Kathmandu: a collection of articles. Kathmandu: American Women of Nepal, 1972? pp.13-23].
Shrine to the Buddhist goddess Tārā in her blue, fierce, sword-bearing form near Sanku. Describes the physical site (includes map) and an associated legend. Emphasizes the artistic merit of the architecture and images.

4551. The tantric universe. Produced by Sheldon Rochlin and Mike Spera. 22 min. 16 and 35 mm. [*Distributed by* Focus International, 505 West End Avenue, New York, New York 10024].
Film portrays and discusses religious life of the Newar community in the Kathmandu valley. Examines ***tāntrika*** concepts of the polarity of the sexes, divine energy and unity in diversity. Compares Hindu and Buddhist concepts. Discusses symbolic aspects of the three deities, Viṣṇu, Śiva and Kālī. Accompanying study guide includes narration text, notes and bibliography. [Unexamined].

(6) Education

4552 SHRESTHA, BIHARI K. Equality of access of women to education in Pokhara: a sociological survey. Kathmandu: Centre for Economic Development and Administration, 1973. 116p.
Results of a sociological survey that focused on socio-economic factors relating to local education for girls, teacher training for women and the extent of migration from surrounding villages and its effect on recruitment of female teachers. Relates female education to local hierarchy, economic condition of family and education of household head. Points to various limitations on female recruitment to teaching profession.

(7) Development and social welfare

4553 DUBERMAN, LUCILE and KOYA AZUMI. Sexism in Nepal. *In* J. of Marriage and the Family 37,4 (1975) 1013-21.
Investigates socio-economic correlates with sexist attitudes in a diverse sample of 521 Kathmandu valley residents in order to explore why women tend to endure second-class status.

4554 GHIMIRE, DURGA, ed. Women and development. Kathmandu: Centre for Economic Development and Administration, Tribhuvan University, 1977. 77p.
Papers and proceedings from a 1975 seminar on women and development in Nepal sponsored by CEDA. Includes introduction, program schedule list of participants, photographs and the following papers, with commentary: "Social Status of Nepali Women" by Durga Ghimire, "Role of Women in Economic Development" by Meena Acharya, "A Daughter's Right to Inherit Paternal Property" by Shilu Singha, "Small Family Norm and the Role of Women" by Chapala

Pandey, "Women and Education" by Lila Devi and "Role of Women [sic] Organization for the Development of Women" by Punya Prabha Devi Dhungana.

4555 JOSHI, ANGUR BABA. Legal Code (sixth amendment) Ordinance, 1975. Kathmandu: Nepal Press Digest, 1975. (Nepal Law Translation Series?).
Considers changes in the Nepali civil code to improve the status of women. Ordinance was enacted in connection with International Women's Year. [Unexamined. Series in ALN].

4556 NEPAL. INTERNATIONAL WOMEN'S YEAR COMMITTEE. The legal status of women. Kathmandu?: Sahayogi Press, 1975.
[Unexamined].

4557 PORAVRELA, DURGĀ, ed. Aiśvarya: śubhajanmotsava viśeṣaṅka. [Kathmandu: the author, 1977. 79p.].
Collected articles on the role of women in Nepal's national development on occasion of Queen Aishwarya's 29th birthday. Four brief articles are in English; remaining articles are in Nepali.

4558 THAKUR, H.N. A demographic quest for family planning in Nepal. *In* J. of Family Welfare 11,1 (1964) 20-8.
Presents statistics on birth rate, food production/consumption and employment opportunities in Nepal to demonstrate need for greater family planning efforts. With suggestions for effective implementation of such a program.

4559 TULADHAR, JAYANTI M., B.B. GUBHAJU and JOHN STOECKEL. Population and family planning in Nepal. Kathmandu: Ratna Pustak Bhandar, 1978. 118p.
[Unexamined. ALN].

4560 VAIDYANATHAN, K.E. and FREDERICK H. GAIGE. Estimates of abridged life tables, corrected sex-age distribution and birth and death rates for Nepal, 1954. *In* Demography India 2,2 (1973) 278-90.
Basic demographic figures based upon "the first census of Nepal to follow modern census procedures."

4560a Women of Nepal: approaches to change; a seminar sponsored by the U.S. International Communication Agency and the Centre for Economic Development and Administration, May 17-18, 1978, Kathmandu. [Kathmandu: Centre for Economic Development and Administration, Tribhuvan University, 1978]. 95p.
Seminar proceedings include opening addresses; papers on the general status of Nepali women, women's organizations and training facilities, political participation and legal status; a statistical profile; a bibliography; workshop recommendations; and a list of participants.

4561 Women's welfare in Nepal. *In* Women on the March 15,3/4 (1971) 30.
Discusses work of the Nepal Mahila Sangathan (i.e., Nepal Women's Organization?) for women. Based upon interview with its president.

(8) Political participation: Queens Ratna and Aishwarya

4562 [AISHWARYA RAJYA LAXMI DEVI, MAHARANI OF NEPAL]. Her majesty Queen Aishwarya Rajya Laxmi Devi Shah: speeches and addresses, 1972-1976. [Kathmandu]: Department of Information, Ministry of Communications, His Majesty's Government of Nepal, 1977. 22p.
Includes messages on the occasion of International Women's Day (8 March), 1972-76; addresses on the occasion of various International Women's Year functions; and a message to the Japanese women's expedition to Mount Sagarmatha.

4563 BHANDARI, ADYA CHARAN RAJ. The coronation book of their majesties King Mahendra Bir Bikram Shaha Deva and Queen Ratna Rajya Lakshmi Devi Shaha of Nepal. Kathmandu: the author, 1956. 1v.
[Unexamined].

4564 Birthday special. *In* Nepalese Perspective 5,47 (23 Aug 1969) 1-9.
Special issue in honor of Queen Ratna's birthday. Has brief articles praising her qualities, leadership and contributions, among which is work for the cause of women in Nepal

4565 Her Majesty's 43rd birthday: special issue. *In* Nepalese Perspective 6.46 (22 Aug 1970) 1-7.
Highlights Queen Ratna's concern with problems and programs relating to Nepali women. Portrays her as the "living symbol of ideal Hindu womanhood, the follower of our glorious tradition and cultural values and a dynamic social reformer," and discusses the various plans for her birthday celebration throughout the country.

4566 Marriage special. Nepalese Perspective 6,21 (28 Feb 1970) 20p.
Special issue in honor of and about the royal wedding of Nepal's Crown Prince Birendra Bickram Shah Deva and Crown Princess Aishwarya Rajya Laxmi Devi Rana in February 1970. Describes the various ceremonies performed, provides biographical sketches of the bride and groom, and discusses marriage customs in Nepal and married life. Photographs. Subsequent issues continue the description of the various ceremonies.

4567 SIMHA, TEEKA. The royal wedding in Nepal, the Himalayan mountain kingdom, and Kathmandu. Kathmandu: n.p., 1971? 1v.
Photo essay. Documents the rites of various stages of the royal wedding in February 1970. The author was allowed to take the photographs as "the only Nepali woman professional photog-

rapher." With brief biographical sketches of the couple and a brief explanation of the various Hindu marriage rites performed in Nepal.

(9) Arts: children's drawings of man, woman and self

4568 SUNDBERG, NORMAN and THOMAS BALLINGER. Comparisons of Nepalese and American children's drawings of man, woman, and self. *In* American Psychologist 17 (1962) 305.
Abstract of paper presented at 1962 meetings of American Psychological Association. [Unexamined].

4569 ________. Nepalese children's cognitive development as revealed by drawings of man, woman, and self. *In* Child Development 39,3 (1968) 969-85.
Compares formal and content properties of samples of drawings from Nepalese and American children. Considers alternate Nepali and American ways of portraying sex differences. Eight drawings reproduced.

(10) Western women in the Himalayas

See also "(11) Mountaineering," entries 4576-87

4570 FISHER, WELTHY. The top of the world. New York: Abingdon Press, 1926? 178p.
Travel, description and social life in the Himalayas and India by a missionary. [Unexamined. NUC].

4571 FLETCHER, GRACE NIES. The fabulous Flemings of Kathmandu: the story of two doctors in Nepal. New York: E.P. Dutton, 1964. 219p.
The story of a doctor and her ornithologist husband and their work in Nepal as medical missionaries. Discusses their early years in the United States, early mission work in India, establishment of the Shanta Bhawan Hospital in Kathmandu and various experiences in Nepal.

4572 A LADY PIONEER [NINA ELIZABETH MAZUCHELLI?]. The Indian Alps and how we crossed them: being a narrative of two years' residence in the eastern Himalaya and two months' tour into the interior. London: Longmans, Green, and Company, 1876. 612p.
Account of an Englishwoman's two-year residence in Darjeeling and tour to the interior originally written "for the exclusive perusal of a family circle" and published anonymously. Records her activities and her impressions of the land and the people. With the author's illustrations.

4573 LEUCHTAG, ERIKA. Erika and the King. New York: Coward-McCann, 1958. 255p. [*Also published as* With a king in the clouds. London: Hutchinson, 1958. 235p. *French ed.* J'ai servi le roi du Népal: récit. Tr. from English by Arlette Rosenblum. Paris: Fasquelle, 1960. 215p.].
Autobiographical account of author's adventures in Nepal in the service of King Tribhuvana. Photographs. [Unexamined. NUC].

4574 NORRISH, ALAN E. Nepal, an opened door. God's challenge to this generation. London: Zenana Bible and Medical Mission, 1956? 39p. (New Challenge Series, 1).
Zenana mission work in Nepal? Illustrations. Portraits. [Unexamined. MRL].

4575 REYMOND, LIZELLE. My life with a brahmin family. Tr. from French by Lucy Norton. London: Rider, 1958. 192p.
Recollections of life "as a member" of an orthodox brahman family of the Himalayan town of Kurmachala (in northernmost Uttar Pradesh?), 1947-53.

(11) Mountaineering

(a) Mrs. Bullock Workman

4576 BULLOCK WORKMAN, FANNY [FANNY (BULLOCK) WORKMAN] and WILLIAM HUNTER WORKMAN. In the ice world of Himalaya: among the peaks and passes of Ladakh, Nubra, Suru, and Baltistan, 2d ed. New York: Cassell and Company, Limited, 1900? 204p.
Account of pioneering Himalayan expeditions made by this couple in the summers of 1898 and 1899. Maps and numerous photographs.

4577 ________. Ice-bound heights of the Mustagh: an account of two seasons of pioneer exploration and high climbing in the Baltistan Himalaya. New York: Charles Scribner's Sons, 1908. 444p.
Account of expeditions in Kashmir in 1902 and 1903. With her ascent of Mount Lungma (22,568 feet), Mrs. Bullock Workman broke her previous altitude record for women of 21,000 feet. Maps and 170 illustrations.

4578 ________. Peaks and glaciers of Nun Kun: a record of pioneer-exploration and mountaineering in the Punjab Himalaya. New York: Charles Scribner's Sons, 1909. 204p.
Report of couple's 1906 exploration of the Nun Kun massif and surrounding area in Kashmir. "By this ascent Mrs Bullock Workman not only broke her last record-ascent for women of 22,568 feet, but won a place with Dr Workman

in the small band of mountaineers who have reached a height of over 23,000 feet." With map and numerous photographs.

4579 ________. The summers in the ice-wilds of eastern Karakoram: the exploration of nineteen hundred square miles. London: T. Fisher Unwin Limited, 1917. 296p.
Report of 1912 expedition to the Siachen or Rose glacier and tributaries in the eastern Karakoram range. Maps and 141 photographs.

4580 MIDDLETON, DOROTHY. The lady pioneers: I. Fanny Bullock Workman, 1859-1925. *In* Geographical Magazine 34,8 (1961) 457-61.
On the travels of an American woman in South Asia. With her husband, she visited Ceylon (now Sri Lanka), bicycled from Cape Comorin to Kashmir and made numerous Himalayan mountain expeditions, the last one in her 53rd year. A striking woman, Mrs. Bullock Workman "was certainly known to have carried a 'Votes for Women' banner into the Himalaya." Photographs.

4581 WORKMAN, WILLIAM HUNTER and FANNY BULLOCK WORKMAN [FANNY (BULLOCK) WORKMAN]. Through town and jungle: 14,000 miles a-wheel among the temples and people of the Indian plain. London: T. Fisher Unwin, 1904. 380p.
Account of bicycle trip from Cape Comorin to the Himalayas begun in 1897. This couple was particularly interested in Buddhist, Hindu and Muslim art and architecture. Map and 202 illustrations. [Unexamined. BMG].

4582 ________. The call of the snowy Hispar: a narrative of exploration and mountaineering on the northern frontier of India. New York: Charles Scribner's Sons, 1911. 297p. [*Also* London: Constable and Company, Ltd.].
Account of the couple's 1908 expedition to the Hispar glacier and its tributaries in the Karakoram range. Maps and numerous photographs.

(b) Others

4583 DAVIES, A. Women's overland Himalayan expedition, 1958. *In* Alpine Journal 64,298 (1959) 83-90.
Illustrated. [Unexamined].

4584 JACKSON, MONICA. The Scottish women's Himalayan expedition. *In* Alpine Journal 61,292 (1956) 60-2.
Illustrated. [Unexamined].

4585 ________ and ELIZABETH STARK. Tents in the clouds: the first women's Himalayan expedition. London: Collins, 1956. 255p.
Expedition led by western women in 1955. Photographs and maps. [Unexamined. NUC].

4586 MIYAZAKI, EIKO. Japanese women's Annapurna III expedition, 1970. *In* Himalayan Journal 30 (1970) 127-8.
Briefly describes schedule and lists and identifies members. Photographs.

4587 SEN GUPTA, SUDIPTA. Ladies' Lahoul expedition, 1970. *In* Himalayan Journal 30 (1970) 221-7.
Account of Indian women's expedition to a virgin peak in Lahoul region of Himachal Pradesh during which one member died. Photographs.

d. Eastern highland tribal cultural region: area of eastern Tibeto-Burman and Mon-Khmer languages

(1) Ethnographic contexts

4588 BURLING, ROBBINS. Rengsanggri: family and kinship in a Garo village. Philadelphia: University of Pennsylvania Press, 1963. 377p.
Women's lives are documented in this ethnographic account of the social organization of a matrilineal hill community of present-day Meghalaya.

4589 CHATTERJI, N. Status of women in the earlier Mizo society. Aizawl: Tribal Research Institute, 1975. 31p. (*Its* Publication 3).
Examines family, courtship and marriage of Lushai women of Mizoram. Neither time implied by "earlier" Mizo society nor sources for study are identified.

4590 GEMINI, PAUL. The place of khadduh: the youngest daughter in Khasi and Synteng society. *In* Vanyajati 4,2 (1956) 82-4.
[Unexamined].

4591 GOSWAMI, M.C. and D.N. MAJUMDAR. A study of women's position among the Garo of Assam. *In* Man in India 45,1 (1965) 27-35.
Discusses power of matrilineally related males in this matrilineal society.

4592 MUKHERJEE, BISHWA NATH. Restrictions on married women's activities and some aspects of husband-wife relations in Khasi culture. *In* Indian Anthropologist 4,2 (1974) 104-30.
Describes and scales types of activities prohibited to rural married Khasi women in Meghalaya. Relates degree of restriction to marital satisfaction and dominating attitudes of wives. Research questions were partially informed by matrilineal structure of Khasi society.

4593 NAKANE, CHIE. Garo and Khasi: a comparative study in matrilineal systems. Paris: Mouton, 1967. 187p. (Cahiers de l'Homme, n.s. 5).
Details the social organization of the Garo and Khasi hill peoples of Assam. Treats marriage, family structure and village organization in these very different matrilineal societies.

4594 SAWAIN, S. Khasi women. *In* Social Welfare 5,7 (1958) 20-2.
The women of this matrilineal community are said to enjoy a generally favorable status. [Unexamined].

4595 WILDE, MRS. FRANK. The Kukis and Nagas of the North Cachar Hills, Assam. *In* T. Athol Joyce and N.W. Thomas, eds. Women of all nations: a record of their characteristics, habits, manners, customs and influence, v3. London: Cassell and Company, 1915? pp.575-84.
Observations on the dress, religion, marriage, dance and work of Kuki and Naga women. The author accompanied her husband on survey work through the hill section of the Assam-Bengal Railway. Photographs.

(2) Fertility and reproduction

4596 BHOWMIK, K.L. et al. Fertility of Zemi women in Nagaland. Calcutta: Institute of Social Studies, 1971. 120p. (Sociology of Fertility Series, 1).
Examination of reproductive lives of women of the Zemi Naga tribal village, Benreu. Considers fertility and differential fertility studies in India; design of present study; socioeconomic features of Benreu; statistics relating to menarche, pregnancy and birth, birth and fertility rates, reproduction rate and menopause; and fertility differentials.

4597 KAR, R.K. and SHYAMALI MAHANTA. Menarche and menopause among the Singpho women of Arunachal Pradesh. *In* Indian J. of Physical Anthropology and Human Genetics 1,1 (1975) 51-7.
Presents data on reported ages of menarche and menopause of 95 Singpho women from several villages of Arunachal Pradesh. Compares findings to those of similar surveys conducted elsewhere in India.

4598 SARMA, JYOTIRMOYEE. Puberty, marriage, and childbirth among the Panggi and Minyong Abor women. *In* Anthropos 55 (1960) 97-113.
Describes and compares behavior related to puberty, courtship, marriage and childbirth of two geographically distinct groups from the Abor Hills of Assam. Relates differences regarding puberty and marriage to differential contact with the plains. Observed no major differences with respect to childbirth.

(3) The political leader Rani Gaidinliu

4599 NAG, AMIT KUMAR. Rani Gaidinliu: a study of the Jadonang movement of the Nagas. Silchar: Tribal Mirror Publications, 1976? 59p.
Story of Naga woman who earned the title "Rani" for her militant leadership of the messianic Jadonang movement against British colonialism. She was imprisoned, was released at independence and afterwards continued to participate in Naga politics.

(4) Western women

4600 BOR, ELEANOR. Adventures of a botanist's wife. London: Hurst and Blackett Ltd., 1952. 204p.
The wife of a forest officer and local administrator recounts their tenure in the Balipara Frontier Tract in the 1930s and 1940s.

4600a BOWER, URSULA GRAHAM. The hidden land. London: John Murray, 1953. 244p.
The wife of the political officer of the newly-formed Subansiri Area recounts their tenure there in the late 1940s in an effort to promote peace among the tribes of the area. Photographs.

4601 CHAPMAN, E. and M. CLARK. Marjorie Sykes, ed. Mizo miracle. Madras: Christian Literature Society, 1968. 192p.
Account of mission work in the South Lushai Hills from 1919 to the authors' retirements in the early 1950s. Discusses prejudice against female missionaries and work among native women, the establishment and early work of the Serkawn Girls' School, other church activities among the Mizo people, close Mizo friends and coworkers and eight adopted Mizo daughters.

4601a GRIMWOOD, ETHEL ST. CLAIR. My three years in Manipur and escape from the recent mutiny. London: Richard Bentley, 1891. 316p.
The wife of the political agent at Manipur details their life there and the local mutiny in 1891 in which her husband was killed.

e. The Diaspora: South Asian women abroad

(1) South Africa

4602 KUPER, HILDA. Indian people in Natal. Natal: University Press, 1960. 305p.
Anthropological account of Indians in the city of Durban. Discusses family structure, kinship categories, role relations, life cycle rites, gods and goddesses, festivals, trance, health problems and other topics. Photographs.

4603 MEER, FATIMA. Portrait of Indian South Africans. Durban: Avon House, 1969. 236p.
Overview of the history and culture of Indians in South Africa. The numerous topics relating to women include marriage and domestic life, domestic life in a slum area, goddess worship and women and the arts.

4604 ________. Women and the family in the Indian enclave in South Africa. *In* Feminist Studies 1,2 (1972) 33-47.
Describes pervasive view that women must be protected. Predicts that increasing female employment opportunities will serve to weaken this view. [Unexamined. BAS].

4604a ROSENTHAL, LEORA N. The definition of female sexuality and the status of women among the Gujerati-speaking Indians of Johannesburg. *In* John Blacking, ed. The anthropology of the body. London: Academic Press, 1977. pp.199-210. (Association of Social Anthropologists Monographs, 15).
Describes various aspects of female sexuality in theory and as in operation among Gujarati speakers of Johannesburg. "The Indian view of female sexual physiology is the opposite of the 'western' view described by Greer, de Beauvoir, Firestone and others, its effects are to surround the woman in a web of restrictions and prohibitions, and to cast suspicion on her every movement."

(2) The Caribbean

4605 BELL, ROBERT R. Marriage and family differences among lower-class Negro and East Indian women in Trinidad. *In* Race 12,1 (1970) 59-73.
"This study shows some sharp differences in a number of marriage and family patterns common to the Negro and Indian sample studies in Trinidad. The differences essentially reflect the patriarchal patterns of the Indians in contrast with the female-family centred patterns of the lower-class Negro women." Considers marriage, sexuality, parenthood, illegitimacy and child rearing.

4606 JAYAWARDENA, CHANDRA. Family organisation in plantations in British Guiana. *In* John Mogey, ed. Family and marriage. Leiden: E.J. Brill, 1963. pp.43-64. (International Studies in Sociology and Social Anthropology, 1). [*Also in* International J. of Comparative Sociology 3,1 (1962) 43-64].
Examines the historical background, family structure and variants, household types and organization, and wider kin groups of plantation communities composed chiefly of immigrants from India. Suggests that black matrifocal family values of the Caribbean have exerted an influence on strikingly different Indian values, as evidenced by husband-wife relations in these plantation communities of present-day Guyana.

4607 ROBERTS, G.W. and L. BRAITHWAITE. Mating among East Indian and non-Indian women in Trinidad. *In* Social and Economic Studies 11,3 (1962) 203-40.
A comparative quantitative investigation of rate of participation in types of unions ("visiting," "common law" or "married" as opposed to "single"), age at entry into unions and union stability. East Indian women tended to be involved in predominantly marital unions, while visiting and common law unions dominated the rest of the Trinidad population sampled. The East Indians tended to enter unions earlier and their unions tended to be relatively unstable.

4608 SMITH, R.T. and C. JAYAWARDENA. Hindu marriage customs in British Guiana. *In* Social and Economic Studies 7,2 (1958) 178-94.
". . . an ethnographic account of the sequence of major ritual events connected with an orthodox (*Sanatan*) wedding in British Guiana [present-day Guyana]."

4609 ________. Family and marriage amongst the East Indians in British Guiana. *In* Social and Economic Studies 8,4 (1959) 321-76.
Presents data on households, family structure and marriage patterns from two sugar plantation areas and a rice-farming district. With background information on Indians in Guyanese society and the structure of the three communities.

(3) Britain

4610 BHATTI, F.M. Language difficulties and social isolation: the case of South Asian women in Britain. *In* New Community 5,1/2 (1976) 115-7.
Discusses problems faced by female South Asian migrants to England who do not know English and their families. Suggests urgency of need for local institutional arrangements for learning English and offers practical suggestions for its implementation.

4611 CRISHNA, SEETHA. Girls of Asian origin in Britain. London: YWCA of Great Britain, 1975. 45p.
Report of study of 16- to 25-year-old women from Bangladesh, India and Pakistan in the Southall area of London and in Bradford, Yorkshire. Considers families, social interaction, employment and education.

4612 DAHYA, ZAYNAB. Pakistani wives in Britain. *In* Race 6,4 (1965) 311-21.
Report of a woman from an Indo-Muslim family of Tanganyika who visited several Pakistani families in Bradford. She contrasts household organization, *pardā* observance and mobility among these families with those found in what was then West Pakistan. Stresses the isolation experienced by Muslim women of Bradford, contrasts it with the mobility of Sikh and Gujarati immigrants and urges further research.

4613 DHANJAL, BERYL. Sikh women in Southall: some impressions. *In* New Community 5,1/2 (1976) 109-14.
Observations on various aspects of women's lives in an immigrant community in Southall, West London: traditional roles, employment, family life and attitudes toward sexuality.

4614 JEFFERY, PATRICIA. Migrants and refugees: Muslim and Christian Pakistani families in Bristol. Cambridge: Cambridge University Press, 1976. 221p.
Report of a study that focused "on the ways in which certain elements of the migrants' culture can be protected and how children may be brought up in a Pakistani domestic setting in Britain . . . . on the social processes involved in non-assimilation and the maintenance of ethnic boundaries." Includes interspersed material on women and men's attitudes toward them with respect to education, dress, employment, mobility and so forth.

4615 MUTHANNA, I.M. The first Indian princess in England: Victoria Gowramma. *In* Modern Review 116,2 (1964) 134-6. [*Also in* Indian Review 63,9 (1964) 315-6.
Brief portrait of the life of Gouramma, the first Indian princess in England, who in 1852 stood by her father in his endeavor to regain his kingdom, the Indian state of Coorg, from the East India Company. The two were unofficial spokespersons for India in England. Queen Victoria took a lively and patronly interest in the princess. She later married Colonel John Campbell who had served in Madras. Photograph.

4616 NIHAL SINGH, SAINT. When the rani lifts her veil in London. *In* Nineteenth Century and After 70,413 (1911) 104-14.
Examines the lives of a number of women from India's royal families who visited England to illustrate how these women have served as the vanguard of a new type of Indian womanhood. Discusses their education, literary work, charitable activities, and forsaking of *pardā*.

4617 POCOCK, D.F. Preservation of the religious life: Hindu immigrants in England. *In* Contributions to Indian Sociology n.s. 10,2 (1976) 341-65.
Examination of a Swami Narayani community in London includes a brief section on "Marriage and the Position of Women." The sect has a tradition of extreme sex-segregation and women are prohibited from many religious activities available to men. Daughters are somewhat peripheral in that they sometimes marry out of the community, acquiring their husbands' identities. Young women experience a schism between the relative freedom of their school lives and orthodoxy of their home lives. Brides born in India are preferred to those born in England.

4618 SAIFULLAH KHAN, VERITY. Asian women in Britain: strategies of adjustment of Indian and Pakistani migrants. *In* Social Action 25,3 (1975) 302-20. [*Reprint in* Alfred de Souza, ed. Women in contemporary India: traditional images and changing roles. Delhi: Manohar Book Service, 1975. pp.164-88].
Discusses the daily routine and general life conditions of women from Asia (primarily Bangladesh, India and Pakistan) in Britain. Considers broader context of British and South Asian socio-political setting.

4619 ________. Pakistani women in Britain. *In* New Community 5,1/2 (1976) 99-108.
Compares *pardā* observance in Pakistan with that of a community of immigrants from Mirpur District residing in the city of Bradford. Discusses continuities and differences and some difficulties the new environment presents.

4620 ________. Purdah in the British situation. *In* Diana Leonard Barker and Sheila Allen, eds. Dependence and exploitation in work and marriage. London: Longman, 1976. pp.224-45.
Relates *pardā* as observed by immigrants from Mirpur District to the seclusion system of their relatives at home in Kashmir.

4621 SHARMA, URSULA, ed. and tr. Rampal and his family. London: Collins, 1971. 222p.
Presents oral life histories of a working-class Panjabi couple who emigrated from peasant villages to Delhi at partition and later to London. Roughly half of the book is devoted to Rampal's story, the other half to his wife Satya's story. Concludes with a brief statement by their daughter. An effort to see "the immigrant's world from within."

4622 STROUD, C.E. and V. MOODY. One hundred mothers: a survey of west Indians in Paddington. *In* Maternal and Child Care 3,26 (1967).
[Unexamined].

4623 UBEROI, NARINDAR. Sikh women in Southall. *In* Race 6,1 (1964) 34-40.
Compares various aspects of Panjabi women's lives prior to and following migration to England. Describes conflicts experienced between the new and the old. Based upon author's casual observations.

4624 WILSON, AMRIT. Finding a voice: Asian women in Britain. London: Virago Ltd., 1978.
Much if not all of this work deals with South Asian women. Examines recurrent themes of loneliness and isolation in the women's lives. Includes much case study material. The book was awarded the Martin Luther King Memorial Prize. [Unexamined].

(4) North America

4625 GAYATRI DEVI. One life's pilgrimage: addresses, letters, and articles by the first Indian woman to teach Vedanta in the West. Cohasset, Massachusetts: Vedanta Centre, 1977. 341p.
Primarily contains interpretations of Vedanta and matters relating to two ashrams in the United States. Also includes numerous photos and "An Autobiographical Sketch." The author, a niece of Swami Vivekananda's disciple Swami Paramananda, joined her uncle in the United States in 1926 as a sister in the Ramakrishna order.

4626 NAIDOO, J.C. South Asian women in Canada. *In* Cannie Stark Adamec, ed. Sex roles: origins, influences and implications for women. St. Albans, Vermont: Eden Press, forthcoming.
Volume contains proceedings of the Inaugural Institute on Women, Ottawa, Canada. [Unexamined].

4627 SRIVASTAVA, RAM P. Family organization and change among the overseas Indians with special reference to Indian immigrant families of British Columbia, Canada. *In* George Kurian, ed. The family in India: a regional view. The Hague: Mouton, 1974. pp.369-91. (Studies in the Social Sciences, 12).
Discusses issues and problems of mate selection and family structure among the predominantly Sikh community of "East Indians" in British Columbia. Conjugal roles are becoming more egalitarian and less differentiated than in traditional Panjabi Sikh families. Most male informants stated that "their attitude towards the status of women did not change *enough* to satisfy their wife."

(5) Middle East

4628 FERNANDES, J.M. Why young Indian women still go to the Middle East. *In* Eve's Weekly 29,28 (12 Jul 1975) 13.
Briefly identifies Indian women who seek employment in the Middle East and describes their reasons for going and some aspects of life there. Based on interviews.

(6) New Zealand

4629 Indian women in New Zealand. *In* Learning about sexism in New Zealand. Wellington: Learmouth Publishers, 1976. pp.95-111.
[Unexamined].

Part Two

Libraries, Archives and Other Local Resources

Libraries, Archives and Other Resources in India for the Study of Women

Geraldine H. Forbes *

My research on women in India has been a tremendously rewarding experience both intellectually and personally. Recalling that time means remembering time spent reading through organizational records (previously pronounced lost) in the private library of a very grand house in Bombay, meeting with grieving *Shī'ah* Muslim women in Hyderabad during *Muḥarram*, listening to Bengali women who were part of the revolutionary movement in the 1930s reminisce about their jail years and experiencing the patience of so many kind people who listened to my questions and tried to help me find the answers. I am unable to suppress my excitement, for in this research I was able to approach history in new ways and with new techniques, as well as to come to understand more about the lives of some of history's most remarkable women.

In this essay I would like to offer some suggestions for those who will go to India to do research on women's topics. My research in India focused on the social and political activities of women in the first half of the twentieth century. In carrying out this research, I traveled extensively, particularly to major cities, in search of libraries, women's organizations and individuals who had private papers. All materials commented on are in English unless otherwise noted. This discussion will bear the mark of a particular research project and can only be a guide. It is my hope that it in no way discourages anyone from doing their own searching and discovering new resource people, libraries and collections.

There are various ways that an essay of this nature might be organized but I have decided to arrange it in terms of the following categories: Major Libraries, Government Archives, Women's Organizations, Newspaper Archives, Private Collections, Resource People and Miscellaneous Sources. While there will necessarily be some overlap, it is hoped that this particular arrangement, rather than one dealing with "types" of material (e.g., private papers, biographies) will be of greater value to the researcher.

MAJOR LIBRARIES

Nehru Memorial Library, New Delhi

The Nehru Library is the place to begin many research projects relating to women in India. It has an excellent collection of secondary sources on women and continues to purchase all the latest books published. From my experience, it is a good place to survey the current literature, check out secondary sources, meet Indian and foreign scholars and discuss one's research interests. Mr. V.C. Joshi, the now retired deputy director, continues to be available and offer help, suggestions, and encouragement to students working on a wide range of topics. Over the last few years, he has worked closely with a number of us interested in women's history. Miss Jolly, a member of the staff, has been intimately involved with collecting, microfilming and cataloguing the records of women. The suggestions one receives from the librarians and other scholars working at the Nehru Library usually make the time spent there well worthwhile.

Designed as a library to house books, documents and private papers primarily from the nationalist period, the Nehru Library is one of the few in India with sophisticated methods of restoring and preserving historical documents. The value of this work becomes clear when one uses any of the private papers they have carefully restored.

The Nehru Library has an ongoing Oral History Project that focuses on both male and female "Freedom Fighters." The interviews are first taped and then the transcript is sent to the interviewee for deletions, additions and, finally, approval. Only then are the transcripts made available to readers. So far the available transcripts include interviews with women such as Vijaya Lakshmi Pandit, Kamaladevi Chattopadhyaya, Nayantara Sahgal, Basanti Devi (wife of C.R. Das), Begam Iftikhar-ud-din, Sucheta Kripalani, Smt. Sharda Mehta, Lakshmi N. Menon, Dr. Sushila Nayar, Miss Rehana Tyabji, Nellie Sen Gupta and Miss Usha Bhat. New transcripts are continually added to the available list although some, such as the interview with Mirabehn, will not be released until after the interviewees' deaths.

Among the private collections that have been placed in the Nehru Library are those of Rajkumari Amrit Kaur, Durgabai Deshmukh, Kulsum Sayani, Sarala Ray and S. Muthulakshmi Reddy. As is true with all private papers, the value of the material included varies from collection to collection. From my perspective material of extraordinary significance can be found among the Muthulakshmi Reddy papers. This fairly large collection includes letters, newspaper clippings and some of her unpublished writings. As a collection, it provides some extremely valuable insights into the life of one of India's tireless female reformers. Of great importance to anyone studying women are the Jawaharlal Nehru papers. These include his correspondence with such women as Sarojini Naidu and Kamaladevi Chattopadhyaya, press statements and miscellaneous items including papers on the Desh Sevikas (women's wing of Indian National Congress volunteers). The Nehru Library's collection of private papers is well worth checking since the staff encourages important individuals to add their private papers to this collection.

The All-India Congress Committee (AICC) files are in the Nehru Library and are a rich source for information on women in the Indian National Congress. These papers include memorials, details on women's suffrage and information about the formation of the Women's Department in 1941. Files of other organizations, notably the Home Rule League and the National Council of Women in India (NCWI), are also available in this library. The NCWI recently allowed microfilming of its biannual meetings and records for deposit in the Nehru Library. This proved a significant gain since this organization, begun in India in 1925, does not have a central office and previously shipped records back and forth across the country whenever there was a change in president. This has meant that records have been lost, destroyed in accidents and misplaced.

For anyone working on women's topics, these materials — the secondary sources on women, the private collections, the AICC records and the Oral History Project — are the Nehru Library's most important offerings. In addition, there is a fine collection of newspapers and journals; of particular value in researching women's topics are ***The Bombay Chronicle, The Tribune*** (Lahore) and the ***Indian Social Reformer***. This library also has an excellent photo collection that includes photographs of many women who became prominent in the nationalist movement. These can be copied upon request. It is also possible to have material at the Nehru Library photocopied and microfilmed on the premises.

Theosophical Society Library, Adyar, Madras

I would place the Theosophical Society Library second in importance for locating many materials on women. Annie Besant, an extremely important leader of the Theosophical Society, was a feminist before she came to India from England. Besant, along with other women from the society, such as Margaret Cousins and Dorothy Jinarajadasa, took a leading role in the early women's movement in India. The Women's Indian Association (established 1917), the first major women's organization with national pretensions, was formed in Madras with Besant as its president and Cousins and Jinarajadasa among its officers. Books by Besant and Cousins and articles by Jinarajadasa can be found in this library as well as a number of rare books and pamphlets relating to the social and political movements among southern women. Some of the annual reports of the WIA can be found in this library. Also available is ***New India***, Besant's newspaper from Madras, which included many articles on women and women's activities.

Less valuable for scholarly purposes are the Theosophical Society Archives, housed in the same building. They reportedly have Annie Besant's papers and some papers belonging to Margaret Cousins but the collection is uncatalogued and it is difficult to ascertain its contents. In addition, the archives are governed by very stringent rules. One must apply to the president of the Theosophical Society in order to use these archives and any notes taken while in the archives must be submitted to the president before they can be taken from the premises. While there may be some valuable items in this collections, the user needs to be forewarned that the archives are in the charge of a devout theosophist and religious concerns may take precedence over scholarly objectives. A pleasant aspect of using the Theosophical Society's library and archives is the pleasant surroundings of the Adyar grounds. It is possible to have material photocopied and microfilmed there.

National Library, Alipore, Calcutta

The National Library in Calcutta is a fine place to look for books published in the nineteenth century that are difficult to locate. The National Library excels in its collection of old and rare books even if one cannot always obtain items listed in the card catalog. The periodical collection of the National Library is also valuable and is housed in the annex adjacent to the National Library and in the archives building near the Esplanade. In the last few years, considerable work has been done restoring newspapers and periodicals and a number of disintegrating newspapers have now been saved. The library has a complete collection of the ***Indian Social Reformer***, which contains considerable information about women's associations and issues. In addition, their collection includes some issues of the rare and valuable ***Indian Ladies' Magazine***, begun by Kamala Ratnam Satthianadhan in 1901, the first English-language periodical for women published by a woman. With contacts all over India, Smt. Satthianadhan was able to include articles about the first female graduates, fledgling organizations and social reform issues; short stories; and debates on women's role. This library also has a few early issues of ***Stri Dharma***, begun in 1917 as the organ of the Women's Indian Association. The collection of English and Bengali newspapers is excellent. The National Library has facilities for microfilming.

Netaji Bhavan Library, Calcutta

The Netaji Bhavan Library contains materials relating to the life and work of Subhas Chandra Bose. For women in Bengal, Subhas Bose emerges as an important figure who worked for women's rights. Not only has he been credited with encouraging women to play an active role in the nationalist movement (he organized the female volunteers for the 1928 Congress session), but his stamp of approval was sought by leaders of activities ranging from pro-franchise demonstrations to acts of terrorism. As part of the Japanese-sponsored Indian National Army during World War II, Subhas Bose organized a women's regiment under the command of Colonel Lakshmi (Swaminathan) Sahgal and sent the regiment to the front in Burma. Among materials in the collection are books and journals that relate to Subhas' various activities. Mrs. Krishna Bose, the wife of Dr. Sisir Bose (Subhas Bose's nephew and the director of the Netaji Research Bureau) has researched and written articles on Subhas and women. She and Dr. Bose are most helpful to scholars and in the past have been eager to help researchers locate materials and contact individuals who might be interviewed.

University of Bombay Library and Asiatic Society Library, Bombay

Poona (now Pune) was the foremost center for social reform in western India in the nineteenth and early twentieth centuries. The reformers were largely male and many of their concerns related to high-caste Marathi women. In the early decades of the twentieth century, a number of institutions and organizations shifted from Poona to Bombay. Issues relating to and activities of Parsi and Gujarati women became prominent during this period in Bombay, which became the center for interest in women in western India.

Both the University of Bombay Library and the Asiatic Society Library have valuable items in their collections. The University of Bombay Library has an excellent collection of books relating to women and an impressive subject card catalog regarding the changing status of women in India. The Asiatic Society Library in the Old Town Hall has a valuable newspaper collection.

Gandhian Libraries: Rajghat, Delhi, and Sabarmati, Ahmedabad

These are not the only Gandhian libraries in India, but they are the only two with which I have personal experience. Rajghat houses the largest collection of sources by and about Gandhi; Sabarmati was his first ashram and has an extensive collection of letters that are not completely catalogued. As one might predict, the unexpected (perhaps a rare biography) often turns up in libraries relating to prominent individuals, but they are most useful for sources relating specifically to the lives of these individuals. Gandhi, a well-known champion of women and women's rights, had more influence than any other individual in bringing about a new consciousness among women of his generation. He wrote frequently about women and women's role and carried on a voluminous correspondence with women attracted to both his movement and his personality.

Rajghat is the largest of the Gandhian libraries but it does not house anything approaching the total collection of his writings and correspondence. At Rajghat can be found all the published books of Gandhi's writings, letters and speeches. Included in this category are books such as ***To the Women*** (collected writings and speeches, entry 1305), ***Letters to Esther*** (Esther Faering) and ***Bapu's Letters to Ashram Sisters*** (Sabarmati Ashram, entry 1307). These are good and valuable collections but they are also easily available elsewhere. The Rajghat collection contains the periodicals from which collections such as ***To the Women*** have been extracted. Even though some of the "collected essays" and "collected writings" publications do contain most of Gandhi's writings on a particular topic, reading the articles as they appeared can create a different impression of what was meant. Of considerable value are the letters — from Gandhi and to Gandhi — that have been collected and preserved. The library at Rajghat houses letters primarily from women who lived and worked in North and Central India. Included are Gandhi's letters to Amrit Kaur, Annie Besant, Kusum Devi, Nirmala Desai, Mirabehn, Rehana Tyabji and Margaret Cousins, along with letters to Gandhi from Amrit Kaur, Rehana Tyabji, Annie Besant and others. Most of the letters are available in bound volumes, well catalogued and easy to use (this library has done an excellent job of caring for materials that might have disintegrated).

While many of the letters focus on personal details and family matters, they reveal Gandhi's impact on the lives of these women. It is unfortunate that a scholarly scrutiny of Gandhi's attitudes and work among women has yet to be done.

The Gandhian library at Sabarmati Ashram houses a large letter collection that is not completely catalogued. The letters in this collection are listed in ledgers, according to the dates they were written. Accompanying the details of when and where and to whom each letter was written is a summary of its contents. All the entries are in English, regardless of a letter's original language. Although this method of cataloguing is awkward, it is of considerable value to anyone unfamiliar with Gujarati. Looking through the entries is tedious but, when followed through a period of time, they give a summary of the topics being discussed. These letters are primarily between Gandhi and women and men who lived in western India.

For anyone using these archives, there is a guesthouse (available at subsidized rates), surroundings with tame peacocks and a kindly staff headed by Sri Kisanbhai Trivedi.

Note on Library Collections

It has been my experience that a number of books published on women in western India or published by Bombay publishers did not find their way into the National Library's collection in Calcutta or that of the Nehru Library in Delhi. The situation is similar with books on southern women and by southern authors — it is difficult to obtain them in the North. For example, I was unable to find anything written by Mrs. Subbarayan, one of the two female delegates appointed to the first Round Table Conference, until I went to Madras. Similarly, it is difficult to obtain all the writings on social reform in western India without using the libraries of Bombay.

GOVERNMENT ARCHIVES

National Archives, New Delhi

While one might hope to find an abundance of information on women's activities in the National Archives, the hope is never quite fulfilled. There are a number of topics dealt with in the ***Proceedings*** of the Home Department that are essentially "women's issues": the age of consent controversy, divorce, female franchise, immoral traffic and prostitution, child marriage and female education. These files have more information on the male response to proposals of social reform than they do on women's attitudes or activities. While the women's organizations consistently argued that they influenced opinion by talking with individuals, presenting petitions and organizing tea parties, there is little evidence in these Home Department files to support their contention.

Among the ***Files*** of the Political Branch of the Home Department are numerous reports on the nationalist movement, some of which include information on women. In some cases, there are "history sheets," essentially biographical sketches, prepared by the Intelligence Division on women who were suspected of the potential for or actual involvement in anti-British activities. Even here there is less information than one would expect, suggesting that the British did not take women's activities very seriously.

The National Archives also include a library, not particularly important in terms of books on women, and some private papers. It would seem that this collection would be most useful to someone studying social reform issues or the political impact of women's issues.

State Archives

I have used state archives in only three states (Maharashtra, Andhra Pradesh and West Bengal) and did not find them particularly helpful for my research. The materials preserved, the state of the records and the cooperation (or lack of cooperation) varies from state to state and undoubtedly from individual to individual. Most of the state archives now sponsor research projects (occasionally providing financial assistance and publishing the results) and it would seem that these lists might be helpful in identifying Indian scholars working on similar projects.

For an example of a study based upon state archives, one should read Alice Clark's "Female Infanticide as a Means of Maintaining Caste Dominance," a paper presented to the fifth Wisconsin Conference on South Asia, 1976. For this paper Dr. Clark relied heavily on the published ***Selections from the Records of the Bombay Government***, which include records at the local (*tālukā*) level. However, Dr. Clark points out that ***Selections*** is also available at other Indian libraries, the India Office Library in London, the Library of Congress and the New York Public Library. One can use a published catalog to gain access to the location of sections on particular topics within the ***Selections*** series. However, Dr. Clark advises that the process can be time consuming as different catalogs handle the material in different ways. In her experience, Settlement Reports at the ***tālukā*** level are a rich source of material on rural women. She cites marriage customs and reproductive rates as typical concerns of local officials that appear in the reports. The reports may be supplemented with relevant selections from earlier reports, correspondence and statistical tables.[1]

WOMEN'S ORGANIZATIONS

Women's Indian Association, Madras

The Women's Indian Association (WIA) was formed in 1917 and became the first women's organization in India to operate on a national level. Saraladevi Choudhurani had attempted to form such an organization, the Bharat Stri Mahamandal, in 1910, but branches were only formed in Bengal and the Punjab. Complete records of the WIA are difficult to assemble. Some of them are available at the library of the All-India Women's Conference (AIWC) (see below) and some are in the Theosophical Society Library at Adyar. Some issues of ***Stri Dharma*** (the magazine of the Women's Indian Association, entry 1264) are in the periodical section of the National Library, Calcutta. However, the bulk of the association's reports and copies of ***Stri Dharma*** are with Mrs. Manda Krishnamurthy, the daughter-in-law of Dr. Muthulakshmi Reddy and the present director of Avvai Homes. The office of Avvai Homes (16 Besant Ave., Adyar, Madras 20), an institution begun by the WIA in the 1930s, contains some of the records of the WIA. Not all of them are available at this location since the WIA became an affiliate of the All-India Women's Conference in 1946. I have not yet located a complete set of either the records of the WIA or ***Stri Dharma***, but have managed to cover most of the years by contacting Mrs. Krishnamurthy and using materials at the National Library, the AIWC Library, and the Theosophical Society Library. Unfortunately Mrs. Krishnamurthy's collection does not include any of the WIA's correspondence or branch records. In the early days of its existence, under the direction of Margaret Cousins, the WIA kept records of the organization and its branches and copies of surveys and studies used by the members to prepare arguments in support of women's causes. Over the years this office relocated several times and somehow most of the files were lost. Some extremely interesting memoranda, branch records, and correspondence are in the Muthulakshmi Reddy papers in the Nehru Library and should be consulted by anyone researching the WIA.

National Council of Women in India

The National Council of Women in India (NCWI), an official branch of the International Council of Women, was established in 1925. However, some of the branches existed considerably earlier without this international affiliation. The Bombay Presidency Women's Council was formed in 1919 to "coordinate and direct all social work concerning women and children in the Presidency of Bombay." In the same year, councils were formed in Bengal, Bihar, Orissa, Delhi and Burma.

As mentioned earlier in this essay, the NCWI did not set up a permanent office, so their records were and continue to be passed back and forth between presidents. At this time, the Nehru Library has microfilmed the ***Reports*** (entry 2347) of the council from the first report in 1926 until 1948. They also have some copies of the ***Bulletin*** (entry 2346), the official organ of the NCWI, but not a complete set. This journal was begun in 1932 and included articles on such topics concerned with women's rights as franchise, social reform, women's movements in other countries and international organizations (e.g., the International Labour Organisation).

Some of the early records of the NCWI remain with Mrs. Tarabai Premchand of Bombay. Mrs. Premchand was a founding member of the council and served in various capacities as one of its officers throughout the years. In her private library she has records of the meetings of the Central Executive Committee of the NCWI, reports of special meetings and some notes and clippings. If there were correspondence between the branches or extensive reports, these papers have not surfaced. What does exist is either at the Nehru Library or in Mrs. Premchand's collection.

Related to these records are the records of the Bombay Presidency Women's Council (now the Maharashtra State Women's Council) located in the Old Town Hall of Bombay. This council, active since 1919, has kept its annual reports since that time. These annual reports are a valuable guide to social work in Bombay.

All-India Women's Conference, New Delhi

The All-India Women's Conference, India's most prestigious women's organization (founded in 1927) has its central offices and library at 6, Bhagawan Das Road, New Delhi. While a new building is under construction the library's fine collection is in storage cabinets and closets. When the library is completed, it should include the following:

1) An excellent collection of books and pamphlets on women and women's issues in India as well as other countries. The intention of the librarian was to build a library where it would be possible to do research on social issues affecting women. In many cases, this research would be tied to social legislation and hence it was necessary to have statistical information, a view of what had been done historically and some information on what had been done in other parts of the world.

2) Files of the AIWC. AIWC materials have been titled, numbered and listed by the staff of the Nehru Library. It is best to consult this list before requesting a particular file from the AIWC. These files, in their present condition, are rapidly being destroyed by white ants, worms and moisture, but are perhaps one of the richest sources on the workings of this important women's organization. The files include private correspondence between officers, membership lists, financial statements, reports of the various committees, reports of the branch organizations and memoranda from the various committees and subcommittees. Whereas the books in the AIWC library and the conference's annual reports exist

elsewhere, these are the only copies of the organization's files.

3) Records of the annual conferences of the AIWC. These have now been microfilmed and are also available in the Nehru Library.

4) ***Roshni***, the journal of the AIWC (entry 2335). This is also available, on microfilm, at the Nehru Library.

Local Associations

The above account deals with an organization that had branches all over India. A great deal of ingenuity is needed to track down branch records. While my efforts have met with consistent failure, Carol Wolkowitz (University of Sussex) was successful in Andhra Pradesh. Ms. Wolkowitz has informed me that the Hyderabad branch of the AIWC was called the Women's Association for Educational and Social Advancement (WAEASA) and that its records are located in the Lady Hydari Recreation Center in Hyderabad City.[2] While one can find some record of the branch activities in reports filed with the parent organization, I would urge researchers to explore all possible angles.

Local associations, that is, organizations that served one area, more frequently kept records. The Saroj Nalini Dutt Memorial Association has a school and office in Calcutta and has preserved some of its reports. In Bombay the Seva Sadan, begun in 1908 to help unfortunate women, has annual reports and a few scattered records on miscellaneous topics. In contrast, Dr. Karve's institution, the Hingne Stree Shikshan Samstha in Pune (formerly Poona), has kept few of its records and is most valuable for its collection of biographies of women who were associated with the organization. One must not overlook social reform organizations run by males while attempting to gain a picture of local efforts concerned with the position of women. For example, in Pune, G.K. Gokhale's Servants of India Society has very carefully maintained its records. Initially male-oriented, the organization later admitted two female members and geared many of its activities towards the uplift of women.

Note on Organizational Records

There is considerable variation regarding which items were preserved by different organizations. I would suggest that anyone interested in local organizations or in the possibility that these records might contain materials relevant to one's research interests should go directly to the organization or one of its present officers. In the case of a defunct organization, one can often locate those individuals whose names were associated with it for a number of years. It is not unusual to find records of associations in private libraries.

Copying these records, when located, can prove challenging. The Nehru Library has been willing to microfilm records of women's organizations that are located in Delhi. However, one must obtain the permission of those individuals in control of the records and they are not always willing to allow microfilming.

Outside of Delhi the situation is more complicated. One must take the materials to private firms with microfilming facilities and film is frequently in short supply. The procedure is often expensive and slow (complicated by power cuts). One can alleviate difficulties by taking microfilm into India, locating a reliable firm and handling borrowed materials with great care.

NEWSPAPER ARCHIVES

While many newspapers ignored women's activities during the first half of the twentieth century others emerged as champions of women's rights. The key seems to be a social reform orientation or nationalist leanings. Those papers that were supportive of women's rights often included information on meetings, organizations and petitions, and the names of people who marched in demonstrations or were jailed by the British. One of the best places to locate newspapers is the libraries of the newspapers themselves. While this may entail much traveling, I feel there are distinct advantages in doing so. The newspaper offices I contacted were more than willing to allow access to their old volumes, their libraries were small and seldom crowded and I was able to use printed volumes instead of microfilms.

PRIVATE COLLECTIONS

In the previous pages I have suggested two private collections of value — that of the WIA held by Mrs. Krishnamurthy and the records of the early NCWI in the library of Mrs. Tarabai Premchand. Locating individuals who have private papers of value can be difficult and time consuming and there is no guarantee that one will be allowed access. In approaching individuals, I would urge tact and sensitivity on the part of the researcher. Not only is it important to respect the individual's right to either grant or deny access to such a collection but, if permitted access, it is particularly important that any restrictions imposed be observed and that the papers in no way be tampered with. I have known cases where the arrogance and carelessness of foreigners using private collections has done irreparable damage to the possibility of future use of these collections.

In most cases the descendants of prominent women have some letters and papers they are willing to share. For example, one of the most important women to contact in eastern India is Mrs. Padmini Sengupta, daughter of Kamala Ratnam Satthianadhan (founder of the ***Indian Ladies' Magazine***) and herself a prominent journalist and author of many books on women. Mrs. Sengupta has written a book about her mother, ***The Portrait of an Indian Woman*** (entry 1394) and has the only complete collection of the ***Indian Ladies' Magazine***, 1901-1934 (entry 1257), that exists. Miss Aroti Sen, daughter of one of Bengal's earliest "suffragettes," Mrinalini Sen, has letters and articles written by her deceased mother. Mrs. Shudha Mazumdar, a prominent Calcutta social worker, has donated her collection of pamphlets and reports from various women's organizations to the University of Illinois Library at Urbana-Champaign. One needs to contact many people to find records but it is a search that frequently pays off. In my experience, women have collected more papers and letters than anyone had previously predicted.

RESOURCE PEOPLE

There are many people in India who can be helpful to the researcher doing a study on Indian women and one should attempt to contact such individuals. The Who's Who in the ***Directory of Indian Women Today, 1976*** (entry 1659) includes addresses and can be of great help in locating prominent Indian women. The women I have listed below have official positions and are quite easy to contact.

Shanta Chenoy of the American International Communication Agency (previously the United States Information Service) in New Delhi was given the task of coordinating activities during International Women's Year (IWY) and is well acquainted with prominent women, women's organizations and the main activities of Indian women. The daughter of Hannah Sen, the first principal of India's first home science college, Lady Irwin College in New Delhi, Mrs. Chenoy knows many of the women who were pioneers in the social and political movements for women.

Sarojini Varadappan, the chairperson of the government's Central Social Welfare Board, New Delhi, is from Madras and well acquainted with women's activities throughout India. During the IWY, the Central Social Welfare Board organized women's seminars in each district to gather information regarding the needs and aspirations of women. Local resolutions were discussed at state level meetings and states submitted their resolutions to the Central Social Welfare Board. Mrs. Varadappan attended many of these meetings and developed a broad understanding of the concerns of women throughout the country.

Dr. Bina Roy, president of the Federation of University Women (an organization whose records are being catalogued) and joint editor of publications, Council for Social Development, New Delhi, is knowledgeable about research being done on Indian women, particularly on the theme of women and development.

Dr. Vina Mazumdar, chief editor of the Indian Council of Social Science Research, New Delhi, and member-secretary of the Committee on the Status of Women in India has been closely connected with contemporary research on women in India.

Mrs. Padma Ramachandran, joint secretary in the Department of Social Welfare of the Ministry of Education, New Delhi, and appointed officer on special duty during IWY, knows about research projects and conferences pertaining to women.

Ivy Khan, national general secretary of the YWCA in New Delhi has been extremely active in encouraging research and writing pertaining to women. The YWCA, begun in India in 1875, is one of the oldest organizations concerned with women that continues to exist. The YWCA has extensive records; its history is currently being written by Padmini Sengupta.

In Bombay, Dr. Neera Desai, director of the Research Unit on Women's Studies at Shreemati Nathibai Damodar Thackersey (SNDT) Women's University, has written and published on Indian women for many years. The research unit is devoted to the study of women and sees its aims as identifying questions and encouraging studies pertaining to women's status and role in society, collecting information about women, building a collection of material on women, acting as liaison between individuals and institutions in India and abroad and helping institutions and associations working for the improvement of the condition of women. The close association of this center with ongoing research and programs makes it an interesting and worthwhile stop for anyone doing research on Indian women in the contemporary setting.

MISCELLANEOUS SOURCES

This essay has omitted a number of sources and persons of which the researcher should be aware. Women's colleges frequently have records of their students and a history of how the institution developed. Labor unions, political parties and literary organizations are other sources of information on women. While the places one searches should be tailored to the particular research topic I would urge an open and creative mind when undertaking research on women. Materials on women are more abundant than we once supposed and it is often well worth following the leads suggested by scholars and others. In preparing this essay, I contacted a number of women who have done research in India and Pakistan with the hope that I might include their insights.

Missionary-Sponsored Colleges

Dr. Michelle Maskiell (University of Pennsylvania), who has written her dissertation on Kinnaird College in Lahore, wrote that former missionary colleges seem to have kept their records even if they have not always organized and catalogued them. She suggests that anyone interested in the missionary women's colleges write to the principal to inquire about possible records. Dr. Maskiell warns that one should not expect an answer with specifics but rather an indication of whether or not records exist.[3] Dr. Gail Minault has informed me that Isabella Thoburn College in Lucknow has a fair library (Mrs. Revis, librarian) with considerable information about missionary efforts for women's education. Marjorie Dimmitt's history of the college, *Isabella Thoburn College* (entry 4278), is available in this library.[4]

Urdu Sources on Muslim Women

While doing my research, I soon became aware that most of the women I was talking to and reading about were Hindu women. When I finally met and talked with Muslim women, I was unable to find out very much about their organizations and journals because I did not know Urdu. Unlike prominent Hindu women who frequently maintained their organizational records and corresponded in English, Muslim women generally used Urdu. Although this essay is primarily concerned with English sources, I asked Dr. Gail Minault (University of Texas, Austin) to share her knowledge concerning Urdu resources regarding women. She has very kindly supplied me with information on such materials in Aligarh and the Lucknow area.

In Aligarh, the Maulana Azad Library of the Aligarh Muslim University (Syed Md. Husain Razvi, librarian) has an outstanding collection of Urdu periodicals, which are listed in a bibliography by Razvi Sahib. Urdu journals for or about women include files of *'Iṣmat, Tahzīb-i-Nisvān, Khātūn, Ẓill-al-Sulṭān, Pardahnashīn* and *Anīs-i-Nisvān*. These journals are valuable sources of information on women's educational and political activities and other concerns. Proceedings of the All-Indian Muhammadan Education Conference (AIMEC) from 1886 until about 1918 are also in the collection. Later proceedings, though not complete, can be had from the headquarters of the AIMEC, Sultan Jahan Manzil, near the Aligarh campus. The library also has an excellent collection of Urdu and English books and a manuscript collection. The staffs of the Urdu and Reference Sections Are competent and sometimes helpful; access for scholars is straightforward. The Aligarh archives are in a separate collection and access to them can be difficult.

The Aligarh Women's College has a separate library, quite small by comparison with the wealth of the university collection. However, they have some interesting items, such as Urdu biographies and writings of Sultan Jahan Begam of Bhopal.

The collection of Begam Mumtaz Haidar (Abdullah Lodge, Marris Road, Aligarh), retired principal of Aligarh Women's College, is also valuable. Begam Mumtaz Haidar is the daughter of Shaikh Abdullah, founder of Aligarh Women's College. Unfortunately, none of his private papers have been preserved. She does, however, have a complete file of his monthly journal, *Khātūn* (1904-1914), which contains information concerning the founding of Aligarh Women's College and other efforts for women's education and reform. She also has some of his published writings.

The Mahmudabad Library is in the possession of Maharaj Kumar Amir Md. Haidar Khan (Mahmudabad House, Kaisarbagh, Lucknow). He is gracious and helpful but should be approached with due deference and, if possible, via someone who knows him. Through him one may gain access to the large private library of the Mahmudabad ***tāluqdārī***, Sitapur District, which contains an occasional jewel. The collection would be especially useful for students of land tenure systems and Muslim League politics, but the raja was also a patron of women's education. A number of writings of Maulvi Karamat Hussain, who in 1946 founded the Karamat Hussain Muslim Girls' College, Lucknow, are in the Mahmudabad Library.[5]

To end this highly personal essay, I will relate a personal experience. In 1969 I was looking for the mansion of Mohun Chand Ghosh (I had found the address on some letters at the Bodleian Library, Oxford) in the Kidderpore area of Calcutta. Accompanied by a Bengali friend, I asked people here and there if they had ever heard of a particular street. The letters had been written in the 1880s and the name of the street had been changed but an elderly gentleman recognized the old name. Declaring that he would take me "to meet a princess," he led the way to a crumbling mansion. This turned out to be the mansion of Mohun Chand Ghosh and the inhabitants were his descendants. They knew little about the ancestors I was interested in but they sent me to visit their aunt, Mrs. Shudha Mazumdar. Mrs. Mazumdar, the family historian, not only had materials relating to her great-uncle but had saved records of various women's organizations, kept a diary for a number of years and written her memoirs until 1930 (entry 3671). It was this acquaintance with Mrs. Mazumdar, which has since developed into a deep and lasting relationship, that led me to my current research on Indian women. This experience left me firmly convinced that poking around, following up leads and asking a lot of questions can not only make one's research experience in India a fascinating one but yield materials of unexpected richness.

---

*Geraldine H. Forbes is Associate Professor of History at State University of New York, College at Oswego, Oswego, New York 13126. The research upon which this essay is based was conducted during 1975 and 1976 as a Faculty Research Fellow of the American Institute of Indian Studies.

[1] Letter from Alice Clark to G. Forbes, 5 July 1978.

[2] Carol Wolkowitz, personal communication, 1978.

[3] Letter from Michelle Maskiell to G. Forbes, 4 May 1978.

[4] Gail Minault. Sources in Urdu on Women's Education. Ms., n.d.

[5] Ibid.

Libraries, Archives and Other Resources in Pakistan for the Study of Women

Emily Hodges *

During the Ayub Khan era, few foreign scholars were allowed to conduct research in Pakistan and scholarly works from this period are primarily those of economists and political scientists. This policy was changed during the early part of Zulfiqar Ali Bhutto's regime and since the early 1970s scholars from many disciplines have carried out significant research in Pakistan. Even so, the number of scholars of South Asia, Pakistani and foreign, who have published research on Pakistan is relatively small. The number who have conducted research on women's topics is smaller still.

Few archives, libraries and collections of private papers in Pakistan have been explored specifically to identify sources that could be used for the study of women. My own research, carried out in Punjab Province from 1974 to 1977, was on the nomadic ecology of southwest Punjab, and I did not personally conduct a search for collections of material relating to women. The information in this essay reflects my own knowledge of general archival and library holdings, and is biased towards material located in the Punjab. I have, however, also included information contributed by other scholars who have done research on women's topics and who have, during the course of their own research, located holdings that deal specifically with women.

Since there has been so little work done in Pakistan on women's topics, I have attempted to identify both collections that are known to contain materials that can be used to study women and collections that are potential sources for the study of women. The material includes both English and vernacular sources and is organized into seven categories: Major Libraries and Research Collections, Government Records, Court Records, Muslim League Papers, Newspaper Holdings, Women's Organizations and Centers and Agencies for Women. I make no claim that this essay is inclusive, but I hope it will generate interest in research on the vitally important but relatively unstudied area of women's studies in Muslim South Asia and will serve as an "explorer's guide" for those who wish to do research on topics relating to the study of the women of Pakistan.

Note on Photocopying, Microfilming and Taping

Commercial facilities for photocopying are available in many smaller towns and in all large cities. In 1977, the cost was ten cents per page. Most photocopying machines use a treated paper that is quite heavy and therefore awkward and expensive to transport. Unless handled gently, the treated surface chips off, taking with it words of the copied text. Lahore and Karachi have a few shops that have imported plain paper copiers and if a large amount of material must be copied, it might be worthwhile to seek out these shops.

There is a microfilm unit at University of the Punjab and scholars have been allowed to have newspaper archives and items from the university's collection filmed by this unit. There is another microfilm unit in Islamabad, which is used by the Quaid-i-Azam Cell in the Ministry of Education, but I do not believe that it can be used to film records not in this archive's possession. A microfilm unit was purchased and installed by the Punjab Government Civil Secretariat Archives in 1977 but as of late 1977 permission to microfilm secretariat records was withheld while the government decided on a policy that would determine which records could be filmed for use by scholars.

Those who have received permission to use private collections or need filmed copies of documents or other materials that are difficult or impossible to transport to reproduction facilities can do their own microfilming. Given the difficulty in getting professionally filmed copies made and the high cost of photocopying, this is often the easiest solution. Equipment necessary for microfilming includes a good 35mm camera, a lightweight tripod, a battery operated electronic flash (with extra batteries for the flash and for the camera if it has a built-in light meter) and either individual cassettes of 35mm low ASA copy film or a bulk loader, empty film cassettes and a good supply of bulk 35mm copy film. (*Do not* purchase regular microfilm; film for a large microfilm unit has no sprocket holes and cannot be used in a 35mm camera.) If microfilming is a new experience, seek advice from a good photographer, test the camera system and practice using it before beginning the actual work. Asking advice, advance testing of the camera and lighting system and a little practice can eliminate many of the difficulties and problems that might otherwise occur when the scholar confronts a stack of documents and unfamiliar equipment.

I found that the use of a cassette tape recorder was the answer to difficulties in securing permission to film government archival holdings. My tape recorder was allowed even where typewriters and pens were forbidden. Inexpensive tapes are available on the market in Pakistan, but more reliable and expensive ones that do not jam or break are recommended.

MAJOR LIBRARIES AND RESEARCH COLLECTIONS

Research Society of Pakistan, Lahore

The Research Society of Pakistan, at 2 Club Road, Lahore, has a small library and a valuable collection of newspapers Files of the ***Inqilāb*** and the ***Zamīndār***, both valuable sources for the study of prepartition politics and women's political activities in Punjab, are available here. The society also has a collection of the ***Risālā***, a monthly journal of Lahore's premier Muslim social reform organization, the Anjuman-i-Himayat-i-Islam.[1]

Permission to use the material at the Research Society can be secured by contacting the director, and is a fairly straightforward process. However, the society is open only until 2:00 P.M., reading space is cramped and the staff is not always cooperative. The Research Society has a series of publications that can be purchased there.

Punjab Public Library, Lahore

This library has both an oriental and a western section. Cataloguing does not always reflect what is available and the holdings of newspapers are haphazard and incomplete. However, the staff is very cordial and helpful, and there are many small rooms where one can work in peace until 6:00 P.M. when the library closes. The library is close to the old campus of University of the Punjab, off the Mall Road in downtown Lahore and just behind the Lahore Museum. It is necessary to apply for a borrower's card and pay a small fee in order to use the library. Books can be checked out and photocopied without difficulty.

University of the Punjab Library, Lahore

Located within walking distance of the Punjab Public Library, this library is located on the old campus of the university. It has some newspapers, including incomplete files of the ***Eastern** Times*. The library has a good collection of printed government documents and it is sometimes easier to locate and use them here than to search for them at the secretariat. Library holdings can be sent to the university's microfilm unit for copying.

Other Libraries and Research Collections

The libraries of the universities in Karachi, Islamabad, Peshawar, Baluchistan and Faisalabad (formerly Lyallpur) as well as that of University of the Punjab should be checked for theses and dissertations regarding women in Pakistan. These holdings probably vary widely in quality and there is no comprehensive listing of the holdings. However, selected theses and dissertations are annotated in *Women in Pakistan and Other Islamic Countries: A Selected Bibliography with Annotations* (entry 16).

In addition to the public and university libraries in major urban centers, there are also public libraries in smaller towns. Although I know no one who has carefully searched through the back rooms of these libraries, some might yield publications of local organizations concerned with social and religious reform activities that were directed toward women, and possibly fiction, biographies and autobiographies by women that were published in small numbers or privately printed and circulated.

Several years ago, the National Institute of Folk Heritage in Islamabad began to record oral traditions from all provinces of Pakistan. I am not familiar with their present collection, but it is possible that some of their holdings include material that could be used to study women's folk traditions.

The Percy Amendment to the US Foreign Assistance Act of 1973 provided for the evaluation of all United States Agency for International Development (USAID) and other development projects for their impact on women. The social impact analyses done under the auspices of USAID/Islamabad often represent pioneering efforts to assess the effectiveness of development projects that are directed toward Pakistani women as either primary or secondary beneficiaries. These studies, as well as other unpublished material relating to women and development, are available in the USAID/Islamabad library, from the appropriate program office at USAID/Islamabad or from USAID offices in Washington.

Other institutions may have unpublished research on family planning and other subjects relating to women and development. The staff of the organizations listed below might be helpful in locating additional materials:

National Research Institute of Fertility Control, Karachi
Pakistan Academy for Rural Development (PARD), Peshawar
Board of Economic Inquiry, Lahore and Peshawar
Training, Research and Evaluation Centre (TREC), Lahore
Pakistan Institute of Development Economics (PIDE), Islamabad
University of Agriculture, Faisalabad (formerly Lyallpur)

Emily Hodges

GOVERNMENT RECORDS

National Archives of Pakistan

Plans have been made for the construction of a national archives building in Pakistan but the archives will not include the type of material found in the Indian National Archives in New Delhi. The Pakistan National Archives are now associated with the Quaid-i-Azam Cell of the Ministry of Education in Islamabad and contain the papers of the All-India Muslim League, Mohammad Ali Jinnah's personal papers and newspaper holdings,[2] as well as a small number of books that are probably duplicated elsewhere. Since the provinces that now constitute Pakistan were administered during the British period by the government of India from London, Calcutta and, later, Delhi, central government records from this period pertaining to the area that is now Pakistan are located in the National Archives in New Delhi and in the India Office Library in London.

Central Government Records, post-1947

The number of files and other records of the central government ministries that relate to women's affairs is probably quite large, but the extent to which these records are available for scholarly research is unclear. As a source for the study of women, these records could be very rich, covering topics as diverse as debates regarding coeducation and women's universities, discussions of social welfare measures for destitute women and women refugees after partition and records detailing internal debates and policy decisions about family planning.[3]

Government of Pakistan archival access regulations do not ordinarily permit the use of post-1940 records by scholars. Permission might possibly be granted for the use of these records when the request concerns a specific issue and a specific research topic. However, this would, I think, be difficult to guarantee and it should not be presumed that permission will be granted. Nevertheless, it cannot hurt to seek permission to use this material and regular inquiries and requests regarding the documents might possibly produce results.

Provincial Archives

Provincial governments' "A" proceedings were printed and are available in London, but "B" proceedings with file notings are available only in the provincial archives. Sind Province was part of Bombay Province until 1935 , and many records dealing with the pre-1935 period are to be found in the Bombay State archives. There are records in the office of the Commissioner of Sind in Karachi, but it is my impression that they contain little that could be used in research on women's topics and access to them is sometimes problematic. Baluchistan and the North-West Frontier Province (NWFP) also have provincial archives, but I have no knowledge of their contents or accessibility.

Of the four provinces, the Punjab provincial archives has the greatest historical depth. Its holdings begin with records from 1849 when the province, which then included parts of what is now NWFP, was taken by the British from the descendents of Ranjit Singh. In the Punjab secretariat archives, the post-1920 records have been heavily weeded. Even so, a careful search of the records should unearth information regarding women's education. The civil lists, together with files from the appropriate departments, could be used to trace the entry of women into educational administration and teaching and into the legal and medical fields, professions open to women because of the requirements of sexual segregation in a *pardā* society. Records pertaining to female infanticide and the British administration's efforts to eliminate this practice are to be found in the Punjab archives. Files about facilities for widows and orphans, women and crime, women's jails and the provision of health care for women, including various plans to train midwives, are also located there.[4] Similar material may be available in other provincial archives.

There is a small press library in the Punjab Secretariat compound in Lahore. It can be used by scholars and has a vast quantity of old press clippings from which the vernacular press reports were written. Its holdings were being catalogued and preserved in 1977. I have not used this library, however, and do not know whether or not it has clipping files that relate to women's issues, including social and religious reform, or to women's participation in politics.

To gain access to these archives, copies of the No-Objection Certificate (NOC), which identifies the holder as a scholar with the Pakistan government's permission to conduct research, and a letter from a Pakistani supervisor are necessary. The requisite sheaf of papers should be taken to the director of the archives and permission to use the records is almost always granted. The level of cooperation of the archive staff varies from province to province. As with central government records, regulations generally do not permit use of post-1940 provincial records. Provincial CID records are not open to scholars and whatever CID material that is available about women politicians in the pre-1947 period will be found in the National Archives in New Delhi or not at all.

Until the central government establishes a policy regarding the filming of provincial archival material, copies of documents can be secured only by paying a rather high fee per page of photocopied or typed material. Permission to microfilm provincial secretariat records is not automatically forthcoming. If filming documents is necessary, one should attempt to obtain permission at the time work in the archives is initiated and allow time to take notes or use a tape recorder in the event permission to film is refused.

Debates of the National and Provincial Legislative Assemblies

National and provincial legislative assembly debates are published by the government and are available in the libraries and archives of the assemblies. The Punjab Legislative Assembly proceedings contain debates about the first, and unsuccessful, attempt to pass a Shariat (Islamic law) Bill in 1932, and record debates and speeches made in the West Punjab Assembly when the bill passed in 1948. Among other materials of interest are the assembly debates regarding the passage of subsequent legislation that affected the status and rights of women. The bills introduced by women members and debated in the provincial and national legislatures are available in the printed proceedings as are speeches by women members of the legislatures. Permission to use the assembly libraries will usually be granted upon application to the speaker's office.

COURT RECORDS

The records of district courts and the provincial high courts are rich sources for the study of women and the legal framework that has either circumscribed or expanded their legal rights to inherit, adopt, own property or divorce. Compilations of high court decisions are available in the holdings of some major law schools in the United States. Extensive collections of such publications are also available in Lahore in the libraries of private law firms. Printed summaries of Privy Council decisions are available in private libraries in Pakistan and possibly at the Punjab Law College library. Lawyers practicing in Lahore, Karachi or other cities should be able to assist in identifying private legal libraries.

It has been my experience, however, that evidence presented in the course of a court hearing can be equally if not more valuable to the scholar than the summaries of a judgement. Evidence presented to the Privy Council in London was printed with the judgement and can be found in the council's printed proceedings located in the library of the Inns of Court and at the India Office Library in London.

Prior to the passage of a Shariat Bill in 1948, the Punjab legal codes governing inheritance were based on compilations of customary law first begun in the 1860s. Customary law did not usually permit women to inherit property. Studies of both customary law as it applied to women and the actual impact on women of the provisions of the Shariat Act, which allowed women to inherit property, are long overdue. Other important changes in family law that affected women's rights, including the right to divorce, have also occurred since 1947 and debate about family law and its provisions that affect women has continued in Pakistan through and beyond International Women's Year in newspapers and seminars.

It is possible, however, that the scholar who wishes to study post-1947 legal developments as they relate to women will have to depend on printed materials and case law, rather than case files from court archives. Theoretically, court records are open only to the persons whose case is recorded in them, to their descendents or to their legal counsel. To the best of my knowledge, no one has requested permission to use post-1947 court records. However, permission for a research scholar to use pre-1947 court records has been granted by at least one provincial high court. Access to both district and high court records must be sought from the chief justice who has jurisdiction over the court whose records are required. A personal appointment with the chief justice is essential. At this meeting, one should present all documentation verifying one's position as a acholar with government clearance to conduct research. Permission to use court records for scholarly research depends entirely on the chief justice's discretion and could be granted in one province and not in another. If permission to use these records is granted, one should keep in mind that it is a rare courtesy.

It is my impression that records of the high courts are extremely well kept. In one case, although it took a week to retrieve them from a district court, files from 1902 were in excellent condition. In older files, evidence may be in handwritten Persian and Urdu. The difficulty in working with handwritten materials may necessitate the use of a research assistant unless one has unusually ample time at one's disposal. A request for permission to have an assistant work is a potential problem. Archivists have been known to forbid the use of an assistant, ruling that records open only to scholars should not be used in any way by a Pakistani who was not a scholar. One possible way around this difficulty is to try to find a retired employee who knows the records well and is willing to work as a research assistant. An inquiry about such a person might properly be made at the time one requests permission to use court records. This strategy might be used at other archives as well.

MUSLIM LEAGUE PAPERS

Of great significance for the study of the political history of the Pakistan Movement are the papers of the All-India Muslim League and the papers of the Quaid-i-Azam Mohammad Ali Jinnah. To the best of my knowledge, complete holdings of provincial Muslim League papers no longer exist, but this is not a categorical statement and a persistent search might unearth some of them. However, their usefulness for the study of women's participation in Muslim League politics is questionable. Of more potential interest are the collections of Muslim League papers, temporarily located at Karachi University Library,[5] and Mr. Jinnah's personal papers in Islamabad.

All-India Muslim League

The papers from the Muslim League office in Delhi are housed in the Freedom Movement Archive at Karachi University until the National Archives building in Islamabad is constructed. The university campus is located quite a distance from downtown Karachi and travel to and from the campus can be very time consuming. However, the staff is quite helpful and the documents have been conveniently arranged by subject and bound into folio-sized books. The holdings in this collection cover the period from 1900 to 1948.

This archive has some material from the post-1938 period when the women's subcommittees of the Muslim League were operating and includes some papers from provincial branches of the league. The formation of the All-India Muslim Women's Subcommittee of the Central Muslim League represents the largest pre-1947 effort to involve Muslim women in the political process. The activities of these subcommittees are relatively unknown. Sarfaraz Hussain Mirza, in ***Muslim Women's Role in the Pakistan Movement*** (entry 1242), has presented an overview of women's participation in the Muslim League. The account contains detailed information on the activities of the Punjab women's subcommittee gathered from newspapers and interviews. Subcommittee records are not cited, and I do not know whether or not such records were kept or still exist. A scholar interested in this topic would do well to contact Begam Jahan Ara Shah Nawaz and Begam Salma Tasadduque Hussain in Lahore and Begam Ra'ana Liaquat Ali Khan in Karachi, along with other women who were involved in both pre- and post-partition politics as members of provincial women's subcommittees and in other capacities.[6]

Papers of Mohammad Ali Jinnah

The personal papers of Mohammad Ali Jinnah from his Bombay home were in the possession of his sister, Miss Fatima Jinnah, for many years. They are now in the Quaid-i-Azam Cell at the Ministry of Education, Islamabad, where they have been catalogued and microfilmed. This collection does include some correspondence with women politicians, but I do not know how much and with whom. The documents can be used only on the film copy and there was at one time a shortage of microfilm readers. It can be somewhat tedious to use these papers as a scholar is allowed to see only the particular document that she or he requests by file or document number and examination of unrequested items on the film is not allowed.

A second collection of Mr. Jinnah's personal papers from his house in New Delhi is in the possession of the sons of Shams-ul-Hassan. These papers are not yet completely catalogued and I do not know how many, if any, deal with women and Muslim League politics. This collection is available on film in Islamabad and the documents themselves can be seen by contacting Mr. Khalid Hassan at the National Bank of Pakistan in Karachi, where he is employed.

Papers of Fatima Jinnah

The papers of Miss Fatima Jinnah would, if they exist, span a long and visible political career. I do not know whether or not she left personal papers or whether they are available to scholars. Very little has been written about Miss Jinnah and her role in the Muslim League in an era when the constraints of ***pardā*** confined many Muslim women to separate women's groups. Some of her speeches and other writings have been collected and published by Salahuddin Khan in *Speeches, Messages and Statements of Madar-i-Millat Mohtarama Fatimah Jinnah (1948-1967)* (entry 2395). A conversation with the director of the Research Society and Mr. Khan might begin to clarify whether or not any of her personal papers have survived.

NEWSPAPER HOLDINGS

A number of newspapers reported to varying degrees on activities by women politicians, on women's issues and on social and religious reform efforts that affected women. No paper would in itself be a major source, but information on women's activities and women's issues can be found in many of them.

Files of *The Tribune* published in Lahore until 1947 and in Ambala in Indian Punjab from 1948, are available in India, England and the United States, but not in Pakistan. *Dawn*, an English-language paper published in Karachi, is also available in the United States. Files of the Urdu-language *Zamīndār* and *Inqilāb*, both from Lahore, are located at the Research Society of Pakistan. The *Civil and Military Gazette*, which began publication from Lahore in 1872 and ceased publication in 1963, was, for several years, in private hands and unavailable to scholars. It was acquired in 1977 by the National Archives, has been microfilmed and is now available there.

Files of the Urdu-language *Rāfiq-i-Hind*, published by Muharram Ali Chisti beginning in 1884, are reportedly in the collection of his papers in the possession of Muhammad Shafi, a journalist in Lahore. These papers have not yet been opened to scholars, although persistent inquiries and requests might lead to securing permission to use them. I know of no other holdings of this paper. *Eastern Times* from Lahore is available at the University of the Punjab Library. Other major newspapers, such as the Urdu-language *Navā-i-Vaqt*, published in Lahore since 1949, have their own archives, as might some of the smaller publications. Permission to use newspaper archives is usually granted.[7]

WOMEN'S ORGANIZATIONS

All Pakistan Women's Association (APWA)

The APWA has worked actively to improve the status of women in Pakistan since its formation in 1949. APWA was established by Begam Ra'ana Liaquat Ali Khan to coordinate and ensure the continuation of services that were hastily organized to meet refugee women's needs in the exceptional circumstances surrounding partition. APWA is the largest organization for women in Pakistan, is affiliated with several international organizations and has many local branches. Headquarters are in Karachi, where organizational records and a library are maintained. Rashida Patel, a lawyer with a particular interest in the legal status of Pakistani women, deposited her own clipping files and personal papers with this library.[8]

APWA sponsors or assists in sponsoring a wide range of social service facilities for women, including educational and vocational training, mother and child health care, child welfare services, rehabilitation of the handicapped and consumer welfare. The organization also sponsors conferences and has served as a lobby group. In the early 1960s, APWA took an aggressive stance against the repeal of the Muslim Family Laws Ordinance (1961), which extended women's legal rights.

The organization has continued its strong advocacy for maintaining and extending the legal rights of women whenever these rights have been challenged or debated in the national political forum.

Pakistan Girl Guides and Pakistan Red Crescent Society

Both of these organizations have had a long and distinguished history in Pakistan. I do not know whether or not either association has records, but Begam Viqar-un-Nissa Noon of Lahore and Begam Liaquat Ali Khan of Karachi have been active in both organizations and might be able to assist a scholar in search of records.

Other Organizations

There are also other and more recently established women's social welfare organizations.[9] The Family Welfare Cooperative in Lahore has an excellent facility that provides maternal and child health care, family planning information and vocational training classes; it also has residential facilities for destitute women. Begam Yavar Ali Shah, among others, has been active in this organization and can be contacted through her father-in-law, Syed Amjad Ali Shah of "Shahdab" on the Canal Bank in Lahore. The Mubarik Botique is a retail outlet for a cooperative that trains poor women to embroider. Founded by Amjad Ali Shah's mother, Mubarik Begam, its training facility is located in her family home in the Faqir Khana inside Bhatti Gate in Lahore's old city. Begam Babar Ali Shah is the family member who is most active in this enterprise and she can be contacted through the Mubarik Botique in the Swedish Flats, FFC Scheme, Lahore. The Behbud Association of Rawalpindi/Islamabad, begun in 1967, has a program that provides many of the same services and facilities to women in the Rawalpindi area that the Family Welfare Cooperative provides in Lahore. Some of these organizations may have records.

CENTERS AND AGENCIES FOR WOMEN

Shirkat Gah/Women's Resource Centre, Karachi

Located at 1/6 Rimpa Sunbeam, 5 Girzi Road in Karachi, this center grew out of activities that took place in 1975 during International Women's Year. This organization is a source of services and information for women on housing, employment opportunities, legal and medical aid and day care facilities. It sponsors research on Pakistani women and structured informal discussion groups. Shirkat Gah has established a hostel for working women in Islamabad and provides temporary residential facilities for women visitors to Islamabad. In 1976, Shirkat Gah sponsored a conference on problems of Pakistani women and established a library that may become an important collection of resource material about women in Pakistan. Aban Marker of the Karachi office, editor of ***Women in Pakistan and Other Islamic Countries: A Selected Bibliography with Annotations***, is knowledgeable about the location of source materials related to women's issues.

Pakistan Women's Institute, Lahore

This organization was founded during International Women's Year at Kinnaird College. The institute maintains a reading room and library, publishes a bimonthly newsletter and also publishes research by women scholars on all topics and by men on topics relating to women. The institute is building up a women's network and could be a congenial place to begin a search for untraditional source material and to locate women actively working to improve the status of Pakistani women.

In addition to the archival and other sources described in this essay, there are many other potential sources for the study of women in Pakistan. Women's colleges and medical schools in all four provinces have kept varying amounts of records. Polling station data and voter's lists have been preserved by the provincial and national Election Commissions from 1971 to the present (however, none of this kind of data seems to be available for elections before 1971). Holdings of old magazines that addressed women's issues, diaries of both famous and ordinary women, collections of letters and other personal papers are as yet unidentified.[10] I trust, however, that this essay has suggested the range of materials available and that it will encourage scholars to begin their own search for "undiscovered" records and documents that can be used to enrich our understanding of the women of Pakistan.

---

*Emily Hodges is a member of the Foreign Service, US Department of State. Much of the information in this essay was collected between 1974 and 1976, while the author was conducting predoctoral research, funded by grants from the Department of Health, Education and Welfare Fulbright program and the American Institute of Pakistan Studies. The views presented herein are those of the author alone, and in no way reflect official or unofficial policies or views of the Foreign Service or the US Department of State.

[1]The Anjuman's central office on Brandreth Road apparently has no archives or papers. The collection of the ***Risālā*** at the Research Society includes issues from 1886 to 1925. The author is indebted to Dr. Gail Minault for this information.

[2]These collections are treated elsewhere in this essay. For the holdings of the National Archives see Pakistan, Department of Archives, ***Microfilms: Holdings of the National Archives of Pakistan*** ([Islamabad]: Department of Archives, Government of Pakistan, 1976-).

[3]The author is grateful to Dr. Hanna Papanek for bringing this potential source of research material to her attention.

[4]Dr. Jack Hume located files about women and health care during the course of his research in Pakistan in 1974-75 and brought them to the attention of the author.

[5]As of 1976, 292 volumes of this collection had been filmed for the National Archives. Pakistan, Department of Archives, ***Microfilms***, vI, p2.

[6]Begam Shah Nawaz comes from a family long active in Lahore and provincial politics and has written about her political career in ***Father and Daughter: A Political Biography*** (entry 1402). Begam Salma Tasadduque Hussain was elected to the Punjab Legislative Assembly in 1946 and remained active in post-1947 politics. Begam Ra'ana Liaquat Ali Khan was active in prepartition Muslim League politics and in women's organizations and activities; she also served both as Pakistan's ambassador to the Netherlands and as governor of Sind. Biographies

and addresses of these and other women politicians, social workers, educators and doctors can be found in ***Biographical Encyclopedia of Pakistan*** (Lahore: Biographical Research Institute Pakistan, 1955) and subsequent editions.

[7]For information about holdings in North America and Great Britain of many newspapers published in the area that is now Pakistan, see Margaret H. Cases's ***South Asian History, 1750-1950: A Guide to Periodicals, Dissertations and Newspapers*** (Princeton, New Jersey: Princeton University Press, 1968), pp.437ff.

[8]The author is indebted to Dr. Hanna Papanek for information about Rashida Patel's papers. For a discussion of APWA see Sylvia A. Chipp, ***The Role of Women Elites in a Modernizing Country*** (entry 2401) and "Tradition vs. change: the All Pakistan Women's Association" (entry 2402).

[9]Molly Mayo, in her "Women's Organizations in Pakistan: A Preliminary Identification," has briefly described other voluntary societies and professional groups concerned with women's issues and women's welfare. Mayo's mimeographed article was prepared with the support of the Ford Foundation in Islamabad (P.O. Box 1043, located at 20 26th Street, Shalimar 6/2, Islamabad, Pakistan). Leads for access to numerous organizations can be obtained from ***Women's Movement in Pakistan*** issued by the All Pakistan Women's Association (entry 2400) and a brief section "Women's Organizations in Pakistan" in Ruth Frances Woodsmall, ***Women and the New East*** (entry 2405).

[10]In addition, the government of Pakistan has recently established a Women's Affairs Division in the Cabinet Secretariat in Islamabad. It has been described as a "central body with considerable powers" (letter from Aban Marker to Carol Sakala, 25 March 1979). Although I am not personally knowledgeable about its powers or mandate, a research scholar might find the division's secretary an excellent resource person.

Libraries, Archives and Other Resources in Bangladesh for the Study of Women

Sirajul Islam*

Bangladesh is extremely rich in archival sources; she has, however, much to learn regarding their collection, preservation, organization and management. From 1947 to 1971 Bangladesh was the province of East Pakistan in the state of Pakistan. Archival collections were maintained in the cities of Karachi and Islamabad, West Pakistan, where most national agencies were headquartered. Before 1947, all official records were housed in the Writer's Building in Calcutta. The National Archives of Bangladesh was established in 1973 with the aim or organizing and developing a modern national archive.

As of yet, no archival depository in Bangladesh has a catalog or index for its preserves; the location and condition of specific material is largely unknown. In preparing this essay, I traveled to various parts of the country and personally examined the contents of many collections. The advantage of this approach was that many materials came to my attention that might have gone unnoticed had I relied on traditional catalogs and indexes.

Space does not allow me to detail the information I have found. I will discuss the general nature and extent of material preserved at various places in order to help researchers locate and further explore the sources regarding the women of Bangladesh. For convenience I have organized the sources of archival information into four categories: Major Libraries, Government Archives, Women's Organizations and Press and Periodicals.

MAJOR LIBRARIES

Dacca University Library, Dacca

The greatest archival asset of the Dacca University Library is a collection of 24,000 manuscripts gathered by the university from private sources. These manuscripts are in Sanskrit, Pali, Arabic, Persian, Urdu and old Bengali languages; most are written on palm leaves, leather bark or homemade cotton paper. The collection includes religious documents, caste controversies, almanacs, marriage and other songs, plays, poems and the writings of scholars and saints. These manuscripts contain interesting information regarding marriage customs, status of women as decreed by the *śāstras*; the role of women in the family and society; social position of women in the caste hierarchy; privileges of husbands; obligations of women to husbands, parents and other relatives; moral guidelines for women; polygamy; *kulīna* practices; *satīs* and the like. They are not indexed, but they have been classified by topic. They offer a tempting opportunity for the study of the women of ancient and medieval Bangladesh.

Another unique preserve of the Dacca University Library is its extensive collection of the weekly Bengali newspaper *Ḍhākā Prakāśa*. No other library has a file of this periodical from its origin in 1863 until it ceased publication in 1962. Published in Dacca by members of the Brahmo Samaj, it was among the most widely circulated of periodicals published in Bengal in the early twentieth century. Its principal aim was social reform, particularly the emancipation of Hindu women. The practices of different forms of female slavery, polygamy, concubinage, prostitution, child marriage, female education and dowries are all topics on which *Ḍhākā Prakāśa* regularly published. An analysis of these articles could provide a description of nineteenth and twentieth century social history of Bengali Hindu women.

Bangla Academy Library, Dacca

The Bangla Academy Library is particularly rich in folk literature. The fundamental feature of folk literature is its unsophisticated description of the experiences of traditional rural life. Poems, rhymes, songs, *ślokas* and folk sayings are used to describe rural joys — and sorrows. Folk literature can provide valuable assistance in studying the role of women in rural society. The Bangla Academy Library maintains a folklore division for the collection and preservation of this literature.

The collection of *pũthi* literature is particularly good. *Pũthi* literature has some affinity with epic literature. It is a poetic narrative of legendary social or political events. *Pũthis* are not meant to be read, but rather to be recited. The composers were conscious of their audience; to suit the taste of a rustic, often illiterate audience they frequently indulged in vulger aphorism and sensual description. Although the exact dates of *pũthis* are not known, scholars date many to the late eighteenth and early nineteenth centuries. Women are the subject matter of many of these works and much can be learned regarding society's attitudes and actions with respect to them. The following *pũthis*, with authors where known, are examples of the Bangla Academy's collection:

Bāramāsī, "Twelve Months" songs about love, crops, weather and other topics, usually sung by women	unknown
Sunābhān, the story of a lady and her adventures	unknown
Nārī Nāmā, "Account of Women"	unknown
Premakathā, "Love Stories"	unknown
Sāiphul Mūlluk Badiujjamān, the story of "Sāiphul Mūlluk and Badiujjamān"	Ābadul Hākim
Jāigun Bibira Lāla Mati Sāiphul Mūllak, "Jāigun Bibi's 'Lāla Mati and Sāiphul Mūlluk'"	Ābadul Hākim
Bibi Āliphāra Yuddha, "War of Lady Āliphā"	unknown
Iusuph Julekhā, story of "Iusuph and Julekhā"	Garīb Phakīr
Madhumālā, "Garland of Honey"	unknown
Sakhināra Jār, "Laments of Sakhinā"	Muhāmmad Khān
Jaya Kālī o Balarāmera Prema, "Romance of Jaya Kālī and Balarāma"	Saiẏad Nasim
Pardā Sambāda, "News of Female Seclusion"	Muhāmmad Ābbās
Premera Gāna, "Songs of Love"	unknown
Rādhikāra Bāramāsī, "Rādhikā's Twelve Months" songs	unknown
Sakhīra Bāramāsī, "A Girl Friend's Twelve Months" songs	unknown

Candra Kalāra Bibāha, "Candrakalā's Marriage"	unknown
Rādhāra Bilāpa, "Laments of Rādhā"	unknown
Prema Taraṅgiṇī, "Waves of Love" between Rādhā and Kṛṣṇa	unknown

Dacca Secretariat Library, Dacca

This library houses almost all of the official publications of the early British period, along with the compiled proceedings of the Legislative Council and the Legislative Assembly. These proceedings and official publications contain the government's policies toward women and public reaction to these policies. The discussion that developed out of the issues of ***satīs***, ***kulīna*** practices, child marriage, age of consent, female education, the dowry system, polygamy and women's enfranchisement is documented in these proceedings and publications.

Dacca National Museum Library, Dacca, and Varendra Research Library and Museum, Rajshahi

These libraries are extremely useful for all research in the arts and humanities. Both maintain extensive collections of literature, ancient and medieval manuscripts, fine arts specimens (e.g., sculptures and terra cottas) and artifacts (e.g., coins, clothing and ornaments). Both have thousands of female images from which scholars can draw various conclusions regarding the cultural life of ancient women. Dr. M. Rahman, director of the Varendra Research Museum, and Dr. Enamul Huq, director general of the Dacca National Museum, will be of great assistance to researchers; both are scholars of ancient and medieval arts and culture and highly qualified to speak about women of historical Bangladesh.

Ram-mala Library, Comilla

This private library is owned by a local businessman and features a large collection of Sanskrit sources. A scholar proficient in Sanskrit can find here a mass of materials regarding social customs, social institutions and the belief systems of ancient and medieval Bangladesh. For example, the collection contains scrolls that describe marriage ceremonies, work to be done by male and female slaves and the behavior of virtuous women. The collection also contains a sale deed in old Bengali detailing the rights and obligations of a slave girl.

Data Banks

In recent years there has been a spate of research on rural life and institutions. The main aim of this research is the development of the rural economy and society. To introduce changes into the traditional life and outlook of the rural society, it has been felt necessary to understand the nature and character of the traditional social system. Aided by the United Nations Development Program (UNDP), Asian Development Bank (ADB), Ford Foundation, UNICEF and many other national and international organizations, numerous research projects have been conducted to collect and preserve data for use in planning change-oriented development projects. This information has usually been collected in the form of questionnaires, which often include questions regarding the role of women in the family and society. This information, preserved on magnetic tape or in its original form, is available at the libraries of the sponsoring institutions. The principal institutions that maintain data banks are:

In Dacca

Bangladesh Institute of Development Studies (BIDS)
Integrated Rural Development Programme (IRDP)
Ministry of Planning, Research Division
Directorate of Family Planning
Bureau of Statistics
Foundation of Manpower
Social Science Research Council
Bangladesh Rural Advancement Committee (BRAC)
Cholera Research Laboratory
Bangladesh Fertility Research Programme
Bangladesh Diabetic Association
Bureau of Economic Research, Dacca University
Institute of Statistical Research and Training, Dacca University
Institute of Nutrition, Dacca University

In Chittagong

Centre of the Study of Rural Economics, Chittagong University

In Rajshahi

Institute of Bangladesh Studies

In Bogra and Comilla

Bangladesh Academy of Rural Development (BARD)

Since most data collected and preserved by these institutions are of a confidential nature, potential users are advised to make contact prior to visiting the individual institutions and obtain necessary permission. Those who do not carry the necessary documents certifying them as academic researchers may not be able to obtain the cooperation of the authorities.

GOVERNMENT ARCHIVES

Dacca Secretariat Record Room, Dacca

This record room is considered to be the most important center for archival sources in Bangladesh. Records available in this archive date from the beginning of British rule in Bengal. All materials have been gathered from various collectorate record rooms and are classified according to district.[1]

In addition to the manuscript records, the Record Room has the printed proceedings of the Bengal government from 1859 when the government first began to print its proceedings.[2]

Problems of women recur with regularity in government proceedings throughout most of the 19th century as important developments regarding the status and condition of women in the society were taking place during this period. Documents regarding slavery, polygamy, *kulīna* practices, *satīs*, infanticide, prostitution, female education, *pardā*, early marriage, dowries and the legal status of women are numerous. The British knew very little about the country when they first established political supremacy in Bengal in the 1760s. To better equip themselves for administration, they tried to understand the customs, traditions, manners, social institutions and social systems of the country; officers were even rewarded for undertaking research on these topics. Thus, we find numerous reports, memoranda, petitions and letters about these subjects in the official proceedings from the early period of British rule.

In the 1820s, with strong anti-*satī* agitation, the age of reform began in Bengal. Various reforms threatened the stability of the traditional social structure. The government's reform policy sharply divided the society into pro- and anti-reform groups. Much of the subsequent controversy appears in the proceedings in the form of minutes, memoranda, petitions and letters. From the 1820s onward, the proceedings contain voluminous discussions of the numerous reform issues relating to women.

A fascinating aspect of the proceedings in the General Department (Emigration Branch) is the emigration of women to overseas British colonies in the nineteenth century. Indentured labor emigration began in the 1840s. The proceedings document district-level emigration, specifying male, female and child emigrants. Many of these indentured laborers never returned home and became the founders of the Indian communities in Fiji, Mauritius, southeastern Africa and the Caribbean.

Many of the various government documents described above are also available at the West Bengal State Archives in Calcutta and the India Office library in London.

District-level Collectorate and Judge Muhafezkhanas

Every district has two archives — the Collectorate Muhafezkhana and the Judge Muhafezkhana. The Collectorate Muhafezkhana contains land records, such as registers of landholders, rent roles, survey reports and miscellaneous papers. The collectorate records are the main source of information for studying land control by women. It should be pointed out that although women in general were not prominent in public matters, many individual women did surpass men in the management of land and social leadership. The great eighteenth century zamindars like Maharani Biṣṇukāmārī of Burdwan, Maharani Bhabānī of Rajshahi, Maharani Sarasbatī of Dinajpur, Begam Rauśānārā of Baldakhal (Comilla) and Sāleha Khātuna of Sandip were sufficiently daring and independent to come into direct conflict with and seriously challenge British rule. The collectorate records contain very interesting information about these women. There were other women of the period, like Rani Sbarṇamayī of Kashimbazar, Munni Jāna of Hughli and Pītāmbarī of Dacca Rajnagar, whose names became household words through their munificence and social leadership. Many others established themselves in the fields of literature, social service and land control throughout the period of British rule. Their annals have never been written. The Collectorate Muhafezkhana is the major source for materials relating to many such persons.

The records of the Judge Muhafezkhana also have interesting documents on women. Judicial records in nearly all Judge Muhafezkhana date from the beginning of the nineteenth century. Many court cases concerned social reform legislation and these records contain case judgements on *satīs*, slavery, age of consent, concubinage and other issues. The judges often made long statements regarding the social practices affecting the lives of women. There is no index for the records. The judgements are written on long winding scrolls and preserved in bundles wrapped in cloth; users must open each bundle individually, and carefully read its contents in the hope of discovering information regarding women.

WOMEN'S ORGANIZATIONS

Many organizations in Bangladesh are concerned with the interests and welfare of women. The most common objectives of these organizations are to offer social and adult education programs, to abolish *pardā* and dependence on men, to teach sewing agricultural skills, to create ideal homes, to help women be better mothers, to work for equal rights, to abolish dowries, to promote family planning and to perform various other types of social work.

Only a few organizations, however, have elaborate structures on a national scale. I am concerned here only with those organizations that have definite constitutions, social and state sanctions and, above all, maintain regular proceedings of their activities. These include:

<u>In Dacca</u>

Jatiya Mahila Samstha (National Organisation of Women), New Bailey Road. A government organization. Aims to cooperate with private women's organizations. Executive committee consists of members drawn from leading women's organizations.
Bangladesh Mahila Samiti (Bangladesh Women's Association), New Bailey Road
Bangladesh Girl Guides Association, New
Bangladesh Women's Rehabilitation and Welfare Foundation (BWRWF), Road No. 3, Dhanmandi
National Women's Federation, 88, Shantinagar
Child Protection Association, 5/6, Gopi Kishore Lane, Wari
Nursery Association, 14, Shekh.Shaheb Bazar
Lioness Club, 9, Shah Shaheb Lane, Narinda
Women for Women, V.I.P. Circuit House
Mahila Parishad (Council of Women), Larmani Street
Bangladesh Lekhika Sangha, Peara Bagh. Organization of female writers.
Women's Rehabilitation Centre, 74, Bijoynagar. Government organization originally established to rehabilitate the women displaced during the war of liberation.

<u>In Chittagong</u>

Bangladesh Mahila Samstha (Association of Bangladesh Women), 37, Dhampora

From the proceedings of these organizations, information regarding the social and familial roles of Bengali women can be gathered.

PRESS AND PERIODICALS

Periodical literature is an important source of information for many research problems of the nineteenth and twentieth centuries. The nineteenth century press was quite articulate regarding various social issues, many of which directly concerned women. However, throughout the 1800s most discussions, debates and disputes about the status of women focused on Hindu women. The papers that participated in the women's movement were most often based in Calcutta and owned by Hindus. The files of these periodicals are available in Indian archives and libraries.

Topics relating to Muslim women became prominent in the Bengali press at the beginning of the twentieth century. Until the end of the nineteenth century, the press was silent about Muslim women. The Muslim press considered it a violation of religious norms to discuss an issue such as female seclusion publicly. In January of 1900 the weekly ***Islām Pracāraka*** raised this issue for the first time. The paper commented that the cause of Islam's present plight was the neglect and contempt shown to women. After this, many Muslim periodicals dealt with women's issues. Until the 1940s the Muslim press published many more features than it did "news" stories. Feature articles and editorials were often devoted to the problems of women, as were many letters to editors. The most common themes were female education, early marriage, ***pardā***, polygamy, ill-treatment of wives, divorce, dowries and unequal rights. Among the periodicals in support of the cause of the emancipation of women were ***Nabanūr, Kahinūr, Āl-Islām, Baṅgīya Musalmān, Sāhitya Patrikā, Muslem Bhārata, Sahacara, Sāmyabādī, Nārī Śakti, Śīkhā, Saogāt, Muyājjīn*** and ***Māsika Muhammadi***. The files of many of these periodicals are available at the Bangla Academy Library. The Varendra Research Library also has some important files of the Muslim press of early twentieth century Bengal.

As in any research, for particular problems an investigator must seek particular private papers, records, resource persons and other materials. I hope that this essay has provided information and suggestions that will help research scholars interested in women of Bangladesh to generate materials appropriate to their particular interests.

---

*Sirajul Islam is Associate Professor of History, Dacca University, Dacca. Funds used to obtain much of the information contained in this essay were provided by the South Asia Council of the Association for Asian Studies.

[1]The districts for which the Record Room maintains records, along with the inclusive dates and number of available volumes, are: Chittagong (1760-1864, 548 volumes), Barisal (1772-1885, 370 volumes), Rangpur (1773-1895, 515 volumes), Rajshahi (1781-1864, 190 volumes), Comilla (1782-1867, 470 volumes), Dacca (1783-1859, 364 volumes), Dinajpur (1786-1875, 883 volumes), Mymensingh (1787-1866, 33 volumes), Pabna (1800-85, 267 volumes), Faridpur (1802-27, 92 volumes), Sylhet (1816-70, 422 volumes) and Noakhali (1841-72, 97 volumes).

[2]Certain departments were not, however, established until the late nineteenth century. The departments were established in the following order: General (1859); Judicial (1859); Legislative (1862); Financial (1868); Revenue (1868); Education (1874); Municipal (1880); Police, Jail and Political (1891); Agricultural (1897).

Library Resources in the United Kingdom for the Study of Women in South Asia

Prepared by

Maureen L.P. Patterson *

With contributions by
Penelope Tuson, Amar Kaur Jasbir Singh,
Rosemary Seton and Mary Thatcher

Comments by Geraldine H. Forbes

Extensive printed and manuscript materials for the study of women in South Asia exist in United Kingdom libraries. Most of these libraries are located in London, although there is one valuable, special archive in Cambridge.[1] The majority of printed and manuscript resources located in the U.K. for the study of women in South Asia were produced by the major British organizations and important British citizens who had lived and served in the subcontinent and who were officially or unofficially involved with the Indian Empire from their home base. These resources may be divided into four main areas of action and concern: 1) official — both civil and military, 2) non-official, non-missionary — private individuals and socio-political reform organizations, 3) missionary — primarily Protestant, of several denominations, and 4) commercial — the large business firms and managing agencies that dominated the import-export trade in India in the large cities and plantations, and to a great extent the major industries of pre-independence India. This paper presents a preliminary survey of the resources of the first three groups, which are located in their respective British depositories. Little if any exploration or description appears yet to have been made of the records of commercial and industrial firms and their relations with India.

In 1977, I spent five weeks in England searching for materials in bookstores and visiting libraries. While there, I made a special point of looking for holdings pertinent to the study of women in South Asia. This report is a composite of my own findings and of several contributions I solicited especially for this volume during my visit. Each of the writers, identified at the appropriate place, has presented her materials in a different style, ranging from the more impersonal description of the India Office materials to the more personal introduction to the "memsahib" records at Cambridge. Comments on specific libraries and archives by Professor Geraldine Forbes (State University of New York, College at Oswego), written in 1978 after her research trip to London, are identified as such and included at pertinent places. Forbes indicates that the place to begin the search for materials in London relating to our topic is the Women's Research and Resources Centre:

> This is not a library but rather a resource center and the first place for a researcher to look for materials. The center has a file on people doing research on women's topics and a list of research projects that are in progress. In addition there is a file of published

and unpublished papers. It is a useful place to register, to look for the addresses of scholars one may have heard of, to read the proposals of others researching South Asian women and to pick up a newsletter full of information on women's seminars and new publications. Seminars are held fortnightly and could provide an opportunity to test ideas.[2]

OFFICIAL DEPOSITORIES — CIVIL AND MILITARY: INDIA OFFICE AND BRITISH MUSEUM

Comprehensive collections of British and Indian government documents (published and unpublished) exist in London in both the British Museum/Library and the India Office Library and Records. Both these libraries also house extensive collections of non-official books and serials, tracts and pamphlets; the India Office Library and Records also has a rapidly growing collection of private papers. While several general and many specialized guides and catalogs to both these collections have been published, the following remarks describe the value of these materials for engaging in research on women in South Asia.

Archival Collections in the India Office Records. Prepared by Penelope Tuson and Amar Kaur Jasbir Singh of the India Office Records, 1977

The archival collections of the India Office Records are the most important official sources relating to South Asia located outside the subcontinent. They consist primarily of the archives of the East India Company, beginning with the granting of its charter in 1600 by Queen Elizabeth I; the archives of the Board of Control, established in 1784 to supervise the company's administration; and the archives of the India Office, which in 1858 assumed the responsibilities formerly held by the company and the board and continued to exercise them until Indian independence in 1947. With certain exceptions,[3] the period beginning with 1858 is most fruitful for studies of the social and political status and activities of women; the departmental records of the India Office and other closely related archive groups contain a wealth of material for such studies.

Before indicating the scope and nature of these sources, one obvious but important reservation must be emphasized in this context: the archives are, of course, British and official, largely created by western imperial administrators who were, without exception, men. Their main activities were not concerned with women's issues, even though many of them were individually fired with the reforming zeal of the nineteenth century which brought about many changes affecting the position of women in society. Consequently, although there is a large quantity of material available, it is not always easy to find and it must be interpreted carefully.

The sources may be divided into two categories, the status of women and women in politics.

Status of women. The most important papers are those relating to reform — education, marriage (divorce, child marriage, female infanticide and *satī*), property rights and other social institutions — and to specific legislative measures aimed either partly or wholly at altering the social and political status of women in society. The legislation and many of the unpublished reports are discussed elsewhere (see "Official Government Papers in the India Office Library and Records and the British Museum Library," below). Of equal interest, however, are the background papers to these measures, the official correspondence and unpublished reports, which generally are to be found in the records of the India Office Public and Judicial Department (IOR:L/P&J),[4] and in the various proceedings of the government of India and of the provinces and presidencies (IOR:P; for example, India Legislative, Judicial, Public and Education proceedings).[5] There are also references in the departmental records of the Legal Adviser and Solicitor (IOR:L/L) to cases in the Court of Wards in which women were involved, particularly in the Indian (princely) states. After the reorganization of India Office departments in 1923, related material appears in the records of other departments. The Services and General Department (IOR:L/S&G/6-7, 1924-48), for example, contains information on the education of women.

During the twentieth century, the status of women was greatly enhanced by their increasing participation in public service and in employment generally. Until 1924, the Public and Judicial Department (IOR:L/P&J) was the India Office department responsible for public service questions affecting India; after this date the Services and General Department files and collections (IOR:L/S&G/6-7) deal with establishment and personnel. However, here again it must be emphasized that public service questions primarily consisted of Indian Civil Service matters and the ICS was a wholly masculine institution. There is material on the employment of women, but it represents only a tiny portion of the information on employment generally and, as always, it is almost entirely confined to the so-called "caring" professions — education, missionary work and medicine. IOR:L/P&J and L/S&G contain material on the employment of women as educators and the Women's Education Service. Records about the medical field are to be found in the Economic and Overseas Department (IOR:L/E/7-9) and, for the Indian Medical Services, in the Military Department (IOR:L/MIL/2-3, 6-7, 9, 14). The Military Department is a source of information on the employment of women in wartime generally and it also has some interesting correspondence on prostitution. For example, material on the operation of the Contagious Diseases Act and related matters from 1873 to 1927 is found in IOR:L/MIL/7/13809-13902.

Women in politics. In the twentieth century women began to play a positive role in the political struggles leading to Indian independence. The files of the Public and Judicial Departments are the main sources of information concerning political and constitutional developments in India during the first half of the twentieth century, and the papers include information on the participation of women in the nationalist movement. They also provide material on the political and public careers of individual women, such as Sarojini Naidu and Vijaya Lakshmi Pandit. To a lesser extent, the files and collections of the Political (External) Department (IOR:L/P&S/12, 1931-50) contain relevant material, as do the Private Office records (IOR:L/PO, circa 1916-47), the Central Government Records: Viceroy's Private Office (IOR:R/3/1) and the Collections of Records of Commissions, Committees and Conferences (IOR:Q), which include papers relating to the Indian Round Table Conference, 1930-32. There is additional material on women from the Indian states (for instance, Rajkumari Amrit Kaur and Rani Rajwade) in the collections of Crown Representative's Records (IOR:R/1) and Residency Records (IOR:R/2). The departmental records generally are adequately indexed; separate index and register volumes are classified under the reference IOR:Z. In addition, detailed lists of many archive groups and section guides are currently in preparation.

This report is intended to introduce some of the pertinent available resources and cannot claim to be exhaustive. For a comprehensive look at all the relevant material, it is advisable for researchers to visit the India Office Records. Such a visit will uncover much additional material useful for scholarship on the subject of women in South Asia. The archives are open to the public subject to the Thirty Year Rule; occasional restrictions may need to be imposed because of the fragility of some material. There are facilities for photocopying.

Private papers in the India Office Library and Records. Prepared by Rosemary Seton, formerly of the India Office Records, 1977

The large and ever-increasing collection of private papers held by the India

Office Library and Records contains much material relevant to the subject of women in South Asia. The collection chiefly comprises letters, diaries and other papers of the British administrators, soldiers, members of the medical and teaching professions, missionaries and businessmen in India during British rule. The papers of their wives and daughters have also been collected; these often contain detailed descriptions of social and family life, comment on leading personalities and reveal a variety of attitudes to India and the Indians.

Also in the collection are the records of some notable Indian women, including some fragmentary writings of Sarojini Naidu (14ff Mss.Eur.A.95) and a substantial number of the papers of Cornelia Sorabji. Miss Sorabji, after taking a degree in law at Oxford, created for herself a role as protector of the rights of women landholders in Bengal, Bihar, Orissa and Assam from 1904 to 1923; from 1923 to 1929, she practised as a barrister in Calcutta. The papers cover all aspects of her life and career and include her writings on the promotion of infant welfare and of maternity and district nursing in India, as well as on the educational work of her sister, Susie Sorabji (15 boxes, Mss.Eur.F.165).

The collection also includes papers of western men and women who were associated with India. Frank Lugard Brayne, who served in the Indian Civil Service from 1905 to 1941, and was Commissioner for Rural Reconstruction in the Punjab from 1933 to 1939, considered any improvement in the standard of living to be impossible without raising the status of Indian women. This idea pervades his writing and correspondence and several files deal exclusively with the subject of women's welfare and status (48 boxes, Mss.Eur.F.152). Annette Beveridge, née Ackroyd, founded the Hindu Mahila Bidyalaya (Hindu Ladies' School) in Calcutta in 1873. Her letters and diaries are to be found in the Beveridge Collection (29 boxes, Mss.Eur.C.176). Other noteworthy items include the papers of Alice, Lady Reading and Vicereine of India from 1921 to 1926, who took an active part in social work in India (2 boxes, Mss.Eur.E.316); miscellaneous letters of Florence Nightingale (dated circa 1866-90), which reveal her informed understanding of Indian affairs; and the unpublished autobiography of Constance Wilson, who nursed in India from 1921 to 1947. Also in the collection are letters of Marjorie Ussher, governess in Hyderabad from 1936 to 1942 (Mss.Eur.D.859); memoranda on the status, condition and education of Indian women by Eleanor Rathbone and others, which are part of the papers of Sir John Simon (Mss.Eur.F.77); two files on women's education, in the papers of Sir Philip Hartog (Mss.Eur.E.221); and a collection of essays, dated circa 1911, by girls of the Poona Widows' and Orphans' Home on the treatment of Hindu widows (Mss.Eur.D.356).[6]

Official Government Publications in the India Office Library and Records and the British Museum Library

Official publications on India include both those of the various British administrations in India (from 1793 to 1947) as well as the reports of the British Parliamentary Debates and House of Commons and House of Lords ***Sessional Papers*** which are "commonly referred to as Parliamentary Papers."[7] The use of these papers for research is greatly facilitated by the ***Annual Lists and General Index of the Parliamentary Papers Relating to the East Indies Published during the Years 1801 to 1907 Inclusive***,[8] and the typescript continuation held in the IOL/R. Among the rubrics in the ***Annual Lists*** under which one can find material of particular relevance to the study of women in India are: Contagious Diseases, Cantonment Acts and Venereal Disease; Hindoo:-Infanticide; Hindoo:-Widows, Custom of Suttee; Marriage and Funeral Customs in Rajputana; Mines:-Women and Children, Employment of; and Sanitary:-Commissions.

In addition to the debates, "Command" Papers (as many of the Parliamentary Papers are called) and those non-parliamentary publications which include volumes of evidence for royal commissions and other official authorities (whose reports were issued with "Command" numbers) are of considerable interest for the study of women. Those published after 1921 are particularly important since publication of materials ancillary to the reports themselves was then curtailed.[9] Such volumes of evidence are being made available and cataloged as "Q" Papers. According to Geraldine Forbes,

> "Q" Papers are not available for all the Royal Commissions, nor has the entire collection been cataloged. I was the first person to use some of the newly cataloged "Q" Papers, and they helped me to gain some insight into how women operated vis à vis the commissions, along with what they said privately. For example, the "Q" Papers from the Indian Franchise Committee include actual statements made during the committee's investigation. Such information often gives a clearer idea of attitudes than a final report.[10]

According to Sims, official publications of the British government of India and of the provincial governments "fall into two broad categories, legislative and departmental." He states:

> The legislative publications include the acts, rules and ordinances of the central and provincial governments and the debates and proceedings of the legislative councils and assemblies. There is a consolidated index to the statute book of India up to the end of 1938 in ***Chronological tables and index of the Indian statutes*** (Delhi, 1939-41, 2 vols.). This includes central and provincial statutes, acts, regulations and ordinances. Departmental publications include the volumes issued by the various surveys of India, the annual reports of governments and departments and many non-serial publications. Among these are reports of committees and commissions appointed in India, monographs on almost every subject, and a large array of procedural manuals and handbooks issued by each department for the guidance of its officers which provide a detailed picture of the administrative development. Bibliographies of non-serial publications . . . are virtually non-existent.[11]

After mentioning the existence of provincial administration reports, gazetteers, settlement reports, census volumes and "Selections from the Records" of both central and provincial governments, Sims reports:

> The India Office Records has the most complete collection in Britain of pre-1947 Indian Official publications. Normally copies of all government publications were sent to the India Office, but some publications considered to be of purely local interest were never forwarded, and from about 1930 the India Office collection is far from complete. The earlier publications are included in the *List of reports and other publications in the Record Department of the India Office up to December 1892* (HMSO, 1894). They are arranged under 511 subject headings and the catalogue gives short title, author and date. The comprehensiveness of the collection gives value to the catalogue as a bibliography, but it is not an entirely accurate guide to the current holdings. A revised catalogue is in preparation.[12]

After the IOL/R, the British Museum (now British Library), Cambridge University Library and the Indian Institute Library at Oxford contain the strongest collections of these materials. As Sims notes, "The British Library's nineteenth century holdings are listed in Frank Campbell, ***Index-catalogue of Indian Official Publications in the Library of the British Museum*** (HMSO, 1899). Its layout is rather fuller than that of the India Office Records catalogue. Many of the entries, particularly of serials, are annotated, and background information on commissions is provided."[13]

In all, then, a vast amount of information on women in the subcontinent is to be found in the multitudinous publications of both the British and Indian governments.

Maureen L.P. Patterson

NON-OFFICIAL, NON-MISSIONARY: RESOURCES OF PRIVATE INDIVIDUALS AND SOCIO-POLITICAL REFORM ORGANIZATIONS

South Asian Archive at Cambridge Centre of South Asian Studies

The Centre of South Asian Studies at the University of Cambridge is building a unique collection of letters, films, taped interviews and other personal items gathered from British men and women who lived and served in the subcontinent during the British Raj. In 1977, I visited Cambridge to see the archive and requested the South Asian Archivist, Miss Mary Thatcher, to describe this unique collection. The information she provides illustrates the richness of this collection for research on women in South Asia.

British women in South Asia during the Raj: records in the Cambridge South Asian Archive — prepared by T. Mary Thatcher, 1977. The Centre of South Asian Studies was established as a distinct institution in May 1964, in accordance with the recommendations of the Hayter Report, to promote teaching and research in South Asia (i.e., India, Pakistan, Ceylon, Burma, Afghanistan and Nepal), to publish the results of completed research and to cooperate with outside organizations in encouraging research in South Asian Studies. The centre is controlled by an Inter-Faculty Committee of Management. In 1966, this committee launched the preliminary exploratory phase of an archive project it had been considering for some time. The committee believed that there still existed papers, diaries, letters, photographs, films and other materials written or collected by those who lived and served in South Asia, which were capable of throwing light on economic, social and political conditions during the period of British rule in the former Indian Empire and Ceylon. Similar original sources pertaining to the colonial world, but excluding the former Indian Empire, were already being collected by the Colonial Records Project in Oxford. Serious collecting at the centre began in May 1967.

In October 1973, the first handlist of the contents of the archive collection (as of June 1972) was published by Mansell as *Cambridge South Asian Archive: Records of the British period in South Asia relating to India, Pakistan, Ceylon, Burma, Nepal and Afghanistan, held in the Centre of South Asian Studies, University of Cambridge*, compiled and edited by Mary Thatcher. It lists 238 written collections, 11 film collections (consisting of 134 films) and 104 tape recordings made in India.

Since June 1972, 138 further collections have been received and catalogued and 7 collections of films (51 reels) have been acquired. More tape recordings have been made in India and in England. I have made 19 recordings by widows of former Indian Civil Service officers, missionaries and tea planters. In addition, I am currently compiling selections from memoirs and letters written by Englishwomen living in India between the years 1900 and 1947. The passages are representative of the life of Englishwomen in India, specifically the wives of ICS officers.

The writings record life in the remote regions of the subcontinent — the North-West Frontier, Assam, the desert of Sind and the forests of the Central Provinces — where wives accompanied their ICS husbands on tour, camping for a month or two at a time and organizing tents, food, and other necessities for themselves and their retinue of necessary servants and coolies. When living in the administrative centres, these women wrote home about their domestic life, especially about their first arrival and adjustment to a new language, unfamiliar food, differences in hygiene and innumerable servants who did not speak English. There was in these centres a considerable amount of mutual help, but young wives a thousand miles from home and relations had to live without airmail service (post typically required a month or more), antibiotics, air conditioning, refrigeration and telephones. They also had to tolerate being separated from children, who from the age of about five were sent home to England to be brought up by relations and friends. "Cruel, cruel," as one woman records in her memoirs, feeling torn between her husband's need for a home in India, where he worked 12 to 14 hours a day, and her sick children's need for care in England.

Women whose outstanding contributions are in the collection include: Mrs. Showers, who wrote a memoir of life as Resident Commissioner's wife in Jaipur and Nepal before 1916, detailing her experiences with hunting, coping with endless visitors and camping; Mrs. Dench, who remained with her husband on the North-Western Frontier in troubled times and in the hot weather, until she was the last woman there; Lady Scott, who walked 15 to 20 miles a day in Assam jungle and bathed in a canvas bath in a tent, while a myriad of curious eyes peered through the slits, watching her every move; Mrs. Hall, who lived in the desert with her children, with the rats climbing over her bedroom furniture; and Lady Anderson, who sat in a boat at dawn waiting for the duck to rise, so that it could be shot for the pot; the list is a long one, indeed.[14]

Comments of an archive user. In 1978, Geraldine Forbes surveyed the Cambridge South Asian Archive and noted that the collection contains three types of materials of interest to those studying the women of South Asia. First of all, there are written materials from the private collections of individuals who lived in India. These include letters, photographs, pamphlets, diaries and other items that are normally included in a collection of private papers. However, Forbes notes that "these papers are more valuable for a study of the British in India than for a study of Indian people. [Many papers] belonging to British women barely mention Indians. While I am certain that one could find some material, these women were memsahibs and spent little time either with Indian women or thinking about their problems."[15]

Secondly, Forbes stresses the value of the film collection. She was "impressed with both the quality and composition of the films . . . anyone interested in doing research on the 1920s and 1930s will very likely find interesting and valuable footage."[16]

In the third place, the transcripts of taped interviews contain some of the most interesting and important information in the Cambridge collection. Though they are mostly interviews with western men and women, there are also recordings of Lakshmiben, Mahatma Gandhi's adopted daughter; Mrs. Hansa Mehta, Indian National Congress leader; and Goshiben Captain, a leader of women's political organizations in Bombay. Forbes comments that "these interviews are first-rate and they in and of themselves make a trip to Cambridge essential."[17]

Fawcett Society Library

The Fawcett Library was inaugurated in 1926 by the London Society for Women's Service (now the Fawcett Society), in honor of Millicent Garrett Fawcett, a leading English suffragist. In 1977, the library was transferred to the City of London Polytechnic, where it is now housed as a special collection. Its fine collection of information and literature on women consists of about 20,000 books and an equal number of pamphlets, as well as periodicals, archives, photographs, letters and press cuttings. A small but important portion of its holdings consists of unique material on women in or associated with South Asia.

Eleanor Rathbone (1872-1946) addressed many social issues of her day. One that she approached with great vigor was the issue of the status of women in India. Her efforts included work for the enfranchisement of Indian women, improvements in their legal status, female education and, especially, the abolition of child marriage (see entry 1028). The material in the Eleanor Rathbone Papers — one of the self-contained archives within the library — supplements, through Rathbone's correspondence concerning Indian women's affairs, the officially published reports and evidence volumes of such royal commissions and committees as those on constitutional reform and franchise in the early 1930s, which can be found in the IOL/R (see "Official Government Publications in the India Office Library and Records and the British Museum Library," above). The following chart of the collection's contents has been assembled from the mimeographed list made available to patrons at the Fawcett Library.

Rathbone Papers relating to Indian Women's Affairs

Correspondent/topic	Dates
(Mrs.) Dr. S. Muthulakshmi Reddy	14 Feb 1929-29 Jul 1936
Mr. Wedgwood Benn	1 Jul 1929-30 Jul 1934
letters to the *Times* on child marriage, correspondence with signatories and others	3 Sep 1929-7 Aug 1936
legislation — child marriage	4 Sep 1929-18 Mar 1935
Lady Hartog's correspondence with E. Rathbone and others	29 Apr 1930-13 Aug 1935
Sir John Simon	10 May 1930
Mrs. K. Radhabai Subbarayan	20 Nov 1930-31 Dec 1936
Lord Sankey, the Lord Chancellor	14 Jan 1931-3 Mar 1933
Rt. Hon. Ramsay Macdonald, the Prime Minister	14 Jan 1931-27 Aug 1932
Mrs. Sri Maya Devi (Gangulee) Butler	13 Aug 1931-27 Aug 1932
Sir Samuel Hoare and R.A. Butler	12 Sep 1931-7 Apr 1936
memoranda and notes, mainly on discussions with government members and on government reports	Sep 1931-5 Mar 1936
Lord Lothian	25 Nov 1931-2 Jul 1935
Dr. J.H. Hutton	9 Jul 1932-18 Apr 1934
press conferences, statements, letters	16 Jul 1932-12 Mar 1935
Indian letters — Sir Tej Bahadur Sapru, Mr. Jayaker, Mr. Joshi and others	28 Jul 1932-17 Apr 1935
correspondence concerning White Paper on Indian Franchise, and other Indian correspondence	8 Sep 1932-7 Jun 1935
Mrs. Hamid Ali	8 Sep 1932-13 May 1935
Begam Shah Nawaz	19 Nov 1932-19 Jun 1936
correspondence with members of Round Table Conference on India	21 Dec 1932
Mrs. P.K. (Sarala) Ray	26 Jan 1933-29 Feb 1934
Mrs. Kailash Srivastava	30 Jan 1933-17 Mar 1933
minutes, papers and correspondence of British Committee for Indian Women's Franchise	3 Apr 1933-23 May 1935
Rajkumari Amrit Kaur	18 Mar 1933-16 Sep 1935
Mrs. S.C. Mukerjee	5 Apr 1933-2 Aug 1935
Joint Select Committee on Indian Constitutional Reform	26 Apr 1933-15 Feb 1934
Lady Macpherson	5 May 1933-9 Jun 1933
Mrs. Mona Hensman	30 May 1933-3 Feb 1936
Dr. and Mrs. Nehru	30 Sep 1933-23 Aug 1934
Mrs. Lakshmi Menon	29 Feb 1934-18 Jul 1935

Correspondent/topic	Dates
reviews, letters, revised third chapter of Rathbone's book on child marriage	3 Apr 1934-24 May 1934
Sir Malcolm Hailey	2 Jun 1934-12 Jul 1934
list prepared for Mrs. How-Martyn (Women's Freedom League) of addresses of persons in India's "useful" for social reform	7 Dec 1934
Mr. N.M. Joshi	3 Jan 1935-5 May 1936
Mr. H.S.L. Polak	17 Jan 1935-23 Jan 1935
women's amendments to Government of India Bill, 1935 (includes letters to Miss Lloyd George, Thelma Cazalet, Dennis Herbert)	Mar 1935
Sir Archibald Carter	17 May 1935-21 May 1935
(Mrs.) Dr. P.K. Sen	23 May 1935-24 Nov 1935
Dowager Nawab-Begam Saheba of Janjiri	28 Sep 1935-13 Mar 1935
Das' Bill to amend the Sarda Act	5 May 1936-24 Jun 1938
Rex v. Abdul Majid	1936
Women's Freedom League	12 May 1937-16 Sep 1937

Geraldine Forbes conducted research in the Fawcett Library in 1978 and concluded that it should be at or near the top of one's list of places to visit in London while researching topics of women in South Asia. According to her, the Fawcett Library is virtually a women's archives, and as such is an excellent place to obtain information concerning ongoing research and other collections of materials on women. Forbes identifies the following materials in the collection as valuable for anyone studying women in India:

1) ***Private papers.*** The library has the private papers of three women who were interested in, and had contact with, Indian women: Maude Royden, Millicent Fawcett and Eleanor Rathbone. The Rathbone Papers, richest in this regard, are particularly important for anyone studying the Indian women's movement.

2) ***Books of biographical news cuttings.*** In the absence of an adequate "Who's Who" on women, these notebooks containing news clippings are valuable for information about British women. Generally, the pages on a particular woman include obituary notices as well as other pertinent items. These notebooks were compiled by volunteers, however, and should be used to supplement information from other sources.

3) ***Magazines and journals.*** The Fawcett Library contains both Indian and British journals on women. Examples of holdings are ***Stri Dharma*** (organ of the Women's Indian Association/WIA, entry 1264) for most of 1925, 1927 and 1928-30; assorted issues of ***Roshni*** (magazine of the All-India Women's Conference/AIWC, entry 2335) from 1946 to 1959; and the British ***Common Cause***, which carried a number of articles on Indian women's franchise.

4) ***Reports of associations.*** Because a number of women who were connected with Millicent Fawcett were interested in India, a number of reports from Indian women's associations are in the library. These include the sixth through ninth ***Report*** of the AIWC, 1931-35; the ***Report*** of the National Council of Women in India (entry 2346) for the years 1928-29, 1936-37 and 1942-44; the ***Report*** of the WIA (entry 1267) for 1928-29, 1930-31, 1932-33 and 1934-36; and the ***Report*** of the Delhi Provincial Council of Women, 1928-29.

5) ***Pamphlet collection.*** There is an extremely valuable collection of pamphlets on the Indian women's franchise issue. The collection con-

tains many rare items.

6) *Books.* The Fawcett collection includes a number of rare and out-of-print books. The holdings are varied and certainly should be checked for materials on women in India.

7) *Josephine Butler Collection.* As yet uncatalogued, the Butler collection takes up almost half of the space allotted to the Fawcett collection. A number of topics relating to India could be researched through materials contained in the Butler Collection. This collection contains, for example, considerable information on Indian rescue homes, including descriptions of the women and girls who were rescued, the reactions of neighbors to a rescue home, the harassment of the women and other community relations problems. There is also some very interesting information on Miss M. Shephard, of the Association for Moral and Social Hygiene, who traveled to India in the 1930s to study concerns of the association and make a report about rescuing women. The Butler Collection includes boxes of material on the working of the Indian Contagious Diseases Act, and still others containing reports of various Indian women's associations devoted to helping women. This collection has not yet been dealt with by a historian working on India, but it would seem to hold considerable promise for such research.[18]

MISSIONARY SOCIETY LIBRARIES

Over a century of British missionary work in South Asia is recorded in the papers, correspondence and publications of numerous church and religious organizations. Groups involved with South Asia were primarily Protestant: Church of England/Anglican and other English denominations whose organization headquarters are in London; Scottish organizations — Church of Scotland/Free Church/Presbyterian — located in Edinburgh; and Welsh groups such as the Presbyterian Church of Wales, with offices in Liverpool.

As Mary Thatcher (Cambridge South Asian Centre) has pointed out, the archives of Roman Catholic orders from the British Isles operating in India are as yet unlocated, unlisted and undescribed in such otherwise comprehensive sources as Wainwright and Matthews' *Guide.* They constitute an untapped resource in an uncharted field. Thatcher noted that since Irish and other orders were responsible for directing many of the famous convent schools that provided a first-rate education for the children of many of India's westernized elite, the records of such schools and their parent organizations would be a significant contribution to the study of India and of Indian female education in particular.[19]

Missionary activities ran the gamut from evangelism and conversion, through general education at all levels, to specialized concerns with medicine, which gave rise to clinics, hospitals and teaching institutions. Church-related groups such as the YWCA, the Association for Moral and Social Hygiene (established by Josephine Butler; see "Fawcett Society Library," above) and the Women's Christian Temperance Union (WCTU, one of many American organizations whose Indian activities deserve study), as well as groups within the Society of Friends (Quakers), were concerned with social problems such as prostitution (including the related issues of contagious diseases and military cantonments), temperance, and opium and other drug traffic. The work of the Society of Friends led to political activities in the 1930s and 1940s through its India Conciliation Group in support of the Indian nationalist movement. Such prominent Quakers as Eleanor Rathbone, M.P., and Agatha Harrison were involved.

Scholars who wish to pursue work on South Asian women and on the character, background and living conditions of the British women who "served" India and its women will find a wealth of information in the various missionary libraries in Great Britain. Both the Collison (information current as of 1969) and the Wainwright and Matthews (as of 1959-61) directories mentioned in note 1 provide detailed descriptions of the holdings of missionary libraries throughout the British Isles (with convenient access through their indexes). While some archives suffered damage from the World War II bombing of London, most appear to be complete and well-organized, and work is continuing in an effort to catalog and increase accessibility. In this regard, the existing guides are not up to date, and a scholar is thus likely to find more rather than less material available for research. Since the "Fifty-Year Rule" is in effect for almost all missionary archives, letters and reports up to 1930 are now (1980) open to bona fide scholars.[20]

The following descriptions of some of the major missionary archives in London are based on notes I made during my 1977 visit, supplemented by information from entries in the Collision and the Wainright and Matthews directories, and also by comments from Geraldine Forbes (1978).

United Society for the Propagation of the Gospel (formerly Society for the Propagation of the Gospel in Foreign Parts)

The Collison directory describes this organization, which was founded in 1701, as follows:

> The United Society for the Propagation of the Gospel (USPG) continues the work formerly undertaken by the Society for the Propagation of the Gospel (SPG) and the Universities' Mission to Central Africa (UMCA). Its Library, which specialises in missionary history in general and in the Anglican Communion in particular, includes a large collection of works on Asia, the Middle East, and the individual regions and territories of that area. The Archives of the Society for the Propagation of the Gospel have been maintained since 1701. In addition to the missionary material, the reports of the early missionaries were often very detailed and contain much historical material.[21]

Since the SPG was an auxiliary branch of the established, "official," Church of England (called "Anglican" in its "High Church" mode), the British government undoubtedly supported its many activities in India. This possibly explains its all-India spread and large staff of men and women, as well as the extensiveness of its archives. In their *Guide*, Wainwright and Matthews show that the SPG files, under the rubric "Women's Work Records," include 33 volumes of "letters received" from India during 1894-1924, and 26 volumes of "letters sent" from 1867 to 1926.[22]

After visiting this library in 1978, Geraldine Forbes noted:

> In my estimation, this library has the richest collection on female British missionaries to India. The Ladies' Association of the Society for the Propagation of the Gospel in Foreign Parts was formed in 1866. It sent single women out as missionaries to teach in zenanas. The records of this society are complete. They include annual reports; letters written by the organizing secretary to India; letters concerning women missionaries received from India; *Grain of Mustard Seed*, a monthly on women in the mission field; a book with biographical notes; and personal dossiers (from the 20th century only), including the applications and reference letters of women who wanted to become missionaries. Because the association was a smaller and more personal operation in the nineteenth century, records from that time are better; but there is a wealth of information for the twentieth century as well.[23]

Church Missionary Society

The CMS of the Church of England was established in 1799 with a stronger evangelical commitment than the more "High Church" SPG. With greater ties to and dependence on "home," the CMS generated a larger number of papers and correspondence than did its counterpart, according to Rosemary Keen, its archivist.[24] During 1962-63, Keen prepared a catalog of the "Papers of the North India Missions, 1812-1914." (A similar work exists for Punjab and Sind.) Papers in the Keen typescript are listed by subject and person. North India includes the Calcutta (later Bengal) mission after 1896. The catalog provides access to such materials as "Correspondence with . . . other societies" (for example, with the Ladies' Society for Native Female Education, Calcutta, from 1820 to 1879); the printed circulars of the Association for the Improvement of the Native Christian Women in the North West Provinces; the 1877-78 letters of Mrs. Annie Jane Briggs, who worked with the Female Education Society in Multan, Punjab; and the letters of the Reverend Henry Davis, regarding the Ladies' Association for Promoting the Education of Females in India and other Heathen Countries.

The CMS Woman Secretary's Department papers include two volumes of minutes of the Women's Foreign Committee, 1895-1901; three volumes of group despatches from missions, 1912-34; and correspondence and papers, 1898-1915. For the study of women in India, the most valuable holdings of the CMS library are the publications and archives of the Church of England Zenana Missionary Society, which amalgamated with the CMS in 1957. Founded in 1880 for work in both India and China, the CEZMS was an offshoot of the Indian Female Normal School and Instruction Society (IFNSIS), which in turn had grown out of the Female Education Society (FES, founded in 1834). In 1899, the CEZMS and IFNSIS again joined forces.

The CMS library holds Female Education Society minutes (1834-99); annual *Reports* (1858-99); finance ledgers and other documents (1860-99); and a complete set of the IFNSIS publication, the *Indian Female Evangelist* (vols. 1-13, 1872-93); as well as the CMS' own publication, *India's Women* (1881-95) and its successors, *India's Women and China's Daughters* (1896-1939) and *Looking East at India's Women and China's Daughters* (1940-57, entry 1586).

The annual *Report* of the CEZMS (entry 1579) provides an immense amount of detail on the life of Englishwomen who "served" in India, including such topics as their medical problems, the local opposition they encountered and their persistence in the face of hardship. All the women who worked in the CEZMS were unmarried during their tenure, and had to leave the society if and when they married. The first annual *Report* promulgated the society's regulations, the second of which was:

> The primary object of the Society shall be, to make known the Gospel of Christ to the women of India, in accordance with the Protestant and Evangelical teaching of the articles and formularies of the Church of England, by means of Normal Schools, Zenana Visitation, medical Missions, Hindu and Mahomedan Female Schools, Bible-women, and such other agencies as may from time to time be determined on . . .[25]

The society established regional committees for Bengal, Punjab and Madras. Some flavor of their work in Bengal is given in the *Report* for 1881-82: "Beside the Hindu schools in Calcutta, Miss Highton is carrying on Zenana work in five neighbouring villages; though the bigotry of Mahomedans is well known, Miss Mulvaney, who recently commenced her work among them, writes that between fifty and sixty houses are open to her."[26] Also noted is the first annual meeting in November 1881 of the Bengali Christian Ladies' Association in Calcutta, attended by "nearly 300 native ladies."[27]

The quarterly *Indian Female Evangelist* described itself as "containing original articles on the past and present condition of Indian women; also recording the progress of true evengelical work amongst them." The size of the volumes attests to the amount of information they contain: the early volumes average 370 pages in length. The following excerpts from IFE articles are samples of the flavor and richness of the publication:

> No persons are fonder of proverbs than the women of India. The writer of this . . . paid women to go into the Zenanas to collect proverbs . . . ; they are often used as riddles, but oftener they help to point those sarcasms which Bengali women in their scoldings are so apt to indulge in; and at times . . . the contest will be carried on by pitching at each other the bitterest and most caustic proverbs. Now what is used for evil might be employed for good; for there are many excellent proverbs.[28]

An article by Reverend W.R. Blackett entitled "Village Women in India" notes the need to go beyond the cities:

> The Zenana Mission has done and is doing a great work. But it hardly goes beyond the cities, and there touches only a few of the richer and more enlightened families. Even in the Zenanas that are open, a large proportion of the time is occupied, not in religious teaching, but in secular matters. The religious teaching must not be made too prominent, lest the Zenanas should be closed, and many Zenanas are being closed just for fear of the religious element in the instruction. Not a few Babus have learnt to value female instruction, so far as they are making efforts to procure it independently of mission agents . . . . But it must not be forgotten that the women shut up in Zenanas are after all but a small part of the women of India. India is a thoroughly aristocratic country, and those interested in India are apt to fall into the way of counting the upper classes alone worthy of attention.[29]

In an article "Twofold Healing for the Women of India," Louisa Clayton, in the course of making a plea for more female doctors, writes:

> The Zenana . . . has not the slightest pretense to be called a ***home***, even in the lowest acceptation of the term; a ***prison*** would really be the most appropriate word, for it is dark and damp, sunlight and air being both excluded. The windows, if any, on the outside are small and high up, so that the inmates can neither see nor hear the sights and sounds of the outer world; and when they do go out which is not often, their faces are veiled, and they are so concealed in their palanquin that they can neither see nor be seen. It is a lifelong captivity, and a most dreary existence, their chief occupation being to dress, eat, and sleep, and their only recreation puerile conversation, varied by quarrelling . . . .
>
> But the utter neglect with which the Indian women are treated in illness is not confined to the middle and poorer classes alone, for even ladies of wealth and position are likewise subjected to the same inhuman treatment . . . .
>
> Is not this an instance where "women's rights" may assert a strong claim ***versus*** "women's wrongs?" There has been of late a loud outspoken demand that our women want work and a sphere.[30]

The well-known Sanskritist, Monier Monier-Williams, contributed an article to the IFE on "Co-ordinate Education in its bearing on the Present Condition of the Women of India," and in it proclaims his bias in regard to women's education when he states:

> The educator who has to do with the training of both sexes must bear in mind that he has presented to him two sets of skulls . . . . the skull of an ordinary woman contains four ounces less brain than that of a man. This difference of weight is an important factor in determining the amount of development that each will bear.[31]

The pages of the IFE also offer insights into missionary organization politics "at home," in particular into the continuing tensions between Nonconformists and members of the Church of England "orthodox missionary societies." (Nonconformists are Methodists, Baptists, Presbyterians and others who do not "conform" to the established Church of England and its tenets.) It appears that even though the CMS proclaimed its readiness to work with Nonconformists within the Indian Female Normal School and Instruction Society, it in fact refused to do so when Lady Kinnaird (a prominent Scottish worker on behalf of women) argued that Dr. Murray Mitchell of Edinburgh should be appointed to some office in the society. This proposal was turned down because he belonged to the Church of Scotland. This sort of tension led to the secession of the "orthodox" group to form the CEZMS in 1880, and to the division of the Indian "field of labour," whereby the IFNSIS retained Bombay Presidency (except Karachi) and the whole of western India, as well as upper India including all the North-Western Provinces except Amritsar in Punjab. This left North India — which seems to have denoted Bengal (along with Bihar) and Orissa in those days — and Central and South India for the CEZMS.

References in the ***Indian Female Evangelist*** mention the existence of Scottish organizations such as the Scottish Ladies' Association for the Advancement of Female Education in India, which was founded in 1836 in Edinburgh, and the Ladies Society for Promoting the Christian Education of the Females of India of the Free Church of Scotland.[32] Among the prominent Scottish scholar-missionaries who lived and wrote in Bombay and other parts of western India, and who were associated with these organizations were Drs. Sinclair Stevenson, John Wilson and Murray Mitchell.

These few notes and sample selections from the records of one organization should make it clear that historical studies on women's education in India and the place of missionary societies in Indian life must make use of the archives of this and other societies. Even though the Fifty-Year Rule is in effect for the archives in this library, for studies of women in India the earlier papers are undoubtedly by far the most important and the richest.

Methodist Missionary Society

The Methodist Missionary Society was established in 1817, although individual missionary work had begun around 1760. For South Asia, the MMS maintained mission stations in India and Ceylon and, according to Wainwright and Matthews' ***Guide***, it has extensive printed and manuscript records, "which are described in a number of inventories, and . . . are open to students" through the period ending fifty years ago. The minutes of the Women's Work Committee include, in one volume for 1858-68, the minutes of the first meeting of the Ladies' Committee for the Amelioration of the Condition of Women in Heathen Countries, Female Education, &c., and comprise 14 volumes for the period 1864-1932.[33]

In his directory, Collison notes that the MMS has "an extensive reference library [which] includes biographical, political, sociological, travel, religious and other works on Asia and the Middle East, and a valuable and extensive collection of archives [that] relates to Ceylon, India, Burma, China, and Hong Kong, from the beginning of the nineteenth century." He further states that nonconfidential sections of these records are open to research by bona fide scholars "thirty years after their dates"[34] (the discrepancy between the Fifty-Year Rule cited by Wainwright and Matthews and the thirty years referred to by Collison may be due to a change in the regulation during the years intervening between the two directories).[35]

Baptist Missionary Society

The Baptist Missionary Society was established in 1792 and began work in Bengal in 1793. Its missions have been primarily in northern and eastern India, as well as in Ceylon. The BMS is best known for its early members — William

Carey, William Ward, and Joshua Marshman — who served at Serampore in Bengal, translating the scriptures, preparing grammers and pioneering in developing printing presses for Indic scripts. Bombing destroyed some London records during World War II, but most survived, have now been sorted and inventoried, and are accessible under the Fifty-Year Rule. Among the BMS holdings are the minutes and agenda books of the Baptist Women's Missionary Association, 1867-1936, and its Indian "Zenana mission matters" for 1866-69.

Society of Friends

The library of the Society of Friends houses the records of the Friends Foreign Mission Association starting from 1860, which are chiefly concerned with medical and educational matters. The library also contains reports of the society's India Committee, which sponsored a school for girls in Hoshangabad, Central Provinces; papers of the India Conciliation Group (1931-50), led by Agatha Harrison and involving leading Quakers such as Hilda Cashmore and Kathleen Lonsdale; minute-books of the Social Purity Association, connected with Josephine Butler's Association for Moral and Social Hygiene through personal links and concerned with such matters as prostitution, white slavery, temperance and other problems associated with military cantonments in India; and complete sets of journals such as the ***British Friend***, the ***Bombay Guardian*** and ***Our Missions***. According to the librarian, "The library also contains private journals of Friends visiting India in which observations on women would surface."[36]

Presbyterian Church of England Overseas Missions Committee

The English Presbyterian mission established a station in the Rajshahi District of Bengal (now in Bangladesh) in 1862. Records exist for the Women's Missionary Association from 1904 to 1943, including minutes, committee records and a historical sketch of the WMA. Forbes reports that these materials are now deposited in the library of the School of Oriental and African Studies (SOAS) of the University of London, and may be consulted after securing written permission from the Council for World Mission in Westminster[37] (see below).

London Missionary Society

The archives of the London Missionary Society, founded in 1795, have been recently amalgamated with records of other missionary groups to form the archives of the Church World Mission, and the united records are now at SOAS, where they have been put onto microfiche by the Inter Documentation Company (IDC) of Zug, Switzerland. These valuable documents, including extensive Indian reports and correspondence as well as the more famous letters of David Livingstone from Africa, will now be available outside of England in libraries which purchase the IDC microform edition. The Center for Research Libraries in Chicago plans to acquire a set for the use of its members throughout North America.

Judging from the Wainwright and Matthews description, the LMS archives are very strong in letters and diaries from South India, both from the British Madras Presidency and the princely state of Travancore.[38] This is most likely to include a great deal of material on women.

This report has described some of the more important research materials for the study of South Asian women that are available in various libraries of the United Kingdom. Further collections of resources on this topic will surely come to light as researchers continue to investigate the many significant questions concerning the women of South Asia.

Addresses of Libraries Mentioned in Report

Women's Research and Resources Centre
27, Clerkenwell Close, London, E.C.1

India Office Library and Records
Orbit House, 197, Blackfriars Road, London, S.E.1

British Museum/Library
Great Russell Street, Bloomsbury, London, W.C.1

South Asian Archive at the Centre of South Asian Studies, University of Cambridge
Laundress Lane, Cambridge

Fawcett Society Library
City of London Polytechnic, Old Castle Street, London, E.1

United Society for the Propagation of the Gospel
15, Tufton Street, London, S.W.1

Church Missionary Society
157, Waterloo Road, London, S.W.1

Methodist Missionary Society
25, Marylebone Road, London, N.W.1

Baptist Missionary Society
93-97, Gloucester Place, London, W.1

Society of Friends
Friends House, Euston Road, London, N.W.1

Presbyterian Church of England Overseas Missions Committee
86, Tavistock Place, London, W.C.1

London Missionary Society
Livingstone House, 11, Carteret Street, London, S.W.1

School of Oriental and African Studies
University of London, London, W.C.1

*Maureen L.P. Patterson is Bibliographer and Head of the South Asian Collection of the Library, and Associate Professorial Lecturer in the Department of South Asian Languages and Civilizations, University of Chicago. A travel grant from the Committee on Southern Asian Studies of the University of Chicago aided her work in Britain.

[1]The most important published directories and general guides to these libraries and manuscript collections are: Robert Collison, comp., ***Directory of Libraries and Special Collections on Asia and North Africa*** (Hamden, Connecticut: Archon Books, 1970) 123p.; M.D. Wainwright and Noel Matthews, comps., ***A Guide to Western Manuscripts and Documents in the British Isles relating to South and South East Asia*** (London: Oxford University Press, 1965) 532p.; Mary Thatcher, comp. and ed., ***Cambridge South Asian Archive: Records of the British Period in South Asia relating to India, Pakistan, Ceylon, Burma, Nepal and Afghanistan held in the Centre of South Asian Studies, University of Cambridge*** (London: Mansell, 1973) 346p.; and J.D. Pearson, ed., ***South Asian Bibliography: A Handbook***

and Guide, comp. by the South Asia Library Group (Hassocks, Sussex: Harvester, 1979) 381p. (entry 5).

[2]Geraldine H. Forbes. "Libraries in England with Materials on South Asian Women," Ms., 1978, p.3.

[3]The Rani of Jhansi is a notable example in the 1850s of a woman forced by circumstances to engage in political activity. There are references to her in IOR:E/4 (Correspondence with India), IOR:F/4 (Board's Collections) and IOR:P (NWP Revenue Proceedings).

[4]For a general description of the classification scheme used by the India Office Records see J.C. Lancaster ***The India Office Records*** (archives vol.10, no. 43, Apr. 1970) and M.I. Moir ***Introduction to the Use of the Records*** (in press).

[5]Much of this material is duplicated in central government departmental records in India.

[6]After using this collection in 1978, Geraldine Forbes wrote: "Materials relating to women in the India Office were more extensive and of greater value than I had anticipated . . . . The private papers contain a wealth of information . . . . One should allocate a number of days to examine them. Much of this material takes time to use, but my experience suggests that it is time well spent." "Libraries in England," p.1.

[7]See J.M. Sims' "Official Publications to 1947" in J.D. Pearson, ed. ***South Asian Bibliography: A Handbook and Guide***, pp.73-79. While collections of the Parliamentary Papers exist in many American and other research libraries, Geraldine Forbes found them particularly easy to use in the IOL/R. "Libraries in England," p.1.

[8](London: His Majesty's Stationery Office, 1909) 194p. If what is wanted cannot be found through the use of this book, one may consult Sims' "Official Publications to 1947."

[9]Ibid., p.74.

[10]"Libraries in England," p.2.

[11]Sims, "Official Publications to 1947," p.75.

[12]Ibid., p.77.

[13]Ibid., pp.77-78.

[14]In view of these documents, Mary Thatcher writes: "Women of today may think they are free and liberated, adventurous and capable . . . . It is surely the case that Englishwomen in India (not to mention the lives of missionaries, which were probably even more adventurous) were just as liberated, just as adventurous and just as capable." She also notes that the experiences of many American educators and missionaries who also spent their lives in the service of another people in another country have yet to be recorded.

[15]"Libraries in England," p.1.

[16]Ibid.

[17]Ibid.

[18]Ibid., pp.2-3.

[19]Personal communication, September 1977.

[20]Visitors to missionary archives should make arrangements in advance with the appropriate offices to use the archives, since they are to a large extent in-house collections for busy, ongoing organizations. A letter, phone call or academic reference should open the doors to serious researchers. Copying facilities are rare, so old-fashioned note taking will be in order.

[21]Collison, *Directory of Libraries and Special Collections*, p.85.

[22]Wainwright and Matthews, *Guide to Western Manuscripts and Documents*, p.252.

[23]"Libraries in England," p.3.

[24]Personal communication, September 1977.

[25]Church of England Zenana Missionary Society, *Report* I (1880-81).

[26]Ibid. 2 (1881-82) p.11.

[27]Ibid., p.18.

[28]"The Use of Oriental Proverbs for Illustrating the Bible in Zenana Teaching" in *Indian Female Evangelist* 4 (1878) p.56.

[29]*Indian Female Evangelist*, vol.4.

[30]Ibid., 4 (1879) pp.203-6.

[31]Ibid., (Jan 1880) p.5.

[32]Ibid., I (1872).

[33]Wainwright and Matthews, *Guide to Western Manuscripts and Documents*, p.153.

[34]Collison further states that photocopying facilities are available at the MMS. *Directory of Libraries and Special Collections*, p.70.

[35]Unfortunately, I did not pay the MMS a personal visit in 1977.

[36]Personal communication, September 1977.

[37]"Libraries in England," p.4.

[38]Wainwright and Matthews, *Guide to Western Manuscripts and Documents*, p.152.

Indexes

Author Index

Abbas, Khwaja Ahmad, 1353, 1365, 2666
Abbasi, Nasreen, 4463
Abbott, John, 2040
'Abd al-Aḥad, 768
Abdul Ali, A.F.M., 769, 771
Abdullah, Tahrunnessa Ahmed, 2303, 3845-6, 3914
Abed, Ayesha, 3850
Aberle, David F., 194
Abeille, Mireille, 211
Abeyesooriya, Samson, 3096
Abhayaratne, O.E.R., 3057-9, 3111
Abidi, Syed Zaheer Hasan, 2772
Abū al-Faẕl ibn Mubārak, 727
Achar, M.R., 1849
Acharekar, M.R., 312
Acharya, Meena, 4554
Acworth, Harry Arbuthnot, 758
Adalene, M., 2276
Adam, Leonhard, 4524
Adam, William, 3630
Adil, Enver, 2505
Adnan, Shapan, 3906
Adyanthaya, N.K., 2163
Adranwala, T.K., 2411
Adult Education Development Board, 4489
Aery, Raj Rani, 4320
Afzal, Mohammad, 3860, 4433-4, 4438
Agarwal, A.K., 4179
Agarwal, Bina, 1755
Agarwal, H.C., 2153
Agarwal, J.S., 3514
Agarwal, R.C., 2308
Agarwal, S.K., 4287
Agarwala, Raj Kumari, 1872
Agarwala, S.N., 1661, 1851, 1963, 1901, 2442, 2477, 2494, 4080
Agency for International Development, 2300
Aggarwal, J.C., 2238
Aggarwal, Partap C., 4165
Agha, Sharkeshwari, 3976
Agnew, Vijay, 1644, 2552
Agnihotri, Harendra Kumar, 4057
Agnihotri, V., 2196
Agnihotri, Vidyadhar, 4310
Agrawal, Chandra P., 477, 1762, 2595, 2914, 4361, 4365
Agrawala, Raj Kumari, 2002
Agrawala, Vasudeva Sharana, 125, 389
Agrawala, V.S., 659
Ahluwalia, Kamla, 2164
Ahluwalia, M.L., 3995
Ahmad, Bashir, 2003
Ahmad, Imtiaz, 1990, 2552a
Ahmad, Khurshid, 2013
Ahmad, Mahbubuddin, 3865
Ahmad, Perveen, 3905
Ahmad, Shadbano, 4267
Ahmad, Shahran, 2835
Ahmad, Zeyauddin, 4201
Aḥmad-ul-'Umrī, 752
Ahmed, Anna Molka, 4509
Ahmed, Fatema, 3926
Ahmed, Ferozi, 1852
Ahmed, Imtiaz. *See* Ahmad, Imtiaz
Ahmed, Kazi Nasir-ud-Din, 2004
Ahmed, Mohiuddin, 3926
Ahmed, Razia Fasih, 2915
Ahmed, Shereen Aziz, 1711
Ahmed, Zeenat Rashid, 2398
Ahuja, Ram, 2437, 4315
Ahuja, S.K., 258
Aishwarya Rajya Laxmi Devi, Maharani of Nepal, 4562
Aitken, Annie, 3927
Aitken, R.H., 956
Aiyappan, A., 1995
Aiyappan, Parvathe, 3320
Aiyar, S. Krishnamurthi, 1181
Akhtar, Halida Hanum, 3935
Akhtar, Hamida, 3905
Akhtar, Jamila, 4427
Akhter, Roushan, 3853, 3888
Akhter, Saleem, 2918
Akkamahādēvi, 583-4
Akram, Muhammad, 2014
Alam, Bilquis A., 3896
Alam, Iqbal, 1853, 2446, 4439, 4463
Alamgir, Jalil, 3947
Alamgir, Susan Fuller, 3847
Alauddin, Talat K., 2301
Albers, A. Christina, 3701
Alexander, A., 3185
Alexander, Meena, 2710, 2832-4
Alexander, Mithrapuram K., 1354
Ali, Ameer, 107, 1768-70
Ali, Fahmida, 4483
Ali, S. Amjad, 2632
Allahakoon, A.W., 3026
Allen, Michael R., 4543-4
All-India Conference on Women, 1975, Trivandrum, 2564

All-India Federation of Educational Associations, 1044
All-India Women's Conference, 800, 2333-5
All-India Women's Conference. Cultural Section, 1045
All-India Women's Conference on Educational Reform, 1046
All Pakistan Women's Association, 1712, 2389-91, 2399-400
Almenas-Lipowsky, Angeles J., 2540
Alphonso-Karkala, John B., 478
Altekar, Anant Sadashiv, 46, 80, 212, 274, 302-3
AmaraSingham, Lorna Rhodes, 3093
Ambannavar, Jaipal P., 2138
Ambedkar, B.R., 413, 1182
Ambrose, Kay, 2589
Ameena Begam, 3332
Ament, G., 3473
American Ramabai Association, 3443
Amin, Rafia Manzurul, 2916
Amjad Ali, Zahida, 1713
Amrita Pritam, 4385-98
Amrit Kaur, Rajkumari, 1187, 1244, 1298, 2309-10, 2365
Anand, K., 1829, 4120, 4288
Anand, Mulk Raj, 33, 47, 313, 759, 2863
Anand, R.L., 1850
Anandamayi Ma, 2094-6
Anandkar, Piroj, 588
Anant, Santokh Singh, 2262
Anantha Krishna Iyer, L.K., 3147, 3236
Anderson, Emma Dean, 4032
Anderson, J.D., 3614
Anderson, Lily Strickland, 1140
Anderson, M.W., 4036
Andhra Mahila Sabha, 3314
Andhra Pradesh. Committee for International Women's Year, 3188
Andhra Pradesh. State Evaluation Committee, 3306, 3308, 3322-3
Andhra Pradesh. Women's Welfare Department, 3188
Andors, Ellen B., 4523-3a
Andrews, Charles Freer, 869
Andrews, Robert Hardy, 1344
Ansari, Dagmar, 4362
Ansari, Ghaus, 4091
Ansari, Khursheed A. Salam, 2392
Ansari, Umer, 1771
Āṇṭāḷ, 577-9
Anthony, D.J., 3095
Anuradha, 1662
Anwar, Seemin, 4458
Anwar, Shamim, 1772
Anwari, Khawaja Arshad Mubeen, 2015
Appadorai, Angadipuram, 1736
Appa Rao, 1188
Appasamy, Jaya, 2583
Appasamy, Paul, 1189
Apurvananda, Swami, 2063
Aravamudan, Gita, 3301
Archer, Mildred, 4343
Archer, William George, 687a, 4151, 4224, 4227, 4340
Ar Cy Dae / Romesh Chunder Dutt, 644
Aries, pseud., 2755. *See also* Dalal, Nergis
Ariyapala, Manikka Badaturu, 550
Armstrong, Ruth Gallup, 2989
Armstrong-Hopkins, Saleni, 1596-7
Arora, Jagdish, 1355
Arora, K.L., 2583
Arunachalam, M., 297, 523
Arundale, George S., 1442
Arya, Subhash C., 1946
Asaf Ali, Aruna, 1270, 1663
Asha, 283
Ashapurna Devi, 3803
Ashby, Lillian Luker, 4054
Ashk, Upendra Nath, 4399
Ashmore, Harriette, 4055
Ashok, 785
Ashraf, Asia, 3900
Ashraf, Mohammad, 706
Ashraf, Muhammad, 2028
Ashworth, M., 1047
Aslam, Muhammad, 2474
Asmar, Samir, 3104
Asmi, Saleem, 2596, 2610
Asnani, Shyam M., 2697, 2790, 2951
Assam. Directorate of Employment and Craftsman Training. State Employment Market Information Unit, 3781
Associated Country Women of the World, 2302
Association of Medical Women in India, 2412
Association of the All-Ceylon Women's Conference, Colombo, 2239
Association of Women's Institutes in Ceylon, 3109-9a
Asthana, Pratima, 889, 920
Aśvaghoṣa, 426
Athalye, Yasavant Vasudev, 3497
Athavale, Parvatibai, 3465
Atkinson, E.T., 3968
Atmaprana, Pravrajika, 1463
Auboyer, Jeannine, 48, 402
Aurobindo, Sri / Aurobindo Ghose, 2075
Auslander, Joseph, 2735
Avalon, Arthur. *See* Woodroffe, John George
Avinashilingam, T.S., 534
Azam, Ikram, 2235
Azeem, Anwer, 2919
Azhar Mohammad, 4438, 4499
Aziz, Wahida, 2226
Aziz Ahmad, 1773
Azmat, Tahera, 108
Azumi, Koya, 4553

Babar, Sarojini, 3531
Babb, Lawrence A., 4239-40
Bachchan, Teji, 2692
Bachman de Mello, Hedwig, 3587
Bader, Clarisse, 61
Badley, Mrs. M.A., 1105
Bagal, Jogesh Chandra, 1225, 3631-4
Bagchee, Moni, 1464
Bagchi, Josodhara, 2667
Bagchi, Probodh Chandra, 3747
Bagga, V., 1873
Bahadur, Umrao, 2864
Bahadurji, G.J., 1245
Bahiṇābāī, 589
Baig, Tara Ali, 831, 1326, 1381, 1664, 1737, 1984
Bajpai, P.C., 4133
Bajracharya, Purna Harsha, 4525
Bake, A.A., 117
Bal, Sharayu, 3545, 3550
Bal, Vidya, 2660
Balakrishna, Sitamraju, 3328
Balaram Iyer, T.G.S., 178
Balasubrahmanyam, K., 3245
Balasubramanian, C., 524
Baldwin, Olivia A., 1019

Balfour, Margaret Ida, 1106, 1180
Ballhatchet, Kenneth, 3376
Ballinger, Thomas O., 4568-9
Baloch, N.A., 2655
Baloch, S.K., 4435
Balse, Mayah, 2042, 2836
Baluch, Akhtar, 4508
Bandopadhyay, Biswanath, 4232
Bandyopadhyay, Asok, 4318
Bandyopadhyay, Pranab, 2690
Bandyopadhyay, Samaresh, 199
Banerjea, Jitendra Nath, 188, 390
Banerjea, Krishna Mohan, 3635
Banerjee, D., 3703, 3726
Banerjee, Gooroodass, 90
Banerjee, Gopa, 3790
Banerjee, Sachchidananda, 4318
Banerjee, Shyamananda, 2098
Banerji, Albion Rajkumar, 3656
Banerji, Brajendranath, 772-3, 777-9, 957, 3636
Banerji, O.N., 34
Banerji, Poresh Nath, 1035
Banerji, Projesh, 2653
Banerji, S.K., 725
Banerji, Sures Chandra, 346
Bang, B.G., 3765
Bangladesh Academy for Rural Development. Pilot Project in Family Planning, 3928
Bangladesh Academy for Rural Development. Women's Education and Home Development Programme, 3915
Bankey Behari, 601
Banningan, John A., 1205
Baptist Missionary Society. Women's Missionary Association, 1574
Baqai, Mohammad Sabihuddin, 4442, 4466
Bardhan, Amita, 1903, 4121
Bardis, Panos D., 2479, 3727
Barlow, Thomas Lambert, 4436
Barnes, Irene H., 1575-6
Barnett, Steve, 1986
Baroda. Committee on Hindu Women's Property Rights, 3427
Barot, Jyoti, 3505
Barr, Pat, 1425
Bartrum, Katherine Mary, 4010
Barua, B.K., 179, 670
Barua, Dipak Kumar, 427-8
Barua, Rabindra Bijoy, 433
Basana Devi, 370
Basavarajappa, K.G., 1902
Baskara Rao, N., 3329
Basu, Anath Nath, 602, 1048
Basu, Anjana, 2710
Basu, Aparna, 1226
Basu, Baman Das, 1049
Basu, Jogiraj, 371
Basu, Krishna, 1752
Basu, Manoje, 3819
Basu, M.N., 3714-5
Basu, Nripendra Kumer, 230, 255
Basu, Sita, 2219
Basu, Tarapada, 3820
Batley, Dorothea Sibella, 1215
Batlivala, Soli S., 1230
Baveja, Malik Ram, 104
Bawa, Ahamadu, 3034
Bawany, Zeb, 3901
Baybasthapana Shangsad Limited, 3929-30
Bazaz, Prem Nath, 35, 593
Beals, Alan R., 3189
Beals, Rose Fairbank, 1107
Bean, Lee L., 1911, 2130, 2506, 4433, 4495
Bean, Susan S., 3228
Beane, Wendell Charles, 154
Beatty, Jerome, 3164
Bebarta, Prafulla Chandra, 1897, 4289
Becher, Augusta Emily Prinsep, 1493
Beck, Brenda E.F., 3190, 3241
Bedekar, Malatibai, 3483
Bedi, Freda, 2311, 2598
Bedi, Rajinder Singh, 2920-1, 4400
Bedi, Sohinder Singh, 4323
Beech, Mary Jane Higdon, 3730, 3782
Begam Akhtar, 2618-20
Bell, Eva Mary, 1164
Bell, Robert R., 4605
Belliappa, N. Meena, 2698, 2818, 2952
Belok, Michael, 2565
Belvalgidad, M.I., 1902
Bengali Academy, 3951
Bennett, Amelia, 4011
Bennett, Lynn, 4515, 4528, 4530-0a, 4541
Benson, R., 3969
Berkeley-Hill, Owen, 1240
Berreman, Gerald D., 2546, 4058, 4096, 4114
Besant, Annie (Wood), 36, 921, 1442-4
Besterman, Theodore, 1445
Beteille, Andre, 1645
Bethune Society, 3637
Beven, Edwin, 3047
Beveridge, Annette S., 720, 726
Bhagavat Sinh Jee / Bhagavat Simhaji, Maharaja of Gondal, 459
Bhagvat, A.R., 3588
Bhagwat, Durga N., 437, 3491
Bhagwati, Jagdish N., 2554
Bhaiji, 2099
Bhalla, P.N., 774
Bhanawat, Mahendra, 2646
Bhandari, Adya Charan Raj, 4563
Bhandari, Arvind, 2256
Bhandarkar, Devadatta Ramakrishna, 286, 372
Bhansali, Kamalini, 3554
Bharadwaj, Aruna, 4251
Bharadwaj, S.K., 62
Bharadwaja, E., 3282
Bharata, 509
Bharatia, L.K., 2191
Bhardwaj, K.S., 4290
Bharucha, Perin, 2837
Bhasin, Kamla, 1738, 1755, 2263
Bhate, G.C., 3395
Bhate, Vaijayanti, 1964, 3570
Bhatia, J.C., 4291-2
Bhatia, Kanta, 1
Bhatia, Krishnan, 1356
Bhatia, Pratima, 1829a
Bhatia, S., 1108
Bhatnagar, Manju, 1931, 4192
Bhatnagar, N.K., 2490
Bhatnagar, Ram Ratan, 2722
Bhatnagar, Vatsala, 4088
Bhatt, Ela R., 2303
Bhatt, Neela, 2354
Bhattacharjee, Surovi, 1842
Bhattacharya, Bhabani, 2865
Bhattacharya, K.K., 1327
Bhattacharya, Pasupati. *See* Pasupati
Bhattacharya, Sibesh, 328
Bhattacharyya, Asutosh, 163-4, 3766-7
Bhattacharyya, Narendra Nath, 126, 131-2, 138, 196-7, 231, 287, 2033
Bhattacharyya, Panchanan, 19

Bhattacharyya, Sivaprasad, 456
Bhatti, A.D., 2506, 4495
Bhatti, F.M., 4610
Bhatty, Idrack, 2219
Bhatty, Zarina, 1755, 1774, 2219, 4071
Bhaumik, Kumud Nath, 1168
Bhavnani, Enakshi, 329-30
Bhawalkar, Vanamala, 401
Bhende, Asha A., 2443, 2480
Bhise, Saroj, 2838
Bhojani, Mahomedalibhoy C., 1961
Bhouraskar, D.M., 2499
Bhowmick, Prabodh Kumar, 3748, 3768, 3793
Bhowmik, Atrayee, 3714-5
Bhowmik, Kanai Lal, 3716, 4596
Bhownaggree, Mancherjee M., 1050
Bilimoria, Najoo, 2312
Billimoria, N.M., 364
Billimoria, Mrs. R.N., 3584
Billings, Martin H., 4252
Billington, Mary Frances, 836, 1405
Bilquees, Faiz, 4458
Bindra, P.S., 1883
Binford, Mira Reym, 2060, 3293
Birjis, Zahida, 4467
Bisen, Malini, 754
Bista, Khem Bahadur, 4542
Biswas, Dilip Kumar, 964
Biswas, Suddhendu, 3509
Biswas, Usha, 1051
Blackwell, Frederick Warn, 277, 2699, 4370
Blackwell, Mary Lilian, 1598
Blaise, Clark, 2828
Blake, Robert Rogers, 4305
Blazé, Ray, 3012, 3125
Bleakley, Ethel, 3674-6
Bloomfield, Maurice, 214, 278
Boaz, G.D., 279
Bodding, Paul Olaf, 4078
Bode, Mabel, 442
Bodley, Rachel, 3418
Boga, Russi, 736
Bogue, Donald J., 2500
Bokil, Kamala, 4180
Bombay (Presidency), 3380-1
Bombay (Presidency). Educational Department, 3404
Bombay (Presidency). Prostitution Committee, 3422
Bombay (Presidency). Women's Council, 3369
Bombay (Province). Education and Industries Department, 3552
Bond, E.C., 3677
Bondrey, Razia, 1714, 4513
Bondurant, Joan V., 1271
Bonnerjea, Biren, 2643
Booth, Mary Warburton, 1599-1603
Booth, Winifred, 3174
Borges, B.C., 2227
Bose, A.B., 4158
Bose, Amlendu, 2723
Bose, Anima, 1299, 3803-4
Bose, Ashish, 2303, 2444
Bose, Kheroth M., 1053
Bose, Koylaschunder, 3638
Bose, Krishna, 3667
Bose, Kunjabihari, 94
Bose, Moni Mohan, 1054
Bose, Nemai Sadhan, 3602
Bose, P.K., 1272
Bose, Pramatha Nath, 818, 959, 996, 1055
Bose, Shib Chunder, 3697
Boserup, Ester, 2140
Bos-Kunst, Emmy, 4505
Boulding, Elise, 2445
Boulger, Demetrius, 960
Bowers, Faubion, 2599
Bradbury, James, 837
Brahme, Sulabha, 3542
Braithwaite, L., 4607
Bramsen, Michèle Bo, 2307
Brayne, Frank Lugard, 3984
Brey, Kathleen Healy, 1929
Bright, Jagat S., 1320
Brij Bhushan, Jamila, 316, 321, 1338
Brinda, Maharani of Kapurthala, 832
Brittain, Vera Mary, 1345
Brittan, Harriette G., 1216, 1604, 3663
Brockway, K. Nora, 3133-5
Brown, Carol A., 2578
Brown, Cheever Mackenzie, 632
Brown, Edith M., 1109-10, 3977-8
Brown, James Howard, 1605
Brown, W. Norman, 227, 391, 694
Bruce, Clara Harding, 3405
Bruce, Judith, 2526
Bryce, Lucy Winifred, 1556, 4081
Buck, H.C., 2292
Bullock Workman, Fanny, 4576-9, 4581-2
Bullough, Vern L., 247, 2423
Burdette, Miriam R., 3678
Burling, Robbins, 4588
Burn, R., 3999
Burnell, A.C., 273
Burnes, Alexander, 3382
Burney, Naushaba, 1715, 2938
Burr, Agnes Rush, 838
Burton, Richard Francis, 4417
Burway, Ramakrishna Ganesh, 1190
Bushby, Henry Jeffreys, 3957
Butler, Clementina, 1606, 3430-1
Butler, Iris, 1479
Butler, Marguerite L., 839, 1056
Buvinić, Mayra, 2307

Cadell, Patrick, 3999
Cakravartī, Mukunda Rāma, 645
Calcott, Lady Maria (Dundas) Graham. *See* Graham, Maria
Camerini, Michael, 2060, 3293
Campbell, A., 4097
Campbell, Mary (Frazer). *See* Monkland, Mrs.
Campbell, Mary Jane, 840, 4032-4
Caplan, Patricia, 4539
Caraka, 460
Carlaw, Raymond W., 3931
Carmichael, Amy Wilson. *See* Wilson-Carmichael, Amy
Carmody, Denise Lardner, 74
Carpenter, Joseph Estlin, 1434
Carpenter, Mary, 1057, 1435-6
Carstairs, G. Morris, 4152-3, 4228
Carter, Lillian, 2979
Carter, Thomas, 3474
Carus-Wilson, Mrs. Ashley / Mary Louisa Georgiana (Petrie) Carus-Wilson, 4403
Case, Mrs. / Adelaide Teague Case, 4012
Castillo, Gelia T., 3013
Caton, Annie Rose, 841, 890-1, 999, 1177
Cattell, Milly, 1148
Cavalier, A.R., 4035
Cave Browne, John, 3383
Central Provinces and Berar. Female Education Committee, 1058

Ceylon. Department of Census and Statistics, 3060
Chaddah, R.P., 2700
Chaddha, Promila, 4293
Chahil, Renu, 2491
Chaina Mall, 963, 2122
Chakladar, Haran Chandra, 373, 511
Chakrabarty, Tapo Nath, 551
Chakrabortty, Krishna, 3783-4
Chakraborty, Usha, 3603-4
Chakravarti, Chandra, 232
Chakravarti, Chintaharan, 638a, 3769
Chakravarti, Prabhat Chandra, 118
Chakravarti, Tripurari, 479
Chakravartti, R., 1894
Chakravartty, Renu, 1246, 2016, 2336, 2563
Chakravarty, Basudha, 1465
Chakravarty, Kumaresh, 2578
Chakravarty, Syam Sunder, 870
Chakravorty, Shanti, 2366, 4253
Chambard, Jean-Luc, 4098
Chamberlain, Mrs. W.I., 1577
Chand, Malini, 2303
Chand, Tek, 1859
Chandar, Krishan, 4371-2
Chandarvaker, Pushker, 3535
Chandavarkar, Ganesh Lakshman, 3451
Chander, Parkash, 2553
Chandna, R.C., 4254
Chandna, Suman, 339
Chandola, Sudha, 4241
Chandra, Jagdish, 316a, 336, 2648
Chandra, Moti. *See* Moti Chandra
Chandra, Pramod, 638
Chandra, Sudhir, 2044
Chandrakant, L.S., 2219
Chandran, Ramesh, 2424
Chandran, Victoria M., 2566
Chandrasekaran, C., 2511, 3567, 3717-8
Chandrasekhar, Sripati, 1925, 1936-7, 2492, 2494, 3330, 3568
Chandrasekharan, K., 2600
Chandrasekharan, K.R., 2773
Chapman, Edith, 4601
Chapman, Mrs. E.F. / Georgiana Charlotte Clive Bayley Chapman, 1287
Chapman, John Alexander, 871
Chapman, Priscilla, 3639
Chappell, Jennie, 3432
Chatfield, Jean, 3347
Chatterjee, A.K., 403
Chatterjee, Bankim Chandra, 1059, 3821-3
Chatterjee, Bishwa Bandhu, 4283
Chatterjee, Heramba, 466-7
Chatterjee, Kamala, 1165
Chatterjee, Krishna Nath, 207
Chatterjee, Margaret, 2710
Chatterjee, Mary, 4181
Chatterjee, Santa, 3805
Chatterjee, Santosh Kumar, 3148
Chatterjee, Sita, 3805
Chatterji, Basu, 2011
Chatterji, N., 4589
Chatterji, Saral Kumar, 1938
Chatterji, Sarat Chandra, 3824-7
Chatterji, Tapan Mohan, 3749
Chattopadhyay, Aparna, 374, 400, 675-7
Chattopadhyay, P.K., 1895
Chattopadhyay, Tushar, 3770
Chattopadhyaya, Kamaladevi, 801, 892, 1228, 1247-8, 1665, 1691, 2313, 2567, 2649, 2652. *See also* Kamaladevi
Chattopadhyaya, Sarat Chandra. *See* Chatterji, Sarat Chandra
Chaubay, Ganesh, 4242
Chaube, Ramghalib, 1996
Chaudhari, D.H., 1877, 1879
Chaudhary, Mrs. A.R., 4486
Chaudhary, Muhammad Anwar, 2017
Chaudhary, Pawan, 2543
Chaudhary, Roop L., 304
Chaudhary, Zafar Hussain, 2018
Chaudhry, Mohammad Iqbal, 4496
Chaudhuri, Buddhadeb, 3757
Chaudhuri, Jatindra Bimal, 288-93, 347, 537, 680
Chaudhuri, K.K., 3714
Chaudhuri, Nani Madhab, 365, 392, 2123
Chaudhuri, Nirad C., 1666, 2133
Chaudhuri, Roma, 49, 81, 295, 347, 1752
Chaudhuri, S., 2413
Chaudhury, Rafiqul Huda, 2303, 3861-2, 3864, 3897
Chauhan, P.S., 2774
Chauhan, Vijay, 4366
Chawdhari, T.P.S., 4255
Chawner, Esther, 4055a
Chemburkar, Jaya, 665
Chen, Lincoln C., 3863, 3867
Chen, Marty, 3850
Chettur, Usha, 2183
Chhabra, R., 4304
Chhabra, Rami, 2660, 4076
Chhaya, Shakti, 2032
Chimnabai II, Maharani of Baroda, 923, 936
Chinnatamby, Siva, 3061
Chintamani, C. Yajneswara, 924
Chiplunkar, Gopal Mahadev, 1060
Chipp, Sylvia A., 2401-2
Chirantanananda, Swami, 3283
Chisolm, Mrs., 1489
Chitale, Venu, 2839
Chitalia, Karsandas Jagjivandas, 3370
Chitnis, Suma, 2380
Chitre, Dilip, 2045, 2612
Chitty, Simon Casie, 354
Choksi, Mithan, 897, 1061, 1357, 3373
Choldin, Harvey M., 3933, 4294
Chopra, Pran Nath, 715
Chaudhrani, Sarala Devi, 1249
Choudhuri, A.S., 2507
Choudhuri, Narendra Nath, 155
Choudhuri, Niren, 4148
Choudhury, A.K.M., 3866
Choudhury, Moqbul A., 3942
Chowdhury, Nuimuddin, 3864
Chowdhury, Suprova, 3640
Chowdhury, Uma, 4092
Christian Medical Association of India, 1557
Christlieb, Marie Luise, 3175, 3179
Chugtai, Ismat, 2887, 2895-900
Chunder, Pratap Chandra, 514
Church, Mrs. Ross. *See* Marryat, Florence
Churchill, Mrs. George / Matilda (Faulkner) Churchill, 3176
Church Missionary Society, 1578
Church of England Zenana Missionary Society, 1579-81
Church of Scotland, 1589
Clapp, Estelle Barnes, 2979a
Clark, Marjorie, 4601
Clark, Mary Mead, 3679
Clark, Muriel, 3433
Clark, Robert, 4404

Clark, T.W., 646
Clarke, Flora, 1607
Clarke, Maureen, 1608
Claus, Peter J., 3286
Clerk, Alice M. (Frere). *See* Frere, Alice M.
Clough, Margaret Morley, 3002
Cobb, Betsey, 1339
Cockburn, W., 2041
Coelho, Marcel Anthony Francis, 842
Colebrooke, H.T., 222
Collet, Sophia Dobson, 964
Condict, Alice Byram, 3979
Conklin, George H., 3255-6
Cook, Nilla Cram, 1494
Cooke, H.R., 3381
Coomaraswamy, Ananda Kentish, 159, 189, 695, 728, 819
Coomaraswamy, Ethel, 2994
Cooper, Elizabeth, 843, 1149
Coopland, Mrs. R.M., 4013
Cooray, G.L., 3003
Cormack, John, 3384
Cormack, Margaret, 1813-4, 2264
Corner, Caroline / Caroline Corner-Ohlmus, 3008
Correia, A.C.G. da Silva, 3423
Costa Benedict, 2425
Cotes, Sara Jeanette (Duncan). *See* Duncan, Sara Jeanette
Cotton, H.E.A., 790
Cottrell, Ann Baker, 2987
Coulson, N.J., 2019-20
Cousins, James Henry, 872, 1446, 1477, 2724
Cousins, Margaret E., 893, 1250, 1382, 1477, 3653
Cowan, Minna Galbraith, 1062
Craske, M. Edith, 873
Crawford, C.W., 3475
Crawford, E.A., 3014
Crishna, Seetha, 4611
Croley, H.T., 3868
Crooke, William, 248, 281, 2124, 2930, 4104
Curjel, Dagmar F., 3654

D., A. / Mrs. A. Deane, 791, 844
Dabholkar, Venu, 3543
Dabrera, A.L.J. Croos, 3048
Da Cunha, J. Gerson, 792
Dadachanji, Faredun K., 3371
Daftary, Sharayu, 2206a
DaGama, A., 1180
Daggett, Mrs. L.H., 1582
Dahya, Zaynab, 4612
Dalal, Nergis, 2754, 2756-8. *See also* Aries
Dall, Caroline Healey, 3419
Damle, Y.B., 1930
Dāmodaragupta, 681
Damodara Menon, Leela, 2381
Dandekar, Kumudini, 1854, 1898, 2459, 2501, 3518, 3569-70
Dandiya, C.K., 4069
Dang, Satyapal, 4256
Dange, A.S., 4281
Daniels, Shouri, 2840
Dar, Rita, 1352
Dar, S.N., 317
Darling, Malcolm Lyall, 4419-20
Das, Bhuban M., 3704
Das, Frieda Hauswirth, 1539-40. *See also* Hauswirth, Frieda
Das, Harihar, 2712-3
Das, Kamala, 2808-13, 2583, 3356-7
Das, Kunja Bihari, 3737
Das, Manmatha Nath, 3622, 3961-2
Das, Nitai Chandra, 3223
Das, P., 3715
Das, Parimal, 2367
Das, Priya Bala, 3704
Das, Rajani Kanta, 1166
Das, R.M., 468
Das, Sisir Kumar, 3738
Das, Sudhendu Kumar, 119
Das, Sudhir Ranjan, 515, 3750, 3874-5
Das, Veena, 1667, 1830, 1972-3, 1985, 4081a, 4166
Das Gupta, Charu Chandra, 337-8
Dasgupta, Jyotiprova, 1063
Dasgupta, Kalpana, 12
Dasgupta, Manashi, 1752
Dasgupta, Mary Ann, 2701, 2710, 2976-7
Dasgupta, N.K., 1466
Das Gupta, Pranab Kumar, 2947
Das Gupta, Rajatananda, 3761
Das Gupta, Shashi Bhusan, 139
Dasgupta, Shibani, 2660
Dash, Bhagwan, 221
Dass, Jarmani, 833
Dass, Rakesh Bhan, 833
Dastur, Aloo J., 101, 1300-1
Datar, Chaya, 2576
Datta, Jatindra Mohan, 1273, 3789
Datta, Kalikinkar, 538, 552, 925
Datta, Nalinee, 3705-6
Davane, G.V., 149
Davidson, Charles James C., 965
Davidson, C.I., 1609
Davidson, Flora Marion, 4405
Davies, A., 4583
Dawson, Edwin Collas, 1610
Dawson, J.E., 1406
Dayananda, James Y., 2866
D'Cunha, S., 2980
De, Sushil Kumar, 233-4, 375, 3641
De Alwis, James, 3036
Deane, Mrs. A. *See* D., A.
Deb, Mahesh Chundra, 3605
Debi, Bharati, 1752
Debnath, Dhirendra, 111
Deepak, Awant Kaur, 4070
de Kleen, Tyra, 2601
de La Valette, John, 3963
Dell, David, 4363
Dengal, Anna, 1111
Denning, Margaret Beahm, 844a, 1419
Denny, J.K.H., 926
Deolalkar, P.V., 1882
Derrett, John Duncan Martin, 37-8, 200, 1191, 1206, 1831, 2530, 3252-4
Desai, Anita, 2691, 2819-24
Desai, A.R., 894
Desai, Arvindrai N., 1962
Desai, Bhadra, 1358
Desai, Chitra, 3549
Desai, Devangana, 696
Desai, Kumud, 1874-5, 1884
Desai, M.M., 2314
Desai, Neera, 570, 895, 2244, 2657, 3372, 3554
Desai, Padma, 2554
Desai, P.B., 2460-1
Desai, S.K., 2766
De Saram, C., 443
de Sélincourt, Agnes, 896
Deshmukh, Durgabai, 2179, 2198, 2261, 2315
Deshmukh, Rajguru, 3510

Deshpande, C., 3506
Deshpande, Dinkar Yashwant, 2569
Deshpande, Gauri, 2841
Deshpande, Kamalabai, 539
Deshpande, Kusumavati, 3595
Deshpande, Vinayak A., 2470
Deshpande, V.V., 259
Deshpande, Y.K., 783
De Silva, C.M. Austin, 3037-9
De Silva, Kingsley, 3070
de Silva, W.A., 172
Desjardins, Arnaud, 2100
De Souza, Alfred, 1669, 1739
de Souza, Eunice, 2953
Deulgaonkar, Sulochana, 927
Devadas, Rajammal P., 1947, 2029, 2368
Devanandan, Paul David, 1974
Devarāja, 682-3
Devgan, A.K., 2513
Devi, Aksaya Kumari, 376
Devi, Charulata, 874
Devi, Indira, 619
Devi, Lila, 4554
Devi, Ritha, 3791
Devi, Sushila, 820
Devi, Sushil Malti, 296
de Viri, Anne, 2990
Dewar, Phebe Rutherford, 1612
De Zoete, Beryl, 2602, 3149
D'Gruyther, W.J., 3958
Dhal, Upendra Nath, 160
Dhamija, Jasleen, 2192, 2652
Dhammadinna, Sister, 3094
Dhanapala, D.B., 3116
Dhanjal, Beryl, 4613
Dhar, Shailendranath, 504
Dharma, P.C., 377, 474, 489
Dharmaraj, Robin, 3952
Dhavalikar, M.K., 165-6
Dhillon, H.S., 2493-4
Dhindsa, Ragwinder Kaur, 1791
Dhirasekara, Jothiya, 414
Dhungana, Punya Prabha Devi, 4554
Diehl, Carl Gustav, 167
Dikshit, Ratnamayidevi, 348
Dimmitt, Marjorie A., 2842, 4278
Dimock, Edward C., Jr., 622-3, 647-8, 3827a
Dissanaike, A., 3064
Diver, Maud / Katherine Helen Maud (Marshall) Diver, 1407, 1480, 1523-29, 4414
Divya, Ambika Prasad, 4373
Diwakar, R.R., 378
Diwaker, R.R., 1302
Dixit, Asha, 4259
Dixit, Ramesh C., 1815
Dixit, S.C., 565
Dixon, Ruth Bronson, 2193-4, 3029
Doctor, Geeta, 3553
Doig, Desmond, 2981
Dongerkery, Kamala Sunderrao, 322, 1383, 2650-2, 2931, 2939
Dongre, Rajas Krishnarao, 3434
Doraiswami, S., 2283, 2315a
Downie, Annie Hershey, 3178
Dowson, John, 712
Drieberg, Trevor, 1359
Driver, Edwin E., 3511
D'Souza, Anthony A., 2134
D'Souza, S.M., 3935
D'Souza, Victor S., 2034, 2141-2, 3237
Dube, Leela, 1646, 1975, 3261, 4134
Dube, Shyama C., 1670, 3191, 4089
Duberly, Mrs. Henry / Frances Isabella (Locke) Duberly, 4014
Duberman, Lucile, 4553
Dubey, Bhagwant Rao, 4159
Dubey, Dinesh Chandra, 1903, 2513, 4121, 4294
Dudley, Rosemary J., 140
Duff, Alexander, 1065
Duff, Mrs. Grant, 3130
Dufferin, Harriot / Hariot Georgina (Hamilton) Hamilton-Temple-Blackwood, Marchioness of Dufferin and Ava, 1112-3, 1481
Duggal, K.S., 2583
Dulai, Surjit Singh, 4398
Dumont, Louis, 1823, 1976, 3207, 4099
Duncan, Sara Jeanette / Sara Jeanette (Duncan) Cotes, 1541
Durai, Mrs. H. Gnana, 3245
Durdin-Robertson, Lawrence, 143
Durga, S.A., 1797
Durrani, Fazal Karim Khan, 1066
Dustoor, Phiroze Edulji, 2725
Dutt, Govin Chunder, 2715
Dutt, Guru Saday, 1384
Dutt, Kalpana, 3668
Dutt, K. Guru, 393
Dutt, Manmatha Nath, 20
Dutt, Mohendra Nath, 802
Dutt, Nalinaksha, 415
Dutt, N.K., 223
Dutt, Prabha, 2660
Dutt, Romesh Chunder. *See* Ar Cy Dae
Dutt, Ruby, 397
Dutt, Saroj Nalini, 3606
Dutt, Sukumar, 429, 434
Dutt, Toru, 2710, 2714-7
Duza, Mohammed Badrud, 1904
Dwarkadas, Kanji, 1395, 3546
Dwivedi, Amar Nath, 2718
Dyer, A. Saunders, 780
Dyer, Helen S., 3435-6, 3476
Dymock, W., 3150
Dyson, Ketaki Kushari, 1426, 2710

Eastman, Alvan Clark, 697
Eden, Emily, 1427-30
Edwardes, Stephen Meredyth, 249, 987
Eglar, Zekiye, 4421
Ehrenfels, Umar Rolf von, 192-3, 1802, 2035-9, 2143, 3262
Eichinger Ferro-Luzzi, Gabriella, 3203-4, 3208, 3229-30
Ekambaram, C.R., 2219
El-Badry, M.A., 3512
Elder, Joseph, 2060, 3293
Ellickson, Jean, 3848
Elliot, H.M., 712
Elmore, Wilbur Theodore, 3287
Elwin, Verrier, 1803, 3759, 4082, 4135
Elwood, Mrs. Colonel / Anne Katherine Curteis Elwood, 1482
Emery, Gladys Winifred, 4036
Engineer, Miss, 3373
Epstein, Scarlett, 3273, 3907
Erikson, Joan, 3536
Erlbeck, Ruth, 2316
Esquer, A., 1070
Evangelical National Society in Sweden, 1613
Everett, Jana Genevieve Matson, 1251-2
Evola, Julius, 127

F., F.E., 845
Fabri, Charles Louis, 318

Falk, Nancy, 415a, 480
Fallaci, Oriana, 1725
Fallon, L., 1614
Fane, Hannah, 82
Farani, Merajuddin, 4449
Faridi, Tazeen, 1716, 2393
Farmer, B.H., 8
Farooki, Nazratun Naeem, 2932
Farooqi, Hafiz Abbadullah, 730, 738
Farooqi, Vimla, 50
Farouk, A., 2303
Faruki, Kemal A., 2021
Fawcett, Fred, 3150, 3247, 3274, 3288
Fawcett, Millicent Garrett, 1020
Feldman, Shelley, 3887
Felton, Monica, 3200
Fernandes, J.M., 4628
Fernando, Dallas F.S., 3030
Fernando, G.P.S., 3107
Fernando, P.T.M., 3031
Fernando, Siromi, 2706
Fernando, Sylvia E.C., 3097-8, 3103
Field, Harry Hubert, 875
Filliozat, Jean, 579
Finner, Stephen L., 4163
Fisher, Frederick Bahn, 928
Fisher, Marguerite J., 2265
Fisher, Marlene, 2867
Fisher, Welthy Honsinger, 2982-3, 4570
Fitzroy, Yvonne, 1483
Fleming, Daniel Johnson, 1071, 3161, 3980
Fletcher, Grace Nies, 4571
Flint, Marcha Prottas, 4083
Foley, Caroline A. / Caroline Augusta (Foley) Rhys Davids, 443
Foll, C.V., 3707
Fonseca, Mabel B., 2005, 3507, 3519
Forbes, Geraldine H., 1254-5, 1274, 2339, 3669, 3671
Forbes, Jehangir Cursetji, 1000-1
Fordyce, Mrs., 3185
Fordyce, John, 3185
Foucaux, Marie. *See* Summer, Mary
Foxe, Barbara, 1467
Franda, Marcus F., 1727
Franks, Horace George, 1114
Fraser, Donald, 1431
Frater, Judy, 3591
Frazer, Heather T., 1728
Freed, Ruth S., 4122, 4229, 4243
Freed, Stanley A., 4122, 4229, 4243
French, Francesca, 3981
Frere, Alice M. / Alice M. (Frere) Clerk, 3009
Friedlander, Eva, 3772
Fruzzetti, Lina Maria, 1986, 3731-2
Fuchs, Stephen, 4167
Fuller, Christopher J., 3263
Fuller, Mrs. Marcus B. / Jenny Frow Fuller, 1558
Fuller, Mary Lucia Bierce, 3437, 3483a, 3490, 3532, 3589-90
Fürer-Haimendorf, Christoph von, 1976, 4516-7, 4540
Futehally, Zeenuth, 2843

Gadgil, D.R., 2166
Gadgil, Gangadhar, 3596
Gaige, Frederick H., 4560
Gajendragadkar, K.B., 1192
Gajendragadkar, P.B., 1207
G.A. Khan, Khudeja, 1401
Galpin, C.A., 3040
Gambhirananda, Swami, 2063a
Ganai, Amarendra, 3773
Ganapati, R., 2613
Gandhi, Ambalal Bhikhabhai, 2022
Gandhi, Indira, 1360-1
Gandhi, Manubehn Jaysukhlal, 1303-4
Gandhi, Mohandas Karamchand / Mahatma Gandhi, 1305-9, 1320-1, 1323
Gandhi, Raj S., 260, 3525
Gangoly, Ordhendra C., 721
Gangrade, K.D., 2514, 2531, 4182-3
Ganguli, J.M., 1410
Ganguli, Kalyan Kumar, 3876
Ganguli, Prabhat Chandra, 964
Ganguli, Tarak Nath, 3828
Ganguly, D.C., 83, 553
Ganguly, H.C., 3788
Ganguly, Narendranath, 967
Ganhar, Janki Nath, 180
Gani, Amna, 4468
Gardezi, Hassan Nawaz, 4497-8
Gardiner, G., 1424
Garg, B.M., 1804
Garg, R.S., 760
Garg, S., 4121
Garga, B.D., 2636
Garza, Joseph M., 3295
Gauba, Kanhaya Lal, 876
Gauri Ma, 2116
Gautam, K., 469
Gayatri Devi, Maharani of Jaipur, 834, 4625
Gedge, Evelyn Clara, 897
Gemini, Paul, 4590
George, Aleyamma, 1752, 2495, 2578
George, M., 2369
George, Molly Kutty, 3224
George, M.V., 3717
Gérard, Renée, 3882, 3916
Germain, Adrienne, 3908
Germon, Maria Vincent Garratt, 4015
Ghaffar, Sayeda, 3869
Ghanananda, Swami, 284, 411-2, 2064, 2117
Gharpure, Jagannath Raghunath, 1193
Ghimire, Durga, 2303, 4554.
Ghosal, Mrs. / Svarna Kumari Devi Ghosal, 3806-10
Ghosal, Samir, 3751
Ghose, Aurobindo. *See* Aurobindo, Sri
Ghose, Grish Chunder, 3655
Ghose, Lotika, 898, 3647
Ghosh, B.N., 3231
Ghosh, Chitra, 1752
Ghosh, Deva Prasad, 314
Ghosh, Molina, 4090
Ghosh, Saral C., 320
Ghosh, Satyavrata, 1229
Ghosh, Shanti, 1949
Ghosha, Pratapachandra, 3774
Ghoshal, U.N., 554, 639
Ghulam, Muhammed, 2403
Ghulam Ali, Anis, 2945
Ghurye, Govind Sadashiv, 318a, 1932, 3484, 3488
Gibson, B.D., 3643
Gibson, Julia Roberts, 846
Gideon, Helen, 4136-41
Gidumal, Dayaram / Dayaram Gidumal Shahani, 822, 899, 3396
Gidwani, N.N., 2, 2265a
Gill, Harjeet Singh, 4084
Gill, Pritam Singh, 112

Giri, Raghunath, 655
Giri, Varahagiri Venkata, 2167
Gisbert, P., 3485
Gist, Noel P., 1832
Gladstone, Soloman W.E., 404
Glover, Jessie R., 4537
Godakumbura, Chandra, 555
Godden, Jon, 1530
Godden, Rumer / Margaret Rumer Godden, 1530-6, 3670
Gode, P.K., 501
Goetz, Hermann, 604
Gokhale, A.R., 3374
Gokhale, Aravind Vishu, 3597
Gokhale, Gopal Krishna, 1072
Gokhale, Neil, 3462
Gokhale, Ram, 3462
Gokulananthan, Karakat Sankaran, 1950
Goldberg, Helen, 3240
Goldstein, Melvyn C., 4529
Goldstein, Rhoda L., 3309-11
Gollock, Georgina Anne, 1495
Gombrich, Richard, 633, 3082
Gonda, Jan, 235, 398
Gooneratne, Yasmine, 2844
Goonesekere, R.K.W., 3049-50
Goonetilleke, William, 3015, 3027, 3065
Goonewardene, E.T., 2059
Gopal, K., 4233
Gopal, Y.S., 3226
Gopalakrishnan, M.S., 133
Gopalakrishnan, T.P., 1880
Gopalakrishna Naidu, G.T., 298
Gopalan, Gopalan V., 3533
Gopinatha Rao, T.A., 261
Gordon, John E., 4137-41, 4163, 4286, 4318a
Gordon-Cumming, Constance Frederica, 3010
Gore, M.S., 1987, 4184, 4202
Gorwaney, Naintara, 4268
Gosal, Gurdev Singh, 2462
Gosha, Jogesachandra, 821
Gosse, Edmund W., 2716, 2732
Goswami, Kewal, 2868
Goswami, M.C., 3712, 4591
Goswami, Praphulladatta, 3794
Gough, E. Kathleen, 194, 3209, 3214, 3220, 3238
Gould, Harold A., 4172
Gould, Ketayun H., 4295
Gour, Hari Singh, 1208, 1939
Govinda, Lama, 75
Gowan, Edna, 1073
Goyal, M.M.L., 2482
Goyal, R.P., 1855
Gracey, Mrs. J.T. / Annie Ryder Gracey, 1584, 1615
Graham, Maria / Lady Maria (Dundas) Graham Calcott, 793
Gray, Hester Alice, 929, 1074, 3407
Gray, Maxwell, pseud. / Mary Gleed Tuttiett, 1543
Gray, Mrs. R.M., 900, 1275
Great Britain. Indian Franchise Committee, 1276
Great Britain. Indian Statutory Commission, 1075
Great Britain. Parliament. House of Commons, 930
Green, Thomas Leslie, 3074
Greenfield, M. Rose, 4037
Gregson, Fanny / Fanny (Gregson) Liesching, 3004
Gribble, James Dunning Baker, 745
Griffiths, Percival, 968
Griffiths, William, 3943
Grimwood, Ethel St. Clair, 4601a
Grover, Anil, 2199
Gründler, O., 1616
Gubhaju, B.B., 4559
Guha, Phulrenu, 901
Guha, Uma, 4210, 4296
Guharaj, Aysha, 4297
Guinness, Lucy E., 1617
Gulati, J.S., 2228
Gulati, Leela, 2144-5, 2188, 2578, 3215, 3302
Gulati, Subhash Chander, 1856, 2463
Gulbadan Begam, 726
Gunawardana, A.M.T., 3104
Gunawardhana, Theja, 3016
Gupta, A.M., 3708
Gupta, A.N., 2726
Gupta, Anand Swarup, 150-1
Gupta, A.R., 1763
Gupta, Bimalendu, 1951
Gupta, B.L., 4313
Gupta, B.R., 2475
Gupta, Giri Raj, 4168
Gupta, L.N., 1671
Gupta, Modusoodun, 1896
Gupta, Nagendranath, 3829
Gupta, Nolini Kanta, 2076
Gupta, Parmeshwari Lal, 168
Gupta, Premlata, 2494
Gupta, Rabindra Nath, 4311
Gupta, Ramesh, 60, 1845
Gupta, Rameshwar, 2727
Gupta, Satish, 2726
Gupta, S.C., 4297
Gupta, Shakti M., 2845
Gupta, Shiva Kumar, 4093
Gupta, S.L., 51
Gupta, Subodh Bhushan, 1447
Gupta, Suniti Bala, 481-2
Gupte, Balkrishna Atmaram, 76, 3498
Gupte, Shankar Vinayak, 2023
Gurupriya Devi, 2102
Guthrie, Anne, 1346

H., G. / George Huddleston, 781
Haas, V., 1965
Habib, Mohammad, 707
Habibullah, A.B.M., 712a
Habibullah, Attia, 1150, 2846
Hagman, Lorri, 508
Hajrah Begam, 1277
Halangoda, John Ashfield, 3051
Haldane, Julia, 4016
Halder, Ajit, 2468
Hamadani, Naseem, 2406
Hamid, S.M. Abdul, 2050
Hamid, T., 2293
Hamid Ali, Mrs., 1115
Hamid Ali, Shareefah, 1178
Hamidullah, Zaib-un-Nissa. *See* Zaib-un-Nissa Hamidullah
Hanbury, C., 4407
Handiqui, Krishnakanta, 379
Handler, Esther, 673
Handoo, Chandra Kumari, 412, 594
Handoo, Jawaharlal, 362
Hanks, Jane (Richardson). *See* Richardson, Jane
Hans, Pushpa, 4279
Hansen, Kathryn, 4368

Haq, Isar-ul, 1793
Haqqi, S.A.H., 4115
Haque, Mozammel, 105
Harband, Beatrice M., 3162, 3177
Hardee, J. Gilbert, 2508, 4499
Hardgrave, Robert L., 3334
Hare, Augustus John Cuthbert, 1484
Harle, James C., 649
Harper, Edward B., 3275-6
Harper, Mary McKibbin. *See* McKibbin-Harper, Mary
Harrex, S.C., 2775
Harris, E.F., 1559
Harris, Katherine, 4017
Harrison, Minnie (Hastings), 2995
Hart, George L., 525-7
Hartley, Lois, 1537, 2954
Hartog, Lady / Mabel Hélène (Kisch) Hartog, 1076, 1241, 1729
Hartog, Philip, 1077
Harvard, William Martin, 1618
Hasan, S. Nurul, 731
Hashmi, M. Iqbal, 4434
Hashmi, Nasiruddin, 2888
Hashmi, Salima, 4474
Hashmi, Sultan S., 2446, 2474
Hassan, Md. Nazmul, 3884
Hastie, M. Lissa, 3438
Hate, Chandrakala Anandrao, 1764, 2494, 3486, 3551
Hauswirth, Frieda, 902, 1501. *See also* Das, Frieda Hauswirth
Hayes, Marie Elizabeth, 4038
Hazra, Rajendra Chandra, 500, 656, 664, 671
Heera, Perviz, 2219
Hehir, Patrick, 1116
Heimsath, Charles H., 84, 903, 1021
Hein, Norvin, 4246
Hemachandra, Narayana, 21
Hendley, Thomas Holbein, 323
Hennessy, Maurice, 781a
Henriques, Fernando, 250
Henry, Edward Oscar, 4105, 4325
Henry, Mary Roblee, 4522
Hershman, Paul, 4208
Hessney, Richard C., 536
Heston, Winifred, 3477
Hiatt, Lester R., 3083
Hiebert, Paul G., 3281
Higginbottom, Ethel Cody, 1619-20
Hildburgh, W.L., 3066
Hima Akhlaq Husain, 1775
Hinchcliffe, Doreen, 1848, 2006
Hingne Stree Shikshan Samstha, 3452-3
Hinkley, Edyth, 3179
Hinton, Mrs. W.H., 3478
Hiranandani, Popti, 4511-2
Hitchcock, John T., 4063
Hitchcock, Olive, 2996
Hivale, Shamrao, 4185
Hoggan, Frances Elizabeth, 1117
Holcomb, Helen Harriet (Howe), 4039-42
Holcomb, James Foote, 4042
Honigmann, John Joseph, 4422-3
Hooja, Swarn Lata, 4112-3
Hopkins, Edward Washburn, 483
Hopkins, Saleni Armstrong. *See* Armstrong-Hopkins, Saleni
Hoque, Naseem, 3917
Horner, Isaline Blew, 416
Hosain, Attia, 2749-50
Hoskins, Mrs. Robert / Charlotte Lewis (Roundey) Hoskins, 4043
Hossain, Monowar, 3909
Hossain, T., 3932
Houghton, Frank, 3169
Huber, Douglas H., 3934
Huddleston, George. *See* H., G.
Hughes-Hallett, Florence, 1621
Hull, E.G., 4408
Human, Grace, 3000
Hume, Elizabeth C., 904
Humphrey, Mrs. E.J., 1288, 1622, 4018
Hunashal, S.M., 585
Hunter, William Wilson, 1036, 1118
Huntsworth, C. Elizabeth, 3110
Huq, Jahanara, 3905, 3909
Husain, A.F.A., 3898
Husain, Imtiazuddin, 4433
Husain, Ishrat Zafar, 1905, 2447
Husain, M. Arshad, 1396
Husain, Mazhar, 2427
Husain, Mirza Kazim, 1887
Husain, Saliha Abid, 2889
Husain, Shahanara, 556-7
Husain, Sheikh Abrar, 4094
Husain, Yusuf Jamal, 1843
Hussain, Asaf, 4479
Hussain, Iqbalunnisa, 828, 2847
Hussain, Salma Tasadduque, 1401
Huston, Perdita, 3017-8
Hutheesing, Krishna Nehru, 313, 1343, 1362, 1377. *See also* Nehru, Krishna
Hyde, H.B., 794
Hyder, Qurratulain, 1717, 1776, 2905-8, 2614, 2638
Hymer, Esther W., 2394

Ibrahim Kunju, A.P., 784
Ievers, R.W., 3044
Ikram Azam, R.M., 2634
Ikramullah, Shaista Akhtar Banu (Suhrawardy), 1397, 1401, 1718-9, 1844, 2890-2
Imtiaz Ali, Surraya, 2940
Inayatullah, Attiya, 1906, 4498
Inden, Ronald B., 42, 3733
India. Age of Consent Committee, 1022-3
India. Bureau of Education, 1079
India. Central Advisory Board of Education. Women's Education Committee, 1080
India. Hindu Law Committee, 1209
India. Home Department, 1002, 3624
India. Laws, Statutes, etc., 1168-70, 1194
India (Dominion). Laws, Statutes, etc., 1858
India (Dominion). University Education Commission, 2266
India (Republic). All India Handicrafts Board, 3303
India (Republic). Census Commission, 1926
India (Republic). Central Bureau of Correctional Services, 2428
India (Republic). Central Social Welfare Board, 2031
India (Republic). Committee for Review and Evaluation of the Programme of "Condensed Courses of Education of Adult Women," 2278
India (Republic). Committee of Differentiation of Curricula for Boys and Girls, 2257
India (Republic). Committee on Adult Education Programmes for Women, 2279
India (Republic). Committee on the Status of Women in India, 1647, 1672, 1704, 1760, 1977, 2168, 2251, 2316a, 2409, 2448, 2532, 2547, 2658

India (Republic). Committee to Look into the Causes for Lack of Public Support Particularly in Rural Areas for Girls' Education and to Enlist Public Cooperation, 2252
India (Republic). Committee to Study the Question of Legalisation of Abortion, 1940
India (Republic). Directorate of National Sample Survey, 1907, 2449-51, 2517
India (Republic). Directorate of Nonformal (Adult) Education, 2280
India (Republic). Education Commission, 2253
India (Republic). Information Services, 2555
India (Republic). Labour Bureau, 2169-71, 2200
India (Republic). Laws, Statutes, etc., 1849-50, 1859-60, 1876-84
India (Republic). Maternal and Child Health Advisory Committee (1968). Targets for Maternal and Child Health Services in Community Health Programmes Sub-committee (1969), 2415
India (Republic). Ministry of Community Development and Cooperation, 2370
India (Republic). Ministry of Education, 2294
India (Republic). Ministry of Education. National Committee on Women's Education, 2254
India (Republic). Ministry of Health and Family Planning. Department of Family Planning, 2503
India (Republic). Office of the Registrar General, 1869, 2452, 2464
India (Republic). Planning Commission, 2146, 2533
India (Republic). Planning, Research, Evaluation and Monitoring Division, 2453
India (Republic). Social and Moral Hygiene Advisory Committee, 2429
India (Republic). Vital Statistics Division, 1908
India (Republic). Women's Welfare Division, 2356
Indian Cooperative Union, 2221
Indian Council of Medical Research, 2201
Indian Council of Social Science Research, 1648
Indian Council of Social Science Research. Advisory Committee on Women's Studies, 2317
Indian National Congress. All India Congress Committee. All India Congress Women's Convention (1960), 1742
Indian National Congress. All India Congress Committee. Women's Department, 2556, 2560-1
Indra, V.V., 63
Indradeva, Shrirama, 39, 64, 128
Ingham, Kenneth, 933
Inglis, Julia Selina, 4019
Inverarity, Rosalind Harriet Maria (Wallace-Dunlop), 4056
Irshad Ali, A.N.M., 3734
Ishvani, 3465a
Islam, Mahmuda, 3899, 3905
Islam, Meherunnessa, 3885, 3916
Islam, Rushidan, 3906
Islam, Shamima, 2303, 3902, 3905, 3918
Israil, Md., 4225
Ivory, James, 1997
Jackson, Abraham Valentine Williams, 262
Jackson, Alice F., 4020
Jackson, Barbara (Ward). *See* Ward, Barbara E.
Jackson, Elva, 3180
Jackson, Monica, 4584-5
Jacob-Pandian, E.T., 3290
Jacobs, Sue-Ellen, 13
Jacobson, Dorothy Ann / Doranne Jacobson, 40, 2318, 4059, 4173-4, 4209, 4211-4, 4248
Jacolliot, Louis, 41, 848-9
Jafarey, S.A., 2508
Ja'far Sharif, 3205
Jaffer, Mehru, 4249
Jafri, Roquyya, 4430
Jafri, S.N.A., 275
Jagannathan, Maithily, 2615
Jahan, Mehraj, 3916
Jahan, Rounaq, 2303, 2385, 3849, 3945
Jahan, Roushan, 355, 3811, 3905
Jahānārā, 737
Jahina, Mehru B., 2518
Jai Lal, 1885
Jain, Anrudh K., 4304
Jain, Devaki, 73, 1650, 2303, 3559
Jain, Jagdish Chandra, 349, 455
Jain, Jasbir, 2776, 2791
Jain, Kamta Prasad, 97
Jain, P.K., 1861
Jain, S.P., 1909-10, 2458
Jain, Sunita, 2848
Jai Prakash, 2172, 2177
Jalal, Khurshid, 3905, 3946
Jambagi, Sadanand, 3233
Jambagi, Sulochana, 3233
Jamdar, Dilip, 2644, 4277
Jameelah, Maryam / Margaret Marcus, 1777
James, Edwin Oliver, 134
James, Ralph C., 3547
James, V., 3210
Jan, Tariq Sajjad, 4438
Janah, Sunil, 1674
Janakiraman, T., 3348
Jasbhai, Manibhai, 3409
Jayadeva (author of ***Gītagovinda***), 624
Jayadeva (author of ***Ratimañjarī***), 684
Jayakanthan, 3349
Jayakar, M.R., 1004
Jayakar, Pupul, 2641, 4341
Jayakar, R.B.K., 2430
Jayal, Shakambari, 475
Jayamani, Kumar N., 2371
Jayawardana, Sita, 3123
Jayawardena, Chandra, 4606, 4608-9
Jayawardena, H.A., 3052
Jayawardena, Junius Richard, 3053
Jayawardena, Kumari, 3114
Jayewardene, C.H.S., 3057-9, 3111
Jayaweera, Swarna, 3019
Jeffery, Mary Pauline, 3165-6
Jeffery, Patricia M., 4215, 4614
Jehangir, Lady Cowasji, 3421
Jensen, Irene Khin Khin, 1347
Jex-Blake, Sophia, 1119
Jha, Akhileshwar, 1765, 2869
Jha, Amarnath, 2729
Jha, Makhan, 181
Jha, Manoranjan, 864
Jha, Ratnadhar, 4342
Jhabvala, Renana, 4269
Jhabvala, Ruth Prawer, 1997, 2955-67
Jhaveri, Vithalbhai K., 1230
Jhirad, J., 1120-1

Jilani, Ghulam, 2289
Jinarajadasa, Curuppumullage, 1448
Jinnah, Fatima, 2395
John, K.T., 1668
John, Mariam, 3239
John Samuel, Gnana Siromoni, 3350
Johnson, Lewis, 3681
Johnson, Rani, 2946
Jolly, Julius, 470
Jones, Clifford, 3278, 3289
Jones, L. Bevan, 1778
Jones, Rex Lee, 4526, 4531-3
Jones, Shirley Kurz, 4532-3
Jones, Violet Stanford, 1778
Jorapur, P.B., 2147, 3296
Jordan-Horstmann, Monika, 4326
Josef, Byron, 3067
Joshi, Angur Baba, 4535, 4555
Joshi, Dina Nath, 2173
Joshi, Hari Ram, 2103
Joshi, Heather, 2158
Joshi, J.R., 169-70, 190
Joshi, Purushottam Balkrishna, 263
Julia, Deaconess, 4049
Jumunabai, J., 2281
Junghare, Indira Y., 3537, 3591
Junnarkar, P.B., 2066
Jussawala, D.C., 3466

K., V.V., 1037
Kabir, Humayun, 2284
Kabir, Khushi, 3850
Kabiraj, Shibnarayan, 1892
Kakar, Sudhir, 1952
Kakar, V.N., 2870
Kakati, Bani Kanta, 182
Kalakdina, Margaret, 1816
Kala Rani, 4260-1
Kale, B.D., 1862, 2288
Kalhan, Promilla, 1378, 1675, 1705
Kalhaṇa, 693
Kalyāṇamalla, 686
Kalyanikutty Amma, Kalamandalum, 3365
Kamal, Mehr, 1720
Kamal, Shoukat, 2295
Kamalā, 680
Kamaladevi, 1227, 1310, 1340. *See also* Chattopadhyaya, Kamaladevi
Kamaliah, K.C., 571
Kamat, A.R., 1966, 2257a
Kamleshwar, 2692
Kamrunnessa Begam, 3873
Kanan Devi, Ma Mahajnana Shri Guru, 3760
Kanapathipillai, Kandasamy, 3084
Kanbargi, Ramesh, 3225
Kane, Pandurang Vaman, 201, 220, 224-5, 246, 251, 264, 285, 305-6.
Kanitkar, Tara, 2443
Kannan, C.T., 1824
Kannan, Lakshmi, 2710
Kannangara, Imogen, 3099
Kannoo Mal, Lala, 236, 699
Kantawala, S.G., 394
Kapadia, Hiralal Rasikdas, 98
Kapadia, Kanailal Motilal, 202
Kapadia, Kundanika, 3600
Kapali Sastri, T.V., 2077
Kapil, Krishan K., 2519
Kapoor, Indira, 2416
Kapoor, Jyotsana, 4236
Kapoor, P.N., 1927
Kapur, Geeta, 2637
Kapur, Promilla, 1676, 1798, 1978, 2159-60, 2184, 2386, 2431, 4262, 4270
Kapur, Rama, 4263
Kapur, Veena, 1799
Kar, R.K., 4597
Kara, Maniben, 2179
Karambelkar, V.W., 640
Karanjia, Rustom Khurshedji, 1365
Karanth, K.S., 3361
Karim, Mehtab S., 4439
Karkal, Malini, 1863, 1941, 3493, 3513
Karkaria, Bachi J., 3487, 3953
Karkaria, Rustomji Pestonji, 3463
Karkhanis, G.G., 3151
Karlekar, Kalyani, 1752
Karlekar, Malavika, 2660
Kurmanadham, K., 2873
Karn, N.E., 1218
Karnataka. Women and Children's Welfare Department, 3316
Karney, E.S., 3005
Karun Krishna, 629
Karve, Anandibai, 3454
Karve, B.D., 3561
Karve, Dhondo Keshav, 1084, 3410, 3455-9
Karve, Irawati, 1677, 3460, 3467, 3534
Kashyap, S.S., 4282
Katona-Apte, Judit, 2417
Katti, A.P., 3331
Katzenstein, Mary Fainsod, 1278
Kaul, Hari Krishen, 2078
Kaul, Inge, 1730, 4203
Kaul, Jayalal / Jai Lal Kaul, 595
Kaul, Mani, 1795
Kaul, T.N., 4284
Kayal, Akshay Kumar, 3795
Kaye, John William, 934
Kazi, Khawar, 4464
Keeble, U., 2893
Keegan, W., 782
Keeler, Orrell, 3682
Kelkar, Manohar Purushottam, 3508
Kelman, Janet Harvey, 1171
Kennedy, Beth C., 1817
Kennedy, Richard Hartley, 3378
Kerala. Bureau of Economics and Statistics, 3192a
Kesavanarayana, B., 3130a
Keshaviah, M., 540
Keshawaji, Hari, 823, 1085
Khan, Abdul Majid, 1348
Khan, Akhter Hameed, 2396, 2528
Khan, A.M., 3933
Khan, Atiqur Rahman, 3934-7
Khan, Ivy, 2342
Khan, Lilian, 4298, 4300-1
Khan, Masihur Rahman, 1911
Khan, Mazhar ul Haq, 2050a
Khan, Mir Alim, 2871
Khan, Mohammad Israil, 152
Khan, Mohammad Shamsul Islam, 3910
Khan, Obaidullah, 2303
Khan, Razia, 2849
Khan, W.A., 4500
Khandavala, Karl J., 2639
Khandwala, Vidyut, 2219, 2240, 2275
Khanna, Adarsh, 4188
Khanna, Girija, 1678, 1812
Khanna, Prem Nath, 1833, 2007
Khare, Ravindra S., 2515, 4169, 4186
Khatana, R.P., 4443
Khatri, A.A., 3516

Khatun, Saleha, 3886
Khatun, Sharifa, 2303, 3873
Khazan Chand, 237
Kher, B.G., 590
Khera, P.N., 1279
Khipple, R.L., 1349
Khokar, Mohan, 3762
Khosla, Gopal Das, 1366, 1679, 1800, 2494, 2583, 2872, 4327
Khullar, S., 1895
Khurshid Ara Begam, 1401
Khwaja, B.A., 4216
Kibe, M.V., 761-2
Kidwai, Mushir Hosain, Shaikh of Gadia, 77, 1005, 1151
Kim, N.I., 2153
Kincaid, Charles Augustus, 22, 4000-1
Kincaid, Dennis, 1411
Kinch, Arne, 3112
King, Mrs. Robert Moss / E. Augusta King, 1485
King, Ursula, 1761
Kingscote, Georgina, 3136
Kini, N.G.S., 3585
Kinikar, Roy, 1749
Kinnaird, Emily, 1432-3
Kinsley, David R., 156-7
Kirkpatrick, Joanna, 1752, 2702, 3850a, 4319
Kirtane, Sumati, 3538
Kirthisinghe, Buddhadasa P., 2997
Kirtikar, K.R., 3517
Kishore, Brij, 757
Kleinman, David S., 1912
Knight, Florence M., 1623
Knight, Henry, 746
Knighton, William, 3986-7
Knipe, David, 2061
Knowles-Foster, Frances G., 3988
Kogekar, S.V., 2557
Kohli, Devindra, 2814-6
Kohli, Suresh, 2583
Kokkoka, 687-7a, 692
Kolenda, Pauline Mahar, 1979-80
Kolhatkar, Wamanrao M., 3397
Kooij, K.R. van, 672
Kopf, David, 3660-1
Korson, J. Henry, 4444-7, 4470
Kosambi, D.D., 1913
Koshy, T.A., 3327
Kothari, Sunil, 245, 3792
Koul, Anand, 596-7, 600
Kramer, Anthony, 2662
Kramrisch, Stella, 144, 2642, 3877
Kripalani, Krishna, 1311
Kripalani, Sucheta, 1385-6
Krippendorf, Sultana, 3903
Krishan, Y., 700
Krishna, Gopal, 1231
Krishnamurthy, K.G., 2483
Krishnamurti, K.S., 1825
Krishnamurti, Y.G., 228
Krishna Rao, Angara Venkata, 2792
Krishna Rao, H., 3332
Krishna Sastry, L.S.R., 2968
Krishna Sastri, Hoskote, 145
Krishnasvami Aiyangar, S., 265
Krishnaswami Aiyar, C.V., 1086
Kuder, Katherine, 3567
Kugler, Anna S., 3146
Kulkarni, G.V., 1024
Kulkarni, V.B., 747, 775, 4002
Kumar, Arvind, 490
Kumar, Jainendra, 4374
Kumar, Pramod, 4312
Kumar, Prem, 4375
Kumara Guru, pseud. / Chandrasekhar Subrahmanya Ayyar, 3242
Kumarappa, J.M., 1172
Kundu, C.L., 4280
Kuper, Hilda, 4602
Kureishi, M., 2258
Kurian, George Thomas, 1981-2, 3216-7, 3239, 3257
Kurup, R.S., 1914
Kusika, pseud. / Appav-aiya Madhav-Aiya, 2874. *See also* Madhaviah, Appavaiya
Kutty, A.R., 3264
Kutty, Krishna, 3265

L., M., 3965
Lago, Mary M., 3830
Lahiri, Subrata, 1953-4
Lajpat Rai, Lala, 52, 878
Lakhanpal, Chandravati, 1038
Lakhanpal, Sarv Krishna, 14
Lakshmana, Ganpat, 935
Lakshmi, C.S., 3337, 3351
Lal / Lal Dyad / Lalīśvarī / Lallā, 598-9
Lal, J.N., 1698
Lal, K.S., 722
Lal, Lakshmi, 785
Lal, Lakshmi Narain, 2693
Lal, Mohan, 2285
Lal, P., 2703
Lal, R.K., 742
Lalitha, N.V., 2320
Lall, Amrit, 2465
Lall, Kesar, 4534
Lalye, P.G., 666
Lam, M. Tata, 1006
Lambat, Ismail A., 3494
Lambert, William W., 4155
Lang, John, 4003
Langdon, Samuel, 2998
Lankester, Dorthea, 2343
Lankester, Grace, 2343
Lateef, Shahida, 1755, 2570
Latham, S.F., 1624
Latif, Khalid, 2902
Latifi, Danial, 1886
Laurent, Emile, 252
Law, Bimala Churn, 418-20, 446
Law, Narendra Nath, 708, 1087
Lawrence, Lady / Rosamond Napier Lawrence, 1486
Lawrence, James Henry, 3266
Laxminarayan, N., 3153
Layard, John, 3248
Lazarus, Hilda, 1122
Leach, Edmund Ronald, 3028, 3045
League of Nations. Commission of Enquiry into Traffic in Women and Children in the East, 1142
Lean, Florence (Marryat) Church. *See* Marryat, Florence
Learmonth, A.T.A., 7-8
Leboyer, Frederick, 1955
Lee, Ada, 2111
Leeson, Francis, 238
Le Grand, Jacob, 3387
Leitch, Margaret W., 3006
Leitch, Mary, 3006
Leith, M.L., 1560

Le Mesurier, C.J.R., 3085
Leonard, John G., 3132
Leonard, Karen Isaksen, 1731, 3258
Leonowens, Anna Hariette (Crawford), 1487
Leslie, Mary E., 3663a, 3682a
Leuchtag, Erika, 4572
Levertov, Denise, 623
Levy, Harold, 2024
Liaquat Ali Khan, Ra'ana / Begam Liaquat Ali Khan, 1721, 2403
Lichtenstadter, Ilse, 1780
Liesching, Fanny (Gregson). *See* Gregson, Fanny
Lindenbaum, Shirley, 3851-2, 3859, 3919
Lipski, Alexander, 2104-5
Lloyd, Harriette, 850
Login, Edith Dalhousie, 1488
Lohani, Mohan, 4520
Long, James, 3644, 3796
Loomis, Charles P., 1794
Lorenzen, David N., 641
Lovett, Richard, 1561
Lovett, Verney H., 969
Lowe, Clara M.S., 1625
Lowe, John, 1562
Luschinsky, Mildred Stroop, 4061, 4204
Lushington, Charles, 3607
Luthra, Bimla, 1341
Lutyens, Emily, 1496
Lutzker, Edythe, 3479
Lytle, Elizabeth, 15

M., C.M. / Clara M. Miner, 1497
M., S., 1437
Macauliffe, M., 606
Macbeth, Madge, 1398
McCandless, Boyd R., 4483
McCarthy, Florence E., 2303, 3852a-3, 3887-8, 3920-1
McCreery, John L., 307
McDougall, Eleanor, 905, 1088-9, 3137-8
MacFarlane, Eileen W. Earlanson, 3193
Machwe, Prabhakar, 2583, 2694
Mackay, Ernest, 366
MacKay, Jean Sinclair, 851
McKenzie, Aline, 3904
MacKenzie, Mrs. Colin / Helen (Douglas) MacKenzie, 4021, 4044-5
McKibbin-Harper, Mary / Mary (McKibbin) Harper, 1123-5
Macleod, Anne C. / Anne Campbell (Macleod) Wilson, 1421, 4046-7
MacMinn, Edwin, 1219
MacMunn, George, 4022
McNair, John Frederick, 4436
McNeill, Ian, 1948
Macnicol, Margaret Grant Campbell, 360
Macnicol, Nicol, 3439
Macy, Joanna Rogers, 453
Madan, Atam Prakash, 308
Madan, Lajwanti, 607
Madan, Triloki Nath, 1988, 4448
Madhava, Anand, 1887
Madhav-Aiya, Appav-aiya. *See* Kusika
Madhavan, Shantha, 3211
Madhavananda, Swami, 23
Madhaviah, Appavaiya, 3352. *See also* Kusika
Madras School of Social Work, 3297
Mahadevan, Meera, 4367
Mahadevan, T.M.P., 580
Mahadeva Sastri, Alladi, 203
Mahajan, Amarjit, 4271
Mahalaksmivala, Cavasji Dhanjibhai, 3411
Mahanta, Shyamali, 4597
Mahapatra, Piyushkanti, 99
Mahar, James Michael, 4175
Maharani of Baroda. *See* Chimnabai II, Maharani of Baroda
Maharashtra. Committee to Examine the Problems Facing Women Employees in Government Service, 3548
Mahawalatenne, S.D., 3032
Mahindra, Indira, 2571
Mahindra, Santosh Kumari, 4318
Mahīpati, 591-2, 608
Mahmood, Hameeduddin, 2668
Mahmood, Shaukat, 2025
Mahmood, Tahir, 2026, 2529
Mahmud, Satnam, 2303
Mahtab Bijay Chand, 3608
Mahtab, Nazmunnessa, 3905
Mair, J.H., 1195
Maitland, Julia Charlotte, 3181
Maitreyi Devi, 3812
Maity, Pradyot Kumar, 171, 3723, 3740
Maity, Sachindra Kumar, 405
Majmudar, Manjulal R., 558, 650, 661-2, 3592
Majumdar, A.K., 243
Majumdar, Bimanbehari, 3831
Majumdar, Chandra, 23
Majumdar, Dhirendra Nath, 1983, 3870, 4116-7, 4299, 4591
Majumdar, Lila, 1680, 3657
Majumdar, Ramesh Chandra, 23, 53, 65, 937, 1468, 4004
Majumdar, S., 1369
Malabari, Behramji Merwanji, 1002, 3396, 3398
Malakar, Chittaranjan, 1864, 3721
Malden, W.W.S., 3005
Malhari Rao, Ş., 3139
Malhotra, L.K., 2616
Malhotra, Madan Lal, 2730, 2793
Malhotra, Prabha, 4300-1
Malik, Amita, 2296
Malik, Ijaz Ilahi, 2008
Malik, M., 2520
Malik, Vijay, 2427
Malleson, G.B., 23a
Mamdani, Mahmood, 4302
Mandelbaum, David Goodman, 1818, 1899, 1915
Mane, Vasudha, 3598-8a
Mangahas, Anna F., 115
Mangeshkar, Lata, 605, 2622
Mangudkar, M.P., 1182
Manickam, J.T., 518
Manickam, Valliappa Subramanium, 528
Manickavasagam, M.E., 529
Manjusri, L.T.P., 3086
Mankekar, Kamala, 1681
Manmohan Kaur, 1232-3, 1449
Mann, R.S., 4072
Mannan, Muhammad Abdul, 3938
Manohar, Sujita, 2544
Manorama Bai, H., 2136
Manto, Saadat Hasan, 2922-3
Manton, Jo, 1438
Manu, 471
Mappilaparambil, Annie, 2185
Marcus, Margaret. *See* Jameelah, Maryam
Marga Institute, 3110a
Marglin, Frédérique Apffel, 3763
Markandaya, Kamala, pseud. / Kamala (Purnaiya) Taylor, 2777-84
Marker, Aban, 16
Marriott, McKim, 42

Marryat, Florence / Mrs. Ross Church / Florence (Marryat) Church Lean, 1413
Marshall, Henry, 2999
Marshall, John, 367
Marshall, John F., 4303
Martelli, E., 1152, 1173
Martin, Mary E.R., 3645
Martius-von Harder, Gudrun, 3889-90
Marulasiddaiah, Hirekumbalagunte Mutt, 3234
Marwah, Mala, 2584
Masani, Mehra, 1706
Masani, Shakuntala, 1707
Masani, Zareer, 1367
Mascarenhas, Marie M., 2516
Maschmann, Melita, 2106
Masud-ul-Hasan, 109
Matheson, Sylvia A., 4424, 4437
Mathew, Anna, 3218
Mathur, A.S., 4313
Mathur, J.C., 4343
Mathur, Manorama, 2222
Mathur, P.R.G., 3277
Mathur, Ramesh, 85
Mathur, Shanta, 4154
Mathur, Yaduvansh Bahadur, 2248
Matthews, David John, 356
Maudoodi, Abul 'Ala, 1153, 1183
Mayhew, Arthur Innes, 1090, 1259
Mayo, Katherine, 866-8, 1007, 1025
Mazuchelli, Nina Elizabeth, 4573
Mazumdar, Amiya Kumar, 1469
Mazumdar, Ammu Menon, 1312
Mazumdar, Lakshmi, 2345
Mazumdar, Shudha, 3671
Mazumdar, Vina, 86, 938, 1651, 1682, 1708, 2241, 2303-4, 2548, 2660
Meer, Fatima, 4603-4
Meer Hassan Ali, Mrs. B., 4062
Meerwarth-Levina, Ludmila, 172
Meghani, J.K., 3499
Mehra, B.N., 2436
Mehra, Pramila, 2934
Mehta, Aban B., 3548a
Mehta, B.H., 2372
Mehta, Chandralekha, 1352
Mehta, Hansa Manubhai, 361, 1008, 1280, 2242
Mehta, H.S., 3571
Mehta, Makrand J., 3388
Mehta, Perin Ḥ., 2219
Mehta, Rama, 1683, 2009, 2267, 2764-5, 4217-8
Mehta, Ramanlal V., 1196
Mehta, Rustam J., 340
Mehta, Sarojini, 631
Mehta, Shakuntala, 2244
Mehta, S.S., 215, 3500-1
Mehta, Sushila, 2268
Mehta, Swarnjit, 2155
Mehta, Usha, 1301, 1388, 2558
Mehta, Vinod, 2663
Mehta, V.V., 1091
Mencher, Joan P., 3240, 3267-8
Menon, C. Achyutha, 3291
Menon, Lakshmi Nandan, 803, 906, 1143, 1234, 1684, 2275, 2494, 2549
Menon Marath, S., 2875
Merchant, Kanchanlal Tribhovandas, 3520
La Mère. *See* The Mother
Meyer, Johann Jakob, 476
Mhatre, Sharayu, 3562-3
Middleton, Dorothy, 4580
Mies, Maria, 1801, 2550
Miles, Kay, 1399
Miller, Alfred Donald, 3480
Miller, Barbara Stoler, 244, 3813
Miller, Basil William, 1627, 3440
Miller, William, 3140
Milne, Louise Jordan, 3041
Minattur, Joseph, 2541
Minault, Gail, 1235
Miner, Clara M. *See* M., C.M.
Minhāj-ud-dīn Abū-'Umar 'Uṣmān / Minhāj Sirāj Juzānī, 713
Minkler, Meredith, 4123
Minturn, Leigh, 4063, 4155
Mir, Ezra, 1845
Mīrābāī, 602-3, 605, 609-14
Mirabehn / Madeleine Slade, 1313
Mir Amiruddin, Begam, 939, 1260
Mirkhan, Pathan, 3522
Mirza, Mohammad Wahid, 541
Mirza, Sarfaraz Hussain, 1242
Mishra, Gopal Chandra, 3797
Mishra, Indra Raj, 4518
Mishra, S.D., 4193
Mishra, Shanti, 4520
Misra, Babagrahi, 2131
Misra, Lakshmi, 2249-50
Misra, Prashanta, 3564
Misra, Rekha, 716
Missionary Settlement for University Women, 3412
Mistri, Jerbanoo, 1144
Mital, Harish Chandra, 1009
Mitchell, Mrs. Murray / Maria Hay (Flyter) Mitchell, 1498, 3182, 3683
Mitra, Asok, 1685, 2148, 2454-5, 2466
Mitra, K.P., 435
Mitra, Sarat Chandra, 216-7, 2132, 3626, 3878, 3948-9, 4124, 4237-8, 4244
Mitra, S.M., 923
Mitra, Subal Chandra, 3658
Mitra, Trailokyanath, 226
Mitra, Veda, 204
Mittal, V.K., 1819
Mitter, Dwarka Nath, 91
Mittra, Kalipada, 3615-6, 3724
Mittra, Peary Chand, 92, 3646
Miyazaki, Eiko, 4586
Mizlaff, Eugenia von, 1220
Moaven, Niloufar, 4547
Mode, Heinz, 341
Modi, Jivanji Jamshedji, 102-3, 208, 218, 266, 3502, 3539, 4230
Mody, Cooverjee Rustomjee, 3389
Mody, Susan N., 3562-3
Mohamed, Syed, 739
Mohan, Anand, 1368
Mohan Brij, 1805
Mohan, Jag, 2583
Mohan, M.C., 2229
Mohanty, S.P., 1942, 2480
Mohinder Kaur, 2223
Mokashi, P.R., 3495
Mokashi-Punekar, Shankar, 2731
Mongia, J.N., 2202
Monkland, Mrs., pseud. / Mary (Frazer) Campbell, 3693-5
Montgomery, Helen Barrett, 1588
Montgomery, R., 3974
Moodgal, Hari Mohan K., 1369
Moody, V., 4622
Mookerjee, Ajit, 120, 3879
Mookerjee, Nanda, 2067

Mookerjee, Sipra, 1752
Mookerji, Radha Kumud, 54
Mookerji, Tapati, 2710
Moor, Edward, 989
Moore, Kate, 4023
Moore, Mrs. P.H. / Jessie Fremont Moore, 3684-7
Moraes, Frank, 1281
Moreland, Elizabeth, 1563
Moreno, H.W.B., 795-6
Morgan, Lady Sydney Owenson, 787
Morling, Olive M. Elliot, 1628
Morrison, William A., 3572-3
Morton, Eleanor, pseud. / Elisabeth Gertrude Stern, 1314
Mosena, Patricia Wimberley, 3939
Moser-Schmitt, Erika, 341a, 4350-9
The Mother / La Mère, 2079-81
Moti Chandra, 141, 161, 253, 625
Motiwala, B.N., 3464
Motwani, Clara, 3108
Mountbatten, Lady / Edwina Ashley Mountbatten, 1236, 1732
M.S. Subbulakshmi, 609, 2621, 2626-8, 2631
Mudholkar, R.N., 1010
Mudiyanse, Nandasena, 421
Mufti, Mumtaz, 2924
Muggeridge, Malcolm, 2985
Muḥammad Riẓā / Nau'ī, 728
Muir-Mackenzie, Lady, 1127
Mukerjee, Radhakamal, 1289, 2203
Mukerjee, Sandhya, 406
Mukerji, Bithika, 2108
Mukerji, Dhan Gopal, 880
Mukerji, D.P., 1686
Mukerji, Krishna Prasanna, 3117
Mukerji, Renuka, 2290
Mukharji, Gita, 1752
Mukherjea, Charulal, 2876, 3752
Mukherjee, Amitabha, 3609. *See also* Mukhopadhyay, Amitabha
Mukherjee, Bharati, 2828-31
Mukherjee, Bishwa Nath, 1652, 1687, 2496, 2521-2, 4592
Mukherjee, Govinda Gopal, 115a
Mukherjee, H.B., 1092
Mukherjee, Ila, 717
Mukherjee, Jogendra Nath, 1154
Mukherjee, Kanak, 2387
Mukherjee, Meenakshi, 2704, 3814
Mukherjee, Nara Nath, 1154
Mukherjee, Prabhati, 87, 407, 457-8
Mukherjee, Ramkrishna, 2504
Mukherjee, S.P., 3703, 3719, 3726
Mukherji, A.B., 3304, 4257
Mukherji, R., 1965
Mukherji, Santosh Kumar, 254
Mukherji, Sashibhushan, 3610
Mukhopadhyay, Amitabha, 3617-8. *See also* Mukherjee, Amitabha
Mukhopadhyaya, Damodar, 3832
Muktānanda, 701
Muktananda Saraswati, Swami, 2418
Mulay, Vijaya, 2660
Mullens, Mrs. / Hannah Catherine (Lacrois) Mullens, 3688-9
Mullens, Joseph, 3690
Müller, Eduard, 447
Müller, F. Max, 940
Mullick, Saroj, 4290
Mundkar, Balaji, 173
Mundri. Lal Singh, 4142
Muni, S.D., 1662
Munshi, Lilavati, 2664
Munson, Arley Isabel, 3183
Murdoch, John, 941, 1564
Murickan, Joseph, 3194
Murthy, K.K., 267
Muske, Carol, 4506
Muter, Mrs. D.D. / Elizabeth McMullin Muter, 4024-5
Muthanna, I.M., 4615
Muthulakshmi Reddy, S., 1093, 1144, 1335-6

Nadarajah, Devapoopathy, 519-21, 530
Nadkarni, Vithal C., 3154
Nag, Amit Kumar, 4599
Nag, Jamuna, 970
Nag, Kalidas, 3647
Nag, Moni, 1916-8, 3720
Nagaraja Rao, M.S., 651
Nāgārjuna Siddha, 688-90
Nagarkar, Mrs. K.C., 1197
Nagaswami, R., 566
Naidoo, J.C., 4626
Naidu, Muthyalayya, 1039
Naidu, P.P., 2373
Naidu, Sarojini, 1328, 2728, 2732-6
Naik, T.B., 3521, 3526
Naji, Ghulamali Ismail, 1782, 1993
Nakane, Chie, 3269, 4593
Nalaswami, J.M., 573
Nallazarilli, Gulshan, 4506
Nambiar, K.C., 2705
Namboodiripad, E.M.S., 2578
Namjoshi, A.N., 2237
Nanavati, S.N., 3417
Nanavutty, Piloo, 78
Nanda, A.K., 2488
Nanda, B.R., 1750
Nanda, Savitri Devi, 3985
Nandakumar, Prema, 2082-3, 2746
Nandi, Leena, 1752
Nandy, Ashis, 43, 971, 3619
Naqui, S.A.H., 2917
Narain, Dhirendra, 1989, 1999, 2010
Narain, Ram, 2877
Narain, Vatsala, 1688
Narang, Sharada, 1174
Narasimhaiah, C.D., 2737
Narasimhan, Raji, 2850
Narasimha Rao, Manthripragada, 3788
Narasimha Reddy, D., 2144
Narayan, Shovana, 2605
Narayana Menon, Vatakke Kurupath, 2606
Narayana Rao, Kolar Surya, 2785-7
Narula, Uma, 2231
Nataraj, P., 3312-3
Natarajan, Bhavani, 1128
Natarajan, Dandipani, 2456, 2467
Natarajan, K., 881, 1389
Natarajan, Swaminath, 942
Natesa Sastri, S.M., 3219
Nath, Kamla, 2149-50, 2161, 2207, 4073
Nath, Kidar, 4194
Nath, Viswa, 3390
Nathubhai, Tribhovandas Manguldas, 3503
National Association for Supplying Female Medical Aid to the Women of India, 1129
National Council for Women's Education, 2255
National Council of Women in India, 1198, 2346-7
National Institute of Public Cooperation and Child Development, 2231a

National Research Institute of Family Planning, 2484
Nau'ī. *See* Muḥammad Riẓā
Navalani, K., 2, 2265a
Nayak, Sharada, 1751
Nayar, K. Kannan, 3221
Nayar, S.B., 4085
Nayyar, Sushila, 1323, 1390
Nazir Ahmad, 2925
Nazir Ahmad, Razia, 2407
Nazmul Karim, A.K., 3880
Nehru, Jawaharlal, 1342-3
Nehru, Krishna, 1376, 2438. *See also* Hutheesing, Krishna Nehru
Nehru, Rameshwari, 1026, 1243, 1391
Nehru, Shyam Kumari, 908, 1011
Nehru, Uma, 909
Nelson, J.A., 3922
Nelson, Nici, 2305
Neog, Maheshwar, 3775
Neogi, Haran Chandra, 368
Nepal. International Women's Year Committee, 4521, 4556
Nepali, Gopal Singh, 4519
Nesiah, Lanka, 3126
Nethercot, Arthur H., 1450-1
Neumann, Alfred K., 4292
Nève, Félix Jean Baptiste Joseph, 485
Nevill, Hugh, 3023
Newell, Harriet Atwood / Mrs. Samuel Newell, 788-9
Newell, William H., 4170
Niaz Hussain, R., 1155
Nicholas, Ralph W., 3733, 3776-7
Nicholson, Sydney, 3232, 3367
Nicolson, Nigel, 1490
Niehoff, Arthur, 1835
Nighat, Ayub, 16
Nihal Singh, Saint, 943, 1452, 3413-4, 4616
Nihshreyasananda, Swami, 491
Nijjar, Bakhshish Singh, 3996
Nikambe, Shevantibai M., 3415, 3442
Nikhilananda, Swami, 2068
Nilakantan Unni, K.S., 582
Nilakanta Sastri, K.A., 24, 542
Nilam, Mrs. A.R.M., 1094
Nilima Devi, 1012
Nilkanth, Lady Ramanbhai, 3375
Nilsson, Usha Saksena, 615, 4364
Nimbkar, Jai, 2851
Nimbkar, Krishnabai, 2282, 2374-6, 2559
Nirmala Devi, 2623-4
Nirodbaran, 2084
Nirvedananda, Swami, 2069
Nischol, K., 2259
Nityananda, Sarasvathi, 3195
Nivedita, Sister / Margaret Elizabeth Noble, 852, 1470-3, 2000, 3648-50, 3778
Nizami, N.H., 4434
Noble, Margaret Elizabeth. *See* Nivedita, Sister
Noorani, M., 2027
Noorunnahar Fyzunnessa, 3905
Noronha, George Eric, 1095
Norris, Douglas, 3865
Norrish, Alan E., 4574
North-Western Provinces, 3966-71
North-Western Provinces. Infanticide Committee, 3972
Nugent, Maria (Skinner), 797
Nunn, G. Raymond, 3
Nuzhat Qureshi, K., 4475

Obeyesekere, Gananath, 3068, 3078-9, 3087
O'Brian, A.J., 3973
O'Flaherty, Wendy Doniger, 657
Ohlmus, Caroline Corner. *See* Corner, Caroline
Ojha, P.N., 718-9
O'Kelly, Elizabeth, 3891
Oliver, B.C., 1261
Oman, John Campbell, 943a
Omananda Puri, Swami, 380
Omar, Kamal, 1783
Omvedt, Gail, 2573-8, 3578-81
Opler, Morris E., 4187
Oppenheimer, Martin, 2578
Orissa. Labour Department, 3786
Orr, Inge C., 2269, 4376
Östör, Ákos, 1986, 3732
Ottman, Nina, 1629
Oturkar, R.V., 756
Ouvry, Matilda H., 4026
Overstreet, Gene D., 1211
Owen, Hugh F., 1453-4
Oza, Ghanshyambhai, 2195

P., F.E.F. / Fanny Emily (Farr) Penny, 3011. *See also* Penny, Fanny Emily (Farr)
Padfield, J.E., 3196
Padhye, K.A., 753
Padmanabhan, Neela, 3353
Padmanabhan, T., 3358
Padmaraju, Palagummi, 3363-4
Padmaśrī, 691
Paget, Mrs. Leopold / Georgiana Theodosia (Fitzmoor-Halsey) Paget, 4027
Paintal, Veena, 2852
Pakistan. Central Bureau of Education, 4476
Pakistan. Information and Broadcasting Division, 2659, 4431, 4465, 4484, 4490-2, 4514
Pakistan. Laws, Statutes, etc., 2027-8
Pakistan. National Manpower Council. Research and Statistics Branch, 2151
Pakistan. Pakistan Women's Rights Committee, 4488
Pakistan Academy for Rural Development. *See* Bangladesh Academy for Rural Development
Pakistan Council for National Integration, Lahore Branch, 2397
Pakistan Women's Institute, 4493
Pakrasi, Kanti, 990-1, 1919, 1968, 2468, 3391-3, 3721
Pal, Bepin Chandra / Bipin Chandra Pal, 1455
Pal, Cora, 2935
Pal, Dhirendra Nath, 824
Pal, P., 3728
Palaniappan, K., 183
Palchoudhuri, Ila, 326
Palit, D.R., 174
Panandikar, Sulabha, 3554
Panchapekesa Ayyar, Aiylam Subramanier, 2878
Pandey, Chapala, 4554
Pandey, Indu Prakash, 4156
Pandey, Rajendra, 4275
Pandey, R.N., 2152
Pandey, S.M., 616
Pandit, M.P., 2085-8
Pandit, S.G., 882
Pandit, Vijaya Lakshmi, 1237, 1350-1, 1957
Pandurang, Dadoba, 823
Panduranga Rao, Ilapavuluri, 491a
Panigrahi, Lalita, 992
Panikkar, K.M., 559

Pant, Chandra, 732
Papanek, Hanna, 1653-4, 2051-4, 2209, 2232, 2303
Pappu, Shyamala, 2542
Paradkar, M.D., 350
Parajuli, Devidatta, 692
Paramatmananda, Swami, 581
Paranjpe, M.R., 3416
Paranjpe, R.P., 3461
Parashar, Om Datt, 4276
Paraṣurāma, 3155
Pareek, Udai, 2458, 4188
Parekh, Kishor, 652
Pares, Lady, 2343
Parikh, R.D., 3594
Parks, Fanny / Fanny (Parks) Parlby, 4055a
Parmar, Yashant Singh, 4117
Parulekar, N.B., 1238
Parulekhar, Godavari S., 3582
Parveen Shaukat Ali, 1402, 1722
Pastner, Carroll McClure, 4452-5, 4457
Pasupati / Pasupati Bhattacharya, 2089
Patankar, Tara, 1900
Patel, Haribhai G., 3492
Patel, M.S., 1315
Patel, Rashida, 4450
Patel, Toni, 748
Pathak, K.B., 1865
Pathak, Lalit P., 2148
Pathak, Saroj, 3601
Pathare Reform Association, 3399
Pati, Pramod, 2329
Patil, B.R., 256
Patil, R.L., 3331
Patil, Sharad, 193a
Patil, Vimla, 245
Patnaik, Bibudhendhra Narayan, 2794
Patterson, Josephine E., 3434
Patterson, Maureen L.P., 4
Pattison, Mattie, 2032
Pattnaik, Bijoylakshmi, 3709
Patwardhan, Daya, 1504
Patwardhan, Lilabai, 3468
Patwardhan, Vasundhara, 3599
Paul, Diana Mary, 431-2
Paul, Glendora B., 910
Paul, S.K., 110
Pavitrananda, Swami, 2070
Payne, Ernest Alexander, 121
Peace, M.L., 25
Pearl, David, 2534, 4451
Pearson, J.D., 5
Peggs, James, 975-6, 993-4
Pehrson, Robert Niel, 4425
Peiris, Edmund, 3042
Peiris, W., 96
Penn, Irving, 4522
Penny, Fanny Emily (Farr), 1518-22, 3186, 3197. *See also* P., F.E.F.
Penzer, N.M., 219, 257, 268, 280
Perera, Simon Gregory, 3033
Perrin, Alice Robinson, 1547-8
Pertold, Otakar, 3088
Peter, Prince of Greece and Denmark, 1870-1
Peterson, P., 512
Phadke, Narayan Sitaram, 1184
Phadke, Sindhu, 2260
Phatak, L.V., 4304
Phillips, Mrs. E.G., 1565
Picken, W.H. Jackson, 3163
Pieris, Ralph, 560
Piggott, R., 1180
Pillai, K.P.R., 2583
Pillay, Alyappin Padmanabbha, 1179-80
Pinch, Trevor, 854
Pinkham, Mildreth Worth, 66, 463
Pipping, Ella, 3696
Pitman, Emma Raymond, 1566
Pizarro de Rayo, Aguedo, 3813
Platt, Kate Anne, 1130, 1422
Plunkett, Frances Taft, 3994
Pocock, David F., 3540, 4617
Podder, Arabinda, 3629
Poffenberger, Shirley B., 3574, 3576
Poffenberger, Thomas, 3574-6
Pollock, John Charles, 1590
Pool, John J., 26
Poravrela, Durgā, 4557
Potter, Robert G., 4125-6
Prabha, pseud., 2055, 4219
Prabhakar, C.L., 663
Prabhu, John Coelho, 1920
Prabhu, R.K., 1324
Prakasa, Sri, 1456
Prasad, Amba, 2377
Prasad, B.G., 4085
Prasad, Baijnath, 4335
Prasad, Tarkeshwar, 4143, 4157
Premchand, pseud. / Dhanpat Rai Srivastava, 4377-80
Prideaux, Edwin, 4245
Prior, Lilian Faith Loveday, 4415
Pritam, Amrita. *See* Amrita Pritam
Przyluski, Jean, 135
Punekar, S.D., 3565
Punekar, Vijaya, 1921
Punjab, 3974
Punjab (India). Board of Economic Inquiry, 4316
Puri, Baij Nath, 369
Puri, Krishna, 2494
Puri, Meenakshi, 2853
Puthenkalam, Joseph, 3270

Qadri, Sayyid Ahmad-Ullah, 749
Qasimi, Ahmad Nadeem, 2926
Quin, Eva Wyndham, 3187
Qurashi, Salma Mustafa, 4477
Qureshi, Mohammed Ahmed, 1888
Qureshi, Sarfaraz Khan, 2303

Radhakrishna Murty, K., 3338-9
Radhakrishnan, S., 505
Radhakrishnan, Sarvepalli, 205
Raghavachari, S., 1913
Raghavacharyulu, K., 543
Raghavan, M.D., 175, 3043, 3089, 3092
Raghavan, V., 351, 544
Raghavan, V., 395
Raghavan, V., 3366
Raghavender Rao, J.V., 3321
Raghunatha Rao, R., 213, 1040
Raghunathji, K., 3424
Ragini Devi, 2594
Ragoonath, R. *See* Raghunatha Rao, R.
Raheem, Ryhana, 2706
Rahim, M.A., 729
Rahman, Fazlur, 2056
Rahman, Makhlisur, 3934
Rahman, Muqaddesur, 269
Rahman, Zebun Nessa, 3924
Rahurkar, V.G., 381
Rai, Ganpat, 1325
Rai, Jamiat, 4426
Rai, Kumari S., 55

Rai, Raghu, 4344
Rai, Usha, 2179
Raikar, Y.A., 567
Raina, Bhushan, 4314
Raina, Bishen Lal, 2494, 4305
Raina, Vimala, 450, 2854
Rainy, Christina, 1630, 3185
Raizada, R.K., 1943, 2585
Raj, Hilda, 2855
Raj, Prakash A., 4520
Raja, C.K., 382
Rajagopal, T.S., 804
Rajagopalachari, Chakravarti, 535
Rajagopalan, C., 4101
Rajagopalan, T.R., 178, 184
Rajah, R.S., 3054
Rajahgopaul, Susan, 3185
Rajalakshmi, C.R., 2941
Rajalakshmi, S., 531
Rajan, Balachandra, 2879
Raja Rao, 2880
Rajlukshmi Debee, 3815
Rajput, A.B., 723, 2942
Rajwade, Lakshmibai, 1131, 1478
Rajwade, Madhav, 763
Rajyalakshmi, P.V., 2738-9
Rakshit, Sipra, 3489
Rallia Ram, Mayavanthi, 1784-6, 2057
Ram, Atma, 2817, 2825
Rama, K.G., 3317
Ramabai Association. *See* American Ramabai Association
Ramabai Mukti Mission, 3444
Ramabai Sarasvati, Pandita, 825, 1558, 3434, 3446-7
Ramachandra, Ragini, 2767
Ramachandran, K.V., 2470
Ramachandran, P., 2162
Ramachandran, Padma, 2388
Ramachandra Rao, Bommatapalli, 2826
Ramachandra Rao, Visarada, 506
Ramachandra Sastry, K., 2523
Rama Devi, B., 1820
Rama Krishna, T., 88
Ramakrishna Vedanta Center, 299
Ramakumar, R., 3226
Ramamritham, L.S., 3354
Raman, M.V., 2524
Ramanan, V.V., 3292
Ramanathan, Jaya, 2440
Ramanujan, A.K., 532, 648
Raman Unni, K., 3271
Rāmaprasāda Ṣena, 642
Rama Rao, G., 2443
Rama Rau, Dhanvanthi, 1392
Ramasubramanian, N., 3368
Ramaswami Aiyar, Chetpat Pattabhirama, 617, 1329, 1457-8
Ramaswamy, E.A., 1924
Rameshwar Rao, Shanta, 2856, 3778a
Rampal, Satendra Nath, 2046
Ramu, G.N., 1841
Ranade, H.G., 461
Ranade, Mahadev Govind, 1027, 1041
Ranade, Meena, 764
Ranade, Ramabai, 3469
Ranade, S.N., 2162, 4258
Ranadive, Vimal, 2174, 2578
Ranasinghe, Anne, 3127-9
Randhawa, Mohindar Singh, 626, 703-4
Rangachari, K., 2275
Ranga Iyer, C.S., 883
Ranganathananda, Swami, 2071
Ranga Rao, M., 3321
Rangaswami Aiyangar, K.V., 472
Rangaswami Aiyer, A., 1459
Rani, Gita, 3886
Rao, Amla R., 4085
Rao, C. Vimala, 2695
Rao, Kamala, 3565
Rao, Kamala Gopal, 2486-7, 2494
Rao, K.V. Lakshman, 436
Rao, Nandini. *See* Rao, Velagapudi Nandini Prakasa
Rao, Sakuntala. *See* Sastri, Shakuntala Rao
Rao, Sharadamba, 4231
Rao, Tirmal, 1085
Rao, Velagapudi Nandini Prakasa, 3295, 3298
Raper, Arthur F., 3923
Rashid, S., 2894
Rashid Ahmad, Zinat, 2943
Rastogi, Sita Ram, 4306
Rathbone, Eleanor F., 884, 1028, 1199
Rathnamal, Sita, 3201
Rathod, Kantilal, 1967
Ratté, Mary Lou, 3611
Rau, M. Chalapathi, 1371
Rau, Santha Rama, 835, 2768-71
Rauf, Abdur, 2881
Ravindra, 2090
Rawlins, T.W., 3970
Rawlinson, H.G., 798
Ray, Annada Sankar, 3833
Ray, Gautam Sankar, 4148
Ray, Lila, 345, 2743-5, 3816
Ray, Renuka, 1175, 1200, 1212, 1262, 1752
Ray, Satyajit, 3736, 3739, 3771, 3785, 3841
Ray, Shreela, 2710
Ray, Sudhansu Kumar, 3753
Raychaudhuri, Arun Kumar, 158
Ray (Choudhury), Jaya, 3710
Raza, Maulvi Hasan, 4144
Raza, S. Musi, 4220
Razdan, C.K., 2669
Reddi, T.S., 1337
Reddy, N.S., 4106
Reejhsinghani, Aroona, 2936
Rees, J.D., 1029, 1132
Rege, Y.M., 805
Rehman, Rakhshinda, 4481
Reith, David Jerome, 2471
Renuka, Y., 1894
Reyes-Hockings, Amelia, 1836
Reymond, Lizelle, 1474, 2072, 4575
Reynolds, Holly Baker, 3250
Richards, Elias Jones, 4048
Richardson, Jane / Jane (Richardson) Hanks, 2992
Richter, Linda K., 2689
Rihani, May, 2306
Ringard, Morten, 2728
Rishabhchand, 2091
Risley, H.H., 3627
Rizvi, Athar Abbas, 709
Rizvi, Najma, 3871
Robb, Peter, 1460
Roberts, Beryl J., 3940, 3943
Roberts, Emma, 1414
Roberts, G.W., 4607
Robertson, John, 1133, 1896
Robinson, A.M., 1215, 1559
Robinson, Edward Jewitt, 855
Robinson, Richard H., 503
Robinson, Warren C., 2509-10

Roche, Paul, 3222
Rocher, Ludo, 473
Rodrigues, Lucio, 3425
Rolleston, Charles J., 1156
Rose, Horace Arthur, 4107, 4145-6, 4437a, 4440-1
Rose, Isabel Brown, 1549-50
Rosenthal, A.M., 865
Rosenthal, E., 3142
Rosenthal, Leora N., 4604a
Roshan Ara Begam, 2625, 2629
Rosner, Victor, 4108
Ross, Aileen D., 2179, 2210, 3259, 3307
Roterberg, H., 1631
Rothermund, Indira, 4321
Rothfeld, Otto, 856, 1145
Rouse, George Henry, 3680
Rout, Savitri, 357
Row, Ksamabai, 67
Rowe, William L., 4176
Rowlands, Jane Helen, 561
Roy, Barnik, 3881
Roy, Bhupendranath, 1475
Roy, Bina, 1690
Roy, Debabrata, 4349
Roy, Dilip Kumar, 618-9
Roy, Juthika, 603
Roy, Manendra Nath, 806
Roy, Manisha, 3698, 3701a-2, 3741
Roy, Mira, 383
Roy, Rammohun, 944, 977-80
Roy, Sarat Chandra, 4147
Roy, Satindra Narayan, 3713, 3758, 3799
Roy, Shibani, 4074
Royal, C.S., 3285
Royal Empire Society, London. Library, 945
Roy Burman, B.K., 2457
Roy Choudhury, P.C., 185
Roy Chowdhury, Bulu, 1238a
Rubenstein, Carol, 2978
Rudolph, Lloyd I., 1316, 4189
Rudolph, Susanne Hoeber, 1316, 4189
Rudra, Ashok, 89
Rugnathdas, Madhowdas, 3400
Ruhela, Satya Pal, 2291
Ruikar, Malathi, 2225
Rukanuddin, Abdul Razzaque, 2469, 2476
Rukhmabai, Dr., 1158
Rukmini, M.A., 384
Rukmini Devi / Rukmini Devi Arundale, 2586
Runganadhan, S.E., 911, 2323
Ruskin, David, 2512
Rustomji, Hilla, 1157
Ruswa, Mirza Muhammad Hadi, 2927
Ryan, Bryce, 3062, 3075, 3103, 3113
Ryder, Emily Brainerd, 1030

S., A.C., 1423
S., C., 885
Sabbah, Saleh, 3853, 3888
Sabra Azam, 4485
Sachchidananda, 1806
Sadiq, Nasim Mahmood, 1866
Saeed, Kishwar, 4459
Saeed, S.A., 4478
Saeed Dehlvi, Mohammed, 2928
Sagant, Philippe, 4527
Saha, Nirmal Kanti, 3742
Saha, Panchanan, 1239
Sahai, Indu, 4171
Sahay, Sachidanand, 315
Sahgal, Nayantara, 1352, 1379-80, 2795-800
Sahi, Abrar Fatima, 4427
Sahu, Kishori Prasad, 710
Sahukar, Mani, 2112
Saibaba, G., 2175
Saifullah Khan, Verity, 4618-20
Sainsara, Gurcharan Singh, 1239a
Saiyed, A.R., 3522
Sakhawat Hossain, Rokeya, 3817
Saksena, Devendra N., 2519, 4127
Saksena, Jogendra, 2645
Saksena, Kashi Prasad, 1878
Saksena, R.N., 4119
Saletore, Rajaram Narayan, 27, 282, 567a
Saltzman, Paul, 1363
Salahuddin, Ahmad, 4510
Samarakkody, Amara, 3063
Samartha, Michael Prakash, 586
Samuel, Getsie R., 3134
Samuel, T.J., 1922
Sandesara, Bhogilal J., 545
Sandesara, Upendraray J., 486
Sanger, Margaret, 1184-5
Sanjeevi, Krishna, 3355
Sankalia, H.D., 176
Sankaran Nair, C., 1201
Sanyal, Nirmal Chandra, 667
Sanyal, Nisikanta, 300
Sanyal, R.K., 2488
Sanyal, Shubhra, 4317
Sarabhai, Bharati, 2747-8
Sarabhai, Mrinalini, 301, 705, 2802-4
Sarada, K., 3324
Saradananda, Swami, 2118
Saradhi, K.P., 2707
Saraf, Suraj, 186
Saran, A.B., 4226
Saran, H.L., 1859
Saran Raksha, 2286, 2324, 2359
Sarangapani, M.P., 1330
Sarangapani Ayyangar, P.S., 3156
Saraswathi, M.E., 574
Sardar, G.B., 2244
Sarkar, Aditi Nath, 3777
Sarkar, Arati, 4148
Sarkar, B.N., 1867
Sarkar, Jadunath, 1476
Sarkar, Jayanta, 3754
Sarkar, Lotika, 1213, 1755, 2535-6
Sarkar, Rashindra Nath, 1169-70, 1881
Sarkar, R.M., 1807
Sarkar, S.S., 3710
Sarkar, Subimal Chandra, 68
Sarkar, Sumit, 946
Sarma, Jyotirmoyee, 3743-4, 4598
Sarma, M.N., 2801
Sarma, N.A., 1691
Sarwal, Amita, 2233
Sastri, Hirananda, 744
Sastri, P.S., 385
Sastri, Shakuntala Rao, 69, 93, 270, 276, 386
Sastri, Sivanath / Sibnath Sastri, 3662
Sastri, T.V.G., 129
Sastry, L. Subrahmanya, 1858, 1860, 1876
Sastry, S.N.S., 1370
Satchidanandam Pillai, S., 575
Satpathy, Nandini, 3800-2
Sat Prem, 2092
Sathyanarayana, R., 332
Sattar, Ellen, 3855, 3892, 3905
Satterthwaite, A.P., 2508
Satthianadhan, Kamala, 56
Satthianadhan, Krupabai / Mrs. S.

Satthianadhan, 1221, 2857
Satyanarayanachar, R.A., 3332
Satyanarayana Raju, N., 2175
Satyarthi, Devendra, 3593, 4149, 4328-31
Savithri, T.S., 3299
Savory, Isabel, 1499
Savur, Manorama, 2578
Sawain, S., 4594
Saxena, G.B., 4128
Saxena, Rajendra Kumar, 3954-5
Sayami, Dhooswan, 4549
Sayeed, S.M., 4322
Scarpa, Antonio, 3024
Scharlieb, Mary Ann Dacomb (Bird), 1134, 3146a
Schermerhorn, Richard A., 1821
Schmidt, Richard, 239
Schneider, David M., 194
Schomer, Karine, 4368
Schomerus, Hilko Wiardo, 572
Schoustra-van Beukering, E.J.E., 3856
Schwartzberg, Joseph E., 6
Schweiger-Lerchenfeld, Amand, 3015
Scindia, Maharani of Gwalior, 1097
Sclater, William Lutley, 799
Scott, David, 620
Scudder, Dorothy Jealous, 3167
Seamands, Ruth, 1632
Seed, Geoffrey, 3620
Seelananda Brahmachari, 422
Seeta, S., 333
Seltzer, William, 2474
Sen, Aditya, 2583
Sen, Asok, 3628
Sen, Dinesh Chandra, 3621, 3950
Sen, D.K., 4129
Sen, Ela, 912, 1290, 1331, 1372
Sen, Gopinath, 3755
Sen, Hannah, 807, 913, 1098
Sen, J.C., 2472
Sen, Jyoti, 2947
Sen, Keshab Chandra, 3651
Sen, M.L.A., 4158
Sen, Mrinalini, 1692
Sen, Nabaneeta Dev, 1752, 3813
Sen, N.B., 2245-6
Sen, Mrs. N.C., 808
Sen, Shipra, 2179
Sen, Snehalata, 3818
Sen, S.P., 1291
Sen, Sukumar, 546, 3844
Sen, Sushama, 1393
Sen, Tulika, 1893, 3711
Senaveratne, Anna P., 547
Seneviratne, Maureen, 548, 3100, 3118
Sengupta, A., 3722
Sen Gupta, Anima K., 1693-4
Sen Gupta, Nares Chandra, 3834
Sengupta, Nilakshi, 210
Sengupta, Padmini, 57, 1292, 1332, 1394, 1695, 2186-7, 2247, 2719, 2858, 2948, 3447a
Sen Gupta, Roshani, 2298
Sen Gupta, Sankar, 44, 363, 2656
Sen Gupta, Santosh Kumar, 1927
Sen Gupta, Sudhir Ranjan, 122
Sen Gupta, Sudipta, 4587
Serajul Haque, 3910
Seshadri, P., 582
Seshadri, Pundi, 947
Sethi, Gargi, 1850
Sethi, Raj Mohini, 4075
Sethna, H.D., 809
Seton, Grace Thompson, 1500
Seymour, Susan, 3745
Shackle, C., 356
Shafi, Mohammad, 4471
Shah, A.B., 3448
Shah, Gunvant B., 1099
Shah, Khalida, 4460, 4472, 4480
Shah, K.K., 3417
Shah, K.T., 2325
Shah, Madhuri R., 2270
Shah, M.H., 3514
Shah, M.S., 2204
Shah, Nasra M., 2303, 4461-3, 4501
Shah, Umakant Premanand, 100, 653
Shahane, Vasant Anant, 2969-71
Shahani, Dayaram Gidumal. *See* Gidumal, Dayaram
Shahani, Kumar, 1834
Shahani, Savitri, 3523
Shahi, Indira, 4154
Shah Nawaz, Jahan Ara / Begam Shah Nawaz, 1263, 1283, 1401-2
Shah Nawaz, Mumtaz, 2859
Shama Shastri, R., 464
Shamim, Ishrat, 3905
Shamim, Mohammad, 4481
Sham Rao, D.P., 2113
Shamsudeen, A.T., 3069, 3124
Shane, Ryland, 1317
Shankar, Anasuya. *See* Triveni
Shankar, Kalyani, 1671
Shankar, Lakshmi, 2623-4, 2630
Shanmugam, T.E., 3279
Shantakumari, S.L., 549, 1753
Shantaram, V., 2670
Sharif, Raihan, 3909
Sharma, Arvind, 18, 451, 2119
Sharma, B.M., 4255
Sharma, Chandrakanta, 228
Sharma, D.D., 352-3
Sharma, Hira Lal, 765
Sharma, I.D., 58
Sharma, J.N., 2177
Sharma, Krishan Datt, 2189
Sharma, Kumud, 1651
Sharma, Madhavi D., 2219
Sharma, Nageswar, 4195
Sharma, Piare Lal, 1373, 2434
Sharma, Pushpendra Kumar, 658
Sharma, Raj Kumar, 643, 1369
Sharma, Ram Sharan, 465
Sharma, Ratan Lal, 4381
Sharma, Revti Saran, 4396a, 4398
Sharma, Sadashiv Ratha, 3764
Sharma, Shakti, 4332
Sharma, Som P., 2882
Sharma, Ursula M., 4221, 4621
Shashi, Shyam Singh, 1808
Shasmal, Kartick Chandra, 3745a
Shastri, Prabhu Dutt, 130
Shastri, Shakuntala Rao. *See* Sastri, Shakuntala Rao
Shaukat Ali, Parveen. *See* Parveen Shaukat Ali
Sheatsley, Clarence Valentine, 857
Sheonarain, Pandit, 1159
Sheikh, Gulam Mohammed, 2637
Sherazee, M.H., 2404
Sher-Gil, Amrita, 2637
Sherring, M.A., 1591
Sherwani, H.K., 750
Sheth, Jyotsna, 1969

Shintri, Sarojini, 1753
Shipstone, Eva I., 2219
Shirin, Mumtaz / Mumtaz Shireen, 2909-13
Shivaraman, Mythily, 2578
Shome, Joy Gobindo, 1013
Shore, John, 948
Shortt, John, 3157
Shreemati Nathibai Damodar Thackersey Women's University, 3555
Shreemati Nathibai Damodar Thackersey Women's University. Research Unit on Women's Studies, 17, 3556
Shrestha, Bihari K., 4552
Shridevi, Sripati, 914, 1318, 2271-2
Shridharani, Krishnalal, 826
Shrinagesh, Shakuntala, 2860
Shujauddin, Mohammad, 733
Shujauddin, Razia, 733
Shunmuga Sundaram, S., 3340
Shyamlal, 2360
Siddiqi, Mohammad Mazheruddin, 1787
Siddiqui, B.B., 3516
Siegel, Lee, 627
Silva, S., 1889
Simha, Teeka, 4567
Simharay, Diana, 28
Simpson, Hassell A., 1538
Simson, R., 3971
Singh, Andrea Menefee, 1655, 2178, 4309
Singh, Arjun, 4252
Singh, Birendra, 2153
Singh, Ganda, 3997-8
Singh, Indera P., 4065
Singh, Jacquelin, 2988
Singh, Jaspal, 4101-2
Singh, Justina Arjun, 2944
Singh, K. Jagjit, 4333
Singh, Mrs. K.P., 2234, 4103
Singh, K.S., 1943
Singh, Mala, 1696
Singh, Nalini, 2303
Singh, Puran, 113
Singh, Rajendra, 4086
Singh, Ram Sevak, 2788, 2827, 2972
Singh, Satindra, 4401
Singh, Shilendra K., 770
Singh, Sirdar Gurdyal, 4150
Singh, Sirdar Jogendra, 734, 3401
Singh, Sohan, 4318a
Singh, Teja, 114
Singh, T.R., 3280, 4161
Singha, P., 1923
Singha, Shilu, 4554
Singhi, Narendra Kumar, 1697
Singhi, Sushila, 1752
Sinha, Bindesawari Prasad, 516
Sinha, G.P., 4258
Sinha, Jadunath, 634
Sinha, J.N., 2144
Sinha, Pratima, 4269
Sinha, Rajeshwar Prasad Narain, 628
Sinha, S.M., 3725
Sinha, S.N., 255
Sinha, Surajit, 4334
Sinha, Umesh Prasad, 4130, 4307
Sirageldin, Ismail, 3865
Sircar, Dineschandra, 29, 116a, 148, 654
Sircar, Mahendra Lal, 1031-2, 1135
Siriwardena, B.S., 3020
Siriwardena, T.A.C., 3107
Sirsikar, V.M., 3586
Sirvya, Bhagwan Das, 309
Sitara Devi, 2607
Sivananda, Swami, 2062
Sivaramamurti, C., 162
Sivaramayya, Bhamidipati, 310, 2537
Sivasankara Pillai, Thakazhi, 3359-60
Slade, Madeleine. *See* Mirabehn
Sleeman, William Henry, 3959
Slocum, W.L., 4427
Slusser, Mary, 4550
Smith, D.J., 1503
Smith, Donald Eugene, 2538
Smith, H. Daniel, 3249
Smith, Raymond T., 4608-9
Smith, Wilfred Cantwell, 1788
Smock, Audrey Chapman, 3857
Smyth, John, 4004a
Sobhan, Salma, 3925
Sohoni, Neera Kuchreja, 2439
Solanki, M.S., 4360
Sonalkar, Wandana, 2578
Soppitt, Mrs., 4028
Sorabji, Cornelia, 810-11, 827, 949, 1014, 1033, 1160-1, 1202-3, 1295-7, 2861, 3670a
Sorabji, S., 3470
Sovani, N.V., 3515
Spann, Gloria Carter, 2979
Spate, O.H.K., 7, 8
Speer, Robert E., 1101
Spink, Walter, 408
Spratt, P., 229
Sreekantaiya, 587
Sreenivasa Murthy, H.V., 179
Sreenivasan, Kasthuri, 2883
Sreenivasan, M.A., 95
Srikantha Sastri, S., 668
Srimany, Adhir K., 2148
Srinivas, Mysore Narasimhachar, 1766, 1811, 1924, 3158, 3206, 3243-4
Srinivasa Iyengar, Kodaganallur Ramaswami, 2093, 2708, 2720, 2740, 2884
Srinivasan, K., 3227
Srinivasan, K.S., 2660
Srinivasa Sastri, V.S., 950
Srivastava, Balram, 146
Srivastava, K.K., 1698
Srivastava, K.N., 2287
Srivastava, Mahesh Chandra Prasad, 142
Srivastava, M.P., 711
Srivastava, Narsingh, 2709
Srivastava, Ram P., 4095, 4627
Srivastava, R.P., 3712
Srivastava, Sahab Lal, 1933
Srivastava, Vinita, 4264, 4272
Staelin, Charlotte Dennett, 3428
Stanford, John Keith, 1415
Stark, Elizabeth, 4585
Stead, William Thomas, 1461
Steel, Flora Annie (Webster), 735, 951, 1424, 1505-17
Stein, Dorothy K., 981
Stern, Elisabeth Gertrude. *See* Morton, Eleanor
Sternbach, Ludwik, 195, 517, 674
Stevenson, Ian, 3072-3, 3235, 3729, 4164
Stevenson, Mabel, 4049
Stevenson, William, 3185
Stewart, Duncan, 1136
Stocks, Mary Danvers, 1284
Stoeckel, John, 3866, 3927, 3939, 3941-2, 4559
Stokes, Olivia, 4077
Storrie, Kate, 3429

Storrow, Edward, 858, 3612
Story, Francis, 3073
Stratton, Alfred William, 4416
Straus, Jacqueline H., 3527
Straus, Murray A., 3527-30
Strickland, Lily, 1146. *See also* Anderson, Lily Strickland
Stroud, C.E., 4622
Stuart, E. Gertrude, 4409
Stutley, James, 147
Stutley, Margaret, 147
Subbarayan, P., 1285
Subrahmanian, N., 522, 533
Subrahmanya Ayyar, Chandrasekhar. *See* Kumara Guru
Subrahmanya Ayyar, P.A., 1333
Subramania Iyer, G., 1016
Subramania Iyer, P.A., 1102
Subramaniam, K., 3341
Subramaniam, Venkateswarier, 423
Subramania Sastri, N., 70
Subramanyam, M., 1042
Subramanyam, Mysore, 1180
Subramanyan, K.G., 2637
Suktankar, Sundarabai, 952
Sukumaran Nair, P.K., 3219a
Sultana, Farrukh, 2929
Sultan Jahan Begam, Nawab of Bhopal, 1162, 3989-91
Summer, Mary, pseud. / Marie Foucaux, 507
Sundaram, Vivan, 2637
Sundaramaiah, R., 2741
Sundarayya, Puchalapalli, 3335
Sundarī, 680
Sundberg, Norman D., 4568-9
Suniti Devi, Maharani of Cooch Behar, 95a, 424, 724, 3665, 3993
Sur, Atul Krishna, 206, 487, 3699
Suri, Kul Bhushan, 2480
Surjit Kaur, 1928, 4308
Surtees, Virginia, 1491
Surya, Rekha, 2617
Suryananda Lakshmi, 2109
Suryanarayan Rao, Bengakuru, 1934
Sushila, pseud., 2862
Suśruta, 462
Swain, Clara A., 4050
Swaminatha, K., 1827
Swaminathan, Mina, 1710, 3198
Swaminathan, V.S., 1265
Swamivadivu, 31
Swann, Darius, 4247
Syed, Sabiha Hassan, 4439a
Sykes, Marjorie, 3135
Symons, Arthur, 2733

T., M.A., 1417
Tadpatrikar, S.N., 669
Tagore, Abanindranath, 3756
Tagore, Protima, 320
Tagore, Rabindranath, 812-3, 1017, 3736, 3827a, 3829, 3835-41
Tahera, B.S., 3912
Tahera, Sayeda, 3894
Tahmankar, Dattatraya Vishwanath, 4005
Taimuri, M.H.R., 4006
Taj, Kokab, 4502
Taleyarkhan, Homi J.H., 2327
Talim, Meena V., 425, 441
Talpallikar, M.B., 3305
Talukdar, Sumita, 1945
Talukder, Alauddin, 3910
Talwar, G.P., 2458
Talwar, Prem P., 1903
Tambiah, Stanley J., 311, 3046, 3076
Tambimuttu / Thurairajah Tambimuttu, 240
Tantia, Rameshwar, 2885
Tapasyananda, Swami, 2073, 2120
Taseer, Christable, 2635
Tata, Herabai A., 1286
Tata, Mithan, 1204
Tatke, R.S., 3561
Tattubhushan, Sitanath, 3613
Tavarkar, Narayan Gopal, 191
Taylor, Kamala (Purnaiya). *See* Markandaya, Kamala
Taylor, Philip Meadows, 751, 4029
Tejasananda, Swami, 2121
Telang, Kashinath Trimbak, 3402
Tellis-Nayak, Jessie, 2363
Temple, Helen F., 1634
Temple, Richard Carnac, 1944, 3960
Thackersey, Premlila Vithaldas, 2247a, 3558
Thakur, Harsha N., 4558
Thakur, Upendra, 271, 568, 4345
Thakur, V.V., 766
Thakur Singh, S.G., 2633
Thankappan Nair, P., 198, 1828, 1935, 3342-3
Thanvi, Ashraf Ali, 1789
Thapar, Romila, 915, 1656
Thapar, Savitri, 2489
Tharakan, Michael, 2578
Tharakan, Sophie M., 2578
Theodorson, George A., 1837
Thergaonkar, D.M., 3561
Thiagarajan, K., 187
Thierry, Solange, 3780
Thoburn, James Mills, 1635
Thomä, Hedwig, 1223
Thomas, M.M., 1974
Thomas, Paul, 59, 241, 488, 1018
Thompson, Edward, 272, 985-6
Thompson, Jemima, 1636
Thomson, Bertha M., 1137
Thurston, Edgar, 3159
Thwaites, Jeanne, 3071
Tikker, Khema, 2012
Tilack, Tara, 1176
Tilak, H.V., 1180
Tilak, Lakshmibai, 3471-2
Tinker, Hugh, 9
Tinker, Irene, 2307
Tinling, Christine Isabel, 3982
Tirumala Rao, Pratury, 1959
Tirumalayya Naidu, C., 3160
Tisdall, Evelyn Earnest Percy, 4030
Tiwari, Udai Narain, 4196
Tod, James, 4066
Tonge, E.M., 4410
Toussaint, J.R., 358
Trakroo, P.L., 562
Tribhuwan, Jyotsna Amrit, 79, 2435
Tripathi, A.D., 2488
Tripathi, Amales, 3659
Tripathi, Govardhanram M., 3504
Tripathi, Harsha J., 1699
Trivedi, G.M., 4087
Trivedi, Harshad R., 1810
Trivedi, Sheela, 4280a
Triveni, pseud. / Anasuya Shankar, 3362
Tsolinas, George, 3566
Tucci, Giuseppe, 123
Tuladhar, Jayanti M., 4559
Tuli. Jitendra, 2047

Turkhud, Alice M., 1416
Turnbull, H.G. Dalway, 886
Tuttiett, Mary Gleed. *See* Gray, Maxwell
Tyabji, F.B., 3426
Tyabji, Rehana, 2587
Tyler, Mary, 2993, 4508
Tytler, Harriet C., 4031

Uberoi, Narindar, 4623
Učida, Norihiko, 3212
Ullrich, Helen E., 3199, 3300, 3344
Underhill, Barbara, 1551, 1637
Underhill, Mrs. L.A., 916
Underhill, Muriel M., 859
UNESCO, 2391
United Free Church of Scotland, 3481
University of Dacca. Institute of Statistical Research and Training, 3872
Unnithan, T.K.N., 3272
Upadhyay, Vasudev, 563
Upadhyaya, Bhagwat Saran, 387
Upadhyaya, Daya Shankar, 4346-7
Upadhyaya, Hari S., 4197-9
Upadhyaya, Krishna Deva, 4336-8
Upadhyaya, Padma, 343
Upadhyaya, S.C., 242
Upreti, H.C., 1838, 4066a
Urquhart, Margaret M., 3735

Vadivelu, A., 3992
Vaid, Krishna Baldev, 4382
Vaidehi Krishnamoorthy, A., 564
Vaidya, G.M., 767, 4007
Vaidya, Narayana Keshava, 995, 1043
Vaidyanathan, K.E., 4560
Vakil, Jafar Ali M., 1961
Vanamamalai, N., 3345
Vanarase, S.J., 3550
Van Doren, Alice B., 1266, 1567-8
Van Meter, Rachel R., 3842
Van Zile, Judy, 334
Varadpande, M.L., 510
Varghese, Mariamma A., 1678
Varma, Bhagwati Charan, 4383-4
Varma, Mahadevi, 4369
Varma, Monika, 2710-1, 2751-3
Varma, Phulmani, 2692
Varma, P.N., 2973
Vashishtha, V.K., 3975
Vasudev, Uma, 1374-5, 1755
Vaswani, J.P., 2114-5
Vaswani, Thanwardas Lilaram, 621
Vatsyayan, Kapila, 335, 2583, 2654
Vātsyāyana, 513
Vatuk, Sylvia Jane, 2058, 4162, 4177-8, 4190, 4200, 4205-6, 4250
Vatuk, Ved Prakash, 4178, 4200, 4250
Vaughan, Kathleen Olga, 1138, 1163
Veen, Klaas W. van der, 3496
Venkanna, T., 1849
Venkatachalam, Govindraj, 2608-9
Venkatarama Dikshitar, T., 294
Venkataraman, Balasubrahmanyam, 743
Venkatarama Sastri, T.R., 388
Venkataratnam Naidu, R., 1147
Venkatarayappa, K.N., 1822
Venkateswaran, Shyamala, 2789
Venkateswara Rao, T., 2458
Vequaud, Yves, 4348
Verghese, J., 3346
Verghese, K.S., 1950
Verma. Amrit, 32
Verma, Babu Ram, 1890
Verma, Dayanand, 2048
Verma, Hari Narain, 32
Verma, K.D., 2886
Verma, K.K., 4131
Verma, Malka, 4265
Verma, Shrikant, 2583
Verma, S.K., 4008
Vetschera, Traude, 3541, 4109
Vickery, K.C., 3449
Vickland, Ellen Elizabeth, 3664, 3700
Vidyāpati, 630
Vidyasagar, Iswar Chandra, 3629
Vijayalakshmi, C., 3843
Vijayalakshmi, P., 2721
Vincent, Gladys, 3666
Vincent, Shelomith I, 1569
Vines, Charlotte S., 4411-3
Vineśa, M.B., 2647
Vinoba / Vinoba Bhave, 45, 1700
Visaria, Pravin M., 2464, 2473
Vishwanath, K., 2604
Viswanathan, K., 2742
Viswanathan, Radha, 2631
Vivekananda, Swami, 814-5
Vreede-de Stuers, Cora, 1839-40, 4100, 4110-1, 4207, 4222-3, 4273-4
Vyas, N.N., 4079
Vyas, Shantikumar Nanooram, 492-8

Wadhera, Kiron, 4266
Wadia, Ardeshir Ruttonji, 816
Wadia, Avabai B., 1701, 2230, 2328
Wadley, Susan Snow, 40, 89a, 4191, 4234, 4339
Wagle, Iqbal, 10
Wagle, N.K., 499
Waheed, Bushra, 2408
Walawalkar, Nibha, 3561
Walker, Alexander, 3380
Wallace-Dunlop, Madeline Anne, 4056
Walter, Margaret, 349
Ward, Barbara E. / Barbara (Ward) Jackson, 1726, 1756
Warne, Francis Wesley, 1638
Warty, S.G., 888
Wasi, Muriel, 1103, 2212, 2219, 2273, 2275
Wasserzug-Traeder, Gertrud, 1592
Watney, Daniel, 1139
Wattal, Pyare Kishen, 1186
Wayman, Alex, 454
Wazir Hasan, Sakinatul Fatima, 829
Weatherley, Ella M., 1639
Weeraratne, Amarasiri, 452
Weerawardana, I.D.S., 3115
Weiss, Eugene M., 4305
Weitbrecht, Mrs. / Martha (Edwards) Weitbrecht, 1224, 1570-1, 1640
Wernher, Hilda, 1502, 1552-3
West, Geoffrey, 1462
West Bengal. Department of Labour, 3787
Western, R.H., 4428
White, Ebe Minerva, 79a
White, Elizabeth Herrick, 4456
White, Rose, 1641
Whitehead, Henry, 3294
Wickramanayake, D., 1702
Wiebe, Paul D., 1841
Wiesinger, Rita, 2001, 4235
Wigram, E.F.E., 1593
Wijayaratne, C.M., 3104
Wijenaike, Punyakante, 2805-7
Wijesekera, N.D., 3021, 3090

Wilbur, Donald N., 1734
Wilde, Mrs. Frank, 4595
Wilkens, W.J., 860
Wille, G.A., 3055-6
Williams, Edith A., 1642
Williams, Gertrude Marvin, 861
Williams, Haydn Moore, 2974-5
Williams, Nancy, 1643
Willman-Grabowska, Helena, 396
Wilson, Amrit, 4624
Wilson, Anne Campbell (Macleod). *See* Macleod, Anne C.
Wilson, Dagmar Curjel, 917
Wilson, Dorothy Clarke, 3168, 3184, 3202, 4051
Wilson, Elizabeth, 3692
Wilson, James, 3652
Wilson, John, 1572, 3394, 3482
Wilson, Margaret, 1554-5
Wilson, Rosalind, 2660
Wilson-Carmichael, Amy, 3170-3
Winkelmann, Dorothea, 3530
Winslow, Myron, 3007
Winternitz, Moritz, 71, 399
Wiser, Charlotte Viall, 1334, 4067-8
Wiser, William, 4068
Witlin, Ray, 3560
Wodeyar, Sadashiva Shivadeva, 786
Women's Christian College, Madras, 3144
Women's Christian Medical College, Ludhiana, 3983
Women's Franchise Union of Ceylon, 3001
Women's Indian Association, 1267, 2348
Wood, Ernest, 887
Wood, Maria Lydia Blane, 1492
Wood, Marjorie R., 3544
Woodroffe, John George / Arthur Avalon, pseud., 124, 136, 635-7
Woodruff, Gertrude M., 3260
Woods, Dorthea E., 2275
Woodsmall, Ruth Frances, 1294, 1573, 1733, 1735, 1790, 2405
Woodward, Frank Lee, 3025
Workman, Fanny. *See* Bullock Workman, Fanny
Workman, William Hunter, 4576-9, 4581-2
Wright, Arnold, 799
Wright, Theodore P., Jr., 3524
Wyckoff, Charlotte Chandler, 1104
Wyon, John B., 4132, 4137-41, 4163, 4286, 4318a

Yadav, S.S., 1868
Yalman, Nur, 2049, 3077, 3080, 3091
Yaravintelimath, C.R., 1753
Yashpal, 4402
Yasodadevi, V., 153, 177
Yaukey, David, 3943-4
Yazdani, G., 410
Yesudas, R.N., 569, 3336
Yocum, Glenn E., 576
Yoosoof, P.M., 3081
Young, Katherine K., 18
Young, Miriam, 4052-3
Young, Ruth, 919, 1106
Younghusband, Francis Edward, 954
Young Women's Christian Association, 2350-1
Young Women's Christian Association, India, 2220, 2275, 2352, 2441
Young Women's Christian Association of India, Burma and Ceylon, 1268
Young Women's Christian Association of India, Burma and Ceylon. National Committee, 1269
Youssef, Nadia H., 2154, 2182
Yousuf, Farhat / Farhat Yusuf, 4503
Yule, Henry, 273
Yusuf Ali, A., 891

Zafar, Emmanuel, 1891
Zaheer, Razia Sajjad, 2903-4
Zaib-un-Nissa Hamidullah, 1724, 2759-63, 2949-50
Zaidi, Muhammad Hasanain, 830
Zaidi, S.M. Hafeez, 4473
Zaidi, Syed M.H., 106
Zain-el-Abidin, 817
Zakaria, Rafiq, 714
Zbavitel, Dušan, 11
Zeb-un-Nisa Hamidullah. *See* Zaib-un-Nissa Hamidullah
Zeidenstein, Laura, 3913
Zeidenstein, Sondra A., 2303, 3846, 3913-4
Zenana Bible and Medical Mission, 1593
Zia-ul-Islam Janjua, 2018
Zīb-un-Nisā, 740-1
Zimmer, Heinrich, 137
Zurayk, Huda C., 4504

Subject Index

Numbers in this gothic type designate bibliographic entries.
Italic numbers designate pages of the volume.
The designation "ad loc." indicates westerners' dates of residence in South Asia.

adolescence. *See* life cycle
Agha, Zubeida (20th cent.), 2634-5
aging. *See* life cycle
Ahalyābāī Holakar, rani of Indore (1725?-95), *20*, 759-67
Aishwarya Rajya Laxmi Devi, badamaharani of Nepal (1949-), 4566-7
Akbar (1542-1605), 727-9
Akhtar, Begam (20th cent.), 2611, 2616-7
Akkamahādēvi (12th cent.), 583-5, 587
alcoholics, 2440
Ali, Mumtaz (b. 19th cent.), 1773
Alkazi, Roshen (b. 1923), 2707
All-India Women's Conference/AIWC (est. 1926), *430, 431-2*, 936, 1185, 1241, 1261-2, 1764, 2333-5, 2339, 2343-4
All Pakistan Women's Association/APWA (est. 1949), *444-5*, 1399, 2398-9, 2401-3, 4490
Ambrose, Ethel Mary Murray (1874-1934), 3478
Amrita Pritam (1919-), 4396-6a, 4398
Amrit Kaur, Rajkumari (1887-1964), *426, 428*, 1309, 1725
Anand, Mulk Raj (b. 1905), 2873
Anandamayi Ma (b. 1896), *22*, 2061, 2094-2109
Anasuyadevi/The Mother (b. 1923), 3282
Andal. *See* Āṇṭāḷ
Anderson, Lady (ad loc. 20th cent.), *461*
Anderson, Mrs. (ad loc. 19th cent.), 3185
Andhra Pradesh, women of. *See* South Indian women
Āṇṭāḷ (8th cent.), *19*, 298, 571-2, 577-81
Antrim, Elza Thronburg, 1626
Aparajita Debi, pseud./Radharani Debi (b. 1904), 3813
Appasamy, Mrs. E.S. (1878-1963), 3143
Armstrong, Ruth Gallup (ad loc. ca. 1960), 2989
Armstrong-Hopkins, Saleni/Saleni (Armstrong) Hopkins (b. 1855), 1596-7
Arthaśāstra of Kautilya, *19*, 457-8, 514-7
arts, *18, 24, 26, 27, 29, 450*, 85, 329, 341, 718, 914, 2580, 2584, 2586, 2588, 2659. *See also* censorship, obscenity; folklore
  architecture, 723, 736, 743, 760
  literature, 11, 113, 240, 344-5, 347-8, 351-61, 373, 379, 421, 423, 450, 502, 508-10, 518-35, 543-4, 571-81, 583-90, 593-621, 623-8, 630-1, 642, 680, 694-5, 724, 730, 732-5, 738, 740-1, 751, 941, 965, 1332, 1396, 1752, 1830, 2055, 2583, 2658, 2690-2929, 3155, 3266, 3347-64, 3415, 3595-3601, 3603, 4029, 4218, 4360-4402, 4511-2. *See also* Sanskrit, Prakrit, Pali literatures; western women in South Asia; *particular classical texts, genres and authors, by name*
  music/dance/drama, 91, 117, 236, 245, 301, 330-5, 423, 450, 509-10, 603, 605, 609, 614, 705, 1219, 1518, 2587, 2589-2631, 2662, 2803, 3148-9. *See also devadāsī*
  painting, drawing, 120, 245, 312, 341a, 404, 501, 625-6, 628, 650, 652, 661-2, 694-5, 697, 699, 702-5, 721, 739, 752, 2632-9a, 4509
  sculpture, 120, 129, 238, 253, 312, 340, 343, 408, 410, 685, 696, 698, 700, 2635, 4373
Arundale, Rukmini Devi. *See* Rukmini Devi Arundale
Ashapurna Devi (b. 1909), 3804
Ashby, Lilian Luker (b. 1876), 4054
Ashmore, Harriette (ad loc. 19th cent.), 4055
Assamese women, *27*, 179-80, 182. *See also* East India, women of highland; East India, women of lowland
associations, programs, 2300, 2302, 2305, 2391. *See also* education; health; missions; social welfare
  Bangladesh, *451, 452-3*, 2303, 2526, 3846, 3850, 3908, 3912-3, 3916-24, 3928
  England, *455-6*
  India, *426, 427, 430-2, 434, 435, 440, 442-6*, 889, 895, 936, 1083, 1105, 1108, 1112-3, 1118, 1129, 1132, 1135, 1139, 1185, 1261-4, 1267-9, 1320, 1383-4, 1432, 1647-8, 1651, 1704-10, 1721, 1733, 1764, 2255, 2282, 2303, 2311, 2328, 2333-54, 2357, 2360, 2362, 2383, 2412-3, 2443, 2579, 2991, 3130-1, 3152, 3314-5, 3374, 3395, 3399, 3407, 3412, 3451-62, 3465, 3469-70, 3559-61, 3602, 3606-7, 3644, 3650, 3660-2, 3665, 3670, 3692, 4283, 4285
  Nepal, 2526, 4523-3a, 4554, 4560a-61
  Pakistan, *444-6*, 1399, 1721, 1735, 2392, 2398-2407, 2526, 4487, 4490-3, 4507
  Sri Lanka, 1740, 2338, 3106, 3109-10a, 3118
astrology, 1825, 1934
Aśvaghoṣa (ca. 2nd cent. C.E.), 503

Athavale, Parvatibai (b. 1870), 3465
Aurobindo Ghose, Sri (1872-1950), 2884, 2886. *See also* The Mother
auspiciousness, 3158, 3250, 3280, 3763
Auvaiyār (ca. 7th cent.), *19*, 534-5
Auzurie, Madam/Anne-Marie Auzurie (b. early 20th cent.), 2596
āyurveda. *See* health

Bābur (1494-1530), 720, 725
Bādshāh Begam of Oudh (early 19th cent.?), 768
Bahiṇābāī (1629?-1700), *19*, 28, 588-9
Bahū Begam/Ammat-uz-Zahrā of Faizabad (1728?-1816), 769-70
Balasaraswati, T. (1918-), 2597, 2600, 2602, 2606, 2609
Baluch, Akhtar (b. ca. 1952), 4508
Baluchi women, *29*. *See* Northwestern Islamic women
Bandaranaike, Sirimavo Dias (1916-), 3022, 3116-8
Banerji, Sevabrata Sasipada (1840-1924), 3656
Bangladesh, women of, *27*, 2303, 2452, 2529, 2655, 2942-3, 3845-3953. *See also* Bengali women; Pakistani women
Bartrum, Katherine Mary (ad loc. 1857), 4010
Basavaṇṇa (1106-67), 586
basavi, *25*, 3147-8, 3150, 3158-9, 3207
Becher, Augusta Emily (Prinsep) (1830-1909), 1493
Begam Akhtar. *See* Akhtar, Begam
Bengali women, *27*, 44, 163, 355, 363, 551-2, 556-7, 561, 622-3, 629, 639, 642, 644, 771-4, 1225, 1255, 1384, 1916, 1986, 2303, 2548. *See also* Bangladesh, women of; East India, women of lowland
Bennett, Amelia (b. 1839), 4011
Bentinck, William Cavendish (1774-1839), 983, 3618, 3620
Besant, Annie (Wood) (1847-1933), *21*, *427*, *428*, 1439-42, 1445-62, 3143
Bethune School (est. 1849) and Bethune College (est. 1878), Calcutta, 3631-4, 3636-7, 3647, 3658-9
Beveridge, Annette (Ackroyd) (1842-1929), *458*
Bhābhī Begam of Faizabad (early 19th cent.?), 770
Bhagvat Sinhjee, maharaja of Gondal (20th cent.), 3414
bhakti. *See* religion
Bhandari, Mannu (b. 1931), 4365
Bharati, Subrahmanya (1882-1921), 3350, 3355
Bharatidasan (20th cent.), 3355
Bhat, Usha (20th cent.), *426*
Bhatt, Ela Ramesh (1933-), 3560
Bhattacharya, Bhabani (1906-), 2865, 2867
Bhavaśaṃkarī of Bhurshut (16th cent.), 783
Bibhavati Devi, rani of Bhowal (b. ca. 1890), 831
Bihar, women of, 185, 315, 2993. *See also* North/Central Indian women
Bīnabāyī (ca. 12th to 15th cent.), 537
birth. *See* child bearing
birth control. *See* population studies
Blackwell, Mary Lilian (d. 1889), 1598
Bleakley, Ethel (ad loc. ca. early 20th cent.), 3674
Booth, Mary Warburton (b. 1872), 1599-1603
Booth, Winifred (ad loc. 20th cent.), 3174
Bor, Eleanor (20th cent.), 4600
Bose, Abala (1865-1951), 1250
Bose, Krishna (20th cent.), *428*
Bose, Sadhona (1914-72), 2605, 2609
Bose, Subhas Chandra/Netaji (1897-1945?), *427-8*, 3667
Bower, Ursula Graham (20th cent.), 4600a
Brand, Evelyn Constance/Granny Brand (1879-1974), 3184
Brayne, Frank Lugard (b. 1882), *458*
Briggs, Annie Jane (ad loc. 1877-78), *466*
Brinda, maharani of Kapurthala (b. ca. 1900), 832
Brockway, Frances Elizabeth (Abbey) (1862-1903), 1605
Brown, Edith Mary (b. 1864), 3981
Buddhism, *17*, *18*, 74-5, 79a, 96, 123, 127, 172, 175, 411, 413-4, 415a-9, 437-41, 453-4, 633, 3082, 3085-94, 3113, 4540
Buddhist women in ancient South Asia, 413-25
  bhikṣuṇīs/bhikkhunīs ("almswomen"), 412, 433-52
  lay women, 426-32
Bullock Workman, Fanny/Fanny (Bullock) Workman (1859-1925), *29*, 4576-82
Butler, Clementina (Rowe) (1820-1913), 1606
Butler, Fanny Jane (1850-89), 4406, 4410

Calcott, Lady Maria (Dundas) Graham. *See* Graham, Maria
Cama, Bhikaji Rustom (1861-1936), 1238a
Campbell, Mary Frazer. *See* Monkland, Mrs.
Campbell, Mary Jane (b. 1865), 4033-4
Cānd Bībī of Ahmadnagar (Niẓām Shāhī queen, 1547?-99?), *20*, 745-51
Caṅkam/Sangam literature, *19*, 523-35
Canning, Charlotte (Stuart), Countess (1817-61), 1484, 1491
Captain, Gosasp Manekji Sorabji (b. 1884), *461*
careers. *See* work
Carmichael, Amy Wilson. *See* Wilson-Carmichael, Amy
Carpenter, Mary (1807-77), *21*, 1434-5, 1437
Carter, Lillian (1898-), 2979
Case, Mrs./Adelaide Teague Case (ad loc. 1857), 4012
case studies. *See* life histories, case studies
castes, communities, 856. *See also* scheduled caste communities; tribal communities; ***religious communities, by name***
  Agarwal, 4184, 4202
  Ambalavasi, 3289
  Anglo-Indian, 795-6, 1821, 4093
  Badaga, 3346
  Bania, 3503
  Banjara, 2930
  Bauri, 3745a
  Bediya, 3961
  Beralakoduva Vakkaliga, 3247
  Bhil, 4079, 4235
  Bhotia, 4095
  Bhumij, 4232
  Birhor, 4147
  brahman, 3238, 3242, 3249, 3352, 3415, 3451-65, 3466-72, 3497, 3701, 3744, 4053, 4161, 4351, 4358-9, 4515, 4528, 4530-30a, 4541
    Anavil, 3496
    Gaur, 4177
    Havik, 3275-6, 3300
    Namboodiri, 3240, 3265, 3277
    Pandit, 4448
    Sanketi, 540
    Vadnagar Nagar, 3488, 3504
  Bugti, 4424, 4437

Chamar, 4126
Chandraseniya Kayastha Prabhu, 3498
Chetri, 4515, 4528, 4530-30a, 4541
Divaru, 3300
Gaddi, 4170
Garo, 2038, 3678, 4588, 4591, 4593
Gond, 4134, 4185
Gujar Bakarwal, 4443
Gurung, 4523-3a, 4537
Jamaati, 3522
Jat, 4126, 4150
Jogati, 3154
Kanbi, 3388, 3390
Kayastha, 3258, 4350, 4352
Khasa, 4066a, 4119
Khasi, 2038, 4590, 4592-4
Khoja, 3426, 3465a
Khond, 3622-3, 3625
Korku, 4167
Kuki, 4595
Kunbi, 3491
Limbu, 4526-7, 4531-3
Lingayat, 3233
Lushai, 4589
Magar, 4524
Mahadev Koli, 3484
Mali, 4353
Mang, 3541
Mappilla/Moplah, 194, 3214, 3237
Maratha, 753, 3491, 3523
Marri Baluch, 4425
Memon, 4468
Meo, 4165
Mina, 4109
Minyong, 4598
Mukkuvan, 3193
Munda, 3757, 4142, 4226
Nadar, 3334, 3336
Naga, 4595-6, 4599
Nayar, 194, 2875, 3207, 3209, 3214, 3220-1, 3240, 3263, 3265-9, 3271-2, 3342-3
Newar, 4516, 4519, 4525, 4534, 4543-4, 4551
Noniya, 4176
Oraon, 4148, 4225-7, 4230
Oswal, 4217-8
Paharia, 4130, 4307
Panggi, 4598
Parayan, 3210, 3222
Pardhan, 4185
Pathare Prabhu, 3399, 3517
Patidar, 3540
Pirzada, 4215
Pulluvan, 3278
Rajput, 568, 3389, 3391-3, 3964, 3993-4, 4063, 4066, 4155, 4189
  Chauhan, 3961
  Jethva, 3380
  Jhareja, 3380, 3382
  Raya, 4162
Rastogi, 4171
Santal, 2876, 3742, 4078, 4092, 4097, 4130-1, 4151, 4224, 4307
Saora, 3759
Saurashtra, 3212
Sherpa, 4517
Singhpo, 4597
Soomra, 3380
Sunni Surati Vohra, 3494
Swami Narayani, 701, 4617
Synteng, 4590
Syrian Christian, 3236, 3257
Telia Nagesia, 4108
Tibetan, 4529
Tiyyar, 194, 3209
Warli, 3485, 3582
caste structure, *448*, 2049, 3525. *See also* prestige, rank
Cennamma, rani of Kittur (1778-1829), 786
censorship, obscenity, 2582-3, 2585, 2668-9
Central Indian women. *See* North/Central Indian women
Ceylon, women of. *See* Sri Lanka, women of
Chakko, Sarah (1905-54), 1223
Chand Bibi. *See* Cānd Bībī
Chand Kaur of Sukherchakia *misal* (b. ca. 1800), 3995
Chaṅkrottu Amma (8th cent.?), 582
Chapman, Edith (b. 1888), 4601
Chatterjee, Bankim Chandra (1838-94), 3842
Chatterji, Sarat Chandra (1876-1938), 3820
Chattopadhyaya, Kamaladevi (1903-), *21*, *426*, 1338-9, 2327
Chenoy, Shanta (20th cent.), *434*
child bearing, 140, 218, 459-62, 688, 690, 1184, 1951, 1986, 1993, 2316, 2414, 2415a, 2418, 3064, 3066, 3069, 3204-5, 3517, 3724, 3732, 3870, 4063, 4131, 4134-6, 4144, 4147-8, 4286, 4596. *See also* female infanticide; health; life cycle; motherhood/child rearing; population studies; social welfare
  abortion, 1936-44, 3225, 3514, 3726-7, 4151, 4291-2, 4296
  barrenness, 1510, 1514, 2497, 2868, 2922, 3377, 3510, 3723, 4124, 4156-7, 4511
  birth, 131, 198, 217, 1114-6, 1179-80, 1929, 1931-3, 1935, 2508, 3093, 3203, 3230-2, 3509, 3513, 3725, 3766, 3868, 3871, 4137-8, 4140-3, 4146, 4149-51, 4208, 4298, 4441, 4497-8
  pregnancy, 214-6, 219, 383, 3065, 3067-8, 3229, 4139, 4145, 4440
child rearing. *See* motherhood/child rearing
Chisholm, Mrs. (ad loc. ca. 19th cent.), 1489
Choudhurani, Sarala Devi (1872-1945), *430*
Christianity, 1757, 1974, 2566, 3095. *See also* missions
Christian women (South Asian), general statements, 844
Christlieb, Marie Luise (b. 1868), 3175, 3179
Chugtai, Ismat (1915-), *24*, 2901-2
Chundawat, Lakshmi Kumari (b. 1916), 4360
Chundra Lela (b. 19th cent.), 2111
Churchill, Mrs. George/Matilda (Faulkner) Churchill (b. 1840), 3176
Church Missionary Society/CMS, Church of England (est. 1799), *466-8*, 1578, 1593, 1621, 4403-4
Church of England Zenana Missionary Society/ CEZMS (est. 1880?), *466*, 1559, 1575-6, 1579-81, 1583, 1609, 3005, 4404, 4407-13, 4428
Cilappatikāram. *See* epics
Clapp, Estelle Barnes (20th cent.), 2979a
Clark, Marjorie (b. 1896), 4601
Clark, Mary Mead (b. 1832), 3679
Clarke, Maureen (ad loc. mid-20th cent.), 1608
class, social, 1650, 1670, 3528-9, 3543, 3655, 3717, 3849
Clerk, Alice M. (Frere). *See* Frere, Alice M.
Clough, Margaret Morley (1803-27), 3002
Committee on the Status of Women in India, *22*, 1647, 1704-10
communalism, *21*, 1240-1, 1243, 4385, 4400-1

community development. *See* development
concubines, 722, 3153, 3565, 3666
Cook, Nilla Cram (ad loc. 20th cent.), 1494
Cooke, Mary Anne/Mrs. Wilson (ad loc. 1824), 3639
Coopland, Mrs. R.M. (ad loc. 1857), 4013
Corner, Caroline/Caroline Corner-Ohlmus (b. 19th cent.), 3008
cosmological principles, feminine (*Śakti, Prakṛti, Māyā, Prajñāparāmitā* et al.), *17, 18*, 84, 89a, 125-31, 137, 453. *See also Śakti* and *Śākta* traditions
costume, beauty, *18, 24, 25, 26, 29, 450*, 313-5, 321, 509, 521, 1842, 2414, 2931-7, 3122, 4417, 4513-4. *See also* arts
  body painting, 2646-7, 4347, 4352
  clothing, 316-20, 753, 2057, 2930, 2938-44, 3334, 3336, 3367, 3876-7, 3879, 3887
  hairstyles, 326-7, 1042
  jewelry, 321-5, 2945-50, 3123-4, 3196, 4248-50
  physical beauty, 85, 312, 337-8, 340-1, 342-3, 408-10
courtesans. *See* prostitution
Cousins, Margaret Elizabeth (1878-1954), *21, 427, 428, 430*, 1282, 1477-8
cows, 1240, 4208
crime, *440*, 2425, 2434, 3548, 3566. *See also* female infanticide; murderers; prison; prostitution; social welfare
Curzon, Mary (Leiter) (1870-1906), 1490

D., A./Mrs. A. Deane (ad loc. 1804-14), 791
dance, dancing ("nautch") girls. *See* arts
Das, Basanti Devi (b. 1880), *426*
Das, Frieda Mathilda (Hauswirth). *See* Hauswirth, Frieda
Das, Kamala (1934-), *29*, 2699, 2707, 2812, 2814-7
Daśakumāracarita of Daṇḍin, 673
Davidson, Flora Marion (b. 1879), 4405
Deane, Mrs. A. *See* D., A.
Delhi Sultanate, *20*, 706, 710-1, 712-4
demography. *See* population studies
Dench, Mrs., *461*
Desai, Anita (1937-), *24*, 2704, 2818, 2824-7
Desai, Neera (1925-), *434*
Desai Nirmala (20th cent.), *428*
Deshmukh, Durgabai (1910-), *426*, 1381
Deshpande, Gauri (1942-), 2707
devadāsī, *18, 21, 25, 27*, 41, 247-50, 256-7, 332, 334, 676, 700, 848, 1335-7, 1810, 2432, 2593-4, 2653, 2803, 2883, 3130a, 3147-9, 3151-60, 3423-5, 3565, 3761-4, 3791, 4545. *See also* arts; *basavi*; prostitution
development, *23*, 1654, 1740, 2192-4, 2300-7, 2526. *See also* associations, programs; education; health; social welfare; work
  Bangladesh, *27, 450*, 3850, 3882, 3884-5, 3891, 3893, 3895, 3902, 3905-9, 3912-3, 3915-7, 3920-3
  India, *23, 26, 28*, 1110, 1250, 1298-9, 1947, 2149-50, 2158, 2165-6, 2179, 2190, 2280-1, 2308, 2312, 2315-8, 2321-3, 2325, 2328-31a, 2344, 2356, 2365-80, 2415, 2428, 2489, 2494, 2502, 2504, 2560, 2777, 2782, 3325-7, 3548, 3984, 4069, 4252
  Nepal, *29*, 4554, 4557
  Pakistan, *23, 29, 439*, 16, 1724, 2301, 2390, 2392-7, 2401, 2506, 2509-10, 4475, 4486, 4495
  Sri Lanka, *25*, 3018
devī. *See* goddesses
deViri, Anne (20th cent.), 2990
Dewar, Phebe Rutherford (1884-1923), 1612
Dhar, Sheila (b. 1929), 2614
dharmaśāstra, *18*, 220, 224-5, 246, 251, 264, 285, 305-6, 467, 470, 473
  Mānava Dharmaśāstra ("Code of Manu"), 457-8, 466, 468-9, 471-2
dharmasūtra, 201, 397
dissertations, sources for, *439*, 12, 16-7
Dolly, Miss/"Mees Dolly" (19th cent.), 4022
domestic sphere, *22, 25, 26, 27, 28, 29*, 81, 839, 1391, 1724, 2235, 3196, 3244, 3697, 3730, 3735, 3782, 3915, 3920, 4604. *See also* kinship; seclusion, modesty, veiling
Dongerkery, Kamala Sunderrao (b. 1909), 1383
Downie, Annie Kennard (1875-1901), 3178
drama. *See* arts; folklore
Draper, Eliza (1744-78), 798-9
Draupadī, 477, 480. *See also* epics
Duberly, Mrs. Henry/Frances Isabella (Locke) Duberly (1829-1903), 4014, 4030
Dufferin, Hariot/Hariot Georgina (Hamilton) Hamilton-Temple-Blackwood, Marchioness of Dufferin and Ava (ad loc. 1884-88), 1481
Dupleix, Jeanne Albert (b. 1708), 792
Durgāvatī of Gondwana (16th cent.), *20*, 775-6
Dutt, Kalpana (20th cent.), 3668
Dutt, Saroj Nalini (1887-1925), 1255, 1384
Dutt, Toru (1856-77), *24*, 1287, 2712, 2718-21, 2730

East India, women of highland, *30*, 546, 4588-4601a
East India, women of lowland, *27*, 546, 3602-3844
Eaton, Emma G. (b. 1869), 1627
economic position, *18, 21, 28, 29*, 306, 1164, 1709, 2193, 2325, 3063, 3551, 3578-81, 4058, 4531, 4533. *See also* kinship; law; work
Eden, Emily (1797-1869), *21*, 1427-30
education, *18, 20, 23, 25, 26, 27, 28, 29*, 295, 371, 708, 718, 889, 914, 1045, 1315, 1703, 1709, 1730, 1740, 2238-55, 2260, 2271, 2313, 2317, 2322, 2391, 3306, 3549, 3641, 3647, 3900, 3902, 3909, 4280, 4475-7. *See also* missions
  associations, *435, 466*, 1078, 1083, 2255, 3407, 3412, 3639, 3644
  fields, 4474
    adult, 2276-83, 2303, 2315a, 2316a, 3308, 3325-7, 3692, 3905, 3916-8, 4280a, 4284, 4489. *See also* associations, programs; development; social welfare
    agriculture, 2190, 3022, 3106
    family life/home science, 1071, 2029-32, 2276, 3904, 3915, 3920-3, 3980, 4489
    health care, 1109, 1116, 1930, 2416, 3977-9, 3981-3
    law, 3101-2, 3105
    physical, 2292, 2294-5, 4483, 4485
    sex, 2289-91, 2430, 2433, 3212
    teaching, 1051, 1057, 2298-9, 4280a, 4552
    vocations, 3692, 4486, 4494
  formal, *435, 446*, 1061-3, 1066, 1068-9, 1074-7, 1079-80, 1082, 1089, 1091, 1096, 1104, 1733, 2244, 2250-1, 2256-75, 2310. 3107-8. 3143, 3145, 3309-11.

3407-7, 3412-3, 3549, 3554, 3651, 3901, 3904, 4474, 4477-8, 4482
institutions, 458, 466, 873, 2237, 2842, 2966, 2995, 2997, 3106, 3134, 3136-7, 3139, 3141-2, 3144, 3161, 3164-8, 3403, 3405-6, 3410, 3413, 3416-7, 3428, 3442, 3453, 3456-8, 3552-8, 3631-4, 3636-7, 3640, 3642, 3647-9, 3658-9, 3746, 3977, 3980, 4277-80, 4601
issues, 1092, 1801, 2235-7, 2280, 3307, 3404, 3905, 4275-6
access, problem groups, 1051, 1064, 1161, 2252, 2276, 2283-7, 2303, 2365-79, 3414, 3430-62, 4284, 4474, 4478, 4552
curricula, 1080, 2257, 2261, 2266, 2278, 3413
effects, correlations, 910, 1752, 1797, 1799-1801, 1862, 1921, 2149, 2207, 2257a, 2264, 2267-9, 2272-3, 2315a, 2490-1, 2944, 3074, 3218, 3256, 3307, 3309-13, 3520, 3538, 3550-1, 3727, 3850a, 3852, 4123, 4188, 4216, 4267-74, 4439a, 4466, 4470, 4475, 4479-81, 4502
housing, student-teacher, 296, 1104, 2441, 3324
sex segregation/coeducation, 1296, 2261-2, 4279, 4483
social reform movement, *20, 24, 25, 27, 28, 429, 435, 436, 440, 450, 456, 457, 458, 461*, 898, 910, 921, 925, 931, 1044-1104, 1434-8, 1463-76, 2251, 2994-8, 3130a, 3133-45, 3200, 3403-17, 3430-65, 3469-70, 3602, 3608-9, 3611, 3613, 3630-52, 3658-60, 3955, 3976-83
textbooks, images in, 2259, 2660, 3903
literacy/illiteracy, 1747, 1856, 1864, 2149, 2251, 2277, 2283, 2288, 2454-5, 2578, 3325-7, 3414, 4252
Elizabeth, Sister (20th cent.?), 3126
Elwood, Mrs. Colonel/Anne Katherine (Curteis) Elwood (ad loc. 1820s), 1482
employment. *See* work
English, creative writing in, 2697-2886. *See also* western women in South Asia
epics, *18, 19*, 463, 465, 474-6
Cilappatikāram, 536, 3084
Mahābhārata, 477-88
Rāmāyaṇa, 181, 489-99, 3092, 3591
eroticism. *See* arts; love; sexuality
ethnicity, 2256
evil, women's. *See* fear of women/women's evil

Falaiseau, Marquise de (née Adelaide de Kerjean) (18th cent.), 792
family. *See* kinship
family planning. *See* population studies
Faridi, Tazeen (20th cent.), 1725
Fawcett, Millicent (1847-1929), *463*
fear of women/women's evil, *18, 25, 27, 28, 29*, 214, 278-80, 417, 681, 1667, 2040-1, 2876, 3273, 3276, 3485, 3757-8, 3878, 4224-6, 4239, 4530a, 4537. *See also* goddesses
female infanticide, *20, 26, 27, 28, 430, 440*, 195, 934, 987-95, 1939. 2467, 3380-94, 3622-5, 3954, 3961-75
feminism, 1752, 2564-79, 3016, 3698
fertility. *See* population studies
film industry, 2583, 2585, 2596, 2660, 2662-70, 2923, 3337, 4372
films depicting women's lives, *460, 461*, 60, 327, 698, 702, 1363-4, 1370, 1668, 1673, 1792, 1795-6, 1826, 1834, 1845, 1847, 1948, 1956, 1967, 1994, 1997, 2011, 2060, 2126, 2135, 2156, 2205, 2211, 2274, 2329, 2340, 2362, 2378-9, 2410, 2421, 2426, 2436, 2497-8, 2512, 2590, 2592, 2597, 2604, 2611, 2636, 2644, 2662, 2933, 2986, 3022, 3153, 3213, 3249, 3278, 3289, 3293, 3462, 3736, 3739, 3771, 3785, 3841, 3952, 4060, 4064, 4277, 4349-59, 4551
Fisher, Welthy Honsinger (b. 1880), 2983, 2986, 4570
Fitzroy, Yvonne (ad loc. 1921-24), 1483
Fleming, Bethel (b. 1901), 4571
folklore, *18, 24, 26, 27, 29, 439, 449*, 39, 44, 336, 339, 362-3, 2642, 2645, 2655-6, 3340, 3342, 3345, 3592, 3699, 3737, 3740, 3794, 3947, 4185, 4323, 4338, 4360, 4376. *See also* arts; costume, beauty; language; religion
dance, 330, 334, 2594, 2653-4
drama, 4200, 4246-7
embroidery, 316, 2648-52, 3303, 3876-7, 3879
handicrafts, 2391, 2581, 2640-1
medicine, 1944
painting, drawing, 2643-7, 3246, 3248-9, 3251, 3746, 3749, 3753, 3755-6, 4340-52, 4354-9, 4568-9
printing, dyeing, 316, 3536
proverbs, folksayings, 3339, 3341, 3343, 3346, 3587, 3795-6, 3798-9, 3844, 4070, 4192
sculpture, 337-8, 342, 409, 3874, 4343, 4354
song, 758, 1238, 1931, 3088, 3212, 3338, 3425, 3490, 3491, 3499, 3501-2, 3531, 3534, 3537, 3588-90, 3591, 3593, 3754, 3772, 3793, 3797, 3827a, 3948-50, 3960, 4104-5, 4111, 4143-4, 4149, 4156-7, 4173, 4192-9, 4241, 4324-6, 4328-34, 4336, 4339, 4441, 4534
tales, 214, 219, 227, 3344, 4336-7. *See also kathā* ("story")
food and commensality, 3080, 3204, 3208, 3229-30, 3871, 3885, 4186. *See also* health; western women in South Asia
Fordyce, Mrs. (ad loc. 19th cent.), 3185
freedom movements. *See* nationalist movements
Frere, Alice M./Alice M. (Frere) Clerk (ad loc. mid-19th cent.), 3009
Fuller, Jenny Frow (1851-1900), 3476

Gaidinliu, Rani (b. 1915), 4599
G.A. Khan, Khudeja (20th cent.), 1401
Gandhi, Indira (1917-), *21*, 1353-9, 1361-75, 1754
Gandhi, Kasturba (1869-1944), *21*, 1290, 1320-5, 1340
Gandhi, Mohandas Karamchand/Mahatma Gandhi (1869-1948), *21, 428-9*, 1182, 1185, 1298-1304, 1310-25, 1348, 1361, 1364, 1391, 1540, 1673, 2310, 2360
Gani, Amna (b. ca. 1921), 4468
Gaurībāī (1759-1809), *19*, 631
Gauri Ma/Gaurimani Devi (1857-1938), 2116
Gayatri Devi (sister in Ramakrishna order, 20th cent.), 4625
Gayatri Devi, maharani of Jaipur (b. 1919), 834, 1725
gender of children, preferred, 220, 383, 832, 1668, 1953-4, 1989, 2468, 2497, 3516,

(gender of children, preferred), 3575, 4391. *See also* child bearing
Germon, Maria Vincent Garratt (19th cent.), 4015
Gibson, Julia Roberts (b. 1877), 846
Gītagovinda of Jayadeva, *19*, 624-8
Gnanananda Sarasvathi, Sadguru Swami Sri/ Sarasvathi Achan (b. 1929), 3284
Goan women, 3303, 3423, 3425
Godden, Jon (b. 1908), 1530
Godden, Rumer/Margaret Rumer Godden (b. 1907), *21*, 1530, 1534, 1537-8
goddesses, *17, 22, 25, 26, 27, 28, 29*, 116-7, 131-47, 164, 176, 179-80, 185, 192, 229, 279, 337-8, 342, 392, 395, 576, 650, 654, 655-72, 810, 2061, 2120, 2122-4, 2127-30, 2132, 3281, 3536, 3626, 3768, 4208, 4234, 4239-41, 4515. *See also* cosmological principles, feminine; religion; *Śakti* and *Śākta* traditions
  Āī, 3775
  apsarā, 190-1, 652
  Araṇyānī, 167, 394
  Bhādu, 3770, 3772
  Bhagavati, 3289
  Caṇḍī, 644-6
  devatā, 188
  Dovār Devī, 4244
  Durgā, 154-5, 642, 649, 659-63, 2126, 3769, 3774, 4243
  Ekānaṁśā, 168
  Ellamma, 3154
  Gaṅgā, 177
  Gaurī, 3500
  grāmadevatā ("village deities"), 3287-8, 3294, 3539, 4242
  Iḍā, 169
  Joginī, 4550
  Kālī/Kāḷi, 154, 156-8, 642, 3291, 3771, 3778, 4551
  Kāmākhyā, 182
  Kaṇṇaki, 3088, 3290
  Kosī, 4245
  Kumārī, 4543-4, 4546-9
  Lakṣmī, 148, 159-62, 3249
  Lakṣmīāī, 3541
  Manasā, 171, 646-8, 3767, 3778a, 3780
  Māriyammaṉ, 3190, 3292
  Melenī, 3773
  Mīnākṣī/Mīṉāṭci, 178, 183-4, 187, 3293
  Olābibi, 3776
  Pattini, 172, 175, 3082-91
  Pṛthivī, 170
  Sapahīdevī, 4244
  saptamātṛkā ("Seven Mothers"), *aṣṭamātṛkā* ("Eight Mothers"), 165, 174, 651
  Sarasvatī, 148-53, 396
  Ṣaṣṭhī, 3766
  Satī, 263
  Siri, 3286
  Sītā, 181
  Śītalā, 163, 166, 2131, 3537, 3765, 3776-7, 4243
  Tārā, 116a
  Umā, 665
  Vāc, 391
  Vaḍucī, 3535
  Vaināyakī, 173
  Vaiṣṇodevī, 186
  yakṣiṇī, 189, 653
  Yamunā, 177
  yoginī, 640, 643
Gollack, Georgina Anne (1861-1940), 1495
Gooneratne, Yasmine (20th cent.), 2706
Gordon-Cummings, Constance Frederica (1837-1924), 3010
Gouramma of Coorg (1841?-64), 1488, 4615
Graham, Maria/Lady Maria (Dundas) Graham Calcott (1785-1842), 793
Great and Little Traditions, 39, 3093, 3587, 4243, 4453
Greenfield, M. Rose (ad loc. mid-19th cent.), 4037
Gregson, Fanny/Fanny (Gregson) Liesching (1865-93), 3004
gṛhyasūtra, 398-9
Grimwood, Ethel St. Clair (ad loc. 1890), 4601a
Guinness, Lucy Evangeline (1865-1906), 1617
Gujarati women, *26-7, 428*, 545, 558, 565, 631, 650, 694, 701, 745, 2548, 4604-4a. *See also* West India, women of
Gulab Kaur (b. 189_), 1239a
Gulbadan Begam (1524-1603), *20*, 720, 726
Gyanamamba, Sri (b. 1895), 3285

Haidar, Mumtaz (20th cent.), *435*
Ḥaidar Mīrzā Dughlāt (16th cent.), 720
hairstyles. *See* costume, beauty
Haldane, Julia (ad loc. 1857), 4016
Hall, Margery (ad loc. 1937-4_), *461*
Hamida Khala, pseud. (b. ca. 1915), 2053
Hanks, Jane (Richardson). *See* Richardson, Jane
Hare, David (1775-1842), 3646
Harper, Mary (McKibbin). *See* McKibbin-Harper, Mary
Harris, Katherine (ad loc. 1857), 4017
Harṣacarita of Bāṇa, 673
Hartog, Philip (b. 1864), *458*
Harvard, Elizabeth (early 19th cent.), 1618
Harvey, Rosalie (b. 1854), 3473-4, 3480
Haryana, women of. *See* North/Central Indian women
Hastings, Mrs. Warren (18th cent.), 794
Hauswirth, Frieda/Frieda Mathilda (Hauswirth) Das (20th cent.), 1501
Hawkins, Mrs. William (later Mrs. Gabriel Towerson, 17th cent.), 798
Hayes, Marie Elizabeth (1875?-1908), 4038
health, *21, 23, 25, 26, 28, 440, 458*, 1106, 1117, 1782, 2313, 2317, 2415a, 2418, 2935-6, 3675, 4506. *See also* child bearing; missions; western women in South Asia
  associations, medical, 1105, 1108, 1112-3, 1118, 1129, 1132, 1135, 1139, 2412-3
  āyurveda ("knowledge of life"), 237, 459-62
  disorders, 1019-20, 1025, 1032, 1034, 2424-5, 2429-30, 2433, 2999, 3318-9, 3654, 3788, 4137-41. *See also* population studies
  education. *See* education
  groups with special needs
    mothers/children, 1114-6, 1179-80, 1335-7, 1927-8, 1946-7, 1949-51, 2362, 2415, 2417, 2912-3, 3066-7, 3325-7, 3421, 3479, 3725, 3867, 3872, 4137-41, 4153, 4318a, 4487, 4489
    rural women, 1110, 1179-80, 2502, 3977
    secluded women, *21*, 1106, 1111, 1119, 1156, 1161, 1163, 3146a
  hospitals, 1557, 3146-6a, 4036, 4043, 4050-1, 4133, 4319
  nutrition, 1947, 1949-50, 2316a, 2417, 3204,

3325-7, 3872, 4318, 4489
Helen (film dancer, 20th cent.), 2662
Henderson, Agnes Elizabeth (1865-1925), 3481
Heston, Winifred (ad loc. ca. 1900), 3477
Higgins, Marie Musaeus (1855-1926), 2997
Himachal Pradesh, women of. *See* North/Central Indian women
Hindi-speaking women, *27-9*. *See* North/Central Indian women
Hinduism, *17, 22*, 74-5, 78, 79a, 92
Hindu women, general statements, *20, 22*, 40, 80-9a, 463, 818-27, 839, 844, 850, 857, 859-60, 931, 1189-90, 1762-6, 1814, 3605, 3612, 3682a, 3697, 3735
Hinkley, Edyth (b. 19th cent.), 3179
historical periodization, 9, 35, 46-60, 80, 107, 210, 241, 284, 895, 902, 1254, 1670, 1681, 1695, 2314, 2492, 2578, 3012, 3604
  "ancient period," general statements, 52, 61-71, 83, 85, 115, 193a, 377, 382, 402-3, 405-7, 455, 483, 520, 522-5, 531, 533
  "medieval period," general statements, 550-64, 706-7, 710-1
Holcomb, Helen Harriet (Howe) (b. 1836), 4041
Holy Mother. *See* Sarada Devi
home furnishings, 1012
home science. *See* education
Hopkins, Saleni Armstrong. *See* Armstrong-Hopkins, Saleni
housing, 296, 2441, 3322-4, 3872
Humāyūn (1508-56), 726
Humphrey, Mrs. E.J. (ad loc. ca. 1860), 1622, 4018
Hussain, Karamat (20th cent.), *436*
Hutheesing, Krishna (Nehru) (1907-67), *21*, 1376-7, 2438
Hutheesing, Shrimati (dancer, 20th cent.), 2609

ideals of South Asian womanhood, 19-32, 34, 39, 844, 1053. *See also* arts; costume, beauty
  Buddhist tradition, 430-2
  Hindu tradition, 81, 85-8, 89a, 94-5a, 352, 355, 476-82, 504, 506-7, 695, 701, 703-5, 820, 852, 1813-4, 1820, 2000, 2062, 2071, 2884, 2886, 3701a
  Jaina tradition, 100, 349, 412
  Muslim tradition, 107-10, 752
Iftikhar-ud-din, Begam (20th cent.), *426*
Ikramullah, Shaista Akhtar Banu (Suhrawardy) (b. 1915), 1397
Indian women, general statements, *20, 22*, 12, 14-5, 17-8, 23, 33-4, 36, 40-1, 43, 45, 72-3a, 240, 800-17, 836-8, 840-4a, 846-9, 851-6, 858, 861-3, 890, 895, 897, 908-9, 924, 941, 1305, 1308, 1334, 1342, 1360, 1470-3, 1558-9, 1567, 1619, 1650, 1652, 1663-1703, 1725, 1727-33, 1737-9, 1741-50, 1752-5, 1757-9, 2071, 2185, 2317, 2454, 2494-5, 2540, 2577
Indus valley civilization, *18*, 192, 364-9, 2932
infanticide. *See* female infanticide
Inglis, Julia Selina (ad loc. 1857), 4019
inheritance. *See* kinship; law
International Women's Year/IWY (1975), *23, 434, 445*, 1740, 2380-8, 4070, 4520
Inverarity, Rosalind Harriet Maria Wallace-Dunlop (ad loc. 1856-57), 4056
Iqbal, Muhammad (1877-1938), 2929
Ishvani (b. 1908), 2702, 3465a

Jackson, Elva (20th cent.), 3180
Jadhav, Mary Clubvala (1908-75), 3143
Jahānārā (1613-83), *20*, 737
Jain, Rama (1917-75), 2692
Jaina women, general statements, 99, 455
Jainism, *17, 18*, 98, 411, 455, 650, 653
Jameelah, Maryam (prev. Margaret Marcus b. 1934?), 2110
Janab Aulia of Oudh (19th cent.), 3987
Japanese women in South Asia, 4562, 4586
jauhar ("valor"), 271, 568
jewelry. *See* costume, beauty
Jhabvala, Ruth Prawer (1927-), 2698, 2951-4, 2968-75
Jijābāī Bhosale (1596?-1674), *20*, 754-6
Jinarajadasa, Dorothy (b. 19th cent.), *427*
Jind Kaur/Rani Jindan of Sukherchakia *misal* (1817-63), 1488, 3996-8
Jinnah, Fatima (1894-1967), *443-4*
Jinnah, Mohammad Ali, Quaid-i-Azam (1876-1948), *443*, 1401
Jinnah, Ruttie (1900?-29?), 1395
Johnson, Begam (1725-1812), 790
Johnson, Hilda Mary (1877-1915), 3681
Joshi, Anandibai (1865-87), 1287, 3418-9
Jussawala, D.C. (b. 19th cent.), 3466

Kādambarī of Bāṇa, 673
Kālidāsa (ca. 400 C.E.), *19*, 503-7
kāmaśāstra. See love
Kaminibai (20th cent.), 3581
Kanan Devi, Ma Mahajnana Shri Guru (20th cent.), 3760
Kannada women, *25-6*, 333, 549, 583-7, 651. *See also* South Indian women
Kāraikkālammaiyār (ca. 5th to 6th cent. C.E.), *19*, 571-5
Karnataka, women of. *See* Kannada women
Karney, Evelyn Storrs (1869-1953), 3003
Karve, Anandibai (1865-1950), 3454
Karve, Dhondo Keshav/Maharshi Karve (1858-1962), *26*, 3451-62
Kashmiri women, *29*, 35, 180, 186, 562, 593-600, 693, 3962-3, 4619-20. *See also* Northwestern Islamic women
kathā ("story"), *19*, 349, 417, 488, 674-9
kāvya, *19*, 502-7, 673
Kerala, women of. *See* Malayali women
Kerkar, Kesarbai (1892-1977?), 2612
Khan, Ivy (20th cent.), *434*
Khatoon, A.R. (20th cent.), 2894
Khurshid Ara Begam Nawab Siddiq Ali Khan (20th cent.), 1401
King, Mrs. Robert Moss/E. Augusta King (ad loc. 1877-82), 1485
Kinnaird, Emily (1885-1947), *21*, 1432-3
Kinnaird, Mary Jane (Hoare) (1816-88), *21*, 1431
kinship, *17, 20, 22, 25, 26, 27, 28, 29, 429, 448, 451, 454, 456*, 59, 499, 514, 557, 560, 1018, 1842, 1971-3, 1975-9, 1981-2, 2319, 2391, 2540, 2569, 3236. *See also* domestic sphere; law; life cycle; social change
  descent, 1972, 2033
    matrilineal, *17, 25*, 193-4, 202, 2036-9, 2875, 3207, 3261-72, 3286, 4588-94
    patrilineal, 3240, 3757, 4170, 4541
  family, 1670, 1730, 2051-2, 2058, 3521,

(family), 3880, 4166, 4446, 4605-6
disruption, 2010, 3519
joint/nuclear, 1004, 1016, 1974, 1979-80, 2515, 2987, 3529-30, 3714, 3720-1, 4184, 4274, 4289
home science, 1071, 2029-32, 2276, 3904, 3915, 3920-3, 3980, 4489
natal/conjugal, 2126, 3490, 3544, 4173-4, 4334
relationships, 1974, 1989, 1995-2001, 3199, 3241-4, 3267-8, 3525-30, 3534, 3588, 3596, 3736-45a, 3748, 4179-4200, 4326
size, 3226, 3575, 3939, 3943
marriage, 79, 90-1, 199-210, 487, 505, 529-30, 825, 1008-9, 1011, 1017, 1779, 1825-6, 1828, 1873-4, 1878-91, 1985, 3032, 3041, 3047-8, 3050-5, 3220, 3310, 3488, 3493-6, 3731, 3994, 4091-5, 4098-9, 4102, 4166, 4270, 4433-4, 4531-3, 4538, 4607. *See also* widowhood
age at, child, ***20, 22, 429, 461-3***, 196, 211-3, 674, 899, 921, 952, 981, 996-7, 999, 1002-3, 1007, 1010, 1013-5, 1019-34, 1335-7, 1555, 1851-68, 1901-2, 1905, 1909, 1915, 2288, 2442, 2454, 2456, 2895, 3029-30, 3061, 3162, 3215, 3217, 3223, 3396, 3398, 3401-2, 3608, 3627, 3860, 3955, 4103, 4132
ceremonies, forms, 207-10, 313, 398-9, 401, 466-7, 1842-5, 2899, 3015, 3034-43, 3196, 3221-2, 3293, 3497-3504, 3713, 4089, 4097, 4104-11, 4168, 4424, 4435-7a, 4524-5, 4527, 4566-7, 4608
disruption, divorce, 225, 473, 1000-1, 1006, 1188, 1872, 1884-8, 1890, 2002-12, 2798, 2905, 2958, 2961, 3465a, 3505-8, 3519, 3745a, 4179, 4210, 4533
economic transactions, 307, 311, 1827-8, 1846-50, 3388, 3859, 4112-3, 4177-8, 4444-5
and employment, 2134-7, 2142, 2159, 2211, 3544-5, 3782, 3785, 3897, 4261-4, 4466
hypergamy, 3091, 3388, 3390
intercommunity, 1824, 1873, 1875-7, 3219a, 3506
networks, alliances, 1667, 4172, 4174-8
polygamy, 494, 996, 1005, 1869-71, 2050a, 2847, 3044-6, 3659, 4114-9, 4129, 4529
reform, 211-3, 899, 903, 935, 940, 952, 981, 996-7, 999-1003, 1006-11, 1013-5, 1018-41, 1043, 1188, 1201, 1335-7, 1823, 1858-60, 1872-91, 1915, 2013-28, 2874, 3130a, 3395-3402, 3463, 3602, 3608, 3613, 3627-9, 3658-9, 3955, 4204
spouse selection, 1013, 1825, 1829-9a, 1830-41, 1934, 1972, 2008, 2329, 3029, 3031, 3034, 3040, 3213-4, 3216, 3218-9, 3255, 3309, 3497, 3504, 4096, 4100-1, 4107, 4109, 4271, 4481, 4526
widow. *See* widowhood
"mother right," 131-2, 192, 193a, 2034-5
property rights, maintenance, ***442, 458***, 79, 90-1, 302-11, 372, 397, 457, 465, 566, 1008, 1164, 1167-70, 1174, 1188, 1848, 1972, 2022-3, 2033, 3045, 3049, 3056, 3076, 3252-4, 3427, 3503, 4457, 4535-6
residence, 1972, 1983
surveys, by community. *See also* castes, communities
Hindu, 998, 1763, 1984-9
Jaina, 97
Muslim, 1990-4, 3206
Koran. *See Qor'ān*
Kripalani, Sucheta (1908-74), ***426***, 1385-6
Krishnamurthy, Manda (1924-), ***430***
Kumari, Meena. *See* Meena Kumari
Kurūr Amma (16th cent.), 582
Kusum Devi (20th cent.), ***428***
Kuṭṭanīmata of Dāmodaragupta, 681

labor force. *See* work
Lakshmibai, rani of Jhansi (1835?-58), ***28***, 28, 3999-4009
Lakshmiben (20th cent.), ***461***
Lakshmipathi, Rukmini (1891-1951), 1382
Lal/Lal Dyad/Lalīśvarī/Lallā (14th cent.), ***19***, 593-9
Lal, Lakshmi Narain (b. 1925), 4370
land tenure, ***452, 458***
language, 328, 486, 3199, 3228, 3368, 3738, 3844, 4190, 4610. *See also* folklore
Lalibai, Sanyasini (b. 1908), 4236
Latham, S.F., 1624
law, ***21, 23***
Bangladesh, ***27, 452***, 2534, 3847, 3924-5
India, ***21, 23, 431, 456, 461***, 12, 79, 895, 1009, 1194, 1196-8, 1200-2, 1204, 1681, 1703, 1709, 1764, 2322, 2328, 2355, 2430, 2494, 2530-42
Age of Consent Act (1891), 1021, 1031
Child Marriage Restraint Act/Sarda Bill (1929), 875, 1022-6, 1859
Child Marriage Restraint (Amendment) Act (1938), 1859
Child Marriage Restraint (Second Amendment) Act (1938), 1859
Child Marriage Restraint (Amendment) Act (1949), 1024, 1858-60
Child Marriage Restraint (Amendment) Act (1952), 1024, 1860
Cinematograph Act (1952), 2669
Constitution (adopted 1949), 2238
Contagious Diseases Act, ***464***
Court of Wards Act (1879, Bengal, Behar and Orissa), 1297
Dissolution of Muslim Marriages Act (1939), 1001, 1887
Dowry Prohibition Act (1961), 1846, 1849-50
Female Infanticide Prevention Act (1870), 992
Government of India Act (1935), 1187, 1199, 1276, 1279, 1283, 1285
Hindu Adoptions and Maintenance Act (1956), 2016, 2023
Hindu Code, ***21***, 1205-14, 2016
Hindu Marriage Act (1955), 1872-4, 1878-84, 2016, 4204
Hindu Succession Act (1956), 304, 310, 2016, 2039, 4204
Hindu Widow's Remarriage Act (1856), 1038, 1043
Hindu Women's Rights to Property Act (1937), 1168-70
Indian and Colonial Divorce Jurisdiction Act (1926), 1000
Indian Christian Marriage Act (1872), 1884, 1889, 1891
Indian Divorce Act (1869), 1000, 1884
Indian Statutory Commission/Simon Report (1930), 841
Legal Practioners (Women) Act (1923), 1204
Maternity Benefit Act (1961), 2220, 3786
Medical Termination of Pregnancy Act (1971),

1937-40, 1942a-3, 3514
Parsi Marriage and Divorce Act (1936), 1884
Sati Regulation (1829, Bengal), 955, 960, 964, 968, 983
Special Marriage Act (1954), 1873, 1875-7, 1884, 2016
Suppression of Immoral Traffic in Women and Girls Act (1956), 2427, 2435, 3320-1
Women's and Children's Institutions (Licensing) Act (1956), 2427
Nepal, 4535-6, 4554, 4556, 4560a
Legal Code (Sixth Amendment) Ordinance (1975), 4555
Pakistan, ***29, 441, 444***, 2534, 4430, 4449-50, 4488
Maternity Benefit Ordinance (1958, West Pakistan), 4471
Muslim Family Laws Ordinance (1961), 2013-5, 2017-21, 2025-8, 4451
Shariat Act (1948, Punjab), ***441-2***
of religious communities (civil and religious law), 79, 1196, 1884, 2532, 2537, 3925
Buddhist, 433, 437-41
Christian, 1889, 1891
Hindu, 37-8, 90-3, 199-207, 210-3, 220, 222-6, 246, 251, 264, 286-94, 302-11, 372, 397, 457-8, 464-73, 566, 674, 1008, 1038, 1041, 1043, 1167-70, 1189-93, 1201, 1205-14, 1252, 1872-4, 1878-84, 2002, 2039, 3427
Muslim, 38, 77, 104-6, 310, 1001, 1767-73, 1775-85, 1787-9, 1848, 1887, 1890, 2003-4, 2403, 2534, 4457
Sri Lanka, ***25***, 2026, 3047-56
Marriage and Divorce Commission, 3050
topics, 1189, 1191, 2531-2, 2535, 3924-5, 4450
abortion, 1936-40, 1942a-3
family and marriage, ***22, 29, 442***, 90-1, 200-4, 220, 225, 246, 306, 458, 473, 674, 1000-1, 1004, 1006, 1008-9, 1011, 1021-7, 1031, 1188, 1848-50, 1858-60, 1872-91, 2002-4, 2006, 2013-28, 2039, 2532, 3047-56, 3252-4, 4449, 4451
female infanticide, 1939
female seclusion, 1154, 1156, 1203
labor, ***23***, 2163, 2171, 2173-4, 2179, 2220, 4471
property rights, maintenance, ***442, 458***, 90-1, 302-11, 372, 397, 457, 465, 566, 1008, 1167-70, 1174, 1848, 2033, 3045, 3056, 3076, 3252-4, 3427, 4457, 4535-6, 4554
prostitution, 251, 2424, 2427, 2430
rape, 2434
satī/suttee, 264, 955, 960, 964, 968, 977, 979, 983
widowhood, 91, 222-6, 303, 458, 1036, 1038-9, 1041, 1043
Lawrence, Honoria (Marshall) (1806-57), 1480, 4414
Lawrence, Lady/Rosamond Napier Lawrence (b. 1878), 1486
Leitch, Margaret W. (ad loc. late 19th cent.), 3006
Leitch, Mary (ad loc. late 19th cent.), 3006
Leonowens, Anna Harriette (Crawford) (b. 1834), 1487
lesbian relationships, 2898, 2909
Leuchtag, Erika (ad loc. mid-20th cent.), 4573
Liaquat Ali Khan, Ra'ana (20th cent.), ***443, 445***, 1398-1400, 1403
libraries, archives, ***425-72***, 5
Liesching, Fanny (Gregson). *See* Gregson, Fanny
life cycle, ***17, 22, 25, 26, 27, 28, 29***, 80, 218, 470, 475-6, 822, 825, 827, 1664, 1812, 1818, 3020, 3023-5, 3203-6, 3264, 3489, 3701-2, 3845, 3856, 3859, 4081a, 4211, 4338, 4596, 4598. *See also* child bearing; kinship; menstruation-menopause; motherhood/child rearing; religion; widowhood
aging, 2409, 2441, 2823, 2885, 2896, 2916, 2926, 3234, 3364, 4162, 4371, 4381-2
puberty, adolescence, 3026, 3208, 3491-2, 4088-90
reincarnation, 3072-3, 3235, 3728-9, 4164
life histories, case studies, ***460, 461***, 953, 965, 1019, 1033, 1347, 1764, 1810, 2053, 2440, 2514, 2552a, 3072-3, 3078-9, 3162-3, 3198, 3235, 3302, 3415, 3562-4, 3669, 3701, 3728-9, 3790, 4076-7, 4152, 4164, 4182-3, 4197, 4209, 4229, 4232, 4261-2, 4270, 4310-3, 4531, 4540, 4621, 4624
literacy. *See* education
literature. *See* arts; folklore
Login, Lady/Lena Campbell Login (1820-1904), 1488
love, 240, 356, 488, 528, 532, 4270, 4375. *See also* myths, legends; sexuality
erotic, 85, 230-4, 236-9, 241-2, 244, 678-9, 681, 696, 698, 700, 703, 2582-3, 2585, 3093, 3813
kāmaśāstra ("science of erotic love"), ***19, 20***, 231, 233-4, 239, 242, 511-3, 682-92, 2046
lover:beloved::devotee:God, 300-1, 623-30, 702, 728, 741, 2118, 4237-8, 4246
romantic, 694, 697, 699, 703-5, 1837, 2854, 3033, 3821
Lutyens, Emily (b. 1874?), 1496

M., C.M./Clara M. Miner (ad loc. 19th cent.), 1497
Ma Anandamayi. *See* Anandamayi Ma
MacKenzie, Mrs. Colin/Helen (Douglas) MacKenzie (ad loc. early 19th cent.), 4044-5
McKibbin-Harper, Mary/Mary (McKibbin) Harper (b. 1873), 1125
Macleod, Anne C./Anne Campbell (Macleod) Wilson (d. 1921), 4046-7
Madhya Pradesh, women of. *See* North/Central Indian women
magazines. *See* serial publications
Mahābhārata. *See* epics
Mahādēviyakka. *See* Akkamahādēvi
Māham Anaga (d. 1562), 729
Maharashtra, women of. *See* Marathi women
Mahāvaṃsa, Cūlavaṃsa, 547-8
Maithili women, 4340-59
Maitland, Julia Charlotte (d. 1864), 3181
Makhijani, Shanti H. *See* Vaswani, Sister Shanti T.
Malabari, Behramji Merwanji (1853-1912), ***26***, 1038, 3396, 3401-2, 3463
Malayali women, ***25-6***, 569, 582, 1926, 2049. *See also* South Indian women
Malgonkar, Manohar (b. 1913), 2866
maṅgalakāvya, 646-8
Maṅkaiyarkkaraciyār (7th cent.), 571, 574
Manoramabai (1881-1921), 3438

Manu. *See dharmaśāstra*
Maratha kingdoms, 753-67
Marathi women, *26, 428,* 539, 567, 588-92, 753, 2548. *See also* West India, women of
Marcus, Margaret. *See* Jameelah, Maryam
Markandaya, Kamala, pseud./Kamala (Purnaiya) Taylor (1924-), *24,* 2698, 2702, 2704, 2772-6, 2785-9
Marker, Aban (20th cent.), *445*
marriage. *See* kinship
Maschmann, Melita (b. 1918), 2106
Mason, Mrs. (ad loc. late 19th cent.), 3677
matriliny. *See* kinship
Mayo, Katherine (1868?-1940), *20,* 864
Mazuchelli, Nina Elizabeth (ad loc. mid-19th cent.), 4572
Mazumdar, Shudha (1899-), *433, 436,* 3671
Mazumdar, Vina (1927-), *434*
media, *24,* 1754, 1791, 2582, 2657-61. *See also* arts; censorship, obscenity; film industry; reading interests; serial publications
Meena Kumari (1932-72), 2434, 2663, 2668
Mehta, Hansa (b. 1897), *461*
Mehta, Sharda (b. 1882), *426*
Mehta, Usha (b. 1920), 1388
men. *See* sex roles
Menaka/Leilavati Sokhey (b. late 19th cent.?), 2601, 2609
Menon, Lakshmi N. (b. 1899), *426*
menstruation-menopause, 102, 140, 196-8, 459, 1782, 1893-6, 1945, 1993, 3024, 3026-8, 3040, 3061, 3203-4, 3207-10, 3211-2, 3489, 3491, 3703-12, 3718, 3935, 4134, 4163, 4295, 4541, 4597
La Mère. *See* The Mother
midwifery. *See* child bearing
military and war, 27, 28, 745-51, 753, 757, 775-83, 1164, 1229, 1721, 2310, 2406-8, 2413, 3096, 3670, 4329, 4491
Miner, Clara M. *See* M., C.M.
Mīrābāī (ca. 1500-46), *19,* 28, 298, 601-21
Mirabehn/Madeleine Slade (b. 1892), *426, 428,* 1306
missions, *20, 21, 25, 26, 27, 28, 29, 457, 464-9,* 873, 896, 905, 910, 926, 933, 941, 1556, 1558-60, 1563-5, 1567-70, 1572-3, 1604, 1607, 1616, 1619-20, 1625, 1630-1, 1641, 2982, 3384, 3676. *See also* western women in South Asia
  converts, *21, 26,* 1215-24, 2111, 3161-3, 3429-40, 3442, 3471-2, 3612, 3663-4
  in fiction, 787, 1550, 1554, 3177
  societies, *464-9,* 1559, 1574-95, 1608-9, 1614, 1621, 1623, 1628, 1633, 1639, 1643, 2984, 3005, 3146, 3407, 3412, 3430-50, 3475, 3481, 3607, 3678, 3682, 4049, 4403-4, 4407-13, 4032-4, 4036, 4428, 4574
  special interest
    educational, *435,* 1053, 1062, 1065, 1088-9, 1101, 1561, 1575-6, 1578, 2276, 2995-6, 3133-5, 3137-8, 3144, 3161, 3417, 3428, 3641, 3644, 3688-90, 3980, 4033, 4035, 4049
    medical, 846, 1106, 1111, 1557, 1561-2, 1574-6, 1580, 1584, 1590, 1595, 1614, 1633, 3146, 3164-8, 3183, 3478, 3481, 3674-5, 4035-6, 4038, 4043, 4049-51, 4406-7, 4409-13, 4428, 4571
    zenana, 1216, 1219, 1561-2, 1566, 1571, 1575-6, 1579-81, 1583, 1586, 1590, 1595, 1599-1603, 1609, 1613-4, 1623-4, 1628, 1633, 1639, 2984, 3005, 3185, 3682a, 3688-90, 3980, 4035, 4037, 4041, 4044-5, 4049, 4404, 4407-13, 4574
Mitchell, Mrs. Murray/Maria Hay (Flyter) Mitchell (d. 1907), 1498, 3182, 3683
Moghal Empire. *See* Mughal Empire
Monkland, Mrs., pseud./Mary Frazer Campbell (1785-1843), *27,* 3693, 3696
Moore, Kate (b. ca. 1840), 4023
Moore, Mrs. P.H./Jessie Fremont Moore (b. 1857), 3684-7
Morrison, Anna Maria (Ward) (1814-38), 4048
mortality. *See* population studies
The Mother/La Mère/Mirra Alfassa (1878-1973), *22,* 2075-8, 2082-93
Mother Earth, 125-6, 128, 131, 170, 389, 1240, 2132, 3827a
motherhood/child rearing, 825, 1782, 1816, 1948, 1951-2, 1958-9, 1989, 2512, 2516, 3071, 3082, 3228, 3872, 4063, 4152, 4154-5, 4487, 4622. *See also* child bearing; gender of children, preferred; health; social welfare
  child care, 1946, 1949-50, 1955, 1957, 1960-1, 3064, 3230-1, 3869, 3948, 4528
  employed mothers, 2220, 2231a, 2233-4, 3545, 3783-4, 3786, 4261-2, 4264, 4471
  religion, images of mothers in, 288, 453, 633
  unwed mothers, 1956, 2409, 2895, 4151
Mother India, *20,* 864-88, 1240
mountaineering, *29,* 4562, 4576-80, 4582-7
Mountbatten, Lady/Edwina Ashley Mountbatten (20th cent.), 1732
Mṛcchakaṭikā of Śūdraka, *19,* 508
M.S. Subbulakshmi (b. 1916), 2613, 2631
Mughal Empire (1526-1765), *20,* 706, 711, 715-41
Muhammadi Begam (b. 19th cent.), 2917
Mukherjee, Bharati (20th cent.), *24,* 2828
Muktābāī (d. 1297), 592
Mulji, Karsondas (1832-71), *26,* 3464
Mullens, Mrs./Hannah Catherine (Lacrois) Mullens (1826-61), 3688-90
Mumtāz Maḥal (1593-1631), *20,* 736
Munnī Begam of Murshidabad (1716-1813), 771-4
Munson, Arley Isabel (b. 1871), 3183
murderers, 2437, 3510, 3626, 4317
music. *See* arts; folklore
Muslim League, Women's Muslim League, *21, 440, 442-4,* 1242, 1721
Muslim women, general statements, *20, 22, 435,* 106-7, 828-30, 844, 904, 1755, 1772, 1774-6, 1778, 1780, 1783, 1787-8, 1790, 2050a, 3192, 3205, 4062, 4071, 4074. *See also* Islam
Muter, Mrs. D.D./Elizabeth McMullin Muter (ad loc. 1857), 4024-5
Muthulakshmi Reddy, S. (1886-1968), *21, 430, 431,* 1335-7, 3143
Mutiny of 1857-58, *28,* 1484, 1492, 1509, 1543, 3999-4031
Muttulakshmi, Lydia (ca. 19th cent.), 3163
myths, legends, 484, 697, 3092, 3241, 4327, 4335. *See also* arts; epics; folklore; goddesses; *purāṇas*; *satī*/suttee
  Rādhā-Kṛṣṇa, *19,* 243-5, 622-30, 632, 702, 2699, 2804, 4246-7

Nacaramma (14th cent.), 540
Naidu, Sarojini (1879-1949), *21, 24, 426, 457, 458*, 1250, 1255, 1326-34, 1340, 2699, 2722-31, 2737-42
Naikīdevī of Anahilapatika (Caulukya queen, 12th cent.), *20*, 745
Nalini, Saroj. *See* Dutt, Saroj Nalini
names. *See* language
Nanda, Savitri Devi (20th cent.), 2702, 3985
Nandkunverba, maharani of Gondal (20th cent.), 3414
National Council of Women in India/NCWI (est. 1925), *426, 431*, 2339, 2346-7
nationalist movements. *See also* Mutiny of 1857-58; partition of India (1947)
  Bangladesh, *27*, 3952-3
  India, *21, 426-9, 433, 438, 442-3, 457*, 826, 893-5, 900-4, 907-8, 912, 914-5, 1225-39a, 1300, 1307, 1312-3, 1326, 1332-3, 1338, 1343-54, 1356-8, 1361-2, 1364, 1366-9, 1371-4, 1376-9, 1383, 1385-6, 1388, 1390, 1402, 1439-41, 1443-9, 1451-69, 1472-6, 2438, 2552, 2573, 2750, 2778, 2795, 2843, 2880, 3130a, 3598a, 3633, 3667-9, 3670a, 3836, 4599
  Khilafat, 1235
  Pakistan, *21, 442-4*, 1241-2, 1396-1403, 1717, 2659
  Sind, 4508
Nātyaśāstra of Bharata, *19*, 509
nautch. *See* arts; prostitution
Nayyar, Sushila (b. 1914), *426*, 1390
Nazmul Karim, A.K. (20th cent.), 3880
Nehru, Jawaharlal (1889-1964), *21, 426*, 1213, 1341, 1361, 1364
Nehru, Kamala (1899-1936), *21*, 1290, 1378
Nehru, Krishna. *See* Hutheesing, Krishna (Nehru)
Nehru, Rameshwari (1886-1966), 1391
Nepali/high Himalayan women, *29-30*, 123, 181, 1662, 1740, 1940, 2303, 4515-87
Newell, Harriet (Atwood) (1793-1812), 788-9
newspapers. *See* serial publications
Nightingale, Florence (1820-1910), *458*
Nīladevī of Nurpur, 785
Nimbkar, Krishnabai (20th cent.), 2559
Nivedita, Sister/Margaret Elizabeth Noble (1867-1911), *21*, 1463-9, 1474-6
North/Central Indian women, *27-9*, 29, 40, 538, 563, 706-11, 715-9, 742, 845, 860, 917, 1826, 1926, 1963, 2189, 3954-4402
Northwestern Islamic women, *29*, 4403-4514
North-West Frontier Province, women of. *See* Northwestern Islamic women
Nugent, Maria (Skinner) (1771?-1834), 797
Nūr Jahān (1577?-1646?), *20*, 730-5

occupations. *See* work
Ohlmus, Caroline Corner. *See* Corner, Caroline
Oriya women, *27*, 357. *See also* East India, women of lowland
Ottman, Nina (ad loc. ca. 1900), 1629
Ouvry, Matilda H. (ad loc. ca. 1857), 4026

Paget, Mrs. Leopold/Georgiana Theodosia (Fitzmoor-Halsey) Paget (d. 1919), 4027
Pahari women, *27-8*. *See* North/Central Indian women
Pakistani women, *21, 22, 23, 24, 29*, 16, 1711-25, 1734-5, 1740, 1780, 1793, 1852-3, 1904, 1906, 1911, 1991, 2006, 2008, 2013-5, 2017-21, 2025-8, 2139, 2258, 2289, 2301, 2303, 2389-2408, 2433, 2446, 2464, 2469, 2473-4, 2476, 2478, 2484-5, 2505-10, 2529, 2611, 2632, 2655, 2659, 2871, 2892, 2932, 2942-3, 2945-50, 4612, 4614. *See also* Northwestern Islamic women
Pandit, Vijaya Lakshmi (1900-), *21, 426, 457*, 1237, 1344-52
Pāṇini (ca. 400 B.C.E.), 400, 436
Panjabi women, *27-9*, 4621, 4623. *See also* North/Central Indian women; Northwestern Islamic women
pardā, pardah. *See* seclusion, modesty, veiling
Parker, Lois Stiles (Lee) (1834-1925), 1638
Parks, Fanny/Fanny (Parks) Parlby (1794-1875), 4055a, 4056a
Parsi women, general statements, 101, 816, 3487
partition of India (1947), 1236, 1241, 1243, 1711, 1713, 1721, 1732
Parulekar Godavari S. (b. 1908), 3582
Patel, Rashida (20th cent.), *444*
Patwardhan, Lilabai (20th cent.), 3468
peasant movements. *See* political participation
Pechey-Phipson, Mary Edith (1845-1908), 3479
Penny, Fanny Emily (Farr) (b. 19th cent.), *21*, 3011, 3186
periodicals. *See* serial publications
Periyapurāṇam of Cēkkiḻār, 573-5
Petrie, Irene Eleanora Verita (d. 1897), 4403
philosophy. *See Śakti* and *Śākta* traditions
politics, *21, 23, 25, 26, 27, 28, 29, 435, 444, 457*, 889, 893, 1270, 1278, 1280-1, 1703, 1709, 2179, 2547-9, 2552a, 2562, 2800, 4321, 4430, 4560a. *See also* associations, programs; nationalist movements; women's movements
  elections, *446*, 1273, 2554, 3001, 3115, 3584-6, 3945
  enfranchisement, *21, 25, 27, 427, 429, 450, 461-3*, 1187, 1250, 1263, 1270, 1272, 1274-6, 1279, 1282-6, 2558, 3001, 3653
  leadership, 2275, 2401, 2550, 2574, 3114
  peasant movements, 2574-9, 3334-6, 3577-83
  political parties, *23, 426, 434*, 1231, 1277, 1334, 2560-3, 3586
  politicians, *441, 443*, 1187, 1271, 1347, 2546, 2548, 2551-9, 3114, 3584, 3945-6, 4320, 4322. *See also* royal families, women of; *particular persons, by name*
  socialism, communism, *23*, 50, 1247, 2174, 2316, 2387, 2569, 3265, 3335
pollution. *See* purity/pollution
population studies, *21, 22, 23, 25, 26, 27, 28, 29, 30*, 1703, 1708-9, 1733, 1735, 2313, 2355-6, 2442-58, 2488, 3013, 3188, 3192a, 3331, 3488, 3511, 3872, 3910, 3936, 4286, 4439, 4558-60a. *See also* child bearing; menstruation-menopause
  education, 2238, 2244, 2247a, 2252, 2265, 2269, 2454-5, 3557, 3900, 4475-7
  elections, 2554, 2556-8
  fertility, *439, 451*, 126, 131, 1897-1900, 1914, 1925, 2319, 2442, 2447, 2450-1, 2483, 2491, 2497, 2499, 2501, 3059, 3062-3, 3226, 3331, 3488-9, 3511, 3570, 3575-6, 3929, 3932, 3942, 4123, 4125-7, 4286, 4299, 4302, 4334
    control, family planning, 221, 383, 1181-6, 1392, 1752, 1936, 2316a, 2477-2529,

(control, family planning), 3018, 3111-3, 3325-33, 3567-76, 3722, 3909-10, 3926-44, 4287-9, 4292-4308, 4495-4504, 4554, 4558-9
rates, 1186, 1866, 1893, 1901-24, 2303, 3024, 3030, 3057-8, 3060-1, 3215, 3223-4, 3227, 3509, 3512-3, 3515, 3530, 3714-21, 3860-6, 4120-2, 4128-32, 4438-9a, 4461, 4529, 4596
marriage, 1827, 1851-7, 1861-8, 3029-30, 3493, 3495
mortality, 1923, 1925, 1927-8, 2417, 2450-1, 2459, 2467-9, 2474-6, 3070, 3859, 3867, 3942, 4133, 4137-41, 4318a
reproductive life, 1893-6, 1926, 1928, 1945, 2499, 2517, 3059, 3061, 3225, 3489, 3725, 3863, 4132, 4596
sex ratio, 922, 2454, 2459-73, 2476, 3789, 4281-2
widowhood, 1963-4, 1966, 1968, 4158
work, 1165, 2138-42, 2144-55, 2157, 2161, 2164, 2171, 2196, 2200, 2204, 2222, 2454-5, 3299, 3542, 3548, 4255
poverty, 1616, 1650, 1669, 2409-10, 2428, 2903, 2912, 3322, 3559, 3562-3, 3908-9, 3916-7, 4309, 4505
Powar, Soonderbai H. (1856-1921), 3429
power, *18, 22, 25,* 241, 282, 497, 526-7, 1898, 1980, 2040, 2049, 2564, 2576, 3241, 3255, 3265, 3273, 3275, 3528-30, 4227, 4239-40, 4454, 4592. *See also Artha-śāstra* of Kauṭilya; *Śakti* and *Śākta* traditions; seclusion, modesty, veiling
Prasad, Jai Shankar (1889-1937), 4370
pregnancy. *See* child bearing
Premābāī, 592
Premchand, pseud./Dhanpat Rai Srivastava (1881-1936), 4376
Premchand, Tara Maneklal (b. 1898), *431*
prestige, rank, 569, 3199, 3238, 3275-6, 3334, 3336, 3496
princely states, ruling families of. *See* royal families, women of
Prior, Lilian Faith Loveday (20th cent.), 4415
prison, 1237, 2409, 2437-9, 2993, 4315-7, 4508
Pritam, Amrita. *See* Amrita Pritam
property. *See* economic position; kinship; law
prostitution, *18, 21, 23, 25, 26, 28, 429, 469,* 237, 247-52, 254-5, 349, 517, 564, 567, 691, 952, 2046, 2423-4, 4538. *See also devadāsī*
call girls, 2431
common prostitutes, *457*, 1810, 2008, 2320, 2409, 2426-30, 2432-3, 2435-6, 2533, 2813, 2862, 3000, 3318, 3320-1, 3422, 3425, 3564-6, 3608, 4310-4. *See also* social welfare
courtesans, 91, 253, 277, 501-2, 508-9, 518, 681, 2927, 3423, 4383
psychodynamics, 43, 229, 1799, 1819, 4152
conflicts, stress, *28*, 1952, 3279, 3362, 3771, 4187, 4227, 4231
aggression, hostility, 2576, 3068, 3547, 4228, 4326
mourning, widows', 1970
oedipal conflict, 158, 3209, 3741, 4399
possession, 2060, 3078-9, 3274-5, 3278, 3286, 4229
pressure to bear sons, 832, 1915, 2922
rape and rejection, 3952-3
role conflict, 1801, 3298, 3784-5, 3825, 3836, 4261-3
suffering, disappointment, 1795, 2830-1, 2922, 3263, 3701a-2, 3850a, 4553
fantasy, creativity, 3083, 3527, 4090, 4143
feminine identity, 1813-7, 1820, 1822, 1952, 2702, 2828, 3698
public life, 891, 905, 2339, 2389, 3669, 3715
Punjab, women of. *See* Panjabi women
purāṇas, 19, 150-1, 463, 465, 500, 537, 562, 632, 634, 655-72
purdah. *See* seclusion, modesty, veiling
purity/pollution, 102-3, 229, 1789, 2049, 3087, 3091, 3203-4, 3276, 3280, 3851, 4089, 4542. *See also* child bearing; menstruation-menopause; sexuality
Pushto women, *29*. *See* Northwestern Islamic women

Qor'ān, 106, 1782, 2056
Qudsia Begam, nawab of Bhopal (1801-81), 3990
Quin, Eva Wyndham (ad loc. late 19th cent.), 3187

Rabee (ca. early 19th cent.), 1224
Rādhā. *See* myths, legends
Radharani Debi. *See* Aparajita Debi
Ragini Devi (20th cent.), 2594
Raja Rao (b. 1909), 2882
Rajasthani women, 601-21, 2645, 3394. *See also* North/Central Indian women
Rājataraṅgiṇī of Kalhana, 693
Rakesh, Mohan (1925-75?), 4370
Ramābāī Peśavā (d. 1771), *20*, 758
Ramabai Sarasvati, Pandita (1858-1922), *26*, 1287, 3430-50, 3454
Ramachandran, Padma (1934-), *434*
Ramakrishna, Sri (1836-86), *22*, 2063, 2116-21
Rama Rau, Dhanvanthi (b. 1893), 1392
Rāmāyaṇa. *See* epics
Ranade, Ramabai (1862-1924), 1250, 3469-70
Rao, Shanta. *See* Shanta Rao
rape, abduction, 246, 493, 1243, 2008, 2425, 2428, 2434, 3335, 3819, 3952-3, 4385, 4400
Rasikapriyā of Keśavadāsa, 695, 703
Rathbone, Eleanor (1872-1946), *458, 461-3,* 1284
Rathnamal, Sita (20th cent.), 3201
Ratna Rajya Lakshmi Devi Shaha, badamaharani of Nepal (b. 1928), 4563-5
Rau, Santha Rama (1923-), *24*, 2698, 2766-8, 2770
Ray, Sarala (20th cent.), *426*
Raẕiyya Sulṭān of Delhi (Mamlūk ruler, d. 1240), *20*, 712-4
Reading, Alice (Cohen) Isaacs, Countess of (ad loc. 1921-25), *458*, 1479
reading interests, 2658, 2660, 2889, 2893, 3603, 3951, 4510. *See also* serial publications
recordings, 603, 605, 609, 614, 2607, 2618-31, 2710, 4324
reform. *See* social reform movement
religion, *17, 18, 19, 20, 21, 22, 25, 26, 27, 28, 29,* 74-9a, 89a, 241, 284, 382, 430-2, 1760-1, 2059, 2062, 2418, 3196, 3483a, 4233, 4235. *See also* cosmological principles, feminine; *devadāsī*; goddesses; *Śakti* and *Śākta* traditions; *particular religions, by name*
asceticism, 81, 235, 278, 283, 412, 433-52, 491, 503, 1218, 1307, 3301, 3456-8, 4383, 4539-40

bhakti tradition, *19*, 333, 359, 570-631
festivals, rites, 285, 1789, 2049, 3083, 3245-6, 3248-9, 3251, 3281, 3699, 3731, 3733, 3747-8, 3750-5, 3874, 3881, 4124, 4211, 4227, 4230, 4351, 4515
calendrical, 3085, 3089-91, 3250, 3532-3, 4187, 4191, 4196, 4234, 4326, 4334, 4358, 4541-2
life cycle, 103, 1813-4, 1892, 3023, 3027, 3247, 4147. *See also* child bearing; kinship; menstruation-menopause
Vedic, 286-94, 372
leaders, specialists, 638a
women and, 413, 423-6, 576, 586, 629, 642, 644, 2060, 2117, 2119, 3538, 3626, 3741
women as, 297-9, 370, 373, 375-6, 379-81, 385, 412, 430-52, 534-5, 537-48, 571-5, 577-85, 587-622, 631, 709, 738-41, 1439-42, 1445-6, 1448-52, 1455-8, 1461-76, 2060-1, 2063-2117, 2121, 2928, 3094, 3282, 3287, 3301, 3485, 3759-60, 4236, 4625
patronage, 429-32, 743, 766, 780, 782
possession, 2060, 3078-9, 3274-5, 3278, 3286
ṣūfī tradition, 593-600, 709, 728, 740-1
worshipped women, 2061, 2122, 2126, 3082, 3095, 3287, 3771, 4543-4, 4546-9
reproduction. *See* child bearing; menstruation-menopause; motherhood/child rearing; population studies
Reymond, Lizelle (ad loc. mid-20th cent.), 4575
Richardson, Jane/Jane (Richardson) Hanks (20th cent.), 2992
rodī, Gurung association, 4523-3a
Roshan Ara Begam (20th cent.), 2610
Rouse, Lydia Miriam (Denham) (1839-84), 3680
Roy, Bina (1914-), *434*
Roy, Rammohun (1772-1833), 964, 970-1, 3618-9
royal families, women of, *20, 27, 28, 457*, 23-9, 108, 429-32, 538-9, 541-2, 546, 549, 693, 716, 720-7, 729-43, 773, 833, 835, 985-6, 1297, 1629, 3192, 3666, 3809, 3986, 3993-4, 4043, 4050-1, 4616. *See also particular persons, by name*
Royden, Agnes Maude (b. 1876), *463*
Rugnathdas, Madhowdas (b. 19th cent.), 3400
Rukhmabai, Dr. (b. 1864), 3420
Rukmini Devi Arundale (b. 1904), 2598, 2600, 2609
Rūpa Bhavānī (1625?-1721), *19*, 600
Rūpamatī of Mandu (K͟haljī queen, 16th cent.), *20*, 752
Rupkala Bhagbanprasad (b. ca. 1850), 4237-8
rural life, 2302-5. *See also* development
Bangladesh, *450-1*, 3845-7, 3850, 3852a-6, 3884, 3888, 3892, 3895, 3906, 3914
India, *21, 22, 430*, 1177-80, 1791-2, 1794-6, 1967, 2155-6, 2283-7, 2365-79, 2863, 2920, 3676, 4057, 4061, 4064-5, 4067-8, 4072-3, 4359
Pakistan, *439*, 1793, 4423, 4458
Sri Lanka, 2805-6, 2998, 3017-8, 3021
Rutnam, Mary (20th cent.), 3125

Sahgal, Lakshmi (Swaminathan) (b. 1914), *428*
Sahgal, Nayantara (1927-), *21, 24, 426*, 1379-80, 1671, 2790-4, 2801
saints. *See* religion
Sakhawat Hossain, Rokeya (1880-1932), 3811
Śakti ("power") and *Śākta* traditions, *17, 19*, 84, 115-6a, 138, 638a, 658, 663-4, 666-9, 671-2, 2061, 2120, 2125. *See also* cosmological principles, feminine; goddesses; power; *tantra*
arts, 120, 123, 639, 661-2, 670
cults, rites, 116a, 636, 638, 639-43, 3779
ethnographic studies, 2040, 4234
myth, 657, 660, 665
philosophy, 117-24, 390, 393, 632, 634-7, 655-6, 659
Sanger, Margaret (1879-1966), 1185
Sanskrit, Prakrit, Pali literatures, *18-20*. *See also particular texts, genres and authors, by name*
female images in, 46, 49, 52-3, 56, 61-71, 81, 83, 92-3, 115a, 118-9, 121, 129, 136, 149, 152, 201-4, 221-6, 237, 250, 277, 286-96, 348-9, 352-3, 403, 456, 464, 1027, 1041
female writers of, 345-7. 350-1, 544, 680
Sarabhai, Bharati (b. 1912), *24*, 2746
Sarada Devi/Sri Ma/the Holy Mother (1853-1920), *22*, 298, 2061, 2063-74
Sarma, Jyotirmoyee (b. 1922), 3744
Sastri, Sivanath (1847-1919), 3660
satī/suttee, *18, 20, 26, 27, 28*, 207, 272, 701, 956, 959, 3954, 3957, 4363. *See also jauhar*
exegesis, 259-60, 265, 958, 3617, 3619
history, 258, 262, 266, 268-71, 273, 388, 568, 3617, 4520
law, 264, 955, 960, 964, 968, 977, 979-80, 983, 1201
legends, accounts, 86, 263, 565, 728, 758, 965-7, 973-4, 976, 982, 1505, 3377-9, 3614, 3621, 3956, 3959-60
memorial stones, 261, 267, 963, 3958
movement to abolish, 925, 933-4, 955, 957-8, 960, 964, 968-86, 1038, 3376, 3379, 3602, 3609, 3611, 3615-6, 3618-20, 3955
Satīgītā of Muktānanda, 701
Sati Godavari Mataji (b. 1914), 2112-3
Satthianadhan, Kamala (1879-1950), *427, 433*, 1394
Satthianadhan, Krupabai (1862-94), 1221
Sāvitrī, 478, 2884, 2886
Sāvitrībāī of Mahur (17th cent.), 783
Savory, Isabel (ad loc. late 19th cent.), 1499
Sayaji Rao III, maharaja of Baroda (b. 1863), 3427
Sayani, Kulsum (b. 1900), *426*
Scharlieb, Mary/Mary Ann Dacomb (Bird) Scharlieb (1845-1930), 3146a
scheduled caste ("harijan," "Dalit," "untouchable") communities, *22*, 1810, 2856, 3302, 3581, 4077, 4311, 4354, 4357, 4359
Scott, Beatrix M. (ad loc. 1911-3_), *461*
Scudder, Ida Belle (b. 1900), *25*, 3167
Scudder, Ida Sophia/Dr. Ida (1870-1960), 3164-8
Seamands, Ruth (b. 1916), 1632
seclusion, modesty, veiling, *18, 21, 22, 28, 29*, 224, 274-6, 400, 707, 1653, 1669, 1719, 2050, 2051-4, 2056-8, 2236, 2239, 3522, 4210-23, 4452-5, 4604-4a, 4619-20. *See also* domestic sphere; life cycle; missions
and development, 2318

and economic position, ***440***, 2154, 2193, 2209, 2232, 3886-7, 3889, 4457, 4468
and education, 1064, 1161, 4267, 4456
and fertility, 4456
and health, ***21***, 1106, 1111, 1119, 1156, 1161, 1163, 3146a
and kinship systems, 2051-5, 2058, 4211-5, 4217-20, 4221, 4223
and legal rights, 1154, 1156, 1195, 1203, 1297
in literature, 1510, 1514, 2055, 2765, 2847, 2859, 2861, 2877, 2898-9, 2909, 3811, 3817, 3836
and politics, 1235, 3945, 4221
separate worlds of women, 1672, 2051, 3730-1, 3735, 4515
harem life, 567a, 722, 727, 3986
zenana life, ***21***, 810, 827, 843, 850, 1160-1, 1416, 1596, 2898, 3163, 3663, 3666, 4055a, 4056a, 4060, 4062
as social reform issue, ***21, 454***, 952, 1016, 1150-9, 1161-3, 1788, 2050a, 2055, 3081, 3426, 4219
Sen, Mrinalini (b. 19th cent.?), ***433***
Sen, Nabaneeta Dev (b. 1938), 3813
Sen, Sushama (b. 1887), 1393
Sen Gupta, Nellie (b. 1886), ***426***
Sengupta, Padmini (1905-), ***433***
serial publications, 5
journals, reports
educational institutions, 2255, 2265a, 2581, 3555, 3637, 3983
mission societies, ***465-9***, 1579, 1583, 1585-7, 1589, 1594-5, 2984, 3441, 3443-5
popular, ***427, 433, 435, 438, 453-4, 463***, 907, 932, 941, 1256-7, 2074, 2097, 2128-30, 2297, 2562, 2572, 2579, 2660, 2671-88, 2889, 2893, 3119-22, 3145, 3337, 3594, 3602-3
scholarly, professional, 1971, 2030, 2127, 2208, 2218, 2319, 2326, 2332, 2412, 2415a, 2449, 2481, 2485, 3316, 3911, 3928, 4487
women's associations, ***427, 430-2, 463***, 1264, 1267-9, 2333-5, 2337-8, 2346-53, 2399, 2412, 2991, 3109, 3314, 3452
newsletters, ***445, 456***, 2382, 3556, 4493
newspapers, ***426-8, 431, 433, 438-9, 440-1, 444, 449, 453-4, 463***
Seton, Grace Thompson (ad loc. 1920s), 1500
sexism, 4553, 4629
sex ratio. *See* population studies
sex roles, 56, 227, 472, 509, 673, 812-3, 1151, 1153, 1670, 1672, 1697, 1726, 1754, 1781, 1815, 1821-2, 1992, 2046, 2232, 2259, 2318, 2380, 2572, 2790, 3022, 3150, 3527, 3592, 3698, 3745, 3782, 3851, 4064, 4200, 4227, 4452, 4520, 4551, 4568-9
feminine in men, 591, 1303, 1316, 2118, 3792, 4237-8
sexuality, ***18, 22, 25, 28, 29***, 198, 232, 235, 237, 246, 487, 502, 514, 519, 567a, 737, 2042-9, 2051-2, 2666, 2784, 3080, 3277, 3290, 3348, 3360, 4088-9, 4166, 4200, 4208-9, 4270, 4295, 4374, 4528, 4538, 4541, 4543-4, 4604a. *See also* censorship, obscentiy; education; film industry; love; prostitution
Shah Jahan Begam, nawab of Bhopal (1838-1901), 3991
Shah Nawaz, Jahan Ara (b. 1896), ***443***, 1401-2
Shah Nawaz, Mumtaz (1912-48), 1396
shakti. *See Śakti* and *Śākta* traditions
Shanta Rao (b. ca. 1927), 2599, 2602-3, 2608-9
Shephard, M. (20th cent.), ***464***
Sher-Gil, Amrita (1913-41), 2636-9a
Showers-Stirling, Christian (ad loc. 1902-15?), ***461***
Shreemati Nathibai Damodar Thackersey (SNDT) Women's University, Poona/Pune (est. 1949; prev. Indian Women's University, est. 1916), ***26, 434***, 2237, 3410, 3413, 3416, 3453, 3458, 3552-8
Siddheshwari Devi (b. 1908), 2615
Sikandar Begam, nawab of Bhopal (d. 1868), 4006
Sikhism, ***17***, 111-4
Sindhi women, ***29***. *See* Northwestern Islamic women
single women, ***22***, 1745, 1754, 1962, 2835, 2881, 2918-9, 3359
Sinhalese women, ***24-5***, 358, 421, 547-8, 555, 560, 2844. *See also* Sri Lanka, women of
Siriwardena, B.S. (20th cent.), 3020
Sītā, 181, 490, 3092. *See also* epics
Sitara Devi (b. 1922), 2595
Śivābāī (d. 1741), 565
Slade, Madeleine. *See* Mirabehn
social change, 833, 1661, 1726, 2391. *See also* development; nationalist movements; social reform movement; women's movements
communities
Hindu, 34, 1766, 3468-72
Muslim, 1784-6, 1790, 4071, 4074
tribal, 1802-3, 1806, 1808
nations
Bangladesh, 3850-50a, 3852, 3906, 3914, 3921
India, 801, 807, 906, 909, 943, 971, 1573, 1664, 1668-9, 1676-7, 1682-4, 1689, 1693-4, 1696, 1698-9, 1728-9, 1733, 1743-5, 1752, 1791, 1794, 1796-7, 2156, 2384, 2494, 2567, 2963, 3199, 3483, 3486, 3604, 3619, 3669, 4072-3, 4203, 4616
Nepal, 4518, 4520
Pakistan, 1713-8, 1720, 1722, 1735, 1780, 2394, 2401, 4447
Sri Lanka, 3012, 3017, 3020, 3022, 3063
social processes, ***22***
industrialization, 3063, 3259, 4202, 4205
Islamization, 4201
modernization, 1786, 1794, 1799, 1816, 2173, 3524, 3585, 4075, 4183, 4268, 4447
Sanskritization, 1766, 1811
urbanization, 1766, 3255-6, 3259-60, 4202, 4254
westernization, 1800, 1811, 3524, 4201
spheres
costume, 2944
education, 2257a-8, 2267, 2274, 3549, 3554
employment, 2198, 2207, 3299, 4460
family planning, 4499
folklore, 2645, 3212
kinship, ***25, 28, 29***, 1829-9a, 1834, 1974, 1978, 2024, 2034, 2038, 2839, 2869, 3074, 3255-60, 3263, 3267-72, 3311, 3467, 3520, 3739, 3744, 3880, 4067, 4101-3, 4171, 4201-7, 4212, 4270, 4442, 4445-7, 4627
media, 2689, 3337, 3831
social reform movement, ***20-1, 24-5, 26, 27-8,***

(social reform movement), *426-7, 428-9, 432-3, 440, 444, 449-52, 454, 456-8, 461-9,* 56, 829, 864-92, 894-9, 901-4, 907-8, 910-54, 1184, 1215, 1257, 1263, 1266, 1295, 1312, 1760, 2311, 2314, 2494, 2573, 2890, 3130-1, 3196, 3200, 3258, 3352, 3355, 3369-75, 3392, 3464, 3483, 3602-13, 3647, 3656-7. *See also* law; missions; nationalist movements; social change; *particular issues, by name*
social structure. *See* castes, communities; caste structure; kinship; prestige, rank
social welfare, *23, 25, 26, 27, 28, 29, 434, 444-5,* 1312, 1381, 1384, 1387, 1389, 1393, 1399-1400, 1709, 1971, 2309-11, 2313-5, 2319, 2321, 2324, 2326-8, 2332, 2342, 2355-6, 2409, 2531, 2533, 2562, 4564-5. *See also* associations, programs; development; missions; *particular problems, by name*
  government policy, programs, 2135, 2156, 2249, 2281, 2316a, 2356, 2359, 2365-71, 2373-9, 3316-8, 3329, 3333, 3561
  institutions, organizations, 2320, 2356, 2358, 2361, 2363, 2400, 2427-8, 3143, 3318, 3369-71, 3373, 3421, 3882
  rescue, rehabilitation, *464, 469,* 2313, 2426, 2428-30, 2433, 2436, 3322-3, 3919
  target groups
    destitute women, 2410, 3916-7
    mothers/children, *431,* 1179-80, 1947, 1949-50, 2316a, 2362, 2415, 2502, 3316-8, 3325-7, 3421, 3911, 4487
    rural women, 1110, 1177-80, 1796, 2365-79, 3984
    tribal women, 1802
  welfare workers, female, 874, 1176, 2179, 2315, 2364, 2366, 2368-72, 2374-5, 2378-9, 3921-3
Sokhey, Leilavati. *See* Menaka
Soppitt, Mrs. (ad loc. 1857), 4028
Sorabji, Cornelia (ca. 1865-1954), *21, 458,* 1287, 1297
Sorabji, Franscina (1833-1910), *21,* 1295
Sorabji, Susie (1868-1931), *21, 458,* 1296
South Asian civilization, feminine in, 82, 84, 115
  Dravidian contributions, 525, 527
South Asian women abroad, *30, 452,* 2770, 4602-29
South Indian women, *25-6,* 24, 145, 193, 542-3, 649, 1826, 1870, 3130-3368
sports, 1499, 2292-7, 4484, 4576-87
Sri Lanka, women of, *24-5,* 172, 175, 307, 354, 358, 421, 547-8, 550, 555, 560, 652, 1574, 1576, 1578, 1581, 1593, 1618, 1662, 1702, 1740, 1916, 2026, 2049, 2338, 2464, 2478, 2706, 2994-3129
Śrīmālāsiṃhanāda Sūtra, 430-2
Srivastava, Dhanpat Rai. *See* Premchand
Steel, Flora Annie (Webster) (1847-1929) *21,* 1504, 1516
Stratton, Anne Booth (ad loc. 1900-02), 4416
strījāti ("genus of women"), 37, 42, 812-3, 3733
strīrājya ("kingdom of women"), legends, 281
Subbalakshmi, Rishiyur Subramania/Sister Subbalakshmi (1886-1969), 3143, 3200
Sultan Jahan Begam, nawab of Bhopal (1858-1930), *435,* 3988, 3992
Sumroo/Le Sombre, Begam Joanna Ziboolnissa, of Sardhana (ca. 1750-1836), *20,* 777-82
Suniti Devi, maharani of Cooch Behar (1864-1932), 1287, 3665
suttee. *See satī*/suttee
Swain, Clara A. (1834-1910), 4043, 4050-1

Tabassum, Vazida (b. 1935), 2914
Tagore, Bala Shoondaree (ca. early 19th cent.), 3612
Tagore, Rabindranath (1861-1941), 1092, 3827a, 3830-1, 3843
Tamil women, *19, 24-6,* 30, 167, 178, 183-4, 187, 209, 261, 297, 354, 518-36, 540, 566, 571-81, 743, 1102, 1986. *See also* South Indian women; Sri Lanka, women of
tantra, 19, 120, 122-3, 127, 132, 454, 634, 636-8a, 640-1, 4551
Tārābāī Bhosale (1675-1761), *20,* 757
Tasadduque Hussain, Salma (b. 1908), *443*
Tata, Mehrbai Dorab (1879-1931), 1387, 1389
Taylor, Kamala (Purnaiya). *See* Markandaya, Kamala
Telugu women, *25-6,* 267. *See also* South Indian women
Temple, Helen F. (20th cent.), 1634
Teresa, Mother (1910-), 2980-1, 2985
Thackersey, Premlila Vithaldas (b. 1894), 3558
Thakkar, Amritlal Vithaldas/Thakkar Bapa (1869-1951), 2360
theses, sources for, *439,* 12, 16-7, 2032, 2301, 2457, 4429
Thoburn, Isabella (1840-1901), 1635
Thomas, George (1756-1802), 781a
Tilak, Lakshmibai (1873-1936), 3471-2
Tilakavatiyār (7th cent.?), 571, 574
Tiruvācakam of Māṇikkavācakar (9th cent.), 576
tribal communities, *22,* 1745, 1752, 1802-9, 2143, 2276, 3201, 3925, 4129, 4135, 4283. *See also* castes, communities
Tyabji, Rehana (20th cent.), *426, 428*
Tyler, Mary (1943-), 2993
Tytler, Harriet Christina (1827-1907), 4031

Umayamma, rani of Venad (fl. 1677-84), 784
unpublished papers, resources for, 5
  manuscripts, *448-50*
  personal papers, *426-9, 431, 433, 436, 442-4, 457-8, 460-6, 469,* 777
  research papers, 16, 1644, 1863, 1900, 1975, 2301, 2306, 2443, 2447, 2457, 2480, 2483, 3194, 3853, 3882, 3929, 3936
upaniṣads, 374-5, 378, 380, 384-5
urban life, *22,* 1798, 3486, 4602. *See also* social change
  kinship, 3259-60, 3525, 4171, 4205-6
  population, 2451, 2465, 2472, 2525
  slum dwellers, 3260, 3302, 3562-3, 4309, 4505
  work, 2157-62, 3897-9
Urdu-speaking women, *27-9,* 356, 1830, 2696, 2887-2929. *See also* North/Central Indian women; Northwestern Islamic women
Ussher, Marjorie (ad loc. 1936-42), *458*
Uttar Pradesh, women of. *See* North/Central Indian women

Vaḍakkēḍattu Naṅga Peṇṇu, 582

Vaiṣṇava-Sahajiyā cult, 622
Varadappan, Sarojini (1921-), *434*
Varma, Mahadevi (1907-), 4368-9
Vasanta Vilāsa, 694
Vāsavadattā of Subhandu, 673
Vaswani, Sister Shanti T. (prev. Shanti H. Makhijani, 1919-69?), 2114-5
Vedas, Vedic literature, *18*, 370-401, 1762
veiling. *See* seclusion, modesty, veiling
Venkamma, Tarikonda (b. 1839), 3283
Verghese, Mary Puthusseril (b. 1925), 3202
Vetra, Vija (20th cent.), 2604
Victoria, queen of Great Britain and Ireland, empress of India (1819-1901), 1488
Vidyāpati (early 15th cent.?), *19*, 630
Vidyasagar, Iswar Chandra (1820-91), 3628-9, 3636, 3658-9
Vines, Charlotte S. (ad loc. early 20th cent.), 4411-3
Viqar-un-Nissa Noon, Begam (20th cent.), *445*
Viresalingam, Kandukuri (1848-1919), 3132
Viswanathan, Radha (20th cent.), 2631
Vivekananda, Swami (1863-1902), 2071

Wallace-Dunlop, Madeline Anne (ad loc. 1856-57), 4056
war. *See* military and war
Weatherley Ella M. (b. 19th cent.), 1639
Weitbrecht, Mrs./Martha (Edwards) Weitbrecht (ca. early 19th cent.), 1640
Wernher, Hilda (1894-1956), 1502
West Bengal, women of. *See* Bengali women
western women in South Asia, *20, 21, 24, 25, 27, 28, 29, 30, 427-8, 457-8, 460-9*, 926, 945, 1293. *See also* missions; Mutiny of 1857-58
  creative writing, 735, 787, 1222, 1502-55, 2743-5, 2951-78, 3127-9, 3177
  domestic management, 1418-24, 1492, 3672, 3673, 3694-5
  as relatives
    of Europeans, 792, 794, 1427-30, 1479-86, 1488-92, 1516, 1530, 1564-5, 1732, 2982, 3002, 3011, 3186, 3677, 3683, 3691, 4014-5, 4024-8, 4030, 4054-6a, 4414, 4416, 4600-600a, 4601a
    of South Asians, 1501, 2951-77, 2987-8, 3127-9
  social life, 799, 1404-16, 1503-4, 2991, 3672a-3, 3693-4, 4055a
  social service
    medical personnel, 846, 1105-7, 1110-3, 1117-21, 1129, 1132, 1135, 1139, 1557, 1561-2, 1574, 1580, 1584, 1590, 1595-7, 1614, 1629, 1633, 1637, 2979, 3146a, 3164-8, 3183, 3477-9, 3481, 3674, 3977-9, 3981-3, 4038, 4043, 4050-1, 4406-7, 4409-13, 4571
    missionaries, 787-9, 846, 1111, 1498, 1556-1643, 2980-1, 2983-6, 2995-6, 3003-7, 3126, 3133-5, 3137-8, 3144, 3146, 3164-80, 3182-5, 3407, 3412, 3473-6, 3478, 3480-2, 3644, 3674, 3678-82a, 3684-90, 4018, 4032-53, 4403-13, 4571, 4574, 4601
    political activists, 1282, 1284, 1313, 1439-41, 1443-9, 1451-69, 1472-6, 1447-8, 2993
    other, 1185, 1434-8, 1463-78, 1489, 3181, 3639, 3666, 3670, 4573
  spiritual pursuits, 1439-42, 1445-6, 1448-52, 1455-8, 1461-76, 1496, 2075-93, 2106, 2110, 4575
  students, 2990
  travelers, 791, 793, 797, 1405, 1480-3, 1487, 1493-5, 1497-1500, 1617, 1622, 2989, 2992, 3009-10, 3187, 4055-6a, 4570, 4572, 4576-85
West India, women of, *26-7*, 3369-3601
widowhood, *20, 22, 25, 26, 28, 440, 458*, 91, 292, 825, 940, 1036-8, 1040, 1042, 1965, 1967, 1969-70, 2409, 2428, 3233-4, 3276, 3873. *See also satī*/suttee
  demography, 1901, 1918, 1963-4, 1966, 1968, 2442, 3488, 4158
  education, 3430-62
  law, 222-6, 303, 458, 1036, 1043, 1848, 3252, 4536
  in literature, 496, 512, 530, 557, 677, 1394, 2864, 2895, 3200, 3352, 3430-40, 3442, 3446-51, 3453-61, 3465, 3823-4, 3832, 4379, 4401
  marriage, 225, 899, 925, 981, 996-7, 999, 1002-3, 1007, 1010, 1014-5, 1035, 1039, 1041, 1043, 1918, 1963, 2442, 3130a, 3132, 3395-3402, 3454, 3457-9, 3464, 3503, 3518, 3602, 3608, 3613, 3627-9, 3658-9, 3955, 4098-9, 4159-61, 4204
Wijenaike, Punyakante (b. 1933), *24*, 2706
Williams, Nancy (ad loc. mid-20th cent.), 1643
Wilson, Mrs. *See* Cooke, Mary Anne
Wilson, Anne Campbell (Macleod). *See* Macleod, Anne C.
Wilson, Constance (ad loc. 1921-47), *458*
Wilson, Margaret (Bayne) (1795-1835), 3482
Wilson-Carmichael, Amy (1867-1951), *25*, 3169-73
Winslow, Harriet Wadsworth (Lathrop) (1796-1833), 3007
witchcraft. *See* fear of women/women's evil
Women's Indian Association/WIA (est. 1917; merged with All-India Women's Conference, 1935), *427, 430-1*, 1264, 1267, 2339, 2344, 2348, 3131
women's liberation. *See* feminism; politics; women's movements
women's movements. *See also* associations, programs; nationalist movements; politics; social reform movements
  Indian, *21, 23, 427, 430-4*, 826, 889-95, 897-8, 900, 907-8, 911, 913, 915, 918-9, 1236, 1244-69, 1318, 1332, 1340, 1383-4, 1391-2, 1752, 1764, 2309, 2311, 2316, 2343, 2372, 2384, 2552, 2564-5, 2567-8, 2570, 2572, 2657, 3130a-1, 3836
  Pakistani, *21, 23, 444-6*, 1722, 2400
women's studies, studying women, *21*, 12, 1651, 1654, 1679, 1731, 1766, 3556, 3846, 3907
  methodology, research experiences, 1646, 1653, 1655, 2446, 2576, 3319, 3331, 3854
  research programs, 1648
  research results, 1644, 1649, 1798, 2275, 3888
  teachers' resources, 1751, 1759
  theory, 407, 1254, 1645, 1647, 1650, 1652, 1656, 1667
Wood, Maria Lydia Blane (1835-89), 1492
work, *21, 23, 25, 26, 27, 28, 29*, 1667, 2051, 2578, 3655, 3882-3, 3909. *See also* arts; *devadāsī*; economic position; politics; prostitution

employment, 1703, 2146-7, 2157, 2163, 2313, 2317, 2322, 2325, 2454-5, 2491, 3097-9, 3295-7, 3299-3300, 3543, 3781, 3898-9, 4203, 4260, 4264, 4306, 4308, 4465, 4469, 4473, 4486, 4628
attitudes toward, 1172, 2133-7, 3310, 4272-3, 4467, 4470
cooperatives, 2193-4, 2221, 2223-4, 3022
and domestic roles, 1801, 2134-7, 2142, 2159, 2175, 2185, 2206a, 2211, 2220, 2231-4, 3255, 3298, 3544-5, 3730, 3782-55, 3897, 4181, 4261-6, 4466, 4468
effects, correlations, 2523, 3862, 4075, 4121, 4123, 4259, 4261-6, 4439a, 4461
and female seclusion, 2154, 2193, 2209, 2232
full-time/part-time, 2162, 2176
income differentials, 3542
legislation, 2163, 2171, 2173-4, 2220, 2540, 3786, 4471
organized/unorganized sectors, 2143, 2149, 2160, 2168, 2178
trade unions, *434*, 2222, 2225, 2336, 4306
unemployment, 3787
vocational guidance, 2226-30, 3100, 4464
labor force participation, *23*, 1730, 1792, 2138-42, 2144, 2148-54, 2207, 2303, 2315a, 2322, 2575, 3096, 4462-3
daily, yearly work cycles, 3198, 3855-6, 3884, 3886, 3892, 4458
rural, 1177, 2155-6, 2188-95, 3104, 3304, 3578-81, 3848, 3855-6, 3884-95, 4252-5, 4257, 4458
urban, 2157-62
occupations, *23, 440, 457*, 1165-6, 1173, 2145, 2155, 2161, 2167, 2179, 2183-7, 2196, 2198, 2200-5, 2206a-8, 2211-2, 2214, 2216, 2218-9, 3108, 3654, 4494
agriculture, *439*, 1792, 2188-90, 2575, 3022, 3104, 3106, 3302, 3304, 3886, 3890, 3893, 3895, 4252-3, 4255, 4257, 4459
business, 2206-6a, 2210, 2214
construction, 4258
cottage industries, handicrafts, 2192, 2391, 2641, 3303, 3536, 4341-2, 4355-6, 4359, 4494
domestic service, 3548a
education, 1051, 1057, 2209, 2298-9, 3324, 4280a, 4552
factories, 2202, 3103
film industry, 2596, 2662-5
government services, 2215, 2366, 2368-72, 2374-5, 2378-9, 3548
home making, 1012, 1792, 2329, 2679, 2936, 3119, 3295, 3884
journalism, 2660-1, 2791-2
jute industry, 3788
legal profession, 1195, 1204, 1297, 2543-5, 3101-2, 3105
medical profession, 1105-39, 1390, 1929, 2209, 2411-3, 2415-6, 2419-22, 2507, 3201-2, 3301, 3418-21, 3675, 3896, 4506
mining industry, 1175, 2199, 3305
police profession, 4251
railway industry, 2213
science, 2217
social work profession, 1176, 2355, 2364
sweeper occupation, 4256
textile industry, 1171, 2197, 3546-7
village industries, 2191-5, 3885, 3894, 4353
problems of working women, 1165, 1171, 1173, 1176, 1801, 2152, 2159-60, 2165, 2172-5, 2178, 2181, 2185, 2188, 2202, 2204, 2206a, 2212, 2231, 2234, 2366, 2441, 3103, 3298, 3305, 3324, 3546-8, 3559-60, 3578-81, 3654, 3783-5, 3788, 3896-7, 4258, 4261-3, 4466, 4469, 4472
Workman, Fanny Bullock. *See* Bullock-Workman, Fanny

Yaśodharā, 424
Yavar Ali Shah, Begam (20th cent.), ***445***
Young, Miriam (ad loc. 20th cent.), 4052-3
Young Women's Christian Association/YWCA, *434*, 1268-9, 1432, 2338, 2344, 2350-3, 3110a, 3692

zenana. *See* seclusion, modesty, veiling
Zenana Bible and Medical Mission, 1590, 1595, 1608, 1614, 1623, 1633, 1639, 1643, 2984, 4036, 4574
Zīb-un-Nisā (1639-1702?), *20*, 28, 738-41
Zoroastrianism, *17*, 218. *See also* Parsi women, general statements